T0184139

Lecture Notes in Computer Science 11800

Commenced Publication in 1973
Founding and Former Series Editors:
Gerhard Goos, Juris Hartmanis, and Jan van Leeuwen

Editorial Board Members

David Hutchison, UK
Josef Kittler, UK
Friedemann Mattern, Switzerland
Moni Naor, Israel
Bernhard Steffen, Germany
Doug Tygar, USA

Takeo Kanade, USA
Jon M. Kleinberg, USA
John C. Mitchell, USA
C. Pandu Rangan, India
Demetri Terzopoulos, USA

Formal Methods

Subline of Lectures Notes in Computer Science

Subline Series Editors

Ana Cavalcanti, *University of York, UK*
Marie-Claude Gaudel, *Université de Paris-Sud, France*

Subline Advisory Board

Manfred Broy, *TU Munich, Germany*
Annabelle McIver, *Macquarie University, Sydney, NSW, Australia*
Peter Müller, *ETH Zurich, Switzerland*
Erik de Vink, *Eindhoven University of Technology, The Netherlands*
Pamela Zave, *AT&T Laboratories Research, Bedminster, NJ, USA*

More information about this series at http://www.springer.com/series/7408

Maurice H. ter Beek · Annabelle McIver ·
José N. Oliveira (Eds.)

Formal Methods – The Next 30 Years

Third World Congress, FM 2019
Porto, Portugal, October 7–11, 2019
Proceedings

 Springer

Editors
Maurice H. ter Beek 🄳
Consiglio Nazionale delle Ricerche
Pisa, Italy

Annabelle McIver 🄳
Macquarie University
Sydney, NSW, Australia

José N. Oliveira 🄳
University of Minho
Braga, Portugal

ISSN 0302-9743   ISSN 1611-3349   (electronic)
Lecture Notes in Computer Science
ISBN 978-3-030-30941-1   ISBN 978-3-030-30942-8   (eBook)
https://doi.org/10.1007/978-3-030-30942-8

LNCS Sublibrary: SL2 – Programming and Software Engineering

© Springer Nature Switzerland AG 2019
This work is subject to copyright. All rights are reserved by the Publisher, whether the whole or part of the material is concerned, specifically the rights of translation, reprinting, reuse of illustrations, recitation, broadcasting, reproduction on microfilms or in any other physical way, and transmission or information storage and retrieval, electronic adaptation, computer software, or by similar or dissimilar methodology now known or hereafter developed.
The use of general descriptive names, registered names, trademarks, service marks, etc. in this publication does not imply, even in the absence of a specific statement, that such names are exempt from the relevant protective laws and regulations and therefore free for general use.
The publisher, the authors and the editors are safe to assume that the advice and information in this book are believed to be true and accurate at the date of publication. Neither the publisher nor the authors or the editors give a warranty, expressed or implied, with respect to the material contained herein or for any errors or omissions that may have been made. The publisher remains neutral with regard to jurisdictional claims in published maps and institutional affiliations.

This Springer imprint is published by the registered company Springer Nature Switzerland AG
The registered company address is: Gewerbestrasse 11, 6330 Cham, Switzerland

Preface

This volume contains the papers presented at the 23rd Symposium on Formal Methods (FM 2019), held in Porto, Portugal, in the form of the Third World Congress on Formal Methods, during October 7–11, 2019. These proceedings also contain five papers selected by the Program Committee (PC) of the Industry Day (I-Day).

FM 2019 was organized under the auspices of Formal Methods Europe (FME), an independent association whose aim is to stimulate the use of, and research on, formal methods for software development. It has been more than 30 years since the first VDM symposium in 1987 brought together researchers with the common goal of creating methods to produce high-quality software based on rigor and reason. Since then the diversity and complexity of computer technology has changed enormously and the formal methods community has stepped up to the challenges those changes brought by adapting, generalizing, and improving the models and analysis techniques that were the focus of that first symposium. The theme for FM 2019, "The Next 30 Years," was a reflection on how far the community has come and the lessons we can learn for understanding and developing the best software for future technologies.

To reflect the fact that it has been 20 years since FM 1999 in Toulouse and 10 years since FM 2009 in Eindhoven, FM 2019 was organized as a World Congress, and we composed a PC of renowned scientists from 42 different countries spread across all continents except for Antarctica. We originally received a stunning total of 185 abstract submissions, which unfortunately resulted in 'only' 129 paper submissions from 36 different countries. Each submission went through a rigorous review process in which 95% of the papers were reviewed by four PC members. Following an in-depth discussion phase lasting two weeks, we selected 37 full papers and 2 short tool papers, an acceptance rate of 30%, for presentation during the symposium and inclusion in these proceedings. The symposium featured keynotes by Shriram Krishnamurthi (Brown University, USA), Erik Poll (Radboud University, The Netherlands), and June Andronick (CSIRO-Data61 and UNSW, Australia). We hereby thank these invited speakers for having accepted our invitation. The program also featured a Lucas Award and FME Fellowship Award Ceremony.

We are grateful to all involved in FM 2019. In particular the PC members and subreviewers for their accurate and timely reviewing, all authors for their submissions, and all attendees of the symposium for their participation. We also thank all the other committees (I-Day, Doctoral Symposium, Journal First Track, Workshops, and Tutorials), itemized on the following pages, and particularly the excellent local organization and publicity teams. In addition to FM 2019 they also managed the FM week consisting of another 8 conferences, 17 workshops, and 7 tutorials, as well as 'X', the secret project of a colloquium in honor of Stefania Gnesi based on a Festschrift to celebrate her 65th birthday.

We are very grateful to our platinum sponsors: Amazon Web Services (AWS), Google, and Sony; our gold sponsors: Springer, Semmle, ASML, and PT-FLAD Chair in Smart Cities & Smart Governance; our silver sponsors: Oracle Labs, Runtime Verification Inc., Standard Chartered, GMV, United Technologies Research Center (UTRC), and Efacec; our bronze sponsors i2S, Foundations of Perspicuous Software Systems Collaborative Research Center, and the Mathematical research center of the University of Porto (CMUP); and our basic sponsors: Natixis and Neadvance.

Finally, we thank Springer for publishing these proceedings in their FM subline and we acknowledge the support from EasyChair in assisting us in managing the complete process from submissions to these proceedings to the program.

August 2019

Maurice H. ter Beek
Annabelle McIver
José N. Oliveira

Organization

General Chair

José N. Oliveira — University of Minho and INESC TEC, Portugal

FM Program Chairs

Maurice H. ter Beek — ISTI–CNR, Italy
Annabelle McIver — Macquarie University, Australia

Industry Day Chairs

Joe Kiniry — Galois Inc., USA
Thierry Lecomte — ClearSy, France

Doctoral Symposium Chairs

Alexandra Silva — University College London, UK
Antónia Lopes — University of Lisbon, Portugal

Journal First Track Chair

Augusto Sampaio — Federal University of Pernambuco, Brazil

Workshop and Tutorial Chairs

Emil Sekerinski — McMaster University, Canada
Nelma Moreira — University of Porto, Portugal

FM Program Committee

Bernhard Aichernig — TU Graz, Austria
Elvira Albert — Complutense University of Madrid, Spain
María Alpuente — Polytechnic University of Valencia, Spain
Dalal Alrajeh — Imperial College, UK
Mário S. Alvim — Federal University of Minas Gerais, Brazil
June Andronick — CSIRO-Data61, Australia
Christel Baier — TU Dresden, Germany
Luís Barbosa — University of Minho and UN University, Portugal
Gilles Barthe — IMDEA Software Institute, Spain
Marcello Bersani — Polytechnic University of Milan, Italy
Gustavo Betarte — Tilsor SA and University of the Republic, Uruguay

Nikolaj Bjørner	Microsoft Research, USA
Frank de Boer	CWI, The Netherlands
Sergiy Bogomolov	Australian National University, Australia
Julien Brunel	ONERA, France
Néstor Cataño	Universidad del Norte, Colombia
Ana Cavalcanti	University of York, UK
Antonio Cerone	Nazarbayev University, Kazakhstan
Marsha Chechik	University of Toronto, Canada
David Chemouil	ONERA, France
Alessandro Cimatti	FBK–IRST, Italy
Alcino Cunha	University of Minho and INESC TEC, Portugal
Michael Dierkes	Rockwell Collins, France
Alessandro Fantechi	University of Florence, Italy
Carla Ferreira	New University of Lisbon, Portugal
João Ferreira	Teesside University, UK
José L. Fiadeiro	Royal Holloway University of London, UK
Marcelo Frias	Buenos Aires Institute of Technology, Argentina
Fatemeh Ghassemi	University of Tehran, Iran
Silvia Ghilezan	University of Novi Sad, Serbia
Stefania Gnesi	ISTI–CNR, Italy
Reiner Hähnle	TU Darmstadt, Germany
Osman Hasan	University of Sciences and Technology, Pakistan
Klaus Havelund	NASA Jet Propulsion Laboratory, USA
Anne Haxthausen	TU Denmark, Denmark
Ian Hayes	University of Queensland, Australia
Constance Heitmeyer	Naval Research Laboratory, USA
Jane Hillston	University of Edinburgh, UK
Thai Son Hoang	University of Southampton, UK
Zhenjiang Hu	National Institute of Informatics, Japan
Dang Van Hung	Vietnam National University, Vietnam
Atsushi Igarashi	Kyoto University, Japan
Suman Jana	Columbia University, USA
Ali Jaoua	Qatar University, Qatar
Einar Broch Johnsen	University of Oslo, Norway
Joost-Pieter Katoen	RWTH Aachen University, Germany
Laura Kovács	TU Vienna, Austria
Axel Legay	UCLouvain, Belgium
Gabriele Lenzini	University of Luxembourg, Luxembourg
Yang Liu	Nanyang Technical University, Singapore
Alberto Lluch Lafuente	TU Denmark, Denmark
Malte Lochau	TU Darmstadt, Germany
Michele Loreti	University of Camerino, Italy
Anastasia Mavridou	NASA Ames, USA
Hernán Melgratti	University of Buenos Aires, Argentina
Sun Meng	Peking University, China
Dominique Méry	LORIA and University of Lorraine, France

Rosemary Monahan	Maynooth University, Ireland
Olfa Mosbahi	University of Carthage, Tunisia
Mohammad Mousavi	University of Leicester, UK
César Muñoz	NASA Langley, USA
Tim Nelson	Brown University, USA
Gethin Norman	University of Glasgow, UK
Colin O'Halloran	D-RisQ Software Systems, UK
Federico Olmedo	University of Chile, Chile
Gordon Pace	University of Malta, Malta
Jan Peleska	University of Bremen, Germany
Marielle Petit-Doche	Systerel, France
Alexandre Petrenko	Computer Research Institute of Montréal, Canada
Anna Philippou	University of Cyprus, Cyprus
Jorge Sousa Pinto	University of Minho and INESC TEC, Portugal
André Platzer	Carnegie Mellon University, USA
Jaco van de Pol	Aarhus University, Denmark
Tahiry Rabehaja	Macquarie University, Australia
Steve Reeves	University of Waikato, New Zealand
Matteo Rossi	Polytechnic University of Milan, Italy
Augusto Sampaio	Federal University of Pernambuco, Brazil
Gerardo Schneider	Chalmers University of Gothenburg, Sweden
Daniel Schwartz Narbonne	Amazon Web Services, USA
Natasha Sharygina	University of Lugano, Switzerland
Nikolay Shilov	Innopolis University, Russia
Ana Sokolova	University of Salzburg, Austria
Marielle Stoelinga	University of Twente, The Netherlands
Jun Sun	University of Technology and Design, Singapore
Helen Treharne	University of Surrey, UK
Elena Troubitsyna	Åbo Akademi University, Finland
Tarmo Uustalu	Reykjavik University, Iceland
Andrea Vandin	TU Denmark, Denmark
R. Venkatesh	TCS Research, India
Erik de Vink	TU Eindhoven and CWI, The Netherlands
Willem Visser	Stellenbosch University, South Africa
Farn Wang	National Taiwan University, Taiwan
Bruce Watson	Stellenbosch University, South Africa
Tim Willemse	TU Eindhoven, The Netherlands
Kirsten Winter	University of Queensland, Australia
Jim Woodcock	University of York, UK
Lijun Zhang	Chinese Academy of Sciences, China

Additional Reviewers

Rui Abreu
Arthur Américo
Hugo Araujo
Myla Archer
Sepideh Asadi
Florent Avellaneda
Eduard Baranov
Davide Basile
Cláudio Belo Lourenço
Philipp Berger
František Blahoudek
Martin Blicha
Jean-Paul Bodeveix
Brandon Bohrer
Ioana Boureanu
Laura Bozzelli
Daniel Britten
James Brotherston
Richard Bubel
Doina Bucur
Juan Diego Campo
Laura Carnevali
Gustavo Carvalho
Davide Cavezza
Xiaohong Chen
Yu-Ting Chen
Robert Colvin
Jesús Correas Fernández
Silvano Dal Zilio
Carlos Diego Damasceno
Quoc Huy Do
Sebastian Ehmes
Santiago Escobar
Marco Faella
Paul Fiterau Brostean
Simon Foster
Maria João Frade
Maciej Gazda
Lorenzo Gheri
Eduardo Giménez
Pablo Gordillo

Gloria Gori
Friedrich Gretz
Jerry den Hartog
Raju Halder
Hossein Hojjat
Karel Horak
Zhe Hou
Thomas Hujsa
Andreas Humenberger
Antti Hyvarinen
Peter Häfner
Fabian Immler
Miguel Isabel
Shaista Jabeen
Phillip James
Seema Jehan
Saul Johnson
Violet Ka I Pun
Eduard Kamburjan
Minh-Thang Khuu
Sascha Klüppelholz
Dimitrios Kouzapas
Robbert Krebbers
Shrawan Kumar
Luca Laurenti
Maurice Laveaux
Corey Lewis
Jianlin Li
Yi Li
Yong Li
Ai Liu
Wanwei Liu
Martin Lukac
Carlos Luna
Lars Luthmann
Joshua Moerman
Hendrik Maarand
Kumar Madhukar
Shahar Maoz
Matteo Marescotti
Bojan Marinkovic

Paolo Masci
Mieke Massink
Franco Mazzanti
Larissa Meinicke
Alexandra Mendes
Stephan Merz
Ravindra Metta
Andrea Micheli
Stefan Mitsch
Alvaro Miyazawa
Carroll Morgan
Mariano Moscato
Toby Murray
David Müller
Koji Nakazawa
Pham Ngoc Hung
Omer Nguena-Timo
Hans de Nivelle
Quentin Peyras
Paul Piho
Danny Bøgsted Poulsen
James Power
Tim Quatmann
Jean-Baptiste Raclet
Markus Roggenbach
Guillermo Román-Díez
Jurriaan Rot
Albert Rubio
Enno Ruijters
Sebastian Ruland
David Sanan
Julia Sapiña
Andy Schürr
Ramy Shahin
Neeraj Singh
Andrew Sogokon
B. Srivathsan
Dominic Steinhöfel
Ivan Stojic
Sandro Stucki
Martin Tappler

Laura Titolo
Andrea Turrini
Ben Tyler
Evangelia Vanezi
Alicia Villanueva

Inna Vistbakka
Matthias Volk
Jingyi Wang
Shuling Wang
Markus Weckesser

Stephan Wesemeyer
Pengfei Yang
Haodong Yao

I-Day Program Committee

M. Antony Aiello   AdaCore, USA
Flemming Andersen   Galois Inc., USA
Stylianos Basagianni   United Technologies Research Centre, Ireland
Roderick Chapman   Protean Code Limited, UK
David Cok   GrammaTech, USA
Alessandro Fantechi   University of Florence, Italy
Chris Hawblitzel   Microsoft, USA
Peter Gorm Larsen   Aarhus University, Denmark
Michael Leuschel   University of Düsseldorf, Germany
Yannick Moy   AdaCore, France
Jan Peleska   Verified Systems International GmbH, Germany
Etienne Prun   ClearSy, France
Kenji Taguchi   CAV Technologies Co., Ltd., Japan
Stefano Tonetta   FBK–IRST, Italy
Daniel Zimmerman   Galois Inc., USA

DS Program Committee

Ana Cavalcanti   University of York, UK
André Platzer   Carnegie Mellon University, USA
Alessandro Fantechi   University of Florence, Italy
Carlo A. Furia   USI, Switzerland
Dalal Alrajeh   Imperial College, UK
Einar Broch Johnson   University of Oslo, Norway
Elvira Albert   Complutense University of Madrid, Spain
Jaco van de Pol   Aarhus University, Denmark
Matteo Rossi   Polytechnic University of Milan, Italy
Stefania Gnesi   ISTI-CNR, Italy
Stephan Merz   Inria, France

JFT Program Committee

Cliff Jones   University of Newcastle, UK
Manfred Broy   TU Munich, Germany

Organizing Committee

Luís Soares Barbosa   University of Minho and INESC TEC, Portugal
José Creissac Campos   University of Minho and INESC TEC, Portugal
João Pascoal Faria   University of Porto and INESC TEC, Portugal
Sara Fernandes   University of Minho and INESC TEC, Portugal
Luís Neves   Critical Software, Portugal
Ana Paiva   University of Porto and INESC TEC, Portugal

Local Organizers

Catarina Fernandes   University of Minho and INESC TEC, Portugal
Paula Rodrigues   INESC TEC, Portugal
Ana Rita Costa   INESC TEC, Portugal

Web Team

Francisco Neves   University of Minho and INESC TEC, Portugal
Rogério Pontes   University of Minho and INESC TEC, Portugal
Paula Rodrigues   INESC TEC, Portugal

FME Board

Ana Cavalcanti   University of York, UK
Lars-Henrik Eriksson   Uppsala University, Sweden
Stefania Gnesi   ISTI–CNR, Italy
Einar Broch Johnsen   University of Oslo, Norway
Nico Plat   Thanos, The Netherlands

Formal Methods for Security Functionality and for Secure Functionality (Invited Presentation)

Erik Poll

Digital Security group, Radboud University Nijmegen, The Netherlands
erikpoll@cs.ru.nl

With cyber security becoming a growing concern, it has naturally attracted the attention of researchers in formal methods. One recent success story here is TLS: the development of the new TLS 1.3 specification has gone hand-in-hand with efforts to verify security properties of formal models [5] and the development of a fully verified implementation [3]. Earlier well-known success stories in using formal methods for security are the verifications of operating system kernels or hypervisors, namely seL4 [7] and Microsoft's Hyper-V [10].

These examples – security protocols and OS kernels – are applications whose primary purpose is to provide security. It is natural to apply formal methods to such systems: they are by their very nature security-critical and they provide some security functionality that we can try to specify and verify.

However, we want *all* our systems to be secure, not just these security systems. There is an important difference between *secure* functionality and *security* functionality, or – given that most functionality and most security problems are down to software – between *software security* and *security software* [11]. Many, if not most, security problems arise in systems that have no specific security objective, say PDF viewers or video players, but which can still be hacked to provide attackers with unwanted functionality they can abuse.

Using formal methods to prove security is probably not on the cards of something as complex as a PDF viewer or video player. Just defining what it would mean for such a system to be secure is probably already infeasible. Still, formal methods can be useful, to prove the absence of certain types of security flaws or simply find security flaws. Successes here have been in the use of static analysis in source code analysers, e.g. tools like Fortify SCA that look for flaws in web applications and tools like Coverity that look for memory vulnerabilities in C(++) code. Another successful application of formal methods is the use of symbolic (or concolic) execution to generate test cases for security testing, as in SAGE [6] or, going one step further, not just automatically finding flaws but also automatically generating exploits, as in angr [16].

Downside of these approaches is that they are post-hoc and can only look for flaws in existing code. The *LangSec* paradigm [4, 9], on the other hand, provides ideas on how to prevent many security problems *by construction*. Key insights are that most security flaws occur in input handling and that there are several root causes in play here. Firstly, the input languages involved (e.g. file formats and network protocols) are complex, very expressive, and poorly, informally, specified. Secondly, there are *many* of these input languages, sometimes nested or stacked. Finally, parsers for these languages are typically hand-written, with parsing code scattered throughout the application code in so-called shotgun parsers [12]. With clearer, formal specifications of input languages and generated parser code much security misery could be avoided. (Recent initiatives in tools for parser generation here include Hammer [1] and Nail [2].) Given that formal languages and parser generation are some of the most basic and established formal methods around, it is a bit of an embarrassment to us as formal methods community that sloppy language specifications and hand-coded parsers should cause so many security problems.

Some security flaws in input handling are not so much caused by *buggy* parsing of inputs, but rather by the *unexpected* parsing of input [13]. Classic examples of this are command injection, SQL injection, and Cross-Site Scripting (XSS). Tell-tale sign that unwanted parsing of input may be happening in unexpected places is the heavy use of strings as data types [14].

Information or data flow analysis can be used to detect such flaws; indeed, this is a standard technique used in the source code analysis tools mentioned above. These flaws can also be prevented by construction, namely by using type systems. A recent example of this is the 'Trusted Types' browser API [8] by Google, where different types are used to track different kinds of data and different trust level of data to prevent XSS vulnerabilities, esp. the DOM-based XSS vulnerabilities that have proved so difficult to root out.

To conclude, formal methods cannot only be used to *prove* security of security-critical applications and components – i.e. the security software –, but they can be much more widely used to *improve* security by ruling out of the root causes behind security flaws in input handling, and do so by construction, and hence improve software security in general. Moreover, some very basic and lightweight formal methods can be used for this: methods that we teach – or should be teaching – our students in the first years of their Bachelor degree, such as regular expressions, finite state machines, grammars, and types. Indeed, in my own research I have been surprised to see how useful the simple notion of finite state machine for describing input sequences is to discover security flaws [15].

That we have not been able to get these basic techniques into common use does not say much for our success in transferring formal methods to software engineering practice. Still, looking at the bright side, it does suggest opportunities for improvement.

References

1. Anantharaman, P., Millian, M.C., Bratus, S., Patterson, M.L.: Input handling done right: building hardened parsers using language-theoretic security. In: Cybersecurity Development (SecDev), pp. 4–5. IEEE (2017)
2. Bangert, J., Zeldovich, N.: Nail: A practical tool for parsing and generating data formats. In: OSDI 2014, pp. 615–628. Usenix (2014)

3. Bhargavan, K., Blanchet, B., Kobeissi, N.: Verified models and reference implementations for the TLS 1.3 standard candidate. In: Security and Privacy (S&P 2017), pp. 483–502. IEEE (2017)
4. Bratus, S., Locasto, M.E., Patterson, M.L., Sassaman, L., Shubina, A.: Exploit programming: from buffer overflows to weird machines and theory of computation. Login, 13–21 (2011)
5. Cremers, C., Horvat, M., Hoyland, J., Scott, S., van der Merwe, T.: A comprehensive symbolic analysis of TLS 1.3. In: SIGSAC Conference on Computer and Communications Security (CCS 2017), pp. 1773–1788. ACM (2017)
6. Godefroid, P., Levin, M.Y., Molnar, D.: SAGE: Whitebox fuzzing for security testing. Commun. ACM **55**(3), 40–44 (2012)
7. Klein, G., et al.: seL4: Formal verification of an OS kernel. In: ACM SIGOPS, pp. 207–220. ACM (2009)
8. Kotowicz, K.: Trusted types help prevent cross-site scripting (2019). https://developers.google.com/web/updates/2019/02/trusted-types. blog
9. LangSec: Recognition, validation, and compositional correctness for real world security (2013). http://langsec.org/bof-handout.pdf. uSENIX Security BoF hand-out
10. Leinenbach, D., Santen, T.: Verifying the microsoft hyper-V hypervisor with VCC. In: Cavalcanti, A., Dams, D.R. (eds.) FM 2009, LNCS, vol. 5850, pp. 806–809. Springer, Heidelberg (2009). https://doi.org/10.1007/978-3-642-05089-3_51
11. McGraw, G.: Software security. IEEE Secur. Priv. **2**(2), 80–83 (2004)
12. Momot, F., Bratus, S., Hallberg, S.M., Patterson, M.L.: The seven turrets of Babel: a taxonomy of LangSec errors and how to expunge them. In: Cybersecurity Development (SecDev 2016), pp. 45–52. IEEE (2016)
13. Poll, E.: LangSec revisited: input security flaws of the second kind. In: Workshop on Language-Theoretic Security (LangSec 2018). IEEE (2018)
14. Poll, E.: Strings considered harmful. Login, **43**(4), 21–26 (2018)
15. Poll, E., de Ruiter, J., Schubert, A.: Protocol state machines and session languages: specification, implementation, and security flaws. In: Workshop on Language-Theoretic Security (LangSec 2015), pp. 125–133. IEEE (2015)
16. Shoshitaishvili, Y., et al.: SoK:(state of) the art of war: offensive techniques in binary analysis. In: Symposium on Security and Privacy (SP 2016), pp. 138–157. IEEE (2016)

Contents

Concurrency

Model Checking Circus

Model Checking

Analysis Techniques

Specification Languages

Reasoning Techniques

Invited Presentations

The Human in Formal Methods

Shriram Krishnamurthi$^{(\boxtimes)}$ and Tim Nelson

Brown University, Providence, RI, USA
{sk,tn}@cs.brown.edu

Abstract. Formal methods are invaluable for reasoning about complex systems. As these techniques and tools have improved in expressiveness and scale, their adoption has grown rapidly. Sustaining this growth, however, requires attention to not only the technical but also the human side. In this paper (and accompanying talk), we discuss some of the challenges and opportunities for human factors in formal methods.

Keywords: Human factors · User Interfaces · Education · Formal methods

1 Humans and Formal Methods

Formal methods are experiencing a long-overdue surge in popularity. This ranges from an explosion in powerful traditional tools, like proof assistants and model checkers, to embeddings of formal methods in program analysis, to a growing recognition of the value to writing formal properties in other settings (like software testing). Whereas traditionally, corporate use was primarily in hardware (e.g., Seger [26]), now major software companies like Amazon [1,7,21], Facebook [6], and Microsoft [3,12] are growing their use of formal methods.

What does it take to support this growth? Researchers will, naturally, continue to work on formal techniques. We believe, however, that not enough attention has been paid to the *humans in the loop*. In this paper and accompanying talk, we discuss some of the challenges and opportunities in this area.

To set a context for what follows, our own work has focused largely on automated methods, specifically *model finding* [18,34], as typified by tools like Alloy [15] and SAT/SMT solvers. This is not to decry the value of other techniques, including deductive methods, which we have worked with in some of our research. However, we find that model-finding tools offer a useful sweet spot:

- Because of their automation, they provide a helpful separation between specification and proof, enabling the user to focus on the former without having to dwell very much on the latter. This separation of concerns is invaluable in training contexts, since it enables us to focus on one skill at a time.
- Because model-finders can be used without properties, they enable *exploration* in addition to verification and proof. Furthermore, this can start with small amounts of partial specification. This idea, which is one aspect of *lightweight formal methods* [16], is a powerful enabler for quickly seeing the value that formal methods can provide.

© Springer Nature Switzerland AG 2019
M. H. ter Beek et al. (Eds.): FM 2019, LNCS 11800, pp. 3–10, 2019.
https://doi.org/10.1007/978-3-030-30942-8_1

– The manifestation of these methods in tools like Alloy proves particularly convenient. An Alloy user can write a small part of a specification and click "Run" (an action already familiar from programming environments), and immediately get at least somewhat useful feedback from the system.

Due to these factors, in our experience, we have found these methods more accessible than others to a broad range of students. Since, in particular, our emphasis is not just on cultivating the small group of "hard core" students but to bring the "other 90%" into the fold, tools that immediately appeal to them—and hold their attention, while they are choosing between courses in formal methods and in other exciting areas such as machine learning—are important.

In the rest of this paper, we focus on two human-facing concerns: the human-factors qualities of model finding tools (Sect. 2), and education (Sect. 3). We believe both are vital: the latter to growing the *number* of people comfortable with formal methods, and the former to their *effectiveness*.

2   User Experience

We believe that the user experience of formal-methods tools has largely been understudied, although there have been promising past venues such as the Workshops on User Interfaces for Theorem Provers (e.g., [2]) and Human-Oriented Formal Methods (e.g., [19]). The majority of this work focuses on interactive tools such as proof assistants, which is to be expected. For instance, in deductive methods, the experience of stating and executing deduction steps is critical. (For early student-facing work, see the efforts of Barker-Plummer, Barwise, and Etchemendy [4]).

However, other formal tools could also benefit from user-focused research. For instance, model finders are often integrated into higher-level tools (with their model output presented in a domain-specific way). Thus, questions of quality and comprehensibility by lay users are key.

Our own work [8] has found that a model finder's choice of output and its presentation can make a major difference in user experience. Experiments with students found that output *minimality*, while intutively appealing, is not necessarily helpful for comprehending systems. Moreover, experiments with users on Amazon's Mechanical Turk crowdsourcing platform seem to suggest that providing a small amount of additional information alongside output can be helpful for comprehension.

3   Education

An equally important—and critically human-centric—problem is thinking about education. Numerous authors have *books* that present different educational viewpoints but, to our knowledge, most of these have not been subjected to any rigorous evaluation of effectiveness. Nevertheless, beyond books and curricula, we believe much more attention should be paid to design methods and student-centric tools. There is a large body of literature on these topics in programming education, but its counterparts are often missing in formal methods education.

We are focusing primarily on the task of *writing specifications*, because:

- It is a near-universal requirement shared between different formal methods—indeed, it is perhaps a defining characteristic of the field.
- Specifications are sufficiently different from programs that we cannot blindly reuse existing knowledge about programming education, though of course there are many problems in common and we should try to port ideas. If anything, we conjecture that the need for formal methods to consider *all* possible behaviors, thanks to attributes like non-determinism, might make it *harder* than programming.
- Specifications are useful even outside traditional formal methods settings, such as in property-based testing, monitoring, etc. Hence, they increasingly affect a growing number of programmers, even ones who don't think of themselves as using traditional formal methods.

We will in turn discuss design methods (Sect. 3.1) and tools (Sect. 3.2).

3.1 A Design Recipe for Writing Specifications

One of the challenges every author faces is the "blank page syndrome" [9]: given a problem statement, they must fill a blank page (or editor) with magical incantations that match the given statement. For many students, this can be a daunting and even overwhelming experience; ones for whom it is not are sometimes merely overconfident in their abilities.

However, in other design disciplines—from electrical engineering to building architecture—designers produce not just one final artifact but a series of intermediate artifacts, using a range of representations with distinct viewpoints that hide some aspects and make others salient. What might that look like in our discipline?

One answer is provided by *How to Design Programs* [9], which breaks down the programming process into a series of steps called the Design Recipe. These steps incrementally build towards a solution, alternating abstract and concrete steps that build on previous ones. For programming, these steps are:

1. Data definitions: translating what is given in the problem statement into abstract descriptions for the computer system.
2. Data examples: constructing examples of each data definition to ensure the student understands it, has created a well-formed definition, and can cover the cases the problem demands.
3. Function outline: translating the function expected in the problem into an abstract computational representation, including type signatures, purpose statements, and a function header.

4. Function examples: constructing input-output examples of the function's use, using the data examples and the function outline components. These ensure the student actually understands the problem before they start working on it. These are usually written using the *syntax* of test cases, so they can eventually be run against the final function, but they are conceptually different: they represent exploration and understanding of the *problem*.
5. Function template: Using the data definition and function outline to create a skeleton of the body based purely on the structure of the data.
6. Function definition: Filling in the template to match the specific function definition, using the examples as a guide.
7. Testing: Constructing tests based on the chosen implementation strategy, checking for implementation-specific invariants. The goal of tests, in contrast to function examples, is to falsify the purported implementation.

There is significant cognitive theory backing the use of this recipe. The process corresponds to Bruner's notion of *scaffolding* [31], while the steps reflect Vygotsky's theory of *zones of proximal development* [29]. The progression from data through examples to code and tests provides a form of *concreteness fading* [13]. Completed sequences form *worked examples* [28] that students can apply to new problems. The templates are a form of *program schema* [22,27] that students can recall and reuse in constructing solutions to new problems.

How can we translate this from writing programs to writing specifications? We believe many of the steps carry over directly (and serve the same purpose), while others need some adaptation, depending on what students are authoring (the process for specifications would look different than that for models given to a model-checker, etc.). For instance, the "function examples" stage translates well to students creating concrete instances of behavior that they believe should or should not satisfy the eventual specification.

We will not go here into the details of how to adapt this process to different settings, especially authoring specifications. However, we believe the basic ideas are fairly universal: of proceeding in a step-wise way with new artifacts building on old artifacts; of proceeding from the concrete to the abstract; of writing illustrative, concrete examples of preceding abstract steps to test well-formedness and understanding; and so on.

3.2   Tools

Researchers and developers have invested significant effort into formal methods tools, many of which are then brought into the classroom. On the one hand, industrial-strength tools tend to be robust and performant, and are endowed with authenticity, which can make a difference for some students. On the other hand, they may expose too much power: they accept full and complex languages that contain features that may confuse students, they produce errors and other feedback with terminology that students may not understand, and so on. In light of this, projects have advocated the use of *language levels* [5,10,14], arguing that students would benefit from a graduated introduction through a sequence of sub-languages (and corresponding tool interfaces), each sub-language presenting an epistemic closure that corresponds to a student's learning at that point.

Beyond this, we argue that educational settings have one key advantage that conventional industrial use does not: the presence of *ground truth*, i.e., someone already knows the answer! In industry, users rarely build a whole new specification that precisely matches one that already exists. In education, however, that is exactly what students do almost all the time. Therefore, we can ask:

How does the presence of a ground truth affect formal tools in education?

We argue that "knowing the answer" especially helps in light of the Design Recipe discussed above, because we can build tools to help with each step. We discuss a concrete manifestation of this below. These should be thought of as training wheels to help beginners become comfortable with formal methods; naturally, we need to study how to wean students so that they can engage in the more authentic experience of writing specifications and models un-aided.

Understanding Before Authoring. A growing body of literature in programming education [17,25,30] shows that students frequently start to write programs before they have understood the problem. As a result they "solve" the wrong problem entirely. Not only is this frustrating, it also leads to learning loss: the stated problem presumably had certain learning goals, which the student may not have met as a result of their misdirection.

Recent work [24,32] has begun to address this issue by devising techniques to make sure students can check their understanding of the problem before they embark on a solution. These critically rely on having intermediate artifacts authored by the student in the process of authoring, precisely matching the intermediate steps proposed by the Design Recipe. In particular, function examples are a valuable way for them to demonstrate their understanding; because they are written in executable form, they can be run against implementations.

We especially draw on the perspective of Politz et al. [23] and Wrenn et al. [33], which think of tests (and examples) as *classifiers*. That is, the quality of a suite of tests or examples can be judged by how well they classify a purported implementation as correct or faulty. If we want a quantitative result, we can compute precision and recall scores to characterize these classifiers. Thus, students can rapidly obtain concrete feedback about how well they are doing in terms of understanding the problem, and our evidence in the context of programming [32] suggests that they take great advantage of this. Initial explorations for specification authoring suggests that this phenomenon carries over.

More Artifacts. More broadly, there are several artifacts that can be produced on both sides for specification-authoring assignments, including:

- Student's concrete examples
- Student's properties
- Student's completed specification

- Instructor's concrete examples
- Instructor's properties
- Instructor's completed specification

the latter three of which are ground truth components. Furthermore, instructional staff can be pressed to produce multiple kinds of each of these, such as correct and faulty specifications to enable classification.

Given this rich set of artifacts, it is instructive to consider all their (at least) pairwise combinations. For example, consider the point where the student believes they have completed their specification. This can now be compared for *semantic difference* [11,20] against the instructor's specification, with the differences presented as concrete examples that the student has to determine how to incorporate to adjust their specification. There are several interesting questions of *mechanism design*, i.e., how to structure rewards and penalties for students using these modes.

4   Conclusion

In sum, we believe there are large human-facing aspects of formal methods that have not yet been explored, and that exploring them is vital for the field to thrive. With enough emphasis, we believe formal methods can be democratized and made accessible to large numbers of users—not only scientists and trained operators, but even the general public, from children to retirees. Even the most non-technical user has to make consequential decisions every time they set a configuration option on a system, and would hence benefit from the specification and state-exploration powers that characterize our field. These problems are intellectually exciting and challenging, and serious progress requires wedding technical results to cognitive and social ones.

Acknowledgements. This work was partially supported by the U.S. National Science Foundation. We are grateful for numerous valuable conversations with Daniel J. Dougherty, Natasha Danas, Jack Wrenn, Kathi Fisler, Daniel Jackson, and Emina Torlak.

References

1. Amazon Web Services: Provable security. https://aws.amazon.com/security/provable-security/. Accessed 5 July 2019
2. Autexier, S., Benzmüller, C. (eds.): User Interfaces for Theorem Provers, Proceedings of UITP 2006, Electronic Notes in Theoretical Computer Science, vol. 174. Elsevier (2007)
3. Ball, T., Cook, B., Levin, V., Rajamani, S.K.: SLAM and static driver verifier: technology transfer of formal methods inside microsoft. In: Boiten, E.A., Derrick, J., Smith, G. (eds.) IFM 2004. LNCS, vol. 2999, pp. 1–20. Springer, Heidelberg (2004). https://doi.org/10.1007/978-3-540-24756-2_1

4. Barker-Plummer, D., Barwise, J., Etchemendy, J.: Language, Proof, and Logic, 2nd edn. Center for the Study of Language and Information/SRI, Stanford (2011)
5. du Boulay, B., O'Shea, T., Monk, J.: The black box inside the glass box. Int. J. Hum.-Comput. Stud. **51**(2), 265–277 (1999)
6. Calcagno, C., et al.: Moving fast with software verification. In: Havelund, K., Holzmann, G., Joshi, R. (eds.) NFM 2015. LNCS, vol. 9058, pp. 3–11. Springer, Cham (2015). https://doi.org/10.1007/978-3-319-17524-9_1
7. Cook, B.: Formal reasoning about the security of amazon web services. In: Chockler, H., Weissenbacher, G. (eds.) CAV 2018. LNCS, vol. 10981, pp. 38–47. Springer, Cham (2018). https://doi.org/10.1007/978-3-319-96145-3_3
8. Danas, N., Nelson, T., Harrison, L., Krishnamurthi, S., Dougherty, D.J.: User studies of principled model finder output. In: Cimatti, A., Sirjani, M. (eds.) SEFM 2017. LNCS, vol. 10469, pp. 168–184. Springer, Cham (2017). https://doi.org/10.1007/978-3-319-66197-1_11
9. Felleisen, M., Findler, R.B., Flatt, M., Krishnamurthi, S.: How to Design Programs, 2nd edn. MIT Press, Cambridge (2018). https://www.htdp.org/
10. Findler, R.B., et al.: DrScheme: a programming environment for Scheme. J. Funct. Prog. **12**(2), 159–182 (2002)
11. Fisler, K., Krishnamurthi, S., Meyerovich, L., Tschantz, M.: Verification and change impact analysis of access-control policies. In: International Conference on Software Engineering, pp. 196–205 (2005)
12. Fogel, A., et al.: A general approach to network configuration analysis. In: Networked Systems Design and Implementation (2015)
13. Fyfe, E.R., McNeil, N.M., Son, J.Y., Goldstone, R.L.: Concreteness fading in mathematics and science instruction: a systematic review. Educ. Psychol. Rev. **26**(1), 9–25 (2014)
14. Holt, R.C., Wortman, D.B.: A sequence of structured subsets of PL/I. SIGCSE Bull. **6**(1), 129–132 (1974)
15. Jackson, D.: Software Abstractions: Logic, Language, and Analysis, 2nd edn. MIT Press, Cambridge (2012)
16. Jackson, D., Wing, J.: Lightweight formal methods. IEEE Comput. (1996)
17. Loksa, D., Ko, A.J.: The role of self-regulation in programming problem solving process and success. In: SIGCSE International Computing Education Research Conference (2016)
18. McCune, W.: Mace4 reference manual and guide. CoRR (2003). https://arxiv.org/abs/cs.SC/0310055
19. Milazzo, P., Varró, D., Wimmer, M. (eds.): STAF 2016. LNCS, vol. 9946. Springer, Cham (2016). https://doi.org/10.1007/978-3-319-50230-4
20. Nelson, T., Ferguson, A.D., Krishnamurthi, S.: Static differential program analysis for software-defined networks. In: Björner, N., de Boer, F. (eds.) FM 2015. LNCS, vol. 9109, pp. 395–413. Springer, Cham (2015). https://doi.org/10.1007/978-3-319-19249-9_25
21. Newcombe, C., Rath, T., Zhang, F., Munteanu, B., Brooker, M., Deardeuff, M.: How amazon web services uses formal methods. Commun. ACM **58**(4), 66–73 (2015)
22. Pirolli, P.L., Anderson, J.R.: The role of learning from examples in the acquisition of recursive programming skills. Canadian Journal of Psychology/Revue canadienne de psychologie **39**(2), 240–272 (1985)
23. Politz, J.G., Krishnamurthi, S., Fisler, K.: In-flow peer-review of tests in test-first programming. In: Conference on International Computing Education Research (2014)

24. Prather, J., et al.: First things first: providing metacognitive scaffolding for interpreting problem prompts. In: ACM Technical Symposium on Computer Science Education (2019)
25. Prather, J., Pettit, R., McMurry, K., Peters, A., Homer, J., Cohen, M.: Metacognitive difficulties faced by novice programmers in automated assessment tools. In: SIGCSE International Computing Education Research Conference (2018)
26. Seger, C.H.: Combining functional programming and hardware verification (abstract of invited talk). In: International Conference on Functional Programming (ICFP) (2000)
27. Spohrer, J.C., Soloway, E.: Simulating Student Programmers. In: IJCAI 1989, pp. 543–549. Morgan Kaufmann Publishers Inc. (1989)
28. Sweller, J.: The worked example effect and human cognition. Learn. Instr. **16**(2), 165–169 (2006)
29. Vygotsky, L.S.: Mind in Society: The Development of Higher Psychological Processes. Harvard University Press, Cambridge (1978)
30. Whalley, J., Kasto, N.: A qualitative think-aloud study of novice programmers' code writing strategies. In: Conference on Innovation and Technology in Computer Science Education (2014)
31. Wood, D., Bruner, J.S., Ross, G.: The role of tutoring in problem solving. J. Child Psychol. Psychiatry **17**, 89–100 (1976)
32. Wrenn, J., Krishnamurthi, S.: Executable examples for programming problem comprehension. In: SIGCSE International Computing Education Research Conference (2019)
33. Wrenn, J., Krishnamurthi, S., Fisler, K.: Who tests the testers? In: SIGCSE International Computing Education Research Conference, pp. 51–59 (2018)
34. Zhang, J., Zhang, H.: SEM: a system for enumerating models. In: International Joint Conference on Artificial Intelligence (1995)

Successes in Deployed Verified Software (and Insights on Key Social Factors)

June Andronick[(✉)]

CSIRO's Data61 and UNSW, Sydney, Australia
june.andronick@data61.csiro.au

Abstract. In this talk, we will share our experience in the successful deployment of verified software in a wide range of application domains, and, importantly, our insights on the key factors enabling such successful deployment, in particular the importance of the social aspects of a group working effectively together.

Our formally verified microkernel, seL4, is now used across the world in a number of applications that keeps growing. Our experience is that such an uptake is enabled not only by a technical strategy, but also by a tight integration of people from multiple disciplines and with both research and engineering profiles. This requires a strong social culture, with well designed processes, for working as one unified team. We share our observations on what concrete social structures have been key for us in creating real-world impact from research breakthroughs.

1 The Dream

Precisely fifty years ago, Tony Hoare, in his seminal paper [1], outlined a dream; a dream where verifying properties of programs can be achieved by purely deductive reasoning; a dream where such reasoning could be applied to non-trivial programs as long as considerably more powerful proof techniques became available; a dream where software systems would not be deployed unless they were formally verified; a dream where verified software would have become the standard produced by industry; a dream where it would be legally considered negligence to deploy unverified software.

We share this dream, and –with many others– have contributed towards it by demonstrating that verified software is feasible and can be deployed on real-world systems. We can, however, observe that, in fifty years, this dream has not been fully achieved yet.

The main reason for verified software not yet being the standard could be phrased as: it has not yet achieved the status of being the *state-of-the-art*. Ten years ago, Hoare was invited to write a retrospective article [2], to share his personal views on progress made since his first article forty years before, and reflect on what he had hoped for back then and what actually happened. One thing he realised he had not predicted correctly was what actually would drive the push for more verified software; he had thought that it would be the fear

© Springer Nature Switzerland AG 2019
M. H. ter Beek et al. (Eds.): FM 2019, LNCS 11800, pp. 11–17, 2019.
https://doi.org/10.1007/978-3-030-30942-8_2

of expensive lawsuits for damages due to software errors. This didn't happen because "the defense of 'state-of-the-art' practice would always prevail".

We thus need to make verified software become the state-of-the-art practice. For this we need (a) to lower the cost (Hoare said "Far more effective is the incentive of reduction in cost" [2]) and (b) to have more success stories, where insights can be shared. Together, these will not only bring economic incentives for all software producers to follow the path of verified software, but lead to 'no more excuses' *not* to follow that path.

Here we share our observations about the social structures and incentives that have allowed us to bring together a large group of people with diverse –sometimes even disjoint– technical backgrounds and to make them work effectively towards a goal that must blend relentlessly formal techniques on the one hand with uncompromising real-world performance on the other. In the last ten years, we have been designing, developing, maintaining, and evolving the world's largest and most verified artefact, ported across multiple hardware platforms, as well as a collection of tools and frameworks for the verification of real-world software. In the last five years, our technology has seen an increasing uptake by companies, governments and the open-source community. This has encouraged a number of initiatives and projects pushing further this pervasive verified software dream. Reflecting on our own experience of what made it possible to push the boundaries of the state-of-the-art into deployed systems, our main insight would be (1) having a single group with both researchers and engineers, and both operating-system (OS) and formal method (FM) experts, all working very closely together, towards a shared vision, and (2) having this vision being not only technical, but also social: making sure this diverse range of people work effectively and efficiently together. We will first give an overview of where our verified software is deployed and the key steps leading to this uptake, and then share our observations on the key social factors that allowed these successes.

2 Successes in Deployed Verified Software

Our story of successfully pushing verified software in deployed systems across a variety of domains contains a few important milestones.

Performance. The first milestone, and starting point, was the research breakthrough making formal program verification scale to an entire operating system kernel, *while maintaining high performance*. This consisted in the formal proof, in the Isabelle/HOL theorem prover [7], of the functional correctness of the seL4 microkernel [3,5], followed by the proof of the security properties of integrity [9] and confidentiality [6] as well as correctness of the binary code [8]. Note that the focus on performance as an equal objective as the correctness was a key factor in the later uptake and deployment; and this was made possible only by the close collaboration between the two disciplines' experts, as we will describe in the next section.

Retrofitting. A second key milestone was to move this research outcome towards a technology transfer in industry by demonstrating the practicality of building whole secure systems on the seL4 trustworthy foundation. We worked with companies to *retrofit* their existing systems into secure architectures, with isolated trusted components, running on seL4 guaranteeing the isolation (as describes in [4]). The key effort that created the most impact was the High-Assurance Cyber Military Systems (HACMS) program, funded by the US Defense Advanced Research Projects Agency (DARPA), where we collaborated with Boeing, Rockwell Collins, Galois, HRL, the University of Minnesota, MIT, University of Illinois, CMU, Princeton University, and US Army's TARDEC to transition the seL4 technology to real-world autonomous vehicles. These included a Boeing-built optionally piloted helicopter and an autonomous US-Army truck, both originally vulnerable to cyber-attack, that we demonstrated to be able to resist these cyber-attacks and others after being re-architected to run on seL4. This kind of work is mainly engineering focused, with a join effort between the systems engineers and the proof engineers, keeping the focus on formal guarantees for the security of the overall system. Such projects are also an important source of input about the real-world requirements that need to be addressed.

Focus on Grand Challenges. This leads to the third key ingredient: keep tackling the grand challenges not yet addressed. Our engineering work, pushing our technology on deployed systems, harvests further requirements calling for still more research advances, such as extending the verification guarantees to timing protection, or concurrent execution on multicore platforms, or increasing the cost-effectiveness of verifying application code or porting the proofs to new platforms. These open questions then constitute our research agenda and roadmap.

Open Source. Finally, the last key contributing factor to the uptake of our technology was the open-sourcing of seL4, both code and proofs, as well as all the infrastructure, tools, and platforms to help building whole secure systems. The first reason why this contributed to the uptake is that a kernel is only a part of the solution, and transitioning to using it requires a retrofit, a re-architecting of an existing system, which is not a decision taken lightly. Being able to explore and 'play' with it before 'buying into it' has been instrumental to people choosing to transition. The second reason open sourcing has been critical is that it builds a community and an ecosystem supporting and extending the technology, infrastructure, libraries, and platforms, helping with the scalability of the support for transitioning. The caveat and challenge is to ensure that the verification guarantees keep being maintained.

These few key milestones have led to an increased uptake of the seL4 kernel and associated technology in real-world systems across a number of domains: automotive (e.g. HRL, TARDEC), aviation (e.g. Boeing, Rockwell), space (e.g. UNSW QB50), military (e.g. Rockwell Soldier Helmet), data distribution (e.g. RTI Connext DDS Micro), Industry 4.0 (e.g. HENSOLDT Cyber), component

OS (e.g. Genode platform), security (e.g. Penten Altrocrypt). Some of these projects are a result of DARPA's call for specific funding to build the seL4 ecosystem, through a number of Small Business Innovation Research (SBIR) grants.

Much work is still to be done (and is ongoing) to lower the bar to transition to seL4-based systems, and to ensure the verification guarantees are maintained and extended, but these successful deployments are contributing to pushing the dream of verified software becoming the default.

3   Insights on Key Social Factors

A major aspect of what we want to communicate here is the importance of social factors, within our group[1], that we have discovered are key contributors to the technical aspects of what we have done. Our experience is that the successful uptake of our technology comes from having a single group hosting both FM and OS people, and both researchers and engineers, working effectively together, as a tightly integrated team. We want to share concrete examples of the social structures that enabled this tight integration for us. Some can be expected and are not unique to our group; we here simply share which ones seem to have been key for us.

Achieving the dream of pervasive verified software requires a combination of academic research and industrial engineering. Today, these mostly live in separated worlds. Industrial engineering brings the real-world requirements, requires usability and performance, but is product-focused and aims at profitability. Hoare said *"The goal of industrial research is (and should always be) to pluck the 'low-hanging fruit'; that is, to solve the easiest parts of the most prevalent problems, in the particular circumstances of here and now."* [2]. Academic research, on the other hand, is innovation-focused, aiming at generic solutions, with a timeframe allowing grand-challenges to be solved in a novel way. Hoare said that *"the goal of the pure research scientist is exactly the opposite: it is to construct the most general theories, covering the widest possible range of phenomena, and to seek certainty of knowledge that will endure for future generations."* [2]. When it comes to verified software, academic research is still crucially needed to increase the scalability and applicability, while industrial engineering is critical to produce specific instances that work.

There have been many studies on the barriers to the adoption of formal methods and the ideas for closing the gaps between academic research and industry practices. These studies paint the world as composed of two separate entities; the formal methods on one side, and the application domain on the other; or the research on one side, and the industrial engineering on the other — with a boundary in between that needs to be crossed, as a 'baton' transferred from one part of the world to the other.

---

[1] the Trustworthy Systems group, in Data61, CSIRO, https://ts.data61.csiro.au.

Our view is that success in deployable verified software comes with having one single world, one single team[2], tightly integrated. It is the notion of *tight* integration that is crucial. That is what prevents the (undesirable) re-creation, within the group, of the binary world we are presently forced to inhabit outside it. If we don't succeed there, then the same boundaries and gaps will be created — where work is 'handed over' by one set of people to another set of people for their consideration. Instead, people need to work hand in hand, day by day, sometimes even hour by hour, sharing their perspective of the issues, solutions, design decisions, all along the way.

In our group, this is illustrated by the fact that 'every project involves every subteam', meaning that the majority of our projects involve *both* OS and FM people and *both* researchers and engineers. Our engineering practices and processes on the OS side and FM side are also tightly integrated; for instance, any change in the code, from any side, starts with a discussion on the implications for the 'other side'; we have a continuous integration process that manages our implementation code base as well as all our proof code base (now more than a million lines of Isabelle/HOL), making sure they are always in sync, that changes to code that is not yet verified can be seamlessly integrated, as well as changes to verified code that happen to not break any proofs, whereas any changes that break the proofs are clearly marked as such and follow a process where a team is allocated to their verification and changes cannot be integrated until the proofs are re-established.

For this tight integration to work, the *frequency* of the personal interactions is crucial. Our group has experienced a few different physical setups, in different locations, and our observation is that having people in the same location, same building, if possible same floor is highly desirable: a proof engineer can just walk up to the OS engineer to check e.g. whether a change in the code to ease verification would have a performance impact; the impromptu encounters at the coffee machine create the opportunity to share a viewpoint on e.g. a desired kernel change; the kind of discussions needed across disciplines work best as face-to-face discussions, with the support of a white board for design brainstorming, or for sharing the knowledge between disciplines.

Another very important social aspect is ensuring *good* communication despite the difference in backgrounds, or even sometimes languages and terminologies. For instance, like many other groups, we run weekly talks and quarterly dive-ins to update the rest of the group on progress in various project or share knowledge in a specific area. Maybe unlike many other research groups, these talks cross discipline boundaries and we strive –and in fact need– to keep them at a level all can understand i.e. the OS-based talks have to be FM-comprehensible, and vice versa. And *everyone* must give one of these talks, on a regular schedule. This way everyone get the opportunity to share their views, to attract interest in their work, and to grow their skills in explaining their work. This fosters a culture inside the group of knowledge sharing and awareness of other people's

---

[2] and if possible, importantly, one single shared coffee machine, surrounded by plenty of whiteboards.

work, which is essential when having to then deliver together on a given project. Being able to effectively communicate technical work to people outside of the field is not easy. To help with this, we run annual 'bootcamps' focusing on training ourselves on communication and presentation skills, and learning how to best adapt to various kinds of audience. This has an important direct impact on getting traction externally to increase the uptake of our technology, and verified software in general. Importantly, it also enables the needed information sharing and productive collaboration within the group.

Creating a one-team culture goes beyond the communication aspect. It requires a technical vision that everyone shares, shapes and contributes to. But it also needs a culture of achieving this vision *together as a team*, where we have the urge to see each other succeed, where we help and support each other in solving hard problems and delivering on projects, and where everyone contributes to creating an environment where everyone can thrive. One way this is achieved in our group is that a lot of activities such as trainings, social events, or cultural awareness initiatives are done *by people from the group*, and tailored to what our groups needs. For instance, our bootcamp mentioned above includes sessions on active listening, mental health, life balance, and all sessions are given by members of the group that have either training or first-hand experience in the topic, and are delivering tailored information and practice that they know are relevant to the type of work we do. The impact of this approach is that the trust that people have in their peers amplifies the impact of the message, the learning experience or the social interaction. It also extends the scope of the collaboration between people from purely technical to all social aspects of the group's life.

All of the above creates and fosters an environment where you can get a unique combination of people with different expertise and profiles that can work well together to achieve their shared mission. Dealing with a truly wonderful mix of personalities, backgrounds and cultures does create a number of challenges, but it also creates the required structure to tackle and solve research grand challenges, while producing systems, tools and frameworks that the world can use and deploy, and while building a community of users, partners and contributors. And this is what is needed to achieve the dream of shifting the whole world's mentality towards accepting verified software as the norm.

Acknowledgements. The author would like to thank Gerwin Klein and Carroll Morgan for their feedback on drafts of this paper.

References

1. Hoare, C.A.R.: An axiomatic basis for computer programming. CACM **12**, 576–580 (1969)
2. Hoare, C.A.R.: Viewpoint - retrospective: an axiomatic basis for computer programming. CACM **52**(10), 30–32 (2009)
3. Klein, G., et al.: seL4: Formal verification of an operating-system kernel. CACM **53**(6), 107–115 (2010)

4. Klein, G., Andronick, J., Kuz, I., Murray, T., Heiser, G., Fernandez, M.: Formally verified software in the real world. CACM **61**, 68–77 (2018)
5. Klein, G., et al.: seL4: Formal verification of an OS kernel. In: SOSP, pp. 207–220. ACM, Big Sky, October 2009
6. Murray, T., et al.: seL4: from general purpose to a proof of information flow enforcement. In: 2013 IEEE Symposium on Security and Privacy, pp. 415–429. IEEE, San Francisco, May 2013
7. Nipkow, T., Wenzel, M., Paulson, L.C. (eds.): Isabelle/HOL. LNCS, vol. 2283. Springer, Heidelberg (2002). https://doi.org/10.1007/3-540-45949-9
8. Sewell, T., Myreen, M., Klein, G.: Translation validation for a verified OS kernel. In: PLDI, pp. 471–481. ACM, Seattle, June 2013
9. Sewell, T., Winwood, S., Gammie, P., Murray, T., Andronick, J., Klein, G.: seL4 enforces integrity. In: van Eekelen, M., Geuvers, H., Schmaltz, J., Wiedijk, F. (eds.) ITP 2011. LNCS, vol. 6898, pp. 325–340. Springer, Heidelberg (2011). https://doi.org/10.1007/978-3-642-22863-6_24

Verification

Provably Correct Floating-Point Implementation of a Point-in-Polygon Algorithm

Mariano M. Moscato[1]([✉]), Laura Titolo[1], Marco A. Feliú[1],
and César A. Muñoz[2]([✉])

[1] National Institute of Aerospace, Hampton, USA
{mariano.moscato,laura.titolo,marco.feliu}@nianet.org
[2] NASA Langley Research Center, Hampton, USA
cesar.a.munoz@nasa.gov

Abstract. The problem of determining whether or not a point lies inside a given polygon occurs in many applications. In air traffic management concepts, a correct solution to the point-in-polygon problem is critical to geofencing systems for Unmanned Aerial Vehicles and in weather avoidance applications. Many mathematical methods can be used to solve the point-in-polygon problem. Unfortunately, a straightforward floating-point implementation of these methods can lead to incorrect results due to round-off errors. In particular, these errors may cause the control flow of the program to diverge with respect to the ideal real-number algorithm. This divergence potentially results in an incorrect point-in-polygon determination even when the point is far from the edges of the polygon. This paper presents a provably correct implementation of a point-in-polygon method that is based on the computation of the winding number. This implementation is mechanically generated from a source-to-source transformation of the ideal real-number specification of the algorithm. The correctness of this implementation is formally verified within the Frama-C analyzer, where the proof obligations are discharged using the Prototype Verification System (PVS).

1 Introduction

PolyCARP (Algorithms for Computations with Polygons) [25, 27] is a NASA developed open source software library for geo-containment applications based on polygons.[1] One of the main applications of PolyCARP is to provide geofencing capabilities to unmanned aerial vehicles (UAV), i.e., detecting whether a UAV is inside or outside a given geographical region, which is modeled using a 2D polygon with a minimum and a maximum altitude. Another application is

---

[1] https://shemesh.larc.nasa.gov/fm/PolyCARP.

Research by the first three authors was supported by the National Aeronautics and Space Administration under NASA/NIA Cooperative Agreement NNL09AA00A.

ⓒ Springer Nature Switzerland AG 2019
M. H. ter Beek et al. (Eds.): FM 2019, LNCS 11800, pp. 21–37, 2019.
https://doi.org/10.1007/978-3-030-30942-8_3

detecting if an aircraft's trajectory encounters weather cells, which are modeled as moving polygons.

PolyCARP implements point-in-polygon methods, i.e., methods for checking whether or not a point lies inside a polygon, that are based on the *winding number* computation. The winding number of a point p with respect to a polygon is the number of times any point traveling counterclockwise along the perimeter of the polygon winds around p. Properties of these methods have been formally verified in the Prototype Verification System (PVS) [28]. A correct implementation of these methods is essential to safety-critical geo-containment applications that rely on PolyCARP.

When an algorithm involving real numbers is implemented using floating-point numbers, round-off errors arising from the difference between real-number computations and their floating-point counterparts may affect the correctness of the algorithm. In fact, floating-point implementations of point-in-polygon methods are very sensitive to round-off errors. For instance, the presence of floating-point computations in Boolean expressions of conditional statements may cause the control flow of the floating-point program to diverge from the ideal real-number program, resulting in the wrong computation of the winding number. This may happen even when the point is far from the edges of the polygon.

This paper presents a formally verified floating-point C implementation of the winding number algorithm. This implementation is obtained by applying a program transformation to the original algorithm. This transformation replaces numerically unstable conditions with more restrictive ones that preserve the control flow of the ideal real number specification. The transformed program is guaranteed to return a warning when real and floating-point flows may diverge. The program transformation used is an extension of the one defined in [32] and it has been implemented within PRECiSA[1] (Program Round-off Error Certifier via Static Analysis), a static analyzer of floating-point programs [24,30].

Frama-C [20] is used to formally verify the correctness of the generated C program. Frama-C is a collaborative platform that hosts several plugins for the verification and analysis of C code. In particular, in this work, an extension of the Frama-C/WP (Weakest Precondition calculus) plugin is implemented to automatically generate verification conditions that can be discharged in PVS.

The rest of this paper is organized as follows. Section 2 presents the definition of the winding number. An extension of the program transformation defined in [30] is presented in Sect. 3. In Sect. 4, the transformed floating-point version of the winding number is introduced. The verification approach used to prove the correctness of the C floating-point implementation of the transformed program is explained in Sect. 5. Related work is discussed in Sect. 6. Finally, Sect. 7 concludes the paper.

---

[1] The PRECiSA distribution is available at https://github.com/nasa/PRECiSA.

2 The Winding Number Algorithm

The winding number of a point s with respect to a polygon P is defined as the number of times the perimeter of P travels counterclockwise around s. For simple polygons, i.e., the ones that do not contain intersecting edges, this function can be used to determine whether s is inside or outside P. In [25], the winding number of s with respect to P is computed by applying a geometric translation that sets s as the origin of coordinates. For each edge e of P, the algorithm counts how many axes e intersects. This contribution can be positive or negative, depending on the direction of the edge e. If the sum of all contributions from all edges is 0 then s is outside the perimeter of P, otherwise, it is inside. Figure 1 shows the edge contributions in the computation of the winding number for two different polygons.

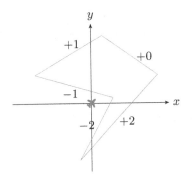

(a) The sum of the contributions is 0 and the point is outside.

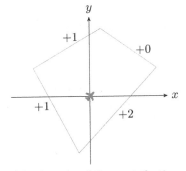

(b) The sum of the contributions is 4 and the point is inside.

Fig. 1. Winding number edge contributions

Mathematical functions that define the winding number algorithm are presented in Fig. 2. Given a point $v = (v_x, v_y)$, the function *Quadrant* returns the quadrant in which v is located. Given the endpoints of an edge e, $v = (v_x, v_y)$ and $v' = (v'_x, v'_y)$, and the point under test $s = (s_x, s_y)$, the function *EdgeContrib*$(v_x, v_y, v'_x, v'_y, s_x, s_y)$ computes the number of axes e intersects in the coordinate system centered in s. This function checks in which quadrants v and v' are located and counts how many axes are crossed by the edge e. If v and v' belong to the same quadrant, the contribution of the edge to the winding number is 0 since no axis is crossed. If v and v' lie in adjacent quadrants, the contribution is 1 (respectively -1) if moving from v to v' along the edge is in counterclockwise (respectively clockwise) direction. In the case v and v' are in opposite quadrants, the determinant is computed to check the direction of the edge. If it is counterclockwise, the contribution is 2; otherwise, it is -2. The function *WindingNumber* takes as input a point $s = (s_x, s_y)$ and a polygon P of size n, which is represented as a couple of arrays $\langle P_x, P_y \rangle$ modeling the coordinates of its vertices $(P_x(0), P_y(0)) \ldots (P_x(n-1), P_y(n-1))$. The size of a polygon is defined as the number of its vertices. The winding number of s with respect to the polygon P is obtained as the sum of the contributions of all the edges in P. The result of the winding number is 0 if and only if the polygon P does not wind around the point s, hence s lies outside P.

$$
\begin{aligned}
Quadrant(v_x, v_y) = \ & if\ v_x \geq 0 \wedge v_y \geq 0\ then\ 1 \\
& elsif\ v_x < 0 \wedge v_y \geq 0\ then\ 2 \\
& elsif\ v_x < 0 \wedge v_y < 0\ then\ 3 \\
& else\ 4
\end{aligned}
$$

$$
\begin{aligned}
EdgeContrib(v_x, v_y, v_x', v_y', s_x, s_y) = \\
& let\ this_x = v_x - s_x, this_y = v_y - s_y, next_x = v_x' - s_x, next_y = v_y' - s_y, \\
& \quad dist_x = next_x - this_x, dist_y = next_y - this_y, \\
& \quad det = dist_x \cdot this_y - dist_y \cdot this_x \\
& \quad q_{this} = Quadrant(this_x, this_y), q_{next} = Quadrant(next_x, next_y)\ in \\
& if\ q_{this} = q_{next}\ then\ 0 \\
& elsif\ q_{next} - 1 = \mathsf{mod}\,(q_{this}, 4)\ then\ 1 \\
& elsif\ q_{this} - 1 = \mathsf{mod}\,(q_{next}, 4)\ then\ -1 \\
& elsif\ det \leq 0\ then\ 2 \\
& else\ -2
\end{aligned}
$$

$$
\begin{aligned}
WindingNumber(P_x, P_y, s_x, s_y, i) = \\
& if\ i < size(P_x) - 1 \\
& then\ EdgeContrib(P_x(i), P_y(i), P_x(i+1), P_y(i+1), s_x, s_y) \\
& \quad + WindingNumber(P_x, P_y, s_x, s_y, i+1) \\
& else\ EdgeContrib(P_x(i), P_y(i), P_x(0), P_y(0), s_x, s_y)
\end{aligned}
$$

Fig. 2. Winding number algorithm

It has been formally verified in PVS, that the algorithm presented in Fig. 2 is equivalent to an alternative point-in-polygon algorithm.[2] The following property is therefore assumed.

Property 1. Given a simple polygon $P = \langle P_x, P_y \rangle$ and a point $s = (s_x, s_y)$, s lies outside P if and only if $WindingNumber(P_x, P_y, s_x, s_y, 0) = 0$.

A formal proof of Property 1 that does not rely on an alternative algorithmic method to check point containment is a hard problem beyond the scope of this paper. In particular, a proof of this statement involving a non-algorithmic definition of containment may require the formal development of fundamental topological concepts such as the Jordan Curve theorem.

---

[2] https://github.com/nasa/PolyCARP.

3   Program Transformation to Avoid Unstable Tests

Floating-point numbers are widely used to represent real numbers in computer programs since they offer a good trade-off between efficiency and precision. A floating-point number can be formalized as a pair of integers $(m, e) \in \mathbb{Z}^2$, where m is called the *significand* and e the *exponent* of the float [7,13]. Henceforth, $\mathbb{F}$ will denote the set of floating-point numbers. A conversion function $R : \mathbb{F} \to \mathbb{R}$ is defined to refer to the real number represented by a given float, i.e., $R((m, e)) = m \cdot b^e$ where b is the base of the representation. According to the IEEE-754 standard [19], each floating-point operation must be computed as if its result is first calculated correct to infinite precision and with unbounded range and then rounded to fit a particular floating-point format.

The main drawback of using floating-point numbers is the presence of *round-off errors* that originate from the difference between the ideal computation in real arithmetic and the actual floating-point computation. Let $\tilde{v}$ be a floating-point number that represents a real number r, the difference $|R(\tilde{v}) - r|$ is called the *round-off error* (or *rounding error*) of $\tilde{v}$ with respect to r. Rounding errors accumulate during the program execution and may affect the evaluation of both arithmetic and Boolean expressions. As a consequence, when guards of if-then-else statements contain floating-point expressions, as in the case of the winding number, the output of a program is not only directly influenced by rounding errors, but also by the error of taking the opposite branch with respect to the real number intended behavior. This problem is known as *test instability*. A conditional statement (or test) *if* $\tilde{\phi}$ *then* S_1 *else* S_2 is said to be *unstable* when $\tilde{\phi}$ evaluates to a different Boolean value than its real-valued counterpart.

In [32], a formally proven[3] program transformation is proposed to detect and correct the effects of unstable tests for a simple language with conditionals and let-in expressions. The output of the transformation is a floating-point program that is guaranteed to return either the result of the original floating-point one, when it can be assured that both the real and its floating-point flows agree, or a warning, when these flows may diverge. In this paper, the transformation defined in [32] has been extended to handle non-recursive function calls and simple for-loops. This extended transformation is then applied to the winding number algorithm.

Henceforth, the symbols $\mathbb{A}$ and $\widetilde{\mathbb{A}}$ denote the domain of arithmetic expressions over real and floating-point numbers, respectively. It is assumed that there is a function $\chi_r : \widetilde{\mathbb{V}} \to \mathbb{V}$ that associates to each floating-point variable $\tilde{x}$ a variable $x \in \mathbb{V}$ representing the real value of $\tilde{x}$. The function $R_{\widetilde{\mathbb{A}}} : \widetilde{\mathbb{A}} \to \mathbb{A}$ converts an arithmetic expression on floating-point numbers to an arithmetic expression on real numbers. This function is defined by simply replacing each floating-point operation with the corresponding one on real numbers and by applying R and χ_r to floating-point values and variables, respectively. By abuse of notation, floating-point expressions are interpreted as their real number evaluation when occurring inside a real-valued expression. The symbols $\mathbb{B}$ and $\widetilde{\mathbb{B}}$ denote

---

[3] The PVS formalization is available at https://shemesh.larc.nasa.gov/fm/PRECiSA.

the domain of Boolean expressions over real and floating-point numbers, respectively. The function $R_{\widetilde{\mathbb{B}}} : \widetilde{\mathbb{B}} \to \mathbb{B}$ converts a Boolean expression on floating-point numbers to a Boolean expression on real numbers. Given a variable assignment $\sigma : \mathbb{V} \to \mathbb{R}$, $eval_{\mathbb{B}}(\sigma, B) \in \{true, false\}$ denotes the evaluation of the real Boolean expression B. Similarly, given $\widetilde{B} \in \widetilde{\mathbb{B}}$ and $\widetilde{\sigma} : \widetilde{\mathbb{V}} \to \mathbb{F}$, $\widetilde{eval_{\widetilde{\mathbb{B}}}}(\widetilde{\sigma}, \widetilde{B}) \in \{true, false\}$ denotes the evaluation of the floating-point Boolean expression $\widetilde{B}$. A program is defined as a set of function declarations of the form $f(\tilde{x}_1, \ldots, \tilde{x}_n) = S$, where S is a program expression that can contain binary and n-ary conditionals, let expressions, arithmetic expressions, non-recursive function calls, for-loops, and a warning exceptional statement ω. Given a set Σ of function symbols, the syntax of program expressions S is given by the following grammar.

$$S ::= \widetilde{A} \mid if\ \widetilde{B}\ then\ S\ else\ S \mid if\ \widetilde{B}\ then\ S\ [elsif\ \widetilde{B}\ then\ S]_{i=1}^m\ else\ S$$
$$\mid let\ \tilde{x} = \widetilde{A}\ in\ S \mid for(i_0, i_n, acc_0, \lambda(i, acc).S) \mid g(\widetilde{A}, \ldots, \widetilde{A}) \mid \omega, \tag{3.1}$$

where $\widetilde{A} \in \widetilde{\mathbb{A}}$, $\widetilde{B} \in \widetilde{\mathbb{B}}$, $\tilde{x}, i, acc \in \widetilde{\mathbb{V}}$, $g \in \Sigma$, $m \in \mathbb{N}^{>0}$, and $i_0, i_n, acc_0 \in \mathbb{N}$. The notation $[elsif\ \widetilde{B}\ then\ S]_{i=1}^m$ denotes a list of m elsif branches. The for expression emulates a for loop where i is the control variable that ranges from i_0 to i_n, acc is the variable where the result is accumulated with initial value acc_0, and S is the body of the loop. For instance, $for(1, 10, 0, \lambda(i, acc).i + acc)$ represents the value $f(1, 0)$, where f is the recursive function $f(i, acc) \equiv if\ i > 10\ then\ acc\ else\ f(i + 1, acc + i)$. The set of program expressions is denoted as $\mathbb{S}$, while the set of programs is denoted as $\mathbb{P}$.

The proposed transformation takes into account round-off errors by replacing the Boolean expressions in the guards of the original program with more restrictive ones. This is done by means of two abstractions $\beta^+, \beta^- : \widetilde{\mathbb{B}} \to \widetilde{\mathbb{B}}$ defined as follows for conjunctions and disjunctions of sign tests, where $\widetilde{expr} \in \widetilde{\mathbb{A}}$ and $\epsilon \in \widetilde{\mathbb{V}}$ is a variable that represents the rounding error of $\widetilde{expr}$ such that $|\widetilde{expr} - R_{\widetilde{\mathbb{A}}}(\widetilde{expr})| \le \epsilon$ and $\epsilon \ge 0$.

$$\beta^+(\widetilde{expr} \le 0) = \widetilde{expr} \le -\epsilon \qquad \beta^-(\widetilde{expr} \le 0) = \widetilde{expr} > \epsilon$$
$$\beta^+(\widetilde{expr} \ge 0) = \widetilde{expr} \ge \epsilon \qquad \beta^-(\widetilde{expr} \ge 0) = \widetilde{expr} < -\epsilon$$
$$\beta^+(\widetilde{expr} < 0) = \widetilde{expr} < -\epsilon \qquad \beta^-(\widetilde{expr} < 0) = \widetilde{expr} \ge \epsilon$$
$$\beta^+(\widetilde{expr} > 0) = \widetilde{expr} > \epsilon \qquad \beta^-(\widetilde{expr} > 0) = \widetilde{expr} \le -\epsilon$$
$$\beta^+(\tilde{\phi}_1 \wedge \tilde{\phi}_2) = \beta^+(\tilde{\phi}_1) \wedge \beta^+(\tilde{\phi}_2) \qquad \beta^-(\tilde{\phi}_1 \wedge \tilde{\phi}_2) = \beta^-(\tilde{\phi}_1) \vee \beta^-(\tilde{\phi}_2)$$
$$\beta^+(\tilde{\phi}_1 \vee \tilde{\phi}_2) = \beta^+(\tilde{\phi}_1) \vee \beta^+(\tilde{\phi}_2) \qquad \beta^-(\tilde{\phi}_1 \vee \tilde{\phi}_2) = \beta^-(\tilde{\phi}_1) \wedge \beta^-(\tilde{\phi}_2)$$
$$\beta^+(\neg\tilde{\phi}) = \beta^-(\tilde{\phi}) \qquad \beta^-(\neg\tilde{\phi}) = \beta^+(\tilde{\phi})$$

Generic inequalities of the form $a < b$ are handled by replacing them with their equivalent sign-test form $a - b < 0$.

The following lemma states that $\beta^+(\tilde{\phi})$ implies both $\tilde{\phi}$ and its real counterpart, while $\beta^-(\tilde{\phi})$ implies both the negation of $\tilde{\phi}$ and the negation of its real counterpart. The proof is available as part of the PVS formalization defined in [32].

Lemma 1. *Given $\tilde{\phi} \in \widetilde{\mathbb{B}}$, let $fv(\tilde{\phi})$ be the set of free variables in $\tilde{\phi}$. For all $\sigma : \{\chi_r(\tilde{x}) \mid \tilde{x} \in fv(\tilde{\phi})\} \to \mathbb{R}, \tilde{\sigma} : fv(\tilde{\phi}) \to \mathbb{F},$ and $\tilde{x} \in fv(\tilde{\phi})$ such that $R(\tilde{\sigma}(\tilde{x})) = \sigma(\chi_r(\tilde{x})), \beta^+$ and β^- satisfy the following properties.*

1. $\widetilde{eval}_{\widetilde{\mathbb{B}}}(\tilde{\sigma}, \beta^+(\tilde{\phi})) \Rightarrow \widetilde{eval}_{\widetilde{\mathbb{B}}}(\tilde{\sigma}, \tilde{\phi}) \wedge eval_{\mathbb{B}}(\sigma, R_{\widetilde{\mathbb{B}}}(\tilde{\phi})).$
2. $\widetilde{eval}_{\widetilde{\mathbb{B}}}(\tilde{\sigma}, \beta^-(\tilde{\phi})) \Rightarrow \widetilde{eval}_{\widetilde{\mathbb{B}}}(\tilde{\sigma}, \neg\tilde{\phi}) \wedge eval_{\mathbb{B}}(\sigma, \neg R_{\widetilde{\mathbb{B}}}(\tilde{\phi})).$

The transformation function $\tau : \mathbb{S} \to \mathbb{S}$ applies β^+ and β^- to the guards in the conditionals. For binary conditional statements, τ is defined as follows.

– If $\tilde{\phi} \neq \beta^+(\tilde{\phi})$ or $\tilde{\phi} \neq \beta^-(\tilde{\phi})$:

$$\tau(if \; \tilde{\phi} \; then \; S_1 \; else \; S_2) =$$
$$if \; \beta^+(\tilde{\phi}) \; then \; \tau(S_1) \; elseif \; \beta^-(\tilde{\phi}) \; then \; \tau(S_2) \; else \; \omega;$$

– If $\tilde{\phi} = \beta^+(\tilde{\phi})$ and $\tilde{\phi} = \beta^-(\tilde{\phi})$:

$$\tau(if \; \tilde{\phi} \; then \; S_1 \; else \; S_2) = if \; \tilde{\phi} \; then \; \tau(S_1) \; else \; \tau(S_2).$$

When the round-off error does not affect the evaluation of the Boolean expression, i.e., $\tilde{\phi} = \beta^+(\tilde{\phi})$ and $\tilde{\phi} = \beta^-(\tilde{\phi})$, the transformation is just applied to the subprograms S_1 and S_2. Otherwise, the *then* branch of the transformed program is taken when $\beta^+(\tilde{\phi})$ is satisfied. From Lemma 1, it follows that both $\tilde{\phi}$ and $R(\tilde{\phi})$ hold and, thus, the *then* branch is taken in both real and floating-point control flows. Similarly, the *else* branch of the transformed program is taken when $\beta^-(\tilde{\phi})$ holds. This means that in the original program the else branch is taken in both real and floating-point control flows. When neither $\beta^+(\tilde{\phi})$ nor $\beta^-(\tilde{\phi})$ is satisfied, a warning ω is issued indicating that floating-point and real flows may diverge. In the case of the for-loop, the transformation is applied to the body of the loop.

$$\tau(for(i_0, i_n, acc_0, \lambda(i, acc).S)) = for(i_0, i_n, acc_0, \lambda(i, acc).\tau(S)). \qquad (3.2)$$

Given a program $P \in \mathbb{P}$, the transformation $\bar{\tau} : \mathbb{P} \to \mathbb{P}$ is defined as follows.

$$\bar{\tau}(P) = \bigcup \{f^{\tau}(\tilde{x}_1, \ldots, \tilde{x}_n, e_1, \ldots, e_m) = \tau(S) \mid f(\tilde{x}_1, \ldots, \tilde{x}_n) = S \in P\}, \quad (3.3)$$

where τ is applied to the body of the function and new arguments $e_1, \ldots, e_m$ are added to represent the round-off error of the arithmetic expressions occurring in each test in the body of S. When either β^+ or β^- is applied to a test in S, e.g. $\widetilde{expr} < 0$, a new fresh variable e is introduced representing the round-off error of the arithmetic expression occurring in the test. This fresh variable becomes a new argument of the function and a pre-condition is imposed stating that $|\widetilde{expr} - R_{\widetilde{\mathbb{A}}}(\widetilde{expr})| \leq e$. In addition, for every function call $g(A_1, \ldots, A_n, e'_1, \ldots, e'_k)$ occurring in S, the error variables of g, $e'_1, \ldots, e'_k$, are added as additional arguments to f.

When a function g is called, it is necessary to check if the returning value is a warning ω. Let $g(A_1, \ldots, A_n)$ be a call to the function $g(x_1, \ldots, x_n) = S$

in the original program with actual parameters $A_1, \ldots, A_n \in \widetilde{\mathbb{A}}$. Additionally, let $g^\tau(x_1, \ldots, x_n, e_1, \ldots, e_m) = \tau(S)$ be the corresponding function declaration in the transformed program such that for all $i = 1 \ldots m$, $\widetilde{expr}_i$ is an arithmetic expression occurring in a transformed test and $|\widetilde{expr}_i - R_{\widetilde{\mathbb{A}}}(\widetilde{expr}_i)| \le e_i$. The transformation of the function call is defined as follows:

$$\tau(g(A_1, \ldots, A_n)) = \textit{if } A_1 = \omega \textit{ then } \omega$$

$$\vdots$$

$$\textit{elsif } A_n = \omega \textit{ then } \omega$$
$$\textit{else } g^\tau(A_1, \ldots, A_n, e'_1, \ldots, e'_m),$$

where for all $i = 1 \ldots m$, e'_i is such that $|\widetilde{expr}_i[x_i/A_i]_{i=1}^n - R_{\widetilde{\mathbb{A}}}(\widetilde{expr}_i[x_i/A_i]_{i=1}^n)| \le e'_i$. In this case, the information regarding the error variables is instantiated with the actual parameters of the function.

The following theorem states the correctness of the program transformation. The transformed program is guaranteed to return either the result of the original floating-point program, when it can be assured that both its real and floating-point flows agree, or a warning ω when these flows may diverge.

Theorem 1 (Program Transformation Correctness). *Given $P \in \mathbb{P}$, for all $f(\tilde{x}_1, \ldots, \tilde{x}_n) = S \in P$, $\sigma : \{x_1 \ldots x_n\} \to \mathbb{R}$, and $\tilde{\sigma} : \{\tilde{x}_1 \ldots \tilde{x}_n\} \to \mathbb{F}$, such that for all $i \in \{1, \ldots, n\}$, $R(\tilde{\sigma}(\tilde{x}_i)) = \sigma(x_i)$:*

$$f^\tau(\tilde{x}_1, \ldots, \tilde{x}_n, e_1, \ldots, e_m) \neq \omega \iff f(x_1, \ldots, x_n) = f^\tau(\tilde{x}_1, \ldots, \tilde{x}_n, e_1, \ldots, e_m)$$

where $f^\tau(\tilde{x}_1, \ldots, \tilde{x}_n, e_1, \ldots, e_m) \in \bar{\tau}(P)$.

Theorem 1 follows from Lemma 1 and the definition of the program transformation $\bar{\tau}$. It has been formally proved in PVS for the particular case of the winding number transformation. A general PVS proof of this statement for an arbitrary program is under development.

4   Test-Stable Version of the Winding Number

The use of floating-point numbers to represent real values introduces test instability in the program defined in Sect. 2. A technique used in PolyCARP to mitigate the uncertainty of floating-point computations in the winding number algorithm is to consider a buffer area around the perimeter of the polygon that is assumed to contain the points that may produce instability. As part of this work, the PRECiSA static analyzer [24,30] is used to validate if a buffer that protects against instability exists. PRECiSA accepts as input a floating-point program and computes a sound over-approximation of the floating-point accumulated round-off error that may occur in each computational path of the program. In addition, the corresponding path conditions are also collected for both stable and

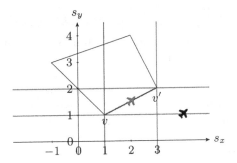

Fig. 3. Points that cause instability in *EdgeContrib* and *WindingNumber*.

unstable cases. When real and floating-point flows diverge, PRECiSA outputs the Boolean conditions under which the instability occurs.

Given the unstable conditions produced by PRECiSA for the winding number algorithm, an over-approximation of the region of instability is generated by using the paving functionality of the Kodiak global optimizer [26]. Concrete examples for these instability conditions are searched in the instability region by using the FPRoCK [29] solver, a tool able to check the satisfiability of mixed real and floating-point Boolean expressions. As an example, consider the edge (v, v'), where $v = (1, 1)$ and $v' = (3, 2)$, in the polygon depicted in Fig. 3. The red lines represent a guaranteed over-approximation of the values for s_x and s_y that may cause instability in the function *EdgeContrib* with respect to the considered edge. The black aircraft denotes a case in which the contribution of the edge (v, v') has a different value in real and floating-point arithmetic. In fact, when $s_x = 4$ and $s_y \approx 1.0000000000000001$, the real function *EdgeContrib* returns -1, indicating that v and v' are located in adjacent quadrants. However, its floating-point counterpart returns 0 meaning that the vertices are located in the same quadrant. The red aircraft represents the point $s_x \approx 2.0000000000000002$, $s_y = 1.5$, for which the main function *WindingNumber* returns 0, i.e., the point is outside, when evaluated with real arithmetics, and it returns 4, i.e., the point is inside, when evaluated in floating-point arithmetic. This figure suggests that simply considering a buffer around the edge is not enough to guarantee the correct behavior of the *EdgeContrib* function since errors in the contribution can happen also when the point is far from the boundaries. It has been conjectured that, for this algorithm, when the checked point is far from the edges of the polygon, the error occurring in one edge is compensated with the error of another edge of the polygon in the computation of the winding number. To the authors' knowledge, no formal proof of this statement exists.

The floating-point program depicted in Fig. 4 is obtained by applying the transformation $\bar{\tau}$ from Sect. 3 to the real-number winding number algorithm presented in Fig. 2. The function *Quadrant*$^\tau$ has two additional arguments, e_x and e_y, modeling the round-off errors of v_x and v_y, respectively. Thus,

$$|v_x - \chi_r(v_x)| \leq e_x, \; |v_y - \chi_r(v_y)| \leq e_y, \text{ and } e_x, e_v \geq 0. \qquad (4.1)$$

The tests are approximated by means of the functions β^+ and β^- by replacing the value 0 with the error variables e_x and e_y.

The function $EdgeContrib^\tau$ contains two calls to $Quadrant^\tau$. Therefore, it is necessary to check if any of these calls return a warning ω. If this is the case, $EdgeContrib^\tau$ also returns ω since a potential instability has been detected in the calculation of $Quadrant^\tau$. The function $EdgeContrib^\tau$ has five additional arguments with respect to its real number counterpart $EdgeContrib$. Besides e_{det} that represents the error of the expression calculating the determinant, the error variables appearing in the calls to $Quadrant^\tau$ are considered: e_{this_x}, e_{this_y}, e_{next_x}, and e_{next_y}. The new parameters are such that:

$$
\begin{aligned}
&|this_x - R_{\widehat{\mathbb{A}}}(this_x)| \leq e_{this_x}, \; |this_y - R_{\widehat{\mathbb{A}}}(this_y)| \leq e_{this_y}, \\
&|next_x - R_{\widehat{\mathbb{A}}}(next_x)| \leq e_{next_x} \; |next_y - R_{\widehat{\mathbb{A}}}(next_y)| \leq e_{next_y} \qquad (4.2) \\
&|det - R_{\widehat{\mathbb{A}}}(det)| \leq e_{det}, \text{ and } e_{this_x}, e_{this_y}, e_{next_x}, e_{next_y}, e_{det} \geq 0.
\end{aligned}
$$

The conditional in the main function $WindingNumber^\tau$ does not introduce any new error variable, therefore just the error parameters in the calls to $EdgeContrib$ are considered. Let $n = size(P_x)$ be the size of the polygon P, and let $fdet$ be the function calculating the determinant, which is defined as follows

$$
\begin{aligned}
fdet(v_x, v_y, v'_x, v'_y, s_x, s_y) = \;\; & ((v_x - s_x) - (v'_x - s_x)) \cdot (v'_y - s_y) \qquad (4.3) \\
& -((v_y - s_y) - (v'_y - s_y)) \cdot (v'_x - s_x).
\end{aligned}
$$

The error variables e_x, e_y, and e_{det} are such that:

$$
\begin{aligned}
&e_x, e_y, e_{det} \geq 0, \\
&\forall i = 0 \ldots n - 1 : \; |(P_x(i) - s_x) - R_{\widehat{\mathbb{A}}}(P_x(i) - s_x)| \leq e_x, \qquad (4.4) \\
&\qquad\qquad\qquad\; |(P_y(i) - s_y) - R_{\widehat{\mathbb{A}}}(P_y(i) - s_y)| \leq e_y, \\
&\forall i = 0 \ldots n - 2 : \; |fdet(P_x(i+1), P_y(i+1), P_x(i), P_y(i), s_x, s_y) \\
&\qquad\qquad\qquad - R_{\widehat{\mathbb{A}}}(fdet(P_x(i+1), P_y(i+1), P_x(i), P_y(i), s_x, s_y))| \leq e_{det}, \\
&\qquad\qquad\qquad |fdet(P_x(0), P_y(0), P_x(n-1), P_y(n-1), s_x, s_y) \\
&\qquad\qquad\qquad - R_{\widehat{\mathbb{A}}}(fdet(P_x(0), P_y(0), P_x(n-1), P_y(n-1), s_x, s_y))| \leq e_{det}.
\end{aligned}
$$

5   Verification Approach

This section presents the approach used to obtain a formally verified test-stable C implementation of the winding number algorithm that uses floating-point numbers. The toolchain is comprised of the PVS interactive prover, the static analyzer PRECiSA, and the Frama-C analyzer [20]. The input is a real-valued program P expressed in the PVS specification language. The output is a C implementation of P that correctly detects and corrects unstable tests. An overview of the approach is depicted in Fig. 5.

$$Quadrant^\tau(v_x, v_y, e_x, e_y) = \text{if } v_x \geq e_x \wedge v_y \geq e_y \text{ then } 1$$
$$\text{elsif } v_x < -e_x \wedge v_y \geq e_y \text{ then } 2$$
$$\text{elsif } v_x < -e_x \wedge v_y < -e_y \text{ then } 3$$
$$\text{elsif } v_x \geq e_x \wedge v_y < -e_y \text{ then } 4$$
$$\text{else } \omega$$

$$EdgeContrib^\tau(v_x, v_y, v'_x, v'_y, s_x, s_y, e_{this_x}, e_{this_y}, e_{next_x}, e_{next_y}, e_{det}) =$$
$$\text{let } this_x = v_x - s_x, this_y = v_y - s_y, next_x = v'_x - s_x, next_y = v'_y - s_y,$$
$$dist_x = next_x - this_x, dist_y = next_y - this_y, det = dist_x \cdot this_y - dist_y \cdot this_x,$$
$$q_{this} = Quadrant^\tau(this_x, this_y, e_{this_x}, e_{this_y}),$$
$$q_{next} = Quadrant^\tau(next_x, next_y, e_{next_x}, e_{next_y}) \text{ in}$$
$$\text{if } q_{this} = \omega \text{ or } q_{next} = \omega \text{ then } \omega$$
$$\text{elsif } q_{this} = q_{next} \text{ then } 0$$
$$\text{elsif } q_{next} - 1 = \mathsf{mod}\,(q_{this}, 4) \text{ then } 1$$
$$\text{elsif } q_{this} - 1 = \mathsf{mod}\,(q_{next}, 4) \text{ then } -1$$
$$\text{elsif } (det \leq -e_{det}) \text{ then } 2$$
$$\text{elsif } (det > e_{det}) \text{ then } -2$$
$$\text{else } \omega$$

$$WindingNumber^\tau(P_x, P_y, s_x, s_y, i, e_x, e_y, e_{det}) =$$
$$\text{if } i < n - 1 \text{ then}$$
$$(\text{if } EdgeContrib^\tau(P_x(i), P_y(i), P_x(i+1), P_y(i+1), s_x, s_y, e_x, e_y, e_x, e_y, e_{det}) = \omega$$
$$\text{then } \omega$$
$$\text{else } EdgeContrib^\tau(P_x(i), P_y(i), P_x(i+1), P_y(i+1), s_x, s_y, e_x, e_y, e_x, e_y, e_{det})$$
$$+ WindingNumber^\tau(P_x, P_y, s_x, s_y, i+1, e_x, e_y, e_x, e_y, e_{det}))$$
$$\text{else}$$
$$(\text{if } EdgeContrib^\tau(P_x(i), P_y(i), P_x(0), P_y(0), s_x, s_y, e_x, e_y, e_x, e_y, e_{det}) = \omega$$
$$\text{then } \omega$$
$$\text{else } EdgeContrib^\tau(P_x(i), P_y(i), P_x(0), P_y(0), s_x, s_y, e_x, e_y, e_x, e_y, e_{det})$$

Fig. 4. Pseudo-code on floating-point arithmetic of the transformed winding number algorithm

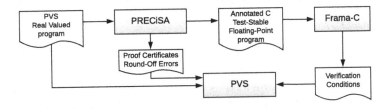

Fig. 5. Verification approach.

As already mentioned, PRECiSA is a static analyzer that computes an over-estimation of the round-off error that may occur in a program. In addition, it automatically generates a PVS proof certificate ensuring the correctness of the computed bound. In this work, PRECiSA is extended to implement the transformation defined in Sect. 3 and to generate the corresponding C code. Given a desired floating-point format (single or double precision), PRECiSA is used to convert the PVS real-number version of the winding-number algorithm defined in Sect. 2 into a floating-point program. This is done by replacing all the real operators with their floating-point counterpart and by approximating the real variables and constants with their floating-point representation. The integer operations, variables, and constants are left unchanged since they do not carry round-off errors. Subsequently, the transformation presented in Sect. 3 is applied. To facilitate the translation from PVS to C syntax, the function $WindingNumber$ has been reformulated using the for-iterate scheme introduced in Eq. (3.1) that emulates an imperative for-loop in a functional setting.

$$
\begin{aligned}
WindingNumber&(P_x, P_y, s_x, s_y, i) = \\
&for(0, size(P_x) - 1, 0, \lambda i, acc. \ \ if \ i < size(P_x) - 2 \\
&\quad then \ acc + EdgeContrib(P_x(i), P_y(i), P_x(i+1), P_y(i+1), s_x, s_y) \\
&\quad else \ \ acc + EdgeContrib(P_x(i), P_y(i), P_x(0), P_y(0), s_x, s_y)).
\end{aligned}
$$
$$(5.1)$$

The result of the transformation is the program shown in Fig. 4 where a for-loop replaces the recursive call in the main function $WindingNumber^\tau$.

The transformed program is then converted in C syntax with ACSL annotations. The ANSI/ISO C Specification Langage (ACSL [1]) is a behavioral specification language for C programs centered on the notion of function contract. For each function in the transformed program, a C procedure is automatically generated. In addition, the functions in the original version of the winding number algorithm, defined in Sect. 2, are rephrased as ACSL axiomatic logic functions. For each function, ACSL preconditions are added to relate C floating-point expressions with their corresponding logic real-valued counterpart through the error variable representing their round-off error. As mentioned in Sect. 4, a fresh error variable e is introduced for each floating-point arithmetic expression $\widetilde{expr}$ occurring in the conditional tests. For each new error variable, a precondition stating that $|\widetilde{expr} - R_{\widetilde{\mathbb{A}}}(\widetilde{expr})| \leq e$ is added.

The loop invariant of the function $WindingNumber^\tau$ is specified as an ACSL annotation before the for-loop as follows

$$
\begin{aligned}
\forall i = 0 \ldots size(P_x). \ \ &if \ acc = 0 \ then \ 0 \\
&else \ acc = WindingNumber^\tau(P_x, P_y, s_x, s_y, i - 1, e_x, e_y, e_{det}).
\end{aligned}
$$

This information is required in order to prove the correctness of each iteration of the for-loop and has to be provided as an input to PRECiSA together with the input program. In addition, PRECiSA identifies the for-loop variant $size(P_x) - i$ that is also needed for the verification of the loop. For each function, a post-condition is added stating that if the result is different from ω, then the result of the C function is the same as the real-valued logic function that corresponds to the initial PVS specification.

To verify the correctness of the C code generated by PRECiSA with respect to the accompanying ACSL contracts, an extension of the Weakest Precondition (WP) plug-in of Frama-C has been developed. This plug-in implements the weakest precondition calculus for ACSL annotations of C programs. For each ACSL annotation, the plug-in generates a set of verification conditions (VCs) that can be discharged by a suite of external provers. In this work, support for generating PVS VCs is added to the Frama-C/WP plug-in. This extension links the generated VCs with the formal certificates generated by PRECiSA regarding the round-off errors and the original PVS formalization of the winding number. Frama-C/WP generates a set of PVS declarations from the ACSL logic definitions. These declarations are proved to be mathematically equivalent to the original winding number PVS formalization (Fig. 2) in the PVS theorem prover. In addition, Frama-C/WP computes a set of verification conditions from the pre and post conditions stating the correctness of the C program with respect to the ACSL logic definitions. The verification conditions generated for the functions $Quadrant^\tau$ and $EdgeContrib^\tau$ are formalized in the following lemmas.

Lemma 2. *Let* $v_x, v_y, e_x, e_y \in \widetilde{\mathbb{V}}$ *such that* $|v_x - \chi_r(v_x)| \leq e_x$ *and* $|v_y - \chi_r(v_y)| \leq e_y$, *if* $Quadrant^\tau(v_x, v_y, e_x, e_y) \neq \omega$, *then* $Quadrant(v_x, v_y) = Quadrant^\tau$ (v_x, v_y, e_x, e_y).

Lemma 3. *Let* $v_x, v_y, v'_x, v'_y, s_x, s_y, e_{this_x}, e_{this_y}, e_{next_x}, e_{next_y}, e_{det} \in \widetilde{\mathbb{V}}$ *such that the inequalities in Eq. (4.2) hold.*

If $EdgeContrib^\tau(v_x, v_y, v'_x, v'_y, s_x, s_y, e_{this_x}, e_{this_y}, e_{next_x}, e_{next_y}, e_{det}) \neq \omega$, *then* $EdgeContrib(v_x, v_y, v'_x, v'_y, s_x, s_y) = EdgeContrib^\tau(v_x, v_y, v'_x, v'_y, s_x, s_y, e_{this_x}, e_{this_y}, e_{next_x}, e_{next_y}, e_{det})$.

The following theorem summarizes the verification conditions generated for the main function $WindingNumber^\tau$. All these verification conditions are proven with the help of the PVS theorem prover[4].

Theorem 2. *Let* $v_x, v_y, v'_x, v'_y, s_x, s_y, e_x, e_y, e_{det} \in \widetilde{\mathbb{V}}$ *and* $P = \langle P_x, P_y \rangle$ *a polygon of size* n *such that for all* $i = 0 \dots n - 1$ $P_x(i), P_y(i) \in \widetilde{\mathbb{V}}$ *and the inequalities in Eq. (4.4) hold.*

If $WindingNumber^\tau(P_x, P_y, s_x, s_y, i, e_x, e_y, e_x, e_y, e_{det}) \neq \omega$, *then* $WindingNumber(P_x, P_y, s_x, s_y, i) = WindingNumber^\tau(P_x, P_y, s_x, s_y, i, e_x, e_y, e_{det})$.

The parameters representing the round-off errors of the arithmetic expressions occurring in the body of each function can be instantiated with concrete numerical values. Given numerical bounds for the input variables, the numerical error values are automatically computed by PRECiSA by means of the Kodiak

---

[4] The PVS verification conditions generated by Frama-C and their proofs can be found at https://shemesh.larc.nasa.gov/fm/PolyCARP.

global optimizer [26]. For example, assuming $P_x(i), s_x \in [-1000, 1000]$ for all $i = 0..size(P_x)$, PRECiSA computes the upper bound $3.637978807091714 \times 10^{-12}$ for the error variable e_x meaning that $|(P_x(i) - s_x) - R_{\tilde{\mathbb{A}}}(P_x(i) - s_x)| \leq 3.637978807091714 \times 10^{-12}$. PRECiSA also emits the proof certificates ensuring that the numerical result computed by Kodiak is a correct over-approximation of the round-off error occurring in the considered expression.

The PRECiSA certificates prove the correctness of the round-off error bounds used in the program transformation. They are essential to ensure that the transformed program is correct, i.e., the Boolean abstractions β^+ and β^- are correctly over-estimating the conditional tests and, thus, Lemma 1 holds. Additionally, they are used to prove the verification conditions generated by Frama-C/WP, for instance, the preconditions on the error defined in Eqs. (4.2) and (4.3).

6   Related Work

Several techniques and tools have been developed to formally verify properties of C programs related to floating-point numbers. Fluctuat [18] and Astrée [12] are commercial tools based on abstract interpretation [11], which have been successfully used to verify and analyze numerical properties for industrial and safety-critical C code, including aerospace software. Fluctuat is a static analyzer that computes round-off error bounds for C programs with annotations. Astrée is a fully-automatic static analyzer that uses sound floating-point abstract domains [9,23] to uncover the presence of run-time exceptions such as division by zero and under and over-flows. Astrée has been applied to automatically check the absence of runtime errors associated with floating-point computations in aerospace control software [2]. For instance, the fly-by-wire primary software of commercial airplanes is verified with the help of Astrée [14]. Moreover, Astrée and Fluctuat have been used in combination to analyze on-board software acting in the Monitoring and Safing Unit of the ATV space vehicle [8]. In contrast to the technique presented in this paper, the above-mentioned approaches do not provide formal proof certificates that can be discharged in an external prover. This is particularly useful for safety-critical systems since the proof certificates improve the trustworthiness of the approach. In addition, in contrast with the tools used in this paper, Fluctuat and Astrée are not open-source.

Caduceus [5,16] is a tool that produces verification conditions from annotated C code with the help of the platform Why [3]. Similarly, in [6], a chain of tools composed of Frama-C, the Jessie plug-in [22], and Why is used to automatically generate verification conditions, which are checked by several external provers. These approaches were used to formally verify wave propagation differential equations [4], a pairwise state-based conflict detection algorithm [17], and numerical properties of industrial software related to inertial navigation [21]. In [31], a combination of Frama-C and PVS was used to verify a numerically improved version of the Compact Position Reporting (CPR) algorithm, a key component of the ADS-B protocol allowing aircraft to share their position. In this case, Frama-C was used to generate verification conditions discharged using the SMT solver Alt-Ergo [10] and the prover Gappa [15]. PVS was employed to prove the equivalence between the original implementation of the CPR algorithm and the improved one. In contrast to [31], the verified C code presented in this paper is automatically generated from the PVS specification. None of the approaches mentioned before tackle the problem of detecting unstable tests.

7   Conclusion

In this paper, a formal approach is proposed to generate and to verify a test-stable version of the winding number algorithm. This version is obtained by applying an extension of the program transformation defined in [30] that over-approximates the Boolean expressions occurring in conditional statements. The over-approximation soundly handles round-off errors that may occur in the numerical computation of the expression. A warning is issued when real and floating-point flows may diverge. Otherwise, the transformed program is guaranteed to return the same output with respect to the original algorithm. The static analyzer PRECiSA [24,30] is enhanced with a module implementing this transformation and with a C/ACSL code generator. Thus, given the PVS program specification of the winding number assuming real numbers arithmetics, PRECiSA automatically generates its test-stable floating-point version in C syntax enriched with ACSL annotations. As a future work, this approach will be extended to handle generic algorithms involving non-recursive function calls, for loops, conditionals, and let-in expressions.

The generated C implementation of the winding number is analyzed within the Frama-C tool suite. In this work, the Frama-C/WP [20] plug-in is extended to generate verification conditions in PVS syntax. These verification conditions state that the transformed floating-point version of the winding number is correct with respect to its real-valued specification, meaning that if the C implementation answers that a point is inside (or outside) a polygon the same answer would be obtained in the ideal real number implementation of the original algorithm. The verification conditions generated by Frama-C are proven correct within the PVS theorem prover.

The verification of the correctness of the transformed C program relies on three different tools: the PVS interactive prover, the Frama-C analyzer, and PRECiSA. All of these tools are based on rigorous mathematical foundations and have been used in the verification of industrial and safety-critical systems. The C floating-point transformed program, the PVS verification conditions, and the round-off errors bounds are automatically generated. However, the verification approach proposed in this work requires some level of expertise for proving the PVS verification conditions generated by Frama-C. In the future, the authors plan to define proof strategies that automatically discharge these PVS verification conditions.

References

1. Baudin, P., et al.: ACSL: ANSI/ISO C Specification Language, version 1.12 (2016)
2. Bertrane, J., et al.: Static analysis and verification of aerospace software by abstract interpretation. Found. Trends Prog. Lang. **2**(2–3), 71–190 (2015)
3. Bobot, F., Filliâtre, J.C., Marché, C., Paskevich, A.: Let's verify this with Why3. Int. J. Softw. Tools Technol. Transf. **17**(6), 709–727 (2015)
4. Boldo, S., Clément, F., Filliâtre, J.C., Mayero, M., Melquiond, G., Weis, P.: Wave equation numerical resolution: a comprehensive mechanized proof of a C program. J. Autom. Reasoning **50**(4), 423–456 (2013)
5. Boldo, S., Filliâtre, J.C.: Formal verification of floating-point programs. In: Proceedings of ARITH18 2007, pp. 187–194. IEEE Computer Society (2007)
6. Boldo, S., Marché, C.: Formal verification of numerical programs: from C annotated programs to mechanical proofs. Math. Comput. Sci. **5**(4), 377–393 (2011)
7. Boldo, S., Muñoz, C.: A high-level formalization of floating-point numbers in PVS. Technical Report CR-2006-214298, NASA (2006)
8. Bouissou, O., et al.: Space software validation using abstract interpretation. In: Proceedings of the International Space System Engineering Conference, Data Systems in Aerospace, DASIA 2009, pp. 1–7. ESA publications (2009)
9. Chen, L., Miné, A., Cousot, P.: A sound floating-point polyhedra abstract domain. In: Ramalingam, G. (ed.) APLAS 2008. LNCS, vol. 5356, pp. 3–18. Springer, Heidelberg (2008). https://doi.org/10.1007/978-3-540-89330-1_2
10. Conchon, S., Contejean, E., Kanig, J., Lescuyer, S.: CC(X): semantic combination of congruence closure with solvable theories. Electron. Notes Theoret. Comput. Sci. **198**(2), 51–69 (2008)
11. Cousot, P., Cousot, R.: Abstract interpretation: a unified lattice model for static analysis of programs by construction or approximation of fixpoints. In: Conference Record of tha 4th ACM Symposium on Principles of Programming Languages, POPL 1977, pp. 238–252. ACM (1977)
12. Cousot, P., et al.: The ASTREÉ analyzer. In: Sagiv, M. (ed.) ESOP 2005. LNCS, vol. 3444, pp. 21–30. Springer, Heidelberg (2005). https://doi.org/10.1007/978-3-540-31987-0_3
13. Daumas, M., Rideau, L., Théry, L.: A generic library for floating-point numbers and its application to exact computing. In: Boulton, R.J., Jackson, P.B. (eds.) TPHOLs 2001. LNCS, vol. 2152, pp. 169–184. Springer, Heidelberg (2001). https://doi.org/10.1007/3-540-44755-5_13
14. Delmas, D., Souyris, J.: Astrée: from research to industry. In: Nielson, H.R., Filé, G. (eds.) SAS 2007. LNCS, vol. 4634, pp. 437–451. Springer, Heidelberg (2007). https://doi.org/10.1007/978-3-540-74061-2_27
15. de Dinechin, F., Lauter, C., Melquiond, G.: Certifying the floating-point implementation of an elementary function using Gappa. IEEE Trans. Comput. **60**(2), 242–253 (2011)
16. Filliâtre, J.-C., Marché, C.: Multi-prover verification of C programs. In: Davies, J., Schulte, W., Barnett, M. (eds.) ICFEM 2004. LNCS, vol. 3308, pp. 15–29. Springer, Heidelberg (2004). https://doi.org/10.1007/978-3-540-30482-1_10
17. Goodloe, A.E., Muñoz, C., Kirchner, F., Correnson, L.: Verification of numerical programs: from real numbers to floating point numbers. In: Brat, G., Rungta, N., Venet, A. (eds.) NFM 2013. LNCS, vol. 7871, pp. 441–446. Springer, Heidelberg (2013). https://doi.org/10.1007/978-3-642-38088-4_31

18. Goubault, E., Putot, S.: Static analysis of numerical algorithms. In: Yi, K. (ed.) SAS 2006. LNCS, vol. 4134, pp. 18–34. Springer, Heidelberg (2006). https://doi.org/10.1007/11823230_3
19. IEEE: IEEE standard for binary floating-point arithmetic. Technical report, Institute of Electrical and Electronics Engineers (2008)
20. Kirchner, F., Kosmatov, N., Prevosto, V., Signoles, J., Yakobowski, B.: Frama-C: a software analysis perspective. Formal Aspects Comput. 27(3), 573–609 (2015)
21. Marché, C.: Verification of the functional behavior of a floating-point program: an industrial case study. Sci. Comput. Prog. 96, 279–296 (2014)
22. Marché, C., Moy, Y.: The Jessie Plugin for Deductive Verification in Frama-C (2017)
23. Miné, A.: Relational abstract domains for the detection of floating-point run-time errors. In: Schmidt, D. (ed.) ESOP 2004. LNCS, vol. 2986, pp. 3–17. Springer, Heidelberg (2004). https://doi.org/10.1007/978-3-540-24725-8_2
24. Moscato, M., Titolo, L., Dutle, A., Muñoz, C.A.: Automatic estimation of verified floating-point round-off errors via static analysis. In: Tonetta, S., Schoitsch, E., Bitsch, F. (eds.) SAFECOMP 2017. LNCS, vol. 10488, pp. 213–229. Springer, Cham (2017). https://doi.org/10.1007/978-3-319-66266-4_14
25. Narkawicz, A., Hagen, G.: Algorithms for collision detection between a point and a moving polygon, with applications to aircraft weather avoidance. In: Proceedings of the AIAA Aviation Conference (2016)
26. Narkawicz, A., Muñoz, C.: A formally verified generic branching algorithm for global optimization. In: Cohen, E., Rybalchenko, A. (eds.) VSTTE 2013. LNCS, vol. 8164, pp. 326–343. Springer, Heidelberg (2014). https://doi.org/10.1007/978-3-642-54108-7_17
27. Narkawicz, A., Muñoz, C., Dutle, A.: The MINERVA software development process. In: 6th Workshop on Automated Formal Methods, AFM 2017 (2017)
28. Owre, S., Rushby, J.M., Shankar, N.: PVS: a prototype verification system. In: Kapur, D. (ed.) CADE 1992. LNCS, vol. 607, pp. 748–752. Springer, Heidelberg (1992). https://doi.org/10.1007/3-540-55602-8_217
29. Salvia, R., Titolo, L., Feliú, M., Moscato, M., Muñoz, C.,Rakamaric, Z.: A mixed real and floating-point solver. In: 11th Annual NASAFormal Methods Symposium (NFM 2019) (2019)
30. Titolo, L., Feliú, M.A., Moscato, M., Muñoz, C.A.: An abstract interpretation framework for the round-off error analysis of floating-point programs. Verification, Model Checking, and Abstract Interpretation. LNCS, vol. 10747, pp. 516–537. Springer, Cham (2018). https://doi.org/10.1007/978-3-319-73721-8_24
31. Titolo, L., Moscato, M.M., Muñoz, C.A., Dutle, A., Bobot, F.: A formally verified floating-point implementation of the compact position reporting algorithm. In: Havelund, K., Peleska, J., Roscoe, B., de Vink, E. (eds.) FM 2018. LNCS, vol. 10951, pp. 364–381. Springer, Cham (2018). https://doi.org/10.1007/978-3-319-95582-7_22
32. Titolo, L., Muñoz, C.A., Feliú, M.A., Moscato, M.M.: Eliminating unstable tests in floating-point programs. In: Mesnard, F., Stuckey, P.J. (eds.) LOPSTR 2018. LNCS, vol. 11408, pp. 169–183. Springer, Cham (2019). https://doi.org/10.1007/978-3-030-13838-7_10

Formally Verified Roundoff Errors Using SMT-based Certificates and Subdivisions

Joachim Bard, Heiko Becker$^{(\boxtimes)}$, and Eva Darulova

MPI-SWS, Saarland Informatics Campus, Saarbrücken, Germany
{jbard,hbecker,eva}@mpi-sws.org

Abstract. When compared to idealized, real-valued arithmetic, finite precision arithmetic introduces unavoidable errors, for which numerous tools compute sound upper bounds. To ensure soundness, providing formal guarantees on these complex tools is highly valuable.

In this paper we extend one such formally verified tool, FloVer. First, we extend FloVer with an SMT-based domain using results from an external SMT solver as an oracle. Second, we implement interval subdivision on top of the existing analyses. Our evaluation shows that these extensions allow FloVer to efficiently certify more precise bounds for nonlinear expressions.

Keywords: Coq · Roundoff error · Finite-precision · SMT · Subdivision

1 Introduction

Floating-point or fixed-point arithmetic are commonly used representations of the reals in today's computers. They necessarily only provide a discrete approximation of infinite-precision reals, resulting in roundoff errors. These errors are introduced by arithmetic operations and are individually small, but can accumulate during the course of a computation. For safety-critical systems, it is thus imperative to soundly bound the overall roundoff error of a program.

A number of automated static analysis tools have been developed in the past for computing roundoff error bounds [4,6,9,10,13,14]. However, their analyses and implementations are complex, raising questions of correctness. Most of these tools thus generate certificates which can be independently and formally verified by a theorem prover such as Coq [1], PVS [12] or HOL4 [2].

One tool to check certificates is FloVer [3], an open source certificate checker for roundoff errors computed using a dataflow static analysis. FloVer's *checker functions* are formally verified in Coq and HOL4 and check roundoff error bounds computed by external tools for floating-point as well as fixed-point arithmetic. The current version of FloVer uses the interval [11] and affine arithmetic (AA) [8] abstract domains, which are efficient and accurate for linear expressions, but which suffer from over-approximations for nonlinear arithmetic programs.

© Springer Nature Switzerland AG 2019
M. H. ter Beek et al. (Eds.): FM 2019, LNCS 11800, pp. 38–44, 2019.
https://doi.org/10.1007/978-3-030-30942-8_4

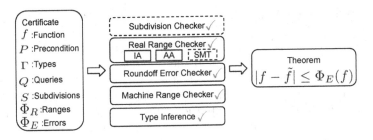

Fig. 1. Overview of FloVer's infrastructure

In this paper, we describe two new approaches to certify tighter error bounds and implement them in FloVer's Coq formalization. First, we implement an SMT-based range estimation [5] (Sect. 2) which computes tighter enclosures for expressions using a trusted SMT solver as an oracle. Second, interval subdivision [4,9] (Sect. 2) further increases analysis precision by splitting input ranges into disjoint subintervals and by analyzing them separately. These techniques are employed by unverified state-of-the-art tools [4,9] but were beyond the scope of formally verified checkers. Our extensions presented in this paper thus close the gap between the errors computed from state-of-the-art tools and what can be certified. Our experimental evaluation (Sect. 3) shows that our extensions increase FloVer's accuracy on a standard benchmark set of nonlinear expressions, while maintaining a reasonable certificate checking time. Our implementation is available online at https://gitlab.mpi-sws.org/AVA/FloVer/tree/SMT_Subdiv.

Related Work. PRECiSA [14], FPTaylor [13], and real2float [10] provide certificate checkers like FloVer, verifying roundoff error bounds encoded by an untrusted static analysis. Certificates of PRECiSA are written in PVS, FPTaylor's in HOL-Light, and real2float's and FloVer's in Coq. Unlike FloVer, their roundoff error verification is based on global optimization. This approach can often verify tighter error bounds than a dataflow analysis, but is currently only applicable to floating-point arithmetic computations and not fixed-point arithmetic. PRECiSA in addition handles loops by widening, and conditional branches by path-by-path error analysis, which are orthogonal to the error estimation of straight-line code which we focus on in this paper.

Gappa [6] is a general purpose finite-precision analysis tool inferring roundoff error bounds, but is not limited to only those. It bounds roundoff errors with a dataflow analysis like FloVer's using intervals as the abstract domain. A certificate in Gappa is encoded as a chain of lemmas proven at checking time, whereas FloVer encodes certificates as a call to a function proven sound once and forall. Gappa already supports subdivisions and, as it emits Coq proofs, we believe that the SMT extension in this paper can also improve its computed error bounds.

2 Extensions to FloVer

Figure 1 illustrates FloVer's *modular* checker structure. Each checker function is first proven correct individually and the separate proofs are then combined into an overall soundness theorem which states that if all checker functions are successful, the roundoff error bound encoded in the certificate is sound. This design facilitates relatively easy extensions, and allows for efficient certificate checking; verifying a certificate does not require any formal proofs at certificate checking time, or formal proof expertise by the user.

FloVer supports arithmetic expressions $(+, -, *, /)$, a fused-multiply-add operation and let-bindings. As other dataflow analysis based tools, FloVer splits checking of roundoff error bounds into checking of real-valued range bounds (Real Range Checker in Fig. 1) and checking of error bounds (Roundoff Error Checker). Roundoff error bounds are checked for mixed-precision programs with 16, 32 and 64 bit floating-points, or arbitrary fixed-point precisions. The type checker (Type Inference) verifies that all mixed-precision type assignments are valid. Component Machine Range Checker checks that evaluation results can be represented in their inferred type, i.e. no overflow occurs.

A certificate checked by FloVer encodes only the minimum necessary information: the analyzed expression f, range (Φ_R) and roundoff error bounds (Φ_E) inferred by a static analysis tool, the precondition constraining input variables (P), a type assignment Γ, the queries to the SMT solver (Q) and the interval subdivisions (S). Our extensions are marked in Fig. 1 by dashed lines. We implement SMT-based range estimation as a real-valued range analysis (Real Range Checker). Interval subdivision is implemented on top of the existing components (Subdivision Checker) and reuses FloVer's existing checker functions internally.

Extension 1: Tighter Ranges using SMT Oracles. Our first extension to FloVer introduces an abstract domain for computing tighter range bounds based on the existing analysis implemented in the static analyzer Daisy [5]. This analysis tracks ranges as plain intervals and achieves better accuracy by using a nonlinear decision procedure provided by an SMT solver to track nonlinear correlations, which cannot be captured by the existing interval and AA-based domains.

Given an expression e, a range bound $[e_{lo}, e_{hi}]$ is first computed using interval arithmetic. Next, the analysis attempts to tighten e_{lo} and e_{hi} separately. For the lower bound, it queries an SMT solver whether e, constrained by the precondition, can take a value which is smaller than some e'_{lo} with $e_{lo} < e'_{lo}$. If the query is unsatisfiable, the tighter bound $[e'_{lo}, e_{hi}]$ is sound, and tightenting repeats a predetermined number of times using a binary search. Tightening of the upper bound is analogous. If the solver times out, the bound is not tightened.

The SMT-based analysis in Daisy makes multiple queries to the SMT solver for tightening a single range. Of these queries, only the last unsatisfiable one for each lower and upper bound is relevant for correctness. We thus instrument Daisy such that these last queries are saved and encoded in a certificate. We do not otherwise modify Daisy.

During certificate checking, we treat the results of SMT queries as oracles. Verifying the query results themselves would require proof reconstruction which current SMT solvers do not support due to the complexity of nonlinear arithmetic. Instead, we trust the SMT solver, but keep the amount of queries that must be trusted to a minimum by storing only the last queries.

We implemented the SMT component of the Real Range Checker from Fig. 1 in the checker function validSMTBounds(f, P, Φ_R, Q) by structural recursion on the AST of the analyzed expression f. For each subexpression of f, a sound interval enclosure is computed first using existing FloVer infrastructure. If Q contains SMT queries which were used to improve the lower or upper bound, validSMTBounds checks first that the queries were correctly encoded by Daisy (we check that the expression and precondition encoded in the query match the currently analyzed expression and the precondition given in the certificate). If this check succeeds, the function checks that the range bound can be tightened to the new bound encoded in the query. Finally, FloVer checks that the inferred range bound is contained in the interval enclosure encoded in the analysis result Φ_R. The soundness proof of validSMTBounds shows that if the checker succeeds, the range bound encoded in Φ_R is valid.

Extension 2: Interval Subdivision. The second analysis we implement in FloVer is interval subdivision, which splits the input domain into equally-sized subdomains. The range and roundoff error analyses are then run on each subdomain separately and joined together into a global analysis result. The overapproximations on each subdomain tend to be smaller, which increases the overall tightness of range and error bounds.

Checker function validSubdivs(f, P, Φ_R, Φ_E, S) implements checking of interval subdivisions, where S is a list of subdomains, represented as quadruples $(P^S, \Phi_R^S, \Phi_E^S, Q^S)$. The checker function checks correctness for each subdomain in S by calling the existing certificate checker on f, P^S, Φ_R^S, Φ_E^S, and Q^S. validSubdivs checks that the global analysis results Φ_R and Φ_E are upper bounds for the current subdivision results Φ_R^S and Φ_E^S for each subexpression of f. Performing this check on every element of S proves correctness of the global analysis results Φ_R and Φ_E.

Finally, validSubdivs checks that the subdomains (P^S) cover the overall input domain (encoded in P), to ensure that Daisy did not forget a subdomain in the roundoff error computation. The check iterates over the free variables of f. For each free variable x and subinterval $[x_{lo}, x_{hi}]$ we check that there exist subdomains where P^S maps x to $[x_{lo}, x_{hi}]$ and the union of these subdomains covers the full global range constraint for all other free variables. This essentially checks for each free variable that Daisy computed the correct cartesian product.

The soundness theorem for both our extensions is:

Theorem 1. *Let f, P, Φ_R, Φ_E, and S be as before. If for all $(P^S, \Phi_R^S, \Phi_E^S, Q^S)$ in S the queries encoded in Q^S are unsatisfiable, and validSubdivs(f, P, Φ_R, Φ_E, S) succeeds, there exists an idealized real-value v_R, a finite-precision value v_F and a precision m, such that f evaluates to v_R under an idealized real-valued semantics, v_F has precision m, and f evaluates to v_F under finite-precision semantics. Furthermore, $\Phi_E(f)$ is an upper bound to the roundoff error $|v_R - v_F|$.*

3 Experiments

We have evaluated our extension of FloVer to check whether it can verify more precise error bounds with reasonable certificate checking times. As neither SMT-based techniques nor interval subdivisions improve precision for linear benchmarks our evaluation focuses on nonlinear ones. For our experiments we used a Debian 9 machine with a 3.3 GHz four-core Intel i5-6600 processor and 16 GB of main memory. Daisy uses Z3 [7] for the SMT-based analysis. When using interval subdivision we split at most 3 input ranges into 5 subintervals each, resulting in at most 125 subdomains.

Table 1. Roundoff errors verified by FloVer and FPTaylor

Benchmark	Interval	Affine	SMT	Subdiv	SMT & Subdiv	Cmp.	FPTaylor
Bspline0	2.41e-16	2.41e-16	2.41e-16	2.41e-16	2.41e-16	1.00	**1.39e-16**
Bspline1	1.52e-15	1.60e-15	1.35e-15	1.28e-15	1.19e-15	0.79	**5.15e-16**
Bspline2	1.41e-15	1.45e-15	1.19e-15	1.26e-15	1.16e-15	0.83	**5.43e-16**
Bspline3	1.30e-16	1.30e-16	1.30e-16	1.30e-16	1.30e-16	1.00	**8.33e-17**
Doppler	6.53e-13	5.61e-12	6.12e-13	3.03e-13	3.03e-13	0.46	**1.22e-13**
DopplerFMA	6.41e-13	5.51e-12	6.00e-13	2.99e-13	2.99e-13	0.47	**1.21e-13**
Floudas26	1.05e-12	1.07e-12	8.13e-13	1.04e-12	$\perp^\%$	0.77	**7.74e-13**
Floudas33	7.29e-13	7.29e-13	**4.93e-13**	7.29e-13	$\perp^\%$	0.68	6.20e-13
Floudas34	3.11e-15	3.11e-15	3.11e-15	3.11e-15	$\perp^\%$	1.00	**2.22e-15**
Floudas46	1.55e-15	1.55e-15	1.55e-15	1.55e-15	$\perp^\%$	1.00	1.55e-15
Floudas47	2.80e-14	2.85e-14	2.30e-14	2.73e-14	$\perp^\%$	0.82	**1.67e-14**
Floudas1	7.29e-13	7.29e-13	**4.93e-13**	7.29e-13	$\perp^\%$	0.68	5.76e-13
Himmilbeau	3.42e-12	3.42e-12	1.50e-12	1.50e-12	1.50e-12	0.44	**1.00e-12**
InvPendulum	5.37e-14	5.37e-14	5.37e-14	5.37e-14	5.37e-14	1.00	**3.84e-14**
JetEngine	$\perp^0$	$\perp^0$	1.67e-08	$\perp^0$	1.87e-10	—	**1.72e-11**
Kepler0	1.85e-13	1.77e-13	1.77e-13	1.70e-13	1.65e-13	0.93	**7.71e-14**
Kepler1	8.97e-13	8.21e-13	8.47e-13	7.07e-13	6.63e-13	0.81	**3.04e-13**
Kepler2	4.13e-12	3.81e-12	3.77e-12	3.75e-12	3.52e-12	0.93	**1.60e-12**
RigidBody1	5.58e-13	5.58e-13	5.58e-13	5.58e-13	5.58e-13	1.00	**2.95e-13**
RigidBody2	6.57e-11	6.57e-11	6.57e-11	6.57e-11	6.57e-11	1.00	**3.61e-11**
Verhulst	8.34e-16	8.34e-16	8.34e-16	7.01e-16	7.01e-16	0.84	**3.24e-16**
PredatorPrey	3.40e-16	3.47e-16	3.40e-16	3.20e-16	3.20e-16	0.94	**1.84e-16**
CarbonGas	5.69e-08	5.67e-08	5.49e-08	2.07e-08	2.03e-08	0.36	**9.13e-09**
Turbine1	1.59e-13	1.59e-13	1.50e-13	6.49e-14	6.32e-14	0.40	**1.67e-14**
Turbine2	2.21e-13	2.23e-13	2.09e-13	5.89e-14	5.64e-14	0.26	**2.00e-14**
Turbine3	1.11e-13	1.11e-13	1.04e-13	2.47e-14	2.43e-14	0.22	**8.69e-15**

Precision Improvements. Table 1 compares the roundoff errors verified by the existing version of FloVer [3] (columns 'Interval' and 'Affine') with those verified by our extensions (columns 'SMT' and 'Subdiv') and those computed by FPTaylor, a state-of-the-art optimization-based analyzer. Column 'SMT & Subdiv' shows roundoff errors computed using both interval subdivision and SMT-based range estimation. All errors are computed for uniform 64-bit floating-point precision.

Table 2. Running times for Daisy and FloVer in seconds

Benchmark	Interval		Affine		SMT		Subdiv		SMT & Subdiv	
	Daisy	Coq	Daisy	Coq	Daisy	Coq	Daisy	Coq	Daisy	Coq
Bsplines	3.00	3.51	2.95	3.55	7.77	3.83	3.71	12.57	10.63	12.82
Doppler	6.04	6.70	2.71	7.36	5.22	4.95	6.1	237.25	86.54	237.86
DopplerFMA	2.57	4.20	2.72	6.99	5.46	4.05	5.29	167.01	86.08	172.64
Floudas	3.93	5.58	4.24	5.68	58.1	11.26	13.04	672.86	$\perp^{\%}$	$\perp^{\%}$
Himmilbeau	2.83	3.21	2.91	3.63	5.96	3.46	3.85	23.77	31.3	25.33
InvPendulum	2.68	3.14	2.71	3.48	4.89	3.46	4.28	50.82	67.65	50.86
JetEngine	$\perp^{0}$	$\perp^{0}$	$\perp^{0}$	$\perp^{0}$	34.28	47.07	$\perp^{0}$	$\perp^{0}$	120.99	1158.97
Kepler	3.21	12.53	3.2	13.44	55.99	13.15	12.38	1326.32	1840.17	1427.25
RigidBody	2.68	3.92	2.74	3.57	11.25	4.07	5.79	138.86	275.19	155.98
Science	2.89	6.87	2.89	420.50	7.73	6.88	3.8	25.99	12.86	26.69
Turbine	3.56	12.98	3.79	19.77	12.89	13.25	14.04	1476.35	331.98	1507.11

Column 'Cmp.' shows the ratio by which our new analyses improve over the roundoff error that could be verified by FloVer before (best new analysis/best previous analysis), values <1.0 mean that a tighter roundoff error bound can be proven. We highlight the smallest roundoff error among all verifiers in bold.

While FPTaylor usually computes the best roundoff error, the errors verified by our extension bring FloVer closer to the state-of-the-art. FloVer further supports fixed-point arithmetic which FPTaylor does not (which is why we perform the comparison in floating-points). For none of our benchmarks the roundoff error has become worse and we further achieve significant improvements where the new roundoff error is up to 4.5 times smaller than the old roundoff error (Turbine3). Verifying SMT-based results also allowed us to compute and verify a roundoff error for the JetEngine benchmark, for which interval and affine arithmetic report a spurious division by zero error (denoted by $\perp^{0}$). For the Floudas benchmarks, Daisy does not compute any roundoff error when using both SMT and subdivision due to a missing check for empty subdomains (denoted by $\perp^{\%}$).

Running Times. We give the overall certificate checking times of FloVer for each benchmark in Table 2. For each of the analyses supported by FloVer, we give the end-to-end running times for both Daisy and FloVer's Coq implementation on the full benchmark file (one file may include multiple functions and thus multiple calls to the certificate checker). The certificate checking times for our extension are higher than those of the baseline as expected, but remain reasonable (below 2 hours for the most complex benchmark). FPTaylor's checking times are in the same order of magnitude as those for SMT with subdivisions.

Summary. Our evaluation has shown that checking certificates with our extension of FloVer is feasible and improves its accuracy. Given the implemented analyses, FloVer now supports the same analyses as the state-of-the-art dataflow-analysis based tool Daisy. FloVers Coq formalization makes it reusable for other tools like Gappa to increase their precision using SMT-based range estimation and interval subdivision.

References

1. The Coq Proof Assistant. https://coq.inria.fr
2. The HOL4 Theorem Prover. https://hol-theorem-prover.org/
3. Becker, H., Zyuzin, N., Monat, R., Darulova, E., Myreen, M.O., Fox, A.: A verified certificate checker for finite-precision error bounds in Coq and HOL4. In: 2018 Formal Methods in Computer Aided Design (FMCAD), pp. 1–10. IEEE (2018)
4. Darulova, E., Izycheva, A., Nasir, F., Ritter, F., Becker, H., Bastian, R.: Daisy - framework for analysis and optimization of numerical programs (tool paper). In: Beyer, D., Huisman, M. (eds.) TACAS 2018. LNCS, vol. 10805, pp. 270–287. Springer, Cham (2018). https://doi.org/10.1007/978-3-319-89960-2_15
5. Darulova, E., Kuncak, V.: Towards a compiler for reals. ACM Trans. Prog. Lang. Syst. (TOPLAS) **39**(2), 8 (2017)
6. De Dinechin, F., Lauter, C.Q., Melquiond, G.: Assisted verification of elementary functions using Gappa. In: ACM Symposium on Applied Computing (SAC) (2006)
7. de Moura, L., Bjørner, N.: Z3: An efficient SMT solver. In: Ramakrishnan, C.R., Rehof, J. (eds.) TACAS 2008. LNCS, vol. 4963, pp. 337–340. Springer, Heidelberg (2008). https://doi.org/10.1007/978-3-540-78800-3_24
8. de Figueiredo, L.H., Stolfi, J.: Affine arithmetic: concepts and applications. Numer. Algorithms **37**(1–4), 147–158 (2004)
9. Goubault, E., Putot, S.: Static analysis of finite precision computations. In: Jhala, R., Schmidt, D. (eds.) VMCAI 2011. LNCS, vol. 6538, pp. 232–247. Springer, Heidelberg (2011). https://doi.org/10.1007/978-3-642-18275-4_17
10. Magron, V., Constantinides, G., Donaldson, A.: Certified roundoff error bounds using semidefinite programming. ACM Trans. Math. Softw. (TOMS) **43**(4), 34 (2017)
11. Moore, R.: Interval Analysis. Prentice-Hall, New Jersey (1966)
12. Owre, S., Rushby, J.M., Shankar, N.: PVS: a prototype verification system. In: Kapur, D. (ed.) CADE 1992. LNCS, vol. 607, pp. 748–752. Springer, Heidelberg (1992). https://doi.org/10.1007/3-540-55602-8_217
13. Solovyev, A., Jacobsen, C., Rakamaric, Z., Gopalakrishnan, G.: Rigorous estimation of floating-point round-off errors with symbolic taylor expansions. In: International Symposium on Formal Methods (FM) (2015)
14. Titolo, L., Feliú, M.A., Moscato, M., Muñoz, C.A.: An abstract interpretation framework for the round-off error analysis of floating-point programs. Verification, Model Checking, and Abstract Interpretation. LNCS, vol. 10747, pp. 516–537. Springer, Cham (2018). https://doi.org/10.1007/978-3-319-73721-8_24

Mechanically Verifying the Fundamental Liveness Property of the Chord Protocol

Jean-Paul Bodeveix[1], Julien Brunel[2], David Chemouil[2(✉)],
and Mamoun Filali[1]

[1] IRIT CNRS UPS, Université de Toulouse, Toulouse, France
{jean-paul.bodeveix,mamoun.filali}@irit.fr
[2] ONERA DTIS, Université de Toulouse, Toulouse, France
{julien.brunel,david.chemouil}@onera.fr

Abstract. Chord is a protocol providing a scalable distributed hash table over an underlying peer-to-peer network. It is very popular due to its simplicity, performance and claimed correctness. However, the original version of the Chord *maintenance* protocol, presented with an informal proof of correctness, was since then shown to be in fact incorrect. It is actually tricky to come up with a provably-correct version as the protocol combines data structures, asynchronous communication, concurrency, and fault tolerance. Additionally, the correctness property amounts to a form of *stabilization*, a particular kind of liveness property. Previous work only addressed automated proofs of safety; and pen-and-paper, or automated but much bounded, proofs of stabilization. In this article, we report on the first mechanized proof of the liveness property for Chord. Furthermore, our proof addresses the full parameterized version of the protocol, weakens previously-devised invariants and operating assumptions, and is essentially automated (requiring limited effort when manual assistance is needed).

Keywords: Chord · Distributed protocol ·
Parameterized verification · Liveness · Stabilization proof

1 Introduction

Chord [10,17,18] is a popular distributed lookup protocol addressing an essential issue of peer-to-peer applications: efficiently localizing some sought data in a dynamically-evolving network. To achieve this, the Chord protocol is designed so as to maintain a *ring* topology, as much as possible, and to fix possible disruptions due to nodes joining or leaving the network, or failing. When it was first introduced, Chord was claimed to be simple, efficient and correct. However, Zave [20] identified some flaws in the *maintenance protocol* (the only aspect we consider in this paper) and proposed some corrections. Since then, Chord has been used as a test-bed for various formal studies [3,5,15,19], using various methods and languages, including an outstanding endeavor by Zave herself [20–23]. However, most work has focused on proofs of safety while the fundamental

© Springer Nature Switzerland AG 2019
M. H. ter Beek et al. (Eds.): FM 2019, LNCS 11800, pp. 45–63, 2019.
https://doi.org/10.1007/978-3-030-30942-8_5

correctness property of Chord is a *stabilization* property, a particular kind of liveness property, saying that *if, from a certain instant, there is no subsequent join, departure or failure, then the network is ensured to recover a ring topology eventually and to keep it.* In her work [23], Zave identified key invariants that are instrumental to make the proof of liveness doable. She was able to check them using Alloy [7] but had to resort to good old pen and paper to provide a proof of liveness (unachievable in Alloy). In [5], some of the authors of the present paper used Electrum [11], a temporal extension of Alloy, to address the liveness proof in an automated way but only for networks of small size.

In this paper, we present a proof of correctness (liveness property) of the Chord maintenance protocol with the following contributions:

- our proof is parametric in the number of nodes in the network and in the number of redundant data used for robustness (so-called "successor lists", cf Sect. 2.1.2);
- we address the problem in a mechanized setting and rely on various abstractions so that most proof obligations are automatically discharged while most manual proofs need only limited manual intervention;
- we develop a proof method to address the specific shape of the liveness property at stake;
- we show that several invariants and operating assumptions made in the literature can be logically weakened.

Our work is performed using the Event-B language [1] and the accompanying tool Rodin [2]. We first use superposition refinement (also called *horizontal refinement*) to build the protocol incrementally. Then technical refinements are introduced to make Rodin produce the wanted proof obligations for stabilization. Thus, we do not really follow a refinement-based method to derive a correct protocol. Rather, we rely on Event-B and Rodin to take advantage of the ability to write specifications in an expressive language that the built-in pivot solver can translate and forward to SMT solvers, with great success in most cases for this work. For this reason, this article is written with the aim of presenting the essential aspects of our approach. Full Event-B models can be found at [4].

In Sect. 2, we present our model of the Chord maintenance protocol and describe our proof methodology. Then, in Sect. 3, we address properties of a Chord network, showing in particular how known operating assumptions and invariants can be weakened. In Sect. 4, we show that the maintenance protocol ensures the liveness property presented above. Finally we present related work in Sect. 5 and discuss future work in Sect. 6.

2   The Chord Protocol

This section presents the Chord network topology forming a ring, Chord data and the protocol itself as a set of guarded symbolic transitions.

2.1   Network Structure

2.1.1   Identifier Space

In a Chord network, every node has an identifier (a hash of its IP address). Pairs of keys and associated data are stored in nodes. In this article, we conflate the notions of a node and its identifier, and thus use a set NODE of node (identifiers).

The *node identifier space* is structured as a ring-shaped directed graph. Intuitively, identifiers are ordered following the usual strict ordering on natural numbers (written $<$ in the following), wrapping around at the largest identifier in order to close the ring. Due to this shape, situating an identifier is advantageously modeled by checking whether it sits *between* two other identifiers: given $n_1, n_2 \in$ NODE, we define the *set of identifiers between n_1 and n_2*, written $n_1 \rightsquigarrow n_2$, by[1]:

$$n_1 \rightsquigarrow n_2 \triangleq \left\{ n \in \text{NODE} \;\middle|\; \begin{array}{ll} n_1 < n < n_2 & \text{if } n_1 < n_2 \\ n_1 < n \text{ or } n < n_2 & \text{otherwise} \end{array} \right\}$$

Given a node $n \in$ NODE, we note $\text{next}(n)$ the next node according to $\rightsquigarrow$, i.e., st $n \rightsquigarrow \text{next}(n) = \emptyset$.

2.1.2   Chord Network

A Chord *network* is thus built over the identifier space. In order for Chord to provide an efficient lookup procedure, *ideally*, the network should also form a ring-shaped digraph at every instant, where every member is in charge of storing some payload (depending on the node identifier) and points to its *nearest successor* among the ring members (see Fig. 1 (left)).

However, as nodes dynamically join and leave the network, this ideal ring shape cannot always be maintained and *appendages* to the ring will appear (see Fig. 1 (middle)). The set of nodes belonging to the Chord network, that is belonging to the Chord ring or to its appendages, is called MEMBERS. Its elements are also called *live* nodes. Non-members are called *dead* nodes. Formally, a node may be dead either because it was live and later failed or left the network, or because it never joined the network.

Thus, the protocol is in fact meant to keep the network in a repairable state and, in the long run, to fix disruptions.

To enhance robustness to failures, every live node holds a fixed-length *successor list* [17, Sect. 5.2] of K pointers to other nodes[2], where K is a parameter of the protocol. This way, if a node leaves the network, its predecessor will still have successors in the network: an assumption is made, stating that every node

---

[1] In our Event-B model, we actually use a pure first-order axiomatization, presented e.g. in [15], which allows SMT solvers to deal with many proofs automatically.

[2] Not to be confused with Chord's *finger tables* whose purpose is to support efficient query routing [17, Sect. 4.3].

always has at least one live node in its successor list (see Sect. 3.2.1). Additionally, every live node also holds a (possibly-null) pointer to its *predecessor* node: this is useful in the execution of maintenance operations.

Thus we end up with the following state variables (prdc is declared as a partial function as it may be undefined for some members).

$$\text{MEMBERS} \subseteq \text{NODE} \quad \text{succ} : \text{MEMBERS} \rightarrow \text{list}_K(\text{NODE})$$
$$\text{prdc} : \text{MEMBERS} \nrightarrow \text{NODE}$$

We also use bestSucc : MEMBERS → MEMBERS to indicate the first live node among the K successors of a member: $\text{bestSucc}(n) \triangleq \text{succ}(n)[i]$ where i is the least index st $\text{succ}(n)[i]$ is alive.

2.2 Chord Operations

2.2.1 Formal Model

We present (end of Sect. 2.2) the Chord operations using a pseudo-code reminiscent of classic formal specification languages. In practice, we relied on the Event-B notation, essentially because we wanted to use the accompanying tool Rodin as a pivot solver for a specification which is parametric in the number of nodes and the length of successor lists. The meaning of our notation (which is *indentation-dependent* for brevity) is as follows:

- events have parameters, a guard (introduced by the keyword **guard**), which is a conjunction of formulas, and an action body (introduced with **do**);
- the execution of the action part of an event is *atomic* and consists in the *simultaneous* execution of all its statements (no sequentiality in actions);
- *interleaving*: at every instant, a single event is fired (proof obligations check that at least one event can be fired at every instant);
- as in Event-B, we do not make any by-default fairness assumption on the execution model, but our proof will suppose strong fairness between two sets of events (see Sect. 2.3);
- instead of using classic function application on nodes (e.g. prdc(n)), we use the dot notation (n.prdc) to emphasize that the variables we consider can be seen as node fields (n.f =⊥ states that f is undefined for n);
- contrary to Event-B, we also have a notion of conditional, where every **then** or **else** branch is *tagged* with a label starting with the @ symbol: this provides a concise way to describe several Event-B events at once[3]

---

[3] An event E with guard g and body **if** c **then** @1 t **else** @2 (**if** c2 **then** @a t2 **else** @b e) will give rise to an Event-B event E1 with guard g **and** c and body t, and to Event-B events E2a (respE2b) with guard g **and not** c **and** c2 and body t2 (resp. with guard g **and not** c **and not** c2 and body e).

Modeling-wise, following [23], an event corresponds to an operation executed by a single node. It may communicate with only one, other node; and there is a time-out such that it allows nodes to detect live or dead nodes. These rules aim at faithfully abstracting the distributed system that Chord is.

2.2.2 Model-Specific State Variables

Apart from the previously-mentioned state variables, our model of the protocol also features two further state variables `Stabilizing` and `Rectifying`:

$$\texttt{Stabilizing} : \text{MEMBERS} \rightarrowtail \text{NODE} \qquad \texttt{Rectifying} \subseteq \text{NODE} \times \text{NODE}$$

The former is used to model the fact that, while an operation, called *stabilize* in Chord, is running on a live node, some significant state changes may happen elsewhere. In our model, as in [23], this operation is split into two in order to allow this "preemption", and if `Stabilizing` is defined for a given member m, then `m.Stabilizing` yields its memory context (the stored identifier of another node).

`Rectifying` is here to account for asynchronous communication. In some contexts, a node may send a message to another node to tell the latter to perform a so-called *rectification*. Intuitively, this binary relation associates a node with the set of messages it has sent and that have not been handled yet. Notice the type of `Rectifying`: we do not consider the order in which messages are sent or received, nor the duplication of messages from a given node to another one. Additionally, not restricting the domain of `Rectifying` to MEMBERS allows us to model a message to a node which has failed since the message was sent.

2.2.3 Events

The Chord operations[4], shown later, follow the presentation by Chord authors in [10,17], Zave [23] and some authors [5] of the present article, with a few variations.

The first two events are `join` and `fail` and are under the control of the environment. The `fail` event models a failure or a voluntary departure. Notice that an operating assumption on `fail` is necessary and presented in Sect. 3.2.1.

In the case of the `join` event, a new node can join the Chord network by taking a well-positioned live node m as its predecessor and taking m's successor list as its list too. Lines 9 to 10, which concern the `Rectifying` field, are here to model a special situation: as explained above, `Rectifying` represents asynchronous communication. When a node m sends a `Rectifying` message to a node n, n may: (1) receive it (and handle it), (2) fail and therefore miss it, *or* (3) fail and

---

[4] We write `++` (resp. `::`) for list concatenation (resp. cons), and `x -= s` (resp. `x += s`) for `x := x \ s` (resp. `x := x ∪ s`). Abusing notation, a singleton set `{s}` is written `s`.

join again fast enough to still receive it. To account for this distributed aspect, instead of modeling a channel explicitly, we keep our simple modeling with the following specificity: when a (previously failed) node joins, *some* Rectifying messages addressed to it are chosen non-deterministically and lost (Line 9).

Maintenance operations aim at compensating disruptions due to nodes joining and failing. The first such operation is *stabilization*. Its purpose is to fix the first successor of a node. As explained in Sect. 2.2.2, to account for possible state changes during its execution, the operation is split into two as in [23]. The first part, stabilizeFromFst, can only happen on a live node if it is not already doing a stabilization (line 15). The node first checks whether its first successor is live. If not, the node updates its successor list by shifting it one step to the left, and padding it at the end with the lowest identifier following its last known successor (line 19). There may be no node corresponding to this identifier but, as it is the lowest possible, it prevents skipping possible live nodes and it can eventually be fixed. Otherwise, the successor list is just updated with fresh data coming from its first successor (line 22). Finally, the node checks whether its first successor's predecessor is better placed than itself. In this case, it decides to update its first successor: as explained above, stabilization is not over yet but, to account for possible changes in parallel, we just memorize that it should continue the operation later with this better successor (line 23). Otherwise, the first successor is sent a message saying that it should update its predecessor.

The second stabilization part, stabilizeFromFstPrdc, precisely continues the operation. It can only be fired if the Stabilizing field is non-null, in which case it holds a well-located, candidate new value for the first successor. Yet, as changes may have happened, this node is tested for being a member. If it is dead, there is nothing to do: the operation is over, the current successor is just sent a message to tell it to update its predecessor. Otherwise, the candidate node is taken as a new successor and similarly asked to update its predecessor.

Finally, *rectification* aims at fixing predecessor pointers. The rectify operation consumes a message sent during the stabilization of a candidate predecessor. If the current predecessor is dead or if the candidate is nearer than the current one, then an update of the predecessor pointer is done, otherwise nothing happens. Finally, the rectifyNull operation can be spontaneously fired. It sets the predecessor pointer to null if the pointed node is dead.

```
1   event join [new, m]
2   guard
3     new ∉ MEMBERS
4     m ∈ MEMBERS
5     new ∈ m ⤳ m.succ[1]
6   do // atomic
7     new.succ := m.succ
8     new.prdc := ⊥
9     choose loss ⊆ NODE then
10      new.Rectifying -= loss
11
12  event stabilizeFromFst [m]
13  guard
14    m ∈ MEMBERS
15    m.Stabilizing = ⊥
16  do // atomic
17    if m.succ[1] ∉ MEMBERS then @1
18      m.succ :=
19        tail(succ) ++ next(m.succ[K])
20    else @2
21      m.succ :=
22        m.succ[1] :: butLast(m.succ[1].succ))
23      if m.succ[1].prdc != ⊥
24        and m.succ[1].prdc ∈ m ⤳ m.succ[1]
25      then @sta
26        m.Stabilizing := m.succ[1].prdc
27      else @rct
28        m.succ[1].Rectifying += m
29
30  event rectifyNull [m]
31  guard
32    m ∈ MEMBERS
33    m.prdc != ⊥
34    m.prdc ∉ MEMBERS
35  do // atomic
36    m.prdc := ⊥
```

```
37  // fail is also subject to an operating
38  // assumption (cf. section 3.2.1)
39  event fail [f]
40  guard
41    f ∈ MEMBERS
42  do
43    MEMBERS -= f
44
45
46
47
48  event stabilizeFromFstPrdc [m, newFst]
49  guard
50    m ∈ MEMBERS
51    m.Stabilizing = newFst
52    newFst ∈ m ⤳ m.succ[1]
53  do // atomic
54    if newFst ∉ MEMBERS then @1
55      m.Stabilizing := ⊥
56      m.succ[1].Rectifying += m
57    else @2
58      m.succ = newFst :: butLast(newFst.succ)
59      m.Stabilizing := ⊥
60      newFst.Rectifying += m
61
62  event rectify [m, newPrdc]
63  guard
64    m ∈ MEMBERS
65    newPrdc ∈ m.Rectifying
66  do // atomic
67    if m.prdc ∉ MEMBERS
68      or newPrdc ∈ m.prdc ⤳ m then @1
69      m.Rectifying -= newPrdc
70      m.prdc := newPrdc
71    else @2
72      m.Rectifying -= newPrdc
```

2.3 Proof Engineering

The proofs of this article have been mechanized thanks to the Rodin framework. The framework is here used as a proof obligation generator and as an environment to discharge generated proofs (through user interaction). The framework contains built-in solvers and is also connected to external SMT solvers. The basic machinery available within Rodin allows for the automatic generation of proof obligations for invariants, event convergence, refinements and theorems. An invariant property is true initially and preserved by each event. Event convergence is established through the introduction of a variant which is an expression yielding a natural number or a finite set. Each *convergent* event must decrease the variant strictly. Event-B also provides *anticipated* events which must not increase the variant. We use these features to generate proof obligations for stabilization.

Since the main property of Chord is stabilization under the hypothesis that the events join and fail do not occur anymore and strong fairness [8] over the other events E in a context H, we propose here proof obligations for establishing the stabilization of a given property Q[5]:

---

[5] Given an event e, $[e](p)$ is the weakest precondition ensuring that e terminates in a state satisfying p.

1. $\bigwedge_{e \in E \setminus C} H \wedge V = v \Rightarrow [e](V \preceq v)$ (generated by Rodin for *anticipated* events): anticipated events do not increase the variant;
2. $\bigwedge_{e \in C} H \wedge V = v \Rightarrow [e](V \prec v)$ (generated by Rodin for *convergent* events): convergent events make the variant decrease;
3. $H \wedge V \neq \emptyset \Rightarrow \bigvee_{e \in C} \text{enabled}(e)$ (manually added as a theorem to be proved): some of the convergent events are enabled while the variant is not empty.
4. $H \wedge V = \emptyset \Rightarrow Q$ (manually added as a theorem to be proved): when the variant is empty, the targetted property is satisfied.

where $C \subseteq E$ is a selected set of convergent events and V is a set expression over state variables (both provided by the user). The correctness of these proof obligations strongly relies on strong fairness between two classes of events: enabled convergent events should eventually be fired for the variant to decrease.

A variation of this proof rule may be used when Q is reached before the variant V becomes empty. Obligation (3) is changed as follows:

3a. $H \wedge \neg Q \Rightarrow \bigvee_{e \in C} \text{enabled}(e)$ (manually added as a theorem to be proved): some of the convergent events are enabled while the targetted property is not reached.
3b. $H \wedge Q \Rightarrow \bigwedge_{e \in E} [e](Q)$ (generated by Rodin if Q is declared invariant): Q is stable.

3   Chord Correctness

In order to formalize a problem, the choice of an appropriate mathematical structure is crucial. Indeed, it can ease not only the specification of properties but also the proof of some of them, in case we can take benefit from meta-properties of the mathematical structure. In our context, an abstract view of a Chord network consists of the total function bestSucc over the set MEMBERS of live nodes. As it is the case for every total function over a finite set, its graph is a directed pseudoforest. Thus, the existence of a *ring* of live nodes that is formed by the bestSucc relation is directly deduced from the representation of the network through a total function, without any additional hypotheses. Similarly, the fact that all the live nodes are located in the ring(s) is equivalent to bestSucc being surjective over MEMBERS. For instance, in the networks on the left-hand side (ideal) and on the right-hand side (loopy) of Fig. 1, all the nodes are in the ring: bestSucc is surjective. This is not the case for the network in the center. The nodes that are not part of the ring form the *appendages*.

A key notion of safe networks identified by [23] distinguishes between the ideal and the loopy networks. This is the notion of *principal* node, which relates the structure of a network (modeled through bestSucc in our case) to the ordering over the node identifier space (↪ in our context). As we will see in the next section, a loopy network does not have any principal node.

In Sect. 3.1 we develop on some results about functions over finite sets, which are not Chord-specific, and in Sect. 3.2 we present the properties of a Chord network.

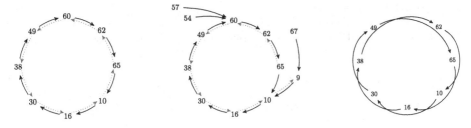

Fig. 1. Some Chord networks: in the ideal state (left), in an arbitrary state (center), loopy (right) (solid edges: bestSucc, dotted edges: prdc)

3.1 Generic Properties

We now present some results about relations and functions over finite sets. These are not Chord-specific, but still useful to prove Chord correctness.

Theorem 1 (Pigeonhole principle). *Given a finite set E, a function $f : E \to E$ is injective if and only if it is surjective.*

A fundamental element in the proof of Chord correctness is the concept of principal nodes, introduced in [23] in the context of a Chord network. We generalize here the definition of a principal node w.r.t. an arbitrary relation r over the identifier space NODE.

Definition 1 (Principal). *Given a binary relation $r \subseteq$ NODE $\times$ NODE over the set of nodes, the set* principals(r) *of principal nodes for r is the set of nodes that are not skipped by any pair in r:*

$$\text{principals}(r) \triangleq \{p \in \text{NODE} \mid \forall \langle n, m \rangle \in r \cdot p \notin n \overset{\frown}{\longrightarrow} m\}$$

The following lemma and theorem will be useful to show that, in the context of a network without appendages, one principal node is enough to ensure that all nodes are correctly located.

Lemma 1. *Given a subset $E \subseteq$ NODE of nodes and a surjective function $f : E \to E$, if a node p is principal for f, then its next neighbour according to $\overset{\frown}{\longrightarrow}$ in E is also principal for f.*

Proof. Suppose that $\text{next}(p)$ is not principal for f. Then, it is between some x and $f(x)$. As p is principal, we have $x = p$. f being surjective, there exists y st $f(y) = \text{next}(p)$. As p is principal, $y = p$. Thus $f(p) = \text{next}(p) = x$, which contradicts the fact that $\text{next}(p)$ is between x and $f(x)$.

Theorem 2 (Principal for a injective (or surjective) total function). *Given a subset $E \subseteq$ NODE of nodes, and a surjective (or injective) total function $f : E \to E$, if there is some principal node in E for f, then every node in E is principal for f.*

Proof. The proof is straightforward using Lemma 1 and the pigeonhole principle.

3.2   Chord Properties

The authors of Chord have provided explicit properties that ensure correct data delivery [10,17]. They define in particular the *ideal state* of a network.

Definition 2 (Ideal state). *A Chord network is in an* ideal *state if:*

1. *the first successor and the predecessor of every live node are alive:*
   $\forall n \in \text{MEMBERS} \cdot n.\text{succ}[1] \in \text{MEMBERS} \wedge n.\text{prdc} \in \text{MEMBERS}$
2. *the successor relation* bestSucc[6] *forms a single ring of nodes (every live node is in the ring):* $\forall n_1, n_2 \in \text{NODE} \cdot n_2 \in n_1.\text{bestSucc}^+ \wedge n_1 \in n_2.\text{bestSucc}^+$, *where* bestSucc$^+$ *is the transitive closure of* bestSucc
3. bestSucc *provides the nearest successor of each node according to the identifier order:* $\forall n \in \text{MEMBERS} \cdot n \frown n.\text{bestSucc} \cap \text{MEMBERS} = \emptyset$
4. prdc *provides the nearest predecessor of each node according to the identifier order:* $\forall n \in \text{MEMBERS} \cdot n.\text{prdc} \frown n \cap \text{MEMBERS} = \emptyset$
5. *the tail of the successor list of each node is equal to the successor list of its first successor (with the last entry removed):*
   $\forall n \in \text{MEMBERS} \cdot \forall i \in 2..K \cdot n.\text{succ}[i] = n.\text{succ}[1].\text{succ}[i-1]$

In the following, we write ideal *for the conjunction of the above five properties defining the ideal state.*

As explained in Sect. 2 informally, the ideal state cannot be continuously ensured because nodes can dynamically join and leave the network. The goal of the maintenance protocol is thus to keep the network in a repairable state so that it will be fixed eventually.

Definition 3 (Correctness). *If eventually no node joins or leaves the network anymore, the network will eventually reach the ideal state and remain in it.*

We will prove the convergence of Chord to the ideal state by relying on inductive invariants (Sect. 3.2.1) and on variants (Sect. 4).

3.2.1   Chord Invariants

In this section, we exhibit an inductive invariant, which is useful to prove the correctness property. It is inspired by Zave's work [23] and consists of three properties. With respect to this pioneering work, the property related to principal nodes is logically weakened and a technical property, related to our model-specific variables, is added.

Property 1 (SomeLiveSuccessor). *A network satisfies* SomeLive Successor *if each live node has a live successor:* $\forall n \in \text{MEMBERS} \cdot \exists i \in 1..K \cdot n.\text{succ}[i] \in \text{MEMBERS}$.

---

[6] Since all the first successors are alive in the ideal state, bestSucc always points to the first successor.

`SomePrincipal` states that there is some principal among the live nodes. Let us first instantiate the definition of principal, from Sect. 3.1, for a Chord network.

Definition 4 (Chord principal). *A Chord principal is a member that is not "skipped" in any successor list. More formally, a node $p \in$ MEMBERS is a Chord principal if, for any node $n \in$ MEMBERS st $n.$succ $= [n_1, \ldots, n_K]$, $p \notin n \rightharpoonup n_1$ and $p \notin n_i \rightharpoonup n_{i+1}$ for $i \in 1..(K-1)$.*

Proposition 1 (Chord principal). *A node is a chord principal iff it is a member that is a principal for the relation* hops, *where :*

$$\text{hops} \triangleq \{\langle m, m.\text{succ}[1]\rangle \mid m \in \text{MEMBERS}\}$$
$$\cup \{\langle m.\text{succ}[i], m.\text{succ}[i+1]\rangle \mid m \in \text{MEMBERS and } i \in 1..(K-1)\}$$

Considering the relation bestSucc instead of the relation hops, i.e., having a more abstract view of the successor relation, we have the following proposition:

Proposition 2 (Principal for bestSucc). *Given a Chord network, if a node n is a Chord principal, i.e., a member that is a principal for* hops, *then it is a principal node for* bestSucc*:* principals(hops) $\subseteq$ principals(bestSucc).

We can now state the property `SomePrincipal`.

Property 2 (`SomePrincipal`). *A Chord network satisfies `SomePrincipal` if there is some live node which is a Chord principal:* principals(hops) $\cap$ MEMBERS $\neq \emptyset$.

Notice this is logically weaker than the property from [23], where the number of principals was required to be greater than the size of successor lists, as discussed above.

The following property is related to the model-specific variable `Stabilizing`, which records the fact that a node n has to take a node m as its future successor

Property 3 (`StabBetterThanSucc`). *A Chord network satisfies `StabBetterThanSucc` if for every live node n having a pending stabilization, the candidate for stabilization is better than the current successor of n[7]:*

$$\forall n : \text{MEMBERS} \cdot n \in \text{dom}(\textbf{Stabilizing}) \Rightarrow \textbf{Stabilizing}(n) \in n \rightharpoonup n.\text{succ}[1]$$

Theorem 3 (Inductive invariant). *The following property is preserved by all of the operations of the Chord protocol, except* fail*:*

SomeLiveSuccessor $\wedge$ SomePrincipal $\wedge$ StabBetterThanSucc

---

[7] dom denotes the domain of a relation or a function.

The proof of this theorem is mechanized with Rodin.

Operating Assumptions. *Our proof of correctness for Chord relies on the critical operating assumptions that no failure "breaks" the invariant*[8]

1. *No failure leaves a node without live node in its successor list.*
2. *No failure leaves the network without any principal node.*

The assumption (1), saying that each successor list always includes a live node, was present in the original Chord article [17]. Indeed, having a list of successors prevents from the failure of a successor as soon as there are other nodes left in the successor list. The assumption (2) comes from Chord property SomePrincipal, which is an adaptation from the invariant property exhibited in [23], where the author explained that when a node joins the network, it becomes a principal as soon as its K preceding nodes are aware of its presence. Assuming the existence of a minimal number of principal nodes ($K + 1$ in [23]) is then reasonable, especially as we assume the existence of only one principal node in this article.

Notice that we also relaxed the assumptions from [23] about the minimal size of the network and about the absence of duplication in successor lists.

3.2.2   Always-True Properties

We now define important structural properties and show that they are actually implied by the inductive invariant.

Property 4 (AtMostOneRing). *A Chord network satisfies the property* AtMostOneRing *if any two ring members can access each other through* bestSucc$^+$.

$$\forall n_1, n_2 \in \text{MEMBERS} \cdot (n_1 \in n_1.\text{bestSucc}^+ \land n_2 \in n_2.\text{bestSucc}^+)$$
$$\Rightarrow (n_1 \in n_2.\text{bestSucc}^+ \land n_2 \in n_1.\text{bestSucc}^+)$$

Theorem 4. *Given a Chord network,* SomePrincipal *implies* AtMostOneRing.

Proof (sketch). Suppose that SomePrincipal is true. Then, there is a Chord principal, which is also a principal node for bestSucc (from Property 2). Also suppose that AtMostOneRing is false. There there are two nodes n_1 and n_2 that are in two unconnected bestSucc-"rings". Considering the first ring, any node outside this ring is necessary "skipped" by bestSucc: all the principal nodes are thus in the first ring. Similarly, we can conclude that all the principal nodes are in the second ring. Contradiction.   □

Property 5. *A Chord network satisfies* DistinctFirstSuccs *if the successor lists include no duplicated node up to the first live node:*

$$\forall n \in \text{NODE} \cdot \forall j \leqslant \mathit{fl}_n \cdot \forall i \in 1..j-1 \cdot n.\text{succ}[i] \neq n.\text{succ}[j]$$

where fl_n *is the index of the first live node in* $n.\text{succ}$.

---

[8] The Chord Property 3 about the Stabilizing function is preserved by failand thus does not impact operating assumptions.

Theorem 5. `SomePrincipal` *implies* `DistinctFirstSuccs`.

Proof (sketch).   Suppose   that   `SomePrincipal`   is   true
and `DistinctFirstSuccs` is false. Then, there is a node n s.t. in n.succ,
there is a duplicated node n' before the first live node in n.succ. Since every
node except n' is in the set $n' \curvearrowright n'$, there cannot be a Chord principal different
from n', which contradicts `SomePrincipal`, because n' is not a member.   □

Property 6. *A Chord network satisfies* `OrderedFirstSuccs` *if the successor
lists are ordered according to* $\curvearrowright$ *up to the first live node in the list:*

$$\forall n \in \text{NODE} \cdot \forall j \leqslant fl_n \cdot \forall i \in 1..j-1 \cdot n.\text{succ}[i] \in n \curvearrowright n.\text{succ}[j]$$

where fl_n is the index of the first live node in n.succ.

Theorem 6. *Given   a   Chord   network,* `SomePrincipal` *implies*
`OrderedFirstSuccs`.

Proof (sketch). Suppose that `SomePrincipal` is true and `OrderedFirst
Succs` is false. Then, there are n, i, j as in the theorem statement st n.succ$[i] \notin
n \curvearrowright n.\text{succ}[j]$. Since these three nodes are distinct (from Theorem 5), we have
$n.\text{succ}[j] \in n \curvearrowright n.\text{succ}[i]$. Then, the properties of $\curvearrowright$ imply that every node
except $n.\text{succ}[i]$ is included in $n \curvearrowright n.\text{succ}[i] \cup n.\text{succ}[i] \curvearrowright n.\text{succ}[j]$. From
`SomePrincipal`, there is a live node p which is principal. Since p is a live node,
it is distinct from $n.\text{succ}[i]$. It is then skipped by some pair in n.succ, which
leads to a contradiction.   □

4 Phase-Based Convergence Proof

We now show that in the absence of `join` and `fail` events, the system eventually reaches the *ideal* state and remains in it. To do so, we introduce four
intermediate macro-states, which are stable[9] under the considered hypothesis
and reached successively:

MS1. `Rectifying` and `prdc` in MEMBERS.
MS2. the first successor is a member: $n.\text{succ}[1] \in$ MEMBERS.
MS3. `Stabilizing` only includes members: `ran(Stabilizing)` $\subseteq$
MEMBERS[10].
MS4. `prdc` is the inverse of `bestSucc` and both `Stabilizing` and
`Rectifying` are empty for members:
$\forall n \in$ MEMBERS$\cdot n.$`Stabilizing` $= \emptyset \wedge n.$`Rectifying` $= \emptyset \wedge$
$n.\text{bestSucc.prdc} = n$
MS6. the tail of the successor list of each node is equal to the successor list of
its first successor (with the last entry removed):
$\forall n \in$ MEMBERS $\cdot \forall i \in 2..K \cdot n.\text{succ}[i] = n.\text{succ}[1].\text{succ}[i-1]$

---

[9] Once a macro-state is reached, the system cannot leave it.
[10] `ran` denotes the range of a relation or a function.

Ideal. We then prove that MS5 implies that the network is ideal.

This phase-based proof allows us to avoid a monolithic convergence proof which would require finding a complex *variant*. Each phase (and sub-phase) relies on a small variant, except the fourth phase (reaching MS4). It relies on the proof method presented in Sect. 2.3 and thus on fairness hypotheses. The proof was mechanized in Rodin from our Event-B model, where the guards of `join` and `fail` were set to `false`[11].

4.1   Reaching MS1: `Rectifying` and `prdc` in Members

This phase is split into two steps: reaching MS1a from a state satisfying the inductive invariant, and reaching MS1b from MS1a.

MS1a.   `ran(Rectifying)` $\subseteq$ MEMBERS

We split the event `rectify` in two events, one guarded by newPrdc $\notin$ members and the other by newPrdc $\in$ members. The variant is the set `Rectifying` \ NODE $\times$ MEMBERS. The event that is guarded by the negative membership condition makes the variant decrease (it is tagged *convergent* in Event-B) while the other events do not make it increase (*anticipated* in Event-B). As long as `Rectifying` includes non members, the convergent event is enabled. So, under the fairness hypothesis, MS1a will be reached eventually.

MS1b.   `prdc` $\in$ MEMBERS $\nrightarrow$ MEMBERS

This property is shown by introducing the variant `prdc`$^{-1}$[NODE \ MEMBERS]. The `rectifyNull` event decreases the variant (and other events do not increase it). It is enabled as long as the variant is not empty, which ensures the convergence from MS1a to MS1b.

4.2   Reaching MS2: The First Successor Is a Member

$$\forall n \in \text{MEMBERS} \cdot n.\mathsf{succ}[1] \in \text{MEMBERS}$$

Notice that this is equivalent to $\forall n \in$ MEMBERS $\cdot n.\mathsf{bestSucc} = n.\mathsf{succ}[1]$. In order to ease the reasoning, given a member node n, we call `zombies`(n) the set of non member nodes preceding $n.\mathsf{bestSucc}$ in its successor list. So, the objective of this phase is to reach a state where the zombie sets are empty. It is split into two steps: reaching MS2a from MS1, and reaching MS2b from MS2a.

MS2a.   each node in the stabilizing state has no zombie successors:
$\forall n \in \mathsf{dom}(\mathtt{Stabilizing}) \cdot \mathsf{zombies}(n) = \emptyset$.
The event `stabilizeFromFstPrdc` is split to introduce the guard `zombies(m)` = $\emptyset$ and its negation. The event with the negative guard makes the variant `dom (Stabilizing)` \ {m | m $\in$MEMBERS $\wedge$ `zombies(m)` = $\emptyset$} decrease while others do not increase it.

---

[11] Technically, we have an Event-B model for each phase defined as a refinement of the Event-B machine modelling the Chord protocol, where the MS of the preceding phase is stated as an invariant of the current phase.

MS2b. each member has no zombie successors: $\forall n \in$ MEMBERS $\cdot$ zombies$(n) =$ $\emptyset$ This property is ensured thanks to the event stabilizeFromFst@1 which removes one element from a non empty zombie set of a member node that has no Stabilizing memory context. In MS1a, this condition is true. For this phase the variant is $\{\langle m, b \rangle \cdot m \in$ MEMBERS $\wedge\, b \in$ zombies$(m)\}$.

4.3 Reaching MS3: Stabilizing only Includes Members

$$\text{ran}(\text{Stabilizing}) \subseteq \text{MEMBERS}$$

We take as variant the set of the pairs (n_1, n_2) in Stabilizing s.t. n_2 is not a member. The sub-event stabilizeFromFstPrdc@1 makes the variant Stabilizing $\cap$ MEMBERS $\times$ (NODE $\setminus$ MEMBERS) decrease. It is enabled while the variant is not empty.

4.4 Reaching MS4: prdc Is the Inverse of bestSucc and the Rectifying and Stabilizing Sets of Each Node Are Empty

$\forall n \in$ MEMBERS $\cdot$ n.Stabilizing $= \emptyset \wedge n$.Rectifying $= \emptyset \wedge n$.bestSucc.prdc $= n$

This property is proved by introducing a complex variant which is the combination of four sets of node pairs. The events of the protocol make the variant decrease by moving some pairs from one of the sets to another one of lower weight, or by removing some pair from the lowest set. Other transitions let the sets unchanged. The following sets are the following in decreasing order of importance (for the variant)[12]:

1. $\{\langle x, y \rangle \mid x \in$ MEMBERS $\wedge y \in$ MEMBERS $\wedge y \in x \rightharpoonup$ bestSucc$(x))\} \setminus$ Stabilizing
2. $\{\langle x, y \rangle \mid x \in$ MEMBERS $\wedge y \in$ MEMBERS $\wedge (y \in$ dom(prdc) $\wedge$ prdc$(y) \in$ MEMBERS $\Rightarrow x \in$ prdc$(y) \rightharpoonup y)\} \setminus$ Rectifying^{-1}
3. Stabilizing $\cap$ Rectifying^{-1}
4. Stabilizing
5. Rectifying^{-1}

The following events make the variant decrease: stabilizeFromFst@ {1,2sta}, stabilizeFromFstPrdc@2, rectify. Besides, the event stabilizeFromFst@2rct must be split to introduce the guard $\langle$m.suc,m$\rangle \notin$ Rectifying. The sub-event having this guard true makes also the variant decrease. The other events do not increase it.

---

[12] In Event-B, this structured variant is encoded as a single set using the Cartesian product and union.

4.5 Reaching MS5: The Tail of the Successor List of Each Node Is Equal to the Successor List of Its First Successor

$$\forall n \in \text{MEMBERS} \cdot \forall i \in 2..K \cdot n.\text{succ}[i] = n.\text{succ}[1].\text{succ}[i-1]$$

In this step, we need to manage the concrete successor list of each member node while its abstraction with bestSucc and a zombie set was sufficient to verify the previous phases. Data refinement is used to replace these two variables by a unique successor list. Verifying its correctness is not automatic as automation is weaker with lists: numerous user-provided case splitting and quantifier instantiations are required.

Then, in order to prove the convergence to MS5, an auxiliary variable E is introduced: it includes the pairs (m, i) such that the successor list of m is correct up to position i. More precisely, E is introduced with the following invariant properties:

$$E \subseteq \text{MEMBERS} \times 1..K \qquad\qquad \text{MEMBERS} \times \{1\} \subseteq E$$
$$\forall m, i \cdot \langle m, i \rangle \in E \land i > 1 \Rightarrow m.\text{succ}[1].\text{succ}[i-1] \in E$$
$$\forall m, i \cdot \langle m, i \rangle \in E \land i > 1 \Rightarrow \{m\} \times 1..i \subseteq E$$
$$\forall m, i \cdot \langle m, i \rangle \in E \land i > 1 \Rightarrow m.\text{succ}[i] = m.\text{succ}[1].\text{succ}[i-1]$$

Thanks to MS4, we can start with MEMBERS $\times$ $\{1\}$. Then, thanks to fairness, the event stabilizeFromFst@2rct which copies the successor list of one node to its predecessor will eventually saturate E. This property is ensured by taking (MEMBERS $\times$ 1..K) \ E as variant and by splitting the selected event s.t. it ensures progress.

4.6 Reaching the Ideal State

By using the results of Sect. 3, we show that the properties of MS5 imply that the network is in the ideal state. Indeed, in MS4, bestSucc is necessarily injective. From the invariant, we have that there is at least one principal node. By Theorem 2 and Proposition 2, all nodes are principal for bestSucc, which means that no node is skipped by bestSucc. Moreover the last property defining the ideal state exactly matches the definition of MS5. The five properties of an ideal state are thus fulfilled.

5 Related Work

Chord is a popular protocol but also, since the seminal work of Zave [20], a popular test-bed for formal verification. However, most work [3,9,15,20–22] has focused on proving *safety*, sometimes with manual proofs only, while the correctness property for Chord maintenance, addressed here, is a liveness property. Zave [23] carried out a manual proof of liveness and discovered the fundamental notion of *principal*. Some of the authors of the present paper analyzed liveness in an automated way using Electrum [5] but for small networks. To the best of our knowledge, this work is the first to address the liveness property of Chord in a parameterized setting and using a much automated, mechanical proof.

Other distributed system protocols have been formally studied using "high-level" specification languages. For instance, Pastry was analyzed using TLA$^+$ [13]; similar work used Event-B [16] or ASM [12] to partly verify other protocols. However, these studies are limited to the verification of safety properties.

Verdi [19] and IronFleet [6] address the question of provably-correct *implementations* of distributed protocols while our approach is markedly at a more abstract level, in particular to favor proof automation. Our work is also focused on a stabilization property for which we developed a specific proof method. Finally, proof automation for liveness of parameterized or even arbitrary infinite-state distributed systems is the subject of recent work such as Ivy [14] but, as far as we know, a fair amount of manual intervention is still needed.

6   Conclusion

In this article, we proposed a mechanized correctness proof of the Chord maintenance protocol. We address a particular form of liveness property (stabilization) over a network of arbitrary size. On the logical side, we weakened the operating assumption related to principal nodes stated in [23], as well as the one requiring a minimal number of nodes in the network. However, the practical consequences of this weakening remain to be assessed quantitatively.

As future work, we intend to develop some automated support to stabilization proofs following the method exhibited in Sect. 4. Another line of work is to refine our model with less abstract types (e.g. FIFO for asynchronous communication). Both directions could contribute to the design of a framework for (1) modelling knowledge in distributed systems, and (2) supporting liveness proofs under fairness assumptions, with an important degree of automation.

Acknowledgements. We warmly thank Pamela Zave for insightful discussions on the protocol and for her thorough reading of this article.

J. Brunel and D. Chemouil were partly financed by the European Regional Development Fund (ERDF) through the Operational Programme for Competitiveness and Internationalisation (COMPETE2020) and by National Funds through the Portuguese funding agency, Fundação para a Ciência e a Tecnologia (FCT) within project POCI-01-0145-FEDER-016826; and within the French Research Agency project FORMEDICIS (ANR-16-CE25-0007).

References

1. Abrial, J.R.: Modeling in Event-B. Cambridge University Press, Cambridge (2009). https://doi.org/10.1017/cbo9781139195881
2. Abrial, J.R., Butler, M., Hallerstede, S., Hoang, T.S., Mehta, F., Voisin, L.: Rodin: an open toolset for modelling and reasoning in Event-B. Int. J. Softw. Tools Technol. Transf. **12**(6), 447–466 (2010). https://doi.org/10.1007/s10009-010-0145-y
3. Bakhshi, R., Gurov, D.: Verification of peer-to-peer algorithms: a case study. Electron. Notes Theor. Comput. Sci. **181**, 35–47 (2007). https://doi.org/10.1016/j.entcs.2007.01.052
4. Bodeveix, J.P., Brunel, J., Chemouil, D., Filali, M.: A model in Event-B of the Chord protocol, July 2019. https://doi.org/10.5281/zenodo.3271455
5. Brunel, J., Chemouil, D., Tawa, J.: Analyzing the fundamental liveness property of the Chord protocol. In: Formal Methods in Computer-Aided Design, Austin, USA, October 2018. https://doi.org/10.23919/fmcad.2018.8603001. https://hal.archives-ouvertes.fr/hal-01862755
6. Hawblitzel, C., et al.: IronFleet: proving practical distributed systems correct. In: Proceedings of the ACM Symposium on Operating Systems Principles (SOSP), ACM –Association for Computing Machinery, October 2015. https://doi.org/10.1145/2815400.2815428
7. Jackson, D.: Software Abstractions: Logic, Language, and Analysis. MIT Press, Cambridge (2012)
8. Lamport, L.: Specifying Systems: The TLA$^+$ Language and Tools for Hardware and Software Engineers. Addison-Wesley Longman Publishing Co., Inc. (2002)
9. Li, X., Misra, J., Plaxton, C.G.: Active and concurrent topology maintenance. In: Guerraoui, R. (ed.) DISC 2004. LNCS, vol. 3274, pp. 320–334. Springer, Heidelberg (2004). https://doi.org/10.1007/978-3-540-30186-8_23
10. Liben-Nowell, D., Balakrishnan, H., Karger, D.: Analysis of the evolution of peer-to-peer systems. In: Proceedings of the Twenty-First Annual Symposium on Principles of Distributed Computing, pp. 233–242. ACM (2002). https://doi.org/10.1145/571860.571863
11. Macedo, N., Brunel, J., Chemouil, D., Cunha, A., Kuperberg, D.: Lightweight specification and analysis of dynamic systems with rich configurations. In: Foundations of Software Engineering (2016). https://doi.org/10.1145/2950290.2950318
12. Marinković, B., Glavan, P., Ognjanović, Z.: Proving properties of the Chord protocol using the ASM formalism. Theor. Comput. Sci. **756**, 64 – 93 (2019). https://doi.org/10.1016/j.tcs.2018.10.025, http://www.sciencedirect.com/science/article/pii/S0304397518306467
13. Merz, S., Lu, T., Weidenbach, C.: Towards verification of the pastry protocol using TLA$^+$. In: 31st IFIP International Conference on Formal Techniques for Networked and Distributed Systems, vol. 6722 (2011). https://doi.org/10.1007/978-3-642-21461-5_16
14. Padon, O., Hoenicke, J., Losa, G., Podelski, A., Sagiv, M., Shoham, S.: Reducing liveness to safety in first-order logic. PACMPL **2**(POPL), 26:1–26:33 (2018). https://doi.org/10.1145/3158114
15. Padon, O., McMillan, K.L., Panda, A., Sagiv, M., Shoham, S.: Ivy: safety verification by interactive generalization. In: Proceedings of the 37th ACM SIGPLAN Conference on Programming Language Design and Implementation, PLDI 2016, Santa Barbara, CA, USA, 13–17 June 2016, pp. 614–630 (2016). https://doi.org/10.1145/2908080.2908118

16. Risson, J., Robinson, K., Moors, T.: Fault tolerant active rings for structured peer-to-peer overlays. In: 2005 The IEEE Conference on Local Computer Networks, 30th Anniversary, pp. 18–25. IEEE (2005). https://doi.org/10.1109/lcn.2005.69

17. Stoica, I., Morris, R., Karger, D., Kaashoek, M.F., Balakrishnan, H.: Chord: a scalable peer-to-peer lookup service for internet applications. ACM SIGCOMM Comput. Commun. Rev. **31**(4), 149–160 (2001). https://doi.org/10.1145/964723.383071

18. Stoica, I., et al.: Chord: a scalable peer-to-peer lookup protocol for Internet applications. IEEE/ACM Trans. Netw. (TON) **11**(1), 17–32 (2003). https://doi.org/10.1109/tnet.2002.808407

19. Wilcox, J.R., et al.: Verdi: a framework for implementing and formally verifying distributed systems. In: Proceedings of the 36th ACM SIGPLAN Conference on Programming Language Design and Implementation, Portland, OR, USA, 15–17 June 2015, pp. 357–368 (2015). https://doi.org/10.1145/2737924.2737958

20. Zave, P.: Why the Chord ring-maintenance protocol is not correct. Technical report, AT&T Research (2011)

21. Zave, P.: Using lightweight modeling to understand Chord. ACM SIGCOMM Comput. Commun. Rev. **42**(2), 49–57 (2012). https://doi.org/10.1145/2185376.2185383

22. Zave, P.: A practical comparison of Alloy and Spin. Formal Aspects Comput. **27**(2), 239 (2015). https://doi.org/10.1007/s00165-014-0302-2

23. Zave, P.: Reasoning about identifier spaces: how to make Chord correct. IEEE Trans. Softw. Eng. **43**(12), 1144–1156 (2017). https://doi.org/10.1109/TSE.2017.2655056

On the Nature of Symbolic Execution

Frank S. de Boer[1,2(✉)] and Marcello Bonsangue[2]

[1] Centrum Wiskunde & Informatica (CWI), Amsterdam, The Netherlands
`f.s.de.boer@cwi.nl`
[2] Leiden Institute Of Advanced Computer Science (LIACS), Leiden, The Netherlands
`m.m.bonsangue@liacs.leidenuniv.nl`

Abstract. In this paper, we provide a formal definition of symbolic execution in terms of a symbolic transition system and prove its correctness with respect to an operational semantics which models the execution on concrete values. We first introduce such a formal model for a basic programming language with a statically fixed number of programming variables. This model is extended to a programming language with recursive procedures which are called by a call-by-value parameter mechanism. Finally, we show how to extend this latter model of symbolic execution to arrays and object-oriented languages which feature dynamically allocated variables.

1 Introduction

Symbolic execution [1] plays a crucial role in modern testing techniques, debugging, and automated program analysis. In particular, it is used for generating test cases [2,3].

Although symbolic execution techniques have improved enormously in the last few years not much effort has been spent on its formal justification. In fact, the symbolic execution community has concentrated most of the effort on effectiveness (improvement in speed-up) and significance (improvement in code coverage) and payed little attention to correctness so far [3].

Further, there exists a pletora of different techniques for one of the major problems in symbolic execution, namely the presence of dynamically allocated program variables, e.g., describing arrays and (object-oriented) pointer structures ("heaps"). For example, in [15] a heap is modeled as a graph, with nodes drawn from a set of objects and updated lazily, whereas [5] introduces a constraint language for the specification of invariant properties of heap structures. In [11] the symbolic state is extended with a heap configuration used to maintain objects which are initialized only when they are first accessed during execution. In the presence of aliasing, the uncertainty on the possible values of a symbolic pointer is treated either by forking the symbolic state or refining the generated path condition into several ones [6]. Powerful symbolic execution tools [7–9] handling arrays exploit various code pre-processing techniques, though formal correctness of the theory behind these tools is acknowledged as a potential problem that might limit the validity of the internal engine, and is validated only

© Springer Nature Switzerland AG 2019
M. H. ter Beek et al. (Eds.): FM 2019, LNCS 11800, pp. 64–80, 2019.
https://doi.org/10.1007/978-3-030-30942-8_6

experimentally by testing [10]. The KeY theorem prover [18] supports symbolic execution of Java programs which is defined in terms of the underlying dynamic logic and which uses an explicit representation of the heap. In all of the above work no explicit formal account of the underlying model of the symbolic execution, and its correctness, is presented.

The main contribution of this paper is a formal definition of symbolic execution in terms of a symbolic transition system and a general definition of its correctness with respect to an operational semantics which models the actual execution on concrete values. Our general starting point is that the basic idea of symbolic execution is to represent the program state, i.e., the assignment of values to program variables, by a corresponding substitution which assigns to each program variable an expression denoting its current value. Further, symbolic execution by its very nature is *syntax-directed* which implies that the *abstraction level* of the symbolic transition system should coincide with that of the programming language. This general requirement implies that symbolic execution operates on substitutions which (only) assign *programming* expressions to the variables (and no other expressions which express properties of the run-time).

The only other approach to a formal modeling of symbolic execution, we are aware of, is the work presented in [4]. A major difference with our approach is that in [4] symbolic execution is defined in terms of a general logic (called "Reachability Logic") for the description of transition systems which abstracts from the specific characteristics of the programming language. A symbolic execution then consists basically of a sequence of logical specifications of the consecutive transitions. On the other hand, a model of the logic defines a concrete transition system. Thus correctness basically follows from the semantics of the logic. In our approach we both model symbolic execution and the concrete semantics (of any language) independently as transition systems. However, in both cases the transitions are directly defined in terms of the program to be executed. This allows to address the specific characteristics of the programming language (like dynamically allocated variables) still in a general manner. In [4], however, these specific characteristics (like arrays) need to be imported in the general framework by corresponding logical theories which require an additional justification.

Detailed Plan of the Paper. In Sect. 2 we introduce a formal model of symbolic execution for a basic programming language with a statically fixed number of programming variables. The concrete transition system for this basic language is standard (and therefore omitted). A configuration of the symbolic transition system consists of the program statement to be executed, a substitution, and a path condition. Correctness then states that for every reachable symbolic configuration and state which satisfies the path condition, there exists a corresponding concrete execution. Conversely, completeness states that for every concrete execution there exists a corresponding symbolic configuration such that the initial state of the concrete execution satisfies the path condition and its final state can be obtained as a composition of the initial state and the generated substitution.

In Sect. 3, we extend the basic theory of symbolic execution to a programming language with recursive procedures which are called by a call-by-value parameter mechanism. This extension requires a formal treatment of local variables stored on the stack of procedure calls.

In Sect. 4 we show how to extend symbolic execution in a strictly syntax-directed manner to an object-oriented language which features dynamically allocated variables. These dynamically allocated variables give rise to an *infinite* number of program variables and corresponding substitutions with an infinite domain. We show how to extend our theory of symbolic execution to such infinite substitutions. Moreover, we introduce for a correct implementation a finite representation of these substitutions, and discuss different strategies for managing aliasing.

In the final technical Sect. 5 (unbounded) arrays, multithreading, and concurrent objects are discussed as a further illustration of the generality of our theory of symbolic execution.

Because of space limitations, in this paper we do not introduce all syntactic details of the programming languages we use, which however should be clear via their transition system semantics.

2   Basic Symbolic Execution

We assume a set of *Var* of program variables $x, y, u, \ldots$, and a set *Ops* of operations $op, \ldots$. We abstract from typing information. The set *Expr* of *programming expressions* e is defined by the following grammar.

$$e := x \mid op(e_1, \ldots, e_n)$$

where $x \in Var$ and $op \in Ops$. A *substitution* σ is a function $Var \rightarrow Expr$ which assigns to each variable an expression. By $e\sigma$ we denote the application of the substitution σ to the expression e, defined inductively by

$$
\begin{aligned}
x\sigma &= \sigma(x) \\
op(e_1, \ldots, e_n)\sigma &= op(e_1\sigma, \ldots, e_n\sigma)
\end{aligned}
$$

A *symbolic configuration* is a triple $\langle S, \sigma, \phi \rangle$ where S denotes the statement to be executed, σ denotes the current substitution, and Boolean condition ϕ denotes the path condition.

Next we describe a transition system for the symbolic execution of a simple programming language which features assignments, sequential composition, a choice and iteration statement.

Assignment

$$- \ \langle x = e; S, \sigma, \phi \rangle \rightarrow \langle S, \sigma[x = e\sigma], \phi \rangle$$

where $\sigma[x = e](y) = \sigma(y)$ if x and y are distinct variables, and $\sigma[x = e](x) = e$ otherwise.

Choice

- $\langle if \ B \ \{S_1\}\{S_2\}; S, \sigma, \phi\rangle \to \langle S_1; S, \sigma, \phi \wedge B\sigma\rangle$
- $\langle if \ B \ \{S_1\}\{S_2\}; S, \sigma, \phi\rangle \to \langle S_2; S, \sigma, \phi \wedge \neg B\sigma\rangle$

Iteration

- $\langle while \ B \ \{S\}; S', \sigma, \phi\rangle \to \langle S; while \ B \ \{S\}; S', \sigma, \phi \wedge B\sigma\rangle$
- $\langle while \ B \ \{S\}; S', \sigma, \phi\rangle \to \langle S', \sigma, \phi \wedge \neg B\sigma\rangle$

We formalize and prove correctness with respect to a concrete semantics. A *valuation* V is a function $Var \to Val$, where Val is a set of *values*. By $V(e)$ we denote the value of the expression e with respect to the valuation V, defined inductively by $V(op(e_1, \ldots, e_n)) = \overline{op}(V(e_1), \ldots, V(e_n))$ where $\overline{op}$ denotes the interpretation of the operation op as provided by the implicitly assumed underlying model. Composition is as usual: $(V \circ \sigma)(x) = V(\sigma(x))$[1].

Lemma 1 (Substitution). $V \circ \sigma(e) = V(e\sigma)$.

Proof (Sketch). The proof of the lemma proceeds by induction on e. We have the following main case:

$$
\begin{aligned}
V \circ \sigma(op(e_1, \ldots, e_n)) &= \overline{op}(V \circ \sigma(e_1), \ldots, V \circ \sigma(e_n)) & \text{(semantics expressions)} \\
&= \overline{op}(V(e_1\sigma), \ldots, V((e_n\sigma)) & \text{(induction hypothesis)} \\
&= V(op(e_1\sigma, \ldots, e_n\sigma)) & \text{(semantics expressions)} \\
&= V(op(e_1, \ldots, e_n)\sigma) & \text{(substitution application)}
\end{aligned}
$$

The concrete semantics of our basic programming language is defined in terms of transitions $\langle S, V\rangle \to \langle S', V'\rangle$. The definition of this transition system is standard and therefore omitted.

Let id be the identity substitution, i.e., $id(x) = x$, for every variable x. We have the following main correctness theorem.

Theorem 1 (Correctness). *If* $\langle S, id, true\rangle \to^* \langle S', \sigma, \phi\rangle$ *and* $V(\phi) = true$ *then*

$$\langle S, V\rangle \to^* \langle S', V \circ \sigma\rangle$$

Proof. Induction on the length of $\langle S, id, true\rangle \to^* \langle S', \sigma, \phi\rangle$ and a case analysis of the last execution step. We consider the following cases.

First, we consider the case of an assignment as the last execution step:

$$\langle S, id, true\rangle \to^* \langle x = e; S', \sigma, \phi\rangle \to \langle S', \sigma[x = e\sigma], \phi\rangle$$

Induction hypothesis (note that $V(\phi) = true$):

$$\langle S, V\rangle \to^* \langle x = e; S', V \circ \sigma\rangle$$

---

[1] In the sequel we omit the parentheses and write $V \circ \sigma(e)$ for the application valuation $V \circ \sigma$ to the expression e (as defined above).

Let $V' = V \circ \sigma$. By the concrete semantics we have

$$\langle S, V \rangle \to^* \langle x = e; S', V' \rangle \to \langle S', V'[x = V'(e)] \rangle$$

where $V'[x = V'(e)](x) = V'(e)$ and $V'[x = V'(e)](y) = V'(y)$, for any other variable y. Suffices to show $V \circ (\sigma[x = e\sigma]) = V'[x = V'(e)]$. We treat the main case:

$$
\begin{aligned}
V \circ (\sigma[x = e\sigma])(x) &= V(\sigma[x = e\sigma](x)) &&(\text{def. } \circ) \\
&= V(e\sigma) &&(\text{def. } \sigma[x = e\sigma]) \\
&= V \circ \sigma(e) &&(\text{substitution lemma}) \\
&= V'(e) &&(V' = V \circ \sigma) \\
&= V'[x = V'(e)](x) &&(\text{def. } V'[x = V'(e)])
\end{aligned}
$$

Next we consider the case when the Boolean guard of a choice construct evaluates to true:

$$\langle S, id, true \rangle \to^* \langle if \ B \ \{S_1\}\{S_2\}; S, \sigma, \phi \rangle \to \langle S_1; S, \sigma, \phi \wedge B\sigma \rangle$$

We have that $V(\phi \wedge B\sigma) = true$ implies $V(\phi) = true$, so by the induction hypothesis we obtain the concrete computation

$$\langle S, V \rangle \to^* \langle if \ B \ \{S_1\}\{S_2\}; S, V \circ \sigma \rangle$$

Since $V \circ \sigma(B) = V(B\sigma) = true$, we derive

$$\langle S, V \rangle \to^* \langle if \ B \ \{S_1\}\{S_2\}; S, V \circ \sigma \rangle \to \langle S_1; S, V \circ \sigma \rangle$$

All other cases are treated similarly.

Theorem 1 guarantees that all possible inputs satisfying a path condition lead to a concrete state with variables conform to the substitution of the corresponding symbolic configuration. Correctness, however, is about coverage [4], meaning that *satisfiable* symbolic execution paths can be simulated by concrete executions. The converse of correctness is completeness and is about precision [4]: every concrete execution can be simulated by a symbolic one. To this end we introduce the following relation between symbolic and the concrete transition systems: Let $\langle S, V \rangle \simeq \langle S, \sigma, \phi \rangle$ denote that $V = V_0 \circ \sigma$ and $V_0(\phi) = true$, for some valuation V_0.

Theorem 2 (Completeness). *The relation $\simeq$ between symbolic and concrete configurations is a simulation relation, i.e., if $\langle S, V \rangle \simeq \langle S, \sigma, \phi \rangle$ then $\langle S, V \rangle \to \langle S', V' \rangle$ implies the existence of a corresponding symbolic transition $\langle S, \sigma, \phi \rangle \to \langle S', \sigma', \phi' \rangle$ such that $\langle S', V' \rangle \simeq \langle S', \sigma', \phi' \rangle$.*

The proof of this theorem proceeds by a straightforward case analysis of the concrete execution steps.

3   Recursion

We extend the basic programming language with procedure declarations $P(\bar{u}) ::$ S and procedure calls $P(\bar{e})$, assuming a call by value parameter passing mechanism. A program then consists of set of procedure declarations and a main statement. We assume absence of name clashes between the global variables of a program and its local variables (e.g., the formal parameters of the procedure declarations). A *symbolic configuration* is of the form $\langle \Sigma, \sigma, \phi \rangle$, where

- Σ denotes the stack of *closures* (τ, S), where τ is a *local* substitution (assigning expressions to formal parameters),
- σ is the current *global* substitution (mapping expressions to global variables),
- ϕ is a Boolean condition denoting the path condition.

In the sequel we indicate by $\perp$ the absence of local variables in a closure $(\perp, S)$ which represents a continuation of the execution of the main statement which does not contain local variables (for technical convenience we do not consider the introduction of local variables by block statements). By $\tau \cup \sigma$ we denote the union of the substitutions τ and σ (defined in terms of their graphs). This is well-defined because of the absence of name clashes between local and global variables of a programs. We have the following symbolic transitions.

Procedure Call. Given the procedure declaration $P(\bar{u}) :: S'$, we have

- $\langle (\tau, P(\bar{e}); S) \cdot \Sigma, \sigma, \phi \rangle \to \langle (\tau', S') \cdot (\tau, S) \cdot \Sigma, \sigma, \phi \rangle$, where $\tau'(\bar{u}) = \bar{e}(\tau \cup \sigma)$.

Procedure Return

- $\langle (\tau, \epsilon) \cdot \Sigma, \sigma, \phi \rangle \to \langle \Sigma, \sigma, \phi \rangle$, where ϵ denotes the empty statement.

Choice

- $\langle (\tau, if\ B\ \{S_1\}\{S_2\}; S) \cdot \Sigma, \sigma, \phi \rangle \to \langle (\tau, S_1; S,) \cdot \Sigma, \sigma, \phi \wedge B(\tau \cup \sigma) \rangle$
- $\langle (\tau, if\ B\ \{S_1\}\{S_2\}; S) \cdot \Sigma, \sigma, \phi \rangle \to \langle (\tau, S_2; S) \cdot \Sigma, \sigma, \phi \wedge \neg B(\tau \cup \sigma) \rangle$

Iteration

- $\langle (\tau, while\ B\ \{S\}; S') \cdot \Sigma, \sigma, \phi \rangle \to \langle (\tau, S; while\ B\ \{S\}; S') \cdot \Sigma, \sigma, \phi \wedge B(\tau \cup \sigma) \rangle$
- $\langle (\tau, while\ B\ \{S\}; S') \cdot \Sigma, \sigma, \phi \rangle \to \langle (\tau, S') \cdot \Sigma, \sigma, \phi \wedge \neg B(\tau \cup \sigma) \rangle$

Assignment Global Variable Let x be a global variable.

- $\langle (\tau, x = e; S) \cdot \Sigma, \sigma, \phi \rangle \to \langle (\tau, S) \cdot \Sigma, \sigma[x = e\theta], \phi \rangle$, where $\theta = \tau \cup \sigma$.

Assignment Local Variable Let x be a local variable.

- $\langle (\tau, x = e; S) \cdot \Sigma, \sigma, \phi \rangle \to \langle (\tau[x = e\theta], S) \cdot \Sigma, \sigma, \phi \rangle$, where $\theta = \tau \cup \sigma$.

Proposition 1. *For any computation* $\langle(\bot, S), id, \text{true}\rangle \rightarrow^* \langle(\tau, S') \cdot \Sigma, \sigma, \phi\rangle$ *where S denotes the main statement, we have that $\tau(x)$, for every local variable x in its domain, and $\sigma(x)$, for every global variable x, does* not *contain local variables.*

Proof. By induction on the length of the computation, using that $e\theta$, for any programming expression e, does not contain local variables, where $\theta = \tau \cup \sigma$ and $\tau(x)$, for every local variable x, and $\sigma(x)$, for every global variable x, does not contain local variables.

Corollary 1. *For any computation* $\langle(\bot\ S), id, \text{true}\rangle \rightarrow^* \langle(\tau, S') \cdot \Sigma, \sigma, \phi\rangle$ *where S denotes the main statement, the generated path condition ϕ does not contain local variables.*

We omit the details of the standard concrete semantics which instead of substitutions is defined in terms of valuations both for the local variables and the global variables, where $V \cup L(e)$ denotes the result of the evaluation of the expression e in the global valuation V and the local valuation L. We have the following correctness theorem of the symbolic execution of recursive programs.

Theorem 3 (Correctness). *If* $\langle(\bot, S), id, \text{true}\rangle \rightarrow^* \langle(\tau, S') \cdot \Sigma, \sigma, \phi\rangle$ *and* $V(\phi) = \text{true}$ *then*

$$\langle(\bot, S), V\rangle \rightarrow^* \langle(V \circ \tau, S') \cdot V \circ \Sigma, V \circ \sigma\rangle$$

where $V \circ \tau'(x) = V(\tau'(x))$, for any local environment τ' and local variable x, and $V \circ \Sigma$ denotes the result of replacing every local environment τ' in Σ by $V \circ \tau'$ (and by $\bot$, in case of the empty local environment $\bot$). Note that by the above proposition and corollary $\tau(x)$ and ϕ do not contain local variables.

Proof. As above, we proceed by induction on the length of the symbolic computation and a case analysis of the last execution step. Given the procedure declaration $P(\bar{u}) :: S'$, we consider the case of a procedure call:

$$\langle(\bot, S), id, \text{true}\rangle \rightarrow^* \langle(\tau, P(\bar{e}); S'') \cdot \Sigma, \sigma, \phi\rangle \rightarrow \langle(\tau', S') \cdot (\tau, ; S'') \cdot \Sigma, \sigma, \phi\rangle$$

where $\tau'(\bar{u}) = \bar{e}(\tau \cup \sigma)$. By the induction hypothesis we obtain the concrete computation

$$\langle(\bot, S), V\rangle \rightarrow^* \langle(V \circ \tau, P(\bar{e}); S'') \cdot V \circ \Sigma, V \circ \sigma\rangle$$

We observe that $V \circ \tau'(\bar{u}) = V(\bar{e}(\tau \cup \sigma)) = V \circ (\tau \cup \sigma)(\bar{e}) = (V \circ \tau \cup V \circ \sigma)(\bar{e})$. So we obtain that

$$\langle(V \circ \tau, P(\bar{e}); S'') \cdot V \circ \Sigma, V \circ \sigma\rangle \rightarrow \langle(V \circ \tau', S') \cdot (V \circ \tau, ; S'') \cdot V \circ \Sigma, V \circ \sigma\rangle$$

As in the basic case, we have a similar completeness result for recursive procedures also expressed in terms of a simulation relation between the symbolic and the concrete transition system.

4   Object Orientation

We distinguish between the global variables appearing in the main statement, the local variables (i.e., the formal parameters of methods, including the keyword *this*), and the instance variables (of the classes) of the given program. For modeling symbolically the dynamic creation of new objects, we assume a (countable) infinite set of global variables. We abstract from the typing information of the variables. We have the following syntax of programming expressions e in class definitions

$$e := x \mid op(e_1, \ldots, e_n)$$

where x is a local or instance variable[2] and op denotes a built-in operation.

The syntax of *heap variables H* and *heap expressions E* is defined by the following grammar:

$$H := x \mid H.y$$
$$E := H \mid op(E_1, \ldots, E_n),$$

where x is a global variable and op an operation. In the last clause defining heap variables we implicitly assume that y is an instance variable of the class of the object represented by H.

A *symbolic heap* σ is a substitution which assigns to each heap variable a heap expression. A *local environment* (of a given method) τ is a substitution which assigns to each formal parameter a general heap expression. Note that thus $\tau(x)$ does not contain local variables.

We have the following inductive definition of the application of a substitution θ which consists of the union $\tau \cup \sigma$ of a symbolic heap σ and a local environment τ to a programming expression e (as above, assuming absence of name clashes between the formal parameters, on the one hand, and the instance and global variables, on the other hand).

$$
\begin{array}{lll}
x\theta & = \tau(x) & \text{local variable} \\
x\theta & = \sigma(\tau(this).x) & \text{instance variable} \\
op(E_1, \ldots, E_n)\theta & = op(E_1\theta, \ldots, E_n\theta)
\end{array}
$$

A *heap update* $\sigma[x = E]$, where x is a global variable, is defined by $\sigma[x = E](x) = E$ and $\sigma[x = E](H) = \sigma(H)$, for any other heap variable H. Next we define a *symbolic heap update* $\sigma[H.x = E]$ by

- $\sigma[H.x = E](H'.x) = if\ \sigma(H') = \sigma(H)\ then\ E\ else\ \sigma(H'.x)\ fi$,
- $\sigma[H.x = E](H') = \sigma(H')$, *for any other heap variable H'.*

It is important to note that the resulting expression in the first clause is a *conditional* heap expression which captures possible aliases. Note further that the case $\sigma[H.x = E](H.x)$ simplifies to E.

---

[2] In the main statement only global variables are used.

Given a program, i.e., a set of class definitions and a main statement, a symbolic configuration is defined as above. We have the following symbolic transitions (the transitions for the assigning local variables, the choice and iteration constructs are as above).

Assignment Global Variable. As above, absence of local variables in the main statement is indicated by $\perp$.

- $\langle (\perp, x = e; S), \sigma, \phi \rangle \rightarrow \langle (\perp, S), \sigma[x = e\sigma], \phi \rangle$
  Note that a closure representing the execution of the main statement is always at the bottom of the stack.

Assignment Instance Variable

- $\langle (\tau, x = e; S) \cdot \Sigma, \sigma, \phi \rangle \rightarrow \langle (\tau, S) \cdot \Sigma, \sigma[\tau(this).x = e\theta], \phi \rangle$, where $\theta = \tau \cup \sigma$.

Object Creation. We describe the assignment of a new object to a local variable[3].

- $\langle (\tau, x = \text{new } C; S) \cdot \Sigma, \sigma, \phi \rangle \rightarrow \langle (\tau[x = y], S) \cdot \Sigma, \sigma', \phi \rangle$

The global variable y (of type C) is *fresh* and σ' results from σ by assigning nil to $y.x$, x an instance variable of C. Freshness is defined with respect to the computation (which thus requires recording the set of new global variables introduced so far, the details of which are straightforward and therefore omitted).

Method Call. Given a method declaration $m(\bar{u})\{S\}$, we have

- $\langle (\tau, y = e_0.m(\bar{e}); S') \cdot \Sigma, \sigma, \phi \rangle \rightarrow \langle (\tau'.S) \cdot (\tau, y =?; S') \cdot \Sigma, \sigma, \phi' \rangle$,
  where $\tau'(\bar{u}) = \bar{e}(\tau \cup \sigma)$ and $\tau'(this) = e_0(\tau \cup \sigma)$. The question mark in the assignment $y =?$ serves as a placeholder of the return expression (see below). Further, ϕ' denotes the path condition $\phi \wedge e_0(\tau \cup \sigma) \neq nil$.

Method Return

- $\langle (\tau, \text{return } e) \cdot (\tau', x =?; S) \cdot \Sigma, \sigma, \phi \rangle \rightarrow \langle (\tau'[x = e\theta], S) \cdot \Sigma, \sigma, \phi \rangle$,
  where $\theta = (\tau \cup \sigma)$. For an assignment of the return expression to an instance variable we have a similar transition.

We have the following basic proposition about the expressions generated by a symbolic computation.

Proposition 2. *For any computation* $\langle (\perp, S), id, true \rangle \rightarrow^* \langle (\tau, S') \cdot \Sigma, \sigma, \phi \rangle$ *where S denotes the main statement, we have that $\tau(x)$ and $\sigma(x)$ do not contain local variables and do not dereference a global variable that does not occur in the main statement (i.e., a global variable used to denote a newly created object).*

Proof. The proof proceeds by a straightforward induction on the length of the symbolic computation.

---

[3] We model a call $x = \text{new } C(\bar{e})$ of a constructor method by the object creation statement $x = \text{new } C$ followed by a method call $x.C(\bar{e})$.

Corollary 2. *For any computation* $\langle (\perp S), id, \text{true} \rangle \rightarrow^* \langle (\tau, S') \cdot \Sigma, \sigma, \phi \rangle$ *where* S *denotes the main statement, the generated path condition* ϕ *does not contain local variables and derefences only global variables appearing in the main statement (in other words, global variables which do not appear in the main statement are not dereferenced).*

In order to define and prove the correctness of the above symbolic transition system for object-oriented programs, we first introduce the notion of a global valuation V which assigns to each heap variable a value (of the corresponding type) and which satisfies the following two conditions:

- $V(H) = V(H')$ implies $V(H.x) = V(H'.x)$, for every heap variables H and H' and instance variable x (belonging to the class of the object).
- $V(x) \neq V(x')$, for any two distinct global variables x and x' which do not appear in the main statement (*unique name assumption*).

A concrete local valuation L assigns to every formal parameter x of the corresponding method a value $L(x)$ (of the appropriate type).

An update $V[x = v]$ of a global valuation V, where x is a global variable and v a value of corresponding type, is defined by $V[x = v](x) = v$ and $V[x = v](H) = V(H)$, for any other heap variable H. On the other hand, an update $V[H.x = v]$ is defined by

- $V[H.x = v](H'.x) = \begin{cases} v & \text{if } V(H') = V(H) \\ V(H'.x) & \text{otherwise} \end{cases}$
- $V[H.x = v](H') = V(H')$, for any other heap variable H'.

An initial configuration $\langle (\perp, S), V \rangle$ of the concrete semantics of a given program consists of the main statement S (as above, $\perp$ indicates the absence of local variables) and an *initial* global valuation V such that for any global variable x which does not appear in the main statement and heap variable H rooted in a global variable we have that $V(x) \neq V(H)$. Any global variable is a heap variable rooted in a global variable, and if H is such a heap variable, so is $H.x$, for any instance variable x. We thus can use these initially unreachable objects in the concrete semantics as a repository of fresh object identities (which are selected non-deterministically, as the fresh global variables in the symbolic semantics). Since every executing object is reachable (from a global variable) we can define the concrete semantics of an assignment $x = e$ to an instance variable e as follows. Given the above update of a global valuation V and a local environment L (which assigns values to the local variables of the executing method), we can define the resulting global valuation of the execution of the assignment $x = e$ by the object $L(this)$ by $V[H.x = v]$, where H is such that $V(H) = L(this)$, and v is the result of evaluating the expression e in the local environment L and the valuation V.

We omit the further details of the standard concrete semantics (which thus, instead of substitutions, is defined in terms of valuations both for the local variables and the heap variables).

We have the following correctness theorem of the symbolic execution of object-oriented programs.

Theorem 4 (Correctness). *Given an object-oriented program with main statement S we have that if $\langle(\bot, S), id, \text{true}\rangle \rightarrow^* \langle(\tau, S') \cdot \Sigma, \sigma, \phi\rangle$ and $V(\phi) = \text{true}$, where V is an initial valuation, then*

$$\langle(\bot, S), V\rangle \rightarrow^* \langle(V \circ \tau, S') \cdot V \circ \Sigma, V \circ \sigma\rangle$$

where $V \circ \tau$ and $V \circ \Sigma$ are defined as above.

Proof. As above, the proof proceeds by induction on the length of the symbolic computation and a case analysis of the last execution step. For the case of an assignment $x = e$ to an instance variable, it suffices to show that

$$V \circ (\sigma[\tau(this).x = e\theta]) = (V \circ \sigma)[\tau(this).x = V(e\theta)]$$

where $\theta = \tau \cup \sigma$. Here we go: First, for any heap variable H not of the form $H'.x$, for some H', we have

$$
\begin{aligned}
V \circ (\sigma[\tau(this).x = e\theta])(H) &= V(\sigma[\tau(this\,).x = e\theta](H)) && (\text{def.} \circ) \\
&= V(\sigma(H)) && (\text{def. update } \sigma[\tau(this).x = e\theta]) \\
&= (V \circ \sigma)(H) && (\text{def.} \circ) \\
&= (V \circ \sigma)[\tau(this).x = V(e\theta)](H) && (\text{def. update}(V \circ \sigma)[\tau(this).x = V(e\theta)]) \,.
\end{aligned}
$$

Further,

$$
\begin{aligned}
&V \circ (\sigma[\tau(this).x = e\theta])(H.x) \\
={}& (\text{def.} \circ) \\
&V(\sigma[\tau(this).x = e\theta](H.x)) \\
={}& (\text{def. update } \sigma[\tau(this).x = e\theta]) \\
&V(\textit{if } \sigma(H) = \sigma(\tau(this)) \textit{ then } e\theta \textit{ else } \sigma(H.x) \textit{ fi}) \\
={}& (\text{semantics of conditional heap expression}) \\
&\textit{if } V(\sigma(H)) = V(\sigma(\tau(this))) \textit{ then } V(e\theta) \textit{ else } V(\sigma(H.x)) \\
={}& (\text{def. update } (V \circ \sigma)[\tau(this).x = V(e\theta)]) \\
&(V \circ \sigma)[\tau(this).x = V(e\theta)](H.x) \,.
\end{aligned}
$$

Again, completeness can be established by means of a simulation relation between the symbolic transition system and the concrete one.

Implementation

An implementation of the above symbolic execution of object-oriented programs requires a finite representation of the generated substitutions (note that we have a countable infinite set of heap variables). As an example, we can represent the generated substitutions by (possibly empty) sequences $\{H_1.x_1 = E_1\}, \ldots, \{H_n.x_n = E_1\}$ of updates of instance variables. Such a sequence ρ simply represents the substitution $\bar{\rho}$ which results from the identity substitution id by applying the updates $[H_1, x_1 = E_1], \ldots, [H_n.x_n = E_n]$, as defined above, consecutively. For such a sequence of updates ρ we define $\rho(H)$ inductively by

- $id(H) = H$,
- $\rho\{H.x = E\}(H'.x) = if \ \rho(H') = \rho(H) \ then \ E \ else \ \rho(H'.x) \ fi$,
- $\rho\{H.x = E\}(H') = \rho(H')$, for any other heap variable H'.

It is easy to prove by induction on the length of the sequence ρ that $\rho(H) = \bar{\rho}(H)$, for every heap variable. We then can define $e(\tau \cup \rho)$ in the same manner as $e(\tau \cup \sigma)$ defined above. Thus we can now define the following transition for an assignment to an instance variable

$$\langle (\tau, x = e; S) \cdot \Sigma, \rho, \phi \rangle \rightarrow \langle (\tau, S) \cdot \Sigma, \rho\{\tau(this).x = e\theta\}, \phi \rangle$$

where ρ is a sequence of updates and $\theta = \tau \cup \rho$. In general, we abstract from the infinite number of heap variables by simply replacing in the symbolic transitions the substitution σ by the sequence of updates ρ. In particular, we have the following adaptation of the transition describing object creation

$$\langle (\tau, x = \text{new } C; S) \cdot \Sigma, \rho, \phi \rangle \rightarrow \langle (\tau[x = y], S) \cdot \Sigma, \rho', \phi \rangle$$

where, as above, the global variable y (of type C) is *fresh* and ρ' results from ρ by adding the updates $\{y.x = nil\}$, for every an instance variable x of C.

Other implementation issues concern the aliasing of heap variables. There are various ways to manage (resolve) aliasing. We briefly describe the following enhancements. First, we can import information from the path condition ϕ into the evaluation of $\rho(H)$:

$$\rho\{H.x = E\}(H'.x) = \begin{cases} E & if \ \phi \vdash \rho(H) = \rho(H') \\ \rho(H'.x) & if \ \phi \vdash \rho(H) \neq \rho(H') \\ if \ \rho(H') = \rho(H) \ then \ E \ else \ \rho(H'.x) \ if & otherwise \end{cases}$$

Here $\vdash$ denotes logical entailment.

Further, there are various ways of branching the symbolic execution by resolving aliasing of heap variables. For example, we can resolve aliasing in the symbolic transition of an assignment $x = e$ as follows:

$$\langle (\tau, x = e; S) \cdot \Sigma, \rho, \phi \rangle \rightarrow \langle (\tau, S) \cdot \Sigma, \rho\{\tau(this).x = E\}, \phi' \rangle$$

where $\langle e(\tau \cup \rho), \phi \rangle \Rightarrow^* \langle E, \phi' \rangle$ and $\Rightarrow^*$ denotes the reflexive, transitive closure of the rewrite system consisting of the rules which resolve conditional expression, like

- $\langle op(\dots, if \ B \ then \ E_1 \ else \ E_2 fi, \dots), \phi \rangle \Rightarrow \langle op(\dots, E_1, \dots), B \wedge \phi \rangle$
- $\langle op(\dots, if \ B \ then \ E_1 \ else \ E_2 \ fi, \dots), \phi \rangle \Rightarrow \langle op(\dots, E_2, \dots), \neg B \wedge \phi \rangle$

In a similar manner, we can resolve aliasing which results from the symbolic evaluation of the Boolean condition of the choice and iteration constructs. For example, we have the following symbolic transition for the choice construct.

$$\langle (\tau, if \ B \ \{S_1\}\{S_2\}; S) \cdot \Sigma, \rho, \phi \rangle \rightarrow \langle (\tau, S_1; S,) \cdot \Sigma, \rho, B' \wedge \phi' \rangle$$

where $\langle B(\tau \cup \rho), \phi \rangle \Rightarrow^* \langle B', \phi' \rangle$.

5   Arrays, Multithreading, and Concurrent Objects

To illustrate the generality of our theory of symbolic execution we discuss the following extensions and applications.

Arrays. Arrays and object structures (i.e., heaps) are similar because both give rise to a (countable) infinite number of program variables. Instead of an infinite number of heap variables, arrays give rise to an infinite number of so-called *subscripted* variables.

To focus on the main ideas, we restrict this discussion to the extension of the basic programming language with one-dimensional arrays. We have the following syntax of *expressions e* in the basic programming language (abstracting from the typing information).

$$e := x \mid a[e] \mid op(e_1, \ldots, e_n),$$

where $x \in Var$, a is an array variable, and op denotes a built-in operation.

A *substitution* then assigns to each (subscripted) variable an expression. An update $\sigma[x = e]$, where x is a program variable, is defined by $\sigma[x = e](x) = e$ and $\sigma[x = e](y) = \sigma(y)$, for any other (subscripted) variable y. Next we define a symbolic update $\sigma[a[e] = e']$ by

- $\sigma[a[e] = e'](a[e'']) = $ *if* $\sigma(e) = \sigma(e'')$ *then* e' *else* $\sigma(a[e''])$ *if*,
- $\sigma[a[e] = e'](y) = \sigma(y)$, for any other (subscripted) variable y.

As above, it is important to note that the resulting expression in the first clause is a *conditional* expression which captures possible aliases.

Given this definition of a symbolic update we can define in a straightforward manner a symbolic transition system for the basic programming language extended with arrays (possibly taking into account symbolically array bounds). Correctness then is defined with respect to the notion of a global valuation V which assigns to each (subscripted) variable a value (of the corresponding type) and which satisfies the following condition:

- $V(e) = V(e')$ implies $V(a[e]) = V(a[e'])$.

It is straightforward to extend Theorem 1. In particular, correctness of a symbolic update of a subscripted variable then can be proved in a similar manner as that of a heap variable. Further, we can apply the same techniques as introduced for heap variables to obtain a finite representation of the generated substitutions and resolve aliasing.

We conclude this discussion on arrays with another approach which consists of a *functional view* of arrays (see [13]). In this view array variables themselves are expressions which denote functions, and a substitution assigns to each array variable an expression which denotes a function. Notably, an *expression* $(a[e] = e')$ denotes the function which results from updating the function denoted by a. Applying a substitution σ then amounts simply to substituting every occurrence of an array variable a by the expression $\sigma(a)$. Similarly, object structures can be viewed as a function h which symbolically represents the heap. However, the abstraction level of such a functional view does not coincide with that of the programming language (it extends the set of programming expressions).

Multithreading. It is straightforward to extend the symbolic transition system introduced above with multithreading: A symbolic configuration $\langle \textit{Threads}, \sigma \rangle$ then consists of a set *Threads* of stacks of closures and local symbolic transitions of a single thread are extended to global transitions by the following rule:

$$\frac{\langle T, \sigma, \phi \rangle \rightarrow \langle T', \sigma', \phi' \rangle}{\langle \{T\} \cup \textit{Threads}, \sigma, \phi \rangle \rightarrow \langle \{T'\} \cup \textit{Threads}, \sigma', \phi' \rangle}$$

where T and T' denote stacks of closures. For a call of the run method of a thread class we need the following separate rule which spawns a new thread.

$$\langle \{(\tau, e.\mathrm{run}; S) \cdot \textit{Stack}\} \cup \textit{Threads}, \sigma, \phi \rangle$$
$$\rightarrow$$
$$\langle \{(\tau, S) \cdot \textit{Stack}, (\tau', S')\} \cup \textit{Threads}, \sigma, \phi \rangle$$

where $\tau'(\textit{this}) = e(\tau \cup \sigma)$ and S' denotes the body of the run method. The proof of correctness is a straightforward extension of the correctness of the symbolic execution of sequential object-oriented programs (as stated by Theorem 4).

Concurrent Objects. We briefly sketch how to extend the symbolic execution of object-oriented programs to the Abstract Behavioral Specification (ABS) language [14] which describes systems of objects that interact via asynchronous method calls. Such a call spawns a corresponding process associated with the called object. Return values are communicated via futures [12]. Each object cooperatively schedules its processes one at a time. The processes of an object can only access their local variables and the instance variables of the object. As in Sect. 4, we assume a main statement that only contains global variables.

Symbolically, a system of concurrent objects in ABS can be described by a configuration $\langle P, \sigma, \phi \rangle$, where P is simply a set of closures (τ, S) which represent the processes, and σ is a substitution, ϕ is a path condition, both as defined in Sect. 4. To model the communication of the return values by futures we introduce for each process a distinguished local variable *dest* which denotes its own future (see below).

We have the following symbolic transition for an asynchronous call $x = e_0!m(\bar{e})$ to a method m with body S:

$$\langle \{(\tau, x = e_0!m(\bar{e}); S)\} \cup P, \sigma, \phi \rangle \rightarrow \langle \{(\tau, x = y; S), (\tau', S')\} \cup P, \sigma[y = \textit{nil}], \phi' \rangle$$

where the newly generated future is symbolically represented by a fresh global variable y which is initialized to *nil* (indicating that the return value has not yet been computed). Further, $\tau'(\bar{u}) = \bar{e}(\tau \cup \sigma)$, $\tau'(\textit{this}) = e_0(\tau \cup \sigma)$, and $\tau'(\textit{dest}) = y$. Finally, ϕ' denotes the path condition $\phi \wedge e_0(\tau \cup \sigma) \neq \textit{nil}$.

For returning a value we have the transition

$$\langle \{(\tau, \mathrm{return}\ e)\} \cup P, \sigma, \phi \rangle \rightarrow \langle P, \sigma[\tau(\textit{dest}) = e(\tau \cup \sigma)], \phi \rangle$$

Obtaining a returned value from a future by means of a "get" operation on a future variable is described by the transition

$$\langle \{(\tau, x = y.\text{get}); S)\} \cup P, \sigma, \phi \rangle \rightarrow \langle \{(\tau[x = \sigma(y)], S)\} \cup P, \sigma, \phi \rangle$$

where $\phi \vdash \sigma(y) \neq nil$ (that is, ϕ entails that $\sigma(y) \neq nil$). Note that this transition thus requires that the return value has been computed as recorded by the path condition.

Scheduling a process that is waiting on a Boolean condition is modeled by

$$\langle \{(\tau, \text{await } e; S)\} \cup P, \sigma, \phi \rangle \rightarrow \langle \{(\tau, S)\} \cup P, \sigma, \phi \wedge e\theta \rangle$$

where $\theta = \tau \cup \sigma$ and e is a Boolean condition. On the other hand, scheduling a process that is waiting on a future is modeled by

$$\langle \{(\tau, \text{await } x?; S)\} \cup P, \sigma, \phi \rangle \rightarrow \langle \{(\tau, S)\} \cup P, \sigma, \phi \rangle$$

where x is a future variable and $\phi \vdash \sigma(y) \neq nil$.

The transitions for the usual statements, e.g., that of assigning an instance variable of an object, are modeled in a straightforward manner after the corresponding transitions in Sect. 4. Assuming that all method bodies start with the awaittrue statement, we can globally constrain the scheduling of processes by the invariant that for each object there exists at most one process with an initial statement different from an await statement.

The concrete transition system for the ABS language can be defined as in Sect. 4 in terms of valuations. Here we use the initially unreachable objects in the concrete semantics additionally as a repository of fresh future identities. Again, the proof of correctness is a straightforward extension of the correctness of the symbolic execution of sequential object-oriented programs.

6   Conclusion

Despite the popularity and success of symbolic execution techniques, to the best of our knowledge, a general theory of symbolic execution is missing which covers in an uniform manner mainstream programming features like arrays and (object-oriented) pointer structures, as well as local scoping as it arises in the passing of parameters in recursive procedure calls. In fact, most existing tools for symbolic execution lack an explicit formal specification and justification.

In this paper we proposed such a general theory which covers the above mainstream programming features, and further illustrated the generality of our approach by its application to both multithreading and concurrent objects. From a practical point of view, we also illustrated how our theory sheds light on major implementation issues related to dynamically allocated variables and aliasing. This point of view we want to further explore by the development of proto-type implementations of the presented formal models of symbolic execution, compare performance with other tools, and investigate optimizations.

Another interesting research direction is the development of a further extension of our theory for concolic execution, mixing symbolic and concrete executions [16], and the symbolic backward execution [17].

Acknowledgements. This work arose out of our *Foundation of Testing* master course (LIACS) in 2018, and we thank the master students for their valuable comments. We thank the anonymous reviewers for their valuable comments.

References

1. King, C.: Symbolic execution and program testing. Commun. ACM **19**(7), 385–394 (1976)
2. Albert, E., Arenas, P., Gómez-Zamalloa, M., Rojas, J.M.: Test case generation by symbolic execution: basic concepts, a CLP-based instance, and actor-based concurrency. In: Bernardo, M., Damiani, F., Hähnle, R., Johnsen, E.B., Schaefer, I. (eds.) SFM 2014. LNCS, vol. 8483, pp. 263–309. Springer, Cham (2014). https://doi.org/10.1007/978-3-319-07317-0_7
3. Baldoni, R., Coppa, E., D'Elia, D.C., Demetrescu, C., Finocchi, I.: A survey of symbolic execution techniques. ACM Comput. Surv. **51**(3), 50:1–50:39 (2018)
4. Lucanu, D., Rusu, V., Arusoaie, A.: A generic framework for symbolic execution: a coinductive approach. J. Symbolic Comput. **80**(1), 125–163 (2017)
5. Braione, P., Denaro, G., Pezzè, M.: Symbolic execution of programs with heap inputs. In: Proceedings of the 10th Joint Meeting on Foundations of Software Engineering (ESEC/FSE 2015), pp. 602–613. ACM (2015)
6. Trtík, M., Strejček, J.: Symbolic memory with pointers. In: Cassez, F., Raskin, J.-F. (eds.) ATVA 2014. LNCS, vol. 8837, pp. 380–395. Springer, Cham (2014). https://doi.org/10.1007/978-3-319-11936-6_27
7. Cadar, C., Ganesh, V., Pawlowski, P.M., Dill, D.L., Engler, D.R.: EXE: automatically generating inputs of death. In: Proceedings of the 13th ACM Conference on Computer and Communications Security (CCS 2006), pp. 322–335. ACM (2006)
8. Cadar, C., Dunbar, D., Engler, D.R.: KLEE: unassisted and automatic generation of high-coverage tests for complex systems programs. In: Proceedings of the 8th USENIX Conference on Operating Systems Design and Implementation (OSDI 2008), pp. 209–224, USENIX Association (2008)
9. Elkarablieh, B., Godefroid, P., Levin, M.Y.: Precise pointer reasoning for dynamic test generation. In: Proceedings of the 18th International Symposium on Software Testing and Analysis (ISSTA 2009), pp. 129–140. ACM (2009)
10. Perry, D.M., Mattavelli, A., Zhang, X., Cadar, C.: Accelerating array constraints in symbolic execution. In Proceedings of the 26th International Symposium on Software Testing and Analysis (ISSTA 2017), pp. 68–78. ACM (2017)
11. Deng, X., Lee, J.: Bogor/Kiasan: a K-bounded symbolic execution for checking strong heap properties of open systems. In: Proceedings of the 21st IEEE/ACM International Conference on Automated Software Engineering (ASE 2006), pp. 157–166 (2006)
12. de Boer, F.S., Clarke, D., Johnsen, E.B.: A complete guide to the future. In: De Nicola, R. (ed.) ESOP 2007. LNCS, vol. 4421, pp. 316–330. Springer, Heidelberg (2007). https://doi.org/10.1007/978-3-540-71316-6_22
13. Gries, D.: The Science of Programming. Texts and Monographs in Computer Science. Springer (1981)

14. Johnsen, E.B., Hähnle, R., Schäfer, J., Schlatte, R., Steffen, M.: ABS: a core language for abstract behavioral specification. In: Aichernig, B.K., de Boer, F.S., Bonsangue, M.M. (eds.) FMCO 2010. LNCS, vol. 6957, pp. 142–164. Springer, Heidelberg (2011). https://doi.org/10.1007/978-3-642-25271-6_8
15. Xie, T., Marinov, D., Schulte, W., Notkin, D.: Symstra: a framework for generating object-oriented unit tests using symbolic execution. In: Halbwachs, N., Zuck, L.D. (eds.) TACAS 2005. LNCS, vol. 3440, pp. 365–381. Springer, Heidelberg (2005). https://doi.org/10.1007/978-3-540-31980-1_24
16. Godefroid, P., Klarlund, N., Sen, K.: DART: directed automated random testing. In: Proceedings of the ACM SIGPLAN Conference on Programming Languages Design and Implementation (PLDI 2005), pp. 213–223. ACM (2005)
17. Chandra, S., Fink, S.J., Sridharan, M.: Snugglebug: a powerful approach to weakest preconditions. In Proceedings of the 30th ACM SIGPLAN Conference on Programming Language Design and Implementation (PLDI 2009), pp. 363–374. ACM (2009)
18. Ahrendt, W., Beckert, B., Bubel, R., Hähnle, R., Schmitt, P.H., Ulbric, M.: Deductive Software Verification - The KeY Book - From Theory to Practice. LNCS, vol. 10001. Springer, Cham (2016). https://doi.org/10.1007/978-3-319-49812-6

Synthesis Techniques

GR(1)*: GR(1) Specifications Extended with Existential Guarantees

Gal Amram, Shahar Maoz$^{(\boxtimes)}$, and Or Pistiner

Tel Aviv University, Tel Aviv, Israel
maoz@cs.tac.ac.il

Abstract. Reactive synthesis is an automated procedure to obtain a correct-by-construction reactive system from its temporal logic specification. GR(1) is an expressive assume-guarantee fragment of LTL that enables efficient synthesis and has been recently used in different contexts and application domains. A common form of providing the system's requirements is through use cases, which are existential in nature. However, GR(1), as a fragment of LTL, is limited to universal properties.

In this paper we introduce GR(1)*, which extends GR(1) with existential guarantees. We show that GR(1)* is strictly more expressive than GR(1) as it enables the expression of guarantees that are inexpressible in LTL. We solve the realizability problem for GR(1)* and present a symbolic strategy construction algorithm for GR(1)* specifications. Importantly, in comparison to GR(1), GR(1)* remains efficient, and induces only a minor additional cost in terms of time complexity, proportional to the extended length of the formula.

1 Introduction

Reactive synthesis is an automated procedure to obtain a correct-by-construction reactive system from its temporal logic specification [36]. Rather than manually constructing an implementation and using model checking to verify it against a specification, synthesis offers an approach where a correct implementation of the system is automatically obtained for a given specification, if such an implementation exists.

GR(1) is a fragment of linear temporal logic [35] (LTL), which has an efficient symbolic synthesis algorithm [6,34] and whose expressive power covers most of the well-known LTL specification patterns of Dwyer et al. [14,28]. GR(1) specifications include assumptions and guarantees about what needs to hold on all initial states, on all states (safety), and infinitely often on every run (justice). GR(1) synthesis has been used and extended in different contexts and for different application domains, including robotics [23,27], scenario-based specifications [33], aspect languages [32], event-based behavior models [13], hybrid systems [17], and device drivers [46], to name a few.

A common form of providing system's requirements is through use cases [1, 19,37]. In contrast to universal behaviors, i.e., which must hold on all possible

© Springer Nature Switzerland AG 2019
M. H. ter Beek et al. (Eds.): FM 2019, LNCS 11800, pp. 83–100, 2019.
https://doi.org/10.1007/978-3-030-30942-8_7

system runs, use cases describe possible, existential behaviors. Use cases are commonly used in the early stages of requirements analysis and specification, as they are natural to define from a user's perspective and as in these stages, invariants may be too strong to be specified correctly. Use cases are useful also in specifying alternative and exceptional behaviors, which, by nature, do not appear in every run, and in specifying examples of behaviors that should not be possible. They are further commonly used again in later stages of development, to prescribe test cases. Despite all the above, to the best of our knowledge, no previous work has proposed efficient reactive synthesis for specifications that include not only universal but also existential properties.

In this work we present GR(1)*, which extends GR(1) specifications and synthesis with existential guarantees over input and output (environment and system) variables. GR(1)* allows engineers to naturally describe use cases as part of the specification and to efficiently synthesize a correct-by-construction controller that guaranties to make them possible.

We formally define GR(1)* and show that it is strictly more expressive than GR(1) (as it can express properties that are in CTL* [16] and outside LTL), see Sect. 3. We show how to solve GR(1)* games using a symbolic fixed-point algorithm, and present a corresponding controller construction, see Sects. 4 and 5. All proofs are provided in an appendix of the archive version of the paper.

Importantly, in comparison to GR(1) [6], GR(1)* induces only a minor additional cost in terms of time complexity, proportional to the extended length of the formula. Specifically, in [6] GR(1) games are solved in time $O(nmN^2)$ (measured in symbolic steps), where n is the number of justice guarantees, m is the number of justice assumptions, and N is the size of the state space $2^{\mathcal{X} \cup \mathcal{Y}}$. The time complexity of our solution for GR(1)* games is $O((nm + \ell r(k'))N^2)$, where l is the number of existential guarantees and $r(k')$ is the length of the longest existential guarantee.

The remainder of the introduction presents a running example and discusses related work.

1.1   Example: Lift Specification

As a motivating example, we enrich a lift specification, inspired by the example in [6], with several existential guarantees.

According to the original specification, the lift moves between n floors and must reach every floor it was called to. The environment controls button presses on every floor through variables $\{b_1, \ldots, b_n\}$. The system controls the lift's location through variables $\{f_1, \ldots, f_n\}$. The lift can move at most one floor in a single step, a button that has been pressed is turned off iff the lift reaches its floor, and the lift is required to reach every floor it was called to. For a complete description see [6]. We now describe example existential guarantees.

First, assume that the requirements document describes a typical use case: the lift is at floor i, button j is pressed, and the lift eventually reaches floor j. The engineer wants to integrate this use case into the specification in order to make sure that the lift will enable it. Thus, in our example, she formalizes the following guarantees and adds them to the specification:

$A_{i,j}$ *Typical use case - the lift is at floor i, button j is pressed, and the lift eventually reaches floor j:* $GE(F(f_i \wedge b_j \wedge F(f_j)))$.

Second, the engineer is aware that sometimes a synthesized controller may achieve its goals by preventing certain events from happening, and she wishes to avoid such vacuous solutions. She thus formalizes and adds the following guarantees to the specification:

B_i *Button i can always be pressed:* $GE(F(b_i))$.

Finally, we present an example of using a negative scenario as a 'test'. Consider new system variables mUp and mDown that model the direction in which the lift should move. The engineer believes that in the presence of pending calls, the specified lift never stays in place. To test this hypothesis, she checks that the specification with the following additional existential guarantee is unrealizable:

C *The lift is in idle mode although there is a pending call:*
$GE(F(\bigvee_{i=1}^{n} b_i \wedge \neg mUp \wedge \neg mDown))$.

1.2   Related Work

LTL synthesis of reactive systems was studied in [36] and shown to be 2EXPTIME-complete [38]. The GR(1) fragment of LTL, which can be solved in time quadratic in the size of the state space, is proposed in [6]. As GR(1)* augments GR(1) with existential requirements, it is in fact a fragment of CTL* [12,16]. Kupferman and Vardi showed that the synthesis problem for CTL* formulas is 2EXPTIME-complete [25]. Recently, Bloem et al. suggested a CTL* synthesis technique [7], and a corresponding synthesis tool. As we show, GR(1)*, like GR(1), is solved in time quadratic in the size of the state space.

Synthesis techniques that consider existential requirements, use cases, and scenarios were suggested in the literature. Harel et al. [18,24] studied synthesis of object systems from universal and existential live sequence charts (LSC). Uchitel et al. [39,40,44,45] studied synthesis of modal transition systems (MTS) from universal and existential message sequence charts (MSC). Besides these papers, discussions about the value of use cases, scenarios, and examples for their use in the specification and analysis of systems can be found in [2,3,42,47]. All these motivated us to extend GR(1) with existential guarantees.

In the context of GR(1), Bloem et al. [5] defined levels of cooperation between the system and the environment. Some of these levels of cooperation require that the justice assumptions hold in an existential manner. Ehlers et al. [15] and Majumdar et al. [26] proposed a synthesis technique for a cooperative GR(1) controller, i.e., a controller that never forces violation of the justice assumptions. Thus, while these papers relate to the justice assumptions as existential guarantees, our technique allows to add any sequence of assertions as existential guarantees. Note that the problem solved in these papers is not a special case of our solution, since [15] and [26] require that the justice assumptions may hold from any reachable state, while we require that the existential guarantees can be satisfied along plays that satisfy the justice assumptions.

2 Preliminaries

2.1 Game Structures and Strategies

Our notations are standard and mostly based on [6]. For a set of Boolean variables $\mathcal{V}$, a *state* is an element $s \in 2^{\mathcal{V}}$, an *assertion* is a Boolean formula over $\mathcal{V}$, and $\models$ is the satisfaction relation between a state and an assertion. true and false are the assertions satisfied by every state and by no state, resp. As an assertion naturally corresponds to the set of states by which it is satisfied, we refer to sets of states as assertions and we may write $s \models A$ instead of $s \in A$. For $\mathcal{Z} \subseteq \mathcal{V}$ and $s \in 2^{\mathcal{V}}$, $s|_{\mathcal{Z}}$ denotes the state $s \cap \mathcal{Z} \in 2^{\mathcal{Z}}$. For a set of variables $\mathcal{V}$, $\mathcal{V}'$ is the set of variables obtained by replacing each $v \in \mathcal{V}$ with v'. Likewise, for $s \in 2^{\mathcal{V}}$ and an assertion a over $\mathcal{V}$, $s' \in 2^{\mathcal{V}'}$ and a' are the state and assertion obtained by replacing each variable v with v'. If $\mathcal{V}_1, \ldots, \mathcal{V}_k$ are pairwise disjoint sets of variables and $s_i \in 2^{\mathcal{V}_i}$, we write $(s_1, \ldots, s_k)$ as an abbreviation for $s_1 \cup \cdots \cup s_k$. Thus, $(s_1, \ldots, s_k)$ is a state over $\mathcal{V} = \mathcal{V}_1 \cup \cdots \cup \mathcal{V}_k$.

A *game structure* is a tuple, $GS = (\mathcal{X}, \mathcal{Y}, \theta^e, \theta^s, \rho^e, \rho^s)$, where $\mathcal{X}, \mathcal{Y}$ are disjoint sets of variables, θ^e is an assertion over $\mathcal{X}$, θ^s is a assertion over $\mathcal{X} \cup \mathcal{Y}$, ρ^e is an assertion over $\mathcal{X} \cup \mathcal{Y} \cup \mathcal{X}'$, and ρ^s is an assertion over $\mathcal{X} \cup \mathcal{Y} \cup \mathcal{X}' \cup \mathcal{Y}'$. Intuitively, a game structure defines how two players, the *environment* and the *system*, choose inputs and outputs repeatedly. θ^e and θ^s set rules for the beginning of the play; the environment chooses an initial input $s_x \models \theta^e$ and, in response, the system chooses an output s_y such that $(s_x, s_y) \models \theta^s$. Afterwards, the players take turns choosing inputs and outputs in compliance with the *safety assumptions and guarantees*, ρ^e and ρ^s, resp. Specifically, from a state $s \in 2^{\mathcal{X} \cup \mathcal{Y}}$, the environment can choose an input $s_x \in 2^{\mathcal{X}}$, such that $(s, s'_x) \models \rho^e$, and the system may respond with an output $s_y \in 2^{\mathcal{Y}}$ if $(s, s'_x, s'_y) \models \rho^s$.

A state s is said to be a *deadlock* for the system if there exists $s_x \in 2^{\mathcal{X}}$ such that $(s, s'_x) \models \rho^e$, but there is no $s_y \in 2^{\mathcal{Y}}$ such that $(s, s'_x, s'_y) \models \rho^s$. Analogously, a deadlock for the environment is a state s for which there is no s_x such that $(s, s'_x) \models \rho^e$. A *play* is a sequence of states $s_0, s_1, s_2, \ldots$, such that (1) for two consecutive states s_i, s_{i+1}, $(s_i, s'_{i+1}) \models \rho^e \wedge \rho^s$, and (2) either it is infinite or it ends in a deadlock.

A *strategy* for the system from $S \subseteq 2^{\mathcal{X} \cup \mathcal{Y}}$ is a partial function $f^s : (2^{\mathcal{X} \cup \mathcal{Y}})^+ \times 2^{\mathcal{X}} \to 2^{\mathcal{Y}}$ such that (1) for $s_0 \in S$, (s_0) is *consistent* with f^s; (2) if $(s_0, \ldots, s_k)$ is consistent with f^s, s_k is not a deadlock for the system, and $(s_k, s'_x) \models \rho^e$ for $s_x \in 2^{\mathcal{X}}$, then $f^s(s_0, \ldots, s_k, s_x)$ is defined, and for $s_y = f^s(s_0, \ldots, s_k, s_x)$, $(s_k, s'_x, s'_y) \models \rho^s$, and the sequence $(s_0, \ldots, s_k, (s_x, s_y))$ is consistent with f^s. We say that an infinite sequence of states is consistent with f^s if any of its finite prefixes is consistent with f^s. A strategy for the environment player is a partial function $f^e : (2^{\mathcal{X} \cup \mathcal{Y}})^+ \to 2^{\mathcal{X}}$ that satisfies the analogous requirements. Consistency of a sequence with f^e is also defined analogously.

A controller determines a strategy from $S \subseteq 2^{\mathcal{X} \cup \mathcal{Y}}$ for the system using a finite memory. Formally, a controller C is a partial function with a set of memory values M. The controller has an initial value m_0, and for some tuples $(s, s_x, m) \in 2^{\mathcal{X} \cup \mathcal{Y}} \times 2^{\mathcal{X}} \times M$ such that $(s, s'_x) \models \rho^e$, $C(s, s_x, m) = (s_y, \hat{m}) \in 2^{\mathcal{Y}} \times M$ such that

$(s, s'_x, s'_y) \models \rho^s$. A controller C, from S, can also be viewed as a partial function over $(2^{\mathcal{X} \cup \mathcal{Y}})^+ \times 2^{\mathcal{X}}$. $C(s_0, \ldots, s_k, s_x) = (s_y, m)$ if, from state s_0, by receiving inputs $s_1|_{\mathcal{X}}, \ldots, s_k|_{\mathcal{X}}, s_x$, the controller replies with $s_1|_{\mathcal{Y}}, \ldots, s_k|_{\mathcal{Y}}, s_y$, and the final value of its memory is m. Formally, we require that the following holds:

- For $s_0 \in S$, (s_0) is *consistent* with C and for every $s_x \in 2^{\mathcal{X}}$ such that $(s_0, s'_x) \models \rho^e$, we require that $C(s_0, s_x, m_0)$ is defined, and if $C(s_0, s_x, m_0) = (s_y, m_1)$, we write $C(s_0, s_x) = (s_y, m_1)$;
- Assume that $(s_0, \ldots, s_k)$ is consistent with C where $s_0 \in S$, and for $s_x \in 2^{\mathcal{X}}$, $C(s_0, \ldots, s_k, s_x) = (s_y, m_{k+1})$. Then, $(s_0, \ldots, s_k, (s_x, s_y))$ is consistent with C, and we require that for every $t_x \in 2^{\mathcal{X}}$ with $((s_x, s_y), t'_x) \models \rho^e$, $C((s_x, s_y), t_x, m_{k+1})$ is defined. Moreover, for $C((s_x, s_y), t_x, m_{k+1}) = (t_y, m_{k+2})$, we write $C(s_0, \ldots, s_k, (s_x, s_y), t_x) = (t_y, m_{k+2})$.

Clearly, a controller C defines a strategy for the system f_C^s, by $f_C^s(s_0, \ldots, s_k, s_x) = s_y$ iff $C(s_0, \ldots, s_k, s_x) = (s_y, m)$ for some $m \in M$.

2.2 Linear Temporal Logic and the GR(1) Fragment

Linear temporal logic (LTL) [35] is a language to specify properties over infinite words. Given a set of variables, $\mathcal{V}$, LTL formulas are generated by the grammar $\varphi = p|\neg\varphi|\varphi \vee \varphi|\varphi \wedge \varphi|X\varphi|F\varphi|G\varphi|\varphi U\varphi$, where p is an assertion over $\mathcal{V}$ and parenthesis may be used to determine the order of operator activations. Given an infinite sequence of states, $\pi \in (2^{\mathcal{V}})^\omega$, π^i denotes the suffix of π that starts from the i-th state in π (counting from zero). The term $\pi \models \varphi$ is defined inductively on the structure of φ: (1) $\pi \models p$ if $\pi(0) \models p$; (2) $\pi \models X\varphi$ if $\pi^1 \models \varphi$; (3) $\pi \models F\varphi$ if $\exists k(\pi^k \models \varphi)$; (4) $\pi \models G\varphi$ if $\forall k(\pi^k \models \varphi)$; (5) $\pi \models \varphi U\psi$ if $\exists k(\pi^k \models \psi \wedge \forall j < k(\pi^j \models \varphi))$; (6) Boolean operators are treated in a standard way.

Given a game structure $GS = (\mathcal{X}, \mathcal{Y}, \theta^e, \theta^s, \rho^e, \rho^s)$, an LTL formula φ, and a play π, π *wins* for the system w.r.t. GS and φ if either it ends in a deadlock for the environment, or it is infinite and $\pi \models \varphi$. Otherwise, it wins for the environment w.r.t. GS and φ. A strategy for the system, f^s, *wins* from $s \in 2^{\mathcal{X} \cup \mathcal{Y}}$ w.r.t. GS and φ if every play from s, consistent with f^s, wins for the system w.r.t. GS and φ. A strategy for the system, f^s is a *winning strategy* w.r.t. GS and φ if for every $s_x \models \theta^e$ there exists $s_y \in 2^{\mathcal{Y}}$ such that $(s_x, s_y) \models \theta^s$ and f^s wins from (s_x, s_y) w.r.t. GS and φ. The *winning region* of the system includes all states, s, for which there exists a strategy for the system that wins from s. The winning region and a winning strategy for the environment are defined analogously.

Among LTL formulas, of special interest to us is the GR(1) fragment [6]. A GR(1) formula is an LTL formula of the form $\bigwedge_{j=1}^m GF(a_j) \to \bigwedge_{i=1}^n GF(g_i)$, where $a_1, \ldots, a_m, g_1, \ldots, g_n$ are assertions. The assertions $a_1, \ldots, a_m$ are called *justice assumptions*, and $g_1, \ldots, g_n$ are called *justice guarantees*.

2.3 μ-calculus over Game Structures

Modal μ-calculus [22] is a modal logic enriched by least and greatest fixed-point (l.f.p. and g.f.p.) operators. Since we are interested in games that model reactive systems, we adopt the form of [6], which uses the controllable predecessor operators $\ocircle$ and $\text{\textcircled{$\Box$}}$. In addition, to deal with possible behaviors, we add to the logic of [6] the predecessor operator $\diamondsuit$.

For a set of variables $\mathcal{V}$, and a set of relational variables $Var = \{X, Y, \ldots\}$, a μ-calculus (in positive form) formula is constructed by the grammar $\phi = p\,|\,X\,|\,\phi \vee \phi\,|\,\phi \wedge \phi\,|\,\ocircle\phi\,|\,\text{\textcircled{$\Box$}}\phi\,|\,\diamondsuit\phi\,|\,\mu X\phi\,|\,\nu X\phi$, where p is an assertion over $\mathcal{V}$. A μ-calculus formula defines a subset of $2^{\mathcal{V}}$. In words, $\ocircle\phi$ defines the set of states from which the system can enforce reaching next a state in the set that ϕ defines, $\text{\textcircled{$\Box$}}\phi$ defines the set of states from which the environment can enforce reaching next a state in the set that ϕ defines, and $\diamondsuit\phi$ is the set of states from which the environment and the system can choose an input and an output to reach a state in the set that ϕ defines. μ and ν denote the l.f.p. and g.f.p. operators, resp.

For a game structure $GS = (\mathcal{X}, \mathcal{Y}, \theta^e, \theta^s, \rho^e, \rho^s)$, a μ-calculus formula ϕ, and a valuation $\mathcal{E} : Var \to 2^{(2^{\mathcal{X} \cup \mathcal{Y}})}$, the semantics of ϕ, $[\![\phi]\!]^{\mathcal{E}}_{GS} \subseteq 2^{\mathcal{X} \cup \mathcal{Y}}$, is defined by a structural induction. We refer the reader to [6] for the exact definition, and add the rule: $[\![\diamondsuit\phi]\!]^{\mathcal{E}}_{GS} = \{s \in 2^{\mathcal{V}} : \exists t \in 2^{\mathcal{X} \cup \mathcal{Y}}(((s, t|'_{\mathcal{X}}, t|'_{\mathcal{Y}}) \models \rho^e \wedge \rho^s) \wedge t \in [\![\phi]\!]^{\mathcal{E}}_{GS})\}$.

If all relational variables in ϕ are bound by fixed-point operators, we omit the notation $\mathcal{E}$, and just write $[\![\phi]\!]_{GS}$. We remark that by Knaster-Tarski theorem [43], $[\![\mu X\phi]\!]^{\mathcal{E}}_{GS}$ and $[\![\nu X\phi]\!]^{\mathcal{E}}_{GS}$ indeed return the l.f.p. and g.f.p. of the function $S \mapsto [\![\phi]\!]^{\mathcal{E}[X \leftarrow S]}_{GS}$. This theorem can be applied since the positive form ensures that the function $S \mapsto [\![\phi]\!]^{\mathcal{E}[X \leftarrow S]}_{GS}$ is monotone, so l.f.p. and g.f.p. exist.

3 GR(1)*: Going Beyond LTL

3.1 GR(1)* Formulas

GR(1)* extends the GR(1) fragment of LTL with existential guarantees of the form $E(F(q_1 \wedge F(q_2 \wedge F(q_3 \wedge \cdots F(q_r) \cdots))))$ that should hold globally, where $q_1, \ldots, q_r$ are assertions over a set of variables $\mathcal{V}$. As in the case of justice guarantees, these guarantees should hold if all justice assumptions are satisfied infinitely often. Therefore, since this formula prescribes a possible behavior, the synthesized controller should either enable reaching $q_1, q_2, \ldots, q_r$ in that order, or enforce the violation of the assumptions.

Definition 1 (GR(1)*). *For $k \in \{1, \ldots, \ell\}$ let $S_k = E(F(q_{(k,1)} \wedge F(q_{(k,2)} \wedge F(q_{(k,3)} \wedge \cdots F(q_{(k,r(k))}) \cdots))))$. A GR(1)* formula over a set of variables $\mathcal{V}$ is a formula of the form*

$$A\Big(\bigwedge_{j=1}^{m} GF(a_j) \to \big(\bigwedge_{i=1}^{n} GF(g_i) \wedge \bigwedge_{k=1}^{\ell} G(S_k) \big) \Big),$$

where $a_1, \ldots, a_m, g_1, \ldots, g_n, q_{(1,1)}, \ldots, q_{(\ell, r(\ell))}$ are assertions over $\mathcal{V}$.

Note that our definition includes existential guarantees but no existential assumptions. Adding such assumptions would only make it easier for the system to win by enforcing violation of the assumptions, which is undesirable. Still, importantly, note that the existential guarantees in GR(1)* may use not only system variables but also environment variables.

Both syntactically and semantically, GR(1)* is a fragment of CTL*, and it is neither a subset of LTL nor of CTL, as illustrated in Fig. 1. For instance, the GR(1)* formula $A(GF(a) \rightarrow (GF(g) \wedge GE(F(q))))$ is expressible neither in LTL nor in CTL. This can be proved using arguments similar to [16].

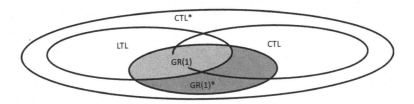

Fig. 1. Relationships between GR(1)* and other subsets of CTL*

3.2   GR(1)* Winning Condition

We now define when a strategy is winning w.r.t. a GR(1)* winning condition. As GR(1)* is a subset of CTL*, we essentially apply the general definition of winning strategies for reactive systems with CTL* winning conditions [25]. That is, roughly, we wish to say that a strategy is winning if it induces a computation tree which satisfies the GR(1)* formula. However, since, in contrast to [25], we consider game structures that restrict the steps that the players can perform, we cannot directly apply the definition of [25], and some technical changes are necessary. Specifically, a strategy may induce a tree that has a branch that is finite (rather than infinite) and ends in a deadlock. Thus, this tree is not a computation tree in the sense of [25], and our formal definition takes this fact into consideration.

Definition 2. *Let* $GS = (\mathcal{X}, \mathcal{Y}, \theta^e, \theta^s, \rho^e, \rho^s)$ *be a game structure, and let* $\psi = A(\bigwedge_{j=1}^{m} GF(a_j) \rightarrow (\bigwedge_{i=1}^{n} GF(g_i) \wedge \bigwedge_{k=1}^{\ell} G(S_k)))$ *be a GR(1)* formula over* $\mathcal{X} \cup \mathcal{Y}$ *where* $S_k = E(F(q_{(k,1)} \wedge F(q_{(k,2)} \wedge F(q_{(k,3)} \wedge \cdots F(q_{(k,r(k))}) \cdots))))$. *A strategy for the system* f^s *wins from a state* $s \in 2^{\mathcal{X} \cup \mathcal{Y}}$ *w.r.t. GS and* ψ, *iff for every play* π *from* s *that is consistent with* f^s, *the following two requirements hold:*

1. *If* π *is finite, then it ends in a deadlock for the environment.*
2. *If* π *is infinite and* $\pi \models \bigwedge_{j=1}^{m} GF(a_j)$, *then:*
   (a) $\pi \models \bigwedge_{i=1}^{n} GF(g_i)$.
   (b) *For every* $i \geq 0$, *and an existential guarantee,* S_k, *the ith prefix of* π, $\pi(0), \ldots, \pi(i)$ *can be extended to a play* $\tilde{\pi}$, *consistent with* f^s, *such that there are indices* $i \leq i_1 \leq i_2 \leq \cdots \leq i_{r(k)}$ *with* $\tilde{\pi}(i_j) \models q_{(k,j)}$.

Further, f^s *is a winning startegy if for every* $s_x \in 2^{\mathcal{X}}$ *with* $s_x \models \theta^e$, *there exists* $s_y \in 2^{\mathcal{Y}}$ *such that* $(s_x, s_y) \models \theta^s$, *and* f^s *wins from* (s_x, s_y).

3.3   Inexpressibility of GR(1)* Winning Conditions in LTL

The fact that GR(1)* is a fragment of CTL* that is expressible neither in LTL nor in CTL (see, Sect. 3.1), does not imply that a GR(1)* winning condition cannot always be replaced with an LTL winning condition. To conclude this form of inexpressibility, we show that the arguments of [16] apply in the context of synthesized reactive systems.

We say that an LTL winning condition φ, is equivalent to a GR(1)* winning condition ψ, if for any game structure GS, and for any strategy for the system f^s, f^s is winning w.r.t. GS and the winning condition φ, iff it is winning w.r.t. GS and the winning condition ψ. Unsurprisingly, the example of [16] works in our context as well, and proves that GR(1)* winning conditions are inexpressible in LTL.

Proposition 1. *GR(1)* winning conditions are inexpressible in LTL.*

The proof of Proposition 1 reveals that even a winning condition as simple as $A(G(EF(y))$ is inexpressible in LTL. Using similar arguments one can show that every existential guarantee from our motivating example (Sect. 1.1) is inexpressible in LTL.

4   Solving GR(1)* Games

In this section, we present a μ-calculus formula that computes the winning region of the system player in GR(1)* games. Consider a game structure $GS = (\mathcal{X}, \mathcal{Y}, \theta^e, \theta^s, \rho^e, \rho^s)$, together with a GR(1)* formula $A(\bigwedge_{j=1}^m GF(a_j) \to (\bigwedge_{i=1}^n GF(g_i) \wedge \bigwedge_{k=1}^\ell G(S_k)))$, where $S_k = E(F(q_{(k,1)} \wedge F(q_{(k,2)} \wedge F(q_{(k,3)} \wedge \cdots F(q_{(k,r(k))}) \cdots))))$. To compute the system's winning region, we present a μ-calculus formula that consists of three components: V, $f(Z)$, and $\{h_k(Z) \colon k = 1, \ldots, \ell\}$, each of which we define next.

First, note that enforcing a violation of the assumptions, if possible, ensures winning. The states from which the system can violate the assumptions are those from which it can win the game whose winning condition is the LTL formula $\bigvee_{j=1}^m FG(\neg a_j)$. These states are characterized by the μ-calculus formula:

$$\mu Y (\bigvee_{j=1}^m \nu X(\bigcirc Y \vee (\neg a_j \wedge \bigcirc X))) \tag{1}$$

Thus, the first component we consider is $V = [\![\mu Y(\bigvee_{j=1}^m \nu X(\bigcirc Y \vee (\neg a_j \wedge \bigcirc X)))]\!]_{GS}$, the set of states computed by the μ-calculus formula in Eq. 1.

The second component we consider is the formula from [6] for solving GR(1) games. The justice assumptions and guarantees part of our GR(1)* formula, $\bigwedge_{j=1}^m GF(a_j) \to \bigwedge_{i=1}^n GF(g_i)$, is solved by the formula in Eq. 2:

$$\nu Z (\bigwedge_{i=1}^n \mu Y (\bigvee_{j=1}^m \nu X((g_i \wedge \bigcirc Z) \vee \bigcirc Y \vee (\neg a_j \wedge \bigcirc X)))) = \nu Z(f(Z)) \tag{2}$$

For the third component, we turn to look at the existential guarantees of the GR(1)* formula, $\{S_k : 1 \leq k \leq \ell\}$. For every such guarantee S_k, and $1 \leq i \leq r(k) + 1$, we define a μ-calculus formula $h_{k,i}(Z)$, parametrized by a set of states Z. This formula characterizes the set of all states in Z from which there is a path in Z that traverses through $q_{(k,i)}, q_{(k,i+1)}, \ldots, q_{(k,r(k))}$. The formulas $h_{k,r(k)}, \ldots, h_{k,1}$ are defined recursively in reverse order as follows:

- $h_{k,r(k)+1}(Z) = Z$;
- $h_{k,i}(Z) = \mu Y((q_{(k,i)} \wedge h_{k,i+1}(Z)) \vee (Z \wedge \Diamond Y))$.

We are interested in the the the outcome of this recursive formula.

$$h_{k,1}(Z) = h_k(Z) \tag{3}$$

The formula in Eq. 3 has k nested μ-operators. However, for $i > j$, the quantified variable of $h_{k,j}$ does not appear in $h_{k,i}$. Therefore, by computing the functions $h_{k,r(k)}(Z), \ldots, h_{k,1}(Z)$ in that order, $[\![h_k(Z)]\!]_{GS}$ is computed in $O(r(k) \cdot N)$ time.

Finally, combining the three components from Eqs. 1-3, we obtain the formula in Eq. 4, which computes the winning region of the system in the GR(1)* game.

$$\nu Z(V \vee (f(Z) \wedge \bigwedge_{k=1}^{\ell} h_k(Z))) \tag{4}$$

Theorem 1 (Realizabilty). $[\![\nu Z(V \vee (f(Z) \wedge \bigwedge_{k=1}^{\ell} h_k(Z)))]\!]_{GS}$ *is the winning region of the system player in the GR(1)* game.*

In the next section, we show how to construct a winning strategy from the set $[\![\nu Z(V \vee (f(Z) \wedge \bigwedge_{k=1}^{\ell} h_k(Z)))]\!]_{GS}$. Hence, to conclude the correctness of Theorem 1, we need to show that the system cannot win from every state in the complementary set of $[\![\nu Z(V \vee (f(Z) \wedge \bigwedge_{k=1}^{\ell} h_k(Z)))]\!]_{GS}$.

Lemma 1. *If* $s \notin [\![\nu Z(V \vee (f(Z) \wedge \bigwedge_{k=1}^{\ell} h_k(Z)))]\!]_{GS}$, *then no strategy for the system wins from* s.

By Theorem 1, a naive approach provides a realizability check for GR(1)* formulas in $O(nmN^3 + lr(k')N^2)$ symbolic steps, where $r(k') = \max\{r(k) : 1 \leq k \leq \ell\}$. As in the case of GR(1), with the technique proposed in [8], this can be improved to $O((nm + lr(k'))N^2)$ steps. We see that extending GR(1) with existential guaranties adds only a minor cost to the realizability check.

5 Strategy Construction

In this section, we present a construction for a GR(1)* controller, which wins the GR(1)* game from the system's winning region W, computed by the formula in Eq. 4. The basic idea behind the construction is very simple, and we start by describing it along with an informal description of a GR(1)* controller construction. Then, we point out that this construction has a significant disadvantage. We therefore suggest a way to improve the construction and present a detailed construction for our improved GR(1)* controller.

5.1   Construction Discussion and Overview

The basic idea is to alternate between two phases. Phase I is the well-known GR(1) strategy from [6]. The GR(1) controller satisfies the justice guarantees $g_1, \ldots, g_n$, one by one, provided that it will fail to satisfy g_i only in case the justice assumptions are violated forever. We add to this phase the requirement that if the controller reaches a state in V, it forces violation of the justice assumptions for the remainder of the play. After satisfying the justice guarantees, the GR(1)* controller proceeds to phase II in which it chooses an existential guarantee S_k, and tries, cooperatively, to reach $q_{(k,1)}, \ldots, q_{(k,r(k))}$.

Although correct, the strategy outlined above suffers from a significant drawback: it forces the violation of the assumptions whenever possible, although in some cases the system can win the game while giving the environment an opportunity to satisfy its assumptions. In the context of GR(1) games, some works suggested to settle this issue by allowing the satisfaction of the assumptions in cases where the justice guaranties can be satisfied as well [5, 15, 26]. In our context of GR(1)*, this approach should be taken carefully, since it is possible that such a strategy will not allow the satisfaction of the existential guarantees. Specifically, by taking this approach, a play can be led into a state from which there is no path that satisfies some existential guarantee, S_k.

To improve the described GR(1)* controller by avoiding unnecessary coercion of justice assumption violation, we note that the existential guarantees can be satisfied from the set $\bigcap_{k=1}^{\ell} [\![h_k(W)]\!]_{GS}$. Hence, we refer to $V' = W \setminus \bigcap_{k=1}^{\ell} [\![h_k(W)]\!]_{GS}$ as the "unsafe" region, from which we must force violation of the assumptions. The following Lemma claims that, indeed, the system can force violation of the assumptions from V'.

Lemma 2. $V' \subseteq V$.

Therefore, we improve the GR(1)* construction described above as follows: in phase I we satisfy the justice guarantees one by one, and in phase II we try to satisfy, cooperatively, an existential guarantee. Whenever the game reaches V', we force violation of the justice assumptions.

5.2   Detailed Construction

We now present the construction in detail. Our GR(1)* controller activates several "sub-controllers", which we describe below: C_V and $C_{(GR(1),1)}, \ldots, C_{(GR(1),n)}$ are activated in phase I; $C_1, \ldots, C_k$ are activated in phase II.

$\mathbf{C_V}$. C_V is a memoryless controller that forces from V the violation of the assumptions so that it wins from V the game whose winning condition is $\bigvee_{j=1}^{m} FG(\neg a_j)$. Clearly, $\bigvee_{j=1}^{m} FG(\neg a_j) \equiv (\bigvee_{j=1}^{m} FG(\neg a_j)) \vee F(\text{false} \wedge \bigcirc V)$. Hence, we apply the results of [20, Lemma 9] and construct C_V using the technique proposed in [6].

Algorithm 1. The controller C_k

$$/* \qquad \text{From state } s \qquad */$$

input: $s_x \in 2^{\mathcal{X}}$ such that $(s, s_x') \models \rho^e$

1: **if** $s \models q_{(k,M)} \wedge q_{(k,M+1)} \wedge \cdots \wedge q_{(k,r(k))}$ **then return** "undefined"
2: **end if**
3: $M \leftarrow \min\{M \leq t \leq r(k) \colon s \models \neg q_{k_t}\}$
4: **return** $C_{k,M}(s, s_x)$

$$/* \text{ The construction of } C_{k,t} \text{ for } t \in \{1, \ldots, r(k)\} */$$

1: $X \leftarrow \{s \in [\![h_k(W)]\!]_{GS} \colon s \models q_{(k,t)}\}$
2: **while** $X \neq [\![h_k(W)]\!]_{GS}$ **do**
3: $\qquad X' \leftarrow \Diamond X \cap [\![h_k(W)]\!]_{GS}$
4: $\qquad$ **for all** $s \in X' \setminus X$ and $s_x \in 2^{\mathcal{X}}$ such that $(s, s_x') \models \rho^e$ **do**
5: $\qquad\qquad$ **if** there exists $s_y \in 2^{\mathcal{Y}}$ s.t. $(s_x, s_y) \in X$ and $(s, (s_x', s_y')) \models \rho^s$ **then**
6: $\qquad\qquad\qquad$ choose $s_y \in 2^{\mathcal{Y}}$ s.t. $(s_x, s_y) \in X$ and $(s, (s_x', s_y')) \models \rho^s$
7: $\qquad\qquad\qquad C_{k,t}(s, s_x) \leftarrow s_y$
8: $\qquad\qquad$ **end if**
9: $\qquad$ **end for**
10: $\qquad X \leftarrow X \cup (\Diamond X \cap [\![h_k(W)]\!]_{GS})$
11: **end while**

$\mathbf{C_{(GR(1),i)}}$. For each $1 \leq i \leq n$, $C_{(GR(1),i)}$ is a memoryless controller that forces from $[\![f(W)]\!]_{GS}$ the satisfaction of the formula $\bigvee_{j=1}^{m} FG(\neg a_j)) \vee F(g_i \wedge \bigcirc W)$. The construction of these controllers is described in [6].

$\mathbf{C_k}$. For $1 \leq k \leq \ell$, C_k is an $r(k)$-memory controller that, from each $s \in [\![h_k(W)]\!]_{GS}$, tries to walk on a path in W that traverses through $q_{(k,1)}, \ldots, q_{(k,r(k))}$. Possibly, for some states $(s, s_x) \in W \times 2^{\mathcal{X}}$, the controller has no defined response, and then the controller returns a designated value "undefined". We present the construction in Algorithm 1. The controller C_k has a memory variable M, which stores values from $\{1, \ldots, r(k)\}$. M is initialized to 1.

Algorithm 2 presents the GR(1)* controller's construction. For clarity of presentation, we present the GR(1)* controller via a simple pseudocode. The translation of the code into a construction of a symbolic controller using BDD [9] operations is straightforward.

In Algorithm 2, we use a 4-field array M for the GR(1)* controller's memory. $M[0]$ specifies the next justice guarantee the controller strives to fulfil, and thus stores values from $\{1, \ldots, n\}$. $M[1]$ specifies the number of the ensuing existential guarantee we aim to satisfy, and thus stores values from $\{1, \ldots, \ell\}$. $M[2]$ is a field used by the controllers $C_1, \ldots, C_\ell$, which require memory of size equal to the number of states the controller is trying to traverse. Hence, $M[2]$ stores values from $\{1, \ldots, r(k')\}$ where $r(k') = \max\{r(k) \colon 1 \leq k \leq \ell\}$. Finally, $M[3]$ indicates which phase we now aim to. When $M[3] = 0$, we want to satisfy the justice guarantee $g_{M[0]}$ (phase I), and when $M[3] = 1$, we are trying, cooperatively, to satisfy the existential guarantee $S_{M[1]}$ (phase II). In line 15, $\oplus 1$ means that we write to $M[1]$ the next value. That is, for $k < \ell$, $k \oplus 1 = k + 1$, and $\ell \oplus 1 = 1$. If the play reaches a V'-state, the GR(1)* controller activates C_V for the remainder of the play.

Algorithm 2. The GR(1)* controller

/*   Initialization   */

    input: $s_x \models \theta^e$

1: $M \leftarrow (1, 1, 1, 0)$

2: **return** s_y, such that $(s_x, s_y) \models (\theta^s \wedge W)$

/*   From state s */

    input: s_x such that $(s, s'_x) \models \rho^e$

1: **if** $s \models V'$ **then return** $C_V(s, s_x)$ // The play reached V'

2: **end if**

3: **if** $M[3] == 0$ **then**   // Phase I: Fulfilling a justice guarantee

4:     $s_y \leftarrow C_{(\mathrm{GR}(1), M[0])}(s, s_x)$

5:     **if** $((s_x, s_y) \models g_{M[0]} \wedge \bigcirc\!\!\!\!W) \wedge (M[0] < n)$ **then** $M[0] \leftarrow M[0] + 1$

6:     **end if**

7:     **if** $((s_x, s_y) \models g_{M[0]} \wedge \bigcirc\!\!\!\!W) \wedge (M[0] = n)$ **then** $M[3] \leftarrow 1$

8:     **end if**

9:     **return** s_y

10: **end if**

11: **if** $M[3] == 1$ **then**   // Phase II: Fulfilling an existential guarantee

12:     $(s_y, M[2]) \leftarrow C_{M[1]}(s, s_x, M[2])$

13:     **if** $s_y \neq$ "undefined" **then return** s_y

14:     **end if**

15:     $(M[0], M[1], M[2], M[3]) \leftarrow (1, M[1] \oplus 1, 1, 0)$

16:     **goto** line 1

17: **end if**

The reader may notice three seemingly problematic issues concerning the construction that require clarification: (1) once the play reaches V', it must never leave, i.e., never reach $2^{\mathcal{X} \cup \mathcal{Y}} \setminus V'$; (2) the controllers $C_{(\mathrm{GR}(1),1)}, \ldots, C_{(\mathrm{GR}(1),n)}$ operate from $[\![f(W)]\!]_{GS}$, but the initialization in Algorithm 2 returns a state in W; (3) phase I ends by reaching a state $s \models g_n \wedge \bigcirc\!\!\!\!W$, from which we want to activate some C_k, which operates from $[\![h_k(W)]\!]_{GS}$. The correctness proof we provide in the appendix settles these three issues as follows: (1) we show that if $s \in V'$ and $(s, s'_x) \models \rho^e$, then $(s_x, C_V(s, s_x)) \in V'$; (2) we show that $W \subseteq [\![f(W)]\!]_{GS}$;[1] (3) we show that $\bigcirc\!\!\!\!W \subseteq W$ and thus, if $s \models \bigcirc\!\!\!\!W$ then either $s \in V'$ and C_V can be activated, or $s \in \bigcap_{k=1}^{\ell} [\![h_k(W)]\!]_{GS}$ and each C_k can be activated.

Theorem 2 (Controller construction). *The controller C as constructed according to Algorithm 2 implements a winning strategy for the system from W with memory of size $2 \cdot n \cdot \ell \cdot r(k')$.*

As a final remark, we note that in lines 5 and 7, the condition $(s_x, s_y) \models g_{M[0]} \wedge \bigcirc\!\!\!\!W$ can be replaced with $(s_x, s_y) \models g_{M[0]}$, for optimization purposes. We now explain the correctness of this replacement. In the proof of Theorem 2, we show that $\bigcirc\!\!\!\!W \subseteq W$. Moreover, Theorem 2 and Lemma 1 ensure that a play

---

[1] In fact, they are equal, but we do not use this observation in the correctness proof of the algorithm.

that is consistent with the GR(1)* controller as constructed in Algorithm 2, never reaches a deadlock for the system, and never leaves W. Hence, for every state s that is reachable by the GR(1)* controller, $s \models \lozenge W$ and there is no reason to test this condition.

6 Implementation and Preliminary Evaluation

We have implemented the realizability check for GR(1)* from Sect. 4 and integrated it in the Spectra language and synthesis environment [30,48], which already includes a GR(1) synthesizer and implementations of several additional analyses. Our implementation uses BDDs [9] via the CUDD 3.0 [41] package.

As a preliminary evaluation for the feasibility of GR(1)* in terms of running times, specifically the cost of adding existential guarantees to a GR(1) specification, we performed the following experiment.

6.1 Setup

We took the lift specification from our motivation example with 40 floors, 40 justice guarantees of the form $GF(\neg b_i)$, effectively meaning that in any infinite run, all requests will be served infinitely often, and 40 justice assumptions of the form $GF(b_i)$, meaning that in any infinite run, every floor will be requested infinitely often. We show the specification in an appendix of the archive version of the paper. This specification is well-separated [29] and realizable. Since the lift can only be positioned at a single floor at a time, we model its location in Spectra by an integer typed variable, which is internally implemented as a $\lceil \log 40 \rceil$-bit variable (and not by a 40-bit array as in [6]). Hence, the size of our example's state space is 2^{46}.

Our goal is to evaluate the cost, in running time, of adding existential guarantees to a GR(1) specification. We thus measured realizability checking times of the baseline specification (without any existential guarantees) and compared it to realizability checking times of the same specification with number of existential guarantees ranging from 2 to 40, and length of existential guarantees (nesting depth of F) ranging from 2 to 40. We generated these existential guarantees by sampling a sequence of assertions of the required length, from some manually written list of assertions. As an example, line 29 in the specification presents (in Spectra syntax) one of the existential guarantees we sampled: **GE** floor = 17 & button[21], floor = 21. In CTL*, this existential guarantee is written $GE(F(\texttt{floor} = 17 \wedge \texttt{button}[21] \wedge F(\texttt{floor} = 21)))$. The length of this CTL* formula, i.e., the number of nested F occurrences, is 2.

Overall, we considered 81 different configurations. For each configuration, we repeated realizability checking 15 times[2], and computed the median running time. We performed the experiments on hardware with Intel Xeon W-2133 processor with 32 GB RAM, running Windows 10.

---

[2] Even though the algorithm is deterministic, we performed multiple runs since JVM garbage collection and the default automatic variable reordering of CUDD add variance to running times.

Table 1. Running times of 81 configurations with additional existential guarantees relative to the baseline specification of a lift with 40 floors, whose running time was 39178 ms.

# ex. gar	Length								
	2	5	10	15	20	25	30	35	40
2	178%	170%	164%	161%	153%	143%	142%	136%	138%
5	162%	154%	150%	139%	124%	124%	119%	142%	135%
10	175%	152%	156%	130%	141%	114%	124%	127%	134%
15	152%	149%	123%	116%	137%	125%	115%	119%	138%
20	137%	128%	125%	155%	142%	123%	142%	131%	137%
25	143%	135%	121%	123%	120%	134%	135%	114%	132%
30	155%	139%	144%	136%	134%	118%	124%	132%	144%
35	136%	137%	153%	133%	138%	148%	126%	128%	135%
40	138%	144%	145%	144%	111%	127%	139%	136%	128%

6.2   Results

The median running time for the realizability check of the baseline was 39178 milliseconds. Table 1 shows the ratios between the running times for the different configurations and the baseline result (e.g., the leftmost cell in the table, reading 178%, means that with 2 existential guarantees of length 2, the median of 15 runs of realizability check took 78% longer than the baseline, i.e., about 70 seconds).

We observe that adding existential guarantees, as expected, has a cost. Yet, the growth in running time seems to be limited. In all 81 configurations, the running time was less than twice the running time of the baseline configuration. We further observe that neither increasing the number of existential guarantees nor extending their length significantly seems to affect running times.

The results of this preliminary evaluation are encouraging, but they are limited to a single specification and experiment setup. Further evaluation with additional specifications is required in order to strengthen the validity of the results.

7   Conclusion

We introduced GR(1)*, which extends GR(1) with existential guarantees. GR(1)* allows engineers to add example use cases to the specification, so as to ensure that the synthesized controller will enable them. We proved that GR(1)* captures CTL* properties that are inexpressible in LTL. We solved the realizability problem and presented a symbolic controller construction for GR(1)*. Importantly, GR(1)* realizability check consumes $O((nm + \ell r(k'))N^2)$-time where n is the number of justice guarantees, m is the number of justice assumptions, ℓ is the number of existential guarantees, and $r(k')$ is the length of the longest existential guarantee, i.e., induces only a minor additional cost in terms of time complexity, proportional to the extended length of the formula.

We consider the following future directions. First, GR(1) has been extended with past LTL operators (already in [6]) and patterns [28]. It would be valuable to carry over these extensions to GR(1)*, specifically supporting the use of past LTL operators and some of the patterns of [14] inside the existential guarantees.

Second, unrealizability is a well-known challenge for reactive synthesis in general and for GR(1) specifications in particular. Researchers have suggested to address GR(1) unrealizability using the concepts of unrealizable core, counter-strategy, and repair, see, e.g., [4,10,11,21,31]. It is interesting to investigate these in the context of GR(1)*. Specifically, counter-strategies for GR(1)* may be more complicated than counter-strategies for GR(1), as they depend not only on each play alone but also on the controller's possible behavior, i.e., a play can be winning for the system w.r.t. one controller, while losing w.r.t. another.

Acknowledgements. This project has received funding from the European Research Council (ERC) under the European Union's Horizon 2020 research and innovation programme (grant agreement No 638049, SYNTECH).

References

1. Alexander, I.F., Maiden, N.: Scenarios, Stories, Use Cases: Through the Systems Development Life-Cycle. 1st edn. Wiley Publishing (2004)
2. Alrajeh, D., Kramer, J., Russo, A., Uchitel, S.: Learning from vacuously satisfiable scenario-based specifications. In: de Lara, J., Zisman, A. (eds.) FASE 2012. LNCS, vol. 7212, pp. 377–393. Springer, Heidelberg (2012). https://doi.org/10.1007/978-3-642-28872-2_26
3. Alrajeh, D., Ray, O., Russo, A., Uchitel, S.: Using abduction and induction for operational requirements elaboration. J. Appl. Logic **7**(3), 275–288 (2009)
4. Alur, R., Moarref, S., Topcu, U.: Counter-strategy guided refinement of GR(1) temporal logic specifications. In: Formal Methods in Computer-Aided Design, FMCAD 2013, Portland, OR, USA, 20–23 October 2013, pp. 26–33. IEEE (2013). https://doi.org/10.1109/FMCAD.2013.6679387
5. Bloem, R., Ehlers, R., Könighofer, R.: Cooperative reactive synthesis. In: Finkbeiner, B., Pu, G., Zhang, L. (eds.) ATVA 2015. LNCS, vol. 9364, pp. 394–410. Springer, Cham (2015). https://doi.org/10.1007/978-3-319-24953-7_29
6. Bloem, R., Jobstmann, B., Piterman, N., Pnueli, A., Sa'ar, Y.: Synthesis of reactive(1) designs. J. Comput. Syst. Sci. **78**(3), 911–938 (2012). https://doi.org/10.1016/j.jcss.2011.08.007
7. Bloem, R., Schewe, S., Khalimov, A.: CTL* synthesis via LTL synthesis. In: Proceedings Sixth Workshop on Synthesis, SYNT@CAV 2017, Heidelberg, Germany, 22 July 2017, pp. 4–22 (2017). https://doi.org/10.4204/EPTCS.260.4
8. Browne, A., Clarke, E.M., Jha, S., Long, D.E., Marrero, W.R.: An improved algorithm for the evaluation of fixpoint expressions. Theor. Comput. Sci. **178**(1–2), 237–255 (1997). https://doi.org/10.1016/S0304-3975(96)00228-9
9. Bryant, R.E.: Graph-based algorithms for Boolean function manipulation. IEEE Trans. Comput. **35**(8), 677–691 (1986). https://doi.org/10.1109/TC.1986.1676819
10. Cavezza, D.G., Alrajeh, D.: Interpolation-based GR(1) assumptions refinement. In: Legay, A., Margaria, T. (eds.) TACAS 2017. LNCS, vol. 10205, pp. 281–297. Springer, Heidelberg (2017). https://doi.org/10.1007/978-3-662-54577-5_16

11. Cimatti, A., Roveri, M., Schuppan, V., Tchaltsev, A.: Diagnostic information for realizability. In: Logozzo, F., Peled, D.A., Zuck, L.D. (eds.) VMCAI 2008. LNCS, vol. 4905, pp. 52–67. Springer, Heidelberg (2008). https://doi.org/10.1007/978-3-540-78163-9_9

12. Clarke, E.M., Emerson, E.A.: Design and synthesis of synchronization skeletons using branching time temporal logic. In: Kozen, D. (ed.) Logic of Programs 1981. LNCS, vol. 131, pp. 52–71. Springer, Heidelberg (1982). https://doi.org/10.1007/BFb0025774

13. D'Ippolito, N., Braberman, V.A., Piterman, N., Uchitel, S.: Synthesizing nonanomalous event-based controllers for liveness goals. ACM Trans. Softw. Eng. Methodol. 22(1), 9 (2013). https://doi.org/10.1145/2430536.2430543

14. Dwyer, M.B., Avrunin, G.S., Corbett, J.C.: Patterns in property specifications for finite-state verification. In: ICSE, pp. 411–420. ACM (1999)

15. Ehlers, R., Könighofer, R., Bloem, R.: Synthesizing cooperative reactive mission plans. In: 2015 IEEE/RSJ International Conference on Intelligent Robots and Systems, IROS 2015, Hamburg, Germany, 28 September - 2 October 2015, pp. 3478–3485. IEEE (2015). https://doi.org/10.1109/IROS.2015.7353862

16. Emerson, E.A., Halpern, J.Y.: "sometimes" and "not never" revisited: on branching versus linear time temporal logic. J. ACM 33(1), 151–178 (1986). https://doi.org/10.1145/4904.4999

17. Filippidis, I., Dathathri, S., Livingston, S.C., Ozay, N., Murray, R.M.: Control design for hybrid systems with tulip: the temporal logic planning toolbox. In: 2016 IEEE Conference on Control Applications, CCA 2016, Buenos Aires, Argentina, 19–22 September 2016, pp. 1030–1041. IEEE (2016). https://doi.org/10.1109/CCA.2016.7587949

18. Harel, D., Kugler, H.: Synthesizing state-based object systems from LSC specifications. Int. J. Found. Comput. Sci. 13(01), 5–51 (2002)

19. Jacobson, I.: Object-Oriented Software Engineering: A Use Case Driven Approach. Addison Wesley Longman Publishing Co. Inc, Redwood City (2004)

20. Kesten, Y., Piterman, N., Pnueli, A.: Bridging the gap between fair simulation and trace inclusion. Inf. Comput. 200(1), 35–61 (2005). http://www.sciencedirect.com/science/article/pii/S0890540105000234

21. Könighofer, R., Hofferek, G., Bloem, R.: Debugging formal specifications: a practical approach using model-based diagnosis and counterstrategies. STTT 15(5–6), 563–583 (2013). https://doi.org/10.1007/s10009-011-0221-y

22. Kozen, D.: Results on the propositional μ-calculus. In: Proceedings of the 9th Colloquium on Automata, Languages and Programming, pp. 348–359. Springer, London (1982). http://dl.acm.org/citation.cfm?id=646236.682866

23. Kress-Gazit, H., Fainekos, G.E., Pappas, G.J.: Temporal-logic-based reactive mission and motion planning. IEEE Trans. Robot. 25(6), 1370–1381 (2009). https://doi.org/10.1109/TRO.2009.2030225

24. Kugler, H., Harel, D., Pnueli, A., Lu, Y., Bontemps, Y.: Temporal logic for scenario-based specifications. In: Halbwachs, N., Zuck, L.D. (eds.) TACAS 2005. LNCS, vol. 3440, pp. 445–460. Springer, Heidelberg (2005). https://doi.org/10.1007/978-3-540-31980-1_29

25. Kupferman, O., Vardi, M.Y.: Synthesis with incomplete information. In: Barringer, H., Fisher, M., Gabbay, D., Gough, G. (eds.) Advances in Temporal Logic, vol. 16, pp. 109–127. Springer, Dordrecht (2000). https://doi.org/10.1007/978-94-015-9586-5_6

26. Majumdar, R., Piterman, N., Schmuck, A.: Environmentally-friendly GR(1) synthesis. CoRR abs/1902.05629 (2019). http://arxiv.org/abs/1902.05629

27. Maniatopoulos, S., Schillinger, P., Pong, V., Conner, D.C., Kress-Gazit, H.: Reactive high-level behavior synthesis for an atlas humanoid robot. In: Kragic, D., Bicchi, A., Luca, A.D. (eds.) 2016 IEEE International Conference on Robotics and Automation, ICRA 2016, Stockholm, Sweden, 16–21 May 2016, pp. 4192–4199. IEEE (2016). https://doi.org/10.1109/ICRA.2016.7487613

28. Maoz, S., Ringert, J.O.: GR(1) synthesis for LTL specification patterns. In: ESEC/FSE, pp. 96–106. ACM (2015). https://doi.org/10.1145/2786805.2786824

29. Maoz, S., Ringert, J.O.: On well-separation of GR(1) specifications. In: Zimmermann, T., Cleland-Huang, J., Su, Z. (eds.) Proceedings of the 24th ACM SIGSOFT International Symposium on Foundations of Software Engineering, FSE 2016, Seattle, WA, USA, 13–18 November 2016, pp. 362–372. ACM (2016). https://doi.org/10.1145/2950290.2950300

30. Maoz, S., Ringert, J.O.: Spectra: a specification language for reactive systems. CoRR abs/1904.06668 (2019). http://arxiv.org/abs/1904.06668

31. Maoz, S., Ringert, J.O., Shalom, R.: Symbolic repairs for GR(1) specifications. In: Mussbacher, G., Atlee, J.M., Bultan, T. (eds.) Proceedings of the 41st International Conference on Software Engineering, ICSE 2019, Montreal, QC, Canada, 25–31 May 2019, pp. 1016–1026. IEEE/ACM (2019). https://dl.acm.org/citation.cfm?id=3339632

32. Maoz, S., Sa'ar, Y.: AspectLTL: an aspect language for LTL specifications. In: AOSD, pp. 19–30. ACM (2011). https://doi.org/10.1145/1960275.1960280

33. Maoz, S., Sa'ar, Y.: Assume-guarantee scenarios: semantics and synthesis. In: France, R.B., Kazmeier, J., Breu, R., Atkinson, C. (eds.) Model Driven Engineering Languages and Systems. MODELS 2012 LNCS, vol. 7590, pp. 335–351. Springer, Heidelberg (2012). https://doi.org/10.1007/978-3-642-33666-9_22

34. Piterman, N., Pnueli, A., Sa'ar, Y.: Synthesis of reactive (1) designs. In: Emerson, E.A., Namjoshi, K.S. (eds.) Verification, Model Checking, and Abstract Interpretation VMCAI 2006. LNCS, vol. 3855, pp. 364–380. Springer, Heidelberg (2005). https://doi.org/10.1007/11609773_24

35. Pnueli, A.: The temporal logic of programs. In: 18th Annual Symposium on Foundations of Computer Science, Providence, Rhode Island, USA, 31 October – 1 November 1977, pp. 46–57. IEEE Computer Society (1977). https://doi.org/10.1109/SFCS.1977.32

36. Pnueli, A., Rosner, R.: On the synthesis of a reactive module. In: POPL, pp. 179–190. ACM Press (1989)

37. Pohl, K.: Requirements Engineering: Fundamentals, Principles, and Techniques, 1st edn. Springer Publishing Company, Incorporated (2010)

38. Rosner, R.: Modular synthesis of reactive systems. Ph.D. thesis, Weizmann Institute of Science (1992)

39. Sibay, G., Uchitel, S., Braberman, V.: Existential live sequence charts revisited. In: Proceedings of the 30th international conference on Software engineering, pp. 41–50. ACM (2008)

40. Sibay, G.E., Braberman, V., Uchitel, S., Kramer, J.: Synthesizing modal transition systems from triggered scenarios. IEEE Trans. Softw. Eng. **39**(7), 975–1001 (2013)

41. Somenzi, F.: CUDD: CU Decision Diagram Package Release 3.0.0 (2015). http://vlsi.colorado.edu/~fabio/CUDD/cudd.pdf

42. Sutcliffe, A.G., Maiden, N.A., Minocha, S., Manuel, D.: Supporting scenario-based requirements engineering. IEEE Trans. Softw. Eng. **24**(12), 1072–1088 (1998)

43. Tarski, A.: A lattice-theoretical fixpoint theorem and its applications. Pac. J. Math. **5**(2), 285–309 (1955). https://doi.org/10.2140/pjm.1955.5.285

44. Uchitel, S., Brunet, G., Chechik, M.: Behaviour model synthesis from properties and scenarios. In: Proceedings of the 29th international conference on Software Engineering, pp. 34–43. IEEE Computer Society (2007)
45. Uchitel, S., Brunet, G., Chechik, M.: Synthesis of partial behavior models from properties and scenarios. IEEE Trans. Softw. Eng. **35**(3), 384–406 (2009)
46. Walker, A., Ryzhyk, L.: Predicate abstraction for reactive synthesis. In: Formal Methods in Computer-Aided Design, FMCAD 2014, Lausanne, Switzerland, 21–24 October 2014, pp. 219–226. IEEE (2014). https://doi.org/10.1109/FMCAD.2014.6987617
47. Zachos, K., Maiden, N., Tosar, A.: Rich-media scenarios for discovering requirements. IEEE Softw. **22**(5), 89–97 (2005)
48. Spectra Website. http://smlab.cs.tau.ac.il/syntech/spectra/

Counterexample-Driven Synthesis for Probabilistic Program Sketches

Milan Češka[1], Christian Hensel[2], Sebastian Junges[2(✉)], and Joost-Pieter Katoen[2]

[1] Brno University of Technology, FIT, IT4I Centre of Excellence, Brno, Czech Republic
[2] RWTH Aachen University, Aachen, Germany
sebastian.junges@cs.rwth-aachen.de

Abstract. Probabilistic programs are key to deal with uncertainty in, e.g., controller synthesis. They are typically small but intricate. Their development is complex and error prone requiring quantitative reasoning over a myriad of alternative designs. To mitigate this complexity, we adopt counterexample-guided inductive synthesis (CEGIS) to automatically synthesise finite-state probabilistic programs. Our approach leverages efficient model checking, modern SMT solving, and counterexample generation at program level. Experiments on practically relevant case studies show that design spaces with millions of candidate designs can be fully explored using a few thousand verification queries.

1 Introduction

With the ever tighter integration of computing systems with their environment, quantifying (and minimising) the probability of encountering an anomaly or unexpected behaviour becomes crucial. This insight has led to a growing interest in probabilistic programs and models in the software engineering community. Henzinger [43] for instance argues that "the Boolean partition of software into correct and incorrect programs falls short of the practical need to assess the behaviour of software in a more nuanced fashion [...]." In [60], Rosenblum advocates taking a more probabilistic approach in software engineering. Concrete examples include quantitative analysis of software product lines [32,40,59,66,67], synthesis of probabilities for adaptive software [19,23], and probabilistic model checking at runtime to support verifying dynamic reconfigurations [20,37].

Synthesis of Probabilistic Programs. Probabilistic programs are a prominent formalism to deal with uncertainty. Unfortunately, such programs are rather intricate. Their development is complex and error prone requiring quantitative reasoning over many alternative designs. One remedy is the exploitation of probabilistic model checking [6] using a *Markov chain* as the operational model of a

This work has been supported by the Czech Science Foundation grant No. GA19-24397S, the IT4Innovations excellence in science project No. LQ1602, the DFG RTG 2236 "UnRAVeL", and the ERC Advanced Grant 787914 "FRAPPANT",.

© Springer Nature Switzerland AG 2019
M. H. ter Beek et al. (Eds.): FM 2019, LNCS 11800, pp. 101–120, 2019.
https://doi.org/10.1007/978-3-030-30942-8_8

program. One may then apply model checking on each design, or some suitable representation thereof [27,32]. Techniques such as parameter synthesis [26,42,58] and model repair [9,31] have been successful, but they only allow to amend or infer transition probabilities, whereas the control structure—the topology of the probabilistic model—is fixed.

Counter-Example-Guided Inductive Synthesis. This paper aims to overcome the existing limitation, by adopting the paradigm of *CounterExample-Guided Inductive Synthesis* (CEGIS, cf. Fig. 1) [1, 3,63,64] to finite-state probabilistic models and programs. The program synthesis challenge is to automatically provide a probabilistic program satisfying all properties, or to return that such a program is non-existing. In the syntax-based setting, we start with a sketch, a program

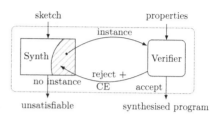

Fig. 1. CEGIS for synthesis.

with holes, and iteratively searches for good—or even optimal—instantiations of these holes. Rather than checking all instantiations, the design space is pruned by potentially ruling out many instantiations (dashed area) at once. From every realisation that was verified and rejected, a counterexample (CE) is derived, e.g., a program run violating the specification. An SMT (satisfiability modulo theory)-based synthesiser uses the CE to prune programs that also violate the specification. These programs are safely removed from the design space. The synthesis and verification step are repeated until either a satisfying program is found or the entire design space is pruned implying the non-existence of such a program.

Problem Statement and Program-Level Approach. This paper tailors and generalises CEGIS to probabilistic models and programs. The input is a sketch—a probabilistic program with holes, where each hole can be replaced by finitely many options—, a set of quantitative properties that the program needs to fulfil, and a budget. All possible realisations have a certain cost and the synthesis provides a realisation that fits within the budget. Programs are represented in the PRISM modelling language [50] and properties are expressed in PCTL (Probabilistic Computational Tree Logic) extended with rewards, as standard in probabilistic model checking [34,50]. Program sketches succinctly describe the design space of the system by providing the program-level structure but leaving some parts (e.g., command guards or variable assignments) unspecified.

Outcomes. To summarise, this paper presents a novel synthesis framework for probabilistic programs that adhere to a given set of quantitative requirements and a given budget. We use families of Markov chains to formalise our problem, and then formulate a CEGIS-style algorithm on these families. Here, CEs are subgraphs of the Markov chains. In the second part, we then generalise the approach to reason on probabilistic programs with holes. While similar in spirit, we rely on program-level CEs [33,71], and allow for a more flexible sketching language. To the best of our knowledge, this is the first lifting of CEGIS to probabilistic programs. The CEGIS approach is sound and complete: either an admissible program does exist and it is computed, or no such program exists and the algorithm reports this. We provide a prototype implementation built on top of the model checker Storm [34] and the SMT-tool Z3 [56]. Experiments with different examples demonstrate scalability: design spaces with millions of realisations can be fully explored by a few thousand verification queries and result in a speedup of orders of magnitude.

Related Work. We build on the significant body of research that employs formal methods to analyse quality attributes of alternative designs, e.g. [8,10, 16,38,65,72]. Enumerative approaches based on Petri nets [54], stochastic models [19,61] and timed automata [44,52], and the corresponding tools for simulation and verification (e.g. Palladio [10], PRISM [50], UPPAAL [44]) have long been used.

For non-probabilistic systems, CEGIS can find programs for a variety of challenging problems [62,63]. Meta-sketches and the *optimal and quantitative synthesis problem* in a non-probabilistic setting have been proposed [17,25,30].

A prominent representation of sets of alternative designs are modal transition systems [5,49,53]. In particular, *parametric* modal transition systems [11] and synthesis therein [12] allow for similar dependencies that occur in program-level sketches. Probabilistic extensions are considered in, e.g. [35], but not in conjunction with synthesis. Recently [36] proposed to exploit relationships between model and specification, thereby reducing the number of model-checking instances. In the domain of quantitative reasoning, sketches and likelihood computation are used to find probabilistic programs that best match available data [57]. The work closest to our approach synthesises probabilistic systems from specifications and parametric templates [39]. The principal difference to our approach is the use of counterexamples. The authors leverage evolutionary optimisation techniques without pruning. Therefore, completeness is only achieved by exploring all designs, which is practically infeasible. An extension to handle parameters affecting transition probabilities (rates) has been integrated into the evolutionary-driven synthesis [21,23] and is available in RODES [22]. Some papers have considered the analysis of sets of alternative designs within the quantitative verification of software product lines [40,59,67]. The typical approach is to analyse all individual designs (product configurations) or build and analyse a single (so-called *all-in-one*) Markov decision process describing all the designs simultaneously. Even with symbolic methods, this hardly scales to large sets of alternative designs. These techniques have recently been integrated into ProFeat [32] and QFLan [66]. An abstraction-refinement scheme has recently been explored in [27]. It iteratively analyses an abstraction of a (sub)set of designs—it is an orthogonal and slightly restricted approach to the inductive method presented here (detailed differences are discussed later). An incomplete method in [45] employs abstraction targeting a particular case study. SMT-based encodings for synthesis in Markov models have been used in, e.g. [24,46]. These encodings are typically monolithic—they do not prune the search space via CEs. Probabilistic CEs have been recently used to ensure that controllers obtained via learning from positive examples meet given safety properties [74]. In contrast, we leverage program-level CEs that can be used to prune the design space.

2   Preliminaries and Problem Statement

We start with basics of probabilistic model checking, for details, see [6,7], and then formalise families of Markov chains. Finally, we define some synthesis problems.

Probabilistic Models and Specifications. A *probability distribution* over a finite set X is a function $\mu\colon X \to [0,1]$ with $\sum_{x \in X} \mu(X) = 1$. Let $Distr(X)$ denote the set of all distributions on X.

Definition 1 (MC).   *A discrete-time Markov chain (MC) D is a tuple (S, s_0, P) with finite set S of states, initial state $s_0 \in S$, and transition probabilities $P\colon S \to Distr(S)$. We write $P(s,t)$ to denote $P(s)(t)$.*

For $S' \subseteq S$, the set $\mathsf{Succ}(S') := \{t \in S \mid \exists s \in S'.\ P(s,t) > 0\}$ denotes the successor states of S'. A *path* of an MC D is an (in)finite sequence $\pi = s_0 s_1 s_2 \ldots$, where $s_i \in S$, and $s_{i+1} \in \mathsf{Succ}(s_i)$ for all $i \in \mathbb{N}$.

Definition 2 (sub-MC). *Let $D = (S, s_0, P)$ be an MC with critical states $C \subseteq S$, $s_0 \in C$. The sub-MC of D, C is the MC $D \downarrow C = (C \cup \mathsf{Succ}(C), s_0, P')$ with: $P'(s,t) = P(s,t)$ for $s \in C$, $P'(s,s) = 1$ for $s \in \mathsf{Succ}(C) \backslash C$, and $P'(s,t) = 0$ otherwise.*

Specifications. For simplicity, we focus on reachability properties $\varphi = \mathbb{P}_{\sim \lambda}(\lozenge G)$ for a set $G \subseteq S$ of goal states, threshold $\lambda \in [0,1] \subseteq \mathbb{R}$, and comparison relation $\sim\ \in \{<, \leq, \geq, >\}$. The interpretation of φ on MC D is as follows. Let $\mathrm{Prob}(D, \lozenge G)$ denote the probability to reach G from D's initial state. Then, $D \models \varphi$ if $\mathrm{Prob}(D, \lozenge G) \sim \lambda$. A specification is a set $\Phi = \{\varphi_i\}_{i \in I}$ of properties, and $D \models \Phi$ if $\forall i \in I.\ D \models \varphi_i$. Upper-bounded properties (with $\sim\ \in \{<, \leq\}$) are safety properties, and lower-bounded properties are liveness properties. Extensions to expected rewards are straightforward.

Families of Markov Chains. We recap an explicit representation of a *family of MCs* using a parametric transition function, as in [27].

Definition 3 (Family of MCs). *A family of MCs is a tuple $\mathfrak{D} = (S, s_0, K, \mathfrak{P})$ with S, s_0 as before, a finite set of parameters K where the domain for each parameter $k \in K$ is $T_k \subseteq S$, and transition probability function $\mathfrak{P}\colon S \to Distr(K)$.*

The transition probability function of MCs maps states to distributions over successor states. For families, this function maps states to distributions over parameters. Instantiating each parameter with a value from its domain yields a "concrete" MC, called a *realisation*.

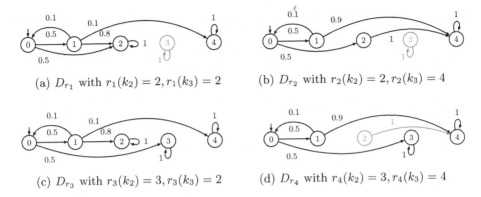

(a) D_{r_1} with $r_1(k_2) = 2, r_1(k_3) = 2$ (b) D_{r_2} with $r_2(k_2) = 2, r_2(k_3) = 4$

(c) D_{r_3} with $r_3(k_2) = 3, r_3(k_3) = 2$ (d) D_{r_4} with $r_4(k_2) = 3, r_4(k_3) = 4$

Fig. 2. The four different realisations of family $\mathfrak{D}$.

Definition 4 (Realisation). *A realisation of a family* $\mathfrak{D} = (S, s_0, K, \mathfrak{P})$ *is a function* $r\colon K \to S$ *where* $\forall k \in K\colon r(k) \in T_k$. *A realisation* r *yields an MC* $D_r := (S, s_0, \mathfrak{P}(r))$, *where* $\mathfrak{P}(r)$ *is the transition probability matrix in which each* $k \in K$ *in* $\mathfrak{P}$ *is replaced by* $r(k)$. *Let* $\mathcal{R}^{\mathfrak{D}}$ *denote the set of all realisations for* $\mathfrak{D}$.

As a family $\mathfrak{D}$ has finite parameter domains, the number of family members (i.e. realisations from $\mathcal{R}^{\mathfrak{D}}$) of $\mathfrak{D}$ is finite, but exponential in $|K|$. While all MCs share their state space, their *reachable* states may differ.

Example 1. Consider the family of MCs $\mathfrak{D} = (S, s_0, K, \mathfrak{P})$ where $S = \{0, \ldots, 4\}$, $s_0 = 0$, and $K = \{k_0, \ldots, k_5\}$ with $T_{k_0} = \{0\}$, $T_{k_1} = \{1\}$, $T_{k_2} = \{2, 3\}$, $T_{k_3} = \{2, 4\}$, $T_{k_4} = \{3\}$ and $T_{k_5} = \{4\}$, and $\mathfrak{P}$ given by:

$$\mathfrak{P}(0) = 0.5\colon k_1 + 0.5\colon k_2 \quad \mathfrak{P}(1) = 0.1\colon k_0 + 0.8\colon k_3 + 0.1\colon k_5 \quad \mathfrak{P}(2) = 1\colon k_3$$
$$\mathfrak{P}(3) = 1\colon k_4 \qquad\qquad\qquad \mathfrak{P}(4) = 1\colon k_5$$

Figure 2 shows the four MCs of $\mathfrak{D}$. Unreachable states are greyed out.

The function $c\colon \mathcal{R}^{\mathfrak{D}} \to \mathbb{N}$ assigns *realisation costs*. Attaching costs to realisations is a natural way to distinguish preferable realisations. We stress the difference with rewards in MCs; the latter impose a cost structure on paths in MCs.

Problem Statement *Synthesis Problems.* Let $\mathfrak{D}$ be a family, and Φ be a set of properties, and $B \in \mathbb{N}$ a budget. Consider the synthesis problems:

1. *Feasibility synthesis:* Find a realisation $r \in \mathcal{R}^{\mathfrak{D}}$ with $D_r \models \Phi$ and $c(r) \leq B$.
2. *Max synthesis:* For given $G \subseteq S$, find $r^* \in \mathcal{R}^{\mathfrak{D}}$ with

$$r^* := \underset{r \in \mathcal{R}_{\mathfrak{D}}}{\arg\max} \{\mathtt{Prob}(D_r, \Diamond G) \mid D_r \models \Phi \text{ and } c(r) \leq B\}.$$

The problem in feasibility synthesis is to determine a realisation satisfying all $\varphi \in \Phi$, or return that no such realisation exists. The problem in max synthesis is to find a realisation that maximises the reachability probability of reaching G. It can analogously be defined for minimising such probabilities. As families are finite, such optimal realisations r^* always exist (if there exists a feasible solution). It is beneficial to consider a variant of the max-synthesis problem in which the realisation r^* is not required to achieve the maximal reachability probability, but it suffices to be close to it. This notion of ε *-maximal synthesis* for a given $0 < \varepsilon \leq 1$ amounts to find a realisation r^* with $\texttt{Prob}(D_{r^*}, \Diamond G) \geq (1-\varepsilon) \cdot \max\limits_{r \in \mathcal{R}^{\mathfrak{D}}} \{\texttt{Prob}(D_r, \phi)\}$.

Problem Statement and Structure. In this paper, we propose novel synthesis algorithms for the probabilistic systems that are based on two concepts, CEGIS [63] and syntax-guided synthesis [3]. To simplify the presentation, we start with CEGIS in Sect. 3 and adopt it for MCs and the feasibility problem. In Sect. 4, we lift and tune CEGIS, in particular towards probabilistic program sketches.

3   CEGIS for Markov Chain Families

We follow the typical separation of concerns as in oracle-guided inductive synthesis [4,39,41]: a *synthesiser* selects single realisations r that have not been considered before, and a *verifier* checks whether the MC D_r satisfies the specification Φ (cf. Fig. 1 on page 1). If a realisation violates the specification, the verifier returns a *conflict* representing the core part of the MC causing the violation.

3.1   Conflicts and Synthesiser

To formalise conflicts, a *partial realisation* of a family $\mathfrak{D}$ is a function $\bar{r} \colon K \to S \cup \{\perp\}$ such that $\forall k \in K. \; \bar{r}(k) \in T_k \cup \{\perp\}$. For any partial realisations $\bar{r}_1, \bar{r}_2$, let $\bar{r}_1 \subseteq \bar{r}_2$ iff $\bar{r}_1(k) \in \{\bar{r}_2(k), \perp\}$ for all $k \in K$.

Definition 5 (Conflict). *Let $r \in \mathcal{R}^{\mathfrak{D}}$ be a realisation with $D_r \not\models \varphi$ for $\varphi \in \Phi$. A partial realisation $\bar{r}_\varphi \subseteq r$ is a* conflict *for the property φ iff $D_{r'} \not\models \varphi$ for each realisation $r' \supseteq \bar{r}_\varphi$. A set of conflicts is called a* conflict set.

To explore all realisations, the synthesiser starts with $Q := \mathcal{R}^{\mathfrak{D}}$ and picks some realisation $r \in Q$.[1] Either $D_r \models \Phi$ and we immediately return r, or a conflict is found: then Q is pruned by removing all conflicts that the verifier found. If Q is empty, we are done: each realisation violates a property $\varphi \in \Phi$.

---

[1] We focus on program-level synthesis, and refrain from discussing important implementation aspects—like how to represent Q—here.

3.2   Verifier

Definition 6. *A verifier is sound and complete, if for family $\mathfrak{D}$, realisation r, and specification Φ, the verifier terminates, the returned conflict set is empty iff $D_r \models \Phi$, and if it is not empty, it contains a conflict $\bar{r}_\varphi \subseteq r$ for some $\varphi \in \Phi$.*

Algorithm 1 outlines a basic verifier. It uses an off-the-shelf probabilistic model-checking procedure CHECK(D_r, φ) to determine all violated $\varphi \in \Phi$. The algorithm then iterates over the violated φ and computes critical sets C of D_r that induce sub-MCs such that $D_r \downarrow C \not\models \varphi$ (line 6). The critical sets for safety properties can be obtained via standard methods [2], and support for liveness properties is discussed at the end of the section.

(a) Fragment of D_{r_1} (b) Sub-MC of D_{r_1} with $C = \{0\}$

Fig. 3. Fragment and corresponding sub-MC that suffices to refute Φ

Algorithm 1. Verifier

1: **function** VERIFY(family $\mathfrak{D}$, realisation r, specification Φ)
2:    Violated $\leftarrow \varnothing$; Conflict $\leftarrow \varnothing$; $D_r \leftarrow$ GENERATEMC($\mathfrak{D}, r$);
3:    **for all** $\varphi \in \Phi$ **do**
4:       **if not** CHECK(D_r, φ) **then** Violated $\leftarrow$ Violated $\cup \{\varphi\}$
5:    **for all** $\varphi \in$ Violated **do**
6:       $C_\varphi \leftarrow$ COMPUTECRITICALSET(D_r, φ)
7:       Conflict $\leftarrow$ Conflict $\cup$ GENERATECONFLICT($\mathfrak{D}, r, C_\varphi$)
8:    **return** Conflict

Example 2. Reconsider $\mathfrak{D}$ from Example 1 with $\Phi := \{\varphi := \mathbb{P}_{\leq 2/5}(\Diamond\{2\})\}$. Assume the synthesiser picks realisation r_1. The verifier builds D_{r_1} and determines $D_{r_1} \not\models \Phi$. Observe that the verifier does not need the full realisation D_{r_1} to refute Φ. In fact, the paths in the fragment of D_{r_1} in Fig. 3a (ignoring the outgoing transitions of states 1 and 2) suffice to show that the probability to reach state 2 exceeds $2/5$. Formally, the fragment in Fig. 3b is a sub-MC $D_{r_1} \downarrow C$ with critical states $C = \{0\}$. The essential property is [70]:

> *If a sub-MC of a MCD refutes a safety property φ, then D refutes φ too.*

Observe that $D_{r_1} \downarrow C$ is part of D_{r_2} too. Formally, the sub-MC of $D_{r_2} \downarrow C$ is isomorphic to $D_{r_1} \downarrow C$ and therefore also violates Φ. Thus, $D_{r_2} \not\models \Phi$.

Finally, the verifier translates the obtained critical set C for realisation r to a conflict $Conflict(C, r) \subseteq r$ and stores it in the conflict set Conflict (line 7). The procedure GENERATECONFLICT($\mathfrak{D}, r, C$) identifies the subset of parameters K that occur in the sub-MCs $D_r \downarrow C$ and returns the corresponding partial realisation. The proposition below clarifies the relation between critical sets and conflicts.

Proposition 1. *If C is a critical set for D_r and φ, with $D_r \not\models \varphi$ then C is also a critical set for each $D_{r'}$, $r' \supseteq Conflict(C, r)$, and furthermore $D_{r'} \not\models \varphi$ holds.*

Example 3. Recall from Example 2 that $D_{r_2} \not\models \Phi$. This can be concluded *without* constructing D_{r_2}. Just considering r_2, $\mathfrak{D}$ and C suffices: First, take all parameters occurring in $\mathfrak{P}(c)$ for any $c \in C$. This yields $\{k_1, k_2\}$. The partial realisation $\bar{r} := \{k_1 \mapsto 1, k_2 \mapsto 2\}$ is a conflict. The values for the other parameters do not affect the shape of the sub-MC induced by C. Realisation $r_2 \supseteq \bar{r}$ only varies from r_1 in the value of k_3, but $\bar{r}(k_3) = \bot$, i.e., k_3 is not included in the conflict. This suffices to conclude $D_{r_2} \not\models \Phi$.

Conflicts for Liveness Properties. To support liveness properties such as $\varphi := \mathbb{P}_{>\lambda}(\lozenge G)$, we first consider a (standard) dual safety property $\varphi' := \mathbb{P}_{<1-\lambda}(\lozenge B)$, where B is the set of all states that do not have a path to G. Observe that B can be efficiently computed using graph algorithms. We have to be careful, however.

Example 4. Consider D_{r_1}, and let $\varphi := \mathbb{P}_{>3/5}(\lozenge\{4\})$. $D_{r_1} \not\models \varphi$. Then, $\varphi' = \mathbb{P}_{<2/5}(\lozenge\{2\})$, which is refuted with critical set $C = \{0\}$ as before. Although $D_{r_2} \downarrow C$ is again isomorphic to $D_{r_1} \downarrow C$, we have $D_{r_2} \models \varphi$. The problem here is that state 2 is in B for D_{r_1} as $r_1(k_3) = 2$, but not in B for D_{r_2}, as $r_2(k_3) = 4$.

To prevent the problem above, we ensure that the states in B cannot reach G in other realisations, by including B in the critical set of φ: Let C be the critical set for the dual safety property φ'. We define $B \cup C$ as critical states for φ. Together, we reach states B with a critical probability mass[2], and never leave B.

Example 5. In D_{r_1}, we compute critical states $\{0, 2\}$, preventing the erroneous reasoning from the previous example. For D_{r_4}, we compute $C' = \{0\} \cup \{3\}$ as critical states, and as $D_{r_4} \downarrow C'$ is isomorphic to $D_{r_3} \downarrow C'$, we obtain that $D_{r_3} \not\models \varphi$.

4   Syntax-Guided Synthesis for Probabilistic Programs

Probabilistic models are typically specified by means of a program-level modelling language, such as PRISM [50], PIOA [73], JANI [18], or MODEST [15]. We propose a *sketching language* based on the PRISM modelling language. A sketch, a syntactic template, defines a high-level structure of the model and represents a-priori knowledge about the system under development. It effectively

---

[2] A good implementation takes a subset of $B' \subseteq B$ by considering the Prob($D, \lozenge B'$).

```
hole X either { XA is 1 cost 3, 2}
hole Y either { YA is 1, 3 }
hole Z either { 1, 2 }
constraint  !(XA && YA);
module rex
s  : [0..3] init 0;
s = 0 -> 0.5: s'=X + 0.5: s'=Y;
s = 1 -> s'=s+Z;
s >= 2 -> s'=s;
endmodule
```

(a) Program sketch $\mathfrak{S}_H$

```
module rex
s  : [0..3] init 0;
s = 0 -> 0.5: s'=1 + 0.5: s'=3;
s = 1 -> s'=3;
s >= 2 -> s'=s;
endmodule
```

(b) Instance $\mathfrak{S}_H(\{X \mapsto 1, Z \mapsto 2, Y \mapsto 3\})$

Fig. 4. Running example

restricts the size of the design space and also allows to concisely add constraints and costs to its members. The proposed language is easily supported by model checkers and in particular by methods for generating CEs [33, 71]. Below, we describe the language, and adapt CEGIS from state level to program level. In particular, we employ so-called *program-level CEs*, rather than CEs on the state level.

4.1 A Program Sketching Language

Let us briefly recap how the model-based concepts translate to language concepts in the PRISM guarded-command language. A PRISM program consists of one or more reactive modules that may interact with each other. Consider a single module. This is not a restriction, every PRISM program can be flattened into this form. A module has a set of bounded variables spanning its state space. Transitions between states are described by guarded commands of the form:

$$\mathtt{guard} \quad \to \quad p_1 : \mathtt{update}_1 + \ldots\ldots + p_n : \mathtt{update}_n$$

The guard is a Boolean expression over the module's variables of the model. If the guard evaluates to true, the module can evolve into a successor state by updating its variables. An update is chosen according to the probability distribution given by expressions $p_1, \ldots, p_n$. In every state enabling the guard, the evaluation of $p_1, \ldots, p_n$ must sum up to one. Overlapping guards yield non-determinism and are disallowed here.

Roughly, a program $\mathcal{P}$ thus is a tuple (Var, E) of variables and commands. For a program $\mathcal{P}$, the *underlying MC* $[\![\mathcal{P}]\!]$ are $\mathcal{P}$'s semantics. We lift specifications: Program $\mathcal{P}$ satisfies a specification Φ, iff $[\![\mathcal{P}]\!] \models \Phi$, etc.

A sketch is a program that contains *holes*. Holes are the program's open parts and can be replaced by one of finitely many options. Each option can *optionally* be named and associated with a cost. They are declared as:

$$\mathtt{hole}\ h\ \mathtt{either}\{x_1\ \mathtt{is}\ \ \mathtt{expr}_1\ \mathtt{cost}\ c_1, \ldots, x_k\ \mathtt{is}\ \ \mathtt{expr}_k\ \mathtt{cost}\ c_k\}$$

where h is the hole identifier, x_i is the option name, $\mathtt{expr}_i$ is an expression over the program variables describing the option, and c_i is the cost, given as expressions over natural numbers. A hole h can be used in commands in a similar

---

Algorithm 2. Synthesiser (feasibility synthesis)

1: **function** SYNTHESIS(program sketch $\mathfrak{S}_H$, specification Φ, budget B)
2:     $\psi \leftarrow$ INITIALISE($\mathfrak{S}_H, B$)
3:     $R \leftarrow$ GETREALISATION(ψ)
4:     **while** $R \neq$ Unsat **do**
5:         $C \leftarrow$ VERIFY($\mathfrak{S}_H(R), \Phi$)
6:         **if** $C = \varnothing$ **then return** R
7:         $\psi \leftarrow \psi \wedge \left(\bigwedge_{\bar{R} \in C}$ LEARNFROMCONFLICT($\mathfrak{S}_H, \bar{R}$)$\right)$
8:         $R \leftarrow$ GETREALISATION(ψ)
9:     **return** Unsat

---

way as a constant, and may occur multiple times within multiple commands, in both guards and updates. The option names can be used to describe constraints on realisations. These propositional formulae over option names restrict realisations, e.g.,

$$\texttt{constraint}(x_1 \vee x_2) \implies x_3$$

requires that whenever the options x_1 or x_2 are taken for some (potentially different) holes, option x_3 is also to be taken.

Definition 7 (Program sketch). *A (PRISM program) sketch is a tuple $\mathfrak{S}_H := (\mathcal{P}_H, \mathsf{Option}_H, \Gamma, \mathsf{cost})$ where $\mathcal{P}_H$ is a program with a set H of holes with options Option_H, Γ are constraints over Option_H, and $\mathsf{cost}\colon \mathsf{Option}_H \to \mathbb{N}$ option-costs.*

Example 6. We consider a small running example to illustrate the main concepts. Figure 4a depicts the program sketch $\mathfrak{S}_H$ with holes $H = \{X, Y, Z\}$. For X, the options are $\mathsf{Option}_X = \{1, 2\}$. The constraint forbids XA and YA both being one; it ensures a non-trivial random choice in state $\mathsf{s=0}$.

Remark 1. Below, we formalise notions previously used on families. Due to flexibility of sketching (in particular in combination with multiple modules), it is *not* straightforward to provide family semantics to sketches, but the concepts are analogous. In particular: holes and parameters are similar, parameter domains are options, and family realisations and sketch realisations both yield concrete instances from a family/sketch. The synthesis problems carry over naturally.

Definition 8 (Realisations of sketches). *Let $\mathfrak{S}_H := (\mathcal{P}_H, \mathsf{Option}_H, \Gamma, \mathsf{cost})$ be a sketch, a sketch realisation on holes H is a function $R\colon H \to \mathsf{Option}_H$ with $\forall h \in H.\ R(h) \in \mathsf{Option}_h$ and that satisfies all constraints in Γ. The sketch instance $\mathfrak{S}_H(R)$ for realisation R is the program (without holes) $\mathcal{P}_H[H/R]$ in which each hole $h \in H$ in $\mathcal{P}_H$ is replaced by $R(h)$. The cost $c(R)$ is the sum of the cost of the selected options, $c(R) := \sum_{h \in H} \mathsf{cost}(R(h))$.*

Example 7. We continue Example 6. The program in Fig. 4b reflects $\mathfrak{S}_H(R)$ for realisation $R = \{X \mapsto 1, Z \mapsto 2, Y \mapsto 3\}$, with $c(R) = 3$ as $\mathsf{cost}(R(X)) = 3$ and all other options have cost zero. For realisation $R' = \{Y, Z \mapsto 1, X \mapsto 2\}$, $c(R') = 0$.

The assignment $\{X, Y, Z \mapsto 1\}$ violates the constraint and is not a realisation. In total, $\mathfrak{S}_H$ represents $6 = 2^3 - 2$ programs and their underlying MCs.

4.2   A Program-Level Synthesiser

Feasibility synthesis. The synthesiser follows the steps in Alglorithm 2. During the synthesis process, the synthesiser stores and queries the set of realisations not yet pruned. These remaining realisations are represented by (the satisfying assignments of) the first-order formula ψ over hole-assignments. Iteratively extending ψ with conjunctions thus prunes the remaining design space.

We give a brief overview, before detailing the steps. INITIALISE($\mathfrak{S}_H, B$) constructs ψ such that it represents *all* sketch realisations that satisfy the constraints in the sketch $\mathfrak{S}_H$ within the budget B. GETREALISATION(ψ) exploits an SMT-solver for linear (bounded) integer arithmetic to obtain a realisation R consistent with ψ, or Unsat if no such realisation exists. As long as new realisations are found, the verifier analyses them (line 5) and returns a conflict set C. If $C = \varnothing$, then $\mathfrak{S}_H(R)$ satisfies the specification Φ and the search is terminated. Otherwise, the synthesiser updates ψ based on the conflicts (line 7). R is always pruned.

INITIALISE($\mathfrak{S}_H, B$): Let hole $h \in H$ have (ordered) options $\text{Option}_h = \{o_h^1, \ldots, o_h^n\}$. To encode realisation R, we introduce integer-valued meta-variables $K_H := \{\kappa_h \mid h \in H\}$ with the semantics that $\kappa_h = i$ whenever hole h has value o_h^i, i.e., $R(h) = o_h^i$. We set $\psi := \psi_{\text{opti}} \wedge \psi_\Gamma \wedge \psi_{\text{cost}}$, where ψ_{opti} ensures that each hole is assigned to some option, ψ_Γ ensures that the sketch's constraints Γ are satisfied, and ψ_{cost} ensures that the budget is respected. These sub-formulae are:

$$\psi_{\text{opti}} := \bigwedge_{h \in H} 1 \leq \kappa_h \leq |\text{Option}_h|, \qquad \psi_\Gamma := \bigwedge_{\gamma \in \Gamma} \gamma[N_h^i/\kappa_h = i],$$

$$\psi_{\text{cost}} := \sum_{h \in H} \omega_h \leq B \wedge \left(\bigwedge_{h \in H} \bigwedge_{i=1}^{|\text{Option}_h|} \kappa_h = i \rightarrow \omega_h = \text{cost}(o_h^i) \right),$$

where $\gamma[N_h^i/\kappa_h = i]$ denotes that in every constraint $\gamma \in \Gamma$ we replace each option name N_h^i for an option o_h^i with $\kappa_h = i$, and ω_h are fresh variables storing the cost for the selected option at hole h.

Example 8. For sketch $\mathfrak{S}_H$ in Fig. 4a, we obtain (with slight simplifications)

$$\psi := 1 \leq \kappa_X \leq 2 \wedge 1 \leq \kappa_Y \leq 2 \wedge 1 \leq \kappa_Z \leq 2 \wedge \neg(\kappa_X = 1 \wedge \kappa_Y = 1) \wedge$$
$$\omega_X + \omega_Y + \omega_Z \leq B \wedge \kappa_X = 1 \rightarrow \omega_X = 3 \wedge \kappa_X = 2 \rightarrow \omega_X = 0 \wedge \omega_Y = 0 = \omega_Z.$$

GETREALISATION(ψ): To obtain a realisation R, we check satisfiability of ψ. The solver either returns Unsat indicating that the synthesiser is finished, or Sat, together with a satisfying assignment $\alpha_R : K_H \rightarrow \mathbb{N}$. The assignment α_R uniquely identifies a realisation R by $R(h) := o_h^{\alpha_R(\kappa_h)}$. The sum over all ω_H gives $c(R)$.

Algorithm 3. Synthesiser (max synthesis)

1: **function** SYNTHESIS($\mathfrak{S}_H$, Φ, B, goal predicate G, tolerance ε)
2:    $\lambda^* \leftarrow \infty$, $R^* \leftarrow$ **Unsat**, $\psi \leftarrow$ INITIALISE($\mathfrak{S}_H, B$)
3:    $R \leftarrow$ GETREALISATION(ψ)
4:    **while** $R \neq$ **Unsat do**
5:        $C, \lambda_{new} \leftarrow$ OPTIMISEVERIFY($\mathfrak{S}_H(R), \Phi, G, \lambda^*, \varepsilon$)
6:        **if** $C = \varnothing$ **then** $\lambda^*, R^* \leftarrow \lambda_{new}, R$
7:        $\psi \leftarrow \psi \wedge \left(\bigwedge_{\bar{R} \in C} \text{LEARNFROMCONFLICT}(\mathfrak{S}_H, \bar{R}) \right)$
8:        $R \leftarrow$ GETREALISATION(ψ)
9:    **return** R^*

```
const int X = 1, Y = 3;                 ...
...                                     module rex
module rex                              s : [0..3] init 0;
s : [0..3] init 0;                      s=0 -> 0.5:s'=X + 0.5:s'=Y;
s=0 -> 0.5: s'=X + 0.5: s'=Y;           s=3 -> s'=3
endmodule                               endmodule
```

(a) CE for upper bound   (b) CE for lower bound

Fig. 5. CEs for (a) $\mathbb{P}_{\leq 0.4}[F\ \text{s=3}]$ and (b) $\mathbb{P}_{>0.6}[F\ \text{s=2}]$.

VERIFY($\mathfrak{S}_H(r), \Phi$): invokes any sound and complete verifier, e.g., an adaption of the verifier from Sect. 3.2 as presented in Sect. 4.3.

LEARNFROMCONFLICT($\mathfrak{S}_H, \bar{R}$): For a conflict[3] $\bar{R} \in C$, we add the formula

$$\neg \left(\bigwedge_{h \in H, \bar{R}(h) \neq \perp} \kappa_h = \alpha_{\bar{R}}(\kappa_h) \right).$$

The formula excludes realisations $R' \supseteq \bar{R}$. Intuitively, the formula states that the realisations remaining in the design space (encoded by the updated ψ) cannot assign the h as in $\bar{R}$ (for holes where $\bar{R}(h) \neq \perp$).

Example 9. Consider ψ from Example 8. The satisfying assignment (for $B \geq 3$) is $\{\kappa_X \mapsto 1, \kappa_Y, \kappa_Z \mapsto 2, \omega_X \mapsto 3, \omega_Y, \omega_Z \mapsto 0\}$ represents R, $c(R) = 3$ from Example 6. Consider $\Phi = \{\mathbb{P}_{\leq 0.4}[\lozenge\ \text{s=3}]\}$. The verifier (for now, magically) constructs a conflict set $\{\bar{R}\}$ with $\bar{R} = \{Y \mapsto 3\}$. The synthesiser updates $\psi \leftarrow \psi \wedge \kappa_Y \neq 2$ (recall that $\kappa_Y = 2$ encodes $Y \mapsto 3$). A satisfying assignment $\{\kappa_X, \kappa_Y, \kappa_Z \mapsto 1\}$ for ψ encodes R' from Example 7. As $\mathfrak{S}_H(R') \models \Phi$, the verifier reports no conflict.

Optimal Synthesis. We adapt the synthesiser to support max synthesis, cf. Alglorithm 3. Recall the problem aims at maximizing the probability of reaching

---

[3] As in Sect. 3.1: A *partial realisation* for $\mathfrak{S}_H$ is a function $\bar{R}: H \rightarrow \text{Option}_H \cup \{\perp\}$ s.t. $\forall h \in H$. $\bar{R}(h) \in \text{Option}_h \cup \{\perp\}$. For partial realisations $\bar{R}_1, \bar{R}_2$, let $\bar{R}_1 \subseteq \bar{R}_2$ iff $\forall h \in H$. $\bar{R}_1(h) \in \{\bar{R}_2(h), \perp\}$. Let R be a realisation s.t. $\mathfrak{S}_H(R) \not\models \varphi$ for $\varphi \in \Phi$. Partial realisation $\bar{R}_\varphi \subseteq R$ is a *conflict* for φ iff $\forall R' \supseteq \bar{R}_\varphi$ $\mathfrak{S}_H(R') \not\models \varphi$.

states described by a predicate G, w.r.t. the tolerance $\varepsilon \in (0,1)$. Algorithm 3 stores in λ^* the maximal probability $\mathsf{Prob}(\mathfrak{S}_H(R), \Diamond G)$ among all considered realisations R, and this R in R^*. In each iteration, an optimising verifier is invoked (line 5) on realisation R. If $\mathfrak{S}_H(R) \models \Phi$ and $\mathsf{Prob}(\mathfrak{S}_H(R), \Diamond G) > \lambda^*$, it returns an empty conflict set *and* $\lambda_{\text{new}} := \mathsf{Prob}(\mathfrak{S}_H(R), \Diamond G)$. Otherwise, it reports a conflict set for $\Phi \cup \{\mathbb{P}_{\geq(1-\varepsilon)\cdot\lambda^*}(\Diamond G)\}$.

4.3 A Program-Level Verifier

We now adapt the state-level verifier from Sect. 3.2 in Alglorithm 1 to use program-level counterexamples [71] for generating conflicts, [68, Appendix] contains details.

GENERATEMC($\mathfrak{S}_H, R$): This procedure first constructs the instance $\mathfrak{S}_H(R)$, i.e., a program without holes, from $\mathfrak{S}_H$ and R, as in Fig. 4b: Constraints in the sketch are removed, as they are handled by the synthesiser. This approach allows us to use any model checker supporting PRISM programs. The realisation is passed separately, the sketch is parsed *once* and then appropriately instantiated. The instance is then translated into the underlying MC $[\![\mathfrak{S}_H(R)]\!]$ via standard procedures, with transitions annotated with their generating commands.

COMPUTECRITICALSET(D, φ) computes program-level CEs as analogue of critical sets. They are defined on commands rather than on states. Let $\mathcal{P} = (\text{Var}, E)$ be a program with commands E. Let $\mathcal{P}_{|E'} := (\text{Var}, E')$ denote the restriction of $\mathcal{P}$ to E' (with variables and initial states as in $\mathcal{P}$). Building $\mathcal{P}_{|E'}$ may introduce deadlocks in $[\![\mathcal{P}_{|E'}]\!]$ (just like a critical set introduces deadlocks). To remedy this, we use the standard operation fixdl, which takes a program and adds commands that introduce self-loops for states without enabled guard.

Definition 9. *For program* $\mathcal{P} = (\text{Var}, E)$ *and specification* Φ *with* $\mathcal{P} \not\models \Phi$, *a program-level CE* $E' \subseteq E$ *is a set of commands, such that for all (non-overlapping) programs* $\mathcal{P}' = (\text{Var}, E'')$ *with* $E'' \supseteq E'$ *(i.e, extending* $\mathcal{P}'$*),* fixdl$(\mathcal{P}') \not\models \Phi$.

Example 10. Reconsider $\Phi = \{\mathbb{P}_{\leq 0.4}[\Diamond\ \mathsf{s}{=}3]\}$. Figure 5a shows a CE for $\mathfrak{S}_H(R)$ in Fig. 4. The probability to reach $\mathsf{s}{=}3$ in the underlying MC is $0.5 > 0.4$.

For safety properties, program-level CEs coincide with high-level CEs proposed in [71], their extension to liveness properties follows the ideas on families. The program-level CEs are computed by an extension of the MaxSat [14] approach from [33], [68, Appendix] contains details and extensions.

GENERATECONFLICT($\mathfrak{S}_H, R, E$) generates conflicts from commands: we map commands in $\mathfrak{S}_H(R)_{|E}$ to the commands from $\mathfrak{S}_H$, i.e., we restore the information about the critical holes corresponding to the part of the design space that can be pruned by CE E. Formally, $Conflict(E, R)(h) = R(h)$ for all $h \in H$ that appear in restriction $\mathfrak{S}_{H|E}$.

Proposition 2. *If E is a CE for $\mathfrak{S}_H(R)$, then E is also a CE for each $\mathfrak{S}_H(R')$, $R' \supseteq Conflict(E, R)$.*

Example 11. The CEs in Fig. 5a contain commands which depend on the realisations for holes X and Y. For these fixed values, the program violates the specification *independent of the value for Z*, so Z is not in the conflict $\{X \mapsto 1, Y \mapsto 3\}$.

5   Experimental Evaluation and Discussion

Implementation. We evaluate the synthesis framework with a prototype[4] using the SMT-solver Z3 [56], and (an extension of) the model checker Storm [34].

Case Studies. We consider the following three case studies:

Dynamic Power Management (DPM). The goal of this adapted DPM problem [13] is to trade-off power consumption for performance. We sketch a controller that decides based on the current workload, inspired by [39]. The fixed environment contains no holes. The goal is to synthesise the guards and updates to satisfy a specification with properties such as φ_1: the expected number of lost requests is below λ, and φ_2: the expected energy consumption is below κ.

Intrusion describes a network (adapted from [51]), in which the controller tries to infect a target node via intermediate nodes. A failed attack makes a node temporarily harder to intrude. We sketched a partial strategy aiming to minimise the expected time to intrusion. Constraints encode domain specific knowledge.

Grid is based on a classical benchmark for solving partially observable MDPs (POMDPs) [48]. To solve POMDPs, the task is to find an observation-based strategy, which is undecidable for the properties we consider. Therefore, we resort to finding a deterministic k-state strategy [55] s.t. in expectation, the strategy requires less than λ steps to the target. This task is still hard: finding a memoryless, observation-based strategy is already NP-hard [29,69]. We create a family describing all k-state strategies (for some fixed k) for the POMDP. Like in [47] actions are reflected by parameters, while parameter dependencies ensure that the strategy is observation-based.

Evaluation. We compare w.r.t. an enumerative approach. That baseline linearly depends on the number of realisations, and the underlying MCs' size. We focus on sketches where all realisations are explored, as relevant for optimal synthesis. For concise presentation we use Unsat variants of feasibility synthesis. Enumerative methods perform mostly independent of the order of enumerating realisations. We evaluate results for *DPM*, and summarise further results. All results are obtained on a Macbook MF839LL/A, within 3 h and using less than 8 GB RAM.

DPM has 9 holes with 260 K realisations, and MCs have 5 K (reachable) states on average, ranging from 2 K to 8 K states. *The performance of CEGIS significantly depends on the specification, namely, on the thresholds appearing in the*

---

[4] https://github.com/moves-rwth/sketching.

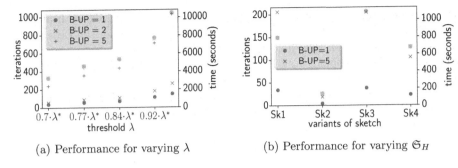

(a) Performance for varying λ (b) Performance for varying $\mathfrak{S}_H$

Fig. 6. Performance (runtime and iterations) on DPM (Color figure online)

properties. Fig. 6a shows how the number of iterations (left axis, green circle) and the runtime in seconds (right axis, blue) change for varying λ for property φ_1 (stars and crosses are explained later). We obtain a speedup of 100× over the baseline for $\lambda = 0.7 \cdot \lambda^*$, dropping to 23× for $\lambda = 0.95 \cdot \lambda^*$, where λ^* is the minimal probabilty over all realisations. The strong dependency between performance and "unsatisfiability" is not surprising. The more unsatisfiable, the smaller the conflicts (as in [33]). Small conflicts have a double beneficial effect. First, the prototype uses an optimistic verifier searching for minimal conflicts; small conflicts are found faster than large ones. Second, small conflicts prune more realisations. A slightly higher number of small conflicts yields a severe decrease in iterations. Thus *the further the threshold from the optimum, the better the performance.*

Reconsider Fig. 6a, crosses and stars correspond to a variant in which we have blown up the state space of the underlying MCs by a factor B-UP. Observe that performance degrades similarly for the baseline and our algorithm, which means that *the speedup w.r.t. the baseline is not considerably affected by the size of the underlying MCs.* This observation holds for various models and specifications.

Varying the sketch tremendously affects performance, cf. Fig. 6b for the performance on variants of the original sketch with some hole substituted by one of its options. The framework performs significantly better on sketches with holes that lie in local regions of the MC. Holes relating to states all-over the MC are harder to prune. Finally, our prototype generally performs better with specifications that have multiple (conflicting) properties: Some realisations can be effectively pruned by conflicts w.r.t. property φ_1, whereas other realisations are easily pruned by conflicts w.r.t., e.g., property φ_2.

Intrusion has 26 holes and 6800 K realisations, the underlying MCs have only 500 states on average. We observe an even more significant effect of the property thresholds on the performance, as the number of holes is larger (recall the optimistic verifier). We obtain a speedup of factor 2200, 250 and 5 over the baseline, for thresholds $0.7 \cdot \lambda^*$, $0.8 \cdot \lambda^*$ and $0.9 \cdot \lambda^*$, respectively. For $0.7 \cdot \lambda^*$, many conflicts contain only 8 holes. Blowing up the model does not affect the obtained speedups. Differences among variants are again significant, albeit less extreme.

Grid is structurally different: only 6 holes in 3 commands and 1800 realisations, but MCs having 100 K states on average. Observe that reaching the targets on expectation below some threshold implies that the goal must almost surely be reached. The MCs' topology and the few commands make pruning hard: our algorithm needs more than 400 iterations. Still, we obtain a 3× speedup for $\lambda = 0.98 \cdot \lambda^*$. Pruning mostly follows from reasoning about realisations that do not reach the target almost surely. Therefore, the speedup is mostly independent of the relation between λ and λ^*.

Discussion. *Optimistic verifiers* search for a minimal CE and thus solve an NP-hard problem [28,71]. In particular, we observed a lot of overhead when the smallest conflict is large, and any small CE that can be cheaply computed might be better for the performance (much like the computation of unsatisfiable cores in SMT solvers). Likewise, reusing information about holes from previous runs might benefit the performance. Improvements in concise sketching, and exploiting the additional structure, will also improve performance.

Sketching. Families are simpler objects than sketches, but their explicit usage of states make them inadequate for modelling. Families can be lifted to a (restricted) sketching class, as in [27]. However, additional features like conflicts significantly ease the modelling process. Consider *intrusion*: Without constraints, the number of realisations grows to $6 \cdot 10^{11}$. Put differently, the constraint allows to discard over 99.99% of the realisations up front. Moreover, constraints can exclude realisations that would yield unsupported programs, e.g, programs with infinite state spaces. While modelling concise sketches with small underlying MCs, it may be hard to avoid such invalid realisations without the use of constraints.

Comparison with CEGAR. We also compared with our CEGAR-prototype [27], which leverages an abstraction-refinement loop for the synthesis. We observed that there are synthesis problems where CEGIS significantly outperforms CEGAR and vice versa. Details, including an evaluation of the strengths and weaknesses of CEGIS compared to CEGAR, are reported in [68, Appendix]. In our future work, we will explore how to effectively combine both approaches to improve the performance and scalability of the synthesis process.

References

1. Abate, A., David, C., Kesseli, P., Kroening, D., Polgreen, E.: Counterexample guided inductive synthesis modulo theories. In: Chockler, H., Weissenbacher, G. (eds.) CAV 2018. LNCS, vol. 10981, pp. 270–288. Springer, Cham (2018). https://doi.org/10.1007/978-3-319-96145-3_15
2. Ábrahám, E., Becker, B., Dehnert, C., Jansen, N., Katoen, J.-P., Wimmer, R.: Counterexample generation for discrete-time Markov models: an introductory survey. In: Bernardo, M., Damiani, F., Hähnle, R., Johnsen, E.B., Schaefer, I. (eds.) SFM 2014. LNCS, vol. 8483, pp. 65–121. Springer, Cham (2014). https://doi.org/10.1007/978-3-319-07317-0_3

3. Alur, R., et al.: Syntax-guided synthesis. In: Dependable Software Systems Engineering, NATO Science for Peace and Security Series, vol. 40, pp. 1–25. IOS Press (2015)
4. Alur, R., Singh, R., Fisman, D., Solar-Lezama, A.: Search-based program synthesis. Commun. ACM **61**(12), 84–93 (2018)
5. Antonik, A., Huth, M., Larsen, K.G., Nyman, U., Wasowski, A.: 20 years of modal and mixed specifications. Bull. EATCS **95**, 94–129 (2008)
6. Baier, C., de Alfaro, L., Forejt, V., Kwiatkowska, M.: Model checking probabilistic systems. Handbook of Model Checking, pp. 963–999. Springer, Cham (2018). https://doi.org/10.1007/978-3-319-10575-8_28
7. Baier, C., Katoen, J.P.: Principles of Model Checking. MIT Press, Cambridge (2008)
8. Balsamo, S., Di Marco, A., Inverardi, P., Simeoni, M.: Model-based performance prediction in software development: a survey. IEEE Trans. Softw. Eng. **30**(5), 295–310 (2004)
9. Bartocci, E., Grosu, R., Katsaros, P., Ramakrishnan, C.R., Smolka, S.A.: Model repair for probabilistic systems. In: Abdulla, P.A., Leino, K.R.M. (eds.) TACAS 2011. LNCS, vol. 6605, pp. 326–340. Springer, Heidelberg (2011). https://doi.org/10.1007/978-3-642-19835-9_30
10. Becker, S., Koziolek, H., Reussner, R.: The Palladio component model for model-driven performance prediction. J. Syst. Softw. **82**(1), 3–22 (2009)
11. Benes, N., Kretínský, J., Larsen, K.G., Møller, M.H., Sickert, S., Srba, J.: Refinement checking on parametric modal transition systems. Acta Inf. **52**(2–3), 269–297 (2015)
12. Beneš, N., Křetínský, J., Guldstrand Larsen, K., Møller, M.H., Srba, J.: Dual-priced modal transition systems with time durations. In: Bjørner, N., Voronkov, A. (eds.) LPAR 2012. LNCS, vol. 7180, pp. 122–137. Springer, Heidelberg (2012). https://doi.org/10.1007/978-3-642-28717-6_12
13. Benini, L., Bogliolo, A., Paleologo, G., Micheli, G.D.: Policy optimization for dynamic power management. IEEE Trans. CAD Integr. Circ. Syst. **8**(3), 299–316 (2000)
14. Biere, A., Heule, M., van Maaren, H., Walsh, T. (eds.): Handbook of Satisfiability, Frontiers in Artificial Intelligence and Applications, vol. 185. IOS Press (2009)
15. Bohnenkamp, H.C., D'Argenio, P.R., Hermanns, H., Katoen, J.P.: MODEST: a compositional modeling formalism for hard and softly timed systems. IEEE Trans. Softw. Eng. **32**(10), 812–830 (2006)
16. Bondy, A.B.: Foundations of Software and System Performance Engineering. Addison Wesley, Boston (2014)
17. Bornholt, J., Torlak, E., Grossman, D., Ceze, L.: Optimizing synthesis with metasketches. In: POPL, pp. 775–788. ACM (2016)
18. Budde, C.E., Dehnert, C., Hahn, E.M., Hartmanns, A., Junges, S., Turrini, A.: JANI: quantitative model and tool interaction. In: Legay, A., Margaria, T. (eds.) TACAS 2017. LNCS, vol. 10206, pp. 151–168. Springer, Heidelberg (2017). https://doi.org/10.1007/978-3-662-54580-5_9
19. Calinescu, R., Ghezzi, C., Johnson, K., et al.: Formal verification with confidence intervals to establish quality of service properties of software systems. IEEE Trans. Reliab. **65**(1), 107–125 (2016)
20. Calinescu, R., Ghezzi, C., Kwiatkowska, M.Z., Mirandola, R.: Self-adaptive software needs quantitative verification at runtime. Commun. ACM **55**(9), 69–77 (2012)

21. Calinescu, R., Češka, M., Gerasimou, S., Kwiatkowska, M., Paoletti, N.: Designing robust software systems through parametric Markov chain synthesis. In: ICSA, pp. 131–140. IEEE (2017)
22. Calinescu, R., Češka, M., Gerasimou, S., Kwiatkowska, M., Paoletti, N.: RODES: a robust-design synthesis tool for probabilistic systems. In: Bertrand, N., Bortolussi, L. (eds.) QEST 2017. LNCS, vol. 10503, pp. 304–308. Springer, Cham (2017). https://doi.org/10.1007/978-3-319-66335-7_20
23. Calinescu, R., Češka, M., Gerasimou, S., Kwiatkowska, M., Paoletti, N.: Efficient synthesis of robust models for stochastic systems. J. Syst. Softw. **143**, 140–158 (2018)
24. Cardelli, L., et al.: Syntax-guided optimal synthesis for chemical reaction networks. In: Majumdar, R., Kunčak, V. (eds.) CAV 2017. LNCS, vol. 10427, pp. 375–395. Springer, Cham (2017). https://doi.org/10.1007/978-3-319-63390-9_20
25. Černý, P., Chatterjee, K., Henzinger, T.A., Radhakrishna, A., Singh, R.: Quantitative synthesis for concurrent programs. In: Gopalakrishnan, G., Qadeer, S. (eds.) CAV 2011. LNCS, vol. 6806, pp. 243–259. Springer, Heidelberg (2011). https://doi.org/10.1007/978-3-642-22110-1_20
26. Češka, M., Dannenberg, F., Paoletti, N., Kwiatkowska, M., Brim, L.: Precise parameter synthesis for stochastic biochemical systems. Acta Inf. **54**(6), 589–623 (2017)
27. Češka, M., Jansen, N., Junges, S., Katoen, J.-P.: Shepherding hordes of Markov chains. In: Vojnar, T., Zhang, L. (eds.) TACAS 2019. LNCS, vol. 11428, pp. 172–190. Springer, Cham (2019). https://doi.org/10.1007/978-3-030-17465-1_10
28. Chadha, R., Viswanathan, M.: A counterexample-guided abstraction-refinement framework for markov decision processes. ACM Trans. Comput. Log. **12**(1), 1:1–1:49 (2010)
29. Chatterjee, K., Chmelik, M., Davies, J.: A symbolic SAT-based algorithm for almost-sure reachability with small strategies in POMDPs. In: AAAI, pp. 3225–3232. AAAI Press (2016)
30. Chaudhuri, S., Clochard, M., Solar-Lezama, A.: Bridging boolean and quantitative synthesis using smoothed proof search. In: POPL. ACM (2014)
31. Chen, T., Hahn, E.M., Han, T., Kwiatkowska, M.Z., Qu, H., Zhang, L.: Model repair for Markov decision processes. In: TASE, pp. 85–92. IEEE (2013)
32. Chrszon, P., Dubslaff, C., Klüppelholz, S., Baier, C.: ProFeat: feature-oriented engineering for family-based probabilistic model checking. Formal Aspects Comput. **30**(1), 45–75 (2018)
33. Dehnert, C., Jansen, N., Wimmer, R., Ábrahám, E., Katoen, J.-P.: Fast debugging of PRISM models. In: Cassez, F., Raskin, J.-F. (eds.) ATVA 2014. LNCS, vol. 8837, pp. 146–162. Springer, Cham (2014). https://doi.org/10.1007/978-3-319-11936-6_11
34. Dehnert, C., Junges, S., Katoen, J.-P., Volk, M.: A *storm* is coming: a modern probabilistic model checker. In: Majumdar, R., Kunčak, V. (eds.) CAV 2017. LNCS, vol. 10427, pp. 592–600. Springer, Cham (2017). https://doi.org/10.1007/978-3-319-63390-9_31
35. Delahaye, B., et al.: Abstract probabilistic automata. Inf. Comput. **232**, 66–116 (2013)
36. Dureja, R., Rozier, K.Y.: More scalable LTL model checking via discovering design-space dependencies (D^3). In: Beyer, D., Huisman, M. (eds.) TACAS 2018. LNCS, vol. 10805, pp. 309–327. Springer, Cham (2018). https://doi.org/10.1007/978-3-319-89960-2_17

37. Filieri, A., Tamburrelli, G., Ghezzi, C.: Supporting self-adaptation via quantitative verification and sensitivity analysis at run time. IEEE Trans. Softw. Eng. **42**(1), 75–99 (2016)
38. Fiondella, L., Puliafito, A. (eds.): Principles of Performance and Reliability Modeling and Evaluation. SSRE. Springer, Cham (2016). https://doi.org/10.1007/978-3-319-30599-8
39. Gerasimou, S., Tamburrelli, G., Calinescu, R.: Search-based synthesis of probabilistic models for quality-of-service software engineering. In: ASE, pp. 319–330. IEEE Computer Society (2015)
40. Ghezzi, C., Sharifloo, A.M.: Model-based verification of quantitative non-functional properties for software product lines. Inf. Softw. Technol. **55**(3), 508–524 (2013)
41. Gulwani, S., Polozov, O., Singh, R.: Program synthesis. Found. Trends Programm. Lang. **4**(1–2), 1–119 (2017)
42. Hahn, E.M., Hermanns, H., Zhang, L.: Probabilistic reachability for parametric markov models. Softw. Tools Technol. Transf. **13**(1), 3–19 (2011)
43. Henzinger, T.A.: Quantitative reactive modeling and verification. Comput. Sci.-Res. Dev. **28**(4), 331–344 (2013)
44. Hessel, A., Larsen, K.G., Mikucionis, M., Nielsen, B., Pettersson, P., Skou, A.: Testing real-time systems using UPPAAL. In: Hierons, R.M., Bowen, J.P., Harman, M. (eds.) Formal Methods and Testing. LNCS, vol. 4949, pp. 77–117. Springer, Heidelberg (2008). https://doi.org/10.1007/978-3-540-78917-8_3
45. Jansen, N., Humphrey, L.R., Tumova, J., Topcu, U.: Structured synthesis for probabilistic systems. CoRR abs/1807.06106, at NFM 2019 (2018, to appear)
46. Junges, S., Jansen, N., Dehnert, C., Topcu, U., Katoen, J.-P.: Safety-constrained reinforcement learning for MDPs. In: Chechik, M., Raskin, J.-F. (eds.) TACAS 2016. LNCS, vol. 9636, pp. 130–146. Springer, Heidelberg (2016). https://doi.org/10.1007/978-3-662-49674-9_8
47. Junges, S., et al.: Finite-state controllers of POMDPs using parameter synthesis. In: UAI, pp. 519–529. AUAI Press (2018)
48. Kaelbling, L.P., Littman, M.L., Cassandra, A.R.: Planning and acting in partially observable stochastic domains. Artif. Intell. **101**(1–2), 99–134 (1998)
49. Křetínský, J.: 30 years of modal transition systems: survey of extensions and analysis. In: Aceto, L., Bacci, G., Bacci, G., Ingólfsdóttir, A., Legay, A., Mardare, R. (eds.) Models, Algorithms, Logics and Tools. LNCS, vol. 10460, pp. 36–74. Springer, Cham (2017). https://doi.org/10.1007/978-3-319-63121-9_3
50. Kwiatkowska, M., Norman, G., Parker, D.: PRISM 4.0: verification of probabilistic real-time systems. In: Gopalakrishnan, G., Qadeer, S. (eds.) CAV 2011. LNCS, vol. 6806, pp. 585–591. Springer, Heidelberg (2011). https://doi.org/10.1007/978-3-642-22110-1_47
51. Kwiatkowska, M.Z., Norman, G., Parker, D., Vigliotti, M.G.: Probabilistic mobile ambients. Theor. Comput. Sci. **410**(12–13), 1272–1303 (2009)
52. Larsen, K.G.: Verification and performance analysis of embedded and cyber-physical systems using UPPAAL. In: MODELSWARD 2014, pp. IS-11 (2014)
53. Larsen, K.G., Thomsen, B.: A modal process logic. In: LICS, pp. 203–210. IEEE Computer Society (1988)
54. Lindemann, C.: Performance modelling with deterministic and stochastic Petri nets. Perf. Eval. Review **26**(2), 3 (1998)
55. Meuleau, N., Kim, K.E., Kaelbling, L.P., Cassandra, A.R.: Solving POMDPs by searching the space of finite policies. In: UAI, pp. 417–426. Morgan Kaufmann Publishers Inc. (1999)

56. de Moura, L., Bjørner, N.: Z3: an efficient SMT solver. In: Ramakrishnan, C.R., Rehof, J. (eds.) TACAS 2008. LNCS, vol. 4963, pp. 337–340. Springer, Heidelberg (2008). https://doi.org/10.1007/978-3-540-78800-3_24

57. Nori, A.V., Ozair, S., Rajamani, S.K., Vijaykeerthy, D.: Efficient synthesis of probabilistic programs. In: PLDI, pp. 208–217. ACM (2015)

58. Quatmann, T., Dehnert, C., Jansen, N., Junges, S., Katoen, J.-P.: Parameter synthesis for Markov models: faster than ever. In: Artho, C., Legay, A., Peled, D. (eds.) ATVA 2016. LNCS, vol. 9938, pp. 50–67. Springer, Cham (2016). https://doi.org/10.1007/978-3-319-46520-3_4

59. Rodrigues, et al.: Modeling and verification for probabilistic properties in software product lines. In: HASE, pp. 173–180. IEEE (2015)

60. Rosenblum, D.S.: The power of probabilistic thinking. In: ASE, p. 3. ACM (2016)

61. Sharma, V.S., Trivedi, K.S.: Quantifying software performance, reliability and security: an architecture-based approach. J. Syst. Softw. **80**(4), 493–509 (2007)

62. Solar-Lezama, A., Jones, C.G., Bodik, R.: Sketching concurrent data structures. In: PLDI, pp. 136–148. ACM (2008)

63. Solar-Lezama, A., Rabbah, R.M., Bodík, R., Ebcioglu, K.: Programming by sketching for bit-streaming programs. In: PLDI, pp. 281–294. ACM (2005)

64. Solar-Lezama, A., Tancau, L., Bodik, R., Seshia, S., Saraswat, V.: Combinatorial sketching for finite programs. In: ASPLOS, pp. 404–415. ACM (2006)

65. Stewart, W.J.: Probability, Markov Chains, Queues, and Simulation: The Mathematical Basis of Performance Modeling. Princeton university press (2009)

66. Vandin, A., ter Beek, M.H., Legay, A., Lluch Lafuente, A.: QFLan: a tool for the quantitative analysis of highly reconfigurable systems. In: Havelund, K., Peleska, J., Roscoe, B., de Vink, E. (eds.) FM 2018. LNCS, vol. 10951, pp. 329–337. Springer, Cham (2018). https://doi.org/10.1007/978-3-319-95582-7_19

67. Varshosaz, M., Khosravi, R.: Discrete time Markov chain families: modeling and verification of probabilistic software product lines. In: SPLC Workshops, pp. 34–41. ACM (2013)

68. Češka, M., Hensel, C., Junges, S., Katoen, J.P.: Counterexample-driven synthesis for probabilistic program sketches. CoRR abs/1904.12371 (2019)

69. Vlassis, N., Littman, M.L., Barber, D.: On the computational complexity of stochastic controller optimization in POMDPs. ACM Trans. Comput. Theor. **4**(4), 12:1–12:8 (2012). https://doi.org/10.1145/2382559.2382563

70. Wimmer, R., Jansen, N., Ábrahám, E., Becker, B., Katoen, J.-P.: Minimal critical subsystems for discrete-time Markov models. In: Flanagan, C., König, B. (eds.) TACAS 2012. LNCS, vol. 7214, pp. 299–314. Springer, Heidelberg (2012). https://doi.org/10.1007/978-3-642-28756-5_21

71. Wimmer, R., Jansen, N., Vorpahl, A., Ábrahám, E., Katoen, J.-P., Becker, B.: High-Level Counterexamples for Probabilistic Automata. In: Joshi, K., Siegle, M., Stoelinga, M., D'Argenio, P.R. (eds.) QEST 2013. LNCS, vol. 8054, pp. 39–54. Springer, Heidelberg (2013). https://doi.org/10.1007/978-3-642-40196-1_4

72. Woodside, M., Petriu, D., Merseguer, J., Petriu, D., Alhaj, M.: Transformation challenges: from software models to performance models. J. Softw. Syst. Model. **13**(4), 1529–1552 (2014)

73. Wu, S., Smolka, S.A., Stark, E.W.: Composition and behaviors of probabilistic I/O automata. Theor. Comput. Sci. **176**(1–2), 1–38 (1997)

74. Zhou, W., Li, W.: Safety-aware apprenticeship learning. In: Chockler, H., Weissenbacher, G. (eds.) CAV 2018. LNCS, vol. 10981, pp. 662–680. Springer, Cham (2018). https://doi.org/10.1007/978-3-319-96145-3_38

Synthesis of Railway Signaling Layout from Local Capacity Specifications

Bjørnar Luteberget[1], Christian Johansen[2], and Martin Steffen[2(✉)]

[1] Railcomplete AS, Oslo, Norway
bjlut@railcomplete.no
[2] Department of Informatics, University of Oslo, Oslo, Norway
{cristi,msteffen}@ifi.uio.no

Abstract. We present an optimization-based synthesis method for laying out railway signaling components on a given track infrastructure to fulfill capacity specifications. The specifications and the optimization method are designed to be suitable for the scope of signaling construction projects and their associated interlocking systems, but can be adapted to related problems in, e.g., highway, tram, or airport runway designs. The main synthesis algorithm starts from an initial heuristic over-approximation of required signaling components and iterates towards better designs using two main optimization techniques: (1) global simultaneous planning of all operational scenarios using incremental SAT-based optimization to eliminate redundant signaling components, and (2) a derivative-free numerical optimization method using as cost function timing results given by a discrete event simulation engine, applied on all the plans from (1).

Synthesizing all of the signaling layout might not always be appropriate in practice, and partial synthesis from an already valid design is a more practical alternative. In consequence, we focus also on the usefulness of the individual optimization steps: SAT-based planning is used to suggest removal of redundant signaling components, whereas numerical optimization of timing results is used to suggest moving signaling components around on the layout, or adding new components. Such changes are suggested to railway engineers using an interactive tool where they can investigate the consequences of applying the various optimizations.

Keywords: Railway signaling · Capacity · On-the-fly synthesis ·
Incremental SAT · Interactive ·
Derivative-free numerical optimization · Discrete event simulation

1 Introduction

Signaling engineering for railway infrastructure consists of setting up signals, train detectors, derailers, and related equipment, and then building a control

The first author was partially supported by the project *RailCons – Automated Methods and Tools for Ensuring Consistency of Railway Designs*, with number 248714 funded by the Norwegian Research Council and Railcomplete AS.

© Springer Nature Switzerland AG 2019
M. H. ter Beek et al. (Eds.): FM 2019, LNCS 11800, pp. 121–137, 2019.
https://doi.org/10.1007/978-3-030-30942-8_9

system called the *interlocking* which ensures that all train movements happen in a safe sequence. Comprehensive regulations and processes have been put in place to ensure the safety of such systems, and standards and authorities "highly recommend" using formal methods (of various kinds) for higher safety integrity levels like SIL4 (cf. [2,6,7,12]).

The precise locations of signaling components on the railway tracks can have crucial impact on the capacity of the railway, i.e., its ability to handle intended operational scenarios in a timely manner. Many details of the signaling layout design can cause operational scenarios to become infeasible or slow, s.a.: signal and detector placement, correct allocation and freeing of resources, track lengths, train lengths, etc. Capacity-related decisions in signaling are closely related to the fields of timetable planning and the implementation of interlocking systems, and although tool support for verification of interlockings [10,15,16] and optimization of timetables [1,13,19] has been thoroughly investigated and developed since the beginnings of computer science (for example, the maximum flow problem was originally formulated to estimate railway network capacity, see [14]) signaling layout design still lacks appropriate modeling and analysis tools.

Consequently, railway construction projects usually rely on informal, vague, or non-existent capacity specifications, and engineers need to make adhoc/manual analyses of how the layout and control system can provide the required capacity. Systematic capacity analysis for railways is typically performed on the scale of national networks, using comprehensive timetables, focusing on delays, congestion, and only after a complete design is finished (cf. [1,9,19]). Large-scale capacity analysis thus assumes railway signaling layouts as low-level details which have already been correctly designed. In contrast, we focus in this paper on specifying and fulfilling capacity measures that make sense in the setting of construction projects, typically for a single or a few stations or railway lines.

In earlier work, we have developed methods for both static [22–24] and dynamic [21] analysis of railway designs and developed tools which run fast enough to be used for immediate feedback in an interactive design process. We have also developed a verification system and a capacity specification language [21] for construction projects, which verifies properties such as running time, train frequency, overtaking and crossing. Building on this verification work, we present in this paper an optimization method where signaling components, i.e., mainly signals and detectors, but also balises, derailers, and catch points, can be moved or removed from the design to improve capacity.

We show how our SAT-based planning procedure can be extended to find redundant signaling equipment, and how a simulator can be extended to move signaling equipment around using continuous-domain mathematical optimization methods and discrete event simulation. With the use of a heuristic initial design algorithm, the optimization procedures can be applied even if the user has not yet supplied any working signaling design, and in this way we get a synthesis algorithm. If a working design is already in place, our method suggests possible design improvements to the user in an interactive style, so that the

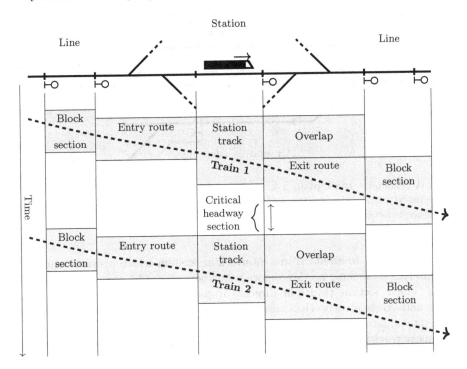

Fig. 1. Blocking time diagram showing two (non-stopping) trains traveling from a line blocking section into a station and back onto a line blocking section. Dashed lines indicate train locations and velocity, and gray boxes indicate the lengths and times of sections exclusively allocated to the trains. Figure adapted from [27].

engineer has the final say in making changes to the design, and can investigate how the changes influence the infrastructure and operational scenarios. Thus, our method can consider some signals fixed, i.e., part of the design, while there rest are amenable to optimization.

These methods are a step towards a railway signaling engineering methodology based on explicit specifications, and using analysis and verification tools every step along the way, which we believe can improve decision-making.

The main contributions of this paper thus are: (1) defining and demonstrating a novel specification-based design methodology for automating the layout of railway signaling components, (2) extending existing planning and simulation methods to make changes in the designs which improve their quality with respect to given specifications, and (3) showing how incremental optimization and partial synthesis can be used in specification-based design through an interactive tool.

2   Background

The basic safety principles used in most railways around the world are based on dividing railway lines into *fixed blocking sections*, and use signals and train

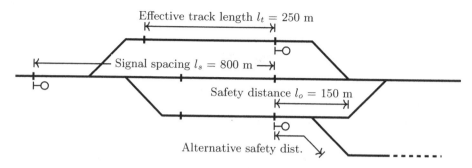

Fig. 2. A schematic track plan, a key artifact in designing the signalling system in a route-based interlocking system. The plan is annotated with signalling components and distances between locations relevant for interlocking safety requirements.

detectors together in an electronic interlocking system which prevents one train from entering a blocking section before it has been cleared by the previous train.

The block section principle directly impacts the maximum frequency of trains, and consequently the *capacity* of the railway, through the interplay between train parameters (length, acceleration, and braking power), track layout (how many tracks are available at which stations), and the location of signalling equipment. The topic of this paper is how to design this infrastructure, specifically how to choose the number and locations of signals and detectors to optimize capacity.

There are two main design methods for deciding signal and detector locations, which have different application areas. The first method is the *blocking time diagram* where a single track on a railway line, or a single path through a railway station, is presented on the horizontal axis, and consecutive trains traveling the same path are plotted with the blocking time of each section shown as rectangles stretching out on the vertical time axis (see Fig. 1).

The second design method is to use a schematic track plan showing the topology of tracks and the locations of signals, detectors, and other signalling system components. The schematic plan is not geographically accurate (for the sake of readability) but is annotated with traveling lengths between relevant locations, such as from one signal to the next signal or detector. This plan is used in the design of *route-based interlocking systems* to make assessments of the effective lengths of station tracks, safety distances from a signal to other tracks (so-called *overlaps*), and more (see Fig. 2).

Observe how the blocking time diagram and the schematic plan provide views in different dimensions: the blocking time diagram provides continuous time and a single spatial dimension but does not treat different choices of path, while the schematic track plan shows all paths at once, but does not directly show how a train would travel in time. The latter concerns *schedulability*, while the former concerns *timing*. For detailed signalling design, the decisions that impact the interaction between these two analysis domains are a complex task where an engineer balances a number of diverse concerns.

2.1   Railway Signalling Layout Design

We define the *railway signalling layout design* problem as follows: given a track plan, and a set of intended operational scenarios, decide on a set of signalling components (signals, detectors, etc.) and their locations, such that it is possible to implement a safe interlocking control system with which the specified operational scenarios can be dispatched efficiently (see example in Fig. 3).

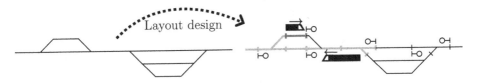

Fig. 3. Railway signalling layout design places a set of signalling components *(as on the right)* on a given track layout *(as on the left)* to ensure that a set of capacity specifications can be fulfilled by dispatching trains in some way.

The main constraints imposed on a signalling design can be classified into four main categories:

1. **Physical infrastructure:** all the trains are guided by the rails and can only travel where the rails guide them. The space that trains move on is a graph with linear connections between nodes.
2. **Allocation of resources:** railway signals are connected to a control system called the interlocking, which ensures mutual exclusion of trains by reading from detectors and ensuring that signals can only signal movement authority when it is safe to do so. This entails that one can only allocate and free resources in certain groupings (see example in Fig. 4).
3. **Limited communication:** the most obvious way to improve capacity on an existing railway line is to install more signals to more finely subdivide the allocation of space so that trains can be traveling more closely on the line.

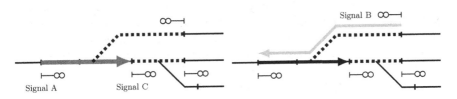

Fig. 4. Allocation and freeing of resources can only be done within the limits of what information the control system can send and receive. In the left figure, a train traveling from Signal A must travel at least until Signal C, and all resources in this path must be allocated and in a safe state before the train can proceed from A. In the right figure, no train can proceed from Signal B because parts of the path require the same resources, meaning elementary routes are conflicting and cannot be used simultaneously.

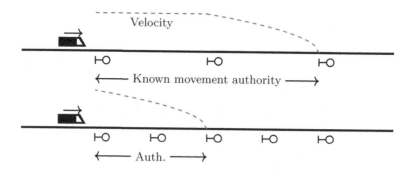

Fig. 5. Signal information only carries across two signals (so-called *distant signals*).

However, since the train driver always has to be able to stop the train within the limits of the currently given length of movement authority, putting signals too close together will lower the speed that the train can travel with. This means that there is a limit to how many signals one can install before the capacity starts to decrease because of this (see Fig. 5).

4. **Laws of motion:** when a train is given a movement authority, this authority has a limited length and a limited maximum velocity. The driver must choose when to accelerate and brake to stay within the given authority.

In the methods for optimization and synthesis proposed below, we assume that the above constraints are absolute. In practice, engineers have subtle work-arounds for each of these constraints whenever the situation requires a non-standard solution. Physical infrastructure (1) can often be modified by taking a step back in the planning process and re-evaluating the track layout together with track engineers. Allocation of resources (2) can be overcome by designing certain movements to be performed as shunting movements, i.e., a second-grade class of movement authority with lower safety requirements. Limited communication (3) can also be overcome by increasing the number of different aspects that the signals can communicate, or by using cab signalling, giving additional communication between the interlocking system and the train driver. The ETCS Level 2 system currently being implemented in many European countries is capable of signalling any number of routes simultaneously through digital radio communication, effectively removing the infrastructure-to-driver communication restriction. Finally, the laws of motion (4) cannot be overcome in themselves, but increasing the requirements for vehicles' acceleration and braking power may improve a layout design's expected performance.

3   Method

The following list is a summary of the components in our work-flow for solving the railway signalling layout design problem automatically and incrementally (Fig. 6):

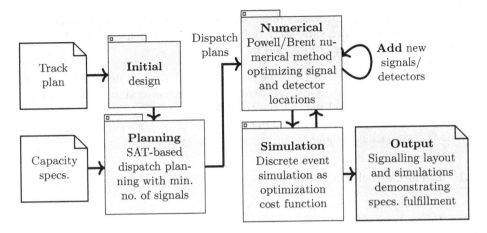

Fig. 6. Synthesis process overview. Track plan and capacity specifications are given as input, and together with an initial design based on a heuristic algorithm they are given to the SAT-based planner for simultaneous dispatch planning of all usage scenarios. A numerical method takes the dispatch plans and adjusts the locations and number of signals and detectors until no better result from simulation is achieved.

1. **Track plan and capacity specification input:** Track plans are graph-like structures with information about track lengths, boundary nodes, switches, and crossings, and are read from the railML format[1]. We use our method from [21] for local capacity specifications in SAT, summarized in Sect. 3.1.

2. **Initial design:** We propose in Sect. 3.2 a heuristic algorithm to over-approximate the signaling components required to plan the set of all possible movements on the given track plan. This forms our initial maximal design.

3. **Planning optimization:** Ignoring all timing aspects, we calculate the smallest set of signals and detectors that are able to dispatch all of the scenarios described in the local capacity specifications. This is done by solving a planning problem where all scenarios are planned simultaneously. An incremental SAT solver derives the plans and optimizes the number of signals that are used. This extends our work from [21], and is detailed in Sect. 3.3.

4. **Numerical optimization:** A measure for the performance of the design is calculated by dispatching all of the planned ways to realize the performance specifications and measuring the difference between the required time and the simulated time. This measure is used as a goal function for a meta-heuristic numerical optimization algorithm for moving the signals around, and when this algorithm converges, each track is tested using Discrete Event **Simulation** for how much improvement would be obtained by adding signals to it and repeating the optimization process. See Sect. 3.4 below.

---

[1] See https://railml.org/.

5. **Output:** After the process is done, the user is left with a design and a set of dispatch plans and simulated train movements which describe how the capacity requirements are fulfilled by this design.

The overall work-flow of our method is thought to be automatic, without manual intervention, unless the user wants to define some signals fixed, which would then be considered part of the track plan input. For this, our synthesis must be incremental, and integrated in the engineers' design tool, offering formal methods automation without requiring any prior knowledge.

3.1 Local Capacity Specifications

To capture typical performance and capacity requirements in construction projects, we have defined in [21] an **operational scenario** $S = (V, M, C)$ as follows:

1. A set of **vehicle types** V, each defined by a length l, a maximum velocity $v_{\max}$, a maximum acceleration a, and a maximum braking deceleration b.
2. A set of **movements** M, each defined by a vehicle type and an ordered sequence of visits. Each visit q is a set of alternative locations $\{l_i\}$ and an optional minimum dwelling time t_d.
3. A set of **timing constraints** C, which are two visits q_a, q_b, and an optional numerical constraint t_c on the minimum time between visit q_a and q_b. The two visits can come from different movements. If the time constraint t_c is omitted, the visits are only required to be ordered, so that $t_{q_a} < t_{q_b}$.

We give here only a simple example of an overtaking requirement. See [21] for further examples[2]. Overtaking as an operational scenario means that two trains traveling in the same direction can be reordered. For example, we specify a passenger train traveling from b1 to b2, and a goods train with the same visits. Timing constraints ensure that the passenger train enters first while the goods train exits first. (Fig. 9 or Fig. 3 contain tracts where this can be performed.)

```
movement passengertrain { visit #p_in [b1]; visit #p_out [b2] }
movement goodstrain { visit #g_in [b1]; visit #g_out [b2] }
timing p_in < g_in; timing g_out < p_out
```

Specifications of this kind can be used to express requirements on running time, train frequency, overtaking, crossing, and similar scenarios which are relevant in railway construction projects. Since we typically only need to refer to locations such as model boundaries and loading/unloading locations, these specifications are not tied to a specific design, and can often be re-used even when the design of the station changes drastically.

---

[2] See complete format: https://luteberget.github.io/rollingdocs/usage.html.

3.2   Initial Design

When starting from an empty set of signalling components, most operational scenarios are not possible to even dispatch, because the railway interlocking safety principles require detectors and signals to have control over movements for safety purposes. Instead of searching for signalling components to add to the design to allow dispatching to happen, we start the synthesis procedure by heuristically over-approximating the components required to perform dispatch. We insert a signal and a detector in front of every trailing switch, and at a set of specified lengths corresponding to the choices of length of safety zone. We also insert a detector in front of every facing switch. See Fig. 7. If more than one train is required on the same track for overtaking or crossing, we can also choose to insert signals at multiples of the trains' lengths. When there are several paths of the specified length leading to a trailing switch, we put signals and detectors at all the relevant locations. This design aims to allow all possible dispatches and we rely on the next stage of the synthesis to remove redundant equipment (Fig. 8).

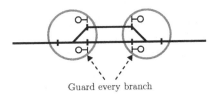

Guard every branch

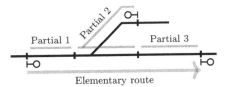

Elementary route

Fig. 7. *Initial design:* put signals in place before every trailing switch, i.e. where tracks join together.

Fig. 8. The planning abstraction of the train dispatch allocates a set of partial routes to each train. Elementary routes are sets of partial routes which must always be allocated together.

3.3   SAT-Based Dispatch Planning

The operational scenarios of the local capacity specifications describe train movements only declaratively, so the first step to analyzing concrete states of the system is to solve a planning problem which gives us a set of dispatch plans, i.e., determining sequences of trains and elementary routes which make the trains end up visiting locations according to the movements specification.

Instead of using a constraint solver system (e.g. SMT solvers) to solve for route dispatching and train dynamics simultaneously, we have chosen to separate the *abstracted planning problem* (i.e. selecting elementary routes to dispatch) from the physical constraints of train dynamics. This choice was made for performance and extensibility reasons (see [21, Sec.III] for details).

We use the encoding from [21, Sec.III(B)] of an instance of the abstracted planning problem into an instance of the Boolean satisfiability problem (SAT,

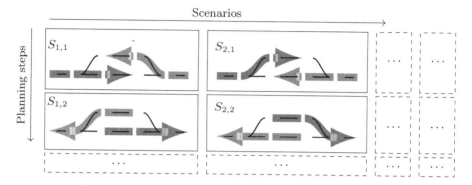

Fig. 9. The planning matrix consists of the occupation status of a set of partial routes for each state required for dispatch planning, and for each scenario in the local capacity requirements. The top left cells show an example dispatch of a crossing movement where green areas show track segments which are currently occupied by a train going from left to right, while the pink areas show track segments which are currently occupied by a train going from right to left. (Color figure online)

see [4] for an overview of SAT techniques). We consider the problem as a model checking problem, and use the technique of bounded model checking (BMC) [3] to unroll the transition relation of the system for a number of steps k, expressing states and transitions using propositional logic. We thus assert the existence of a plan, so that when the corresponding SAT instance is satisfiable, it proves the fulfillment of the performance requirements and gives an example plan for it. When unsatisfiable, we are ensured that there is no plan within the number of k steps. Interlocking features such as elementary routes, partial route release, flank protection, overlaps, overlap timeouts, and swinging overlaps, can be converted into our representation for solving the abstract planning problem.

To find a subset of the signaling components from the initial design that is sufficient to successfully plan all the dispatches, we extend the planning approach described above by adding a set of signal usage Booleans u indicating whether the signal is needed. The set of occupancy status Booleans o_r^i (for route r in state i, taking values either *Free* or a train t) is repeated once for each operational scenario, resulting in a SAT instance with parallel execution of each scenario on copies of the same infrastructure (see Fig. 9). We link the signal usage status u to each copy of the state so that the signal is marked as needed if it is used independently of other signals:

$$\forall i \in \text{State} : \forall s \in \text{Signal} : \forall t \in \text{Train} : \quad \neg u_s \Rightarrow$$
$$\bigvee \left\{ \left(o_r^i \neq t \land o_r^{i+1} = t \right) \mid \text{exit}(r) = s \right\} \Rightarrow$$
$$\bigvee \left\{ \left(o_r^i \neq t \land o_r^{i+1} = t \right) \mid \text{entry}(r) = s \right\} .$$

Similar approaches are taken for other signaling component types.

Now we find the smallest set of signaling equipment which is sufficient to allow dispatching all scenarios. We minimize the number of signals by: taking the sum of u variables as a unary-encoded number (see [5]) and then solving SAT incrementally with a binary search on the upper bound of the sum.

3.4 Numerical Optimization

When we have a design where dispatching is possible, we have fulfilled the discrete part of the dispatch plan. Timing constraints, however might not yet be fulfilled, and we might also want to improve on the total execution time of the various dispatch plans. To improve on the basic design found by the planner, we solve a numerical optimization problem with a cost function f defined as a weighted sum of dispatch timing measures:

$$ f_b(x) = \sum_s w_s \left(\frac{1}{n_s} \sum_d t_{b+x}(d) \right), $$

where x is a vector with components representing the location of each signal and detector, s indexes operational scenarios from the set of capacity specifications, w_s is weight assigned to the operational scenario, d indexes the set of n_s alternative dispatch plans derived by the planning algorithm for each operational scenario, and $t_{b+x}(d)$ is the time measure calculated by executing the dispatch plan d using the discrete event simulation component (described in Sect. 3.5) on an infrastructure constructed by adding the signal and detector locations x to the base track plan infrastructure b.

We define two basic operations for optimizing the timing performance of a signalling layout:

1. Searching for the optimal signalling component locations x for a fixed set of components located on a fixed set of tracks in a fixed order using Powell's method and Brent's method of derivative-free numerical optimization.
2. Adding a new signal or detector to any track.

Powell's Method and Brent's Method. Since we use simulation to measure the cost of a design, we do not have an expression for the derivative of the cost function f_b, and this function is not even guaranteed to be continuous. Even so, it is possible to use numerical methods for local optimization without taking derivatives. We use Brent's method for minimization in the single-parameter case, with the generalization to multivariate functions by Powell's method.

Powell's method works as follows: given a domain $D \subset \mathbb{R}^n$, an initial point $x_0 \in D$, and a cost function $f : D \to \mathbb{R}$, create a set of search vectors V initially containing each of the unit vectors aligned with each axis of $\mathbb{R}^n$. Iterate through the search vectors $v_i \in V$ and do a line search for the parameter α giving the optimal point of $x_{i+1} = f(x_i + \alpha v_i)$. After updating x using each search vector, remove the search vector which yielded the highest α and add instead the unit vector in the direction of $x - x_0$. See [8] for details.

Brent's method for optimization is used for the line search sub-routine in Powell's method. It takes a range of α values for which $x_i + \alpha v_i$ is inside D, and does a robust line search which finds a local minimum even for non-smooth and discontinuous functions. The method keeps a set of the three best points seen so far and fits a quadratic polynomial with the three best function values as parameters (called *inverse quadratic interpolation*). If the predicted optimum by the quadratic fit falls within an expected range, it used as the new best guess, otherwise the method falls back to golden-section search. See [8, 26] for details.

To simplify the use of the numerical algorithms, we map each signalling component's position to an intrinsic coordinate in the interval $[0, 1]$, so that the vector x keeps within $D = [0, 1]^n$. For a component with position p relative to the start of its track, if the component is the only component on a track, we define its intrinsic coordinate as

$$ x = \frac{p - (l_a + l_{min})}{(l_b - l_{min}) - (l_a + l_{min})}, $$

where $l_a = 0$, l_b is the length of the track, and l_{min} is the minimum spacing between components. When there are several components on the same track, we convert the coordinates by processing the components in order of increasing p, and adjusting l_a to correspond to the location of the previous component on the track. In this way the whole of $[0, 1]^n$ represents valid component positions and we do not have to apply constraints to the search space by other methods.

See Fig. 10 for an example of signalling compoments being moved.

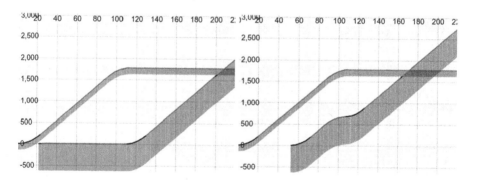

Fig. 10. Partial screen capture from our interactive design tool showing before (left) and after (right) improving signal and detector locations for a two-track station on an overtaking scenario. Note that the time axis is horizontal in this example. A signal at $x \approx 0$ m is moved to $x \approx 700$ m so that the overtaking train is unblocked at an earlier time, lowering the overall time taken to perform the operation

Adding New Components. When the above optimization has converged for a fixed set of components x, we iterate over each track (and each direction), adding a new component and including its dimensions in x, re-running optimization, and see which track, if any, most benefits from adding a signal or detector.

3.5   Discrete Event Simulation

The time measure used in the optimization loop (of Sect. 3.4) is calculated by simulation on a fixed infrastructure, which is a well-established method in railway capacity research. For this we use the custom simulator which we developed in [21, Sec.III], not described here, (see [28] for a methodological overview, and [9,17,18] for discrete events simulation for railway applications). Commercial railway simulation software can also be used instead of custom solutions.

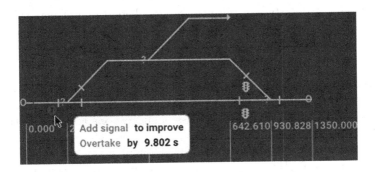

Fig. 11. Partial screen capture from our interactive design tool showing suggestions for design improvement to the user, inspired by integrated development environments used for programming. The individual optimization steps run their calculations as a background process, showing an information symbol where the algorithm is able to provide an improvement over the current design. The user can decide to implement it or to dismiss this change and similar changes from future suggestions.

We also use an automated derivation procedure for interlocking specifications to adjust the behavior of the control system after making changes in the infrastructure, similar to the procedure described in [29].

4   Local Optimizations and Interactive Improvement

In practice, synthesis from-scratch may well be ill-suited. The principle reason for this is the incompleteness of our synthesis method, which implies several inadequacies including, e.g., failing to recognize key concerns the design should be based upon, or if its calculation time prohibits practical use. But even if the specification successfully captures the capacity requirements, and the synthesis algorithm can come up with designs with good capacity, there are in practice often other constraints which can make a full from-scratch synthesis ill-suited. For example, in upgrade construction projects, it might be more useful to search for and suggest small changes which would be the most effective remedies for bottlenecks in a station's capacity. In fact, in such interactive verification and synthesis situations like ours, incompleteness is not a concern since we know that the problem is too difficult for automation and we only aim for the formal tool to provide help to the human. In that case we are mainly interested in the *correctness* of the method, i.e., the help that it provides should be useful help and not spurious suggestions; whereas incompleteness only means that there are some solutions that the tool cannot find, thus becoming the responsibility of the human. So we instead strive for good coverage of the solution space.

Our method and tool[3] can be used in several ways, i.e.: we consider each optimization step as described below as a possible incremental step towards a better design, which can be performed by a user interactively. Using a computer-assisted design program for railway (s.a. RailComplete) with semantic information about railway objects and rail network topology, the user gets suggestions for small changes to their design and can investigate how applying these changes affects the various scenarios (e.g., see Fig. 11).

Local optimization steps suggested to the user are the following:

- **Redundant equipment:** if removing a single object from the drawing can still be made to satisfy all local capacity requirements, the program suggests that the object is redundant. This class of suggestions is based on the SAT-based component minimization technique described above.
- **Local move of equipment:** if moving a single object or a set of nearby objects can improve the overall capacity measure on the station, the program suggests moving the object (or set of objects). This class of suggestions is based on the numerical timing optimization technique described above.
- **Adding equipment:** if adding a single piece of equipment (and performing local moves of equipment afterwards) can improve timing, the program suggests this to the user. This class of suggestions is based on the numerical timing optimization technique described above.

When accepting any of these changes, a user can investigate how the dispatch plans and the timings change. The tool meanwhile calculates new suggestions based on the new layout. We have developed a prototype tool which can calculate and suggest such changes to a user while they are editing their layout, and we are currently starting testing of this tool in an industrial setting together with railway engineers to investigate how useful such suggestions are, and how often they can be used compared to a from-scratch synthesis.

5   Conclusions, Related and Further Work

We have presented a method for partially or fully automating signalling layout design using SAT-based planning and discrete event simulation. The automation of verification, optimization, and synthesis relies on specifications tailored to the relevant scope, and we hope that this is a step on the way to integrating explicit formal specifications into the layout design process. More details can be found in the PhD thesis of the first author [20, Chap. 4].

---

[3] Usage details of our tool can be found on the project's web page: https://www.mn. uio.no/ifi/english/research/projects/railcons/index.html#Tools.

Our planning algorithm uses fixed blocks, so it handles conventional lamp signalling and the European standard ERTMS/ETCS Level 2, while handling Level 3 (which uses moving block) would require changes to the planning algorithm.

The simulation paradigm is imperative, progressing by calculating train trajectories forward in time. This makes the overall synthesis easily extensible with timing-related details, such as engine and braking power models, resistance models, operational regulations, automatic train control systems, etc., which do not impact the applicability of the dispatch plan but impact the timing performance.

For the local incremental operations above we consider useful running times to be under one second, so the method can be used integrated inside engineers' design tools, offering instant feedback.

5.1   Related Works

Although the literature is comprehensive on the safety-critical implementation of railway interlockings and operational analysis of large-scale railway networks, the signalling layout problem in itself has little coverage. We are only aware of the following works: Mao et al. [25] presented a genetic algorithm solution to signal placement, but the method is limited to the one-dimensional railway line, and does not handle signal placements inside stations/interlockings. Dillmann and Hähnle [11] describe a heuristic algorithm for upgrading German conventional signalling systems to an ETCS system, aiming to replicate the behavior and capacity of the existing system.

5.2   Further Work

Although our method is capable of making good design choices in several industrial standard models, we are aware of several limitations. Firstly, the method is not complete – we cannot guarantee finding an optimum because of the following: (1) the initial design does not guarantee maximum possible schedulability, (2) although the global simultaneous planning is exact in finding the smallest subset of the initial plan which can dispatch the operational scenarios, this set might not be the optimal starting point for timing optimization, and (3) the cost that we use for numerical optimization can have multiple local optima, especially when summing the score for competing operational scenarios, in which case the method described above is not guaranteed to find the global optimum.

However, incomplete methods are often very useful in practice, and for us it remains to thoroughly test how much gains our formal automation brings to the engineers. We also need to evaluate empirically the quality of the resulting signal placement as a crucial factor for industrial adoption.

We have also identified the following concerns for scalability of the method: (1) the specification language is practical to use for passing tracks, junctions, and medium-sized terminal stations, but on large-sized terminals and larger-scale analysis across multiple stations, the language is not easy to use because it specifies single movements separately, (2) optimizing the number of detectors in the SAT problem requires quantifying over all paths, which will cause scaling problems on larger track plans with many path choices, and (3) the algorithm for adding new signals to improve performance is naive, and will be expensive for track plans with a large number of tracks.

However, for such large-scale analysis it is already common to use commercial tools like OpenTrack[4] or LUKS[5], whereas our method is meant to be used on smaller scales as in the design phase, aiming to help the engineer to reduce the amount of errors the commercial tools would later find.

References

1. Abril, M., Barber, F., Ingolotti, L., Salido, M., Tormos, P., Lova, A.: An assessment of railway capacity. Transp. Res. Part E: Logistics Transp. Rev. **44**(5), 774–806 (2008). https://doi.org/10.1016/j.tre.2007.04.001
2. Basile, D., et al.: On the industrial uptake of formal methods in the railway domain. In: Furia, C.A., Winter, K. (eds.) IFM 2018. LNCS, vol. 11023, pp. 20–29. Springer, Cham (2018). https://doi.org/10.1007/978-3-319-98938-9_2
3. Biere, A., Cimatti, A., Clarke, E.M., Strichman, O., Zhu, Y.: Bounded model checking. Adv. Comput. **58**(11), 117–148 (2003). https://doi.org/10.1016/S0065-2458(03)58003-2
4. Biere, A., Heule, M., van Maaren, H., Walsh, T. (eds.): Handbook of Satisfiability, Frontiers in Artificial Intelligence and Applications, vol. 185. IOS Press (2009)
5. Björk, M.: Successful SAT encoding techniques. J. Sat. Boolean Model. Comput. **7**(4), 189–201 (2011). https://satassociation.org/jsat/index.php/jsat/article/view/153/118
6. Borälv, A., Stålmarck, G.: Formal verification in railways. In: Hinchey, M.G., Bowen, J.P. (eds.) Industrial-Strength Formal Methods in Practice, pp. 329–350. Springer (1999), https://doi.org/10.1007/978-1-4471-0523-7_15
7. Boulanger, J.L.: CENELEC 50128 and IEC 62279 Standards. Wiley-ISTE, March 2015
8. Brent, R.P.: Algorithms for Minimization Without Derivatives. Dover Publications, Mineola (2002)
9. Büker, T., Seybold, B.: Stochastic modelling of delay propagation in large networks. J. Rail Transp. Plan. Manag. **2**(1–2), 34–50 (2012). https://doi.org/10.1016/j.jrtpm.2012.10.001
10. Cimatti, A., et al.: Formal verification and validation of ERTMS industrial railway train spacing system. In: Madhusudan, P., Seshia, S.A. (eds.) CAV 2012. LNCS, vol. 7358, pp. 378–393. Springer, Heidelberg (2012). https://doi.org/10.1007/978-3-642-31424-7_29
11. Dillmann, S., Hähnle, R.: Automated planning of ETCS tracks. In: Collart-Dutilleul, S., Lecomte, T., Romanovsky, A. (eds.) RSSRail 2019. LNCS, vol. 11495, pp. 79–90. Springer, Cham (2019). https://doi.org/10.1007/978-3-030-18744-6_5
12. Fantechi, A.: Twenty-five years of formal methods and railways: what next? In: Counsell, S., Núñez, M. (eds.) SEFM 2013. LNCS, vol. 8368, pp. 167–183. Springer, Cham (2014). https://doi.org/10.1007/978-3-319-05032-4_13
13. Hansen, I.A., Pachl, J.: Railway Timetabling and Operations. Eurailpress (2014)

---

[4] "OpenTrack: Simulation of railway networks" 2018. http://www.opentrack.ch/.
[5] "LUKS: Analysis of lines and junctions" 2018. http://www.via-con.de/development/luks.

14. Harris, T., Ross, F.S.: Fundamentals of a method for evaluating rail net capacities. Technical report, RM-1573, Rand Corporation (1955)
15. Hartonas-Garmhausen, V., Campos, S.V.A., Cimatti, A., Clarke, E.M., Giunchiglia, F.: Verification of a safety-critical railway interlocking system with real-time constraints. Sci. Comput. Program. 36(1), 53–64 (2000). https://doi.org/10.1016/S0167-6423(99)00016-7
16. Haxthausen, A.E., Peleska, J., Kinder, S.: A formal approach for the construction and verification of railway control systems. Formal Aspects Comput. 23(2), 191–219 (2011). https://doi.org/10.1007/s00165-009-0143-6
17. Hürlimann, D.: Objektorientierte Modellierung von Infrastrukturelementen und Betriebsvorgängen im Eisenbahnwesen. Ph.D. thesis, ETH Zurich (2002). https://www.research-collection.ethz.ch/handle/20.500.11850/47957
18. Kamburjan, E., Hähnle, R., Schön, S.: Formal modeling and analysis of railway operations with active objects. Sci. Comput. Program. 166, 167–193 (2018). https://doi.org/10.1016/j.scico.2018.07.001
19. Landex, A.: Methods to estimate railway capacity and passenger delays. Ph.D. thesis, Technical University of Denmark (DTU) (2008). https://orbit.dtu.dk/en/publications/id(f5578206-74c3-4c94-ba0d-43f7da82bf95).html
20. Luteberget, B.: Automated Reasoning for Planning Railway Infrastructure. Ph.D. thesis, Faculty of Mathematics and Natural Sciences, University of Oslo (2019)
21. Luteberget, B., Claessen, K., Johansen, C.: Design-time railway capacity verification using SAT modulo discrete event simulation. In: Bjørner, N., Gurfinkel, A. (eds.) Formal Methods in Computer Aided Design (FMCAD), pp. 1–9. IEEE (2018). https://doi.org/10.23919/FMCAD.2018.8603003
22. Luteberget, B., Johansen, C.: Efficient verification of railway infrastructure designs against standard regulations. Formal Methods Syst. Des. 52(1), 1–32 (2018). https://doi.org/10.1007/s10703-017-0281-z
23. Luteberget, B., Johansen, C., Feyling, C., Steffen, M.: Rule-based incremental verification tools applied to railway designs and regulations. In: Fitzgerald, J., Heitmeyer, C., Gnesi, S., Philippou, A. (eds.) FM 2016. LNCS, vol. 9995, pp. 772–778. Springer, Cham (2016). https://doi.org/10.1007/978-3-319-48989-6_49
24. Luteberget, B., Johansen, C., Steffen, M.: Rule-based consistency checking of railway infrastructure designs. In: Ábrahám, E., Huisman, M. (eds.) IFM 2016. LNCS, vol. 9681, pp. 491–507. Springer, Cham (2016). https://doi.org/10.1007/978-3-319-33693-0_31
25. Mao, B., Liu, J., Ding, Y., Liu, H., Ho, T.K.: Signalling layout for fixed-block railway lines with real-coded genetic algorithms. Hong Kong Inst. Eng. Trans. 13(1), 35–40 (2006). https://eprints.qut.edu.au/38260/
26. Nocedal, J., Wright, S.J.: Numerical Optimization, 2nd edn. Springer, Heidelberg (2006). https://doi.org/10.1007/978-0-387-40065-5
27. Pachl, J.: Railway Operation and Control. VTD Rail Publishing (2015)
28. Robinson, S.: Simulation: The Practice of Model Development and Use. John Wiley & Sons Inc., New York (2004)
29. Vu, L.H., Haxthausen, A.E., Peleska, J.: A domain-specific language for railway interlocking systems. In: Schnieder, E., Tarnai, G. (eds.) Proceedings of the 10th Symposium on Formal Methods for Automation and Safety in Railway and Automotive Systems, (FORMS/FORMAT). pp. 200–209. TU Braunschweig (2014)

Pegasus: A Framework for Sound Continuous Invariant Generation

Andrew Sogokon[1,2]([envelope]) [ORCID], Stefan Mitsch[1]([envelope]) [ORCID], Yong Kiam Tan[1]([envelope]) [ORCID],
Katherine Cordwell[1]([envelope]) [ORCID], and André Platzer[1,3]([envelope]) [ORCID]

[1] Computer Science Department, Carnegie Mellon University, Pittsburgh, USA
{asogokon,smitsch,yongkiat,kcordwel,aplatzer}@cs.cmu.edu
[2] School of Informatics, University of Edinburgh, Edinburgh, UK
[3] Fakultät für Informatik, Technische Universität München, München, Germany

Abstract. *Continuous invariants* are an important component in deductive verification of hybrid and continuous systems. Just like discrete invariants are used to reason about correctness in discrete systems without unrolling their loops forever, continuous invariants are used to reason about differential equations without having to solve them. *Automatic generation* of continuous invariants remains one of the biggest practical challenges to automation of formal proofs of safety in hybrid systems. There are at present many disparate methods available for generating continuous invariants; however, this wealth of diverse techniques presents a number of challenges, with different methods having different strengths and weaknesses. To address some of these challenges, we develop *Pegasus*: an automatic continuous invariant generator which allows for combinations of various methods, and integrate it with the KeYmaera X theorem prover for hybrid systems. We describe some of the architectural aspects of this integration, comment on its methods and challenges, and present an experimental evaluation on a suite of benchmarks.

Keywords: Invariant generation · Continuous invariants ·
Ordinary differential equations · Theorem proving

1 Introduction

Safety verification problems for ordinary differential equations (ODEs) are continuous analogues to Hoare triples: the objective is to show that an ODE cannot evolve into a designated set of unsafe states from any of its designated initial

This material is based upon work supported by the National Science Foundation under Award CNS-1739629 and under Graduate Research Fellowship Grant No. DGE-1252522, by AFOSR under grant number FA9550-16-1-0288, and by the Alexander von Humboldt Foundation. The third author was supported by A*STAR, Singapore. Any opinions, findings, and conclusions or recommendations expressed in this material are those of the authors and do not necessarily reflect the views of any sponsoring institution, the U.S. government or any other entity.

© Springer Nature Switzerland AG 2019
M. H. ter Beek et al. (Eds.): FM 2019, LNCS 11800, pp. 138–157, 2019.
https://doi.org/10.1007/978-3-030-30942-8_10

states. The role of continuous invariants is therefore analogous to that of inductive invariants in discrete program verification. The problem of automatically generating invariants (also known as *invariant synthesis*) is one of the greatest practical challenges in deductive verification of both continuous and discrete systems. In theory, it is even the *only* challenge for hybrid systems safety [35, 39].

The proliferation of published techniques [4, 24, 29, 36, 42, 44, 51, 58, 60] for continuous invariant generation – targeting various classes of systems, and having different strengths and weaknesses – presents a challenge: ideally, one does not want to be restricted by the limitations of one particular generation technique (or a small family of techniques). Instead, it is far more desirable to have a framework that accommodates existing generation methods, allows for their combination, and is extensible with new methods as they become available. In this paper we (partially) meet the above challenge by developing a single framework which allows us to combine invariant generation methods into novel invariant generation *strategies*. In our work, we are guided by the following considerations:

1. Specialized invariant generation methods are effective only when the problem falls within their domain; their use must therefore be targeted.
2. A combination of invariant generation methods can be more practical than any of the methods considered in isolation. A flexible mechanism for combining these methods is thus highly desirable.
3. Reasoning with automatically generated invariants needs to be done in a *sound* fashion: any deficiencies in the generation procedure must not compromise the final verification result.

Our interest in automatic invariant generation is motivated by the pressing need to enhance the level of proof automation in deductive verification tools for hybrid systems. In this work we target the KeYmaera X theorem prover [15].

Contributions. In this paper we describe the design and implementation of a continuous invariant generator[1] – Pegasus – and its integration into KeYmaera X. We outline some of the basic principles in this coupling, the techniques used to generate invariants, and the mechanism used for combining them into more powerful invariant generation strategies. We evaluate this integration on a set of verification benchmarks – with very promising results.

Coloured versions of all figures are available online.

---

[1] **An etymological note on naming conventions.** The KeY [3] prover provided the foundation for developing KeYmaera [37], an interactive theorem prover for hybrid systems. The name KeYmaera was a pun on *Chimera*, a hybrid monster from Classical Greek mythology. The tactic language of the new KeYmaera X prover [15] is called Bellerophon [14] after the hero who defeats the Chimera in the myth. In keeping with an established tradition, the invariant generation framework is called Pegasus because the aid of this winged horse was crucial to Bellerophon in his feat.

2   Preliminaries

Ordinary Differential Equations. An n-dimensional autonomous system of first-order ODEs has the form: $x' = f(x)$, where $x = (x_1, \ldots, x_n) \in \mathbb{R}^n$ is a vector of state variables, $x' = (x_1', \ldots, x_n')$ denotes their time-derivatives, i.e. $\frac{dx_i}{dt}$ for each $i = 1, \ldots, n$, and $f(x) = (f_1(x), \ldots, f_n(x))$ specify the RHS of the equations that these time-derivatives must obey along solutions to the ODEs. Geometrically, such a system of ODEs defines a *vector field* $f : \mathbb{R}^n \to \mathbb{R}^n$, associating to each point $x \in \mathbb{R}^n$ the vector $f(x) = (f_1(x), \ldots, f_n(x)) \in \mathbb{R}^n$. Whenever the state of the system is required to be confined within some prescribed set of states $Q \subseteq \mathbb{R}^n$, which is known as the *evolution constraint*[2], we will write $x' = f(x) \ \& \ Q$. If no evolution constraint is specified, Q is assumed to be $\mathbb{R}^n$. A *solution* to the initial value problem for the system of ODEs $x' = f(x)$ with initial value $x_0 \in \mathbb{R}^n$ is a differentiable function $x(x_0, t) : (a, b) \to \mathbb{R}^n$ defined for all times $t \in (a, b) \subseteq \mathbb{R} \cup \{\infty, -\infty\}$ where $a < 0 < b$, and such that $x(x_0, 0) = x_0$ and $\frac{d}{dt} x(x_0, t) = f(x(x_0, t))$ for all $t \in (a, b)$. Given a continuously differentiable function $p : \mathbb{R}^n \to \mathbb{R}$, the Lie derivative of p with respect to vector field f equals the time-derivative of p evaluated along the solutions to the system $x' = f(x)$; this Lie derivative is denoted by p' and formally defined as $p' \equiv \sum_{i=1}^{n} \frac{\partial p}{\partial x_i} f_i$.

Semi-algebraic Sets. A set $S \subseteq \mathbb{R}^n$ is *semi-algebraic* iff it is characterized by a finite Boolean combination of polynomial equations and inequalities:

$$\bigvee_{i=1}^{l} \left(\bigwedge_{j=1}^{m_i} p_{ij} < 0 \ \wedge \ \bigwedge_{j=m_i+1}^{M_i} p_{ij} = 0 \right) \tag{1}$$

where $p_{ij} \in \mathbb{R}[x_1, \ldots, x_n]$ are polynomials. By quantifier elimination, every first-order formula of real arithmetic characterizes a semi-algebraic set and can be put into standard form (1) (see e.g. Mishra [32, §8.6]). With a slight abuse of notation, this paper uses formulas and the sets they characterize interchangeably.

Continuous Invariants in Verification. Safety specifications for ODEs and hybrid dynamical systems can be rigorously verified in formal logics, such as *differential dynamic logic* (dL) [34,35] as implemented in the KeYmaera X proof assistant [15] and *hybrid Hoare logic* [28] as implemented in the HHL prover [61]. The use of appropriate continuous invariants is key to these verification approaches as they allow the complexities of the continuous dynamics to be handled rigorously even for ODEs without closed-form solutions. For example, the dL formula $Init \to [x' = f(x) \ \& \ Q] \, Safe$ states that the safety property *Safe* is satisfied throughout the continuous evolution of the system $x' = f(x) \ \& \ Q$ whenever the system begins its evolution from a state satisfying *Init*. The main dL reasoning principle for verifying such a safety property is given by the following sound rule

---

[2] Evolution domain constraints are also called *mode invariants* in the context of hybrid automata. We avoid this name to prevent confusion with generated invariants.

of inference, with three premises above the bar and the conclusion below:

$$\text{(Safety)} \quad \frac{Init \rightarrow I \qquad I \rightarrow [\boldsymbol{x}' = f(\boldsymbol{x}) \,\&\, Q]\, I \qquad I \rightarrow Safe}{Init \rightarrow [\boldsymbol{x}' = f(\boldsymbol{x}) \,\&\, Q]\, Safe}.$$

In this rule, the first and third premiss respectively state that the initial set *Init* is contained within the set I, and that I lies entirely inside the safe set of states *Safe*. The second premiss states that I is a *continuous invariant*, i.e. I is maintained throughout the continuous evolution of the system whenever it starts inside I, that is, the following dL formula is true in all states:

$$I \rightarrow [\boldsymbol{x}' = f(\boldsymbol{x}) \,\&\, Q]\, I. \tag{2}$$

Thus, the problem of verifying safety properties of ODEs reduces to finding an invariant I that can be *proved* to satisfy all three premisses. Semantically, a continuous invariant can also be defined as follows:

Definition 1 (Continuous invariant). *Given a system* $\boldsymbol{x}' = f(\boldsymbol{x}) \,\&\, Q$, *the set* $I \subseteq \mathbb{R}^n$ *is a continuous invariant iff the following statement holds:*

$$\forall \boldsymbol{x}_0 \in I \; \forall t \geq 0 : \left((\forall \tau \in [0,t] : \boldsymbol{x}(\boldsymbol{x}_0, \tau) \in Q) \implies \boldsymbol{x}(\boldsymbol{x}_0, t) \in I \right).$$

For any given set of initial states *Init* $\subseteq \mathbb{R}^n$, a continuous invariant I such that *Init* $\subseteq I$ provides a *sound over-approximation* of the states reachable by the system from *Init* by following the solutions to the ODEs within the domain constraint Q. Indeed, the exact set of states reachable by a continuous system from *Init* provides the *smallest* such invariant.[3] While the definition above features the solution $\boldsymbol{x}(\boldsymbol{x}_0, t)$, which may not be available explicitly, a crucial advantage afforded by continuous invariants is the possibility of checking whether a given set is a continuous invariant *without computing the solution*, i.e. by working *directly with the ODEs*.

3   Sound Invariant Checking and Generation

The problem of *checking* whether a semi-algebraic set $I \subseteq \mathbb{R}^n$ is a continuous invariant of a polynomial system of ODEs $\boldsymbol{x}' = f(\boldsymbol{x}) \,\&\, Q$ was shown to be *decidable* by Liu, Zhan, and Zhao [29]. This decision procedure, henceforth referred to as LZZ, provides a way of automatically checking continuous invariants (2) by exploiting facts about higher-order Lie derivatives of multivariate polynomials appearing in the syntactic description of I and the Noetherian property of the ring $\mathbb{R}[\boldsymbol{x}]$ [18,29]; its implementation requires an algorithm for constructing Gröbner bases [9], as well as a decision procedure for the universal fragment of real arithmetic [47]. A logical alternative for invariant checking is provided by the complete dL axiomatization for differential equation invariants [39]. Whereas using LZZ results in a yes/no answer to an invariance question (2), dL makes it possible to construct a *formal proof of invariance* from a small set of ODE axioms [39] whenever the property holds (or a refutation when it does not).

---

[3] Unfortunately, reachable sets rarely have a simple description as semi-algebraic sets.

3.1   Invariant Generation with Template Enumeration

Given a means to perform invariant checking with real arithmetic, an obvious solution to the invariant generation problem (which has been suggested by numerous authors [29,36,55]) involves the so-called *method of template enumeration*, which yields a theoretically complete semi-algorithm (in the sense that it terminates with a positive answer iff that is possible). All it takes *in theory* is to exhaustively enumerate parametric templates for all real arithmetic formulas describing all semi-algebraic sets, and use a quantifier elimination algorithm (such as CAD [8]) to identify whether choices for the template parameters exist that meet the required arithmetic constraints. While templates make this British Museum Algorithm-like approach more successful than, e.g. exhaustively enumerating all proofs [21], the method is nevertheless quite impractical when used with real quantifier elimination.[4] In practice, invariant generation is usually achieved by using incomplete – but more efficient – generation methods. These methods are numerous and vary considerably in their strengths and limitations, creating a wide spectrum of possible trade-offs in performance, the quality, and the form of invariants that one can generate. Effectively navigating this spectrum is an important practical challenge that we seek to address.

3.2   Soundness: Proof Assistants and Invariant Generation

There are a number of design decisions that can be exercised in how reasoning with continuous invariants is performed within a deductive verification framework. A fundamental design decision is how tightly (i) continuous invariance checking and (ii) continuous invariant generation are to be coupled with the implementation of a proof assistant. This space of design choices is exemplified by the HHL prover and KeYmaera X.

The HHL prover [7,61] implements (i) the LZZ decision procedure for invariant checking and (ii) the method of template enumeration for invariant generation based on real quantifier elimination. From the perspective of the HHL prover, these are *trusted external oracles* for checking the validity of statements about continuous invariance; trusting the output of the HHL prover includes trusting the implementation of its LZZ procedure and the invariant generator.

In contrast, KeYmaera X [15] pursues an LCF-style approach, seeking to minimize the soundness-critical code that needs to be trusted in its output. For continuous invariants, it achieves this by (i) checking invariance within the axiomatic framework of dL (rather than trusting external checking procedures) and (ii) accepting *conjectured invariants* generated from a variety of sources but *separately checking* the result. Invariant checking in KeYmaera X is automatic, which is made possible by the use of specialized proof *tactics* [14]; these additionally allow it to use a variety of other (incomplete, but computationally inexpensive) methods for proving continuous invariance [18].

---

[4] Quantifier elimination algorithms used in practice have doubly-exponential time complexity in the number of variables [43]. Template enumeration introduces a fresh variable per monomial coefficient, so the approach quickly hits scalability barriers.

Remark 1. The difference between these two approaches is broadly analogous to the use of trusted decision procedures in PVS [12] and oracles in HOL [5,63] on the one hand, and proof reconstruction (e.g. in Isabelle [62]) on the other.

4   Invariant Generation Methods in Pegasus

Pegasus is a continuous invariant generator implemented in the Wolfram Language with an interface accessible through both *Mathematica* and KeYmaera X.[5] When KeYmaera X is faced with a continuous safety verification problem that it is unable to prove directly, it automatically invokes Pegasus to help find an appropriate invariant (if possible). As mentioned earlier, KeYmaera X checks *all* the invariants it is supplied with – *including those provided by Pegasus* (see Fig. 1).

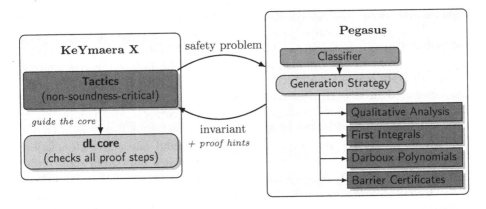

Fig. 1. Sound invariant generation: invariant generator analyses safety problem to provide invariants and proof hints to tactics; the invariants are formally verified to be correct within the soundness-critical dL core

This design ensures that correctness of Pegasus is not integral to the soundness of KeYmaera X. It also presents implementation opportunities for Pegasus:

1. It can freely integrate numerical procedures and heuristic methods while providing *best-effort* guarantees of correctness. Final correctness checks for the generated invariants are left to the purview of KeYmaera X.[6]
2. It records *proof hints* corresponding to various methods that were used to generate continuous invariants. These hints enable KeYmaera X to build more efficient shortcut proofs of continuous invariance [18].

---

[5] Pegasus (http://pegasus.keymaeraX.org/) is linked to KeYmaera X through the Mathematica interface of KeYmaera X, which translates between the internal data structures of the prover core and the Mathematica data structures.

[6] Naturally, the output from Pegasus can also be checked using a trusted implementation of the LZZ decision procedure before anything is returned. When used with KeYmaera X, though, this additional (soundness-critical) check is unnecessary.

Pegasus currently implements an array of powerful invariant generation methods, which we describe below, beginning with a large family of related methods that are based on *qualitative analysis*, which can be best explained using the machinery of *discrete abstraction* of continuous systems. We first briefly recall the main idea behind this approach.

4.1   Exact Discrete Abstraction

Discrete abstraction has been the subject of numerous works [1,57,59]. Briefly, the steps are: (i) discretize the continuous state space of a system by defining *predicates* that correspond to discrete states, (ii) compute a (local) transition relation between the discrete states obtained from the previous step, yielding a discrete transition system which abstracts the behaviour of the original continuous system, and finally (iii) compute reachable sets in the discrete abstraction to obtain an over-approximation of the reachable sets of the original system.

The discrete abstraction is *sound* iff the relation computed in step (ii) has a transition between two discrete states whenever there is a corresponding continuous trajectory of the original system between the two sets corresponding to those discrete states. The abstraction is *exact* iff these are the *only* transitions computed in step (ii). Soundness of the discrete abstraction guarantees that any invariant extracted from the discretization corresponds to an invariant for the original system. Figure 2 illustrates a discretization of a system of ODEs (Fig. 2a), which results in 9 discrete states in a sound and exact abstraction (Fig. 2b). The state space is discretized using predicates built from sign conditions on polynomials, $p_1, p_2 \in \mathbb{R}[x_1, x_2]$. The discrete states of the abstraction are given by formulas such as $S_1 \equiv p_1 < 0 \wedge p_2 = 0$, $S_2 \equiv p_1 < 0 \wedge p_2 > 0$, and so on.

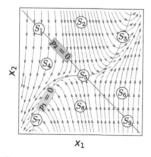

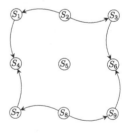

(a) Discretization with p_1, $p_2 \sim 0$ (b) Sound discrete abstraction

Fig. 2. Discrete abstraction of a two-dimensional system

The ability to construct sound and exact discrete abstractions [51] has an important consequence: if an appropriate semi-algebraic continuous invariant I exists at all, it can always be extracted from a discrete abstraction built from discretizing the state space using sign conditions on the polynomials describing I. The problem of (semi-algebraic) invariant generation therefore reduces to finding appropriate polynomials whose sign conditions can yield suitable discrete abstractions and computing reachable states in these abstractions.

Remark 2. Reachable sets (from the initial states) in discrete abstractions are the smallest invariants with respect to $\subseteq$ (set inclusion) that one can extract. The smallest invariant is the most informative because it allows one to prove the most safety properties, but it may not be the most useful invariant in practice. In particular, one often wants to work with invariants that have low descriptive complexity *and are easy to prove in the formal proof calculus.* This leads naturally to consider alternative ways of extracting invariants. Pegasus is able to extract reachable sets of discrete abstractions, but favours less costly techniques, such as *differential saturation* [36], which often succeed in quickly extracting more conservative invariants.

Finding "good" polynomials that can abstract the system in useful ways and allow proving properties of interest is generally difficult. While abstraction using predicates that are extracted from the verification problem itself can be surprisingly effective, in certain cases useful predicates may not be syntactically extracted from the problem statement. In order to improve the quality of discrete abstractions, Pegasus employs a separate *classifier*, which extracts features from the verification problem which can then be used to suggest polynomials that are more tailored to the problem at hand. Certain systems have structure that, to a human expert, might suggest an "obvious" choice of good predicates. Below we sketch some basic examples of what is currently possible.

4.2   Targeted Qualitative Analysis

As a motivating example, consider the class of one-dimensional ODEs $x' = f(x)$, where $f \in \mathbb{R}[x]$. A standard way of studying qualitative behaviour in these systems is to inspect the graph of the function $f(x)$ [54]. Figure 3 illustrates such a graph of $f(x)$, along with a vector field induced by such a system on the real line. By computing the real roots of the polynomial in the right-hand side, i.e. the real

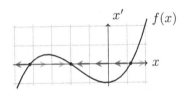

Fig. 3. Qualitative analysis of one-dimensional ODEs $x' = f(x)$

roots $r_1, \ldots, r_k \in \mathbb{R}$ of $f(x)$, we may form a list of polynomials $x - r_1, \ldots, x - r_k$ that can be used for an *algebraic decomposition* of $\mathbb{R}$ into invariant cells corresponding to real intervals from which an over-approximation of the reachable set can be constructed. Such an algebraic decomposition can be further refined by augmenting the list of polynomials with $x - b_{i1}, \ldots, x - b_{il}$, where $b_{i1}, \ldots, b_{il} \in \mathbb{R}$ are the boundary points of the initial set in the safety specification. From this augmented list, one can exactly construct the *reachable set* of the system by computing the reachable set of the corresponding exact abstraction.

Remark 3. Knowledge of the fact that $x' = f(x)$ is one-dimensional allows one to exploit another useful fact: every one-dimensional system is a *gradient system,* i.e. its motion is generated by a *potential function* $F(x)$ which can be computed directly by integrating $-f(x)$ with respect to x, i.e. $F(x) = -\int f(x)\,dx$. For any $k \in \mathbb{R}$, $F(x) \leq k$ defines a continuous invariant of the system $x' = f(x)$.

In higher dimensions, the behaviour of *linear* systems $x' = Ax$ can be studied qualitatively by examining the stability of the fixed point at the origin [2]. The *strongest* algebraic invariants for such systems can be computed for algebraic initial conditions [44]. Pegasus implements methods targeted at linear systems that takes advantage of facts such as these to suggest useful abstractions from which invariants (not necessarily algebraic) can be extracted. This strategy is similar in spirit to the abstraction methods proposed in the work of Tiwari [56].

Example 1. The linear systems in Fig. 4 exhibit different qualitative behaviours. The invariants (shown in blue), demonstrate unreachability of the unsafe states (shown in red) from the initial states (shown as green discs in Fig. 4).

$$x_1' = -4x_2, \qquad x_1' = 2x_1 - x_2, \qquad x_1' = -2x_1 + x_2,$$
$$x_2' = x_1, \qquad x_2' = -3x_1 + x_2, \qquad x_2' = x_1 - 3x_2.$$

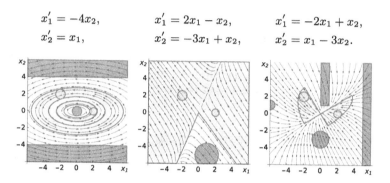

Fig. 4. Automatically generated invariants for linear systems.

In the leftmost system, all eigenvalues of the system matrix A are purely imaginary. Pegasus generates annular invariants containing the green discs because trajectories of such systems are always elliptical. For the middle system, the (asymptotic) behaviour of its trajectories is determined by the eigenvectors of its system matrix (eigenvalues are real and of opposite sign [2]). Pegasus uses these eigenvectors to generate two invariant half-planes, one for each green disc. Invariant half-planes are also generated for the rightmost system which is asymptotically *stable* (all real parts of eigenvalues are negative [2]). Pegasus further refines these half-planes with elliptical regions containing the green discs because elliptical regions are invariants for such systems.

4.3 Qualitative Analysis for Non-linear Systems

General non-linear polynomial systems present a hard class of problems for invariant generation. A number of useful heuristics can be applied to partition the continuous state space, in hopes that the resulting abstraction exhibits a suitable invariant. For example, by factorizing to find polynomials p such that

$p = 0$ implies $x_i' = 0$ for some x_i, the flow along the level curve $p = 0$ vanishes in the x_i direction. This information can be used to cheaply approximate the transition relation in the discrete abstraction and to efficiently extract *invariant candidates*. For the non-linear ODE in Fig. 2, the discretization polynomials p_1, p_2 are chosen such that $x_2' = 0$ and $x_1' = 0$ on their respective level curves. This yields a useful discrete abstraction e.g. S_4 is an invariant for the resulting abstraction (Fig. 2b). Other useful sources of polynomials for qualitative analysis of non-linear systems are found in e.g. the summands and irreducible factors of the right-hand sides of the ODEs, the Lie derivatives of the factors, and physically meaningful quantities such as the *divergence* of the system's vector field.

4.4   General-Purpose Methods

Beyond qualitative analysis, Pegasus implements several general-purpose invariant generation techniques which represent *restricted, but tractable fragments* of the general method of template enumeration. The search for symbolic parameters in these methods is *not* performed using real quantifier elimination, but instead takes place in more tractable theories. We recall these techniques briefly.

First Integrals. The polynomial $p \in \mathbb{R}[x]$ is a *first integral* [19, 2.4.1] of the system $x' = f(x)$ iff its Lie derivative p' with respect to the vector field f is the zero polynomial. First integrals are also known as *conserved quantities* because they have the important property that for any

Fig. 5. Discrete abstraction with first integrals $p - k$ $(k \in \mathbb{R})$

$k \in \mathbb{R}$, $p = k$ defines an invariant of the system. For a single first integral p, if one were to use the polynomial $p - k$ to build an abstraction, the abstract state space would not feature any transitions between its states (illustrated in Fig. 5). Thus, one has the freedom to choose value(s) k for which the resulting discrete abstraction suitably partitions the state space. For example, if the initial states lie entirely within $p < k$ and the unsafe ones within $p > k$, then $p < k$ is an invariant separating those sets. Pegasus can search for *all* polynomial first integrals up to a configurable degree bound by solving a system of *linear equations* whose solutions provide the coefficients of the bounded degree polynomial template for the first integral; the solutions are efficiently found using linear algebra [19,49].

Darboux Polynomials. *Darboux polynomials* were first introduced in 1878 [11] to study integrability of polynomial ODEs. Polynomial $p \in \mathbb{R}[x]$ is a *Darboux polynomial* for the system $x' = f(x)$ iff $p' = \alpha p$ for some cofactor polynomial $\alpha \in \mathbb{R}[x]$. Like first integrals, discrete abstractions produced with Darboux polynomials result in three states with no transitions between them (as illustrated in Fig. 5, but with $k = 0$). Unlike first integrals, only $p = 0$ is guaranteed to be an invariant of the system. Darboux polynomials have been used for predicate abstraction of continuous systems by Zaki et al. [65], who successfully applied them to verify electrical circuit designs. Automatic generation of Darboux polynomials is an active area of research, with several algorithms proposed within the verification community [24,42,49]. Owing to the importance of Darboux polynomials in the *Prelle-Singer method* [41] for computing elementary closed-form solutions to ODEs, sophisticated algorithms for Darboux polynomial generation were developed earlier in the computer algebra community, e.g. two algorithms were reported by Man [31]. Indeed, we have found these algorithms to be the most practical and implement them in Pegasus.

Barrier Certificates. The method of *barrier certificates* is a popular technique for safety verification of continuous and hybrid systems [40]. Barrier certificates p define an invariant region $p \leq 0$ which separates the initial states (wholly contained within $p \leq 0$) from the unsafe states (wholly contained within $p > 0$) when the Lie derivative p' satisfies certain criteria (e.g. $p' \leq 0$). Generating barrier certificates using the method of template enumeration is possible using both sum-of-squares (SOS) [40] and linear programming (LP) [64] techniques. A number of generalizations of the barrier certificate approach have been developed, which differ in the kinds of conditions that ensure the invariance of $p \leq 0$, e.g. *exponential-type* [25] and *general* barrier certificates [10]. A unified understanding of these generalizations [53] based on classical *comparison systems* [45, Ch II, §3, Ch. IX] leads to a yet more general notion of *vector barrier certificates*. Pegasus is able to search for convex [40], exponential-type [25], and vector barrier certificates [53] using both SOS and LP techniques. However, the resulting barrier certificates often suffer from numerical inaccuracies arising from the use of semi-definite solvers and interior point methods [46]. Pegasus currently uses a simple rounding heuristic on the numerical result and explicitly checks invariance for the resulting (exact) barrier certificate candidates using real quantifier elimination.

5   Strategies for Invariant Generation

The implementation of all the aforementioned invariant generation methods in a single framework is a significant undertaking in itself. The overall goal behind Pegasus, however, is to enable these heterogeneous methods to be effectively deployed and fruitfully combined into *strategies* for invariant generation that are tailored to specific classes of verification problems. Different invariant generation strategies are invoked in Pegasus, depending on the classification of the input problem it receives from the problem *classifier*. In this section, and for the evaluation, we focus on the most challenging and general class of *non-linear* systems in which no further structure is known or assumed beyond the fact that the right-hand sides of the ODEs are polynomials.

The main invariant generation strategy Pegasus uses for general non-linear systems is based on a *differential saturation* procedure [36]. Briefly, the procedure loops through a prescribed *sequence* of invariant generation methods and *successively* attempts to strengthen the domain constraint using invariants found by those methods until the desired safety condition is proved.[7] Notably, this loop allows Pegasus to exploit the strengths of different invariant generation methods, even if it is a priori unclear whether one is better than the other. The precise sequencing of invariant generation methods is also important in this strategy to avoid redundancy. In particular, Pegasus currently orders the methods by computational efficiency, e.g. it first searches for first integrals, followed by Darboux polynomials and barrier certificates. This sequencing allows later (slower) methods to exploit invariants that are quickly generated by earlier methods.

Example 2. The synergy between individual methods exploited by differential saturation is illustrated in Fig. 6 using an example from our benchmarks.

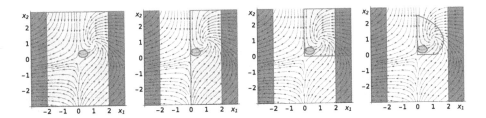

Fig. 6. Invariant synthesis using the differential saturation loop in Pegasus.

Initially (leftmost plot), the entire plane (in blue) is under consideration and Pegasus wants to show the safety property that trajectories from the initial states (in green) never reach the unsafe states (in red). In the second plot, Pegasus confines its search to the domain $x_1 > 0$ using the generated Darboux polynomial x_1. In the third plot, using $x_1 > 0$, qualitative analysis finds the invariant $x_2 > 0$ which further confines the evolution domain. Finally (rightmost plot), Pegasus finds a barrier certificate (of polynomial degree 2) that suffices to show the safety property within the strengthened domain (which, by construction, is invariant). The final invariant region *cannot* be directly obtained from a polynomial barrier certificate, but incorporates invariants discovered earlier by other means.

6   Evaluation

We tested Pegasus and its interaction with the ODE proving tactics of KeYmaera X on a benchmark suite of 90 non-linear continuous safety verification problems drawn from the literature [4,10,17,20,22–24,29,48,52,64,65]. The suite consists of 53 two-dimensional systems, 11 three-dimensional systems, 12 higher-dimensional (≥ 4) systems, and 14 *product systems* that were formed by randomly combining pairs of two- and three-dimensional systems. The benchmark was run

---

[7] Pegasus analyses problems according to variable dependencies present in their differential equations [36]. For $x_1' = x_1, x_2' = x_1 + x_2$, for example, Pegasus first searches for invariants involving only x_1, before searching for those involving both x_1 and x_2.

on commodity hardware: 2.4 GHz Intel Core i7 with 16 GB memory. We compare the differential saturation strategy to the performance of each invariant generation method in isolation, measuring the duration of generating invariants, duration of checking the generated invariants, and the total proof duration.

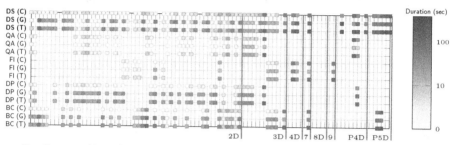

Non-linear problems (dimension: 2D-9D, followed by 4D and 5D product systems)

Fig. 7. Comparison of invariant generation methods. Each column represents one benchmark problem and the colour encodes duration (lighter is faster). Empty columns are unsolved. Legend: the combined Differential Saturation (DS) strategy against Qualitative Analysis (QA), First Integrals (FI), Darboux Polynomials (DP), and Barrier Certificates (BC), on total proof duration (T), generation duration (G), and checking duration (C).

Benchmark results for each of the problems are in Fig. 7. Several experimental insights can be drawn from these results: (i) different invariant generation methods generally solve different subsets of the problems, (ii) invariant generation generally dominates overall proof duration although invariant checking becomes more expensive as problem dimension increases, (iii) when multiple methods solve a problem, qualitative analysis and first integrals are often quickest, followed by Darboux polynomials and then barrier certificates, (iv) the differential saturation strategy effectively combines invariant generation methods; it solves all but one[8] problem that can be solved by individual methods. It additionally solves 8 problems (of which 5 are product systems) that no individual method solves by itself. Differential saturation is especially effective on product systems because each part of the product may be only solvable using a specific method.

To further evaluate the effectiveness of combining methods by differential saturation, Fig. 8 plots the accumulated duration for solving the fastest n problems. The main insights here are: (i) differential saturation solves the largest number of problems per accumulated time, which means that, despite sequential execution, it often succeeds in trying out the most efficient method first and fails fast when earlier methods fail to apply, (ii) the performance of generating versus checking first integrals is inconclusive and depends on the specific example

---

[8] For this high-dimensional (9D) problem, differential saturation runs out of time trying qualitative analysis methods before attempting to find first integrals.

(see also Fig. 7), (iii) checking barrier certificates and Darboux polynomials is much faster than generating them, and (iv) qualitative analysis is less expensive for generation than other methods.

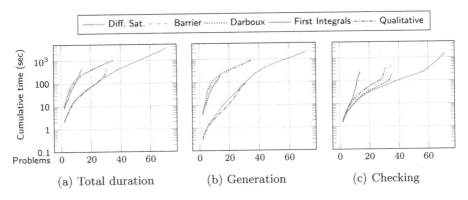

Fig. 8. Cumulative logarithmic time (in seconds) taken to solve the fastest n problems (more problems solved and flatter is better)

7   Related Work

Techniques developed for *qualitative simulation* have been applied to prove temporal properties of continuous systems in the work of Shults and Kuipers [50], as well as Loeser, Iwasaki and Fikes [30]. Zhao [66] developed a tool, MAPS, to automatically identify significant features of dynamical systems, such as stability regions, equilibria, and limit cycles. Since our ultimate goal is sound invariant generation, we are less interested in a full qualitative analysis of the state space. In the verification community, discrete abstraction of hybrid systems was studied by Alur et al. [1]. The case of systems whose continuous motion is governed by non-linear ODEs was studied in the work of Tiwari and Khanna [57,59]. Tiwari further studied reachability of linear systems [56], using information from real eigenvectors and ideas from qualitative abstraction to generate invariants. Zaki et al. [65] were the first to apply Darboux polynomials to verification of continuous systems using discrete abstraction. Numerous works employ barrier certificates for verification [10,25,40,53,64]. Since we implement many of the above techniques as methods for invariant generation in our framework, our work draws heavily upon ideas developed previously in the verification and hybrid systems communities. Previously [51], we introduced a construction of exact abstractions and applied rudimentary methods from qualitative analysis to compute invariants; in certain ways, our present work also builds on this experience, incorporating some of the techniques as special methods in a more general framework. The coupling between KeYmaera X and Pegasus that we pursue in our work is quite distinct from the use of trusted oracles in the work of Wang et al. [61] (for the HHL prover) and provides a *sound* framework for reasoning with continuous invariants that is significantly less exposed to soundness issues in external tools.

8   Outlook and Challenges

The improvements in continuous invariant generation have a significant impact on the overall proof automation capabilities of KeYmaera X and serve to increase overall system usability and user experience. Improved proof automation will certainly also be useful in future applications of provably correct runtime monitoring frameworks, such as ModelPlex [33], as well as frameworks for generating verified controller executables, such as VeriPhy [6].

Some interesting directions for extending our work include implementation of reachable set computation algorithms for all classes of problems where this is possible. For instance, semi-algebraic reachable sets may be computed for diagonalizable classes of linear systems with tame eigenvalues [16, 26]. The complexity of invariants obtained using these methods may not always make them practical, but they would provide a valuable fallback in cases where simpler invariants cannot be obtained using our currently implemented methods.

A more pressing challenge lies in expanding the collection of safety verification problems for continuous systems. While we have done our best to find compelling examples from the literature, a larger corpus of problems would allow for a more comprehensive empirical evaluation of invariant generation strategies and could reveal interesting new insights that can suggest more effective strategies.

Correctness of decision procedures for real arithmetic is another important challenge. KeYmaera X currently uses Mathematica's implementation of real quantifier elimination to close first-order real arithmetic goals, primarily due to the impressive performance afforded by this implementation (compared to currently existing alternatives). Removing this reliance by efficiently building fully formal proofs of real arithmetic formulas within dL (e.g. through exhibiting appropriate *witnesses* [27,38]) is an important task for the future.

9   Conclusion

Among verification practitioners, the amount of manual effort required for formal verification of hybrid systems is one of the chief criticisms leveled against the use of deductive verification tools. Manually crafting continuous invariants often requires expertise and ingenuity, just like manually selecting support function templates for reachability tools [13], and presents the major practical hurdle in the way of wider industrial adoption of this technology. In this paper, we describe our development of a system designed to help overcome this hurdle by automating the discovery of continuous invariants. To our knowledge, this work represents the first large-scale effort at combining continuous invariant generation methods into a single invariant generation framework and making it possible to create more powerful invariant generation strategies. The approach we pursue is unique in its integration with a theorem prover, which provides formal guarantees that the generated invariants are indeed correct (in the form of dL proofs, *automatically*). The results we observe in our evaluation are highly encouraging and suggest that invariant discovery can be improved considerably, opening many exciting avenues for applications and extensions.

Acknowledgements. The authors would like to thank the anonymous reviewers for their feedback.

References

1. Alur, R., Henzinger, T.A., Lafferriere, G., Pappas, G.J.: Discrete abstractions of hybrid systems. Proc. IEEE **88**(7), 971–984 (2000). https://doi.org/10.1109/5.871304
2. Arrowsmith, D., Place, C.M.: Dynamical Systems: Differential Equations, Maps, and Chaotic Behaviour, vol. 5. CRC Press, Boca Raton (1992)
3. Beckert, B., et al.: The KeY system 1.0 (deduction component). In: Pfenning, F. (ed.) CADE 2007. LNCS (LNAI), vol. 4603, pp. 379–384. Springer, Heidelberg (2007). https://doi.org/10.1007/978-3-540-73595-3_26
4. Sassi, M.A.B., Girard, A., Sankaranarayanan, S.: Iterative computation of polyhedral invariants sets for polynomial dynamical systems. In: CDC 2014, pp. 6348–6353. IEEE (2014). https://doi.org/10.1109/CDC.2014.7040384
5. Böhme, S., Weber, T.: Fast LCF-style proof reconstruction for Z3. In: Kaufmann, M., Paulson, L.C. (eds.) ITP 2010. LNCS, vol. 6172, pp. 179–194. Springer, Heidelberg (2010). https://doi.org/10.1007/978-3-642-14052-5_14
6. Bohrer, B., Tan, Y.K., Mitsch, S., Myreen, M.O., Platzer, A.: VeriPhy: verified controller executables from verified cyber-physical system models. In: Foster, J.S., Grossman, D. (eds.) PLDI 2018, pp. 617–630. ACM (2018). https://doi.org/10.1145/3192366.3192406
7. Chen, M., et al.: MARS: a toolchain for modelling, analysis and verification of hybrid systems. In: Hinchey, M.G., Bowen, J.P., Olderog, E.-R. (eds.) Provably Correct Systems. NMSSE 2017, pp. 39–58. Springer, Cham (2017). https://doi.org/10.1007/978-3-319-48628-4_3
8. Collins, G.E.: Quantifier elimination for real closed fields by cylindrical algebraic decompostion. In: Brakhage, H. (ed.) GI-Fachtagung 1975. LNCS, vol. 33, pp. 134–183. Springer, Heidelberg (1975). https://doi.org/10.1007/3-540-07407-4_17
9. Cox, D.A., Little, J., O'Shea, D.: Ideals, Varieties, and Algorithms. UTM 2015. Springer, Cham (2015). https://doi.org/10.1007/978-3-319-16721-3
10. Dai, L., Gan, T., Xia, B., Zhan, N.: Barrier certificates revisited. J. Symb. Comput. **80**, 62–86 (2017). https://doi.org/10.1016/j.jsc.2016.07.010
11. Darboux, J.G.: Mémoire sur les équations différentielles algébriques du premier ordre et du premier degré. Bull. Sci. Math. **2**(1), 151–200 (1878)
12. Denman, W., Muñoz, C.: Automated real proving in PVS via MetiTarski. In: Jones, C., Pihlajasaari, P., Sun, J. (eds.) FM 2014. LNCS, vol. 8442, pp. 194–199. Springer, Cham (2014). https://doi.org/10.1007/978-3-319-06410-9_14
13. Frehse, G., et al.: SpaceEx: scalable verification of hybrid systems. In: Gopalakrishnan, G., Qadeer, S. (eds.) CAV 2011. LNCS, vol. 6806, pp. 379–395. Springer, Heidelberg (2011). https://doi.org/10.1007/978-3-642-22110-1_30
14. Fulton, N., Mitsch, S., Bohrer, B., Platzer, A.: Bellerophon: tactical theorem proving for hybrid systems. In: Ayala-Rincón, M., Muñoz, C.A. (eds.) ITP 2017. LNCS, vol. 10499, pp. 207–224. Springer, Cham (2017). https://doi.org/10.1007/978-3-319-66107-0_14
15. Fulton, N., Mitsch, S., Quesel, J.-D., Völp, M., Platzer, A.: KeYmaera X: an axiomatic tactical theorem prover for hybrid systems. In: Felty, A.P., Middeldorp, A. (eds.) CADE 2015. LNCS (LNAI), vol. 9195, pp. 527–538. Springer, Cham (2015). https://doi.org/10.1007/978-3-319-21401-6_36

16. Gan, T., Chen, M., Li, Y., Xia, B., Zhan, N.: Reachability analysis for solvable dynamical systems. IEEE Trans. Autom. Control **63**(7), 2003–2018 (2018). https://doi.org/10.1109/TAC.2017.2763785

17. Ghorbal, K., Platzer, A.: Characterizing algebraic invariants by differential radical invariants. In: Ábrahám, E., Havelund, K. (eds.) TACAS 2014. LNCS, vol. 8413, pp. 279–294. Springer, Heidelberg (2014). https://doi.org/10.1007/978-3-642-54862-8_19

18. Ghorbal, K., Sogokon, A., Platzer, A.: A hierarchy of proof rules for checking positive invariance of algebraic and semi-algebraic sets. Comput. Lang. Syst. Struct. **47**, 19–43 (2017). https://doi.org/10.1016/j.cl.2015.11.003

19. Goriely, A.: Integrability and Nonintegrability of Dynamical Systems. World Scientific, Hackensack (2001). https://doi.org/10.1142/3846

20. Gulwani, S., Tiwari, A.: Constraint-based approach for analysis of hybrid systems. In: Gupta, A., Malik, S. (eds.) CAV 2008. LNCS, vol. 5123, pp. 190–203. Springer, Heidelberg (2008). https://doi.org/10.1007/978-3-540-70545-1_18

21. Herbrand, J.: Recherches sur la théorie de la démonstration. Ph.D. thesis, Université de Paris, Faculté des Sciences (1930)

22. Immler, F., et al.: ARCH-COMP18 category report: continuous and hybrid systems with nonlinear dynamics. In: Frehse, G., Althoff, M., Bogomolov, S., Johnson, T.T. (eds.) ARCH 2018. EPiC Series in Computing, vol. 54, pp. 53–70. EasyChair (2018)

23. Kapinski, J., Deshmukh, J.V., Sankaranarayanan, S., Arechiga, N.: Simulation-guided Lyapunov analysis for hybrid dynamical systems. In: Fränzle, M., Lygeros, J. (eds.) HSCC 2014, pp. 133–142. ACM (2014). https://doi.org/10.1145/2562059.2562139

24. Kong, H., Bogomolov, S., Schilling, C., Jiang, Y., Henzinger, T.A.: Safety verification of nonlinear hybrid systems based on invariant clusters. In: Frehse, G., Mitra, S. (eds.) HSCC 2017, pp. 163–172. ACM (2017). https://doi.org/10.1145/3049797.3049814

25. Kong, H., He, F., Song, X., Hung, W.N.N., Gu, M.: Exponential-Condition-based barrier certificate generation for safety verification of hybrid systems. In: Sharygina, N., Veith, H. (eds.) CAV 2013. LNCS, vol. 8044, pp. 242–257. Springer, Heidelberg (2013). https://doi.org/10.1007/978-3-642-39799-8_17

26. Lafferriere, G., Pappas, G.J., Yovine, S.: Symbolic reachability computation for families of linear vector fields. J. Symb. Comput. **32**(3), 231–253 (2001). https://doi.org/10.1006/jsco.2001.0472

27. Li, W., Passmore, G.O., Paulson, L.C.: Deciding univariate polynomial problems using untrusted certificates in Isabelle/HOL. J. Autom. Reasoning **62**(1), 69–91 (2019). https://doi.org/10.1007/s10817-017-9424-6

28. Liu, J., et al.: A calculus for hybrid CSP. In: Ueda, K. (ed.) APLAS 2010. LNCS, vol. 6461, pp. 1–15. Springer, Heidelberg (2010). https://doi.org/10.1007/978-3-642-17164-2_1

29. Liu, J., Zhan, N., Zhao, H.: Computing semi-algebraic invariants for polynomial dynamical systems. In: Chakraborty, S., Jerraya, A., Baruah, S.K., Fischmeister, S. (eds.) EMSOFT 2011, pp. 97–106. ACM (2011). https://doi.org/10.1145/2038642.2038659

30. Loeser, T., Iwasaki, Y., Fikes, R.: Safety verification proofs for physical systems. In: Proceedings of the 12th International Workshop on Qualitative Reasoning, pp. 88–95 (1998)

31. Man, Y.: Computing closed form solutions of first order ODEs using the Prelle-Singer procedure. J. Symb. Comput. **16**(5), 423–443 (1993). https://doi.org/10.1006/jsco.1993.1057

32. Mishra, B.: Algorithmic Algebra. Springer, Cham (1993). https://doi.org/10.1007/978-1-4612-4344-1

33. Mitsch, S., Platzer, A.: ModelPlex: verified runtime validation of verified cyber-physical system models. Formal Methods Syst. Des. **49**(1–2), 33–74 (2016). https://doi.org/10.1007/s10703-016-0241-z

34. Platzer, A.: Differential dynamic logic for hybrid systems. J. Autom. Reasoning **41**(2), 143–189 (2008)

35. Platzer, A.: The complete proof theory of hybrid systems. In: LICS 2012, pp. 541–550. IEEE (2012). https://doi.org/10.1109/LICS.2012.64

36. Platzer, A., Clarke, E.M.: Computing differential invariants of hybrid systems as fixedpoints. Formal Methods Syst. Des. **35**(1), 98–120 (2009). https://doi.org/10.1007/s10703-009-0079-8

37. Platzer, A., Quesel, J.-D.: KeYmaera: a hybrid theorem prover for hybrid systems (system description). In: Armando, A., Baumgartner, P., Dowek, G. (eds.) IJCAR 2008. LNCS (LNAI), vol. 5195, pp. 171–178. Springer, Heidelberg (2008). https://doi.org/10.1007/978-3-540-71070-7_15

38. Platzer, A., Quesel, J.-D., Rümmer, P.: Real world verification. In: Schmidt, R.A. (ed.) CADE 2009. LNCS (LNAI), vol. 5663, pp. 485–501. Springer, Heidelberg (2009). https://doi.org/10.1007/978-3-642-02959-2_35

39. Platzer, A., Tan, Y.K.: Differential equation axiomatization: the impressive power of differential ghosts. In: Dawar, A., Grädel, E. (eds.) LICS 2018, pp. 819–828. ACM (2018). https://doi.org/10.1145/3209108.3209147

40. Prajna, S., Jadbabaie, A.: Safety verification of hybrid systems using barrier certificates. In: Alur, R., Pappas, G.J. (eds.) HSCC 2004. LNCS, vol. 2993, pp. 477–492. Springer, Heidelberg (2004). https://doi.org/10.1007/978-3-540-24743-2_32

41. Prelle, M.J., Singer, M.F.: Elementary first integrals of differential equations. Trans. Am. Math. Soc. **279**(1), 215–229 (1983)

42. Rebiha, R., Moura, A.V., Matringe, N.: Generating invariants for non-linear hybrid systems. Theor. Comput. Sci. **594**, 180–200 (2015). https://doi.org/10.1016/j.tcs.2015.06.018

43. Renegar, J.: Recent progress on the complexity of the decision problem for the reals. In: Goodman, J.E., Pollack, R., Steiger, W. (eds.) Discrete and Computational Geometry: Papers from the DIMACS Special Year, vol. 6, pp. 287–308. DIMACS/AMS (1990)

44. Rodríguez-Carbonell, E., Tiwari, A.: Generating polynomial invariants for hybrid systems. In: Morari, M., Thiele, L. (eds.) HSCC 2005. LNCS, vol. 3414, pp. 590–605. Springer, Heidelberg (2005). https://doi.org/10.1007/978-3-540-31954-2_38

45. Rouche, N., Habets, P., Laloy, M.: Stability Theory by Liapunov's Direct Method. Applied Mathematical Sciences. Springer, Heidelberg (1977). https://doi.org/10.1007/978-1-4684-9362-7

46. Roux, P., Voronin, Y., Sankaranarayanan, S.: Validating numerical semidefinite programming solvers for polynomial invariants. Formal Methods Syst. Des. **53**(2), 286–312 (2018). https://doi.org/10.1007/s10703-017-0302-y

47. Roy, M.F.: Basic algorithms in real algebraic geometry and their complexity: from Sturm's theorem to the existential theory of reals. De Gruyter Expositions Math. **23**, 1–67 (1996)

48. Sankaranarayanan, S.: Automatic invariant generation for hybrid systems using ideal fixed points. In: Johansson, K.H., Yi, W. (eds.) HSCC 2010, pp. 221–230. ACM (2010). https://doi.org/10.1145/1755952.1755984

49. Sankaranarayanan, S., Sipma, H.B., Manna, Z.: Constructing invariants for hybrid systems. Formal Methods Syst. Des. **32**(1), 25–55 (2008). https://doi.org/10.1007/s10703-007-0046-1

50. Shults, B., Kuipers, B.: Proving properties of continuous systems: qualitative simulation and temporal logic. Artif. Intell. **92**(1–2), 91–129 (1997). https://doi.org/10.1016/S0004-3702(96)00050-1

51. Sogokon, A., Ghorbal, K., Jackson, P.B., Platzer, A.: A method for invariant generation for polynomial continuous systems. In: Jobstmann, B., Leino, K.R.M. (eds.) VMCAI 2016. LNCS, vol. 9583, pp. 268–288. Springer, Heidelberg (2016). https://doi.org/10.1007/978-3-662-49122-5_13

52. Sogokon, A., Ghorbal, K., Johnson, T.T.: Non-linear continuous systems for safety verification. In: Frehse, G., Althoff, M. (eds.) ARCH 2016. EPiC Series in Computing, vol. 43, pp. 42–51. EasyChair (2016)

53. Sogokon, A., Ghorbal, K., Tan, Y.K., Platzer, A.: Vector barrier certificates and comparison systems. In: Havelund, K., Peleska, J., Roscoe, B., de Vink, E. (eds.) FM 2018. LNCS, vol. 10951, pp. 418–437. Springer, Cham (2018). https://doi.org/10.1007/978-3-319-95582-7_25

54. Strogatz, S.H.: Nonlinear Dynamics And Chaos. Studies in Nonlinearity. Westview Press, Boulder (2001)

55. Sturm, T., Tiwari, A.: Verification and synthesis using real quantifier elimination. In: Schost, É., Emiris, I.Z. (eds.) ISSAC 2011, pp. 329–336. ACM (2011). https://doi.org/10.1145/1993886.1993935

56. Tiwari, A.: Approximate reachability for linear systems. In: Maler, O., Pnueli, A. (eds.) HSCC 2003. LNCS, vol. 2623, pp. 514–525. Springer, Heidelberg (2003). https://doi.org/10.1007/3-540-36580-X_37

57. Tiwari, A.: Abstractions for hybrid systems. Formal Methods Syst. Des. **32**(1), 57–83 (2008). https://doi.org/10.1007/s10703-007-0044-3

58. Tiwari, A.: Generating box invariants. In: Egerstedt, M., Mishra, B. (eds.) HSCC 2008. LNCS, vol. 4981, pp. 658–661. Springer, Heidelberg (2008). https://doi.org/10.1007/978-3-540-78929-1_58

59. Tiwari, A., Khanna, G.: Series of abstractions for hybrid automata. In: Tomlin, C.J., Greenstreet, M.R. (eds.) HSCC 2002. LNCS, vol. 2289, pp. 465–478. Springer, Heidelberg (2002). https://doi.org/10.1007/3-540-45873-5_36

60. Tiwari, A., Khanna, G.: Nonlinear systems: approximating reach sets. In: Alur, R., Pappas, G.J. (eds.) HSCC 2004. LNCS, vol. 2993, pp. 600–614. Springer, Heidelberg (2004). https://doi.org/10.1007/978-3-540-24743-2_40

61. Wang, S., Zhan, N., Zou, L.: An improved HHL prover: an interactive theorem prover for hybrid systems. In: Butler, M., Conchon, S., Zaïdi, F. (eds.) ICFEM 2015. LNCS, vol. 9407, pp. 382–399. Springer, Cham (2015). https://doi.org/10.1007/978-3-319-25423-4_25

62. Weber, T.: Integrating a SAT solver with an LCF-style theorem prover. Electron. Notes Theor. Comput. Sci. **144**(2), 67–78 (2006). https://doi.org/10.1016/j.entcs.2005.12.007

63. Weber, T.: SMT solvers: new oracles for the HOL theorem prover. STTT **13**(5), 419–429 (2011). https://doi.org/10.1007/s10009-011-0188-8

64. Yang, Z., Huang, C., Chen, X., Lin, W., Liu, Z.: A linear programming relaxation based approach for generating barrier certificates of hybrid systems. In: Fitzgerald, J., Heitmeyer, C., Gnesi, S., Philippou, A. (eds.) FM 2016. LNCS, vol. 9995, pp. 721–738. Springer, Cham (2016). https://doi.org/10.1007/978-3-319-48989-6_44

65. Zaki, M.H., Denman, W., Tahar, S., Bois, G.: Integrating abstraction techniques for formal verification of analog designs. J. Aeros. Comp. Inf. Com. **6**(5), 373–392 (2009). https://doi.org/10.2514/1.44289
66. Zhao, F.: Extracting and representing qualitative behaviors of complex systems in phase space. Artif. Intell. **69**(1–2), 51–92 (1994). https://doi.org/10.1016/0004-3702(94)90078-7

Concurrency

A Parametric Rely-Guarantee Reasoning Framework for Concurrent Reactive Systems

Yongwang Zhao[1,2]([✉]), David Sanán[3], Fuyuan Zhang[4], and Yang Liu[3]

[1] School of Computer Science and Engineering, Beihang University, Beijing, China
[2] Beijing Advanced Innovation Center for Big Data and Brain Computing,
Beihang University, Beijing, China
zhaoyw@buaa.edu.cn
[3] School of Computer Science and Engineering, Nanyang Technological University,
Singapore, Singapore
[4] MPI-SWS, Kaiserslautern, Germany

Abstract. Reactive systems are composed of a well defined set of event handlers by which the system responds to environment stimulus. In concurrent environments, event handlers can interact with the execution of other handlers such as hardware interruptions in preemptive systems, or other instances of the reactive system in multicore architectures. The rely-guarantee technique is a suitable approach for the specification and verification of reactive systems. However, the languages in existing rely-guarantee implementations are designed only for "pure programs", simulating reactive systems makes the program and rely-guarantee conditions unnecessary complicated. In this paper, we decouple the system reactions and programs using a rely-guarantee interface, and develop *PiCore*, a parametric rely-guarantee framework for concurrent reactive systems. *PiCore* has a two-level inference system to reason on events and programs associated to events. The rely-guarantee interface between the two levels allows the reusability of existing languages and their rely-guarantee proof systems for programs. In this work we show how to integrate in *PiCore* two existing rely-guarantee proof systems. This work has been fully mechanized in Isabelle/HOL. As a case study, we have applied *PiCore* to the concurrent buddy memory allocation of a real-world OS, providing a verified low-level specification and revealing bugs in the C code.

1 Introduction

Nowadays high-assurance systems are often designed as *concurrent reactive systems* (CRSs) [3]. CRSs react to their computing environment by executing a

This work has been supported in part by the National Natural Science Foundation of China (NSFC) under the Grant No.61872016, and the National Satellite of Excellence in Trustworthy Software Systems and the Award No. NRF2014NCR-NCR001-30, funded by NRF Singapore under National Cyber-security R&D (NCR) programme.

ⓒ Springer Nature Switzerland AG 2019
M. H. ter Beek et al. (Eds.): FM 2019, LNCS 11800, pp. 161–178, 2019.
https://doi.org/10.1007/978-3-030-30942-8_11

sequence of commands under an input event. Some examples of CRSs are operating systems (OSs), control systems, and communication systems, which implementation follow an event-driven paradigm. The rely-guarantee technique [16] represents a fundamental approach to compositional reasoning of *concurrent programs* with shared variables, where programs are represented in imperative languages with extensions for concurrency. Whilst rely-guarantee provides a general framework and can certainly be applied for CRSs, the languages in existing mechanizations of rely-guarantee (e.g. [18, 20, 23, 24, 28]) are imperative and designed only for pure programs, i.e, programs following a flow of procedure calls from an entry point. Examples of reactive systems mentioned above are far more complex than pure programs because they involve many different agents and also heavy interactions with their environment. Without dedicated statements for such system behavior, we often use imperative programs to simulate them, making the formal specification cumbersome, in particular the rely-guarantee conditions. A more detailed motivation will be presented in detail in Sect. 2.

In this paper, we propose *PiCore*, a two-level event-based rely-guarantee framework for CRSs (Sect. 3). *PiCore* detaches the specification and the logic of the reactive aspect of systems from event behaviours. Rather than creating yet another framework for modelling and reasoning on events behaviour, *PiCore* allows to reuse existing rely-guarantee frameworks. The top level introduces the notion of "events" [2,6] into the rely-guarantee method for system reactions. This level defines the events composing a system, and how and when they are triggered. It specifies the language, semantics, and mechanisms to reason on sequences of events and their execution conditions. The second level focuses on the specification and reasoning of the behaviour of the events composing the first level. *PiCore* parametrizes the second level using a rely-guarantee interface, allowing to easily reuse existing rely-guarantee frameworks. This design allows *PiCore* to be independent of the language used to model the behaviour of events.

We have integrated two existing languages and their rely-guarantee proof systems into the *PiCore* framework. As a result we create two instances of *PiCore*: πIMP and πCSimpl (Sect. 4). πIMP integrates the *HOL-Hoare_Parallel* library in Isabelle/HOL that uses a general imperative language [23]. πCSimpl integrates the *CSimpl* language in [24]. *CSimpl* is a generic and realistic imperative language by extending *Simpl* [25] and providing a rely-guarantee proof system in Isabelle/HOL. *Simpl* is able to represent a large subset of C99 code and has been applied to the formal verification of seL4 OS kernel [17] at C code level.

We have developed the *PiCore* framework and its integration with the two languages in Isabelle/HOL, the sources are available at https://lvpgroup.github. io/picore/. As a case study, we have applied *PiCore* to the formal specification and mechanized proof of the concurrent buddy memory allocation of a real-world OS, Zephyr RTOS [1] (Sect. 5). The formal specification represented in πIMP is fine-grained providing a high level of detail. It closely follows the Zephyr C code, covering all the data structures and imperative statements present in the implementation. We use the rely-guarantee proof system in πIMP for the formal verification of functional correctness and invariant preservation in the model, revealing three bugs in the C code.

2   Motivation and Approach Overview

Reactive systems respond to continuous stimulus from their computing environment [12] by changing their state and, in turn, affecting their environment by sending back signals to it or initiating other operations. We consider *concurrent reactive systems (CRSs)*, which may involve many different competitive agents executing concurrently with shared resources due to multicore setting, task preemption or embedded interrupts, e.g. concurrent OS kernels [7,27] and interrupt driven control systems, where the execution of handlers is not atomic. Moreover, the configuration and context of the underlying hardware of systems are not usually encoded in programs, which represent only a portion of the whole system behaviour. For instance, although interrupt handlers (e.g. kernel services and scheduling) in OS kernels are programmed in the C language, when and how interrupts are triggered and which handlers are invoked to react with an interrupt are out of the handler code.

In the setting of imperative languages, CRSs are usually modelled as the parallel composition of reactive systems, each of which is simulated by a *while(true)* loop program sharing data with its environment and invoking the relevant handlers in the loop body (e.g. [4]). First, The environment non-deterministically decides which event handler is triggered and what are the arguments of the handler for this triggering. Second, some critical properties, such as noninterference of OS kernels [21], concern execution traces of reaction sequences rather than program states only. Without native support in the language semantics, the *while* loop programs have to use auxiliary logical/program variables to simulate the two non-determinisms together and store the event context of each reactive system. This will make the program and the rely-guarantee conditions unnecessary complicated, in particular for realistic CRSs with many event handlers.

The cause of the above problems is the lack of a rely-guarantee approach for system reactions and, as a result, the mixture of system and program behavior together. In this paper, we take the level of abstraction and reusability of the rely-guarantee method a step further by decoupling the two levels using a rely-guarantee interface. The result is a flexible rely-guarantee framework for CRSs, which is able to integrate existing rely-guarantee implementations at program level while being unchanged. At the system reaction level, we consider a reactive system as a set of event handlers called *event systems* responding to stimulus from the environment. Fig. 1 illustrates an *event*, which has an event name, a list of input parameters, a guard condition to determine the conditions triggering the event, and an imperative program as its body. In addition to the input parameters, an event has a additional parameter κ which indicates the execution context, e.g. the thread invoking the service and the external devices

EVENT alloc [Ref p, Nat size, Int tout] @ κ
WHEN
   $p \in$ ´mem-pools $\wedge$ timeout ≥ -1
THEN
   ......
   IF timeout > 0 THEN
     ´endt := ´endt(t := ´tick + timeout)
   FI;
   ......
END

Fig. 1. An example of event

triggering the interrupt. The execution of an event system concerns the continuous evaluation of guards of the events with their input arguments. From the set of events for which their associated guard condition holds in the current state, one event is non-deterministically selected to be triggered, and its body executed. After the event finishes, the evaluation of guards starts again looking for the next event to be executed. We call the semantics of event systems *reactive semantics*, where the event context shows the event currently being executed. A CRS is modeled as the *parallel composition* of event systems that are concurrently executed.

As shown in the Zephyr case study in Sect. 5, the formal specification of CRSs with support for reactions and their composition is much simpler than those represented by pure programs. Furthermore, *PiCore* supports verifying total correctness of events, whose execution is usually assumed to be terminating, as well as the properties of event systems, whose execution is often non-terminating.

3   *PiCore*: The Rely-guarantee Framework

This section introduces the event language in *PiCore* as well as its rely-guarantee proof system, the soundness of proof rules and invariant verification.

3.1   The Event Language

Event:

$$\mathcal{E} ::= \textbf{Event}\,(l, g, P) \qquad (Basic\ Event)$$
$$| \lfloor P \rfloor \qquad\qquad (Triggered\ Event)$$

Event System:

$$\mathcal{S} ::= \{\mathcal{E}_0, ..., \mathcal{E}_n\} \qquad (Event\ Set)$$
$$| \mathcal{E} \triangleright \mathcal{S} \qquad\qquad (Event\ Sequence)$$

Parallel Event System:

$$\mathcal{PS} ::= \mathcal{K} \to \mathcal{S}$$

Fig. 2. Abstract syntax of *PiCore*

The abstract syntax of *PiCore* and its semantics are shown in Figs. 2 and 3 respectively. The syntax for events distinguishes basic events pending to be triggered from already triggered events that are under execution. A basic event is defined as **Event** (l, g, P), where l is the event name, g the guard condition, and P the body of the event. When **Event** (l, g, P) is triggered, its body begins to be executed (BASICEVT rule in Fig. 3) and it becomes a triggered event $\lfloor P \rfloor$. The execution of $\lfloor P \rfloor$ just simulates the program P (see TRGDEVT rule in Fig. 3). $\bot$ is the notation to represent the termination of programs. Instead of defining a language for programs, *PiCore* reuses existing languages and their rely-guarantee proof systems, which will be discussed in Sect. 4. Events are parametrized in the meta-logic as "$\lambda(plist, \kappa)$. **Event** (l, g, P)", where $plist$ is the list of input parameters, and κ is the event system identifier that the event belongs to. These parameters are not part of the syntax of events to make the guard g and the event body P, as well as the rely and guarantee relations, more flexible, allowing to define different instances of the relations for different values of $plist$ and κ.

An event system has two forms that we call *event sequence* and *event set*. Event sequences model a sequential execution of events, and event sets model

[BASICEVT]
$$\frac{body(\alpha) \neq \perp \quad s \in guard(\alpha) \quad x' = x(\kappa \mapsto \textbf{Event } \alpha)}{\Sigma \vdash (\textbf{Event } \alpha, s, x) \xrightarrow{\textbf{Event } \alpha @ \kappa}_e (\lfloor body(\alpha) \rfloor, s, x')}$$

[TRGDEVT]
$$\frac{\Sigma \vdash (P, s) \longrightarrow_p (P', s')}{\Sigma \vdash (\lfloor P \rfloor, s, x) \xrightarrow{c@\kappa}_e (\lfloor P' \rfloor, s', x)}$$

[EVTSET]
$$\frac{i \leq n \quad \Sigma \vdash (\mathcal{E}_i, s, x) \xrightarrow{\mathcal{E}_i @ \kappa}_e (\mathcal{E}'_i, s, x')}{\Sigma \vdash (\{\mathcal{E}_0, ..., \mathcal{E}_n\}, s, x) \xrightarrow{\mathcal{E}_i @ \kappa}_{es} (\mathcal{E}'_i \triangleright \{\mathcal{E}_0, ..., \mathcal{E}_n\}, s, x')}$$

[EVTSEQ1]
$$\frac{\Sigma \vdash (\mathcal{E}, s, x) \xrightarrow{t@\kappa}_e (\mathcal{E}', s', x') \quad \mathcal{E}' \neq \lfloor \perp \rfloor}{\Sigma \vdash (\mathcal{E} \triangleright S, s, x) \xrightarrow{t@\kappa}_{es} (\mathcal{E}' \triangleright S, s', x')}$$

[EVTSEQ2]
$$\frac{\Sigma \vdash (\mathcal{E}, s, x) \xrightarrow{t@\kappa}_e (\lfloor \perp \rfloor, s', x')}{\Sigma \vdash (\mathcal{E} \triangleright S, s, x) \xrightarrow{t@\kappa}_{es} (S, s', x')}$$

[PAR]
$$\frac{\Sigma \vdash (\mathcal{PS}(\kappa), s, x) \xrightarrow{t@\kappa}_{es} (S', s', x') \quad \mathcal{PS}' = \mathcal{PS}(\kappa \mapsto S')}{\Sigma \vdash (\mathcal{PS}, s, x) \xrightarrow{t@\kappa}_{pes} (\mathcal{PS}', s', x')}$$

Fig. 3. Operational semantics of $PiCore$

the continuous execution of events from the evaluation of the guards of the events in the set. When the system is not executing any event, one event whose guard condition holds in the current state is non-deterministically chosen to be triggered (EVTSET rule) and its body P executed (EVTSEQ1 rule). After P finishes, the evaluation of the guards starts again looking for the next event to be executed (EVTSEQ2 rule). A CRS is modeled by a parallel composition of event systems with shared states. It is a function from $\mathcal{K}$ to event systems, where $\mathcal{K}$ indicates the identifiers of event systems. This design is more general and could be applied to track executing events. For instance, we use $\mathcal{K}$ to represent the core identifier in multicore systems.

The semantics of $PiCore$ is defined via transition rules between configurations. We define a configuration $\mathcal{C}$ in $PiCore$ as a triple $(\sharp, s, x)$ where $\sharp$ is a specification, s is a state, and $x : \mathcal{K} \to \mathcal{E}$ is an event context. The event context indicates which event is currently being executed in an event system κ. Transition rules in events, event systems, and parallel event systems have the form $\Sigma \vdash (\sharp_1, s_1, x_1) \xrightarrow{\delta}_\square (\sharp_2, s_2, x_2)$, where $\delta = t@\kappa$ is a label indicating the type of transition, the subscript "$\square$" ($_e$, $_{es}$ or $_{pes}$) indicates the transition objects, and Σ is used for some static configuration for programs (e.g. an environment for procedure declarations). Here t indicates a program action c or an occurrence of an event $\mathcal{E}$. $@\kappa$ means that the action occurs in event system κ. The program transition is denoted as $\longrightarrow_p$ in the TRGDEVT rule. Environment transition rules have the form $\Sigma \vdash (\sharp, s, x) \xrightarrow{env}_\square (\sharp, s', x)$. Intuitively, a transition made by the environment may change the state but not the event context nor the specification. The parallel composition of event systems is fine-grained since small steps in events are interleaved in the semantics of $PiCore$. This design relaxes the atomicity of events in other approaches (e.g., Event-B [2]).

A *computation* of $PiCore$ is a sequence of transitions. We define the set of computations of all parallel event systems with static information Σ as $\Psi(\Sigma)$, which is a set of lists of configurations inductively defined as follows. The singleton list is always a computation (1). Two consecutive configurations are part of a computation if they are the initial and final configurations of an environment

(2) or action transition (3). The operator $\#$ in $e\#l$ represents the insertion of element e in list l.

$$
\begin{cases}
(1)[(\mathcal{PS}, s, x)] \in \Psi(\Sigma) \\
(2)(\mathcal{PS}, s_1, x_1)\#cs \in \Psi(\Sigma) \implies (\mathcal{PS}, s_2, x_2)\#(\mathcal{PS}, s_1, x_1)\#cs \in \Psi(\Sigma) \\
(3)\Sigma \vdash (\mathcal{PS}_2, s_2, x_2) \xrightarrow{\delta}_{pes} (\mathcal{PS}_1, s_1, x_1) \wedge (\mathcal{PS}_1, s_1, x_1)\#cs \in \Psi(\Sigma) \\
\quad\quad \implies (\mathcal{PS}_2, s_2, x_2)\#(\mathcal{PS}_1, s_1, x_1)\#cs \in \Psi(\Sigma)
\end{cases}
$$

Computations for events and event systems are defined in a similar way. We use $\Psi(\Sigma, \mathcal{PS})$ to denote the set of computations of a parallel event system $\mathcal{PS}$. The function $\Psi(\Sigma, \mathcal{PS}, s, x)$ denotes the computations of $\mathcal{PS}$ starting up from an initial state s and event context x.

3.2   Rely-Guarantee Proof System

We consider the verification of two different kinds of properties in the rely-guarantee proof system for reactive systems: pre and post conditions of events and invariants in the fine-grained execution of events. We use the former for the verification of functional correctness of the event, where the pre and post conditions have to be respectively satisfied only before and after the execution of the event. The latter is used on the verification of safety properties concerning the small steps inside events and that must be preserved by any internal step of the event. For instance, in the case of Zephyr RTOS, a safety property is that memory blocks do not overlap each other even during internal steps of the *alloc* and *free* services. Other critical properties can also be defined considering the execution trace of events, e.g. noninterference [19,21,22].

A rely-guarantee specification in *PiCore* is a quadruple $\langle pre, R, G, pst \rangle$, where *pre* is the precondition, R is the rely condition, G is the guarantee condition, and *pst* is the post condition. The assumption and commitment functions are denoted by A and C respectively. For each computation $\varpi \in \Psi(\Sigma, \mathcal{E})$, we use ϖ_i to denote the configuration at index i. $\natural_{\varpi_i}$, s_{ϖ_i}, and x_{ϖ_i} represent the projection of each component in the tuple $\varpi_i = (\natural, s, x)$.

$$
A(\Sigma, pre, R) \equiv \{\varpi \mid s_{\varpi_0} \in pre \wedge (\forall i < len(\varpi) - 1. (\Sigma \vdash \varpi_i \xrightarrow{env} \varpi_{i+1}) \longrightarrow (s_{\varpi_i}, s_{\varpi_{i+1}}) \in R)\}
$$

$$
C(\Sigma, G, pst) \equiv \{\varpi \mid (\forall i < len(\varpi) - 1. (\Sigma \vdash \varpi_i \xrightarrow{\delta}_e \varpi_{i+1}) \longrightarrow (s_{\varpi_i}, s_{\varpi_{i+1}}) \in G)
$$
$$
\wedge (\natural_{last(\varpi)} = \lfloor \perp \rfloor \longrightarrow s_{\varpi_n} \in pst)\}
$$

We define validity of rely-guarantee specification for events as

$$
\Sigma \models \mathcal{E} \textbf{ sat } \langle pre, R, G, pst \rangle \equiv \forall s, x. \, \Psi(\Sigma, \mathcal{E}, s, x) \cap A(\Sigma, pre, R) \subseteq C(\Sigma, G, pst)
$$

Intuitively, validity represents that the set of computations *cpts* starting at the configuration $(\mathcal{E}, s, x)$, with $s \in pre$ and environment transitions in a computation $cpt \in cpts$ belonging to the rely relation R, is a subset of the set of computations where action transitions belong to the guarantee relation G and

[BASICEVT]

$$\frac{\Sigma \vdash body(\alpha) \text{ sat } \langle pre \cap guard(\alpha), R, G, pst\rangle \quad stable(pre, R) \quad \forall s. (s, s) \in G}{\Sigma \vdash \textbf{Event } \alpha \text{ sat } \langle pre, R, G, pst\rangle}$$

[CONSEQ]

$$\frac{pre \subseteq pre' \quad R \subseteq R' \quad G' \subseteq G \quad pst' \subseteq pst \quad \Sigma \vdash \natural \text{ sat } \langle pre', R', G', pst'\rangle}{\Sigma \vdash \natural \text{ sat } \langle pre, R, G, pst\rangle}$$

[TRGEVT]

$$\frac{\Sigma \vdash P \text{ sat } \langle pre, R, G, pst\rangle}{\Sigma \vdash (\lfloor P \rfloor) \text{ sat } \langle pre, R, G, pst\rangle}$$

[EVTSEQ]

$$\frac{\Sigma \vdash \mathcal{E} \text{ sat } \langle pre, R, G, m\rangle \quad \Sigma \vdash S \text{ sat } \langle m, R, G, pst\rangle}{\Sigma \vdash (\mathcal{E} \triangleright S) \text{ sat } \langle pre, R, G, pst\rangle}$$

[EVTSET]

$$\frac{\begin{array}{l} (1)\forall i \leq n. \ \Sigma \vdash \mathcal{E}_i \text{ sat } \langle pres_i, Rs_i, Gs_i, psts_i\rangle \quad (2)\forall i, j \leq n. \ psts_i \subseteq pres_j \\ (3)\forall i \leq n. \ pre \subseteq pres_i \quad (4)\forall i \leq n. \ R \subseteq Rs_i \quad (5)\forall i \leq n. \ Gs_i \subseteq G \\ (6)\forall i \leq n. \ psts_i \subseteq pst \quad (7)stable(pre, R) \quad (8)\forall s. (s, s) \in G \end{array}}{\Sigma \vdash (\{\mathcal{E}_0, \ ..., \ \mathcal{E}_n\}) \text{ sat } \langle pre, R, G, pst\rangle}$$

[PAR]

$$\frac{\begin{array}{l} (1)\forall \kappa. \ \Sigma \vdash \mathcal{PS}(\kappa) \text{ sat } \langle pres_\kappa, Rs_\kappa, Gs_\kappa, psts_\kappa\rangle \quad (2)\forall \kappa. \ pre \subseteq pres_\kappa \quad (3)\forall \kappa. \ R \subseteq Rs_\kappa \\ (4)\forall \kappa. \ Gs_\kappa \subseteq G \quad (5)\forall \kappa. \ psts_\kappa \subseteq pst \quad (6)\forall \kappa, \kappa'. \ \kappa \neq \kappa' \longrightarrow Gs_\kappa \subseteq Rs_{\kappa'} \end{array}}{\Sigma \vdash \mathcal{PS} \text{ sat } \langle pre, R, G, pst\rangle}$$

Fig. 4. Rely-guarantee proof rules for *PiCore*

if an event terminates, then the final states belongs to *pst*. Validity for event systems and parallel event systems are defined in a similar way.

Next, we present the rely-guarantee proof rules in *PiCore* and their soundness w.r.t validity. The proof rules are shown in Fig. 4, which give us a relational proof method for concurrent systems. We first define $stable(f, g) \equiv \forall x, y. \ x \in f \wedge (x, y) \in g \longrightarrow y \in f$. Thus, $stable(pre, rely)$ means that the precondition is stable when the rely condition holds. Rules may assume stability of the precondition with regards to the rely relation $stable(pre, R)$ to ensure that the precondition holds after environment transitions.

The TRGDEVT inference rule says that a triggered event $\lfloor P \rfloor$ satisfies the rely-guarantee specification if the program P satisfies the specification. This rule is directly derived from the semantics for triggered events in Fig. 3, where triggered events modifies the state according to how the program modifies the state. A basic event satisfies its rely-guarantee specification (inference rule BASICEVNT) if its body satisfies the rely-guarantee strengthening the precondition with the guard of the event. Since the occurrence of an event does not change the state, it is necessary that the guarantee relation includes the identity relation to accept stuttering transitions.

Regarding the proof rules for event systems, sequential composition of events is modeled by EVTSEQ rule, which is similar to that of the sequential command in imperative languages. In order to prove that an event set satisfies its rely-guarantee specification, we have to prove eight premises (EVTSET rule in Fig. 4). It is necessary that each event together with its specification is derivable in the system (Premise 1). Since the event set behaves as itself after an event finishes, each event postcondition has to imply each event precondition (Premise

2), and the precondition for the event set has to imply the preconditions of all events (Premise 3). An environment transition for the event set corresponds to a transition from the environment of any event i in the event set (Premise 4). The guarantee condition Gs_i of each event must be in the guarantee condition of the event set, since an action transition of the event set is performed by one of its events (Premise 5). The postcondition of each event must be in the overall postcondition (Premise 6). The last two refer to stability of the precondition and identity of the guarantee relation.

The parallel rule in Fig. 4 establishes compositionality of the proof system, where verification of the parallel specification can be reduced to the verification of individual event systems and then to the verification of individual events. It is necessary that each event system $\mathcal{PS}(\kappa)$ satisfies its specification $\langle pres_\kappa, Rs_\kappa, Gs_\kappa, psts_\kappa \rangle$ (Premise 1). The precondition for the parallel composition implies all the event system's preconditions (Premise 2). An environment transition Rs_κ for the event system κ corresponds to a transition from the overall environment R (Premise 3). Since an action transition of the concurrent system is performed by one of its event system, the guarantee condition Gs_κ of each event system must be a subset of the overall guarantee condition G (Premise 4). The overall postcondition must be a logical consequence of all postconditions of event systems (Premise 5). An action transition of an event system κ should be defined in the rely condition of another event system κ', where $\kappa \neq \kappa'$ (Premise 6).

Finally, the soundness theorem for a specification $\natural$ relates rely-guarantee specifications proven on the proof system with its validity.

Theorem 1 (Soundness). $\Sigma \vdash \natural$ **sat** $\langle pre, R, G, pst \rangle \implies \Sigma \models \natural$ **sat** $\langle pre, R, G, pst \rangle$

3.3   Invariant Verification

In many cases, we would like to show that CRSs preserve certain data invariants. Since CRSs may not be closed systems, i.e. their environment may change the system state that is represented by rely conditions of CRSs, the reachable states of CRSs are dependent on both the initial states and the environment. We define as follows that a CRS $\mathcal{PS}$ with static information Σ, starting up from a set of initial states $init$ under an environment R, preserves an invariant inv when its reachable states satisfy the predicate:

$$\forall s_0\, x_0\, \varpi.\ \varpi \in \Psi(\Sigma, \mathcal{PS}, s_0, x_0) \cap A(\Sigma, init, R) \longrightarrow (\forall i < len(\varpi).\ inv(s_{\varpi_i}))$$

In this definition, ϖ denotes an arbitrary computation of $\mathcal{PS}$ from a set of initial states $init$ and under an environment R. It requires that all states in ϖ satisfy the invariant inv. $\{s \mid P(s)\}$ denotes the set of states s satisfying P.

To show that inv is preserved by a system $\mathcal{PS}$, it suffices to show the invariant verification theorem as follows. This theorem indicates that (1) the system satisfies its rely-guarantee specification $\langle init, R, G, post \rangle$, (2) inv initially holds in the set of initial states, and (3) each action transition as well as each environment transition preserve *inv*. Later, by the proof system of *PiCore*, invariant verification is decomposed to the verification of individual events.

Theorem 2 (Invariant Verification). *For formal specification* $\mathcal{PS}$ *and* Σ, *a state set init, a rely condition R, and inv, if*

- $\Sigma \vdash \mathcal{PS}$ **sat** $\langle init, R, G, post \rangle$.
- $init \subseteq \{s \mid inv(s)\}$.
- $stable(\{s \mid inv(s)\}, R)$ *and* $stable(\{s \mid inv(s)\}, G)$ *are satisfied*.

then inv is preserved by $\mathcal{PS}$ *w.r.t. init and R.*

4 Integrating Concrete Languages

We present the rely-guarantee interface of *PiCore* framework in this section as well as the integration of the *IMP* and *CSimpl* languages.

4.1 Rely-Guarantee Interface of *PiCore* Framework

To implement a flexible integration of languages for programs on event bodies, *PiCore* provides a rely-guarantee interface that program languages must respect. The interface is an abstraction for common rely-guarantee components required by *PiCore* (Fig. 5). These components are represented as a set of *parameters* and *assumptions* to guarantee the correctness of the proof system, since the language, semantics, proof rules and soundness proof of *PiCore* in Sect. 3 are developed using this interface.

Following this interface, third-party languages and their rely-guarantee proof systems are embedded into *PiCore* as *interpretations* using an *adapter* that implements the interface. Since these languages may have existed for years, they are not necessary completely consistent with the *PiCore* interface. Hence, for each language that we want to integrate in *PiCore* it is necessary to provide a *rely-guarantee adapter* to bridge the differences of rely-guarantee components between *PiCore* and the languages. The adapter implements the interface by delegating functionality of the event language to the integrated language. This architecture makes it possible to integrate existing languages without modifying their specification, semantics, and rely-guarantee inference system.

The interface requires specifications and assumptions for four differentiated elements: language definition (syntax and semantics), rely-guarantee definitions (computation and rely-guarantee validity), rely-guarantee proof rules, and their soundness.

As a parametric framework, *PiCore* does not define the syntax for languages of programs. It only requires a notation to represent the termination of programs, which is denoted as $\perp$ in *PiCore* (Parameter 1 in Table 1). *PiCore* also needs the transition relations representing the event behaviour (event action) and the environment (Parameters 2 and 3). To reason about event behaviors, *PiCore*

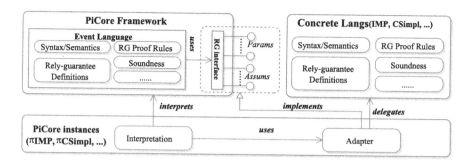

Fig. 5. *PiCore* framework and its integration with imperative languages

assumes that (1) program ⊥ cannot take a step to another state (Assumption 1 in Table 2), (2) if a program P takes an action transition, the program is changed in the next configuration (Assumption 2), and (3) environment transitions do not change the program itself (Assumption 3).

Since the body of events in *PiCore* is specified using external languages, computations and the reasoning of events are dependent on those languages. *PiCore* requires the specification for *computation* of programs (Parameters 4 and 5) and assumes that (1) a computation of any program is not empty (Assumption 4), (2) if ϖ is a computation of a language and the program of its first configuration is P, then ϖ is a computation for the program P (Assumption 5), and (3) there are three constructions for computation of programs (Assumption 6), which is similar to the definition of events we have presented in Sect. 3.

Finally, the interface requires the components related to the validity of rely-guarantee specification and the proof rules (Parameters 6–9). The definitions of the assume/commit functions and validity are similar to those in *PiCore* (see Sect. 3), and are relaxed to be not necessarily equivalent. *PiCore* requires that the rely-guarantee proof rules in languages are sound (Assumption 10). Other rely-guarantee components, such as rely and guarantee condition, are defined in the above parameters at the same time.

Table 1. Parameters of *PiCore*

No.	Name	Notation	No.	Name	Notation
(1)	Terminating statement	⊥	(2)	Program transition	$\Sigma \vdash (P, s) \longrightarrow_p (Q, t)$
(3)	Environment transition	$\Sigma \vdash (P, s) \xrightarrow{env}_p (Q, t)$	(4)	Computations	$\Psi(\Sigma)$
(5)	Computations of a program	$\Psi(\Sigma, P)$	(6)	Assume	$A(\Sigma, pre, R)$
(7)	Commit	$C(\Sigma, G, pst)$	(8)	Validity	$\Sigma \models P \ \mathbf{sat} \ \langle pre, R, G, pst \rangle$
(9)	Proof rule	$\Sigma \vdash P \ \mathbf{sat} \ \langle pre, R, G, pst \rangle$			

Table 2. Assumptions of parameters

(1)	$\neg(\Sigma \vdash (\bot, s) \longrightarrow_p (P, t))$	(2)	$\neg(\Sigma \vdash (P, s) \longrightarrow_p (P, t))$
(3)	$\Sigma \vdash (P, s) \xrightarrow{env}_p (Q, t) \Longrightarrow P = Q$	(4)	$[] \notin \Psi(\Sigma)$
(5)	$\varpi_0 = (P, s) \wedge \varpi \in \Psi(\Sigma) \Longrightarrow \varpi \in \Psi(\Sigma, P)$		
(6)	$(\exists P\ s.\ \varpi = [(P, s)]) \vee (\exists P\ t\ xs\ s.\ \varpi = (P, s)\#(P, t)\#xs \wedge (P, t)\#xs \in \Psi(\Sigma)) \vee$ $(\exists P\ s\ Q\ t\ xs.\ \varpi = (P, s)\#(Q, t)\#xs \wedge \Sigma \vdash (P, s) \longrightarrow_p (Q, t) \wedge (Q, t)\#xs \in \Psi(\Sigma)))$ $\Longrightarrow \varpi \in \Psi(\Sigma)$		
(7)	$\Sigma \models P\ \textbf{sat}\ \langle pre, R, G, pst \rangle \Longrightarrow \forall s.\ \Psi(\Sigma, P, s) \cap A(\Sigma, pre, R) \subseteq C(\Sigma, G, pst)$		
(8)	$(\forall i < len(\varpi) - 1.\ (\Sigma \vdash \varpi_i \xrightarrow{env}_p \varpi_{i+1}) \longrightarrow (s_{\varpi_i}, s_{\varpi_{i+1}}) \in R) \wedge s_{\varpi_0} \in pre$ $\Longrightarrow \varpi \in A(\Sigma, pre, R)$		
(9)	$\varpi \in C(\Sigma, G, pst) \Longrightarrow (\forall i < len(\varpi) - 1.\ (\Sigma \vdash \varpi_i \longrightarrow_p \varpi_{i+1}) \longrightarrow (s_{\varpi_i}, s_{\varpi_{i+1}}) \in G)$ $\wedge\ (\sharp_{last(\varpi)} = \lfloor \bot \rfloor \longrightarrow s_{\varpi_n} \in pst)$		
(10)	$\Sigma \vdash P\ \textbf{sat}\ \langle pre, R, G, pst \rangle \Longrightarrow \Sigma \models P\ \textbf{sat}\ \langle pre, R, G, pst \rangle$		

4.2 Integrating the *IMP* and *CSimpl* languages

To integrate a language and its rely-guarantee framework into *PiCore*, we first create an adapter for the language providing the *PiCore* interface. For each parameter in the interface, there is a corresponding definition (or function) in the adapter instantiating the parameter. Moreover, the adapter provides the necessary set of lemmas and theorems to show that the instances of the interface specifications satisfy the interface assumptions.

In the mechanized implementation of *PiCore* in Isabelle/HOL, we use *locales* to create the framework, where parameters and assumptions of *PiCore* are represented as *parameters* and *assumptions* of locales. Locales are the Isabelle's approach for dealing with parametric theories. Using *locale interpretations*, they may be instantiated by assigning concrete data to parameters, and conclusions of locales will be propagated to the current theory or the current proof context. Using the notion of locales, we create *PiCore* instances by interpreting the *PiCore* locale using adapters for *IMP* and *CSimpl*.

Since the definitions of rely-guarantee components in *IMP* [23] are consistent with the *PiCore* interface, except that there is no static information Σ in *IMP*, the adapter for *IMP* is straightforward from its rely-guarantee specification, we omit the details here and the interested reader can refer to the Isabelle/HOL sources.

More interesting is *CSimpl* that supports most of the features of real world programming languages including exceptions, and is substantially more complex than *IMP*. Here, we show the adapter for *CSimpl*. The language and its rely-guarantee proof system are presented in detail in [24]. The abstract syntax of *CSimpl* is defined as in Fig. 6 in terms of states, of type *'s*; a set of fault types, of type *'f*, a set of procedure names of type *'p*, and a set of simulation events *'e* (simulation events are not addressed in this work). Type *('s, 'p, 'f, 'e) config* defines the configuration used in its transition semantics and *('s, 'p, 'f, 'e) body* denoted as Γ defines the procedure declarations as mapping from procedure

datatype $('s, 'p, 'f, 'e)$ *com* = *Skip* | *Throw* | *Basic* $'s$ $'e$ ⇒ $'s$ | *Spec* $('s \times 's)$ *set* $'e$
| *Seq* $('s, 'p, 'f, 'e)$ *com* $('s, 'p, 'f, 'e)$ *com* | *Await* $'s$ *bexp* $'e$ $('s, 'p, 'f, 'e)$ *com*
| *Cond* $'s$ *bexp* $('s, 'p, 'f, 'e)$ *com* $('s, 'p, 'f, 'e)$ *com*
| *While* $'s$ *bexp* $('s, 'p, 'f, 'e)$ *com* | *Call* $'p$ | *DynCom* $'s$ ⇒ $('s, 'p, 'f, 'e)$ *com*
| *Guard* $'f$ $'s$ *bexp* $('s, 'p, 'f, 'e)$ *com* | *Catch* $('s, 'p, 'f, 'e)$ *com* $('s, 'p, 'f, 'e)$ *com*

datatype $('s, 'f)$ *xstate* = *Normal* $'s$ | *Abrupt* $'s$ | *Fault* $'f$ | *Stuck*
type-synonym$('s, 'p, 'f, 'e)$ *config* = $('s, 'p, 'f, 'e)$*com* $\times$ $('s, 'f)$ *xstate*
type-synonym $('s, 'p, 'f, 'e)$ *body* = $'p$ ⇒ $('s, 'p, 'f, 'e)$ *com option*
type-synonym $('s, 'p, 'f, 'e)$ *confs* = $('s, 'p, 'f, 'e)$ *body* $\times(('s, 'p, 'f, 'e)$ *config*) *list*

Fig. 6. Syntax and state definition of the CSimpl Language [24]

names to *CSimpl* programs. $('s, 'p, 'f, 'e)$ *confs* defines the type of computations. To support reasoning about procedure invocations, *CSimpl* uses the notation Θ to maintain the rely-guarantee specification for procedures. The validity in *CSimpl* requires that each procedure satisfies its specification.

In the adapter, we first use the pair (Γ, Θ) to instantiate the environment Σ in *PiCore*. We instantiate the termination statement as the *Skip* command in *CSimpl*. The program transition in *CSimpl* is $\Gamma \vdash_c (P, s) \longrightarrow (Q, t)$, and it is adapted as $(\Gamma, \Theta) \vdash_{cI} (P, s) \longrightarrow (Q, t) \equiv \Gamma \vdash_c (P, s) \longrightarrow (Q, t)$. *CSimpl* semantics for programs can transit from a *Normal* state to a different type. However, it does not allow transitions from a non *Normal* state to any other state. Therefore, the environment transition in *CSimpl* is defined as follows.

$$\begin{cases} \Gamma \vdash_c (P, Normal\ s) \longrightarrow_{env} (P, t) \\ (\forall t'.\ t \neq Normal\ t') \Longrightarrow \Gamma \vdash_c (P, t) \longrightarrow_{env} (P, t) \end{cases}$$

To adapt the restricted environment transition, we first define the environment transition in the adapter as $(\Gamma, \Theta) \vdash_{cI} (P, s) \longrightarrow_{env} (P, t)$, which allows any state transition and is compatible with that in the interface. Then, we restrict the rely condition in the definition of proof rules in the adapter to bridge this difference, which will be discussed later. Based on the transition functions, the computation function Ψ of the adapter is defined in the same form as in *CSimpl*.

The rely-guarantee specification in *CSimpl* is in the form $[p, R, G, (q, a)]$, where the postcondition (q, a) is a pair of state sets. The set q constrains the final state if the program terminates as *Skip* representing a normal state, whilst a constrains abrupt terminations in an exception with the command *Throw*. The assume and commit functions in *CSimpl* are like *PiCore*, but considering the fault states and abrupt termination. The validity function of *CSimpl* is defined in the same form as in *PiCore*. For procedure invocations, *CSimpl* defines another validity function using the general one, which also requires that each procedure satisfies its rely-guarantee specification.

We define the *assume, commit* and *validity* functions in the adapter as the same form as in *PiCore*. In *CSimpl* preconditions are over normal states. For type consistency *PiCore* does not impose that restriction, but rather it is enforced by the adapter to bridge the difference, which will be discussed later. *PiCore* does restrict the final statement to *Skip* thus exceptions have to be handled at program level. This restriction is motivated by the second assumption in the rule EVTSET for *PiCore* proof system in Fig. 4, since postconditions of events must imply their preconditions, and preconditions in *CSimpl* are sets of normal states, a final configuration of an event cannot throw an exception.

Finally, based on the definition of the proof rules $\Gamma, \Theta \vdash_{/F} P$ sat $[q, R, G, q, a]$ in *CSimpl*, we define proof rules in the adapter as follows. (1) The validity in *CSimpl* only concerns preconditions of *Normal* states, so we restrict the precondition p to *Normal*. (2) Programs of an event body cannot throw exceptions to the event level, so final states when reaching the final statement *Skip* are *Normal*. Thus, we restrict the postcondition q to *Normal*. (3) Events assume the normal execution of their program body, and furthermore the program cannot fall into a *Fault* state. So we assume the *Fault* set F to be empty. In addition, the program P should satisfy its rely-guarantee specification in *CSimpl*. (4) The environment transition in *CSimpl* does not allow transitions from a non *Normal* state to a different state, we represent it in the rely condition R. (5) Finally, the rely-guarantee specification for each procedure in Θ has to be satisfied.

$$(\Gamma, \Theta) \vdash_I P \; sat_p \; [p, \; R, \; G, \; q] \equiv \overbrace{(p \subseteq Normal \; ` \; UNIV)}^{(1)} \wedge \overbrace{(q \subseteq Normal \; ` \; UNIV)}^{(2)} \wedge$$

$$\overbrace{(\Gamma, \Theta \vdash_{/\{\}} P \; sat \; [\{s \mid Normal \; s \in p\}, \; R, \; G, \; \{s \mid Normal \; s \in q\}, \; UNIV])}^{(3)} \wedge$$

$$\overbrace{(\forall \, (s,t) \in R. \; s \notin Normal \; ` \; UNIV \longrightarrow s = t)}^{(4)} \wedge \overbrace{(\forall \, (c,p,R,G,q,a) \in \Theta. \; \Gamma, \{\} \vdash_{/\{\}} (Call \; c) \; sat \; [p, \; R, \; G, \; q,a])}^{(5)}$$

To interpret the *PiCore* framework using the adapter, we have to show that the assumptions in Table 2 are preserved on the adapted definitions. The preservation of assumptions 1–9 are straightforward. To show assumption 10, we prove that

$$(\Gamma, \Theta) \vdash_I P \; sat_p \; [p, \; R, \; G, \; q] \implies (\Gamma, \Theta) \models_I P \; sat_p \; [p, \; R, \; G, \; q]$$

5   Concurrent Memory Management of Zephyr RTOS

In this section, we use πIMP, the instantiation of *PiCore* with *IMP*, to formally specify and verify the concurrent memory management of Zephyr RTOS (for more detail refer to [29]). During the formal verification, we found 3 bugs in the C code of Zephyr: *an incorrect block split*, *an incorrect return*, and *non-termination of a loop* in the $k\_mem\_pool\_alloc$ service. The first two bugs are critical and have been repaired in the latest release of Zephyr.

The buddy memory allocation can split large blocks into smaller ones to fit as best as possible the requested size. This allows blocks of different sizes to be allocated and released efficiently while limiting memory fragmentation concerns. The memory is organized by levels, each "level n" block is a quad-block that can be split into four smaller "level (n+1)" blocks of equal size. This process is repeated until blocks reach a minimum level for which splitting is not possible. In our formal specification, we define the structure of a memory pool as illustrated in Fig. 7. The top of the figure shows the real memory of the first block at level 0.

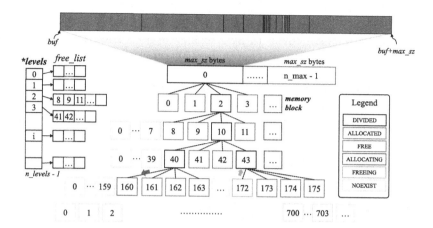

Fig. 7. Structure of memory pools

Thread preemption and fine-grained locking make kernel execution of memory services concurrent. Zephyr provides two kernel services $k\_mem\_pool\_alloc$ and $k\_mem\_pool\_free$, for memory allocation and release respectively. When an application requests a memory block, Zephyr first computes a value $free\_l$ that is the lowest level containing free memory blocks. Due to concurrency, when a service tries to allocate a free block blk from level $free\_l$, blocks at that level may be allocated or merged into a bigger block by other concurrent threads. In such a case the service will back out to retry. Allocation supports a *timeout* parameter to allow threads waiting for that pool for a period of time when the call does not succeed. If the allocation fails and the timeout is not K_NO_WAIT, the thread is suspended and the context is switched to another thread.

We define a rich set of *invariants* on the kernel state clarifying the constraints and consistency of quad trees, free block lists, memory pool configuration, and waiting threads. From the well-shaped properties of quad trees, we derive a critical property to prevent memory leaks: memory blocks cover the whole memory address of the pool, but do not overlap each other. Memory blocks of a memory pool mp are a partition of the pool where for any memory address $addr$ in the address space of a memory pool, i.e. $addr < n\_max * max\_sz$, there is one and only one memory block whose address space contains $addr$. The predicate is defined as follows.

addr-in-block mp $addr$ i j $\equiv$
$i < length\ (levels\ mp) \wedge j < length\ (bits\ (levels\ mp\ !\ i))$
$\wedge\ (is\_memblock(bits\ (levels\ mp\ !\ i)\ !\ j))$
$\quad \wedge\ addr \in \{x \mid j * (max\text{-}sz\ mp\ div\ (4\ \hat{}\ i)) \leqslant x < Suc\ j * (max\text{-}sz\ mp\ div\ (4\ \hat{}\ i))\}$
mem-part $s \equiv \forall p \in mem\text{-}pools\ s.$ **let** $mp = mem\text{-}pool\text{-}info\ s\ p$ **in**
$\quad\quad (\forall\ addr < n\text{-}max\ mp * max\text{-}sz\ mp.\ (\exists!(i,j).\ addr\text{-}in\text{-}block\ mp\ addr\ i\ j)\ )$

From the invariants of the well-shaped bitmap, we derive the general property for the memory partition.

Theorem 3 (Memory Partition). *For any kernel state s, If the memory pools in s are consistent in their configuration, and their bitmaps are well-shaped, the memory pools satisfy the partition property in s:*

$$inv\_mempool\_info\ s \land inv\_bitmap\ s \land inv\_bitmap0\ s \land inv\_bitmapn\ s \implies mem\_part\ s$$

In the formal specification, we consider a scheduler $\mathcal{S}$ and a set of threads $t_1, ..., t_n$. Each user thread t_i invokes allocation and release services, thus the event system for t_i is

$$esys_{t_i} \equiv (\bigcup blk.\ \{mem\_pool\_free[blk]@t_i\}) \cup$$

$$(\bigcup (p, sz, tmout).\ \{mem\_pool\_alloc[p, sz, tmout]@t_i\})$$

which is a set of *alloc* and *free* events, where the input parameters for these events correspond with the arguments of the service implementation in the C code. Events are parametrized by a thread identifier t_i used to control access to the execution context of the thread invoking it. Together with the threads we model the event service for the scheduler $esys_{sched}$ consisting of a unique event *sched* whose argument is a thread t to be scheduled when it is in the *READY* state. The formal specification of the memory management is thus defined as: Sys-Spec $\equiv \lambda$ k. case k of $(\mathcal{T}\ t_i) \Rightarrow esys_{t_i} \mid \mathcal{S} \Rightarrow esys_{sched}$. This is much simpler than the specification obtained from a non-event oriented language.

Using the compositional reasoning of πIMP, correctness of Zephyr memory management can be specified and verified with the rely-guarantee specification of each event. The functional correctness of a kernel service is specified by its pre/post conditions. The preservation of invariants, memory configuration, and separation of local variables is specified in the guarantee condition of each service. Although *IMP* does not have proof rules for loop termination, we use a logical variable α to parametrize the loop invariants and prove the termination of loop statements in Zephyr by finding a convergent relation to show that the number of iterations is finite.

The guarantee condition for both memory services is defined as:

$$\text{Mem-pool-free-guar}\ t \equiv \overbrace{Id}^{(1)} \cup (\overbrace{gvars\_conf\_stable}^{(2)} \cap$$

$$\overbrace{\{(s,r).\ (\overbrace{cur\ s \neq Some\ t}^{(3.1)} \longrightarrow gvars\text{-}nochange\ s\ r \land lvars\text{-}nochange\ t\ s\ r\ )}$$

$$\land\ (\overbrace{cur\ s = Some\ t}^{(3.2)} \longrightarrow inv\ s \longrightarrow inv\ r\ ) \land (\overbrace{\forall t'.\ t' \neq t}^{(4)} \longrightarrow lvars\text{-}nochange\ t'\ s\ r\ )\ \})$$

This relation states that a step from *alloc* or *free* may not change the state (1), e.g., selecting a branch on a conditional statement. If it changes the state then: (2) static configuration of memory pools in the model does not change; (3.1) if the scheduled thread is not the thread invoking the event then its local variables do not change; (3.2) if it is, then the relation preserves the memory invariant; (4) a thread does not change the local variables of other threads.

Using *PiCore* and *IMP* proof rules we verify that the invariant is preserved by all the events. Additionally, we prove that when starting in a valid memory configuration given by the invariant, and if the service does not return an error code, then it returns a valid memory block with size bigger or equal to the requested capacity.

6   Evaluation and Conclusion

Evaluation. We use Isabelle/HOL as the specification and verification system. All derivations of our proofs have passed through the Isabelle proof kernel. We use ≈9,200 lines of specification and proof (*LOSP*) to develop the *PiCore* framework. The *IMP* language and its rely-guarantee proof system consist of ≈2,400 *LOSP*, and *CSimpl* ≈15,000 *LOSP*. The two parts of specification and proof are completely reused in *πIMP* and *πCSimpl* respectively. The adapter of *IMP* is ≈650 *LOSP* including new proof rules and their soundness as well as a concrete syntax. The adapter of *CSimpl* is ≈400 *LOSP*. Finally, we develop ≈17,600 *LOSP* for the Zephyr case study, 40 times more than the lines of the C code due to the in-kernel concurrency, where invariant proofs represent the largest part.

Related Works. The rely-guarantee approach has been mechanized in Isabelle/HOL (e.g. [13,14,23,24,26]) and Coq (e.g. [18,20]). In [13,14], an abstract algebra of atomic steps is developed, and rely/guarantee concurrency is an interpretation of the algebra. To allow a meaningful comparison of rely-guarantee semantic models, two abstract models for rely-guarantee are developed and mechanized in [26]. None of both work consider any concrete imperative languages for rely-guarantee. The works [20,23] mechanize the rely-guarantee approach for simple imperative languages. Later, a rely-guarantee proof system is developed in Isabelle/HOL for *CSimpl* [24], a generic and realistic concurrent imperative language by extending the sequential language *Simpl* [25]. These mechanizations focus on imperative languages for pure programs, of which two of them [23,24] have been integrated in *PiCore*.

Refinement of reactive systems [5] and the subsequent Event-B approach [2] propose a refinement-based formal method for system-level modeling and analysis. In [15], an Event-B model is created to mimic rely-guarantee style reasoning for concurrent programs, but not to provide a rely-guarantee framework for Event-B. The rely-guarantee reasoning for event-based applications has been studied in [8–11]. The definition of events is similar to *PiCore*. They extend a simple, sequential, imperative language by primitives for announcing and consuming events, *announce(e)* and *consume(e(x))* where *e* is an event. Therefore, events are triggered by imperative programs in another event. This is very different from the reactive semantics in *PiCore* where the system is non-deterministically executed simulating a real reactive system. Moreover, the language to specify events in these works is a simple imperative language, whilst *PiCore* has an open interface for the integration and reusability of different languages and frameworks.

Conclusion and Future Work. In this paper, we propose an event-based rely-guarantee framework for concurrent reactive systems. This approach is open to the specification of event behaviours. It provides an interface to integrate systems for specification and reasoning at that level that eases formal methods reusability. We have mechanized the integration of the *IMP* and *CSimpl* languages and their proof systems into *PiCore* in the Isabelle/HOL theorem prover. We show the simplicity of events to represent concurrent reactive systems and the usefulness of *PiCore* for realistic systems in the verification of the concurrent buddy memory allocation of Zephyr RTOS. As future work, we plan to extend *PiCore* to support more event structures and step-wise refinement.

References

1. The Zephyr Project. https://www.zephyrproject.org/. Accessed December 2018
2. Abrial, J.R., Hallerstede, S.: Refinement, decomposition, and instantiation of discrete models: application to event-B. Fundamenta Informaticae **77**(1–2), 1–28 (2007)
3. Aceto, L., Ingólfsdóttir, A., Larsen, K., Srba, J.: Reactive Systems - Modeling, Specification and Verification. Cambridge University Press, Cambridge (2007)
4. Andronick, J., Lewis, C., Morgan, C.: Controlled Owicki-Gries concurrency: reasoning about the preemptible eChronos embedded operating system. In: Proceedings Workshop on Models for Formal Analysis of Real Systems MARS, pp. 10–24 (2015)
5. Back, R.J., Sere, K.: Superposition Refinement of Reactive Systems. Formal Aspects Comput. **8**(3), 324–346 (1996)
6. Back, R.J., Sere, K.: Stepwise refinement of action systems. Struct. Program. **12**, 17–30 (1991)
7. Chen, H., Wu, X., Shao, Z., Lockerman, J., Gu, R.: Toward compositional verification of interruptible OS kernels and device drivers. In: 37th ACM SIGPLAN Conference on Programming Language Design and Implementation (PLDI), pp. 431–447. ACM (2016)
8. Dingel, J., Garlan, D., Jha, S., Notkin, D.: Towards a formal treatment of implicit invocation using rely/guarantee reasoning. Formal Aspects Comput. **10**(3), 193–213 (1998)
9. Fenkam, P., Gall, H., Jazayeri, M.: Composing specifications of event based applications. In: Pezzè, M. (ed.) FASE 2003. LNCS, vol. 2621, pp. 67–86. Springer, Heidelberg (2003). https://doi.org/10.1007/3-540-36578-8_6
10. Fenkam, P., Gall, H., Jazayeri, M.: Constructing deadlock free event-based applications: a rely/guarantee approach. In: Araki, K., Gnesi, S., Mandrioli, D. (eds.) FME 2003. LNCS, vol. 2805, pp. 636–657. Springer, Heidelberg (2003). https://doi.org/10.1007/978-3-540-45236-2_35
11. Garlan, D., Jha, S., Notkin, D., Dingel, J.: Reasoning about implicit invocation. In: Proceedings of the 6th ACM SIGSOFT International Symposium on Foundations of Software Engineering (FSE), pp. 209–221. ACM, New York (1998)
12. Harel, D., Pnueli, A.: On the development of reactive systems. In: Apt, K.R. (ed.) Logics and Models of Concurrent Systems. NATO ASI Series (Series F: Computer and Systems Sciences), vol. 13, pp. 477–498. Springer, Heidelberg (1985). https://doi.org/10.1007/978-3-642-82453-1_17
13. Hayes, I.J.: Generalised rely-guarantee concurrency: an algebraic foundation. Formal Aspects Comput. **28**(6), 1057–1078 (2016)

14. Hayes, I.J., Colvin, R.J., Meinicke, L.A., Winter, K., Velykis, A.: An algebra of synchronous atomic steps. In: Fitzgerald, J., Heitmeyer, C., Gnesi, S., Philippou, A. (eds.) FM 2016. LNCS, vol. 9995, pp. 352–369. Springer, Cham (2016). https://doi.org/10.1007/978-3-319-48989-6_22
15. Hoang, T.S., Abrial, J.-R.: Event-B decomposition for parallel programs. In: Frappier, M., Glässer, U., Khurshid, S., Laleau, R., Reeves, S. (eds.) ABZ 2010. LNCS, vol. 5977, pp. 319–333. Springer, Heidelberg (2010). https://doi.org/10.1007/978-3-642-11811-1_24
16. Jones, C.B.: Tentative steps toward a development method for interfering programs. ACM Trans. Program. Lang. Syst. 5(4), 596–619 (1983)
17. Klein, G., et al.: seL4: formal verification of an OS kernel. In: Proceedings of ACM SIGOPS 22nd Symposium on Operating Systems Principles, SOSP 2009, Big Sky, Montana, USA, pp. 207–220. ACM Press (2009)
18. Liang, H., Feng, X., Fu, M.: A rely-guarantee-based simulation for verifying concurrent program transformations. In: 39th Annual ACM SIGPLAN-SIGACT Symposium on Principles of Programming Languages (POPL), pp. 455–468. ACM Press (2012)
19. Mantel, H., Sands, D., Sudbrock, H.: Assumptions and guarantees for compositional noninterference. In: 24th Computer Security Foundations Symposium (CSF), pp. 218–232. IEEE Press (2011)
20. Moreira, N., Pereira, D., de Sousa, S.M.: On the mechanisation of rely-guarantee in Coq. Universidade do Porto, Technical report (2013)
21. Murray, T., Matichuk, D., Brassil, M., Gammie, P., Klein, G.: Noninterference for operating system kernels. In: Hawblitzel, C., Miller, D. (eds.) CPP 2012. LNCS, vol. 7679, pp. 126–142. Springer, Heidelberg (2012). https://doi.org/10.1007/978-3-642-35308-6_12
22. Murray, T., Sison, R., Pierzchalski, E., Rizkallah, C.: Compositional verification and refinement of concurrent value-dependent noninterference. In: 29th IEEE Computer Security Foundations Symposium (CSF). IEEE Press (2016)
23. Nieto, L.P.: The rely-guarantee method in Isabelle/HOL. In: Degano, P. (ed.) ESOP 2003. LNCS, vol. 2618, pp. 348–362. Springer, Heidelberg (2003). https://doi.org/10.1007/3-540-36575-3_24
24. Sanán, D., Zhao, Y., Hou, Z., Zhang, F., Tiu, A., Liu, Y.: CSimpl: a rely-guarantee-based framework for verifying concurrent programs. In: Legay, A., Margaria, T. (eds.) TACAS 2017. LNCS, vol. 10205, pp. 481–498. Springer, Heidelberg (2017). https://doi.org/10.1007/978-3-662-54577-5_28
25. Schirmer, N.: Verification of Sequential Imperative Programs in Isabelle/HOL. Ph.D. thesis, Technical University Munich (2006)
26. van Staden, S.: On rely-guarantee reasoning. In: Hinze, R., Voigtländer, J. (eds.) MPC 2015. LNCS, vol. 9129, pp. 30–49. Springer, Cham (2015). https://doi.org/10.1007/978-3-319-19797-5_2
27. Xu, F., Fu, M., Feng, X., Zhang, X., Zhang, H., Li, Z.: A practical verification framework for preemptive OS kernels. In: Chaudhuri, S., Farzan, A. (eds.) CAV 2016. LNCS, vol. 9780, pp. 59–79. Springer, Cham (2016). https://doi.org/10.1007/978-3-319-41540-6_4
28. Xu, Q., de Roever, W.P., He, J.: The rely-guarantee method for verifying shared variable concurrent programs. Formal Aspects Comput. 9(2), 149–174 (1997)
29. Zhao, Y., Sanán, D.: Rely-guarantee reasoning about concurrent memory management in Zephyr RTOS. In: Dillig, I., Tasiran, S. (eds.) CAV 2019. LNCS, vol. 11562, pp. 515–533. Springer, Cham (2019). https://doi.org/10.1007/978-3-030-25543-5_29

Verifying Correctness of Persistent Concurrent Data Structures

John Derrick[1], Simon Doherty[1], Brijesh Dongol[2(✉)], Gerhard Schellhorn[3], and Heike Wehrheim[4]

[1] University of Sheffield, Sheffield, UK
[2] University of Surrey, Guildford, UK
b.dongol@surrey.ac.uk
[3] University of Augsburg, Augsburg, Germany
[4] Paderborn University, Paderborn, Germany

Abstract. Non-volatile memory (NVM), aka persistent memory, is a new paradigm for memory preserving its contents even after power loss. The expected ubiquity of NVM has stimulated interest in the design of *persistent* concurrent data structures, together with associated notions of correctness. In this paper, we present the first formal proof technique for *durable linearizability*, which is a correctness criterion that extends linearizability to handle crashes and recovery in the context of NVM. Our proofs are based on refinement of IO-automata representations of concurrent data structures. To this end, we develop a generic procedure for transforming any standard sequential data structure into a durable specification. Since the durable specification only exhibits durably linearizable behaviours, it serves as the abstract specification in our refinement proof. We exemplify our technique on a recently proposed persistent memory queue that builds on Michael and Scott's lock-free queue.

1 Introduction

Recent technological advances indicate that future architectures will employ some form of *non-volatile memory* (NVM) that retains its contents after a system crash (e.g., power outage). NVM is intended to be used as an intermediate layer between traditional *volatile memory* (VM) and secondary storage and has the potential to vastly improve system speed and stability. Software that uses NVM has the potential to be more robust; in case of a crash, a system state before the crash may be recovered using contents from NVM, as opposed to being restarted from secondary storage. However, because the same data is stored in both a volatile and non-volatile manner, and because NVM is updated at a slower rate than VM, recovery to a consistent state may not always be possible. This is particularly true for concurrent systems, where coping with NVM requires introduction of additional synchronisation instructions into a program.

Derrick, Dongol and Doherty are supported by EPSRC grants EP/R032351/1, EP/R032556/2, EP/R019045/2; Wehrheim by DFG grant WE 2290/12-1.

© Springer Nature Switzerland AG 2019
M. H. ter Beek et al. (Eds.): FM 2019, LNCS 11800, pp. 179–195, 2019.
https://doi.org/10.1007/978-3-030-30942-8_12

Recently, researchers have developed *persistent* extensions to existing concurrent objects (e.g., concurrent data structures or transactional memory). This work has been accompanied by extensions to known notions of consistency, such as linearizability and opacity that cope with crashes and subsequent recovery.

In this paper, we examine correctness of the recently developed persistent queue by Friedman et al. [11], against the (also) recently developed notion of *durable linearizability* [14]. Friedman et al.'s queue extends the well-known Michael-Scott queue [20], whereas durable linearizability extends the standard notion of linearizability [12] so that completed executions are guaranteed to survive a system crash.

Our verification follows a well-established methodology: (1) we develop an operational model of durable linearizability that is parameterised by a generic sequential object (e.g., a queue data structure with enqueue and dequeue operations), (2) we prove that this operational model is sound, and (3) we establish a series of refinements between the operational model and the concrete implementation. The final (and most complex) of these steps, which establishes that the implementation refines the operational model, is fully mechanised in the KIV theorem prover [10]. It is important to note that the operational model is generic and for any particular verification one needs therefore just to establish step (3) in order to show that a particular algorithm is durable linearizable.

Ours is the first paper to address formal verification of persistent data structures. We consider the development of our sound operational characterisation of durable linearizability and the refinement proofs, including mechanisation in KIV, to be the main contributions of this paper. The mechanisation and the full version of the paper may be accessed from [17].

We present Friedman et al.'s queue in Sect. 2, durable linearizability in Sect. 3, an operational characterisation of durable linearizability in Sect. 4, and address correctness of the queue in Sect. 5.

2   A Persistent Queue

The persistent queue of Friedman et al. [11] is an extension of the Michael-Scott queue (MSQ) [20] to cope with NVM (see Algorithms 1 and 2). The MSQ uses a linked list of nodes with global head and tail pointers. The first node is a sentinel that simplifies handling of empty queues. The MSQ is initialised by allocating a dummy node with a null next pointer, then setting the global head and tail pointers to this dummy node.

The enqueue operation creates a new node that is inserted at the end of the linked list. The insertion is performed using an atomic compare-and-swap (CAS) instruction that atomically updates the *next* pointer of the last node provided this next pointer hasn't changed since it was read at the beginning of the enqueue operation. The CAS returns true if it succeeds and false otherwise. Immediately after a new node is inserted, the tail pointer is *lagging* one node behind the true tail of the queue, and hence, must be updated to point to the last node in a separate step.

Algorithm 1. Constructors

```
1: class NODE                        1: class DURABLEQUEUE
2: T val;                            2: Node* head;
3: Node* next;                       3: Node* tail;
4: int deqID;                        4: T* RVals[MAX];
5: Node(T k):                        5: DURABLEQUEUE()
6:    val(k), deqID(-1), next(null); 6:    T* node := new Node(T());
                                     7:    flush(node);
                                     8:    head := node;
                                     9:    flush(&head);
                                    10:    tail := node;
                                    11:    flush(&tail);
                                    12:    RVals[i] := null; //all i
                                    13:    flush(&RVals[i]);
```

The dequeue operation returns empty if the head and tail pointer both point to the sentinel node and the tail is not lagging. If the queue is not empty, the dequeue reads from the value of the node immediately after the sentinel and atomically swings the head pointer to this next node provided it has not changed. Thereby, the next node becomes the new sentinel node of the queue.

A key feature of MSQ is a *helping mechanism* where a different thread from the original enqueue may advance the tail pointer if it is lagging. In the case of a dequeue, this only occurs if head and tail pointers are equal, but the queue is not empty.

Friedman et al. [11] adapt MSQ to a system comprising both VM and NVM. In such systems, computations take place in VM as normal, but data is periodically flushed to NVM by the system. In addition to system controlled flushes, a programmer may introduce explicit **flush** events that transfer data from VM to NVM. Only data in NVM persists after a crash (e.g., power loss). A persistent data structure must enable recovery from such an event, as opposed to a full system restart. In doing this, it must ensure some notion of consistency in the presence of crashes and a subsequent recovery operation. Following Friedman et al. [11], the notion of consistency we use is durable linearizability (see Sect. 3).

The persistent queue uses the same underlying data structure as MSQ (see Algorithm 1), but nodes contain an additional field, deqID (initialised to -1), which holds the ID of the thread that removed the node from the queue. In addition to the head and tail pointers, it uses an array of pointers, RVals, with one index for each thread, containing either null (which is the initial value), of a pointer to a cell which itself either contains empty (which signifies that the thread last saw an empty queue), or a value (which is the value that was last dequeued). Unlike MSQ, the persistent dequeue operation does not return a value; instead the returned value for tid is stored in the cell pointed to by RVals[tid].

Persistent Enqueue. The basic structure (see Algorithm 2) is the same as the enqueue of MSQ. In addition, to ensure that the linked list data structure

Algorithm 2. Enqueue and dequeue methods of Friedman et al. [11]

```
1: procedure ENQ(T val)                  1: procedure DEQ(int tid)
2: Node* node := new Node(val);          2: T* newRVal := new T();
3: flush(node);                          3: flush(newRVal);
4: while true do                         4: RVals[tid] := newRVal;
5:   Node* last := tail;                 5: flush(&RVals[tid]);
6:   Node* nxt := last→next;             6: while true do
7:   if (last = tail)                    7:   Node* first := head;
8:    if (nxt = null)                    8:   Node* last := tail;
9:     if CAS(&last→next,nxt,node)       9:   Node* nxt := first→next;
10:       flush(&last→next);            10:   if (first = head)
11:       CAS(&tail, last, node);       11:    if (first = last)
12:       return;                       12:     if (nxt = null)
13:    else                             13:      *RVals[tid] := empty;
14:       flush(&last→next);            14:      flush(RVals[tid]);
15:       CAS(&tail, last, nxt);        15:      return;
                                        16:     flush(&last→next);
                                        17:     CAS(&tail, last, nxt);
                                        18:    else
                                        19:     T val := nxt→val;
                                        20:     if CAS(&nxt→deqID,-1,tid)
                                        21:      flush(&nxt→deqID);
                                        22:      *RVals[tid] := val;
                                        23:      flush(RVals[tid]);
                                        24:      CAS(&head, first, nxt);
                                        25:      return;
                                        26:     else
                                        27:      T* addr:=RVals[nxt→deqID];
                                        28:      if (head = first)
                                        29:       flush(&nxt→deqID);
                                        30:       *addr := val;
                                        31:       flush(addr);
                                        32:       CAS(&head,first,nxt);
```

is recoverable after a crash, nodes and next pointers have to be persisted after being modified in VM.

This is achieved by using three **flush** operations in lines 3, 10 and 14. The first ensures that the node is persisted before it is inserted into the queue; the second and third ensure that the next pointer of a lagging tail pointer is persisted before the tail is advanced. Note that updates to tail do not need to be explicitly flushed because it can be recomputed during recovery by traversing the persistent list.

Persistent Dequeue. The basic structure of the dequeue operation also resembles the dequeue of MSQ. In addition it uses variables RVals and deqID to guarantee durable linearizability. RVals is an array of pointers to cells that are used to store the value returned by each dequeue. A dequeue creates a new cell at

Line 2, then flushes it at Line 3. The pointer to this cell is stored in `RVals` at Line 4, and this pointer is made persistent at Line 5.

The `deqID` field is used to logically mark nodes that are dequeued, which occurs at the successful CAS at Line 20. This logical dequeue is made persistent by flushing the `deqID` at Line 21. After a node has been logically dequeued, the dequeued value is stored in the cell pointed to by `RVals[tid]` (see Line 22) where `tid` is the thread ID of the dequeuing thread. This dequeued value is made persistent at Line 23. A dequeue by thread `tid` stores `empty` in `RVals[tid]` if the queue is empty in Line 13, and this value is made persistent at Line 14.

The persistent dequeue operation employs an additional helping mechanism to ensure that these new fields are made persistent in the correct order. In particular, a node that has been logically dequeued in VM must be made persistent before another dequeue is allowed to succeed. Therefore, if a thread recognises that `deqID` is not −1 at Line 20, it helps the other thread by flushing the `deqID` field, writing the dequeued value into the cell pointed to by `RVals[nxt→tid]`, flushing this cell, and finally advancing the head pointer. Note that the helping thread may be delayed between the read at Line 27 and the write at Line 30, and the original thread `tid` may begin a new dequeue operation in this interval. In this case, since `tid` allocates a fresh cell at Line 2, the helping thread's write at Line 30 will harmlessly modify a previous cell.

After a crash, and prior to resuming normal operation, persistent data structures must perform a *recovery* operation that restores the state of the data structure in VM from NVM. The recovery procedure proposed by Friedman et al. is multithreaded (and complex), so we elide its details here. Instead, we provide a simpler single-threaded recovery operation (see Sect. 5.1).

3   Durable Linearizability

We now define *durable linearizability* [14], a central correctness condition for persistent concurrent data structures. Like linearizability, durable linearizability is defined over *histories* recording the *invocation* and *response* events of operations executed on the concurrent data structure. Unlike linearizability, durably linearizable histories include crash events.

Formally, we let Σ be the set of operations. For a queue, $\Sigma = \{\mathtt{Enq}, \mathtt{Deq}\}$. A history is a sequence of events, each of which is either (a) an invocation of an operation op by a thread $t \in T$ with values $\boldsymbol{v}$, written $inv_t(op, \boldsymbol{v})$, (b) responses of op in thread t with value v, written $res_t(op, v)$, or (c) a system-wide crash c.

Given a history h, we let $ops(h)$ denote h restricted to non-crash events, and $h_{|t}$ denote h restricted to (non-crash) events of thread $t \in T$. The crash events partition a history into $h = h_0 c_1 h_1 c_2 ... h_{n-1} c_n h_n$, such that n is the number of crash events in h, c_i is the ith crash event and $ops(h_i) = h_i$ (i.e., h_i contains no crash events). We call the subhistory h_i the i-th era of h. For a history h and events e_1, e_2, we write $e_1 <_h e_2$ whenever $h = h_0 e_1 h_1 e_2 h_2$.

A history h is said to be *sequential* iff every invocation event (except if it is the last event in h) is immediately followed by its corresponding response event;

it is *well formed* if and only if (a) $h_{|t}$ is sequential for every thread t and (b) each thread id appears in at most one era. Any invocation that is not followed by its response event is called a *pending* invocation. We consider well-formed histories only. A history h defines a *happens-before* ordering on the events occuring in h by letting $e_1 \prec_h e_2$ iff $e_1 <_h e_2$ and e_1 is a response and e_2 an invocation event. Linearizability (and durable linearizability) requires a notion of a *legal history*, which we define using a sequential object. Every history of a sequential object is both sequential and legal.

Definition 1 (Sequential Object). *A sequential object over a base type Val is a 5-tuple* $(\Sigma, S, s_0, in, \rho)$ *where*

- Σ *is an* alphabet *of operations,* S *is a set of states and* s_0 *the initial state,*
- $in : \Sigma \to \mathbb{N}$ *is an input function telling us the number of inputs an operation* $op \in \Sigma$ *takes, and*
- $\rho : S \times \Sigma \times Val^* \to S \times (Val \cup \{\texttt{empty}, \bot\})$ *is a partial* transition function.

We assume outputs of operations to consist of a single value which possibly is the symbol $\texttt{empty}$ or no value denoted by $\bot$. In the following we let $\boldsymbol{v} = v_1 v_2 \ldots v_n$ denote a string of n elements and write $\#\boldsymbol{v}$ to denote its length n. We write $inv_t(op, \boldsymbol{v})$ for an invocation of the operation op with $n = \#\boldsymbol{v}$ inputs by thread t and let Inv be the set of all such invocations. Similarly, we let Res be the set of all responses.

The *legal* histories of a sequential object $\mathbb{S} = (\Sigma, S, s_0, in, \rho)$ are defined as follows. We write $s \xrightarrow{inv_t(op,v)res_t(op,v)} s'$ for $\rho(s, op, \boldsymbol{v}) = (s', v)$ and $t \in T$. For a sequence w of invocations and responses, we write $s \xrightarrow{w} s'$ iff either $w = \langle\rangle$ and $s = s'$, or $w = u \circ w'$ and there exists an s'' such that $s \xrightarrow{u} s''$ and $s'' \xrightarrow{w'} s'$. The set of *legal histories* of $\mathbb{S}$ is given by $legal_\mathbb{S} = \{w \in (Inv \cup Res)^* \mid \exists s \in S.\, s_0 \xrightarrow{w} s\}$.

Example 2. A sequential queue, $\mathbb{Q}$, storing elements of type V is defined by $\Sigma = \{\texttt{Enq}, \texttt{Deq}\}$, $in(\texttt{Enq}) = 1$, $in(\texttt{Deq}) = 0$, $q_0 = \langle\rangle$, and

$$\rho = \{\big((q, \texttt{Enq}, v), (q \cdot v, \bot)\big) \mid v \in V \land q \in V^*\} \cup$$
$$\{\big((v \cdot q, \texttt{Deq}, \varepsilon), (q, v)\big) \mid v \in V \land q \in V^*\} \cup \{\big((\langle\rangle, \texttt{Deq}, \varepsilon), (\langle\rangle, \texttt{empty})\big)\}$$

where ε is the empty string, $\langle\rangle$ is the empty sequence and $\cdot$ is used for sequence concatenation. For $\mathbb{Q}$, the history h below is sequential and legal

$$h = \langle inv_1(\texttt{Enq}, a), res_1(\texttt{Enq}, \bot), inv_2(\texttt{Deq}, \varepsilon), res_2(\texttt{Deq}, a)\rangle$$

whereas the history $h \cdot \langle inv_3(\texttt{Deq}, \varepsilon), res_3(\texttt{Deq}, b)\rangle$ is sequential but not legal.

For the definition of durable linearizability some more notation is needed. We write $h \equiv h'$ if $h_{|t} = h'_{|t}$ for all threads t. We let $compl(h)$ (the completion) be the set of histories that can be obtained from h by appending (some) missing responses at the end, and use $trunc(h)$ to remove pending invocations from a history h (or a set of histories). Following Herlihy and Wing [12], h is *linearizable* if there is some $h' \in trunc(compl(h))$ and some legal sequential history h_S such that (i) $h' \equiv h_S$ and (ii) $\forall e_1, e_2 \in h' : e_1 \prec_{h'} e_2 \Rightarrow e_1 \prec_{h_S} e_2$.

For durable linearizability, this definition is now simply lifted to histories with crashes.

Definition 3 (Durable Linearizability [14]). *A history h is* durably linearizable *if it is well formed and $ops(h)$ is linearizable.*

Informally, durable linearizability guarantees that even after a crash the state of the concurrent object remains consistent with the abstract specification. This means that the effect of any operations that completed before a crash are preserved after the crash. The effect of operations that did not complete before a crash may or may not be preserved. For example, the concurrent history

$$hc = \langle inv_1(\mathsf{Enq}, a), inv_3(\mathsf{Deq}, \varepsilon), res_1(\mathsf{Enq}, \perp), c, inv_2(\mathsf{Deq}, \varepsilon), res_2(\mathsf{Deq}, a) \rangle$$

is durably linearizable since $ops(hc) = \langle inv_1(\mathsf{Enq}, a), inv_3(\mathsf{Deq}, \varepsilon), res_1(\mathsf{Enq}, \perp), inv_2(\mathsf{Deq}, \varepsilon), res_2(\mathsf{Deq}, a) \rangle$ is linearizable with respect to the history h in Example 2. On the other hand the history

$$\langle inv_1(\mathsf{Enq}, a), inv_3(\mathsf{Enq}, b), res_1(\mathsf{Enq}, \perp), c, inv_2(\mathsf{Deq}, \varepsilon), res_2(\mathsf{Deq}, \mathtt{empty}) \rangle$$

is not durably linearizable since the effect of the completed operation $\mathsf{Enq}(a)$ is not preserved after the crash.

Our methodology for proving durable linearizability does not use Definition 3 directly; instead it uses the following characterisation, which defines the set of all durably linearizable histories for a sequential object. We let $\mathrm{LIN}(\mathbb{S})$ be the set of histories linearizable wrt. the legal histories of sequential object $\mathbb{S}$ and define

$$\mathrm{DURLIN}(\mathbb{S}) = \{h \in (Inv \cup Res \cup \{c\})^* \mid ops(h) \in \mathrm{LIN}(\mathbb{S})\}$$

For a given concurrent durable data structure implementing a sequential object $\mathbb{S}$, proving its correctness thus amounts to showing that all histories of the implementation are in $\mathrm{DURLIN}(\mathbb{S})$. To this end, for a given $\mathbb{S}$, we develop an operational model $\mathrm{DURAUT}(\mathbb{S})$ whose behaviours generate $\mathrm{DURLIN}(\mathbb{S})$. We then use a standard refinement approach to show that the implementation model is a refinement of $\mathrm{DURAUT}(\mathbb{S})$. This is enough to guarantee that the original implementation is durably linearizable.

4   An Operational Model for Durable Linearizability

The operational model for durable linearizability is formalised in terms of an *Input/Output automaton (IOA)* [18]. This framework is often used for proving linearizability via refinement [9].

$inv_t(op, \boldsymbol{v})$
Pre: $pc(t) = ready$
　　$\#\boldsymbol{v} = in(op)$
Eff: $pc(t) := inv(op)$
　　$\boldsymbol{val}(t) := \boldsymbol{v}$

$do_t(op)$
Pre: $pc(t) = inv(op)$
Eff: $pc(t) := res(op)$
　　$(s, out(t)) := \rho(s, op, \boldsymbol{val}(t))$

$res_t(op, v)$
Pre: $pc(t) = res(op)$
　　$v = out(t)$
Eff: $pc(t) := ready$

run_t
Pre: $pc(t) = idle$
Eff: $pc(t) := ready$

$crash$
Pre: $true$
Eff: $pc := \lambda t : T.\mathbf{if}\ pc(t) \neq idle\ \mathbf{then}\ crashed\ \mathbf{else}\ pc(t)$

$states(A) : pc : T \rightarrow \{idle, ready, crashed\} \cup \{inv(op), res(op) \mid op \in \Sigma\}$
$s : S$ (the state of the sequential object)
$\boldsymbol{val} : T \rightarrow Val^*$ (values of inputs)
$out : T \rightarrow Val$ (the value of the output)
$start(A) : \forall t \in T : pc(t) = idle \wedge \boldsymbol{val}(t) = \epsilon \wedge out(t) = \epsilon \wedge s = s_0$

Fig. 1. Durable automaton $A = \textsc{DurAut}(\mathbb{S})$ for $\mathbb{S} = (\Sigma, S, s_0, in, \rho)$

Definition 4. *An IOA is a labeled transition system A with*

- *a set of states $states(A)$,*
- *a set of start states $start(A) \subseteq states(A)$,*
- *a set of actions $acts(A)$, and*
- *a transition relation $trans(A) \subseteq states(A) \times acts(A) \times states(A)$ (so that the actions label the transitions).*

The set $acts(A)$ is partitioned into *internal* actions, $internal(A)$ and *external* actions, $external(A)$.[1] The internal actions represent events of the system that are not visible to the environment, whereas the external actions represent the automaton's interactions with its environment.

An *execution* of an IOA A is a sequence $\sigma = s_0 a_1 s_1 a_2 s_2 a_3 \ldots$ of alternating states and actions such that $s_0 \in start(A)$ and for each i, $(s_i, a_{i+1}, s_{i+1}) \in trans(A)$. A *reachable* state of A is a state appearing in an execution of A. An *invariant* of A is any superset of the reachable states of A (equivalently, any predicate satisfied by all reachable states of A). A *trace* of A is any sequence of (external) actions obtained by projecting onto the external actions of any execution of A. The set of traces of A, $traces(A)$, represents A's externally visible behaviour. If every trace of an automaton C is also a trace of an automaton A, then we say that C *implements* or *refines* A.

For an arbitrary sequential object $\mathbb{S}$, we next construct a durable automaton $\textsc{DurAut}(\mathbb{S})$ (see Fig. 1) whose traces are histories in $\textsc{DurLin}(\mathbb{S})$ only. This automaton can serve as a specification automaton in a refinement proof. The state of this automaton incorporates the state s of the sequential object $\mathbb{S}$, plus for every thread $t \in T$:

---

[1] In the standard IOA setting, external actions are further subdivided into input and output actions; this distinction is not needed for this current work.

- a program counter fixing whether the thread is still *idle*, is *ready* to be started, is *crashed* (i.e., has been active during a crash), or is currently executing an operation,
- possible input values of the thread's operations and a possible output value.

The transition relation of the automaton is – as usual – given in the form of pre- and postconditions of actions. For every operation op in the sequential object, the automaton has actions $inv(op)$, $do(op)$ and $res(op)$, where $do(op)$ corresponds to execution of the abstract operation op, potentially changing the state of the sequential object. We use $inv_t(op, v)$ and $res_t(op, v)$ for $inv(op)_t(v)$ and $res(op)_t(v)$, respectively. Any step of the implementation that refines $do(op)$ is a step that persists the corresponding operation op (i.e., a *persistence point*, see Sect. 5). Persistence points in durable linearizability are analogous to linearization points in linearizability [9]. Note that a thread may only invoke an operation if it is *ready*. We furthermore have a dedicated *crash* action that may be executed at any time that sets all active threads to *crashed*. To ensure that crashed threads are confined to a single era, we use a separate action *run* that enables idle threads to become *ready*. While $inv(op)$, $res(op)$ and *crash* are external actions, *run* and $do(op)$ are internal.

The theorem below ensures that traces of the durable automaton are the durably linearizable histories of $\mathbb{S}$.

Theorem 5. *If $\mathbb{S}$ is a sequential object, then $traces(\textsc{DurAut}(\mathbb{S})) \subseteq \textsc{DurLin}(\mathbb{S})$.*

Proof. Let $\sigma = cs_0 a_1 cs_1 \ldots a_n cs_n$ be an execution of $\textsc{DurAut}(\mathbb{S})$ and let $cs_i.s$, $cs_i.out$ etc. be the components of state cs_i. Let tr be the trace of σ. We construct the history h by making the following changes to tr (in this order).

Completion For every a_i being a do action $do_t(op)$ in σ without matching $res_t(op)$, we add $res_t(op, v)$ such that $v = cs_i.out(t)$ to the end of tr.

Truncation We remove all $inv_t(op, v)$ without matching response.

Next, we need to construct a legal sequential history h_S such that $ops(h) \equiv h_S$. Let $i_1, \ldots, i_k$ be the indices of σ such that a_{i_j} is a do action $do_t(op)$. Then $\rho(cs_{i_{j-1}}.s, op, v) = (cs_{i_j}.s, cs_{i_j}.out(t))$ by definition of the durable automaton. We set

$$w_{i_j} = inv_t(op, v)\, res_t(op, cs_{i_j}.out(t)) \ .$$

We let $h_S = w_{i_1} \ldots w_{i_k}$ and $h_S \in legal(\mathbb{S})$.

Now assume $e_1 \prec_h e_2$. By definition, $e_1 = res_t(op, v)$ and $e_2 = inv_{t'}(op', v)$ for some $t, t' \in T$. Then e_1 has not been added to the trace tr by completion since responses are added to the end. By construction of the durable automaton threads execute inv, do and res operations in this ordering only. Hence the execution σ contains an action $do_t(op)$ prior to e_1 and an action $do_{t'}(op')$ following e_2. Hence $e_1 \prec_{h_S} e_2$. □

In fact, we believe that the two sets in Theorem 5 are equal. However, we do not need this property for our proof methodology.

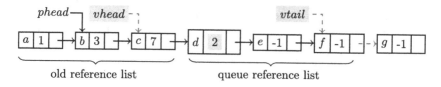

old reference list   queue reference list

Fig. 2. Possible state of persistent queue; volatile data represented using shading and volatile pointers represented using dashed arrows

5   Correctness of the Persistent Queue

In this section we present a formal verification of the persistent queue. In Section 5.1, we describe a model of the queue. In Sect. 5.2 we describe the application of the refinement-based verification to this example, where we establish the relationship between an intermediate automaton and the durable automaton. Section 5.3 describes the persistence points in the concrete implementation that are used in the proof, and Sect. 5.4 describes the main invariants and abstraction relations.

5.1   Modelling the Persistent Queue

To verify durable linearizability we need to model the persistent queue. The persistent queue contains two versions of each variable: one in VM and one in NVM. We model this in the automaton by two mappings $ps, vs : Loc \rightarrow X$, where Loc is a set of locations and X is a generic set that contains enqueued values, references, thread ids, etc. Mappings ps and vs represent the persistent and volatile states, respectively. A flush of location k updates the value of $ps(k)$ to $vs(k)$, while recovery moves data from $ps(k)$ to $vs(k)$. All other operations take place in $vs(k)$.

In order to help illustrate the structure of the queue, Fig. 2 depicts a possible state of the persistent queue. Each node contains three values: a data value, a thread id (possibly -1, which is the initial value), and a next pointer. Variables *phead* and *vhead* are the persistent and volatile head pointers, respectively, and *vtail* is the volatile tail pointer. In the KIV model $phead = ps(head)$, $vhead = vs(head)$, etc. The values depicted by shading and the dashed arrows in the figure are volatile; in Fig. 2, these are the `deqID` of node d and the next pointer of node f, as well as the volatile head and tail pointers. Here enqueues for nodes labelled a to f have all taken place and persisted, whereas node labelled g has been partly enqueued but not yet persisted. Nodes labelled a to c have been dequeued and persisted, but the node labelled d has been marked for dequeue, but not persisted. Here, the *phead* is lagging behind *vhead*; in an execution, *phead* may be lagging by an arbitrary amount as the flush of *vhead* is controlled by the system as opposed to an explicit flush statement in the program code.

The persistent contents of the queue (which we refer to as the *queue reference list*) corresponds to the abstract queue $\langle d, e, f \rangle$. In addition, our proof makes use

$inv_t(op, \boldsymbol{v})$
Pre: $pc(t) = ready$
   $\#\boldsymbol{v} = in(op)$
Eff: $pc(t) := inv(op)$
   $\boldsymbol{val}(t) := \boldsymbol{v}$
   $obsEmp(t) := false$

$do_t(op)$
Pre: $pc(t) = inv(op)$
Eff: $pc(t) := res(op)$
   $(q, out(t)) := \rho(q, op, \boldsymbol{val}(t))$

$res_t(Enq)$
Pre: $pc(t) = res(Enq)$
Eff: $pc(t) := ready$

$res_t(Deq, v)$
Pre: $pc(t) = res(Deq)$
   $v = out(t)$
Eff: $pc(t) := ready$

$do_t(Deq)$
Pre: $pc(t) = inv(Deq)$
   $obsEmp(t)$
Eff: $pc(t) := res(Deq)$
   $out(t) := \textbf{empty}$

$checkEmp_t$
Pre: $pc(t) = inv(Deq)$
   $q = \langle\rangle$
Eff: $obsEmp(t) := true$

run_t
Pre: $pc(t) = idle$
Eff: $pc(t) := ready$

$crash$
Pre: $true$
Eff: $pc := \lambda t : T.\textbf{if } pc(t) \neq idle \textbf{ then } crashed \textbf{ else } pc(t)$

$states(IDQ) : pc : T \to \{idle, ready, crashed\} \cup \{inv(op), res(op) \mid op \in \Sigma\}$

$q : V^*$ (the state of the sequential queue)

$val : T \to V^*$ (values of inputs)

$out : T \to V \cup \{\bot\}$ (the value of the output)

$obsEmp : T \to \mathbb{B}$

Fig. 3. The intermediate automaton IDQ

of the so called old reference list, which are elements that had been persistently enqueued, but have also been persistently dequeued.

5.2 Refinement-Based Verification

As outlined in Sect. 3, we verify durable linearizability by proving refinement between the implementation model and DURAUT($\mathbb{Q}$) using the IO automata formalism introduced in Sect. 4. Refinement can be proven via *forward* or *backward simulations* [19]; such simulations allow a step-by-step comparison between the operations using an abstraction relation. In our proof, we establish a backward simulation between the intermediate automaton and DURAUT($\mathbb{Q}$) as well as a forward simulation between the implementation of the persistent queue and the intermediate automaton. The proof uses an intermediate automaton that resolves non-determinism at the abstract level as used in existing proofs of MSQ [8,9]. Since refinement guarantees trace inclusion, this is sufficient to show that the persistent queue is durably linearizable.

The intermediate automaton IDQ, presented in Fig. 3, is similar to the durable automaton for the queue datatype, DURAUT($\mathbb{Q}$) (see Fig. 1 instantiated for the queue from Example 2). As with DURAUT($\mathbb{Q}$), it has variables pc, val and out, which play the same role, and variable q instantiates the state s.

Furthermore, all its actions except for *checkEmp* are also actions of $\text{DurAut}(\mathbb{Q})$, and have essentially the same effect. For *IDQ* we get the following property[2].

Theorem 6. $traces(IDQ) \subseteq traces(\text{DurAut}(\mathbb{Q}))$.

The additional features of *IDQ* exist to model a behaviour where a dequeue thread first *observes* that the queue is empty, and later decides to return empty, at a point when the queue may no longer *be* empty. The observation is modelled by a $checkEmp_t$ action, which records in the $obsEmp_t$ variable the fact that the queue was empty during the execution of t's dequeue operation. In this automaton, it is possible for a thread t to execute a $do_t(Deq)$ transition and set the output value to empty whenever $obsEmp(t)$ has been set to *true*. We note that the queue may not actually be empty when this transition takes place, but this does not affect soundness of the proof method since $obsEmp(t)$ being set to *true* indicates that the queue has been empty at *some point* during the operation's execution. Further details of this technique, in the context of linearizability, may be found in [4,8,9].

5.3   Identification of Persistence Points

To match executions of the concrete implementation with the abstract level, we must identify the *persistence points* of the implementation, which are atomic events whose execution causes the effect of the corresponding operations to take effect at the abstract level. These are analogous to standard linearizability, where proofs proceed via identification of *linearization points* [9]. In durable linearizability, persistence points are typically statements (flush events) that cause the operation under consideration to become durable. Thus these statements must be simulated by the abstract *do* operation. Note that persistent points must occur after an operation has taken effect in NVM, but before the operation returns.

In MSQ, the enqueue operation linearizes upon successful execution of the CAS at line 9. However, in the persistent queue, this line is not the persistence point of the operation, rather it is the first operation that *flushes the effect of this CAS*, i.e., the first flush of the next pointer to the enqueued element. This may occur in line 10 of the same thread, line 14 executed by another thread, or due to a system-controlled flush. Despite there being several possible choices for the persistence point, it is possible to prove forward simulation with respect to the *do(Enq)* operation of the intermediate automaton *IDQ*.

The verification of the empty dequeue follows a similar pattern to the verification of the empty dequeue of MSQ. The persistence point is conditional on the future execution of the operation, thus we refer to the persistence point as a *potential persistence point* (this is similar to the concept of potential linearization points [4,8,9]). The empty dequeue potentially takes effect at line 9 if the value

---

[2] For the proof, see the full paper at [17].

loaded for **nxt** is **null**, but this decision is not resolved until later in the operation (line 12). Using the intermediate automaton (Fig. 3), it allows the proof to proceed via forward simulation, like earlier proofs of linearizability [8,9].

A non-empty dequeue linearizes in VM when the node that is dequeued is marked for deletion by updating its **deqID** field at line 20. Like the enqueue, the persistence point of the dequeue is the first flush of this **deqID** field. This may occur either at line 21 of the same thread, line 29 of another thread, or a system flush. Again, we show that each of these steps simulates the *do(Deq)* operation of the intermediate automaton.

5.4 Key Invariants and Abstraction Relation

There are several key properties that the persistent queue must maintain in order to ensure correctness. These are formalised as invariants in our proof. Here we describe them in plain English:

1. We keep track of two sublists: *old reference list*, which are elements that have been dequeued, and *queue reference list*, which are elements that form the current queue. Formalising the structure of these lists and ensuring global correctness of the invariant is one of the most difficult parts of the proof. This is particularly true for steps that correspond to persistence points (see below) since the volatile pointers can be "lagging" immediately after persistence.
2. All nodes of the queue must be reachable in NVM (i.e., *ps*) from *phead*. This means that the nodes including the next pointers must be made persistent prior to inserting a new node.
3. All nodes in the old reference list must have a **deqID** field different from -1 in *ps*, indicating that they have been dequeued.
4. All nodes in the queue reference list must have a **deqID** field value -1 in *ps*.
5. Only the first node in queue reference list may have a **deqID** field value different from -1 in *vs*.
6. Pointers *phead* and *ptail* may be lagging behind *vhead* and *vtail*, respectively. However, *vhead* may not overtake *vtail*.

We now describe the state of the queue after execution of some key steps of the algorithm.

Dequeue Persistence Point. A node is considered to be dequeued if its logical deletion is flushed, i.e., the **deqID** marked by a thread id is flushed. For the queue depicted in Fig. 2, the queue immediately after the volatile **deqID** of node *d* is flushed is as follows.

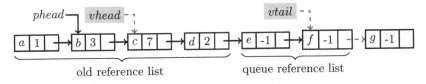

The abstract queue corresponding to this queue is $\langle e, f \rangle$. Note that in the queue above, *vhead* pointer is now lagging and must be updated to point to the new sentinel node d.

Enqueue Persistence Point. A node is considered to be enqueued if it can be reached from *phead* in NVM, and its `deqID` field in persistent memory is -1. Consider again the queue in Fig. 2. The queue immediately after the next pointer of f becomes persistent is as follows.

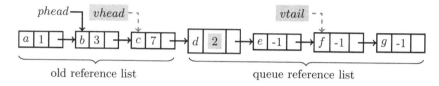

old reference list   queue reference list

Note that this transformation must be performed before moving *vtail*, otherwise the nodes after g could be lost upon system crash. In the queue above *vtail* is lagging, and hence, must be updated before a new node can be enqueued. As soon as the next pointer of f becomes persistent, the node g is considered to be part of the queue, i.e., the abstract queue corresponding to the queue above is $\langle d, e, f, g \rangle$.

Crash and Recovery. Finally, consider the queue in Fig. 2 after a crash and recovery:

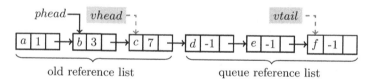

old reference list   queue reference list

The volatile `deqID` value for node d is restored from persistent memory, but the node g is lost.

Abstraction Relation and Mechanisation in KIV. These invariants enable us to prove a refinement between the implementation and *IDQ* in Fig. 3. The main part of the abstraction relation states that the abstract queue corresponds to values in the queue reference list. For an enqueue, the first flush that persists the next pointer (i.e., the effect of line 9) must match $do_t(op)$ with $op = Enq$. For a non-empty dequeue, the first flush that persists `deqID` must match $do_t(op)$ with $op = Deq$ in Fig. 3. An empty dequeue must match $checkEmp_t$ when it loads nxt at line 9 and $do_t(Deq)$ if the test at line 12 succeeds.

This refinement has been interactively, mechanically proven in the KIV theorem prover [10] (see [17] for the KIV proof and the encodings), which has been used extensively in the verification of concurrent data structures (e.g., [4,24]). The proof of the invariant in KIV is simplified via the use of a *rely condition* [15] that captures interference from a thread's environment in an abstract manner. Roughly speaking, a rely condition is a relation over the states of an automaton that must preserve the invariant of each transaction, and that must abstract the transitions of each transaction. Similar techniques have been used in previous proofs of concurrent algorithms [6].

6   Conclusion

There are numerous approaches to proving (standard) linearizability of concurrent data structures (e.g., [1, 24, 27]; see [9] for an overview), including specialisations to cope with weak memory models (e.g., [2, 5, 7, 22, 25, 26]). The recent development of NVM has been accompanied by persistent versions of well-known concurrent constructs, including concurrent objects [3, 11], synchronisation primitives [13, 21] and transactional memory [16]. This paper has focussed on a persistent queue [11], against the recently developed notion of durable linearizability [14].

Development of objects implemented for NVM presents a similar challenge to weak memory, in the sense that there are multiples levels of memory to consider. Moreover, caches and registers are volatile, while cache flush instructions allow reordering with store instructions in accordance with the memory model of the system (e.g., [23]). Correctness in the presence of crashes and recovery can be affected by the order in which elements are persisted, which necessitates the use of programmer-controlled flush operations, increasing complexity. Unfortunately, proofs of correctness (e.g., of durable linearizability) are either given informally or are entirely lacking. This gives little confidence in the correctness of the underlying persistent objects.

Verification of persistent memory algorithms is inherently more complex than in the standard setting. Since an operation only takes effect after a flush event, helping is inevitably required to bring the data structure into a consistent state and for an operation to take effect. For proofs by refinement, these additional helping steps have to be considered in the simulation proof. This ultimately complicates the invariant since the helping is performed by another thread (including a system thread). Moreover, since the state of the data structure can be "lagging" immediately after helping is performed, precisely formalising the underlying helping mechanism further complicates the invariant. Future work will consider how best to manage this additional proof complexity.

Acknowledgements. We thank Lindsay Groves for comments that have helped improve this paper.

References

1. Abdulla, P.A., Haziza, F., Holík, L., Jonsson, B., Rezine, A.: An integrated specification and verification technique for highly concurrent data structures. In: Piterman, N., Smolka, S.A. (eds.) TACAS 2013. LNCS, vol. 7795, pp. 324–338. Springer, Heidelberg (2013). https://doi.org/10.1007/978-3-642-36742-7_23
2. Batty, M., Dodds, M., Gotsman, A.: Library abstraction for C/C++ concurrency. In: Giacobazzi, R., Cousot, R. (eds.) Symposium on Principles of Programming Languages, POPL, pp. 235–248. ACM (2013). https://doi.org/10.1145/2429069.2429099

3. Cohen, N., Aksun, D.T., Larus, J.R.: Object-oriented recovery for non-volatile memory. PACMPL **2**(OOPSLA), 153:1–153:22 (2018)
4. Derrick, J., Schellhorn, G., Wehrheim, H.: Verifying linearisability with potential linearisation points. In: Butler, M., Schulte, W. (eds.) FM 2011. LNCS, vol. 6664, pp. 323–337. Springer, Heidelberg (2011). https://doi.org/10.1007/978-3-642-21437-0_25
5. Derrick, J., Smith, G., Groves, L., Dongol, B.: A proof method for linearizability on TSO architectures. In: Hinchey, M.G., Bowen, J.P., Olderog, E.-R. (eds.) Provably Correct Systems. NMSSE, pp. 61–91. Springer, Cham (2017). https://doi.org/10.1007/978-3-319-48628-4_4
6. Doherty, S., Dongol, B., Derrick, J., Schellhorn, G., Wehrheim, H.: Proving opacity of a pessimistic STM. In: OPODIS, LIPIcs, vol. 70, pp. 35:1–35:17. Schloss Dagstuhl - Leibniz-Zentrum fuer Informatik (2016)
7. Doherty, S., Dongol, B., Wehrheim, H., Derrick, J.: Making linearizability compositional for partially ordered executions. In: Furia, C.A., Winter, K. (eds.) IFM 2018. LNCS, vol. 11023, pp. 110–129. Springer, Cham (2018). https://doi.org/10.1007/978-3-319-98938-9_7
8. Doherty, S., Groves, L., Luchangco, V., Moir, M.: Formal verification of a practical lock-free queue algorithm. In: de Frutos-Escrig, D., Núñez, M. (eds.) FORTE 2004. LNCS, vol. 3235, pp. 97–114. Springer, Heidelberg (2004). https://doi.org/10.1007/978-3-540-30232-2_7
9. Dongol, B., Derrick, J.: Verifying linearisability: a comparative survey. ACM Comput. Surv. **48**(2), 19:1–19:43 (2015). https://doi.org/10.1145/2796550
10. Ernst, G., Pfähler, J., Schellhorn, G., Haneberg, D., Reif, W.: KIV–overview and verifythis competition. Softw. Tools Technol. Transf. (STTT) **17**(6), 677–694 (2015)
11. Friedman, M., Herlihy, M., Marathe, V.J., Petrank, E.: A persistent lock-free queue for non-volatile memory. In: Krall, A., Gross, T.R. (eds.) ACM SIGPLAN Symposium on Principles and Practice of Parallel Programming, PPoPP, pp. 28–40. ACM (2018). https://doi.org/10.1145/3178487.3178490
12. Herlihy, M., Wing, J.M.: Linearizability: a correctness condition for concurrent objects. ACM TOPLAS **12**(3), 463–492 (1990)
13. Huang, Y., Pavlovic, M., Marathe, V.J., Seltzer, M., Harris, T., Byan, S.: Closing the performance gap between volatile and persistent key-value stores using cross-referencing logs. In: USENIX Annual Technical Conference, pp. 967–979. USENIX Association (2018)
14. Izraelevitz, J., Mendes, H., Scott, M.L.: Linearizability of persistent memory objects under a full-system-crash failure model. In: Gavoille, C., Ilcinkas, D. (eds.) DISC 2016. LNCS, vol. 9888, pp. 313–327. Springer, Heidelberg (2016). https://doi.org/10.1007/978-3-662-53426-7_23
15. Jones, C.B.: Tentative steps toward a development method for interfering programs. ACM Trans. Program. Lang. Syst. **5**(4), 596–619 (1983). https://doi.org/10.1145/69575.69577
16. Joshi, A., Nagarajan, V., Cintra, M., Viglas, S.: DHTM: durable hardware transactional memory. In: ISCA, pp. 452–465. IEEE Computer Society (2018)
17. KIV proofs for the durable linearizable queue (2019). http://www.informatik.uni-augsburg.de/swt/projects/Durable-Queue.html
18. Lynch, N.A., Tuttle, M.R.: Hierarchical correctness proofs for distributed algorithms. In: PODC, pp. 137–151. ACM, New York (1987). https://doi.org/10.1145/41840.41852

19. Lynch, N., Vaandrager, F.W.: Forward and backward simulations part I: untimed systems. Inf. Comput. Inf. Control - IANDC **121**, 214–233 (1995). https://doi.org/10.1006/inco.1995.1134

20. Michael, M.M., Scott, M.L.: Simple, fast, and practical non-blocking and blocking concurrent queue algorithms. In: Proceedings of 15th ACM Symposium on Principles of Distributed Computing, pp. 267–275 (1996)

21. Pavlovic, M., Kogan, A., Marathe, V.J., Harris, T.: Brief announcement: persistent multi-word compare-and-swap, In: PODC, pp. 37–39. ACM (2018)

22. Raad, A., Doko, M., Rozic, L., Lahav, O., Vafeiadis, V.: On library correctness under weak memory consistency: specifying and verifying concurrent libraries under declarative consistency models. PACMPL **3**(POPL), 68:1–68:31 (2019). https://dl.acm.org/citation.cfm?id=3290381

23. Raad, A., Vafeiadis, V.: Persistence semantics for weak memory: integrating epoch persistency with the TSO memory model. PACMPL **2**(OOPSLA), 137:1–137:27 (2018)

24. Schellhorn, G., Derrick, J., Wehrheim, H.: A sound and complete proof technique for linearizability of concurrent data structures. ACM Trans. Comput. Logic **15**(4), 31:1–31:37 (2014). https://doi.org/10.1145/2629496

25. Travkin, O., Mütze, A., Wehrheim, H.: SPIN as a linearizability checker under weak memory models. In: Bertacco, V., Legay, A. (eds.) HVC 2013. LNCS, vol. 8244, pp. 311–326. Springer, Cham (2013). https://doi.org/10.1007/978-3-319-03077-7_21

26. Travkin, O., Wehrheim, H.: Verification of concurrent programs on weak memory models. In: Sampaio, A., Wang, F. (eds.) ICTAC 2016. LNCS, vol. 9965, pp. 3–24. Springer, Cham (2016). https://doi.org/10.1007/978-3-319-46750-4_1

27. Vafeiadis, V.: Automatically proving linearizability. In: Touili, T., Cook, B., Jackson, P. (eds.) CAV 2010. LNCS, vol. 6174, pp. 450–464. Springer, Heidelberg (2010). https://doi.org/10.1007/978-3-642-14295-6_40

Compositional Verification of Concurrent Systems by Combining Bisimulations

Frédéric Lang[1(✉)], Radu Mateescu[1], and Franco Mazzanti[2]

[1] Univ. Grenoble Alpes, Inria, CNRS,
Grenoble INP (Institute of Engineering Univ. Grenoble Alpes), LIG,
38000 Grenoble, France
Frederic.Lang@inria.fr
[2] ISTI-CNR, Pisa, Italy

Abstract. One approach to verify a property expressed as a modal μ-calculus formula on a system with several concurrent processes is to build the underlying state space compositionally (i.e., by minimizing and recomposing the state spaces of individual processes, keeping visible only the relevant actions occurring in the formula), and check the formula on the resulting state space. It was shown previously that, when checking the formulas of the L_μ^{dsbr} fragment of μ-calculus (consisting of weak modalities only), individual processes can be minimized modulo divergence-preserving branching (divbranching) bisimulation. In this paper, we refine this approach to handle formulas containing both strong and weak modalities, so as to enable a combined use of strong or divbranching bisimulation minimization on concurrent processes depending whether they contain or not the actions occurring in the strong modalities of the formula. We extend L_μ^{dsbr} with strong modalities and show that the combined minimization approach preserves the truth value of formulas of the extended fragment. We implemented this approach on top of the CADP verification toolbox and demonstrated how it improves the capabilities of compositional verification on realistic examples of concurrent systems.

1 Introduction

We consider the problem of verifying a temporal logic property on a concurrent system $P_1 \parallel ... \parallel P_n$ consisting of n processes composed in parallel. We work in the action-based setting, the property being specified as a formula φ of the modal μ-calculus (L_μ) [18] and the processes P_i being described in a language with process algebraic flavour. A well-known problem is the state-space explosion that happens when the system state space exceeds the available computer memory.

Compositional verification is a set of techniques and tools that have proven efficient to palliate state-space explosion in many situations [11]. These techniques may be either independent of the property, i.e., focus only on the construction of the system state space, such as compositional state space construction [14,19,22,29,31–33]. Alternatively, they may depend on the property, e.g.,

© Springer Nature Switzerland AG 2019
M. H. ter Beek et al. (Eds.): FM 2019, LNCS 11800, pp. 196–213, 2019.
https://doi.org/10.1007/978-3-030-30942-8_13

verification of the property on the full system is decomposed in the verification of properties on (expectedly smaller) sub-systems, such as in compositional reachability analysis [4,36], assume-guarantee reasoning [28], or partial model checking [1].

Nevertheless, the frontier between property-independent and property-dependent techniques is loose. In compositional state space construction, to be able to reduce the system size, a set of actions is selected and a suitable equivalence relation (e.g., strong bisimulation, branching bisimulation, or divergence-preserving branching bisimulation—divbranching for short) is chosen, restricting the set of properties preserved after hiding the selected actions and reducing the system w.r.t. the selected relation. Therefore, there is still a dependency between the state space construction and the set of properties that can be verified. Given a formula φ of L_μ to be verified on the system, Mateescu and Wijs [24] have pushed this idea and shown how to extract a maximal hiding set of actions and an equivalence relation (either strong or divbranching bisimulation) automatically from φ, thus inviting the compositional state space construction technique to the table of property-dependent reductions. To select the equivalence relation from the formula, they have identified an L_μ fragment named L_μ^{dsbr}, which is adequate with divbranching bisimulation [24]. This fragment consists of L_μ restricted to *weak* modalities, which match actions preceded by arbitrary sequences of hidden actions, as opposed to traditional strong modalities $\langle \alpha \rangle\, \varphi_0$ and $[\alpha]\, \varphi_0$, which match only a single action satisfying α. If φ belongs to L_μ^{dsbr}, then the system can be reduced for divbranching bisimulation; otherwise, it can be reduced for strong bisimulation, the weakest equivalence relation preserving full L_μ.

In this paper, we revisit and refine this approach to accommodate L_μ formulas containing both strong and weak modalities. To do so, we define a logic named $L_\mu^{strong}(A_s)$, which extends L_μ^{dsbr} with strong modalities matching only the actions belonging to a given set A_s of *strong* actions. The set A_s induces a partition of the processes $P_1 \parallel ... \parallel P_n$ into those containing at least one strong action, and those that do not. We show that a formula φ of $L_\mu^{strong}(A_s)$ is still preserved if the processes containing strong actions are reduced modulo strong bisimulation and the other ones modulo divbranching bisimulation. We also provide guidelines for extracting the set A_s from particular L_μ formulas encoding the operators of widely-used temporal logics, such as CTL [5], ACTL [26], PDL [9], and PDL-Δ [30]. This combined use of bisimulations to reduce different parts of the same system makes possible a fine-tuning of the compositional state space construction by going smoothly from strong bisimulation (when all modalities are strong) to divbranching bisimulation (when A_s is empty, as in the previous approach based on L_μ^{dsbr}). We implemented this approach on top of the CADP verification toolbox [12], and demonstrated how it improves the capabilities of compositional verification on two realistic case studies, namely the TFTP plane-ground communication protocol specified in [13] and the parallel CTL benchmark of the RERS'2018 challenge.

The paper is organized as follows. Section 2 recalls some definitions. Section 3 defines $L_\mu^{strong}(A_s)$ and proves the main result of its adequacy with the combined use of strong and divbranching bisimulations. Section 4 presents the experimental results obtained on the two case studies. Finally, Sect. 5 contains concluding remarks and directions of future work. Formal proofs and code of case studies are available at https://doi.org/10.5281/zenodo.2634148.

2 Background

2.1 LTS Compositions and Reductions

We consider systems whose behavioural semantics can be represented using an LTS (*Labelled Transition System*).

Definition 1 (LTS). *Let $\mathcal{A}$ denote an infinite set of actions, including the invisible action τ, which denotes internal behaviour. All other actions are called visible. An LTS is a tuple $(\Sigma, A, \longrightarrow, p_{init})$, where Σ is a set of states, $A \subseteq \mathcal{A}$ is a set of actions, $\longrightarrow \subseteq \Sigma \times A \times \Sigma$ is the (labelled) transition relation, and $p_{init} \in \Sigma$ is the initial state. We write $p \xrightarrow{a} p'$ if $(p, a, p') \in \longrightarrow$ and $p \xrightarrow{\tau^*} p'$ if there is a (possibly empty) sequence of τ-transitions from p to p', i.e., states $p_0, \dots, p_n$ $(n \geq 0)$ such that $p = p_0$, $p' = p_n$, and $p_i \xrightarrow{\tau} p_{i+1}$ for $i = 0, \dots, n-1$.*

LTS can be composed in parallel and their actions can be abstracted away using the parallel composition and hiding operators defined below. Prior to hiding, an action mapping operator is also introduced for the generality of the approach.

Definition 2 (Parallel composition of LTS). *Let $P = (\Sigma_P, A_P, \longrightarrow_P, p_{init})$, $Q = (\Sigma_Q, A_Q, \longrightarrow_Q, q_{init})$, and $A_{sync} \subseteq \mathcal{A} \setminus \{\tau\}$. The parallel composition of P and Q with synchronization on A_{sync}, "$P \, |[A_{sync}]| \, Q$", is defined as $(\Sigma_P \times \Sigma_Q, A_P \cup A_Q, \longrightarrow, (p_{init}, q_{init}))$, where $(p, q) \xrightarrow{a} (p', q')$ if and only if either (1) $p \xrightarrow{a} p'$, $q' = q$, and $a \notin A_{sync}$, or (2) $p' = p$, $q \xrightarrow{a} q'$, and $a \notin A_{sync}$, or (3) $p \xrightarrow{a} p'$, $q \xrightarrow{a} q'$, and $a \in A_{sync}$.*

Definition 3 (Action mapping). *Let $P = (\Sigma_P, A_P, \longrightarrow_P, p_{init})$ and a total function $\rho : A_P \to 2^{\mathcal{A}}$. We write $\rho(A_P)$ for the image of ρ, defined by $\bigcup_{a \in A_P} \rho(a)$. We write $\rho(P)$ for the action mapping ρ applied to P, defined as the LTS $(\Sigma_P, \rho(A_P), \longrightarrow'_P, p_{init})$ where $\longrightarrow'_P = \{(p, a', p') \mid p \xrightarrow{a}_P p' \wedge a' \in \rho(a)\}$. An action mapping ρ is admissible if $\tau \in A_P \implies \rho(\tau) = \{\tau\}$.*

Action mapping enables a single action a to be mapped onto the empty set of actions, onto a single action a', or onto more than one actions $a'_0, \dots, a'_{n+1}$ $(n \geq 0)$. In the first case, every transition labelled by a is removed. In the second case, a is renamed into a'. In the third case, every transition labelled by a is replaced by $n + 2$ transitions with same source and target states, labelled by $a'_0, \dots, a'_{n+1}$. Action hiding is a special case of admissible action mapping.

Definition 4 (Action hiding). *Let $P = (\Sigma_P, A_P, \longrightarrow_P, p_{init})$ and $A \subseteq \mathcal{A} \setminus \{\tau\}$. We write "$\textbf{hide } A \textbf{ in } P$" for the LTS $\rho(P)$, where ρ is the admissible action mapping defined by $(\forall a \in A_P \cap A) \, \rho(a) = \{\tau\}$ and $(\forall a \in A_P \setminus A) \, \rho(a) = \{a\}$.*

Parallel composition and admissible action mapping subsume all abstraction and composition operators encodable as *networks of LTS* [7,11,20], such as the parallel composition, hiding, renaming, and cut (or restriction) operators of CCS [25], CSP [2], mCRL [15], LOTOS [16], E-LOTOS [17], and LNT [3], as well as synchronization vectors[1]. In the sequel, we write $P_1 \parallel \ldots \parallel P_n$ for any expression composing $P_1, \ldots, P_n$ using these operators. Given any partition of $P_1, \ldots, P_n$ into arbitrary subsets $\mathcal{P}_1$ and $\mathcal{P}_2$, it is always possible to rewrite $P_1 \parallel \ldots \parallel P_n$ in the form $(\parallel_{P_i \in \mathcal{P}_1} P_i) \parallel (\parallel_{P_j \in \mathcal{P}_2} P_j)$, even for non-associative parallel composition operators (e.g., $|[\ldots]|$), using appropriate action mappings[2].

LTS can be compared and reduced with respect to well-known bisimulation relations. In this paper, we consider strong bisimulation [27] and divbranching bisimulation, which itself derives from branching bisimulation [34,35].

Definition 5 (Bisimulations). *A strong bisimulation is a symmetric relation $R \subseteq \Sigma \times \Sigma$ such that if $(p_1, p_2) \in R$ then: for all $p_1 \xrightarrow{a} p_1'$, there exists p_2' such that $p_2 \xrightarrow{a} p_2'$ and $(p_1', p_2') \in R$. A branching bisimulation is a symmetric relation $R \subseteq \Sigma \times \Sigma$ such that if $(p_1, p_2) \in R$ then: for all $p_1 \xrightarrow{a} p_1'$, either $a = \tau$ and $(p_1', p_2) \in R$, or there exists a sequence $p_2 \xrightarrow{\tau^*} p_2' \xrightarrow{a} p_2''$ such that $(p_1, p_2') \in R$ and $(p_1', p_2'') \in R$. A divergence-preserving branching bisimulation (divbranching bisimulation for short) is a branching bisimulation R such that if $(p_1^0, p_2^0) \in R$ and there is an infinite sequence $p_1^0 \xrightarrow{\tau} p_1^1 \xrightarrow{\tau} p_1^2 \xrightarrow{\tau} \ldots$ with $(p_1^i, p_2^0) \in R$ for all $i \geq 0$, then there is an infinite sequence $p_2^0 \xrightarrow{\tau} p_2^1 \xrightarrow{\tau} p_2^2 \xrightarrow{\tau} \ldots$ such that $(p_1^i, p_2^j) \in R$ for all $i, j \geq 0$. Two states p_1 and p_2 are strongly (resp. branching, divbranching) bisimilar, written $p_1 \sim p_2$ (resp. $p_1 \sim_{br} p_2$, $p_1 \sim_{dsbr} p_2$), if there exists a strong (resp. branching, divbranching) bisimulation R such that $(p_1, p_2) \in R$. Two LTS P_1 and P_2 are strongly (resp. branching, divbranching) bisimilar, written $P_1 \sim P_2$ (resp. $P_1 \sim_{br} P_2$, $P_1 \sim_{dsbr} P_2$), if their initial states are strongly (resp. branching, divbranching) bisimilar.*

Strong, branching, and divbranching bisimulations are congruences for parallel composition and admissible action mapping. This allows reductions to be applied at any intermediate step during the state space construction, thus potentially reducing the overall cost of reduction. However, since processes may constrain each other by synchronization, composing LTS two by two following the algebraic structure of the composition expression and applying reduction after each composition can be orders of magnitude less efficient than other strategies in terms of the largest intermediate LTS. Finding an optimal strategy is difficult. One generally relies on heuristics to select a subset of LTS to compose at each step of the compositional reduction. In this paper, we will use the *smart reduction* heuristic [6,11], which is implemented within the SVL [10] tool of CADP [12].

---

[1] For instance, the composition of P and Q where action a of P synchronizes with either b or c of Q, can be written as $\rho(P) |[b, c]| Q$, where ρ maps a onto $\{b, c\}$.

[2] For instance, $P_1 |[a]| (P_2 |[]| P_3)$ is equivalent to $\rho_0((\rho_1(P_1) |[a_1]| \rho_2(P_2)) |[a_2]| \rho_3(P_3))$ —observe the different associativity— where ρ_1 maps a onto $\{a_1, a_2\}$, ρ_2 renames a into a_1, ρ_3 renames a into a_2, and ρ_0 renames a_1 and a_2 into a.

This heuristic tries to find an efficient composition order by analysing the synchronization and hiding structure of the composition expression.

2.2   Temporal Logics

Definition 6 (Modal μ-calculus [18]**).** *The modal μ-calculus (L_μ) is built from action formulas α and state formulas φ, whose syntax and semantics w.r.t. an LTS $P = (\Sigma, A, \longrightarrow, p_{init})$ are defined as follows:*

$$
\begin{aligned}
\alpha ::= \; & a & & [\![a]\!]_A = \{a\} \\
\mid \; & \text{false} & & [\![\text{false}]\!]_A = \emptyset \\
\mid \; & \alpha_1 \vee \alpha_2 & & [\![\alpha_1 \vee \alpha_2]\!]_A = [\![\alpha_1]\!]_A \cup [\![\alpha_2]\!]_A \\
\mid \; & \neg\alpha_0 & & [\![\neg\alpha_0]\!]_A = A \setminus [\![\alpha_0]\!]_A
\end{aligned}
$$

$$
\begin{aligned}
\varphi ::= \; & \text{false} & & [\![\text{false}]\!]_P\delta = \emptyset \\
\mid \; & \varphi_1 \vee \varphi_2 & & [\![\varphi_1 \vee \varphi_2]\!]_P\delta = [\![\varphi_1]\!]_P\delta \cup [\![\varphi_2]\!]_P\delta \\
\mid \; & \neg\varphi_0 & & [\![\neg\varphi_0]\!]_P\delta = \Sigma \setminus [\![\varphi_0]\!]_P\delta \\
\mid \; & \langle\alpha\rangle\,\varphi_0 & & [\![\langle\alpha\rangle\,\varphi_0]\!]_P\delta = \{s \in \Sigma \mid \exists s \xrightarrow{a} s'.a \in [\![\alpha]\!]_A \wedge s' \in [\![\varphi_0]\!]_P\delta\} \\
\mid \; & X & & [\![X]\!]_P\delta = \delta(X) \\
\mid \; & \mu X.\varphi_0 & & [\![\mu X.\varphi_0]\!]_P\delta = \bigcup_{k\geq 0} \Phi_{0\,P,\delta}^{\,k}(\emptyset)
\end{aligned}
$$

where $X \in \mathcal{X}$ are propositional variables denoting sets of states, $\delta : \mathcal{X} \to 2^\Sigma$ is a context mapping propositional variables to sets of states, $[\,]$ is the empty context, $\delta[U/X]$ is the context identical to δ except for variable X, which is mapped to state set U, the functional $\Phi_{0\,P,\delta} : 2^\Sigma \to 2^\Sigma$ associated to the formula $\mu X.\varphi_0$ is defined as $\Phi_{0\,P,\delta}(U) = [\![\varphi_0]\!]_P\delta[U/X]$, and Φ^k means k-fold application. We write $P \models \varphi$ (read P satisfies φ) for $p_0 \in [\![\varphi]\!]_P[\,]$.

Action formulas α are built from actions and boolean operators. State formulas φ are built from boolean operators, the possibility modality $\langle\alpha\rangle\,\varphi_0$ denoting the states with an outgoing transition labeled by an action satisfying α and leading to a state satisfying φ_0, and the minimal fixed point operator $\mu X.\varphi_0$ denoting the least solution of the equation $X = \varphi_0$ interpreted over 2^Σ.

The usual derived operators are defined as follows: boolean connectors $\text{true} = \neg\text{false}$ and $\varphi_1 \wedge \varphi_2 = \neg(\neg\varphi_1 \vee \neg\varphi_2)$; necessity modality $[\alpha]\,\varphi_0 = \neg\langle\alpha\rangle\,\neg\varphi_0$; and maximal fixed point operator $\nu X.\varphi_0 = \neg\mu X.\neg\varphi_0[\neg X/X]$, where $\varphi_0[\neg X/X]$ is the syntactic substitution of X by $\neg X$ in φ_0. Syntactically, $\langle\rangle$ and $[]$ have the highest precedence, followed by $\wedge$, then $\vee$, and finally μ and ν. To have a well-defined semantics, state formulas are syntactically monotonic [18], i.e., in every subformula $\mu X.\varphi_0$, all occurrences of X in φ_0 fall in the scope of an even number of negations. Thus, negations can be eliminated by downward propagation.

Although L_μ subsumes most action-based logics, its operators are rather low-level and lead to complex formulas. In practice, temporal logics or extensions of L_μ with higher-level operators are used, avoiding (or at least reducing) the use of fixed point operators and modalities. We review informally some of these logics (whose operators can be translated to L_μ), which will be useful in the sequel.

Propositional Dynamic Logic with Looping. The logic PDL-Δ [30] introduces the modalities $\langle \beta \rangle \, \varphi_0$ and $\langle \beta \rangle \, @$, where β is a regular formula defined as follows:

$$\beta ::= \varphi? \mid \alpha \mid \beta_1 \cdot \beta_2 \mid \beta_1 \mid \beta_2 \mid \beta_0^*$$

Regular formulas β denote sets of transition sequences in an LTS: the testing operator $\varphi?$ denotes all zero-step sequences consisting of states satisfying φ; α denotes all one-step sequences consisting of a transition labeled by an action satisfying α; the concatenation $\beta_1 \cdot \beta_2$, choice $\beta_1 \mid \beta_2$, and transitive-reflexive closure β_0^* operators have their usual semantics transposed to transition sequences.

The regular diamond modality $\langle \beta \rangle \, \varphi_0$ denotes the states with an outgoing transition sequence satisfying β and leading to a state satisfying φ_0. The infinite looping operator $\langle \beta \rangle \, @$ denotes the states having an outgoing transition sequence consisting of an infinite concatenation of subsequences satisfying β.

Action Computation Tree Logic. The logic ACTL\X (ACTL without next operator) [26] introduces four temporal operators, whose semantics can be found in terms of L_μ formulas in [8,24], where α_1, α_2 are interpreted over visible actions:

$$\mathsf{E}(\varphi_1 \, _{\alpha_1} \mathsf{U} \, \varphi_2), \mathsf{E}(\varphi_1 \, _{\alpha_1} \mathsf{U}_{\alpha_2} \, \varphi_2), \mathsf{A}(\varphi_1 \, _{\alpha_1} \mathsf{U} \, \varphi_2), \mathsf{A}(\varphi_1 \, _{\alpha_1} \mathsf{U}_{\alpha_2} \, \varphi_2)$$

A transition sequence satisfies the path formula $\varphi_1 \, _{\alpha_1} \mathsf{U}_{\alpha_2} \, \varphi_2$ if it contains a visible transition whose action satisfies α_2 and whose target state satisfies φ_2, whereas at any moment before this transition, φ_1 holds and all visible actions satisfy α_1. A sequence satisfies $\varphi_1 \, _{\alpha_1} \mathsf{U} \, \varphi_2$ if it contains a state satisfying φ_2 and at any moment before, φ_1 holds and all visible actions satisfy α_1. A state satisfies $\mathsf{E}(\varphi_1 \, _{\alpha_1} \mathsf{U}_{\alpha_2} \, \varphi_2)$ (resp. $\mathsf{E}(\varphi_1 \, _{\alpha_1} \mathsf{U} \, \varphi_2)$) if it has an outgoing sequence satisfying $\varphi_1 \, _{\alpha_1} \mathsf{U}_{\alpha_2} \, \varphi_2$ (resp. $\varphi_1 \, _{\alpha_1} \mathsf{U} \, \varphi_2$). It satisfies $\mathsf{A}(\varphi_1 \, _{\alpha_1} \mathsf{U}_{\alpha_2} \, \varphi_2)$ (resp. $\mathsf{A}(\varphi_1 \, _{\alpha_1} \mathsf{U} \, \varphi_2)$) if all its outgoing sequences satisfy the corresponding path formula. The following abbreviations are often used:

$$\mathsf{EF}_\alpha(\varphi_0) = \mathsf{E}(\mathsf{true} \, _{\mathsf{true}} \mathsf{U}_\alpha \, \varphi_0) \qquad \mathsf{AG}_\alpha(\varphi_0) = \neg \mathsf{EF}_{\neg\alpha}(\mathsf{true}) \wedge \neg \mathsf{E}(\mathsf{true} \, _{\mathsf{true}} \mathsf{U} \, \neg\varphi_0)$$

A state satisfies $\mathsf{EF}_\alpha(\varphi_0)$ if it has an outgoing sequence leading to a transition whose action satisfies α and target state satisfies φ_0. A state satisfies $\mathsf{AG}_\alpha(\varphi_0)$ if none of its outgoing sequences leads to a transition labeled by an action not satisfying α or to a state not satisfying φ_0.

Computation Tree Logic. The logic CTL [5] contains the following operators:

$$\mathsf{E}(\varphi_1 \, \mathsf{U} \, \varphi_2), \mathsf{A}(\varphi_1 \, \mathsf{U} \, \varphi_2), \mathsf{E}(\varphi_1 \, \mathsf{W} \, \varphi_2), \mathsf{A}(\varphi_1 \, \mathsf{W} \, \varphi_2), \mathsf{EF}(\varphi_0), \mathsf{AG}(\varphi_0), \mathsf{AF}(\varphi_0), \mathsf{EG}(\varphi_0)$$

A state satisfies $\mathsf{E}(\varphi_1 \, \mathsf{U} \, \varphi_2)$ (resp. $\mathsf{A}(\varphi_1 \, \mathsf{U} \, \varphi_2)$) if some of (resp. all) its outgoing sequences lead to states satisfying φ_2 after passing only through states satisfying φ_1. It satisfies $\mathsf{E}(\varphi_1 \, \mathsf{W} \, \varphi_2)$ (resp. $\mathsf{A}(\varphi_1 \, \mathsf{W} \, \varphi_2)$) if some of (resp. all) its outgoing sequences either contain only states satisfying φ_1, or lead to states satisfying φ_2 after passing only through states satisfying φ_1. A state satisfies $\mathsf{EF}(\varphi_0)$ (resp. $\mathsf{AF}(\varphi_0)$) if some of (resp. all) its outgoing sequences lead to states satisfying φ_0. A state satisfies $\mathsf{EG}(\varphi_0)$ (resp. $\mathsf{AG}(\varphi_0)$) if some of (resp. all) its outgoing sequences contain only states satisfying φ_0.

2.3 Compositional Property-Dependent LTS Reductions

Given a formula $\varphi \in L_\mu$ and a composition of processes $P_1 \parallel \ldots \parallel P_n$, [24] shows two results that allow an LTS equivalent to $P_1 \parallel \ldots \parallel P_n$ to be reduced compositionally, while preserving the truth value of φ. The first result is a procedure, called *maximal hiding*, which extracts systematically from φ a set of actions $H(\varphi)$ that are not discriminated by any action formula occurring in φ. It is shown that $P_1 \parallel \ldots \parallel P_n \models \varphi$ if and only if **hide** $H(\varphi)$ **in** $(P_1 \parallel \ldots \parallel P_n) \models \varphi$. The second result is the identification of a fragment of L_μ, called L_μ^{dsbr}, which is strictly more expressive than $\mu\text{ACTL}\backslash\text{X}^3$ and adequate with divbranching bisimulation. This fragment is defined as follows.

Definition 7 (Modal μ-calculus fragment L_μ^{dsbr} [24]). *By convention, we use the symbols α_τ and α_a to denote action formulas such that $\tau \in \llbracket \alpha_\tau \rrbracket_A$ and $\tau \notin \llbracket \alpha_a \rrbracket_A$. The fragment L_μ^{dsbr} of L_μ is defined as the set of formulas that are semantically equivalent to some formula of the following language:*

$$\varphi ::= \mathsf{false} \mid \varphi_1 \vee \varphi_2 \mid \neg\varphi_0 \mid X \mid \mu X.\varphi_0$$
$$\mid \langle(\varphi_1?.\alpha_\tau)^*\rangle\, \varphi_2 \mid \langle(\varphi_1?.\alpha_\tau)^*.\varphi_1?.\alpha_a\rangle\, \varphi_2 \mid \langle\varphi_1?.\alpha_\tau\rangle\, @$$

The ultra-weak modality $\langle(\varphi_1?.\alpha_\tau)^*\rangle\, \varphi_2$, weak modality $\langle(\varphi_1?.\alpha_\tau)^*.\varphi_1?.\alpha_a\rangle\, \varphi_2$, and weak infinite looping modality $\langle\varphi_1?.\alpha_\tau\rangle\, @$ are shorthand notations for the respective L_μ formulas $\mu X.\varphi_2 \vee (\varphi_1 \wedge \langle\alpha_\tau\rangle X)$, $\mu X.\varphi_1 \wedge (\langle\alpha_a\rangle \varphi_2 \vee \langle\alpha_\tau\rangle X)$, and $\nu X.\varphi_1 \wedge \langle\alpha_\tau\rangle X$. Derived operators are also defined as follows:

$$[(\varphi_1?.\alpha_\tau)^*]\, \varphi_2 = \neg\langle(\varphi_1?.\alpha_\tau)^*\rangle \neg\varphi_2$$
$$[\varphi_1?.\alpha_\tau]\, \dashv = \neg\langle\varphi_1?.\alpha_\tau\rangle\, @$$
$$[(\varphi_1?.\alpha_\tau)^*.\varphi_1?.\alpha_a]\, \varphi_2 = \neg\langle(\varphi_1?.\alpha_\tau)^*.\varphi_1?.\alpha_a\rangle \neg\varphi_2$$

Depending on the L_μ fragment φ belongs to, it is thus possible to determine whether the system can or cannot be reduced for divbranching bisimulation.

3 Combining Bisimulations Compositionally

The above approach is a *mono-bisimulation* approach: either the formula is in L_μ^{dsbr} and then the system is entirely reduced for divbranching bisimulation, or it is not and then the system is entirely reduced for strong bisimulation. We show in this section that, even if the formula is not in L_μ^{dsbr}, it may still be possible to reduce some processes among the parallel processes $P_1, \ldots, P_n$ for divbranching instead of strong bisimulation. This approach relies on the fact that, in general, an arbitrary temporal logic formula φ may be rewritten in a form that contains both weak modalities, as those present in L_μ^{dsbr}, and non-weak modalities of L_μ (called *strong modalities* in this context).

---

[3] $\mu\text{ACTL}\backslash\text{X}$ denotes $\text{ACTL}\backslash\text{X}$ plus fixed points. The authors of [24] claim that L_μ^{dsbr} is as expressive as $\mu\text{ACTL}\backslash\text{X}$, but they omit that the $\langle\varphi_1?.\alpha_\tau\rangle\, @$ weak infinite looping modality cannot be expressed in $\mu\text{ACTL}\backslash\text{X}$.

To do so, we characterize a family of fragments of L_μ, each of which is written $L_\mu^{strong}(A_s)$, where A_s is the set of actions that can be matched by strong modalities. We then prove that if φ belongs to $L_\mu^{strong}(A_s)$ and some process P_i does not contain any action from the set A_s, then P_i can be reduced for divbranching bisimulation. Throughout this section, we assume that the concurrent system $P_1 \parallel \ldots \parallel P_n$ is fixed, and we write A for the set of actions occurring in the system.

3.1 The $L_\mu^{strong}(A_s)$ Fragments of L_μ

Definition 8 ($L_\mu^{strong}(A_s)$). *Let $A_s \subseteq A$ be a fixed set of actions, called strong actions, and let α_s denote any action formula such that $[\![\alpha_s]\!]_A \subseteq A_s$, called a strong action formula. The fragment $L_\mu^{strong}(A_s)$ of L_μ is defined as the set of formulas that are semantically equivalent to some formula of the following language:*

$$\varphi ::= \mathsf{false} \mid \varphi_1 \vee \varphi_2 \mid \neg\varphi_0 \mid \langle \alpha_s \rangle \varphi_0 \mid X \mid \mu X.\varphi_0$$
$$\mid \langle (\varphi_1?.\alpha_\tau)^* \rangle \varphi_2 \mid \langle (\varphi_1?.\alpha_\tau)^*.\varphi_1?.\alpha_a \rangle \varphi_2 \mid \langle \varphi_1?.\alpha_\tau \rangle @$$

We call $\langle \alpha_s \rangle \varphi_0$ a *strong modality*. $L_\mu^{strong}(A_s)$ is the fragment of L_μ consisting of formulas expressible in a form where strong modalities match only actions in A_s. Its formal relationship with L_μ^{dsbr} and L_μ is given in Theorem 1.

Theorem 1. *The following three propositions hold trivially: $L_\mu^{strong}(\emptyset) = L_\mu^{dsbr}$, $L_\mu^{strong}(A) = L_\mu$, and if $A_s \subset A_s'$ then $L_\mu^{strong}(A_s) \subset L_\mu^{strong}(A_s')$.*

Given $\varphi \in L_\mu$, there exists a (not necessarily unique, see Theorem 3 page 10) minimal set A_s such that $\varphi \in L_\mu^{strong}(A_s)$. Obviously, $L_\mu^{strong}(A_s)$ is not adequate with divbranching bisimulation when A_s is not empty, as illustrated by the following example.

Example 1. Consider the LTS P, P', Q, and Q' depicted in Fig. 1. P' (resp. Q') denotes the minimal LTS equivalent to P (resp. Q) for divbranching bisimulation. The formula $\varphi = [(\mathsf{true}?.\mathsf{true})^*.\mathsf{true}?.a_1][a_2]\mathsf{false}$ of $L_\mu^{strong}(\{a_2\})$ (which

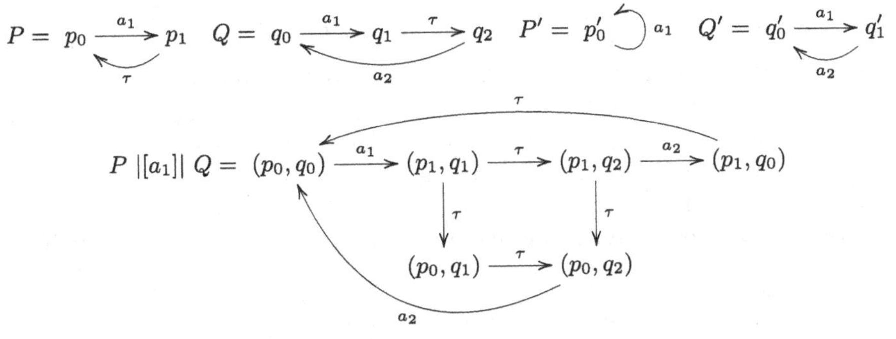

Fig. 1. LTS used in Examples 1 and 2

is equivalent to the PDL formula [true$^*.a_1.a_2$] false) expresses that the system does not contain two successive transitions labelled by a_1 and a_2 respectively. φ does not belong to L_μ^{dsbr}. Indeed, $P \,||[a_1]|\, Q$ satisfies φ because a_1 is necessarily followed by a τ transition, but $P' \,||[a_1]|\, Q'$ (which is isomorphic to Q') does not.

3.2 Applying Divbranching Bisimulation to Selected Components

The following theorem states the main result of this paper, namely that every component process containing no strong action can be replaced by any divbranching equivalent process, without affecting the truth value of the formula[4].

Theorem 2. Let $P = (\Sigma_P, A_P, \rightarrow_P, p_{init})$, $Q = (\Sigma_Q, A_Q, \longrightarrow_Q, q_{init})$, $Q' = (\Sigma_{Q'}, A_{Q'}, \longrightarrow_{Q'}, q'_{init})$, $A_{sync} \subseteq \mathcal{A}$, and $\varphi \in L_\mu^{strong}(A_s)$. If $A_Q \cap A_s = \emptyset$ and $Q \sim_{dsbr} Q'$, then $P \,||[A_{sync}]|\, Q \models \varphi$ if and only if $P \,||[A_{sync}]|\, Q' \models \varphi$.

Proof. The proof looks like the one in [24], showing that divbranching bisimulation preserves the properties of L_μ^{dsbr}, but reasoning concerns product states and additionally handles the case of strong modalities. ☐

Note that τ may belong to A_s. If so, every P_i containing τ cannot be reduced for divbranching bisimulation. On the contrary, processes that do not contain strong actions do not contain τ. Reducing them for divbranching bisimulation is thus allowed, but coincides with strong bisimulation reduction. In the end, all τ-transitions of the system are preserved, as expected for the truth value of formulas containing strong modalities matching τ to be preserved.

Example 2. In Example 1, P does not contain a_2, the only strong action of the system. Thus, φ can be checked on $P' \,||[a_1]|\, Q$ (which is isomorphic to Q and has only 3 states) instead of $P \,||[a_1]|\, Q$ (6 states), while preserving its truth value.

Theorem 2 is consistent with Andersen's *partial model checking* [1] and the mono-bisimulation approach [24]. Given $P \,||\, Q$ such that the strong actions of φ occur only in P, one can observe that the quotient $\varphi // P$ (defined in [1,21]) belongs to L_μ^{dsbr}, because quotienting removes all strong modalities, leaving only weak modalities in the quotiented formula. It follows that Q, on which $\varphi // P$ has to be checked, can be reduced for divbranching bisimulation. This observation could serve as an alternative proof of Theorem 2.

3.3 Identifying Strong Actions in Derived Operators

In the general case, identifying a minimal set of strong actions is not easy, if even feasible. One cannot reasonably assume that formulas are written in the obscure $L_\mu^{strong}(A_s)$ syntax (see Example 1) and that the remaining strong modalities cannot be turned to weak ones. Instead, users shall continue to use "syntactic sugar" extensions of L_μ, with operators of e.g., CTL, ACTL, PDL, or PDL-Δ. In Lemma 1, we provide patterns that can be used to prove that a formula written using one of those operators belongs to a particular instance of $L_\mu^{strong}(A_s)$.

---

[4] Theorem 2 generalizes easily to more general compositions $P \,||\, Q$ (with admissible action mappings) if Q does not contain any action that maps onto a strong action.

Lemma 1. *Let* $\varphi_0, \varphi_1, \varphi_2 \in L_\mu^{strong}(A_s)$, $\tau \in \llbracket \alpha_\tau \rrbracket_A$, $\tau \notin \llbracket \alpha_a \rrbracket_A$, $\llbracket \alpha_s \rrbracket_A \subseteq A_s$, *and* $\alpha_0, \alpha_1, \alpha_2$ *be any action formulas. The following formulas belong to* $L_\mu^{strong}(A_s)$ *(the list may be not exhaustive):*

1. **Modal μ-calculus:**

   $\langle \alpha_s \rangle \varphi_0$ $\qquad$ $[\alpha_s] \varphi_0$ $\qquad$ $\neg \varphi_0$ $\qquad$ $\varphi_1 \vee \varphi_2$ $\qquad$ $\varphi_1 \wedge \varphi_2$ $\qquad$ $\varphi_1 \Rightarrow \varphi_2$

2. **Propositional Dynamic Logic:**

   $\langle \alpha_\tau^* \rangle \varphi_0$ $\qquad$ $[\alpha_\tau^*] \varphi_0$ $\qquad$ $\langle \alpha_\tau^* \cdot \alpha_a \rangle \varphi_0$ $\qquad$ $[\alpha_\tau^* \cdot \alpha_a] \varphi_0$ $\qquad$ $\langle \alpha_\tau \rangle @$ $\qquad$ $[\alpha_\tau] \dashv$

3. **Action Computation Tree Logic:**

   $A(\varphi_1 \ _{\alpha_1} U \ \varphi_2)$ $\qquad$ $A(\varphi_1 \ _{\alpha_1} U_{\alpha_2} \ \varphi_2)$ $\qquad$ $AG_{\alpha_0}(\varphi_0)$

   $E(\varphi_1 \ _{\alpha_1} U \ \varphi_2)$ $\qquad$ $E(\varphi_1 \ _{\alpha_1} U_{\alpha_2} \ \varphi_2)$ $\qquad$ $EF_{\alpha_0}(\varphi_0)$

4. **Computation Tree Logic:**

   $A(\varphi_1 \ U \ \varphi_2)$ $\qquad$ $A(\varphi_1 \ W \ \varphi_2)$ $\qquad$ $AG(\varphi_0)$ $\qquad$ $AF(\varphi_0)$

   $E(\varphi_1 \ U \ \varphi_2)$ $\qquad$ $E(\varphi_1 \ W \ \varphi_2)$ $\qquad$ $EF(\varphi_0)$ $\qquad$ $EG(\varphi_0)$

   $A([\alpha_a] \varphi_1 \ U \ \varphi_2)$ $\qquad$ $A([\alpha_a] \varphi_1 \ W \ \varphi_2)$ $\qquad$ $AG([\alpha_a] \varphi_0)$ $\qquad$ $EF(\langle \alpha_a \rangle \varphi_0)$

   $AG(\varphi_1 \vee [\alpha_a] \varphi_2)$ $\qquad$ $EF(\varphi_1 \wedge \langle \alpha_a \rangle \varphi_2)$

Example 3. Let a_1, a_2, and a_3 be visible actions and recall that A denotes the set of all actions of the system. Lemma 1 allows the following to be shown (this is left as an exercise):

$\langle true^*.a_1.(\neg a_2)^*.a_3 \rangle true \in L_\mu^{strong}(\emptyset)$ $\qquad\qquad$ $[true] false \in L_\mu^{strong}(A)$

$A(\langle a_1 \rangle true \ _{\neg a_2} U_{a_3} \ true) \in L_\mu^{strong}(\{a_1\})$ $\qquad$ $AG([a_1] false) \in L_\mu^{strong}(\emptyset)$

$E(true \ _{true} U_\tau \ true) \in L_\mu^{strong}(A)$ $\qquad\qquad$ $\langle a_1^*.a_2 \rangle true \in L_\mu^{strong}(\{a_1, a_2\})$

$E(true \ _{true} U \ \langle \tau \rangle true) \in L_\mu^{strong}(\{\tau\})$ $\qquad\qquad$ $[a_1.a_2] false \in L_\mu^{strong}(\{a_1, a_2\})$

$EF(\langle a_1 \rangle true \wedge \langle a_2 \rangle true) \in L_\mu^{strong}(\{a_1\})$ $\qquad$ $EF(\langle a_1 \rangle \langle a_2 \rangle true) \in L_\mu^{strong}(\{a_2\})$

$EF(\langle a_1 \rangle true \wedge \langle a_2 \rangle true) \in L_\mu^{strong}(\{a_2\})$ $\qquad$ $EF(\langle \neg a_1 \rangle true) \in L_\mu^{strong}(A \setminus \{a_1\})$

Theorem 3. *There is not a unique minimal set A_s such that $\varphi \in L_\mu^{strong}(A_s)$.*

Proof. $EF(\langle a_1 \rangle true \wedge \langle a_2 \rangle true) \in L_\mu^{strong}(\{a_1\}) \cap L_\mu^{strong}(\{a_2\})$, because it is semantically equivalent to both formulas $EF(\langle(\langle a_1 \rangle true?.true)^*.\langle a_1 \rangle true?.a_2 \rangle true)$ and $EF(\langle(\langle a_2 \rangle true?.true)^*.\langle a_2 \rangle true?.a_1 \rangle true)$. Yet, it is not in $L_\mu^{strong}(\emptyset)$ as it has not the same truth value on the divbranching equivalent LTS P and P' below:

Thus, $\{a_1\}$ and $\{a_2\}$ are non-unique minimal sets of strong actions. $\qquad$ □

4 Applications

We consider two examples to illustrate our new verification approach combining strong and divbranching bisimulation and show how it can reduce both time and memory usage when associated to the smart reduction heuristic. In both examples, the aim is to perform a set of verification tasks, each consisting in checking a formula φ on a system of parallel processes $P_1 \parallel \ldots \parallel P_n$. Since our approach can only improve the verification of formulas containing both strong and weak modalities, we consider only the pairs of formulas and systems such that the formula is part of $L_\mu^{strong}(A_s)$ for some minimal A_s that is not empty and that is strictly included in the set of visible actions of the system[5]. For each verification task, we compare the largest LTS size, the verification time, and the memory peak obtained using the following two approaches:

Mono-bisimulation approach: φ is verified on **hide** $H(\varphi)$ **in** $(P_1 \parallel \ldots \parallel P_n)$ (where $H(\varphi)$ is the maximal hiding set mentioned in Sect. 2.3) reduced compositionally for strong bisimulation (since φ is not in L_μ^{dsbr}) using the smart reduction heuristic.

Refined approach combining bisimulations: The set $\{P_1, \ldots, P_n\}$ is partitioned in two groups $\mathcal{P}_s$ and $\mathcal{P}_w$ such that $P_i \in \mathcal{P}_s$ if it contains actions in A_s and $P_i \in \mathcal{P}_w$ otherwise, so that $P_1 \parallel \ldots \parallel P_n$ can be rewritten in the equivalent form $(\parallel_{P_i \in \mathcal{P}_s} P_i) \parallel (\parallel_{P_j \in \mathcal{P}_w} P_j)$. The set A_I of actions on which at least one process of $\mathcal{P}_s$ and one process of $\mathcal{P}_w$ synchronize (*inter-group* synchronization) is then identified. Using the smart reduction heuristic, **hide** $H(\varphi) \setminus A_I$ **in** $\parallel_{P_i \in \mathcal{P}_s} P_i$ (corresponding to the processes containing strong actions) is reduced compositionally for strong bisimulation, leading to a first LTS P_s, and **hide** $H(\varphi) \setminus A_I$ **in** $\parallel_{P_j \in \mathcal{P}_w} P_j$ (corresponding to the processes containing no strong action) is reduced compositionally for divbranching bisimulation, leading to a second LTS P_w. Finally, φ is verified on **hide** $H(\varphi) \cap A_I$ **in** $(P_s \parallel[A_I]\parallel P_w)$ reduced for strong bisimulation.

All experiments were done on a 3GHz/12GB RAM/8-core Intel Xeon computer running Linux, using the specification languages and 32-bit versions of tools provided in the CADP toolbox [12] version 2019-a "Pisa".

4.1 Trivial File Transfer Protocol

The TFTP (*Trivial File Transfer Protocol*) case-study[6] addresses the verification of an avionic communication protocol between a plane and the ground [13]. It comprises two instances (A and B) of a process named TFTP, connected through a FIFO buffer. Since the state space is very large in the general case, the authors defined five scenarios named A, B, C, D, and E, depending on whether each instance may write and/or read a file. The system corresponding to each scenario is a parallel composition of eight processes. The requirements consist of 29 properties parameterized by the identity of a TFTP instance, defined in MCL [23] (an implementation of the alternation-free modal μ-calculus including PDL-Δ modalities and macro definitions enabling the construction of libraries of

---

[5] Otherwise, our approach coincides with the mono-bisimulation approach of [24]. In all the examples addressed in this section, there is always a unique minimal set A_s, whose identification is made easy using Lemma 1.

[6] Specification available at ftp://ftp.inrialpes.fr/pub/vasy/demos/demo_05.

Table 1. TFTP properties (strong action formulas are highlighted)

Nr.	Property
08	$[\text{true}^* \cdot a_1 \cdot \boxed{a_2}]$ false
09	$[\text{true}^* \cdot a_1 \cdot \boxed{a_2} \cdot ((\boxed{a_3} \cdot (\neg a_4)^* \cdot a_5)|(\boxed{a_6} \cdot (\neg a_7)^* \cdot a_8))]$ false
14	$[\text{true}^* \cdot a_1 \cdot \boxed{a_2} \cdot (\neg a_3)^* \cdot a_4 \cdot \boxed{a_5}]$ false
16	$[(\neg a_1)^* \cdot a_2 \cdot (\neg a_3)^* \cdot a_4] \langle ((\neg a_5)^* \cdot a_6 \cdot \boxed{a_7}) \cdot ((\neg a_5)^* \cdot a_6 \cdot \boxed{a_7}) \rangle$ true
17	Same shape as property Nr. 16

operators), 24 of which belong to L_μ^{dsbr}. The remaining five, namely properties 08, 09, 14, 16, and 17, contain both weak and strong modalities. The shape of these properties is described in Table 1, where we do not provide the details of the action formulas, but instead denote them by letters $a_1, a_2, \ldots$, where $\tau \notin [\![a_i]\!]_A$ for all i. Strong action formulas are highlighted and one shows easily that the other are weak using Lemma 1-2.

We consider 31 among a potential of 50 verification tasks (five properties, five scenarios, and two instances) as some properties are not relevant to every TFTP instance and scenario (e.g., in a scenario where one TFTP instance only receives messages, checking a property concerning a message emission is irrelevant). All 31 verification tasks return true and the strong actions occur in only three (although not the same three) out of the eight parallel processes.

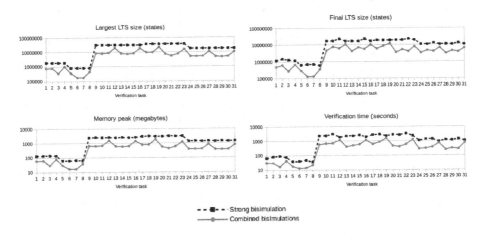

Fig. 2. Experimental results of the TFTP case-study

Figure 2 shows that the refined approach always reduces LTS size (for both intermediate and final LTS), memory and time following similar curves, up to a factor 7 (the vertical axis is on a logarithmic scale). Time does not include LTS generation of the component processes from their LNT specification, which takes

Table 2. RERS 2018 properties (strong action formulas are highlighted)

Nr.	Property	Result
101#21	AG([A21] [A23] [A4] [true] false)	false
101#22	AG([A3] AF(⟨A2⟩ true))	false
101#23	AG(⟨A20⟩ true ⇒ ⟨A20⟩ A([A23] false W ⟨A8⟩ true))	true
102#21	EF(AG([A5] false))	true
102#22	EG([A35] E([A23] false U ⟨A35⟩ true))	false
102#23	AG([A22] A([A8] false U ⟨A22⟩ true))	false
103#21	AG([A11] A([A2] false W ⟨A6⟩ true) ⇒ [A11] A([A5] false W ⟨A6⟩ true))	true
103#22	EG([A14] false ∧ (⟨A18⟩ true ⇒ [A18] EG([A21] false ∧ EF(⟨A19⟩ true)))) = EG([A14] false ∧ [A18] EG([A21] false ∧ EF(⟨A19⟩ true)))	true
103#23	AG(⟨A34⟩ true ⇒ [A34] A([A68] false W ⟨A59⟩ true)) = AG([A34] A([A68] false W ⟨A59⟩ true))	false

only a few seconds and is common to both approaches. In these experiments, time is dominated by the last step of generation and minimization, whereas memory usage is dominated by minimization.

4.2   Parallel Benchmark of the RERS 2018 Challenge

The RERS (Rigorous Examination of Reactive Systems)[7] challenge is an international competition on a benchmark of verification tasks. Since 2018 (8th edition), the challenge features a set of parallel problems where systems are synchronizing LTS and properties are expressed using CTL and modalities. This section illustrates the benefits of our approach on these problems.

The benchmark comprises three specifications of concurrent systems, numbered 101, 102, and 103, each accompanied by three properties to be checked, numbered $p\#21$, $p\#22$, and $p\#23$, where p is the system number. Thus, nine verification tasks have to be solved. The properties are presented in Table 2, where the strong action formulas are highlighted. One easily shows that all other action formulas are weak using Lemmas 1-1 and 1-4. However, for 103#22 and 103#23, the identity $(\langle\alpha\rangle\ \text{true} \Rightarrow [\alpha]\ \varphi) = ([\alpha]\ \text{false} \vee [\alpha]\ \varphi) = [\alpha]\ \varphi$ (because $[\alpha]\ \text{false} \implies [\alpha]\ \varphi$ for all φ) was applied to obtain the simplified formulas occurring after the = sign in the table. For 102#23, this simplification allowed us to prove that $A34$ is not a strong action, unlike what appears at first sight.

Table 3 gives, for each of the nine verification tasks, the number #act of actions in the system, the number #hide of actions in the maximal hiding set, the number #sact of strong actions, the number #proc of parallel processes, the number #sproc of processes in the strong group, the number #sync of inter-group actions, and the best reduction relation among strong bisimulation, divbranching bisimulation, or a combination of both. We observe that:

– The set of weak actions of 101#21 is empty due to the presence of the "true" strong action formula, whereas the set of strong actions of 102#21 is empty,

---

[7] http://rers-challenge.org.

Table 3. Some numbers about the RERS 2018 parallel benchmark

Task	#act	#hide	#sact	#proc	#sproc	#sync	Relation
101#21	24	21	24	9	9	-	Strong
101#22	24	22	1	9	4	11	Combination
101#23	24	21	2	9	3	9	Combination
102#21	28	27	0	20	0	-	Divbranching
102#22	28	26	2	20	10	14	Combination
102#23	28	26	1	20	4	12	Combination
103#21	70	66	2	34	8	12	Combination
103#22	70	66	3	34	6	18	Combination
103#23	70	67	1	34	7	10	Combination

i.e., the property belongs to L_μ^{dsbr}. In both cases, our approach coincides with the mono-bisimulation approach. The verification of 101#21 (reduced for strong bisimulation) takes 75 s, with a memory peak of 11 MB and a largest LTS of $83,964$ states and $374,809$ transitions. The verification of 102#21 (reduced for divbranching bisimulation) takes 261 s, with a memory peak of 22 MB and a largest LTS of 243 states and 975 transitions.

- 101#22, 101#23, 102#22, 102#23, 103#21, 103#22, and 103#23 contain both weak and strong actions. They are used to evaluate our approach.

Table 4 compares the performance of verifying the latter seven verification tasks using the approaches described above. LTS sizes are given in kilostates, memory in megabytes, and time in seconds. Tasks using more than 3 GB of memory were aborted. We see that our approach reduces both time and memory usage and allows all problems of the challenge to be solved, whereas using strong bisimulation alone fails in five out of those seven tasks.

Table 4. Experimental results of the RERS 2018 parallel benchmark

Task	Strong bisimulation				Combined bisimulations			
	Kstates		Verif.		Kstates		Verif.	
	Largest	Final	MB	Sec.	Largest	Final	MB	Sec.
101#22	84	77	10	77	1.4	1.4	10	72
101#23	84	77	11	80	0.5	0.5	8	73
102#22	-	-	-	-	611	585	57	295
102#23	-	-	-	-	17	9.8	22	260
103#21	-	-	-	-	734	313	101	604
103#22	-	-	-	-	14,143	14,141	1575	2533
103#23	-	-	-	-	122	122	35	566

The negligible reductions in time and memory usage observed for tasks 101#22 and 101#23 are due to the fact that time and memory usage are dominated by the algorithm in charge of selecting a sub-set of processes to be composed and reduced (implemented in smart reduction). The complexity of this algorithm does not depend on the state space size, but on the number of actions and parallel processes, which is almost the same using both approaches. When considering larger examples, memory usage gets dominated by minimisation. In particular, for tasks 102#22, 102#23, 103#21, and 103#23 (and likely also 103#22), memory usage is reduced by several orders of magnitude.

Note that some of these tasks can be verified more efficiently using non-compositional approaches, such as on-the-fly model checking, in cases where proofs or counter-examples can be detected much before having explored the full state space. The main drawback of maximal hiding is that the generated counter-examples are given only in terms of the actions visible in the formula, which abstracts out a lot of intermediate transitions. However, this is the price to pay for being able to verify most of the tasks, such as 103#21, for which on-the-fly verification aborts due to memory exhaustion.

5   Conclusion and Future Work

In this paper, we proposed a compositional verification approach that extends the state of the art [24] and consists of three steps: First, so-called strong actions are identified, corresponding to those actions of the system that the formula cannot match using weak modalities in the sense of the L_μ fragment L_μ^{dsbr} adequate with divbranching bisimulation. These actions are used to partition the parallel processes into those containing strong actions and the others. Second, maximal hiding and compositional reduction are used to minimize the composition of processes not containing strong actions for divbranching bisimulation, and the other processes for strong bisimulation. Finally, the property is verified on the reduced system.

The originality of this approach is to combine strong and divbranching bisimulation, as opposed to the mono-bisimulation approach of [24]. We proved it correct by characterizing a family of fragments of the logic L_μ, called $L_\mu^{strong}(A_s)$, parameterized by the set A_s of strong actions. We also showed under which conditions action-based branching-time temporal logic formulas containing well-known operators from the logics CTL, ACTL, PDL, and PDL-Δ are part of $L_\mu^{strong}(A_s)$ when A_s is fixed. In the future, it might be worth investigating whether more operators can be considered, e.g., from the linear-time logic LTL.

This approach may significantly improve the verification performance for systems containing both processes with and without strong actions, as illustrated by two case-studies. In particular, it allowed the whole parallel CTL benchmark of the RERS 2018 challenge to be solved on a standard computer.

Identifying (close to minimal) sets of strong actions for arbitrary formulas manually is a cumbersome task, prone to errors. We shall investigate ways to compute such sets automatically. As illustrated by verification task 103#23 of

RERS 2018, the problem is not purely syntactic: considering non-trivial semantic equivalences may prove useful to eliminate actions that appear strong at first sight. Yet, we trust that the presented approach has potential to be implemented in automated software tools, such as those available in the CADP toolbox.

References

1. Andersen, H.R.: Partial model checking. In: Proceedings of the 10th Annual IEEE Symposium on Logic in Computer Science LICS, San Diego, California, USA, pp. 398–407. IEEE Computer Society Press, June 1995
2. Brookes, S.D., Hoare, C.A.R., Roscoe, A.W.: A Theory of communicating sequential processes. J. ACM **31**(3), 560–599 (1984)
3. Champelovier, D., et al.: Reference manual of the LNT to LOTOS translator (Version 6.7), INRIA, Grenoble, France, July 2017
4. Cheung, S.C., Kramer, J.: Enhancing compositional reachability analysis with context constraints. In: Proceedings of the 1st ACM SIGSOFT International Symposium on the Foundations of Software Engineering, Los Angeles, CA, USA, pp. 115–125. ACM Press, December 1993
5. Clarke, E.M., Emerson, E.A., Sistla, A.P.: Automatic verification of finite-state concurrent systems using temporal logic specifications. ACM Trans. Program. Lang. Syst. **8**(2), 244–263 (1986)
6. Crouzen, P., Lang, F.: Smart reduction. In: Giannakopoulou, D., Orejas, F. (eds.) FASE 2011. LNCS, vol. 6603, pp. 111–126. Springer, Heidelberg (2011). https://doi.org/10.1007/978-3-642-19811-3_9
7. de Putter, S., Wijs, A., Lang, F.: Compositional Model Checking is Lively – Extended Version 2018. Submitted to Science of Computer Programming (2018)
8. Fantechi, A., Gnesi, S., Ristori, G.: From ACTL to μ-calculus (extended abstract). In: Proceedings of the Workshop on Theory and Practice in Verification. ERCIM (1992)
9. Fischer, M.J., Ladner, R.E.: Propositional dynamic logic of regular programs. J. Comput. Syst. Sci. **18**(2), 194–211 (1979)
10. Garavel, H., Lang, F.: SVL: a scripting language for compositional verification. In: Kim, M., Chin, B., Kang, S., Lee, D. (eds.) FORTE 2001. IFIP, vol. 69, pp. 377–392. Springer, Boston, MA (2002). https://doi.org/10.1007/0-306-47003-9_24
11. Garavel, H., Lang, F., Mateescu, R.: Compositional verification of asynchronous concurrent systems using CADP. Acta Informatica **52**(4), 337–392 (2015)
12. Garavel, H., Lang, F., Mateescu, R., Serwe, W.: CADP 2011: a toolbox for the construction and analysis of distributed processes. Int. J. Softw. Tools Technol. Transf. (STTT) **15**(2), 89–107 (2013)
13. Garavel, H., Thivolle, D.: Verification of GALS systems by combining synchronous languages and process calculi. In: Păsăreanu, C.S. (ed.) SPIN 2009. LNCS, vol. 5578, pp. 241–260. Springer, Heidelberg (2009). https://doi.org/10.1007/978-3-642-02652-2_20
14. Graf, S., Steffen, B.: Compositional minimization of finite state systems. In: Clarke, E.M., Kurshan, R.P. (eds.) CAV 1990. LNCS, vol. 531, pp. 186–196. Springer, Heidelberg (1991). https://doi.org/10.1007/BFb0023732
15. Groote, J.F., Ponse, A.: The Syntax and Semantics of μCRL. CS-R 9076. Centrum voor Wiskunde en Informatica, Amsterdam (1990)

16. ISO/IEC. LOTOS - A Formal Description Technique Based on the Temporal Ordering of Observational Behaviour. International Standard 8807, International Organization for Standardization - Information Processing Systems - Open Systems Interconnection, Geneva, September 1989
17. ISO/IEC. Enhancements to LOTOS (E-LOTOS). International Standard 15437:2001, International Organization for Standardization - Information Technology, Geneva, September 2001
18. Kozen, D.: Results on the propositional μ-calculus. Theoret. Comput. Sci. **27**, 333–354 (1983)
19. Krimm, J.-P., Mounier, L.: Compositional state space generation from Lotos programs. In: Brinksma, E. (ed.) TACAS 1997. LNCS, vol. 1217, pp. 239–258. Springer, Heidelberg (1997). https://doi.org/10.1007/BFb0035392
20. Lang, F.: Exp.Open 2.0: a flexible tool integrating partial order, compositional, and on-the-fly verification methods. In: Romijn, J., Smith, G., van de Pol, J. (eds.) IFM 2005. LNCS, vol. 3771, pp. 70–88. Springer, Heidelberg (2005). https://doi.org/10.1007/11589976_6
21. Lang, F., Mateescu, R.: Partial model checking using networks of labelled transition systems and boolean equation systems. Log. Methods Comput. Sci. **9**(4), 1–32 (2013)
22. Malhotra, J., Smolka, S.A., Giacalone, A., Shapiro, R.: A tool for hierarchical design and simulation of concurrent systems. In: Proceedings of the BCS-FACS Workshop on Specification and Verification of Concurrent Systems, Stirling, Scotland, UK, pp. 140–152. British Computer Society, July 1988
23. Mateescu, R., Thivolle, D.: A model checking language for concurrent value-passing systems. In: Cuellar, J., Maibaum, T., Sere, K. (eds.) FM 2008. LNCS, vol. 5014, pp. 148–164. Springer, Heidelberg (2008). https://doi.org/10.1007/978-3-540-68237-0_12
24. Mateescu, R., Wijs, A.: Property-dependent reductions adequate with divergence-sensitive branching bisimilarity. Sci. Comput. Program. **96**(3), 354–376 (2014)
25. Milner, R.: Communication and Concurrency. Prentice-Hall, Upper Saddle River (1989)
26. De Nicola, R., Vaandrager, F.: Action versus state based logics for transition systems. In: Guessarian, I. (ed.) LITP 1990. LNCS, vol. 469, pp. 407–419. Springer, Heidelberg (1990). https://doi.org/10.1007/3-540-53479-2_17
27. Park, D.: Concurrency and automata on infinite sequences. In: Deussen, P. (ed.) GI-TCS 1981. LNCS, vol. 104, pp. 167–183. Springer, Heidelberg (1981). https://doi.org/10.1007/BFb0017309
28. Pnueli, A.: In transition from global to modular temporal reasoning about programs. Log. Models Concurr. Syst. **13**, 123–144 (1984)
29. Sabnani, K.K., Lapone, A.M., Ümit Uyar, M.: An algorithmic procedure for checking safety properties of protocols. IEEE Trans. Commun. **37**(9), 940–948 (1989)
30. Streett, R.: Propositional dynamic logic of looping and converse. Inf. Control **54**, 121–141 (1982)
31. Tai, K.-C., Koppol, P.V.: An incremental approach to reachability analysis of distributed programs. In: Proceedings of the 7th International Workshop on Software Specification and Design, Los Angeles, CA, USA, pp. 141–150, Piscataway, NJ, December 1993. IEEE Press (1993)
32. Tai, K.-C., Koppol, P.V.: Hierarchy-based incremental reachability analysis of communication protocols. In: Proceedings of the IEEE International Conference on Network Protocols, San Francisco, CA, USA, pp. 318–325. IEEE Press, Piscataway, NJ, October 1993 (1993)

33. Valmari, A.: Compositional state space generation. In: Rozenberg, G. (ed.) ICATPN 1991. LNCS, vol. 674, pp. 427–457. Springer, Heidelberg (1993). https:// doi.org/10.1007/3-540-56689-9_54

34. van Glabbeek, R.J., Weijland, W.P.: Branching-time and abstraction in bisimulation semantics (extended abstract). CS R8911, Centrum voor Wiskunde en Informatica, Amsterdam 1989. Also in Proceedings IFIP 11th World Computer Congress, San Francisco (1989)

35. van Glabbeek, R.J., Weijland, W.P.: Branching time and abstraction in bisimulation semantics. J. ACM 43(3), 555–600 (1996)

36. Yeh, W.J., Young, M.: Compositional reachability analysis using process algebra. In: Proceedings of the ACM SIGSOFT Symposium on Testing, Analysis, and Verification (SIGSOFT 1991), Victoria, British Columbia, Canada, pp. 49–59. ACM Press, October 1991 (1991)

Model Checking Circus

Towards a Model-Checker for *Circus*

Artur Oliveira Gomes[1]($\boxtimes$) and Andrew Butterfield[2]

[1] Universidade Federal de Mato Grosso do Sul, Corumbá, Brazil
artur.gomes@ufms.br
[2] School of Computer Science and Statistics,
Trinity College Dublin, Dublin 2, Ireland
butrfeld@tcd.ie

Abstract. Among several approaches aiming at the correctness of systems, model-checking is one technique to formally assess system models regarding their desired/undesired behavioural properties. We aim at model-checking the *Circus* notation that combines Z, CSP, and Morgan's refinement calculus, based on the Unifying Theories of Programming. In this paper, we experiment with approaches for capturing *Circus* processes in CSP, and for each approach, we evaluate the impact of our decisions on the state-space explored as well as the time spent for such a checking using FDR. We also experimented with the consequences of model-checking CSP models that capture both state invariants and pre-conditions of *Circus* models.

1 Introduction

The use of formal methods provides a way to rigorously specify, develop, and verify complex systems. Among several approaches aiming at the correctness of systems, model-checking formally assesses given systems regarding their desired/undesired behavioural properties, through exhaustive checking of a finite model of that system.

Woodcock and Cavalcanti defined *Circus* [38], which is a formal language that combines structural aspects of a system using the Z language [40] and the behavioural aspects using CSP [36], along with the refinement calculus [23] and Dijkstra's guarded commands [10]. Its semantics is based on the *Unifying Theories of Programming (UTP)* [18]. In addition, a refinement calculus for *Circus* was developed by Oliveira [27], currently considered the de-facto reference for *Circus*, using tool support with ProofPower-Z [28]. More recently, Foster *et al.* introduced Isabelle/UTP, supporting *Circus* [11]. Moreover, *Circus* has a refinement calculator, CRefine [8], and an animator for *Circus*, Joker [26]. However, for model-checking, *Circus* is usually translated by hand to machine-readable CSP (CSP_M) [35] and then FDR [14] is used. We applied that method in our response to the Haemodialysis case study for ABZ'16 [16]. Model checking through FDR allows the user to perform a wide range of analysis, such as checks for refinement, deadlock, livelock, determinism, and termination.

© Springer Nature Switzerland AG 2019
M. H. ter Beek et al. (Eds.): FM 2019, LNCS 11800, pp. 217–234, 2019.
https://doi.org/10.1007/978-3-030-30942-8_14

Some related work on techniques for model-checking *Circus* was presented by Freitas [12] where a refinement model checker based on automata theory [19] and the operational semantics of *Circus* [39] was formalised in Z/Eves [34]. He also prototyped a model checker in Java. Moreover, Nogueira *et al.* [24] also presented a prototype of a model checker based on the operational semantics of *Circus* within the Microsoft FORMULA [21] framework. However, they could not provide a formal proof of the soundness of their approach, since FORMULA does not have an available formal semantics. Yet another approach for model-checking *Circus* was defined by Ye and Woodcock [41], who defined a link from *Circus* to $CSP\|B$ with model-checking using ProB [31]. Finally Beg [4] prototyped and investigated an automatic translation that supports a subset of *Circus* constructs.

Since CSP_M does not have a notion of variables for state as in Z, *Circus* or even the B-Method, we have to somehow capture them in order to obtain a CSP_M model as similar as possible to the original *Circus* one. Therefore, one could either use a memory model [25,30] in order to manage the values of the state variables, or else, to adopt the idea of *state-variable parametrised processes* [4].

Following the results presented in ABZ'16 [16], which involved manual translation, we decided to develop *Circus2CSP* [1], an automatic translator from *Circus* into CSP_M, aiming at model-checking with FDR. Our tool was then built based on the strategy presented in Sect. 5.3 of Deliverable 24.1 [29], from the COMPASS project [37], that defines a rigorous but manual translation strategy aiming at obtaining CSP_M specifications from *Circus*.

This paper reports design decisions regarding different approaches for model checking and experimental results obtained for *Circus* specifications. Such experiments were enough to identify an effective general form for any CSP_M model derived from *Circus*, where FDR could perform refinement checks with reduced time and memory consumption compared to existing approaches from the literature.

2   *Circus* Background

A *Circus* specification is in some sense an extension of Z [40] in that it takes the paragraphs of Z and adds new paragraph forms that can define *Circus* channels, processes and actions. Channels correspond to CSP events:

channel $c : T$

Circus actions can be considered as CSP processes extended with the ability to read and write shared variables, usually defined using a Z schema:

$$LocVars \mathrel{\widehat{=}} [v_1 : T_1, \ldots, v_n : T_n]$$

---

[1] See https://bitbucket.org/circusmodelcheck/circus2csp.

A *Circus process* is an encapsulation of process-local shared variables and *Circus actions* that access those local variables, along with a 'main' action.

$$\textbf{process } ProcName \; \widehat{=} \; \textbf{begin}$$
$$\textbf{state } PState == LocVars$$
$$PBody \; \widehat{=} \; \langle \text{action defn.} \rangle$$
$$PInit \; \widehat{=} \; \langle \text{action defn.} \rangle$$
$$PMain \; \widehat{=} \; PInit; PBody$$
$$\bullet \; PMain$$
$$\textbf{end}$$

Circus processes can only communicate with the external environment via channels, while *Circus* actions can also communicate via the local variables of their containing process. Processes can be modified and combined with each other, using the following CSP operators: sequential composition (;), non-deterministic choice ($\sqcap$), external choice ($\square$), alphabetised parallel ($[\![\ldots]\!]$), interleaving ($|||$), iterated versions of the above (e.g., $\sqcap_{e \in E} \bullet \ldots$), and hiding ($\setminus$).

Circus actions can be built with the CSP operators detailed above, as well as the following CSP constructs: termination (Skip), deadlock (Stop), abort(Chaos), event prefix ($\rightarrow$), guarded action ($\&$), and recursion (μ). In addition a *Circus* action can be defined by a Z schema, or Dijkstra-style guarded commands, including variable assignment ($:=$). Note that actions cannot be defined as standalone entities at the top level of a *Circus* specification.

Parallel composition of *Circus* actions differs from that in CSP, in that we need to also specify which variables each side is allowed to modify. Parallel action composition, written as $A_1 [\![ns_1 \, | \, cs \, | \, ns_2]\!] A_2$ states that action A_i may only modify variables listed in ns_i, where ns_1 and ns_2 are disjoint, and both actions must synchronise on events listed in cs. The semantics is that each side runs on its own copy of the shared variables, and the final state is obtained by merging the (disjoint) changes when both sides have terminated.

Circus also allows the use of local declarations in a variety of both process and action contexts. For actions, we can declare local variables, using **var** $x : T \bullet A$ which introduces variable v of type T which is only in scope within A. Variations of these can be used to define parameterised actions, of which the most relevant here is one that supports read-write parameters.

Finally, there is a refinement calculus for *Circus*, which is a fusion of those for both Z and CSP (failures-divergences)[27].

3   Translating *Circus* to CSP_M using *Circus2CSP*

Our first attempt to model check the *Circus* haemodialysis (HD) specification [16], was to manually translate it into CSP_M, and adjust its state-space until the desired checks could be successfully completed. This manual translation was error-prone, and this motivated the development of a mechanised translator. Our plan was to provide a high degree of automation to minimise error-prone human interventions, in such a way that we have a basis for arguing for its correctness.

We started the development based on the *Circus*-to-CSP_M translation strategy developed for the EU COMPASS project and described in deliverable D24.1 [29, Section 5]. It specifies the translation in two parts: a function Ω that maps a *Circus* specification to an equivalent *Circus* specification using only the CSP subset of the *Circus* language; and a function Υ that translates CSP-as-*Circus* into machine-readable CSP_M (Fig. 1).

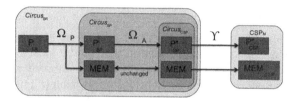

Fig. 1. Mapping *Circus* into CSP_M (derived from [29, Fig. 7, p77])

Function Ω has two phases: Ω_P and Ω_A. Function Ω_P extracts mutable state from the input state-rich ($Circus_{SR}$) process P_{SR} and gathers it in a new *Memory* action, while replacing direct references to state in P_{SR} with appropriate "get" and "set" messages that communicate with that *Memory*, to obtain a state-poor ($Circus_{SP}$) process P'_{SP}. Function Ω_A then translates P'_{SP} into its CSP equivalent P''_{SP}, by replacing *Circus*-specific actions by CSP-as-*Circus* ($Circus_{CSP}$) equivalents. All of the transformations done by Ω_P and Ω_A are valid *Circus* refinement steps, each of which are in fact equivalences, defined in D24.1 [29, §5.3 and App. A].

3.1   The Memory Model

The need for a memory model arises from the fact that CSP does not naturally capture the notion of *mutable state*. One solution for that is to produce a state-poor process that communicates with a Memory model [25] that stores the values of state components and local variables from the original state-rich processes. Initially, our memory model was very similar to that in D24.1, with some differences in naming conventions. In our approach, we defined a notation for renaming the variables allowing the user to easily identify which are (global) state components, or local variables. Variables are renamed by adding a prefix $sv\_$ or $lv\_$ indicating respectively a state or local variable.

As part of the translation strategy, the CSP_M environment is redefined in terms of the type system. Based on the work of Mota *et al.* [25], D24.1 defined a union type $UNIVERSE$ containing any type defined in the specification. When translated into CSP_M, use is made of the **subtype** facility of that language to manage the universe construction. Moreover, the names of every state component and local variable are defined as elements of a type $NAME$.

$$NAME ::= sv\_v_1 | sv\_v_2 | \ldots | sv\_v_n | lv\_l_1 | \ldots | lv\_l_k$$

The approach makes use of a set of bindings, $BINDING$, which maps all the names, $NAME$, into the $UNIVERSE$ type. In [29], a function δ is defined as a mapping between each variable in $NAME$ and its type, where each type (T_i is a subtype of $UNIVERSE$), and is used to define $Memory$.

$$BINDING == NAME \rightarrow UNIVERSE$$
$$\delta == \{sv\_v_1 \mapsto T_1, sv\_v_2 \mapsto T_2, \ldots, sv\_v_n \mapsto T_3, \ldots, lv\_l_k \mapsto T_m\}$$

As a result of applying the Ω functions, the state of a *Circus* process is replaced by a $Memory$ action parameterised by a read/write binding (**vres** b), which manages the mutable state, offering $mget$ and $mset$ channels carrying name/value pairs ($n.v$).

$Memory \mathrel{\widehat{=}} \textbf{vres } b : BINDING \bullet$

  $(\Box n : \operatorname{dom} b \bullet mget.n!b(n) \rightarrow Memory(b))$

  $\Box \ (\Box n : \operatorname{dom} b \bullet mset.n?nv : (nv \in \delta(n)) \rightarrow Memory(b \oplus \{n \mapsto nv\}))$

  $\Box \ terminate \rightarrow \text{Skip}$

Note, that while syntactically a *Circus* action, $Memory$ uses only the CSP subset of *Circus* Such a $Memory$ process runs in parallel with the main action of the translated *Circus* process, communicating through the channels $mget$ and $mset$. Moreover, the process execution ends when the $terminate$ signal is triggered. The above three channels compose the MEM_I channel set: **channelset** $MEM_I ==$ $\{\!| mget, mset, terminate |\!\}$.

The final specification puts the original process after Ω-translation in parallel with the memory model, synchronising on the MEM_I channels, which are themselves hidden at the top-level, with the binding as a top-level parameter. Note that the semantics of this at the top-level involves a non-deterministic choice[2] of the values in the initial binding b. This results in the following CSP form:

$$\sqcap b : BINDING \bullet \left(\begin{array}{c} (\Omega_A(P); terminate \rightarrow \text{Skip}) \\ \|_{MEM_I} \ Memory(b) \end{array} \right) \backslash MEM_I$$

Deliverable D24.1 contains manual proofs of the correctness of the translation [29, Appendix K].

4   Upgrading the Memory Model

With the initial version of the tool, we took examples from D24.1 (e.g. the ringbuffer example [29, Appendix D.2, p163]) and automatically translated them and

---

[2] A non-deterministic choice of values means that the bindings are picked randomly among the possible combinations of bindings.

then succesfully performed FDR checks. However, when we turned our attention to the somewhat larger HD model, we immediately uncovered some limitations of the basic translation, which were overcome by changing the memory model.

4.1   Limitation 1: Z Types vs. CSP_M Types

The use of the $UNIVERSE$ type, the CSP_M subtype feature, and a function written in CSP_M to map a name to its specific type, worked fine if all the types in $UNIVERSE$ were a sub-type of one supertype. In the D24.1 examples, all types were sub-types of the natural numbers. However, in the HD model we were developing, we had a mixture of natural sub-types, and enumerations. The type system in CSP_M does not consider enumeration types to be isomorphic to subtypes of any sufficiently large number type. We could have generated those isomorphisms, but these would have complicated the back-annotation problem, whenever a counter-example was found using FDR. Instead, we partitioned $UNIVERSE$ and $BINDING$ into the distinct supertypes present in the *Circus* model.

$$Memory \cong \mathbf{vres}\ b_{T_1} : BINDING_{T_1}, \ldots, b_{T_k} : BINDING_{T_k}$$

$$\bullet \left(\begin{array}{l} (\Box n_1 : \mathrm{dom}\ b_1 \bullet mget.n_1!b_1(n_1) \to Memory(b_1, \ldots, b_k)) \\ \Box \left(\begin{array}{l} \Box n_1 : \mathrm{dom}\ b_1 \bullet mset.n_1?nv : (nv \in \delta(n_1)) \\ \qquad \to Memory(b_1 \oplus \{n_1 \mapsto nv\}, \ldots, b_k) \end{array} \right) \\ \Box \ldots \Box (\Box n_k : \mathrm{dom}\ b_k \bullet mget.n_k!b_k(n_k) \to Memory(b_1, \ldots, b_k)) \\ \Box \left(\begin{array}{l} \Box n_k : \mathrm{dom}\ b_k \bullet mset.n_k?nv : (nv \in \delta(n_k)) \\ \qquad \to Memory(b_1, \ldots, b_k \oplus \{n_k \mapsto nv\}) \end{array} \right) \\ \Box\ terminate \to \mathrm{Skip} \end{array} \right)$$

We then changed the top-level view to have a non-deterministic choice over all the distinct bindings.

$$\sqcap b_{T_1} : BINDING_{T_1}, \ldots, b_{T_k} : BINDING_{T_k}$$

$$\bullet \left(\begin{array}{l} (\Omega_A(P); terminate \to \mathrm{Skip}) \\ \|_{MEM_I} Memory(b_{T_1}, \ldots, b_{T_k}) \end{array} \right) \setminus MEM_I$$

4.2   Limitation 2: FDR Time/Space Explosion

We quickly discovered that using this translation, we could only check *Circus* models with a small number of state variables, usually less than ten, with even the hand-translation of the HD model done for the original case-study being more effective. We proceeded to experiment with transformations to the memory model, justified by the *Circus* refinement laws.

Variables Have Non-deterministic Start Values. We first changed the top-level non-deterministic choice over the various bindings by replacing it with parameters.

$$\textbf{var } b_{T_1} : BINDING_{T_1}, \dots, b_{T_k} : BINDING_{T_k} \bullet$$
$$\left(\begin{array}{c} (\Omega_A(P); terminate \rightarrow \text{Skip}) \\ \|_{MEM_I} \; Memory(b_{T_1}, \dots, b_{T_k}) \end{array} \right) \backslash MEM_I$$

This is an equivalence, as $(\textbf{var } x : T \bullet A(x)) = (\sqcap x : T \bullet A(x))$. However, FDR treats the latter as being parameterised by x and requires it to be given an initial value. This means that we can only check a very strong proper refinement, rather than the full equivalence. However, we argue that in the safety-critical domain in general, it is always mandatory to initialise all variables. If *Init* is an action that initialises each variable precisely once with a constant value, with no intervening participation in events, then, regardless of the assignment ordering or any arbitrary initial value of any variable, the outcome is always the same: $s' = S_0$, where S_0 is the assignment of those constants to the coprresponding variables. If we insist on proper initialisation, then equivalence is restored. Given that the main usage of model-checking takes place in safety critical domains, we consider this a reasonable trade-off, particularly because it resulted in FDR performance improvements. However, our experiments revealed that a process translated this way, with more than ten state variables, still could not be checked with FDR in a reasonable time.

Distributed Memory Model. The final step, was to do more partitioning, moving to a situation were every variable gets its own memory process. The supertype bindings were retained at the top-level, but each variable's memory process was parameterised by the relevant binding with its domain restricted to just the name of that variable. So, for example, if variable n_i has a type whose supertype is T, then we first define a binding b_T for that supertype, and use it to parameterise a memory action for all variables of that supertype, which is itself the parallel composition of a memory process for each such variable, all synchronising on *terminate*, but interleaving all the *mget* and *mset* events:

$$MemoryT(b_T) \; \widehat{=}$$
$$[\![\{|terminate|\}]\!] n : \text{dom } b_T \bullet MemoryTVar(n, \{n\} \lhd b_T)$$

Here $N \lhd \mu$ restricts the domain of map μ to set N. We then define a parameterised process that represents a single variable:

$$MemoryTVar(n, b) \; \widehat{=}$$
$$\quad mget.n.b(n) \rightarrow MemoryTVar(n, b)$$
$$\quad \Box \; mset.n?nv : \delta(n) \rightarrow MemoryTVar(n, b \oplus n \mapsto nv)$$
$$\quad \Box \; terminate \rightarrow \text{Skip}$$

The entire memory is constructed by putting the memories for each supertype in parallel, in the same way as for the individual variable processes.

$$Memory(b_{T_1}, \dots, b_{T_k}) \; \widehat{=}$$
$$MemoryT_1(b_{T_1}) [\![\{|terminate|\}]\!] \dots [\![\{|terminate|\}]\!] MemoryT_k(b_{T_k})$$

This last transformation produced a marked improvement in the time and memory consumption of FDR when checking models.

In the next section we describe and discuss our experiments on the HD machine mode comparing some of approaches above. Moreover, we also compare the results obtained using other tools as a way of assessing our results.

5   Experimental Results

In this section we present the tests we performed using our tool, *Circus2CSP*, exploring ways of overcoming any limitations from FDR, as well as comparing our approach with others from the literature. Firstly, we explore the interference of invariants and preconditions in CSP_M. Then, we compare *Circus2CSP* with the model from [16]. We also the effects of using some compression techniques available in FDR. Finally, we compare different approaches for modeling the Ring Buffer case study.

One of the requirements when model-checking a system is to produce a model whose range of values is enough for covering any condition imposed by an operation. However, when including the state invariant, we are also restricting the range of values permitted to be used within the system. From the example of the chronometer [27], we know that both *min* and *sec* was declared as natural numbers. However, while thinking of a chronometer in the real world, we know that neither a second, nor a minute goes beyond 59 units, without flipping the next unit counter. Therefore, it is safe to restrict the range of *min* and *sec* to $0 \ldots 60$, where 60 is an unexpected value in the system.

We experimented with the impact of explicitly including invariant and precondition checks using the example of the Chronometer [27], with a new process *Chrono*. When using the translation rules presented in [29], we noticed that it is hard for FDR to check the model: it was translated using the conversion from normalised schemas to specification statements and from there, to the appropriate rules that introduce a condition that checks if *pre* is satisfied. If satisfied, it behaves as a non-deterministic choice of values from the state variables that satisfies both invariant and precondition, followed by updating these values in the memory model. Otherwise, if *pre* is not satisfied, it behaves like *Chaos*.

Our example of the chronometer has only two state variables and the results obtained using FDR are enough to show how the invariant checks throughout the specification increase the time spent during the assertion check in FDR. We deliberately modified the original model with the inclusion of the state invariant restricting both *min* and *sec* to values below 60, in order to experiment with the translated model in FDR.

process *Chrono* $\hat{=}$ **begin**

    state *AState* $\hat{=}$ $[sec, min : \mathbb{N} \mid min < 60 \wedge sec < 60]$

    AInit $\hat{=}$ $[AState' \mid sec' = 0; \; min' = 0]$

    IncSec $\hat{=}$ $[\Delta AState \mid sec' = (sec + 1) \bmod 60]$

    IncMin $\hat{=}$ $[\Delta AState \mid min' = (min + 1) \bmod 60]$

$$Run \; \hat{=} \; \left(\begin{array}{l} tick \rightarrow \big(IncSec\big) \; ; \; \Big(\big(sec = 0\big) \; \& \; \big(IncMin\big) \; \Box \; \big(sec \neq 0\big) \; \& \; \text{Skip} \Big) \\ \Box \; time \rightarrow out!(min, sec) \rightarrow \text{Skip} \end{array} \right)$$

    $\bullet$ *AInit* ; $(\mu X \bullet Run \; ; \; X)$

end

We illustrate our experiment in Table 1 while exploring the inclusion of state invariants and precondition verification in the chronometer model, and used the following derived models[3]:

    D241 Model manually translated using the approach from [29] without invariants and preconditions, using a non-deterministic choice of any set of bindings.

    D241Inv Model manually translated using the approach from [29] including the invariants as a restriction to the bindings set.

    D241Pre Model manually translated using the approach from [29] which includes precondition checks before the operations, but no invariants in the main action.

D241InvPre Combination of *D241Inv* and *D241Pre*.

    CTOC Model translated using our improved translation rules, the result from our tool *Circus2CSP*, as discussed in Sect. 4 (no invariant checks).

  CTOCPre Extension of *CTOC* model where pre-condition checks, as done for *D241Pre*, are entered manually.

From the models above, our tool is able to automatically generate *CTOC*, *CTOCPre* was obtained by manually modifying *CTOC*, while the others were generated by hand. We performed checks for deadlock freedom[4] using the translated models in the six variants above, combined with a different range of values for natural numbers, ranging from $\ldots 3$ to $0 \ldots 60$. For example, in a specification where the values for natural numbers are restricted to the range $0 \ldots 10$, the process state was defined as $[min, sec : 0 \ldots 10 \mid min < 10 \wedge sec < 10]$.

We noticed a first difference between models *D241* and *D241Inv*, on one hand, and *CTOC* and *CTOCPre* on the other. The number of states visited for checks with the models *D241* and *D241Inv* was over 10-fold larger than for *CTOC* and *CTOCPre*. However, the influence of a precondition check within an operation makes a significant reduction in the state exploration, but with the price of spending more time computing preconditions, as seen in Table 1, between *CTOC* and *CTOCPre*. Moreover, we also observed that the checks

---

[3] The files used in this experiment can be found in the tool repository at https://bit.ly/2ONnk2T.

[4] The tests were performed using *Intel Core i7* 2.8 GHz CPU with 16GB of RAM.

Table 1. Interference of invariants and preconditions in CSP_M—Deadlock freedom checks (in seconds unless indicated otherwise)

Values range	CTOC		CTOCPre		D241		D241Inv		D241InvPre		D241Pre	
	Exec time	States visited	Exec time	States visited	Exec time	States visited	Exec time	States visited	Exec time	States visited	Exec time	States visited
0..3	0.116	68	0.134	21	0.206	1085	0.177	610	0.173	190	0.187	337
0..6	0.242	260	0.373	42	0.416	12734	0.35	9355	0.393	1513	0.428	2059
0..9	0.559	578	1.4	63	1.158	57791	1.138	46810	1.826	5104	1.955	6301
0..12	1.246	1022	4.197	84	2.714	172706	2.57	147157	5.22	12097	5.45	14197
0..15	2.533	1592	9.867	105	5.846	407537	5.452	358186	11.988	23626	12.6	26881
0..60	3m27s	25262	22m29s	1024	2h48	99M	1h40	91M	52m28s	3.7M	1h05	3.8M

for invariants has a weaker effect on states visited, when comparing the results between $D241InvPre$ and $D241Pre$. We also noticed that all variants of $D241$ were executed in a much larger time frame than the approaches using the translation from our tool, Circus2CSP. However, the models generated by our tool do not include either invariants or preconditions.

Finally, as a way of experimenting with the real world example of the chronometer, we examined the models with numbers ranging from 0 up to 60, as presented in the last row of Table 1. We see a significant difference among the results from the approaches evaluated, where the model using $CTOC$ was evaluated (3 min) by FDR, which is 97% less time than the time spent to check the model using $D241Inv$ (over 1h40) and 94% less than $D241Pre$ (1h05). In general, the CSP_M models ($CTOC$) translated using our tool were evaluated by FDR using a much smaller state space and were checked in less time than all the other models we tried. Such a result shows how different models of the same system can be affected by the checks of invariants and preconditions, as well as how optimising the memory model can result in much smaller state exploration when using FDR. Finally, we observed no correlation between time and state visited, in spite of the use (or not) of compression by default in FDR.

5.1 Haemodialysis (HD) Machine Experiments

The manual translation (herein byHand) of the Circus [16] HD model resulted in a CSP_M specification with twice as many lines as the Circus model. Using the CTOC translation results in CSP_M with approximately 75% fewer lines than the corresponding Circus file.

Our reference Circus model was that of the HD machine running in parallel with a model of one of the case study requirements (**R-1** [2, Section 4.2, p11]). The requirement model is effectively a monitor that observes the machine model, checking that it is satisfied, and deadlocking if it observes a violation. We then check the proposition that the HD model is correct w.r.t **R-1** by showing that the combination is deadlock free. In addition to comparing various translation schemes, we also explored the effect of changing the size of our "natural number" type: $NatValue == 0..N$, in order to estimate the number of states visited in FDR.

We explored the byHand and CTOC translation schemes with four ranges of *NatValue* size, with N up to a maximum of 90, as shown in Table 2. The only case where we could compare the two approaches was our first case, with $N = 2$: it resulted in 9,409 states visited using byHand, in contrast with 811 states visited using CTOC, demonstrating a reduction of 91% in terms of states explored. Moreover, the execution time with the model generated using CTOC was equally reduced by 91% compared to the model using byHand. The "Plys" column indicates how deep the breadth-first search algorithm used by FDR went while checking. This is larger for the byHand model, and is independent of the value of N. Interestingly, after waiting more than 2 h, we were unable to obtain results from the model generated with byHand when we increased the N to 3. However, the model generated with CTOC, when tested using $n = 90$, was executed in 35 s, which is still quicker than byHand with $N = 2$. We also note that amount of memory used was constant, at 240 MB approx.

Table 2. Time for asserting deadlock freedom of the HD Machine in FDR4

Approach	NatValue range	Result	States visited	Transitions visited	Plys visited	Exec. time
CTOC	0..1	Passed	811	1,800	39	0.375 s
	0..2	Passed	1,761	3,786	39	0.407 s
	0..10	Passed	21,169	44,586	39	0.937 s
	0..90	Passed	1,369,809	1,369,809	39	35.097 s
byHand	0..1	Passed	9,409	301,617	47	40.826 s
	0..2	Incomplete	?	?	?	>2 h

We could not get results here for the D241 scheme as its translation of the HD model resulted in type errors being reported by FDR.

In addition to experiments that varied N above, we also explored how the *number* of variables, rather than the size of their datatypes, influenced the checking time. Using a hypothetical example having 12 state variables, checks using D241 were performed in 35 min, compared to 76 ms using CTOC. We observed segmentation faults using D241 with a more than 12 variables. However, checks using CTOC in an example with 42 state variables and $NatValue = 0..30$, were performed in 870 ms. What is clear is that with the CTOC translation scheme, namely one memory-process per state-variable, we can now handle *Circus* models of considerable complexity.

5.2 Ring-Buffer Experiments

Another interesting example was to take the *Circus* specification of the bounded reactive ring buffer, RB, from D24.1 [29, Appendix D.2, p. 163], based on the model presented in [7]. We compared the CTOC translation of this using *Circus2CSP* (RB_{CTOC}), with the by-hand translation in D24.1 [29, Appendix D.4,

Table 3. *RingBuffer* checks: deadlock and livelock freedom, and determinism.

Test	Model	Result	States visited	Transitions	Plys	Exec. time
Deadlock free	RB_{byH}	Passed	8,297,025	16,805,249	44	26.657 s
	RB_{CTOC}	Passed	1,628	3,109	38	0.145 s
Livelock free	RB_{byH}	Passed	8,297,025	16,805,249	44	25.476 s
	RB_{CTOC}	Passed	1,628	3,109	38	0.151 s
Deterministic	RB_{byH}	Passed	9,869,889	19,852,673	69	54.863 s
	RB_{CTOC}	Passed	2,012	3,853	63	0.159 s

Table 4. Refinement checks between models of the Ring Buffer example

	Refinement check	Result	States visited	Transitions visited	Plys visited	Exec. time
1	$RB_{byH} \sqsubseteq_{FD} RB_{CTOC}$	Passed	1,628	3,109	38	58.019 s
2	$RB_{CTOC} \sqsubseteq_{FD} RB_{byH}$	Passed	8,297,025	16,805,249	44	42.543 s

p166] (RB_{CTOC}). We firstly perform the usual tests like deadlock freedom and termination checks for *the*RB_{CTOC} and for the RB_{CTOC} specifications, as illustrated in Table 3.

We can see a clear difference between the states visited between the three approaches, notably those between RB_{byH} and RB_{CTOC} where the number of states and transitions visited was reduced considerably, as well as the amount of time spent by FDR4 to check the assertions.

We also experimented to check the failures-divergences refinement ($P \sqsubseteq_{FD} Q$) between the three approaches, each pair in both directions. Since we know that the specification RB_{CTOC} is a translation from the same *Circus* model of the handmade translation of RB_{byH}, we expect that RB_{byH} and RB_{CTOC} are equivalent to each other, $RB_{byH} \sqsubseteq_{FD} RB_{CTOC}$ and $RB_{CTOC} \sqsubseteq_{FD} RB_{byH}$, which is true, as seen below in row 1 and 3.

Interestingly, if we compare the states and transitions visited, as well as the execution time from Tables 3 with 4, given a refinement $A \sqsubseteq_{FD} B$, the states and transitions visited are almost the same as when checking B for deadlock freedom.

During our experiments, we also compared our *Circus2CSP* model with the Ring Buffer model RB_{KW}, based on [40, Chapter 22], produced using the approach of Ye and Woodcock [41] for translating *Circus* into CSP||B, for model checking using ProB [22]. Such an approach is similar [29, p. 116] but makes use of Z schemas as *Circus* actions that are currently not available in our translation scheme. In our experiments, we observed that the model RB_{KW} is refined by both RB_{CTOC} and RB_{byH}, but the refinement in the reverse direction does not hold, *i.e.*, RB_{KW} is not a refinement of neither RB_{CTOC} nor RB_{byH}, as it is a more abstract model since its data aspects of specification are defined in B.

Unfortunately, the structure defined for our translation strategy is not fully supported by ProB, which was used to test RB_{KW} [42]. ProB is another model-checker, which like FDR, also allows the user to animate specifications. It was originally developed for the B language, but it has been extended and now it supports other formal languages such as CSP, Z, Event-B [1], as well as combined languages such as CSP||B. We observed that the use of subtype, in our models, is not fully supported by the ProB tool, causing some commands like "model-check" to result in errors. However, we were able to animate our translated specification using ProB, and to execute the same assertion check, as in FDR: we obtained similar results to those when running FDR.

On the other side, the tests performed with the CSP_M specification of RB_{KW} using FDR failed the checks for deadlock freedom and determinism. The results obtained from ProB can be related to what we obtained in FDR in terms of the behavior of the system: the counterexample given can be used to animate the CSP||B model in ProB, causing the same effect: deadlock. However, we have no way to fully compare both approaches since CSP||B takes into account the system state in ProB, whereas we only have the CSP_M side of the model, which captures the behavior of the system, but does not captures the system state. The most obvious explanation for the deadlock in RB_{KW} is that the state (modeled in B) influences control-flow that results in deadlock situations being avoided.

5.3 Compression Experiments

An important aspect when using FDR is the availability of compression techniques [33] in order to reduce the number of states, reducing the time spent for refinement checking. A compression transforms a labelled-transition system (LTS) into a corresponding one, which is expected to be smaller and more efficient whilst using it for checks in FDR. Currently, FDR applies compressions in parallel compositions by default, which is the main structure we use in our memory model. We explored a few other compression tecniques, such as *sbisim*, which determines the maximal strong bisimulation [5], and *wbisim*, which computes the maximal weak bisimulation. Depending on the compression used, the number of states visited, were indeed reduced, as illustrated in Table 5.

Table 5. Experimenting CSP_M compression techniques with the HD Machine

Values range	sbisim+diamond		No compression		sbisim		wbisim	
	States visited	Exec time (seconds)	States visited	Exec time (seconds)	States visited	Exec time (seconds)	States visited	Exec time (seconds)
0..10	77	0.499	21,169	0.458	302	0.479	87	0.56
0..120	77	25.096	2,416,749	18.805	302	21.793	87	35.839
0..240	77	114.845	9,556,509	84.803	302	100.112	87	175.846
0..360	77	327.815	21,419,469	235.236	302	269.414	Killed	286.079
0..480	77	668.437	38,005,629	467.602	302	523.825	Killed	525.889

Although the states/transitions/plys visited were considerably reduced using the compression techniques mentioned above, there was little impact on overall execution time, and the number of states visited are independent of the size of *NatValue*, while the number of transitions grows slowly. However, the results obtained here are related to the model of the HD machine, and it is difficult to identify which compression technique will be most effective in a general case, and indeed, further experiments are required.

6   Future Work

Our plans for future work include exploring other industrial-scale case studies [3,15,17], as a way of identifying the kind of *Circus* constructs that would be suitable to have available in our translation tool. We have a particular interest in specifying a translation strategy for Z schemas used as *Circus* actions within a process. The best approach would be to use Z Refinement Calculus [6]. For now, our tool deals only with those schemas that in fact can be translated into assignments. We intend to explore the operators for Z schemas and the refinement laws that can be applied accordingly.

In addition, we also plan to establish a link between *Circus2CSP* and Isabelle/UTP [11], so that we can use their mechanised UTP semantics for *Circus* to verify the correctness of our Haskell implementation. Moreover, our tool also has a *Circus* refinement "calculator" embedded in it, which implements the laws listed in Appendix A of the Deliverable 24.1 [29, p.147], which can easily be extended to the other refinement laws proved by Oliveira [27] in the near future.

We can eliminate the use of CSP_M subtyping in CTOC (the process-per-variable model), and simplify "get" and "set" prefixes of the forms *mget.n.v* and *mset.n.v* to *get_n.v* and *set_n.v* respectively, where we now have dedicated channels per variable. However, the relationship of this new form to CTOC is no longer a simple equivalence as there are now different events in the two models.

Finally, in terms of improvement of our tool, compared to other approaches [9], it would also be interesting to review the parser of Z and *Circus* from *Circus2CSP* in order to rewrite it to be in conformance with the International Standards Organization (ISO) standards, ISO/IEC 13568:2002 [20], which describes the syntax, type system and semantics of Z formal notation. Moreover, we would like to include the *libcspm* library[5] into *Circus2CSP* in order to be able to parse the relevant code included in our definition of the *assertion* LATEX environment. Such an attempt would help a *Circus2CSP* user wishing to review any fault in the CSP_M specification translated from *Circus*.

Finally, we can envisage work in the future that might extend the benefits gained here to the wider model-checking community. One possibility is extending the translator to target model-checkers other than FDR. This would require us to have either a rigorously defined embedding, of the subset of CSP that we produce, into the modelling language of the proposed checker, or have a way of linking the semantics of the target modelling language to *Circus* and/or CSP to verify the correctness of direct output in that language. The second aspect

---

[5] https://github.com/tomgr/libcspm

concerns the possibility that our approach can be adapted to work within another model-checking eco-system entirely. ne key advantage in having a state-rich form is the ability to easily describe state changes that only modify small parts of the state (compare $P = w := y - x; Q$ with $P(u, v, w, x, y, z) = Q(u, v, y - x, x, y, z)$). We note that the CADP system, which is based on LOTOS (state-poor), has already moved in this direction, with tools now working with LTN (LOTOS New Technology, state-rich), using a LTN to LOTOS translator [13]. Do other modelling notations have state-rich forms that are hard to check, but have good checkers for state-poor forms?

7   Conclusions

In this paper we evaluated possible approaches for translating *Circus* into CSP_M, for model checking using FDR. Our main concern was how the state of a *Circus* process could be captured in CSP_M in such a way that FDR could handle a large amount of state variables and an even larger range of values. We then produced several models of CSP_M specifications translated from *Circus* and also explored the consequences of including both state invariants and preconditions of *Circus* actions in the CSP_M models. Such a research resulted in the development of *Circus2CSP*, a tool for model checking *Circus*, through the automatic translation from *Circus* to CSP_M, and therefore, being able to use FDR for refinement checks. *Circus2CSP* development was developed in 24 months, and has a total of over 26 thousand lines of Haskell code.

We observed that a distributed memory model, rather than a centralised one, as proposed by Mota *et al.* [24] is beneficial for larger states. Moreover, the time spent as well as the state exploration from FDR's refinement checks is larger when capturing preconditions and state invariants. Another observation from our experiments is that we were able to reduce the state exploration even more by refining our model to one where the bindings were explicitly defined by *Circus2CSP*, rather than considering a non-deterministic choice over such bindings, as per the original manual translation. This is justified by assuming that every state variable should be initialised prior to its use in the process. The outcome is that we now have a mechanised translator from *Circus* to CSP_M that produces tractable models, and allows the use of FDR on larger case studies than has been possible up to now.

We should clarify that our approach to produce parametrised processes is not an attempt to use the bindings *data-independently* [32, p. 453]. That is solving a different problem, namely finding a finite size of a type that is suitable to demonstrate the correctness for any finite or even infinite size of such type. Moreover, to date, our approach is unable to generate counterexamples or any kind of back annotation to the *Circus* models, and thus is in our plans for future work.

We used the HD machine and the ring buffer case studies as examples in order to test the capabilities of our tool whilst model checking the automatically translated models in FDR. Our aim was to contribute to reducing FDR's workload in order to model check larger systems. We learned that a practical implementation/mechanisation of a theory may reveal difficulties that could not otherwise be discovered without extensive use of a tool prototype, especially when applying it to larger case studies.

Acknowledgments. This work was funded by CNPq (Brazilian National Council for Scientific and Technological Development) within the Science without Borders programme, Grant No. 201857/2014-6, and partially funded by Science Foundation Ireland grant 13/RC/2094.

References

1. Abrial, J.R.: Modeling in Event-B: System and Software Engineering, 1st edn. Cambridge University Press, New York (2010)
2. Mashkoor, A.: The hemodialysis machine case study. In: Butler, M., Schewe, K.-D., Mashkoor, A., Biro, M. (eds.) ABZ 2016. LNCS, vol. 9675, pp. 329–343. Springer, Cham (2016). https://doi.org/10.1007/978-3-319-33600-8_29
3. Beg, A., Butterfield, A.: Linking a state-rich process algebra to a state-free algebra to verify software/hardware implementation. In: Proceedings of the 8th International Conference on Frontiers of Information Technology - FIT 2010, pp. 1–5 (2010). http://portal.acm.org/citation.cfm?doid=1943628.1943675
4. Beg, A., Butterfield, A.: Development of a prototype translator from Circus to CSPm. In: Proceedings of ICOSST 2015–2015 International Conference on Open Source Systems and Technologies, pp. 16–23, December 2016
5. Boulgakov, A., Gibson-Robinson, T., Roscoe, A.W.: Computing maximal weak and other bisimulations. Form. Asp. Comput. **28**(3), 381–407 (2016). https://doi.org/10.1007/s00165-016-0366-2
6. Cavalcanti, A., Woodcock, J.C.P.: ZRC - a refinement calculus for Z. Form. Asp. Comput. **10**(3), 267–289 (1998). http://link.springer.com/10.1007/s001650050016, https://doi.org/10.1007/s001650050016
7. Cavalcanti, A.L.C., Sampaio, A.C.A., Woodcock, J.C.P.: A refinement strategy for Circus. Form. Asp. Comput. **15**, 146–181 (2003). https://doi.org/10.1007/s00165-003-0006-5
8. Conserva Filho, M., Oliveira, M.V.M.: Implementing tactics of refinement in CRefine. In: Eleftherakis, G., Hinchey, M., Holcombe, M. (eds.) SEFM 2012. LNCS, vol. 7504, pp. 342–351. Springer, Heidelberg (2012). https://doi.org/10.1007/978-3-642-33826-7_24
9. CZT Partners: Community Z tools, October 2006. czt.sourceforge.net/
10. Dijkstra, E.W.: Guarded commands, nondeterminacy and formal derivation of programs. Commun. ACM **18**(8), 453–457 (1975). http://portal.acm.org/citation.cfm?doid=360933.360975%5Cn
11. Foster, S., Zeyda, F., Woodcock, J.: Isabelle/UTP: a mechanised theory engineering framework. In: Naumann, D. (ed.) UTP 2014. LNCS, vol. 8963, pp. 21–41. Springer, Cham (2015). https://doi.org/10.1007/978-3-319-14806-9_2
12. Freitas, L.: Model checking Circus. Ph.D. thesis, Department of Computer Science, The University of York, UK (2005)
13. Garavel, H., Lang, F., Serwe, W.: From LOTOS to LNT. In: Katoen, J.-P., Langerak, R., Rensink, A. (eds.) ModelEd, TestEd, TrustEd. LNCS, vol. 10500, pp. 3–26. Springer, Cham (2017). https://doi.org/10.1007/978-3-319-68270-9_1

14. Gibson-Robinson, T., Armstrong, P., Boulgakov, A., Roscoe, A.W.: FDR3 – a modern model checker for CSP. Tools Algorithms Constr. Anal. Syst. **8413**, 187–201 (2014). http://www.cs.ox.ac.uk/projects/fdr/manual/

15. Gomes, A.O.: Formal Specification of the ARINC 653 Architecture Using Circus (2012). http://etheses.whiterose.ac.uk/id/eprint/2683

16. Gomes, A.O., Butterfield, A.: Modelling the haemodialysis machine with *Circus*. In: Butler, M., Schewe, K.-D., Mashkoor, A., Biro, M. (eds.) ABZ 2016. LNCS, vol. 9675, pp. 409–424. Springer, Cham (2016). https://doi.org/10.1007/978-3-319-33600-8_34

17. Gomes, A.O., Oliveira, M.V.M.: Formal specification of a cardiac pacing system. In: Cavalcanti, A., Dams, D.R. (eds.) FM 2009. LNCS, vol. 5850, pp. 692–707. Springer, Heidelberg (2009). https://doi.org/10.1007/978-3-642-05089-3_44

18. Hoare, C., He, J.: Unifying Theories of Programming. Prentice-Hall, Upper Saddle River (1998)

19. Hopcroft, J.E., Motwani, R., Ullman, J.D.: Introduction to Automata Theory, Languages, and Computation - International Edition, 2nd edn. Addison-Wesley, Boston (2003)

20. ISO/IEC: ISO/IEC 13568:2002 Information Technology - Z formal specification notation - Syntax, type system and semantics. Technical report (2002). http://standards.iso.org/ittf/PubliclyAvailableStandards/c021573_ISO_IEC_13568_2002 (E).zip

21. Jackson, E.K., Levendovszky, T., Balasubramanian, D.: Reasoning about meta-modeling with formal specifications and automatic proofs. In: Whittle, J., Clark, T., Kühne, T. (eds.) MODELS 2011. LNCS, vol. 6981, pp. 653–667. Springer, Heidelberg (2011). https://doi.org/10.1007/978-3-642-24485-8_48

22. Leuschel, M., Butler, M.: ProB: a model checker for B. In: Araki, K., Gnesi, S., Mandrioli, D. (eds.) FME 2003. LNCS, vol. 2805, pp. 855–874. Springer, Heidelberg (2003). https://doi.org/10.1007/978-3-540-45236-2_46

23. Morgan, C.: Programming from Specifications. Prentice Hall International Series in Computer Science, vol. 16, 2nd edn. Prentice Hall, Upper Saddle River (1994). https://dl.acm.org/citation.cfm?id=184737

24. Mota, A., Farias, A., Didier, A., Woodcock, J.: Rapid prototyping of a semantically well founded *Circus* model checker. In: Giannakopoulou, D., Salaün, G. (eds.) SEFM 2014. LNCS, vol. 8702, pp. 235–249. Springer, Cham (2014). https://doi.org/10.1007/978-3-319-10431-7_17

25. Nogueira, S., Sampaio, A., Mota, A.: Test generation from state based use case models. Form. Asp. Comput. **26**(3), 441–490 (2014)

26. Oliveira, D., Oliveira, M.V.M.: Joker: an animation framework for formal specications. In: SBMF 2011 - Short Papers, pp. 43–48. ICMC/USP, September 2011

27. Oliveira, M.V.M.: formal derivation of state-rich reactive programs using Circus. Ph.D. thesis, University of York, UK (2005). http://ethos.bl.uk/OrderDetails.do?uin=uk.bl.ethos.428459

28. Oliveira, M.V.M., Cavalcanti, A., Woodcock, J.C.P.: Unifying theories in ProofPower-Z. Form. Asp. Comput. **25**, 133–158 (2013). https://doi.org/10.1007/s00165-007-0044-5

29. Oliveira, M.V.M., Sampaio, A., Antonino, P., Ramos, R., Cavalcanti, A., Woodcock, J.C.P.: Compositional analysis and design of CML models. Technical report D24.1, COMPASS Deliverable (2013). http://www.compass-research.eu/Project/Deliverables/D241.pdf

30. Oliveira, M.V.M., Sampaio, A.C.A., Conserva Filho, M.S.: Model-checking *Circus* state-rich specifications. In: Albert, E., Sekerinski, E. (eds.) IFM 2014. LNCS, vol. 8739, pp. 39–54. Springer, Cham (2014). https://doi.org/10.1007/978-3-319-10181-1_3

31. Plagge, D., Leuschel, M.: Validating Z specifications using the PROB animator and model checker. In: Davies, J., Gibbons, J. (eds.) IFM 2007. LNCS, vol. 4591, pp. 480–500. Springer, Heidelberg (2007). https://doi.org/10.1007/978-3-540-73210-5_25

32. Roscoe, A.W.: The Theory and Practice of Concurrency. Prentice Hall PTR, Upper Saddle River (1973)

33. Roscoe, A.W., Gardiner, P.H.B., Goldsmith, M.H., Hulance, J.R., Jackson, D.M., Scattergood, J.B.: Hierarchical compression for model-checking CSP or how to check 10^{20} dining philosophers for deadlock. In: Brinksma, E., Cleaveland, W.R., Larsen, K.G., Margaria, T., Steffen, B. (eds.) TACAS 1995. LNCS, vol. 1019, pp. 133–152. Springer, Heidelberg (1995). https://doi.org/10.1007/3-540-60630-0_7

34. Saaltink, M., Meisels, I., Saaltink, M.: The Z/EVES reference manual (for version 1.5). Reference manual, ORA Canada, pp. 72–85 (1997). http://dl.acm.org/citation.cfm?id=647282.722913

35. Scattergood, B.: The semantics and implementation of machine-readable CSP, pp. 1–179 (1998). http://ethos.bl.uk/OrderDetails.do?uin=uk.bl.ethos.299037

36. Schneider, S.: Concurrent and Real-Time Systems. Wiley, Chichester (2000)

37. Woodcock, J.C.P., Bryans, J., Canham, S., Foster, S.: The COMPASS modelling language: timed semantics in UTP, pp. 1–32 (2014)

38. Woodcock, J.C.P., Cavalcanti, A.: The semantics of Circus. In: ZB 2002: formal specification and development in Z and B. In: 2nd International Conference of B and Z Users Grenoble (2002)

39. Woodcock, J., Cavalcanti, A., Freitas, L.: Operational semantics for model checking Circus. In: Fitzgerald, J., Hayes, I.J., Tarlecki, A. (eds.) FM 2005. LNCS, vol. 3582, pp. 237–252. Springer, Heidelberg (2005). https://doi.org/10.1007/11526841_17

40. Woodcock, J.C.P., Davies, J.: Using Z, Specification, Refinement, and Proof. Prentice Hall International Series in Computer Science. Prentice-Hall Inc., Upper Saddle River (1996)

41. Ye, K.: Model checking of state-rich formalisms. Ph.D. thesis, University of York (2016)

42. Ye, K., Woodcock, J.C.P.: Model checking of state-rich formalism Circus by linking to CSP——B. Int. J. Softw. Tools Technol. Transf. **19**(1), 73–96 (2017). https://doi.org/10.1007/s10009-015-0402-1

Circus2CSP: A Tool for Model-Checking *Circus* Using FDR

Artur Oliveira Gomes[1]([⊠]) and Andrew Butterfield[2]

[1] Universidade Federal de Mato Grosso do Sul, Corumbá, Brazil
artur.gomes@ufms.br
[2] School of Computer Science and Statistics, Trinity College Dublin, Dublin, Ireland
butrfeld@tcd.ie

Abstract. In this paper, we introduce *Circus2CSP*, a tool that automatically translates *Circus* into CSP_M, with an implementation based on a published manual translation scheme. This scheme includes new and modified translation rules that emerged as a result of experimentation. We addressed issues with FDR state-space explosion, by optimising our models using the *Circus* Refinement Laws. We briefly describe the usage of *Circus2CSP* along with a discussion of some experiments comparing our tool with the literature.

1 Introduction

Among the range of verification techniques, model checking is used for exploring all the possible states a reactive system can reach. The focus of model-checking is on the system's behaviour rather than how the model would manage its data. Therefore, a system whose behaviour strongly relies on its data may become difficult to check, since the data may range over infinite domains.

There has been an effort from the community in order to design a systematic approach for model-checking *Circus*, which due to its combination of formalisms, is quite a challenge. *Circus* [33] is a formal language that combines structural aspects of a system using the Z language [35] and the behavioural aspects using CSP [31], along with the refinement calculus [22] and Dijkstra's guarded commands [7]. Its semantics is based on the *Unifying Theories of Programming (UTP)* [15]. As an initial attempt to model-check *Circus*, we participated in the ABZ'16 haemodialysis case study [12], producing a *Circus* specification, manually translating it into CSP_M, which we then checked with FDR [9]. Moreover, when translating *Circus* into CSP, we adapted the *Circus* model to map the structural Z parts into appropriate CSP.

Unlike in *Circus* processes, an explicit notion of state variables is not present in CSP processes. Therefore, in order to translate *Circus* state, we would either translate it into a memory process [17,23,29], allowing other processes to read and write the values by synchronising on memory 'get' and 'put' events, or to transform the state variables into process parameters, as used by Beg [4]. For instance, we captured the state-based features of *Circus* in CSP using a memory

© Springer Nature Switzerland AG 2019
M. H. ter Beek et al. (Eds.): FM 2019, LNCS 11800, pp. 235–242, 2019.
https://doi.org/10.1007/978-3-030-30942-8_15

process synchronising on channels for reading and updating the values of the state variables. Such an approach was also used while model checking [10] the ARINC 653 [2] architecture.

In this paper, we present *Circus2CSP*[1] [13], a tool capable of model-checking specifications designed in *Circus* using FDR. It was developed by extending JAZA [32], a Z animator written in Haskell, in order to cover the *Circus* abstract syntax. The rest of the paper is organized as follows: In Sect. 2, we discuss the main goal of this work. A brief description of some experiments using *Circus2CSP* is presented in Sect. 3. The paper is concluded in Sect. 4.

2   *Circus2CSP*: Requirements and Goals

Our translation is based on that developed by Oliveira in the Compass project [26,27], which is based on repeated application of carefully selected *Circus* refinement laws, all of which happen to be equivalences. Such a translation uses set of rules for refining state-rich *Circus* into stateless processes that can be mapped into CSP_M.

Our focus while model-checking *Circus* is to produce a model in CSP_M where FDR can evaluate using as little computing resources as possible. As such, we provide a refined model from the strategy presented by Oliveira *et al.* [26], where our tool is capable of producing CSP_M models from larger specifications and making it possible for model-checking them using FDR. We highlight that because FDR is a refinement checker, it is not possible to perform temporal logic checks, which is further discussed by Lowe [20].

The entire toolset is developed as an extension of JAZA, which parses Z specifications written in LaTeX, the same input used by the Community Z Tools. Our goal was to produce a framework using the infrastructure available from JAZA, where the parser for Z was extended and now supports *Circus*, and from there, we include new modules like the translation tool and the refinement calculator for *Circus*. Moreover, our tool is linked to FDR, and may also be integrated with other tools in the future. Our contribution here is mainly related to the fulfilment of a tool for automatically model-checking *Circus*.

The reason we adopted the translation presented by Oliveira *et al.*, is that, even though it is a manual translation, with no tool support involved, each translation step is justified by the *Circus* refinement laws, which have been formally proved to be correct. Currently, their approach covers a subset of *Circus*. However, our investigation [14] through experiments with the implementation of such rules demonstrated that such an initial and theoretical approach was restricted to a subset of the possible *Circus* specifications: those dealing with only one same type for all variables within the state of those processes. Thus, we had to implement not only a tool for the translation but also to refine that translation strategy in order to support a more realistic set of specifications: those using mixed types among their state variables.

---

[1] https://bitbucket.org/circusmodelcheck/circus2csp.

We also experimented with the efficiency of FDR concerning the scale of the specifications. For such, we used the haemodialysis case study [3,12], a complex system which behaves according to the values of dozens of state variables. Thus, we refined the memory model in order to optimise the task of reading and updating the state variables from the *Circus* processes.

The outcome is that we now have a mechanised translator from *Circus* to CSP_M that produces tractable models, and allows the use of FDR on larger case studies than have been possible up to now. The new developed approach, as described in this paper, is sound since we were able to prove, by hand as well as using FDR as a refinement checker, that the memory model from Oliveira *et al.* is refined by the model discussed here [11, p. 77].

Our tool has an automatic refinement calculator for *Circus2CSP*, which handles a selected set of *Circus* refinement laws used according to [26, Appendix A, p. 147]. Moreover, we experimented with a strategy for refining Z schemas into "schema-free" *Circus* actions using Z Refinement Calculus [6].

Deliverables. In summary, our research towards model checking *Circus* resulted in the following contributions:

- **A tool for automatically translating a subset of** *Circus* **into** CSP_M**:** Implementation of a tool based on the work of Oliveira *et al.* [26] where one is able to translate *Circus* models written in LATEX into CSP_M, and then, be able to perform model-checking and refinement checks using FDR.
- **An automatic** *Circus* **refinement calculator:** As part of the translation strategy, the *Circus* refinement laws are applied to the processes and actions. In order to automate the translation as much as possible, we provide an automatic *Circus* refinement calculator.
- **A transformation of some Z schemas into appropriate** *Circus* **constructs for translating into** CSP_M**:** The translation approach presented by Oliveira does not handle Z schemas directly, but only after normalisation. However, such a translation was not yet formally proved to be correct. We explored ways of translating Z schemas into *Circus* actions, specifically, those schemas where the translation results in a set of assignments.
- **An improved** *Circus* **model that supports multiple types within a specification:** The generated CSP_M model from Oliveira *et al.* using multiple types is not supported by FDR, since it contains some auxiliary functions that are seen by FDR as polymorphic functions, which are not supported by such a tool. We, however, introduce a new data structure that treats each type with its own set of auxiliary functions.
- **A refinement of the memory model from Oliveira** *et al.* **[26]:** We provide a refined memory model with distributed memory cells updating and retrieving the values of the state variables, allowing FDR to handle a large number of state variables in a process, optimizing FDR's effort to check such models.

- **New rules for mapping** *Circus* **to** CSP_M**:** We extended the mapping functions for expressions and predicates from Z, as well as mapping functions for those actions specifically related to the Memory model.
- **A mechanism that integrates** *Circus2CSP* **with FDR:** We connected our tool to the "terminal-mode" interface of FDR, in order to be able to run checks straight from our tool. Unfortunately, we have no direct access to the code of FDR, and thus, we have to manually parse the results from the execution of FDR's "refine" command.
- **An automatic assertion generator for checking with FDR:** Our tool is able to generate assertion checks for refinement, deadlock, livelock and determinism checks for the loaded specification.

Tool Restrictions. Our tool expects *Circus* specifications as input, written in LATEX, very similar to the way Z paragraphs are written in LATEX, which is a *de facto* standard for writing *Circus* specifications. We assume that the *Circus* document is already type checked by existing tools [21].

Our tool supports most of the *Circus* syntax, avoiding those constructs not handled in [26, p. 78] such as: no writting to input variables; external choice only among prefixed actions (those guaranteed to participate in an event before doing anything else, such as assignment); and no miraculous specifications.

Furthermore, some features are not yet supported such as: dealing with state invariants or preconditions in the Z schemas; non-determinism of data is not supported; and the consequences of nested parallelism and hiding with non-disjoint name sets have not been handled yet. These are a consequence of this being an automated translation, rather than the manual one prescribed in [26]. Finally, the translation of Z schemas used as *Circus* actions is restricted to those resulting in assignments.

3   Experiments with *Circus2CSP*

During our research we performed tests using our tool, *Circus2CSP*, exploring ways of overcoming any limitations from FDR, as well as comparing our approach with others from the literature.

Firstly, we explore the interference of invariants and preconditions in CSP_M, using the chronometer model from Oliveira [25, pp. 34–41], comparing the model from *Circus2CSP* with the translation from Oliveira [26]. We identified that using *Circus2CSP*, the time spent by FDR to check for deadlock freedom, for example, with a model with the natural numbers ranging from zero to sixty (0..60), was of around 3 min. However, using Oliveira's approach it took nearly three hours. In general, the CSP_M models translated using our tool were evaluated by FDR using a much smaller state space and were checked in up to 95% less time than all the other models we tried derived from Oliveira's. However, we observed no correlation between time and state visited.

Then, we compare the translation of the HD model using *Circus2CSP* with the model from [12]. We observed a reduction of over 91% of the state explored, as well as the execution time. Moreover, the manual translation didn't allow us to run FDR with a larger range of values for natural numbers, usually ranging from 0 up to 2. However, with *Circus2CSP*, we were able to go beyond the range 0 up to 90 in less than a minute. Such a result demonstrated that our approach is capable of handling large-scale case studies like the haemodialysis machine [12] and the ring buffer [26,37].

We also evaluated the effects of using some compression techniques available in FDR using the HD model as an example. Although the states/transitions/plys visited were considerably reduced using the compression techniques such as *sbisim*, which determines the maximal strong bisimulation [5], and *wbisim*, which computes the maximal weak bisimulation, there was little impact on overall execution time, and the number of states visited are independent of the range of natural numbers used, while the number of transitions grows slowly. However, it is difficult to identify which compression technique will be most effective in a general case, and indeed, further experiments are required.

Finally, we compare different approaches for modeling the Ring Buffer case study [26,37], using FDR, in order to test the capabilities of our tool while model-checking the translated models, in contrast to the limitations of ProB [19]. Unfortunately, the structure defined for our translation strategy is not fully supported by ProB, which was used to test the model generated with the translation strategy from Ye [37]. ProB is another model-checker, which was originally developed for the B language, and was extended to support CSP, Z, Event-B [1], as well as combined languages such as CSP||B. We observed that some of the constructs used in our CSP_M model, such as subtype, are not yet supported by ProB. Nevertheless, we were able to use ProB's animator and to execute the same assertion check, as in FDR, obtaining similar results.

However, the tests performed with the CSP_M specification of Ye using FDR failed to checks for deadlock freedom and determinism. The results obtained from ProB can be related to what we obtained in FDR in terms of the behavior of the system: the counterexample given from FDR can be used to animate the CSP||B model in ProB, causing the same effect: deadlock. Although, our experiment was limited since CSP||B takes into account the system state in ProB. In such model, the CSP_M file generated from Ye captures only the behavior of the system, but does not captures the system state. We reckon that the deadlock was caused because the state (modeled in B) can interfere in the system behavior in order to avoid deadlocks.

4   Conclusions

In this paper, we briefly introduced *Circus2CSP*, a tool capable of model-checking *Circus* specifications using FDR, through a translation strategy from *Circus* into CSP_M. It comprises a series of translation rules, combined with *Circus* refinement laws. One can perform refinement checks using FDR directly from *Circus2CSP*'s command-line. The tool can be downloaded freely from https:// bitbucket.org/circusmodelcheck/.

We improved Oliveira's [26] translation strategy in a few ways: handling a wider mix of datatypes; translating Z schemas easily "compiled" to assignments; coping better with potentially large state spaces; and close integration with FDR. Some of the equivalence laws used in the translation have side-conditions that lead to proof obligations. Our tool does not discharge these, leaving them to the user to handle by other means.

The modifications for the memory model developed for our tool are similar to what was presented by Mota *et al.* [24], where interleaving between processes, one for each state variable, was proposed. In fact, the memory model used in [26] was based on the one by Mota *et al.*, and was expanded with the inclusion of a *terminate* signal, and, rather than one process for each variable, it would offer all possible *mget* and *mset* for all state variables at the same time.

A key principle in critical software development methods is that all global variables should be intialised pretty much immediately [2]. In a *Circus* context, if all the assignments are done are before any observable event occurs, then its behaviour is that of a (simultaneous) assignment $s' = s_{init}$, where s is the (aggregated) global state. This allows us to introduce an additional translation step that replaces a non-deterministic choice over all possible starting values of s by one arbitrary choice of starting value for s. This is normally a proper refinement, but with initialisation as above, results in being an equivalence. This trick dramatically improved the performance of FDR.

Some related work on techniques for model-checking *Circus* was presented by Freitas [8] where a refinement model checker based on automata theory [16] and the operational semantics of *Circus* [34] was formalised in Z/Eves [30]. However, Freita's *Circus* model checker is restricted to a subset of *Circus* actions and does not support the notion of *Circus* processes. Moreover, Nogueira *et al.* [23] also presented a prototype of a model checker for *Circus* within the Microsoft FORMULA [18] framework. However, they could not provide a formal proof of the soundness of their approach, since FORMULA does not have an available formal semantics. Model-checking *Circus* was investigated by Ye and Woodcock [36], who defined a link from *Circus* to $CSP \| B$ with model-checking using ProB [28]. However, ProB is a limited tool not supporting multiprocessors nor multithreading. Finally, Beg [4] prototyped an automatic translation that supports a subset of *Circus* constructs, supporting only *Skip*, prefixing action, sequential composition, assignments, if statements, and guards with simple predicates.

For future work, we have plans for specifying a translation strategy for Z schemas used as *Circus* actions within a process. The best approach would be to use Z Refinement Calculus [6]. For now, our tool deals only with those schemas that in fact can be translated into assignments. We intend to explore the operators for Z schemas and the refinement laws that can be applied accordingly.

Acknowledgements. This work was funded by CNPq (Brazilian National Council for Scientific and Technological Development) within the Science without Borders programme, Grant No. 201857/2014-6, and partially funded by Science Foundation Ireland grant 13/RC/2094.

References

1. Abrial, J.R.: Modeling in Event-B: System and Software Engineering, 1st edn. Cambridge University Press, New York (2010)
2. Aeronautical Radio, I.A.: ARINC 653: Avionics Application Standard Software Interface, November 2006
3. Mashkoor, A.: The hemodialysis machine case study. In: Butler, M., Schewe, K.-D., Mashkoor, A., Biro, M. (eds.) ABZ 2016. LNCS, vol. 9675, pp. 329–343. Springer, Cham (2016). https://doi.org/10.1007/978-3-319-33600-8_29
4. Beg, A., Butterfield, A.: Development of a prototype translator from Circus to CSPm. In: 2015 International Conference on Open Source Systems and Technologies, Proceedings, ICOSST 2015, pp. 16–23, December 2016
5. Boulgakov, A., Gibson-Robinson, T., Roscoe, A.W.: Computing maximal weak and other bisimulations. Formal Aspects Comput. **28**(3), 381–407 (2016). https://doi.org/10.1007/s00165-016-0366-2
6. Cavalcanti, A., Woodcock, J.C.P.: ZRC - a refinement calculus for Z. Formal Aspects Comput. **10**(3), 267–289 (1998). https://doi.org/10.1007/s001650050016
7. Dijkstra, E.W.: Guarded commands, nondeterminacy and formal derivation of programs. Commun. ACM **18**(8), 453–457 (1975). http://portal.acm.org/citation.cfm doid=360933.360975%5Cn
8. Freitas, L.: Model checking circus. Ph.D. thesis, Department of Computer Science, The University of York, UK (2005)
9. Gibson-Robinson, T., Armstrong, P., Boulgakov, A., Roscoe, A.W.: FDR3 - a modern model checker for CSP. Tools Algorithms Constr. Anal. Syst. **8413**, 187–201 (2014). https://www.cs.ox.ac.uk/projects/fdr/manual/
10. Gomes, A.O.: Formal Specification of the ARINC 653 Architecture Using Circus (2012). https://etheses.whiterose.ac.uk/id/eprint/2683
11. Gomes, A.O.: Model-checking circus with FDR using Circus2CSP. Ph.D. thesis, Trinity College Dublin (2019). https://www.tara.tcd.ie/handle/2262/86009
12. Gomes, A.O., Butterfield, A.: Modelling the haemodialysis machine with circus. In: Butler, M., Schewe, K.-D., Mashkoor, A., Biro, M. (eds.) ABZ 2016. LNCS, vol. 9675, pp. 409–424. Springer, Cham (2016). https://doi.org/10.1007/978-3-319-33600-8_34
13. Gomes, A.O., Butterfield, A.: Circus2CSP - a translator from circus to CSPm (2018). https://bitbucket.org/circusmodelcheck/circus2csp
14. Gomes, A.O., Butterfield, A.: Towards a model-checker for circus. In: 3rd World Congress on Formal Methods. Springer, Berlin (2019)
15. Hoare, C., He, J.: Unifying Theories of Programming. Prentice-Hall, Upper Saddle River (1998)
16. Hopcroft, J.E., Motwani, R., Ullman, J.D.: Introduction to Automata Theory, Languages, and Computation - International Edition, 2nd edn. Addison-Wesley, Boston (2003)
17. Hopkins, D., Roscoe, A.W.: SVA, a tool for analysing shared-variable programs. Electronic Notes in Theoretical Computer Science, pp. 1–5 (2007). https://www.cs.ox.ac.uk/people/bill.roscoe/publications/119.pdf
18. Jackson, E.K., Levendovszky, T., Balasubramanian, D.: Reasoning about meta-modeling with formal specifications and automatic proofs. In: Whittle, J., Clark, T., Kühne, T. (eds.) MODELS 2011. LNCS, vol. 6981, pp. 653–667. Springer, Heidelberg (2011). https://doi.org/10.1007/978-3-642-24485-8_48
19. Leuschel, M., Butler, M.: ProB: an automated analysis toolset for the B method. Int. J. Softw. Tools Technol. Transf. **10**(2), 185–203 (2008)

20. Lowe, G.: Specification of communicating processes: temporal logic versus refusals-based refinement. Formal Aspects Comput. **20**(3), 277–294 (2008). https://link.springer.com/content/pdf/10.1007%2Fs00165-007-0065-0.pdf
21. Malik, P., Utting, M.: CZT: a framework for Z tools. In: Treharne, H., King, S., Henson, M., Schneider, S. (eds.) ZB 2005. LNCS, vol. 3455, pp. 65–84. Springer, Heidelberg (2005). https://doi.org/10.1007/11415787_5. http://czt.sourceforge.net
22. Morgan, C.: Programming from Specifications. Prentice Hall International Series in Computer Science, 2nd edn. vol. 16. Prentice Hall (1994). https://dl.acm.org/citation.cfm?id=184737
23. Mota, A., Farias, A., Didier, A., Woodcock, J.: Rapid prototyping of a semantically well founded circus model checker. In: Giannakopoulou, D., Salaün, G. (eds.) SEFM 2014. LNCS, vol. 8702, pp. 235–249. Springer, Cham (2014). https://doi.org/10.1007/978-3-319-10431-7_17
24. Nogueira, S., Sampaio, A., Mota, A.: Test generation from state based use case models. Formal Aspects Comput. **26**(3), 441–490 (2014)
25. Oliveira, M.V.M.: Formal derivation of state-rich reactive programs using circus. Ph.D. thesis, University of York, UK (2005). https://ethos.bl.uk/OrderDetails.do?uin=uk.bl.ethos.428459
26. Oliveira, M.V.M., Sampaio, A., Antonino, P., Ramos, R., Cavalcanti, A., Woodcock, J.C.P.: Compositional analysis and design of CML models. Technical report D24.1, COMPASS Deliverable (2013). https://www.compass-research.eu/Project/Deliverables/D241.pdf
27. Oliveira, M.V.M., Sampaio, A.C.A., Conserva Filho, M.S.: Model-checking circus state-rich specifications. In: Albert, E., Sekerinski, E. (eds.) IFM 2014. LNCS, vol. 8739, pp. 39–54. Springer, Cham (2014). https://doi.org/10.1007/978-3-319-10181-1_3
28. Plagge, D., Leuschel, M.: Validating Z specifications using the ProB animator and model checker. In: Davies, J., Gibbons, J. (eds.) IFM 2007. LNCS, vol. 4591, pp. 480–500. Springer, Heidelberg (2007). https://doi.org/10.1007/978-3-540-73210-5_25
29. Roscoe, A.W.: The Theory and Practice of Concurrency. Prentice Hall PTR, Upper Saddle River (1973)
30. Saaltink, M., Meisels, I., Saaltink, M.: The Z/EVES Reference Manual (for Version 1.5). Reference Manual, ORA Canada, pp. 72–85 (1997). https://dl.acm.org/citation.cfm?id=647282.722913
31. Schneider, S.: Concurrent and Real-Time Systems. Wiley, Chichester (2000)
32. Utting, M.: Jaza User Manual and Tutorial, June 2005
33. Woodcock, J., Cavalcanti, A.: The semantics of circus. In: Bert, D., Bowen, J.P., Henson, M.C., Robinson, K. (eds.) ZB 2002. LNCS, vol. 2272, pp. 184–203. Springer, Heidelberg (2002). https://doi.org/10.1007/3-540-45648-1_10
34. Woodcock, J., Cavalcanti, A., Freitas, L.: Operational semantics for model checking circus. In: Fitzgerald, J., Hayes, I.J., Tarlecki, A. (eds.) FM 2005. LNCS, vol. 3582, pp. 237–252. Springer, Heidelberg (2005). https://doi.org/10.1007/11526841_17
35. Woodcock, J.C.P., Davies, J.: Using Z, Specification, Refinement, and Proof. Prentice Hall International Series in Computer Science. Prentice Hall Inc., Upper Saddle River (1996)
36. Ye, K.: Model checking of state-rich formalisms. Ph.D. thesis, University of York (2016)
37. Ye, K., Woodcock, J.C.P.: Model checking of state-rich formalism circus by linking to CSP—B. Int. J. Softw. Tools Technol. Transf. **19**(1), 73–96 (2017). https://doi.org/10.1007/s10009-015-0402-1

Model Checking

How Hard Is Finding Shortest Counter-Example Lassos in Model Checking?

Rüdiger Ehlers[✉]

Clausthal University of Technology, Clausthal-Zellerfeld, Germany
`ruediger.ehlers@tu-clausthal.de`

Abstract. Modern model checkers help system engineers to pinpoint the reason for the faulty behavior of a system by providing counter-example traces. For finite-state systems and ω-regular specifications, they come in the form of lassos. Lassos that are unnecessarily long should be avoided, as they make finding the cause for an error in a trace harder.

We give the first thorough characterization of the computational complexity of finding the shortest and approximately shortest counter-example lassos in model checking for the full class of ω-regular specifications. We show how to build (potentially exponentially larger) *tight automata* for arbitrary ω-regular specifications, which can be used to reduce finding shortest counter-example lassos for some finite-state system to finding a shortest accepting lasso in a (product) Büchi automaton. We then show that even approximating the size of the shortest counter-example lasso is an NP-hard problem for any polynomial approximation function, which demonstrates the hardness of obtaining short counter-examples in practical model checking. Minimizing only the length of the lasso cycle is however possible in polynomial time for a fixed but arbitrary upper limit on the size of strongly connected components in specification automata.

1 Introduction

With *model checking*, we can exhaustively test if a reactive system (or a model of it) satisfies a given specification. A key feature of most model checking tools is that they provide a *counter-example* whenever this is not the case. Counter-examples are helpful for the system engineer to understand the reason for non-satisfaction and to find out whether the model is erroneous and hence needs to be fixed, or whether the design itself has an error, which necessitates refining the design. For safety properties, such a counter-example can be a finite trace, where the violation of the property becomes apparent with the last state of the trace. For a specification outside of the set of safety properties such as a *liveness property*, a finite trace cannot show the absence of a specification violation in

---

This work was supported by the German Science Foundation (DFG) under Grant No. 322591867. It was inspired by discussions at Dagstuhl seminar 19081.

© Springer Nature Switzerland AG 2019
M. H. ter Beek et al. (Eds.): FM 2019, LNCS 11800, pp. 245–261, 2019.
https://doi.org/10.1007/978-3-030-30942-8_16

the model. In this case, an infinite trace is needed, and if and only if a finite-state system does not satisfy an ω-regular specification, there is a *lasso-shaped counter-example* that can be presented to the engineer. Such lassos consist of a *handle* that shows how the system initially evolves, followed by a *cycle* that shows repetitive behavior that the system can follow indefinitely long. The trace consisting of following the handle once and cycle infinitely often is then the counter-example.

To fulfill the promise of helping the system engineer with revising the model of the design, a counter-example needs to be *understandable*. While a full formalization of this requirement is difficult, it is commonly agreed on that counter-examples should be *short*, as deriving the core reason for the violation of overly long counter-examples is cumbersome. The length of counter-example lassos can be defined both over the lengths of the handle and the cycle, but the most common definition is the sum of these. Finding a shortest counter-example lasso in a *Büchi automaton* that models the intersection between the complement of the specification and the traces that the system permits is computationally easy as polynomial-time algorithms are known for this task [11,18]. The intersection Büchi automaton in this context is built from a finite-state machine description of the system and a Büchi automaton representation of the specification. This means that the syntactic structure of the latter influences the length of the counter-example lassos in the product, and hence finding a shortest lasso in it does not mean that the lasso's projection on the system FSM yields a shortest lasso in the FSM alone. Hence, following this approach can lead to unnecessarily long counter-examples.

When the specification of the system is given as a *linear temporal logic* (LTL) property, this problem can however be avoided [17]. The translation from LTL to a Büchi automaton can be made *tight*, i.e., such that it ensures that lassos in the finite-state machine system description along which a specification is violated give rise to lassos in the product automaton of the same size. In this way, shortest counter-example lassos are present in the product automaton. The construction is however bound to LTL and algorithms that post-process specification Büchi automata to reduce their size or improve their amenability for model checking [19] can break tightness. Since such post-processing procedures have been shown to be important for good model checking performance, computing shortest counter-example lassos for LTL specifications remains practically more difficult than computing *any* counter-example. Even more important, novel specification logics such as *linear dynamic logic* (LDL, [4]) and *property specification logic* (PSL, [7]) have recently been proposed to achieve full ω-regular expressivity and to support the industrial adoption of model checking techniques. The results from Schuppan and Biere [17] do not carry over to these logics, hence leaving a gap for the question of how difficult the problem of obtaining shortest counter-example lassos for these logics and ω-regular specifications in general is.

In this paper, we revisit the computational hardness of the problem of computing shortest counter-example lassos for arbitrary ω-regular specifications. We start by showing that by applying two constructions by Calbrix et al. [2] and

Farzah et al. [9] in succession, we can translate an arbitrary Büchi automaton into an equivalent tight automaton. The construction leads to an exponential blow-up while already for the safety case, the lower bound identified by Kupferman and Vardi [14] is also exponential. While a tight Büchi automaton can be used to find a shortest counter-example lasso, the automaton blow-up leads to the question if there is a more efficient way to compute shortest counter-example lassos with specification automata that are not tight. To study this question, we define the problem of finding a short *component lasso* in a Büchi automaton that is the product of a specification automaton and a finite-state machine. While it is relatively easy to show that the problem is NP-complete, we mainly examine the approximation hardness of the problem, as approximately shortest counter-example lassos may also suffice in practical applications. Unfortunately, it turns out that the problem is also NP-hard to approximate within any polynomial approximation function. On the positive side, we give a polynomial-time construction for minimizing the lassos cycle length for specification Büchi automata with small strongly connected components (of a fixed maximal size), which are common when model checking against liveness properties.

The hardness results that we present provide an a-posteriori justification for heuristic approaches to finding short counter-example lassos in model checking.

1.1   Related Work

Minimizing the size of counter-example traces or lassos is a classical problem in the model checking literature. Standard depth-first search Büchi automaton language emptiness checking algorithms commonly implemented in explicit-state model checkers such as spin [12] are not guaranteed to yield shortest counter-examples. A simple improvement is to minimize the lasso cycle length in the product automaton between the system and the specification automaton, which can be done in time polynomial in the sizes of the automata. Gastin et al. [10] give an approach to find shortest counter-examples in explicit-state model checking without increasing memory usage substantially. Edelkamp et al. [5] give an approach for doing so in explicit-state model checking when using external memory for storing states. In symbolic model checking using binary decision diagrams (BDDs), lasso cycle length minimization comes as a side effect of the typically implemented algorithms. Clarke et al. [3] showed that adding fairness requirements to the lasso to be found (such as in the acceptance condition of *generalized Büchi automata*) makes the problem of finding shortest accepting lassos NP-hard, even in the product automata used in model checking.

All approaches mentioned so far can however still compute unnecessarily long counter-examples as they search for short counter-example lassos in the product automaton. As an alternative, Schuppan and Biere [17] showed how to compute *tight* specification automata for linear time temporal logic (LTL). Such specification automata ensure that shortest counter-example lassos in the finite-state machine modeling the system to be tested induce shortest lassos in the product automaton, enabling the application of an approach to obtain short accepting lassos in Büchi automata [10,11,18] to compute shortest counter-example lassos. Post-processing such specification automata by simulation-based automaton minimization [8], as usually done in practical model checking, can break this property, though, requiring the specification automata to remain unaltered after their construction.

For the safety fragment of the ω-regular specifications, Kupferman and Vardi gave a construction to build tight automata [14]. Starting with a non-deterministic Büchi automaton, their construction leads to an exponential blowup in the specification automaton size, which they show to be unavoidable.

For general ω-regular properties and for every system to be checked, the liveness-to-reachability reduction from [16] can be applied to obtain a Büchi automaton that is, in a sense, tight enough not to miss the shortest counter-example in the product. The necessary blow-up depends on the *diameter* of the system to be checked (or alternatively some refinement of this concept), and hence the approach cannot be used to compute one Büchi automaton that can be used for finding shortest counter-examples for *all* finite-state systems. We improve upon this result in this paper by giving a construction to obtain not only "tight-enough" Büchi automata, but completely tight automata, for which the diameter of the system to be checked does not need to be known.

An alternative type of counter-example has been defined by Kupferman and Sheinvald [13], where the goal is to find the shortest lasso-shaped *input/output word* that the system can read and emit during a counter-example lasso. They call such lasso-shaped words *witnesses* (for the violation of a specification by a system). While these can be much more compact than counter-example lassos (for instance when the output of the system is always the same along a non-trivial counter-example lasso), even approximating the size of the shortest such counter-example word within any polynomial approximation function is NP-hard [6] for specifications in all commonly used automata types. Hence, abstracting from the concrete system states adds complexity to the problem, which is a motivation to revisit the simpler counter-example lassos in this work.

2   Preliminaries

Words and Graphs: Given an alphabet Σ, we denote the set of finite words over Σ as Σ^*, and the set of infinite words as Σ^ω. A word in Σ^ω is called *ultimately periodic* if it is of the form uv^ω for some $u, v \in \Sigma^*$, where the ω operator denotes infinite repetition of the operand. The empty word is denoted by ϵ. A graph is a two-tuple (V, E) consisting of a set of vertices V and an edge relation $E \subseteq V \times V$.

Automata over Finite Words: An automaton over finite words is a tuple $\mathcal{A} = (Q, \Sigma, \delta_{\mathcal{A}}, Q_0, F)$ with the finite set of states Q, the finite alphabet Σ, the transition relation $\delta_{\mathcal{A}} \subseteq Q \times \Sigma \times Q$, the set of initial states $Q_0 \subseteq Q$, and the set of accepting states $F \subseteq Q$. We say that $\mathcal{A}$ is *deterministic* if for every $q \in Q$ and $x \in \Sigma$, there is only at most one $q' \in Q$ with $(q, x, q') \in \delta_{\mathcal{F}}$, and furthermore Q_0 contains exactly one element. A *run* for a finite word $w = w_0 \ldots w_{n-1} \in \Sigma^*$

is a sequence $\pi = \pi_0 \ldots \pi_n$ with $\pi_0 \in Q_0$ and for all $1 \leq i \leq n$, we have $\pi_i \in \delta_{\mathcal{A}}(\pi_{i-1}, x_{i-1})$. We say that $\mathcal{A}$ accepts a finite word $w \in \Sigma^*$ if there exists an accepting *run* $\pi = \pi_0 \ldots \pi_n$ for w, i.e., for which $\pi_n \in F$. The set of words accepted by $\mathcal{A}$ is also called its *language* and denoted by $\mathcal{L}(\mathcal{A})$. The size of an automaton, written as $|\mathcal{A}|$ is defined to be the sum of the number of states and the number of transitions.

Büchi Automata: A (non-deterministic) Büchi automaton is a tuple $\mathcal{A} = (Q, \Sigma, \delta_{\mathcal{A}}, Q_0, F)$ with the same structure as an automaton over finite words, the same definitions of determinism and the size of an automaton, and the same definition of runs, except that they can be infinitely long, as Büchi automata represent languages over Σ^ω. We say that $\mathcal{A} = (Q, \Sigma, \delta_{\mathcal{A}}, Q_0, F)$ accepts a word $w \in \Sigma^\omega$ if and only if there exists an *accepting run* $\pi = \pi_0 \pi_1 \ldots$ of $\mathcal{A}$ for w. A run is accepting if for infinitely many $i \in \mathbb{N}$, we have $\pi_i \in F$. The set of accepted words again forms the language $\mathcal{L}(\mathcal{A})$ of $\mathcal{A}$. We define the reachability relation $R_{\mathcal{A}} \subseteq Q \times Q$ of $\mathcal{A}$ as the transitive closure of $\{(q, q') \in Q^2 \mid \exists x \in \Sigma, (q, x, q') \in \delta\}$. We say that a set of states $Q' \subseteq Q$ forms a *strongly connected component* (SCC) of $\mathcal{A}$ if for every $q, q' \in Q'$, we have that $(q, q') \in R_{\mathcal{A}}$. We say that $\mathcal{A}$ encodes a *safety language* if every word that is not in the language has a prefix all of whose extensions are also not in the language.

Regular and ω-regular Expressions: Such expressions are a way to represent languages over finite and infinite words. Starting from elements in Σ, they are composed using the *concatenation* ($\cdot$), *union* ($\cup$), *intersection* ($\cap$), and *finite repetition* ($*$) operators. The "$\cdot$" operator is often omitted when clear from the context. In case of ω-regular expressions, the additional $^\omega$ operator denotes infinite repetition. No sub-expression can be concatenated to the right of such an operator application. The set of properties over infinite words representable by ω-regular expressions is called the ω *-regular languages*. It is known that these are exactly the properties representable by non-deterministic Büchi automata.

Finite-State Machines: A *finite-state machine* (FSM) is a tuple $\mathcal{F} = (S, \Sigma, \delta_{\mathcal{F}}, s_0, L)$ with the finite set of states S, the alphabet Σ, the transition relation $\delta_{\mathcal{F}} \subseteq S \times S$, the initial state s_0, and the labeling function L. A trace of $\mathcal{F}$ is an (infinite) sequence $\rho = \rho_0 \rho_1 \ldots \in S^\omega$ such that $\rho_0 = s_0$ and for every $i \in \mathbb{N}$, we have $(\rho_i, \rho_{i+1}) \in \delta_{\mathcal{F}}$. The trace *induces a word* $w = w_0 w_1 \ldots \in \Sigma^\omega$ with $w_i = L(\rho_i)$ for all $i \in \mathbb{N}$.

Model Checking: Given an FSM $\mathcal{F}$ and an *error specification* in the form a Büchi automaton $\mathcal{A}$ over the same alphabet, the model checking problem is to test if $\mathcal{F}$ has a trace that induces a word in the language of $\mathcal{A}$. Whenever this is the case, we are interested in a *counter-example* of $\mathcal{F}$ that proves that it has a run whose word is in the language of $\mathcal{A}$. Such a counter-example has the form of a *lasso*, i.e., is of the shape $((c_1, \ldots, c_m), (c'_1, \ldots, c'_n))$, where $c_1, \ldots, c_m$ is the *lasso handle* and $c'_1, \ldots, c'_n$ is the *lasso cycle*. They fulfill the following conditions:

- All elements $c_1, \ldots, c_m, c'_1, \ldots, c'_n$ are in S (the lasso elements are states).
- For all $1 < i \leq m$, we have $(c_{i-1}, c_i) \in \delta$, and for all $1 < i \leq n$, we have $(c'_{i-1}, c'_i) \in \delta$ (the lasso parts describe state transitions).

– We have $c_m = c'_1$ (lasso handle and lasso cycle are connected) and $(c'_n, c'_1) \in \delta_{\mathcal{F}}$ (the lasso cycle is closed).

The lasso $((c_1, \ldots, c_m), (c'_1, \ldots, c'_n))$ represents the trace $c_1, \ldots, c_{m-1}(c'_1, \ldots, c'_n)^\omega$, i.e., on which the lasso cycle is repeated an infinite number of times. We say that this lasso is a counter-example for $\mathcal{A}$ if the word induced by the trace is in the language of $\mathcal{A}$. The constants m and n are also called the *handle length* and *cycle length* of a lasso. The *combined length* of a lasso is defined to be $m + n - 1$, where the subtraction by one comes from counting the state shared by the handle and the cycle only once.

We say that a lasso in $\mathcal{F}$ is a counter-example to some state q in $\mathcal{A}$ if there exists a counter-example lasso for $\mathcal{F}$ and $\mathcal{A}$, where state q is assumed to be the sole initial state in $\mathcal{A}$. We say that a lasso cycle is a counter-example lasso cycle if it can be completed to a counter-example lasso with a single-state handle (which is then part of the cycle itself).

Product Büchi Automaton for Model Checking: A finite-state machine $\mathcal{F} = (S, \Sigma, \delta_{\mathcal{F}}, s_0, L)$ has a trace (a *counter-example*) that induces a word in the language represented by an (error) specification in the form of a Büchi automaton $\mathcal{A} = (Q, \Sigma, \delta_{\mathcal{A}}, Q_0, F)$ if and only if there exists a counter-example lasso for the FSM. Testing if such a lasso exists can be done by testing the *product Büchi automaton* of $\mathcal{F}$ and $\mathcal{A}$ for language emptiness. Formally, we define this product automaton as $\mathcal{P} = (Q_{\mathcal{P}}, \Sigma, \delta_{\mathcal{P}}, Q_{\mathcal{P},0}, F_{\mathcal{P}})$ with $Q_{\mathcal{P}} = Q \times S$, $Q_{\mathcal{P},0} = Q_0 \times \{s_0\}$, $F_{\mathcal{P}} = F \times S$, and the transition relation is defined as

$$\delta_{\mathcal{P}} = \{((q, s), x, (q', s')) \in Q_{\mathcal{P}} \times \Sigma \times Q_{\mathcal{P}} \mid (s, s') \in \delta_{\mathcal{F}}, q' \in \delta(q, L(s))\}.$$

A lasso in $\mathcal{P}$ is defined in the same way as in a finite-state machine. A lasso in $\mathcal{P}$ is *accepting* if its cycle contains at least one state from $F_{\mathcal{P}}$. Since a Büchi automaton has a non-empty language exactly if and only if such a lasso can be found, $\mathcal{P}$ can be used to model check $\mathcal{F}$ against $\mathcal{A}$.

Tight Automata: While a product Büchi automaton $\mathcal{P}$ between an FSM $\mathcal{F}$ and a Büchi automaton can be used to check if a counter-example for $\mathcal{F}$ and $\mathcal{A}$ exists, the combined length of the shortest accepting lasso in $\mathcal{P}$ may be higher than the length of the shortest counter-example lasso for $\mathcal{A}$ in $\mathcal{F}$. Intuitively, the reason for this difference is that $\mathcal{P}$ incorporates the structure of $\mathcal{A}$, whereas the definition of a counter-example lasso in $\mathcal{F}$ does not. However, the structure of $\mathcal{A}$ may be suitable to avoid this issue. We say that $\mathcal{A}$ is *tight* if for every counter-example lasso for every FSM $\mathcal{F}$, there is an accepting lasso in $\mathcal{P}$ of the same length. Since $\mathcal{P}$ is the product of $\mathcal{A}$ and $\mathcal{F}$, it is easy to obtain a counter-example lasso from an accepting lasso in $\mathcal{P}$ such that both are of the same length. This allows using $\mathcal{P}$ to find shortest counter-example lassos, and since it is known that finding shortest accepting lassos in $\mathcal{P}$ is solvable in polynomial time [11,18], so is the former problem.

Satisfiability Problem: The *satisfiability* problem is to check if a Boolean formula in conjunctive normal form over some set of Boolean variables $\{v_1, \ldots, v_n\}$ has a satisfying assignment. The conjuncts of the formula are called its *clauses*, and the number of clauses is also denoted by $|\psi|$. The satisfiability problem often serves as the canonical NP-complete problem. We write $c \in \psi$ for some clause c if c is a clause in ψ.

3   Tightening Büchi Automata

With a tight specification automata, computing shortest counter-examples is (computationally) easy. We will show in this section that by utilizing two previous constructions from Calbrix et al. [2] and Farzah et al. [9], we can translate an arbitrary Büchi automaton into an equivalent tight automaton. The first construction is captured by the following theorem:

Theorem 1 ([2], Section 5). *Given a non-deterministic Büchi automaton $\mathcal{A}$ over an alphabet Σ with n states, we can build a deterministic finite-state automaton $\mathcal{A}'$ over the alphabet $\Sigma \cup \{\$\}$ of size exponential in n that accepts exactly the words $u\$w$ with $u, w \in \Sigma^*$ for which uv^ω is accepted by $\mathcal{A}$. Building $\mathcal{A}'$ does not take more time than polynomial in the combined input and output sizes.*

Two Büchi automata accept the same language if they accept the same ultimately periodic words [2]. Since these are captured by the automaton $\mathcal{A}'$, that automaton encodes the essence of an ω-regular language. Since $\mathcal{A}'$ is a deterministic automaton over finite words (*DFA*), it can also be minimized in polynomial time.

The automaton $\mathcal{A}'$ can now be translated back to an automaton $\mathcal{A}''$ with the same language as $\mathcal{A}$ with only polynomial blow-up. A construction for this step has been given by Farzah et al. [9], whose properties needed in this section we distill into the following proposition:

Proposition 1 ([9]). *Let $\mathcal{A}' = (Q', \Sigma \cup \{\$\}, \delta', Q'_0, F')$ be a DFA that accepts exactly the words $u\$v$ with $u, v \in \Sigma^*$ for which uv^ω is a word in some ω-regular language L. We can compute, in polynomial time, a set of pairs P of regular languages such that*

$$L = \bigcup_{(A,B)\in P} AB^\omega. \tag{1}$$

Furthermore, (1) P is of cardinality quadratic in $|Q'|$, (2) for every $(A, B) \in P$, the languages A and B are representable by DFAs with at most $|Q'| + 1$ states, and (3) for every word $u\$v$ in the language of $\mathcal{A}'$, there exists some $(A, B) \in P$ with $u \in \mathcal{L}(A)$ and $v \in \mathcal{L}(B)$.

This characterization enables the efficient construction of a non-deterministic Büchi automaton for an ω-regular language from a DFA accepting its ultimately periodic words. While the core idea of the following construction was already suggested in a footnote in [9], we changed it substantially to make the resulting automaton tight.

Lemma 1. *Let* $\mathcal{A}' = (Q', \Sigma \cup \{\$\}, \delta', Q'_0, F')$ *be a DFA that accepts exactly the words* $u\$v$ *with* $u, v \in \Sigma^*$ *for which* uv^ω *is a word in some* ω-*regular language* L. *Let* $P = \{P_1, \ldots, P_n\}$ *be the set of pairs of regular languages described in Proposition 1. Let furthermore* $\mathcal{A}_i^A = (Q_i^A, \Sigma, \delta_i^A, Q_{0,i}^A, F_i^A)$ *and* $\mathcal{A}_i^B = (Q_i^B, \Sigma, \delta_i^B, Q_{0,i}^B, F_i^B)$ *be the DFAs for the elements* $P_i = (A_i, B_i)$ *for* $1 \leq i \leq n$, *where w.l.o.g, all states in the these automata have distinct names. We can build a non-deterministic Büchi automaton* $\hat{\mathcal{A}} = (\hat{Q}, \Sigma, \hat{\delta}, \hat{Q}_0, \hat{F})$ *capturing* L *with the following components:*

$$\hat{Q} = \bigcup_{1 \leq i \leq n} Q_i^A \cup (Q_i^B \times \mathbb{B})$$

$$\hat{Q}_0 = \left(\bigcup_{1 \leq i \leq n} Q_{0,i}^A \right) \cup \bigcup_{1 \leq i \leq n, Q_{0,i}^A \cap F_i^A \neq \emptyset} Q_{0,i}^B \times \mathbb{B}$$

$$\hat{\delta} = \bigcup_{1 \leq i \leq n} \delta_i^A \cup \{((q,b), x, (q', b')) \mid (q, x, q') \in \delta_i^B, b' = (q' \in F_i^B)\}$$

$$\cup \bigcup_{1 \leq i \leq n} \{(q, x, (q', b)) \mid q \in Q_i^A, x \in \Sigma, \exists q'' \in F_i^A, (q, x, q'') \in \delta_i^A,$$

$$q' \in Q_{0,i}^B, b \in \mathbb{B}\}$$

$$\cup \bigcup_{1 \leq i \leq n} \{((q,b), x, (q', \mathbf{true})) \mid q \in Q_i^B, x \in \Sigma, \exists q'' \in F_i^B, (q, x, q'') \in \delta_i^B,$$

$$q' \in Q_{0,i}^B, b \in \mathbb{B}\}$$

$$\hat{F} = \bigcup_{1 \leq i \leq n} Q_{0,i}^B \times \{\mathbf{true}\}$$

The construction in the lemma essentially defines a Büchi automaton implementing Eq. 1, with the modification that states in the automata $\mathcal{A}_i^B$ have been duplicated by attaching a Boolean flag. Due to the changes (which are necessary to derive Corollary 1 later), a proof of correctness is in order:

Proof. Since a Büchi automaton $\hat{\mathcal{A}}$ captures an ω-regular language L if the language of $\hat{\mathcal{A}}$ has exactly the same ultimately periodic words as the ones in L, we can restrict our attention to those.

First proof direction: Let uv^ω be an ultimately periodic word in L. Then, by Theorem 1, we have that $u\$v \in \mathcal{L}(\mathcal{A}')$. By Proposition 1, we have that $u \in A_i$ and $v \in \mathcal{L}(B_i)$ for some $(A_i, B_i) \in P$. We can now construct an accepting lasso for uv^ω in $\hat{\mathcal{A}}$. Since $u = u_1 \ldots u_k \in \mathcal{L}(A_i)$, there exits a accepting run $\pi_A = \pi_0 \ldots \pi_k$ for u in A_i.

By the construction of $\hat{\mathcal{A}}$, there exists a prefix run $\pi_0 \ldots \pi_{k-1}$ for the same word in $\hat{\mathcal{A}}$. Furthermore, if $k > 0$, then there exist a transition $(\pi_{k-1}, u_k, (q, \mathbf{true}))$ for some $q \in Q_{0,i}^B$. If u is the empty word, then $(q, \mathbf{true})$ is an initial state. Hence, in both cases every state in $Q_{0,i}^B \times \{\mathbf{true}\}$ is reached by some run in $\hat{\mathcal{A}}$ after reading u.

Since $v \in \mathcal{L}(B_i)$, there exists a run $\pi'_0 \ldots \pi'_r$ with $\pi'_0 \in Q^B_{0,i}$ and $\pi'_r \in F^B_i$ for $v = v_1 \ldots v_r$. By the construction of $\hat{A}$, the (prefix) run $\pi'_0 \ldots \pi'_{r-1}$ exists in $\hat{A}$ as well, except that every state element is labeled by whether the last visited state is accepting, where the label for π'_0 can also be **true**. From the last such state (π'_{r-1}, b) for some $b \in \mathbb{B}$, the construction of $\hat{A}$ furthermore ensures that $((\pi'_{r-1}, b), v_r, (\pi'_0, \textbf{true})) \in \hat{\delta}$. This closes a cycle in $\hat{A}$. Since the cycle can be repeated indefinitely long when reading v^ω and it contains at least one accepting state, namely $(\pi'_0, \textbf{true})$, we constructed an accepting infinite run in $\hat{A}$ for uv^ω, proving its acceptance.

Second proof direction: Let $w_1 w_2 \ldots = uv^\omega$ be a word accepted by $\hat{A}$. Since $\hat{A}$ has a finite number of states, there exists an accepting run of the shape $\pi = \pi_0 \ldots \pi_{k-1} (\pi_k \ldots \pi_{r-1})^\omega$ for it such that at least one state in $\hat{F}$ occurs in $\pi_k \ldots \pi_{r-1}$. Without loss of generality, we can also assume that $\pi_k \in \hat{F}$, as the prefix of the lasso can always be extended slightly to rotate the cycle.

Due to the construction of $\hat{A}$, the complete run π takes place in a part of $\hat{A}$ generated by one element (A_i, B_i) in P (as there are no transitions between these parts). Let s be the index in π at which π reaches the states in $Q^B_i \times \mathbb{B}$ for the first time. We have that $w_1 \ldots w_s$ is a word in the language of A_i by the fact that such a switch is only possible in $\hat{A}$ after reading a word in $\mathcal{L}(A_i)$. By the fact that π_k is an accepting state and the construction of $\hat{A}$, we have that $w_{s+1} \ldots w_k$ is a word in $\mathcal{L}(B_i)$ (if non-empty), as $\pi_s \ldots \pi_k$ simulates the Q^B_i component of a run from an initial state in B_i to an accepting state, except that π_k is replaced by a state in $(Q^B_{0,i}, \textbf{true})$. As such states can only be reached when reaching an accepting state for $w_{s+1} \ldots w_k$ in B_i, it follows that $w_{s+1} \ldots w_k \in \mathcal{L}(B_i)$.

For the same reason and since π is an accepting lasso, we have that the word $w_{k+1} \ldots w_r$ is accepted by B_i as well. Since π is a lasso for the word w, this actually means that $w_{r+j \cdot (r-k)+1} \ldots w_{r+(j+1) \cdot (r-k)}$ is the same word for every $j \in \mathbb{N}$. This observation allows us to overall decompose w as follows:

$$w = \underbrace{w_0 w_1 \ldots w_s}_{\in \mathcal{L}(A_i)} \underbrace{w_{s+1} \ldots w_k}_{\in \mathcal{L}(B_i) \text{ if not } \epsilon} \underbrace{w_{k+1} \ldots w_r}_{\in \mathcal{L}(B_i)} \underbrace{w_{r+1} \ldots w_{2r-k}}_{\in \mathcal{L}(B_i)} \cdots$$

This proves that $w \in L$ by Proposition 1. $\qquad \square$

Corollary 1. *Let $\hat{A}$ be a Büchi automaton built from some DFA $\mathcal{A}' = (Q', \Sigma \cup \{\$\}, \delta', Q'_0, F')$ that accepts exactly the words $u\$v$ with $u, v \in \Sigma^*$ for which uv^ω is a word in some ω-regular language L using the construction from Lemma 1. We have that $\hat{A}$ is a tight automaton.*

Proof. The first direction of the proof of the preceding lemma proves the existence of an accepting lasso of length $|u| + |v| - 1$ in $\hat{A}$ for every word uv^ω in L. $\qquad \square$

By applying the constructions from Theorem 1 and Lemma 1 in succession, we can thus obtain a tight Büchi automaton from an arbitrary Büchi automaton. Since the construction from Lemma 1 has only a polynomial blow-up in the automaton size, we obtain an overall size exponential in the size of the original Büchi automaton. Since Kupferman and Vardi [14] gave an exponential lower bound for the safety case, this construction is complexity-theoretically optimal on a large scale. On a finer scale, our approach yields automata of size $2^{O(n^2)}$, while the lower bound by Kupferman and Vardi's for the safety case is only $O(2^n)$, leaving a small gap to be filled in future work.

4   Component Lassos – Negative Result

While we have seen above that in general, tight Büchi automata need to be exponentially larger than (the smallest) equivalent arbitrary Büchi automata, this does not automatically mean that finding shortest counter-example lassos for arbitrary specification Büchi automata is not possible in polynomial time.

In previous work [6], we showed that the smallest value of $|u| + |v|$ for some ultimately periodic word uv^ω in the language of a Büchi automata is NP-hard to approximate within any polynomial approximation function p. Under the assumption that $NP \neq P$, this means that no polynomial-time algorithm exists that given a non-deterministic Büchi automaton always outputs a value between $|u| + |v|$ and $p(|u| + |v|)$ for some ultimately periodic word uv^ω in the language of the automaton with minimal $|u| + |v|$. The result does not apply to the problem of finding shortest counter-example lassos as it adds the requirement that some state is reached twice after $|u| + |v|$ steps. Even if that problem is still NP-complete, its approximation hardness could be lower, which would be useful for the practical application of model checking. We show that, unfortunately, this is not the case. The following proof transfers the main ideas from [6] to the *component lasso* setting.

Proposition 2. *Approximating the length of the shortest lasso of a finite-state machine $\mathcal{F}$ that is accepted by a non-deterministic Büchi automaton $\mathcal{A}$ within any polynomial approximation function p is NP-hard.*

Proof. We reduce the NP-hard *satisfiability* problem to the (approximation) problem at hand. Let p be a polynomial function and ψ be a satisfiability problem in conjunctive normal form over the set of variables $\mathcal{V} = \{v_1, \ldots, v_n\}$, where we assume that every solution has $v_1 = \mathbf{false}$. The satisfiability is still NP-hard under this restriction, as it is easy to extend a SAT instance by one variable and to add a clause that requires the additional variable to have a **false** value.

We build a Büchi automaton over the language $\Sigma = \{\mathbf{false}, \mathbf{true}\}$ that implements the following language:

$$L = \bigodot_{c \in \psi} \Big(\underbrace{\bigcup_{x_1, \ldots, x_n \in \mathbb{B}^n, (v_1 = x_1, \ldots, v_n = x_n) \models c} (x_1 \ldots x_n)}_{enc_c} \Big)^{p(n)+1} \cdot \Sigma^\omega$$

In this equation, the $\odot$ operator refers to taking the concatenation of the elements in its scope. Here, the operator ranges over all clauses in the SAT instance

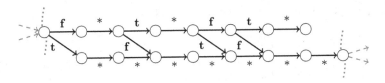

Fig. 1. Example automaton part for $n = 8$ and a clause $c_1 \vee \neg c_3 \vee c_5 \vee \neg c_6$, where **f** is an abbreviation for **false**, **t** is an abbreviation for **true**, and $*$ captures both characters.

ψ, where the order does not matter for the scope of this proof. Note that while the union operator in the equation ranges over a set of size exponential in n, a Büchi automaton part for one element enc_c is of size at most $2n$, as we demonstrate in Fig. 1. We furthermore consider a finite-state machine $\mathcal{F}$ with $2n - 1$ states of the shape given in Fig. 2. To prove the approximation hardness result, we show that:

1. the Büchi automaton for L can be built in time polynomial in the number of clauses in ψ, n, and $p(n)$ and is of size polynomial in ψ, n, and $p(n)$;
2. if ψ has a solution, then there exists a counter-example lasso in $\mathcal{F}$ of size n;
3. if there exists a counter-example lasso of size at most $p(n)$, then we can obtain a solution to ψ from the lasso.

(1) Note that L can be represented by concatenating $|\psi| \cdot (p(n)+1)$ many automaton parts with $2n$ states each (as shown in Fig. 1). The final Σ^ω component needs a single accepting state. Overall, the number of states of the resulting automaton is $(p(n) + 1) \cdot 2n \cdot |\psi| + 1$.

(2) Let $x_1, \ldots, x_n$ be a solution to ψ (where $x_1 = $ **false** by the assumption above). The word $(x_1, \ldots, x_n)^\omega$ induces a counter-example lasso starting in the initial state of the FSM, proceeding to the states labeled by $x_2, \ldots, x_n$, and looping back to the initial state afterwards. Since we have $x_1, \ldots, x_n \models \psi$, we know that $x_1, \ldots, x_n$ is a word in enc_c for every $c \in \psi$. Hence, $(x_1, \ldots, x_n)^\omega$ is accepted by $\bigodot_{c \in \psi} (enc_c)^m$ for any $m \in \mathbb{N}$ and by the subsequent Σ^ω component of L.

(3) Let $w = uv^\omega$ be a counter-example lasso of size at most $p(n)$. Note that $|v|$ needs to be a multiple of n for the lasso to be correct. We rewrite w slightly to $u'v'^\omega$ by unrolling the lasso until the length of u' is also a multiple of n (with $|v'| = |v|$). Let $x_1 \ldots x_n$ be the first n characters of v'. Since u' and v' are of sizes that are multiples of n, for every c, we have that v' needs to be accepted by enc_c. This is because as every enc_c is repeated $p(n) + 1$ times, v' is not long enough to have $x_1 \ldots x_n$ miss all $p(n) + 1$ repetitions. Due to the construction of enc_c, we have that $x_1 \ldots x_n$ is a model of the clause c. Since this line of reasoning holds for all clauses c, we know that $x_1, \ldots, x_n$ is a model of the whole formula ψ. □

Note that the automaton built in Proposition 2 is actually deterministic, hence showing the hardness of the problem even for deterministic Büchi automata.

5 Component Lassos – Positive Result

Now that we know that finding shortest counter-example lassos for general ω-regular properties is computationally difficult (even for any reasonable approximation version of the problem), the question arises whether there are at least some easy classes of properties and/or finite-state machines. While we have seen in the previous section that the determinism of a specification automaton does not change the computational complexity, other properties of the specification automaton can be used to derive a more detailed characterization of the complexity of finding shortest counter-example lassos.

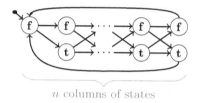

Fig. 2. Finite-state machine shape for the proof of Proposition 2, where **f** is an abbreviation for **false** and **t** is an abbreviation for **true**.

An interesting structural property of specification automata is the *maximal size of the strongly connected components* (SCCs) in the automata. For instance, if all SCCs of a specification automaton have a size of at most 1, we call such an automaton *very-weak* or *one-weak*. Intuitively, this means that all loops in the automaton are self-loops. This subset of the set of non-deterministic Büchi automata has been identified to characterize the set of properties of reactive systems whose complements are representable by both LTL and computation tree logic with only universal path quantifiers (ACTL), where in the LTL case the formula is checked along all executions of the system [15]. Very-weak automata have been used to derive heuristically shorter counter-example lassos [1] with the model checker **spin**. We extend this previous positive result on a more fundamental level by giving a polynomial-time algorithm to find guaranteed shortest *counter-example lasso cycles* for specification automata with a fixed upper bound on the size of the SCCs. We hence no longer require the SCCs to have a size of at most 1 and give an algorithm that is guaranteed to find shortest counter-examples.

The main idea of the following construction is that if an SCC is small enough, we can keep track of multiple runs of the specification automaton from *all* SCC states in parallel while traversing a lasso cycle in the FSM. When the lasso cycle in the FSM is closed, we then check if transitions of the specification automaton can be stitched together to form an accepting cycle for the lasso cycle of the FSM. Doing so requires time exponential in the number states in an SCC. Switches between SCCs do not have to be taken into consideration here due to the fact that we are only interested in minimizing the length of lasso cycles. We start by defining a graph that is suitable for searching for shortest component lassos.

Definition 1. *Let $\mathcal{A} = (Q, \Sigma, \delta_{\mathcal{A}}, Q_0, F)$ be a Büchi automaton and $\mathcal{F} = (S, \Sigma, \delta_{\mathcal{F}}, s_0, L)$ be a finite-state machine. Let $\mathcal{S}_1, \ldots, \mathcal{S}_m$ be the state sets of the (maximal) strongly connected components of $\mathcal{A}$ that contain at least one accepting state each.*

For each $1 \leq k \leq m$, we define the lasso-searching graph *of $\mathcal{S}_k$ and $\mathcal{F}$ as a tuple $(V, E_0 \cup E_1)$ with the set of vertices V, the normal edges E_0, and the closing edges E_1. These are defined as:*

$$V = S \times \mathcal{S}_k \times \{\mathcal{S}_k \to (\mathcal{S}_k \times \mathbb{B} \cup \bot)\}$$
$$E_0 = \{((s, \bar{q}, f), (s', \bar{q}, f') \in V \times V \mid \exists x \in \Sigma : (s, x, s') \in \delta_{\mathcal{F}}$$
$$\wedge \, \forall q \in \mathcal{S}_k : f'(q) = \bot \vee \exists q', q'' \in \mathcal{S}_k, b \in \mathbb{B} : f(q) = (q', b)$$
$$\wedge \, (q', x, q'') \in \delta_{\mathcal{A}} \wedge f'(q) = (q'', b \vee (q'' \in F))\}$$
$$E_1 = \{(s, \bar{q}, f), (s, \bar{q}, f) \in V \times V : \exists q_1, \ldots, q_l \in \mathcal{S}_k : q_1 = \bar{q},$$
$$\forall 2 \leq i \leq l, f(q_{i-1})|_Q = q_i, f(q_n)|_Q = q_1,$$
$$\exists 1 \leq j \leq l, f(q_j)|_{\mathbb{B}} = \mathbf{true}\}$$

Note that the SCC decomposition of an automaton can be computed in time linear in its number of states and transitions [20]. Hence, $\mathcal{S}_1, \ldots, \mathcal{S}_m$ can be easily obtained and for every strongly connected component $\mathcal{S}_k$, the graph $(V, E_0 \cup E_1)$ can be built in time polynomial in the sizes of $\mathcal{A}$ and $\mathcal{F}$ and exponential in $|\mathcal{S}_k|$. The first component of a state $(s, \bar{q}, f)$ tracks the state in the FSM, and the second one denotes an *anchor* state of the specification automaton, which never changes along graph edges. The third component keeps track of from which SCC state which other state can be reached for the labels along the cycle part in $\mathcal{F}$ traversed so far.

Lemma 2. *If and only if some state $(s, \bar{q}, f)$ is reachable from itself in $n+1 \in \mathbb{N}$ steps using first only edges from E_0 and then closing the cycle with an edge in E_1, there exists an accepting lasso cycle from FSM state s for the specification automaton $\mathcal{A}$ of length n, using $\bar{q}$ as the first state of the lasso cycle.*

Proof. $\Leftarrow$: Let $s_1 \ldots s_n$ be some counter-example lasso cycle for some state $q \in \mathcal{A}$ with the labels $x_1, \ldots, x_n$ along the cycle. In this case, there exists an accepting cycle $q_1 q_2 \ldots \in Q^\omega$ of the specification automaton for the same (suffix) trace of the system. Without loss of generality, we can assume that this cycle is ultimately periodic and that when the same state occurs for the second time at a position that is a multiple of n, the cycle is closed. Let us consider the pairs $(q_{nk+1}, q_{n(k+1)})$. By the assumption, all such pairs have distinct left elements, and let their number be $l \in \mathbb{N}$. Let $q_1^j, \ldots, q_{n+1}^j$ be the states of the cycle in $\mathcal{A}$ (for $1 \leq j \leq l$) between the state pairs, where for all $1 \leq j \leq l$, we have $q_1^j = q_{n+1}^j$.

We show that there is a loop in $(V, E_0 \cup E_1)$ from state $v = (s_1, q_1, f)$ with $f(q_1^j) = (q_1^j, b)$ for some $b \in \mathbb{N}$ for all states q_1^j for $1 \leq j \leq l$, and $f(q') = \bot$

for all other states q'. We can obtain this loop by successively transitioning, for each step $1 \leq i \leq n + 1$, to state $v_i = (s_j, q, f_i)$ for $f_i(q_i^j) = (q_i^j, b)$ for some $b \in \mathbb{N}$ for all states q_i^j for $1 \leq j \leq l$, and $f_i(q') = \bot$ for all other states $q' \in \mathcal{S}_k$. By the assumption that $q_1^j, \ldots, q_{n+1}^j$ is a valid transition sequence in $\mathcal{A}$ for $x_1, \ldots, x_n$, the construction of $(V, E_0 \cup E_1)$ includes these edges. Furthermore, by the assumption that the lasso is accepted by $\mathcal{A}$, along one of these l sequences, an accepting state is visited. By the construction of E_0, this means that one of the Boolean values encoded by f_n has a **true** value. Since the parts $q_1^j, \ldots, q_n^j$ (for $1 \leq j \leq l$) can be stitched together to form an accepting cycle, the definition of E_1 ensures that a suitable closing edge exists.

$\Rightarrow$: Let $v_1, \ldots, v_{n+1}$ be a path in $(V, E_0 \cup E_1)$ ending with an edge in E_1. We know from the construction of the graph that (1) the FSM loops under the label sequence $x_1, \ldots, x_{n-1}$ used for deriving the cycle, and (2) for every $q \in \mathcal{S}_k$ and $v_i = (s_i, \bar{q}, f_i)$ (for $1 \leq i \leq n + 1$) with $f_i(q) \neq \bot$, we have that there exists a transition sequence between $f_1(q)|_Q$ and $f_n(q)|_Q$ for $x_1, \ldots, x_n$. Furthermore, $f_n(q)|_{\mathbb{B}}$ is **true** if and only if along the way, an accepting state is visited. This allows us to construct an accepting lasso cycle for $x_1, \ldots, x_{n-1}$ by taking $f_1(\bar{q})|_Q, f_2(\bar{q})|_Q, \ldots, f_n(\bar{q})|_Q, f_1(f_n(\bar{q})|_Q)|_Q, f_2(f_n(\bar{q})|_Q)|_Q, \ldots, f_n(f_n(\bar{q})|_Q)|_Q, \ldots$ until the cycle is closed after a multiple of n states. Since the closing edge from E_1 can only be taken if the lasso cycle is closed and one Boolean flag has a **true** value, this part of the proof follows. □

Since finding shortest paths in a graph is computationally easy by performing a breadth-first search, and adapting breadth-first search to use E_1 as final transitions (back to the initial state) during the search is also simple, we can iterate over all states in $(V, E_0 \cup E_1)$ and search for shortest loops back the same state in time polynomial in $|E_0 \cup E_1|$. This allows us to derive the following corollary:

Corollary 2. *For every fixed $c \in \mathbb{N}$, we can label every state in $S \times Q$ by the shortest lasso cycle length of a counter-example lasso in time polynomial in the sizes of $\mathcal{A}$ and $\mathcal{F}$ if all SCCs of $\mathcal{A}$ have sizes of at most c.*

Proof. For every SCC $\mathcal{S}_k$, we build the graph defined above, label every state by the shortest lasso, and then take $\min_{f \in Q \to Q \times \mathbb{B} \cup \bot}(s, \bar{q}, f)$ as the length of the shortest counter-example lasso cycle from $(s, \bar{q})$. □

As a final step of our construction, we need to compute which lasso cycles are actually reachable from (q_0, s_0) for some $q_0 \in Q_0$. By performing a depth-first search in the classical product automaton, we can identify those states (q, s) that are reachable and then select one with a shortest cycle. The actual counter-example lasso can be obtained by taking the path in the product automaton up to the selected state (q, s) as the lasso handle, and taking the FSM state component of a cycle in the graph $(V, E_0 \cup E_1)$ that witnesses the length of the shortest counter-example lasso cycle as lasso cycle. Taking all parts of the construction together, we obtain:

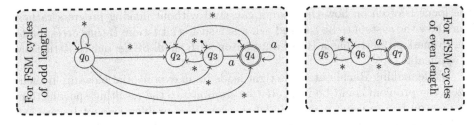

Fig. 3. A tight automaton for the alphabet $\Sigma = \{a, b\}$ and the specification that at infinitely many even positions, the letter in a word is a.

Corollary 3. *Given a FSM $\mathcal{F}$ and a specification Büchi automaton $\mathcal{A}$ in which every strongly connected component has at most $c \in \mathbb{N}$ states, we can compute a counter-example lasso for $\mathcal{F}$ and $\mathcal{A}$ that minimizes the cycle length in time polynomial in $|\mathcal{F}| \cdot |\mathcal{A}|$ and exponential in c.*

Note that the overall construction can be computationally streamlined. For instance, a search for a shortest lasso cycle can also keep the anchor state $\bar{q}$ implicit, reducing the size of the graph. For the simplicity of presenting the main idea of our approach, we did not apply such improvements here.

Note that the approach cannot be generalized to minimize the combined length of a counter-example lasso. The automata built from satisfiability problem instances in the hardness proof of Sect. 4 only have a single strongly connected component each, and these components only have a single state each. Hence, finding counter-example lassos with a minimal combined length is hard even the in the case of very-weak Büchi automata.

6   Conclusion

In this paper, we revisited the problem of obtaining shortest counter-example lassos for ω-regular specifications. Interestingly, it was open before this paper whether finding (approximately) shortest counter-example lassos is NP-hard or not for specifications given as non-deterministic Büchi automata. Our main result is negative: even approximating the (combined) length of the shortest counter-example lasso is NP-hard within any reasonable approximation function, let alone approximation factor. This is unfortunate, as approximate shortest counter-example lassos could be interesting for the model checking practitioner.

On the positive side, we showed how by using two existing automaton translations, we can make an arbitrary non-deterministic Büchi automaton tight, which enables the use of approaches for finding shortest accepting lassos in product automata to also find shortest counter-example lassos. Furthermore, we looked at the *parameterized complexity* of finding shortest counter-example lasso cycles and showed that for specification automata with small strongly connected components (SCCs), finding counter-example lassos with shortest cycles is possible in polynomial time for arbitrary (but fixed) SCC size limits. This result is interesting for the case of tracking down *starvation bugs* in models – in such situations, the focus is often on how the system can stall without making progress rather than how the system to be checked can reach such a situation. If the corresponding liveness property has a Büchi automaton with small SCCs, our construction is applicable.

While making Büchi automata tight leads to an exponential blow-up in their sizes, the problem could be mitigated by *minimizing* the resulting specification automaton before using it in a model checker. This problem cannot be tackled with previous simulation-based minimization approaches as we have to take care that loops with an accepting state are only removed if there are other loops of the same length that together accept the lasso cycles captured by the removed loop. We visualize this observation in Fig. 3, which shows a tight automaton that is only tight because it has different SCCs for lasso cycles with even and odd lengths. Suitable minimization algorithms for tight automata that retain such redundancies in the specification automata still have to be developed, and we leave this challenge to future work.

References

1. Adabala, K., Ehlers, R.: A fragment of linear temporal logic for universal very weak automata. In: Lahiri, S.K., Wang, C. (eds.) ATVA 2018. LNCS, vol. 11138, pp. 335–351. Springer, Cham (2018). https://doi.org/10.1007/978-3-030-01090-4_20
2. Calbrix, H., Nivat, M., Podelski, A.: Ultimately periodic words of rational w-languages. In: Brookes, S., Main, M., Melton, A., Mislove, M., Schmidt, D. (eds.) MFPS 1993. LNCS, vol. 802, pp. 554–566. Springer, Heidelberg (1994). https://doi.org/10.1007/3-540-58027-1_27
3. Clarke, E.M., Grumberg, O., McMillan, K.L., Zhao, X.: Efficient generation of counterexamples and witnesses in symbolic model checking. In: 32nd Conference on Design Automation (DAC), pp. 427–432. ACM Press (1995)
4. De Giacomo, G., Vardi, M.Y.: Linear temporal logic and linear dynamic logic on finite traces. In: 23rd International Joint Conference on Artificial Intelligence (IJCAI), pp. 854–860. IJCAI/AAAI (2013)
5. Edelkamp, S., Sulewski, D., Barnat, J., Brim, L., Simecek, P.: Flash memory efficient LTL model checking. Sci. Comput. Program. **76**(2), 136–157 (2011)
6. Ehlers, R.: Short witnesses and accepting lassos in ω-Automata. In: Dediu, A.-H., Fernau, H., Martín-Vide, C. (eds.) LATA 2010. LNCS, vol. 6031, pp. 261–272. Springer, Heidelberg (2010). https://doi.org/10.1007/978-3-642-13089-2_22
7. Eisner, C., Fisman, D.: A Practical Introduction to PSL. Series on Integrated Circuits and Systems. Springer, Heidelberg (2006)
8. Etessami, K., Wilke, T., Schuller, R.A.: Fair simulation relations, parity games, and state space reduction for Büchi automata. SIAM J. Comput. **34**(5), 1159–1175 (2005)
9. Farzan, A., Chen, Y.-F., Clarke, E.M., Tsay, Y.-K., Wang, B.-Y.: Extending automated compositional verification to the full class of omega-regular languages. In: Ramakrishnan, C.R., Rehof, J. (eds.) TACAS 2008. LNCS, vol. 4963, pp. 2–17. Springer, Heidelberg (2008). https://doi.org/10.1007/978-3-540-78800-3_2
10. Gastin, P., Moro, P., Zeitoun, M.: Minimization of counterexamples in SPIN. In: Graf, S., Mounier, L. (eds.) SPIN 2004. LNCS, vol. 2989, pp. 92–108. Springer, Heidelberg (2004). https://doi.org/10.1007/978-3-540-24732-6_7

11. Groce, A., Visser, W.: What went wrong: explaining counterexamples. In: Ball, T., Rajamani, S.K. (eds.) SPIN 2003. LNCS, vol. 2648, pp. 121–136. Springer, Heidelberg (2003). https://doi.org/10.1007/3-540-44829-2_8
12. Holzmann, G.J.: The model checker SPIN. IEEE Trans. Softw. Eng. **23**(5), 279–295 (1997)
13. Kupferman, O., Sheinvald-Faragy, S.: Finding shortest witnesses to the nonemptiness of automata on infinite words. In: Baier, C., Hermanns, H. (eds.) CONCUR 2006. LNCS, vol. 4137, pp. 492–508. Springer, Heidelberg (2006). https://doi.org/10.1007/11817949_33
14. Kupferman, O., Vardi, M.Y.: Model checking of safety properties. In: Halbwachs, N., Peled, D. (eds.) CAV 1999. LNCS, vol. 1633, pp. 172–183. Springer, Heidelberg (1999). https://doi.org/10.1007/3-540-48683-6_17
15. Maidl, M.: The common fragment of CTL and LTL. In: 41st Annual Symposium on Foundations of Computer Science (FOCS), pp. 643–652 (2000)
16. Schuppan, V., Biere, A.: Efficient reduction of finite state model checking to reachability analysis. STTT **5**(2–3), 185–204 (2004)
17. Schuppan, V., Biere, A.: Shortest counterexamples for symbolic model checking of LTL with past. In: Halbwachs, N., Zuck, L.D. (eds.) TACAS 2005. LNCS, vol. 3440, pp. 493–509. Springer, Heidelberg (2005). https://doi.org/10.1007/978-3-540-31980-1_32
18. Schwoon, S., Esparza, J.: A note on on-the-fly verification algorithms. In: Halbwachs, N., Zuck, L.D. (eds.) TACAS 2005. LNCS, vol. 3440, pp. 174–190. Springer, Heidelberg (2005). https://doi.org/10.1007/978-3-540-31980-1_12
19. Sebastiani, R., Tonetta, S.: "more deterministic" vs. "smaller" Büchi automata for efficient LTL model checking. In: 12th IFIP WG 10.5 Advanced Research Working Conference (CHARME), Correct Hardware Design and Verification Methods, pp. 126–140 (2003)
20. Tarjan, R.E.: Depth-first search and linear graph algorithms. SIAM J. Comput. **1**(2), 146–160 (1972)

From LTL to Unambiguous Büchi Automata via Disambiguation of Alternating Automata

Simon Jantsch[ID], David Müller[(✉)][ID], Christel Baier[ID], and Joachim Klein[ID]

Technische Universität Dresden, Dresden, Germany
david.mueller2@tu-dresden.de

Abstract. This paper proposes a new algorithm for the generation of unambiguous Büchi automata (UBA) from LTL formulas. Unlike existing tableau-based LTL-to-UBA translations, our algorithm deals with very weak alternating automata (VWAA) as an intermediate representation. It relies on a new notion of unambiguity for VWAA and a disambiguation procedure for VWAA. We introduce optimizations on the VWAA level and new LTL simplifications targeted at generating small UBA. We report on an implementation of the construction in our tool `Duggi` and discuss experimental results that compare the automata sizes and computation times of `Duggi` with the tableau-based LTL-to-UBA translation of the `SPOT` tool set. Our experiments also cover the analysis of Markov chains under LTL specifications, which is an important application of UBA.

1 Introduction

Translations from linear temporal logic (LTL) to non-deterministic Büchi automata (NBA) have been studied intensively as they are a core ingredient in the classical algorithmic approach to LTL model checking (see, e.g. [4,9,37]). In the worst case, such translations produce automata that are exponentially larger than the input formula. However, a lot of effort has been put into optimizing the general case, which has turned LTL-to-NBA translations feasible in practice. Two classes of algorithms have emerged as being especially well suited: tableau-based decomposition of the LTL formula into an automaton (see, e.g. [11,18]), as represented by the `SPOT` family of tools [15], and translations via very weak alternating automata (VWAA) [17], where `LTL3BA` [3] is the leading tool currently.

A property that has been studied in many areas of automata theory is *unambiguity* [10]. It allows non-deterministic branching but requires that each

The authors are supported by the DFG through the Collaborative Research Centers CRC 912 (HAEC), the DFG grant 389792660 as part of TRR 248, the DFG-project BA-1679/12-1, the Cluster of Excellence EXC 2050/1 (CeTI, project ID 390696704, as part of Germany's Excellence Strategy), and the Research Training Group QuantLA (GRK 1763).

© Springer Nature Switzerland AG 2019
M. H. ter Beek et al. (Eds.): FM 2019, LNCS 11800, pp. 262–279, 2019.
https://doi.org/10.1007/978-3-030-30942-8_17

input word has at most one accepting run. Prominent cases in which unambiguity can be utilized include the universality check for automata ("Is every word accepted?") on finite words, which is PSPACE-complete for arbitrary nondeterministic finite automata (NFA), but in P for unambiguous finite automata (UFA) [34]. Another example is model checking of Markov chains, which is in P if the specification is given as an unambiguous Büchi automaton (UBA) [5], and PSPACE-hard for arbitrary NBA [35]. Thus, using UBA leads to a single-exponential algorithm for LTL model checking of Markov chains, whereas using deterministic automata always involves a double-exponential lower bound in time complexity.

Every ω-regular language is expressible by UBA [1], but NBA may be exponentially more succinct than UBA [24] and UBA may be exponentially more succinct than any deterministic automaton [7]. Universality and language inclusion are in P for subclasses of UBA [7,22], but the complexity is open for general UBA.

Although producing UBA was not the goal of the early translation from LTL to NBA by Vardi and Wolper [37], their construction is asymptotically optimal and produces *separated* automata, a subclass of UBA where the languages of the states are pairwise disjoint. Separated automata can express all ω-regular languages [8], but UBA may be exponentially more succinct [7]. LTL-to-NBA translations have been studied intensively [13,16–18], but the generation of UBA from LTL formulas has not received much attention so far. We are only aware of three approaches targeted explicitly at generating UBA or subclasses. The first approach by Couvreur et al. [12] adapts the algorithm of [37], but still generates separated automata. LTL-to-UBA translations that attempt to exploit the advantages of UBA over separated automata have been presented by Benedikt et al. [6] and Duret-Lutz [14]. These adapt tableau-based LTL-to-NBA algorithms ([18] in the case of [6] and [11] in the case of [14]) and rely on transformations of the form $\varphi \vee \psi \rightsquigarrow \varphi \vee (\neg\varphi \wedge \psi)$ to enforce that splitting disjunctive formulas generates states with disjoint languages, thus ensuring unambiguity.

To the best of our knowledge, the only available tool that supports the translation of LTL formulas to UBA is ltl2tgba, which is part of the SPOT tool set and implements the LTL-to-UBA algorithm of [14].

You can find an extended version of this paper at [23] with further details and proofs.

Contribution. We describe a novel LTL-to-UBA construction. It relies on an intermediate representation of LTL formulas using VWAA and adapts the known translation from VWAA to NBA by Gastin and Oddoux [17]. We introduce a notion of unambiguity for VWAA, show that the subsequent translation steps preserve it and that checking whether a VWAA is unambiguous is PSPACE-complete (Sect. 3). To the best of our knowledge, unambiguity for alternating automata has not been considered before.

We present a disambiguation procedure for VWAA that relies on intermediate unambiguity checks to identify ambiguous states and local disambiguation transformations for the VWAA (Sect. 4). It has the property that an already

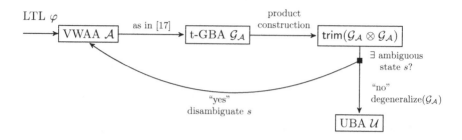

Fig. 1. The LTL-to-UBA step. A sequence of unambiguity checks and disambiguation transformations are applied and ultimately a UBA is returned. We use $\text{trim}(\mathcal{G}_\mathcal{A} \otimes \mathcal{G}_\mathcal{A})$ to check whether unambiguity is achieved or more iterations are necessary.

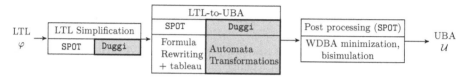

Fig. 2. Overview of the general LTL-to-UBA generation algorithm. The LTL simplification step, the actual LTL-to-UBA translation step, and the automaton post processing step can be combined freely. We propose novel rewriting rules for LTL and a LTL-to-UBA translation, both implemented in our tool `Duggi`.

unambiguous VWAA is not changed. Figure 1 gives an overview of our LTL-to-UBA algorithm. Apart from the main construction, we introduce novel LTL rewrite rules and a heuristic, both of which are aimed at producing small UBA and may also benefit existing tools (see Fig. 2). The heuristic is targeted at states with a certain structure, defined using the concepts of *purely-universal* and *alternating* formulas (Sect. 5). Finally, we report on an implementation of our construction in our tool `Duggi` and compare it to the existing LTL-to-UBA translator `ltl2tgba`. We also compare `Duggi` with `ltl2tgba` in the context of Markov chain analysis under LTL specifications (Sect. 6).

2   Preliminaries

This section introduces our notation and standard definitions. The set of infinite words over a finite alphabet Σ is denoted by Σ^ω and we write $w[i]$ to denote the i-th position of an infinite word $w \in \Sigma^\omega$, and $w[i..]$ to denote the suffix $w[i]w[i+1]\ldots$. We write $\mathcal{B}^+(X)$ to denote the set of positive Boolean formulas over a finite set of variables X. A *minimal model* of a formula $f \in \mathcal{B}^+(X)$ is a set $M \subseteq X$ such that $M \models f$, but no $M' \subset M$ satisfies $M' \models f$. LTL is defined using $\mathcal{U}$ ("Until")and $\bigcirc$ ("Next"). Additionally we use syntactical derivations $\Diamond$ ("Finally"), $\Box$ ("Globally"), and $\mathcal{R}$ ("Release") (see [4,19] for details).

Alternating Automata on Infinite Words. An alternating ω-automaton $\mathcal{A}$ is a tuple $(Q, \Sigma, \Delta, \iota, \Phi)$ where Q is a non-empty, finite set of states, Σ is a finite alphabet, $\Delta : Q \times \Sigma \to \mathcal{B}^+(Q)$ is the transition function, $\iota \in \mathcal{B}^+(Q)$ is the initial condition and Φ is the acceptance condition. Additionally, we define the function $\delta : Q \times \Sigma \to 2^{2^Q}$ which assigns to a pair $(q, a) \in Q \times \Sigma$ the set of minimal models of $\Delta(q, a)$ and the set $I \subseteq 2^Q$ as the set of minimal models of ι. We denote by $\mathcal{A}(\iota')$ the automaton $(Q, \Sigma, \delta, \iota', \Phi)$ and we write $\mathcal{A}(Q_0)$ for $\mathcal{A}(\bigwedge_{q \in Q_0} q)$, if $Q_0 \subseteq Q$. We call the number of the reachable states of an automaton $\mathcal{A}$ its size.

A run of $\mathcal{A}$ for $w \in \Sigma^\omega$ is a directed acyclic graph (DAG) (V, E) [28], where

1. $V \subseteq Q \times \mathbb{N}$, and $E \subseteq \bigcup_{0 \leq l} (Q \times \{l\}) \times (Q \times \{l+1\})$,
2. $\{q : (q, 0) \in V\} \in I$,
3. for all $(q, l) \in V : \{q' : ((q, l), (q', l+1)) \in E\} \in \delta(q, w[l])$,
4. for all $(q, l) \in V \setminus (Q \times \{0\})$ there is a q' such that $((q', l-1), (q, l)) \in E$.

We define $V(i) = \{s : (s, i) \in V\}$, called the i-th *layer* of V. A run is called accepting if every infinite path in it meets the acceptance condition.

A word is accepted by $\mathcal{A}$ if there exists an accepting run for it. We denote the set of accepted words of $\mathcal{A}$ by $\mathcal{L}(\mathcal{A})$. We distinguish between Büchi, generalized Büchi and co-Büchi acceptance conditions. A Büchi condition is denoted by $\text{Inf}(Q_f)$ for a set $Q_f \subseteq Q$. An infinite path $\pi = q_0 q_1 \ldots$ meets $\text{Inf}(Q_f)$ if $Q_f \cap \inf(\pi) \neq \varnothing$, where $\inf(\pi)$ denotes the set of infinitely occurring states in π. A co-Büchi condition is denoted by $\text{Fin}(Q_f)$ and π meets $\text{Fin}(Q_f)$ if $Q_f \cap \inf(\pi) = \varnothing$. An infinite path π meets a generalized Büchi condition $\bigwedge_{i \in F} \text{Inf}(Q_i)$ if it meets $\text{Inf}(Q_i)$ for all $i \in F$. A *transition-based* acceptance condition uses sets of transitions $T \subseteq Q \times \Sigma \times Q$ instead of sets of states to define acceptance of paths.

We call a subset $C \subseteq Q$ a configuration and say that C is reachable if it is a layer of some run. A configuration C is reachable from a state q, also written as $q \longrightarrow^* C$, if C is a reachable configuration of $\mathcal{A}(q)$. Analogously, $C' \subseteq Q$ is reachable from $C \subseteq Q$, or $C \longrightarrow^* C'$, if C' is a reachable configuration of $\mathcal{A}(C)$. A configuration C is *reachable via* u if there is a run (V, E) for a word uw, with $u \in \Sigma^*, w \in \Sigma^\omega$, such that $C = V(|u|)$. We extend this notion to reachability from states and configurations via finite words in the expected way and write $q \xrightarrow{u}^* C'$ and $C \xrightarrow{u}^* C'$. We define $\mathcal{L}(C) = \mathcal{L}(\mathcal{A}(C))$.

The *underlying graph* of $\mathcal{A}$ has vertices Q and edges $\{(q, q') : \exists a \in \Sigma. \exists S \in \delta(q, a). q' \in S\}$. We say that $\mathcal{A}$ is *very weak* if every strongly connected component of its underlying graph consists of a single state and $\mathcal{A}$ has a co-Büchi acceptance. If $|C_0| = 1$ for every $C_0 \in I$, and $|C_\delta| = 1$ for every $C_\delta \in \delta(q, a)$ with $(q, a) \in Q \times \Sigma$, we call $\mathcal{A}$ non-deterministic. As a non-deterministic automaton has only singleton successor sets, its runs are infinite sequences of states. Finally, an automaton $\mathcal{A}$ is *trimmed* if $\mathcal{L}(q) \neq \varnothing$ holds for every state q in $\mathcal{A}$, and we write $\text{trim}(\mathcal{A})$ for the automaton that we get by removing all states with empty language in $\mathcal{A}$. For the non-alternating automata types that we consider, $\text{trim}(\mathcal{A})$ can be computed in linear time using standard graph algorithms.

From LTL to NBA. We use the standard translation from LTL to VWAA where the states of the VWAA correspond to subformulas of φ and the transition relation follows the Boolean structure of the state and the LTL expansion laws [31,36]. It has been used as a first step in an LTL-to-NBA translation in [17], whose construction we follow. Additionally, we use the optimizations proposed in [3]. We also maintain the following invariant, as proposed in [17]: for all $(q, a) \in Q \times \Sigma$ and successor sets $S_1, S_2 \in \delta(q, a)$, such that $S_1 \neq S_2$, it holds that $S_1 \not\subseteq S_2$.

A VWAA $\mathcal{A}$ can be transformed into a transition-based generalized Büchi automaton (t-GBA) by a powerset-like construction, where the non-deterministic choices of $\mathcal{A}$ are captured by non-deterministic choices of the t-GBA, and the universal choices are captured by the powerset.

Definition 1. *Let $\mathcal{A} = (Q, \Sigma, \Delta, \iota, \mathrm{Fin}(Q_f))$ be a VWAA. The t-GBA $\mathcal{G}_\mathcal{A}$ is the tuple $(2^Q, \Sigma, \delta', I, \bigwedge_{f \in Q_f} \mathrm{Inf}(\mathcal{T}_f))$, where*

- *$\delta'(C, a) = \bigotimes_{q \in C} \delta(q, a)$, where $T_1 \otimes T_2 = \{C_1 \cup C_2 \;:\; C_1 \in T_1, C_2 \in T_2\}$*
- *$\mathcal{T}_f = \{(C, a, C') \;:\; f \notin C'$ or there exists $Y \in \delta(f, a)$ and $f \notin Y \subseteq C'\}$*

Theorem 2 (Theorem 2 of [17]). *Let $\mathcal{A}$ be a VWAA and $\mathcal{G}_\mathcal{A}$ be as in Definition 1. Then, $\mathcal{L}(\mathcal{A}) = \mathcal{L}(\mathcal{G}_\mathcal{A})$.*

The size of $\mathcal{G}_\mathcal{A}$ may be exponential in $|Q|$ and the number of Büchi conditions of $\mathcal{G}_\mathcal{A}$ is $|Q_f|$. Often a Büchi automaton with a (non-generalized) Büchi acceptance is desired. For this step we follow the construction of [17], which translates $\mathcal{G}_\mathcal{A}$ into an NBA $\mathcal{N}_{\mathcal{G}_\mathcal{A}}$ of at most $|Q_f| \cdot 2^{|Q|}$ reachable states.

3   Unambiguous VWAA

In this section we introduce a notion of unambiguity for VWAA and show that unambiguous VWAA are translated to UBA by the translation presented in Sect. 2. We define unambiguity in terms of configurations of the VWAA, which are strongly related to the states of the resulting NBA. Let $\mathcal{A} = (Q, \Sigma, \Delta, \iota, \mathrm{Fin}(Q_f))$ be a fixed VWAA for the rest of this section.

Definition 3. *$\mathcal{A}$ is unambiguous if it has no distinct configurations C_1, C_2 that are reachable via the same word $u \in \Sigma^*$ and such that $\mathcal{L}(C_1) \cap \mathcal{L}(C_2) \neq \varnothing$.*

The standard definition of unambiguity is that an automaton is unambiguous if it has at most one accepting run for any word. In our setting runs are DAG's and we do allow multiple accepting runs for a word, as long as they agree on the configurations that they reach for each prefix. In this sense it is a weaker notion. However, the notions coincide on non-deterministic automata as the edge relation of the run is then induced by the sequence of visited states.

Theorem 4. *Let $\mathcal{N}_{\mathcal{G}_\mathcal{A}}$ be the NBA for $\mathcal{A}$, obtained by the translation from Sect. 2. If $\mathcal{A}$ is unambiguous, then $\mathcal{N}_{\mathcal{G}_\mathcal{A}}$ is unambiguous.*

We show that every step in the translation from VWAA to NBA preserves unambiguity. First, we establish the following correspondance:

Lemma 5. *If $\mathcal{A}$ is unambiguous, then for every accepting run $r = Q_0 Q_1 \ldots$ of $\mathcal{G}_\mathcal{A}$ for $w \in \Sigma^\omega$ there exists an accepting run $\rho = (V, E)$ of $\mathcal{A}$ for w such that $Q_i = V(i)$ for all $i \geq 0$.*

Table 1. The adapted expansion laws for $\mathcal{U}$ and $\mathcal{R}$ are the result of applying the disjunction rule to the classic expansion laws.

	Expansion law	Adapted expansion law
$\varphi \mathcal{U} \psi$	$\Gamma \equiv \psi \vee (\varphi \wedge \bigcirc \Gamma)$	$\Gamma \equiv \psi \vee (\varphi \wedge \neg \psi \wedge \bigcirc \Gamma)$
$\varphi \mathcal{R} \psi$	$\Gamma \equiv \psi \wedge (\varphi \vee \bigcirc \Gamma)$	$\Gamma \equiv \psi \wedge (\varphi \vee (\neg \varphi \wedge \bigcirc \Gamma))$

Intuitively, the lemma states that if $\mathcal{A}$ is unambiguous, then every accepting run r of $\mathcal{G}_\mathcal{A}$ can be matched by an accepting run ρ of $\mathcal{A}$ such that the states of r are the layers of ρ. The proof is not immediate and requires $\mathcal{A}$ to be unambiguous.

A direct consequence of Lemma 5 is that if $\mathcal{A}$ is unambiguous, then so is $\mathcal{G}_\mathcal{A}$. The degeneralization construction in [17] makes $|Q_f| + 1$ copies of $\mathcal{G}_\mathcal{A}$. As the next copy is uniquely determined by the current state and word label, it preserves unambiguity. In combination with Lemma 7 we obtain Theorem 4.

We now show that deciding whether a VWAA is unambiguous is PSPACE-complete. The idea for proving hardness is to reduce LTL satisfiability, which is known to be PSPACE-hard, to VWAA emptiness (this follows directly by the LTL $\to$ VWAA translation) and VWAA emptiness to VWAA unambiguity. The second step uses the following trick: a VWAA $\mathcal{A}$ accepts the empty language if and only if the disjoint union of $\mathcal{A}$ with itself is unambiguous.

To check wether VWAA is unambiguous we first show that for every accepting run of $\mathcal{A}$, we find a matching accepting run of $\mathcal{G}_\mathcal{A}$, which follows directly from the definition of $\mathcal{G}_\mathcal{A}$:

Lemma 6. *For every accepting run $\rho = (V, E)$ of $\mathcal{A}$ for $w \in \Sigma^\omega$ there exists an accepting run $r = Q_0 Q_1 \ldots$ of $\mathcal{G}_\mathcal{A}$ for w, such that $Q_i = V(i)$ for all $i \geq 0$.*

Lemmas 5 and 6 give us the following:

Lemma 7. *$\mathcal{A}$ is unambiguous if and only if $\mathcal{G}_\mathcal{A}$ is unambiguous.*

However, checking whether $\mathcal{G}_\mathcal{A}$ is unambiguous can be done in space polynomial in the size of $\mathcal{A}$, and we conclude:

Theorem 8. *Deciding whether a VWAA is unambiguous is PSPACE-complete.*

4   Disambiguating VWAA

Our disambiguation procedure is inspired by the idea of "separating" the language of successors for every non-deterministic branching. A disjunction $\varphi \vee \psi$ is transformed into $\varphi \vee (\neg \varphi \wedge \psi)$ by this principle. The rules for $\mathcal{U}$ and $\mathcal{R}$ are derived by applying the disjunction rule to the expansion law of the corresponding operator (see Table 1). These rules are applied by ltl2tgba in its tableau-based algorithm to guarantee that the resulting automaton is unambiguous, and have also been proposed in [6].

In our approach we define corresponding transformations for non-deterministic branching in the VWAA. Furthermore, we propose to do this in an "on-demand" manner: instead of applying these transformation rules to every non-deterministic split, we identify ambiguous states during the translation and only apply the transformations to them. This guarantees that we return the automaton produced by the core translation, without disambiguation, in case it is already unambiguous.

The main steps of our disambiguation procedure are the following:

1. A preprocessing step that computes a complement state $\tilde{s}$ for every state s.
2. A procedure that identifies ambiguous states.
3. Local transformations that remove the ambiguity.

If no ambiguity is found in step 2, the VWAA is unambiguous. The high-level overview is also depicted in Fig. 1. In what follows we fix a VWAA $\mathcal{A} = (Q, \Sigma, \Delta, \iota, \text{Fin}(Q_f))$ and assume that it has a single initial state.

Complement States. The transformations we apply for disambiguation rely on the following precondition: for every state s of $\mathcal{A}$ there should be another state $\tilde{s}$ such that $\mathcal{L}(\tilde{s}) = \overline{\mathcal{L}(s)}$. We compute these complement states in a preprocessing step and add them to $\mathcal{A}$. Complementing alternating automata can be done without any blow up by dualizing both the acceptance condition and transition structure, as shown by Muller and Schupp [32]. As dualizing the acceptance condition and complementing the set of final states yields an equivalent VWAA, we can keep the co-Büchi acceptance when complementing.

The complement automaton has the same underlying graph and is therefore also very weak. Furthermore, no state s is reachable from its own complement state $\tilde{s}$, which is an invariant that we maintain and which ensures that very weakness is preserved in the construction.

Source Configurations and Source States. To characterize ambiguous situations we define *source configurations* and *source states*. A source configuration of $\mathcal{A}$ is a reachable configuration C such that there exist two different configurations C_1, C_2 that are reachable from C via some $a \in \Sigma$ and $\mathcal{L}(C_1) \cap \mathcal{L}(C_2) \neq \emptyset$. By definition, $\mathcal{A}$ is not unambiguous if a source configuration exists.

Let C be a source configuration of $\mathcal{A}$ and let C_1, C_2 be the successor configurations as described above. A source state of C is a state $s \in C$ with two transitions $S_1, S_2 \in \delta(s, a)$ such that $S_i \subseteq C_i$, for $i \in \{1, 2\}$, $S_1 \neq S_2$ and $(S_1 \cup S_2) \setminus (C_1 \cap C_2) \neq \emptyset$. The last condition ensures that either S_1 or S_2 contains a state that is not common to C_1 and C_2. By Definition 1, $C_i = \bigcup_{q \in C} S_q$ with $S_q \in \delta(a, q)$ for all $q \in C$, and thus C must contain a source state.

Ambiguity Check and Finding Source States. For the analysis of source configurations and source states we use the standard product construction $\mathcal{G}_1 \otimes \mathcal{G}_2$, which returns a t-GBA such that $\mathcal{L}(\mathcal{G}_1 \otimes \mathcal{G}_2) = \mathcal{L}(\mathcal{G}_1) \cap \mathcal{L}(\mathcal{G}_2)$ for two given t-GBA $\mathcal{G}_1$ and $\mathcal{G}_2$. Specifically, we consider the self product $\mathcal{G}_\mathcal{A} \otimes \mathcal{G}_\mathcal{A}$ of $\mathcal{G}_\mathcal{A}$. It helps to identify ambiguity: $\mathcal{G}_\mathcal{A}$ is not unambiguous if and only if there exists a reachable state (C_1, C_2) in $\text{trim}(\mathcal{G}_\mathcal{A} \otimes \mathcal{G}_\mathcal{A})$ with $C_1 \neq C_2$.

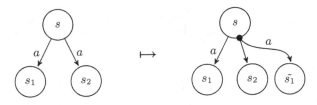

Fig. 3. Disambiguation scheme for a source state s with successors s_1 and s_2 in the VWAA. Transitions with successor set of size ≥ 1 are conjoined by a •.

The pair of configurations (C_1, C_2) is a witness to ambiguity of $\mathcal{A}$. We look for a symbol $a \in \Sigma$ and a configuration C such that $(C, C) \xrightarrow{a} (C_1', C_2') \rightarrow^* (C_1, C_2)$ is a path in $\mathsf{trim}(\mathcal{G}_\mathcal{A} \otimes \mathcal{G}_\mathcal{A})$ and $C_1' \neq C_2'$. Such a configuration must exist as we have assumed that $\mathcal{A}$ has a single initial state q_i, which implies that $\mathsf{trim}(\mathcal{G}_\mathcal{A} \otimes \mathcal{G}_\mathcal{A})$ has a single initial state $(\{q_i\}, \{q_i\})$. C is a source configuration and therefore must contain a source state which we can find by inspecting all pairs of transitions of states in C.

Disambiguating a Source State. The general scheme for disambiguating source states is depicted in Fig. 3. Assume that we have identified a source state s with successor sets S_1 and S_2 as explained above. The LTL-to-VWAA construction guarantees $S_1 \not\subseteq S_2$ and $S_2 \not\subseteq S_1$. We need to distinguish the looping successor sets (i.e. those S_i that contain s) from the non-looping. Technically, we consider two cases: either S_1 or S_2 do not contain s or both sets contain s. In the first case we assume, w.l.o.g., that $s \notin S_1$. The successor set S_2 is split into the $|S_1|$ new successor sets $\{(S_2 \cup \{\tilde{s}_1\}) : s_1 \in S_1\}$. The new sets of states are added to $\delta(s, a)$ and the successor set S_2 is removed. If both S_1 and S_2 contain s, we proceed as in the first case but do not add the successor set $S_2 \cup \{\tilde{s}\}$ to $\delta(s, a)$.

This transformation does not guarantee that s is not a source state anymore. However, it removes the ambiguity that stems from the non-deterministic choice of transitions $S_1, S_2 \in \delta(a, s)$. If s is still a source state it will be identified again for another pair of transitions. After a finite number of iterations all successor sets of s for any symbol in Σ will accept pairwise disjoint languages, in which case s cannot be a source state anymore. The transformation preserves very weakness as it only adds transitions from s to complement states of successors of s and by assumption there is no path between a state and its complement state.

Iterative Algorithm. Putting things together, our algorithm works as follows: it searches for source configurations of $\mathcal{A}$ (using $\mathcal{G}_\mathcal{A}$), applies the local disambiguation transformations to $\mathcal{A}$ as described and recurses (see Fig. 1). As rebuilding the t-GBA may become costly, in our implementation we identify which part of the t-GBA has to be recomputed due to the changes in $\mathcal{A}$, and rebuild only this part. If no source configuration is found, we know that both $\mathcal{A}$ and $\mathcal{G}_\mathcal{A}$ are unambiguous and we can apply degeneralization to obtain a UBA.

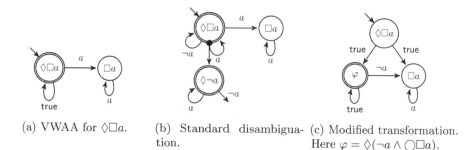

(a) VWAA for $\Diamond\Box a$.

(b) Standard disambiguation.

(c) Modified transformation. Here $\varphi = \Diamond(\neg a \wedge \bigcirc\Box a)$.

Fig. 4. Three VWAA for $\Diamond\Box a$. The automaton in (b) is the result of standard disambiguation and (c) is the result of the modified transformation applied to (a). The automaton in (c) is non-deterministic and has two looping states, whereas (b) is not non-deterministic and has three looping states.

Complexity of the Procedure. The VWAA-to-t-GBA translation that we adapt produces a t-GBA $\mathcal{G}_{\mathcal{A}}$ of size at most 2^n for a VWAA $\mathcal{A}$ of size n. In our disambiguation procedure we enlarge $\mathcal{A}$ by adding complement states for every state in the original automaton, yielding a VWAA of size $2n$. Thus, a first size estimate of $\mathcal{G}_{\mathcal{A}}$ in our construction is 4^n. However, no state in trim($\mathcal{G}_{\mathcal{A}}$) can contain both s and $\tilde{s}$ for any state s of $\mathcal{A}$. The reason is that the language of a state in $\mathcal{G}_{\mathcal{A}}$ is the intersection of the languages of the VWAA-states it contains, and $\mathcal{L}(s) \cap \mathcal{L}(\tilde{s}) = \varnothing$. Thus, trim($\mathcal{G}_{\mathcal{A}}$) has at most 3^n states.

The amount of ambiguous situations that we identify is bounded by the number of non-deterministic splits in the VWAA, which may be exponential in the length of the input LTL formula. In every iteration we check ambiguity of the new VWAA, which can be done in exponential time. Thus, our procedure computes a UBA in time exponential in the length of the formula.

5   Heuristics for Purely-Universal Formulas

In this section we introduce alternative disambiguation transformations for special source states representing formulas $\varphi\mathcal{U}\nu$, where ν is *purely-universal*. The class of purely-universal formulas is a syntactically defined subclass of LTL-formulas with suffix-closed languages. These transformations reduce the size of the resulting UBA and often produce automata of a simpler structure. The idea is to decide whether ν holds whenever moving to a state representing $\varphi\mathcal{U}\nu$ and, if not, finding the *last* position where it does not hold.

Example 9. Consider the formula $\Diamond\Box a$. A VWAA for it is shown in Fig. 4a. It is ambiguous, as a word satisfying $\Box a$ may loop in the initial state for an arbitrary amount of steps before moving to the next state.

In the standard disambiguation transformation the state $\Diamond\neg a$ is added to the self loop of the initial state (Fig. 4b). The automaton in Fig. 4c, on the other hand, makes the following case distinction: either a word satisfies $\Box a$, in which case we move to that state directly, or there is a suffix that satisfies $\neg a$ and $\bigcirc \Box a$. The state φ is used to find the *last* occurrence of $\neg a$, which is unique.

To generalize this idea and identify the situations where it is applicable we use the syntactically defined subclasses of *purely-universal* (ν), *purely-eventual* (μ) and *alternating* (ξ) formulas ([3,16]). In the following definition φ ranges over arbitrary LTL formulas:

$$\nu ::= \Box\varphi \mid \nu \vee \nu \mid \nu \wedge \nu \mid \bigcirc\nu \mid \nu\mathcal{U}\nu \mid \varphi\mathcal{R}\nu \mid \Diamond\nu$$
$$\mu ::= \Diamond\varphi \mid \mu \vee \mu \mid \mu \wedge \mu \mid \bigcirc\mu \mid \varphi\mathcal{U}\mu \mid \mu\mathcal{R}\mu \mid \Box\mu$$
$$\xi ::= \Box\mu \mid \Diamond\nu \mid \xi \vee \xi \mid \xi \wedge \xi \mid \bigcirc\xi \mid \varphi\mathcal{U}\xi \mid \varphi\mathcal{R}\xi \mid \Diamond\xi \mid \Box\xi$$

Formulas that fall into these classes define suffix closed (ν), prefix closed (μ) and prefix invariant (ξ) languages respectively:

Lemma 10 ([3,16]). *For all $u \in \Sigma^*$ and $w \in \Sigma^\omega$:*

- *If ν is purely-universal, then $uw \models \nu \implies w \models \nu$.*
- *If μ is purely-eventual, then $w \models \mu \implies uw \models \mu$.*
- *If ξ is alternating, then $w \models \xi \iff uw \models \xi$.*

Let ν be purely-universal. We want to find a formula $\mathfrak{g}(\nu)$, called the *goal* of ν, that is simpler than ν and satisfies $\mathfrak{g}(\nu) \wedge \bigcirc\nu \equiv \nu$. If ν does not hold initially for some word w we can identify the last suffix $w[i..]$ where it does not hold, given that such an i exists, by checking if $w[i..]$ satisfies $\neg\mathfrak{g}(\nu) \wedge \bigcirc\nu$.

It is not clear how to define $\mathfrak{g}(\nu)$ for purely-universal formulas of the form $\nu_1 \vee \nu_2$ or $\nu_1\mathcal{U}\nu_2$. We therefore introduce the concept of *disjunction-free* purely-universal formulas in which all occurrences of $\vee$ and $\mathcal{U}$ appear in the scope of some $\Box$. As $\varphi\mathcal{R}\nu \equiv \nu$ if ν is purely-universal, we assume that all occurences of $\mathcal{R}$ are also in the scope of some $\Box$ for purely-universal formulas.

Lemma 11. *Every purely-universal formula ν can be rewritten into a formula $\nu_1 \vee \ldots \vee \nu_n$, where ν_i is disjunction-free for all $1 \leq i \leq n$.*

Disjunction-free purely-universal formulas have a natural notion of "goal".

Definition 12. *Let ν be a disjunction-free and purely-universal formula. We define $\mathfrak{g}(\nu)$ inductively as follows:*

$$\mathfrak{g}(\Box\varphi) = \varphi \qquad\qquad \mathfrak{g}(\bigcirc\nu) = \bigcirc\mathfrak{g}(\nu)$$
$$\mathfrak{g}(\nu_1 \wedge \nu_2) = \mathfrak{g}(\nu_1) \wedge \mathfrak{g}(\nu_2) \quad \mathfrak{g}(\Diamond\nu) = \text{true}$$

The reason for defining $\mathfrak{g}(\Diamond\nu)$ as true is that $\Diamond\nu$ is an alternating formula and checking its validity can thus be temporarily suspended. Indeed, the definition satisfies the equivalence that we aimed for:

Lemma 13. *Let ν be a disjunction-free and purely-universal formula. Then $\mathfrak{g}(\nu) \wedge \bigcirc\nu \equiv \nu$.*

In Example 9 $\neg\mathfrak{g}(\nu) \wedge \bigcirc \nu$ corresponds to $\neg a \wedge \bigcirc \Box a$, which is realized by the transition from state φ to state $\Box a$ in Fig. 4c.

Lemma 14 shows the general transformation scheme (applied left to right). It introduces non-determinism, but we show that it is not a cause of ambiguity as the languages of the two disjuncts are disjoint. An important difference to the known rule for $\mathcal{U}$ is that the left-hand side of the $\mathcal{U}$-formula stays unchanged. This is favorable as it is the left-hand side that may introduce loops in the automaton.

Lemma 14. *Let ν be a disjunction-free and purely-universal formula. Then*

$$1.\ \varphi\mathcal{U}(\nu \vee \psi) \equiv \nu \vee \gamma \quad and \quad 2.\ \mathcal{L}(\nu) \cap \mathcal{L}(\gamma) = \varnothing$$

where $\gamma = \varphi\mathcal{U}\left(((\varphi \wedge \neg\mathfrak{g}(\nu) \wedge \bigcirc\nu) \vee (\psi \wedge \neg\nu))\right)$.

LTL formulas may become larger when applying this transformation. However, they are comparable to the LTL formulas produced by the standard disambiguation transformations in terms of the number of subformulas. If all occurrences of $\bigcirc$ in ν are in the scope of some $\Box$, then no subformulas are added. Otherwise, $\mathfrak{g}(\nu)$ and $\bigcirc\nu$ may introduce new $\bigcirc$-subformulas.

6   Implementation and Experiments

The tool `Duggi` is an LTL-to-UBA translator based on the construction introduced in the foregoing sections.[1] It reads LTL formulas in a prefix syntax and produces (unambiguous) automata in the HOA format [2]. In the implementation we deviate from or extend the procedure described above in the following ways:

- We make use of the knowledge given by the VWAA-complement states in the translation steps to t-GBA $\mathcal{G}_\mathcal{A}$ and the product $\mathcal{G}_\mathcal{A} \otimes \mathcal{G}_\mathcal{A}$. It allows an easy emptiness check: if s and $\tilde{s}$ are present in some $\mathcal{G}_\mathcal{A}$ or $\mathcal{G}_\mathcal{A} \otimes \mathcal{G}_\mathcal{A}$ state, then it accepts the empty language and does not have to be further expanded.
- We have included the following optimization of the LTL-to-VWAA procedure: when translating a formula $\Box\mu$, where μ is purely-eventual, we instead translate $\Box \bigcirc \mu$. This results in an equivalent state with fewer transitions. It is close to the idea of suspension as introduced in [3], but is not covered by it.
- Additionally, `Duggi` features an LTL rewriting procedure that uses many of the LTL simplification rules in the literature [3,16,30,33]. We have included the following rules that are not used by `SPOT`:

$$\text{I } (\Box\Diamond\varphi) \wedge (\Diamond\Box\psi) \mapsto \Box\Diamond(\varphi \wedge \Box\psi) \qquad \text{II } (\Diamond\Box\varphi) \vee (\Box\Diamond\psi) \mapsto \Diamond\Box(\varphi \vee \Diamond\psi)$$

These rewrite rules are more likely to produce formulas of the form $\Diamond\Box\varphi$, to which the heuristic of Sect. 5 can be applied. They stem from [30], where the reversed rules have been used to achieve a normal form.

---

[1] `Duggi` and the `PRISM` implementation, together with all experimental data, are available at https://wwwtcs.inf.tu-dresden.de/ALGI/TR/FM19-UBA/.

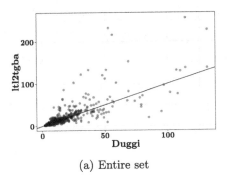
(a) Entire set

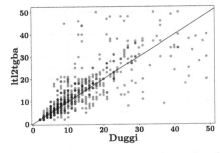
(b) Instances where both tools produced automata with at most 50 states

Fig. 5. Non-WDBA-recognizable fragment of LTLSTORE (948 formulas). Every point stands for a formula where the according automaton size for Duggi is the abcissa, the automaton size of ltl2tgba the ordinate. Points above the line stand for formulas where Duggi performed better.

LTL Benchmarks from the Literature. We now compare the UBA sizes for LTL formulas of the benchmark set LTLSTORE [25]. It collects formulas from various case studies and tool evaluation papers in different contexts. We include the negations of all formulas and filter out duplicates, leaving 1419 formulas.

Languages that are recognizable by *weak deterministic Büchi automata* (WDBA) can be efficiently minimized [27] and ltl2tgba applies this algorithm as follows: it computes the minimal deterministic Büchi automaton and the UBA and returns the one with fewer states. Our formula set contains 472 formulas that are WDBA-recognizable and for which we could compute the minimal WDBA within the bounds of 30 min and 10 GB of memory using ltl2tgba. Of these 472 formulas we found 11 for which the UBA generated by either Duggi or ltl2tgba was smaller than the minimal WDBA, and only two where the difference was bigger than 3 states. On the other hand, the minimal WDBA were smaller than the UBA produced by ltl2tgba (Duggi) for 164 (203) formulas. This supports the approach by ltl2tgba to apply WDBA minimization when possible and in what follows we focus on the fragment of the LTLSTORE that does not fall into this class. In [14] it was noted that WDBA minimization often leads to smaller automata than the LTL-to-NBA translation of ltl2tgba.

We consider the following configurations: Duggi is the standard configuration, $\text{Duggi}_{\backslash(R,H)}$ is Duggi without the new rewrite rules I and II (R) and/or without the heuristic introduced in Sect. 5 (H). For SPOT, ltl2tgba is the standard configuration that produces UBA without WDBA-minimization, which is switched on in ltl2tgba$_{\text{WDBA}}$. We use simulation-based postprocessing as provided by SPOT in all Duggi-configurations (they are enabled by default in ltl2tgba). We use SPOT with version 2.7.2. All computations, including the PMC experiments, were performed on a computer with two Intel E5-2680 8 cores at 2.70 GHz running Linux, with a time bound of 30 min and a memory bound of 10 GB.

Table 2. Cumulative results on the LTLSTORE benchmark set.

	Non-WDBA-recognizable				WDBA-recognizable			
	States	∅ States	Time in s	Timeouts	States	∅ States	Time in s	Timeouts
Duggi	16,169	20.702	38,932	167	6,866	16.308	5,958	51
Duggi$_{\backslash R}$	15,450	20.196	37,803	183	6,857	16.287	5,978	51
Duggi$_{\backslash RH}$	14,415	19.323	39,772	202	6,882	16.346	5,758	51
ltl2tgba	19,547	24.618	6,089	154	9,250	20.240	3,965	15
ltl2tgba$_{WDBA}$	19,411	24.539	7,309	157	7,632	16.700	3,814	15

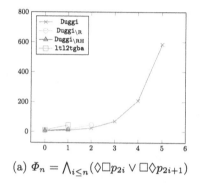   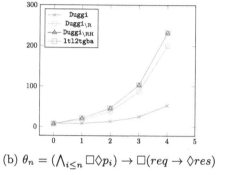

(a) $\Phi_n = \bigwedge_{i \leq n}(\Diamond\Box p_{2i} \vee \Box\Diamond p_{2i+1})$ (b) $\theta_n = (\bigwedge_{i \leq n}\Box\Diamond p_i) \rightarrow \Box(req \rightarrow \Diamond res)$

Fig. 6. UBA sizes for two sets of parametrized formulas.

Scatter plots comparing the number of states of UBA produced by ltl2tgba and Duggi are shown in Fig. 5. Table 2 gives cumulative results of different configurations on these formulas. All configurations of Duggi use more time than ltl2tgba, but produce smaller automata on average. One reason why Duggi uses more time is the on-demand nature of algorithm, which rebuilds the intermediate t-GBA several times while disambiguating. The average number of disambiguation iterations per formula of Duggi on the entire LTLSTORE was 9.5.

LTL Rewrites and the Purely-Universal Heuristic. A formula that benefits from using the rewrite rules I and II is $\Phi_n = \bigwedge_{i \leq n}\Diamond\Box p_{2i} \vee \Box\Diamond p_{2i+1}$, which describes a *strong fairness* condition. Here ltl2tgba applies the rule $\Diamond\varphi \vee \Box\Diamond\psi \mapsto \Diamond(\varphi \vee \Box\Diamond\psi)$ which yields $\bigwedge_{i \leq n}\Diamond(\Box p_{2i} \vee \Box\Diamond p_{2i+1})$. Applying rule II yields the formula $\Psi_n = \Diamond\Box(\bigwedge_{i \leq n} p_{2i} \vee \Diamond p_{2i+1})$. Figure 6a shows that Duggi produces smaller automata for Φ_n. Figure 6b shows the corresponding results for the parametrized formula $\theta_n = (\bigwedge_{i \leq n}\Box\Diamond p_i) \rightarrow \Box(req \rightarrow \Diamond res)$ which is a request/response pattern under fairness conditions.

A property that profits from the "on-demand" disambiguation is: "b occurs k steps before a". We express it with the formula $\varphi_k^{steps} = \neg a \; \mathcal{U} \; (b \wedge \neg a \wedge \bigcirc\neg a \wedge \ldots \wedge \bigcirc^{k-1}\neg a \wedge \bigcirc^k a)$. Both Duggi and ltl2tgba produce the minimal UBA, but ltl2tgba produces an exponential-sized automaton in an intermediate step, because it does not realize that the original structure is already unambiguous. This leads to high run times for large k (see Fig. 7a).

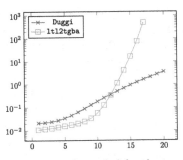
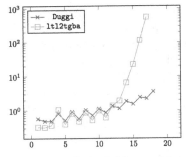

(a) Time in seconds needed for the translation of φ_k^{steps} into a UBA.

(b) Time in seconds needed for model checking the BRP model with φ_k^{steps}.

Fig. 7. Time consumption for translating and model checking φ_k^{steps} (which includes building the automaton).

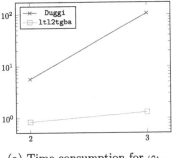
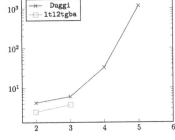

(a) Time consumption for φ_k.

(b) Time consumption for ψ_k.

Fig. 8. Model checking times for the cluster protocol with φ_k and ψ_k.

Use Case: Probabilistic Model Checking. Now we look at an important application of UBA, the analysis of Markov chains. We compare run times of an implementation of [5] for Markov chain model checking with UBA, using PRISM (version 4.4) and either Duggi or ltl2tgba as automata generation backends. We take two models of the PRISM benchmark suite [26], the bounded retransmission protocol, and the cluster working protocol [21].

The bounded retransmission protocol (BRP) is a message transmission protocol, where a sender sends a message and receives an acknowledgment if the transmission was successful. We set the parameter N (the number of the message parts) to 16, and MAX (the number of maximal retries) to 128. We reuse φ_k^{steps}, which now means: "k steps before an acknowledgment there was a retransmit", where we replace a by ack_received and b by retransmit. As expected, the faster automaton generation leads to lower model checking times when using Duggi (Fig. 7b). The reason for the spikes in Fig. 7b is that the probability of the property is zero in the BRP model for odd k. This makes the model checking (which uses the numeric procedure of [5]) easier. For bigger k the automaton generation uses a bigger share of the time, making this effect less pronounced.

As second model we analyse the cluster working model with the LTL properties presented in [20]. It consists of a workstation cluster with two sub-clusters that are connected by a backbone and have $n = 16$ participants each. Let fct_i denote the number of functional working stations in sub-cluster i. We define $\varphi_{\Box\Diamond} = \Box\Diamond(\text{fct}_1 = n)$, which expresses that the first cluster stays functional on the long run and $\varphi_{\Diamond\Box} = \bigvee_{i\in\{0,\ldots,k\}}\Diamond\Box(\text{fct}_2 = n - i)$, which expresses the property that from some point, the second cluster contains at least $n - k$ functional working stations. We check the two formula patterns $\varphi_k = \varphi_{\Box\Diamond} \wedge \varphi_{\Diamond\Box}$ and $\psi_k = \varphi_{\Box\Diamond} \vee \varphi_{\Diamond\Box}$. We leave out a third property described in [20], which is WDBA-recognizable (see the full version [23] for further details).

The results for φ_k are depicted in Fig. 8a. Both tools have a time-out at $k = 4$, although, for smaller k, the time consumption of Duggi was bigger than ltl2tgba. Comparing the automata size, Duggi produces smaller automata for both $k = 2$ and $k = 3$, e.g., 32 (Duggi) vs. 137 (ltl2tgba) states for $k = 3$. The results for ψ_k can be seen in Fig. 8b. Duggi performed better than ltl2tgba, as Duggi reached the time-out at $k = 6$ (vs. $k = 4$ for ltl2tgba). However, if no time-out was reached, ltl2tgba consumed less time. Nevertheless, for $k \leqslant 3$, model checking time of both tools was below 7 s. Still, Duggi produced smaller automata, e.g., 25 (Duggi) vs. 59 (ltl2tgba) states for $k = 3$.

7   Conclusion

In this paper we have presented a novel LTL-to-UBA translation. In contrast to other LTL-to-UBA translations [6,12,14] we use alternating automata as an intermediate representation. To adapt the VWAA-to-NBA construction of [17] for the unambiguity setting, we introduced a notion of unambiguity for VWAA and a corresponding disambiguation procedure. This may be of independent interest when considering unambiguity for different types of alternating automata. We devise heuristics that exploit structural properties of purely-universal and alternating formulas for disambiguation. Furthermore, we identify LTL rewriting rules that benefit the construction of UBA.

Experimental analysis on a big LTL benchmark set shows that our tool Duggi produces smaller automata on average than the existing tools. In particular, formulas containing nested $\Diamond$ and $\Box$ benefit from our heuristics and rewrite rules. Such formulas occur often, for example when modelling fairness properties. Experiments on Markov chain model checking indicate that the positive properties of our approach carry over to this domain.

Our approach opens up many possibilities for optimization, for example by processing multiple source states at once, or in a certain order. This would let us decrease the number of disambiguation steps, and thus the run time. It would be interesting to investigate intermediate strategies in our framework that allow for a trade-off between automata sizes and computation times. Another promising direction is to identify more patterns on LTL or VWAA that allow special disambiguation transformations. As many interesting properties stem from the safety-/cosafety-class, a combination of our approach with the ideas of the UFA generation described in [29] seems to be beneficial. The application of simulation-based automata reductions to UBA is also an open question. Whereas bisimulation preserves unambiguity, it is unclear whether there exist simulation relations targeted specifically at shrinking unambiguous automata.

References

1. Arnold, A.: Deterministic and non ambiguous rational ω-languages. In: Nivat, M., Perrin, D. (eds.) LITP 1984. LNCS, vol. 192, pp. 18–27. Springer, Heidelberg (1985). https://doi.org/10.1007/3-540-15641-0_20
2. Babiak, T., et al.: The Hanoi omega-automata format. In: Kroening, D., Păsăreanu, C.S. (eds.) CAV 2015. LNCS, vol. 9206, pp. 479–486. Springer, Cham (2015). https://doi.org/10.1007/978-3-319-21690-4_31
3. Babiak, T., Křetínský, M., Řehák, V., Strejček, J.: LTL to Büchi automata translation: fast and more deterministic. In: Flanagan, C., König, B. (eds.) TACAS 2012. LNCS, vol. 7214, pp. 95–109. Springer, Heidelberg (2012). https://doi.org/10.1007/978-3-642-28756-5_8
4. Baier, C., Katoen, J.P.: Principles of Model Checking. MIT Press, Cambridge (2008)
5. Baier, C., Kiefer, S., Klein, J., Klüppelholz, S., Müller, D., Worrell, J.: Markov chains and unambiguous Büchi automata. In: Chaudhuri, S., Farzan, A. (eds.) CAV 2016. LNCS, vol. 9779, pp. 23–42. Springer, Cham (2016). https://doi.org/10.1007/978-3-319-41528-4_2
6. Benedikt, M., Lenhardt, R., Worrell, J.: LTL model checking of interval Markov chains. In: Piterman, N., Smolka, S.A. (eds.) TACAS 2013. LNCS, vol. 7795, pp. 32–46. Springer, Heidelberg (2013). https://doi.org/10.1007/978-3-642-36742-7_3
7. Bousquet, N., Löding, C.: Equivalence and inclusion problem for strongly unambiguous Büchi automata. In: Dediu, A.-H., Fernau, H., Martín-Vide, C. (eds.) LATA 2010. LNCS, vol. 6031, pp. 118–129. Springer, Heidelberg (2010). https://doi.org/10.1007/978-3-642-13089-2_10
8. Carton, O., Michel, M.: Unambiguous Büchi automata. Theor. Comput. Sci. **297**(1–3), 37–81 (2003)
9. Clarke, E.M., Grumberg, O., Peled, D.A.: Model Checking. MIT Press, Cambridge (2001)
10. Colcombet, T.: Unambiguity in automata theory. In: Shallit, J., Okhotin, A. (eds.) DCFS 2015. LNCS, vol. 9118, pp. 3–18. Springer, Cham (2015). https://doi.org/10.1007/978-3-319-19225-3_1
11. Couvreur, J.-M.: On-the-fly verification of linear temporal logic. In: Wing, J.M., Woodcock, J., Davies, J. (eds.) FM 1999. LNCS, vol. 1708, pp. 253–271. Springer, Heidelberg (1999). https://doi.org/10.1007/3-540-48119-2_16
12. Couvreur, J.-M., Saheb, N., Sutre, G.: An optimal automata approach to LTL model checking of probabilistic systems. In: Vardi, M.Y., Voronkov, A. (eds.) LPAR 2003. LNCS (LNAI), vol. 2850, pp. 361–375. Springer, Heidelberg (2003). https://doi.org/10.1007/978-3-540-39813-4_26
13. Duret-Lutz, A.: Manipulating LTL formulas using spot 1.0. In: Van Hung, D., Ogawa, M. (eds.) ATVA 2013. LNCS, vol. 8172, pp. 442–445. Springer, Cham (2013). https://doi.org/10.1007/978-3-319-02444-8_31

14. Duret-Lutz, A.: Contributions to LTL and ω-automata for model checking. Habilitation thesis, Université Pierre et Marie Curie (Paris 6), February 2017
15. Duret-Lutz, A., Lewkowicz, A., Fauchille, A., Michaud, T., Renault, É., Xu, L.: Spot 2.0—a framework for LTL and ω-automata manipulation. In: Artho, C., Legay, A., Peled, D. (eds.) ATVA 2016. LNCS, vol. 9938, pp. 122–129. Springer, Cham (2016). https://doi.org/10.1007/978-3-319-46520-3_8
16. Etessami, K., Holzmann, G.J.: Optimizing Büchi automata. In: Palamidessi, C. (ed.) CONCUR 2000. LNCS, vol. 1877, pp. 153–168. Springer, Heidelberg (2000). https://doi.org/10.1007/3-540-44618-4_13
17. Gastin, P., Oddoux, D.: Fast LTL to Büchi automata translation. In: Berry, G., Comon, H., Finkel, A. (eds.) CAV 2001. LNCS, vol. 2102, pp. 53–65. Springer, Heidelberg (2001). https://doi.org/10.1007/3-540-44585-4_6
18. Gerth, R., Peled, D., Vardi, M.Y., Wolper, P.: Simple on-the-fly automatic verification of linear temporal logic. In: Dembiński, P., Średniawa, M. (eds.) Protocol Specification, Testing and Verification XV, PSTV 1995. IFIP Advances in Information and Communication Technology, vol. 38, pp. 3–18. Springer, Boston (1996). https://doi.org/10.1007/978-0-387-34892-6_1
19. Grädel, E., Thomas, W., Wilke, T. (eds.): Automata Logics, and Infinite Games: A Guide to Current Research. LNCS, vol. 2500. Springer, Heidelberg (2002). https://doi.org/10.1007/3-540-36387-4
20. Hahn, E.M., Li, G., Schewe, S., Turrini, A., Zhang, L.: Lazy probabilistic model checking without determinisation. In: 26th International Conference on Concurrency Theory (CONCUR 2015), Leibniz International Proceedings in Informatics (LIPIcs), vol. 42, pp. 354–367. SchlossDagstuhl–Leibniz-Zentrum fuer Informatik, Dagstuhl (2015)
21. Haverkort, B.R., Hermanns, H., Katoen, J.P.: On the use of model checking techniques for dependability evaluation. In: 19th IEEE Symposium on Reliable Distributed Systems (SRDS), pp. 228–237. IEEE Computer Society (2000)
22. Isaak, D., Löding, C.: Efficient inclusion testing for simple classes of unambiguous ω-automata. Inf. Process. Lett. **112**(14–15), 578–582 (2012)
23. Jantsch, S., Müller, D., Baier, C., Klein, J.: From LTL to unambiguous Büchi automata via disambiguation of alternating automata. Technical report, Technische Universität Dresden (2019). https://arxiv.org/abs/1907.02887/
24. Karmarkar, H., Joglekar, M., Chakraborty, S.: Improved upper and lower bounds for Büchi disambiguation. In: Proceedings of the 11th International Symposium on Automated Technology for Verification and Analysis (ATVA), pp. 40–54 (2013)
25. Kretínský, J., Meggendorfer, T., Sickert, S.: LTL store: repository of LTL formulae from literature and case studies. CoRR abs/1807.03296 (2018). http://arxiv.org/abs/1807.03296
26. Kwiatkowska, M.Z., Norman, G., Parker, D.: The PRISM benchmark suite. In: Proceedings of the 9th International Conference on Quantitative Evaluation of SysTems (QEST), pp. 203–204. IEEE Computer Society (2012)
27. Löding, C.: Efficient minimization of deterministic weak ω-automata. Inf. Process. Lett. **79**(3), 105–109 (2001)
28. Loding, C., Thomas, W.: Alternating automata and logics over infinite words. In: van Leeuwen, J., Watanabe, O., Hagiya, M., Mosses, P.D., Ito, T. (eds.) TCS 2000. LNCS, vol. 1872, pp. 521–535. Springer, Heidelberg (2000). https://doi.org/10.1007/3-540-44929-9_36
29. Mohri, M.: On the disambiguation of finite automata and functional transducers. Int. J. Found. Comput. Sci. **24**(6), 847–862 (2013)

30. Müller, D., Sickert, S.: LTL to deterministic Emerson-Lei automata. In: Proceedings of the 8th International Symposium on Games, Automata, Logics and Formal Verification (GandALF). Electronic Proceedings in Theoretical Computer Science, vol. 256, pp. 180–194. Open Publishing Association (2017)
31. Muller, D.E., Saoudi, A., Schupp, P.E.: Weak alternating automata give a simple explanation of why most temporal and dynamic logics are decidable in exponential time. In: Proceedings of the Third Annual Symposium on Logic in Computer Science (LICS), pp. 422–427 (1988)
32. Muller, D.E., Schupp, P.E.: Alternating automata on infinite trees. Theor. Comput. Sci. **54**, 267–276 (1987)
33. Somenzi, F., Bloem, R.: Efficient Büchi automata from LTL formulae. In: Emerson, E.A., Sistla, A.P. (eds.) CAV 2000. LNCS, vol. 1855, pp. 248–263. Springer, Heidelberg (2000). https://doi.org/10.1007/10722167_21
34. Stearns, R.E., Hunt, H.B.: On the equivalence and containment problem for unambiguous regular expressions, grammars, and automata. SIAM J. Comput. **14**, 598–611 (1985)
35. Vardi, M.Y.: Automatic verification of probabilistic concurrent finite-state programs. In: Proceedings of the 26th IEEE Symposium on Foundations of Computer Science (FOCS), pp. 327–338. IEEE Computer Society (1985)
36. Vardi, M.Y.: Nontraditional applications of automata theory. In: Hagiya, M., Mitchell, J.C. (eds.) TACS 1994. LNCS, vol. 789, pp. 575–597. Springer, Heidelberg (1994). https://doi.org/10.1007/3-540-57887-0_116
37. Vardi, M.Y., Wolper, P.: An automata-theoretic approach to automatic program verification (preliminary report). In: Proceedings of the 1st Symposium on Logic in Computer Science (LICS), pp. 332–344. IEEE Computer Society Press (1986)

Generic Partition Refinement
and Weighted Tree Automata

Hans-Peter Deifel, Stefan Milius, Lutz Schröder, and Thorsten Wißmann[✉]

Friedrich-Alexander-Universität Erlangen-Nürnberg, Erlangen, Germany
{hans-peter.deifel,stefan.milius,lutz.schroeder,thorsten.wissmann}@fau.de

Abstract. Partition refinement is a method for minimizing automata and transition systems of various types. Recently, we have developed a partition refinement algorithm that is generic in the transition type of the given system and matches the run time of the best known algorithms for many concrete types of systems, e.g. deterministic automata as well as ordinary, weighted, and probabilistic (labelled) transition systems. Genericity is achieved by modelling transition types as functors on sets, and systems as coalgebras. In the present work, we refine the run time analysis of our algorithm to cover additional instances, notably weighted automata and, more generally, weighted tree automata. For weights in a cancellative monoid we match, and for non-cancellative monoids such as (the additive monoid of) the tropical semiring even substantially improve, the asymptotic run time of the best known algorithms. We have implemented our algorithm in a generic tool that is easily instantiated to concrete system types by implementing a simple refinement interface. Moreover, the algorithm and the tool are modular, and partition refiners for new types of systems are obtained easily by composing pre-implemented basic functors. Experiments show that even for complex system types, the tool is able to handle systems with millions of transitions.

1 Introduction

Minimization is a basic verification task on state-based systems, concerned with reducing the number of system states as far as possible while preserving the system behaviour. It is used for equivalence checking of systems and as a pre-processing step in further system analysis tasks, such as model checking.

In general, minimization proceeds in two steps: (1) remove unreachable states, and (2) identify behaviourally equivalent states. Here, we are concerned with the second step, which depends on which notion of equivalence is imposed on states; we work with notions of *bisimilarity* and generalizations thereof. Classically, bisimilarity for labelled transition systems obeys the principle "states x and y are bisimilar if for every transition $x \to x'$, there exists a transition $y \to$

Work by S. Milius, L. Schröder, and T. Wißmann forms part of the DFG project COAX (MI 717/5-2 and SCHR 1118/12-2).

© Springer Nature Switzerland AG 2019
M. H. ter Beek et al. (Eds.): FM 2019, LNCS 11800, pp. 280–297, 2019.
https://doi.org/10.1007/978-3-030-30942-8_18

y' with x' and y' bisimilar". It is thus given via a fixpoint definition, to be understood as a *greatest* fixpoint, and can therefore be iteratively approximated from above. This is the principle behind *partition refinement* algorithms: Initially all states are tentatively considered equivalent, and then this initial partition is iteratively refined according to observations made on the states until a fixpoint is reached. Unsurprisingly, such procedures run in polynomial time. Its comparative tractability (in contrast, e.g. trace equivalence and language equivalence of nondeterministic systems are PSPACE complete [24]) makes miminization under bisimilarity interesting even in cases where the main equivalence of interest is linear-time, such as word automata.

Kanellakis and Smolka [24] in fact provide a minimization algorithm with run time $\mathcal{O}(m \cdot n)$ for ordinary transition systems with n states and m transitions. However, even faster partition refinement algorithms running in $\mathcal{O}((m+n) \cdot \log n)$ have been developed for various types of systems over the past 50 years. For example, Hopcroft's algorithm minimizes deterministic automata for a fixed input alphabet A in $\mathcal{O}(n \cdot \log n)$ [22]; it was later generalized to variable input alphabets, with run time $\mathcal{O}(n \cdot |A| \cdot \log n)$ [17,26]. The Paige-Tarjan algorithm minimizes transition systems in time $\mathcal{O}((m+n) \cdot \log n)$ [27], and generalizations to labelled transition systems have the same time complexity [13,23,33]. Minimization of weighted systems is typically called *lumping* in the literature, and Valmari and Franchescini [35] have developed a simple $\mathcal{O}((m+n) \cdot \log n)$ lumping algorithm for systems with rational weights.

In earlier work [14,37] we have developed an efficient *generic* partition refinement algorithm that can be easily instantiated to a wide range of system types, most of the time either matching or improving the previous best run time. The genericity of the algorithm is based on modelling state-based systems as coalgebras following the paradigm of universal coalgebra [30], in which the branching structure of systems is encapsulated in the choice of a functor, the *type functor*. This allows us to cover not only classical relational systems and various forms of weighted systems, but also to combine existing system types in various ways, e.g. nondeterministic and probabilistic branching. Our algorithm uses a functor-specific *refinement interface* that supports a graph-based representation of coalgebras. It allows for a generic complexity analysis, and indeed the generic algorithm has the same asymptotic complexity as the above-mentioned specific algorithms; for Segala systems [32] (systems that combine probabilistic and non-deterministic branching, also known as Markov decision processes), it even improves on the best known run time and matches the run time of a recent algorithm [19] discovered independently and almost at the same time.

The new contributions of the present paper are twofold. On the theoretical side, we show how to instantiate our generic algorithm to weighted systems with weights in a monoid (generalizing the group-weighted case considered previously [14,37]). We then refine the complexity analysis of the algorithm, making the complexity of the implementation of the type functor a parameter $p(n, m)$, where n and m are the numbers of nodes and edges, respectively, in the graph representation of the input coalgebra. In the new setup, the previous analysis becomes the special case where $p(n, m) = 1$. Under the same structural assumptions on the type functor and the refinement interface as previously, our algorithm runs in time $\mathcal{O}(m \cdot \log n \cdot p(n, m))$. Instantiated to the case of weighted systems over non-cancellative monoids (with $p(n, m) = \log(n)$), such as the additive monoid $(\mathbb{N}, \max, 0)$ of the tropical semiring, the run time of the generic algorithm is $\mathcal{O}(m \cdot \log^2 m)$, thus markedly improving the run time $\mathcal{O}(m \cdot n)$ of previous algorithms for weighted automata [9] and, more generally, (bottom-up) weighted tree automata [20] for this case. In addition, for cancellative monoids, we again essentially match the complexity of the previous algorithms [9,20].

Our second main contribution is a generic and modular implementation of our algorithm, the *Coalgebraic Partition Refiner* (CoPaR). Instantiating CoPaR to coalgebras for a given functor requires only to implement the refinement interface. We provide such implementations for a number of basic type functors, e.g. for non-deterministic, weighted, or probabilistic branching, as well as (ranked) input and output alphabets or output weights. In addition, CoPaR is *modular*: For any type functor obtained by composing basic type functors for which a refinement interface is available, CoPaR automatically derives an implementation of the refinement interface. We explain in detail how this modularity is realized in our implementation and, extending Valmari and Franchescini's ideas [35], we explain how the necessary data structures need to be implemented so as to realize the low theoretical complexity. We thus provide a working efficient partition refiner for all the above mentioned system types. In particular, our tool is, to the best of our knowledge, the only available implementation of partition refinement for many composite system types, notably for weighted (tree) automata over non-cancellative monoids. The tool including source code and evaluation data is available at https://git8.cs.fau.de/software/copar.

2   Theoretical Foundations

Our algorithmic framework [14,37] is based on modelling state-based systems abstractly as *coalgebras* for a (set) *functor* that encapsulates the transition type, following the paradigm of *universal coalgebra* [30]. We proceed to recall standard notation for sets and maps, as well as basic notions and examples in coalgebra. We fix a singleton set $1 = \{*\}$; for every set X we have a unique map $! \colon X \to 1$. We denote composition of maps by $(-) \cdot (-)$, in applicative order. Given maps $f \colon X \to A$, $g \colon X \to B$ we define $\langle f, g \rangle \colon X \to A \times B$ by $\langle f, g \rangle(x) = (f(x), g(x))$. We model the transition type of state based systems using *functors*. Informally, a functor F assigns to a set X a set FX of structured collections over X, and an F-coalgebra is a map c assigning to each state x in a system a structured collection $c(x) \in FX$ of successors. The most basic example is that of transition systems, where F is powerset, so a coalgebra assigns to each state a set of successors. Formal definitions are as follows.

Definition 2.1. A *functor* $F \colon \mathsf{Set} \to \mathsf{Set}$ assigns to each set X a set FX, and to each map $f \colon X \to Y$ a map $Ff \colon FX \to FY$, preserving identities and composition ($F\mathrm{id}_X = \mathrm{id}_{FX}$, $F(g \cdot f) = Fg \cdot Ff$). An F-*coalgebra* (C, c) consists of a set C

of *states* and a *transition* structure $c\colon C \to FC$. A *morphism* $h\colon (C,c) \to (D,d)$ of F-coalgebras is a map $h\colon C \to D$ that preserves the transition structure, i.e. $Fh \cdot c = d \cdot h$. Two states $x, y \in C$ of a coalgebra $c\colon C \to FC$ are *behaviourally equivalent* ($x \sim y$) if there exists a coalgebra morphism h with $h(x) = h(y)$.

Example 2.2. (1) The *finite powerset* functor $\mathcal{P}_\omega$ maps a set X to the set $\mathcal{P}_\omega X$ of all *finite* subsets of X, and a map $f\colon X \to Y$ to the map $\mathcal{P}_\omega f = f[-]\colon \mathcal{P}_\omega X \to \mathcal{P}_\omega Y$ taking direct images. $\mathcal{P}_\omega$-coalgebras are finitely branching (unlabelled) transition systems. and two states are behaviourally equivalent iff they are bisimilar.

(2) For a fixed finite set A, the functor given by $FX = 2 \times X^A$, where $2 = \{0,1\}$, sends a set X to the set of pairs of boolean values and functions $A \to X$. An F-coalgebra (C, c) is a deterministic automaton (without an initial state). For each state $x \in C$, the first component of $c(x)$ determines whether x is a final state, and the second component is the successor function $A \to X$ mapping each input letter $a \in A$ to the successor state of x under input letter a. States $x, y \in C$ are behaviourally equivalent iff they accept the same language in the usual sense.

(3) For a commutative monoid $(M, +, 0)$, the *monoid-valued* functor $M^{(-)}$ sends each set X to the set of maps $f\colon X \to M$ that are finitely supported, i.e. $f(x) = 0$ for almost all $x \in X$. An F-coalgebra $c\colon C \to M^{(C)}$ is, equivalently, a finitely branching M-weighted transition system: For a state $x \in C$, $c(x)$ maps each state $y \in C$ to the weight $c(x)(y)$ of the transition from x to y. For a map $f\colon X \to Y$, $M^{(f)}\colon M^{(X)} \to M^{(Y)}$ sends a finitely supported map $v\colon X \to M$ to the map $y \mapsto \sum_{x \in X, f(x) = y} v(x)$, corresponding to the standard image measure construction. As the notion of behavioural equivalence of states in $M^{(-)}$-coalgebras, we obtain weighted bisimilarity (cf. [9,25]), given coinductively by postulating that states $x, y \in C$ are behaviourally equivalent ($x \sim y$) iff

$$\sum_{z' \sim z} c(x)(z') = \sum_{z' \sim z} c(y)(z') \qquad \text{for all } z \in C.$$

For the Boolean monoid $(2 = \{0,1\}, \vee, 0)$, the monoid-valued functor $2^{(-)}$ is (naturally isomorphic to) the finite powerset functor $\mathcal{P}_\omega$. For the monoid of real numbers $(\mathbb{R}, +, 0)$, the monoid-valued functor $\mathbb{R}^{(-)}$ has $\mathbb{R}$-weighted systems as coalgebras, e.g. Markov chains. In fact, finite Markov chains are precisely finite coalgebras of the *finite distribution functor*, i.e. the subfunctor $\mathcal{D}_\omega$ of $\mathbb{R}_{\geq 0}^{(-)}$ (and hence of $\mathbb{R}^{(-)}$) given by $\mathcal{D}_\omega(X) = \{\mu \in \mathbb{R}_{\geq 0}^{(X)} \mid \sum_{x \in X} \mu(x) = 1\}$. For the monoid $(\mathbb{N}, +, 0)$ of natural numbers, the monoid-valued functor is the bag functor $\mathcal{B}_\omega$, which maps a set X to the set of finite multisets over X.

3   Generic Partition Refinement

We recall some key aspects of our generic partition refinement algorithm [14, 37], which *minimizes* a given coalgebra, i.e. computes its quotient modulo behavioural equivalence; we center the presentation around the implementation and use of our tool.

The algorithm [37, Algorithm 4.5] is parametrized over a type functor F, represented by implementing a fixed *refinement interface*, which in particular allows for a representation of F-coalgebras in terms of nodes and edges (by no means implying a restriction to relational systems!). Our previous analysis has established that the algorithm minimizes F-coalgebras with n nodes and m edges in time $\mathcal{O}(m \cdot \log n)$, assuming $m \geq n$ and that the operations of the refinement interface run in linear time. In the present paper, we generalize the analysis, establishing a run time in $\mathcal{O}(m \cdot \log n \cdot p(n, m))$, where $p(n, m)$ is a factor in the time complexity of the operations implementing the refinement interface, and depends on the functor at hand. In many instances, $p(n, m) = 1$, reproducing the previous analysis. In some cases, $p(n, m)$ is not constant, and our new analysis still applies in these cases, either matching or improving the best known run time in most instances, most notably weighted systems over non-cancellative monoids.

We proceed to discuss the design of the implementation, including input formats of our tool CoPaR for composite functors built from pre-implemented basic blocks and for systems to be minimized (Sect. 3.1). The refinement interface and its implementation are described in Sect. 3.2.

3.1 Generic System Specification

CoPaR accepts as input a file that represents a finite F-coalgebra $c: C \to FC$, and consists of two parts. The first part is a single line specifying the functor F. Each of the remaining lines describes one state $x \in C$ and its one-step behaviour $c(x)$. Examples of input files are shown in Fig. 1.

Functor Specification. Functors are specified as composites of basic building blocks; that is, the functor given in the first line of an input file is an expression determined by the grammar

$$T ::= \mathsf{X} \mid F(T, \dots, T) \qquad (F \colon \mathsf{Set}^k \to \mathsf{Set}) \in \mathcal{F}, \qquad (1)$$

where the character X is a terminal symbol and $\mathcal{F}$ is a set of predefined symbols called *basic functors*, representing a number of pre-implemented functors

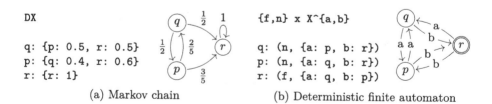

DX

q: {p: 0.5, r: 0.5}
p: {q: 0.4, r: 0.6}
r: {r: 1}

(a) Markov chain

{f,n} x X^{a,b}

q: (n, {a: p, b: r})
p: (n, {a: q, b: r})
r: (f, {a: q, b: p})

(b) Deterministic finite automaton

Fig. 1. Examples of input files with encoded coalgebras

of type $F\colon \mathsf{Set}^k \to \mathsf{Set}$. Only basic functors need to be implemented explicitly (Sect. 3.2); for composite functors, the tool derives instances of the algorithm automatically (Sect. 3.3). Basic functors currently implemented include (finite) powerset $\mathcal{P}_\omega$, the bag functor $\mathcal{B}_\omega$, monoid-valued functors $M^{(-)}$, and polynomial functors for finite many-sorted signatures Σ, based on the description of the respective refinement interfaces given in our previous work [14, 37] and, in the case of $M^{(-)}$ for unrestricted commutative monoids M (rather than only groups) the newly developed interface described in Sect. 5. Since behavioural equivalence is preserved and reflected under converting G-coalgebras into F-coalgebras for a subfunctor G of F [37, Proposition 2.13], we also cover subfunctors, such as the finite distribution functor $\mathcal{D}_\omega$ as a subfunctor of $\mathbb{R}^{(-)}$. With the polynomial constructs $+$ and $\times$ written in infix notation as usual, the currently supported grammar is effectively

$$T ::= \mathtt{X} \mid \mathcal{P}_\omega T \mid \mathcal{B}_\omega T \mid \mathcal{D}_\omega T \mid M^{(T)} \mid \Sigma$$

$$\Sigma ::= C \mid T + T \mid T \times T \mid T^A \qquad C ::= \mathbb{N} \mid A \qquad A ::= \{s_1, \ldots, s_n\} \qquad (2)$$

where the s_k are strings subject to the usual conventions for C-style identifiers, exponents F^A are written $\mathtt{F}\verb|^|\mathtt{A}$, and M is one of the monoids $(\mathbb{Z}, +, 0)$, $(\mathbb{R}, +, 0)$, $(\mathbb{C}, +, 0)$, $(\mathcal{P}_\omega(64), \cup, \emptyset)$ (i.e. the monoid of 64-bit words with bitwise or), and $(\mathbb{N}, \max, 0)$ (the additive monoid of the tropical semiring). Note that C effectively ranges over at most countable sets, and A over finite sets. A term T determines a functor $F\colon \mathsf{Set} \to \mathsf{Set}$ in the evident way, with $\mathtt{X}$ interpreted as the argument, i.e. $F(\mathtt{X}) = T$. It should be noted that the implementation treats composites of polynomial (sub-)terms as a single functor in order to minimize overhead incurred by excessive decomposition, e.g. $\mathtt{X} \mapsto \{0, 1\} + \mathcal{P}_\omega(\mathbb{R}^{(\mathtt{X})}) + \mathtt{X} \times \mathtt{X}$ is composed from the basic functors $\mathcal{P}_\omega$, $\mathbb{R}^{(-)}$ and the 3-sorted polynomial functor $\Sigma(X, Y, Z) = \{0, 1\} + X + Y \times Z$.

Coalgebra Specification. The remaining lines of an input file define a finite F-coalgebra $c\colon C \to FC$. Each line of the form $x\colon t$ defines a state $x \in C$, where x is a C-style identifier, and t represents the element $t = c(x) \in FC$. The syntax for t depends on the specified functor F, and follows the structure of the term T defining F; we write $t \in T$ for a term t describing an element of FC:

- $t \in \mathtt{X}$ iff t is one of the named states specified in the file.
- $t \in T_1 \times \cdots \times T_n$ is given by $t ::= (t_1, \ldots, t_n)$ where $t_i \in T_i$, $i = 1, \ldots, n$.
- $t \in T_1 + \cdots + T_n$ is given by $t ::= \mathtt{inj\_}i\mathtt{\_}t_i$ where $i = 1, \ldots, n$ and $t_i \in T_i$.
- $t \in \mathcal{P}_\omega T$ and $t \in \mathcal{B}_\omega T$ are given by $t ::= \{t_1, \ldots, t_n\}$ with $t_1, \ldots, t_n \in T$.
- $t \in M^{(T)}$ is given by $t ::= \{t_1\colon\mathtt{\_}m_1, \ldots, t_n\colon\mathtt{\_}m_n\}$ with $m_1, \ldots, m_n \in M$ and $t_1, \ldots, t_n \in T$, denoting $\mu \in M^{(TC)}$ with $\mu(t_i) = m_i$ and $\mu(t) = 0$ otherwise.

For example, for the functor F given by the term $T = \mathcal{P}_\omega(\{a, b\} \times \mathbb{R}^{(\mathtt{X})})$, the one-line declaration $\mathtt{x}\colon \{(\mathtt{a}, \{\mathtt{x}\colon 2.4\}), (\mathtt{a}, \{\}), (\mathtt{b}, \{\mathtt{x}\colon \text{-}8\})\}$ defines an F-coalgebra with a single state x, having two a-successors and one b-successor, where successors are elements of $\mathbb{R}^{(X)}$. One a-successor is constantly zero, and the other assigns weight 2.4 to x; the b-successor assigns weight -8 to x. Two more examples are shown in Fig. 1.

Parsing Input Files. After reading the functor term T, the tool builds a parser for the functor-specific input format and parses an input coalgebra specified in the above syntax into an intermediate format described in Sect. 3.2. In the case of a composite functor, the parsed coalgebra then undergoes a substantial amount of preprocessing that also affects how transitions are counted; we defer the discussion of this point to Sect. 3.3, and assume for the time being that $F\colon \mathsf{Set} \to \mathsf{Set}$ is a basic functor with only one argument.

3.2   Refinement Interfaces

New functors are added to the framework by implementing a *refinement interface* (Definition 3.2). The interface relates to an abstract encoding of the functor and its coalgebras in terms of nodes and edges:

Definition 3.1. An *encoding* of a functor F consists of a set A of *labels* and a family of maps $\flat\colon FX \to \mathcal{B}_\omega(A \times X)$, one for every set X. The *encoding* of an F-coalgebra $c\colon C \to FC$ is given by the map $\langle F!, \flat \rangle \cdot c\colon C \to F1 \times \mathcal{B}_\omega(A \times C)$ and we say that the coalgebra has $n = |C|$ states and $m = \sum_{x \in C} |\flat(c(x))|$ edges.

An encoding does by no means imply a reduction from F-coalgebras to $\mathcal{B}_\omega(A \times (-))$-coalgebras, i.e. the notions of behavioural equivalence for $\mathcal{B}_\omega(A \times (-))$ and F, respectively, can be radically different. The encoding just fixes a representation format, and $\flat$ is not assumed to be natural (in fact, it fails to be natural in all encodings we have implemented except the one for polynomial functors). Encodings typically match how one intuitively draws coalgebras of various types as certain labelled graphs. For instance for Markov chains (see Fig. 1), i.e. coalgebras for the distribution functor $\mathcal{D}_\omega$, the set of labels is the set of probabilities $A = [0, 1]$, and $\flat\colon \mathcal{D}_\omega X \to \mathcal{B}_\omega([0, 1] \times X)$ assigns to each finite probability distribution $\mu\colon X \to [0, 1]$ the bag $\{(\mu(x), x) \mid x \in X, \mu(x) \neq 0\}$.

   The implementation of a basic functor contains two ingredients: (1) a parser that transforms the syntactic specification of an input coalgebra (Sect. 3.1) into the encoded coalgebra, and (2) the implementation of the refinement interface.

   To understand the motivation behind the definition of a refinement interface, suppose that the generic partition refinement has already computed some block of states $B \subseteq C$ in its partition and that states in $S \subseteq B$ have different behaviour than those in $B \setminus S$. From this information, the algorithm has to infer whether states $x, y \in C$ that are in the same block and have successors in B exhibit different behaviour and thus have to be separated. For example, in the classical Paige-Tarjan algorithm [27], i.e. for $F = \mathcal{P}_\omega$, x and y can stay in the same block provided that (a) x has a successor in S iff y has one and (b) x has a successor in $B \setminus S$ iff y has one. Equivalently, $\mathcal{P}_\omega \langle \chi_S, \chi_{B \setminus S} \rangle (c(x)) = \mathcal{P}_\omega \langle \chi_S, \chi_{B \setminus S} \rangle (c(y))$, where $\chi_S\colon C \to 2$ is the usual characteristic function of the subset $S \subseteq C$. In the example

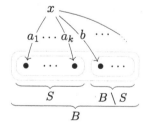

Fig. 2. Splitting a block

of Markov chains, i.e. $F = \mathcal{D}_\omega$, $x, y \in C$ can stay in the same block if $\sum_{x' \in S} c(x)(x') = \sum_{y' \in S} c(y)(y')$ and $\sum_{x' \in B \setminus S} c(x)(x') = \sum_{y' \in B \setminus S} c(y)(y')$, i.e. if $\mathcal{D}_\omega \langle \chi_S, \chi_{B \setminus S} \rangle (c(x)) = \mathcal{D}_\omega \langle \chi_S, \chi_{B \setminus S} \rangle (c(y))$. Note that the element $(1, 1)$ is not in the image of $\langle \chi_S, \chi_{B \setminus S} \rangle \colon C \to 2 \times 2$. Since, moreover, $S \subseteq B$, we can equivalently consider the map

$$\chi_S^B \colon C \to 3, \quad \chi_S^B(x \in S) = 2, \quad \chi_S^B(x \in B \setminus S) = 1, \quad \chi_S^B(x \in C \setminus B) = 0. \quad (3)$$

That is, two states $x, y \in C$ can stay in the same block in the refinement step provided that $F\chi_S^B(c(x)) = F\chi_S^B(c(y))$. Thus, it is the task of a refinement interface to compute $F\chi_S^B \cdot c$ efficiently and incrementally.

Definition 3.2. Given an encoding $(A, \flat)$ of the set functor F, a *refinement interface* for F consists of a set W of *weights* and functions

$$\text{init} \colon F1 \times \mathcal{B}_\omega A \to W \qquad \text{and} \qquad \text{update} \colon \mathcal{B}_\omega A \times W \to W \times F3 \times W$$

satisfying the following coherence condition: There exists a family of *weight maps* $w \colon \mathcal{P}X \to (FX \to W)$ such that for all $t \in FX$ and all sets $S \subseteq B \subseteq X$,

$$w(X)(t) = \text{init}\big(F!(t), \mathcal{B}_\omega \pi_1(\flat(t))\big)$$
$$(w(S)(t), F\chi_S^B(t), w(B \setminus S)(t)) = \text{update}\big(\{a \mid (a, x) \in \flat(t), x \in S\}, w(B)(t)\big).$$

Note that the comprehension in the first argument of update is to be read as a *multiset* comprehension. In contrast to init and update, the function w is not called by the algorithm and thus does not form part of the refinement interface. However, its existence ensures the correctness of our algorithm. Intuitively, X is the set of states of the input coalgebra (C, c), and for every $x \in C$, $w(B)(c(x)) \in W$ is the overall weight of edges from x to the block $B \subseteq C$ in the coalgebra (C, c). The axioms in Definition 3.2 assert that init receives in its first argument the information which states of C are (non-)terminating, in its second argument the bag of labels of all outgoing edges of a state $x \in C$ in the graph representation of (C, c), and it returns the total weight of those edges. The operation update receives a pair consisting of the bag of labels of all edges from some state $x \in C$ into the set $S \subseteq C$ and the weight of all edges from x to $B \subseteq C$, and from only this information (in particular update does not know x, S, and B explicitly) it computes the triple consisting of the weight $w(S)(c(x))$ of edges from x to S, the result of $F\chi_S^B \cdot c(x)$ and the weight $w(B \setminus S)(c(x))$ of edges from x to $B \setminus S$ (e.g. in the Paige-Tarjan algorithm, the number of edges from x to S, the value for the three way split, and the number of edges from x to $B \setminus S$, cf. Fig. 2). Those two computed weights are needed for the next refinement step, and $F\chi_S^B \cdot c(x)$ is used by the algorithm to decide whether or not two states $x, y \in C$ that are contained in the same block and have some successors in B remain in the same block for the next iteration.

For a given functor F, it is usually easy to derive the operations init and update once an appropriate choice of the set W of weights and weight maps w is made, so we describe only the latter in the following; see [14,37] for full definitions.

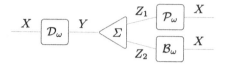

Fig. 3. Visualization of $FX = \mathcal{D}_\omega(\Sigma(\mathcal{P}_\omega X, \mathcal{B}_\omega X))$ for $\Sigma(Z_1, Z_2) = \mathbb{N} \times Z_1 \times Z_1$

Example 3.3. (1) For $F = \mathbb{R}^{(-)}$ we can take $W = \mathbb{R}^2$, and $w(B)(t)$ records the accumulated weight of $X \setminus B$ and B: $w(B)(t) = \left(\sum_{x \in X \setminus B} t(x), \sum_{x \in B} t(x)\right)$, i.e. $w(B) = F\chi_B \colon FX \to F2$.

(2) More generally, let F be one of the functors $G^{(-)}, \mathcal{B}_\omega, \Sigma$ where G is a group and Σ a signature with bounded arity, represented as a polynomial functor. Then we can take $W = F2$ (e.g. $W = \mathbb{R}^2$ for $F = \mathbb{R}^{(-)}$ as above) and $w(B) = F\chi_B \colon FX \to F2$.

(3) For $F = \mathcal{P}_\omega$, we need $W = 2 \times \mathbb{N}$, and $w(B)(t) = (|t \setminus B| \geq 1, |t \cap B|)$ records whether there is an edge to $X \setminus B$ and counts the numbers of edges into B.

In order to ensure that iteratively splitting blocks using $F\chi_S^B$ in each iteration correctly computes the minimization of the given coalgebra, we require that the type functor F is *zippable*, i.e. the evident maps $\langle F(X+!), F(!+Y)\rangle \colon F(X+Y) \longrightarrow F(X+1) \times F(1+Y)$ are injective [37, Definition 5.1]. All functors mentioned in Example 2.2 are zippable, and zippable functors are closed under products, coproducts, and subfunctors [37, Lemma 5.4] but not under functor composition; e.g. $\mathcal{P}_\omega \mathcal{P}_\omega$ fails to be zippable [37, Example 5.9].

The main correctness result [37] states that for a zippable functor equipped with a refinement interface, our algorithm correctly minimizes the given coalgebra. The low time complexity of our algorithm hinges on the time complexity of the implementations of init and update. We have shown previously [37, Theorem 6.22] that if both init and update run in linear time in the input list (of type $\mathcal{B}_\omega A$) *alone* (independently of n, m), then our generic partition refinement algorithm runs in time $\mathcal{O}((m+n) \cdot \log n)$ on coalgebras with n states and m edges. In order to cover instances where the run time of init and update depends also on n, m, we now generalize this to the following new result:

Theorem 3.4. *Let F be a zippable functor equipped with a refinement interface. Suppose further that $p(n, m)$ is a function such that in every run of the partition refinement algorithm on F-coalgebras with n states and m edges,*

(1) all calls to init and update on $\ell \in \mathcal{B}_\omega A$ run in time $\mathcal{O}(|\ell| \cdot p(n, m))$;
(2) all comparisons of values of type W run in time $\mathcal{O}(p(n, m))$.

Then the algorithm runs in overall time $\mathcal{O}((m+n) \cdot \log n \cdot p(n, m))$.

Obviously, for $p(n, m) \in \mathcal{O}(1)$, we obtain the previous complexity. Indeed, for the functors $G^{(-)}, \mathcal{P}_\omega, \mathcal{B}_\omega$, where G is an abelian group, we can take $p(n, m) = 1$; this follows from our previous work [37, Examples 6.4 and 6.6]. For a *ranked alphabet* Σ, i.e. a signature with arities of operations bounded by, say, r, we can take $p(m,n) = r \in \mathcal{O}(1)$ if Σ (or just r) is fixed. We will discuss in Sect. 5 how Theorem 3.4 instantiates to weighted systems, i.e. to monoid-valued functors $M^{(-)}$ for unrestricted commutative monoids M.

3.3   Combining Refinement Interfaces

In addition to supporting genericity via direct implementation of the refinement interface for basic functors, our tool is *modular* in the sense that it automatically derives a refinement interface for functors built from the basic ones according to the grammar (1). In other words, for such a functor the user does not need to write a single line of new code. Moreover, when the user implements a refinement interface for a new basic functor, this automatically extends the effective grammar.

For example, our tool can minimize systems of type $FX = \mathcal{D}_\omega(\mathbb{N} \times \mathcal{P}_\omega X \times \mathcal{B}_\omega X)$. To achieve this, a given F-coalgebra is transformed into one for the functor $F'X = \mathcal{D}_\omega X + (\mathbb{N} \times X \times X) + \mathcal{P}_\omega X + \mathcal{B}_\omega X$. This functor is obtained as the sum of all basic functors involved in F, i.e. of all the nodes in the visualization of the functor term F (Fig. 3). Then the components of the refinement interfaces of the four involved functors $\mathcal{D}_\omega$, Σ, $\mathcal{P}_\omega$, and $\mathcal{B}_\omega$ are combined by disjoint union $+$. The transformation of a coalgebra $c\colon C \to FC$ into a F'-coalgebra introduces a set of intermediate states for each edge in the visualization of the term F in Fig. 3. E.g. Y contains an intermediate state for every $\mathcal{D}_\omega$-edge, i.e. $Y = \{(x,y) \mid \mu(x)(y) \neq 0\}$. Successors of such intermediate states in Y lie in $\mathbb{N} \times Z_1 \times Z_2$, and successors of intermediate states in Z_1 and Z_2 lie in $\mathcal{P}_\omega X$ and $\mathcal{B}_\omega X$, respectively. Overall, we obtain an F'-coalgebra on $X + Y + Z_1 + Z_2$, whose minimization yields the minimization of the original F-coalgebra. The correctness of this construction is established in full generality in [37, Section 7].

CoPaR moreover implements a further optimization of this procedure that leads to fewer intermediate states in the case of polynomial functors Σ: Instead of putting the refinement interface of Σ side by side with those of its arguments, CoPaR includes a systematic procedure to combine the refinement interfaces of the arguments of Σ into a single refinement interface. For instance, starting from $FX = \mathcal{D}_\omega(\mathbb{N} \times \mathcal{P}_\omega X \times \mathcal{B}_\omega X)$ as above, a given F-coalgebra is thus transformed into a coalgebra for the functor $F''X = \mathcal{D}_\omega X + \mathbb{N} \times \mathcal{P}_\omega X \times \mathcal{B}_\omega X$, effectively inducing intermediate states in Y as above but avoiding Z_1 and Z_2.

3.4   Implementation Details

Our implementation is geared towards realizing both the level of genericity and the efficiency afforded by the abstract algorithm. Regarding genericity, each basic functor is defined (in its own source file) as a single Haskell data type that implements two type classes: a class that directly corresponds to the refinement interface given in Definition 3.2 with its methods `init` and `update`, and a parser that defines the coalgebra syntax for the functor. This means that new basic functors can be implemented without modifying any of the existing code, except for registering the new type in a list of existing functors (refinement interfaces are in src/Copar/Functors).

A key data structure for the efficient implementation of the generic algorithm are refinable partitions, which store the current partition of the set C of states of the input coalgebra during the execution of the algorithm. This data structure has to provide constant time operations for finding the size of a block, marking a state and counting the marked states in a block. Splitting a block in marked and unmarked states must only take linear time in the number of marked states of this block. In CoPaR, we use such a data structure described (for use in Markov chain lumping) by Valmari and Franceschinis [35].

Our abstract algorithm maintains two partitions P, Q of C, where P is one transition step finer than Q; i.e. P is the partition of C induced by the map $Fq \cdot c \colon C \twoheadrightarrow FQ$, where $q \colon C \twoheadrightarrow Q$ is the canonical quotient map assigning to every state the block which contains it. The key to the low time complexity is to choose in each iteration a *subblock*, i.e. a block S in P whose surrounding *compound block*, i.e. the block B in Q such that $S \subseteq B$, satisfies $2 \cdot |S| \le |B|$, and then refine Q (and P) as explained in Sect. 3.2 (see Fig. 2). This idea goes back to Hopcroft [22], and is also used in all other partition refinement algorithms mentioned in the introduction. Our implementation maintains a queue of subblocks S satisfying the above property, and the termination condition $P = Q$ of the main loop then translates to this queue being empty.

One optimization that is new in CoPaR in relation to [35,37] is that weights for blocks of exactly one state are not computed, as those cannot be split any further. This has drastic performance benefits for inputs where the algorithm produces many single-element blocks early on, e.g. for nearly minimal systems or fine grained initial partitions, see [11] for details and measurements.

4   Instances

Many systems are coalgebras for functors composed according to the grammar (2). In Table 1, we list various system types that can be handled by our algorithm, taken from [14,37] except for weighted tree automata, which are new in the present paper. In all cases, m is the number of edges and n is the number of states of the input coalgebra, and we compare the run time of our generic algorithm with that of specifically designed algorithms from the literature. In most instances we match the complexity of the best known algorithm. In the one case where our generic algorithm is asymptotically slower (LTS with unbounded alphabet), this is due to assuming a potentially very large number of alphabet letters – as soon as the number of alphabet letters is assumed to be polynomially bounded in the number n of states, the number m of transitions is also polynomially bounded in n, so $\log m \in \mathcal{O}(\log n)$. This argument also explains why '<' and '=', respectively, hold in the last two rows of Table 1, as we assume Σ to be (fixed and) finite; the case where Σ is infinite and unranked is more complicated. Details on the instantiation to weighted tree automata are discussed in Sect. 5. We comment briefly on some further instances and initial partitions:

Further System Types can be handled by our algorithm and tool by combining functors in various ways. For instance, general Segala systems are coalgebras for the functor $\mathcal{P}_\omega \mathcal{D}_\omega(A \times (-))$, and are minimized by our algorithm in time $\mathcal{O}((m + n) \cdot \log n)$, improving on the best previous algorithm [2]; other type functors for various species of probabilistic systems are listed in [3], including the ones for reactive systems, generative systems, stratified systems, alternating systems, bundle systems, and Pnueli-Zuck systems.

Initial Partitions: Note that in the classical Paige-Tarjan algorithm [27], the input includes an initial partition. Initial partitions as input parameters are covered via the genericity of our algorithm: Initial partitions on F-coalgebras are accomodated by moving to the functor $F'X = \mathbb{N} \times FX$, where the first component of a coalgebra assigns to each state the number of its block in the initial partition. Under the optimized treatment of the polynomial functor $\mathbb{N} \times (-)$ (Sect. 3.3), this transformation does not enlarge the state space and also leaves the complexity parameter $p(n, m)$ unchanged [37]; that is, the asymptotic run time of the algorithm remains unchanged under adding initial partitions.

5   Weighted Tree Automata

We proceed to take a closer look at weighted tree automata as a worked example. In our previous work, we have treated the case where the weight monoid is a group; in the present paper, we extend this treatment to unrestricted monoids. As indicated previously, it is this example that mainly motivates the refinement of the run time analysis discussed in Sect. 3.2, and we will see that in the case of non-cancellative monoids, the generic algorithm improves on the run time of the best known specific algorithms in the literature.

Weighted tree automata simultaneously generalize tree automata and weighted (word) automata. A partition refinement construction for weighted automata (w.r.t. weighted bisimilarity) was first considered by Buchholz [9, Theorem 3.7]. Högberg et al. first provided an efficient partition refinement algorithm for tree automata [21], and subsequently for weighted tree automata [20]. Generally, tree automata differ from word automata in replacing the input alphabet, which may be seen as sets of unary operations, with an algebraic signature Σ:

Definition 5.1. Let $(M, +, 0)$ be a commutative monoid. A (bottom-up) *weighted tree automaton* (WTA) (over M) consists of a finite set X of states, a finite signature Σ, an output map $f \colon X \to M$, and for each $k \geq 0$, a transition map $\mu_k \colon \Sigma_k \to M^{X^k \times X}$, where Σ_k denotes the set of k-ary input symbols in Σ; the maximum arity of symbols in Σ is called the *rank*.

A weighted tree automaton is thus equivalently a finite coalgebra for the functor $M \times M^{(\Sigma)}$ (where $M^{(\Sigma)}(X) = M^{(\Sigma X)}$) where $\Sigma \colon \mathsf{Set} \to \mathsf{Set}$ is a polynomial functor. Indeed, we can regard the output map as a transition map for a constant symbol, so it suffices to consider just the functor $M^{(\Sigma)}$ (and in fact the

Table 1. Asymptotic complexity of the generic algorithm (2017/2019) compared to specific algorithms, for systems with n states and m transitions, respectively $m_{\mathcal{P}_\omega}$ nondeterministic and $m_{\mathcal{D}_\omega}$ probabilistic transitions for Segala systems. For simplicity, we assume that $m \geq n$ and, like [20,22], that A, Σ are finite.

System	Functor	Run-time		Specific algorithm (Year)	
DFA	$2 \times (-)^A$	$n \cdot \log n$	$=$	$n \cdot \log n$	1971 [22]
Transition systems	$\mathcal{P}_\omega$	$m \cdot \log n$	$=$	$m \cdot \log n$	1987 [27]
Labelled TS	$\mathcal{P}_\omega(\mathbb{N} \times -)$	$m \cdot \log m$	$=$	$m \cdot \log m$	2004 [15]
			$>$	$m \cdot \log n$	2009 [33]
Markov chains	$\mathbb{R}^{(-)}$	$m \cdot \log n$	$=$	$m \cdot \log n$	2010 [35]
Segala systems	$\mathcal{P}_\omega(A \times -) \cdot \mathcal{D}$	$m_{\mathcal{D}_\omega} \cdot \log m_{\mathcal{P}_\omega}$	$<$	$m \cdot \log n$	2000 [2]
			$=$	$m_{\mathcal{D}_\omega} \cdot \log m_{\mathcal{P}_\omega}$	2018 [19]
Colour refinement	$\mathcal{B}_\omega$	$m \cdot \log n$	$=$	$m \cdot \log n$	2017 [5]
Weighted tree automata	$M \times M^{(\Sigma(-))}$	$m \cdot \log^2 m$	$<$	$m \cdot n$	2007 [20]
	$M \times M^{(\Sigma(-))}$ (M cancellative)	$m \cdot \log m$	$=$	$m \cdot \log n$	2007 [20]

output map is ignored in the notion of backward bisimulation used by Högberg et al. [20]). For weighted systems, *forward* and *backward* notions of bisimulation are considered in the literature [9,20]; we do not repeat the definitions here but focus on backward bisimulation, as it corresponds to behavioural equivalence:

Proposition 5.2. *Backward bisimulation of weighted tree automata coincides with behavioural equivalence of $M^{(\Sigma)}$-coalgebras.*

Since $M^{(\Sigma)}$ is a composite of $M^{(-)}$ and a polynomial functor Σ, the modularity of our approach implies that it suffices to provide a refinement interface for $M^{(-)}$. For the case where M is a group, a refinement interface with $p(n, m) = 1$ has been given in our previous work. For the general case, we distinguish, like Högberg et al. [20], between cancellative and non-cancellative monoids, because we obtain a better complexity result for the former.

5.1   Cancellative Monoids

Recall that a commutative monoid $(M, +, 0)$ is *cancellative* if $a+b = a+c$ implies $b = c$. It is well-known that every cancellative commutative monoid M embeds into an abelian group G via the Grothendieck construction. Hence, we can convert $M^{(-)}$-coalgebras into $G^{(-)}$-coalgebras and use the refinement interface for $G^{(-)}$ from our previous work, obtaining

Theorem 5.3. *On weighted tree automata with n states, k transitions and rank r over a cancellative monoid, our algorithm runs in time $\mathcal{O}((rk+n) \cdot \log(k+n) \cdot r)$.*

Note that rk may be replaced with the number m of edges of the corresponding coalgebra. Thus, for a fixed signature and $m \geq n$, we obtain the bound in Table 1.

5.2   Non-cancellative Monoids

The refinement interface for $G^{(-)}$ for a group G (in which the cancellative monoid M in Sect. 5.1 is embedded) crucially makes use of inverses for the fast computation of the weights returned by update. For a non-cancellative monoid $(M, +, 0)$, we instead need to maintain bags of monoid elements and consider subtraction of bags. For the encoding of $M^{(-)}$, we take labels $A = M_{\neq 0} = M \setminus \{0\}$, and $\flat(f) = \{ (f(x), x) \mid x \in X, f(x) \neq 0 \}$ for $f \in M^{(-)}$. The refinement interface for $M^{(-)}$ has weights $W = M \times \mathcal{B}(M_{\neq 0})$ and

$$w(B)(f) = \left(\sum_{x \in X \setminus B} f(x), \ (m \mapsto |\{x \in B \mid f(x) = m\}|) \right) \in M \times \mathcal{B}(M_{\neq 0});$$

that is, $w(B)(f)$ returns the total weight of $X \setminus B$ under f and the bag of non-zero elements of M occurring in f. The interface functions init: $M^{(1)} \times \mathcal{B}_\omega M_{\neq 0} \to W$, update: $\mathcal{B}_\omega M_{\neq 0} \times W \to W \times M^{(3)} \times W$ are

$$\mathsf{init}(f, \ell) = (0, \ell)$$
$$\mathsf{update}(\ell, (r, c)) = ((r + \Sigma(c - \ell), \ell), (r, \Sigma(c - \ell), \Sigma(\ell)), (r + \Sigma(\ell), c - \ell)),$$

where for $a, b \in \mathcal{B}Y$, the bag $a - b$ is defined by $(a - b)(y) = \max(0, a(y) - b(y))$; $\Sigma \colon \mathcal{B}M \to M$ is the canonical summation map defined by $\Sigma(b) = \sum_{m \in M} b(m) \cdot m$; and we denote elements of $M^{(3)}$ as triples over M.

We implement the bags $\mathcal{B}(M_{\neq 0})$ used in $W = M \times \mathcal{B}(M_{\neq 0})$ as balanced search trees with keys $M_{\neq 0}$ and values $\mathbb{N}$, following Adams [1]. In addition, we store in every node the value $\Sigma(b)$, where b is the bag encoded by the subtree rooted at that node. Hence, for every bag b, the value $\Sigma(b)$ is immediately available at the root node of the search tree encoding b. It is not difficult to see that maintaining those values in the nodes only adds a constant overhead into the operations of our data structure for bags and that the size of the search trees is bounded by $\min(|M|, m)$. Thus, we obtain:

Proposition 5.4. *The above function* update$(\ell, (r, c))$ *can be computed in* $\mathcal{O}(|\ell| \cdot \log \min(|M|, m))$, *where m is the number of all edges of the input coalgebra.*

Corollary 5.5. *On a weighted tree automaton with n states, k transitions, and rank r over an (unrestricted) monoid M, our algorithm runs in time* $\mathcal{O}((rk + n) \cdot \log(k + n) \cdot (\log k + r))$, *respectively* $\mathcal{O}((rk + n) \cdot \log(k + n) \cdot r)$ *if M is finite.*

More precisely, the analysis using Theorem 3.4 shows that rk can be replaced with the number m of edges of the input coalgebra. Assuming $m \geq n$ we thus obtain the bound given in Table 1. In addition to guaranteeing a good theoretical complexity, our tool immediately yields an efficient implementation. For the case of non-cancellative monoids, this is, to the best of our knowledge, the only available implementation of partition refinement for weighted tree automata.

Table 2. Processing times (in seconds) t_p for parsing and t_a for partition refinement on maximal weighted tree automata with n states and $50 \cdot n$ random transitions fitting into 16 GB of memory. File sizes range from 117 MB to 141 MB, and numbers m of edges from 11 million to 17 million.

$\Sigma X=$	$4 \times X$			$4 \times X^2$			$4 \times X^3$			$4 \times X^4$			$4 \times X^5$		
M	n	t_p	t_a	n	t_p	t_a	n	t_p	t_a	n	t_p	t_a	n	t_p	t_a
2	132177	53	188	98670	46	243	85016	47	187	59596	41	146	49375	38	114
$\mathbb{N}$	113957	61	141	92434	55	175	69623	49	152	57319	47	140	48962	45	112
2^{64}	114888	58	100	95287	54	138	70660	49	107	62665	48	92	49926	44	72

5.3   Evaluation and Benchmarking

We report on a number of benchmarks that illustrate the practical scalability of our algorithm instantiated for weighted tree automata. Previous studies on the practical performance of partition refinement on large labelled transition systems [33,34] show that memory rather than run time seems to be the limiting factor. Since labelled transition systems are a special case of weighted tree automata, we expect to see similar phenomena. Hence, we evaluate the maximal automata sizes that can be processed on a typical current computer setup: We randomly generate weighted tree automata for various signatures and monoids, looking for the maximal size of WTAs that can be handled with 16 GB of RAM, and we measure the respective run times of our tool, compiled with GHC version 8.4.4 on a Linux system and executed on an Intel® Core™ i5-6500 processor with 3.20 GHz clock rate. We fix $|\Sigma| = 4$ and evaluate all combinations of rank r and weight monoid M for r ranging over $\{1, \ldots, 5\}$ and M over $2 = (2, \vee, 0)$, $\mathbb{N} = (\mathbb{N}, \max, 0)$ (the additive monoid of the tropical semiring), and $2^{64} = (2, \vee, 0)^{64} \cong (\mathcal{P}_\omega(64), \cup, \emptyset)$. We write n for the number of states, k for the number of transitions, and m for the number of edges in the graphical presentation; in fact, we generate only transitions of the respective maximal rank r, so $m = k(r+1)$. Table 2 lists the maximal values of n that fit into the mentioned 16 GB of RAM when $k = 50 \cdot n$, and associated run times. For $M = (2, \vee, 0)$, the optimized refinement interface for $\mathcal{P}_\omega$ needs less memory, allowing for higher values of n, an effect that decreases with increasing rank r. We restrict to generating at most 50 different elements of M in each automaton, to avoid situations where all states are immediately distinguished in the first refinement step. In addition, the parameters are chosen so that with high likelihood, the final partition distinguishes all states, so the examples illustrate the worst case. The first refinement step produces in the order of $|\Sigma| \cdot \min(50, |M|)^r$ subblocks (cf. Sect. 3.4), implying earlier termination for high values of $|M|$ and r and explaining the slightly longer run time for $M = (2, \vee, 0)$ on small r. We note in summary that WTAs with well over 10 million edges are processed in less than five minutes, and in fact the run time of minimization is of the same order of magnitude as that of input parsing. Additional evaluations on DFAs, Segala Systems, and benchmarks for the Prism model checker [28], as well as a comparison with existing specific tools by Valmari [35] and from the mCRL2 toolset [10] are in the full version of this paper [12].

6 Conclusion and Future Work

We have instantiated a generic efficient partition refinement algorithm that we introduced in recent work [14,37] to weighted (tree) automata, and we have refined the generic complexity analysis of the algorithm to cover this case. Moreover, we have described an implementation of the generic algorithm in the form of the tool CoPaR, which supports the modular combination of basic system types without requiring any additional implementation effort, and allows for easy incorporation of new basic system types by implementing a generic refinement interface.

In future work, we will further broaden the range of system types that our algorithm and tool can accomodate, and provide support for base categories beyond sets, e.g. nominal sets, which underlie nominal automata [8,31].

Concerning genericity there is an orthogonal approach by Ranzato and Tapparo [29] that is generic over *notions of process equivalence* but fixes the system type to standard labelled transition systems; see also [18]. Similarly, Blom and Orzan [6,7] present *signature refinement*, which covers, e.g. strong and branching bisimulation as well as Markov chain lumping, but requires adapting the algorithm for each instance. These algorithms have also been improved using symbolic techniques (e.g. [36]). Moreover, many of the mentioned approaches and others [4,6,7,16,36] focus on parallelization. We will explore in future work whether symbolic and distributed methods can be lifted to coalgebraic generality. A further important aim is genericity also along the axis of process equivalences.

References

1. Adams, S.: Efficient sets - a balancing act. J. Funct. Program. **3**(4), 553–561 (1993)
2. Baier, C., Engelen, B., Majster-Cederbaum, M.: Deciding bisimilarity and similarity for probabilistic processes. J. Comput. Syst. Sci. **60**, 187–231 (2000)
3. Bartels, F., Sokolova, A., de Vink, E.: A hierarchy of probabilistic system types. In: Coagebraic Methods in Computer Science, CMCS 2003, ENTCS, vol. 82, pp. 57–75. Elsevier (2003)
4. Bergamini, D., Descoubes, N., Joubert, C., Mateescu, R.: BISIMULATOR: a modular tool for on-the-fly equivalence checking. In: Halbwachs, N., Zuck, L.D. (eds.) TACAS 2005. LNCS, vol. 3440, pp. 581–585. Springer, Heidelberg (2005). https://doi.org/10.1007/978-3-540-31980-1_42
5. Berkholz, C., Bonsma, P.S., Grohe, M.: Tight lower and upper bounds for the complexity of canonical colour refinement. Theory Comput. Syst. **60**(4), 581–614 (2017)
6. Blom, S., Orzan, S.: Distributed branching bisimulation reduction of state spaces. In: Parallel and Distributed Model Checking, PDMC 2003, ENTCS, vol. 89, pp. 99–113. Elsevier (2003)

7. Blom, S., Orzan, S.: A distributed algorihm for strong bisimulation reduction of state spaces. J. Softw. Tools Technol. Transf. **7**(1), 74–86 (2005)
8. Bojańczyk, M., Klin, B., Lasota, S.: Automata theory in nominal sets. Log. Methods Comput. Sci. **10**(3) (2014)
9. Buchholz, P.: Bisimulation relations for weighted automata. Theor. Comput. Sci. **393**, 109–123 (2008)
10. Bunte, O., et al.: The mCRL2 toolset for analysing concurrent systems. In: Vojnar, T., Zhang, L. (eds.) TACAS 2019. LNCS, vol. 11428, pp. 21–39. Springer, Cham (2019). https://doi.org/10.1007/978-3-030-17465-1_2
11. Deifel, H.-P.: Implementation and evaluation of efficient partition refinement algorithms. Master's thesis, Friedrich-Alexander Universität Erlangen-Nürnberg (2019). https://hpdeifel.de/master-thesis-deifel.pdf
12. Deifel, H.-P., Milius, S., Schröder, L., Wißmann, T.: Generic partition refinement and weighted tree automata (2019). https://arxiv.org/abs/1811.08850
13. Derisavi, S., Hermanns, H., Sanders, W.: Optimal state-space lumping in Markov chains. Inf. Process. Lett. **87**(6), 309–315 (2003)
14. Dorsch, U., Milius, S., Schröder, L., Wißmann, T.: Efficient coalgebraic partition refinement. In: Concurrency Theory, CONCUR 2017, LIPIcs, pp. 32:1–32:16. Schloss Dagstuhl - Leibniz-Zentrum für Informatik (2017)
15. Dovier, A., Piazza, C., Policriti, A.: An efficient algorithm for computing bisimulation equivalence. Theor. Comput. Sci. **311**(1–3), 221–256 (2004)
16. Garavel, H., Hermanns, H.: On combining functional verification and performance evaluation using CADP. In: Eriksson, L.-H., Lindsay, P.A. (eds.) FME 2002. LNCS, vol. 2391, pp. 410–429. Springer, Heidelberg (2002). https://doi.org/10.1007/3-540-45614-7_23
17. Gries, D.: Describing an algorithm by Hopcroft. Acta Informatica **2**, 97–109 (1973)
18. Groote, J., Jansen, D., Keiren, J., Wijs, A.: An $O(m \log n)$ algorithm for computing stuttering equivalence and branching bisimulation. ACM Trans. Comput. Log. **18**(2), 13:1–13:34 (2017)
19. Groote, J., Verduzco, J., de Vink, E.: An efficient algorithm to determine probabilistic bisimulation. Algorithms **11**(9), 131 (2018)
20. Högberg, J., Maletti, A., May, J.: Bisimulation minimisation for weighted tree automata. In: Harju, T., Karhumäki, J., Lepistö, A. (eds.) DLT 2007. LNCS, vol. 4588, pp. 229–241. Springer, Heidelberg (2007). https://doi.org/10.1007/978-3-540-73208-2_23
21. Högberg, J., Maletti, A., May, J.: Backward and forward bisimulation minimization of tree automata. Theor. Comput. Sci. **410**, 3539–3552 (2009)
22. Hopcroft, J.: An $n \log n$ algorithm for minimizing states in a finite automaton. In: Theory of Machines and Computations, pp. 189–196. Academic Press (1971)
23. Huynh, D., Tian, L.: On some equivalence relations for probabilistic processes. Fund. Inf. **17**, 211–234 (1992)
24. Kanellakis, P., Smolka, S.: CCS expressions, finite state processes, and three problems of equivalence. Inf. Comput. **86**(1), 43–68 (1990)
25. Klin, B., Sassone, V.: Structural operational semantics for stochastic and weighted transition systems. Inf. Comput. **227**, 58–83 (2013)
26. Knuutila, T.: Re-describing an algorithm by Hopcroft. Theor. Comput. Sci. **250**, 333–363 (2001)
27. Paige, R., Tarjan, R.: Three partition refinement algorithms. SIAM J. Comput. **16**(6), 973–989 (1987)
28. PRISM: Benchmarks FMS and WLAN. http://www.prismmodelchecker.org/casestudies/fms.php, wlan.php. Accessed 16 Nov 2018

29. Ranzato, F., Tapparo, F.: Generalizing the Paige-Tarjan algorithm by abstract interpretation. Inf. Comput. **206**, 620–651 (2008)
30. Rutten, J.: Universal coalgebra: a theory of systems. Theor. Comput. Sci. **249**, 3–80 (2000)
31. Schröder, L., Kozen, D., Milius, S., Wißmann, T.: Nominal automata with name binding. In: Esparza, J., Murawski, A.S. (eds.) FoSSaCS 2017. LNCS, vol. 10203, pp. 124–142. Springer, Heidelberg (2017). https://doi.org/10.1007/978-3-662-54458-7_8
32. Segala, R.: Modelling and verification of randomized distributed real-time systems. Ph.D. thesis, MIT (1995)
33. Valmari, A.: Bisimilarity minimization in $o(m \log n)$ time. In: Franceschinis, G., Wolf, K. (eds.) PETRI NETS 2009. LNCS, vol. 5606, pp. 123–142. Springer, Heidelberg (2009). https://doi.org/10.1007/978-3-642-02424-5_9
34. Valmari, A.: Simple bisimilarity minimization in $O(m \log n)$ time. Fund. Inform. **105**(3), 319–339 (2010)
35. Valmari, A., Franceschinis, G.: Simple $O(m \log n)$ time Markov chain lumping. In: Esparza, J., Majumdar, R. (eds.) TACAS 2010. LNCS, vol. 6015, pp. 38–52. Springer, Heidelberg (2010). https://doi.org/10.1007/978-3-642-12002-2_4
36. van Dijk, T., van de Pol, J.: Multi-core symbolic bisimulation minimization. J. Softw. Tools Technol. Transf. **20**(2), 157–177 (2018)
37. Wißmann, T., Dorsch, U., Milius, S., Schröder, L.: Efficient and modular coalgebraic partition refinement (2019). https://arxiv.org/abs/1806.05654

Equilibria-Based Probabilistic Model Checking for Concurrent Stochastic Games

Marta Kwiatkowska[1], Gethin Norman[2]($\boxtimes$), David Parker[3], and Gabriel Santos[1]

[1] Department of Computing Science, University of Oxford, Oxford, UK
[2] School of Computing Science, University of Glasgow, Glasgow, UK
gethin.norman@glasgow.ac.uk
[3] School of Computer Science, University of Birmingham, Birmingham, UK

Abstract. Probabilistic model checking for stochastic games enables formal verification of systems that comprise competing or collaborating entities operating in a stochastic environment. Despite good progress in the area, existing approaches focus on zero-sum goals and cannot reason about scenarios where entities are endowed with different objectives. In this paper, we propose probabilistic model checking techniques for concurrent stochastic games based on Nash equilibria. We extend the temporal logic rPATL (probabilistic alternating-time temporal logic with rewards) to allow reasoning about players with distinct quantitative goals, which capture either the probability of an event occurring or a reward measure. We present algorithms to synthesise strategies that are subgame perfect social welfare optimal Nash equilibria, i.e., where there is no incentive for any players to unilaterally change their strategy in any state of the game, whilst the combined probabilities or rewards are maximised. We implement our techniques in the PRISM-games tool and apply them to several case studies, including network protocols and robot navigation, showing the benefits compared to existing approaches.

1 Introduction

Probabilistic model checking is a technique for formally verifying systems that exhibit uncertainty or feature randomisation. Quantitative system requirements, which express, e.g., safety, reliability or performance, are formally specified in temporal logic. These are then automatically checked against a probabilistic model, such as a Markov chain, capturing the possible behaviour of the system being verified. Closely related is strategy synthesis, which uses probabilistic models with nondeterminism, for example Markov decision processes (MDPs), to automatically generate policies or controllers which guarantee that pre-specified system requirements are satisfied. Thanks to mature tool support [20,27], the methods have been successfully applied to many domains, from autonomous vehicles, to computer security, to task scheduling.

Stochastic games are a modelling formalism that incorporates probability, nondeterminism and multiple players, who can compete or collaborate to

© Springer Nature Switzerland AG 2019
M. H. ter Beek et al. (Eds.): FM 2019, LNCS 11800, pp. 298–315, 2019.
https://doi.org/10.1007/978-3-030-30942-8_19

achieve their goals. A variety of verification algorithms for these models have been devised, e.g., [2,3,13,14,45]. More recently, probabilistic model checking and strategy synthesis techniques for stochastic games have been proposed [6,17,25,28] and implemented in the PRISM-games tool [31]. This has allowed modelling and verification of stochastic games to be used for a variety of non-trivial applications, in which competitive or collaborative behaviour between entities is a crucial ingredient, including computer security and energy management.

Initial work in this direction focused on *turn-based* stochastic games (TSGs), where each state is controlled by a single player [17], and proposed the logic rPATL, an extension of the well known logic ATL [4]. The logic can specify that a coalition of players is able to achieve a quantitative objective regarding the probability of an event's occurrence or the expectation of a reward measure, regardless of the strategies of the other players. Recently [28], this was extended to *concurrent* stochastic games (CSGs), in which players make decisions simultaneously. This allows more realistic modelling of interactive agents operating concurrently. In another direction, *multi-objective* model checking of TSGs [6,18] enabled reasoning about coalitions aiming to satisfy a *Boolean combination* of objectives, regardless of the remaining players' behaviour.

A limitation of these approaches is that they focus on *zero-sum* properties, in which a coalition aims to satisfy some requirement or to optimise some objective, while the remaining players have the directly opposing goal. In this paper, we consider CSGs in which two coalitions of players have distinct quantitative objectives. For this, we use the notion of subgame perfect *Nash equilibria* [37], i.e., scenarios in which it is not beneficial for any player to unilaterally change their strategy in any state. Furthermore, amongst these, we consider *social welfare* optimal equilibria, which maximise the sum of the objectives of the players.

We propose an extension to rPATL which allows reasoning about subgame perfect social welfare optimal Nash equilibria between two coalitions of players, with respect to probabilistic or reward objectives, expressed using a variety of temporal operators. We then give a model checking algorithm for the logic against CSGs which employs a combination of backwards induction (for finite-horizon operators) and value iteration (for infinite-horizon operators). A key ingredient of the computation is finding social welfare optimal Nash equilibria for bimatrix games, which we perform using labelled polytopes [32] and a reduction to SMT. We implement our techniques as an extension of the PRISM-games [31] model checker and develop a selection of case studies, including robot navigation, communication protocols and power control, to evaluate its performance and applicability. We show that we are able to synthesise strategies that outperform those derived using existing techniques.

Related Work. Game-theoretic models are used in many contexts within verification, as summarised above. In addition, the existence of and the complexity of finding Nash equilibria for stochastic games are studied in [16,45], but without practical algorithms. In [40], a learning-based algorithm for finding Nash equilibria for discounted properties of CSGs is presented and evaluated. Similarly, [33] studies Nash equilibria for discounted properties and introduces iterative algorithms for strategy synthesis. A theoretical framework for price-taking equilibria of CSGs is given in [5], where players try to minimise their costs which include a price common to all players and dependent on the decisions of all players. A notion of strong Nash equilibria for a restricted class of CSGs is formalised in [21] and an approximation algorithm for checking the existence of such equilibria for discounted properties is introduced and evaluated. We also mention [9], which studies the existence of stochastic equilibria with imprecise deviations for CSGs and proposes a PSPACE algorithm to compute such equilibria.

For non-stochastic games, model checking tools such as PRALINE [10], EAGLE [44] and EVE [24] support Nash equilibria, as does MCMAS-SLK [11] via strategy logic. General purpose tools such as Gambit [34] can compute a variety of equilibria but, again, not for stochastic games.

2   Preliminaries

We first provide some background material on game theory and stochastic games. We let $Dist(X)$ denote the set of probability distributions over set X.

Definition 1 (Normal form game). *A (finite, n-person) normal form game (NFG) is a tuple* $\mathsf{N} = (N, A, u)$ *where:* $N = \{1, \ldots, n\}$ *is a finite set of players;* $A = A_1 \times \cdots \times A_n$ *and* A_i *is a finite set of actions available to player* $i \in N$; $u = (u_1, \ldots, u_n)$ *and* $u_i \colon A \to \mathbb{R}$ *is a utility function for player* $i \in N$.

For an NFG N, the players choose actions at the same time, where the choice for player $i \in N$ is over the action set A_i. When each player i choose a_i, the utility received by player j equals $u_j(a_1, \ldots, a_n)$. A (mixed) strategy σ_i for player i is a distribution over its action set. A *strategy profile* $\sigma = (\sigma_1, \ldots, \sigma_n)$ is a tuple of strategies for each player and the expected utility of player i under σ is:

$$u_i(\sigma) \stackrel{\text{def}}{=} \sum_{(a_1, \ldots, a_n) \in A} u_i(a_1, \ldots, a_n) \cdot \left(\prod_{j=1}^{n} \sigma_j(a_j) \right).$$

For profile $\sigma = (\sigma_1, \ldots, \sigma_n)$ and player i strategy σ_i', we define the sequence $\sigma_{-i} = (\sigma_1, \ldots, \sigma_{i-1}, \sigma_{i+1}, \ldots, \sigma_n)$ and profile $\sigma_{-i}[\sigma_i'] = (\sigma_1, \ldots, \sigma_{i-1}, \sigma_i', \sigma_{i+1}, \ldots, \sigma_n)$. For player i and strategy sequence σ_{-i}, a *best response* for player i to σ_{-i} is a strategy $\sigma_i^\star$ for player i such that $u_i(\sigma_{-i}[\sigma_i^\star]) \geqslant u_i(\sigma_{-i}[\sigma_i])$ for all strategies σ_i of player i. We now introduce the concept of *Nash equilibria* and a particular variant called *social welfare optimal*, which are equilibria that maximise the total utility, i.e. maximise the sum of players' individual utilities.

Definition 2 (Nash equilibrium). *For NFG* N, *a strategy profile* $\sigma^\star$ *is a Nash equilibrium (NE) if* $\sigma_i^\star$ *is a best response to* $\sigma_{-i}^\star$ *for all* $i \in N$. *Furthermore* $\sigma^\star$ *is a social welfare optimal NE (SWNE) if* $u_1(\sigma^\star) + \cdots + u_n(\sigma^\star) \geqslant u_1(\sigma) + \cdots + u_n(\sigma)$ *for all Nash equilibria* σ *of* N.

A two-player NFG is *constant-sum* if there exists $c \in \mathbb{R}$ such that $u_1(\alpha) + u_2(\alpha) = c$ for all $\alpha \in A$ and *zero-sum* if $c = 0$. For general two-player NFGs, we have a *bimatrix game* which can be represented by two distinct matrices $Z_1, Z_2 \in \mathbb{R}^{l \times m}$ where $A_1 = \{a_1, \ldots, a_l\}$, $A_2 = \{b_1, \ldots, b_m\}$, $z_{ij}^1 = u_1(a_i, b_j)$ and $z_{ij}^2 = u_2(a_i, b_j)$.

Example 1. We consider a stag hunt game [38] where, if players decide to cooperate, this can yield a large payoff, but, if the others do not, then the cooperating player gets nothing while the remaining players get a small payoff. A scenario with 3 players, where two form a coalition, yields a bimatrix game:

$$Z_1 = \begin{array}{c} \\ a_0 \\ a_1 \end{array} \begin{array}{ccc} b_0 & b_1 & b_2 \\ \left(\begin{array}{ccc} 2 & 2 & 2 \\ 0 & 4 & 6 \end{array}\right) \end{array} \qquad Z_2 = \begin{array}{c} \\ a_0 \\ a_1 \end{array} \begin{array}{ccc} b_0 & b_1 & b_2 \\ \left(\begin{array}{ccc} 4 & 2 & 0 \\ 4 & 6 & 9 \end{array}\right) \end{array}$$

where a_0 and a_1 represent player 1 not cooperating and cooperating respectively and b_i that i players in the coalition cooperate. There are three Nash equilibria:

- player 1 and the coalition select a_0 and b_0, respectively with utilities $(2, 4)$;
- player 1 selects a_0 and a_1 with probabilities $5/9$ and $4/9$ and the coalition selects b_0 and b_2 with probabilities $2/3$ and $1/3$ with utilities $(2, 4)$;
- player 1 and the coalition select a_1 and b_2 respectively with utilities $(6, 9)$.

For instance, in the first case, neither player 1 nor the coalition thinks the other will cooperate: the best they can do is act alone. The third is the only SWNE.

Concurrent Stochastic Games. In this paper, we use CSGs, in which players repeatedly make simultaneous (probabilistic) choices that update the game state.

Definition 3 (Concurrent stochastic game). *A concurrent stochastic multi-player game (CSG) is a tuple* $\mathsf{G} = (N, S, \bar{S}, A, \Delta, \delta, AP, L)$ *where:*

- $N = \{1, \ldots, n\}$ *is a finite set of players;*
- S *is a finite set of states and* $\bar{S} \subseteq S$ *is a set of initial states;*
- $A = (A_1 \cup \{\bot\}) \times \cdots \times (A_n \cup \{\bot\})$ *where* A_i *is a finite set of actions available to player* $i \in N$ *and* $\bot$ *is an idle action disjoint from the set* $\cup_{i=1}^n A_i$;
- $\Delta \colon S \to 2^{\cup_{i=1}^n A_i}$ *is an action assignment function;*
- $\delta \colon S \times A \to Dist(S)$ *is a probabilistic transition function;*
- AP *is a set of atomic propositions and* $L \colon S \to 2^{AP}$ *is a labelling function.*

A CSG G starts in an initial state $\bar{s} \in \bar{S}$ and, when in state s, each player $i \in N$ selects an action from its available actions $A_i(s)$ given by $\Delta(s) \cap A_i$ if this set is non-empty and $\{\bot\}$ otherwise. Supposing player i selects action a_i, the state of the game is updated according to the distribution $\delta(s, (a_1, \ldots, a_n))$. We augment CSGs with *reward structures* of the form $r = (r_A, r_S)$ where $r_A \colon S \times A \to \mathbb{R}_{\geqslant 0}$ is an action reward function and $r_S \colon S \to \mathbb{R}_{\geqslant 0}$ is a state reward function.

Definition 4 (End component). *An end component of a CSG* G *is a pair* (S', δ') *comprising a subset* $S' \subseteq S$ *of states and a partial probabilistic transition function* $\delta' \colon S' \times A \to Dist(S)$ *satisfying the following conditions:*

- (S', δ') *defines a sub-CSG of* G, *i.e., for all* $s' \in S'$ *and* $\alpha \in A$, *if* $\delta'(s', \alpha)$ *is defined, then* $\delta'(s', \alpha) = \delta(s', \alpha)$ *and* $\delta'(s', \alpha)(s) = 0$ *for all* $s \in S \backslash S'$;
- *the underlying graph of* (S', δ') *is strongly connected.*

It is non-terminal *if* $\delta(s, \alpha)(s') > 0$ *for some* $s \in S'$, $\alpha \in A$ *and* $s' \in S \backslash S'$.

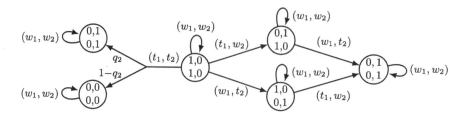

Fig. 1. CSG model of a medium access control problem.

A path of G represents a resolution of both the players' and probabilistic choices and is given by a sequence $\pi = s_0 \xrightarrow{\alpha_0} s_1 \xrightarrow{\alpha_1} \cdots$ such that $s_i \in S$, $\alpha_i = (a_1^i, \ldots, a_n^i) \in A$, $a_j^i \in A_j(s_i)$ for $j \in N$ and $\delta(s_i, \alpha_i)(s_{i+1}) > 0$ for all $i \geqslant 0$. For a path π, the $(i+1)$th state is denoted $\pi(i)$, the $(i+1)$th action $\pi[i]$, and if π is finite, the final state by $last(\pi)$. The sets of finite and infinite paths (starting in state s) are given by $FPaths_G$ and $IPaths_G$ ($FPaths_{G,s}$ and $IPaths_{G,s}$).

CSG Strategies and Equilibria. A *strategy* for player i in a CSG G resolves the player's choices. More precisely, it is a function $\sigma_i : FPaths_G \to Dist(A_i \cup \{\bot\})$ such that if $\sigma_i(\pi)(a_i) > 0$, then $a_i \in A_i(last(\pi))$. We denote by Σ_G^i the set of strategies of player i.

As for NFGs, a *strategy profile* for G is a tuple $\sigma = (\sigma_1, \ldots, \sigma_n)$ of strategies for all players and, for a player i strategy σ_i', we define the sequence σ_{-i} and profile $\sigma_{-i}[\sigma_i']$ in the same way. For strategy profile σ and state s, we let $IPaths_{G,s}^\sigma$ denote the infinite paths from s under the choices of σ. We can define a probability measure $Prob_{G,s}^\sigma$ over the infinite paths $IPaths_{G,s}^\sigma$ [26] and, for random variable $X : IPaths_G \to \mathbb{R}_{\geqslant 0}$, the expected value $\mathbb{E}_{G,s}^\sigma(X)$ of X in s with respect to σ.

An *objective* (or utility function) for player i of G is a random variable $X_i : IPaths_G \to \mathbb{R}_{\geqslant 0}$. This can encode, e.g., the probability or expected cumulative reward for reaching a target. NE for CSGs can be defined as for NFGs. Since our model checking algorithm is based on backwards induction [35,42], we restrict attention to *sub-game perfect* NE [37], which are NE in *every state* of the CSG. In addition, for infinite-horizon objectives, the existence of NE is an open problem [8] so, for such objectives, we use ε-NE, which exist for any $\varepsilon > 0$.

Definition 5 (Subgame perfect ε-NE). *For CSG G and $\varepsilon > 0$, a strategy profile $\sigma^\star$ is a subgame perfect ε-Nash equilibrium for objectives $\langle X_i \rangle_{i \in N}$ if and only if $\mathbb{E}_{G,s}^{\sigma^\star}(X_i) \geqslant \sup_{\sigma_i \in \Sigma_i} \mathbb{E}_{G,s}^{\sigma_{-i}^\star[\sigma_i]}(X_i) - \varepsilon$ for all $i \in N$ and $s \in S$.*

Social welfare optimal variants of these equilibria (SWNEs and ε-SWNEs) are defined for CSGs as for NFGs above (see Definition 2).

Example 2. In [10] a deterministic concurrent game is used to model medium access control. Two users with limited energy share a wireless channel and choose to transmit (t) or wait (w) and, if both transmit, the transmissions fail due to interference. We extend this to a CSG by assuming that transmissions succeed with probability q_2 if both transmit. Figure 1 presents a CSG where each user has energy for one transmission (the first value of tuples labelling states represents if a user has energy and the second if it has successfully transmitted).

If the objectives are to maximise the probability of a successful transmission, there are two SWNEs when one user waits for the other to transmit and then transmits. This means both successfully transmit. If the objectives are to maximise the probability of being one of the first to transmit, then there is only one SWNE corresponding to both immediately trying to transmit.

3   Extending rPATL with Nash Formulae

We now extend the logic rPATL, previously proposed for zero-sum properties of both TSGs [28] and CSGs [28], to allow the analysis of equilibria-based properties. Since we are limited to considering ε-SWNE for infinite-horizon properties, we assume some ε has been fixed in advance when considering such properties.

Definition 6 (Extended rPATL syntax). *The syntax of our extended version of* rPATL *is given by the grammar:*

$$\phi := \texttt{true} \mid \texttt{a} \mid \neg\phi \mid \phi\wedge\phi \mid \langle\!\langle C\rangle\!\rangle\texttt{P}_{\sim q}[\psi] \mid \langle\!\langle C\rangle\!\rangle\texttt{R}^r_{\sim x}[\rho] \mid \langle\!\langle C{:}C'\rangle\!\rangle_{\max\sim x}(\theta)$$
$$\theta := \texttt{P}[\psi]+\texttt{P}[\psi] \mid \texttt{R}^r[\rho]+\texttt{R}^r[\rho]$$
$$\psi := \texttt{X}\,\phi \mid \phi\,\texttt{U}^{\leqslant k}\,\phi \mid \phi\,\texttt{U}\,\phi$$
$$\rho := \texttt{I}^{=k} \mid \texttt{C}^{\leqslant k} \mid \texttt{F}\,\phi$$

where a *is an atomic proposition, C and C' are coalitions of players such that $C' = N\backslash C$, $\sim\,\in\,\{<,\leqslant,\geqslant,>\}$, $q\,\in\,[0,1]$, $x\,\in\,\mathbb{R}$, r is a reward structure and $k\in\mathbb{N}$.*

The logic rPATL is a branching-time temporal logic that combines the probabilistic operator P of PCTL [23], PRISM's reward operator R [27], and the coalition operator $\langle\!\langle C\rangle\!\rangle$ of ATL [4]. The formula $\langle\!\langle C\rangle\!\rangle\texttt{P}_{\geqslant q}[\psi]$ states that the coalition C has strategies which, when followed, regardless of the strategies of $N\backslash C$, guarantee that the probability of satisfying path formula ψ is at least q. Such properties are inherently *zero-sum* in nature as one coalition tries to maximise an objective (here the probability of ψ) and the other to minimise it.

We extend rPATL with the ability to reason about *equilibria* through *Nash formulae* of the form $\langle\!\langle C{:}C'\rangle\!\rangle_{\max\sim x}(\theta)$. In addition to the usual state (ϕ), path (ψ) and reward (ρ) formulae, we distinguish *non-zero sum* formulae (θ), which comprise a sum of probability or reward objectives. The formula $\langle\!\langle C{:}C'\rangle\!\rangle_{\max\sim x}(\theta)$ is satisfied if there exists a subgame perfect SWNE strategy profile between coalitions C and $C'(=N\backslash C)$ under which the *sum* of the two objectives in θ is $\sim x$. As is common for probabilistic temporal logics, we allow numerical queries of the form $\langle\!\langle C{:}C'\rangle\!\rangle_{\max=?}[\theta]$ which return the sum of SWNE values.

For probabilistic objectives ($\theta = \texttt{P}[\psi^1]+\texttt{P}[\psi^2]$), each ψ^i can be a "next" (X), "bounded until" ($\texttt{U}^{\leqslant k}$) or "until" (U) operator, with the usual equivalences such as $\texttt{F}\,\phi \equiv \texttt{true}\,\texttt{U}\,\phi$. For reward objectives ($\theta = \texttt{R}^{r_1}[\rho^1]+\texttt{R}^{r_2}[\rho^2]$), each ρ^i refers to the expected reward with respect to reward structure r_i: the instantaneous reward after k steps ($\texttt{I}^{=k}$); the reward accumulated over k steps ($\texttt{C}^{\leqslant k}$); or the reward accumulated until a state satisfying ϕ is reached (F ϕ).

Example 3. Recall the medium access control CSG of Example 2. Formula $\langle\langle p_1{:}p_2\rangle\rangle_{\max\geqslant 2}(\mathsf{P}[\,\mathsf{F}\,\mathsf{send}_1\,]+\mathsf{P}[\,\mathsf{F}\,\mathsf{send}_2\,])$ means players p_1 and p_2 send their packets with probability 1, while $\langle\langle p_1{:}p_2\rangle\rangle_{\max=?}(\mathsf{P}[\,\neg\mathsf{send}_2\,\mathsf{U}\,\mathsf{send}_1\,]+\mathsf{P}[\,\neg\mathsf{send}_1\,\mathsf{U}\,\mathsf{send}_2\,])$ asks what is the sum of subgame perfect SWNE values when the objectives are to maximise the probability of being one of the first to successfully transmit.

Before we give the semantics, we define *coalition games* which, given a CSG and coalition (set of players), reduce the CSG to a two-player CSG. Without loss of generality we assume the coalition of players is of the form $C = \{1, \ldots, n'\}$.

Definition 7 (Coalition game). *For CSG* $\mathsf{G} = (N, S, \bar{s}, A, \Delta, \delta, AP, L)$ *and coalition* $C = \{1, \ldots, n'\} \subseteq N$, *the* coalition game $\mathsf{G}^C = (\{1, 2\}, S, \bar{s}, A^C, \Delta, \delta^C, AP, L)$ *is a two-player game where:* $A^C = A_1^C \times A_2^C$, $A_1^C = (A_1 \cup \{\perp\}) \times \cdots \times (A_{n'} \cup \{\perp\})$, $A_2^C = (A_{n'+1} \cup \{\perp\}) \times \cdots \times (A_n \cup \{\perp\})$ *and for any* $s \in S$, $a_1^C = (a_1, \ldots, a_{n'}) \in A_1^C$ *and* $a_2^C = (a_{n'+1}, \ldots, a_n) \in A_2^C$ *we have* $\delta^C(s, (a_1^C, a_2^C)) = \delta(s, (a_1, \ldots, a_n))$.

Furthermore, for a reward structure r *of* G, *by abuse of notation we use* r *for the corresponding reward structure of* G^C *which is constructed similarly.*

Definition 8 (Extended rPATL semantics). *The satisfaction relation* $\models$ *of our rPATL extension is defined inductively on the structure of the formula. The propositional logic fragment* (true, a, $\neg$, $\wedge$) *is defined in the usual way. For temporal operators and a state* $s \in S$ *in CSG* G, *we have:*

$$s \models \langle\langle C\rangle\rangle\mathsf{P}_{\sim q}[\,\psi\,] \Leftrightarrow \exists\sigma_1 \in \Sigma^1.\forall\sigma_2 \in \Sigma^2.\mathit{Prob}_{\mathsf{G}^C,s}^{\sigma_1,\sigma_2}\{\pi \in \mathit{IPaths}_{\mathsf{G}^C,s}^{\sigma_1,\sigma_2} \mid \pi \models \psi\} \sim q$$

$$s \models \langle\langle C\rangle\rangle\mathsf{R}_{\sim x}^r[\,\rho\,] \Leftrightarrow \exists\sigma_1 \in \Sigma^1.\forall\sigma_2 \in \Sigma^2.\mathbb{E}_{\mathsf{G}^C,s}^{\sigma_1,\sigma_2}[\mathit{rew}(r,\rho)] \sim x$$

$$s \models \langle\langle C{:}C'\rangle\rangle_{\max\sim x}(\theta) \Leftrightarrow \exists\sigma_1^\star \in \Sigma^1, \sigma_2^\star \in \Sigma^2.\left(\mathbb{E}_{\mathsf{G}^C,s}^{\sigma_1^\star,\sigma_2^\star}(X_1^\theta) + \mathbb{E}_{\mathsf{G}^C,s}^{\sigma_1^\star,\sigma_2^\star}(X_2^\theta)\right) \sim x$$

and $(\sigma_1^\star, \sigma_2^\star)$ *is a subgame perfect SWNE[1] for the objectives* (X_1^θ, X_2^θ) *in* G^C *where, for* $1 \leqslant i \leqslant 2$ *and* $\pi \in \mathit{IPaths}_{\mathsf{G}^C,s}^{\sigma_1,\sigma_2}$:

$$X_i^{\mathsf{P}[\psi^1]+\mathsf{P}[\psi^2]}(\pi) = 1 \text{ if } \pi \models \psi^i \text{ and } 0 \text{ otherwise}$$

$$X_i^{\mathsf{R}^{r_1}[\rho^1]+\mathsf{R}^{r_2}[\rho^2]}(\pi) = \mathit{rew}(r_i,\rho^i)(\pi)$$

$$\pi \models \mathsf{X}\,\phi \Leftrightarrow \pi(1) \models \phi$$

$$\pi \models \phi_1\,\mathsf{U}^{\leqslant k}\,\phi_2 \Leftrightarrow \exists i \leqslant k.(\pi(i) \models \phi_2 \wedge \forall j < i.\pi(j) \models \phi_1)$$

$$\pi \models \phi_1\,\mathsf{U}\,\phi_2 \Leftrightarrow \exists i \in \mathbb{N}.(\pi(i) \models \phi_2 \wedge \forall j < i.\pi(j) \models \phi_1)$$

$$\mathit{rew}(r, \mathtt{I}^{=k})(\pi) = r_S(\pi(k))$$

$$\mathit{rew}(r, \mathtt{C}^{\leqslant k})(\pi) = \sum_{i=0}^{k-1}\left(r_A(\pi(i),\pi[i]) + r_S(\pi(i))\right)$$

$$\mathit{rew}(r, \mathsf{F}\,\phi)(\pi) = \begin{cases} \infty & \text{if } \forall j \in \mathbb{N}.\pi(j) \not\models \phi \\ \sum_{i=0}^{k_\phi}\left(r_A(\pi(i),\pi[i]) + r_S(\pi(i))\right) & \text{otherwise} \end{cases}$$

and $k_\phi = \min\{k-1 \mid \pi(k) \models \phi\}$.

---

[1] In the case of infinite-horizon properties, this is a subgame perfect ε-SWNE.

4 Model Checking CSGs Against Nash Formulae

Since rPATL is a branching-time logic, the basic model checking algorithm works by recursively computing the set $Sat(\phi)$ of states satisfying formula ϕ over the structure of ϕ. So, to extend the existing rPATL model checking algorithm for CSGs [28] to the logic from Sect. 3, we need only consider Nash formulae $\langle\langle C:C' \rangle\rangle_{\max\sim x}(\theta)$. This requires computation of subgame perfect SWNE values of the objectives (X_1^θ, X_2^θ) and a comparison of their sum to the threshold x.

We first explain how we compute SWNE values in bimatrix games, then subgame perfect SWNE values for finite-horizon objectives and lastly approximate subgame perfect ε-SWNE values for infinite-horizon objectives. We also discuss how to synthesise SWNE profiles. Our algorithm requires the following assumption on CSGs, which can be checked using standard graph-based methods. Without this assumption the presented value iteration algorithms are not guaranteed to converge (for further details, see [29]).

Assumption 1. *For any infinite-horizon probabilistic properties, there are no non-terminal end components. For infinite-horizon reward properties, the targets are reached with probability 1 under all strategy profiles.*

Computing SWNE Values of Bimatrix Games. Finding Nash equilibria in bimatrix games is in the class of *linear complementarity* problems (LCPs). More precisely, a profile (σ_1, σ_2) is a Nash equilibrium of the bimatrix game $Z_1, Z_2 \in \mathbb{R}^{l \times m}$ where $A_1 = \{a_1, \ldots, a_l\}$, $A_2 = \{b_1, \ldots, b_m\}$ if and only if there exists $u, v \in \mathbb{R}$ such that, for the column vectors $x \in \mathbb{R}^l v$ and $y \in \mathbb{R}^m$ where $x_i = \sigma_1(a_i)$ and $y_j = \sigma_2(b_j)$ for $1 \leqslant i \leqslant l$ and $1 \leqslant j \leqslant m$, we have:

$$x^T(1u - Z_1 y) = 0, \quad y^T(1v - Z_2^T x) = 0, \quad 1u - Z_1 y \geqslant 0, \quad 1v - Z_2^T x \geqslant 0$$

and 0 and 1 are vectors or matrices with all components 0 and 1, respectively.

The Lemke-Howson algorithm [32] can be applied for finding Nash equilibria and is based on the method of *labelled polytopes* [36]. Other well-known methods include those based on *support enumeration* [39] and *regret minimisation* [41].

SWNE via Labelled Polytopes. Given a bimatrix game $Z_1, Z_2 \in \mathbb{R}^{l \times m}$, we denote the sets of deterministic strategies of players 1 and 2 by $I = \{1, \ldots, l\}$ and $M = \{1, \ldots, m\}$ and define $J = \{l+1, \ldots, l+m\}$ by mapping $j \in M$ to $l+j \in J$. A *label* is then defined as element of $I \cup J$. The sets of strategies for players 1 and 2 can be represented by:

$$X = \{x \in \mathbb{R}^l \mid 1x = 1 \wedge x \geqslant 0\} \quad \text{and} \quad Y = \{y \in \mathbb{R}^m \mid 1y = 1 \wedge y \geqslant 0\}.$$

The strategy set Y is then divided into regions $Y(i)$ and $Y(j)$ (polytopes) for $i \in I$ and $j \in J$ such that $Y(i)$ contains strategies for which the deterministic strategy i of player 1 is a best response and $Y(j)$ contain strategies which choose action j with probability zero:

$$Y(i) = \{y \in Y \mid \forall k \in I. \, Z_1(i, :)y \geqslant Z_1(k, :)y\} \quad \text{and} \quad Y(j) = \{y = Y \mid y_{j-l} = 0\}$$

where $Z_1(i,:)$ is the ith row vector of Z_1. A vector y is then said to have label k if $y \in Y(k)$, for $k \in I \cup J$. The strategy set X is divided analogously into regions $X(j)$ and $X(i)$ for $j \in J$ and $i \in I$ and a vector x has label k if $x \in X(k)$, for $k \in I \cup J$. A pair of vectors $(x, y) \in X \times Y$ is *completely labelled* if the union of the labels of x and y equals $I \cup J$. The Nash equilibria of the game equal the vector pairs that are completely labelled [32,43].

Once all completely labelled vector pairs have been computed, one can calculate the corresponding set of values through matrix-vector multiplication. The pairs that maximise the sum of values correspond to SWNE strategies. In case of multiple SWNEs, we choose the values that are maximal for the first player, unless both players can get equal payoff, in which case we choose these.

Computing Values of Nash Formulae. For a formula $\langle\!\langle C{:}C' \rangle\!\rangle_{\max\sim x}(\theta)$, if the objectives of the non-zero sum formula θ are both finite-horizon, we can use *backwards induction* [35,42] to compute (precise) subgame perfect SWNE values. Below, we give the cases for bounded probabilistic reachability and bounded cumulative reward objectives; the remaining cases can be found in [29]. If both of the objectives are infinite-horizon, we use *value iteration* [15] to approximate subgame perfect SWNE values. Since there is not necessarily a unique pair of such values, the convergence criterion is applied to the sum of the two values computed, which *is* unique. Below, we give details for probabilistic and expected reachability objectives; the remaining cases can be found in [29]. Finally, for cases where there is a combination of finite- and infinite-horizon objectives, we convert to having both infinite-horizon by modifying the game and formula in a standard manner for probabilistic model checking; see [29] for the construction. The two key aspects of the value iteration algorithm are using SWNE to ensure uniqueness and solving an MDP when the target of one player has been reached.

We use the notation $V_{G^C}(s, \theta)$ for SWNE values of the objectives (X_1^θ, X_2^θ) in state s of G^C. We also use $P_{G,s}^{\max}(\psi)$ and $R_{G,s}^{\max}(r, \rho)$ for the maximum probability of satisfying ψ and maximum expected reward for the random variable $rew(r, \rho)$, respectively, in state s when all players collaborate. These can be computed through standard MDP model checking [1,7].

Bounded Probabilistic Reachability. If $\theta = P[F^{\leq k_1} \phi^1] + P[F^{\leq k_2} \phi^2]$, then we compute values of the objectives for the formulae $\theta_{n+n_1,n+n_2} = P[F^{\leq n+n_1} \phi^1] + P[F^{\leq n+n_2} \phi^2]$ for $0 \leq n \leq k$ recursively, where $k = \min\{k_1, k_2\}$, $n_1 = k_1 - k$ and $n_2 = k_2 - k$. For state s, if $n = 0$:

$$V_{G^C}(s, \theta_{n_1,n_2}) = \begin{cases} (\eta_{\phi^1}(s), \eta_{\phi^2}(s)) & \text{if } n_1 = n_2 = 0 \\ (\eta_{\phi^1}(s), P_{G,s}^{\max}(F^{\leq n_2} \phi^2)) & \text{else if } n_1 = 0 \\ (P_{G,s}^{\max}(F^{\leq n_1} \phi^1), \eta_{\phi^2}(s)) & \text{otherwise} \end{cases}$$

and if $n > 0$:

$$V_{G^C}(s, \theta_{n+n_1,n+n_2}) = \begin{cases} (1, 1) & \text{if } s \in Sat(\phi^1) \cap Sat(\phi^2) \\ (1, P_{G,s}^{\max}(F^{\leq n+n_2} \phi^2)) & \text{else if } s \in Sat(\phi^1) \\ (P_{G,s}^{\max}(F^{\leq n+n_1} \phi^1), 1) & \text{else if } s \in Sat(\phi^2) \\ val(Z_1, Z_2) & \text{otherwise} \end{cases}$$

where $\eta_{\phi^i}(s)$ equals 1 if $s \in Sat(\phi^i)$ and 0 otherwise for $1 \leqslant i \leqslant 2$, and $val(Z_1, Z_2)$ equals SWNE values of the bimatrix game $(Z_1, Z_2) \in \mathbb{R}^{l \times m}$:

$$z_{i,j}^l = \sum_{s' \in S} \delta(s, (a_i, b_j))(s') \cdot v_{(n-1)+n_l}^{s',l}$$

$1 \leqslant l \leqslant 2$ and $(v_{(n-1)+n_1}^{s',1}, v_{(n-1)+n_2}^{s',2}) = \mathsf{V}_{\mathsf{G}^c}(s', \theta_{(n-1)+n_1,(n-1)+n_2})$ for all $s' \in S$.

Bounded Cumulative Rewards. If $\theta = \mathbb{R}^{r_1}[\,\mathsf{C}^{\leqslant k_1}\,] + \mathbb{R}^{r_2}[\,\mathsf{C}^{\leqslant k_2}\,]$, then we compute values of the objectives for the formulae $\theta_{n+n_1,n+n_2} = \mathbb{R}^{r_1}[\,\mathsf{C}^{\leqslant n+n_1}\,] + \mathbb{R}^{r_2}[\,\mathsf{C}^{\leqslant n+n_2}\,]$ for $0 \leqslant n \leqslant k$ recursively, where $k = \min\{k_1, k_2\}$, $n_1 = k_1 - k$ and $n_2 = k_2 - k$. For state s, if $n = 0$:

$$\mathsf{V}_{\mathsf{G}^c}(s, \theta_{n_1,n_2}) = \begin{cases} (0,0) & \text{if } n_1 = n_2 = 0 \\ (0, \mathsf{R}_{\mathsf{G},s}^{\max}(r_2, \mathsf{C}^{\leqslant n_2})) & \text{else if } n_1 = 0 \\ (\mathsf{R}_{\mathsf{G},s}^{\max}(r_1, \mathsf{C}^{\leqslant n_1}), 0) & \text{otherwise} \end{cases}$$

and if $n > 0$, then $\mathsf{V}_{\mathsf{G}^c}(s, \theta_{n+n_1,n+n_2})$ equals SWNE values of the bimatrix game $(Z_1, Z_2) \in \mathbb{R}^{l \times m}$:

$$z_{i,j}^l = r_S^l(s) + r_A^l(s, (a_i, b_j)) + \sum_{s' \in S} \delta(s, (a_i, b_j))(s') \cdot v_{(n-1)+n_l}^{s',l}$$

$1 \leqslant l \leqslant 2$ and $(v_{(n-1)+n_1}^{s',1}, v_{(n-1)+n_2}^{s',2}) = \mathsf{V}_{\mathsf{G}^c}(s', \theta_{(n-1)+n_1,(n-1)+n_2})$ for all $s' \in S$.

Probabilistic Reachability. If $\theta = \mathsf{P}[\,\mathsf{F}\,\phi^1\,] + \mathsf{P}[\,\mathsf{F}\,\phi^2\,]$, values can be computed through value iteration as the limit $\mathsf{V}_{\mathsf{G}^c}(s, \theta) = \lim_{n \to \infty} \mathsf{V}_{\mathsf{G}^c}(s, \theta, n)$ where:

$$\mathsf{V}_{\mathsf{G}^c}(s, \theta, n) = \begin{cases} (1,1) & \text{if } s \in Sat(\phi^1) \cap Sat(\phi^2) \\ (1, \mathsf{P}_{\mathsf{G},s}^{\max}(\mathsf{F}\,\phi^2)) & \text{else if } s \in Sat(\phi^1) \\ (\mathsf{P}_{\mathsf{G},s}^{\max}(\mathsf{F}\,\phi^1), 1) & \text{else if } s \in Sat(\phi^2) \\ (0,0) & \text{else if } n = 0 \\ val(Z_1, Z_2) & \text{otherwise} \end{cases}$$

where $val(Z_1, Z_2)$ equals SWNE values of the bimatrix game $(Z_1, Z_2) \in \mathbb{R}^{l \times m}$:

$$z_{i,j}^l = \sum_{s' \in S} \delta(s, (a_i, b_j))(s') \cdot v_{n-1}^{s',l}$$

$1 \leqslant l \leqslant 2$ and $(v_{n-1}^{s',1}, v_{n-1}^{s',2}) = \mathsf{V}_{\mathsf{G}^c}(s', \theta, n-1)$ for all $s' \in S$.

Expected Reachability. If $\theta = \mathbb{R}^{r_1}[\,\mathsf{F}\,\phi^1\,] + \mathbb{R}^{r_2}[\,\mathsf{F}\,\phi^2\,]$, values can be computed through value iteration as the limit $\mathsf{V}_{\mathsf{G}^c}(s, \theta) = \lim_{n \to \infty} \mathsf{V}_{\mathsf{G}^c}(s, \theta, n)$ where:

$$\mathsf{V}_{\mathsf{G}^c}(s, \theta, n) = \begin{cases} (0,0) & \text{if } s \in Sat(\phi^1) \cap Sat(\phi^2) \text{ or } n = 0 \\ (0, \mathsf{R}_{\mathsf{G},s}^{\max}(r_2, \mathsf{F}\,\phi^2)) & \text{else if } s \in Sat(\phi^1) \\ (\mathsf{R}_{\mathsf{G},s}^{\max}(r_1, \mathsf{F}\,\phi^1), 0) & \text{else if } s \in Sat(\phi^2) \\ val(Z_1, Z_2) & \text{otherwise} \end{cases}$$

where $val(Z_1, Z_2)$ equals SWNE values of the bimatrix game $(Z_1, Z_2) \in \mathbb{R}^{l \times m}$:

$$z_{i,j}^l = r_S^l(s) + r_A^l(s, (a_i, b_j)) + \sum_{s' \in S} \delta(s, (a_i, b_j))(s') \cdot v_{n-1}^{s',l}$$

$1 \leqslant l \leqslant 2$ and $(v_{n-1}^{s',1}, v_{n-1}^{s',2}) = \mathsf{V}_{\mathsf{G}^c}(s', \theta, n-1)$ for all $s' \in S$.

Strategy Synthesis. In addition to property verification, it is usually beneficial to perform *strategy synthesis*, that is, construct a witness of the satisfaction of a property. In the case of a formula $\langle\!\langle C{:}C'\rangle\!\rangle_{\max\sim x}(\theta)$, we can return a subgame perfect SWNE for the objectives (X_1^θ, X_2^θ). This is achieved using the approach above, both keeping track of a SWNE for the bimatrix game solved in each state and, when computing optimal values for MDPs, also performing strategy synthesis [30] (a strategy of the MDP is equivalent to a strategy profile of the CSG). We can then combine these generated profiles to yield a subgame perfect SWNE. The synthesised strategies require randomisation and memory. Memory is needed since choices change after a path formulae becomes true or a target reached and is required for finite-horizon properties. For infinite-horizon properties, the use of value iteration means only approximate ε-NE profiles are synthesised. However, for the case studies in Sect. 6, we find that all synthesised profiles are NE.

Correctness and Complexity. The proof of correctness is given in the extended version of the paper [29] and shows that the values computed during value iteration correspond to subgame perfect SWNE values of finite game trees, and the values of these game trees converge uniformly and are bounded from below and above by the finite approximations of G^C and actual values of G^C, respectively. A limitation of our approach, as for standard value iteration [22,25], is that convergence of the values does not give guarantees on the precision. Complexity is linear in the size of the formula, while finding NE for reachability objectives is EXPTIME [12]. Value iteration requires solving an LCP problem of size $|A|$ for each state at every iteration, with the number of iterations depending on the convergence criterion. Section 6 reports on efficiency in practice.

5   Implementation and Tool Support

We have extended PRISM-games [31] with support for modelling and verification of CSGs against equilibria-based properties, building upon the CSG extension of [28]. The tool and files for the case studies of Sect. 6 are available from [46].

Modelling. CSGs are specified using an extension of the PRISM modelling language, in which behaviour is defined using probabilistic guarded commands of the form $[a]\ g \to u$, where a is an action label, g is a guard (a predicate over states) and u is a probabilistic state update. If it is enabled (i.e., g is true), an a-labelled transition can probabilistically update the model's state.

This language is adapted to CSGs in [28] by assigning modules to players and, in any state, letting each player choose between enabled commands of the corresponding modules (if no command is enabled, the player idles). One requirement of [28] was that the updates of all player were independent of each other; we extend the language to remove this requirement, by allowing commands to be labelled with lists of actions $[a_1, \ldots, a_n]$, and thus represent behaviour dependent on other players' choices. Rewards are extended similarly so that an individual player's rewards can depend on the choices taken by multiple players.

Table 1. Statistics for a representative set of CSG verification instances.

Case study & property [parameters]	Param. values	CSG statistics				Constr. time(s)	Verif. time (s)	
		Players	States	Choices	Trans.		MDP	CSG
Aloha $\mathrm{P}[\,\mathrm{F}\,sent_1\,]+\mathrm{P}[\,\mathrm{F}\,sent_{2,3}\,]$ $[b_{max},D]$	2,8	3	17,057	19,713	42,654	0.6	0.6	21.4
	3,8	3	89,114	97,326	264,172	2.2	2.1	32.8
	4,8	3	449,766	474,898	1,655,479	10.9	10.6	49.9
	5,8	3	2,308,349	2,385,537	10,362,711	97.7	90.0	121.7
Robot coordination $\mathrm{P}[\,\mathrm{F}^{\leqslant k}goal_1\,]+\mathrm{P}[\,\mathrm{F}^{\leqslant k}goal_2\,]$ $[l,k]$	10,10	3	9,802	66,514	543,524	1.4	2.0	27.2
	15,15	3	50,177	375,549	3,175,539	5.0	19.8	131.8
	20,20	3	159,202	1,249,434	10,738,004	15.4	136.3	928.7
	25,25	3	389,377	3,142,669	27,267,419	48.3	548.8	4,837.0
Medium access control $\mathrm{R}^{r_1}[\,\mathrm{C}^{\leqslant k}\,]+\mathrm{R}^{r_2}[\,\mathrm{C}^{\leqslant k}\,]$ $[e_{max},k]$	10,20	2	441	1,600	2,759	0.1	–	17.2
	20,40	2	1,681	6,400	11,119	0.2	–	127.5
	40,80	2	6,561	25,600	44,639	0.7	–	991.7
	80,160	2	25,921	102,400	178,879	1.3	–	6,937.0
Power control $\mathrm{R}^{r_1}[\,\mathrm{F}\,e_1{=}0\,]+\mathrm{R}^{r_2}[\,\mathrm{F}\,e_2{=}0\,]$ $[e_{max},k]$	4,20	2	2,346	6,802	13,574	0.2	0.2	3.0
	4,40	2	10,746	30,700	60,854	0.4	1.0	12.7
	8,20	2	4,010	14,545	31,654	0.3	0.4	5.2
	8,40	2	32,812	119,694	260,924	1.2	3.9	64.8

Implementation. We have implemented model construction of CSGs for the language described above, and the model checking and strategy synthesis algorithms of Sect. 4, extending the PRISM-games implementation of rPATL verification [28]. We build on PRISM's Java-based 'explicit' engine which uses sparse matrices, and add an SMT-based implementation for solving bimatrix games using Z3 [19]. The set of all Nash equilibria for a bimatrix game are found by progressively querying the SMT solver for new profiles until the model becomes unsatisfiable. Structuring the problem using labelled polytopes, which can be expressed through conjunctions, disjunctions and linear inequalities, avoids non-linear arithmetic. As an optimisation, we also search for and filter out *dominated strategies* as a precomputation step to reduce the calls to the solver.

6 Case Studies and Experimental Results

We now present case studies and results to demonstrate the applicability of our approach and implementation, as well as the benefits of using equilibria.

Efficiency and Scalability. Before describing the case studies, we first discuss the performance of the implementation. In Table 1, we show experiments run on a 2.10 GHz Intel Xeon using 16 GB RAM. The table includes model statistics (players, states and transitions) and the time to construct the CSG and verify it; the latter is split between CSG verification (including solving the bimatrix games) and the instances of MDP verification. Our tool can analyse models with over 2 million states and 20 million transitions; all are solved in under 2 h and most are considerably quicker. However, for models where players have choices in almost all states, only models with up to tens of thousands of states can be verified within 2 h. The majority of the time is spent solving bimatrix games, and therefore it is the number of choices of each coalition, rather than the number of players, that affects performance.

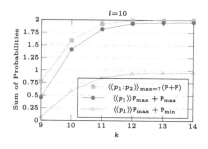
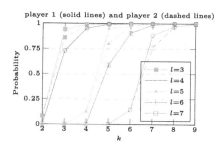

Fig. 2. Robot coordination: $\langle\!\langle p_1{:}p_2 \rangle\!\rangle_{\max=?}(P[\,F^{\leqslant k}\ goal_1\,] + P[\,F^{\leqslant k}\ goal_2\,])$ $(q = 0.1)$

Investigating the Benefits of Equilibria Properties. In each case study, we compare our results with the corresponding zero-sum properties [28]. E.g., for $\langle\!\langle C{:}C' \rangle\!\rangle_{\max=?}(P[\,F\ \phi_1\,] + P[\,F\ \phi_2\,])$, we compute the value and an optimal strategy σ_C for coalition C of the formula $\langle\!\langle C \rangle\!\rangle P_{\max=?}[\,F\ \phi_1\,]$, and then find the value of an optimal strategy for the coalition C' for $P_{\min=?}[\,F\ \phi_2\,]$ and $P_{\max=?}[\,F\ \phi_2\,]$ in the MDP induced by CSG when C follows σ_C. The aim is to showcase the advantages of cooperation as, in many real-world applications, agents' goals are not strictly opposed. As will be seen, all the presented results demonstrate that by using equilibrium properties at least one of the players gains and in almost all cases neither player loses (in the one case study where this is not the case the gains far outweigh the losses). The individual SWNE values for players need not be unique and, for all case studies (except Aloha in which the players goals are not symmetric), the values can be swapped to give alternative SWNE values.

Robot Coordination. Our first case study models a scenario in which two robots move concurrently over a grid of size $l \times l$. The robots start in diagonally opposite corners and try to reach the corner from which the other starts. A robot can move either diagonally, horizontally or vertically towards its goal and when it moves there is a probability (q) that it instead moves in an adjacent direction. E.g., if a robot moves north east, then with probability $q/2$ it will move north or east. If the robots enter the same cell, they crash and are unable to move again.

We suppose the robots try to maximise the probability of reaching their individual goals eventually and within a given number of steps (k). If there is no bound and $l \geqslant 4$, the SWNE strategies allow each robot to reach its goal with probability 1 (as time is not an issue, they can collaborate to avoid crashing). For the bounded case, in Fig. 2 we have plotted both the sum of the probabilities for a grid of size 10 (left) and the probabilities of the individual players for different grid sizes (right) as k varies. When there is only one route to each goal within the bound (along the diagonal), i.e. when $k = l - 1$, the SWNE strategies of both robots take this route. In odd grids, there is a high chance of crashing, but also a chance one will deviate and the other reaches their goal. Initially, as the bound k increases, for odd grids the SWNE values for the players are not equal (see Fig. 2 right). Here, it is better overall for one to follow the diagonal and the

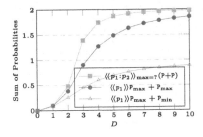
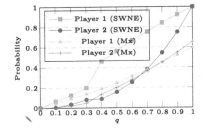

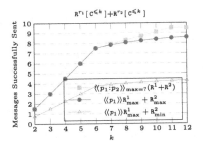
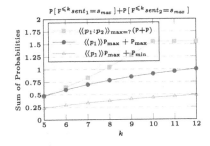

Fig. 3. Aloha: $\langle\!\langle p_1 : \{p_2, p_3\}\rangle\!\rangle_{\max=?}(\mathrm{P}[\,\mathrm{F}\,(sent_1 \wedge t \leqslant D)\,] + \mathrm{P}[\,\mathrm{F}\,(sent_2 \wedge sent_3 \wedge t \leqslant D)\,])$

Fig. 4. Medium access control ($e_{max} = 5$, $s_{max} = 5$, $q_1 = 0.9$ and $q_2 = 0.75$)

other to take a longer route, as if both took the diagonal route, the chance of crashing increases, decreasing the chance of reaching their goals.

Aloha. This case study concerns three users trying to send packets using the slotted ALOHA protocol. In a time slot, if a single user tries to send a packet, there is a probability (q) that the packet is sent; as more users try and send, then the probability of success decreases. If sending a packet fails, the number of slots a user waits before resending is set according to an exponential backoff scheme. More precisely, each user maintains a backoff counter which it increases each time there is a failure (up to b_{max}) and, if the counter equals k, randomly chooses the slots to wait from $\{0, 1, \ldots, 2^k - 1\}$.

We suppose three users try to maximise the probability of sending packets before a deadline D, with users 2 and 3 forming a coalition. Figure 3 presents total values as D varies (left) and individual values as q varies (right). Through synthesis, we find the collaboration is dependent on D and q. Given more time there is more chance for the users to collaborate sending in different slots, while if q is large it is unlikely users need to repeatedly send, so again can send in different slots. As the coalition has more messages to send, their probabilities are lower. However, even for two users, the probabilities are different, since, although it is advantageous to collaborate and only one user tries first, if transmission fails, then both users try to send as this is the best option for their individual goals.

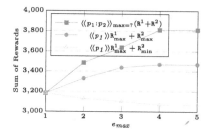 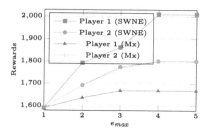

Fig. 5. Power Control: $\langle\langle p_1{:}p_2 \rangle\rangle_{\max=?}(\mathtt{R}^{r_1}[\,\mathtt{F}\ e_1 = 0\,] + \mathtt{R}^{r_2}[\,\mathtt{F}\ e_2 = 0\,])$

Medium Access Control. Our third case study extends the CSG model from Example 2 by assuming the probability of a successful transmission when a single user tries to transmit equals q_1 and the energy of each user is bounded by e_{max}.

We consider two Nash properties for this model, both bounded by the number of time slots (k). The goal for each user in the first property is to maximise their expected number of successful transmissions and the second to maximise the probability of successfully transmitting a certain number (s_{max}) of messages. Figure 4 presents results for these properties as the bound k varies. For both properties, the SWNE strategies yield equal values for the players. Synthesising strategies we see that for small values of k there is not sufficient time to collaborate (both users always try and transmit); however, as k increases there is time for the users to collaborate and try to transmit in different slots, and hence improve their values. Since the users have limited energy, Fig. 4 shows that eventually adding steps does not increase the reward or probability.

Power Control. Our final case study is based on a model of power control in cellular networks from [10]. In the model, phones emit signals over a cellular network and the signals can be strengthened by increasing the power level up to a bound (pow_{max}). A stronger signal can improve transmission quality, but uses more energy and lowers the quality of other transmissions due to interference. We extend this model by adding a failure probability (q_{fail}) when a power level is increased and assume each phone has a limited battery capacity (e_{max}). Based on [10], we associate a reward structure with each phone representing transmission quality dependent both on its power level and that of other phones due to interference.

We consider two players, each trying to maximise their reward before their battery is empty. Figure 5 presents, for $p_{max} = 5$ and $e_{max} = 5$, the sum of the SWNE values (left) and the values of the individual players (right) as the battery capacity varies. The values of the players are different because if one increases their power level this increases the overall reward (their reward increases, while the other's decreases by a lesser amount due to interference), whereas if both increase the overall reward decreases (both rewards decrease due to interference).

7 Conclusions

We have presented a logic, algorithms and tool for model checking and strategy synthesis of concurrent stochastic games using Nash equilibria-based properties. In comparison to existing methods, which support only zero-sum properties, we demonstrate, on a range of case studies, that our approach produces strategies that are collectively more beneficial for all players in the game. Future work will investigate other techniques for Nash equilibria synthesis, non-coalitional multi-player games and mechanism design.

Acknowledgements. This work is partially supported by the EPSRC Programme Grant on Mobile Autonomy and the PRINCESS project, under the DARPA BRASS programme. We would like to thank the reviewers of an earlier version of this paper for finding a flaw in the correctness proof.

References

1. de Alfaro, L.: Computing minimum and maximum reachability times in probabilistic systems. In: Baeten, J.C.M., Mauw, S. (eds.) CONCUR 1999. LNCS, vol. 1664, pp. 66–81. Springer, Heidelberg (1999). https://doi.org/10.1007/3-540-48320-9_7
2. de Alfaro, L., Henzinger, T., Kupferman, O.: Concurrent reachability games. Theor. Comput. Sci. **386**(3), 188–217 (2007)
3. de Alfaro, L., Majumdar, R.: Quantitative solution of omega-regular games. J. Comput. Syst. Sci. **68**(2), 374–397 (2004)
4. Alur, R., Henzinger, T.A., Kupferman, O.: Alternating-time temporal logic. J. ACM **49**(5), 672–713 (2002)
5. Arslan, G., Yüksel, S.: Distributionally consistent price taking equilibria in stochastic dynamic games. In: Proceedings of CDC 2017, pp. 4594–4599. IEEE (2017)
6. Basset, N., Kwiatkowska, M., Wiltsche, C.: Compositional strategy synthesis for stochastic games with multiple objectives. Inf. Comput. **261**(3), 536–587 (2018)
7. Bianco, A., de Alfaro, L.: Model checking of probabilistic and nondeterministic systems. In: Thiagarajan, P.S. (ed.) FSTTCS 1995. LNCS, vol. 1026, pp. 499–513. Springer, Heidelberg (1995). https://doi.org/10.1007/3-540-60692-0_70
8. Bouyer, P., Markey, N., Stan, D.: Mixed Nash equilibria in concurrent games. In: Proceedings of FSTTCS 2014, LIPICS, vol. 29, pp. 351–363. Leibniz-Zentrum für Informatik (2014)
9. Bouyer, P., Markey, N., Stan, D.: Stochastic equilibria under imprecise deviations in terminal-reward concurrent games. In: Proceedings of GandALF 2016, EPTCS, vol. 226, pp. 61–75. Open Publishing Association (2016)
10. Brenguier, R.: PRALINE: a tool for computing nash equilibria in concurrent games. In: Sharygina, N., Veith, H. (eds.) CAV 2013. LNCS, vol. 8044, pp. 890–895. Springer, Heidelberg (2013). https://doi.org/10.1007/978-3-642-39799-8_63
11. Čermák, P., Lomuscio, A., Mogavero, F., Murano, A.: MCMAS-SLK: a model checker for the verification of strategy logic specifications. In: Biere, A., Bloem, R. (eds.) CAV 2014. LNCS, vol. 8559, pp. 525–532. Springer, Cham (2014). https://doi.org/10.1007/978-3-319-08867-9_34
12. Chatterjee, K.: Nash equilibrium for upward-closed objectives. In: Ésik, Z. (ed.) CSL 2006. LNCS, vol. 4207, pp. 271–286. Springer, Heidelberg (2006). https://doi.org/10.1007/11874683_18

13. Chatterjee, K.: Stochastic ω-regular games. Ph.D. thesis, University of California at Berkeley (2007)
14. Chatterjee, K., de Alfaro, L., Henzinger, T.: Strategy improvement for concurrent reachability and turn-based stochastic safety games. J. Comput. Syst. Sci. **79**(5), 640–657 (2013)
15. Chatterjee, K., Henzinger, T.A.: Value iteration. In: Grumberg, O., Veith, H. (eds.) 25 Years of Model Checking. LNCS, vol. 5000, pp. 107–138. Springer, Heidelberg (2008). https://doi.org/10.1007/978-3-540-69850-0_7
16. Chatterjee, K., Majumdar, R., Jurdziński, M.: On Nash equilibria in stochastic games. In: Marcinkowski, J., Tarlecki, A. (eds.) CSL 2004. LNCS, vol. 3210, pp. 26–40. Springer, Heidelberg (2004). https://doi.org/10.1007/978-3-540-30124-0_6
17. Chen, T., Forejt, V., Kwiatkowska, M., Parker, D., Simaitis, A.: Automatic verification of competitive stochastic systems. Formal Methods Syst. Des. **43**(1), 61–92 (2013)
18. Chen, T., Forejt, V., Kwiatkowska, M., Simaitis, A., Wiltsche, C.: On stochastic games with multiple objectives. In: Chatterjee, K., Sgall, J. (eds.) MFCS 2013. LNCS, vol. 8087, pp. 266–277. Springer, Heidelberg (2013). https://doi.org/10.1007/978-3-642-40313-2_25
19. de Moura, L., Bjørner, N.: Z3: an efficient SMT solver. In: Ramakrishnan, C.R., Rehof, J. (eds.) TACAS 2008. LNCS, vol. 4963, pp. 337–340. Springer, Heidelberg (2008). https://doi.org/10.1007/978-3-540-78800-3_24
20. Dehnert, C., Junges, S., Katoen, J.-P., Volk, M.: A **Storm** is coming: a modern probabilistic model checker. In: Majumdar, R., Kunčak, V. (eds.) CAV 2017. LNCS, vol. 10427, pp. 592–600. Springer, Cham (2017). https://doi.org/10.1007/978-3-319-63390-9_31
21. Fernando, D., Dong, N., Jegourel, C., Dong, J.S.: Verification of strong Nash-equilibrium for probabilistic BAR systems. In: Sun, J., Sun, M. (eds.) ICFEM 2018. LNCS, vol. 11232, pp. 106–123. Springer, Cham (2018). https://doi.org/10.1007/978-3-030-02450-5_7
22. Haddad, S., Monmege, B.: Interval iteration algorithm for MDPs and IMDPs. Theor. Comput. Sci. **735**, 111–131 (2018)
23. Hansson, H., Jonsson, B.: A logic for reasoning about time and reliability. Formal Aspects Comput. **6**(5), 512–535 (1994)
24. Gutierrez, J., Najib, M., Perelli, G., Wooldridge, M.: **EVE**: a tool for temporal equilibrium analysis. In: Lahiri, S.K., Wang, C. (eds.) ATVA 2018. LNCS, vol. 11138, pp. 551–557. Springer, Cham (2018). https://doi.org/10.1007/978-3-030-01090-4_35
25. Kelmendi, E., Krämer, J., Křetínský, J., Weininger, M.: Value iteration for simple stochastic games: stopping criterion and learning algorithm. In: Chockler, H., Weissenbacher, G. (eds.) CAV 2018. LNCS, vol. 10981, pp. 623–642. Springer, Cham (2018). https://doi.org/10.1007/978-3-319-96145-3_36
26. Kemeny, J., Snell, J., Knapp, A.: Denumerable Markov Chains. Springer, New York (1976). https://doi.org/10.1007/978-1-4684-9455-6
27. Kwiatkowska, M., Norman, G., Parker, D.: PRISM 4.0: verification of probabilistic real-time systems. In: Gopalakrishnan, G., Qadeer, S. (eds.) CAV 2011. LNCS, vol. 6806, pp. 585–591. Springer, Heidelberg (2011). https://doi.org/10.1007/978-3-642-22110-1_47
28. Kwiatkowska, M., Norman, G., Parker, D., Santos, G.: Automated verification of concurrent stochastic games. In: McIver, A., Horvath, A. (eds.) QEST 2018. LNCS, vol. 11024, pp. 223–239. Springer, Cham (2018). https://doi.org/10.1007/978-3-319-99154-2_14

29. Kwiatkowska, M., Norman, G., Parker, D., Santos, G.: Equilibria-based probabilistic model checking for concurrent stochastic games (2018). http://arxiv.org/abs/1811.07145
30. Kwiatkowska, M., Parker, D.: Automated verification and strategy synthesis for probabilistic systems. In: Van Hung, D., Ogawa, M. (eds.) ATVA 2013. LNCS, vol. 8172, pp. 5–22. Springer, Cham (2013). https://doi.org/10.1007/978-3-319-02444-8_2
31. Kwiatkowska, M., Parker, D., Wiltsche, C.: PRISM-games: verification and strategy synthesis for stochastic multi-player games with multiple objectives. Softw. Tools Technol. Transf. **20**(2), 195–210 (2018)
32. Lemke, C., Howson Jr., J.: Equilibrium points of bimatrix games. J. Soc. Ind. Appl. Math. **12**(2), 413–423 (1964)
33. Lozovanu, D., Pickl, S.: Determining Nash equilibria for stochastic positional games with discounted payoffs. In: Rothe, J. (ed.) ADT 2017. LNCS (LNAI), vol. 10576, pp. 339–343. Springer, Cham (2017). https://doi.org/10.1007/978-3-319-67504-6_24
34. McKelvey, R., McLennan, A., Turocy, T.: Gambit: software tools for game theory, version 16.0.1 (2016). gambit-project.org
35. von Neumann, J., Morgenstern, O., Kuhn, H., Rubinstein, A.: Theory of Games and Economic Behavior. Princeton University Press, Princeton (1944)
36. Nisan, N., Roughgarden, T., Tardos, E., Vazirani, V.: Algorithmic Game Theory. Cambridge University Press, Cambridge (2007)
37. Osborne, M., Rubinstein, A.: An Introduction to Game Theory. Oxford University Press, Oxford (2004)
38. Pacheco, J., Santos, F., Souza, M., Skyrms, B.: Evolutionary dynamics of collective action. In: Chalub, F., Rodrigues, J. (eds.) The Mathematics of Darwin's Legacy, pp. 119–138. Springer, Basel (2011). https://doi.org/10.1007/978-3-0348-0122-5_7
39. Porter, R., Nudelman, E., Shoham, Y.: Simple search methods for finding a Nash equilibrium. In: Proceedings of AAAI 2004, pp. 664–669. AAAI Press (2004)
40. Prasad, H., Prashanth, L., Bhatnagar, S.: Two-timescale algorithms for learning Nash equilibria in general-sum stochastic games. In: Proceedings of AAMAS 2015, pp. 1371–1379. IFAAMAS (2015)
41. Sandholm, T., Gilpin, A., Conitzer, V.: Mixed-integer programming methods for finding Nash equilibria. In: Proceedings of AAAI 2005, pp. 495–501. AAAI Press (2005)
42. Schwalbe, U., Walker, P.: Zermelo and the early history of game theory. Games Econ. Behav. **34**(1), 123–137 (2001)
43. Shapley, L.: A note on the Lemke-Howson algorithm. In: Balinski, M.L. (ed.) Pivoting and Extension. Mathematical Programming Studies, vol. 1, pp. 175–189. Springer, Heidelberg (1974). In Honor of A.W. Tucker
44. Toumi, A., Gutierrez, J., Wooldridge, M.: A tool for the automated verification of nash equilibria in concurrent games. In: Leucker, M., Rueda, C., Valencia, F.D. (eds.) ICTAC 2015. LNCS, vol. 9399, pp. 583–594. Springer, Cham (2015). https://doi.org/10.1007/978-3-319-25150-9_34
45. Ummels, M.: Stochastic multiplayer games: theory and algorithms. Ph.D. thesis, RWTH Aachen University (2010)
46. Supporting material. prismmodelchecker.org/files/fm19nash/

Analysis Techniques

Abstract Execution

Dominic Steinhöfel(⊠)🆔 and Reiner Hähnle🆔

Department of Computer Science, TU Darmstadt, Darmstadt, Germany
{steinhoefel,haehnle}@cs.tu-darmstadt.de

Abstract. We propose a new static software analysis principle called *Abstract Execution*, generalizing Symbolic Execution: While the latter analyzes all possible execution paths of a *specific program*, Abstract Execution analyzes a *partially unspecified program* by permitting *abstract symbols* representing unknown contexts. For each abstract symbol, we faithfully represent each possible concrete execution resulting from its substitution with concrete code. There is a wide range of applications of Abstract Execution, especially for verifying *relational properties* of schematic programs. We implemented Abstract Execution in a deductive verification framework and proved correctness of eight well-known statement-level refactoring rules, including two with loops. For each refactoring we characterize the preconditions that make it semantics-preserving. Most preconditions are not mentioned in the literature.

1 Introduction

Reasoning about *abstract programs*, i.e. programs containing an abstract context represented by placeholder symbols, is required whenever one aims to rigorously analyze program transformation techniques. Notably in compiler validation, to argue that a specific compilation or optimization step preserves the meaning of any input program is a standard task. An established approach to this problem formalizes the abstract syntax and the semantics of the target programming language as a set of inductive definitions, then proves properties of abstract programs via structural induction over the program syntax [7]. Early work relied on pen-and-paper proofs [22,24]. Recently, interactive theorem provers are used to mechanize correctness proofs, e.g., in CompCert [21] and CakeML [31]. The main drawback is the very high effort required to mechanize a programming language and to perform interactive proofs. In this paper we take a different approach to reason about abstract programs that is automatic and based on symbolic execution. To make it work, we need to answer two questions: (i) Can one specify abstract program contexts sufficiently without giving full inductive definitions? (ii) If yes, which specification constructs are needed for abstract contexts?

We propose a new static software analysis principle called Abstract Execution (AE) that allows to *automatically* reason about *abstract* sequential programs with *side effects*. An essential component of AE is a specification language for

This work was funded by the Hessian LOEWE initiative within the Software-Factory 4.0 project.

© Springer Nature Switzerland AG 2019
M. H. ter Beek et al. (Eds.): FM 2019, LNCS 11800, pp. 319–336, 2019.
https://doi.org/10.1007/978-3-030-30942-8_20

abstract program contexts. This permits, in contrast to prior work [13,14,18, 29], to specify irregular termination behavior (exceptions, etc.) and fine-grained assumptions on abstract programs. Here we target sequential JAVA programs, but the principles of AE are equally applicable to other sequential languages.

Abstract Execution generalizes Symbolic Execution (SE) [5,8,17]. Symbolic Execution means to execute programs with symbolic expressions as input values. When SE is embedded into a program logic [1], these symbolic values are represented by first-order Skolem constants. Skolem symbols can also be viewed as *abstract* symbols whose concrete domain value is not specified. In this sense, SE is already abstract and it amounts to execution of *abstract* programs that permit variables and fields to be initialized with unknown values. For example, *symbolic* execution of a program "i++;" amounts to execution of the *abstract* program "i_0++;", where i_0 is a fresh Skolem symbol of type int.

AE in addition permits not only abstract *values*, but whole *programs* to appear as undefined expressions. In the program "if (i > 0) p_0 else p_1", for example, the placeholders p_i can be substituted with *arbitrary* concrete programs, as long as the result is well-formed. From a semantic point of view, the difference between abstract values and abstract programs is that (i) an abstract program may change the value of arbitrary variables and fields, and (ii) its execution may terminate abruptly, i.e., by returning, throwing an exception, or continuing or breaking out of a loop. In other words, an abstract program can be seen as an unknown partial function between execution states, i.e. its big-step semantics $[\![p]\!]$. In logic, such a function can be represented by a *second-order* Skolem symbol. Therefore, AE amounts to a limited form of second-order reasoning: let p be an abstract program and φ a first-order formula. Then $\vdash_{ae} [p]\varphi$ holds iff the weakest precondition of p w.r.t. φ is first-order derivable. For example:

$$\vdash_{ae} [\texttt{int i; boolean b} = b_0; \texttt{ if (b) } p_0 \texttt{ else i = 0;}](b_0 \doteq \text{FALSE} \rightarrow i \doteq 0)$$

To check the relation $\vdash_{ae}$ *automatically*, we must provide a technical solution to the following question: how can one implement weakest precondition reasoning over *abstract* programs such that the result is a *first-order* formula? These are the main building blocks of our solution to realize limited second-order inference over programs in terms of first-order deduction: (1) *second-order* Skolemization to represent the effects of placeholders like p_0 on local variables and the heap, (2) explicit modeling of all possible ways of irregular termination in separate SE branches, (3) over-approximation of returned values and thrown exceptions by first-order Skolemization, and (4) a specification language to describe the possible effect of second-order Skolem symbols as well as to define conditions when irregular termination of concrete instances for abstract programs can happen.

Applications of Abstract Execution. AE is applicable to many problems involving reasoning about abstract programs. It can be instantiated to (at least) the following tasks: (1) Execution of abstract method calls [6], a special case of AE; (2) automatic soundness proofs of program transformation and of (3) rule-based compilation [29]; (4) sound, automatic ("lazy") symbolic execution over programs with loops and calls, (5) incremental program development and synthesis [28]; (6) a modular version of *proof carrying code* [26], where the contract of called methods needs not to be known to the certificate provider. It is impossible to discuss all these in this paper. Therefore, we focus on program transformation—task (2). We study refactoring rules as described in Fowler's well-known books [11,12]. We model refactoring techniques as abstract programs, formalize assumptions under which a refactoring is sound, and prove behavioral equivalence of the original and refactored version for all concrete programs satisfying the abstract context.

The paper is structured as follows. In Sect. 2 we describe how to construct *abstract* JAVA programs. Section 3 expounds our logic for AE. Section 4 contains our case study about proving correctness of refactoring techniques. Section 5 discusses related work, Sect. 6 concludes and gives an outlook to the future. An appendix with more material is available at key-project.org/papers/ae/.

2   Specifying Abstract Programs

An abstract JAVA program is a program containing at least one *Abstract Placeholder Statement (APS)* symbol. The syntax to declare an APS is:

```
abstract_statement P;
```

The symbol P is an identifier for an abstract statement. Semantically, every APS with the same identifier occurring in a program or proof represents the same program. The above APS may be substituted with any *concrete* JAVA program accessing and assigning arbitrary fields and local variables, except that it is not allowed to declare local variables visible outside. Additionally, a concrete program may (1) throw any type of exception, (2) return from the method it executes, (3) break to any surrounding block label, (4) continue to and break from a surrounding loop, (5) continue to the label of a surrounding loop.

The possible behaviors of an APS are constrained by an *abstract specification*. The syntax of the specification language extends *block contracts* [1,19] of the JAVA Modelling Language (JML). JML [20] is a specification language for JAVA used to describe the behavior of JAVA classes and methods. JML specifications are embedded into JAVA code via comment lines starting with an "@" sign. *An APS is the declaration of an abstract placeholder symbol together with all specification clauses that constrain it.* We explain the involved concepts by specifying a variant of Fowler's *Consolidate Duplicate Conditional Fragments* refactoring [11] step-by-step. The result, a fully specified program after refactoring is shown in Listing 3 (on p. 5). Table 1 summarizes all specification constructs that may be used in an APS.

Figure 1 shows an unconstrained formalization of the refactoring. The abstract code uses an idiom to formalize abstract *expressions*: it introduces a variable representing the abstract expression (in this case, the boolean b) and precedes it with the APS Init that assigns to b an unknown value. The idiom works as expected if Init is constrained so it assigns a value exactly

Table 1. Specification constructs for APSs

Spec. Construct	Explanation
`locals(P)`	Refers to the Skolem (abstract) location set of local variables of an APS with symbol P visible from outside.
`declares` *skLocs*;	Specifies that an APS/method declares a list *skLocs* of Skolem location set specifiers `locals(·)`, opt. wrapped in `final(·)` modifiers, which can be used in APSs in the visible scope afterwards.
`assignable` *locs*;	Declares the location set *locs* to be assignable by the APS. *locs* is a list of variables, fields, and Skolem location set specifiers, optionally wrapped in a `hasTo(·)` modifier.
`accessible` *locs*;	Declares *locs* to be accessible by the APS.
`return_behavior requires` φ;	Specifies that the APS returns iff φ holds.
`exceptional_behavior requires` φ;	Spec. that the APS throws an exc. iff φ holds.
`break_behavior requires` φ; `continue_behavior requires` φ;	Specifies that the APS breaks/continues during loop execution iff φ holds.
`break_behavior` (*lbl*) `requires` φ; `continue_behavior` (*lbl*) `requires` φ;	Specifies that the APS breaks/continues to the (loop) label *lbl* iff φ holds.

Listing 1: Before

```
abstract_statement Init;
if (b) {
  abstract_statement P;
  abstract_statement Q1;
} else {
  abstract_statement P;
  abstract_statement Q2;
}
```

Listing 2: After

```
abstract_statement P;

abstract_statement Init;
if (b) {
  abstract_statement Q1;
} else {
  abstract_statement Q2;
}
```

Fig. 1. Unconstrained formalization of the "Consolidate Duplicate Conditional Fragments" Refactoring, "Pullout Prefix" variant [11]

to b and not to any other variable. JML uses the **assignable** clause to specify which locations can be assigned a value, but does not *enforce* the assignment. Hence, we extend JML with the **hasTo**(·) keyword. The specification "//@ **assignable hasTo**(b);" enforces that the specified abstract code assigns a value *exactly* to b.

Observe that the refactoring is unsound, whenever the APS P influences the value of b. If, for instance, P sets b to **true**, the **else** branch of the **if** statement in the refactored program is never reached. A drastic solution is to specify "//@ **assignable \nothing**;" for P which excludes any assignment. This, however, restricts the refactoring rule too severely to be useful. Assume the depicted program fragments occur in the scope of a method with a variable result that is returned at the end. Then we might constrain P with "//@ **assignable** result;" which forbids assignments to b (because it allows assignments *exactly* to result),

Listing 3. Fully specified abstract program for the refactored version

```
//@ axiom mutex{throwsExc(P),              if (b) {
//@              throwsExc(Init), returns(P)};      //@ declares    locals(Q1);
                                               //@ assignable \everything;
//@ declares   locals(P);                      //@ accessible \everything;
//@ assignable locals(P), result;              abstract_statement Q1;
//@ accessible locals(P), result, args;    } else {
//@ return_behavior requires returns(P);       //@ declares    locals(Q2);
//@ exceptional_behavior requires throwsExc(P); //@ assignable \everything;
abstract_statement P;                          //@ accessible \everything;
                                               abstract_statement Q2;
//@ assignable hasTo(b);                    }
//@ accessible args;
//@ return_behavior requires false;
//@ exceptional_behavior requires throwsExc(Init);
abstract_statement Init;
```

but renders P still useful. But this is not restrictive enough: The abstract program Init that initializes b may still *access* arbitrary locations and assign them to b. Thus, P can indirectly influence the control flow by assigning a value to the variable result which could then affect Init's choice for b. To address this issue we proceed as follows:

We add to all APSs in Fig. 1 (except Init) a "**declares**" annotation. It declares abstract "Skolem" location sets that can be instantiated with arbitrary concrete local variable declarations visible from outside. For example, to P we add the annotation "//@ **declares locals**(P);". To specify that a method containing APSs receives an unknown set "args" of parameters, we annotate it with "//@ **declares** args;". Abstract location sets in declarations can be declared final by surrounding them with "**final**(·)". This prevents them from occurring in **assignable** clauses. Continuing the example, we add to P the annotation "//@ **assignable locals**(P), result;" , to Init "//@ **accessible** args;".

Proving correctness of the refactoring still fails, however, for two reasons. The first is: we have not excluded that Init contains a **return** statement. Since Init's only task is to initialize b, this should never happen. We add the annotation "//@ **return_behavior requires false**;" to Init, specifying that a **return** requires the specified condition—here falsity—which excludes returning.

The second reason why the refactoring is not yet correct is that Init might raise an exception. This is entirely possible and a real problem: If we permit P to return or throw an exception, but Init may also throw an exception, then the refactored and the original program have different behavior. We have two options: (i) We deny Init to throw an exception by adding the annotation "//@ **exceptional_behavior requires false** ;" or, more generally, (ii) we enforce that *if* Init throws an exception, then P can neither throw an exception nor can it return. The latter is achieved with the help of the abstract functions **throwsExc**(Init), **throwsExc**(P), and **returns**(P) of *Boolean* type. They qualify the **requires** clauses that restrict exceptional and returning behavior of Init and P. A global **axiom** declares them to be mutually exclusive.

Listing 3 shows the specified refactored program. Similar annotations apply to the original version. For Q1 and Q2, we permit assigning/accessing all locations ("**\everything**"). This is default, so these declarations can be left out. The annotation "//@ **declares final**(args);" would have to be added to the surrounding method declaration. With the specification in Listing 3 we can prove *equivalence* of the original and refactored program for *any concrete instance* matching the abstract program structurally and satisfying its I/O and control flow constraints. Having proved equivalence, the refactoring can be applied in either direction. This is relevant: many of Fowler's refactorings are bi-directional. We continue with formalizing AE over constrained APSs in a program logic.

3   Abstract Execution Logic

Our implementation of AE is realized on top of the symbolic execution framework of the deductive verification system KeY [1]. It is based on JAVA Dynamic Logic (JavaDL), a program logic for the JAVA language.

3.1   Principles of JavaDL

JavaDL extends sorted First-Order Logic (FOL). JAVA programs appear inside logical formulas as *modalities*, of which there are two types: The box modality $[p]\varphi$ expresses that *if* program p terminates, then the postcondition φ holds in any final state (partial correctness). The diamond modality $\langle p \rangle \varphi$ additionally requires p to terminate (total correctness). To prove the validity of formulas, i.e. $[p]\varphi$ or $\langle p \rangle \varphi$ holds in any initial state, JavaDL has a sequent calculus comprising FOL and theory-specific rules, as well as rules realizing SE of JAVA programs. A Hoare triple $\{\psi\}\,p\,\{\varphi\}$ is equivalent to the JavaDL formula $\psi \to [p]\varphi$.

The SE rules of the JavaDL calculus reduce a JAVA statement to first-order assumptions and a separate syntactic category called symbolic *updates* representing symbolic state transitions. The atomic building blocks of updates are the empty update *Skip*, representing the identity state transition, and the *elementary update* x := t for the state transition where variable x is assigned the value of term t. Two updates $\mathcal{U}_1, \mathcal{U}_2$ can be combined into a *parallel* update $\mathcal{U}_1 \,||\, \mathcal{U}_2$: the state changes of $\mathcal{U}_1$ and $\mathcal{U}_2$ are executed *simultaneously*; in case both assign to the same variable, the assignment in $\mathcal{U}_2$ "wins". Only in the absence of such "conflicts", parallel composition is commutative. Updates are applied to terms t and formulas φ: $\{\mathcal{U}\}t$ and $\{\mathcal{U}\}\varphi$ represent the value of term t and truth value of formula φ after the state change effected by $\mathcal{U}$, respectively. Parallel update composition $\{\mathcal{U}_1 \,||\, \mathcal{U}_2\}\varphi$ is different from sequential composition $\{\mathcal{U}_1\}\{\mathcal{U}_2\}\varphi$. In the sequential case, right-hand sides of $\mathcal{U}_2$ are interpreted in the state resulting from $\mathcal{U}_1$. In the parallel case, they are interpreted in the *same* pre-state. The formula $\{\mathcal{U}_1\}\{\mathcal{U}_2\}\varphi$ is equivalent to $\{\mathcal{U}_1 \,||\, \{\mathcal{U}_1\}\mathcal{U}_2\}\varphi$.

$$\text{assignment} \quad \frac{\Gamma \vdash \{\mathcal{U}\}\{x := e\}[\pi\,\omega]\varphi, \Delta}{\Gamma \vdash \{\mathcal{U}\}[\pi\ \text{x=e;}\ \omega]\varphi, \Delta} \quad e \text{ is side effect-free}$$

Fig. 2. SE rule for variable assignment

Figure 2 depicts an SE rule using an update to represent the effect of an assignment of an expression without side effects to variable x. As usual, sequent calculus rules are read "bottom-up", i.e. the rule symbolically executes the assignment by turning it into a symbolic update. SE rules operate on the first active (i.e. executable) statement of a program, here the assignment. The remaining program is contained in $\pi\,\omega$, where the prefix π consists of opening braces, labels, try-blocks, etc., and the postfix ω of closing braces, blocks, and remaining statements. The program $\pi\,\omega$ is a well-formed JAVA program. Sequent calculus rules have zero or more premises (sequents on top of the rule); zero premises characterize a rule that closes a proof case, more than *one* premise causes a proof to split. An example of the latter is the rule for an **if**-statement (see web appendix). The conclusion (bottom part) of a rule consists of exactly one sequent. A rule is *sound* if the correctness of the conclusion follows from the correctness of all premises. A sequent $\Gamma \vdash \Delta$ is correct if the conjunction of the formulas in the set Γ implies the disjunction of those in Δ. Details are in [1].

We need a recently introduced concept of JavaDL for reasoning about loops: *loop scopes* [30]. A loop scope $\circlearrowright_x p\,_x\circlearrowright$ is a scope for a loop body p. It results from SE of a loop **while**(b){p}. The boolean flag x encodes *completion information* about the loop: it is set to TRUE if the loop is *exited* (either normally or by irregular termination) and to FALSE if it *continues* with another iteration. Using the value of x, a postcondition can distinguish both cases.

3.2   Formalization of Abstract Execution

We first give a definition of the domain of *locations* used in **declares**, **accessible** and **assignable** specifications of APSs. The symbol "*allLocs*" is introduced for the "**\everything**" specifier in **accessible** and **assignable** specifications.

Definition 1. *The set $Locs^{Concr}$ of concrete locations consists of program variables x and, for an object o and field identifier f, field locations (o, f). The set $Locs^{Sk}$ of Skolem location sets consists of uninterpreted functions loc^{Sk} representing arbitrary sets of concrete locations $Locs^{Concr}$. We define $Locs = Locs^{Concr} \cup Locs^{Sk} \cup \{allLocs\}$, where the symbol allLocs represents all concrete locations $Locs^{Concr}$. The set of assignable locations is defined as $Locs^{Assgn} = Locs \cup \{loc^! \mid loc \in Locs \setminus \{allLocs\}\}$ which also includes "have-to" locations $loc^!$.*

In Sect. 2, we introduced the specification elements of APSs. These are formalized in the subsequent definition of the logic representation of an APS.

Definition 2. *Let id be an identifier symbol, decls $\subseteq Locs^{Sk}$, assignables $\subseteq Locs^{Assgn}$ and accessibles $\subseteq Locs$. An* Abstract Placeholder Statement *is a tuple*

$$(id, decls, assignables, accessibles, specs)$$

where "specs" represents behavioral specifications and is a tuple of the form:

$$(returnsSpec, excSpec, continuesSpec,$$
$$breaksSpec, continuesSpecLbl, breakSpecLbl)$$

The elements returnsSpec, excSpec, continuesSpec, breaksSpec are optional: they are the empty set or a singleton of a formula specifying when an APS returns, throws an exception, continues, and breaks, respectively. Elements breakSpecLbl, continuesSpecLbl are partial functions from labels to formulas, specifying when an APS continues a labeled loop or breaks from a labeled block or loop.

We write "APS P" short for "the APS with identifier symbol P". Abstract Execution reasons about the behavior of *all possible concrete programs* with which APSs "legally" may be instantiated, formally:

Definition 3. *Let p_a be an abstract program with occurrences of APS symbols $P_1, \ldots P_n$. We call the substitution with concrete programs P_i^0 for each P_i a legal instantiation iff (1) the result from substituting all occurrences of P_i by P_i^0 in p_a is a compilable JAVA program, and (2) all P_i^0 satisfy all constraints of the APSs declaring the P_i.*

Example 1. We substitute P in Listing 3 with "**int** z=result++;". This is legal if z is undeclared in the visible scope. The substitution instantiates the location set "**locals**(P)" with $\{z\}$, affecting further instantiations referring to it. The substitution of "y=z;" for P is illegal: First, it *assigns* a variable which is not contained in its assignable set; second, if z is not contained in the instantiation of args, it *accesses* an undeclared variable z; third, the program is not *compilable* if y and z are undeclared. Let param be in the instantiation of args. Substituting P with "**int** z=result/param;" and Init with b=result/param;" is illegal since *both* could throw an exception, contradicting the axiom.

SE of an APS must over-approximate the behavior of *all* legal instantiations. To model this in the logic, we use second-order *Skolemization*. Given an APS (P, *decls, assignables, accessibles, specs*), we create what we call a *Skolem update* "$\mathcal{U}_P(assignables :\approx accessibles)$" with *Skolem path condition* "$C_P(accessibles)$" fresh for P. The term "fresh for" means that the symbols $\mathcal{U}_P$, C_P are created freshly (as usual for Skolemization) when P first occurs in a proof context, but are re-used each time when P re-occurs. This ensures that each occurrence of an APS symbol represents the *same* program. We define the meaning of Skolem update and Skolem path condition by extending the notion of legal instantiation. In the definition we assume all Skolem location sets in $Locs^{Sk}$ to be instantiated with concrete locations.

$$\text{simpleAERule} \quad \frac{\Gamma \vdash \{\mathcal{U}\}\{\mathcal{U}_P(allLocs :\approx allLocs)\}(C_P(allLocs) \rightarrow [\pi\,\omega]\varphi), \Delta}{\Gamma \vdash \{\mathcal{U}\}[\pi\ \texttt{abstract\_statement}\ \text{P};\ \omega]\varphi, \Delta}$$

Fig. 3. Simple AE rule without abrupt termination

Definition 4. *Let an APS* P *with assignables* $\subseteq Locs^{Assgn} \setminus Locs^{Sk}$, *accessibles* $\subseteq Locs \setminus Locs^{Sk}$ *be given. An abstract update* $\mathcal{U}_P(assignables :\approx accessibles)$ *may be instantiated with any concrete update* $x_1 := t_1 \,\|\, \ldots \,\|\, x_n := t_n$ *for which the following conditions hold: (1) either* $allLocs \in accessibles$ *or the* t_i *depend at most on locations in* accessibles*; (2) either* $allLocs \in assignables$ *or for each* x_i *one of* $x_i \in assignables$ *or* $x_i^! \in assignables$*; (3) for all* $x^! \in assignables$*, there is an* i *such that* $x = x_i$*. An abstract path condition* $C_P(accessibles)$ *may be instantiated with any closed formula* φ *depending at most on locations in* accessibles*.*

Definition 5. *Abstract JavaDL extends JavaDL syntax as follows: (1) updates can be Skolem updates; (2) Skolem path conditions are also formulas; (3) programs can be abstract. Abstract sequents and sequent rules are defined as before, but range over abstract JavaDL formulas.*

A JavaDL sequent calculus rule is *sound* if the validity of the conclusion follows from the validity of all premises [1]. We can leave this definition *unchanged* provided that we define validity of abstract sequents suitably:

Definition 6. *A sequent* S^0 *is a* legal instantiation *of an abstract sequent* S *if* S^0 *results from substituting all Skolem updates, Skolem path conditions and APS symbols in* S *with legal instantiations. An abstract sequent is* valid *iff all its legal instantiations are valid in JavaDL.*

One of the simplest possible AE rules (first mentioned in [29]) is shown in Fig. 3. It is only applicable for an APS whose specification and legal instantiations exclude irregular termination.

Theorem 1. *The Abstract Execution rule* simpleAERule *(Fig. 3) is sound.*

Proof. Let P^0 be any legal instantiation of P. Since P^0 cannot terminate irregularly, symbolic execution transforms the sequent $\Gamma \vdash \{\mathcal{U}\}[\pi\ P^0\ \omega]\varphi, \Delta$ to one of the shape $\Gamma \vdash \{\mathcal{U}\}\{\mathcal{U}^0\}(C^0 \rightarrow [\pi\,\omega]\varphi), \Delta$.[1] Assume the premise of simpleAERule is valid (otherwise, the rule is trivially sound). The instantiations $\mathcal{U}^0$ of $\mathcal{U}_P$ and C^0 of C_P are legal (the *allLocs* location allows reading and writing arbitrary locations). So, by assumption, $\Gamma \vdash \{\mathcal{U}\}\{\mathcal{U}^0\}(C^0 \rightarrow [\pi\,\omega]\varphi), \Delta$ is valid and, by soundness of SE, also the conclusion. Since P^0 was chosen arbitrarily, the abstract sequent in the conclusion of simpleAERule is valid.   □

---

[1] If the statement causes a split, like an **if** statement, we still can combine the arising sequents to a single one by state merging [27].

nonVoidLoopAERule

$\Gamma \vdash \{\mathcal{U}\}\{\mathcal{U}_{\mathsf{P}}(assignables :\approx accessibles)\}$
$\qquad \{\texttt{returns} := returns_0 \,\|\, \texttt{result} := result_0 \,\|\, \texttt{exc} := exc_0 \,\|\,$
$\qquad\quad \texttt{breaks} := breaks_0 \,\|\, \texttt{continues} := continues_0 \,\|\,$
$\qquad\quad \texttt{breaksToLbl\_1} := breaksToLabel1_0 \,\|\, \cdots \,\|\,$
$\qquad\quad \texttt{breaksToLbl\_n} := breaksToLabeln_0\}$

$($ $C_{\mathsf{P}}(accessibles)$
$\quad \wedge\; mutex\,(\texttt{returns}, \texttt{exc} \neq \texttt{null}, \texttt{breaksToLbl\_1}, \cdots, \texttt{breaksToLbl\_n})$
$\quad \wedge\; (\texttt{returns} \doteq \mathrm{TRUE} \leftrightarrow returnsSpec)^? \;\wedge\; (\texttt{exc} \neq \texttt{null} \leftrightarrow excSpec)^?$
$\quad \wedge\; (\texttt{breaks} \doteq \mathrm{TRUE} \leftrightarrow breaksSpec)^?$
$\quad \wedge\; (\texttt{continues} \doteq \mathrm{TRUE} \leftrightarrow continuesSpec)^?$
$\quad \wedge\; (\texttt{breaksToLbl\_1} \doteq \mathrm{TRUE} \leftrightarrow breaksLbl1Spec)^? \;\wedge\; \cdots$
$\quad \wedge\; (\texttt{breaksToLbl\_n} \doteq \mathrm{TRUE} \leftrightarrow breaksLblnSpec)^?$
$\to [\pi\; l_1 : \{\cdots\{\; l_n : \{$
$\qquad \circlearrowleft_x$ `if (returns) return result; if (exc != null) throw exc;`
$\qquad$ `if (breaks) break;` $\qquad$ `if (continues) continue;`
$\qquad$ `if (breaksToLbl_1) break` $l_1;$ $\cdots$ `if (breaksToLbl_n) break` $l_n;$
$\qquad Rest_1 \;_x\circlearrowleft$
$\quad Rest_2 \;\}\} \cdots \} \;\omega]\varphi), \Delta$

$\Gamma \vdash \{\mathcal{U}\}[\pi\; l_1 : \{\cdots\{l_n : \{$
$\qquad \circlearrowleft_x$ `abstract_statement` P; $Rest_1 \;_x\circlearrowleft Rest_2$
$\qquad \}\} \cdots \} \;\omega]\varphi, \Delta$

Fig. 4. AE rule for an APS within a loop scope.

The simpleAERule rule is unsatisfactory: it is too restrictive on irregular termination. It is also too abstract, because the abstract update and path condition in the premise may write and read any location. The abstract update can erase all variables and the whole heap, which prevents proving interesting properties. More useful rules can be obtained for *specific contexts* in which an APS occurs in the conclusion. Depending on the context, legal instantiations can lead to different ways of irregular termination.

Figure 4 shows a rule for AE within a loop scope and a non-void method, but outside the scope of *loop* labels. In contrast to simpleAERule, nonVoidLoopAERule uses the *assignables/accessibles* specifications of the APS syntax. Irregular termination is modeled by **if** statements inside the loop scope in the premise. The conditionals depend on variables initialized with fresh constants in the update after the abstract update. E.g., `returns` is initialized with a constant $returns_0$.

Without a specific context, SE will split at each **if** statement and follow both branches, e.g., one where P returns and one where it does not. Using the behavior specification, this can be fine-tuned: For example, in the path condition in the premise, there is an optional (marked with $^?$) conjunct "$(\texttt{returns} \doteq \mathrm{TRUE} \leftrightarrow returnsSpec)^?$". This lets one control the value of the guard `returns` with the formula *returnsSpec*. The behavior specifications stem from the specifications of the abstract symbol P in the conclusion as detailed in Sect. 2. The function *mutex* is interpreted such that at most one of its arguments is true at any time: here this specifies that there is not more than one reason for a program to terminate irregularly. [2] A proof of the following Theorem 2 is provided in the web appendix.

Theorem 2. *The Abstract Execution rule nonVoidLoopAERule (Fig. 4) is sound.*

Design Principles for AE Rules. The principles underlying the above rules apply to other sequential languages than JAVA as well. To create a new AE rule, we proceed as follows. Given a context in which an APS declaration is the active statement (a loop, method, labeled block, etc.), we model possible side effects of that APS with separate, conditioned SE branches in the premise. For soundness it is crucial not to miss any irregular termination cases. We point out that instead of performing exhaustive structural induction, we merely distinguish *different paths of program completion.* For paths depending on values (as for a **return** or exception), Skolem constants are introduced. The conditioned premises depend on flags that establish a link to the APS's specification; abstract updates and path conditions are added as in nonVoidLoopAERule. AE rules are not specific to the target application of this paper (correctness of refactoring rules), but can be used in any of the areas mentioned in the introduction.

3.3   Abstract Update Simplification

The JavaDL calculus comes with many simplification rules for concrete updates: $\{\mathcal{U}_1\}\{\mathcal{U}_2\}\varphi$ simplifies to $\{\mathcal{U}_1 \,\|\, \{\mathcal{U}_1\}\mathcal{U}_2\}\varphi$, updates applied to formulas without program variables are removed, etc. In addition, spurious updates, such as those assigning variables not occurring in their scope, are removed. To reason about abstract programs, we need corresponding rules for abstract updates.

We designed a set of simplification rules for abstract updates (see Table 2): (1) Remove spurious updates: From the *assignables* part of an abstract update, delete those not occurring in the scope or that are overwritten before being read; (2) two rules handle the interplay between concrete and abstract updates; (3) two rules handle *concatenation* of abstract updates: When we cannot further simplify a formula $\{\mathcal{U}_1\}\{\mathcal{U}_2\}\varphi$, we connect the abstract updates by a concatenation operator, resulting in $\{\mathcal{U}_1 \circ \mathcal{U}_2\}\varphi$. This is not needed for concrete updates which are directly simplified as shown above. Within a concatenation, abstract updates can be commuted if their assignable/accessible specifications do not interfere.

4   Proving the Correctness of Refactoring Techniques

We studied five refactoring techniques from Fowler's classic book [11] and three from the second edition [12]. We choose refactorings operating at the statement

---

[2] It is possible that, for instance, during *returning* an exception is thrown: this simply means that *exception* is the reason for termination.

Table 2. Simplification rules for abstract updates

Simplification Scheme	Description
$\{\mathcal{U}_{\mathsf{P}}(x, \boxed{y} :\approx \ldots)\}\varphi(x) \rightsquigarrow$ $\{\mathcal{U}_{\mathsf{P}}(x :\approx \ldots)\}\varphi(x)$	Ineffective assignables are removed, abstract updates with no assignables dropped.
$\{x_1 := t_1 \mid\mid \boxed{x_2 := t_2} \mid\mid \ldots\}$ $\{\mathcal{U}_{\mathsf{P}}(\ldots, x_1, \ldots :\approx$ $\ldots, \boxed{x_2}, \ldots)\}\varphi \rightsquigarrow$ $\{x_1 := t_1 \mid\mid \ldots\}$ $\{\mathcal{U}_{\mathsf{P}}(\ldots, x_1, \ldots :\approx$ $\ldots, \boxed{t_2}, \ldots)\}\{x_2 := t_2\}\varphi$	Applies variable assignments to the accessibles of the abstract update and pushes down elementary updates not assigned by the abstract update. Elementary updates that *have to* be assigned (overwritten) are dropped later.
$\{\mathcal{U}_{\mathsf{P}}(\ldots, \boxed{y}, \ldots :\approx \ldots)\}$ $\{\ldots \mid\mid \boxed{x := y} \mid\mid \ldots\}\varphi(x) \rightsquigarrow$ $\{\mathcal{U}_{\mathsf{P}}(\ldots, \boxed{x}, \ldots :\approx \ldots)\}$ $\{\ldots \mid\mid \ldots\}\varphi(x)$	Eliminates a renaming substitution "y for x": Since the concrete update assigns to x a value chosen by $\mathcal{U}_{\mathsf{P}}$ (which *has to* assign y), the abstract update can as well directly choose that value. Sound because y is not contained in φ.
$\{\mathcal{U}_{\mathsf{P}}\}\{\mathcal{U}_{\mathsf{Q}}\}\varphi \rightsquigarrow \{\mathcal{U}_{\mathsf{P}} \circ \mathcal{U}_{\mathsf{Q}}\}\varphi$	Sequential to "concatenated" update application.
$\mathcal{U}_{\mathsf{P}}(assgn_1 :\approx access_1)\circ$ $\mathcal{U}_{\mathsf{Q}}(assgn_2 :\approx access_2) \rightsquigarrow$ $\mathcal{U}_{\mathsf{Q}}(assgn_2 :\approx access_2)\circ$ $\mathcal{U}_{\mathsf{P}}(assgn_1 :\approx access_1)$	Abstract updates within concatenations can be commuted if their assignable and accessible specifiers are *independent*; i.e., $assgn_1$ has to be disjoint from $assgn_2$ and $access_2$, and similarly vice versa.

level, because they are directly expressible in JavaDL and—for the time being—exclude techniques that reorganize class hierarchies, rename constructs, or move methods. For each of the eight techniques we formalized the starting point and the result of the refactoring as a suitably specified abstract program (see Sect. 2), and then proved their *equivalence* with the AE calculus discussed in Sect. 3. Thus, we obtain soundness of, for example, *Extract Method* at the same time as of its inverse, *Inline Method*. All proofs are fully mechanized in KeY [1].

Methodology. For each refactoring, we create a JAVA class `Refactor` with two public methods: `before` contains an abstract program representing the input to the refactoring, `after` the refactored result. We start with minimal annotations in the occurring APSs including **declares** directives and standard return and assignable specifications for the abstract expressions idiom. The following JavaDL formula performs AE of an abstract program p on a `Refactor` object o and records the result ("Flag" in the postcondition is explained later):

$$\text{AE}(p, \text{Flag}) = \{\text{result} := result_0 \mid\mid \ldots\}$$
$$\langle \textbf{try} \; \{\text{result=o.p(result,}\ldots\text{)@Refactor;}\}$$
$$\textbf{catch} \; (\text{Throwable t}) \; \{\text{result=t;}\}\rangle Post(\text{result}, \text{Flag}) \tag{1}$$

Equivalence of the original and the refactored program is established by proving the formula "AE(`before`, TRUE) $\leftrightarrow$ AE(`after`, TRUE)". This is loaded into KeY and an automatic proof is started. In all but one refactoring technique (first

Listing 4: Before	Listing 5: After
| ```
done = false; i = 0;
while (!done && i < threshold) {
  if (condition) {
    abstract_statement Body;
    done = true;
  }
  i++;
}
return result;
``` | ```
i = 0;
while (i < threshold) {
  if (condition) {
    abstract_statement Body;
    break;
  }
  i++;
}
return result;
``` |

Fig. 5. The *Remove Control Flag* Refactoring Technique

in Table 3), the proof cannot be finished and open goals remain. The reason is—quite simply—that Fowler's refactoring techniques are not sound in general [10]. As he points out, they rely on robust test suites and a "try-compile-and-test" loop trusted to unveil potential faults introduced by a refactoring.

In our setting we have the opportunity to restrict the programs that can be soundly refactored via suitable annotations of the APSs used to describe refactoring source and target. Fowler in most cases does not mention these restrictions. Fortunately, inspection of uncloseable proof goals provides clear hints on the nature of the required annotations.

A typical example is when all open proof goals expect an APS P to throw an exception (assumption exc $\neq$ null occurs in each unprovable goal). This is addressed by adding a constraint on P that forbids to throw exceptions. Another common situation concerns too liberal **accessible/assignable** specifications. These lead to open goals that contain a sequent of the form $\{\mathcal{U}\}\varphi \vdash \{\mathcal{U}'\}\varphi$ that becomes valid when the abstract updates $\mathcal{U}$ and $\mathcal{U}'$ are identical. Any differences give hints on possible annotations that permit to close the proof.

Once a proof is complete, the formalization of a refactoring should be checked for validity, i.e. whether the intention of the refactoring technique has been faithfully captured. Specifications should not be more restrictive than necessary and permit substituting non-trivial programs for APSs. For example, it is easy, but useless, to find a proof with "**assignable \nothing**;" specifications. For each behavioral restriction, there should be a convincing justification. We discovered non-trivial and justifiable restrictions for almost all the investigated refactoring techniques (summarized in Table 3). Source code samples are in the appendix.

Complexity of Checking Legal Substitutions. A closed equivalence proof about abstract programs asserts that those programs behave equivalently for all legal substitutions of concrete programs for APS symbols (Definition 3). Consequently, for each concrete program one must check that all the constraints specified in APSs are satisfied. These include syntactic restrictions (e.g., when inlining a method, there are no recursive calls in the body) as well as behavioral ones. The latter are not necessarily automatically checkable or even decidable. For example, to decide whether a program throws an exception, is equivalent to reachability. Even so, a formalized and proven refactoring technique makes its

Table 3. Studied refactoring techniques and discovered behavioral constraints.

Refactoring Technique	Discovered Restrictions	Justification & Remarks
Consolidate duplicate conditional fragments (Extract Postfix) [11]	none	—
Consolidate duplicate conditional fragments (Extract Prefix) [11]	• **if** guard may only throw exc. if prefix terminates normally; • pulled out statement may assign heap and parameters iff guard does not access it.	Irregular termination in both guard and prefix affect final result. Influence on accessibles of guard can change control flow (whether **if** or **else** is taken).
Consolidate duplicate conditional fragments (Postfix of **try-catch** to **finally**) [11]	• Program in **try** block may not return; • program in **catch** block may not return or throw exception.	A **finally** block is always executed, even after a return. This changes the returned result before and after the refactoring.
Consolidate duplicate conditional fragments (Postfix of **try-catch**, no **finally**) [11]	none	Fowler talks about moving the postfix "to the final block", leaving unspecified whether this refers to the **finally** block or to the statements after **try**. Only in the latter case no restrictions apply.
Decompose Conditional [11]	Special case of "Extract Method", see below.	
Extract Method [11]	Extracted fragment • must not return; • may only assign heap and a local variable.	A return after extraction does not affect the top-level method.
Replace Exception with Test [11]	There has to be a "rollback" program in the **catch/else** block, program in **try/if** may only assign variables reset by that program.	The program in **try/if** may change part of the state before throwing an exception, therefore the result after the exception/test can differ.
Move Statements to Callers [12]	Neither the moved statement nor the remaining program may return.	If the remaining program in the called method returns early, the moved one is not executed after, but before refactoring.
Slide Statements [12]	All programs participating in the sliding, i.e. the swapped parts and the one in the middle • must not return or throw an exception; • must be *independent*.	*Independent* means the participating programs write to locations that the others do not access. Abrupt termination would change the result.
Split Loop [12]	Explained in text.	Example with loop.
Remove Control Flag [11]	Explained in text.	Example with loop.

requirements *explicit* that before were mentioned only informally (if at all). Not in general, but in practice quite often, constraints can be proven in KeY.

Multiple Specifications. It can make sense to create *multiple* formalizations of the same refactoring technique. The restrictions that ensure soundness can differ depending on (1) the program *context* (inside/outside a loop or labeled block), and (2) the termination mode (normal, exceptional, break, etc.). The "consolidate duplicate conditional fragments" technique in Table 3 exemplifies this.

Programs with Loops. We studied two refactoring techniques involving loops: *Remove Control Flag* [11] and *Split Loop* [12]. To handle loops we make use of the Flag in formula (1) to separate runs leaving the loop from those leading to further executions of the loop body. The value of Flag is controlled by the loop scope parameter (the invariant rule in Fig. 7 in the appendix contains details).

The *Remove Control Flag* refactoring in Fig. 5 is interesting, because the number of runs of the loop before and after the refactoring differs by one (the guard needs to be executed one extra time before). This complicates the proof since we obtain $Post(\_result, \text{FALSE})$ for one case and $Post(\_result, \text{TRUE})$ for the other. We solve this by harmonizing the iteration structure via an *unrolling technique* [16] and an intermediate refactoring. Alternatively, one can code the unrolling inside a modified loop invariant rule (Fig. 9 in the appendix).

The *Split Loop* refactoring splits a loop with two independent parts into two successive loops. We had to supply several annotations to the APSs. For instance, the first part of the loop body must not break or continue (since otherwise, the second part is skipped, which is not the case after the refactoring), while the second part must not return, throw an exception, or break, since then we would have to relate runs continuing loop iteration with others exiting the loop.

Performance. All proofs are performed automatically in KeY without user interaction. For the refactorings with loops, currently small proof scripts ($\approx$ 40 lines) are needed for loop coupling. The proofs have 2,900–40,000 nodes (median: 7,100) and take 6–300 s (median: 29 s) to complete. All problem files with detailed statistics, together with a KeY version implementing AE, are available at key-project.org/papers/ae/.

5   Related Work

The idea of Abstract Execution was first mentioned in our earlier work [29], where it is used to formalize the correctness of compilation rules of a JAVA-to-LLVM IR compiler. There, APSs could not be annotated and irregular termination was excluded; also, every APS can assign and access any location. In the present paper we lift these restrictions, provide an implementation and a case study. Abstract execution of APSs can be seen as a generalization of *abstract operation contracts* [6,15] to abstract *block* contracts. In the former, contracts are abstract, but programs concrete; we generalize this to abstract *programs*. This amounts to encoding limited second-order inference (no induction, no higher-order quantification) over programs into first-order (dynamic) logic.

The principal use cases for AE reside in the area of *relational verification* [4], which includes, but is not limited to: general-purpose relational proofs about programs [2,16], correctness proofs for refactorings [13], regression verification [14], proven-correct compilation [21,31] and compiler optimizations [18,23], program synthesis [28], information flow properties (e.g., by self-composition [3,9]).

There are several approaches to prove relational properties of *concrete* programs (e.g., LLRÊVE [16]). Barthe et al. [2] propose the construction of *product programs* from two variable-disjoint programs as a general-purpose technique for verifying relational program properties. After execution of the product program, the result is checked for correctness, i.e. equality. This works even for structurally different programs. Instead, we execute both programs in isolation in an equivalence proof. This has the drawback of requiring a certain structural similarity of the programs and explicit loop coupling, but it is more resilient in the presence of irregular or non-termination. Product programs and AE are not mutually exclusive: One can create a *product* of *abstract* programs.

Garrido and Meseguer [13] prove correctness of three JAVA refactoring techniques based on an executable Maude semantics of JAVA. They focus on refactorings not targeted by us (e.g., *Pull Up Field*). It is unclear whether this approach works for statement-based refactorings including loops. Alive [23] permits proving automatically the correctness of "peephole optimizations" for LLVM. While this approach reasons about classes of programs, it is parametric only in register names and imposes other serious restrictions (e.g., no loops). Eilertsen et al. [10] generate semantic correctness assertions that ensure preservation of program semantics after refactoring. They work on concrete programs and perform run-time, not static checking.

Godlin and Strichman [14] perform "Regression Verification" by transforming loops into recursive functions and replacing recursive calls with uninterpreted function symbols. The latter are similar to APSs, however, side effects or irregular termination cannot be modeled, because functions are pure. Mechtaev et al. [25] propose a mechanism for proving existential second-order properties based on symbolic functions. Their goal is to find existential witnesses for those functions by synthesis from a user-specified grammar. In contrast, we aim at *universal* properties, and APSs represent statements (with side effects), not functions. The PEC system [18] for proving the correctness of compiler optimizations uses *meta variables* ranging over expressions, variables and statements. The latter are "single-entry-single-exit", whereas APSs can have multiple exit points, including irregular termination. In addition, we permit annotations that constrain possible behavior. The property to be proven in [18] is a certain bisimulation relation which is somewhat inflexible and requires lockstep execution.

6 Conclusion and Future Work

We proposed *Abstract Execution* of programs that contain APS symbols, a new software analysis principle extending symbolic execution. AE permits to *auto-*

matically reason about partially unspecified programs. APSs allow irregular termination and include specification of assignable and accessible locations as well as of termination behavior. This generalizes other approaches going into similar directions. We implemented our method and applied it to eight JAVA refactoring techniques, of which two require reasoning about loops. Our formalization of the refactoring techniques makes implicit requirements explicit. It helps to better understand and safely apply refactorings. We plan to investigate how to support structurally different programs (e.g., comparing iterative and recursive versions of the same algorithm), concurrent programs, and we intend to look at other application areas. To prove the correctness of compiler optimizations automatically using AE is a natural follow-up to our work on refactoring techniques.

References

1. Ahrendt, W., Beckert, B., Bubel, R., Hähnle, R., Schmitt, P., Ulbrich, M. (eds.): Deductive Software Verification-The KeY Book: From Theory to Practice. LNCS, vol. 10001. Springer, Heidelberg (2016). https://doi.org/10.1007/978-3-319-49812-6

2. Barthe, G., Crespo, J.M., Kunz, C.: Relational verification using product programs. In: Butler, M., Schulte, W. (eds.) FM 2011. LNCS, vol. 6664, pp. 200–214. Springer, Heidelberg (2011). https://doi.org/10.1007/978-3-642-21437-0_17

3. Barthe, G., D'Argenio, P.R., Rezk, T.: Secure information flow by self-composition. In: 17th IEEE Computer Security Foundations Workshop, CSFW-17, Pacific Grove, CA, USA, pp. 100–114. IEEE Computer Society (2004)

4. Beckert, B., Ulbrich, M.: Trends in relational program verification. In: Principled Software Development - Essays Dedicated to Arnd Poetzsch-Heffter on the Occasion of his 60th Birthday, pp. 41–58 (2018)

5. Boyer, R.S., Elspas, B., Levitt, K.N.: SELECT–a formal system for testing and debugging programs by symbolic execution. ACM SIGPLAN Not. **10**(6), 234–245 (1975)

6. Bubel, R., Hähnle, R., Pelevina, M.: Fully abstract operation contracts. In: Margaria, T., Steffen, B. (eds.) ISoLA 2014. LNCS, vol. 8803, pp. 120–134. Springer, Heidelberg (2014). https://doi.org/10.1007/978-3-662-45231-8_9

7. Burstall, R.M.: Proving properties of programs by structural induction. Comput. J. **12**(1), 41–48 (1969)

8. Burstall, R.M.: Program proving as hand simulation with a little induction. In: Information Processing 1974, pp. 308–312. Elsevier/North-Holland (1974)

9. Darvas, Á., Hähnle, R., Sands, D.: A theorem proving approach to analysis of secure information flow. In: Hutter, D., Ullmann, M. (eds.) SPC 2005. LNCS, vol. 3450, pp. 193–209. Springer, Heidelberg (2005). https://doi.org/10.1007/978-3-540-32004-3_20

10. Eilertsen, A.M., Bagge, A.H., Stolz, V.: Safer refactorings. In: Proceedings of 7th International Symposium on Leveraging Applications of Formal Methods, ISoLA, pp. 517–531 (2016)

11. Fowler, M.: Refactoring: Improving the Design of Existing Code. Object Technology Series. Addison-Wesley (1999)

12. Fowler, M.: Refactoring: Improving the Design of Existing Code. Addison-Wesley Signature Series, 2nd edn. Addison-Wesley Professional (2018)

13. Garrido, A., Meseguer, J.: Formal specification and verification of Java refactorings. In: Proceedings of 6th IEEE International Workshop on Source Code Analysis and Manipulation, SCAM 2006, pp. 165–174. IEEE Computer Society (2006)
14. Godlin, B., Strichman, O.: Regression verification: proving the equivalence of similar programs. Softw. Test. Verif. Reliab. **23**(3), 241–258 (2013)
15. Hähnle, R., Schaefer, I., Bubel, R.: Reuse in software verification by abstract method calls. In: Bonacina, M.P. (ed.) CADE 2013. LNCS (LNAI), vol. 7898, pp. 300–314. Springer, Heidelberg (2013). https://doi.org/10.1007/978-3-642-38574-2_21
16. Kiefer, M., Klebanov, V., Ulbrich, M.: Relational program reasoning using compiler ir - combining static verification and dynamic analysis. J. Autom. Reas. **60**(3), 337–363 (2018)
17. King, J.C.: Symbolic execution and program testing. Commun. ACM **19**(7), 385–394 (1976)
18. Kundu, S., Tatlock, Z., Lerner, S.: Proving optimizations correct using parameterized program equivalence. Proc. PLDI **2009**, 327–337 (2009)
19. Lanzinger, F.: A divide-and-conquer strategy with block and loop contracts for deductive program verification. Bachelor thesis, Institute of Theoretical Informatics, Karlsruhe Institute of Technology, April 2018
20. Leavens, G.T., et al.: JML reference manual, draft revision 2344, May 2013. http://www.eecs.ucf.edu/leavens/JML//OldReleases/jmlrefman.pdf
21. Leroy, X.: Formal verification of a realistic compiler. Commun. ACM **52**(7), 107–115 (2009)
22. London, R.L.: Correctness of a compiler for a LISP subset. In: Proceedings of ACM Conference on Proving Assertions About Programs, pp. 121–127. ACM (1972)
23. Lopes, N.P., Menendez, D., Nagarakatte, S., Regehr, J.: Practical verification of peephole optimizations with alive. Commun. ACM **61**(2), 84–91 (2018)
24. McCarthy, J., Painter, J.: Correctness of a compiler for arithmetic expressions. Math. Aspects Comput. Sci. **1**, 33–41 (1967)
25. Mechtaev, S., Griggio, A., Cimatti, A., Roychoudhury, A.: Symbolic execution with existential second-order constraints. In: Proceedings of 2018 Joint Meeting on European Software Engineering Conference and Symposium on the Foundations of Software Engineering, pp. 389–399 (2018)
26. Necula, G.C.: Proof-carrying code. In: Proceedings of 24th ACM Symposium on Principles of Programming Languages, Paris, France, pp. 106–119. ACM Press, January 1997
27. Scheurer, D., Hähnle, R., Bubel, R.: A general lattice model for merging symbolic execution branches. In: Ogata, K., Lawford, M., Liu, S. (eds.) ICFEM 2016. LNCS, vol. 10009, pp. 57–73. Springer, Cham (2016). https://doi.org/10.1007/978-3-319-47846-3_5
28. Srivastava, S., Gulwani, S., Foster, J.S.: From program verification to program synthesis. In: Proceedings of 37th POPL, pp. 313–326 (2010)
29. Steinhöfel, D., Hähnle, R.: Modular, correct compilation with automatic soundness proofs. In: Margaria, T., Steffen, B. (eds.) ISoLA 2018. LNCS, vol. 11244, pp. 424–447. Springer, Cham (2018). https://doi.org/10.1007/978-3-030-03418-4_25
30. Steinhöfel, D., Wasser, N.: A new invariant rule for the analysis of loops with nonstandard control flows. In: Polikarpova, N., Schneider, S. (eds.) IFM 2017. LNCS, vol. 10510, pp. 279–294. Springer, Cham (2017). https://doi.org/10.1007/978-3-319-66845-1_18
31. Tan, Y.K., Myreen, M.O., Kumar, R., Fox, A., Owens, S., Norrish, M.: A new verified compiler backend for CakeML. In: Proceedings of 21st International Conference on Functional Programming, pp. 60–73. ACM (2016)

Static Analysis for Detecting High-Level Races in RTOS Kernels

Abhishek Singh[2], Rekha Pai[1(✉)], Deepak D'Souza[1], and Meenakshi D'Souza[2]

[1] Indian Institute of Science, Bangalore, India
{rekhapai,deepakd}@iisc.ac.in
[2] International Institute of Information Technology, Bangalore, Bangalore, India .
abhishek.singh1@iiitb.org, meenakshi@iiitb.ac.in

Abstract. We propose a static analysis based approach for detecting high-level races in RTOS kernels popularly used in safety-critical embedded software. High-Level races are indicators of atomicity violations and can lead to erroneous software behaviour with serious consequences. Hitherto techniques for detecting high-level races have relied on model-checking approaches, which are inefficient and apriori unsound. In contrast we propose a technique based on static analysis that is both efficient and sound. The technique is based on the notion of disjoint blocks recently introduced in Chopra et al. [5]. We evaluate our technique on three popular RTOS kernels and show that it is effective in detecting races, many of them harmful, with a high rate of precision.

Keywords: Static analysis · RTOS kernel ·
Interrupt-driven programs · High-level data races

1 Introduction

In a multi-threaded program, a high-level race occurs when two user-specified pieces of code (or "critical accesses"), which are meant to access a common set of variables or data-structures mutually exclusively, end up "overlapping" or being interleaved with one another in an execution. High-Level races are often the cause of atomicity violations and unexpected erroneous behaviour of the software.

Our focus in this paper is on high-level races that occur in the kernel API functions of Real-Time Operating Systems (RTOSs), which are often used in embedded software. The kernel APIs of an RTOS are typically invoked by multiple task threads or Interrupt Service Routines (ISRs) of an application, in an interleaved fashion on a single processor core. Detecting high-level races in the kernel APIs of an RTOS is at once important and challenging. Important because these kernels are often used in safety-critical embedded applications in aerospace, automotive, and medical domains. High-Level races here may lead to serious undesirable consequences. Also, a single race in the kernel (as against an application) could potentially impact *many* applications that use it. Finally,

© Springer Nature Switzerland AG 2019
M. H. ter Beek et al. (Eds.): FM 2019, LNCS 11800, pp. 337–353, 2019.
https://doi.org/10.1007/978-3-030-30942-8_21

the problem is challenging because these kernels invariably make use of non-standard synchronization mechanisms like disabling/enabling interrupts, suspending the scheduler, and often rely on the relative scheduling priorities of specialized threads like callbacks and software interrupts (SWIs).

Previous techniques for finding high-level races in embedded kernels have typically relied on model-checking based approaches, where it is easier to model the ad-hoc synchronization and context-switching semantics. Here one constructs a model for a "most general" application A that non-deterministically exercises all the kernel API functions, and uses the model-checker to exhaustively search for high-level races. While this is a precise approach with a very low rate of false positives, it has some inherent drawbacks. Firstly, the most general application A must fix *a priori* the number of threads of each type (task, ISR, etc). This choice, unless backed by an intricate, RTOS-specific, meta-argument proving sufficiency of this choice, as in [14], may lead to unsoundness of the analysis in the following sense: it could be that A uses 2 task threads, while a certain high-level race needs 3 or more task threads to orchestrate it. The model-checker would thus unsoundly declare that such a race does not occur. Secondly, even for a fixed number of threads, the state-space may prove to be prohibitively large for the model-checker to complete its search [14].

In this paper we propose a sound and efficient technique based on static analysis of code, to solve this problem. Our technique is based on the notion of *disjoint-blocks* proposed recently in [5]. Much like two pieces of code in a classical multi-threaded program that occur between the acquire and release of a common lock, two patterns of code form a pair of disjoint-blocks if they are guaranteed never to "overlap" in any execution of the program. Our high-level race detection algorithm essentially does a disjoint-block analysis of the kernel API functions, and then checks for each pair of conflicting critical accesses whether they are "covered" by some pair of disjoint-blocks.

We have implemented and evaluated our approach on three important contemporary RTOS kernels. The first is an ARINC 653 based proprietary RTOS of an Indian aeronautics major, which is used to manage navigation systems of its aircraft. This RTOS, which we call "P-RTOS" for confidentiality reasons, is characterized by its use of *callback* routines, which are threads of priority in between tasks and ISRs. The other two are among the most popular open-source RTOSs – TI-RTOS [13] from Texas Instruments, and FreeRTOS [4] from Real-Time Engineers. TI-RTOS is distinguished by its use of software interrupts (SWIs). Our analysis finds several harmful high-level races in each of these RTOSs in a running time of a few seconds, and with a low rate of false positives. We have been in touch with the developers of these RTOSs and many of these are issues they would like to fix.

2   Overview

We begin with an overview of our contributions with an illustrative example from the P-RTOS kernel. A P-RTOS application can create a bunch of task, callback, and ISR threads, which execute in an interleaved manner, subject to some restrictions. Firstly, callbacks need to be "activated" before they can execute. Threads may pre-empt each other, subject to the following rules: (a) a task cannot be preempted by another task if `LockPreemption` is in force, (b) callbacks cannot execute when `LockPreemption` is in force, and (c) ISRs and callbacks cannot be preempted – once begun, they run to completion.

Figure 1 shows a part of the P-RTOS kernel code. The kernel API function `ProcessResume` is invoked with a pointer to the Process Control Block (PCB) of a task, and the routine first makes sure the given task is in the delayed queue (`WAITING` state). It then goes on to move the task from the delayed queue to the ready queue. This latter part is done in the scope of a `LockPreemption` command. The `Tick_ISR` is an ISR thread that services the timer interrupt. Its main job is to increment the tick count, and then activate the `TimeDelay` callback. The `TimeDelay` callback essentially scans through the delayed queue, moving tasks whose time-to-awake has past, to the ready queue.

As a developer, we may mark the lines 3–9 in `ProcessResume` as a *critical access A*. This piece of code accesses kernel structures like the delayed and ready queue, and clearly must be done "exclusively" from other critical accesses to one of these structures, failing which the data structures may end up in an inconsistent or erroneous state. Similarly the lines 2–16 in `TimeDelay` may be considered as a critical accesss B to the delayed and ready queues, as well as the tick count variable.

We say a high-level race involving the critical accesses A and B occurs, if there is an execution of some application program which exercises these kernel routines in such a way that the critical accesses end up interleaving (or overlapping) in the execution.

Consider now a P-RTOS application with two tasks P and Q. Let us say the current tick count (recorded in the kernel variable `Tick_Count`) has value 100, and task Q is in the delayed queue with a time-to-awake of 101. Task P which is currently running, invokes the `ProcessResume` kernel routine with task Q as the argument. The check in line 3 passes since Q is in the delayed queue and its state is `WAITING`. However, just before it can lock preemption in line 5, a timer interrupt arrives and the `Tick_ISR` runs, incrementing the tick count to 101 and activating the `TimeDelay` callback. Since preemption has not yet been locked, the `TimeDelay` routine runs and moves task Q from the delayed to the ready queue. When execution switches back to task P, it tries to remove Q from the delayed list in line 7. Since it is trying to remove a task not present in the list, this causes an exception.

This scenario exhibits a high-level race involving the critical accesses A and B (notice that the code segments A and B overlap in time in this scenario). Moreover, this race is a *harmful* one, since we reach a system state (namely with the exception condition) which cannot be reached in any execution in which the two critical accesses are done *serially* (i.e. without overlap).

We now describe our technique to report high-level races. The two colored blocks comprising lines 6–9 in `ProcessResume` and lines 1–16 in `TimeDelay`, constitute a pair of *disjoint-blocks*, since by the execution semantics they can *never* overlap in an execution. This is because the first block is in the scope of a lock preemption and hence cannot be interrupted by a callback thread. Similarly, the second block – being part of a callback thread – cannot be interrupted by any thread. Our race detection algorithm essentially checks whether the critical accesses A and B are "covered" by pairs of disjoint blocks (see Sect. 5 for details). In this case they are not, and we declare A and B to be potentially high-level racy.

We note that a better programming discipline would have put the lock preemption just before line 3 instead of line 5. In this case the critical accesses would have been covered by disjoint-blocks, and our algorithm would have reported the pair to be safe.

```
ProcessResume(struct Pcb_t* Pcb){        TimeDelay(void){
1. int eRet = VALID_MODE;                1. ···
   ...                                   2. Ptr_delayq = delayq.HeadPtr;
2. // Task must be in WAITING state      3. while (Ptr_delayq != NULL){
3. if(Pcb->eState == WAITING){           4.   if(Ptr_delayq->Pcb->TimeoutTicks
4.   // Disable process scheduling                              <=Tick_Count){
5.   LockPreemption();                   5.     Pcb = Ptr_delayq->Pcb;
6.   Pcb->TimeoutTicks = 0;              6.     RemoveFromDelayQ(Pcb);
7.   RemoveFromDelayQ(Pcb);              7.     Pcb->TimeoutTicks = 0;
8.   Pcb->eState = READY_TO_RUN;         8.     Pcb->TimeoutFlag = TRUE;
9.   InsertToReadyQueue(Pcb);            9.     Pcb->eState = READY_TO_RUN;
10.  UnlockPreemption();                 10.    InsertToReadyQueue(Pcb);
11.}                                     11.    Ptr_delayq = Ptr_delayq->Next_ptr;
12.···                                   12.  }
}                                        13. else
                                         14.    Ptr_delayq = NULL;
Tick_ISR(void){                          15. }
1. ···                                   16.}
2. Tick_Count++;                         17.···
3. // Activate TimeDelay callback        }
4. Activate(&TimeDelay);
5. ···
}
```

Fig. 1. An example adapted from the P-RTOS kernel exhibiting a high level race.

3   Interrupt-Driven Programs with Callbacks

We describe a multi-threaded programming language that is meant to capture the semantics of a P-RTOS application with calls to the kernel routines inlined. We abstract away from priorities among tasks as they play no role in our analysis of the P-RTOS kernel routines. We refer to programs in this language as Interrupt-Driven Programs with Callbacks (or IDC programs for short).

IDC programs have a fixed finite number of threads and a fixed number of global variables. Each thread is of one of three types: *task* threads that are like standard threads, *ISR* threads that represent interrupt service routines, and *callback* threads are activated by ISR threads. There is a *main* thread, which is a task thread and is the only task thread enabled initially. The *main* thread can initialize variables and then invoke the `start` command to enable the scheduler and begin execution.

Task threads can be preempted by other task threads (whenever interrupts are not disabled and the scheduler is not suspended) or by ISR threads (whenever interrupts are not disabled) or by callback threads (whenever interrupts are not disabled and the scheduler is not suspended). Callback threads are initially disabled, and can be enabled by an `activate` command from an ISR. Activated callbacks can execute whenever interrupts are not disabled, and the scheduler is not suspended. ISR and callback threads cannot be preempted, and must run to completion. A callback thread gets disabled after its execution and can be enabled again by an activate command from an ISR.

The threads access a set of shared global variables some of which are used as "synchronization flags", using a standard set of commands like assignment statements of the form `x := e`, conditional statements (`if-then-else`), loop statements (`while`), etc. The threads can also use commands like `lockpreem`, `unlockpreem` (to suspend and resume the scheduler, respectively) and `disableint`, `enableint` (to disable and enable interrupts, respectively). Table 1 shows the set of basic statements $cmd_{V,T}$ over a set of variables V and a set of threads T.

Table 1. Basic IDC program statements $cmd_{V,T}$ over variables V and threads T

Command	Description
`skip`	Do nothing
`x := e`	Assign the value of expression e to variable $x \in V$
`assume(b)`	Enabled only if expression b evaluates to *true*, acts like `skip`
`start`	Enable task and ISR threads for execution
`activate(t)`	Enable callback thread t for execution
`disableint`	Disable interrupts and context switches
`enableint`	Enable interrupts and context switches
`lockpreem`	Suspend the scheduler (callbacks and task threads cannot preempt the current thread)
`unlockpreem`	Resume the scheduler

Formally we represent an IDC program P as a tuple $P = (V, T)$ where V is a finite set of integer variables and T is a finite set of named threads. Each thread $t \in T$ has a *type* which is one of *task* or *ISR* or *callback*, and an associated control flow graph of the form $G_t = (L_t, s_t, inst_t)$ where L_t is a finite set of *locations* of thread t, $s_t \in L_t$ is the *start* location of thread t, $inst_t \subseteq L_t \times cmd_{V,T} \times L_t$ is a finite set of *instructions* of thread t. For an instruction $\iota = \langle l, c, l' \rangle \in inst_t$, we refer to l and l' as the source and target location of ι respectively and $tid(\iota)$ to mean the thread t. For a function $f : A \to B$, we define $f[a \mapsto b]$ as a function $g : A \to B$ where $g(a') = f(a')$ if $a' \neq a$ and $g(a) = b$. For a Boolean or an arithmetic expression e over the set of variables V, and a valuation $\phi : V \to \mathbb{Z}$, we define $[\![e]\!]_\phi$ to be the value obtained by evaluating e under the valuation ϕ.

Figure 2 shows an example IDC program with a `main` thread, a task thread called `cons`, an ISR thread called `service-packet`, and a callback thread `prod`. The ISR thread runs whenever an interrupt corresponding to a packet arrives. It activates the `prod` callback, which transfers the packets into items. The `cons` thread consumes the items, making sure to lock preemption while it does so.

We define the operational semantics of an IDC program using a labeled transition system (LTS). Let $P = (V, T)$ be a program. We define an LTS $\mathcal{T}_P = (Q, \Sigma, s, \Rightarrow)$ corresponding to P where,

- Q is a set of states of the form $(pc, enab, rt, it, id, pl, \phi)$ where $pc \in T \to L$ is the program counter giving the current location of each thread, $\phi \in V \to \mathbb{Z}$ is a valuation for the variables, $enab \subseteq T$ is the set of enabled threads, $rt \in T$ is the currently running thread, $it \in T$ is the task thread which is interrupted when the scheduler is suspended; and id and pl are Boolean values telling us whether interrupts are disabled ($id = true$) or not ($id = false$) and whether the scheduler is suspended ($pl = true$) or not ($pl = false$).
- The set of labels Σ is the set of instructions $inst_P$ of P.
- The initial state s is $(\lambda t.s_t, \{main\}, main, main, true, true, \lambda x.0)$. In the initial state, all the threads are at their entry locations, only the $main$ thread is enabled and running, the interrupted task is set to $main$ (this is a dummy value as it is used only when the scheduler is suspended), interrupts are disabled, the scheduler is suspended and the initial environment sets all variables to 0.
- For an instruction $\iota = \langle l, c, l' \rangle$ in $inst_P$, with $tid(\iota) = t$, we define $(pc, enab, rt, it, id, pl, \phi) \Rightarrow_\iota (pc', enab', rt', it', id', pl', \phi')$ iff the following conditions are satisfied:
  - $t \in enab$;
  - if rt is an ISR or callback thread then $t = rt$;
  - if rt is a task thread, the conditions on t are defined in Table 2 for different values of id and pl.
  - Based on the command c, the following conditions must be satisfied:
    * If c is the `skip` command then $\phi' = \phi$, $id' = id$ and $pl' = pl$.
    * If c is the `start` command then $t = main$ and $\phi' = \phi$.
    * If c is a command of the form `assume(b)` then $[\![b]\!]_\phi = true$, $\phi' = \phi$, $id' = id$ and $pl' = pl$.
    * If c is an assignment statement of the form x := e then $\phi' = \phi[x \mapsto [\![e]\!]_\phi]$, $id' = id$ and $pl' = pl$.
    * If c is a `activate(u)` command then t must be an ISR thread, u must be a callback thread, $\phi' = \phi$, $id' = id$, and $pl' = pl$.
    * If c is a `disableint` command then $\phi' = \phi$, $id' = true$ and $pl' = pl$.
    * If c is a `enableint` command then $\phi' = \phi$, $id' = false$ and $pl' = pl$.
    * If c is a `lockpreem` command then $\phi' = \phi$, $id' = id$, and $pl' = true$.
    * If c is a `unlockpreem` command then $\phi' = \phi$, $id' = id$, and $pl' = false$.

* The program counter pc and the set of enabled threads $enab$ are updated as follows. If c is $\texttt{activate(u)}$, $enab' = enab \cup \{u\}$, $pc' = pc$. If c is the last statement of t, a callback, $enab' = enab \setminus \{t\}$, $pc' = pc[t \mapsto s_t]$. If c is the last statement of t, an ISR, $enab' = enab$, $pc' = pc[t \mapsto s_t]$. In all other cases, $enab' = enab$, $pc' = pc[t \mapsto l']$.

• In addition, the transitions set the new running thread rt' and interrupted task it' as follows. If t is an ISR thread, pl is true, and ι is the first instruction of t then $it' = rt$, $rt' = t$. If t is an ISR or callback thread and ι is the last instruction of t then $it' = it$, $rt' = it$. In all other cases, $rt' = t$ and $it' = it$. For simplicity we assume that no instruction is both the first and last instruction of a thread.

Table 2. Conditions on thread t for state transition

id	pl	Constraints on t
False	False	No restriction on t
False	True	$t = rt$, $t = ISR$
True	False	$t = rt$
True	True	$t = rt$

An execution σ of P is a finite sequence of transitions $\sigma = \tau_0, \tau_1, \ldots, \tau_n$, $(n \geq 0)$, such that there exists a sequence of states $q_0, q_1, \ldots, q_{n+1}$ from Q, with $q_0 = s$ and $\tau_i = (q_i, \iota_i, q_{i+1}) \in \Rightarrow$ for each $0 \leq i \leq n$. We say that a state $q \in Q$ is *reachable* in program P if there is an execution of P leading to state q.

4   High-Level Races

In this section we describe the notion of a high-level race in the context of IDC programs. A *critical access* in a program P is a finite non-empty path π in the CFG of P. We say a critical access π is a *write* to a variable v, if it contains a statement that writes to v. Similarly, we say π is *read* access of v if it contains a statement that reads v. Critical accesses are a subjective, user-given input, that represent portions of code that the user expects to run "atomically" or "exclusively" with regard to other critical accesses to the same variables.

For example, in the program of Fig. 2, we may mark lines 4–9 of the cons thread as a critical access A which both reads and writes the items variable. Similarly, lines 1–4 of the prod thread may be considered a critical access B that reads and writes items and packets. We follow the convention that whenever the path segment defining the critical access contains a loop, then we treat the path as representing the (infinite) family of paths that enter the loop zero times, once, twice, etc.

Finally, we say two critical accesses are *conflicting* if they access a common variable and at least one of them writes to the variable.

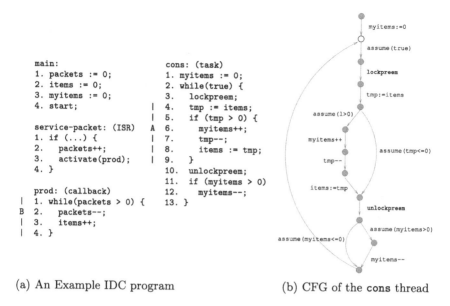

```
main:                       cons: (task)
1. packets := 0;            1. myitems := 0;
2. items := 0;              2. while(true) {
3. myitems := 0;            3.   lockpreem;
4. start;                 | 4.   tmp := items;
                          | 5.   if (tmp > 0) {
service-packet: (ISR)   A | 6.     myitems++;
1. if (...) {             | 7.     tmp--;
2.    packets++;          | 8.     items := tmp;
3.    activate(prod);     | 9.   }
4. }                        10.  unlockpreem;
                            11.  if (myitems > 0)
prod: (callback)            12.    myitems--;
 | 1. while(packets > 0) {  13. }
 B 2.   packets--;
 | 3.   items++;
 | 4. }
```

(a) An Example IDC program   (b) CFG of the **cons** thread

Fig. 2. An example program and the CFG representation of one of its threads.

We say that two conflicting critical access π and ρ in a program P are involved in a *high-level race* (or are simply *racy*) if there is an execution of P in which they *overlap* in time; that is, one critical access begins somewhere in between the beginning and ending of the other. Going back to the example of Fig. 2a, the critical accesses A and B are conflicting (they both write **items**), but they are *not* racy since they can never overlap in any execution of the program. However if the **lockpreem** and **unlockpreem** statements in the **cons** task were removed, the two accesses could now overlap, and they would be racy.

We classify a race involving critical accesses A and B as *harmful* if there is an execution in which they overlap and the execution reaches a state which *cannot* be reached by executing the two critical accesses one after the other in a serial manner. Some papers (see [9]) also refer to this condition as an atomicity violation.

5   High-Level Race Detection Using Disjoint Blocks

We now propose a static analysis based algorithm to soundly detect high-level races in IDC programs. The algorithm is based on the notion of disjoint-blocks introduced in [5], which we describe next.

Disjoint-Blocks. We recall from [5] that *disjoint-blocks* are statically identifiable pairs of path segments in the CFGs of different threads, which are guaranteed by the execution semantics of the class of programs never to overlap in an execution of the program. We have worked out a set of disjoint-blocks for the class of IDC programs, which we list in Fig. 3.

As an example, let us look at the pair in part (g) of Fig. 3. The first block in the pair (marked S) represents the portion of code between a `lockpreem` and an `unlockpreem`, while the second block (labelled C) represents the entire code of a callback thread. These two blocks are clearly disjoint, in that in any execution of an IDC program containing two such blocks, these blocks of code will never overlap in time. Going back to our running example of Fig. 2a, the lines 4–9 of `cons` would correspond to an S block, while lines 1–4 of `prod` would correspond to a C block, thereby forming a pair of disjoint-blocks according to pattern (g).

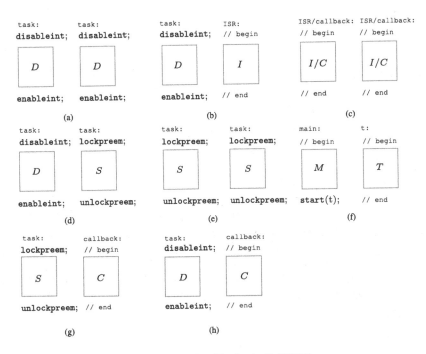

Fig. 3. Disjoint blocks in P-RTOS

Race Detection Algorithm. Algorithm 1 shows the outline of our race-detection algorithm. We begin by explaining some of the terms used in the algorithm. By a disjoint-block analysis we mean the following. Recall from Fig. 3 that there are six different patterns of blocks, labelled D, I, C, S, M, and T. We first do a data-flow analysis on each thread of the given IDC program P, to compute for each statement s, the set of blocks it *must* be a part of. We say a statement s is *must-part-of* a block F, if along every initial path in the thread's CFG that reaches s, s is always contained in an F-block. Finally, we say a pair of blocks (F, G) *covers* a pair of critical accesses (A, B), if every statement in A is must-part-of block F and every statement in B is must-part-of block G; or vice-versa.

Algorithm 1. Detecting High-Level Races

1: **procedure** DETECT HIGH-LEVEL RACES
Require: IDC Program P and a set CA of critical accesses in P.
Ensure: Set H of potential high-level races
2:     $H := \emptyset$;
3:     Perform a disjoint-block analysis on each thread in P;
4:     **for** each conflicting pair (A, B) of critical accesses in CA **do**
5:         **if** $\exists$ a pair of disjoint-blocks (F, G) s.t. (F, G) covers (A, B) **then**
6:             Declare (A, B) to be non-racy;
7:         **else**
8:             Declare (A, B) to be potentially racy;
9:             $H := H \cup \{(A, B)\}$;
        return H

For example, in the program of Fig. 2a, the critical accesses A and B are covered by an (S, C) disjoint-block.

It is fairly immediate to see that if two critical accesses A and B are covered by a pair of disjoint blocks (F, G), then A and B can *never* be involved in a high-level race. Algorithm 1 is thus *sound* in that if it declares that two critical accesses cannot race then they indeed cannot.

6   Analyzing the P-RTOS Kernel

Let us return to the problem of finding high-level races in the kernel APIs of P-RTOS. Suppose that the developer has marked out a set of critical accesses in the API functions. We are interested in knowing whether there is a high-level race involving the marked critical accesses, in the sense that there is *some* P-RTOS application which invokes the kernel APIs, and *some* execution of this application in which two conflicting critical accesses overlap.

We can solve this problem using the framework for IDC programs developed so far, as follows. For any natural number n, we can create a *most general (P-RTOS) application* (MGA) P_n, which is an IDC program with the following structure. It has a main thread that initializes the kernel variables, and then starts the scheduler; n task threads, each of which non-deterministically invokes one of the task API functions, in an overall loop; a callback thread which non-deterministically calls one of the callback API functions; and an ISR thread that simply invokes the

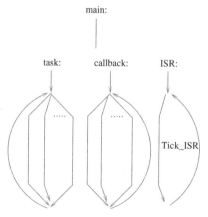

Tick_ISR routine (once again in a loop). P-RTOS has 45 API functions that can be called from task threads, and 23 API functions that may be called from

callbacks. P-RTOS does not use ISRs in general (except for the `Tick_ISR`) and instead relies on periodic tasks to poll IO buffers. The figure alongside depicts the MGA P_1. It is reasonably clear that if *some* P-RTOS application with n task threads has an execution exhibiting a high-level race involving two critical accesses, then a similar race can be orchestrated by the MGA P_n.

We need one more step to get rid of the dependence on the number of task threads n. We essentially analyze the MGA P_1, with a small change to Algorithm 1. Instead of looking for pairs of critical accesses in *different* threads in Line 4, we also allow to form pairs *within* the task thread. This gives us a sound algorithm for detecting high-level races in the P-RTOS kernel.

7 TI-RTOS and FreeRTOS

In this section we briefly describe the other RTOSs we handle.

TI-RTOS allows applications to create three sets of threads: tasks, software interrupts (swi), and hardware interrupts (hwi). Task threads are the normal threads, swi threads are triggered programmatically (by any thread), and hwi threads are ISRs, triggered by hardware. The *main* thread is a task thread in which the TI-RTOS application starts running. The *main* thread initialises global variables and invokes `start` command to enable the task and swi schedulers and also the interrupts. Only task and hwi threads are enabled initially for execution. The task thread can be preempted by other task threads (whenever the task scheduler is not disabled), or by swi threads (whenever the swi scheduler is not disabled), or by hwi threads (whenever the interrupts are not disabled). Swi threads can be preempted by other swi threads (whenever swi scheduler is not disabled) or by hwi threads (whenever interrupts are not disabled). Hwi threads can be preempted by other hwi threads. Swi and hwi threads run to completion. Every thread starts and ends with a distinct `skip` command.

In addition to the basic commands introduced in Sect. 3, TI-RTOS threads use commands like `taskdisable` and `taskenable` to disable and enable task schedulers, respectively. The `swidisable` and `swienable` commands are used to disable and enable swi schedulers and the threads can use `hwidisable` and `hwienable` commands to disable and enable interrupts. These are the commands used by the threads to enforce mutual exclusion. More details of the program model and disjoint-blocks are available in https://bitbucket.org/rekhapai/hlr-tool/downloads/.

The FreeRTOS kernel allows task threads and ISR threads, and has a designated set of kernel API functions that can be invoked by each type of thread. For more details of the modelling of FreeRTOS we refer the reader to the recent paper [5], which contains details of the program model and the disjoint-block patterns identified.

8 Experimental Evaluation

We now describe our experimental evaluation of the race detection algorithm for our three RTOS kernel case studies. We used the current version of P-RTOS,

TI-RTOS version 2.21.01.08, and FreeRTOS version 10.0.0 for our analysis. We considered all the significant APIs from each of these libraries for our analysis. The number of APIs analyzed in each of the RTOSs is given in Table 3.

We first prepared the kernel API functions for analysis by moving some of the code from functions that are actually initialization code (for example the first time a task or queue is created, many kernel variables are initialized), to the initialization part of the main thread. In the initialization phase the scheduler is not yet started and hence the accesses to these variables do not result in race. Also all helper function calls made inside the top-level functions were inlined.

We now describe how we marked out critical accesses. For this one needs an understanding of main kernel data structures and how they are modified by the kernel API functions. The key kernel data structures for each of the kernels are depicted in Fig. 4. All the three kernels have structures like a ready queue (for processes ready to execute), delay queue (for the processes that are delayed), task lists with their pointers, timer variables, etc. P-RTOS being ARINC653-compliant also has several partitions, but we focus on the code within a partition. For TI-RTOS, in addition to task state depicted in the figure, there are similar components for software interrupts and for hardware interrupts. These variables and structures constitute the "variables of interest" for us.

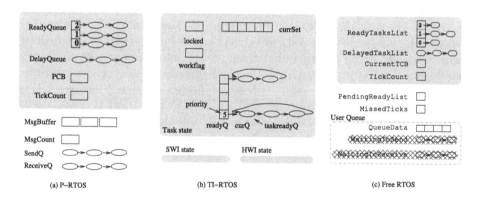

Fig. 4. Kernel structures of three RTOSs

A block of code, in an API, accessing any variable of interest that we believe should be executed atomically, is marked to be a critical access. For each critical access we also need to annotate the variables it accesses and the type of access (read/write). While this information can be automatically inferred in most cases, sometimes this is difficult to infer automatically. For a critical write access to variable x, the function call begin("w:", x);[1] is added at the beginning of the access and end ("w:", x);(see footnote 1) at its end. For example, the vTaskResume API in FreeRTOS removes a task from $xSuspendedTaskList$ and

---

[1] This is a variable length argument function we have defined.

inserts into *pxReadyTasksLists*. This is accomplished using a sequence of code, which we have marked as a critical access of these lists. At the start of this critical access we add begin("w:w:", *xSuspendedTaskList*, *pxReadyTasksLists*). The string "w:w:" is to be interpreted as write access to *xSuspendedTaskList* and *pxReadyTasksLists*. The end of the critical access is identified by a call to end("w:w:", *xSuspendedTaskList*, *pxReadyTasksLists*). (A read access is denoted by the string "r:".) The critical accesses are marked manually. It took around 130 and 100 person-hours, to understand the FreeRTOS and TI-RTOS kernels, respectively. Identifying critical accesses took around 10 person-hours each for these kernels. Details regarding the number of critical accesses marked are given in Table 3.

Next, we describe the implementation of our disjoint-block analysis. For each block in the set of disjoint-blocks, we associate a lock, which is acquired at the beginning of the block and released at the end of it. For instance, we insert an acquire(S) statement after a lockpreem, and a release(S) statement just before a unlockpreem. We now use the classical lockset analysis [17] to compute the set of locks that are must-held at each statement. At program entry it is assumed that no locks are held. When a call to acquire(l) is encountered, the analysis adds the lock l at the *out* point of the call. When a call to release(l) is encountered the lockset at the *out* point of the call is the lockset computed at the *in* point with the lock l removed. For any other statement, the lockset from the *in* point of the statement is copied to its *out* point. The *join* operation is the simple intersection of the input locksets. The disjoint-block analysis was implemented in the CIL framework [15].

Once the disjoint-block analysis is done, we can do our high-level race analysis. For every pair of conflicting critical accesses, we check whether the two accesses are covered by a pair of disjoint-blocks, as described in Sect. 5, and if not we flag it as a potential race.

The evaluation was conducted on an Intel Core i7 machine with 32 GB RAM running Ubuntu 16.04. We implement Algorithm 1 using the CIL framework [15] and other scripts that we have written.

Table 3 provides details about the number of potential races. Each of these were manually classified by us as being false positives (not racy in the actual unabstracted system), and among the true positives, harmful or benign. We give some representative examples from P-RTOS for each of these classifications. We begin with an example of a false positive. The tool reports a race between the API functions ProcessCreate and TimeDelay which both access the eState structure of a task. However, it turns out that ProcessCreate can only be called by the main thread during initialization (during which the TimeDelay callback is not active), and hence they are not racy in the actual system. In FreeRTOS code, we had abstracted data-structures (like *pxDelayedTaskList*) by a variable. Hence, even if the accesses were to disjoint parts of the structures, our analysis reports them as racy. This resulted in many false positives in FreeRTOS.

An example of a true positive but benign race in P-RTOS is the critical access in the SetEvent function. Event objects are used as a signalling mechanism between tasks. A task calls the `SetEvent` function to signal to other tasks that some data is ready for consumption. The function checks if the `flag` field of the event object is unset, and if so goes on to lock preemption, sets the flag, resets the task queue associated with the event, and unlocks preemption. The whole of this function (including the check on `flag`) is marked as a critical access. There is clearly a race between these accesses in `SetEvent`. However, it does not lead to any atomicity violation as the effect of interleaving these critical accesses is the same as doing them serially. Finally, as an example of a harmful race, we have the critical accesses in the `BufferSend` function and the `Tick_ISR`. When a periodic task invokes `BufferSend` to send a message to a full queue, the function checks whether the next activation time of the task is beyond the tick count, and only then puts the task in the delayed queue. Now this check is done without disabling interrupts, and the `Tick_ISR` may run soon after and increment the tickcount. Consider the case when the current tick count is 99 and the next activation time of the task is 100. The tick ISR now increments the time to 100. When control switches back to `SendBuffer` it goes ahead and puts the task in the delayed queue. As a result, when the scheduler tries to run the periodic task next, it finds it in the delayed queue instead of the ready queue. This is a state that cannot be reached by any serial execution of these two critical accesses.

Table 3. Result summary

	#APIs Analyzed	LoC	#Critical Accesses (CA)	#Confl. CA Pairs	#Potential Races	Time (s)	#False Pos	#Harm. Races
PRTOS	45	9.6K	945	6117	187	4.90	19	3
TI-RTOS	45	5.0K	83	1005	61	1.56	6	3
FreeRTOS	49	3.7K	181	3154	63	1.46	25	18

We have been in touch with the developers of these kernels regarding the harmful races. All 3 issues in P-RTOS have been fixed. In TI-RTOS some of the harmful races involve accesses made in the task delete function. The kernel developers expect the programmer not to call other task APIs when a task is deleted. In Freertos, some issues were fixed independent of our work. The other races mostly involve a queue registery which they consider unnecessary to fix.

The entire implementation code and the modified source code of TI-RTOS and FreeRTOS is available at https://bitbucket.org/rekhapai/hlr-tool/src/master/.

9   Related Work

Classical Lockset Based Analysis. Artho et al. [3] coined the term "high-level datarace" and gave an informal definition of it in terms of accessing a set of shared variables atomically. They define a notion of a thread's *view* of the set of shared variables, and flag potential races whenever two threads have inconsistent views. They provide a lock-set based algorithm for detecting view inconsistencies dynamically along an execution. von Praun and Gross [22] and Pessanha et al. [6] extend the view-based approach of [3] to carry out a static analysis to detect high-level races. Lockset-based static analysis for data races in classical concurrent programs [1,8,20,23] could in principle be extended to handle high-level races. However none of the above techniques apply to interrupt-driven programs due to the ad hoc nature of the synchronization mechanisms and non-standard switching semantics.

Static Analysis for Interrupt-Driven Programs. Regehr and Cooprider [16] describe a source-to-source translation of an interrupt-driven program to a standard multi-threaded program, and analyze the translated program for data races. However their translation is inadequate for our setting. We refer the reader to [5] for the inherent problems with such an approach. Schwarz et al. [18,19] provide a precise data-flow analysis for checking races in interrupt-driven applications that handles flag-based synchronization and interrupt-driven scheduling. While the technique is capable of detecting all races, it is applicable only to a given application rather than a kernel library. Sung and others [21] consider interrupt-driven applications in the form of ISRs with different priorities, and perform interval-based static analysis for checking assertions. They do not handle libraries. Wang et al. [24] analyze interrupt-driven applications for races using a combination of symbolic and dynamic analysis. This is a bug-detection approach and cannot guarantee to detect all possible races. Finally, Chopra et al. [5] propose the notion of disjoint-blocks to detect data races and carry out data-flow analysis for Free-RTOS-like interrupt-driven kernels. Our work extends the use of disjoint-blocks to handle high-level races, and also identifies disjoint-block patterns for new classes of interrupt-driven programs with callbacks and software interrupts.

Model-Checking Based Approaches. Several researchers have used model-checking tools like Slam, Blast, and Spin to precisely model various kinds of control-flow and synchronization mechanisms and detect errors exhaustively [2,7,10–12,25]. All these approaches are for specific application programs rather than libraries. Finally, the closely related work [14] uses a model-checking approach to find all high-level races in v6.1.1 of the FreeRTOS kernel. They use a meta-argument tailored for this software to bound the number of threads needed to orchestrate a race. They handle only 25 API functions and have a total running time of close to 2 h. In comparison, our approach needs no kernel-specific argument and runs in a few seconds.

10   Conclusion

In this paper we have given the first comprehensive static analysis based approach for detecting high-level races in RTOS kernels. The approach is sound, efficient, and has a low rate of false positives. We believe that the approach is widely applicable to the space of interrupt-driven kernels, where there appear to be many specialized and proprietory kernels in use.

In future work, we would like to investigate extending this approach to kernels that use multiple cores (like TI-RTOS) and multiple partitions (in the sense of a separation kernel) like P-RTOS.

References

1. Abadi, M., Flanagan, C., Freund, S.N.: Types for safe locking: static race detection for Java. ACM Trans. Program. Lang. Syst. (TOPLAS) **28**(2), 207–255 (2006)
2. Alur, R., McMillan, K.L., Peled, D.A.: Model-checking of correctness conditions for concurrent objects. Inf. Comput. **160**(1–2), 167–188 (2000)
3. Artho, C., Havelund, K., Biere, A.: High-level data races. J. Softw. Test. Verif. Reliab. **13**, 207–227 (2003)
4. Barry, R.: The FreeRTOS kernel, v10.0.0 (2017). https://freertos.org
5. Chopra, N., Pai, R., D'Souza, D.: Data races and static analysis for interrupt-driven kernels. In: Caires, L. (ed.) ESOP 2019. LNCS, vol. 11423, pp. 697–723. Springer, Cham (2019). https://doi.org/10.1007/978-3-030-17184-1_25
6. Dias, R.J., Pessanha, V., Lourenço, J.M.: Precise detection of atomicity violations. In: Biere, A., Nahir, A., Vos, T. (eds.) HVC 2012. LNCS, vol. 7857, pp. 8–23. Springer, Heidelberg (2013). https://doi.org/10.1007/978-3-642-39611-3_8
7. Elmas, T., Qadeer, S., Tasiran, S.: Precise race detection and efficient model checking using locksets. Technical Report MSR-TR-2005-118. Microsoft Research (2005)
8. Engler, D., Ashcraft, K.: RacerX: effective, static detection of race conditions and deadlocks. SIGOPS Oper. Syst. Rev. **37**(5), 237–252 (2003)
9. Flanagan, C., Qadeer, S.: A type and effect system for atomicity. In Proceedings ACM SIGPLAN Programming Language Design and Implementation (PLDI), pp. 338–349 (2003)
10. Havelund, K., Lowry, M.R., Penix, J.: Formal analysis of a space-craft controller using SPIN. IEEE Trans. Softw. Eng. **27**(8), 749–765 (2001)
11. Havelund, K., Skakkebæk, J.U.: Applying model checking in Java verification. In: Dams, D., Gerth, R., Leue, S., Massink, M. (eds.) SPIN 1999. LNCS, vol. 1680, pp. 216–231. Springer, Heidelberg (1999). https://doi.org/10.1007/3-540-48234-2_17
12. Henzinger, T.A., Jhala, R., Majumdar, R.: Race checking by context inference. In: Proceedings of ACM SIGPLAN Programming Language Design and Implementation (PLDI), pp. 1–13 (2004)
13. Texas Instruments: TI-RTOS: A Real-Time Operating System for Microcontrollers. http://www.ti.com/tool/ti-rtos, 2017
14. Mukherjee, S., Kumar, A., D'Souza, D.: Detecting all high-level dataraces in an RTOS kernel. In: Bouajjani, A., Monniaux, D. (eds.) VMCAI 2017. LNCS, vol. 10145, pp. 405–423. Springer, Cham (2017). https://doi.org/10.1007/978-3-319-52234-0_22
15. Necula, G.: CIL - infrastructure for C Program Analysis and Transformation (v. 1.3.7) (2002). http://people.eecs.berkeley.edu/~necula/cil/
16. Regehr, J., Cooprider, N.: Interrupt verification via thread verification. Electr. Notes Theor. Comput. Sci. **174**(9), 139–150 (2007)
17. Savage, S., Burrows, M., Nelson, G., Sobalvarro, P., Anderson, T.E.: Eraser: a dynamic data race detector for multithreaded programs. ACM Trans. Comput. Syst. **15**(4), 391–411 (1997)

18. Schwarz, M.D., Seidl, H., Vojdani, V., Apinis, K.: Precise analysis of value-dependent synchronization in priority scheduled programs. In: McMillan, K.L., Rival, X. (eds.) VMCAI 2014. LNCS, vol. 8318, pp. 21–38. Springer, Heidelberg (2014). https://doi.org/10.1007/978-3-642-54013-4_2
19. Schwarz, M.D., Seidl, H., Vojdani, V., Lammich, P., Müller-Olm, M.: Static analysis of interrupt-driven programs synchronized via the priority ceiling protocol. In Proceedings of ACM SIGPLAN-SIGACT Principles of Programming Languages (POPL), pp. 93–104 (2011)
20. Sterling, N.: WARLOCK - a static data race analysis tool. In: Proceedings of Usenix Winter Technical Conference, pp. 97–106 (1993)
21. Sung, C., Kusano, M., Wang, C.: Modular verification of interrupt-driven software. In: Proceedings of the 32nd IEEE/ACM International Conference on Automated Software Engineering, ASE 2017, pp. 206–216 (2017)
22. von Praun, C., Gross, T.R.: Static detection of atomicity violations in object-oriented programs. J. Object Technol. **3**(6), 103–122 (2004)
23. Voung, J.W., Jhala, R., Lerner, S.: RELAY: static race detection on millions of lines of code. In: Proceedings of ESEC/SIGSOFT Foundations of Software Engineering (FSE), pp. 205–214 (2007)
24. Wang, Y., Wang, L., Yu, T., Zhao, J., Li, X.: Automatic detection and validation of race conditions in interrupt-driven embedded software. In: Proceedings of the 26th ACM SIGSOFT International Symposium on Software Testing and Analysis, ISSTA 2017, pp. 113–124. ACM (2017)
25. Zeng, R., Sun, Z., Liu, S., He, X.: McPatom: a predictive analysis tool for atomicity violation using model checking. In: Donaldson, A., Parker, D. (eds.) SPIN 2012. LNCS, vol. 7385, pp. 191–207. Springer, Heidelberg (2012). https://doi.org/10.1007/978-3-642-31759-0_14

Parallel Composition and Modular Verification of Computer Controlled Systems in Differential Dynamic Logic

Simon Lunel[1,2], Stefan Mitsch[3], Benoit Boyer[1], and Jean-Pierre Talpin[2(✉)]

[1] Mitsubishi Electric R&D Centre Europe,
1 allée de Beaulieu, CS 10806, 35708 Rennes CEDEX 7, France
b.boyer@fr.merce.mee.com
[2] Inria, Centre de recherche Rennes - Bretagne - Atlantique,
Campus universitaire de Beaulieu, 35042 Rennes Cedex, France
jean-pierre.talpin@inria.fr
[3] Computer Science Department, Carnegie Mellon University, Pittsburgh, PA, USA
smitsch@cs.cmu.edu

Abstract. Computer-Controlled Systems (CCS) are a subclass of hybrid systems where the periodic relation of control components to time is paramount. Since they additionally are at the heart of many safety-critical devices, it is of primary importance to correctly model such systems and to ensure they function correctly according to safety requirements. Differential dynamic logic $d\mathcal{L}$ is a powerful logic to model hybrid systems and to prove their correctness. We contribute a component-based modeling and reasoning framework to $d\mathcal{L}$ that separates models into components with timing guarantees, such as reactivity of controllers and controllability of continuous dynamics. Components operate in parallel, with coarse-grained interleaving, periodic execution and communication. We present techniques to automate system safety proofs from isolated, modular, and possibly mechanized proofs of component properties parameterized with timing characteristics.

1 Introduction

A computer-controlled system (CCS) is a hybrid system with discrete hardware-software components that control a specific physical phenomenon, *e.g.* the water level of a tank in a water-recycling plant. CCSs are widely used in industry to monitor time-critical and safety-critical processes. While CCS defines a large class of hybrid systems, systems mixing physical phenomena and natural discrete interactions (*e.g.* a bouncing-ball) are neither CCSs nor the focus of this work, although most could easily be given verification models in $d\mathcal{L}$. Tools to model, verify, and design CCSs need to capture mixed discrete and continuous dynamics,

This material is based upon work supported by the United States Air Force and DARPA under Contract No. FA8750-18-C-0092.

© Springer Nature Switzerland AG 2019
M. H. ter Beek et al. (Eds.): FM 2019, LNCS 11800, pp. 354–370, 2019.
https://doi.org/10.1007/978-3-030-30942-8_22

as well as mixed logical, discretized real-time and continuous time in, resp., computer programs, electronics, and physics models.

CCSs are difficult to model since they subsume the problem of designing a software controller and its real-timed hardware. Our aim is to develop a *component-based approach* to engineer such systems in a modular manner while accounting for time domain boundaries across components. In component-based design, a system is constructed from smaller elements that are modeled and individually verified, then assembled and checked for consistency to form larger components and subsystems. The CCS components typically execute in parallel, and concurrency must be accounted for in the envisioned verification framework.

In this paper, we contribute a component-based verification technique that aims at the definition of a bottom-up and modular verification methodology through a *correct-by-construction* system design methodology, in which component *contracts* formalize the domain, timing, and invariants of components. The proof of a system model is built by assembling the contracts of its components through formally defined composition mechanisms. Contracts-based approaches have been successfully implemented for several paradigms such as programming languages [16] or automata [2], because contracts are very efficient to make proofs easier scalable. Following the component-based design widely used for CCS, contracts provide a natural way to get modularity and abstraction in proofs.

To meet the time-criticality requirements of CCSs, we start from earlier compositionality results in $d\mathcal{L}$ [7] to elaborate a timed model of parallel composition as the foundation of our modeling and verification framework. In Sect. 3, we detail modeling and verification in our framework on a simple system where only one reactive controller monitors a plant. In Sect. 4, we generalize it to systems where multiple controllers monitor multiple parallel plants; we show how to compose: multiple reactive controllers into a component called Multi-Choice Reactive Controllers (**MRCtrl**, see Sect. 4.1); multiple controllable plants together (see Sect. 4.2); **MRCtrl** with controllable plants to form Multi Computer-Controlled Systems (**MCCS**, see Sect. 4.3); and finally how **MCCS** compose (see Sect. 4.4).

2 Differential Dynamic Logic

This section briefly recalls *differential dynamic logic* ($d\mathcal{L}$ [13]) and its proof system, which is implemented in the theorem prover KeYmaera X [3].

In $d\mathcal{L}$, hybrid programs are used as a programming language for expressing the combined discrete and continuous dynamics of hybrid systems (the programs operate over mathematical reals). The syntax and semantics of hybrid programs is summarized in Table 1. The set of reachable states from state ν by hybrid program α is noted $\rho_\nu(\alpha)$, and $[\![x]\!]_\nu$ denotes the value of x at state ν. Hybrid programs include discrete assignment $x := \theta$ and tests $?\phi$, as well as combinators for non-deterministic choice ($\alpha \cup \beta$), sequential composition ($\alpha; \beta$), and non-deterministic repetition (α^*). The notation $\{x' = \theta \ \& \ H\}$ denotes an ordinary differential equation (ODE) system (derivatives with respect to time) of the

Table 1. Syntax and semantics of hybrid programs

Program	Semantics
$?\phi$	Test whether formula ϕ is true, abort if false: $\rho_\nu(?\varphi) = \{\nu \mid \nu \models \varphi\}$
$x := \theta$	Assign value of term θ to variable x: $\rho_\nu(x := \theta) = \{\omega \mid \omega = \nu \text{ except that } [\![x]\!]_\omega = [\![\theta]\!]_\nu\}$
$\{x' = \theta \ \& \ H\}$	Evolve ODE $x' = \theta$ for any time $t \geqslant 0$ with evolution domain constraint H true throughout: $\rho_\nu(\{x' = \theta \ \& \ H\}) = \{f(r) \mid f(0) = \nu \text{ and for any duration } r \geqslant 0$ $f(r) \models x' = \theta \text{ and } f(r) \models H\}$
$\alpha; \beta$	Run α followed by β on resulting state(s): $\rho_\nu(\alpha; \beta) = \bigcup_{\omega \in \rho_\nu(\alpha)} \rho_\omega(\beta)$
$\alpha \cup \beta$	Run either α or β non-deterministically: $\rho_\nu(\alpha \cup \beta) = \rho_\nu(\alpha) \cup \rho_\nu(\beta)$
α^*	Repeat α n times, for any $n \in \mathbb{N}$: $\rho(\alpha^*) = \bigcup_{n \in \mathbb{N}} \rho(\alpha^n) \text{ with } \alpha^0 = ?\top \text{ and } \alpha^{n+1} = \alpha^n; \alpha$

form $x'_1 = \theta_1, \ldots, x'_n = \theta_n$ within evolution domain H. For example, the ODE $\{t' = 1 \ \& \ t \geqslant 0\}$ describes that variable t evolves with constant slope 1, where $t \geqslant 0$ discards any negative values. Formulas of $d\mathcal{L}$ formalize properties, Definition 1.

Definition 1 ($d\mathcal{L}$ formulas). *The formulas ϕ, ψ of $d\mathcal{L}$ relevant in this paper consist of the following operators:*

$$\phi, \psi ::= \phi \wedge \psi \mid \phi \vee \psi \mid \phi \to \psi \mid \neg\phi \mid \theta_1 \sim \theta_2 \mid \forall x \ \phi \mid \exists x \ \phi \mid [\alpha]\phi$$

Connectives $\phi \wedge \psi$, $\phi \vee \psi$, $\phi \to \psi, \neg\phi$, $\forall x \ \phi$, and $\exists x \ \phi$ are according to classical first-order logic. Formula $\theta_1 \sim \theta_2$ are any comparison operator $\sim \in \{\leqslant, <, =, \neq, >, \geqslant\}$ and θ_i are real-valued terms in operators $\{+, -, \cdot, /\}$. The modal operator $[\alpha]\phi$ is true iff ϕ holds in all states reachable by program α.

The notion of *free and bound variables* is defined in the static semantics of $d\mathcal{L}$ [13] and useful to characterize the interaction of a program α with its context. It is computed from the syntactic structure of programs: the bound variables $\mathrm{BV}(\alpha)$ can be updated by assignments (*e.g.* $x := 10$) or ODEs (*e.g.* $x' = 3$) in α, whereas free variables $\mathrm{FV}(\alpha)$ are those that the program depends on. For example, in program $\alpha \equiv (v := a \cup v := 2); \{x' = v \ \& \ x \leqslant 5\}$ the free variables are $\mathrm{FV}(\alpha) = \{a, x\}$ (the variable v is not free, because it is bound on all paths of α and so the result of α does not depend on the initial value of v; even though also modified, variable x is free because the result of α depends on the initial value of x) and the bound variables are $\mathrm{BV}(\alpha) = \{v, x\}$ (variable a is not bound because it is not modified anywhere in the program). We use $\mathrm{V}(\alpha)$ to denote $\mathrm{BV}(\alpha) \cup \mathrm{FV}(\alpha)$.

In [7], a component model $C_i = (\mathbf{disc}_i \cup \mathbf{cont}_i)^*$ is evaluated as the non-deterministic interleaving of its discrete specifications $\mathbf{disc}_i$ and ODE $\mathbf{cont}_i = \{x'_i = \theta_i \ \& \ H_i\}$. For $i \in \{1, 2\}$, the parallel composition of C_1 and C_2 builds a component of the same structure, *i.e.* the dicrete parts $\mathbf{disc}_1$ and $\mathbf{disc}_2$ are non-deterministically interleaved within the evolution of the ODE obtained from the mathematical composition of $\mathbf{cont}_1$ and $\mathbf{cont}_2$. In $d\mathcal{L}$, it is defined by

$$C_1 \otimes C_2 = (\mathbf{disc}_1 \cup \mathbf{disc}_2 \cup \{x_1' = \theta_1, x_2' = \theta_2 \ \& \ H_1 \wedge H_2\})^* \qquad (1)$$

The logic $d\mathcal{L}$ further enjoys a proof calculus [12–14] based on uniform substitution from axioms. Its base axioms are those of a classical first-order sequent calculus, augmented with syntactical deconstruction of hybrid programs α for goals of the form $[\alpha]\phi$ and for iteration and ODEs [15].

3 Computer-Controlled Systems

We present a component-based approach to model and verify Computer Controlled Systems (CCS) based on the parallel composition pattern proposed in [7]. We construct the proof of a CCS from the isolated sub-proofs of its components by *syntactically* decomposing the CCS using the axioms of $d\mathcal{L}$, so that the theorems presented here can be implemented as tactics in the theorem prover KeYmaera X. This enables automation to reduce the proof complexity of analyzing a CCS to that of modularly analyzing its components.

In this section, we introduce the necessary concepts to adapt the framework of [7] to systematically model CCSs modularly. We achieve modularity by limiting the ways in which the free and bound variables of different components may overlap, and by taking into account the timing constraints of CCSs. The idea is to analyze the *controllability* of the plant, *i.e.* the period of time it can evolve safely without intervention of a controller, and the *reactivity* of the controller, *i.e.* the execution period of the controller. These concepts satisfy the associativity property of parallel composition and the ability to retain contracts from [7].

3.1 Modeling CCS

A CCS is classically composed of a *controller* and a *plant*. The controller measures the state of the plant through sensing and regulates the behavior of the plant through actuation. For example, the controller in the water tank regulates the water level by opening or closing a faucet. The key trait of a CCS is the periodic execution of the controller to regulate the plant. We associate periodic values δ and Δ with the controller and the plant, respectively: Control *reactivity* δ models the period in which control is guaranteed to happen. Plant *controllability* Δ models how long a plant can evolve safely without control intervention.

Time. To make timed reasoning available to any component, we use the ODE $\mathbf{Time}(t) \doteq \{t' = 1 \ \& \ t \geqslant 0\}$. The hence defined global variable t represents time passing with constant slope 1, initialized to 0.

Controller. The functional behavior of a controller is provided as a discrete program *ctrl* and the associated *reactivity* δ. The controller acts at least every δ units of time, see Definition 2.

Definition 2 (Reactive Controller). *A* reactive controller $\boldsymbol{RCtrl}(ctrl, \delta)$ *with* reactivity boundary δ *and fresh timestamp* τ *has the program shape*

$$\boldsymbol{RCtrl}(ctrl, \delta) \doteq (?t \leqslant \tau + \delta; \ ctrl; \ \tau := t)$$

Execution periodicity is ensured by a *fresh* variable τ time stamping ($\tau := t$) the last execution of *ctrl*. The prefixing guard $?t \leqslant \tau + \delta$ forces *ctrl* to be executed within δ time since its last execution τ. This pattern models control frequency, since all runs not satisfying a test are aborted, see Sect. 2.

Example 1 (Water-level Controller). We consider the water level controller in a water plant[1]. When the level reaches a maximum (resp. minimum) threshold, we close the inlet faucet *fin* (resp. we open the inlet faucet). The resulting controller has the program shape $\boldsymbol{RCtrl}(wlctrl, \delta_{wlctrl})$ i.e. ($?t \leqslant \tau + \delta_{wlctrl}; \ wlctrl; \ \tau := t$), where $\delta_{wlctrl} = 0.05$ s ensures a control frequency of at least 20 Hz. The controller:

$$wlctrl \doteq wlm := wl; \left((?wlm \geqslant 6.5; fin := 0) \cup (?wlm \leqslant 3.5; fin := 1)\right)$$

measures the water level using $wlm := wl$ and then sets *fin* depending on whether the water level exceeds the minimum threshold 3.5 or the maximum threshold 6.5. This controller makes implicit assumptions on the maximum inflow and outflow of the water tank through the relation between its reactivity δ_{wlctrl} and the thresholds on wlm.

Plant. The functional behavior of the plant is provided as an ODE system $\{x' = \theta \ \& \ H\}$ with $t \notin V(x' = \theta)$ and the *controllability bound* Δ. Controllability is implemented by adding the formula $t \leqslant \Delta$ to the evolution domain, see Definition 3.

Definition 3 (Controllable Plant). *A* controllable plant $\boldsymbol{CPlant}(\{x' = \theta \ \& \ H\}, \Delta)$ *with* controllability bound Δ *is a differential equation system of the shape* $\boldsymbol{CPlant}(\{x' = \theta \ \& \ H\}, \Delta) \doteq \{x' = \theta \ \& \ H \wedge t \leqslant \Delta\}$, *combined with time defined by* $\boldsymbol{Time}(t)$.

Example 2 (Water-level). The evolution of the water level wl in the tank is determined by the difference between the inlet flow *fin* and the outlet flow *fout*. The water level is always non-negative ($H \doteq wl \geqslant 0$), and so the controllable water level is the ODE with controllability $\Delta_{wl} = 0.2$ s:

$$\{wl' = fin - fout, t' = 1 \ \& \ t \geqslant 0 \wedge wl \geqslant 0 \wedge t \leqslant \Delta_{wl}\}$$

We compose the plant with the controller to a full system with repeated interaction between the plant and the controller.

---

[1] Adapted from http://symbolaris.com/info/KeYmaera-guide.html#watertank.

Full System. The full system is obtained by applying parallel composition as defined in (1) to the plant and the controller, but with one important change: the formula $t \leqslant \Delta$ is replaced by the formula $t \leqslant \tau + \delta$ to ensure that the plant suspends when the controller is expected to run, see Definition 4.

Definition 4 (Computer-Controlled System). *A computer-controlled system CCS is a parallel composition of a reactive controller $RCtrl(ctrl, \delta)$ and a controllable plant $CPlant(\{x' = \theta \ \& \ H\}, \Delta)$ with $\delta \leqslant \Delta$ and the resulting hybrid program shape, assuming $Time(t)$ and, initially, $\tau = t$:*

$$CCS \doteq \left(\{x' = \theta \ \& \ H \wedge \underbrace{t \leqslant \tau + \delta}_{\delta \leqslant \Delta}\} \cup RCtrl(ctrl, \delta)\right)^*$$

Execution between the controller and the plant switches based on the variable τ. At the beginning of each loop iteration, we have $t \geqslant \tau$. The difference $t - \tau$ grows according to the evolution of time until the point $t - \tau = \delta$. At the latest, then, the controller must act before the plant can continue. Safety requires $\delta \leqslant \Delta$, *i.e.* the reactivity of the controller is at most the controllability of the plant. Otherwise, there may be runs of the whole system where the controller executes too late for the plant to stay safe.

Example 3 (Water-tank). We compose the water level with its controller to obtain the water tank system with the following behavior:

$$\left(\begin{array}{l} \{wl' = fin - fout, t' = 1 \ \& \ t \geqslant 0 \wedge wl \geqslant 0 \wedge t \leqslant \tau + \delta_{wlctrl}\} \\ \cup \ (?t \leqslant \tau + \delta_{wlctrl}; wlctrl; \tau := t) \end{array} \right)^*$$

The composition is possible because the reactivity of the controller ($\delta_{wlctrl} = 0.05s$) does not exceed the controllability of the plant ($\Delta_{wl} = 0.2\,\text{s}$).

3.2 Modular Verification of a CCS

Based on the modular modeling capabilities offered by the concepts of Sect. 3.1 and through [7, Thm. 2], we provide techniques to verify the safety of a complete system from safety proofs of its components (which can be reactive controllers, controllable plants, or subsystems built from those following the computer-controlled systems composition). The proofs of our theorems are syntactic using the axioms of $d\mathcal{L}$ (as opposed to the semantic proofs in [7]) and are, thus, implementable as tactics in the theorem prover KeYmaera X [3].

Environment. A description of the global system environment $\mathcal{E}$ characterizing constants (either as exact values or through their relevant characteristics) is necessary. We require that $FV(\mathcal{E}) \cap BV(\alpha) = \varnothing$ for all system components α to ensure that the environment variables are constants: these constants are not controlled, but can be read by all components. (*e.g.*, gravity constant g).

Example 4 (Water tank environment). In the water tank example, the environment $\mathcal{E}_{wt} \doteq fout = 0.75 \wedge \delta_{wlctrl} = 0.05 \wedge \Delta_{wl} = 0.2$ is the outlet flow *fout* of 0.75, plant controllability Δ_{wl} of 0.2 s, and controller reactivity δ_{wlctrl} of 0.05 s.

Contracts. A designer specifies the assumptions A_{ctrl} and guarantees G_{ctrl} of the controller as well as the assumption A_{plant} and guarantees G_{plant} of the plant. In order to be compositional, the guarantees of the controller must not refer to outputs of the plant and inversely ($\mathrm{FV}(G_{ctrl}) \cap \mathrm{BV}(plant) = \varnothing$ and $\mathrm{FV}(G_{plant}) \cap \mathrm{BV}(ctrl) = \varnothing$). A component α satisfies its contract (A_α, G_α) in environment $\mathcal{E}$ under starting conditions $Init_\alpha$ if formula $(\mathcal{E} \wedge A_\alpha \wedge Init_\alpha) \rightarrow [\alpha^*]G_\alpha$ is valid (*e.g.*, proved using the $d\mathcal{L}$ proof calculus). Unlike the environment $\mathcal{E}$, the initial conditions $Init_\alpha$ and assumptions A_α of a component α can mention assumptions about the state of other components.

Example 5 (Water tank contracts). The water-level controller assumes that the actual water level in the tank ranges over the interval $[3, 7]$ (as guaranteed by the tank), and itself guarantees to drain the tank when the measured water level approaches the upper threshold 6.5, and fill the tank when below the lower threshold 3.5. The tank contract assumes that the tank is instructed correctly to drain or fill, and then guarantees to keep the water level in the limits $[3, 7]$.

$$\begin{cases} A_{wlctrl} : G_{wl} \\ G_{wlctrl} : wlm \leqslant 3.5 \rightarrow fin = 1 \\ \qquad\quad 6.5 \leqslant wlm \rightarrow fin = 0 \\ \qquad\quad (3.5 \leqslant wlm \leqslant 6.5) \rightarrow (fin = 0 \vee fin = 1) \end{cases} \qquad \begin{cases} A_{wl} : G_{wlctrl} \\ G_{wl} : 3 \leqslant wl \leqslant 7 \end{cases}$$

These contracts assume that the measured water level is correct, *i.e.* it corresponds to the true water level in the tank, so $Init_{ctrl} \equiv wl = wlm$ and also $Init_{plant} \equiv wl = wlm$. As we compose the controller and plant components to a full system, where the plant evolves for some time between controller runs (and thus measurements), we will need to find a condition that describes the relationship between the true water level evolution and the measured water level.

Full System. The contract $(A_{ctrl} \wedge A_{plant}, G_{ctrl} \wedge G_{plant})$ for the full system is the conjunction of the assumptions and of the guarantees.

Composition Invariant. In the full system, the controller and the plant will run in a quasi-parallel fashion, so time passes between controller runs and thus in turn between measurements of the true plant values. With a composition invariant J_{cmp} we describe the relationship between the true values of the plant and the measured values in the controller. The formula J_{cmp} is a composition invariant for two components α and β if the formulas $J_{cmp} \rightarrow [\alpha]J_{cmp}$ and $J_{cmp} \rightarrow [\beta]J_{cmp}$ are valid (components maintain the composition invariant), and $Init_\alpha \wedge Init_\beta \rightarrow J_{cmp}$ is valid (composition invariant is initially satisfied).

Each component is responsible for satisfying its own guarantees and can assume that others will satisfy its assumptions. We also require that other components do not interfere with a component's guarantees. This notion of non-interference ensures that contracts focus on the behavior of their own component (but nothing else), as intuitively expected.

Definition 5 (Non-interfering Controller and Plant). *A controller ctrl and plant* $\{x' = \theta \,\&\, H\}$ *are* non-interfering *if they do not influence the guarantees of the respective other component, so* $FV(G_{ctrl}) \cap BV(\{x' = \theta \,\&\, H\}) = \varnothing$ *and* $FV(G_{plant}) \cap BV(ctrl) = \varnothing$, *and if they do not share the same outputs, so* $BV(ctrl) \cap BV(\{x' = \theta \,\&\, H\}) = \varnothing$.

For composition it is important that contracts are compatible, meaning that they mutually satisfy their assumptions from their respective guarantees.

Definition 6 (Compatible Contracts). *Contracts* (A_α, G_α) *and* (A_β, G_β) *of components* α *and* β *with composition invariant* J_{cmp} *are* compatible *if the formulas* $A_\alpha \rightarrow [\beta](G_\beta \wedge J_{cmp} \rightarrow A_\alpha)$ *and* $A_\beta \rightarrow [\alpha](G_\alpha \wedge J_{cmp} \rightarrow A_\beta)$ *are valid.*

Theorem 1 (Composition of Controller and Plant). *Let* $\mathbf{RCtrl}(ctrl, \delta)$ *be a reactive controller satisfying its contract* (A_{ctrl}, G_{ctrl}) *and* $\mathbf{CPlant}(\{x' = \theta \,\&\, H\}, \Delta)$ *be a controllable plant satisfying its contract* (A_{plant}, G_{plant}). *Further let the components* $\mathbf{RCtrl}(ctrl, \delta)$ *and* $\mathbf{CPlant}(\{x' = \theta \,\&\, H\}, \Delta)$ *be non-interfering, the contracts* (A_{ctrl}, G_{ctrl}) *and* (A_{plant}, G_{plant}) *be compatible, and* J_{cmp} *be a composition invariant. Then, the parallel composition* $\mathbf{CCS}$ *is safe, i.e.,* $(\mathcal{E} \wedge A_{ctrl} \wedge Init_{ctrl} \wedge A_{plant} \wedge Init_{plant}) \rightarrow [\mathbf{CCS}](G_{ctrl} \wedge G_{plant})$ *is valid.*

Proof. Adapts [7, Thm. 2] to a syntactic $d\mathcal{L}$ proof with loop invariant $A_{ctrl} \wedge G_{ctrl} \wedge A_{plant} \wedge G_{plant} \wedge J_{cmp}$ with differential refinement to replace δ with Δ, see long version [8] for details. $\square$

Example 6 (Water-tank contract). The controller and the water-level are non-interfering, their contracts compatible, and the controller is fast enough to keep the plant safe ($\delta_{wlctrl} \leqslant \Delta_{wl}$). We apply Theorem 1 with the composition invariant $J_{cmp} \doteq wl = (fin - fout)(t - \tau) + wlm$ to obtain that the composition is safe, *i.e.* formula $\mathcal{E} \wedge Init_{wl} \wedge Init_{wlctrl} \wedge A_{wl} \wedge A_{wlctrl} \rightarrow [\mathbf{Water\text{-}tank}](G_{wl} \wedge G_{wlctrl})$ is valid. The composition invariant says how the true value wl deviates from the last measured value wlm according to the flow $fin - fout$ as time $t - \tau$ passes.

Outlook. We adapted parallel composition of [7] to model and prove computer-controlled systems composed of two components, a reactive controller and a controllable plant. Next, we extend this concept to arbitrarily nested combinations of controllers and plants with a systematic integration of timed constraints.

4   Parallel Composition

We want to extend the integration of temporal considerations for every component in a timed framework. The previous section shows the importance of temporal considerations in CCS. Industrial systems combine CCS in parallel and it is necessary to have a framework to handle temporal properties.

In order to reason about parallel execution of control software sharing computation resources, models of different costs (controllability, performance, latency, etc) become important. For example, when two programs execute quasi-parallel on a single CPU core, their computation resources are shared and execution may mutually preempt. As a result, the worst-case execution times of the programs sum up to the total worst-case execution time of the composed system. This requires designing plants with sufficiently longer controllability periods, and controllers that react further in advance.

Based on the parallel composition pattern in [7] and the concepts of reactive controller and controllable plant introduced above, here we present parallel compositions of component hierarchies, including composition of multiple reactive controllers, multiple controllable plants, and mixed compositions. We retain the algebraic properties of [7], commutativity and associativity, and present theorems guaranteeing that the conjunction of contracts is preserved through composition.

Controllable plants are already hierarchically compositional per Definition 3. The particular structure to enclose control programs with temporal guards in reactive controllers, however, makes it necessary to extend the definition of reactive controller (Definition 2) to a *multi-choice reactive controller* that combines choices of each of its constituting atomic reactive controllers nondeterministically. We associate a *fresh variable* τ_i with each atomic reactive controller $ctrl_i$. It is used to specify the time stamp of the controller in an execution cycle.

Definition 7 (Multi-choice Reactive Controller). *A multi-choice reactive controller* $\boldsymbol{MRCtrl}\left(\bigcup_{1\leqslant i\leqslant n} ctrl_i, \delta\right)$ *with* n *control choices and overall reactivity bound* δ *has the program shape*

$$\boldsymbol{MRCtrl}\left(\bigcup_{1\leqslant i\leqslant n} ctrl_i, \delta\right) \doteq \left(\bigcup_{1\leqslant i\leqslant n} \boldsymbol{RCtrl}(ctrl_i, \delta)\right).$$

The parallel composition follows cases for purely discrete components, purely continuous components or a mix of both, which we detail in the subsections below. We illustrate each case with an example with two connected water-tanks, one where the inlet flow of one is the outlet flow of the other, with respective reactive controllers to ensure that they remain within a pre-defined range. The first controller actuates on the inlet flow of the first tank, whereas the second actuates on the outlet valve of the second tank.

4.1   Parallel Composition of Multi-choice Reactive Controllers

We refine the parallel composition operator for multi-choice reactive controllers to consider the controllability and reactivity bounds Δ and δ of its components. By definition, the controllability bound of composed components α and β is always $\min(\Delta_\alpha, \Delta_\beta)$ of their individual bounds $\Delta_\alpha, \Delta_\beta$. The reactivity bound depends on the physical architecture that composes α and β. It is overapproximated by a max+ cost function $\mathcal{C} : \mathbb{R}^2 \to \mathbb{R}$ such that $\mathcal{C}(\delta_\alpha, \delta_\beta) = \max(\delta_\alpha, \delta_\beta)$ if α and β have controllers running independently (e.g. two ECUs or PLCs), or else $\delta_\alpha + \delta_\beta$, if both controllers execute on one resource. Notice that such a definition is associative and commutative with respect to composition.

Modeling. We first define the parallel composition of discrete components, which are multi-choice reactive controllers $\mathbf{MRCtrl}(\bigcup_{1\leqslant i\leqslant n} ctrl_i, \delta)$. To the definition in [7], we add the cost model $\mathcal{C}$ to combine individual bounds δ as that of the composed system. The parallel composition is the non-deterministic choice between all control choices in multi-choice reactive controllers $\mathbf{MRCtrl}(\bigcup_{1\leqslant i\leqslant n_\alpha} \alpha_i, \delta_\alpha)$ and $\mathbf{MRCtrl}(\bigcup_{1\leqslant j\leqslant n_\beta} \beta_j, \delta_\beta)$, but with the individual δ_α and δ_β replaced by the cost model $\mathcal{C}(\delta_\alpha, \delta_\beta)$. Interleaving of controller executions occurs through embedding the non-deterministic choice in the loop of a full system, see Theorem 2.

Definition 8 (Parallel Composition of Multi-choice Controllers). *Let α and β be multi-choice reactive controllers of shapes* $\textbf{MRCtrl}(\bigcup_{1\leqslant i\leqslant n_\alpha} \alpha_i, \delta_\alpha)$ *and* $\textbf{MRCtrl}(\bigcup_{1\leqslant j\leqslant n_\beta} \beta_j, \delta_\beta)$. *Their parallel composition $\alpha \otimes \beta$ has shape:*

$$\textit{MRCtrl}\left(\bigcup_{1\leqslant i\leqslant n_\alpha} \alpha_i \cup \bigcup_{1\leqslant j\leqslant n_\beta} \beta_j, \mathcal{C}(\delta_\alpha, \delta_\beta) \right).$$

Example 7 (Composition of two water-level controllers). We compose two reactive water-level controllers $wlctrl_1$ (reactivity $\delta_{wlctrl_1} = 0.05\,\mathrm{s}$) and $wlctrl_2$ (reactivity $\delta_{wlctrl_2} = 0.02\,\mathrm{s}$) on one CPU. The multi-choice reactive controller resulting from cost model $\mathcal{C}(\delta_{wlctrl_1}, \delta_{wlctrl_2}) = \delta_{wlctrl_1} + \delta_{wlctrl_2}$ is:

$$\begin{aligned}
&\mathbf{MRCtrl}\,(wlctrl_1 \cup wlctrl_2, \delta_{wlctrl_1} + \delta_{wlctrl_2}) \\
&= \mathbf{RCtrl}(wlctrl_1, \delta_{wlctrl_1} + \delta_{wlctrl_2}) \cup \mathbf{RCtrl}(wlctrl_2, \delta_{wlctrl_1} + \delta_{wlctrl_2}) \\
&= \quad (?t \leqslant \tau_1 + \delta_{wlctrl_1} + \delta_{wlctrl_2};\ wlctrl_1;\ \tau_1 := t) \\
&\quad \cup (?t \leqslant \tau_2 + \delta_{wlctrl_1} + \delta_{wlctrl_2};\ wlctrl_2;\ \tau_2 := t)
\end{aligned}$$

where $wlctrl_1$ follows Example 1 and
$wlctrl_2 \doteq wlm_2 := wl;\, \big((?wlm_2 \geqslant 9.7; fout_2 := 1) \cup (?wlm_2 \leqslant 2.3; fout_2 := 0)\big).$

Algebraic Properties. We retain commutativity and associativity of the parallel composition operator defined in [7]. Commutativity implies that we are able to decompose a system and associativity ensures that we can build it step-by-step. The proof, detailed in the long version [8], relies on the commutativity and associativity of both non-deterministic choice and cost model $\mathcal{C}$.

Modular Verification. We adapt [7, Thm. 2] by adding the condition that the individual reactivity bound δ_α of a controller α must neither occur in its functional behavior $\bigcup_{1\leqslant i\leqslant n_\alpha} \alpha_i$ nor in its guarantees. Failing to do so may prevent to re-use a component proof.

Definition 9 (Non-interfering Controllers). *Two controllers α and β are non-interfering if they do not modify the same variables, i.e. the outputs are separated ($BV(\alpha) \cap BV(\beta) = \varnothing$), and if they do not influence the guarantees of the other component ($FV(G_\alpha) \cap BV(\alpha) = \varnothing$ and $FV(G_\beta) \cap BV(\beta) = \varnothing$).*

Theorem 2 (Composition of Multi-choice Reactive Controllers). *Let*
α *and* β *be non-interfering multi-choice reactive controllers with program shape*
MRCtrl$(\bigcup_{1\leqslant i\leqslant n_\alpha} \alpha_i, \delta_\alpha)$ *and* ***MRCtrl***$(\bigcup_{1\leqslant j\leqslant n_\beta} \beta_j, \delta_\beta)$ *satisfying their compat-*
ible contracts (A_α, G_α) *and* (A_β, G_β) *and let* J_{cmp} *be a composition invariant.*
Then the parallel composition $\alpha \otimes \beta$ *is safe, i.e.,* $(\mathcal{E} \wedge A_\alpha \wedge Init_\alpha \wedge A_\beta \wedge Init_\beta) \rightarrow$
$[(\alpha \otimes \beta)^*](G_\alpha \wedge G_\beta)$ *is valid.*

Proof. Similar to Theorem 1 using the additional condition that δ_α (resp. δ_β)
does not appear in the functional behavior $\bigcup_{1\leqslant i\leqslant n_\alpha} \alpha_i$ (resp. $\bigcup_{1\leqslant j\leqslant n_\beta} \beta_j$) of
the controller, nor in its guarantee G_α (resp. G_β). See long version [8]. □

Non-interference of controllers and compatibility of contracts are standard
requirements when modeling a system compositionally and safely.

Example 8 (Safe composition of two water-level controllers). The contract of
the first reactive controller $wlctrl_1$ is the same as in Example 5 with necessary
changes. The contract for the second controller is:

$$
\begin{cases}
A_{wlctrl_2} : \top \\
G_{wlctrl_2} : wlm_2 \leqslant 2.3 \rightarrow fout_2 = 0 \\
\qquad\quad 9.7 \leqslant wlm_2 \rightarrow fout_2 = 1 \\
\qquad\quad (2.3 \leqslant wlm_2 \leqslant 9.7) \rightarrow (fout_2 = 0 \vee fout_2 = 1)
\end{cases}
$$

The controller actuates the outlet valve of the system ($fout_2$). It is open if
the real water-level of the second tank is too close to the maximum threshold
(10 here) to drain the tank and closed in order to fill the tank if too close to the
minimum threshold (2). The two controllers are non-interfering, the contracts
are compatible and they both satisfy their contracts (verified using the proof
calculus of $d\mathcal{L}$). Hence, Theorem 2 guarantees that the parallel composition is
safe, *i.e.* that the contract $(A_{wlctrl_1} \wedge A_{wlctrl_2}, G_{wlctrl_1} \wedge G_{wlctrl_2})$ is valid.

4.2 Parallel Composition of Controllable Plants

When composing two continuous components in parallel, the controllability of
the resulting system is the minimum of their individual controllability bounds
(which is obvious from the semantics of ODEs listed in Table 1: safety proofs
hold for any non-negative duration, so also for smaller durations).

Modeling. Non-interference of controllable plants ensures that their combined
continuous dynamics stays true to the isolated dynamics, and that they do not
interfere with the guarantees of the respective other component.

Definition 10 (Non-interfering Plants). *Two controllable plants* α *and* β
with ***CPlant***$(\{x' = \theta \,\&\, H\}, \Delta_\alpha)$ *and* ***CPlant***$(\{y' = \eta \,\&\, Q\}, \Delta_\beta)$ *and contracts*
(A_α, G_α) *and* (A_β, G_β) *are non-interfering if* $BV(\{x' = \theta \,\&\, H\}) \cap FV(\eta) = \varnothing$
and $BV(\{y' = \eta \,\&\, Q\}) \cap FV(\theta) = \varnothing$, *and if* $BV(\{x' = \theta \,\&\, H\}) \cap FV(G_\beta) = \varnothing$
and $BV(\{y' = \eta \,\&\, Q\}) \cap FV(G_\alpha) = \varnothing$.

Note that non-interference implies $BV(\{x' = \theta \ \& \ H\}) \cap BV(\{y' = \eta \ \& \ Q\}) = \varnothing$.

Definition 11 (Parallel Composition of Controllable Plants). *Let α and β be non-interfering controllable plants $CPlant(\{x' = \theta \ \& \ H\}, \Delta_\alpha)$ and $CPlant(\{y' = \eta \ \& \ Q\}, \Delta_\beta)$. The parallel composition $\alpha \otimes \beta$ is an ODE system of the shape $CPlant(\{x' = \theta, y' = \eta \ \& \ H \wedge Q\}, min(\Delta_\alpha, \Delta_\beta))$.*

Example 9 (Composition of two water-level). Here, we compose the water level dynamics of two tanks ($\{wl_1' = fin - fout_1, t' = 1 \ \& \ wl_1 \geqslant 0 \wedge t \leqslant \Delta_{wl_1}\}$ and $\{wl_2' = fout_1 - fout_2, t' = 1 \ \& \ wl_2 \geqslant 0 \wedge \Delta_{wl_2}\}$) to obtain a controllable plant modeling the evolution of both water levels simultaneously. Their respective controllability bounds are $\Delta_{wl_1} = 0.2\,\mathrm{s}$ and $\Delta_{wl_2} = 0.15\,\mathrm{s}$. The controllable plant resulting from the parallel composition expands to $\{wl_1' = fin - fout_1, wl_2' = fout_1 - fout_2, t' = 1 \ \& \ wl_1 \geqslant 0 \wedge wl_2 \geqslant 0 \wedge t \leqslant min(\Delta_{wl_1}, \Delta_{wl_2})\}$.

Algebraic Properties. Commutativity and associativity of the parallel composition pattern defined in [7] are preserved. The proof, detailed in the long version [8], follows from commutativity and associativity of "," in ODEs and of operator min.

Modular Verification. The conjunction of contracts is retained for parallel composition of continuous components, similar to parallel composition of controllers.

Theorem 3 (Composition of Controllable Plants). *Let α and β be two non-interfering controllable plants $CPlant(\{x' = \theta \ \& \ H\}, \Delta_\alpha)$, $CPlant(\{y' = \eta \ \& \ Q\}, \Delta_\beta)$ satisfying their respective compatible contracts (A_α, G_α), (A_β, G_β), and let J_{cmp} be a composition invariant. Then the parallel composition $\alpha \otimes \beta$ is safe, i.e., $(\mathcal{E} \wedge A_\alpha \wedge Init_\alpha \wedge A_\beta \wedge Init_\beta) \rightarrow [(\alpha \otimes \beta)^*](G_\alpha \wedge G_\beta)$ is valid.*

Proof. Similar to Theorem 1 after separating the non-interfering plants using the inverse direction of the differential ghost axiom [13], see long version [8].   □

Example 10 (Safe composition of two water-level). The contract for the first water level is the same as in Example 5 with necessary changes. We guarantee that the water level of the second tank is within 2 and 10, provided that there is a controller which reacts appropriately. Its contract is:

$$\begin{cases} A_{wl_2} : G_{wlctrl_2} \\ G_{wl_2} : 2 \leqslant wl_2 \leqslant 10 \end{cases}$$

We apply Theorem 3 to guarantee that the controllable plant modeling the evolution of water levels in distinct connected tanks is safe, *i.e.* it satisfies the contract $(Awl_1 \wedge A_{wl_2}, G_{wl_1} \wedge G_{wl_2})$.

4.3 Parallel Composition of Multi-choice Reactive Controllers and Controllable Plants

We present the composition of a multi-choice reactive controller with a controllable plant that may result from the composition of several atomic controllable plants. We lift the definition of **CCS** (Sect. 3) to a general integration of controllability and reactivity.

Modeling. We define a multi computer-controlled system **MCCS** as the parallel composition of a multi-choice reactive controller with a controllable plant.

Definition 12 (Multi Computer-Controlled System). *A multi computer-controlled system is a parallel composition of a multi-choice reactive controller* **MRCtrl**$(\bigcup_{1 \leqslant i \leqslant n} ctrl_i, \delta)$ *and a controllable plant* **CPlant**$(\{y' = \theta \ \& \ H\}, \Delta)$. *The parallel composition* **MCCS** *has the hybrid program shape:*

$$
\left(\{y' = \theta, t' = 1 \ \& \ H \wedge \underbrace{\bigwedge_{1 \leqslant i \leqslant n} t \leqslant \tau_i + \delta\}}_{\delta \leqslant \Delta} \cup \textbf{\textit{MRCtrl}} \left(\bigcup_{1 \leqslant i \leqslant n} ctrl_i, \delta \right) \right)^*
$$

The formula $\bigwedge_{1 \leqslant i \leqslant n} t \leqslant \tau_i + \delta$ is the conjunction of the reactivity bounds of all the n sub-controllers $ctrl_i$.

Modular Verification. Corollary 1 lifts Theorem 1 (for a single controller and a single plant) to multi computer-controlled systems of possibly many controllers with a controllable plant representing multiple simultaneous evolutions.

Corollary 1 (Composition of Multi-Choice Reactive Controller and Controllable Plant). *Let* **MRCtrl**$(\bigcup_{1 \leqslant i \leqslant n} ctrl_i, \delta)$ *be a multi-choice reactive controller non-interfering with the controllable plant* **CPlant**$(\{x' = \theta \ \& \ H\}, \Delta)$ *satisfying their compatible contracts* (A_{ctrl}, G_{ctrl}) *and* (A_{plant}, G_{plant}). *Further let* J_{cmp} *be a composition invariant. Then,* **MCCS** *is safe, i.e.,* $(\mathcal{E} \wedge A_{ctrl} \wedge Init_{ctrl} \wedge A_{plant} \wedge Init_{plant}) \rightarrow [\textbf{\textit{MCCS}}](G_{ctrl} \wedge G_{plant})$ *is valid.*

Proof. Similar to the proof of Theorem 1, but with multi-choice reactive controller instead of a single reactive controller. $\square$

4.4 Parallel Composition of Multi Computer-Controlled Systems

When composing multi computer-controlled systems, the combined reactivity of all controllers must not exceed the combined (minimum) controllability bounds of the plants. Otherwise, safety cannot be guaranteed, as elaborated next.

Modeling. The parallel composition of two multi computer-controlled systems is similar to the composition of a multi-choice reactive controller with a controllable plant to obtain a multi computer-controlled system **MCCS**, but with extra care for the combined reactivity bounds obtained from the physical cost model $\mathcal{C}$.

Definition 13 (Parallel Composition of Multi Computer-Controlled Systems). *Let* α *and* β *be two multi computer-controlled systems with shapes* $\alpha \doteq \left(\{x' = \theta, t' = 1 \ \& \ H \wedge \bigwedge_{1 \leqslant i \leqslant n} t \leqslant \tau_i + \delta_\alpha\} \cup \textbf{\textit{MRCtrl}}(\bigcup_{1 \leqslant i \leqslant n} \alpha_i, \delta_\alpha) \right)^*$, $\beta \doteq \left(\{y' = \eta, t' = 1 \ \& \ Q \wedge \bigwedge_{1 \leqslant j \leqslant m} t \leqslant \tau_j + \delta_\beta\} \cup \textbf{\textit{MRCtrl}}(\bigcup_{1 \leqslant j \leqslant m} \beta_j, \delta_\beta) \right)^*$.

The parallel composition $\alpha \otimes \beta$ has the hybrid program shape:

$$
\left(
\begin{array}{c}
\boldsymbol{MRCtrl}(\bigcup_{1 \leqslant i \leqslant n} \alpha_i, \mathcal{C}(\delta_\alpha, \delta_\beta)) \cup \boldsymbol{MRCtrl}(\bigcup_{1 \leqslant j \leqslant m} \beta_j, \mathcal{C}(\delta_\alpha, \delta_\beta)) \\
\cup \{ x' = \theta, y' = \eta, t' = 1 \ \& \ H \wedge Q \\
\wedge \underbrace{\displaystyle\bigwedge_{1 \leqslant i \leqslant n} t \leqslant \tau_i + \mathcal{C}(\delta_\alpha, \delta_\beta) \ \wedge \ \bigwedge_{1 \leqslant j \leqslant m} t \leqslant \tau_j + \mathcal{C}(\delta_\alpha, \delta_\beta) \}}_{\mathcal{C}(\delta_\alpha, \delta_\beta) \leqslant min(\Delta_\alpha, \Delta_\beta)}
\end{array}
\right)^*
$$

Algebraic Properties. We retain the commutativity and associativity properties (under the condition that the provided max+ cost function $\mathcal{C}$ is commutative and associative), essential for a modular component-based approach.

Proposition 1 (Commutativity and Associativity). *Let α, β and γ be multi computer-controlled systems. Then:*

$$
\begin{array}{lll}
\alpha \otimes \beta & = \beta \otimes \alpha & \textit{(Commutativity)} \\
(\alpha \otimes \beta) \otimes \gamma = \alpha \otimes (\beta \otimes \gamma) & & \textit{(Associativity)}
\end{array}
$$

Proof. Follows from Definition 13, see long version [8] for details.   □

Modular Verification. We retain also the respective contracts through the parallel composition. We assume that the individual reactivity bound δ_α of the controller does not occur in its functional behavior, nor in its guarantees.

Theorem 4 (Composition of Multi Computer-Controlled Systems).
Let α and β be non-interfering multi computer-controlled systems (with program shape $\boldsymbol{MCCS}_\alpha$ and $\boldsymbol{MCCS}_\beta$ per Definition 12) satisfying their respective compatible contracts (A_α, G_α) and (A_β, G_β), and let J_{cmp} be a composition invariant. Then the parallel composition $\alpha \otimes \beta$ is safe, i.e., $(\mathcal{E} \wedge A_\alpha \wedge Init_\alpha \wedge A_\beta \wedge Init_\beta) \to [\alpha \otimes \beta](G_\alpha \wedge G_\beta)$ is valid.

Proof. We use the commutativity and associativity of operator $\otimes$ to group the multi-choice reactive controllers into a single discrete fragment and the controllable plants into a single continuous fragment. We prove contracts are retained for the discrete fragment by Theorem 2 and for the continuous fragment by Theorem 3. Finally, contracts are retained for the composition of discrete fragment to the continuous fragment using Corollary 1, see long version [8].   □

Outlook. In this section, we presented how to extend our previous component-based approach to take into account the timing constraints inherent in the design of a Computer-Controlled System. We have proved that we retain the commutativity and associativity, essential to scale up to realistic systems. Finally, we state and prove theorems to retain contracts through the parallel composition. Theses results give us confidence in the ability of our approach to be adapted to new challenges that will arise when applied to realistic industrial systems.

5   Related Work

Recent component-based verification techniques [10,11] proposed a composition operator in $d\mathcal{L}$ based on the modeling pattern $(ctrl; plant)^*$ to split verification of systems into more manageable pieces. It focuses on separating self-contained components (a controller monitoring its own plant) instead of separating discrete and continuous fragments. This paper extends previous work [7] with capabilities to handle timing relations of CCS upon composition (using max+ cost functions) and syntactic proofs to facilitate implementation of the proposed techniques as tactics in the theorem prover KeYmaera X.

Hybrid automata [1] are a popular formalism to model hybrid systems, but composition of automata results in an exponential product automaton which is intractable to analyze in practice. *I/O hybrid automata* [9] is an extension of hybrid automata with explicit inputs and outputs. Assume-guarantee reasoning [4] on such automata tackles composability to prevent state-space explosion. Yet, use is in practice restricted to linear hybrid automata. Differential Dynamic Logic handles systems with ODEs (and not just linear ODEs), thus our approach is more expressive.

Hybrid Communicating Sequential Processes (HCSP) [5] is a hybrid extension of the CSP framework. It features a native parallel composition operator and communicating primitives in addition to standard constructs for hybrid systems (sequences, loops, ODEs) and a proof calculus has been proposed in [6]. In contrast, our parallel composition operator is not native and relies on usual constructs of $d\mathcal{L}$. The benefit is that we do not have to extend $d\mathcal{L}$ and check the soundness of such extension, but it requires additional effort to mechanize it into the theorem prover KeYmaera X. Also, our approach provides engineering support for timing aspects and modular verification principles.

6   Conclusion

We presented a component-based verification technique for modularly designing and verifying computer-controlled systems with special focus on timing constraints (reactivity and controllability) and modular verification. Our concepts enable systematic modeling of CCS in a modular way while maintaining algebraic properties of composition patterns and preserving contract proofs through composition. We additionally support reasoning on non-functional properties (reactivity, controllability) through multiple compositions of reactive controllers and plants. This paves the way to ultimately model complex cyber-physical systems (several controllers running in parallel according to a generic max+ cost function that monitor different plants) from only simple, atomic components. Verification of safety properties for the global system reduces to component safety proofs with only mild assumptions on the reactivity of controllers (does not exceed the controllability of plants) and compatibility between contracts.

As future work, we intend to allow more aggressive compositions to lift restrictions of the techniques presented here: allow some interference in the parallel composition of controllable plants and reactive controllers with additional compatibility proofs (lift non-interference restriction of Corollary 1); allow time and reactivity in the predictions and guarantees of controllers with refactoring techniques to strengthen control choices upon composition (lift restriction of Theorem 4 that does not grant controllers to exploit their reactivity bounds δ for control decisions); and support fine-grained communication going beyond shared variables with communication channels as in Hybrid Communicating Sequential Processes. For proof automation, we intend to implement the theorems of this paper as tactics in the KeYmaera X theorem prover.

References

1. Alur, R., Courcoubetis, C., Henzinger, T.A., Ho, P.-H.: Hybrid automata: an algorithmic approach to the specification and verification of hybrid systems. In: Grossman, R.L., Nerode, A., Ravn, A.P., Rischel, H. (eds.) HS 1991-1992. LNCS, vol. 736, pp. 209–229. Springer, Heidelberg (1993). https://doi.org/10.1007/3-540-57318-6_30
2. Benveniste, A., et al.: Contracts for system design. Technical report (2012)
3. Fulton, N., Mitsch, S., Quesel, J.-D., Völp, M., Platzer, A.: KeYmaera X: an axiomatic tactical theorem prover for hybrid systems. In: Felty, A.P., Middeldorp, A. (eds.) CADE 2015. LNCS (LNAI), vol. 9195, pp. 527–538. Springer, Cham (2015). https://doi.org/10.1007/978-3-319-21401-6_36
4. Henzinger, T.A., Minea, M., Prabhu, V.: Assume-guarantee reasoning for hierarchical hybrid systems. In: Di Benedetto, M.D., Sangiovanni-Vincentelli, A. (eds.) HSCC 2001. LNCS, vol. 2034, pp. 275–290. Springer, Heidelberg (2001). https://doi.org/10.1007/3-540-45351-2_24
5. Jifeng, H.: From CSP to hybrid systems. In: A Classical Mind, pp. 171–189. Prentice Hall International (UK) Ltd. (1994)
6. Liu, J., et al.: A calculus for hybrid CSP. In: Ueda, K. (ed.) APLAS 2010. LNCS, vol. 6461, pp. 1–15. Springer, Heidelberg (2010). https://doi.org/10.1007/978-3-642-17164-2_1
7. Lunel, S., Boyer, B., Talpin, J.-P.: Compositional proofs in differential dynamic logic. In: Legay, A., Schneider, K. (eds.) ACSD (2017)
8. Lunel, S., Mitsch, S., Boyer, B., Talpin, J.-P.: Parallel composition and modular verification of computer controlled systems in differential dynamic logic. CoRR, abs/1907.02881, July 2019
9. Lynch, N.A., Segala, R., Vaandrager, F.W.: Hybrid I/O automata. Inf. Comput. **185**(1), 105–157 (2003)
10. Müller, A., Mitsch, S., Retschitzegger, W., Schwinger, W., Platzer, A.: A component-based approach to hybrid systems safety verification. In: Ábrahám, E., Huisman, M. (eds.) IFM 2016. LNCS, vol. 9681, pp. 441–456. Springer, Cham (2016). https://doi.org/10.1007/978-3-319-33693-0_28
11. Müller, A., Mitsch, S., Retschitzegger, W., Schwinger, W., Platzer, A.: Tactical contract composition for hybrid system component verification. STTT **20**(6), 615–643 (2018). Special issue for selected papers from FASE 2017
12. Platzer, A.: The complete proof theory of hybrid systems. In: LICS, pp. 541–550. IEEE (2012)
13. Platzer, A.: A complete uniform substitution calculus for differential dynamic logic. J. Autom. Reas. **59**(2), 219–265 (2017)

14. Platzer, A.: Logical Foundations of Cyber-Physical Systems. Springer, Cham (2018). https://doi.org/10.1007/978-3-319-63588-0
15. Platzer, A., Tan, Y.K.: Differential equation axiomatization: the impressive power of differential ghosts. In: Dawar, A., Grädel, E. (eds.) LICS, pp. 819–828. ACM, New York (2018)
16. Signoles, J., Cuoq, P., Kirchner, F., Kosmatov, N., Prevosto, V., Yakobowski, B.: Frama-C: a software analysis perspective. Form. Asp. Comput. **27**, 573–609 (2012)

An Axiomatic Approach to Liveness
for Differential Equations

Yong Kiam Tan$^{(\boxtimes)}$ ⓘ and André Platzer$^{(\boxtimes)}$ ⓘ

Computer Science Department, Carnegie Mellon University, Pittsburgh, USA
{yongkiat,aplatzer}@cs.cmu.edu

Abstract. This paper presents an approach for deductive liveness verification for ordinary differential equations (ODEs) with differential dynamic logic. Numerous subtleties complicate the generalization of well-known discrete liveness verification techniques, such as loop variants, to the continuous setting. For example, ODE solutions may blow up in finite time or their progress towards the goal may converge to zero. Our approach handles these subtleties by successively refining ODE liveness properties using ODE invariance properties which have a well-understood deductive proof theory. This approach is widely applicable: we survey several liveness arguments in the literature and derive them all as special instances of our axiomatic refinement approach. We also correct several soundness errors in the surveyed arguments, which further highlights the subtlety of ODE liveness reasoning and the utility of our deductive approach. The library of common refinement steps identified through our approach enables both the sound development and justification of new ODE liveness proof rules from our axioms.

Keywords: Differential equations · Liveness · Differential dynamic logic

1 Introduction

Hybrid systems are mathematical models describing discrete and continuous dynamics, and interactions thereof [6]. This flexibility makes them natural models of cyber-physical systems (CPSs) which feature interactions between discrete computational control and continuous real world physics [2,19]. Formal verification of hybrid systems is of significant practical interest because the CPSs they model frequently operate in safety-critical settings. Verifying properties of the continuous dynamics is a key aspect of any such endeavor.

This paper focuses on deductive liveness verification for continuous dynamics described by ordinary differential equations (ODEs). We work with differential dynamic logic (dL) [16,17,19], a logic for *deductive verification* of hybrid systems, which compositionally lifts our results to the hybrid systems setting. Methods for proving liveness in the discrete setting are well-known: loop variants show that discrete loops eventually reach a desired goal, while temporal logic is used to

© Springer Nature Switzerland AG 2019
M. H. ter Beek et al. (Eds.): FM 2019, LNCS 11800, pp. 371–388, 2019.
https://doi.org/10.1007/978-3-030-30942-8_23

Table 1. Surveyed ODE liveness arguments with our corrections highlighted in blue. The referenced corollaries are our corresponding (corrected) derived proof rules.

Source	Without domain constraints		With domain constraints	
[15]	OK	(Corollary 5)	if open/closed, initially false	(Corollary 13)
[22,23]	[23, Remark 3.6] is incorrect		if conditions checked globally	(Corollary 19)
[24]	if compact	(Corollary 12)	if compact	(Corollary 15)
[25]	OK	(Corollary 9)	OK	(Corollary 16)
[27]	if globally Lipschitz	(Corollary 7)	if globally Lipschitz	(Corollary 14)

specify and study liveness properties in concurrent and infinitary settings [12,13]. In the continuous setting, *liveness* for an ODE means that its solutions eventually enter a desired goal region in finite time without leaving the domain of allowed (or safe) states.[1] Deduction of such ODE liveness properties is hampered by several difficulties: *(i)* solutions of ODEs may converge towards a goal without ever reaching it, *(ii)* solutions of (non-linear) ODEs may blow up in finite time leaving insufficient time for the desired goal to be reached, and *(iii)* the goal may be reachable but only by leaving the domain constraint. In contrast, *invariance* properties for ODEs are better understood [9,11] and have a complete dL axiomatization [20]. Motivated by the aforementioned difficulties, we present dL axioms enabling step-by-step refinement of ODE liveness properties with a sequence of ODE invariance properties. This brings the full deductive power of dL's ODE invariance proof rules to bear on liveness proofs. Our approach is a general framework for understanding ODE liveness arguments. We use it to survey several arguments from the literature and derive them all as (corrected) dL proof rules, see Table 1. This logical presentation has two key benefits:

- The proof rules are *derived* from sound axioms of dL, guaranteeing their correctness. Many of the surveyed arguments contain subtle soundness errors, see Table 1. These errors do not diminish the surveyed work. Rather, they emphasize the need for an axiomatic, uniform way of presenting and analyzing ODE liveness arguments rather than ad hoc approaches.
- The approach identifies common refinement steps that form a basis for the surveyed liveness arguments. This library of building blocks enables sound development and justification of new ODE liveness proof rules, e.g., by generalizing individual refinement steps or by exploring different combinations of those steps. Corollaries 8, 10, and 18 are examples of new ODE liveness proof rules that can be derived and justified using our uniform approach.

All proofs are in the companion report [28], together with counterexamples for the soundness errors listed in Table 1. Colored versions of all figures are available online.

---

[1] This property has also been called, e.g., *eventuality* [23,25] and *reachability* [27]. To minimize ambiguity, this paper refers to the property as *liveness*, with a precise formal definition in Sect. 2. Other advanced notions of liveness for ODEs are discussed in Sect. 6, although their formal deduction is left for future work.

2   Background

This section reviews the syntax and semantics of dL, focusing on its continuous fragment which has a complete axiomatization for ODE invariants [20]. Full presentations of dL, including its discrete fragment, are available elsewhere [17,19].

2.1   Syntax

The grammar of dL terms is as follows, where $v \in \mathbb{V}$ is a variable and $c \in \mathbb{Q}$ is a rational constant. These terms are polynomials over the set of variables $\mathbb{V}$:

$$p, q ::= v \mid c \mid p + q \mid p \cdot q$$

The grammar of dL formulas is as follows, where $\sim \in \{=, \neq, \geq, >, \leq, <\}$ is a comparison operator and α is a hybrid program:

First-order formulas of real arithmetic P, Q
$$\phi, \psi ::= \overbrace{p \sim q \mid \phi \wedge \psi \mid \phi \vee \psi \mid \neg \phi \mid \forall v\, \phi \mid \exists v\, \phi} \\ \mid [\alpha]\phi \mid \langle \alpha \rangle \phi$$

The notation $p \succcurlyeq q$ (resp. $\preccurlyeq$) is used when the comparison operator can be either $\geq$ or $>$ (resp. $\leq$ or $<$). Other standard logical connectives, e.g., $\rightarrow$, $\leftrightarrow$, are definable as in classical logic. Formulas not containing the modalities $[\cdot], \langle \cdot \rangle$ are formulas of first-order real arithmetic and are written as P, Q. The box ($[\alpha]\phi$) and diamond ($\langle \alpha \rangle \phi$) modality formulas express dynamic properties of the hybrid program α. We focus on *continuous* programs, where α is given by a system of ODEs $x' = f(x)\,\&\,Q$. Here, $x' = f(x)$ is an n-dimensional system of differential equations, $x_1' = f_1(x), \ldots, x_n' = f_n(x)$, over variables $x = (x_1, \ldots, x_n)$, where the LHS x_i' is the time derivative of x_i and the RHS $f_i(x)$ is a polynomial over variables x. The domain constraint Q specifies the set of states in which the ODE is allowed to evolve continuously. When there is no domain constraint, i.e., Q is the formula *true*, the ODE is written as $x' = f(x)$.

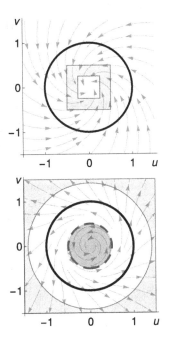

Fig. 1. Visualization of α_l (above) and α_n (below). Solutions of α_l globally spiral towards the origin. In contrast, solutions of α_n spiral inwards within the inner red disk (dashed boundary), but spiral outwards otherwise. For both ODEs, solutions starting on the black unit circle eventually enter their respective shaded green goal regions.

Two running example ODEs are visualized in Fig. 1 with directional arrows corresponding to their RHS evaluated at points on the plane. The first ODE,

$\alpha_l \equiv u' = -v - u, v' = u - v$, is *linear* because its RHS depends linearly on u, v. The second ODE, $\alpha_n \equiv u' = -v - u(\frac{1}{4} - u^2 - v^2), v' = u - v(\frac{1}{4} - u^2 - v^2)$, is *non-linear*. The non-linearity of α_n results in more complex behavior for its solutions, e.g., the difference in spiraling behavior shown in Fig. 1. In fact, solutions of α_n blow up in finite time iff they start outside the disk characterized by $u^2 + v^2 \leq \frac{1}{4}$. Finite time blow up is impossible for linear ODEs like α_l [5, 29].

When terms (or formulas) appear in contexts involving ODEs $x' = f(x)$, it is sometimes necessary to restrict the set of free variables they are allowed to mention. These restrictions are always stated explicitly and are also indicated as arguments[2] to terms (or formulas), e.g., $p()$ means the term p does not mention any of $x_1, \ldots, x_n$ free, while $P(x)$ means the formula P may mention all of them.

2.2 Semantics

States $\omega : \mathbb{V} \to \mathbb{R}$ assign real values to each variable in $\mathbb{V}$; the set of all states is written $\mathbb{S}$. The semantics of polynomial term p in state $\omega \in \mathbb{S}$ is the real value $\omega[\![p]\!]$ of the corresponding polynomial function evaluated at ω. The semantics of formula ϕ is the set of states $[\![\phi]\!] \subseteq \mathbb{S}$ in which that formula is true. The semantics of first-order logical connectives are defined as usual, e.g., $[\![\phi \wedge \psi]\!] = [\![\phi]\!] \cap [\![\psi]\!]$.

For ODEs, the semantics of the modal operators is defined directly as follows.[3] Let $\omega \in \mathbb{S}$ and $\boldsymbol{\varphi} : [0, T) \to \mathbb{S}$ (for some $0 < T \leq \infty$), be the unique, right-maximal solution [5, 29] to the ODE $x' = f(x)$ with initial value $\boldsymbol{\varphi}(0) = \omega$:

$\omega \in [\![[x' = f(x) \,\&\, Q]\phi]\!]$ iff for all $0 \leq \tau < T$ where $\boldsymbol{\varphi}(\zeta) \in [\![Q]\!]$ for all $0 \leq \zeta \leq \tau$:

$$\boldsymbol{\varphi}(\tau) \in [\![\phi]\!]$$

$\omega \in [\![\langle x' = f(x) \,\&\, Q\rangle\phi]\!]$ iff there exists $0 \leq \tau < T$ such that:

$$\boldsymbol{\varphi}(\tau) \in [\![\phi]\!] \text{ and } \boldsymbol{\varphi}(\zeta) \in [\![Q]\!] \text{ for all } 0 \leq \zeta \leq \tau$$

Informally, $[x' = f(x) \,\&\, Q]\phi$ is true in initial state ω if *all* states reached by following the ODE from ω while remaining in the domain constraint Q satisfy postcondition ϕ. Dually, the *liveness* property $\langle x' = f(x) \,\&\, Q\rangle\phi$ is true in initial state ω if *some* state which satisfies the postcondition ϕ is eventually reached in *finite* time by following the ODE from ω while staying in domain constraint Q. For the running example, Fig. 1 suggests that formulas[4] $\langle \alpha_l \rangle (\frac{1}{4} \leq \|(u, v)\|_\infty \leq \frac{1}{2})$ and $\langle \alpha_n \rangle u^2 + v^2 \geq 2$ are true for initial states ω on the unit circle. These liveness properties are rigorously proved in Examples 6 and 11 respectively.

Variables $y \in \mathbb{V} \setminus \{x\}$ not occurring on the LHS of ODE $x' = f(x)$ remain constant along solutions $\boldsymbol{\varphi} : [0, T) \to \mathbb{S}$ of the ODE, with $\boldsymbol{\varphi}(\tau)(y) = \boldsymbol{\varphi}(0)(y)$ for all $\tau \in [0, T)$. Since only the values of $x = (x_1, \ldots, x_n)$ change along the solution $\boldsymbol{\varphi}$ it may also be viewed geometrically as a trajectory in $\mathbb{R}^n$, dependent on the

---

[2] This understanding of variable dependencies is made precise using function and predicate symbols in dL's uniform substitution calculus [17].

[3] The semantics of dL formulas is defined compositionally elsewhere [17, 19].

[4] Here, $\|(u, v)\|_\infty$ denotes the L^∞ norm. The inequality $\|(u, v)\|_\infty \leq \frac{1}{2}$ is expressible in first-order real arithmetic as $u^2 \leq \frac{1}{4} \wedge v^2 \leq \frac{1}{4}$ (similarly for $\frac{1}{4} \leq \|(u, v)\|_\infty$).

initial values of the constant *parameters* y. Similarly, the value of terms and formulas depends only on the values of their free variables [17]. Thus, terms (or formulas) whose free variables are all parameters for $x' = f(x)$ also have constant (truth) values along solutions of the ODE. For formulas ϕ that only mention free variables x, $[\![\phi]\!]$ can also be viewed geometrically as a subset of $\mathbb{R}^n$. Such a formula is said to *characterize* a (topologically) open (resp. closed, bounded, compact) set with respect to variables x iff the set $[\![\phi]\!] \subseteq \mathbb{R}^n$ is topologically open (resp. closed, bounded, compact) with respect to the Euclidean topology. These topological conditions are used as side conditions for some of the axioms and proof rules in this paper. In the report [28], a more general definition of these side conditions is given for formulas ϕ that mention parameters y. These side conditions are decidable [3] when ϕ is a formula of first-order real arithmetic and there are simple syntactic criteria for checking if they hold [28].

Formula ϕ is valid iff $[\![\phi]\!] = \mathbb{S}$, i.e., ϕ is true in all states. In particular, if the formula $I \to [x' = f(x) \,\&\, Q]I$ is valid, the formula I is an *invariant* of the ODE $x' = f(x) \,\&\, Q$. Unfolding the semantics, this means that from any initial state ω satisfying I, all states reached by the solution of the ODE $x' = f(x)$ from ω while staying in the domain constraint Q satisfy I.

2.3 Proof Calculus

All derivations are presented in a classical sequent calculus with usual rules for manipulating logical connectives and sequents. The semantics of *sequent* $\Gamma \vdash \phi$ is equivalent to the formula $(\bigwedge_{\psi \in \Gamma} \psi) \to \phi$ and a sequent is valid iff its corresponding formula is valid. Completed branches in a sequent proof are marked with $*$. First-order real arithmetic is decidable [3] so we assume such a decision procedure and label proof steps with ℝ when they follow from real arithmetic. An axiom (schema) is *sound* iff all instances of the axiom are valid. Proof rules are *sound* iff validity of all premises (above the rule bar) entails validity of the conclusion (below the rule bar). Axioms and proof rules are *derivable* if they can be deduced from sound dL axioms and proof rules. Soundness of the base dL axiomatization ensures that derived axioms and proof rules are sound [17,19,20].

The dL proof calculus (briefly recalled below) is *complete* for ODE invariants [20], i.e., any true ODE invariant expressible in first-order real arithmetic can be proved in the calculus. The proof rule dI$_\succcurlyeq$ (below) uses the *Lie derivative* of polynomial p with respect to the ODE $x' = f(x)$, which is defined as $\mathcal{L}_{f(x)}(p) \overset{\text{def}}{=} \sum_{x_i \in x} \frac{\partial p}{\partial x_i} f_i(x)$. Higher Lie derivatives $\dot{p}^{(i)}$ are defined inductively: $\dot{p}^{(0)} \overset{\text{def}}{=} p, \dot{p}^{(i+1)} \overset{\text{def}}{=} \mathcal{L}_{f(x)}(\dot{p}^{(i)}), \dot{p} \overset{\text{def}}{=} \dot{p}^{(1)}$. Syntactically, Lie derivatives $\dot{p}^{(i)}$ are polynomials in the term language. They are provably definable in dL using differentials [17]. Semantically, the value of Lie derivative $\dot{p}$ is equal to the time derivative of the value of p along solution φ of the ODE $x' = f(x)$.

Lemma 1 (Axioms and proof rules of dL [17,19,20]). *The following are sound axioms and proof rules of* dL.

$\langle \cdot \rangle$ $\langle \alpha \rangle P \leftrightarrow \neg[\alpha]\neg P$ K $[\alpha](R \to P) \to ([\alpha]R \to [\alpha]P)$

$$\text{dI}_{\succcurlyeq} \quad \frac{Q \vdash \dot{p} \geq \dot{q}}{\Gamma, p \succcurlyeq q \vdash [x' = f(x) \,\&\, Q] p \succcurlyeq q} \quad \text{(where } \succcurlyeq \text{ is either } \geq \text{ or } >\text{)}$$

$$\text{dC} \quad \frac{\Gamma \vdash [x' = f(x) \,\&\, Q]C \quad \Gamma \vdash [x' = f(x) \,\&\, Q \wedge C]P}{\Gamma \vdash [x' = f(x) \,\&\, Q]P}$$

$$\text{dW} \quad \frac{Q \vdash P}{\Gamma \vdash [x' = f(x) \,\&\, Q]P} \qquad \text{dGt} \quad \frac{\Gamma, t = 0 \vdash \langle x' = f(x), t' = 1 \,\&\, Q \rangle P}{\Gamma \vdash \langle x' = f(x) \,\&\, Q \rangle P}$$

$$\text{M}['] \quad \frac{Q, R \vdash P \quad \Gamma \vdash [x' = f(x) \,\&\, Q]R}{\Gamma \vdash [x' = f(x) \,\&\, Q]P} \qquad \text{M}\langle' \rangle \quad \frac{Q, R \vdash P \quad \Gamma \vdash \langle x' = f(x) \,\&\, Q \rangle R}{\Gamma \vdash \langle x' = f(x) \,\&\, Q \rangle P}$$

Axiom $\langle \cdot \rangle$ expresses the duality between the box and diamond modalities. It is used to switch between the two in proofs and to dualize axioms between the box and diamond modalities. Axiom K is the modus ponens principle for the box modality. Differential invariants $\text{dI}_{\succcurlyeq}$ says that if the Lie derivatives obey the inequality $\dot{p} \geq \dot{q}$, then $p \succcurlyeq q$ is an invariant of the ODE. Differential cuts dC says that if we can separately prove that formula C is always satisfied along the solution, then C may be assumed in the domain constraint when proving the same for formula P. In the box modality, solutions are restricted to stay in the domain constraint Q; differential weakening dW says that postcondition P is always satisfied along solutions if it is already implied by the domain constraint. Liveness arguments are often based on analyzing the duration that solutions of the ODE are followed. Rule dGt is a special instance of the more general differential ghosts rule [17,19,20] which allows *new* auxiliary variables to be introduced for the purposes of proof. It augments the ODE $x' = f(x)$ with an additional differential equation, $t' = 1$, so that the (fresh) variable t, with initial value $t = 0$, tracks the progress of time. Using dW,K,$\langle \cdot \rangle$, the final two monotonicity proof rules M$[']$,M$\langle' \rangle$ for differential equations are derivable. They strengthen the postcondition from P to R, assuming domain constraint Q, for the box and diamond modalities respectively.

Throughout this paper, we present proof rules, e.g., dW, that discard all assumptions Γ on initial states when moving from conclusion to the premises. Intuitively, this is necessary for soundness because the premises of these rules internalize reasoning that happens *along solutions* of the ODE $x' = f(x) \,\&\, Q$ rather than in the initial state. On the other hand, the truth value of constant assumptions $P()$ do not change along solutions, so they can be soundly kept across rule applications [19]. These additional constant contexts are useful when working with assumptions on symbolic parameters e.g., $v() > 0$ to represent a (constant) positive velocity.

3   Liveness via Box Refinements

Suppose we already know an initial liveness property $\langle x' = f(x) \,\&\, Q_0 \rangle P_0$ for the ODE $x' = f(x)$. How could this be used to prove a desired liveness property $\langle x' = f(x) \,\&\, Q \rangle P$ for that ODE? Logically, this amounts to proving:

$$\langle x' = f(x) \,\&\, Q_0 \rangle P_0 \rightarrow \langle x' = f(x) \,\&\, Q \rangle P \tag{1}$$

Proving implication (1) *refines* the initial liveness property to the desired one. Our approach is built on refinement axioms that conclude such implications from box modality formulas. The following are two basic derived refinement axioms:

Lemma 2 (Diamond refinement axioms). *The following* $\langle \cdot \rangle$ *refinement axioms are derivable in* dL.

$$\text{DR}\langle \cdot \rangle \quad [x' = f(x)\,\&\,R]Q \to (\langle x' = f(x)\,\&\,R \rangle P \to \langle x' = f(x)\,\&\,Q \rangle P)$$

$$\text{K}\langle \& \rangle \quad [x' = f(x)\,\&\,Q \wedge \neg P]\neg G \to (\langle x' = f(x)\,\&\,Q \rangle G \to \langle x' = f(x)\,\&\,Q \rangle P)$$

In axiom $\text{K}\langle \& \rangle$, formula $[x' = f(x)\,\&\,Q \wedge \neg P]\neg G$ says the solution cannot get to G before getting to P as G never happens while $\neg P$ holds. In axiom $\text{DR}\langle \cdot \rangle$, formula $[x' = f(x)\,\&\,R]Q$ says that the ODE solution never leaves Q while staying in R, so the solution getting to P within R implies that it also gets to P within Q. These axioms prove implication (1) in just one refinement step. Logical implication is transitive though, so we can also chain a longer sequence of such steps to prove implication (1). This is shown in (2), with neighboring implications informally chained together for illustration:

$$\overbrace{\langle x' = f(x)\,\&\,Q_0 \rangle P_0 \to}^{\text{DR}\langle \cdot \rangle \text{ with } [x'=f(x)\,\&\,Q_1]Q_0} \overbrace{\langle x' = f(x)\,\&\,Q_1 \rangle P_0 \to}^{\text{K}\langle \& \rangle \text{ with } [x'=f(x)\,\&\,Q_1 \wedge \neg P_1]\neg P_0} \langle x' = f(x)\,\&\,Q_1 \rangle P_1$$
$$\to \cdots \to \langle x' = f(x)\,\&\,Q \rangle P \tag{2}$$

The chain of refinements (2) proves the desired implication (1), but to formally conclude the liveness property $\langle x' = f(x)\,\&\,Q \rangle P$, we still need to prove the hypothesis $\langle x' = f(x)\,\&\,Q_0 \rangle P_0$ on the left of the implication. The following axioms provide a means of formally establishing such an initial liveness property:

Lemma 3 (Existence axioms). *The following existence axioms are sound. In both axioms, $p()$ is constant for the ODE $x' = f(x), t' = 1$. In axiom GEx, the ODE $x' = f(x)$ is globally Lipschitz continuous. In axiom BEx, the formula $B(x)$ characterizes a bounded set over variables x.*

$$\text{GEx} \quad \langle x' = f(x), t' = 1 \rangle t > p()$$

$$\text{BEx} \quad \langle x' = f(x), t' = 1 \rangle (\neg B(x) \vee t > p())$$

Axioms GEx,BEx are stated for ODEs with an explicit time variable t, where $x' = f(x)$ does not mention t. Within proofs, these axioms can be accessed after using rule dGt to add a fresh time variable t. Solutions of globally Lipschitz ODEs exist for all time so axiom GEx says that along such solutions, the value of time variable t eventually exceeds that of the constant term $p()$.[5] This global Lipschitz continuity condition is satisfied e.g., by α_l, and more generally by linear ODEs of the form $x' = Ax$, where A is a matrix of (constant) parameters [5]. Global Lipschitz continuity is a strong requirement that does not hold even for simple

---

[5] It is important for soundness that $p()$ is constant for the ODE, e.g., instances of axiom GEx with postcondition $t > 2t$ are clearly not valid.

non-linear ODEs like α_n, which only have short-lived solutions (see Fig. 1). This phenomenon, where the right-maximal ODE solution φ is only defined on a finite time interval $[0, T)$ with $T < \infty$, is known as *finite time blow up of solutions* [5]. Axiom BEx removes the global Lipschitz continuity requirement but weakens the postcondition to say that solutions must either exist for sufficient duration or blow up and leave the *bounded* set characterized by formula $B(x)$.

Refinement with axiom $\mathrm{DR}\langle\cdot\rangle$ requires proving the formula $[x' = f(x) \& R]Q$. Naïvely, we might expect that adding $\neg P$ to the domain constraint should also work, i.e., the solution only needs to be in Q while it has not yet gotten to P:

$$\mathrm{DR}\langle\cdot\rangle \text{\textlightning} \; [x' = f(x) \& R \wedge \neg P]Q \rightarrow \left(\langle x' = f(x) \& R \rangle P \rightarrow \langle x' = f(x) \& Q \rangle P \right)$$

This conjectured axiom is unsound (indicated by $\text{\textlightning}$) as the solution could sneak out of Q when it crosses from $\neg P$ into P. In continuous settings, the language of topology makes precise what this means. The following topological refinement axioms soundly restrict what happens at the crossover point:

Lemma 4 (Topological refinement axioms). *The following topological $\langle\cdot\rangle$ refinement axioms are sound. In axiom COR, P, Q either both characterize topologically open or both characterize topologically closed sets over variables x.*

$$\mathrm{COR} \; \neg P \wedge [x' = f(x) \& R \wedge \neg P]Q \rightarrow \left(\langle x' = f(x) \& R \rangle P \rightarrow \langle x' = f(x) \& Q \rangle P \right)$$

$$\mathrm{SAR} \; [x' = f(x) \& R \wedge \neg(P \wedge Q)]Q \rightarrow \left(\langle x' = f(x) \& R \rangle P \rightarrow \langle x' = f(x) \& Q \rangle P \right)$$

Axiom COR is the more informative topological refinement axiom. Like the (unsound) axiom candidate $\mathrm{DR}\langle\cdot\rangle\text{\textlightning}$, it allows formula $\neg P$ to be assumed in the domain constraint when proving the box refinement. For soundness though, axiom COR has additional topological side conditions on formulas P, Q so it can only be used when these conditions are met. Axiom SAR applies more generally but only assumes the less informative formula $\neg(P \wedge Q)$ in the domain constraint for the box modality formula in the refinement. Its proof crucially relies on Q being a formula of real arithmetic so that the set it characterizes has tame topological behavior [3], see the proof in the report [28] for more details.[6]

4   Liveness Without Domain Constraints

This section presents proof rules for liveness properties of ODEs $x' = f(x)$ without domain constraints, i.e., where Q is the formula *true*. Errors and omissions in the surveyed techniques are <u>highlighted in blue</u>.

---

[6] By topological considerations similar to COR, axiom SAR is also sound if it requires that the formula P (or resp. Q) characterizes a topologically closed (resp. open) set over the ODE variables x. These additional cases are also proved in the report [28] without relying on the fact that Q is a formula of real arithmetic.

4.1 Differential Variants

A fundamental technique for verifying liveness of discrete loops is the identification of a loop variant, i.e., a quantity that decreases monotonically across each loop iteration. Differential variants [15] are their continuous analog:

Corollary 5 (Atomic differential variants [15]). *The following proof rules (where $\succcurlyeq$ is either $\geq$ or $>$) are derivable in* dL. *Terms $\varepsilon(), p_0()$ are constant for ODE $x' = f(x), t' = 1$. In rule $dV_{\succcurlyeq}$, $x' = f(x)$ is globally Lipschitz continuous.*

$$dV_{\succcurlyeq}^* \quad \frac{\neg(p \succcurlyeq 0) \vdash \dot{p} \geq \varepsilon()}{\Gamma, p = p_0(), t = 0, \langle x' = f(x), t' = 1 \rangle \big(p_0() + \varepsilon()t > 0\big) \vdash \langle x' = f(x), t' = 1 \rangle p \succcurlyeq 0}$$

$$dV_{\succcurlyeq} \quad \frac{\neg(p \succcurlyeq 0) \vdash \dot{p} \geq \varepsilon()}{\Gamma, \varepsilon() > 0 \vdash \langle x' = f(x) \rangle p \succcurlyeq 0}$$

Proof Sketch ([28]). Rule $dV_{\succcurlyeq}^*$ derives by using axiom $K\langle\&\rangle$ with the choice of formula $G \equiv p_0() + \varepsilon()t > 0$:

$$K\langle\&\rangle \quad \frac{\Gamma, p = p_0(), t = 0 \vdash [x' = f(x), t' = 1 \& \neg(p \succcurlyeq 0)]p_0() + \varepsilon()t \leq 0}{\Gamma, p = p_0(), t = 0, \langle x' = f(x), t' = 1 \rangle \big(p_0() + \varepsilon()t > 0\big) \vdash \langle x' = f(x), t' = 1 \rangle p \succcurlyeq 0}$$

Monotonicity $M[']$ strengthens the postcondition to $p \geq p_0() + \varepsilon()t$ with the domain constraint $\neg(p \succcurlyeq 0)$. A subsequent use of $dI_{\succcurlyeq}$ completes the derivation:

$$\frac{\dfrac{\neg(p \succcurlyeq 0) \vdash \dot{p} \geq \varepsilon()}{dI_{\succcurlyeq} \quad \Gamma, p = p_0(), t = 0 \vdash [x' = f(x), t' = 1 \& \neg(p \succcurlyeq 0)]p \geq p_0() + \varepsilon()t}}{M['] \quad \Gamma, p = p_0(), t = 0 \vdash [x' = f(x), t' = 1 \& \neg(p \succcurlyeq 0)]p_0() + \varepsilon()t \leq 0}$$

Rule $dV_{\succcurlyeq}$ is derived in the report [28] as a corollary of rule $dV_{\succcurlyeq}^*$. It uses the global existence axiom GEx and rule dGt to introduce the time variable. □

The premises of both rules require a constant (positive) lower bound on the Lie derivative $\dot{p}$ which ensures that the value of p strictly increases along solutions to the ODE, eventually becoming non-negative. Soundness of both rules therefore crucially requires that ODE solutions exist for sufficiently long for p to become non-negative. This is usually left as a soundness-critical side condition in liveness proof rules [15,25], but such a side condition is antithetical to approaches for minimizing the soundness-critical core in implementations [17] because it requires checking the (semantic) condition that solutions exist for sufficient duration. The conclusion of rule $dV_{\succcurlyeq}^*$ formalizes this side condition as an assumption while rule $dV_{\succcurlyeq}$ uses global Lipschitz continuity of the ODEs to show it. All subsequent proof rules can also be presented with sufficient duration assumptions like $dV_{\succcurlyeq}^*$ but these are omitted for brevity.

Example 6. Rule $dV_{\succcurlyeq}$ enables a liveness proof for the linear ODE α_l as suggested by Fig. 1. The proof is shown on the left below and visualized on the right. The first monotonicity step $M\langle'\rangle$ strengthens the postcondition to the inner blue circle $u^2 + v^2 = \frac{1}{4}$ which is contained within the green goal region. Next, since solutions satisfy $u^2 + v^2 = 1$ initially (black circle), the $K\langle \& \rangle$ step expresses an intermediate value property: to show that the *continuous* solution eventually reaches $u^2 + v^2 = \frac{1}{4}$, it suffices to show that it eventually reaches $u^2 + v^2 \leq \frac{1}{4}$ (see Corollary 7). The postcondition is rearranged before $\mathrm{dV}_{\succcurlyeq}$ is used with $\varepsilon() = \frac{1}{2}$. Its premise proves with $\mathbb{R}$ because the Lie derivative of $\frac{1}{4} - (u^2 + v^2)$ with respect to α_l is $2(u^2 + v^2)$, which is bounded below by $\frac{1}{2}$ with assumption $\frac{1}{4} - (u^2 + v^2) < 0$.

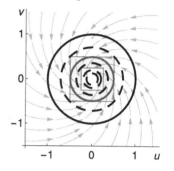

$$
\begin{array}{c}
\mathbb{R} \quad \dfrac{*}{\frac{1}{4} < u^2 + v^2 \vdash 2(u^2 + v^2) \geq \frac{1}{2}} \\[2pt]
\dfrac{\frac{1}{4} - (u^2 + v^2) < 0 \vdash 2(u^2 + v^2) \geq \frac{1}{2}}{} \\[2pt]
\mathrm{dV}_{\succcurlyeq} \quad \dfrac{}{u^2 + v^2 = 1 \vdash \langle \alpha_l \rangle \frac{1}{4} - (u^2 + v^2) \geq 0} \\[2pt]
\dfrac{u^2 + v^2 = 1 \vdash \langle \alpha_l \rangle u^2 + v^2 \leq \frac{1}{4}}{} \\[2pt]
K\langle \& \rangle \quad \dfrac{}{u^2 + v^2 = 1 \vdash \langle \alpha_l \rangle u^2 + v^2 = \frac{1}{4}} \\[2pt]
M\langle ' \rangle \quad \dfrac{}{u^2 + v^2 = 1 \vdash \langle \alpha_l \rangle \left(\frac{1}{4} \leq \|(u, v)\|_\infty \leq \frac{1}{2} \right)}
\end{array}
$$

The Lie derivative calculation shows that the value of $u^2 + v^2$ decreases along solutions of α_l, as visualized by the shrinking (dashed) circles. However, the rate of shrinking converges to zero as solutions approach the origin, so solutions *never* reach the origin in finite time! This is why $\mathrm{dV}_{\succcurlyeq}^*, \mathrm{dV}_{\succcurlyeq}$ need a *constant* positive lower bound on the Lie derivative $\dot{p} \geq \varepsilon()$ instead of merely requiring $\dot{p} > 0$.

It is instructive to examine the chain of refinements (2) underlying the proof. The first $\mathrm{dV}_{\succcurlyeq}$ step refines the initial liveness property from GEx, i.e., that solutions exist globally (so, for at least $\frac{3}{4} / \frac{1}{2} = \frac{3}{2}$ time), to the property $u^2 + v^2 \leq \frac{1}{4}$. Subsequent refinement steps can be read off from the proof steps above:

$$
\langle \alpha_l, t' = 1 \rangle t > \frac{3}{2} \xrightarrow{\mathrm{dV}_{\succcurlyeq}} \langle \alpha_l \rangle u^2 + v^2 \leq \frac{1}{4} \xrightarrow{K\langle \& \rangle} \langle \alpha_l \rangle u^2 + v^2 = \frac{1}{4} \xrightarrow{M\langle ' \rangle} \langle \alpha_l \rangle \left(\frac{1}{4} \leq \|(u, v)\|_\infty \leq \frac{1}{2} \right)
$$

The latter two steps illustrate the idea behind the next two surveyed proof rules. In the original presentation [27], the ODE $x' = f(x)$ is only assumed to be locally Lipschitz continuous, which is insufficient for global existence of solutions, making the original rules unsound. See the report [28] for counterexamples.

Corollary 7 (Equational differential variants [27]). *The following proof rules are derivable in* dL. *Term* $\varepsilon()$ *is constant for ODE* $x' = f(x)$ *and the ODE is globally Lipschitz continuous for both rules.*

$$
\mathrm{dV}_= \; \frac{p < 0 \vdash \dot{p} \geq \varepsilon()}{\Gamma, \varepsilon() > 0, p \leq 0 \vdash \langle x' = f(x) \rangle p = 0}
\qquad
\mathrm{dV}_=^M \; \frac{p = 0 \vdash P \quad p < 0 \vdash \dot{p} \geq \varepsilon()}{\Gamma, \varepsilon() > 0, p \leq 0 \vdash \langle x' = f(x) \rangle P}
$$

The view of $\mathrm{dV}_{\succcurlyeq}$ as a refinement of GEx immediately yields generalizations to higher Lie derivatives. For example, it suffices that *any* higher Lie derivative $\dot{p}^{(k)}$ is bounded below by a positive constant rather than just the first:

Corollary 8 (Atomic higher differential variants). *The following proof rule (where $\succcurlyeq$ is either $\geq$ or $>$) is derivable in* dL. *Term $\varepsilon()$ is constant for ODE $x' = f(x)$ and the ODE is globally Lipschitz continuous.*

$$\mathrm{dV}^k_{\succcurlyeq} \quad \frac{\neg(p \succcurlyeq 0) \vdash \overset{\cdot(k)}{p} \geq \varepsilon()}{\Gamma, \varepsilon() > 0 \vdash \langle x' = f(x) \rangle p \succcurlyeq 0}$$

Proof Sketch ([28]). Since $\overset{\cdot(k)}{p}$ is strictly positive, the (lower) Lie derivatives of p all eventually become positive. This derives using a sequence of dC,dI$_{\succcurlyeq}$ steps. $\quad\square$

4.2   Staging Sets

The idea behind *staging sets* [25] is to use an intermediary staging set formula S that *can only be left by entering the goal region P*. This staging property is expressed by the box modality formula $[x' = f(x) \,\&\, \neg P]S$ and is formally justified as a refinement using axiom $K\langle\&\rangle$ with $G \equiv \neg S$.

Corollary 9 (Staging sets [25]). *The following proof rule is derivable in* dL. *Term $\varepsilon()$ is constant for ODE $x' = f(x)$, which is globally Lipschitz continuous.*

$$\mathrm{SP} \quad \frac{\Gamma \vdash [x' = f(x) \,\&\, \neg P]S \quad S \vdash p \leq 0 \wedge \dot{p} \geq \varepsilon()}{\Gamma, \varepsilon() > 0 \vdash \langle x' = f(x) \rangle P}$$

In rule SP, the staging set formula S provides a choice of intermediary between the differential variant p and the desired postcondition P. Proof rules can be significantly simplified by choosing S with desirable topological properties. All proof rules derived so far either have an explicit sufficient duration assumption (like $\mathrm{dV}^*_{\succcurlyeq}$) or use axiom GEx by assuming that ODEs are globally Lipschitz. To make use of axiom BEx, an alternative is to choose staging set formulas $S(x)$ that characterize a bounded (or even compact) set over the variables x.

Corollary 10 (Bounded/compact staging sets). *The following proof rules are derivable in* dL. *Term $\varepsilon()$ is constant for $x' = f(x)$. In rule SP_b, formula S characterizes a bounded set over variables x. In rule SP_c, it characterizes a compact, i.e., closed and bounded, set over those variables.*

$$\mathrm{SP}_b \, \frac{\Gamma \vdash [x' = f(x) \,\&\, \neg P]S \quad S \vdash \dot{p} \geq \varepsilon()}{\Gamma, \varepsilon() > 0 \vdash \langle x' = f(x) \rangle P} \qquad \mathrm{SP}_c \, \frac{\Gamma \vdash [x' = f(x) \,\&\, \neg P]S \quad S \vdash \dot{p} > 0}{\Gamma \vdash \langle x' = f(x) \rangle P}$$

Proof Sketch ([28]). Rule SP_b derives using BEx and differential variant p to establish a time bound. Rule SP_c is an arithmetical corollary of SP_b, using the fact that continuous functions on a compact domain attain their extrema. $\quad\square$

Example 11. Liveness for the non-linear ODE α_n (as suggested by Fig. 1) is proved using rule SP_c by choosing the staging set formula $S \equiv 1 \le u^2 + v^2 \le 2$ (blue annulus) and the differential variant $p = u^2 + v^2$. The Lie derivative $\dot{p}$ with respect to α_n is $2(u^2 + v^2)(u^2 + v^2 - \frac{1}{4})$, which is bounded below by $\frac{3}{2}$ in S. Thus, the right premise of SP_c closes trivially. The left premise (abbreviated ①) requires proving that S is an invariant within the domain constraint $\neg(u^2 + v^2 \ge 2)$. Intuitively, this is true because the blue annulus can only be left by entering $u^2 + v^2 \ge 2$. Its (elided) invariance proof is easy [20].

$$\text{SP}_c \frac{① \qquad {}^{\mathbb{R}}\dfrac{*}{S \vdash \dot{p} > 0}}{u^2 + v^2 = 1 \vdash \langle \alpha_n \rangle u^2 + v^2 \ge 2}$$

$$\text{cut,}{}^{\mathbb{R}}① : \frac{\dfrac{*}{S \vdash [\alpha_n \,\&\, \neg(u^2 + v^2 \ge 2)]S}}{u^2 + v^2 = 1 \vdash [\alpha_n \,\&\, \neg(u^2 + v^2 \ge 2)]S}$$

There are two subtleties to highlight in this proof. First, S characterizes a compact, hence bounded, set (as required by rule SP_c). Solutions of α_n can blow up in finite time which necessitates the use of BEx for proving its liveness properties. Second, S is cleverly chosen to *exclude* the red disk (dashed boundary) characterized by $u^2 + v^2 \le \frac{1}{4}$. As mentioned earlier, solutions of α_n behave differently in this region, e.g., the Lie derivative $\dot{p}$ is *non-positive* in this disk. The chain of refinements (2) behind this proof can be seen from the derivation of rules SP_b, SP_c in the report [28]. It starts from the initial liveness property BEx (with time bound $1 / \frac{3}{2} = \frac{2}{3}$) and uses two $K\langle\&\rangle$ refinement steps, first showing that the staging set is left ($\langle \alpha_n \rangle \neg S$), then showing the desired liveness property:

$$\langle \alpha_n, t' = 1 \rangle (\neg S \vee t > \frac{2}{3}) \overset{K\langle\&\rangle}{\rightarrow} \langle \alpha_n \rangle \neg S \overset{K\langle\&\rangle}{\rightarrow} \langle \alpha_n \rangle u^2 + v^2 \ge 2$$

The use of axiom BEx is subtle and is sometimes overlooked in surveyed liveness arguments. For example, [23, Remark 3.6] incorrectly claims that their liveness argument works without assuming that the relevant sets are bounded. The following proof rule derives from SP_c and adapts ideas from [24, Theorem 2.4, Corollary 2.5], but formula K in the original presentation is only assumed to characterize a closed rather than compact set; the proofs (correctly) assume that the set is bounded but this assumption is not made explicit [24].

Corollary 12 (Set Lyapunov functions [24]). *The following proof rule is derivable in* dL. *Formula K characterizes a* compact set *over variables x, while formula P characterizes an* open set *over those variables.*

$$\text{SLyap} \frac{p \ge 0 \vdash K \qquad \neg P, K \vdash \dot{p} > 0}{\Gamma, p \not\succcurlyeq 0 \vdash \langle x' = f(x) \rangle P}$$

5   Liveness with Domain Constraints

This section presents proof rules for liveness properties $x' = f(x) \,\&\, Q$ with domain constraint Q. Axiom DR$\langle\cdot\rangle$ provides direct generalizations of the proof rules from Sect. 4 with the following derivation choosing $R \equiv true$:

$$\text{DR}\langle\cdot\rangle \frac{\Gamma \vdash [x' = f(x)]Q \quad \Gamma \vdash \langle x' = f(x)\rangle P}{\Gamma \vdash \langle x' = f(x) \,\&\, Q\rangle P}$$

This extends all chains of refinements (2) from Sect. 4 with an additional step:

$$\cdots \rightarrow \langle x' = f(x)\rangle P \xrightarrow{\text{DR}\langle\cdot\rangle} \langle x' = f(x) \,\&\, Q\rangle P$$

Liveness arguments become much more intricate when attempting to generalize beyond DR$\langle\cdot\rangle$, e.g., recall the unsound conjecture DR$\langle\cdot\rangle\notslash$. Indeed, unlike the technical glitches of Sect. 4, our survey uncovers subtle soundness-critical errors here. With our deductive approach, these intricacies are isolated to the topological axioms (Lemma 4) which have been proved sound once and for all. As before, errors and omissions in the surveyed techniques are <u>highlighted in blue</u>.

5.1   Topological Proof Rules

The first proof rule generalizes differential variants to handle domain constraints:

Corollary 13 (Atomic differential variants with domains [15]). *The following proof rule (where $\succcurlyeq$ is either $\geq$ or $>$) is derivable in* dL. *Term $\varepsilon()$ is constant for the ODE $x' = f(x)$ and the ODE is globally Lipschitz continuous. Formula Q characterizes a closed (resp. open) set when $\succcurlyeq$ is $\geq$ (resp. $>$).*

$$\text{dV}_{\succcurlyeq}\& \frac{\Gamma \vdash [x' = f(x) \,\&\, \neg(p \succcurlyeq 0)]Q \quad \neg(p \succcurlyeq 0), Q \vdash \dot{p} \geq \varepsilon()}{\Gamma, \varepsilon() > 0, \neg(p \succcurlyeq 0) \vdash \langle x' = f(x) \,\&\, Q\rangle p \succcurlyeq 0}$$

Proof Sketch ([28]). The derivation uses axiom COR choosing $R \equiv true$, noting that $p \geq 0$ (resp. $p > 0$) characterizes a topologically closed (resp. open) set so the appropriate topological requirements of COR are satisfied:

$$\text{COR} \frac{\Gamma \vdash [x' = f(x) \,\&\, \neg(p \succcurlyeq 0)]Q \quad \dfrac{\neg(p \succcurlyeq 0), Q \vdash \dot{p} \geq \varepsilon()}{\cdots \atop \Gamma, \varepsilon() > 0 \vdash \langle x' = f(x)\rangle p \succcurlyeq 0}}{\Gamma, \varepsilon() > 0, \neg(p \succcurlyeq 0) \vdash \langle x' = f(x) \,\&\, Q\rangle p \succcurlyeq 0}$$

The right premise follows similarly to dV$_{\succcurlyeq}$ although it uses an intervening dC step to add Q to the antecedents.   □

The original presentation of rule $dV_{\succ}^*$ [15] omits the highlighted assumption $\neg(p \succcurlyeq 0)$. This premise is needed for the COR step and the rule is unsound without it. In addition, it uses a form of syntactic weak negation [15], which is also unsound for open postconditions, as pointed out earlier [25]. See the report [28] for counterexamples. Our presentation of $dV_{\succ}\&$ recovers soundness by adding topological restrictions on the domain constraint Q.

The next two corollaries similarly make use of COR to derive the proof rule $dV_{=}^{M}\&$ [27] and the adapted rule SLyap& [24]. They respectively generalize $dV_{=}^{M}$ and SLyap from Sect. 4 to handle domain constraints. The technical glitches in their original presentations [24,27], which were identified in Sect. 4, remain highlighted here:

Corollary 14 (Equational differential variants with domains [27]). *The following proof rules are derivable in* dL. *Term* $\varepsilon()$ *is constant for the ODE* $x' = f(x)$ *and the ODE is globally Lipschitz continuous in both rules. Formula* Q *characterizes a closed set over variables* x.

$$dV_{=}\& \quad \frac{\Gamma \vdash [x' = f(x) \,\&\, p < 0]Q \quad p < 0, Q \vdash \dot{p} \geq \varepsilon()}{\Gamma, \varepsilon() > 0, p \leq 0, Q \vdash \langle x' = f(x) \,\&\, Q\rangle p = 0}$$

$$dV_{=}^{M}\& \quad \frac{Q, p = 0 \vdash P \quad \Gamma \vdash [x' = f(x) \,\&\, p < 0]Q \quad p < 0, Q \vdash \dot{p} \geq \varepsilon()}{\Gamma, \varepsilon() > 0, p \leq 0, Q \vdash \langle x' = f(x) \,\&\, Q\rangle P}$$

Corollary 15 (Set Lyapunov functions with domains [24]). *The following proof rule is derivable in* dL. *Formula* K *characterizes a* compact set *over variables* x, *while formula* P *characterizes an open set over those variables.*

$$\text{SLyap\&} \quad \frac{p \geq 0 \vdash K \quad \neg P, K \vdash \dot{p} > 0}{\Gamma, p > 0 \vdash \langle x' = f(x) \,\&\, p > 0\rangle P}$$

The staging sets with domain constraints proof rule SP& [25] uses axiom SAR:

Corollary 16 (Staging sets with domains [25]). *The following proof rule is derivable in* dL. *Term* $\varepsilon()$ *is constant for ODE* $x' = f(x)$ *and the ODE is globally Lipschitz continuous.*

$$\text{SP\&} \quad \frac{\Gamma \vdash [x' = f(x) \,\&\, \neg(P \wedge Q)]S \quad S \vdash Q \wedge p \leq 0 \wedge \dot{p} \geq \varepsilon()}{\Gamma, \varepsilon() > 0 \vdash \langle x' = f(x) \,\&\, Q\rangle P}$$

The rules derived in Corollaries 13–16 demonstrate the flexibility of our refinement approach for deriving surveyed liveness arguments as proof rules. Our approach is not limited to these surveyed arguments because refinement steps can be freely mixed-and-matched for specific liveness questions.

Example 17. The liveness property $u^2 + v^2 = 1 \rightarrow \langle \alpha_n \rangle u^2 + v^2 \geq 2$ was proved in Example 11 using the staging set formula $S \equiv 1 \leq u^2 + v^2 \leq 2$. Since S and $u^2 + v^2 \geq 2$ both characterize closed sets, axiom COR extends the chain of refinements (2) from Example 11 to show a stronger liveness property for α_n:

$$\langle \alpha_n, t' = 1\rangle(\neg S \vee t > \tfrac{2}{3}) \xrightarrow{\text{K}\langle\&\rangle} \langle \alpha_n \rangle \neg S \xrightarrow{\text{K}\langle\&\rangle} \langle \alpha_n \rangle u^2 + v^2 \geq 2 \xrightarrow{\text{COR}} \langle \alpha_n \,\&\, S\rangle u^2 + v^2 \geq 2$$

Formula $\widetilde{S} \equiv 1 \leq u^2 + v^2 < 2$ also proves Example 11 but does *not* character-ize a closed set. Thankfully, the careful topological restriction of COR prevents us from unsoundly concluding the property $u^2 + v^2 = 1 \to \langle \alpha_n \,\&\, \widetilde{S} \rangle u^2 + v^2 \geq 2$. This latter property is unsatisfiable because $\widetilde{S}$ does not overlap with $u^2 + v^2 \geq 2$.

The refinement approach also enables discovery of new, general liveness proof rules by combining refinement steps in alternative ways. As an example, the following chimeric proof rule combines ideas from Corollaries 8, 10, and 16:

Corollary 18 (Combination proof rule). *The following proof rule is deriv-able in* dL. *Formula S characterizes a compact set over variables* x.

$$\mathrm{SP}^k_c\& \quad \frac{\Gamma \vdash [x' = f(x) \,\&\, \neg(P \wedge Q)]S \quad S \vdash Q \wedge \dot{p}^{(k)} > 0}{\Gamma \vdash \langle x' = f(x) \,\&\, Q \rangle P}$$

Our logical approach derives even complicated proof rules like $\mathrm{SP}^k_c\&$ from a small set of sound logical axioms, which ensures their correctness. The proof rule $\mathrm{E}_c\&$ below derives from $\mathrm{SP}^k_c\&$ (for $k = 1$) and is an adapted version of the liveness argument from [23, Theorem 3.5]. In the original presentation, addi-tional restrictions are imposed on the sets characterized by Γ, P, Q, and different conditions are given compared to the left premise of $\mathrm{E}_c\&$ (highlighted below). These original conditions are overly permissive as they are checked on a smaller set than necessary for soundness. See the report [28] for counterexamples.

Corollary 19 (Compact eventuality [23]). *The following proof rule is deriv-able in* dL. *Formula $Q \wedge \neg P$ characterizes a compact set over variables* x.

$$\mathrm{E}_c\& \quad \frac{\Gamma \vdash [x' = f(x) \,\&\, \neg(P \wedge Q)]Q \quad Q, \neg P \vdash \dot{p} > 0}{\Gamma \vdash \langle x' = f(x) \,\&\, Q \rangle P}$$

6   Related Work

Liveness Proof Rules. The liveness arguments surveyed in this paper were orig-inally presented in various notations, ranging from proof rules [15,25,27] to other mathematical notation [22–25]. All of them were justified directly through semantical (or mathematical) means. We unify (and correct) all of these argu-ments and present them as dL proof rules which are syntactically derived with our refinement-based approach from dL axioms.

Other Liveness Properties. The liveness property studied in this paper is the con-tinuous analog of *eventually* [12] or *eventuality* [23,25] from temporal logics. In discrete settings, temporal logic specifications give rise to a zoo of liveness prop-erties [12]. In continuous settings, *weak eventuality* (requiring *almost all* initial states to reach the goal region) and *eventuality-safety* have been studied [22,23]. In (continuous) adversarial settings, *differential game variants* [18] enable proofs of (Angelic) winning strategies for differential games. In dynamical systems and controls, the study of *asymptotic stability* requires both stability (an invariance property) with asymptotic attraction towards a fixed point or periodic orbit (an eventuality-like property) [5,24]. For hybrid systems, various authors have proposed generalizations of classical asymptotic stability, such as *persistence* [26], *stability* [21], and *inevitability* [7]. *Controlled* versions of these properties are also of interest, e.g., *(controlled) reachability and attractivity* [1,27]. Eventuality(-like) properties are fundamental to all of these advanced liveness properties. The formal understanding of eventuality in this paper is therefore a key step towards enabling formal analysis of more advanced liveness properties.

Automated Liveness Proofs. Automated reachability analysis tools [4,8] can also be used for liveness verification. For an ODE and initial set $\mathcal{X}_0$, computing an over-approximation $\mathcal{O}$ of the reachable set $\mathcal{X}_t \subseteq \mathcal{O}$ at time t shows that *all* states in $\mathcal{X}_0$ reach $\mathcal{O}$ at time t [26] (if solutions do not blow up). Similarly, an under-approximation $\mathcal{U} \subseteq \mathcal{X}_t$ shows that *some* state in $\mathcal{X}_0$ eventually reaches $\mathcal{U}$ [10] (if $\mathcal{U}$ is non-empty). Neither approach handles domain constraints directly [10,26] and, unlike deductive approaches, the use of reachability tools limits them to concrete time bounds t and bounded initial sets $\mathcal{X}_0$. Deductive liveness approaches can also be automated. Lyapunov functions guaranteeing (asymptotic) stability can be found by sum-of-squares (SOS) optimization [14]. Liveness arguments can be similarly combined with SOS optimization to find suitable differential variants [22,23]. Other approaches are possible, e.g., a constraint solving-based approach can be used for finding so-called *set Lyapunov functions* [24]. Crucially, automated approaches must be based on sound liveness arguments. The correct justification of these arguments is precisely what our approach enables.

7   Conclusion

This paper presents a refinement-based approach for proving liveness for ODEs. Exploration of new ODE liveness proof rules is enabled by piecing together refinement steps identified through our approach. Given its wide applicability and correctness guarantees, our approach is a suitable framework for justifying ODE liveness arguments, even for readers less interested in the logical aspects.

Acknowledgments. We thank Katherine Cordwell, Frank Pfenning, Andrew Sogokon, and the anonymous reviewers for their feedback on this paper. This material is based upon work supported by the Alexander von Humboldt Foundation and the AFOSR under grant number FA9550-16-1-0288. The first author was also supported by A*STAR, Singapore.

References

1. Abate, A., D'Innocenzo, A., Benedetto, M.D.D., Sastry, S.: Understanding deadlock and livelock behaviors in hybrid control systems. Nonlinear Anal. Hybrid Syst. **3**(2), 150–162 (2009). https://doi.org/10.1016/j.nahs.2008.12.005
2. Alur, R.: Principles of Cyber-Physical Systems. MIT Press, Cambridge (2015)

3. Bochnak, J., Coste, M., Roy, M.F.: Real Algebraic Geometry. Springer, Heidelberg (1998). https://doi.org/10.1007/978-3-662-03718-8

4. Chen, X., Ábrahám, E., Sankaranarayanan, S.: Flow*: an analyzer for non-linear hybrid systems. In: Sharygina, N., Veith, H. (eds.) CAV. LNCS, vol. 8044, pp. 258–263. Springer, Heidelberg (2013). https://doi.org/10.1007/978-3-642-39799-8_18

5. Chicone, C.: Ordinary Differential Equations with Applications, 2nd edn. Springer, New York (2006). https://doi.org/10.1007/0-387-35794-7

6. Doyen, L., Frehse, G., Pappas, G.J., Platzer, A.: Verification of hybrid systems. In: Clarke, E.M., Henzinger, T.A., Veith, H., Bloem, R. (eds.) Handbook of Model Checking, pp. 1047–1110. Springer, Cham (2018). https://doi.org/10.1007/978-3-319-10575-8_30

7. Duggirala, P.S., Mitra, S.: Lyapunov abstractions for inevitability of hybrid systems. In: Dang, T., Mitchell, I.M. (eds.) HSCC, pp. 115–124. ACM, New York (2012). https://doi.org/10.1145/2185632.2185652

8. Frehse, G., et al.: SpaceEx: scalable verification of hybrid systems. In: Gopalakrishnan, G., Qadeer, S. (eds.) CAV. LNCS, vol. 6806, pp. 379–395. Springer, Heidelberg (2011). https://doi.org/10.1007/978-3-642-22110-1_30

9. Ghorbal, K., Platzer, A.: Characterizing algebraic invariants by differential radical invariants. In: Ábrahám, E., Havelund, K. (eds.) TACAS. LNCS, vol. 8413, pp. 279–294. Springer, Heidelberg (2014). https://doi.org/10.1007/978-3-642-54862-8_19

10. Goubault, E., Putot, S.: Forward inner-approximated reachability of non-linear continuous systems. In: Frehse, G., Mitra, S. (eds.) HSCC, pp. 1–10. ACM, New York (2017). https://doi.org/10.1145/3049797.3049811

11. Liu, J., Zhan, N., Zhao, H.: Computing semi-algebraic invariants for polynomial dynamical systems. In: Chakraborty, S., Jerraya, A., Baruah, S.K., Fischmeister, S. (eds.) EMSOFT, pp. 97–106. ACM, New York (2011). https://doi.org/10.1145/2038642.2038659

12. Manna, Z., Pnueli, A.: The Temporal Logic of Reactive and Concurrent Systems - Specification. Springer, New York (1992). https://doi.org/10.1007/978-1-4612-0931-7

13. Owicki, S.S., Lamport, L.: Proving liveness properties of concurrent programs. ACM Trans. Program. Lang. Syst. 4(3), 455–495 (1982). https://doi.org/10.1145/357172.357178

14. Papachristodoulou, A., Prajna, S.: On the construction of Lyapunov functions using the sum of squares decomposition. In: CDC, vol. 3, pp. 3482–3487. IEEE (2002). https://doi.org/10.1109/CDC.2002.1184414

15. Platzer, A.: Differential-algebraic dynamic logic for differential-algebraic programs. J. Log. Comput. 20(1), 309–352 (2010). https://doi.org/10.1093/logcom/exn070

16. Platzer, A.: Logics of dynamical systems. In: LICS, pp. 13–24. IEEE (2012). https://doi.org/10.1109/LICS.2012.13

17. Platzer, A.: A complete uniform substitution calculus for differential dynamic logic. J. Autom. Reas. 59(2), 219–265 (2017). https://doi.org/10.1007/s10817-016-9385-1

18. Platzer, A.: Differential hybrid games. ACM Trans. Comput. Log. 18(3), 19:1–19:44 (2017). https://doi.org/10.1145/3091123

19. Platzer, A.: Logical Foundations of Cyber-Physical Systems. Springer, Cham (2018). https://doi.org/10.1007/978-3-319-63588-0

20. Platzer, A., Tan, Y.K.: Differential equation axiomatization: the impressive power of differential ghosts. In: Dawar, A., Grädel, E. (eds.) LICS, pp. 819–828. ACM, New York (2018). https://doi.org/10.1145/3209108.3209147

21. Podelski, A., Wagner, S.: Model checking of hybrid systems: from reachability towards stability. In: Hespanha, J.P., Tiwari, A. (eds.) HSCC. LNCS, vol. 3927, pp. 507–521. Springer, Heidelberg (2006). https://doi.org/10.1007/11730637_38

22. Prajna, S., Rantzer, A.: Primal-dual tests for safety and reachability. In: Morari, M., Thiele, L. (eds.) HSCC. LNCS, vol. 3414, pp. 542–556. Springer, Heidelberg (2005). https://doi.org/10.1007/978-3-540-31954-2_35

23. Prajna, S., Rantzer, A.: Convex programs for temporal verification of nonlinear dynamical systems. SIAM J. Control Optim. **46**(3), 999–1021 (2007). https://doi.org/10.1137/050645178

24. Ratschan, S., She, Z.: Providing a basin of attraction to a target region of polynomial systems by computation of Lyapunov-like functions. SIAM J. Control Optim. **48**(7), 4377–4394 (2010). https://doi.org/10.1137/090749955

25. Sogokon, A., Jackson, P.B.: Direct formal verification of liveness properties in continuous and hybrid dynamical systems. In: Bjørner, N., de Boer, F.S. (eds.) FM. LNCS, vol. 9109, pp. 514–531. Springer, Cham (2015). https://doi.org/10.1007/978-3-319-19249-9_32

26. Sogokon, A., Jackson, P.B., Johnson, T.T.: Verifying safety and persistence in hybrid systems using flowpipes and continuous invariants. J. Autom. Reas. (2018, to appear). https://doi.org/10.1007/s10817-018-9497-x

27. Taly, A., Tiwari, A.: Switching logic synthesis for reachability. In: Carloni, L.P., Tripakis, S. (eds.) EMSOFT, pp. 19–28. ACM, New York (2010). https://doi.org/10.1145/1879021.1879025

28. Tan, Y.K., Platzer, A.: An axiomatic approach to liveness for differential equations. CoRR abs/1904.07984 (2019)

29. Walter, W.: Ordinary Differential Equations. Springer, New York (1998). https://doi.org/10.1007/978-1-4612-0601-9

Local Consistency Check in Synchronous Dataflow Models

Dina Irofti$^{(\boxtimes)}$ (iD) and Paul Dubrulle (iD)

CEA, LIST, 91191 Gif-sur-Yvette Cedex, France
{dina.irofti,paul.dubrulle}@cea.fr

Abstract. Dataflow graphs are typically used to model signal processing applications. Consistency is a necessary condition for the existence of a dataflow graph schedule using bounded memory. Existing methods to check this property are based on a static analysis. At every modification on the dataflow graph, the consistency property has to be checked again and on the entire graph, after its construction. In this paper, we argue that for each modification, the consistency can be checked only on the modified graph elements, and during its construction. We propose an alternative method, that can be applied either on the entire graph, or locally, at each modification of a dataflow graph. For both cases, we analyse our algorithm's advantages, and compare its performance to an existing algorithm. For the experimental setup, we generate random graphs with worst-case instances and realistic instances. Our theoretical analysis shows that the proposed algorithm can reduce the number of operations required for the consistency verification, even on entire graphs. The experimental results show that our algorithm outperforms the state-of-the-art algorithm on the considered benchmark.

1 Introduction

In the last few decades, dataflow graphs have been used to describe the behaviour of signal processing applications, as they provide execution semantics adequate to analyse their performance. The most common criteria for the performance analysis are directly related to buffer sizing, throughput or latency optimization. A first step in solving these optimization problems is verifying a couple of properties, such as the existence of an upper bound for the buffer sizes (the consistency property) and the absence of deadlocks (also called the liveness property). For Synchronous dataflow (SDF) model [11], whether a dataflow graph satisfies these properties is decidable, in general. These properties are usually decidable for most models extending the SDF model, e.g. Cyclo-static dataflow (CSDF) [5], Parameterized dataflow (PSDF) [3], Scenario-aware dataflow (SADF) [15]. We note that SDF and CSDF are considered static dataflow models, as opposed to PSDF and SADF, which include some limited dynamic behaviour. However, similar techniques are used for all these models to decide upon the consistency property. In this paper, we focus on the consistency property for SDF graphs. The methods used for the consistency check are based on a static analysis and

© Springer Nature Switzerland AG 2019
M. H. ter Beek et al. (Eds.): FM 2019, LNCS 11800, pp. 389–405, 2019.
https://doi.org/10.1007/978-3-030-30942-8_24

require the construction of the entire graph describing the application. This requirement may be restrictive in some cases. For instance, some performance optimization techniques need to generate random dataflow graphs. In this context, the cost of state-of-the-art techniques is prohibitive, as the consistency is checked many times and on the entire graph during the generation process. In this paper, we propose an incremental approach that can be applied during the graph construction. Thus, the construction of an inconsistent graph is stopped as soon as an inconsistent element has been identified. Another example is the construction of modular applications. Suppose we would like to extend an existing consistent dataflow application describing an autonomous car radar. We would like to obtain a collision avoidance system by connecting the radar to another consistent dataflow graph describing a camera extension. In this case, we say that we add a camera module to the radar system. With the existing methods, the extended dataflow application has to be rechecked on the entire graph, despite the fact that the initial radar application and the camera module were already verified in advance. The alternative method we propose is able to locally check the consistency in the graph: it only checks the new changes when the dataflow graph suffers some modifications, such as adding a module, and can thus reduce the number of operations required for the consistency check. The efficiency gain obtained by our method is particularly important for complex applications represented by large graphs with very dynamic topology.

2   Synchronous Dataflow Models

Generally, a dataflow program consists in a number of tasks, called *actors*, connected by a number of communication channels. A dataflow graph describes a dataflow program structure: the actors are represented by vertices, and the communication channels by edges. Every actor in the dataflow graph has a set of ports. A *port* represents a communication channel endpoint. Actors generally have a cyclic behaviour, called *firing*: they read data from their input ports, execute their tasks, and put data on their output ports. A firing can take place only when the actor has enough information on its input ports. The quantity of data sent on the output or received from the input ports is specified by a number of tokens. The *production (consumption) rates* represent how many tokens an actor can send (receive) when it fires. In a *synchronous dataflow*, all actors have constant consumption and production rates, and these rates are known when defining the graph. The nodes in the dataflow graph can be mapped on different computational units, so that the tasks can be executed following a certain order. This procedure is called *scheduling*. We note that the scheduling can be done statically (at compile time), or dynamically (at run-time). An SDF program can be scheduled statically because we know that every given actor in the graph produces and consumes the same amount of data every time it fires. Moreover, a periodic schedule can be constructed for an SDF program, given that all consumption and production rates are fixed. In a valid *periodic schedule*, each actor fires a certain number of times before the graph returns to its initial state, with the same number of tokens as initially on the channels. A valid *repetition vector* has to be found when scheduling an SDF program. The repetition vector is a positive, integer vector of size equal to the number of actors in the dataflow graph. Every element in the vector corresponds to an actor and specifies the number of times the actor fires in a periodic schedule. More than one repetition vector can be found for a given SDF graph. The minimal repetition vector has the minimum norm and corresponds to a minimal periodic schedule.

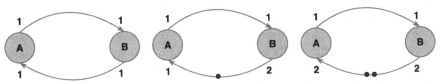

(a) Example of a consistent SDF graph. The repetition vector is (1 1). The graph is not live because there are no initial tokens on the channels. The graph is deadlocked.

(b) Example of a deadlock-free SDF graph. The graph is not consistent, as the tokens will continue to accumulate on the bottom channel. No repetition vector can be found.

(c) Example of a consistent graph without deadlock. The repetition vector is (1 1). A periodic schedule can be found: after one firing of each actor, the graph returns in its initial state.

$$\Gamma = \begin{bmatrix} 1 & -1 \\ -1 & 1 \end{bmatrix}$$

(d) Topology matrix of Figure 1(a) graph.

$$\Gamma = \begin{bmatrix} 1 & -1 \\ -1 & 2 \end{bmatrix}$$

(e) Topology matrix of Figure 1(b) graph.

$$\Gamma = \begin{bmatrix} 1 & -1 \\ -2 & 2 \end{bmatrix}$$

(f) Topology matrix of Figure 1(c) graph.

Fig. 1. Consistency and liveness properties illustrated on SDF graphs with two actors.

To find a valid periodic scheduling of a dataflow program, two properties are essential: the consistency property and the absence of deadlocks; the repetition vector is important for both of them. A graph where the tokens do not accumulate on the channels over several execution periods satisfies the *consistency property*. It has been proven in [12] that the existence of a non-zero repetition vector is a necessary condition for an SDF graph to be consistent, i.e. to have a valid periodic schedule. For example, the graph in Fig. 1(a) is consistent, because no token accumulates on the channels: actor A produces a token, which is consumed by actor B; then actor B fires and produces one token, and this token is consumed by actor A, and so on. The repetition vector corresponding to the graph depicted in Fig. 1(a) is (1 1), which means that each actor, A and B, fire once before the graph returns to its initial state. However, the graph in Fig. 1(a) is not free of deadlocks: there is no initial token on the channels, which means that neither actor A, nor actor B can start firing. The deadlock absence and the consistency properties are independent. For example, the graph depicted in Fig. 1(b) has no deadlock, but it is not consistent: the channel (B → A) contains one initial token; actor A consumes the initial token, and produces another token, which is consumed by actor B; then, actor B produces two tokens per firing, so that actor A will have enough tokens on its inputs to continue to fire, but the tokens will continue to accumulate at its inputs, as actor A cannot consume them as fast as actor B produces. No repetition vector can be found for this graph, which means that it is not consistent. A graph that satisfies both the consistency property and has no deadlock is depicted in Fig. 1(c): actor A consumes the two initial tokens on its input, and produces one token on its output; then, actor B consumes one token and produces two tokens on its output, which means that the graph returns in its initial state. The repetition vector corresponding to the graph depicted in Fig. 1(c) is (1 1). The existence of such a (non-zero) vector means that the graph is consistent. Then, one way to check the deadlock absence, as proposed in [12], is to fire each node the number of times specified by the repetition vector. If the SDF program has no deadlock during this test, then the SDF graph is deadlock free. We note that the deadlock absence is sometimes referred to as the liveness property in the literature [2,8].

Existing Framework for Consistency Property in SDF Graphs

The consistency property is important because if a repetition vector cannot be found for a given graph, then any schedule for this graph will end up either in deadlock, or in unbounded buffer sizes (as in the example depicted in Fig. 1(b)). The formalism typically used in the literature for the consistency check is based on the computation of the *topology matrix*. This formalism was first proposed by Lee and Messerschmitt [10–12] for SDF graphs, and was further adapted to other models derived from SDF model, e.g. CSDF [2,5], Boolean dataflows [6], PSDF [3], Variable rate dataflows [17], Variable phased dataflows [18], SADF [15]. The topology matrix is usually denoted by Γ. Every actor in the dataflow graph has a column assigned in the topology matrix, and every channel is assigned to a row. Thus, the $(i,j)^{\text{th}}$ entry of Γ matrix is the production or consumption rate of node j on channel i. By convention, the consumption rates take negative values in the topology matrix. The topology matrices corresponding to the graphs depicted in Fig. 1(a–c) are represented in Fig. 1(d–f). Finding a non-zero repetition vector, usually denoted by q, by solving the matrix equation

$$\Gamma q = \overrightarrow{0}, \tag{1}$$

where $\overrightarrow{0}$ is a vector full of zeros, is a necessary and sufficient condition for the buffer sizes to remain bounded. This result is proven in [12]. We notice that the minimal repetition vector solving Eq. (1) is $q^T = (1\ 1)$ for the graphs depicted in Fig. 1(a) and (c), and that there is no vector q solving equation (1), except $q = \overrightarrow{0}$, for the graph depicted in Fig. 1(b). The examples illustrated in Fig. 1 are didactic. The reader can refer, for example, to [4] for a more realistic example of a dataflow graph with 16 actors describing a modem application, for which the repetition vector is computed in a similar way.

3   A New Approach for Consistency Check

In this section, we argue that when a dataflow graph is subject to modifications, the consistency can be checked only on the modified graph elements. Even for

Algorithm 1. Consistency check for SDF graphs. Connect the ith element of x' vector to the jth element of x'' vector.

Require: x' and x'' repetition vectors corresponding to two graphs; i the index of the ith element of vector x'; j the index of the jth element of vector x''; r_i the production rate corresponding to x'_i; r_j the consumption rate corresponding to x''_j.

Ensure: x the repetition vector corresponding to the new graph; the inconsistent connexions are marked

1: **if** $r_i x'_i = r_j x''_j$ **then**
2:     c_flag $\leftarrow$ true   ▷ the new connection is consistent
3: **if** x' and x'' are two distinct vectors **then** ▷ connect two actors from two different graphs
4:     **if** c_flag is true **then**
5:         $x \leftarrow [x' \ x'']$
6:         STOP
7:     **else**

8:     $m \leftarrow lcm(r_i, r_j)$
9:     $d \leftarrow gcd(x'_i, x''_j)$
10:     $c_i \leftarrow \frac{m}{d}\frac{x''_j}{r_i}$
11:     $c_j \leftarrow \frac{m}{d}\frac{x'_i}{r_j}$
12:     $d \leftarrow gcd(c_i, c_j)$
13:     $c_i \leftarrow \frac{c_i}{d}$
14:     $c_j \leftarrow \frac{c_j}{d}$
15:     $x \leftarrow [c_i x' \ c_j x'']$
16:     STOP
17: **else** ▷ connect two actors of the same graph
18:     **if** c_flag is true **then**
19:         $x \leftarrow x'$
20:         STOP
21:     **else**
22:         Mark this connection as not consistent
23:         Optional: Send error message
24:         STOP

---

graphs that are not subject to modifications, the consistency check can be made at their construction. We consider by **convention** that when an actor is created, a repetition vector is associated to it; this associated repetition vector has only one component, equal to one. The approach we propose for locally checking the consistency property is based on Algorithm 1, and can be used either at the graph construction, or when the graph suffers a modification. We note that the proposed algorithm also provides the minimal repetition vector corresponding to the resulting SDF graph. In the following, we give the proof of correctness for Algorithm 1, as well as three illustrating examples important for some steps of the algorithm. Algorithm 1 proof makes use of the following proposition and its corollary.

Proposition 1. *If a graph* **G** *is consistent and has a valid repetition vector* x, *then* kx *is also a valid repetition vector* $\forall k \in \mathbb{N}$.

The proof is based on the fact that a valid repetition vector x satisfies $\Gamma x = \overrightarrow{0}$.

Corollary 1. *Consider a consistent graph with* n *actors and a valid repetition vector* $x = [x_1 \ x_2 \ldots x_n]$. *Suppose that, due to an additional design constraint, the* i^{th} *component of vector* x *has to be changed. We denote* x_i^* *the new value of the* i^{th} *component of vector* x. *Then, in order to keep the graph consistent, all other* x *vector components* x_j, $j = 1 \ldots n$, $j \neq i$, *have to be multiplied by* $\frac{x_i^*}{x_i}$.

Proof of Correctness for Algorithm 1. We consider the general case where we connect two actors i and j, with the production and consumption rates r_i and r_j, respectively. We denote the values corresponding to their position in their repetition vector by x_i' and x_j''. Algorithm 1 takes into account two cases. The case where the two actors come from two different repetition vectors is treated on line 3 of the algorithm: vector x' is associated to actor i and the repetition vector x'' corresponds to actor j. If the two actors have the same corresponding repetition vector, then $x' \equiv x''$ (line 17 of Algorithm 1). Given a consistent SDF graph and its corresponding repetition vector x, we note that a consistent connection between actors i and j of the graph satisfies the equation

$$r_i x_i = r_j x_j. \tag{2}$$

This equation ensures that after x_i activations of actor i and x_j activations of actor j, the channel returns at its initial state. In order to avoid unnecessary operations, we first verify if the new connection is consistent. In this case, we make the consistency flag true on line 2. Then, we consider two cases: the case where the two actors come from two different repetition vectors, i.e. there is no path between the two actors before the new connection is made (line 3), and the case where the two actors come from the same graph, i.e. they have the same repetition vector (line 17). If the two actors come from two different repetition vectors, and the new connection is consistent, then we concatenate the two repetition vectors x' and x'' into a new repetition vector, denoted by x. This corresponds to lines 3–6 of Algorithm 1. If the initial consistency condition (2) does not hold before the new connection is made (line 7), we use Proposition 1 and claim that a newly created channel connecting actor i to actor j is consistent if we can find two coefficients $c_i, c_j \in \mathbb{N}$ satisfying

$$c_i r_i x_i' = c_j r_j x_j''. \tag{3}$$

We remark that coefficients c_i and c_j play a role in updating the repetition vectors x' and x'' after the connection. In the following, we present how to choose c_i and c_j coefficients so that they satisfy Eq. (3) for the general case in which we connect two actors. If we choose $c_i = \frac{x_j''}{r_i}$ and $c_j = \frac{x_i'}{r_j}$, and replace them in Eq. (3), then we obtain $\frac{x_j''}{r_i} r_i x_i' = \frac{x_i'}{r_j} r_j x_j''$, which is always true. We note that this choice of parameters does not guarantee positive integer values for c_i and c_j. Because we are searching for $c_i, c_j \in \mathbb{N}$, we multiply the equation above by $\frac{m}{d}$, where[1]

$$m = lcm(r_i, r_j), \qquad \text{and} \qquad d = gcd(x_i', x_j'').$$

Thus, we obtain the coefficients $c_i = \frac{m}{d} \frac{x_j''}{r_i}$, and $c_j = \frac{m}{d} \frac{x_i'}{r_j}$, satisfying the consistency condition (3). If we are looking for the minimal repetition vector, we have

---

[1] *lcm* stands for the least common multiple, and *gcd* stands for the greatest common divisor.

to make sure that we multiply the initial elements of the repetition vector only by the coefficients divided by their greatest common divisor:

$$c_i = \frac{\frac{m}{d}\frac{x_j''}{r_i}}{gcd\left(\frac{m}{d}\frac{x_j''}{r_i}, \frac{m}{d}\frac{x_i'}{r_j}\right)}, \quad \text{and} \quad c_j = \frac{\frac{m}{d}\frac{x_i'}{r_j}}{gcd\left(\frac{m}{d}\frac{x_j''}{r_i}, \frac{m}{d}\frac{x_i'}{r_j}\right)}. \quad (4)$$

We remark that c_i and c_j coefficients defined by (4) satisfy Eq. (3). If the two actors are coming from two distinct repetition vectors and the initial consistency condition (2) is not satisfied, then we compute c_i and c_j given by (4) on lines 8–14 of Algorithm 1. Then, the resulting repetition vector x is updated on line 15, using Proposition 1 and its Corollary 1. If the two actors we would like to connect come from the same repetition vector (line 17) and the consistency flag is true (line 18), then we have nothing more to verify: the new repetition vector is identical to the original one (lines 19–20). Otherwise (line 21), the connection is not consistent, i.e. the resulting graph is not consistent (lines 22–24).   □

Example 1. We consider that the graph depicted in Fig. 1(c) is modified, such that a new actor is added. The resulting graph is depicted in Fig. 2. We note that this modification can be seen either as an alteration of the initial graph depicted in Fig. 1(c), or as a step in the construction of the graph depicted in Fig. 2. In both cases, the modification actually consist in adding a new connection between actor B and actor C. In this case, $x_i = 1$ and corresponds to the second element of repetition vector associated to the initial graph, and $x_j = 1$ by convention. On the new channel, actor B produces one token, which means $r_i = 1$, and actor C consumes two tokens, which means $r_j = 2$. We know that the repetition vector corresponding to the initial graph is (1 1), and we would like to compute the new repetition vector resulting after the connection is made. For this, we only need to find the c_i and c_j coefficients. We replace the known variables in Eq. (3), and we obtain $c_i = 2c_j$. If we search the minimal repetition vector, we choose $c_i = 2$ and $c_j = 1$. Thus, the values corresponding to the actors B and C in the new repetition vector will be $x_i^* = c_i x_i = 2$, and $x_j^* = c_j x_j = 1$, respectively. In this case, the consistency property is preserved by Proposition 1. However, the repetition vector element corresponding to actor A also changes, as indicated in Corollary 1. Thus, after connecting actors B and C, the new repetition vector is (2 2 1) and it corresponds to the graph depicted in Fig. 2.

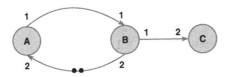

Fig. 2. A consistent and live graph obtained after including a new actor, denoted by actor C, to the graph depicted in Fig. 1(c). The corresponding repetition vector is (2 2 1).

Remark 1. We note that, for Example 1, the computation of a new Γ matrix is not necessary in order to find a valid repetition vector. We only need to find the coefficients c_i and c_j and then apply Corrolary 1. However, we remark that the repetition vector we find $x = (2\ 2\ 1)$ satisfies Eq. (1), where

$$\Gamma = \begin{bmatrix} 1 & -1 & 0 \\ -2 & 2 & 0 \\ 0 & 1 & -2 \end{bmatrix}, \text{ and } q = x.$$

The minimal repetition vector is unique, given the particular structure of Γ matrix (only two non-zero elements per row, as a channel only has two end-points). This means that Algorithm 1 finds the same (minimal) repetition vector as other state-of-the-art methods based on the framework presented in Sect. 2.

Example 2. We apply Algorithm 1 at the construction of the graph depicted in Fig. 3. When actors A, B, C, and D are created, each of them have a repetition vector $x = (1)$. The connections are made in the following order: $(A \rightarrow B)$, $(A \rightarrow C)$, $(B \rightarrow D)$, $(C \rightarrow D)$. After the connection $(A \rightarrow B)$, Algorithm 1 gives $c_i = 3$, $c_j = 2$, and $x = (3\ 2)$, as the two actors come from two different repetition vectors. In a similar way, $c_i = 1$, $c_j = 3$, and $x = (3\ 2\ 3)$ when the connection $(A \rightarrow C)$ is made. Connection $(B \rightarrow D)$ emphasizes the importance of lines 12–14 in Algorithm 1: before line 12, $c_i = c_j = 2$; using these coefficients, we do not obtain a minimal repetition vector when updating x as on line 15, hence, the role of dividing the coefficients by d. The case expressed on the lines 17 and 18 in Algorithm 1 illustrates the connection $(C \rightarrow D)$: the repetition vector does not change, it is the same as after connection $(C \rightarrow D)$, $x = (3\ 2\ 3\ 1)$.

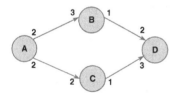

Fig. 3. A graph with a split-join configuration.

Example 2 illustrates how to apply the Algorithm 1 on a given graph. From this example, we observe that lines 8–14 guarantee a set of integer coefficients necessary to obtain a minimal repetition vector. However, the local consistency check has another important feature, namely it can reduce the number of operations required, especially in the case of modular applications.

Example 3. We consider a modular dataflow application, in which a dataflow program described by the graph depicted in Fig. 3 is added to an existing dataflow program described by Fig. 2 graph. The resulting graph is depicted in Fig. 4. As the consistency property has been already checked for the two graphs, only the new connection between B_1 actor of the first graph and B_2 actor of the second graph needs to be checked. We apply Algorithm 1 with the inputs $x' = (2\ 2\ 1)$, $x'' = (3\ 2\ 3\ 1)$, $i = 2$, $j = 2$, $r_i = 1$, $r_j = 5$, and obtain $c_i = 5$ and $c_j = 1$. The repetition vector given by Algorithm 1 output is $x = (10\ 10\ 5\ 3\ 2\ 3\ 1)$. We note that the three first elements of vector x correspond to repetition vector x' and have been multiplied by c_i.

Remark 2. Example 3 shows that Algorithm 1 can locally check the consistency property: when two consistent graphs are connected, the user does not have to recheck their consistency. The proposed algorithm checks only the new connections in this case, and deduces the resulting repetition vector from the two initial repetition vectors. This is one important advantage when compared to the classical method used in the literature, for which a new topology matrix has to be computed and a new matrix equation of type (1) has to be solved.

Remark 3. Example 3 gives some insights into the advantages of locally checking the consistency property. The modular application described by this example, can also be seen as the construction of a graph: first, three actors are created and linked, then other four actors are created and linked, and finally the two subgraphs are connected. For example, this is how graphs are constructed in the SDF[3] open source tool [14], starting from an *xml* file where the actors and the connections are given in a random order. More details are given in Subsect. 4.1.

The examples and remarks presented above emphasize the advantages of locally checking the consistency property. On the considered examples, we can see that the computation of the topology matrix is not necessary, and that the minimal repetition vector can be found in a more efficient way. Another advantage of our approach is that the inconsistent elements can be identified, and not the entire graph is needed in order to decide on the graph consistency. Algorithm 1 basically describes how the consistency can be checked on a connection, and can be applied incrementally during the dataflow graph construction. It can be also applied after the graph construction, on each channel of the graph. This means that graphs with many connections need more time for the consistency check. We define **fully connected graphs** as dataflow graphs where all actors are connected to all actors. Moreover, we remark that, for fully connected graphs, Algorithm 1 efficiency also depends on the order in which the channels are checked for consistency. When channels connecting actors from different graphs are first read, more operations are executed in Algorithm 1, as lines 3–16 contains more instructions than lines 17–24. This way of reading the channels on fully connected graphs represent the **worst-case execution scenario** for Algorithm 1, and can be avoided by changing the order of reading. For a given fully connected graph under the worst-case execution scenario, we neglect the complexity for *gcd* and *lcm* functions, as they are difficult to predict, and we estimate Algorithm 1 complexity to

$$c = \sum_{i=1}^{n-1} (2i + 5) + 24(n - 1) + 16 \left[n^2 - (n - 1) \right] = 17n^2 + 12n - 18, \quad (5)$$

where n is the number of actors in the graph. Because of space restrictions, we give only some insights into why the Eq. (5) is quadratic: in a fully connected graph with n actors, the number of connections is n^2. In the next section, we experimentally verify these observations by testing our algorithm on a few thousands graphs, of different size and topology.

4   Experimental Results

4.1   Implementation in the SDF3 Open Source Tool

SDF[3] tool is written in C/C++ and provides analysis, random generation and implementation techniques for SDF graphs and other similar models. In particular, it contains a function to check the consistency for SDF graphs. The algorithm used by the consistency check function in the SDF[3] tool is based on the recursive algorithm presented in Section IV.D from [11]. It basically consists in one graph traversal to compute a fraction corresponding to each node in the graph. These fractions are then reduced to integer numbers by using Euclid's algorithm to find the least common multiple of all denominators. These integer numbers are actually the components of the smallest repetition vector. In the remaining part of this paper, we denote this algorithm by **SDF3 algorithm**. Even if the technique presented in Sect. 2 is the most commonly used for the consistency study in the models extending the SDF model, SDF3 algorithm is more efficient as it only involves a single graph traversal instead of solving a matrix equation.

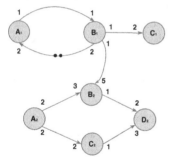

Fig. 4. A modular dataflow graph obtained by adding a connection between two modules. The first module is the graph depicted in Fig. 2, and the second module is the graph illustrated in Fig. 3. The connection between the two modules is the $(B_1 \rightarrow B_2)$ connection.

In short, we have chosen the SDF[3] tool for our experimental setup because it provides the right framework to generate thousands of graphs on which we can test Algorithm 1, and because it provides a consistency check function to which we can compare our algorithm performance. The machine on which we conduct the experimental tests is an Intel(R) Xeon(R) CPU E5-2620 v4 @ 2.10 GHz running Ubuntu 16.1 Linux 4.4.0-135-generic. We used only one core for the measurements in our experiments. We define the running time of an algorithm as the time measured by calls to *clock_gettime* on $CLOCK\_PROCESS\_CPUTIME\_ID$ around the function call.

We have included an additional function to SDF[3], implementing Algorithm 1. In our experiments, we compare the running times necessary for the consistency check for the two algorithms, SDF3 algorithm and Algorithm 1. We have also included a function that checks and thus guarantees, in our experiments, that Algorithm 1 provides the same results and the same repetition vector as the consistency check function implemented in the SDF[3] tool. This function experimentally confirms the observation made at the end of Remark 1. Moreover, we have added and adapted a few functions to the considered benchmark, as presented in the following subsection.

4.2   Benchmark

There is no standard benchmark set of SDF graphs. However, there are a few graphs describing some typical applications in the literature, such as a modem, a satellite receiver, a sample-rate converter or an MP3 decoder (see [9] and references therein). Models extending the SDF model have been used to describe, for instance, a speech compression application [3] and an MP3 play-back application [7]. In this work, we have chosen to evaluate our algorithm on a very large number of graphs, and we preferred to generate a benchmark of random graphs by using the SDF^3 tool. More precisely, we consider three sets of graphs, denoted in the remaining part of the paper by the notation in bold.

Homogeneous Graphs. We use this benchmark to compare the experimental results to the theoretical complexity (5) computed for Algorithm 1 in the worst-case execution scenario of fully connected graphs. With this benchmark we measure the run-time without taking into account the *gcd* and *lcm* functions. Considering fully connected homogeneous synchronous dataflow graphs (HSDF) allows us to neglect these functions, since all production and consumption rates are equal to one. This benchmark contains 10 graphs. The number of actors of each graph varies between 100 and 1000, with a step of 100. We implemented an additional function that changes the order in which the channels are read in the SDF^3 tool, to simulate the worst-case execution scenario. We precise that we use this additional function only for the homogeneous graph benchmark. We note that in the original form of the SDF^3 tool the channels are read in a random order.

Fully Connected Graphs. We consider fully connected graphs with the number of actors varying between 10 and 300 with a step of 10. We generate 100 different consistent graphs of size s, with the number of actors s varying between 10 and 300, with random rates on the channels. We set in the SDF^3 generator the rate average 2, the minimum acceptable rate 1, the maximum acceptable rate 3, the rates variance 1, and the repetition vector sum equal to 9 times the number of nodes in the generated graph. This fully connected graph benchmark contains 3000 graphs in total.

Practical Graphs. In practical applications, dataflow programs are very rarely represented by fully connected graphs; in general, less connections are involved. Practical applications usually contains actors connected in a linear way mixed with actors connected in a split-join configuration, as the one depicted in Fig. 3, but with more actors of type B and C in the middle. For our experimental setup, we estimate that in practical applications the average number of connections of an actor to other actors in the graph is equal to 4. For instance, in the illustrative modem example presented in [4], we can see that the average number of connections per actor is close to 3. In this work, we suppose that for more realistic and complex applications, the average is around 4. We generate with the SDF^3 generator 30 sets of 100 consistent graphs, each set of a size between 10 and 300 nodes with a step of 10. In the generator, we set the average number of actor connections to 4, the rate average 2, the minimum rate 1, the maximum rate 3, the rates variance 1, and the repetition vector sum 9 times the number of nodes in the generated graph. This benchmark totals 3000 graphs. We have implemented a verification function in SDF[3], and checked that all graphs generated for this benchmark have the average connection close to 4.

We have also encountered some problems when we generated the benchmark with the SDF[3] tool. One difficulty was that sometimes the rate average and range do not satisfy the generator settings. Some graphs have very large production and consumption rates, but they are limited by the sum of the repetition vector settings. Another major problem was that, even if it should generate only consistent graphs, the generator sometimes fails to do so for large-size graphs. We have remarked that for graphs with more than 100 nodes, the SDF[3] generator has a 3% error probability: 3 out of 100 generated graphs of size larger than 100 nodes are not consistent. We have fixed this problem by replacing the nonconsistent graphs with other, newly generated, consistent graphs. We verified that each graph considered in our benchmark is consistent by checking it with both our algorithm and SDF3 algorithm and comparing the results. We have also verified that for all considered graphs, SDF[3] and our algorithm provide the same minimal repetition vector. Also, the number of actors considered for our benchmark is reasonable, similar, for instance, to some applications implemented in StreamIt language [16].

4.3 Results Obtained on the Experimental Setup

Throughout this section, we experimentally validate Algorithm 1 and compare it to the SDF3 algorithm.

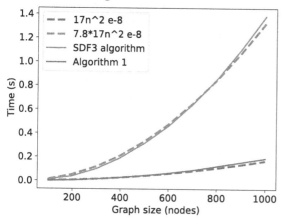

We first validate the implementation of Algorithm 1 in SDF[3] by analysing the experimental results obtained on the homogeneous graph benchmark. We cancel all compiler optimization (only for our experiments on the homogeneous graph benchmark), and we measure the run-time necessary for the SDF3 algorithm and for Algorithm 1 to check the consistency on the homogeneous benchmark. The result is depicted in Fig. 5, where the continuous curves correspond to the experimental results, the blue one to Algorithm 1, and the orange one to SDF3 algorithm. The dotted, purple curve in Fig. 5 represents the polynomial $17n^2$, with n the number of nodes in the graph, multiplied by a constant 10^{-8}. We estimated this constant so that the dotted purple curve

Fig. 5. Experimental results obtained on homogeneous graph benchmark.

fits the experimental blue curve. We note that $17n^2$ corresponds to complexity (5); this means that the experimental curve given by Algorithm 1 has the same slope as the estimated complexity (5). The dotted green curve in Fig. 5 is only a translation of the purple curve: it is obtained by multiplying the polynomial giving the purple curve by 7.8. These experimental results suggest that Algorithm 1 performs between 7 and 8 times better than SDF3 algorithm on fully connected graphs under the worst-case execution scenario. We remark that locally checking the consistency property can be advantageous, especially for large-size graphs, as the time needed for Algorithm 1 is smaller than the time needed for SDF3 algorithm.

In Fig. 6(a), we compare the results obtained with Algorithm 1 (blue triangles) to the results obtained with SDF3 algorithm (orange dots) on the fully connected graph benchmark. For each size of a fully connected graph we plot 100 points corresponding to the time needed for SDF3 algorithm (in orange dots) and for Algorithm 1 (in blue triangles). We can remark that our algorithm performs better. We can also remark a time variation, especially for the results obtained by SDF3 algorithm. We recall that the 100 graphs of size s, with s varying between 10 and 300 in this benchmark, have exactly the same topology (the same number of actors, the same number of connections), but different rates on the channels. Thus, one possible explanation for this variation is the fact that the production and consumption rates are different for the same topology considered for the 100 points plotted for a given graph size. Another source of variation can be linked to the compiler optimization and to the order in which the channels are read by the SDF^3 tool. We note that randomly reading the channels means avoiding the worst-case scenario execution. Overall, the experimental results presented in Fig. 6(a) show that locally checking the consistency outperforms the SDF^3 technique in the case of graphs with a very high average number of connections per actor.

Next, we present the experimental results obtained on the practical graph benchmark. We measure the running time needed for both algorithms on this benchmark and plot the results in Fig. 6, where the orange dots correspond to SDF3 algorithm and the blue triangles correspond to Algorithm 1. We remark that in this case, the two algorithm performance is similar; Algorithm 1 performs a bit better, though. A difference, when compared to the fully connected graphs results, is that the results obtained with our algorithm also varies, even if the variation is less important than the one produced by SDF3 algorithm. An explanation for this variation is also the production and consumption rate variation determined by the SDF^3 graph generator. For example, we have noticed that the graphs in the practical graph benchmark contains a larger interval for their channels' rates, as opposed to the graphs in the fully connected graph benchmark, which contains many unitary rates generated by SDF^3. We note that a large variation of rates will induce different results of the time measured for gcd and lcm functions for Algorithm 1. However, we consider that this variation is reasonable.

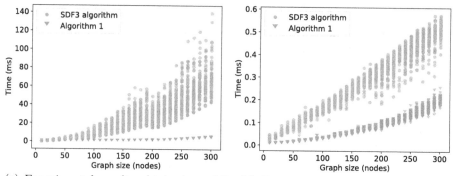

(a) Experimental results obtained on fully connected graph benchmark.

(b) Experimental results obtained on practical graph benchmark.

Fig. 6. Experimental results on fully connected and practical graph benchmark. (Color figure online)

One major advantage of our approach of locally checking the consistency property is illustrated on the following experiment concerning modular applications. Because of space limitation, we illustrate only the *add* operation for modular applications, i.e. two modules are connected. However, our approach can be generalized for the *remove* operation (e.g. a module elimination), and for a *changing rate* operation (composed by an add and a remove operation). For this experiment, we consider two fully connected graphs G_1 and G_2, with n_1 and n_2 actors, respectively. We suppose that n_2 is comparable to n_1: either $n_2 = n_1$, or $n_2 = n_1 + 10$. We would like to check the consistency of a modular application described by a fully connected graph $G_3 = G_1 \bigcup G_2$. In other words, we connect all actors from G_1 to all actors of G_2 and obtain G_3 graph. We propose two strategies to check the graph G_3 consistency.

Strategy 1: apply Algorithm 1 on G_3.

Strategy 2: apply Algorithm 1 on G_1, then apply Algorithm 1 on G_2, and then use Algorithm 1 to verify only the new connections made when the modular graph G_3 is created.

We note that for this experiment we have implemented an additional functionality in the SDF^3 tool, corresponding to Strategy 2. Moreover, we have created a new benchmark for this experiment, by using 50 graphs of each size up to 150 nodes from the fully connected graph benchmark for G_1 graph, and another 50 graphs for the G_2 graph. In Fig. 7(a), we compare the time needed for Strategy 1 (orange dots) and Strategy 2 (blue triangles) to merge two graphs G_1 and G_2, and obtain a modular application G_3 of various size represented on the horizontal axis. We remark that Strategy 2 outperforms Strategy 1. We note also that the results summarized in Fig. 7(a) include only one merge of two possible applications. We can extrapolate by saying that Strategy 2 will perform even better when more applications are merged into one graph. This statement is confirmed by the experiment depicted in Fig. 7(b), where the two strategies

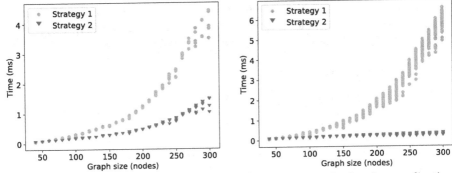

(a) Connection of two dataflow modules of similar size.

(b) Connection of a dataflow application to a module of size 10.

Fig. 7. Experimental results on modular applications. The graph size represented on the horizontal axis is the size of the resulting dataflow graph. (Color figure online)

are compared for n_1 varying from 30 to 290 with a step of 10, and $n_2 = 10$ is fixed. We note that for this experiment we have used 100 graphs of each size up to 290 from the fully connected graph benchmark for G_1, and all 100 graphs of size 10 from the same benchmark for G_2. The horizontal axis in Fig. 7(b) represents the size of the resulting dataflow graph G_3, and the vertical axis represents the measured run-time for the two strategies. We remark that, in this case, Strategy 2 clearly outperforms Strategy 1. We can conclude by saying that one major contribution of Algorithm 1 is that it allows the implementation of Strategy 2, which is not the case for any existing consistency check techniques in the dataflow literature, as far as we know.

5   Related Work

Generally, the technique presented in Sect. 2 is the most commonly used for SDF graphs and models extending the SDF model [3,5,11,15]. The same method is used in Berkley's Ptolemy Project [13], ΣC language [1] and StreamIt language and compiler. For all these models, the consistency is checked by solving a matrix equation. However, the SDF3 algorithm is more efficient than solving Eq. (1), as solving this matrix equation is generally an operation of complexity order three. In the cited models, the consistency check technique does not identify the inconsistent elements in the graph. However, a small modification can be made to the SDF3 algorithm to identify the inconsistent elements and stop the algorithm when such an element is found, as our algorithm do. Moreover, Algorithm 1 has another advantage when compared to these techniques: it is more efficient for modular dataflow application, as the modules put together do not have to be checked again; checking only the new connections between the modules is sufficient. Thus, our algorithm and Strategy 2 can significantly decrease the time needed for consistency check in modular applications in which a topology exploration is performed (i.e. where many random graphs are generated). Algorithm 1 can be generalized for other models extending the SDF model.

6 Concluding Remarks

We have proposed a new approach and method for consistency check in synchronous dataflow graphs. This approach has two main differences when compared to state-of-the-art methods. Firstly, we propose checking the consistency during the dataflow graph construction, and not after the construction, i.e. on the entire graph. Secondly, we propose locally checking the consistency, meaning checking the consistency on every modification suffered by the graph starting to its construction, and thus immediately identifying the inconsistent connections. We have proposed an algorithm using this approach, and implemented it in an existing open source tool. We have generated an experimental benchmark totalling more than six thousands dataflow graphs, and we have tested our algorithm on this benchmark. We have also validated the results obtained with our algorithm, as they are identical to the results given by the state of the art consistency check algorithm implemented in the open source tool. We have compared the time performance given by our algorithm to the time needed by the existing algorithm, and found out that our algorithm performs better on the considered benchmark. The experimental results we obtained show that our algorithm has the advantage of being extremely efficient for complex systems represented by dataflow applications build from several modules and with highly dynamic topology. For future work, we consider to model an Industry 4.0 supply chain using the SDF model, and apply the proposed approach to simulate and control reconfigurable production processes. For such complex systems, the efficiency gain provided by our algorithm and Strategy 2 is significant.

Acknowledgements. Many thanks to Jason Lecerf for its attentive reading and suggestions. We thank Loïc Cudennec and Thierry Goubier for our discussions.

References

1. Aubry, P., et al.: Extended cyclostatic dataflow program compilation and execution for an integrated manycore processor. In: Alchemy 2013-Architecture, Languages, Compilation and Hardware Support for Emerging ManYcore Systems, vol. 18, pp. 1624–1633 (2013)
2. Benazouz, M., Munier-Kordon, A., Hujsa, T., Bodin, B.: Liveness evaluation of a cyclo-static dataflow graph. In: 2013 50th ACM/EDAC/IEEE on Design Automation Conference (DAC), pp. 1–7. IEEE (2013)
3. Bhattacharya, B., Bhattacharyya, S.S.: Parameterized dataflow modeling for DSP systems. IEEE Trans. Signal Process. **49**(10), 2408–2421 (2001). https://doi.org/10.1109/78.950795
4. Bhattacharyya, S.S., Murthy, P.K., Lee, E.A.: Synthesis of embedded software from synchronous dataflow specifications. J. VLSI Signal Process. Syst. Signal Image Video Technol. **21**(2), 151–166 (1999)

5. Bilsen, G., Engels, M., Lauwereins, R., Peperstraete, J.: Cycle-static dataflow. IEEE Trans. Signal Process. **44**(2), 397–408 (1996). https://doi.org/10.1109/78.485935

6. Buck, J.T., Lee, E.A.: Scheduling dynamic dataflow graphs with bounded memory using the token flow model. In: 1993 IEEE International Conference on Acoustics, Speech, and Signal Processing, ICASSP 1993, vol. 1, pp. 429–432. IEEE (1993). https://doi.org/10.1109/ICASSP.1993.319147

7. Geilen, M., Tripakis, S., Wiggers, M.: The earlier the better: a theory of timed actor interfaces. In: Proceedings of the 14th International Conference on Hybrid Systems: Computation and Control, pp. 23–32. ACM (2011)

8. Ghamarian, A.H., Geilen, M., Basten, T., Theelen, B.D., Mousavi, M.R., Stuijk, S.: Liveness and boundedness of synchronous data flow graphs. In: 2006 Formal Methods in Computer Aided Design, FMCAD 2006, pp. 68–75. IEEE (2006)

9. Ghamarian, A.H., et al.: Throughput analysis of synchronous data flow graphs. In: 2006 Sixth International Conference on Application of Concurrency to System Design. ACSD 2006, pp. 25–36. IEEE (2006)

10. Lee, E.A.: Consistency in dataflow graphs. IEEE Trans. Parallel Distrib. Syst. **2**(2), 223–235 (1991). https://doi.org/10.1109/71.89067

11. Lee, E.A., Messerschmitt, D.G.: Synchronous data flow. Proc. IEEE **75**(9), 1235–1245 (1987). https://doi.org/10.1109/PROC.1987.13876

12. Lee, E.A., Messerschmitt, D.G.: Static scheduling of synchronous data flow programs for digital signal processing. IEEE Trans. Comput. **100**(1), 24–35 (1987). https://doi.org/10.1109/TC.1987.5009446

13. Ptolemaeus, C.: System Design, Modeling, and Simulation: Using Ptolemy II, vol. 1. Ptolemy.org, Berkeley (2014)

14. Stuijk, S., Geilen, M., Basten, T.: SDF^3: SDF for free. In: 2006 Sixth International Conference on Application of Concurrency to System Design, ACSD 2006, pp. 276–278. IEEE (2006). https://doi.org/10.1109/ACSD.2006.23

15. Theelen, B.D., Geilen, M.C., Basten, T., Voeten, J.P., Gheorghita, S.V., Stuijk, S.: A scenario-aware data flow model for combined long-run average and worst-case performance analysis. In: 2006 Fourth ACM and IEEE International Conference on Formal Methods and Models for Co-Design, MEMOCODE 2006, Proceedings, pp. 185–194. IEEE (2006). https://doi.org/10.1109/MEMCOD.2006.1695924

16. Thies, W., Amarasinghe, S.: An empirical characterization of stream programs and its implications for language and compiler design. In: Proceedings of the 19th International Conference on Parallel Architectures and Compilation Techniques, pp. 365–376. ACM (2010)

17. Wiggers, M.H., Bekooij, M.J., Smit, G.J.: Buffer capacity computation for throughput constrained streaming applications with data-dependent inter-task communication. In: 2008 Real-Time and Embedded Technology and Applications Symposium, RTAS 2008, pp. 183–194. IEEE (2008). https://doi.org/10.1109/RTAS.2008.10

18. Wiggers, M.H., Bekooij, M.J., Smit, G.J.: Buffer capacity computation for throughput-constrained modal task graphs. ACM Trans. Embed. Comput. Syst. (TECS) **10**(2), 17 (2010)

Gray-Box Monitoring of Hyperproperties

Sandro Stucki[1]([⊠]) [iD], César Sánchez[2] [iD], Gerardo Schneider[1] [iD],
and Borzoo Bonakdarpour[3] [iD]

[1] University of Gothenburg, Gothenburg, Sweden
sandro.stucki@gu.se, gerardo@cse.gu.se
[2] IMDEA Software Institute, Madrid, Spain
cesar.sanchez@imdea.org
[3] Iowa State University, Ames, USA
borzoo@iastate.edu

Abstract. Many important system properties, particularly in security and privacy, cannot be verified statically. Therefore, runtime verification is an appealing alternative. Logics for hyperproperties, such as Hyper-LTL, support a rich set of such properties. We first show that *black-box* monitoring of HyperLTL is in general unfeasible, and suggest a *gray-box* approach. Gray-box monitoring implies performing analysis of the system at run-time, which brings new limitations to monitorability (the feasibility of solving the monitoring problem). Thus, as another contribution of this paper, we refine the classic notions of *monitorability*, both for trace properties and hyperproperties, taking into account the computability of the monitor. We then apply our approach to monitor a privacy hyperproperty called *distributed data minimality*, expressed as a HyperLTL property, by using an SMT-based static verifier at runtime.

1   Introduction

Consider a *confidentiality* policy φ that requires that every pair of separate executions of a system agree on the position of occurrences of some proposition a. Otherwise, an external observer may learn some sensitive information about the system. We are interested in studying how to build runtime monitors for properties like φ, where the monitor receives independent executions of the system under scrutiny and intend to determine whether or not the system satisfies the property. While no such monitor can determine whether the system satisfies φ—as it cannot determine whether it has observed the whole (possibly infinite) set of traces—it may be able to detect violations. For example, if the monitor receives finite executions $t_1 = \{a\}\{\}\{\}\{a\}\{\}$ and $t_2 = \{a\}\{a\}\{\}\{\}\{a\}$, then it is

This research has been partially supported by the United States NSF SaTC Award 1813388, by the Swedish Research Council (*Vetenskapsrådet*) under Grant 2015-04154 "PolUser", by the Madrid Regional Government under Project S2018/TCS-4339 "BLOQUES-CM", by EU H2020 Project 731535 "Elastest", and by Spanish National Project PGC2018-102210-B-100 "BOSCO".

© Springer Nature Switzerland AG 2019
M. H. ter Beek et al. (Eds.): FM 2019, LNCS 11800, pp. 406–424, 2019.
https://doi.org/10.1007/978-3-030-30942-8_25

straightforward to see that the pair (t_1, t_2) violates φ (the traces do not agree on the truth value of a in the second, fourth, and fifth positions).

Now, if we change the policy to φ' requiring that, for every execution, there must exist a different one that agrees with the first execution on the position of occurrences of a, the monitor cannot even detect violations of φ'. Indeed, it is not possible to tell at run-time whether or not for each execution (from a possibly infinite set), there exists a related one. Such properties for which no monitor can detect satisfaction or violation are known as *non-monitorable*.

Monitorability was first defined in [26] as the problem of deciding whether any extension of an observed trace would violate or satisfy a property expressed in LTL. We call this notion *semantic black-box monitorability*. It is semantic because it defines a decision problem (the existence of a satisfying or violating trace extension) without requiring a corresponding decision procedure. In settings like LTL the problem is decidable and the decision procedures are well-studied, but in other settings, a property may be semantically monitorable even though no algorithm to monitor it exists. This notion of monitorability is "black-box" because it only considers the temporal logic formula to determine the plausibility of an extended observation that violates or satisfies the formula. This is the only sound assumption without looking inside the system. Many variants of this definition followed, mostly for trace logics [17] (see also [4]).

The definition of semantic monitorability is extended in [1] to the context of *hyperproperties* [10]. A hyperproperty is essentially a set of sets of traces, so monitoring hyperproperties involves reasoning about multiple traces simultaneously. The confidentiality example discussed above is a hyperproperty. The notion of monitorability for hyperproperties in [1] also considers whether extensions of an observed trace, or of other additional observed traces, would violate or satisfy the property. An important drawback of these notions of monitorability is that they completely ignore the role of the system being monitored and the possible set of executions that it can exhibit to compute a verdict of a property.

In this paper, we consider a landscape of monitorability aspects along three dimensions, as depicted in Fig. 1. We explore the ability of the monitor to reason about multiple traces simultaneously (the trace/hyper dimension). We first show that a large class of hyperproperties that involve quantifier alternations are non-monitorable. That is, no matter the observation, no verdict can ever be declared. We then propose a solution based on a combination of static analysis and runtime verification. If the analysis of the system is completely precise, we call it *white-box* monitoring. *Black-box* monitoring refers to the classic approach of ignoring the system and crafting general monitors that provide sound verdicts for every system. In *gray-box* monitoring, the mon-

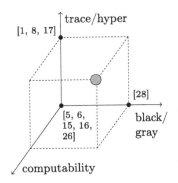

Fig. 1. The monitorability cube.

itor uses an approximate set of executions, given for example as a model, in addition to the observed finite execution. The combination of static analysis and runtime verification allows to monitor hyperproperties of interest, but it involves reasoning about possible executions of the system (the black/gray dimension in Fig. 1). This, in turn, forces us to consider the computability limitations of the monitors themselves as programs (the computability dimension).

We apply this approach to monitoring a complex hyperproperty of interest in privacy, namely, *data minimization*. The principle of data minimization (introduced in Article 5 of the EU General Data Protection Regulation [13]) from a software perspective requires that only data that is semantically used by a program should be collected and processed. When data is collected from independent sources, the property is called *distributed data minimization* (DDM) [3,24]. Our approach for monitoring DDM is as follows. We focus on detecting violations of DDM (which we express in HyperLTL using one quantifier alternation). We then create a gray-box monitor that collects dynamically potential witnesses for the existential part. The monitor then invokes an oracle (combining symbolic execution trees and SMT solving) to soundly decide the universally quantified inner sub-formula. Our approach is sound but approximated, so the monitor may give an inconclusive answer, depending on the precision of the static verification.

Contributions. In summary, the contributions of this paper are the following:

(1) Novel richer definitions of monitorability that consider trace and hyperproperties, and the possibility of analyzing the system (gray-box monitoring). This enables the monitoring, via the combination of static analysis and runtime verification, of properties that are non-monitorable in a black-box manner. Our novel notions of monitorability also cover the computability limitations of monitors as programs, which is inevitable once the analysis is part of the monitoring process.
(2) We express DDM as a hyperproperty and study its monitorability within the richer landscape defined above. We then apply the combined approach where the static analysis in this case is based on symbolic execution (Sect. 4).

Full proofs as well as a detailed description of our proof-of-concept implementation and its empirical evaluation can be found in the extended version of this paper [27]. The source code of our implementation is freely available online.[1]

2   Background

Let AP be a finite set of *atomic propositions* and $\Sigma = 2^{AP}$ be the finite *alphabet*. We call each element of Σ a *letter* (or an *event*). Throughout the paper, Σ^ω denotes the set of all infinite sequences (called *traces*) over Σ, and Σ^* denotes the set of all finite traces over Σ. For a trace $t \in \Sigma^\omega$ (or $t \in \Sigma^*$), $t[i]$ denotes the ith element of t, where $i \in \mathbb{N}$. We use $|t|$ to denote the length (finite or infinite) of

---

[1] At https://github.com/sstucki/minion/.

trace t. Also, $t[i,j]$ denotes the subtrace of t from position i up to and including position j (or ϵ if $i > j$ or if $i > |t|$). In this manner $t[0,i]$ denotes the prefix of t up to and including i and $t[i,..]$ denotes the suffix of t from i (including i).

Given a set X, we use $\mathcal{P}(X)$ for the set of subsets of X and $\mathcal{P}_{fin}(X)$ for the set of finite subsets of X. Let u be a finite trace and t a finite or infinite trace. We denote the concatenation of u and t by ut. Also, $u \preceq t$ denotes the fact that u is a prefix of t. Given a finite set U of finite traces and an arbitrary set W of finite or infinite traces, we say that W extends U (written $U \preceq W$) if, for all $u \in U$, there is a $v \in W$, such that $u \preceq v$. Note that every trace in U is extended by some trace in W (we call these *trace extensions*), and that W may also contain additional traces with no prefix in U (we call these *set extensions*).

2.1   LTL and HyperLTL

We now briefly introduce LTL and HyperLTL. The syntax of LTL [25] is:

$$\varphi ::= a \mid \neg\varphi \mid \varphi \vee \varphi \mid \bigcirc \varphi \mid \varphi \,\mathcal{U}\, \varphi$$

where $a \in \mathsf{AP}$. The semantics of LTL is given by associating to a formula the set of traces $t \in \Sigma^\omega$ that it accepts:

$t \models p$	iff	$p \in t[0]$
$t \models \neg\varphi$	iff	$t \not\models \varphi$
$t \models \varphi_1 \vee \varphi_2$	iff	$t \models \varphi_1$ or $t \models \varphi_2$
$t \models \bigcirc\varphi$	iff	$t[1,..] \models \varphi$
$t \models \varphi_1 \,\mathcal{U}\, \varphi_2$	iff	for some i, $t[i,..] \models \varphi_2$ and for all $j < i, t[j,..] \models \varphi_1$

We will also use the usual derived operators ($\Diamond\varphi \equiv true\,\mathcal{U}\,\varphi$) and ($\Box\varphi \equiv \neg\Diamond\neg\varphi$). All properties expressible in LTL are *trace properties* (each individual trace satisfies the property or not, independently of any other trace). Some important properties, such as information-flow security policies (including confidentiality, integrity, and secrecy), cannot be expressed as trace properties but require reasoning about two (or more) independent executions (perhaps from different inputs) simultaneously. Such properties are called *hyperproperties* [10]. HyperLTL [11] is a temporal logic for hyperproperties that extends LTL by allowing explicit quantification over execution traces. The syntax of HyperLTL is:

$$\varphi ::= \forall\pi.\varphi \mid \exists\pi.\varphi \mid \psi \qquad \psi ::= a_\pi \mid \neg\psi \mid \psi \vee \psi \mid \bigcirc\psi \mid \psi\,\mathcal{U}\,\psi$$

A trace assignment $\Pi : \mathcal{V} \to \Sigma^\omega$ is a partial function mapping trace variables in $\mathcal{V}$ to infinite traces. We use $\Pi_\varnothing$ to denote the empty assignment, and $\Pi[\pi \to t]$ for the same function as Π, except that π is mapped to trace t. The semantics of HyperLTL is defined by associating formulas with pairs (T, Π), where T is a set of traces and Π is a trace assignment:

$T, \Pi \models \forall\pi.\varphi$	iff	for all $t \in T$ the following holds $T, \Pi[\pi \to t] \models \varphi$
$T, \Pi \models \exists\pi.\varphi$	iff	there exists $t \in T$ such that $T, \Pi[\pi \to t] \models \varphi$
$T, \Pi \models \psi$	iff	$\Pi \models \psi$

The semantics of the temporal inner formulas is defined in terms of the traces associated with each path (here $\Pi[i,..]$ denotes the map that assigns π to $t[i,..]$ if $\Pi(\pi) = t$):

$$
\begin{array}{llll}
\Pi \models a_\pi & \text{iff} & a \in \Pi(\pi)[0] \\
\Pi \models \psi_1 \vee \psi_2 & \text{iff} & \Pi \models \psi_1 \text{ or } \Pi \models \psi_2 \\
\Pi \models \neg\psi & \text{iff} & \Pi \not\models \psi \\
\Pi \models \bigcirc\psi & \text{iff} & \Pi[1..] \models \psi \\
\Pi \models \psi_1 \,\mathcal{U}\, \psi_2 & \text{iff} & \text{for some } i, \Pi[i,..] \models \psi_2, \text{ and for all } j < iT, \Pi[j,..] \models \psi_1
\end{array}
$$

We say that a set T of traces satisfies a HyperLTL formula φ (denoted $T \models \varphi$) if and only if $T, \Pi_\varnothing \models \varphi$.

Example 1. Consider the HyperLTL formula $\varphi = \forall\pi.\forall\pi'.\Box(a_\pi \leftrightarrow a_{\pi'})$ and $T = \{t_1, t_2, t_3\}$, where $t_1 = \{a, b\}\{a, b\}\{\}\{b\}\cdots$, $t_2 = \{a\}\{a\}\{b\}\cdots$ and $t_3 = \{\}\{a\}\{b\}\cdots$ Although traces t_1 and t_2 together satisfy φ, t_3 does not agree with the other two, i.e., $a \in t_1(0), a \in t_2(0)$, but $a \notin t_3(0)$. Hence, $T \not\models \varphi$.

2.2 Semantic Monitorability

Runtime verification (RV) is concerned with (1) generating a monitor from a formal specification φ, and (2) using the monitor to detect whether or not φ holds by observing events generated by the system at run time. *Monitorability* refers to the possibility of monitoring a property. Some properties are non-monitorable because no finite observation can lead to a conclusive verdict. We now present some abstract definitions to encompass previous notions of monitorability in a general way. These definitions are made concrete by instantiating them for example to traces (for trace properties) or sets of traces (for hyperproperties), see Example 2 below.

– **Observation.** We refer to the finite information provided dynamically to the monitor up to a given instant as an *observation*.
  We use O and P to denote individual observations and $\mathcal{O}$ to denote the set of all possible observations, equipped with an operator $O \preceq P$ that captures the extension of an observation.
– **System behavior.** We use $\mathcal{B}$ to denote the universe of all possible *behaviors* of a system. A behavior $B \in \mathcal{B}$ may, in general, be an infinite piece of information. By abuse of notation, $O \preceq B$ denotes that observation $O \in \mathcal{O}$ can be extended to a behavior B.

Example 2. When monitoring trace properties such as LTL, we have $\mathcal{O} = \Sigma^*$, an observation is a finite trace $O \in \Sigma^*$, $O \preceq O'$ is the prefix relation on finite strings, and $\mathcal{B} = \Sigma^\omega$. When monitoring hyperproperties such as HyperLTL, an observation is a finite set of finite traces $O \subset \Sigma^*$, that is, $\mathcal{O} = \mathcal{P}_{fin}(\Sigma^*)$. The relation $\preceq$ is the prefix for finite sets of finite traces defined above. That is, $O \preceq P$ whenever for all $t \in O$ there is a $t' \in P$ such that $t \preceq t'$. Finally, $\mathcal{B} = \mathcal{P}(\Sigma^\omega)$.

We say that an observation $O \in \mathcal{O}$ *permanently satisfies* a formula φ, if every $B \in \mathcal{B}$ that extends O satisfies φ:

$$O \models^s \varphi \quad \text{iff} \quad \text{for all } B \in \mathcal{B} \text{ such that } O \preceq B, \, B \models \varphi$$

where $\models$ denotes the satisfaction relation in the semantics of the logic. Similarly, we say that an observation $O \in \mathcal{O}$ *permanently violates* a formula φ, if every extension $B \in \mathcal{B}$ violates φ:

$$O \models^v \varphi \quad \text{iff} \quad \text{for all } B \in \mathcal{B} \text{ such that } O \preceq B, \, B \not\models \varphi$$

Monitoring a system for satisfaction (or violation) of a formula φ is to decide whether a finite observation permanently satisfies (resp. violates) φ.

Definition 1 (Semantic Monitorability). *A formula φ is* (semantically) monitorable *if every observation O has an extended observation $P \succeq O$, such that $P \models^s \varphi$ or $P \models^v \varphi$.*

A similar definition of monitorability only for satisfaction or only for violation can be obtained by considering only $P \models^s \varphi$ or only $P \models^v \varphi$. Instantiating this definition of monitorability for LTL and finite traces as observations ($\mathcal{O} = \Sigma^*$ and $\mathcal{B} = \Sigma^\omega$) leads to the classic definitions of monitorability for LTL by Pnueli and Zaks [26] (see also [17]). Similarly, instantiating the definitions for HyperLTL and observations as finite sets of finite traces leads to monitorability as introduced by Agrawal and Bonakdarpour [1].

Example 3. The LTL formula $\Box \Diamond a$ is not (semantically) monitorable since it requires an infinite-length observation, while formulas $\Box a$ and $\Diamond a$ are monitorable. Similarly, $\forall \pi. \forall \pi. \Box(a_\pi \leftrightarrow \neg a_{\pi'})$ is monitorable, but $\forall \pi. \exists \pi. \Box(a_\pi \leftrightarrow \neg a_{\pi'})$ is not, as it requires an observation set of infinite size. We will prove this claim in detail in Sect. 3.

3   The Notion of Gray-Box Monitoring

Most of the previous definitions of monitorability make certain assumptions: (1) the logics are trace logics, i.e. do not cover hyperproperties, (2) the system under analysis is black-box in the sense that every further observation is possible, (3) the logics are tractable, in that the decision problems of satisfiability, liveness, etc. are decidable. We present here a more general notion of monitorability by challenging these assumptions.

3.1   The Limitations of Monitoring Hyperproperties

Earlier work on monitoring hyperproperties is restricted to the quantifier alternation-free fragment, that is either $\forall^*.\psi$ or $\exists^*.\psi$ properties. We establish now an impossibility result about the monitorability of formulas of the form $\forall \pi. \exists \pi'. \Box F$, where F is a state predicate. That is, F is formed by atomic propositions, a_π or

$a_{\pi'}$ and Boolean combinations thereof, and can be evaluated given two valuations of the propositions from AP, one from each path π and π' at the current position. For example, the predicate $F = (a_\pi \leftrightarrow \neg a_{\pi'})$ for AP $= \{a\}$ depends on the valuation of a at the first state of paths π and π'. We use v and v' in $F(v, v')$ to denote that F uses two copies of the variables v (one copy from π and another from π'). A predicate F is *reflexive* if for all valuations $v \in 2^{AP}$, $F(v, v)$ is true. A predicate F is *serial* if, for all v, there is a v' such that $F(v, v')$ is true.

Theorem 1. *A HyperLTL formula of the form* $\psi = \forall \pi.\exists \pi'.\Box F$ *is non-monitorable if and only if* F *is non-reflexive and serial.*

Proof (Sketch). For the "$\Leftarrow$" direction, it is easy to see that seriality implies that Σ^ω is a model of φ. Also, non-reflexivity means any observation can be extended to a non-model by adding v to every trace, so that $\neg F(v, v)$. Since every observation can be extended to a model and a non-model, φ is non-monitorable.

For the "$\Rightarrow$" direction, we prove that reflexivity or non-seriality imply monitorability. Reflexivity implies that φ is vacuously true by taking the same trace for π and π'. Then, assume non-seriality, and append to one path in the observation v such that for no v, $F(v, v')$, generating a permanent violation.   □

The fragment of $\forall\exists$ properties captured by Theorem 1 is very general (and this result can be easily generalized to $\forall^+\exists^+$ hyperproperties). First, the temporal operator is just safety (the result can be generalized for richer temporal formulas). Also, every binary predicate can be turned into a non-reflexive predicate by distinguishing the traces being related. Moroever, many relational properties, such as non-interference and DDM, contain a tacit assumption that only distinct traces are being related. Seriality simply establishes that F cannot be falsified by only observing the local valuation of one of the traces. Intuitively, a predicate that is not serial can be falsified by looking only at one of the traces, so the property is not a proper hyperproperty. The practical consequence of Theorem 1 is that many hyperproperties involving one quantifier alternation cannot be monitored.

3.2 Gray-Box Monitoring. Sound and Perfect Monitors

To overcome the negative non-monitorability result, we exploit knowledge about the set of traces that the system can produce (gray-box or white-box monitoring). Given a system that can produce the set of system behaviors $\mathcal{S} \subseteq \mathcal{B}$, we parametrize the notions of permanent satisfaction and permanent violation to consider only behaviors in $\mathcal{S}$:

$$O \models^s_{\mathcal{S}} \varphi \quad \text{iff} \quad \text{for all } B \in \mathcal{S} \text{ such that } O \preceq B, B \models \varphi$$
$$O \models^v_{\mathcal{S}} \varphi \quad \text{iff} \quad \text{for all } B \in \mathcal{S} \text{ such that } O \preceq B, B \not\models \varphi$$

First, we extend the definition of monitorability (Definition 1 above) to consider the system under observation.

Definition 2 (Semantic Gray-Box Monitorability). *A formula* φ *is semantically gray-box monitorable for a system* $\mathcal{S}$ *if every observation O has an extended observation $P \succeq O$ in $\mathcal{S}$, such that $P \models_{\mathcal{S}}^{s} \varphi$ or $P \models_{\mathcal{S}}^{v} \varphi$.*

In this definition, monitors must now analyze and decide properties of extended observations which is computationally not possible with full precision for sufficiently rich system descriptions.

We now introduce a novel notion of monitors that consider $\mathcal{S}$ and the computational power of monitors (the diagonal dimension in Fig. 1). A *monitor* for a property φ and a set of traces $\mathcal{S}$ is a *computable* function $M_{\mathcal{S}} \colon \mathcal{O} \to \{\top, \bot, ?\}$ that, given a finite observation O, decides a *verdict* for φ: $\top$ indicates success, $\bot$ indicates failure, and ? indicates that the monitor cannot declare a definite verdict given only u. To avoid clutter, we write M instead of $M_{\mathcal{S}}$ when the system is clear from the context. The following definition captures when a monitor for a property φ can give a definite answer.

Definition 3 (Sound monitor). *Given a property φ and a set of behaviors $\mathcal{S}$, a monitor M is sound whenever, for every observation $O \in \mathcal{O}$,*

1. *if $O \models_{\mathcal{S}}^{s} \varphi$, then $M(O) = \top$ or $M(O) = ?$,*
2. *if $O \models_{\mathcal{S}}^{v} \varphi$, then $M(O) = \bot$ or $M(O) = ?$,*
3. *otherwise $M(O) = ?$.*

If a monitor is not sound then it is possible that an extension of O forces M to change a $\top$ to a $\bot$ verdict, or vice-versa. The function that always outputs ? is a sound monitor for any property, but this is the least informative monitor. A *perfect monitor* precisely outputs whether satisfaction or violation is inevitable, which is the most informative monitor.

Definition 4 (Perfect Monitor). *Given a property φ and a set of traces $\mathcal{S}$, a monitor M is perfect whenever, for every observation $O \in \mathcal{O}$,*

1. *if $O \models_{\mathcal{S}}^{s} \varphi$ then $M(O) = \top$,*
2. *if $O \models_{\mathcal{S}}^{v} \varphi$ then $M(O) = \bot$,*
3. *otherwise $M(O) = ?$.*

Obviously, a perfect monitor is sound. Similar definitions of perfect monitor only for satisfaction (resp. violation) can be given by forcing the precise outcome only for satisfaction (resp. violation).

A black-box monitor is one where every behavior is potentially possible, that is $\mathcal{S} = \mathcal{B}$. If the monitor uses information about the actual system, then we say it is *gray-box* (and we use *white-box* when the monitor can reason with absolute precision about the set of traces of the system). In some cases, for example to decide instantiations of a $\forall$ quantifier, a satisfaction verdict that is taken from $\mathcal{S}$ can be concluded for all over-approximations (dually under-approximations for violation and for $\exists$). For space limitations, we do not give the formal details here.

Using Definitions 3 and 4, we can add the computability aspect to capture a stronger definition of monitorability. Abusing notation, we use $O \in S$ to say that observation O can be extended to a trace allowed by the system.

Definition 5 (Strong Monitorability). *A property φ is strongly monitorable for a system S if there is a sound monitor M s.t. for all observations $O \in \mathcal{O}$, there is an extended observation $P \in S$ for which either $M(P) = \top$ or $M(P) = \bot$.*

A property is strongly monitorable for satisfaction if the extension with $M(P) = \top$ always exists (and analogously for violation). In what follows we will use the term *monitorability* to refer to strong monitorability whenever no confusion may arise. It is easy to see that if a property is not semantically monitorable, then it is not strongly monitorable, but in rich domains, some semantically monitorable properties may not be strongly monitorable. One trivial example is termination for deterministic programs (that is, the halting problem). Given a prefix of the execution of a deterministic program, either the program halts or it does not, so termination is monitorable in the semantics sense. However, it is not possible to build a monitor that decides the halting problem.

Lemma 1. *If φ is strongly monitorable, then φ is semantically monitorable.*

A property may not be monitorable in a black-box manner, but monitorable in a gray-box manner. In the realm of monitoring of LTL properties, strong and semantic monitorability coincide for finite state systems (see [28]) both black-box and gray-box (for finite state systems), because model-checking and the problem of deciding whether a state of a Büchi automaton is live are decidable.

Following [8] we propose to use a combination of static analysis and runtime verification to monitor violations of $\forall^+\exists^+$ properties (or dually, satisfactions of $\exists^+\forall^+$). The main idea is to collect candidates for the outer $\exists$ part dynamically and use static analysis at runtime to over-approximate the inner $\forall$ quantifiers.

4   Monitoring Distributed Data Minimality

In this section, we describe how to monitor DDM, which can be expressed as a hyperproperty of the form $\forall^+\exists^+$. In the particular case of DDM, although we mainly deal with the input/output relation of functions and are not concerned with infinite temporal behavior, we still need to handle possibly infinite set extensions S for black-box monitoring.

In the remainder of this section, we discuss the following, seemingly contradictory aspects of DDM:

(P1) DDM is not semantically *black-box* monitorable,
(P2) DDM is semantically *white-box* monitorable (for programs that are not DDM),
(P3) checking DDM statically is undecidable,

(P4) DDM is strongly gray-box monitorable for violation, and we give a *sound monitor*.

The apparent contradictions are resolved by careful analysis of DDM along the different dimensions of the monitorability cube (Fig. 1).

We will show how to monitor DDM and similar hyperproperties using a gray-box approach. In our approach, a monitor can decide at run time the existence of traces using a limited form of static analysis. The static analyzer receives the finite observation O collected by the monitor, but not the future system behavior. Instead it must reason under the assumption that any system behavior in S that is compatible with O, may eventually occur. For example, given an $\exists\forall$ formula, the outer existential quantifier is instantiated with a concrete set U of runtime traces, while possible extensions of U provided by static analysis can be used to instantiate the inner universal quantifier.

4.1 DDM Preliminaries

We briefly recapitulate the formal notion of data-minimality from [3]. Given a function $f: I \to O$, the problem of data minimization consists in finding a *preprocessor* function $p: I \to I$, such that $f = f \circ p$ and $p = p \circ p$. The goal of p is to limit the information available to f while preserving the behavior of f.

There are many possible such preprocessors (e.g. the identity function), which can be ordered according to the information they disclose, that is, according to the subset relation on their *kernels*. The kernel $\ker(p)$ of a function p is defined as the equivalence relation $(x, y) \in \ker(p)$ iff $p(x) = p(y)$. The smaller $\ker(p)$ is, the more information p discloses. The identity function is the worst preprocessor since it discloses all information (its kernel is equality—the least equivalence relation). An optimal preprocessor, or *minimizer*, is one that discloses the least amount of information.

A function f is *monolithic data-minimal* (MDM), if it fulfills either of the following equivalent conditions:

1. the identity function is a minimizer for f,
2. f is injective.

Condition 1. is an information-flow-based characterization that can be generalized to more complicated settings in a straightforward fashion. Condition 2. is a purely logical or *data-based* characterization more suitable for implementation in e.g. a monitor.

MDM is the strongest form of data minimality, where one assumes that all input data is provided by a single source and thus a single preprocessor can be used to minimize the function. If inputs are provided by multiple sources (called a distributed setting) and access to the system implementing f is restricted, it might be impossible to use a single preprocessor. For example, consider a web-based auction system that accepts bids from n bidders, represented by distinct input domains $I_1, \ldots, I_n$, and where concrete bids $x_k \in I_k$ are submitted remotely. The auction system must compute the function

$m(x_1, \ldots, x_n) = \max_k\{x_k\}$, which is clearly non-injective and, hence, non-MDM. In this case, a single, monolithic minimizer cannot be used since different bidders need not have any knowledge of each other's bids. Instead, bidders must try to minimize the information contained in their bid locally, in a distributed way, before submitting it to the auction.

The problem of *distributed data minimization* consists in building a collection $p_1, \ldots, p_n$ of n independent preprocessors $p_k \colon I_k \to I_k$ for a given function $f \colon I_1 \times \cdots \times I_n \to O$, such that their parallel composition $p(x_1, \ldots, x_n) = (p_1(x_1), \ldots, p(x_n))$ is a preprocessor for f. Such composite preprocessors are called *distributed*, and a distributed preprocessor for f that discloses the least amount of information is called a *distributed minimizer* for f. Then, one can generalize the (information-flow) notion of data-minimality to the distributed setting as follows. The function f is *distributed data-minimal* (DDM) if the identity function is a distributed minimizer for f. Returning to our example, the maximum function m defined above is DDM. As for MDM, there is an equivalent, data-based characterization of DDM defined next.

Definition 6 (distributed data minimality [3,23]**).** *A function f is* distributed data-minimal (DDM) *if, for all input positions k and all $x, y \in I_k$ such that $x \neq y$, there is some $z \in I$, such that $f(z[k \mapsto x]) \neq f(z[k \mapsto y])$.*

We use Definition 6 to explore how to monitor DDM. In the following, we assume that the function $f \colon I_1 \times \cdots \times I_n \to O$ has at least two arguments ($n \geq 2$). Note that for unary functions, DDM coincides with MDM. Since MDM is a $\forall^+$-property (involving no quantifier alternations), most of the challenges to monitorability discussed here do not apply [24]. We also assume, without loss of generality, that the function f being monitored has only nontrivial input domains, i.e. $|I_k| \geq 2$ for all $k = 1, \ldots n$. If I_k is trivial then this constant input can be ignored. Finally, note that checking DDM statically is undecidable (P3) for sufficiently rich programming languages [3].

4.2 DDM as a Hyperproperty

We consider data-minimality for total functions $f \colon I \to O$. Our alphabet, or set of events, is the set of possible *input-output (I/O) pairs* of f, i.e. $\Sigma_f = I \times O$. Since a single I/O pair $u = (u_{in}, u_{out}) \in \Sigma_f$ captures an entire run of f, we restrict ourselves to observing singleton traces, i.e. traces of length $|u| = 1$. In other words, we ignore any temporal aspects associated with the computation of f. This allows us to use first-order predicate logic—without any temporal modalities—as our specification logic.

DDM is a hyperproperty, expressed as a predicate over sets of traces, even though the traces are I/O pairs. The set of observable behaviors $\mathcal{O}_f$ of a given f consists of all *finite sets* of I/O pairs $\mathcal{O}_f = \mathcal{P}_{fin}(\Sigma_f)$. The set of all possible system behaviors $\mathcal{B}_f = \mathcal{P}(\Sigma_f)$ additionally includes *infinite sets* of I/O pairs.

Example 4. Let $f \colon \mathbb{N} \times \mathbb{N} \to \mathbb{N}$ be the addition function on natural numbers, $f(x, y) = x + y$. Then $I = \mathbb{N} \times \mathbb{N}$, $O = \mathbb{N}$, and a valid trace $u \in \Sigma_f$ takes the form

$u = ((x, y), z)$, where x, y and z are all naturals. Both $U = \{((1,2),3), ((2,1),3)\}$ and $V = \{((1,1),3)\}$ are considered observable behaviors $U, V \in \mathcal{O}_f$, even though V does not correspond to a valid system behavior since $f(1,1) \neq 3$. Remember that we do not discriminate between valid and invalid system behaviors in a black-box setting.

We now express DDM as a hyperproperty, using HyperLTL, but with only state predicates (no temporal operators). Given a tuple $x = (x_1, x_2, \ldots, x_n)$, we write $\mathrm{proj}_i(x)$ or simply x_i for its i-th projection. Given an I/O pair $u = (x, y)$ we use u_{in} for the input component and u_{out} for the output component (that is $u_{in} = x$ and $u_{out} = y$). Given trace variables π, π', we define

$$\mathrm{output}(\pi, \pi') \stackrel{\mathrm{def}}{=} \pi_{out} = \pi'_{out} \qquad\qquad \pi \text{ and } \pi' \text{ agree on their output,}$$

$$\mathrm{same}_i(\pi, \pi') \stackrel{\mathrm{def}}{=} \mathrm{proj}_i(\pi_{in}) = \mathrm{proj}_i(\pi'_{in}) \qquad \pi \text{ and } \pi' \text{ agree on the } i\text{-th input,}$$

$$\mathrm{almost}_i(\pi, \pi') \stackrel{\mathrm{def}}{=} \bigwedge_{k \neq i} \mathrm{proj}_k(\pi_{in}) = \mathrm{proj}_k(\pi'_{in}) \qquad \begin{array}{l} \pi \text{ and } \pi' \text{ agree on all but the} \\ i\text{-th input} \end{array}$$

Example 5. Let $u = ((1,2),3)$, $u' = ((2,1),3)$, and $\Pi = \{\pi \mapsto u, \pi' \mapsto u'\}$. Then $\Pi \models \mathrm{output}(\pi, \pi')$, but $\Pi \not\models \mathrm{same}_1(\pi, \pi')$ and $\Pi \not\models \mathrm{almost}_1(\pi, \pi')$.

We define DDM for input argument i as follows:

$$\varphi_i \;=\; \forall \pi. \forall \pi'. \exists \tau. \exists \tau'. \, \neg\, \mathrm{same}_i(\pi, \pi') \rightarrow \left(\begin{array}{l} \mathrm{same}_i(\pi, \tau) \wedge \mathrm{same}_i(\pi', \tau') \wedge \\ \mathrm{almost}_i(\tau, \tau') \wedge \neg\, \mathrm{output}(\tau, \tau') \end{array} \right)$$

In words: given any pair of traces π and π', if π_{in} and π'_{in} differ in their i-th position, then there must be some common values z for the remaining inputs, such that the outputs of f for $\tau_{in} = z[i \mapsto \mathrm{proj}_i(\pi_{in})]$ and $\tau'_{in} = z[i \mapsto \mathrm{proj}_i(\pi'_{in})]$ differ. Note that z does not appear in φ_i directly, instead it is determined implicitly by the (existentially quantified) traces τ and τ'. Finally, *distributed data minimality* for f is defined as

$$\varphi_{\mathsf{dm}} \;=\; \bigwedge_{i=1}^{n} \varphi_i.$$

The property φ_{dm} follows the same structure as the logical characterization of DDM from Sect. 4.1. The universally quantified variables range over the possible inputs at position i, while the existentially quantified variables τ and τ' range over the other inputs and the outputs. Note also that, given the input coordinates of π, π', and τ, all the output coordinates, as well as the input coordinates of τ', are uniquely determined.[2]

---

[2] For simplicity, even though φ_{dm} is not in prenex normal form, it is a finite conjunction of $\forall\forall\exists\exists$ formulas in prenex normal form so a finite number of monitors can be built and executed in parallel, one per input argument.

Example 6. Consider again $U = \{((1,2),3),((2,1),3)\}$ and $V = \{((1,1),3)\}$ from Example 4. Then, $V \models \varphi_{\text{dm}}$ trivially holds, but $U \not\models \varphi_{\text{dm}}$ because when $\Pi(\pi) \neq \Pi(\pi')$ there is no choice of $\Pi(\tau), \Pi(\tau') \in U$ for which $\Pi \models \neg\,\text{output}(\tau, \tau')$ holds.

Note that, in the above example, $V \models \varphi_{\text{dm}}$ holds despite the fact that V is not a valid behavior of the example function $f(x,y) = x + y$. Indeed, whether or not $U \models \varphi_{\text{dm}}$ holds for a given U is independent of the choice of f. In particular, $\Sigma_f \models \varphi_{\text{dm}}$, for any choice of f regardless of whether f is data-minimal or not. This is already a hint that the notion of semantic black-box monitorability is too weak to be useful when monitoring φ_{dm}. Since Σ_f is a model of φ_{dm}, no observation U can have an extension that permanently violates φ_{dm}. As we will see shortly, gray-box monitoring does not suffer from this limitation. Monitorability of DDM for violations becomes possible once we exclude potential models such as Σ_f which do not correspond to valid system behaviors.

Remark. Note that though our definition and approach work for general (reactive) systems, the DDM example is admittedly a non-reactive system with traces of length 1. This, however, is not a limitation of the approach. Extending DDM for reactive systems is left as future work.

4.3   Properties of DDM

Since φ_{dm} is a $\forall^+\exists^+$ property, it should not come as a surprise that it is *not* semantically black-box monitorable in general (P1). Although DDM is not a temporal property, the proof of non-monitorability follows the same basic structure as that of Theorem 1 [27]. In particular, since $\Sigma_f \models \varphi_{\text{dm}}$ for any f, no set of I/O pairs U can permanently violate φ_{dm}. In other words, φ_{dm} is clearly not black-box monitorable for violations.

However, and perhaps surprisingly, φ_{dm} is semantically white-box monitorable for violations (P2). That is, if f is not DDM, there is hope to detect it. To make this statement more precise, we first need to identify the set of valid system behaviors $\mathcal{S}_f$ of f. We define $\Sigma_f^{\#} = \{(x,y) \mid f(x) = y\}$ to be the set of I/O pairs that correspond to executions of f. Then $\mathcal{S}_f = \mathcal{P}(\Sigma_f^{\#})$ precisely characterizes the set of valid system behaviors.

Example 7. Define $g\colon \mathbb{N} \times \mathbb{N} \to \mathbb{N}$ as $g(x,y) = x$, i.e. g simply ignores its second argument. Then $\Sigma_g^{\#} = \{((x,y),x) \mid x,y \in \mathbb{N}\}$. It is easy to show that DDM is white-box monitorable for g. Any finite set of valid traces U can be extended to include a pair of traces u, u' that only differ in their second input value, e.g. $u = ((1,1),1)$ and $u' = ((1,2),1)$. Now, consider any $T \in \mathcal{S}_f$ that extends $U \cup \{u, u'\}$. Clearly, T cannot contain any trace v for which $\text{proj}_1(v_{in}) = 1$ but $v_{out} \neq 1$ as that would constitute an invalid system behavior. But T would have to contain such a trace to be a model of φ_2. Hence, $T \not\models \varphi_{\text{dm}}$ for any such T, which means $U \cup \{u, u'\}$ permanently violates φ_{dm}.

Note the crucial use of information about g in the above example: it is the restriction to *valid* extensions $T \in \mathcal{S}_f$ that excludes trivial models such as Σ_f and thereby restores (semantic) monitorability for violations. The apparent conflict between (P1) and (P2) is thus resolved.

With the extra information that gray-box monitoring affords, we can make more precise claims about properties like DDM: whether or not a property is monitorable may, for instance, depend on whether the property actually holds for the system under scrutiny. Concretely, for the case of DDM, we show the following.

Theorem 2. *Given a function* $f: I \to O$, *the formula* φ_{dm} *is semantically gray-box monitorable in* $\mathcal{S}_f$ *if and only if either* f *is distributed non-minimal or the input domain* I *is finite.*

Proof (Sketch). If I is finite, $\Sigma_f^{\#} \in \mathcal{S}_f$ is a finite extension of any U and also permanently satisfies or violates φ_{dm}. If, instead, I is infinite and f is not distributed minimal, then there must be some input position i and some pair of distinct inputs $x \neq x' \in I_i$, such that $f(z[i \mapsto x]) = f(z[i \mapsto x'])$ for any choice of $z \in I$. Any set U extended by a pair of traces featuring these inputs at position i (permanently) violates φ_{dm}. The proof for the case where I is infinite and f is distributed minimal uses a similar idea to construct counterexamples to permanent satisfaction of φ_{dm}. (See our tech-report for the full proof [27].)   □

Intuitively, this means that f cannot be monitored for satisfaction. Note that the semantic monitorability property established by Theorem 2 is independent of whether we can actually decide DDM for the given f. We address the question of strong monitorability later on in this section.

If I is finite, it is easy to strengthen Theorem 2 by providing a perfect monitor M_{dm} for φ_{dm}. Since f is assumed to be a total function with a finite domain, we can simply check the validity of φ_{dm} for every trace $U \subseteq \Sigma_f^{\#}$ and tabulate the result. To do so, the $\exists$ and $\forall$ quantifiers in φ_{dm} can be converted into conjunctions and disjunctions over U.

Corollary 1. *For* $f : I \to O$ *with finite* I, φ_{dm} *is strongly monitorable in* $\mathcal{S}_f$.

If I is infinite, then φ_{dm} is not semantically monitorable for satisfaction, but we can still hope to build a sound monitor for violation of φ_{dm}.

4.4   Building a Gray-Box Monitor for DDM

In what follows, we assume a computable function capable of deciding DDM only for some instances. This function, that we call oracle, will serve as the basis for a *sound* monitor for DDM (P4). This monitor will detect some, but not all, violations of DDM when given sets of observed traces, thus resolving the apparent tension between (P3) and (P4).

Given $f\colon I_1 \times \cdots \times I_n \to O$, we define the predicate φ_f as

$$\varphi_f(i, x, y) = \exists z \in I.\, f(z[i \mapsto x]) \neq f(z[i \mapsto y]),$$

and assume a total computable function $N_{f,i}\colon I_i \times I_i \to \{\top, \bot, ?\}$ such that

$$N_{f,i}(x, y) = \begin{cases} \top \text{ or } ? & \text{if } \varphi_f(i, x, y) \text{ holds,} \\ \bot \text{ or } ? & \text{otherwise.} \end{cases}$$

The function $N_{f,i}$ acts as our oracle to instantiate the existential quantifiers in φ_{dm}. As discussed earlier, such oracles may be implemented by statically analyzing the system under observation (here, the function f). In our proof-of-concept implementation, we extract $\varphi_f(i, x, y)$ from f using *symbolic execution*, and use an SMT solver to compute $N_{f,i}(x, y)$ [27].

We now define a monitor M_{dm} for φ_{dm} as follows:

$$M_{\mathsf{dm}}(U) = \begin{cases} ? & \text{if } f(u_{in}) \neq u_{out} \text{ for some } u \in U, \\ ? & \text{if } \bigwedge_{i=1}^{n} \bigwedge_{u,u' \in U} N_{f,i}(\mathrm{proj}_i(u_{in}), \mathrm{proj}_i(u'_{in})) \neq \bot, \\ \bot & \text{otherwise.} \end{cases}$$

Intuitively, the monitor $M_{\mathsf{dm}}(U)$ checks the set of traces U for violations of DDM by verifying two conditions: the first condition ensures the *consistency* of U, i.e. that every trace in U does in fact correspond to a valid execution of f; the second condition is necessary for U *not* to permanently violate φ_{dm}. Hence, if it fails, U must permanently violate φ_{dm}. Since $N_{f,i}$ is computable, so is M_{dm}. Note that M_{dm} never gives a positive verdict $\top$. This is a consequence of Theorem 2: if f is DDM, then φ_{dm} is not monitorable in $\mathcal{S}_f$. In other words, DDM is not monitorable for satisfaction.

The second condition in the definition of M_{dm} is an approximation of φ_{dm}: the universal quantifiers are replaced by conjunctions over the finite set of input traces U, while the existential quantifiers are replaced by a single quantifier ranging over all of $\Sigma_f^{\#}$ (not just U). This approximation is justified formally by the following theorem [27].

Theorem 3 (soundness). *The monitor M_{dm} is sound. Formally,*

1. *$U \models_{\mathcal{S}_f}^s \varphi_{\mathsf{dm}}$ if $M_{dm}(U) = \top$, and*
2. *$U \models_{\mathcal{S}_f}^v \varphi_{\mathsf{dm}}$ if $M_{dm}(U) = \bot$.*

4.5   Proof-of-Concept Implementation

We have implemented the ideas described above in a proof-of-concept monitor for data minimization called `minion`. The monitor uses the symbolic execution API and the SMT backend of the KeY deductive verification system [2,18] to extract logical characterizations of Java programs (their *symbolic execution trees*). It then extends them to first-order formulas over sets of observed traces, and checks the result using the state-of-the-art SMT solver Z3 [20,21]. The `minion` monitor is written in Scala and provides a simple command-line interface (CLI). Its source code is freely available online at https://github.com/sstucki/minion/. A detailed description of `minion`, including examples, appears in the extended version of this paper [27].

5   Related Work

LTL Monitorability. Pnueli and Zaks [26] introduced monitorability as the existence of extension of the observed traces that permanently satisfy or violate an LTL property. It is known that the set of monitorable LTL properties is a superset of the union of safety and co-safety properties [5,6] and that it is also a superset of the set of obligation properties [14,15]. Havelund and Peled [17] introduce a finer-grained taxonomy distinguishing between *always* finitely satisfiable (resp. refutable), and *sometimes* finitely satisfiable where only some prefixes are required to be monitorable (for satisfaction). Their taxonomy also describes the relation between monitorability and classical safety properties. This is a new dimension in the monitorability cube in Fig. 1 which we will study in the future. While all the notions mentioned above ignore the system, predictive monitoring [28] considers the traces allowed in a given finite state system.

Monitoring HyperLTL. Monitoring hyperproperties was first studied in [1], which introduces the notion of monitorability for HyperLTL [11] and gives an algorithm for a fragment of alternation-free HyperLTL. This is later generalized to the full fragment of alternation-free formulas using formula rewriting in [9], which can also monitor alternating formulas but only with respect to a fixed finite set of finite traces. Finally, [16] proposes an automata-based algorithm for monitoring HyperLTL, which also produces a monitoring verdict for alternating formulas, but again for a fixed trace set. The complexity of monitoring different fragments of HyperLTL was studied in detail in [7]. The idea of gray-box monitoring for hyperproperties, as a means for handling non-monitoriable formulas, was first proposed in [8].

Data Minimization. A formal definition of *data minimization* and the concept of *data minimizer* as a preprocessor appear in [3], which introduces the monolithic and distributed cases. Minimality is closely related to information flow [12]. Malacaria et al. [19] present a symbolic execution-based verification of non-interference security properties for the *OpenSSL* library. In our paper, we have focused on a version of distributed minimization which is not monitorable in general. For stronger versions (cf. [3]), Pinisetty et al. [23,24] show that monitorability for satisfaction is not possible, but it is for violation. (the paper also introduces an RV approach for similar safety hyperproperties for deterministic programs).

6   Conclusions

We have rephrased the notion of monitorability considering different dimensions, namely (1) whether the monitoring is black-box or gray-box, (2) whether we consider trace properties or hyperproperties, and (3) taking into account the computatibility aspects of the monitor as a program. We showed that many hyperproperties that involve quantifier alternation are non-monitorable in a black-box manner and proposed a technique that involves inspecting the behavior of the system. In turn, this forces to consider the computability limitations of the monitor, which leads to a more general notion of monitorability.

We have considered distributed data minimality (DDM) and expressed this property in HyperLTL, involving one quantifier alternation. We then presented a methodology to monitor violations of DDM, based on a model extracted from the program being monitored in the form of its symbolic execution tree, and an SMT solver. We have implemented a tool (`minion`) and applied it to a number of representative examples to assess the feasibility of our approach [27].

As future work, we plan to extend the proposed methodology for other hyperproperties, particularly in the concurrent and distributed setting. We are also planning to use bounded model checking as our verifier at run-time by combining over- and under-approximated methods to deal with universal and existential quantifiers in HyperLTL formulas. Another interesting problem is to apply gray-box monitoring for hyperproperties with real-valued signals (e.g., HyperSTL [22]). Finally, we intend to extend the definition and results of data minimality in order to capture reactivity, and study monitorability in this setting.

References

1. Agrawal, S., Bonakdarpour, B.: Runtime verification of k-safety hyperproperties in HyperLTL. In: Proceedings of the IEEE 29th Computer Security Foundations (CSF 2016), pp. 239–252. IEEE CS Press (2016)
2. Ahrendt, W., Beckert, B., Bubel, R., Hähnle, R., Schmitt, P.H., Ulbrich, M. (eds.): Deductive Software Verification - The KeY Book - From Theory to Practice. LNCS, vol. 10001. Springer, Heidelberg (2016). https://doi.org/10.1007/978-3-319-49812-6
3. Antignac, T., Sands, D., Schneider, G.: Data minimisation: a language-based approach. In: De Capitani di Vimercati, S., Martinelli, F. (eds.) SEC 2017. IAICT, vol. 502, pp. 442–456. Springer, Cham (2017). https://doi.org/10.1007/978-3-319-58469-0_30
4. Bartocci, E., Falcone, Y., Francalanza, A., Reger, G.: Introduction to runtime verification. In: Bartocci, E., Falcone, Y. (eds.) Lectures on Runtime Verification. LNCS, vol. 10457, pp. 1–33. Springer, Cham (2018). https://doi.org/10.1007/978-3-319-75632-5_1
5. Bauer, A., Leucker, M., Schallhart, C.: Runtime verification for LTL and TLTL. ACM T. Softw. Eng. Meth. **20**(4), 14 (2011)
6. Bauer, A., Leucker, M., Schallhart, C.: The good, the bad, and the ugly, but how ugly is ugly? In: Sokolsky, O., Taşiran, S. (eds.) RV 2007. LNCS, vol. 4839, pp. 126–138. Springer, Heidelberg (2007). https://doi.org/10.1007/978-3-540-77395-5_11

7. Bonakdarpour, B., Finkbeiner, B.: The complexity of monitoring hyperproperties. In: CSF 2018, pp. 162–174. IEEE CS Press (2018)

8. Bonakdarpour, B., Sanchez, C., Schneider, G.: Monitoring hyperproperties by combining static analysis and runtime verification. In: Margaria, T., Steffen, B. (eds.) ISoLA 2018. LNCS, vol. 11245, pp. 8–27. Springer, Cham (2018). https://doi.org/10.1007/978-3-030-03421-4_2

9. Brett, N., Siddique, U., Bonakdarpour, B.: Rewriting-based runtime verification for alternation-free hyperLTL. In: Legay, A., Margaria, T. (eds.) TACAS 2017. LNCS, vol. 10206, pp. 77–93. Springer, Heidelberg (2017). https://doi.org/10.1007/978-3-662-54580-5_5

10. Clarkson, M.R., Schneider, F.B.: Hyperproperties. J. Comput. Secur. 18(6), 1157–1210 (2010)

11. Clarkson, M.R., Finkbeiner, B., Koleini, M., Micinski, K.K., Rabe, M.N., Sánchez, C.: Temporal logics for hyperproperties. In: Abadi, M., Kremer, S. (eds.) POST 2014. LNCS, vol. 8414, pp. 265–284. Springer, Heidelberg (2014). https://doi.org/10.1007/978-3-642-54792-8_15

12. Cohen, E.: Information transmission in computational systems. SIGOPS Oper. Syst. Rev. 11(5), 133–139 (1977)

13. European Commission: Proposal for a Regulation of the European Parliament and of the Council on the protection of individuals with regard to the processing of personal data and on the free movement of such data (GDPR). Technical Report 2012/0011 (COD), European Commission, January 2012

14. Falcone, Y., Fernandez, J.-C., Mounier, L.: Runtime verification of safety-progress properties. In: Bensalem, S., Peled, D.A. (eds.) RV 2009. LNCS, vol. 5779, pp. 40–59. Springer, Heidelberg (2009). https://doi.org/10.1007/978-3-642-04694-0_4

15. Falcone, Y., Fernandez, J.C., Mounier, L.: What can you verify and enforce at runtime? Int. J. Softw. Tools Technol. Transfer (STTT) 14(3), 349–382 (2012)

16. Finkbeiner, B., Hahn, C., Stenger, M., Tentrup, L.: Monitoring hyperproperties. In: Lahiri, S., Reger, G. (eds.) RV 2017. LNCS, vol. 10548, pp. 190–207. Springer, Cham (2017). https://doi.org/10.1007/978-3-319-67531-2_12

17. Havelund, K., Peled, D.: Runtime verification: from propositional to first-order temporal logic. In: Colombo, C., Leucker, M. (eds.) RV 2018. LNCS, vol. 11237, pp. 90–112. Springer, Cham (2018). https://doi.org/10.1007/978-3-030-03769-7_7

18. KeY contributors: The KeY project. https://www.key-project.org. Accessed 5 November 2018

19. Malacaria, P., Tautchning, M., DiStefano, D.: Information leakage analysis of complex c code and its application to openSSL. In: Margaria, T., Steffen, B. (eds.) ISoLA 2016. LNCS, vol. 9952, pp. 909–925. Springer, Cham (2016). https://doi.org/10.1007/978-3-319-47166-2_63

20. Microsoft Research: The Z3 theorem prover. https://github.com/Z3Prover/z3. Accessed 5 Nov 2018

21. de Moura, L., Bjørner, N.: Z3: an efficient smt solver. In: Ramakrishnan, C.R., Rehof, J. (eds.) TACAS 2008. LNCS, vol. 4963, pp. 337–340. Springer, Heidelberg (2008). https://doi.org/10.1007/978-3-540-78800-3_24

22. Nguyen, L.V., Kapinski, J., Jin, X., Deshmukh, J.V., Johnson, T.T.: Hyperproperties of real-valued signals. In: Proceedings of the 15th ACM-IEEE International Conference on Formal Methods and Models for System Design (MEMOCODE 2017), pp. 104–113. ACM (2017)

23. Pinisetty, S., Antignac, T., Sands, D., Schneider, G.: Monitoring data minimisation. Technical Report, CoRR-arXiv.org (2018). http://arxiv.org/abs/1801.02484

24. Pinisetty, S., Sands, D., Schneider, G.: Runtime verification of hyperproperties for deterministic programs. In: Proceedings of the 6th Conference on Formal Methods in Software Engineering (FormaliSE@ICSE 2018), pp. 20–29. ACM (2018)
25. Pnueli, A.: The temporal logic of programs. In: Proceedings of the 18th IEEE Symposium on Foundations of Computer Science (FOCS 1977), pp. 46–67. IEEE Computer Society Press (1977)
26. Pnueli, A., Zaks, A.: PSL model checking and run-time verification via testers. In: Misra, J., Nipkow, T., Sekerinski, E. (eds.) FM 2006. LNCS, vol. 4085, pp. 573–586. Springer, Heidelberg (2006). https://doi.org/10.1007/11813040_38
27. Stucki, S., Sánchez, C., Schneider, G., Bonakdarpour, B.: Gray-box monitoring of hyperproperties (extended version). Technical Report, CoRR-arXiv.org (2019). http://arxiv.org/abs/1906.08731
28. Zhang, X., Leucker, M., Dong, W.: Runtime verification with predictive semantics. In: Goodloe, A.E., Person, S. (eds.) NFM 2012. LNCS, vol. 7226, pp. 418–432. Springer, Heidelberg (2012). https://doi.org/10.1007/978-3-642-28891-3_37

Quantitative Verification of Numerical Stability for Kalman Filters

Alexandros Evangelidis[(⊠)] and David Parker

School of Computer Science, University of Birmingham, Birmingham, UK
{a.evangelidis,d.a.parker}@cs.bham.ac.uk

Abstract. Kalman filters are widely used for estimating the state of a system based on noisy or inaccurate sensor readings, for example in the control and navigation of vehicles or robots. However, numerical instability may lead to divergence of the filter, and establishing robustness against such issues can be challenging. We propose novel formal verification techniques and software to perform a rigorous quantitative analysis of the effectiveness of Kalman filters. We present a general framework for modelling Kalman filter implementations operating on linear discrete-time stochastic systems, and techniques to systematically construct a Markov model of the filter's operation using truncation and discretisation of the stochastic noise model. Numerical stability properties are then verified using probabilistic model checking. We evaluate the scalability and accuracy of our approach on two distinct probabilistic kinematic models and several implementations of Kalman filters.

1 Introduction

Estimating the state of a continuously changing system based on uncertain information about its dynamics is a crucial task in many application domains ranging from control systems to econometrics. One of the most popular algorithms for tackling this problem is the *Kalman filter* [16], which essentially computes an optimal state estimate of a noisy linear discrete-time system, under certain assumptions, with the optimality criterion being defined as the minimisation of the mean squared estimation error.

However, despite the robust mathematical foundations underpinning the Kalman filter, developing an operational filter in practice is considered a very hard task since it requires a significant amount of engineering expertise [20]. This is because the underlying theory makes assumptions which are not necessarily met in practice, such as there being precise knowledge of the system and the noise models, and that infinite precision arithmetic is used [12,24]. Avoidance of numerical problems, such as round-off errors, remains a prominent issue in filter implementations [11,12,24,26]. Our goal in this paper is to develop techniques that allow the detection of possible failures in filters due to numerical instability arising as a result of these assumptions.

The Kalman filter repeatedly performs two steps. The first occurs before the next measurements are available and relies on prior information. This is called

© Springer Nature Switzerland AG 2019
M. H. ter Beek et al. (Eds.): FM 2019, LNCS 11800, pp. 425–441, 2019.
https://doi.org/10.1007/978-3-030-30942-8_26

the *time update* (or prediction step) and propagates the "current" state estimate forward in time, along with the uncertainty associated with it. These variables are defined as the a priori state estimate $\hat{x}^-$ and estimation-error covariance matrix P^-, respectively. The second step is called the *measurement update* (or correction step) and occurs when the next state measurements are available. The Kalman filter then uses the newly obtained information to update the a priori $\hat{x}^-$ and P^- to their a posteriori counterparts, denoted $\hat{x}^+$ and P^+, which are adjusted using the so-called optimal *Kalman gain* matrix K.

The part of the filter that could hinder its numerical stability, and so cause it to produce erroneous results, is the propagation of the estimation-error covariance matrix P in the time and measurement updates [4,12,20]. This is because the computation of the Kalman gain depends upon the correct computation of P and round-off or computational errors could accumulate in its computation, causing the filter either to diverge or slow its convergence [12]. While, from a mathematical point of view, the estimation-error covariance matrix P should maintain certain properties such as its symmetry and positive semidefiniteness to be considered valid, subtle numerical problems can destroy those properties resulting in a covariance matrix which is theoretically impossible [17]. Out of the two update steps in which the filter operates, the covariance update in the correction step is considered to be the *"most troublesome"* [20]. In fact, the covariance update can be expressed with three different but algebraically equivalent forms, and all of them can result in numerical problems [4].

To address the aforementioned challenges, we present a general framework for modelling and verifying different filter implementations operating on linear discrete-time stochastic systems. It consists of a modelling abstraction which maps the system model whose state is to be estimated and a filter implementation to a discrete-time Markov chain (DTMC). This framework is general enough to handle the creation of various different filter variants. The filter implementation to be verified is specified in a mainstream programming language (we use Java) since it needs access to linear algebra data types and operations.

Once the DTMC has been constructed, we verify numerical stability properties of the Kalman filter being modelled using properties expressed in a reward-based extension [10] of the temporal logic PCTL (probabilistic computation tree logic) [13]. This requires generation of non-trivial reward structures for the DTMC computed using linear algebra computations on the matrices and vectors used in the execution of the Kalman filter implementation. The latter is of more general interest in terms of the applicability of our approach to analyse complex numerical properties via probabilistic model checking.

We have implemented this framework within a software tool called VerFilter, built on top of the probabilistic model checker PRISM [18]. The tool takes the filter implementation, a description of the system model being estimated and several extra parameters: the maximum time the model will run, the number of intervals the noise distribution will be truncated into, and the numerical precision, in terms of the number of decimal places, to which the floating-point numbers which are used throughout the model will be rounded.

The decision to let the user specify these parameters is particularly important in the modelling and verification of stochastic linear dynamical systems, where the states of the model, which comprise of floating-point numbers, as well as the labelling of the states, are the result of complex numerical linear algebra operations. Lowering the numerical precision usually means faster execution times at the possible cost of affecting the accuracy of the verification result. This decision is further motivated by the fact that many filter implementations run on embedded systems with stringent computational requirements [24], and being able to produce performance guarantees is crucial.

We demonstrate the applicability of our approach by verifying two distinct filter implementations: the conventional Kalman filter and the Carlson-Schmidt square-root filter. This allows us to evaluate the trade-offs of one versus the other. In fact, our tool has been tested on five implementations, but we restrict our attention to these two due to space restrictions. For the system models, we use *kinematic state models*, since they are used extensively in the areas of navigation and tracking [4,19]. We evaluate our approach with two distinct models. We demonstrate that our approach can successfully analyse a range of useful properties relating to the numerical stability of Kalman filters, and we evaluate the scalability and accuracy of the techniques.

Related Work. Studies of Kalman filter numerical stability outside of formal verification are discussed above and in more detail in the next section. To the best of our knowledge, there is no prior work applying probabilistic model checking to the verification of Kalman filters. Perhaps the closest is the use of non-probabilistic model checking on a variant of the filter algorithm is the work by [21], which applied model checking to target estimation algorithms in the context of antimissile interception. In general, applying formal methods in state estimation programs is an issue which has concerned researchers over the years. For example, [23,25] combined program synthesis with property verification in order to automate the generation of Kalman filter code based on a given specification, along with proofs about specific properties in the code. Other work relevant to the above includes [22], which used the language ACL2 to verify the loop invariant of a specific instance of the Kalman filter algorithm.

2   Preliminaries

2.1   The Kalman Filter

The Kalman filter tracks the state of a linear stochastic discrete-time system of the following form:

$$x_{k+1} = F_k x_k + w_k \qquad z_k = H_k x_k + v_k \qquad (1)$$

where x_k is the $(n \times 1)$ system state vector at discrete time instant k, F_k is a square $(n \times n)$ state transition matrix, which relates the system state vector x_k

between successive time steps in the absence of noise. In addition, z_k is the $(m \times 1)$ measurement vector, H_k is the $(m \times n)$ measurement matrix, which relates the measurement with the state vector. Finally, w_k and v_k represent the process and measurement noises, with covariance matrices Q_k and R_k, respectively. Given the above system and under certain assumptions, the Kalman filter is an optimal estimator in terms of minimising the mean squared estimation error.

The task of the Kalman filter is to find the optimal Kalman gain matrix K_k in terms of minimising the sum of estimation-error variances, which can be obtained by summing the elements of the main diagonal of the a posteriori estimation-error covariance matrix P^+. The estimation process begins by initialising $\hat{x}_0^+ = \mathbb{E}[x_0]$, and $P_0^+ = \mathbb{E}[(x_0 - \hat{x}_0^+)(x_0 - \hat{x}_0^+)^T]$. Then, the conventional Kalman filter algorithm proceeds by iterating between two steps. The time update is given as:

$$\hat{x}_{k+1}^- = F_k \hat{x}_k^+ \qquad P_{k+1}^- = F_k P_k^+ F_k^T + Q_k \qquad (2)$$

The measurement update is given as:

$$y_{k+1} = z_{k+1} - H_{k+1}\hat{x}_{k+1}^- \qquad S_{k+1} = H_{k+1}P_{k+1}^- H_{k+1}^T + R_{k+1} \qquad (3)$$

$$K_{k+1} = P_{k+1}^- H_{k+1}^T S_{k+1}^{-1} \qquad (4)$$

$$\hat{x}_{k+1}^+ = \hat{x}_{k+1}^- + K_{k+1}y_{k+1} \qquad P_{k+1}^+ = (I - K_{k+1}H_{k+1})P_{k+1}^- \qquad (5)$$

2.2 Numerical Instability of the Kalman Filter

In order for P to be statistically valid it must be (symmetric) positive definite. Briefly, this means that all of its eigenvalues are positive real numbers. This is for two reasons. First, from a modelling perspective, if its eigenvalues were zero, this would translate to a filter which completely trusts its estimates and consequently would avoid taking into account the subsequent measurements, placing all of its "belief" in the system model [4]. Second, from a numerical stability perspective, it does not suffice for the eigenvalues of P to be greater than zero, because if they are in close proximity to zero, then round-off errors could cause them to become negative, rendering it totally invalid [2,12,15].

In fact, the three equivalent forms to express the covariance measurement update are susceptible to numerical errors [4] and cannot guarantee the numerical stability of P. For example, the covariance update $P_k^+ = (I - K_kH_k)P_k^-$ is generally not preferred because it is too sensitive to round-off errors [4], which means neither the symmetry nor the positive definiteness of P_k can be guaranteed. That is because this update takes the product of nonsymmetric and symmetric matrices, a form which has been characterised as undesirable [20].

Alternatively, changing the covariance measurement update equation to $P_k^+ = P_k^- - K_kS_kK_k^T$ could potentially pose a "serious numerical problem" [20], such as P_k losing positive definiteness. Finally, while *Joseph's stabilised form* [8], given by $P_k^+ = (I - K_kH_k)P_k^-(I - K_kH_k)^T + K_kR_kK_k^T$, is considered to preserve the numerical robustness of P^+, it is not totally insensitive to numerical errors [4]. An additional disadvantage is the high computational complexity, which is $O(n^3)$ [12,20], since the number of arithmetic operations such as additions and multiplications is considerably higher compared to the simpler form.

To ameliorate these numerical problems, an alternative form of expressing the covariance time and measurement updates is using so-called *square-root filters.* These are generally considered superior to conventional filter implementations mainly because of their ability to increase the numerical stability of the propagation of the estimation-error covariance matrix P, and have often been described as outstanding [17,20]. It should be noted that the term square-root filter is mostly used to refer to the measurement update of the Kalman filter algorithm, since it is this part that can cause numerical problems [11]. They were motivated by the need for increased numerical precision because of word lengths of limited size in the 1960s [24] and by the concern with respect to the numerical accuracy of P in the measurement update of the Kalman filter equations [11]. Potter [5] proposed the idea of the so-called square-root filters and this idea has evolved ever since. The idea, which was limited to noiseless systems, is that P is factored into its square root C, such that $P = CC^T$, and as a result C is propagated through the measurement update equations, instead of P. Replacing P with its square-root factor C has the effect of doubling the numerical precision of the filter, thus making it particularly suitable for matrices which are not well-conditioned or when increased precision cannot be obtained from the hardware [11,12,20,24].

2.3   The Carlson-Schmidt Square-Root Filter

The Carlson-Schmidt filter is a form of a square-root filter which relies on the decomposition of P into its Cholesky factors in the time and measurement update equations. The Carlson part of the filtering algorithm, originally given by Carlson [9], corresponds to the measurement update, while the Schmidt part corresponds to the time update of the Kalman filter equations, respectively. Carlson's algorithm is capable of handling noise and, like Potter's algorithm, processes measurements as scalars. It factors P into the product of an upper-triangular Cholesky factor and its transpose such that $P = CC^T$. Note that unlike Potter's initial square-root filter where the factor C is not required to be triangular, in Carlson's square-root implementation the Cholesky factor C is an upper-triangular matrix. Maintaining C in upper-triangular form has been shown to provide several advantages in terms of storage and computational speed compared to Potter's algorithm [9,20]. While the choice between a lower and upper-triangular Cholesky factor C is arbitrary [20], Carlson motivated the preference to choose an upper-triangular Cholesky factor by the fact that in the time update part of the algorithm, fewer retriangularisation operations are required especially when someone designs a filter to be applied in a tracking or in a navigation problem, respectively [9].

3   Quantitative Verification of Kalman Filters

In this section, we describe our approach to modelling and verifying the numerical stability of Kalman filter implementations. This is based on the construction and analysis of a probabilistic model (a discrete-time Markov chain) representing the behaviour of a particular Kalman filter executing in the context of estimating the state of a linear stochastic discrete-time system. The probabilistic model is automatically constructed based on a specification of the filter and the system whose state it is trying to estimate. Numerical stability properties are then verified using probabilistic model checking queries. We describe these phases in the following two sections.

3.1   Constructing Probabilistic Models of Kalman Filter Execution

We define a high-level modelling abstraction which can be instantiated to construct models of various different Kalman filter implementations. The modelling abstraction comprises three components: the first and second correspond to the system and measurement models along with their associated noise distributions; the third is the Kalman filter implementation itself used to estimate the state of the system model in the presence of uncertainty. The first two of these are defined mathematically along the lines described in Sect. 2.1. The third is specified in detail using a mainstream programming language, since it requires linear algebra data types and operations. Our implementation (see Sect. 4) uses Java and associated numerical libraries.

The DTMC which represents the evolution of the system model along with the filter estimates is not a *static* process. Rather it occurs in a *dynamic* fashion, involving the interaction of several components. For example, we do not assume that the measurements emitted from the system model are already given to us or that the filter estimates are already predetermined. Rather, as the system model evolves from state to state, the Kalman filter executes and tries to estimate its true state, imitating a real-time tracking scenario.

DTMC States and Transitions. The variables which define the Markov chain's states correspond to the system, measurement and filter models. All of these variables can be made independent of the filter implementations. For example, in a square-root filter implementation, C^+ can be either reconstructed or not in each time step, before being passed into the Markov chain's state, which demonstrates the modularity and extensibility of our approach.

The evolution of the states of the Markov chain corresponds to the system model perturbed by different noise values. Each of the Markov chain's states stores the "true" values of the system model's state and the noisy measurements emitted at each time step k. These variables, along with the a posteriori state estimate and the estimation-error covariance, are included in the state of the Markov chain because they are needed for verification purposes. Then, before the Markov chain transitions to the next state (between time k and $k+1$), the time update of the corresponding filter variant is invoked. Both of the a priori variables depend on their a posteriori counterparts.

Specifically, once we are in a state for time instant k, our goal is to compute in the next state at time $k+1$ both the system model's updated state vector and the a posteriori variables of the respective filter, $\hat{x}^+$ and P^+. The a priori variables of the Kalman filter types are encapsulated between these two updates as an intermediate step. Note that $\hat{x}$ and P are essentially the same variables which are used in the computation of both the a priori and a posteriori state estimates and estimation-error covariance matrices, respectively. What distinguishes x's semantics is whether the measurement z has been processed. This allows us to concretely define the notion of time k in each of the Markov chain's states.

In particular, a time instant k in the Markov chain can be thought of as encompassing: (i) state variables *before* the measurement is processed; and (ii) state variables *after* the measurement has been processed. Combining this temporal order into one state allows us to save storage by merging what would otherwise require two states to be represented.

The number of outgoing transitions and their probability values are determined by a *granularity level* of the noise, that we denote gLevel. The Gaussian distribution of the noise is discretised into gLevel disjoint intervals. The intervals used for each granularity level are shown in Table 1.

The measure used to determine these intervals is the standard deviation σ, which is a common practice in statistical contexts; see for example the so-called 68–95–99.7 rule, which states that, assuming the data are normally distributed, then 68%, 95% and 99.7% of them will fall between one, two and three standard deviations of the mean, respectively. This statement can be expressed probabilistically as well by computing the cumulative distribution function (CDF) of a normally distributed random variable X, usually by converting it to its *standard* counterpart and using the so-called standard normal tables. While computing the probability that a noise value will fall inside an interval is relatively easy, the computation of its expected value is slightly more difficult. This is because we can choose to either truncate the distribution to intervals which contain the mean value of the distribution, which is the easier case, or to intervals which do not. For the first case, the expected value will be 0, which is the mean of distribution; for the second, this is not true.

Usually, for those cases, one might use a simple heuristic such as dividing the sum of the two endpoints of the interval by two, which is actually quite common. However, this might not be representative of the actual expected value since it does not weigh the values lying inside the interval according to the corresponding value of the density correctly. In other words, since the mean is also interpreted as the *"centre of gravity"* of the distribution [6], in the case of truncated intervals which do not contain the mean, more accurate techniques are needed. The probabilities of the Markov chain for a given granularity level are computed by first standardising the random variable, the noise in our case, and then evaluating its CDF at the two endpoints of the corresponding interval. Then, by subtracting them, we obtain the probability that it will fall within a certain interval.

Table 1. Intervals according to the granularity level.

gLevel	Intervals
2	$[-\infty..\mu], [\mu..+\infty]$
3	$[-\infty.. - 2\sigma], [-2\sigma.. + 2\sigma], [+2\sigma.. + \infty]$
4	$[-\infty.. - 2\sigma], [-2\sigma..\mu], [\mu.. + 2\sigma], [+2\sigma.. + \infty]$
5	$[-\infty.. - 2\sigma], [-2\sigma.. - \sigma], [-\sigma.. + \sigma], [+\sigma.. + 2\sigma], [+2\sigma.. + \infty]$
6	$[-\infty.. - 2\sigma], [-2\sigma.. - \sigma], [-\sigma..\mu], [\mu.. + \sigma], [+\sigma.. + 2\sigma], [+2\sigma.. + \infty]$

Once the probabilities have been computed, it remains to find the expected value of the random variable for the corresponding intervals. In order to avoid the situation described earlier, and obtain the mean in a more accurate way, we have used the *truncated normal distribution* to compute the mean for the respective intervals. Formally, if a normal random variable X is normally distributed and lies within an interval $[a..b]$, where $-\infty \leq a \leq b \leq +\infty$, then X conditioned on $a < X < b$ has a truncated normal distribution. The PDF of a normally truncated random variable X is characterised by four parameters: (i-ii) the mean μ and standard deviation σ of the *original* distribution and (iii-iv) the lower and upper truncation points, a and b. Compactly, the mean value of the noise for a corresponding interval can be expressed as the conditional mean, $E[X|a < X < b]$, given by the following formula [14]:

$$E[X|a < X < b] = \mu + \sigma \frac{\phi(\frac{a-\mu}{\sigma}) - \phi(\frac{b-\mu}{\sigma})}{\Phi(\frac{b-\mu}{\sigma}) - \Phi(\frac{a-\mu}{\sigma})} \tag{6}$$

Note that in the expression above, ϕ and Φ denote the PDF and CDF of the standard normal distribution, respectively. Also note that the denominator has already been computed in the previous step, when the transition probabilities were computed. As a result, the computation of the transition probabilities and the conditional mean values for each of the corresponding intervals can be done in a unified manner.

3.2   Verification of Numerical Stability

Next, we discuss how to capture numerical stability properties for our Kalman filter models (see the earlier summary in Sect. 2) using the probabilistic temporal logic [10] of the PRISM model checker [18]. We explain the properties below, as we introduce them, and refer the reader to [10] for full details of the logic.

Verifying Positive Definiteness. In order to construct this property, we perform an eigenvalue-eigenvector decomposition of P^+ into the matrices $[V, D]$. The eigenvalues are obtained from the diagonal matrix D, and their positivity is determined and used to label each state of the Markov chain accordingly: we use an atomic proposition *isPD* for states in which P^+ is positive definite.

We can then specify the probability that the matrix remains positive definite for the duration of execution of the filter using the formula $P_{=?}[\,\Box\ isPD\,]$, where the temporal logic operator $\Box$, which is often referred to as "always" or "globally", is used to represent invariance.

Examining the Condition Number of the Estimation-Error Covariance Matrix. The verification of certain numerical properties, such as those related to positive definiteness, is a challenging task and should be treated with caution. This is because, while convenient, focusing the verification on whether an event will occur or not, might not capture inherent numerical difficulties related to the numerical stability of state estimation algorithms. In other words, it does not suffice to check whether P^+ is positive definite or not by checking its eigenvalues because, as mentioned earlier, if they are in close proximity to zero, then round-off errors could cause them to become negative [12].

For example, it is often the case that estimation practitioners want to detect matrices that are close to becoming *singular*, a concept which is often referred to as *"detecting near singularity"* [7]. In other words, since a positive definite matrix is nonsingular, one wants to determine the "goodness" of P^+ in terms of its "closeness" to singularity, within some level of tolerance, usually the machine precision [12]. A matrix is said to be *well-conditioned* if it is "far" from singularity, while *ill-conditioned* describes the opposite. In order to quantify the goodness of P^+, we use the so-called *condition number*, which is a concept used in numerical linear algebra to provide an indication of the sensitivity of the solution of a linear equation (e.g. $Ax = b$), with respect to perturbations in b [12,20]. In our case, this concept is used to obtain a measure of goodness of P^+.

The condition number of P^+ is given as $\kappa(P^+) = \sigma_{max}/\sigma_{min}$, where σ_{max} and σ_{min} are the maximum and minimum singular values, respectively [11,20]. These can be obtained by performing the singular value decomposition (SVD) of P^+. A "small" condition number indicates that the matrix is well-conditioned and nonsingular, while a "large" condition number indicates the exact opposite. Note that the smallest condition number is 1 when $\sigma_{max} = \sigma_{min}$.

We express this property as the formula $R_{=?}^{cond}[\,\mathtt{I}^{=k}\,]$, which gives the expected value of the condition number after k time steps. We assign the condition number to each state of the DTMC using a reward function *cond* and we set k to be `maxTime`, the period of time for which we verify the respective filter variant.

Providing Bounds on Numerical Errors. Another useful aspect of the condition number is that it can be used to obtain an estimate of the precision loss that numerical computations could cause to P^+. For instance, for a single precision and a double precision floating-point number format, the precision is about 7 and 16 decimal digits, respectively. Since our computations take place in the decimal number system, the logarithm of the condition number (e.g. $log_{10}(\kappa(P^+))$), gives us the ability to define more concretely when a condition number will be considered "large" or "small" [3,20,24]. For example, a $log_{10}(\kappa(P^+)) > 6$ and a $log_{10}(\kappa(P^+)) > 15$ could cause numerical problems in the estimation-error covariance computation and render P^+ as ill-conditioned when implemented in a single and a double precision floating-point number format, respectively.

Table 2. User inputs for each of the models.

Input	Description	Used in:	Type
$\hat{x}_0^+$	A posteriori state estimate vector	Filter	`RealVector`
P_0^+	A posteriori estimation-error covariance matrix	Filter	`RealMatrix`
x	State vector	System	`RealVector`
w	Process noise vector	System	`RealVector`
v	Measurement noise vector	System	`RealVector`
F	State transition matrix	Shared	`RealMatrix`
Q	Process noise covariance matrix	Filter	`RealMatrix`
H	Measurement matrix	Shared	`RealMatrix`
R	Measurement noise covariance matrix	Shared	`RealMatrix`
`gLevel`	Granularity of the noise	Shared	`int`
`decPlaces`	Number of decimal places	Shared	`int`
`maxTime`	Maximum time the model will run	Shared	`int`
`filterType`	Type of filter variant	Shared	`int`

So, to verify this property we construct a closed interval whose endpoints will be based on the appropriate values of the numerical quantity of $log_{10}(\kappa(P^+))$. This lets us label states whose $log_{10}(\kappa(P^+))$ value will fall within "acceptable" values in the interval, when, for instance, double precision is used. We then use the property $\mathsf{P}_{=?}[\,\square\,isCondWithin\,]$, in a similar fashion to the first property above, where *isCondWithin* labels the "acceptable" states. A probability value of less than 1 should raise an alarm that numerical errors may be encountered.

4   Tool Support: VerFilter

Next, we provide some details about the tool, VerFilter, which is the software implementation of the framework defined in Sect. 3. The VerFilter tool is written in the Java programming language in order to be seamlessly integrated with the PRISM libraries, which are written in Java as well. The tool and supporting files for the results in the next section are available from [27].

VerFilter Inputs. In Table 2 we show the user inputs available to VerFilter, by distinguishing which of those refer to the system and measurement model, which refer specifically to the filter models and which are shared between them. The `RealVector` and `RealMatrix` shown in Table 2 are implemented as one-dimensional and two-dimensional arrays of type `double`, respectively. VerFilter also takes as inputs four extra parameters: (i) `gLevel` which takes an integer between 2 and 6, and has been discussed in Sect. 3.1; (ii) `decPlaces` which allows the user to specify an integer between 2 and 15, the number of decimal places, to which the numerical values used in the computations will be rounded; (iii) `maxTime` which is an integer and determines the maximum time the model will run; and (iv) `filterType` which is the type of filter to be executed.

VerFilter Algorithms. In this paper, we focus on two of our filter variants: the conventional Kalman filter (`CKFilter`) and the Carlson-Schmidt square-root filter (`SRFilter`). In VerFilter, several of the numerical linear algebra computations for implementing Kalman filters are done using the Apache Commons Math library [1], while other parts have been manually implemented. In `CKFilter`, for example, the library is used for "basic" matrix operations and for the eigen and singular value decomposition of P. For `SRFilter`, algorithms implemented manually include the upper-triangular Cholesky factorisation and Carlson's measurement update with Schmidt's time update using *Householder transformations*.

5   Experimental Results

We now illustrate results from the implementation of our techniques on the two filters `CKFilter` and `SRFilter` mentioned above. For the system models in our experiments, we use two distinct *kinematic state models* which describe the motion of objects as a function of time. For the first, the *discrete white noise acceleration model* (DWNA), the initial estimation-error covariance matrix P_0^+ is defined as $\begin{bmatrix} 10 & 0 \\ 0 & 10 \end{bmatrix}$. Defining P_0^+ as a diagonal matrix is quite common, since it is initially unknown whether the state variables are correlated to each other. The process noise covariance matrix is given by $Q = \Gamma \sigma_w^2 \Gamma^T$ where the noise gain matrix $\Gamma = [\frac{1}{2}\Delta t^2 \ \Delta t]^T$ is initialised by setting the sampling interval Δt to 1, which results in $\Gamma = [0.5 \ 1]^T$. The variance σ_w^2 is set to 0.001 initially. For the second model, the *continuous white noise acceleration model* (CWNA), σ_w^2 is initially set to 0.001. Note that each of these models results in a different process noise covariance matrix Q. For more details on these models, see [27].

5.1   Verification of Kalman Filter Implementations

In the first set of experiments, shown in Fig. 1, we analyse the condition number of P^+, in order to verify that it remains well-conditioned in terms of maintaining its nonsingularity as it is being propagated forward in time (as discussed in Sect. 3.2). This property is verified against two inputs which we vary; the first is the numerical precision in terms of the number of decimal places, which we vary from 3 to 6 inclusive. The second input is the time horizon of the model which in our case is measured in discrete time steps and is varied from 2 to 20.

Our goal is twofold. Firstly, we examine whether an increase in the numerical precision has a meaningful effect on how accurately the condition number is computed. This is important since, as we show in Sect. 5.2, a decrease in the numerical precision usually makes verification more efficient. Being able to consider an appropriate threshold above which an increase in the numerical precision will not have an effect on the property to be verified can determine the applicability of these verification mechanisms in realistic settings. Secondly, we examine whether letting the model evolve for a greater amount of time could have an impact on the property that is being verified.

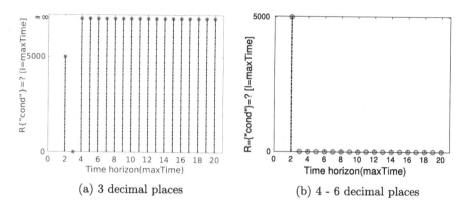

Fig. 1. Condition number of $P+$ over time under various degrees of precision.

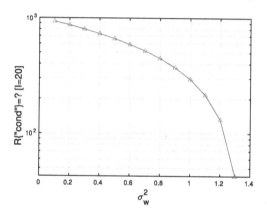

Fig. 2. Verifying goodness of P^+

The first observation between Fig. 1a and b is that the increased numerical precision actually determines the verification result. For example, we note that for `maxTime` values in the range of [4–20], when the input to our model for the numerical precision is 3 decimal places, the instantaneous reward jumps to infinity. An infinite reward in this case means that the condition number of P^+ is $\approx1.009\text{e}+16$, which practically means that P^+ is "computationally" singular and consequently positive definiteness is not being preserved. Conversely, when we increase the numerical precision to a value >4, positive definiteness is preserved and the instantaneous reward assigned to the states fluctuates around small values close to zero. Another interesting observation is that the instantaneous rewards stabilise to a value of ≈3, irrespective of whether the numerical precision is 4, 5 or 6. In fact, the actual absolute difference of the rewards over the states in which positive definiteness is preserved between a numerical precision of 5 and 6 decimal places, is ≈0.1.

Table 3. Comparison between two filter variants.

CKFilter $P_{=?}[\,\square\, isPD\,]$	SRFilter $P_{=?}[\,\square\, isPD\,]$	CKFilter $R^{cond}_{=?}[\,I^{=maxTime}\,]$	SRFilter $R^{cond}_{=?}[\,I^{=maxTime}\,]$
1	1	5001	69.88
1	1	6.85	2.48
0	1	$+\infty$	2.01
0	1	$+\infty$	1.94
0	1	$+\infty$	1.94
0	1	$+\infty$	1.94

In the second set of experiments the system model is a CWNA kinematic model. Our goal is to examine how VerFilter can be used to examine heuristic-based approaches and ad-hoc methods such as artificial noise injection in terms of their usefulness in correcting potential numerical problems in P^+. This is also helpful in situations where it is challenging to determine the elements of Q, by performing an automatic search over those values which will produce an optimal performance, in this case in terms of the numerical robustness of P.

To this end, we verify whether P^+ will remain well-conditioned or not, by varying the elements of Q. The noise variance σ_w^2, which determines the elements of Q, is the input to our model, P^+ is being verified against. We do not vary the maximum time; rather, we let the Markov chain evolve to a fixed maxTime value of 20 time steps, which corresponds to $\approx 1 \times 10^6$ states.

In Fig. 2 we show the effects of increasing the variance of the noise by small increments, which is then multiplied with the elements of Q. The first point of the plot $(0.1, 1000)$, means that for a value of $\sigma_w^2 = 0.1$, the corresponding instantaneous reward which corresponds to the condition number of P^+ in a set of states where maxTime=20, is 1000. As we increase σ_w^2, the "quality" of P^+ increases, reaching a condition number of ≈ 43.

In summary, for this particular example, the optimal $\sigma_w^2 = 1.3$. It is important to note that when performing verification on Markov chains whose trajectories evolve over multiple states, to verify that the positive definiteness of P^+ is not destroyed between successive states (i.e. successive time steps). To this end, it is advisable to use a property of the form $P_{=?}[\,\square\, isPD\,]$ and reject models in which the previous property is not satisfied with probability one.

In Table 3 we compare two of the filter variants available in VerFilter; the CKFilter and the SRFilter. In this set of experiments, the setup is similar to the first one. First, our purpose is to demonstrate the correctness of our approach by comparing the condition numbers of P^+ and C^+, respectively. The superiority of the SRFilter compared to CKFilter, is demonstrated from the fact that for the same set of parameters the numerical robustness of P^+ is preserved. This can be seen by comparing the computed results of the reward-based properties as shown in the third and fourth column of Table 3. We note that when choosing the

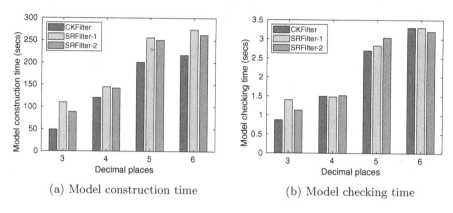

(a) Model construction time   (b) Model checking time

Fig. 3. Time comparisons between three filters.

CKFilter, the reward value shoots up to $+\infty$, representing an estimation-error covariance matrix in which the PD property is destroyed, while in the SRFilter case the corresponding reward value settles around the small value of 1.94. This is also evident by observing the first and second columns of Table 3 which tell us whether the PD invariant will be maintained in all the states of the model. Notably, the PD property in the CKFilter does not hold for every state, in fact the probability is zero, while for the SRFilter the PD property holds for every state with probability one.

5.2   Scalability Analysis

In this section, we report on the scalability of our approach in terms of the model construction and model checking time, across three filter variants. The model has been generated by letting the Markov chain evolve to a fixed maxTime value of 20 time steps, which corresponds to $\approx 1 \times 10^6$ states. The rationale behind this section is to emphasise the careful analysis that needs to be performed to systematically evaluate the trade-offs between the accuracy of the verification result and the fastness of the verification algorithms.

In Fig. 3 we show the time comparisons, for varying degrees of precision, between a model which encodes the conventional Kalman filter (CKFilter), and our two implementations of the Carlson-Schmidt square-root filter with (SRFilter-1) and without (SRFilter-2) reconstruction of the estimation-error covariance matrix, respectively. The model checking time refers to the total time it takes to verify the first and second property of Sect. 3.2. These sets of experiments were run on a 16 GB RAM machine with an i7 processor at 1.80 GHz, running Ubuntu 18.04.

By observing Fig. 3a it is apparent that the increased numerical precision affects the construction time of the models. The average model construction time of the three filter variants increased by a factor of ≈ 3 from 3 to 6 decimal places. Specifically, the average time is ≈ 83 s for 3 decimal places compared to ≈249 s, when 6 decimal places were used. Moreover, the construction of the `CKFilter` was the fastest in all the degrees of precision considered, however, as it was noted in Sect. 5.1 it produces an inaccurate verification result when the number of decimal places is 3.

Conversely, the construction times of the two square-root filters were about the same, and it seems that the extra computational step $(P = CC^T)$ did not have a significant effect on the performance of the model construction. However, it should be borne in mind that these experiments were conducted on systems represented by two-dimensional matrices. The model checking times are shown in Fig. 3b and one can observe that they follow a similar pattern with the model construction times shown earlier, in terms of the increase in time from 3 to 6 decimal places. For instance, the average model checking time increases by a factor of ≈3 when 6 decimal places are used, compared to 3.

Another observation is that the model checking time appears to be independent of the type of the filter used. This can be seen from the limited variability the model checking time experiences between the three filter variants, since for the degrees of precision considered, it remains at approximately the same level. This is in contrast to the model construction time which appears to be affected by the filter type, since it is considerably less for the `CKFilter` compared to its square-root variants. In fact, for a precision of 6 decimal places, and once `CKFilter` is chosen as an input we experience a drop in the model construction time of about 53 s. However, for the same amount of precision, the time it takes to model check all the three filters is around 3 s.

6   Conclusion

We have presented a framework for the modelling and verification of Kalman filter implementations. It is general enough to analyse a variety of different implementations, and various system models, and to study a range of numerical issues which may hinder the effective deployment of the filters in practice. We have implemented the techniques in a tool and illustrated its applicability and scalability with a range of experiments. Due to space limitations, we showed results for two filters, the conventional Kalman filter and for the Carlson-Schmidt square-root filter, but our implementation already supports three others.

In general, the evaluation of Kalman filters in terms of their performance has attracted considerable attention, since the early days of their development. However, formal methods such as probabilistic model checking have not been used for their verification. This is, to the best of our knowledge, the first work where these types of problems are applied to a probabilistic verification setting. Our main contribution in this work is that we show that probabilistic verification can be a promising alternative in verifying these types of systems.

Acknowledgements. This work has been partially supported by an EPSRC-funded Ph.D. studentship (award ref: 1576386) and the PRINCESS project (contract FA8750-16-C-0045) funded by the DARPA BRASS programme.

References

1. Math - Commons-Math: The Apache Commons Mathematics Library. http://commons.apache.org/math/
2. Anderson, B., Moore, J.: Optimal Filtering. Dover Books on Electrical Engineering. Dover Publications, New York (2012)
3. Bar-Shalom, Y.: Tracking and Data Association. Academic Press Professional Inc., San Diego (1987)
4. Bar-Shalom, Y., Li, X.R.: Estimation with Applications to Tracking and Navigation. Wiley, New York (2001). https://doi.org/10.1002/0471221279
5. Battin, R.H.: Astronautical Guidance. McGraw-Hill, New York (1964). Electronic sciences
6. Bertsekas, D., Tsitsiklis, J.: Introduction to Probability. Athena Scientific, Athena Scientific optimization and computation series (2008)
7. Bierman, G.J.: Factorization Methods for Discrete Sequential Estimation (1977)
8. Bucy, R.S., Joseph, P.D.: Processes with Applications to Guidance. Interscience Publishers, New York (1968)
9. Carlson, N.A.: Fast triangular formulation of the square root filter. AIAA J. **11**(9), 1259–1265 (1973). https://doi.org/10.2514/3.6907
10. Forejt, V., Kwiatkowska, M., Norman, G., Parker, D.: Automated verification techniques for probabilistic systems. In: Bernardo, M., Issarny, V. (eds.) SFM 2011. LNCS, vol. 6659, pp. 53–113. Springer, Heidelberg (2011). https://doi.org/10.1007/978-3-642-21455-4_3
11. Gibbs, B.P.: Advanced Kalman Filtering, Least Squares and Modeling: A Practical Handbook. Wiley, New York (2011). https://doi.org/10.1002/9780470890042
12. Grewal, M.S., Andrews, A.P.: Kalman Filtering: Theory and Practice Using MATLAB, 4th edn. Wiley-IEEE Press, New York (2014)
13. Hansson, H., Jonsson, B.: A logic for reasoning about time and reliability. Formal Aspects Comput. **6**(5), 512–535 (1994). https://doi.org/10.1007/BF01211866
14. Johnson, N.L., Kotz, S., Balakrishnan, N.: Continuous univariate distributions. Wiley, New York (1994)
15. Kailath, T.: Linear Systems. Prentice-Hall, Englewood Cliffs (1980)
16. Kalman, R.E.: A new approach to linear filtering and prediction problems. ASME J. Basic Eng. **82**, 35–45 (1960)
17. Kaminski, P., Bryson, A., Schmidt, S.: Discrete square root filtering: a survey of current techniques. IEEE Trans. Autom. Control **16**(6), 727–736 (1971). https://doi.org/10.1109/TAC.1971.1099816
18. Kwiatkowska, M., Norman, G., Parker, D.: PRISM 4.0: verification of probabilistic real-time systems. In: Gopalakrishnan, G., Qadeer, S. (eds.) CAV 2011. LNCS, vol. 6806, pp. 585–591. Springer, Heidelberg (2011). https://doi.org/10.1007/978-3-642-22110-1_47
19. Li, X.R., Jilkov, V.P.: Survey of maneuvering target tracking part. i. dynamic models. IEEE Trans. Aerosp. Electron. Syst. **39**(4), 1333–1364 (2003). https://doi.org/10.1109/TAES.2003.1261132
20. Maybeck, P.S.: Stochastic Models, Estimation, and Control: Mathematics in Science and Engineering, vol. 1. Elsevier Science, Burlington (1982)
21. Moulin, M., Gluhovsky, L., Bendersky, E.: Formal verification of maneuvering target tracking. In: AIAA Guidance, Navigation, and Control Conference and Exhibit (2003). https://doi.org/10.2514/6.2003-5716

22. R. Gamboa, J. Cowles, J.V.B.: On the verification of synthesized kalman filters. In: 4th International Workshop on the ACL2 Theorem Prover and Its Applications (2003)

23. Roşu, G., Venkatesan, R.P., Whittle, J., Leuştean, L.: Certifying optimality of state estimation programs. In: Hunt, W.A., Somenzi, F. (eds.) CAV 2003. LNCS, vol. 2725, pp. 301–314. Springer, Heidelberg (2003). https://doi.org/10.1007/978-3-540-45069-6_30

24. Simon, D.: Optimal State Estimation: Kalman, H Infinity, and Nonlinear Approaches. Wiley, New York (2006)

25. Whittle, J., Schumann, J.: Automating the implementation of kalman filter algorithms. ACM Trans. Math. Softw. **30**(4), 434–453 (2004). https://doi.org/10.1145/1039813.1039816

26. Zarchan, P., Musoff, H.: Fundamentals of Kalman filtering : A Practical Approach, 4th edn. American Institute of Aeronautics and Astronautics, Reston (2015)

27. Supporting material. www.prismmodelchecker.org/files/fm19kf/

Concolic Testing Heap-Manipulating Programs

Long H. Pham[1(✉)], Quang Loc Le[2], Quoc-Sang Phan[3], and Jun Sun[4]

[1] Singapore University of Technology and Design, Singapore, Singapore
longph1989@gmail.com
[2] School of Computing & Digital Technologies, Teesside University,
Middlesbrough, UK
[3] Synopsys, Inc., Mountain View, USA
[4] Singapore Management University, Singapore, Singapore

Abstract. Concolic testing is a test generation technique which works effectively by integrating random testing generation and symbolic execution. Existing concolic testing engines focus on numeric programs. Heap-manipulating programs make extensive use of complex heap objects like trees and lists. Testing such programs is challenging due to multiple reasons. Firstly, test inputs for such programs are required to satisfy non-trivial constraints which must be specified precisely. Secondly, precisely encoding and solving path conditions in such programs are challenging and often expensive. In this work, we propose the first concolic testing engine called CSF for heap-manipulating programs based on separation logic. CSF effectively combines specification-based testing and concolic execution for test input generation. It is evaluated on a set of challenging heap-manipulating programs. The results show that CSF generates valid test inputs with high coverage efficiently. Furthermore, we show that CSF can be potentially used in combination with precondition inference tools to reduce the user effort.

1 Introduction

Unit testing is essential during the software development process. To automate unit testing effectively, we are required to generate *valid* test inputs which exercise program behaviors *comprehensively* and *efficiently*. Many techniques for automating unit testing have been proposed, including random testing [18] and symbolic execution [45]. A recent development is the concolic testing technique [32,40]. Concolic testing works by integrating random testing and symbolic execution to overcome their respective limitations [46]. It has been shown that concolic testing often works effectively [47].

Existing concolic testing engines focus on numeric programs, i.e., programs which take numeric type variables as inputs. In contrast, *heap-manipulating* programs make extensive use of heap objects and their inputs are often dynamically allocated data structures. Test input generation for heap-manipulating programs

© Springer Nature Switzerland AG 2019
M. H. ter Beek et al. (Eds.): FM 2019, LNCS 11800, pp. 442–461, 2019.
https://doi.org/10.1007/978-3-030-30942-8_27

is hard for two reasons. Firstly, the test inputs are often heap objects with complex structures and strict requirements over their shapes and sizes. Secondly, the inputs have unbounded domains. Ideally, test generation for heap-manipulating programs must satisfy three requirements.

1. *(Validity)*. It must generate valid test inputs.
2. *(Comprehensiveness)*. It must exercise program behaviors comprehensively, e.g., maximizing certain code coverage.
3. *(Efficiency)*. It must be efficient.

Existing approaches often overlook one or more of the requirements. The state-of-the-art approaches are based on classical symbolic execution [26] with lazy initialization [45]. To achieve comprehensiveness and efficiency, lazy initialization postpones the initialization of reference type symbolic variables and fields until they are accessed. However, lazy initialization has limited support to capture constraints on the shapes of the input data structures. As a result, invalid test inputs are generated, which are not only wasteful but also lead to the exploration of infeasible program paths. Furthermore, because the values of un-accessed fields are not initialized, the generated test inputs need to be further concretized. Subsequent works on improving lazy initialization [15,16,21,45] share the same aforementioned problems. To address the validity requirement, Braione *et al.* [11] introduced a logic called HEX as a specification language for the input data structures. However, HEX has limited expressiveness and thus cannot describe many data structures (unless using additional user-provided methods called *triggers*).

Inspired by the recent success of concolic execution (e.g., [1,41]), we aim to develop a concolic execution engine for heap-manipulating programs. Developing a concolic execution engine which achieves validity, comprehensiveness and efficiency is however highly non-trivial. For validity, we need a specification language which is expressive enough to capture constraints over the shapes and sizes of heap objects. We thus adopt a recently proposed fragment of separation logic which is shown to be expressive and decidable [30]. For comprehensiveness and efficiency, we propose a novel concolic testing strategy which combines specification-based testing and concolic execution. That is, we first generate test inputs according to the specification in a black-box manner and then apply concolic execution to cover those uncovered program parts.

In summary, we make the following contributions. Firstly, we propose a concolic execution engine for heap-manipulation programs based on separation logic. Secondly, we combine specification-based testing with concolic execution in order to reduce the cost of constraint solving. Thirdly, we implement the proposal in a tool called Concolic StarFinder (CSF) and evaluate it in multiple experiments.

The rest of this paper is organized as follows. Section 2 illustrates our approach through an example. Section 3 describes our specification language and specification-based test input generation. Next, we present our concolic execution engine in Sect. 4. We show the implementation and experiments in Sect. 5. Section 6 discusses related works and finally Sect. 7 concludes.

```
 1  public class BinarySearchTree {
      public BinaryNode root;
 3    public void remove(int x) {
        root = remove(x, root);
 5    }
      private BinaryNode remove(int x, BinaryNode t) {
 7      if (t == null) return t;
        if (x < t.element)
 9        t.left = remove(x, t.left);
        else if (x > t.element)
11        t.right = remove(x, t.right);
        else if (t.left != null && t.right != null){
13        t.element = findMin(t.right).element;
          t.right = remove(t.element, t.right);
15      } else
          t = (t.left != null) ? t.left : t.right;
17      return t;
      }
19    private BinaryNode findMin(BinaryNode t) {
        if (t == null) return null;
21      else if (t.left == null) return t;
        return findMin(t.left);
23    }
    }
25
    public class BinaryNode {
27    int element; BinaryNode left; BinaryNode right;
    }
```

Fig. 1. Sample program

2   Approach at a Glance

We illustrate our approach using method *remove* in class *BinarySearchTree* from the SIR repository [7]. The method is shown in Fig. 1. It checks if a binary search tree object contains a node with a specific value and, if so, removes the node. To test the method, we must generate two inputs, i.e., a *valid* binary search tree object t and an integer x, and then execute *t.remove(x)*. Note that a valid binary search tree object must satisfy strict requirements. Firstly, all *BinaryNode* objects must be structured in a binary tree shape. Secondly, for any *BinaryNode* object in the tree, its *element* value must be greater than all the *element* values of its *left* sub-tree and less than those of the *right* sub-tree. One way to define valid binary search tree objects is through programming a *repOK* method [9,45].

If a *repOK* method is provided, we can use the black-box enumeration (BBE) approach [45] to generate test inputs. BBE performs symbolic execution with lazy initialization on the *repOK* method. Although BBE can generate valid test inputs, it also generates many invalid ones, e.g., the generated input is a cyclic graph instead of a tree[1]. In our experiment with BBE for this method, a total of 225 test inputs are generated and only 9 of them are valid. Moreover, because

---

[1] When BBE runs, we count the structures that the *repOK* method returns **true** as valid ones, and the structures that the *repOK* method returns **false** as invalid ones.

Formula	$\Phi ::= \Delta \mid \Phi_1 \vee \Phi_2$	
Symbolic heap	$\Delta ::= \exists \bar{v}. \, (\kappa \wedge \pi)$	
Spatial formula	$\kappa ::= \mathtt{emp} \mid x \mapsto c(\bar{v}) \mid \mathtt{P}(\bar{v}) \mid \kappa_1 * \kappa_2$	
Pure formula	$\pi ::= \mathtt{true} \mid \alpha \mid \neg \pi \mid \pi_1 \wedge \pi_2$	$\alpha ::= a_1 = a_2 \mid a_1 \leq a_2$
	$a ::= \mathtt{null} \mid k \mid v \mid k \times a \mid a_1 + a_2 \mid -a$	
Data structure	$Node ::= \mathtt{data}\, c_i \{ \tau_{i_1}\, f_{i_1}; ...; \tau_{i_n}\, f_{i_n} \}$	$\tau ::= \mathtt{bool} \mid \mathtt{int} \mid c$
Predicate definition	$Pred ::= \mathtt{pred}\, \mathtt{P}_i(\bar{v}_i) \equiv \Phi_i$	

Fig. 2. Specification language, where k is a 32-bit integer constant, $\bar{v}$ is a sequence of variables

BBE generates test inputs based on the $repOK$ method only, it may not generate a high coverage test suite.

One way to obtain a high coverage test suite is to use the white-box enumeration approach [45]. First, white-box enumeration performs symbolic execution on the method under test to create some partially initialized data structures. Then, these data structures are used as initial inputs to perform symbolic execution with the $repOK$ method. However, because the approach still uses lazy initialization, many invalid test inputs may be generated. Moreover, white-box enumeration requires the availability of a conservative $repOK$ method in the first step, which is not easy to derive. Another approach is to use the HEX logic [12] as a language to specify valid data structures. During lazy initialization, the exploration is pruned when the heap configuration violates the specification. However, HEX has limited expressiveness, e.g., HEX cannot capture the property that the nodes in the binary search tree are sorted due to the lack of arithmetic constraints.

In comparison, our approach works as follows. We use separation logic to define a predicate $\mathtt{bst}(\mathtt{root}, minE, maxE)$, which specifies valid binary search trees where $\mathtt{root}$ is the root of the tree and $minE$ (resp. $maxE$) is the minimum (resp. maximum) bound of the *element* values of the tree. We refer the readers to Sect. 3 for details of the definition. The precondition of method *remove* is then specified as $\mathtt{bst}(this\_root, minE, maxE)$. With the specification, we first apply specification-based testing based on the precondition in a black-box manner. That is, we generate the test inputs according to the precondition using a constraint solver without exploring the method body. After this step, we generate 22 test inputs and they cover 14 over 15 feasible branches of the method *remove* (including auxiliary method $findMin$). The only branch which is not covered is the *else* branch at line 21. We then perform concolic execution with the generated test inputs to identify a feasible path which leads to the uncovered branch. After solving that path condition, we obtain the test inputs for 100% branch coverage.

3   Specification-Based Testing

Our approach takes as input a heap-manipulating program which has a precondition specified using a language recently developed in [14,30]. In the follow-

---

Algorithm 1: genFromSpec(Γ, n)

1 **if** $n = 0$ **then**
2 | $tests \leftarrow \emptyset$
3 | **foreach** $\Delta \in \Gamma$ **do**
4 | | $r, \texttt{model} \leftarrow \texttt{sat}(\Delta)$
5 | | **if** $r = \texttt{SAT}$ **then**
6 | | | $tests \leftarrow tests \cup \texttt{toUnitTest}(\texttt{model})$
7 | **return** $tests$
8 **else**
9 | $\Gamma' \leftarrow \emptyset$
10 | **foreach** $\Delta \in \Gamma$ **do**
11 | | $\Gamma' \leftarrow \Gamma' \cup \texttt{unfold}(\Delta)$
12 | **return** genFromSpec($\Gamma', n - 1$)

---

ing, we introduce the language and present the first step of our approach, i.e., specification-based testing based on the provided precondition.

Specification Language. The language we adopt supports separation logic, inductive predicates and arithmetical constraints, which is expressive to specify many data structures [14,30]. Its syntax is shown in Fig. 2. In general, the precondition is a disjunction of one or more symbolic heaps. A symbolic heap is an existentially quantified conjunction of a heap formula κ and a pure formula π. While a pure formula is a constraint in the form of the first-order logic, the heap formula is a conjunction of heap predicates which are connected by separating operation $*$. A heap predicate may be the empty predicate **emp**, a points-to predicate $x \mapsto c(\bar{v})$ or an inductive predicate $\mathsf{P}(\bar{v})$. Reference types are annotated by the keyword **data**. Variables may have type τ as boolean **bool** or 32-bit integer **int** or user-defined reference type **c**.

Inductive predicates are supplied by the users with the keyword **pred**. They are used to specify constraints on recursively defined data structures like linked lists or trees. Inductive predicates are defined in the same language. For instance, the inductive predicate $\mathsf{bst}(\mathbf{root}, minE, maxE)$ introduced in Sect. 2 is defined as follows

$$\mathbf{pred}\ \mathsf{bst}(\mathbf{root}, minE, maxE) \equiv (\mathbf{emp} \wedge \mathbf{root} = \mathbf{null})$$
$$\vee\ (\exists elt, l, r.\ \mathbf{root} \mapsto BinaryNode(elt, l, r)\ *$$
$$\mathsf{bst}(l, minE, elt) * \mathsf{bst}(r, elt, maxE) \wedge minE < elt \wedge maxE > elt),$$

where **root** is the root of the tree and $minE$ (resp. $maxE$) is the minimum (resp. maximum) bound of the *element* values of the tree. Using this definition with *this_root* as symbolic value for field *root* in class *BinarySearchTree*, the precondition of method *remove* in the preceding section is then specified as $\mathsf{bst}(this\_root, minE, maxE)$.

1. $\mathtt{emp} \wedge this\_root = \mathtt{null}$
2. $\exists elt, l, r.\ this\_root \mapsto BinaryNode(elt, l, r) * \mathtt{bst}(l, minE, elt) * \mathtt{bst}(r, elt, maxE) \wedge$
   $minE < elt \wedge maxE > elt$
3. $\exists elt, l, r.\ this\_root \mapsto BinaryNode(elt, l, r) * \mathtt{bst}(r, elt, maxE) \wedge l = \mathtt{null} \wedge$
   $minE < elt \wedge maxE > elt$
4. $\exists elt, l, r, elt1, l1, r1.\ this\_root \mapsto BinaryNode(elt, l, r) * l \mapsto BinaryNode(elt1, l1, r1) *$
   $\mathtt{bst}(r, elt, maxE) * \mathtt{bst}(l1, minE, elt1) * \mathtt{bst}(r1, elt1, elt) \wedge$
   $minE < elt \wedge maxE > elt \wedge minE < elt1 \wedge elt > elt1$
5. $\exists elt, l, r.\ this\_root \mapsto BinaryNode(elt, l, r) * \mathtt{bst}(l, minE, elt) \wedge r = \mathtt{null} \wedge$
   $minE < elt \wedge maxE > elt$
6. $\exists elt, l, r, elt2, l2, r2.\ this\_root \mapsto BinaryNode(elt, l, r) * r \mapsto BinaryNode(elt2, l2, r2) *$
   $\mathtt{bst}(l, minE, elt) * \mathtt{bst}(l2, elt, elt2) * \mathtt{bst}(r2, elt2, maxE) \wedge$
   $minE < elt \wedge maxE > elt \wedge elt < elt2 \wedge maxE > elt2$

Fig. 3. Unfoldings

Specification-Based Testing. If we follow existing concolic testing strategies [18], we would first generate random test inputs before applying concolic execution. However, it is unlikely that randomly generated heap objects are valid due to the strict precondition. Thus, we apply specification-based testing to generate test inputs based on the user-provided precondition instead.

The details are shown in Algorithm 1. The inputs are a set of formulae Γ and a bound on n. The initial value of Γ contains only the precondition of the program under test. The output is a set of test inputs which are both *valid* and *fully initialized*. Algorithm 1 has two phases.

In the first phase, from line 8 to 12, procedure $\mathtt{unfold}$ is applied to each symbolic heap Δ in Γ (at line 11) to return a set of unfolded formulae. Recall that a symbolic heap is a conjunction of a heap constraint κ and a pure constraint π. If the heap constraint κ contains no inductive predicates (i.e., it is a base formula), κ is returned as it is. Otherwise, each inductive predicate $P_i(\bar{t}_i)$ in κ is unfolded using its definition. Note that the definition of $P_i(\bar{t}_i)$ is a disjunction of multiple base cases and inductive cases. During unfolding, κ is split into a set of formulae, one for each disjunct in the definition of every inductive predicate $P_i(\bar{t}_i)$ in κ. The process ends when n reaches 0.

Procedure $\mathtt{unfold}$ is formalized as follows. Given an inductively predicate definition $\mathtt{pred}\ P_i(\bar{v}_i) \equiv \Phi_i$ and a formula constituted with this predicate, e.g., $\Delta_i * P_i(\bar{t}_i)$, $\mathtt{unfold}$ proceeds in two steps. First, it replaces the occurrences of the inductive predicate with its definition as: $\mathtt{unfold}(\Delta_i * P_i(\bar{t}_i), P_i(\bar{t}_i)) \equiv \Delta_i * (\Phi_i[\bar{t}_i/\bar{v}_i])$. After that, it applies the following axioms to normalizes the formula into the grammar in Fig. 2:

$$(\kappa_1 \wedge \pi_1) * (\kappa_2 \wedge \pi_2) \equiv (\kappa_1 * \kappa_2) \wedge (\pi_1 \wedge \pi_2)$$
$$(\exists \bar{w}.\ \Delta_1) * (\exists \bar{v}.\ \Delta_2) \equiv \exists \bar{w}, \bar{v}'.\ (\Delta_1 * \Delta_2[\bar{v}'/\bar{v}])$$

The correctness of these axioms could be found in [23,38]. We then use $\mathtt{unfold}(\Delta) \equiv \bigcup_{i=1}^{n} \mathtt{unfold}(\Delta, P_i(\bar{t}_i)), P_i(\bar{t}_i) \in \Delta$. For example, given the above-specified precondition for method *remove*, we obtain 6 formulae shown in Fig. 3 after unfolding twice.

```
public void test_remove1() throws Exception {
  BinarySearchTree obj = new BinarySearchTree();
  obj.root = null; int x = 0;
  obj.remove(x);
}

public void test_remove2() throws Exception {
  BinarySearchTree obj = new BinarySearchTree();
  obj.root = new BinaryNode();
  BinaryNode left_2 = null; BinaryNode right_3 = null;
  int element_1 = 0; int x = 0; obj.root.element = element_1;
  obj.root.left = left_2; obj.root.right = right_3;
  obj.remove(x);
}
```

Fig. 4. Two test inputs

$$datat ::= \mathbf{data}\ c\ \{\ (type\ v;)^*\ \}$$
$$type ::= \mathbf{bool} \mid \mathbf{int} \mid c$$
$$prog ::= stmt^*$$
$$stmt ::= v := e \mid v.f_i := e \mid \mathbf{goto}\ e \mid \mathbf{assert}\ e \mid \mathbf{if}\ e_0\ \mathbf{then\ goto}\ e_1\ \mathbf{else\ goto}\ e_2$$
$$\mid v := \mathbf{new}\ c(v_1, ..., v_n) \mid \mathbf{free}\ v$$
$$e ::= k \mid v \mid v.f_i \mid e_1\ op_b\ e_2 \mid op_u\ e \mid \mathbf{null}$$

Fig. 5. A core intermediate language

Unit Test Generation. After unfolding, Γ contains a set of formulae, each of which satisfies the precondition. In the second phase, at lines 1–7, these formulae are transformed into test inputs. First, we check the satisfiability of each formula using a satisfiability solver $\mathsf{S2SAT_{SL}}$ [28,30] at line 4. The result of the solver is a pair $(\mathbf{r}, \mathbf{model})$ where $\mathbf{r}$ is a *decision* of satisfiability and $\mathbf{model}$ is a symbolic model which serves as the evidence of the satisfiability. Intuitively, a symbolic model is a base formula where every variable is assigned a *symbolic* value. Formally, a symbolic model is a quantifier-free base formula Δ_m where Δ_m is satisfiable and for each variable v in Δ_m, if v has a reference type, Δ_m contains $v \mapsto c(...)$, or $v = v'$, or $v = \mathbf{null}$; otherwise, Δ_m contains $v = k$ with k is either a boolean or 32-bit integer constant.

At line 6, the symbolic model is transformed into a test input using procedure $\mathtt{toUnitTest}$, which initializes the variables according to the symbolic model (e.g., for each points-to predicate $v \mapsto c(...)$, a new object of type c is created and assigned to v). Figure 4 shows two test inputs generated for the example shown in Fig. 1. These two test inputs correspond to the first two formulae shown in Fig. 3 (where x is assigned the default value 0).

The correctness of the algorithm, i.e., each generated test input is a valid one, is straightforward as each symbolic model obtained from the unfolding satisfies the original precondition, since each one is an under-approximation of a Δ in Γ.

4   Concolic Execution

Specification-based testing allows us to generate test inputs which cover some parts of the program. Some program paths however are unlikely to be covered with such test inputs without exploring the program code [46]. Thus, the second step of our approach is to apply concolic execution to cover the remaining parts of the program.

We take a program, a set of test inputs and a constraint tree as inputs. The constraint tree allows us to keep track of both explored nodes and unexplored nodes. Informally, the concolic execution engine executes the test inputs, expands the tree and then generates new test inputs to cover the unexplored parts of the tree. This process stops when there are no unexplored nodes in the tree or it times out.

For simplicity, we present our concolic engine based on a general core intermediate language. The syntax of the language is shown in Fig. 5, which covers common programming language features. A program in our core language includes several data structures and statements. Our language supports boolean and 32-bit integer as primitive types. Program statements include assignment, memory store, goto, assertion, conditional goto, memory allocation, and memory deallocation. Expressions are side-effect free and consist of typical non-heap expressions and memory load. We use op_b to represent binary operators, e.g., addition and subtraction, and op_u to represent unary operators, e.g., logical negation. k is either a boolean or 32-bit integer constant.

We assume the program is in the form of static single assignments (SSA) and omit the type-checking semantics of our language (i.e., we assume programs are well-typed in the standard way). Note that our prototype implementation is for Java bytecode, which in general can be translated to the core language (with unsupported Java language features are abstracted during the translation). The core language is easily extended to interprocedural scenario with method calls.

Execution Engine. Our concolic execution engine incrementally grows the constraint tree. Formally, the constraint tree is a pair (V, E) where V is a finite set of nodes and E is a set of labeled and directed edges (v, l, v') where v' is a child of v. Having edge (v, l, v') means that we can transit from v to v' via an execution rule l. Each node in the tree is a concolic state in the form of a 6-tuple $\langle \Sigma, \Delta, s, pc, flag \rangle \iota$ where Σ is the list of program statements; Δ is the symbolic state (a.k.a. the path condition); s is the current valuation of the program variables (i.e., the stack); pc is the program counter; $flag$ is a flag indicating whether the current node has been explored or not and ι is the current statement. Note that Σ and s are mapping functions, i.e., Σ maps a number to a statement, and s maps a variable to its value.

Initially, the constraint tree has only one node $\langle \Sigma, \mathtt{pre}, \emptyset, 0, \mathtt{true} \rangle \iota_0$ where $\emptyset$ denotes an empty mapping function and ι_0 is the initial statement. Note that the initial symbolic state is the precondition. We start with executing the program concretely, with some initial test inputs (at least one), and build the constraint tree along the way. The initial test inputs may come from specification-based testing or be provided by the users. Before each execution, s is initialized with values according to the test input. In the execution process, given a node, our engine systematically identifies an applicable rule (based on the current statement) to generate one or more new nodes. If no rule matches (e.g., accessing a dangling pointer), the execution halts. Note that some of the generated nodes are marked explored whereas some are marked unexplored (depending on the outcome of the concrete execution).

After executing all initial test inputs, the engine searches for unexplored nodes in the tree. If there is one such node with symbolic state Δ, the engine solves Δ using a solver [28,30]. If Δ is satisfiable, the unexplored path is feasible and the symbolic model generated by the solver is transformed into a new test input (as shown in the Sect. 3). The new test input is then executed and the constraint tree is expanded accordingly. If Δ is unsatisfiable, the node is pruned from the tree. This process is repeated until there are no more unexplored nodes or it times out.

The growing of the tree is governed by the execution rules, which effectively defines the semantics of our core language. The detailed execution rules are presented in Fig. 6. One or more rules may be defined for each kind of statements in our core language. Each rule, applied based on syntactic pattern-matching, is of the following form.

$$\frac{\text{conditions}}{\text{current\_state} \rightsquigarrow \text{end\_state}_1, ..., \text{end\_state}_n}$$

Intuitively, if the conditions above the line is satisfied, a node matching the current_state generates multiple children nodes.

In the following, we explain some of the rules in detail. In the rule [C–ASSIGN] which assigns the value evaluated from expression e to variable v, for the concrete state our system first evaluates the value of e based on the concrete state s prior to updating the state of v with the new value. For the symbolic state, it substitutes the current value of v to a fresh symbol v' prior to conjoining the constraint for the latest value of v. In the rule [C–NEW] which assigns new allocated object to variable v, for the concrete state our system updates the stack with an assignment of the variable to a fresh location. For the symbolic state, it substitutes the current value of v to a fresh symbol v' prior to spatially conjoining the points-to predicate for the latest value of v.

In the rule [C–LOAD] (resp. [C–STORE]) which reads from (resp. writes into) the field f_i of an object v, in the concrete state we implicitly assume that the corresponding variable of the field is $l.f_i$ where l is the concrete address of v and proceed accordingly. For the symbolic states, checking whether a variable has been allocated before accessed is much more complicated as the path condition (with the precondition) may include occurrences of inductive predicates (which represent unbounded heaps), so our system keeps the constraints with the field-access form (i.e., $v.f_i$) and field-assign form (i.e., $v.f_i := e$) and will eliminate them before sending these formulae to the solver.

In the rule [C–TCOND], two new nodes denoting the **then** branch and the **else** branch of the condition are added into the tree with the current node is

$$[\text{C-CONST}]\,\frac{}{s \vdash k \Downarrow k} \quad [\text{C-VAR}]\,\frac{}{s \vdash v \Downarrow k} \quad [\text{C-NULL}]\,\frac{}{s \vdash \texttt{null} \Downarrow \texttt{null}}$$

$$[\text{C-UNOP}]\,\frac{s \vdash e \Downarrow k}{s \vdash op_u\, e \Downarrow op_u\, k} \quad [\text{C-BINOP}]\,\frac{s \vdash e_1 \Downarrow k_1 \quad s \vdash e_2 \Downarrow k_2}{s \vdash e_1\, op_b\, e_2 \Downarrow k_1\, op_b\, k_2}$$

$$[\text{C-LOAD}]\,\frac{s \vdash v \Downarrow l \quad s \vdash l.f_i \Downarrow k}{s \vdash v.f_i \Downarrow k} \quad [\text{C-FREE}]\,\frac{s \vdash v \Downarrow l \quad s' = s \setminus \{l.f_i \mapsto \_\}\,\forall i = 1..n \quad \iota = \Sigma(pc+1)}{\langle \Sigma, \Delta, s, pc, \texttt{true}\rangle \texttt{free}\ v \rightsquigarrow \langle \Sigma, \Delta, s', pc+1, \texttt{true}\rangle \iota}$$

$$[\text{C-ASSIGN}]\,\frac{s \vdash e \Downarrow k \quad s' = s[v \leftarrow k] \quad \text{fresh}\ v' \quad e' = e[v'/v] \quad \Delta' \equiv \exists v'.\Delta[v'/v] \land v = e' \quad \iota = \Sigma(pc+1)}{\langle \Sigma, \Delta, s, pc, \texttt{true}\rangle v := e \rightsquigarrow \langle \Sigma, \Delta', s', pc+1, \texttt{true}\rangle \iota}$$

$$[\text{C-NEW}]\,\frac{\begin{array}{c}\text{fresh}\ l \quad \text{fresh}\ v' \quad \Delta' \equiv \exists v'.\Delta[v'/v] * v \mapsto c(v_1, ..., v_n)\\ s'_1 = s[l.f_i \leftarrow (s \vdash v_i)]\,\forall i = 1..n \quad s' = s'_1[v \leftarrow l] \quad \iota = \Sigma(pc+1)\end{array}}{\langle \Sigma, \Delta, s, pc, \texttt{true}\rangle v = \texttt{new}\ c(v_1, ..., v_n) \rightsquigarrow \langle \Sigma, \Delta', s', pc+1, \texttt{true}\rangle \iota}$$

$$[\text{C-STORE}]\,\frac{s \vdash v \Downarrow l \quad s \vdash e \Downarrow k \quad s' = s[l.f_i \leftarrow k] \quad \Delta' \equiv \Delta \land v.f_i := e \quad \iota = \Sigma(pc+1)}{\langle \Sigma, \Delta, s, pc, \texttt{true}\rangle v.f_i = e \rightsquigarrow \langle \Sigma, \Delta', s', pc+1, \texttt{true}\rangle \iota}$$

$$[\text{C-GOTO}]\,\frac{s \vdash e \Downarrow k \quad \iota = \Sigma(k)}{\langle \Sigma, \Delta, s, pc, \texttt{true}\rangle \texttt{goto}\ e \rightsquigarrow \langle \Sigma, \Delta, s, k, \texttt{true}\rangle \iota}$$

$$[\text{C-ASSERT}]\,\frac{s \vdash e \Downarrow \texttt{true} \quad \Delta' \equiv \Delta \land e \quad \iota = \Sigma(pc+1)}{\langle \Sigma, \Delta, s, pc, \texttt{true}\rangle \texttt{assert}(e) \rightsquigarrow \langle \Sigma, \Delta', s, pc+1, \texttt{true}\rangle \iota}$$

$$[\text{C-TCOND}]\,\frac{s \vdash e_0 \Downarrow \texttt{true} \quad s \vdash e_1 \Downarrow k_1 \quad s \vdash e_2 \Downarrow k_2 \quad \Delta_1 \equiv \Delta \land e_0 \quad \Delta_2 \equiv \Delta \land \neg e_0 \quad \iota_1 = \Sigma(k_1) \quad \iota_2 = \Sigma(k_2)}{\begin{array}{c}\langle \Sigma, \Delta, s, pc, \texttt{true}\rangle \texttt{if}\ e_0\ \texttt{then goto}\ e_1\ \texttt{else goto}\ e_2 \rightsquigarrow \\ \langle \Sigma, \Delta_1, s, k_1, \texttt{true}\rangle \iota_1, \langle \Sigma, \Delta_2, s, k_2, \texttt{false}\rangle \iota_2\end{array}}$$

$$[\text{C-FCOND}]\,\frac{s \vdash e_0 \Downarrow \texttt{false} \quad s \vdash e_1 \Downarrow k_1 \quad s \vdash e_2 \Downarrow k_2 \quad \Delta_1 \equiv \Delta \land e_0 \quad \Delta_2 \equiv \Delta \land \neg e_0 \quad \iota_1 = \Sigma(k_1) \quad \iota_2 = \Sigma(k_2)}{\begin{array}{c}\langle \Sigma, \Delta, s, pc, \texttt{true}\rangle \texttt{if}\ e_0\ \texttt{then goto}\ e_1\ \texttt{else goto}\ e_2 \rightsquigarrow \\ \langle \Sigma, \Delta_1, s, k_1, \texttt{false}\rangle \iota_1, \langle \Sigma, \Delta_2, s, k_2, \texttt{true}\rangle \iota_2\end{array}}$$

Fig. 6. Execution rules: $\Sigma[x \leftarrow k]$ updates the mapping Σ by setting x to be k; fresh is used as an overloading function to return a new variable/address; $s \vdash e \Downarrow k$ denotes the evaluation of expression e to a concrete value k in the current context s

their parent. The symbolic states (path conditions) of both nodes are updated accordingly (Δ_1 and Δ_2). The concrete state s helps to identify that the execution is going to follow the **then** branch and marks this branch as explored. The remaining node is marked as unexplored. The rule [C-FCOND] is interpreted similarly.

For example, Fig. 7 show the constraint trees constructed during the concolic execution of the example in Fig. 1 with two initial test inputs in Fig. 4. The input of the first test case is an empty tree. The condition of the if − statement at line 21 evaluates to **true**, satisfying the rule [C-TCOND]. The constraint tree in Fig. 7(a) is constructed. The input of the second test case is a tree with one node and x is 0. Thus the node is to be removed as its *element* is 0. The rule [C-FCOND] is applied, which results in the tree in Fig. 7(b). The condition $x < t.element$ is then used to generate a new test input with $x = 0$ and $t.element = 1$. Executing this new test input triggers the rule [C-TCOND] at line 9, and updates the constraint tree as in Fig. 7(c).

Path Condition Transformation. Note that the path conditions generated according to the execution rules may contain field-access and field-assign expres-

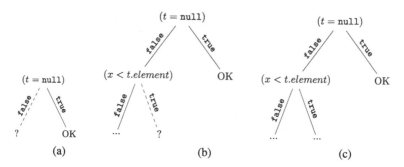

Fig. 7. Constraint trees construction: a question mark represents an unexplored path and OK denotes the execution terminates without error

sions which are beyond the syntax in Fig. 2 and the support of the solver [28,30]. Thus, these expressions need to be eliminated. The details of the transformation are presented in the Algorithm 2. The input of the algorithm is a path condition which may contain field-access and field-assign expressions. The output are multiple path conditions, i.e., a disjunction of path conditions, without field-access and field-assign expressions.

The algorithm begins by recording all symbolic values for all fields of points-to predicates (lines 1–3). Then it considers each conjunct, which in form of a binary expression with left-hand side and right-hand side, in the path condition (line 4). In general, the field-access expression is substituted by symbolic value of the field. For each field-access expression $v.f_i$ in the conjunct (line 5), if the current path condition implies v is $\mathtt{null}$, the path condition is unsatisfiable and is discarded (lines 6–7). In case the path condition implies v is constrained by a points-to predicate, it substitutes $v.f_i$ with the corresponding symbolic name for the field in the predicate (lines 8–9). Otherwise, if v is constrained by an inductive predicate, it unfolds the predicate to find points-to predicate for v (lines 10–14). In the last case (lines 15–16), it considers the current path condition does not have enough information to resolve $v.f_i$ and simply returns empty. For field-assign expression $v.f_i := e$, after transforming the expression with above steps, it substitutes the left-hand side with a fresh symbolic name f_i', update the mapping from $v.f_i$ (or $x.f_i$ in case $\Delta \Longrightarrow x = v$) to f_i', then change := to = (lines 17–20). Note that the update at line 19 may override the update at line 9 for left-hand side. Similar to Algorithm 1, the correctness of Algorithm 2 follows from the fact that each final path condition is an under-approximation of the original path condition because of the unfolding process. For instance, the path condition $\mathtt{bst}(this\_root, minE, maxE) \wedge t = this\_root \wedge t \neq \mathtt{null} \wedge x < t.element$ has field-access expression $t.element$ which need to be transformed. Using Algorithm 2, we get the final path condition which can be passed to the solver:

$$\exists elt, l, r.\ this\_root \mapsto BinaryNode(elt, l, r) * \mathtt{bst}(l, minE, elt) * \mathtt{bst}(r, elt, maxE) \wedge$$
$$minE < elt \wedge maxE > elt \wedge t = this\_root \wedge t \neq \mathtt{null} \wedge x < elt$$

Concolic Testing Heap-Manipulating Programs

Algorithm 2: preprocess(Δ)

---

1   $map \leftarrow \emptyset$
2   **foreach** $v \mapsto c(v_1, ..., v_n) \in \Delta$ **do**
3      $map \leftarrow map \cup \{v.f_i \leftarrow v_i\}$
4   **foreach** $(lhs\ op\ rhs) \in \Delta$ **do**
5   **foreach** $v.f_i \in (lhs\ op\ rhs)$ **do**
6   **if** $\Delta \Longrightarrow v = \mathtt{null}$ **then**
7   **return** $\emptyset$
8   **else if** $map(v.f_i) = v_i\ \|\ map(x.f_i) = v_i\ \&\&\ \Delta \Longrightarrow v = x$ **then**
9                $(lhs\ op\ rhs) \leftarrow (lhs\ op\ rhs)[v_i/v.f_i]$
10   **else if** $\mathtt{P}(\bar{v}) \in \Delta\ \&\&\ (v \in \bar{v}\ \|\ x \in \bar{v}\ \&\&\ \Delta \Longrightarrow v = x)$ **then**
11               $\Delta_s \leftarrow \mathtt{unfold}(\Delta, \mathtt{P}(\bar{v})),\ \Gamma \leftarrow \emptyset$
12   **foreach** $\Delta_i \in \Delta_s$ **do**
13                    $\Gamma \leftarrow \Gamma \cup \mathtt{preprocess}(\Delta_i)$
14   **return** Γ
15   **else**
16   **return** $\emptyset$
17   **if** $op\ is\ :=$ **then**
18   Substitute lhs with a fresh symbolic name
19   Update the field in map to the new name
20   Substitute $:=$ with $=$
21 **return** $\{\Delta\}$

The solver verifies that the path condition is satisfiable and then returns a model which is a *BinarySearchTree* with 1 node. The *element* field of the node has value 1 and the value of parameter x is 0.

5   Implementation and Experiments

We have implemented our proposal in a tool, named Concolic StarFinder (CSF), with 6770 lines of Java code as a module inside the Java PathFinder framework. In the following, we conduct three experiments and contrast CSF's performance with existing approaches. All experiments are conducted on a laptop with 2.20 GHz and 16 GB RAM.

First Experiment. In this experiment, we assume CSF is used as a standalone tool to generate test inputs for heap-manipulating programs. That is, the users provide a program and a precondition, then apply CSF to automatically generate a set of test inputs. The experimental subject is a comprehensive set of benchmark programs collected from previous publications, which includes *Singly-Linked List* (SLL), *Doubly-Linked List* (DLL), *Stack*, *Binary Search Tree* (BST), *Red Black Tree* (RBT) from SIR [7], *AVL Tree*, *AA Tree* (AAT) from

Sireum/Kiasan [8], *Tll* from [27], the motivation example from SUSHI [10], the TSAFE project [17], and the Gantt project [3]. In total, we have 74 methods whose line of codes range from dozens to more than one thousand. For each method, the precondition according to the original publication is adopted for generating test inputs using CSF. In the specification-based testing stage, CSF is configured to generate all test inputs with a depth of 1 (e.g., unfolding the precondition once).

We compare CSF with two state-of-the-art tools, e.g., JBSE [12] and BBE [45]. JBSE uses HEX for specifying the invariants of valid test inputs and generates test inputs accordingly. We use the same invariants reported in [12] in our experiments. Note that because the HEX invariants for *SLL*, *Stack*, *BST*, *AA Tree* and *Tll* are not available[2], we skip running JBSE with these test subjects. BBE is explained in Sect. 2. In the following, we answer multiple research questions (RQ) through experiments.

RQ1: Does CSF generate valid test inputs? We apply CSF to generate test inputs for the 74 methods. To check whether the generated test inputs are valid, we validate the generated test inputs with the *repOK* method in the data structures. The results are shown in the columns named *#Tests* in Table 1 for each test subject. The entries for JBSE and BBE are in the form of the number of valid test inputs over the total number of test inputs. As expected, all test inputs generated by CSF are valid. In comparison, JBSE generates 4.65% valid test inputs and BBE generates 7.83% valid test inputs. The reason for the poor results of JBSE and BBE is that the reference variables/fields are initialized with the wrong values or never initialized if they are not accessed. Note that by default, JBSE generates partially initialized test inputs, so we additionally call method *repOK* to concretize them. CSF solves the path conditions, which contain the precondition, to generate test inputs, which are guaranteed to be valid. We thus conclude that using an expressiveness language is important in achieving validity.

RQ2: Can CSF achieve high code coverage? We use JaCoCo [4] to measure the branch coverage of the generated test inputs. The results are shown in the subcolumns named *Cov.(%)* (which is the coverage achieved by valid test inputs) and *NCov.(%)* (which is the coverage achieved by all test inputs including the invalid ones) in Table 1. The winners are highlighted in bold. Note that for CSF, because all the test inputs are valid, we omit the column *NCov.(%)*. The results show that CSF achieves nearly 100% branch coverage for almost all programs except TSAFE, whose coverage is 59.46%. For 70 out of 74 methods, CSF can obtain 100% branch coverage (including branches for auxiliary methods and excluding infeasible branches). CSF fails to cover 1 branch in two methods (i.e., *remove* for *RBT* and *remove* for *AAT*) and 3 branches in one method (i.e., *put* for *RBT*). The reason is that although the path conditions leading to those branches are satisfiable, the solver times out. For method *TS_R_3*, CSF

---

[2] and it is unclear to us whether HEX is capable to specify them.

Table 1. Experiment 1 & 2: Results

Program	CSF				JBSE				BBE			
	#Tests	Cov.(%)	#Calls	T(s)	#Tests	Cov.(%)	NCov.(%)	T(s)	#Tests	Cov.(%)	NCov.(%)	T(s)
DLL	75	100	40/58	32	121/5146	56	100	206	0/35	0	21	21
AVL	62	100	36/654	274	76/295	100	100	48	17/117	70	89	69
RBT	133	99	14/1106	2403	137/291	87	91	38	14/380	26	53	333
SUSHI	5	100	3/38	8	0/900	0	100	24	2/27	25	25	8
TSAFE	16	59	1/595	1190	0/32	0	5	10	0/1	0	0	1
Gantt	22	100	2/156	25	17/887	55	90	24	0/6	0	5	2
SLL	29	100	21/8	11	-	-	-	-	16/50	66	71	19
Stack	18	100	16/2	7	-	-	-	-	11/14	84	84	6
BST	47	100	16/33	14	-	-	-	-	19/260	69	86	131
AAT	46	99	21/352	277	-	-	-	-	3/166	6	43	111
Tll	6	100	2/4	2	-	-	-	-	1/4	38	50	2
Math	320	88	576/0	73	-	-	-	-	128/320	75	79	95

achieves 59.46% branch coverage because in the execution, some native methods are invoked and applying symbolic execution to those paths are infeasible. Moreover, some of the path conditions contain string constraints which are not supported by the solver. For JBSE and BBE, the average coverage is 68.54% and 37.85% respectively if we consider valid test inputs only. If all test inputs are considered, the average coverage increases to 95.59% for JBSE and 54.66% for BBE. Note that the coverage is inflated with invalid test inputs.

RQ3: Is CSF sufficiently efficient? We measure the time needed to generate test inputs (sub-columns $T(s)$ in the Table 1). The results show that CSF needs 57.34 s on average for each program. The numbers for JBSE and BBE are 8.75 and 9.50 s respectively. Both JBSE and BBE are faster than CSF since they solve simpler constraints (e.g., without inductive predicates). However, their efficiency has a cost in term of the validity of the generated test inputs and the achieved code coverage. To conclude, we believe CSF is sufficiently efficient to be used in practice. We further show the number of solver calls used in CSF, i.e., the sub-column #*Calls* in the Table 1. The results are represented in form of the number of solver calls for specification-based testing over that of concolic execution. The results show that CSF needs 43 calls in average. Note that the number of solver calls in the specification-based testing stage varies according to the number of disjuncts in the precondition.

Second Experiment. One infamous limitation of symbolic execution testing approach is it cannot handle programs with complex numerical conditions. On the other hand, specification-based testing approach does not suffer this limitation because it generates test inputs independently of programs under test. In this experiment, we aim to show the usefulness of specification-based testing in CSF, especially for programs with complex numerical conditions. To do that, we systematically compose a set of programs which travel a singly-linked list, apply a method from *java.lang.Math* library to the list elements, and check if the result satisfies some condition. One example is shown in Fig. 8 with method

```
public boolean withCos(Node root) {
  while (root != null) {
    if (Math.cos(root.elem) == 1) return true;
    root = root.next; }
  return false;
}
```

Fig. 8. An example in the second experiment

cos, which returns the cosin value of an integer. In total, we have 32 programs with 32 different methods from *java.lang.Math* library. We run CSF with only specification-based testing (to generate 10 test inputs) and compare the results with BBE. We cannot compare with JBSE because we do not have the HEX invariant for singly-linked list. However, we note that JBSE is a symbolic execution engine, which means it has difficulties in handling complex numerical conditions. The list elements has random values from -32 to 31 for all the tools. Due to randomness, we repeat the experiment 10 times for each program.

In average, while CSF obtains 88.28% branch coverage, BBE obtains 75.31%. The average number of solver calls is 18 and the average time is 2.27 s for each program. For BBE, it generates 10 test inputs for each program but only 4 of them satisfy *repOK* in 2.97 s. From the results, we conclude that the specification-based testing phase is useful, especially for programs with complex numerical conditions.

Third Experiment. Although having a specification language based on separation logic allows us to precisely specify preconditions of the programs under test and generate valid test inputs, it could be non-trivial for ordinary users to use such a language. This problem has been recognized by the community and there have been multiple approaches to solve this problem [2,27,31,39]. One noticeable example which has made industrial impact is the Infer static analyzer [2], which infers preconditions of programs through bi-abduction [13]. In this experiment, we show that CSF can be effectively combined with Infer so that CSF can be applied without user-specified preconditions.

We first apply Infer to generate preconditions of the programs under test and then apply CSF to generate test inputs accordingly. The test subject is PLEXIL [5], i.e., NASA's plan automation and execution framework. Specifically, we analyze its verification environment PLEXIL5 [6] with Infer, and collect 88 methods that have explicit preconditions returned by Infer.

The experimental results are shown in Table 2, which are categorized based on the number of initial test inputs generated from Infer's preconditions (column *#Init Tests*). The second column *#Methods* shows the number of methods in the category. The column *#Tests* shows the number of generated test inputs and the column *#Exceptions* shows the number of exceptions in the category. Lastly, two columns *#Calls* and *Time(s)* show the number of solver calls and the time needed to generate the test inputs respectively. In summary, CSF generates 292 test inputs in 344 s which achieved 58.36% branch coverage in average. Our

Table 2. Experiment 3 with Infer: Results

#Init Tests	#Methods	#Tests	#Exceptions	#Calls	Time (s)
1	8	10	10	8/14	16
2	51	130	119	102/206	167
3	29	152	132	87/254	161

```
public void test_integerValue1() throws Exception {
  PlexilTreeParser obj = new PlexilTreeParser();
  plexil.PlexilASTNode _t = new plexil.PlexilASTNode();
  obj.ASTNULL = new antlr.ASTNULLType();
  int ttype_1 = 0;
  plexil.PlexilASTNode right_3 = null;
  plexil.PlexilASTNode down_2 = null;
  _t.ttype = ttype_1; _t.down = down_2; _t.right = right_3;
  obj.integerValue(_t);
}
```

Fig. 9. A test input which leads to *RuntimeException*

investigation shows that all of these test inputs are valid according to the inferred preconditions. Interestingly, 261 out of the 292 test inputs (i.e., 89%) lead to *RuntimeException* during execution. The interpretation can be either (1) the inferred preconditions are too weak to capture all the necessary conditions for valid test inputs generation, or (2) there are potential bugs in the programs.

To give an example, method *integerValue* receives an Abstract Syntax Tree (AST) as input and the AST must contain an *INT* token. The inferred precondition only says that the input should not be `null`. One of the test inputs generated by CSF is shown in Fig. 9. The execution result is *RuntimeException* because the value of field *ttype* does not match with the value of *INT* token, which is 108.

It would be interesting to develop a full integration of CSF and the recent bi-abduction for erroneous specification inference [39] so that we can generate meaningful test inputs automatically to witness bugs for any program.

6   Related Work

We review closely related work in the following, emphasis is given to approaches that generate test inputs for heap-manipulating programs.

Concolic Testing Programs with Heap Inputs. This work is the first work that uses separation logic for concolic testing. The engineering design of our tool is based on that of JDart [32]. However, JDart, like most concolic execution engines, e.g., [18,19,24,33,42], does not support data structures as symbolic input for testing methods. Our work is related to CUTE [40] and Pex [43]. CUTE [40] does support data structures as input by using the so-called *logical input map* to keep track of input memory graph. However, CUTE cannot handle unbounded inputs nor capture the shape relations between pointers, which leads to imprecision. Pex [43] uses a type system [44] to describe disjointness of memory regions. But again, Pex cannot handle unbounded inputs. Moreover, the type system can only reason about the *global* heap, which leads to complex constraints and hence poor scalability. In comparison, our work handles unbounded inputs and shape relations are well-captured by separation logic predicates.

Lazy Initialization. As far as we know, lazy initialization [25] is the only way to handle unbounded inputs. However, most works in this direction, e.g., [15,16,21,45], did not address the problem of generating invalid test inputs due to the lack of constraints on the shapes of the input data structures. This work is related to the tool JSF presented in [35,36]. While JSF uses separation logic for specifying preconditions and apply classical symbolic execution, ours relies on concolic execution. Moreover, to support memory access, JSF unfolds those heaps accessed by reference variables in advance, our work prepares heap accesses via lazy unfolding which helps to encode both executed/not-yet-executed paths and heap accesses together. Another related work is [11] by Braione *et al.*, which we have discussed extensively in previous sections. The logic presented in [11], HEX, is not expressive enough to describe many popular data structures, including the binary search tree in our motivating example.

Specification-Based Testing has been an active research area for decades. Depending on the testing goals, different types of logic have been used as the specification languages to generate test inputs, for example Alloy [34], Java predicates [9], and temporal logic [20,22]. However, we are not aware of any existing work that generate test inputs from the specification in separation logic like ours.

Separation Logic. Research in separation logic focuses on static verification [13, 14,27,29,37], which may return false positives and are not able to generate test inputs.

7   Conclusion

We have presented a novel concolic execution engine for heap-manipulating programs based on separation logic. Our engine starts with generating a set of initial test inputs based on preconditions. It concretely executes, monitors the executions and generates new inputs to drive the execution to unexplored code. We have implemented the proposal in CSF and evaluated it over benchmark programs. The experimental results show CSF's effectiveness and practical applications.

Acknowledgments. This research is supported by MOE research grant MOE2016-T2-2-123.

References

1. A Fuzzer and a Symbolic Executor Walk into a Cloud. https://blog.trailofbits. com/2016/08/02/engineering-solutions-to-hard-program-analysis-problems/
2. Facebook Infer. https://fbinfer.com/
3. GanttProject. https://github.com/bardsoftware/ganttproject
4. JaCoCo. https://www.eclemma.org/jacoco/
5. PLEXIL. http://plexil.sourceforge.net
6. PLEXIL5. https://github.com/nasa/PLEXIL5
7. SIR. http://sir.unl.edu/portal/index.php
8. Sireum. https://code.google.com/archive/p/sireum/downloads
9. Boyapati, C., Khurshid, S., Marinov, D.: Korat: automated testing based on Java predicates. In: Frankl, P.G. (ed.) ISSTA 2002, pp. 123–133. ACM (2002). https:// doi.org/10.1145/566172.566191
10. Braione, P., Denaro, G., Mattavelli, A., Pezzè, M.: Combining symbolic execution and search-based testing for programs with complex heap inputs. In: Bultan, T., Sen, K. (eds.) ISSTA 2017, pp. 90–101. ACM (2017). https://doi.org/10.1145/ 3092703.3092715
11. Braione, P., Denaro, G., Pezzè, M.: Symbolic execution of programs with heap inputs. In: Nitto, E.D., Harman, M., Heymans, P. (eds.) FSE 2015, pp. 602–613. ACM (2015). https://doi.org/10.1145/2786805.2786842
12. Braione, P., Denaro, G., Pezzè, M.: JBSE: A symbolic executor for Java programs with complex heap inputs. In: Zimmermann, T., Cleland-Huang, J., Su, Z. (eds.) FSE 2016, pp. 1018–1022. ACM (2016). https://doi.org/10.1145/2950290.2983940
13. Calcagno, C., Distefano, D., O'Hearn, P.W., Yang, H.: Compositional shape analysis by means of bi-abduction. JACM **58**(6), 26:1–26:66 (2011). https://doi.org/ 10.1145/2049697.2049700
14. Chin, W.N., David, C., Nguyen, H.H., Qin, S.: Automated verification of shape, size and bag properties via user-defined predicates in separation logic. Sci. Comput. Program. **77**(9), 1006–1036 (2012). https://doi.org/10.1016/j.scico.2010.07.004
15. Deng, X., Lee, J., Robby: Bogor/Kiasan: a k-bounded symbolic execution for checking strong heap properties of open systems. In: ASE 2006, pp. 157–166. IEEE Computer Society (2006). https://doi.org/10.1109/ASE.2006.26
16. Deng, X., Robby, Hatcliff, J.: Towards a case-optimal symbolic execution algorithm for analyzing strong properties of object-oriented programs. In: SEFM 2007. IEEE Computer Society (2007). https://doi.org/10.1109/SEFM.2007.43
17. Dennis, G.D.: TSAFE : building a trusted computing base for air traffic control software. Master's thesis, Massachusetts Institute of Technology, USA (2003)
18. Godefroid, P., Klarlund, N., Sen, K.: DART: directed automated random testing. In: Sarkar, V., Hall, M.W. (eds.) PLDI 2005, pp. 213–223. ACM (2005). https:// doi.org/10.1145/1065010.1065036
19. Godefroid, P., Levin, M.Y., Molnar, D.: SAGE: whitebox fuzzing for security testing. Queue **10**(1), 20:20–20:27 (2012). https://doi.org/10.1145/2090147.2094081
20. Heimdahl, M.P.E., Rayadurgam, S., Visser, W., Devaraj, G., Gao, J.: Auto-generating test sequences using model checkers: a case study. In: Petrenko, A., Ulrich, A. (eds.) FATES 2003. LNCS, vol. 2931, pp. 42–59. Springer, Heidelberg (2004). https://doi.org/10.1007/978-3-540-24617-6_4
21. Hillery, B., Mercer, E., Rungta, N., Person, S.: Exact heap summaries for symbolic execution. In: Jobstmann, B., Leino, K.R.M. (eds.) VMCAI 2016. LNCS, vol. 9583, pp. 206–225. Springer, Heidelberg (2016). https://doi.org/10.1007/978-3-662-49122-5_10

22. Hong, H.S., Lee, I., Sokolsky, O., Ural, H.: A temporal logic based theory of test coverage and generation. In: Katoen, J.-P., Stevens, P. (eds.) TACAS 2002. LNCS, vol. 2280, pp. 327–341. Springer, Heidelberg (2002). https://doi.org/10.1007/3-540-46002-0_23

23. Ishtiaq, S.S., O'Hearn, P.W.: BI as an assertion language for mutable data structures. In: Hankin, C., Schmidt, D. (eds.) POPL 2001, pp. 14–26. ACM (2001). https://doi.org/10.1145/360204.375719

24. Jayaraman, K., Harvison, D., Ganesh, V., Kiezun, A.: jFuzz: a concolic whitebox fuzzer for Java. In: Denney, E., Giannakopoulou, D., Pasareanu, C.S. (eds.) NFM 2009, pp. 121–125 (2009)

25. Khurshid, S., Păsăreanu, C.S., Visser, W.: Generalized symbolic execution for model checking and testing. In: Garavel, H., Hatcliff, J. (eds.) TACAS 2003. LNCS, vol. 2619, pp. 553–568. Springer, Heidelberg (2003). https://doi.org/10.1007/3-540-36577-X_40

26. King, J.C.: Symbolic execution and program testing. Commun. ACM 19(7), 385–394 (1976). https://doi.org/10.1145/360248.360252

27. Le, Q.L., Gherghina, C., Qin, S., Chin, W.-N.: Shape analysis via second-order bi-abduction. In: Biere, A., Bloem, R. (eds.) CAV 2014. LNCS, vol. 8559, pp. 52–68. Springer, Cham (2014). https://doi.org/10.1007/978-3-319-08867-9_4

28. Le, Q.L., Sun, J., Chin, W.-N.: Satisfiability modulo heap-based programs. In: Chaudhuri, S., Farzan, A. (eds.) CAV 2016. LNCS, vol. 9779, pp. 382–404. Springer, Cham (2016). https://doi.org/10.1007/978-3-319-41528-4_21

29. Le, Q.L., Sun, J., Qin, S.: Frame inference for inductive entailment proofs in separation logic. In: Beyer, D., Huisman, M. (eds.) TACAS 2018. LNCS, vol. 10805, pp. 41–60. Springer, Cham (2018). https://doi.org/10.1007/978-3-319-89960-2_3

30. Le, Q.L., Tatsuta, M., Sun, J., Chin, W.-N.: A decidable fragment in separation logic with inductive predicates and arithmetic. In: Majumdar, R., Kunčak, V. (eds.) CAV 2017. LNCS, vol. 10427, pp. 495–517. Springer, Cham (2017). https://doi.org/10.1007/978-3-319-63390-9_26

31. Le, X.D., Le, Q.L., Lo, D., Le Goues, C.: Enhancing automated program repair with deductive verification. In: ICSME 2016, pp. 428–432. IEEE Computer Society (2016). https://doi.org/10.1109/ICSME.2016.66

32. Luckow, K., et al.: JDART: a dynamic symbolic analysis framework. In: Chechik, M., Raskin, J.-F. (eds.) TACAS 2016. LNCS, vol. 9636, pp. 442–459. Springer, Heidelberg (2016). https://doi.org/10.1007/978-3-662-49674-9_26

33. Marinescu, P.D., Cadar, C.: Make test-zesti: a symbolic execution solution for improving regression testing. In: Glinz, M., Murphy, G.C., Pezzè, M. (eds.) ICSE 2012, pp. 716–726. IEEE Computer Society (2012). https://doi.org/10.1109/ICSE.2012.6227146

34. Marinov, D., Khurshid, S.: TestEra: a novel framework for automated testing of Java programs. In: ASE 2001, pp. 22–31. IEEE Computer Society (2001). https://doi.org/10.1109/ASE.2001.989787

35. Pham, L.H., Le, Q.L., Phan, Q.S., Sun, J., Qin, S.: Enhancing symbolic execution of heap-based programs with separation logic for test input generation. In: ATVA 2019. To appear

36. Pham, L.H., Le, Q.L., Phan, Q.S., Sun, J., Qin, S.: Testing heap-based programs with Java StarFinder. In: Chaudron, M., Crnkovic, I., Chechik, M., Harman, M. (eds.) ICSE 2018, pp. 268–269. ACM (2018). https://doi.org/10.1145/3183440.3194964

37. Piskac, R., Wies, T., Zufferey, D.: Automating separation logic using SMT. In: Sharygina, N., Veith, H. (eds.) CAV 2013. LNCS, vol. 8044, pp. 773–789. Springer, Heidelberg (2013). https://doi.org/10.1007/978-3-642-39799-8_54

38. Reynolds, J.: Separation logic: a logic for shared mutable data structures. In: LICS 2002, pp. 55–74. IEEE Computer Society (2002). https://doi.org/10.1109/LICS.2002.1029817

39. Santos, J.F., Maksimović, P., Sampaio, G., Gardner, P.: JaVerT 2.0: compositional symbolic execution for JavaScript. PACMPL 3(POPL), 66:1–66:31 (2019). https://doi.org/10.1145/3290379

40. Sen, K., Marinov, D., Agha, G.: CUTE: a concolic unit testing engine for C. In: Wermelinger, M., Gall, H.C. (eds.) FSE 2005, pp. 263–272. ACM (2005). https://doi.org/10.1145/1081706.1081750

41. Stephens, N., et al.: Driller: augmenting fuzzing through selective symbolic execution. In: NDSS 2016. The Internet Society (2016)

42. Tanno, H., Zhang, X., Hoshino, T., Sen, K.: TesMa and CATG: automated test generation tools for models of enterprise applications. In: Bertolino, A., Canfora, G., Elbaum, S.G. (eds.) ICSE 2015, pp. 717–720. IEEE Computer Society (2015). https://doi.org/10.1109/ICSE.2015.231

43. Tillmann, N., de Halleux, J.: Pex–white box test generation for.NET. In: Beckert, B., Hähnle, R. (eds.) TAP 2008. LNCS, vol. 4966, pp. 134–153. Springer, Heidelberg (2008). https://doi.org/10.1007/978-3-540-79124-9_10

44. Vanoverberghe, D., Tillmann, N., Piessens, F.: Test input generation for programs with pointers. In: Kowalewski, S., Philippou, A. (eds.) TACAS 2009. LNCS, vol. 5505, pp. 277–291. Springer, Heidelberg (2009). https://doi.org/10.1007/978-3-642-00768-2_25

45. Visser, W., Păsăreanu, C.S., Khurshid, S.: Test input generation with java PathFinder. In: Avrunin, G.S., Rothermel, G. (eds.) ISSTA 2004, pp. 97–107. ACM (2004). https://doi.org/10.1145/1007512.1007526

46. Wang, X., Sun, J., Chen, Z., Zhang, P., Wang, J., Lin, Y.: Towards optimal concolic testing. In: Chaudron, M., Crnkovic, I., Chechik, M., Harman, M. (eds.) ICSE 2018, pp. 291–302 (2018). https://doi.org/10.1145/3180155.3180177

47. Yun, I., Lee, S., Xu, M., Jang, Y., Kim, T.: QSYM : a practical concolic execution engine tailored for hybrid fuzzing. In: Enck, W., Felt, A.P. (eds.) USENIX Security 2018, pp. 745–761. USENIX Association (2018)

Specification Languages

Formal Semantics Extraction from Natural Language Specifications for ARM

Anh V. Vu[✉] and Mizuhito Ogawa

Japan Advanced Institute of Science and Technology, Nomi, Japan
{anhvv,mizuhito}@jaist.ac.jp

Abstract. This paper proposes a method to systematically extract the formal semantics of ARM instructions from their natural language specifications. Although ARM is based on RISC architecture and the number of instructions is relatively small, an abundance of variations diversely exist under various series including Cortex-A, Cortex-M, and Cortex-R. Thus, the semi-automatic semantics formalisation of rather simple instructions results in reducing tedious human efforts for tool developments e.g., the symbolic execution. We concentrate on six variations: M0, M0+, M3, M4, M7, and M33 of ARM Cortex-M series, aiming at covering IoT malware. Our systematic approach consists of the semantics interpretation by applying translation rules, augmented by the sentences similarity analysis to recognise the modification of flags. Among 1039 collected specifications, the formal semantics of 662 instructions have been successfully extracted by using only 228 manually prepared rules. They are utilised afterwards to preliminarily build a dynamic symbolic execution tool for Cortex-M called CORANA. We experimentally observe that CORANA is capable of effectively tracing IoT malware under the presence of obfuscation techniques like indirect jumps, as well as correctly detecting dead conditional branches, which are regarded as opaque predicates.

Keywords: Semantics formalisation · Dynamic symbolic execution · Iot malware analysis · Natural language processing · ARM Cortex-M

1 Introduction

Symbolic execution [1] is an old, powerful, and popular technique to analyse and/or verify software. It has been developed mainly for high-level programming languages, such as C and Java. Recently, the number of symbolic execution tools for binaries has gradually increased (e.g., MCVETO [2], MIASM [3], MAYHEM [4], KLEE-MC [5], CODISASM [6], BE-PUM [7], and ANGR [8]); however, most of them target x86 architecture. When analysing the dynamic behaviour of malware, the major obstacles are obfuscated codes (e.g., indirect jumps, opaque predicates, self-modification), which can be effectively solved by applying dynamic symbolic execution (also known as concolic testing). In particular, the concolic testing is able to dynamically explore the hidden destination of indirect jumps, whilst

© Springer Nature Switzerland AG 2019
M. H. ter Beek et al. (Eds.): FM 2019, LNCS 11800, pp. 465–483, 2019.
https://doi.org/10.1007/978-3-030-30942-8_28

the symbolic execution can discover dead conditional branches, which will be eventually ignored. Considering the evolving threats of IoT malware, extending such tools to disparate architectures (e.g., ARM, MIPS, and PowerPC) becomes highly desired. There are two existing approaches to interpreting machine codes:

- Translating to an intermediate representation (e.g., LLVM in KLEE-MC and VEX in ANGR), where the coverage performance basically depends on the translators, such as VALGRIND [9] in KLEE-MC and CAPSTONE [10] in ANGR.
- Interpreting directly from binary codes, such as MCVETO and BE-PUM (x86).

When the obfuscations exist, the former shares the difficulties with syntax-based disassemblers (e.g., IDA [11] and CAPSTONE), which typically fail to disassemble malware [12]. We adopt the latter approach, which is more powerful; however, since it heavily requires a platform-wise implementation, an expensive engineering effort must be paid (e.g., 3155 instructions for x86-64 are counted in [13]). Contrary to a general impression on the intricacy of binaries, the good news is:

- IoT malware is mainly an user-mode sequential program without floating-point arithmetic. Avoiding multi-threads, weak memory models, and floating-point arithmetic allows us to consider a simple semantics framework as the transitions on the environment made by *memory*, *stack*, *registers*, and *flags*.
- Each instruction set officially contains a rigid natural language specification.
- Since various debuggers and emulation environments are available, the ambiguity occurring in the natural language processing can be resolved by testing.

This intuitively suggests the feasibility of semi-automatically formalising the semantics of rather simple instructions from their natural language specifications.

ARM is based on RISC architecture, thus, it has relatively few instructions ($\simeq$ 60–300). However, various series diversely exist such as Cortex-A for rich operating systems (e.g., Android OS), Cortex-R for real-time systems (e.g., LTE modems), and Cortex-M for micro-controllers (e.g., IoT devices). Moreover, each of them has numerous variations (e.g., 16 in Cortex-A, 5 in Cortex-R, and 9 in Cortex-M), which have been steadily increasing. Our study intentionally focuses on ARM Cortex-M, aiming at covering IoT malware. After collecting the official specifications of Cortex-M instructions on ARM developer website [14], their formal semantics are extracted by a systematic method, and the obtained semantics are utilised afterwards to preliminarily develop a dynamic symbolic execution tool for Cortex-M called CORANA (<u>Co</u>rtex <u>Ana</u>lyser) [15]. Note that, instead of trying to provide a fully automatic approach, our ultimate goal is significantly reducing tedious human efforts by automatically handling rather simple but many instructions, thus enables human to mainly concentrate on most complex parts.

Extraction Overview. Figure 1 briefly illustrates an overview of the semantics extraction, where manually prepared tasks are bounded with dashed boxes. For each instruction i, among 5 sections from its natural language specification

(Sect. 2.1), 3 sections are utilised: *syntax* (name and arguments of *i*), *operation* (an informal interpretation of *i*), and *flags-update* (describing whether flags are modified after *i* is executed). Given a sentence S, after normalising its syntax (Sect. 3) (I), if S comes from the *operation* section, the semantics interpretation (II) based on rewriting rules translates the normalised syntax tree to a Java code statement (Sect. 4). If S is from the *flags-update* section, the similarity analysis (III) recognises whether the flags are modified (Sect. 5). Thereafter, a Java method is automatically generated by instantiating the interpreted data into a pre-defined template, which represents the semantics framework as a transition on the environment. The correctness of generated methods is then verified using a conformance testing by comparing the execution results with a trusted emulator (Sect. 6). By instantiating the extracted semantics into a prepared framework, CORANA is created (Sect. 7). Our experiments on the sampled IoT malware reported in Sect. 8 show that CORANA is capable of dynamically handling conditional data instructions and indirect jumps, as well as detecting dead branches, which are regarded as typical obfuscation techniques in IoT malware.

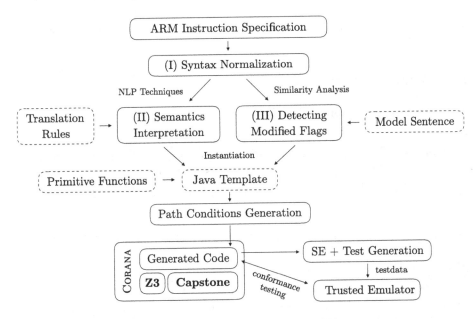

Fig. 1. A high-level overview of our semantics extraction approach

Related Work. There are several works focusing on extracting the specification from natural language descriptions. Nevertheless, they are mostly for human understanding (e.g., the requirements [16] and UML [17]), rather than the formal semantics of binaries. An interesting approach for the synthesis of x86-64 semantics is by learning formulas on BitVectors [18]. They confirmed the correctness by random testing, in which the results between their STRATA [18] and STOKE [19] are compared. Alternatively, an expensive human effort must be paid to describe the formal semantics, such as 3155 x86-64 instructions in the K-framework [13].

In fact, the formal semantics implicitly appears in the implementation of numerous binary emulators (e.g., μVision [20]) and symbolic execution tools (e.g., MCVETO [2], MIASM [3], MAYHEM [4], KLEE-MC [5], CODISASM [6], BE-PUM [7], and ANGR [8]). Whilst MIASM, MAYHEM, ANGR, and KLEE-MC first translate machine codes into an intermediate representation, MCVETO, CODIS-ASM, and BE-PUM directly interpret x86 binaries. Except for MCVETO and MIASM, they support the dynamic symbolic execution. BE-PUM would be the first study of applying the binary semantics extraction from the natural language specifications [21]. After a three-year effort of the manual implementation, BE-PUM roughly supported 250 instructions. Thereafter, the automatic extraction successfully generated 299 among 530 collected specifications, and 5 semantics bugs in the manual implementation were reported. At the moment, BE-PUM covers around 400 instructions in total. Since the pseudocodes of x86 instructions are explicitly included in the Intel Developer Manuals, the semantics extraction was pretty simple by preparing roughly 30 primitive functions appearing in the pseudocodes. In contrast, the specifications of ARM instructions are given entirely in natural language, which makes the formalisation process [22] become more challenging.

2   Formal Semantics of ARM

2.1   Natural Language Specification

The specification of a Cortex-M instruction collected from the official ARM developer website [14] consists of five sections: *mnemonic, description, syntax, operation,* and *flags-update.* Table 1 shows an example of the rigid natural language specification (given in English) of the instruction UMAAL in ARM Cortex-M7.

Table 1. The natural language specification of UMAAL in ARM Cortex-M7

Mnemonic	UMAAL
Description	Signed multiply with accumulate long
Syntax	UMAAL{cond} RdLo, RdHi, Rn, Rm
Operation	The UMAAL instruction multiplies the two unsigned 32-bit integers in the first and second operands. Adds the unsigned 32-bit integer in RdHi to the 64-bit result of the multiplication. Adds the unsigned 32-bit integer in RdLo to the 64-bit result of the addition. Writes the top 32-bits of the result to RdHi. Writes the lower 32-bits of the result to RdLo
Flags-update	This instruction does not affect the condition code flags

2.2 Operational Semantics

The implementation of numerous binary analysis tools (e.g., binary emulators, binary symbolic execution engines) implicitly contains the formal semantics of instructions, which have been formally defined in several recent studies (e.g., for x86 [13,23,24]). Although the semantics of binaries is seemingly intricate for human, the semantics framework for sequential programs is rather simple, which rigidly consists of a tuple of four ingredients: *registers, flags, memory*, and *stack*.

Definition 1. *The environment model* $E = \langle F, R, M, S \rangle$ *of the 32-bit ARM Cortex-M binaries consists of:*

- *F: a set of 6 flags:* $F = \{N, Z, C, V, Q, GE\}$
- *R: a set of 17 registers:*

$$R = \{r_0, r_1, r_2, r_3, r_4, r_5, r_6, r_7, r_8, r_9, r_{10}, r_{11}, r_{12}, sp, lr, pc, apsr\}$$

  where apsr is a special register storing the values of all flags N, Z, C, V (also includes Q, GE in some particular versions of ARM).
- *M: a set of n contiguous memory locations: $M = \{m_0, m_1, \ldots, m_{n-1}\}$*
- *S($\subseteq M$): a set of k contiguously allocated memory to store the stack:*
  $S = \{s_0, s_1, \ldots, s_{k-1}\}$ with $k < n$.

Since our target (IoT malware) is mainly a sequential user-mode process, the weak memory models and multi-threads are omitted. Accordingly, the execution of an instruction i is simply regarded as a transition t_i on a quadruplet in Fig. 2:

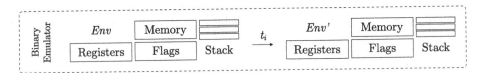

Fig. 2. The semantics transition t_i while executing an instruction i

For instance, the formal semantics of UMAAL is described in the SOS style [25]:

$$\frac{R_{pc} = k; instr(k) = umaal\ rdlo\ rdhi\ rn\ rm; R_{rdlo} = lo; R_{rdhi} = hi;}{R_{rn} = n; R_{rm} = m; a = m * n + lo + hi; hi' = a \gg 32; lo' = (a \ll 32) \gg 32;} \text{[UMAAL]}$$
$$\langle F, R, M, S \rangle \rightarrow \langle F, R[pc \leftarrow k + |\ instr(k)\ |; R_{rdlo} \leftarrow lo'; R_{rdhi} \leftarrow hi'], M, S \rangle$$

2.3 Java Specification as Formal Semantics

The formal semantics of an instruction i, which is considered as a transition t_i on the environment, is represented by a Java specification built on top of a customised class `BitVec` – a pair $\langle bs, s \rangle$ where bs is a `BitSet` value (a 32-bit BitVector supported in Java by default) and s is a string. After executing i, the concrete result of the operators is stored in *bs* whilst the corresponding symbolic formula (in SMT format of BitVector theory) is represented by *s* (an example is shown in Sect. 7.1). In particular, this formal specification is technically obtained by instantiating the missing parameters into a pre-defined Java template:

```java
public void $name($params, Character suffix) {
    arithmeticMode = $arithmeticMode;
    char[] flags = new char[]{$flags};
    BitVec result = null;
    $execCode
    if (suffix != null && suffix == 's') {
        if (result != null) {
            updateFlags(flags, result);
        }
    }
}
```

where:

1. The parameters that need to be instantiated: **params** (the missing arguments of this method), **name** (the instruction name), **arithmeticMode** (to specify whether the floating-point arithmetic is required), **execCode** (the main formal interpreted operations), and **flags** (the list of flags that might be modified).
2. Default arguments: **suffix** (if the suffix s occurs, the flags appearing in **flags** might be optionally updated based on the result of operators in **execCode**).
3. Manually prepared methods: **updateFlags** (update flags occurring in **flags**).

For instance, the generated Java method representing the semantics of UMAAL is described as follows, where dashed boxes indicate the instantiated parameters:

```java
public void UMAAL(Character l, Character h, Character n,
    Character m, Character suffix) {
    arithmeticMode = ArithmeticMode.BINARY;            syntax
    char[] flags = new char[]{};        ⟵ flags-update
    BitVec result = null;
    result = mul(val(n),val(m));
    result = add(result,val(h));
    result = add(result,val(l));
    write(h,shift(result,Mode.RIGHT,32));
    write(l,shift(shift(result,Mode.LEFT,32),Mode.RIGHT,32));
    if (suffix != null && suffix == 's') {
        if (result != null) {                          operation
            updateFlags(flags, result);
        }
    }
}
```

To interpret the Java specifications, 35 simple primitive functions are manually prepared, including arithmetic operators (e.g., **add**, **sub**, **mul**), logical operators (e.g., **and**, **or**, **xor**), and IO operators (e.g., **write**, **load**, **store**). Note that, some pre-defined functions do not have any corresponding representations in SMT format by default, thus their macros must be additionally declared (e.g., bvmin, bvmax, bvabs, bvclz). Among them, some instructions especially contain loops, which must be unfolded to be acceptable by theorem provers. A representative instance is the clz r instruction, which aims at counting the number of leading zeros of the value stored in the register r. Whilst its standard implementations normally require executing a loop, considering a 32-bit architecture, its macro in SMT format can be unfolded by iterating up to 32 times as indicated below:

```
(declare-const r0 (_ BitVec 32))
(declare-const c0 (_ BitVec 32))
... same declarations for r1,c1 ... r31,c31 ...
(declare-const r32 (_ BitVec 32))
(declare-const c32 (_ BitVec 32))
(declare-const z (_ BitVec 32))
(declare-const m (_ BitVec 32))
(define-fun clz ((x (_ BitVec 32))) (_ BitVec 32)
(if (and
  (= r0 x) (= z #x00000000) (= m #x00000001) (= c0 #x00000020)
  (= c1 (ite (bvsgt (bvashr r0 m) z) (bvsub c0 m) c0))
  (= r1 (ite (bvsgt (bvashr r0 m) z) (bvashr r0 m) r0))
  ... same declarations for c2,r2 ... c31,r31 ...
  (= c32 (ite (bvsgt (bvashr r31 m) z) (bvsub c31 m) c31))
  (= r32 (ite (bvsgt (bvashr r31 m) z) (bvashr r31 m) r31))
) c32 #x00000021))
```

3   Syntax Normalisation

Before proceeding further analyses, each raw sentence in the *operation* section is sequentially normalised by *parsing*, *lemmatisation*, and *words refinement*. In the implementation, we utilise *parsing* and *lemmatisation* modules provided in an open library namely NLTK [26]. Figure 3 illustrates an example of the normalisation applied on the first sentence in the *operation* section of the *UMAAL* specification: S – *"The UMAAL instruction multiplies the two unsigned 32-bit integers in the first and second operands"*, which contains three sequential steps.

(1) Parsing. Parsing is applied for transforming each sentence to its structured syntax tree along with the corresponding labels in the grammatical categories (e.g., NP – Noun Phrase, DT – Determiner) based on the context-free grammar.

(2) Lemmatisation. Words written in English might have various expressions, such as conjugations and plural forms. Lemmatisation aims at unifying them to their standardised state. For instance, in Fig. 3, the words bounded with dashed boxes at the leaves of the syntax tree are the normalised results of this lemmatisation: *multiplies* → *multiply*, *integers* → *integer*, and *operands* → *operand*.

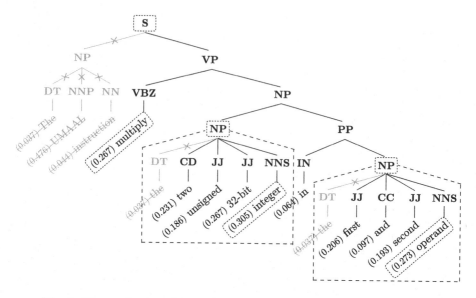

Fig. 3. The syntax tree, lemmatisation results, and TF·IDF of words in S

(3) Words Refinement. The popular measure TF·IDF [27] is utilised to effectively refine unimportant words in each sentence. For instance, the TF·IDF of words in S are put along with the leaves of the syntax tree. By setting a threshold $h = 0.05$, the strikethrough words in Fig. 3 are deleted and the removal recursively propagates to the root. Note that, the instruction name is also removed.

4   Semantics Interpretation by Translation Rules

Our semantics interpretation adopts a *rule-based* approach, which utilises the normalised syntax tree of sentences as the input. The key intuitive idea is: a *less* number of manually prepared rules can cover a *large* number of instructions. Firstly, we extract some popular phrases from the normalised syntax trees, which we named *NP-Phrases* (Sect. 4.1). Thereafter, a set of appropriate instructions is carefully selected to obtain an *optimal trade-off* – the ratio between the number of rules needed and the number of covered instructions (Sect. 4.2). Next, the translation rules are manually described by a recursive process (Sect. 4.3). Eventually, by employing these prepared rewriting rules, the formal semantics of instructions are interpreted in a *bottom-up* manner (Sect. 4.4). Note that, since our method is *sentence-wise*, the interpretation proceeds in sequence. Therefore, if an operation description is constituted of multiple sentences, the actual order of generated Java statements rigidly corresponds to the order of these sentences.

4.1   NP-Phrases Extraction

As a result of the syntax normalisation in Sect. 3, all unimportant terms in the syntax trees are finally removed. We now extract some particular phrases by concentrating on sub-trees with the root label "NP". An *NP-Term* is a flattened string of a sub-tree in the normalised syntax tree in which only the root is labelled "NP". An *NP-Phrase* is either an NP-Term or the flattened string of the whole normalised syntax tree after substituting each NP-Term by an indexed blank hole $\square_i$. For instance, in Fig. 3, the sub-trees surrounded by dashed lines are NP-Terms, and the extracted NP-Phrases are: *"two unsigned 32-bit integer"*, *"first and second operand"*, and *"multiply $\square_2$ in $\square_1$"*. These NP-Phrases are further utilised as the input of the instruction selection strategy described in Sect. 4.2.

4.2   Instructions Selection Strategy

We observe: (1) an instruction may carry various semantics in different variations (e.g., the instruction UASX appears both in M33 and M4, but the *flag-updates* sections are slightly different), and (2) since some instructions are presented by long and complex descriptions though appearing only once among all variations, they do not pay off the effort for preparing the corresponding rules (e.g., STLEX, VLLDM, and LDAEX only appear in M33). Thus, we aim to seek a set of appropriate candidates to obtain an *optimal trade-off*. The very high-level strategy is:

> *The importance of an instruction i is measured by the sum of TF·IDF scores of NP-Phrases in i. Select k instructions that maximise the sum divided by k.*

To be more specific, for a list of k chosen candidates, we use $\varphi(k)$ to measure the efficiency of the selection strategy over all instructions in six variations. The greater $\varphi(k)$, the better selected candidates. Let I is the set of all n instructions:

$$I = \{i_1, i_2, \ldots, i_n\}$$

where an instruction i consists of a set T_i including w NP-Terms:

$$T_i = \{\langle t_1, f_1 \rangle, \langle t_2, f_2 \rangle, \ldots, \langle t_w, f_w \rangle\}$$

where t_j is the jth NP-Term, and f_j is the frequency of t_j in i. Let $p(t_j)$ is the proportional occurrence of t_j over all NP-Terms in I, the importance of i over I is defined as:

$$m_i = \sum_{j=1}^{w} p(t_j) \cdot f_j$$

Let M is the sorted set (descending) of all m:

$$M = sorted(m_1, m_2, \ldots, m_{n-1}, m_n)$$

Let M_q is the qth value of M, k is the number of expected candidates, $\varphi(k)$ is then defined as:

$$\varphi(k) = \frac{1}{k} \sum_{q=1}^{k} M_q$$

Now, given k, this strategy can effectively obtain an optimal trade-off by taking the first k candidates in M to make $\varphi(k)$ as large as possible. Obeying to this strategy, 692 instructions are selected. After combining similar NP-Phrases as conditional terms, 228 selected NP-Phrases become a set of left-hand side (LHS) candidates, which is further utilised as the input of the rules preparation process.

4.3   Translation Rules Preparation

A semantics interpretation rule translates a left-hand side (LHS) – an NP-Phrase, to a right-hand side (RHS) – a Java code statement. Note that, the LHS candidates, which are automatically selected by the strategy presented in Sect. 4.2, are classified into 2 categories: NP-Phrase LHS (e.g., *"first and second operand"*) and Context-Based LHS (e.g., *"multiply $\square_2$ in $\square_1$"*). Additionally, a conditional LHS can be used to combine LHSes carrying similar semantics (e.g., *"halfword data"* and *"halfword value"*: ⟨*halfword data* | *halfword value*⟩). The RHSes are systematically prepared by a flow depicted in Fig. 4, including 5 following steps:

1. The set of LHS candidates (C) is sorted (descending) by their frequency.
2. The highest frequency LHS $c \in C$ is completed as a rule $r : c \rightarrow u$ (u is the corresponding RHS which is directly interpreted by manually checking the specifications consisting of c).
3. $R = R \cup \{r\}$; $C = C \setminus \{c\}$.
4. Rules in R then rewrite remaining LHSes in C. When a substitution to $\square$ in $c_i \in C$ occurs, the LHS of c_i is updated.
5. Continue until $C = \varnothing$, a set of rules R is completely obtained.

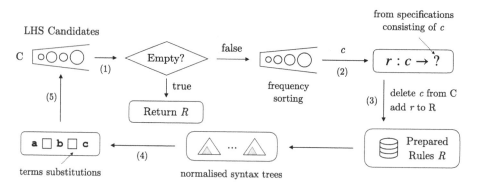

Fig. 4. Recursive rewriting rules preparation

In our experiment, 228 LHSes are automatically extracted. Thereafter, 228 rewriting rules are manually prepared, which is constituted of 208 NP-Phrase rules and 20 Context-Based rules. The number of rules containing conditional LHSes is 85.

4.4   A Comprehensive Example

Recall the sentence S in the Sect. 3. After sequentially normalising the syntax tree, a set of NP-Phrases is obtained $C = \{c_1, c_2, c_3\}$ where c_1 : *first and second operand*, c_2 : *two unsigned 32-bit integer*, and c_3 : *multiply $\square_2$ in $\square_1$*. Note that c_3 is obtained by substituting c_2 and c_1 in "*multiply two unsigned 32-bit integer in first and second operand*" by $\square_2$ and $\square_1$, respectively. Since in the syntax tree, lower-degree nodes are practically more likely to occur than higher ones, the frequency ordering is: $c_1 > c_2 > c_3$. Three rules are then prepared as follows:

1. Select c_1 and manually prepare r_1 : *first and second operand* $\rightarrow$ *rn, rm*. By r_1, c_2 is kept unchanged and c_3 is rewritten to $c_3' = $ *multiply $\square_2$ in rn,rm*.
2. Select c_2 and manually prepare r_2 : *two unsigned 32-bit integer* $\rightarrow$ *val($\square_3$), val($\square_4$)*. By r_2, c_3' is rewritten to c_3'' : *multiply val($\square_3$), val($\square_4$) in rn, rm*.
3. Select c_3 and manually prepare r_3 : *multiply (val$\square_3$), val($\square_4$) in rn, rm* $\rightarrow$ *mul(val(rn), val(rm))*. Expected rules r_1, r_2, r_3 are now completely obtained.

Note that, if some rules already exist, the preparation simply reuses them. Eventually, when all the rules are prepared, the formal semantics of S represented by a Java statement is interpreted in a bottom-up manner as illustrated in Fig. 5:

multiply two unsigned 32-bit integer in <u>first and second operand</u>
$\xrightarrow{r_1}$ multiply <u>two unsigned 32-bit integer</u> in rn, rm
$\xrightarrow{r_2}$ <u>multiply val($\square_3$), val($\square_4$) in rn, rm</u>
$\xrightarrow{r_3}$ mul(val(rn), val(rm))

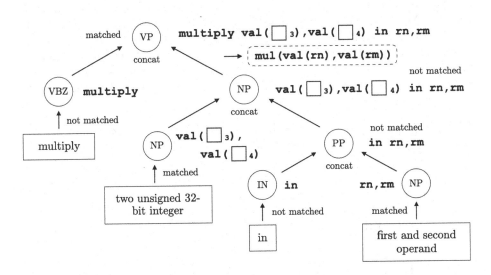

Fig. 5. Semantics interpretation in a bottom-up manner

5   Detecting Modified Flags

Detecting the modification of flags in instructions is practically not straightforward since (1) their descriptions are written totally in natural language and (2) synonyms are diversely used in the *flags-update* sections as indicated in Table 2.

Table 2. The diversity of *flags-update* descriptions

Flags-update descriptions	Implications
This instruction does not change the flags	
This instruction does not affect the condition code flags	Flags are unchanged
The V flag is left unmodified	
This instruction updates the N, Z, C and V flags according to the result	
Updates the N and Z flags according to the result. Does not affect the C and V flags	Modify specific flags

Figure 6 briefly illustrates our proposed solution. Instead of employing a rule-based approach, we adopt a sentences similarity analysis by utilising a well-known topic modeling method called Latent Dirichlet Allocation (LDA) [28]. To train an LDA model, each sentence is firstly represented as a frequency vector of words. Thereafter, when all parameters of the model have already been trained, a *topic* is considered as a distribution of words and a *sentence* is represented as a distribution of topics, which gives their classification based on a similarity measure. Note that, before training the model, each sentence from the *flags-update* section is sequentially normalised by *lemmatisation* and *words refinement* (previously mentioned in Sect. 3). After training (unsupervised) the model by all sentences (1), the topic distribution of a targeted sentence s and the model sentence $m =$ *"update affect set change modify"* are estimated as two dimensional

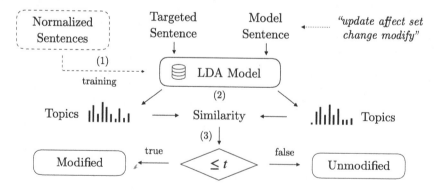

Fig. 6. Detecting modified flags by applying a sentences similarity analysis

real-number vectors $\vec{v_s}$, $\vec{v_m}$, respectively (2). In fact, m is reasonably chosen since it caries a strong meaning of *modified*. The similarity between s and m is then evaluated by calculating the Cosine similarity between $\vec{v_s}$ and $\vec{v_m}$ (3). If the result does not exceed a threshold t, s is considered as *modified*, otherwise *unmodified*. Our module utilises an LDA implementation provided in Sklearn [29], in which the hyperparameters are set: $\alpha = 0.1, \beta = 0.1, ntopics = 10, twords = 10, niters = 2000$, and $t = 0.85$. The major advantage behind this approach is that, when extending our method to other architectures, we solely need to redefine t and a new model sentence m, then the algorithm handles the rest. Comparing with rule-based approaches in case applied, this method is obviously more generalised.

6   Conformance Testing

To verify the correctness of a generated Java specification m, we first apply JDART [30] – a dynamic symbolic execution engine built on top of Java Path-finder [31], to generate a set of test inputs T which covers all feasible execution paths of m. The conformance testing is then performed by *comparing* the execution results of T by m and μVision [20] – a trusted binary emulator supporting numerous ARM variations. Figure 7 illustrates how our conformance testing works:

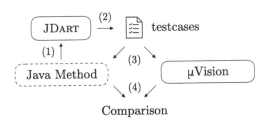

Fig. 7. Conformance testing on the generated Java methods

where: (1) applying dynamic symbolic execution on m, (2) all possible test cases T are generated by JDART, (3) each test case in T is simultaneously executed by m and μVision, and (4) two environments after execution are compared. Finally, if all the test results are passed, it is argued that the correctness of m is verified.

7   The CORANA Tool

The extraction of the formal semantics explicitly implies the generation of a dynamic symbolic execution tool for ARM Cortex-M. By utilising the extracted Java methods, a preliminary version of this tool called CORANA [15] has been developed, which is able to directly interpret and trace obfuscated IoT malware. CORANA takes the advantages of existing powerful engines: CAPSTONE [10] as the single-step disassembler, and Z3 Solver [32] as the back-end theorem prover.

7.1 CORANA Architecture

Figure 8 depicts a high-level architecture of CORANA, as well as describes how it precisely traces and incrementally reconstructs the Control Flow Graph (CFG) of obfuscated ARM binaries. CORANA is constituted of two main components: (I) An execution kernel provides the semantics framework and the path condition generation, and (II) A symbolic executor, which consists of the generated Java methods built on top of primitive functions, dynamically executes inputted instructions and generates the CFG based on the (in)feasibility of tracing results.

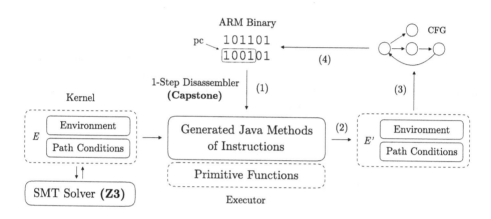

Fig. 8. CORANA architecture

(1) Single-step disassembles the ARM binary file starting from the program counter register *pc* to obtain an instruction *i*.
(2) Symbolically executes *i*, updates the environment and path conditions.
(3) The feasible paths are traced and tested in the depth-first manner, which incrementally generates the CFG.
(4) Repeats disassembling until reaching the end of the binary file or obtaining an unsupported instruction.

To be more specific, step (3) has two main objectives: exploring the destination of indirect jumps, and decrypting self-modifying codes (if exist). Although current IoT malware infrequently contains self-modification, indirect jumps widely occur.

7.2 Path Conditions Generation

By introducing the customised class `BitVec`, the environment transformations is implicitly *embedded* inside the `BitVec` operators. Since `BitVec` computations are totally declared within the primitive functions, the environment is updated without paying an extra effort. As a result, the path conditions are also generated. For instance, the instruction $i : subs\ r_1, r_0, r_1$ sets r_1 by $r_0 - r_1$ and updates flags based on the subtraction. Let r_1, r_0, z are BitVec values: $r_1 = \langle x; a \rangle$, $r_0 = \langle y; b \rangle$, $z = \langle z_0; c \rangle$, where x, y, z_0 are BitSet values and a, b, c are symbolic values. The semantics transitions on the register r_0, r_1 and the flag z are produced as follows:

$$r_0 : \langle y; b \rangle \xrightarrow{i} \langle y; b \rangle$$
$$r_1 : \langle x; a \rangle \xrightarrow{i} \langle y - x ; (bvsub \ b \ a) \rangle$$
$$z : \langle z_0; c \rangle \xrightarrow{i} \langle (y - x) == 0 ; (= (bvsub \ b \ a) \ 0) \rangle$$

where $bvsub$ is the subtraction operator supported in BitVector theory by default. When a conditional branch occurs at a conditional jump (e.g., *bne*) or a conditional data instruction (e.g., *addne*), CORANA symbolically executes this instruction and generates the new path conditions by taking the conjunctions of the pre-condition and the new suffixes at both *true* and *false* branches. For instance, if an instruction *bne* occurs right after the $i : subs \ r_1, r_0, r_1$, CORANA adds the suffix *ne* and its negation $\neg ne$ to the current path condition ψ (pre-condition) of *true* and *false* branches, respectively: $(\psi\_true = \psi \wedge (not \ (= (bvsub \ b \ a) \ 0)))$ and $(\psi\_false = \psi \wedge (= (bvsub \ b \ a) \ 0))$ to obtain the post-conditions (in ARM, the conditional suffix *ne* means checking $\neg z$). While executing another instruction i' that constitutes of more complex semantics (e.g., UMALL), the environment transforming and path condition generating become seemingly complicated, but since i' is a *combination* of primitive functions, it will be automatically handled.

8   Experiments

8.1   Semantics Extraction

Table 3 shows the experimental result of the semantics formalisation. Among 1039 collected ARM instructions over 6 variations, the Java specifications of 692 instructions (66.60%) are generated by using only 228 rewriting rules (approximately 0.33 rules are needed to cover an instruction) and 662 of them (63.72%) have passed the conformance testing. We observed two reasons causing failures:

Incorrect Modified Flags Detection. The presence of relatively complex synonym phrases such as *"left unmodified"* confuses our sentences similarity analysis. For instance, the descriptions of *flags-update* sections in the instruction RORS (Cortex-M0 and Cortex-M0+) contain a sentence *"The V flag is left unmodified"*, which is challenging to be correctly distinguished by our method at the moment.

Inappropriate Sentences Ordering in the Operation Sections. Our method interprets in a sentence-wise manner, which follows the ordering of sentences in the *operation* section. Thus, if the sentences have an inappropriate order, failures occur. For instance, the instruction STRB (Cortex-M7) is described as *"STRB instruction store a register value into memory. Unsigned byte, zero extend to 32 bits on loads"*, but the correct semantics should be defined in the opposite order: *"STRB instruction zero-extend an unsigned byte value then store into memory"*.

Table 3. The number of successfully extracted semantics over six variations

Variation	Collected	Selected	Generated	Verified
Cortex-M0	63	44 (69.84%)	44 (69.84%)	41 (65.08%)
Cortex-M0+	63	44 (69.84%)	44 (69.84%)	41 (65.08%)
Cortex-M3	129	80 (62.02%)	80 (62.02%)	74 (57.36%)
Cortex-M4	244	167 (68.44%)	167 (68.44%)	161 (65.98%)
Cortex-M7	261	178 (68.20%)	178 (68.20%)	172 (65.90%)
Cortex-M33	279	179 (64.16%)	179 (64.16%)	173 (62.00%)
Total	1039	692 (66.60%)	692 (66.60%)	662 (63.72%)

8.2 Dynamically Handling Jumps by CORANA

Since IoT malware rarely contains self-modifications, typical disassemblers (e.g., CAPSTONE and IDA) are able to correctly disassemble them. Nevertheless, when control structures matter, such as VM-aware malware [33] and trigger-based behaviour [34,35], revealing the hidden destination of jumps becomes immensely essential. We describe how CORANA traces obfuscated IoT malware by sampling 37c81e – a Linux.Mirai detected by VirusTotal [36], taken from VirusShare [37].

Conditional Jumps. Figure 9 illustrates the presence of a conditional jump beq at 0x37648, where CORANA adds eq and ¬eq to the path conditions of *true* and *false* branches, respectively. Afterwards, CORANA detects that these paths are both *feasible* by checking the satisfiability of their symbolic constraints. As a result, instead of solely executing the next instruction at 0x3764C, CORANA additionally traces the *true* branch at 0x37658, which presents a correct execution behaviour.

Dead Conditional Jumps. Figure 10 depicts an example of a conditional jump bne at 0x5C354, where CORANA detects that the path constraints of the *true* and the *false* branches are *unsatisfiable* and *satisfiable*, respectively. In other words, the *true* branch will be never executed and hence, this jump will be eventually ignored. This is regarded as the opaque predicates obfuscation in IoT malware.

Indirect Jumps. Figures 11 and 12 describe how CORANA dynamically handles indirect jumps. At 0x00058, when a conditional indirect jump bxeq lr occurs, CORANA adds eq and ¬eq to the path conditions of *true* and *false* branches, respectively. It then checks the feasibility of these branches and detects that both of them are *feasible*. Especially, by testing with a satisfiable instance at 0x00058, CORANA identifies a possible hidden destination stored in lr: 0x0004.

```
...
0x37640 cmp  r5,r1
0x37644 str  r2,[r3]
0x37648 beq  #0x37658
0x37658 ldr  r3,[pc,#0x138]
0x3765C ldr  r0,[sp,#8]
...
```

Fig. 9. Conditional jump handling

```
...
0x5C34C cmp  r4,r0
0x5C350 moveq r2,r5
0x5C354 bne  #0x5c330
0x5C358 b    #0x5c334
0x5C35C andeq lr,ip,ip,ror r0
...
```

Fig. 10. Dead jump detection

```
...
0x00050 ldr  r1,[r3,r2]
0x00054 cmp  r1,#0
0x00058 bxeq lr
0x0005C b    #0x60
0x00060 muleq fp,r4,pc
...
```

Fig. 11. Disassembled indirect jump

```
...
0x00050 ldr  r1,[r3,r2]
0x00054 cmp  r1,#0
0x00058 bxeq lr
0x00004 bl   #0x44
0x00044 ldr  r3,[pc,#0x14]
...
```

Fig. 12. Indirect jump traced by CORANA

9   Conclusion

Through our study, the feasibility of extracting the formal semantics from natural language specifications has been investigated. To demonstrate this possibility, we present an approach to systematically formalise the semantics of ARM Cortex-M instructions from their official specifications over six variations. Note that, instead of aiming to provide a fully automatic method, our ultimate goal is effectively reducing a large amount of tedious human effort on the implementation of tools relying on formal methods. Additionally, by instantiating the extracted semantics into a prepared framework, a dynamic symbolic execution tool for Cortex-M called CORANA has been preliminarily developed, which is able to correctly trace IoT malware under the presence of obfuscation techniques such as indirect jumps and opaque predicates. We expect our method can be practically extended to other architectures in the same manner without adding complicated modifications. Furthermore, we do hope our work enlightens the ability to leverage the benefits of adopting natural language processing and machine learning to automate rather simple but tedious tasks in the development of formal methods.

Future Directions. Beyond six previously mentioned variations, the proposed method is being considered to apply on other architectures such as MIPS and other ARM Cortex series. Contrary to Cortex-M, the specifications of

Cortex-A and Cortex-R are not structurally documented (only PDF files are available on ARM Developer Website at the moment). After parsing the structured data from these PDFs, our approach can be feasibly applied for them in the same manner.

Acknowledgments. We are grateful to Nao Hirokawa, Le Minh Nguyen, and the anonymous reviewers of FM'19 for their insightful feedback and invaluable comments. We sincerely thank Xuan Tung Vu, Thi Hai Yen Vuong, and Lam Hoang Yen Nguyen for their constructive discussions, as well as Thu Trang Hoang for her sharp comments on some grammatical issues. This study is partially supported by JSPS KAKENHI Grant-in-Aid for Scientific Research (B) 19H04083.

References

1. King, J.C.: Symbolic execution and program testing. Commun. ACM **19**(7), 385–394 (1976)
2. Thakur, A., et al.: Directed proof generation for machine code. In: Tayssir, T., Byron, C., Paul, J. (eds.) CAV 2010. LNCS, vol. 6174, pp. 288–305. Springer, Heidelberg (2010). https://doi.org/10.1007/978-3-642-14295-6_27
3. Desclaux, F.: MIASM: Framework de reverse engineering. In: Actes du SSTIC (2012)
4. Cha, S.K., Avgerinos, T., Rebert, A., Brumley, D.: Unleashing MAYHEM on binary code. In: IEEE S and P 2012, pp. 380–394 (2012)
5. Anthony, R.: Methods for binary symbolic execution. In: Ph.D. Dissertation, Stanford University (December 2014)
6. Bonfante, G., Fernandez, J., Marion, J.Y., Rouxel, B., Sabatier, F., Thierry, A.: CODISASM: medium scale concatic disassembly of self-modifying binaries with overlapping instructions. In: CCS 2015, pp. 745–756 (2015)
7. Hai, N.M., Ogawa, M., Tho, Q.T.: Obfuscation code localization based on CFG generation of malware. In: Garcia-Alfaro, J., Kranakis, E., Bonfante, G. (eds.) FPS 2015. LNCS, vol. 9482, pp. 229–247. Springer, Cham (2016). https://doi.org/10.1007/978-3-319-30303-1_14
8. Shoshitaishvili, Y., et al.: (State of) the art of war: offensive techniques in binary analysis. In: IEEE S and P 2016, pp. 138–157 (2016)
9. Nethercote, N., Seward, J.: VALGRIND: a framework for heavyweight dynamic binary instrumentation. In: ACM PLDI 2007, pp. 89–100 (2007)
10. CAPSTONE Engine. http://capstone-engine.org. Accessed 9 July 2019
11. IDA. https://hex-rays.com/products/ida. Accessed 9 July 2019
12. Krishnamoorthy, N., Debray, S., Fligg, K.: Static detection of disassembly errors. In: IEEE WCRE 2009, pp. 259–268 (2009)
13. Dasgupta, S., Park, D., Kasampalis, T., Adve, V.S., Rosu, G.: A complete formal semantics of x86-64 user-level instruction set architecture. In: ACM PLDI 2019, pp. 1133–1148 (2019)
14. ARM Developer. https://developer.arm.com. Accessed 9 July 2019
15. The CORANA TOOL. https://anhvvcs.github.io/corana. Accessed 9 July 2019
16. Robeer, M., Lucassen, G., van der Werf, J.M.E., Dalpiaz, F., Brinkkemper, S.: Automated extraction of conceptual models from user stories via NLP. In: IEEE RE 2016, pp. 196–205 (2016)
17. Yue, T., Briand, L.C., Labiche, Y.: aToucan: an automated framework to derive UML analysis models from use case models. ACM TOSEM **24**(3), 13:1–13:52 (2015)

18. Heule, S., Schkufza, E., Sharma, R., Aiken, A.: Stratified synthesis: automatically learning the x86-64 instruction set. In: ACM PLDI 2016, pp. 237–250 (2016)
19. Schkufza, E., Sharma, R., Aiken, A.: Stochastic superoptimization. In: ASPLOS 2013, pp. 305–316 (2013)
20. μVision. http://keil.com/mdk5/uvision. Accessed 9 July 2019
21. Yen, N.L.H.: Automatic extraction of x86 formal semantics from its natural language description. In: Master's Thesis, School of Information Science, JAIST (March 2018)
22. Anh, V.V.: Formal semantics extraction from natural language specifications for ARM. In: Master's Thesis, School of Information Science, JAIST (December 2018)
23. Bonfante, G., Marion, J.Y., Reynaud-Plantey, D.: A computability perspective on self-modifying programs. In: SEFM 2009, pp. 231–239 (2009)
24. Degenbaev, U.: Formal specification of the x86 instruction set architecture. In: Ph.D. Dissertation, Universitat des Saarlandes (February 2012)
25. Aceto, L., Fokkink, W., Verhoef, C.: Structural operational semantics. Handbook of Process Algebra, pp. 197–292 (2001)
26. Loper, E., Bird, S.: NLTK: the natural language toolkit. In: ACL (2004)
27. Robertson, S.: Understanding inverse document frequency: on theoretical arguments for IDF. J. Documentation **60**(5), 503–520 (2004)
28. Blei, D.M., Ng, A.Y., Jordan, M.I.: Latent Dirichlet allocation. J. Mach. Learn. Res. **3**, 993–1022 (2003)
29. Pedregosa, F., et al.: Scikit-learn: machine learning in Python. J. Mach. Learn. Res. **12**, 2825–2830 (2011)
30. Luckow, K., et al.: JDART: a dynamic symbolic analysis framework. In: Chechik, M., Raskin, J.-F. (eds.) TACAS 2016. LNCS, vol. 9636, pp. 442–459. Springer, Heidelberg (2016). https://doi.org/10.1007/978-3-662-49674-9_26
31. Visser, W., Havelund, K., Brat, G., Park, S., Lerda, F.: Model checking programs. Autom. Softw. Eng. **10**(2), 203–232 (2003)
32. de Moura, L., Bjørner, N.: Z3: an efficient SMT solver. In: Ramakrishnan, C.R., Rehof, J. (eds.) TACAS 2008. LNCS, vol. 4963, pp. 337–340. Springer, Heidelberg (2008). https://doi.org/10.1007/978-3-540-78800-3_24
33. Kirat, D., Vigna, G., Kruegel, C.: BAREBOX: efficient malware analysis on bare-metal. In: ACSAC 2011, pp. 403–412 (2011)
34. Brumley, D., Hartwig, C., Liang, Z., Newsome, J., Song, D., Yin, H.: Automatically identifying trigger-based behavior in malware. In: Wenke L., Cliff W., David D. (eds.) Botnet Detection 2008, ADIS, vol. 36, pp. 65–88. Springer, Heidelberg (2008). https://doi.org/10.1007/978-0-387-68768-14
35. Fleck, D., Tokhtabayev, A., Alarif, A., Stavrou, A., Nykodym, T.: PyTrigger: a system to trigger & extract user-activated malware behavior. In: AERES 2013, pp. 92–101 (2013)
36. Virus Total. https://www.virustotal.com. Accessed 9 July 2019
37. Virus Share. https://virusshare.com. Accessed 9 July 2019

GOSPEL—Providing OCaml
with a Formal Specification Language

Arthur Charguéraud[1], Jean-Christophe Filliâtre[2], Cláudio Lourenço[2],
and Mário Pereira[3(✉)]

[1] Inria Nancy - Grand Est, Strasbourg, France
[2] Inria Saclay - Île de France, Palaiseau, France
[3] NOVA LINCS & DI, FCT, Universidade Nova de Lisboa, Lisbon, Portugal
mjp.pereira@fct.unl.pt

Abstract. This paper introduces GOSPEL, a behavioral specification
language for OCaml. It is designed to enable modular verification of data
structures and algorithms. GOSPEL is a contract-based, strongly typed
language, with a formal semantics defined by means of translation into
Separation Logic. Compared with writing specifications directly in Separation Logic, GOSPEL provides a high-level syntax that greatly improves
conciseness and makes it accessible to programmers with no familiarity
with Separation Logic. Although GOSPEL has been developed for specifying OCaml code, we believe that many aspects of its design could
apply to other programming languages. This paper presents the design
and semantics of GOSPEL, and reports on its application for the development of a formally verified library of general-purpose OCaml data
structures.

1 Introduction

Functional programming languages are particularly suited for producing formally
verified code. For example, the formally verified C compiler CompCert [26] is
written in the applicative subset common to OCaml and Coq [35]. As another
example, the verified microkernel seL4 [21] features components that are written
and verified in Haskell, and then translated into C. The main reason for this
adequacy is that most functional language constructs directly map to logical
counterparts. In Coq, purely functional programs may be directly viewed as
logical definitions. Thus, writing specifications for a purely functional program
simply amounts to stating a lemma relating input and output values.

Functional programming is not, however, limited to purely applicative programming. The use of effectful features such as arrays and mutable records is
necessary to implement efficient data structures and algorithms. For example,
OCaml allows writing clean and concise code for functional and imperative data
structures and algorithms. The OCaml language (excluding its object-oriented

---

This research was partly supported by the French National Research Organization
(project VOCAL ANR-15-CE25-008).

© Springer Nature Switzerland AG 2019
M. H. ter Beek et al. (Eds.): FM 2019, LNCS 11800, pp. 484–501, 2019.
https://doi.org/10.1007/978-3-030-30942-8_29

features) provides a straightforward semantics for its constructs that facilitates the verification process, compared with other languages that pervasively use more complex features such as dynamic dispatch or inheritance. Thus, programming in an effectful functional language such as OCaml can be an interesting route to producing verified, relatively efficient code.

Unlike purely functional code that may be mapped directly to logical definitions, effectful code needs additional infrastructure to write specifications. Indeed, one needs means of describing the scope and the nature of side effects. For each function, it is necessary to specify what part of the mutable state it may access, modify, create, and destroy. Prior work has proposed Separation Logic [32] for reasoning about imperative programs, including those featuring nontrivial manipulations of the mutable state. Although it is very expressive, Separation Logic suffers from two downsides that, we believe, limit its wide adoption. First, Separation Logic specifications are fairly verbose in practice. Second, its standard presentation often appears fairly technical.

In this work, we present GOSPEL, a specification language for OCaml interfaces whose semantics is defined in terms of Separation Logic. Compared with Separation Logic, GOSPEL greatly improves conciseness and accessibility. The GOSPEL acronym stands for "Generic Ocaml SPEcification Language". In particular, the word "Generic" underlines the fact that this specification language is not tied to a specific verification tool, but rather intended to be used for different purposes, such as verification, testing, or even informal documentation.

GOSPEL fits in the tradition of other behavioral specification languages [15] such as SPARK [3], JML [23], or ACSL [1]. In contrast with these languages, GOSPEL features permissions as in Separation Logic. Unlike other tools based on Separation Logic, such as VeriFast [17] or Viper [27], GOSPEL implicitly associates permissions with data types, thereby significantly improving concision.

The contributions of this paper are as follows. First, we introduce GOSPEL through examples (Sect. 2). Second, we propose a formal semantics by means of a translation into Separation Logic (Sect. 3). Third, we report on an implementation of GOSPEL and its application to the verification of an OCaml library (Sect. 4). We finish by discussing related (Sect. 5) and future work (Sect. 6).

2 An Overview of GOSPEL

2.1 Basic Operations on a Mutable Queue

We first present a GOSPEL specification for a mutable queue data structure. This specification covers operations exposed by an OCaml interface for mutable queues, independently of any specific implementation (which could be based, e.g., on doubly-linked lists, ring buffer, etc.). In OCaml, an abstract interface is described in an .mli file. Within such a file, the GOSPEL specifications appear in comments that begin with the @ symbol. Such comments are ignored by the OCaml compiler, but can be parsed and processed by a verification tool.

The abstract data type `'a t` represents a parameterized queue storing elements of type `'a`. To begin with, we provide a `mutable model` annotation for this type, to associate a *model field* called `view` with every value of type `'a t`.

```
type 'a t
(*@ mutable model view: 'a seq *)
```

For a given queue q, the projection `q.view` describes the mathematical sequence of elements stored in the queue. The model field `view` has type `'a seq`, which corresponds to the type of purely applicative sequences (*i.e.*, logical sequences). This type `'a seq` is defined in the GOSPEL standard library.

The `view` field is tagged `mutable` to account for the fact that the sequence of elements stored in a queue may change over time. In general, a given OCaml type may feature several model fields, each being mutable or not. For example, a fixed-capacity mutable queue would typically feature an immutable model field describing its maximum capacity, in addition to the mutable model field describing the sequence of its elements.

Let us now declare and specify the operation that pushes an element of type `'a` to the front of a queue of type `'a t`. We first write the OCaml type, then the GOSPEL specification.

```
val push: 'a -> 'a t -> unit
(*@ push v q
    modifies q
    ensures  q.view = v :: old q.view *)
```

The GOSPEL specification first names the two arguments with v and q. Next, it indicates that q might be mutated during a call to `push` using the `modifies` clause. Last, it features an `ensures` clause describing the postcondition. In this case, it asserts that the updated sequence of elements in the queue (`q.view`) consists of the sequence of elements before the call (`old q.view`), extended with the new element v added at the front. We choose arbitrarily to model the queue with insertion at the front of the sequence and removal at the end of it.

Here, the type of q features a single mutable model field, thus the clause `modifies q` is equivalent to `modifies q.view`. In the case of a type featuring several model fields, the `modifies` clause may include only a subset of the fields, capturing the fact that the fields which are not mentioned remain unchanged.

We next present three more functions from the interface of mutable queues to illustrate other features of GOSPEL. The function `pop` extracts an element from the back of a nonempty queue. This function includes a `requires` clause, to express the precondition asserting that the queue must be nonempty. Note that the first line of the GOSPEL specification assigns the name v to the return value, so that it may be referred to in the postcondition.

```
val pop: 'a t -> 'a
(*@ v = pop q
    requires q.view <> empty
    modifies q
    ensures  old q.view = q.view ++ v :: nil *)
```

The next function, `is_empty`, tests whether a queue is empty. This function does not mutate the queue, as reflected by the absence of a `modifies` clause.

```
val is_empty: 'a t -> bool
(*@ b = is_empty q
    ensures b <-> q.view = empty *)
```

The function `create` below, returns a fresh queue data structure, with empty contents. It is specified as follows.

```
val create: unit -> 'a t
(*@ q = create ()
    ensures q.view = empty *)
```

The fact that the function returns a queue distinct from any previously-allocated queue is implicit because the type `'a t` has been declared with a mutable model field. This design choice is motivated by the fact that writing a function that returns a non-fresh, mutable data structure is considered bad practice in OCaml.

2.2 Destructive and Nondestructive Operations

We next explain how to specify functions that involve more than one mutable value, by presenting three concatenation functions for mutable queues. The first function, called `in_place_concat`, receives two (distinct) queues as arguments. It migrates the contents of the first queue to the front of the second queue, then clears the contents of the first queue.

```
val in_place_concat: 'a t -> 'a t -> unit
(*@ concat q1 q2
    modifies q1, q2
    ensures  q1.view = empty
    ensures  q2.view = old q1.view ++ old q2.view *)
```

The clause `modifies q1, q2` asserts that both queues are updated. The first `ensures` clause describes the new state of q1 as the empty sequence. The second `ensures` clause describes the new state of q2 as the result of the concatenation of the two original sequences. The queues q1 and q2 are implicitly required to be separated, that is, not aliased. This implicit assumption is another deliberate design choice of GOSPEL. Only arguments that are read-only may be aliased.

The next function, specified below, is similar to `in_place_concat`, with the difference that it destroys the queue q1 instead of emptying it. In other words, after the call, q1 cannot be used anymore. To describe the loss of the queue q1, we replace `modifies q1` with the clause `consumes q1`, as shown below.

```
val in_place_destructive_concat: 'a t -> 'a t -> unit
(*@ concat q1 q2
    consumes q1  modifies q2
    ensures  q2.view = old q1.view ++ old q2.view *)
```

Note that the ensures clause may only refer to old q1.view, but not to
q1.view, since there is no "valid new state" for q1. Note also that an implementation of in_place_destructive_concat is allowed to performed arbitrary
side effects on q1, which gets discarded after the call.

The third function, called nondestructive_concat, takes two queues as
read-only arguments, and produces a fresh queue with the concatenation of the
contents of the two input queues. It is specified as follows.

```
val nondestructive_concat: 'a t -> 'a t -> 'a t
(*@ q3 = concat q1 q2
    ensures q3.view = q1.view ++ q2.view *)
```

The absence of a modifies clause implicitly asserts that the arguments are read-
only. When arguments are read-only, it is safe to alias them. For example, a call
of the form non_destructive_concat q q is allowed.

2.3   Higher-Order Functions

In OCaml, iterations over containers are typically implemented using a higher-
order function. For example, map f q produces a fresh queue whose elements are
the pointwise applications of the function f to the elements from the queue q.
Although Separation Logic does support the general case where the function f
may perform arbitrary side effects [5,6], we cover in this paper only the simpler
case where f is a pure function. In this case, we specify map as follows:

```
val map: ('a -> 'b) -> 'a t -> 'b t
(*@ r = map f q
    ensures length r.view = length q.view
    ensures forall i. 0 <= i < length q.view ->
                      r.view[x] = f q.view[i] *)
```

We leave the generalization to the general case of an effectful f to future work.

2.4   Ghost Variables

Ghost arguments and ghost return values may be used to specify a function.
In GOSPEL syntax, ghost entities appear within square brackets in a function
prototype. Consider the example below of a function that computes the largest
power of two no greater than a given integer n. The ghost return value k is a
convenient means of specifying that r is a power of two.

```
val power_2_below: int -> int
(*@ r, [k: integer] = power_2_below n
    requires n >= 1
    ensures  r = power 2 k && r <= n < 2 * r *)
```

In GOSPEL, the type of a ghost variable must be provided. Here, k is declared
with type integer, which denotes the GOSPEL type of mathematical integers.

2.5   Non-visible Side Effects

We next discuss operations that may modify the internal state of a data structure without modifying the value of the model fields. Simply pretending that the operation does not modify the structure would be unsound, as it would suggest that the structure is read-only.

As a first example, consider a random generator module. Type `rand_state` represents the internal state of a generator (*i.e.*, the current value of the seed). We do not wish to expose the implementation of the state, yet we wish to expose in the specification the fact that there exists an internal state. To achieve this, we associate with the type `rand_state` a mutable model field of type `unit`.

```
type rand_state
(*@ mutable model internal: unit *)
```

The function `random_init` takes as argument a seed and produces a fresh random generator state of type `rand_state`. This function needs no specification.

```
val random_init: int -> rand_state
```

The function `random_int` takes as argument a state s and an integer m, and returns a pseudo-random integer smaller than m. This function performs a side effect on the state s, hence the clause `modifies s`.

```
val random_int: rand_state -> int -> int
(*@ n = random_int s m
    requires m > 0  modifies s  ensures  0 <= n < m *)
```

Similarly to the mutable queue example, here the clause `modifies s` is equivalent to `modifies s.internal`. Even though there is only one possible value of type `unit` for this model field, the fact that it is declared in the `modifies` clause is important because it specifies that internal side effects may be performed. If no `modifies` clause were provided, the argument s would be implicitly assumed to be read-only: no side effects would be allowed, even internally.

As a second and more challenging example, consider a union-find data structure that maintains disjoint sets using a pointer-based representation of a reverse forest. Each element of a union-find is represented as a value of type `elem`, an abstract data type. Operations on a union-find instance perform path compression, hence they modify the internal state of the structure, even when the exposed logical state remains unchanged. To account for the fact that an operation performed on a given element does not alter only this element, but potentially all the elements in the union-find instance, we do not associate any mutable model field to the type `elem`. Instead, we introduce a ghost type named `uf_instance`, meant to describe the state of all the elements in the union-find instance.

The ghost type `uf_instance` features three mutable model fields: a domain `dom` describing the set of elements in the current instance; a logical map `rep` that binds each element to its representative; and a model field called `internal` of type `unit`. The latter is used to describe the internal side effects performed by operations such as `find` which exposes no visible side effect.

We impose several well-formedness invariants on these fields. These invariants must hold for any value of type `uf_instance`, before and after any call to a function from the interface. The GOSPEL specification is as follows.

```
type elem
(*@ type uf_instance *)
(*@ mutable model dom: elem set *)
(*@ mutable model rep: elem -> elem *)
(*@ mutable model internal: unit *)
(*@ invariant forall x. mem x dom -> mem (rep x) dom *)
(*@ invariant forall x. mem x dom -> rep (rep x) = rep x *)
```

The function `equiv` below takes as arguments a ghost value `uf` of type `uf_instance` and two elements of type `elem` from the domain of the instance. It tests whether the two elements belong to the same class. The `modifies` `uf.internal` clause indicates that side effects may be performed on the internal state.

```
val equiv: elem -> elem -> bool
(*@ b = equiv [uf: uf_instance] e1 e2
    requires mem e1 uf.dom && mem e2 uf.dom
    modifies uf.internal
    ensures  b <-> uf.rep e1 = uf.rep e2 *)
```

The ghost function `create_instance`, specified below, enables creating a fresh and empty instance of union-find.

```
(*@ val create_instance: unit -> uf_instance *)
(*@ uf = create_instance ()
    ensures uf.dom = {} *)
```

The function `make` populates a given instance with a fresh element. It updates the union-find instance to reflect the extension of its domain with the new element.

```
val make: unit -> elem
(*@ e = make [uf: uf_instance] ()
    modifies uf
    ensures  not (mem e (old uf.dom))
    ensures  uf.dom = union (old uf.dom) (singleton e)
    ensures  uf.rep = update (old uf.rep) e e *)
```

The full union-find interface may be found in the VOCaL library—see Sect. 4.

3   Semantics

In this section, we provide a formal semantics for GOSPEL, by means of a translation into Separation Logic. First, we describe the source and the target languages of this translation. Then, we illustrate the translation using functions from Sect. 2. Finally, we present the general translation scheme.

3.1 General Form of GOSPEL Specifications

In the following, we say that a type is *represented* if its type declaration features one or more mutable model fields. By extension, we say that an argument of a function is represented if its type is represented. Otherwise, we say that it is *non-represented*. The terminology reflects the fact that such arguments get, or do not get, represented as predicates in Separation Logic.

A GOSPEL specification consists of the prototype of a function, followed with a list of clauses. The prototype indicates the name of the function, of its arguments, and of its return values, including ghost arguments and ghost return values within square brackets. The list of clauses include one or several of each `requires`, `modifies`, `consumes`, and `ensures`.

The `requires` clause consists of a proposition that may refer to the model fields of represented arguments and to the names of the non-represented arguments, whether they are ghost or not. The `consumes` clause consists of a list of represented arguments. The `modifies` clause consists of a list of mutable model fields associated with represented arguments. These arguments must not already appear in the `consumes` clause. If the name of an argument appears in the `modifies` clause without a projection, it is interpreted as the list of mutable model fields associated with that arguments. The `ensures` clauses consists of a proposition that may refer to the same entities as the `requires` clause, minus the arguments listed in the `consumes` clause, plus the "old versions" of the fields listed in the `modifies` clause. If several `requires` (or `ensures`) clauses appear, they can be grouped using a conjunction. If several `consumes` (or `modifies`) clause appear, they can be grouped by appending their contents.

3.2 Basics of Separation Logic

A heap predicate, written H, is a predicate over the mutable state. If `Heap` denotes the type of states, and `Prop` denotes the type of logical propositions, then a heap predicate H has type `Heap` $\rightarrow$ `Prop`.

We write $^{\mathsf{HOARE}}\{H\}\, t\, \{\lambda x.H'\}$ to denote a Hoare triple [16] for a program term t, with precondition H and postcondition H', where x binds a name for the result produced by t. In total correctness, the interpretation of such a triple is: "if the predicate H holds in the input state, then the evaluation of t terminates and produces a value x for which the predicate H' holds in the output state".

In Hoare logic, H and H' describe the whole input and output states. In contrast, Separation Logic allows specifying only the fragment of the state that is relevant to the execution of the program. For this purpose, Separation Logic introduces the *star* operator: $H_1 \star H_2$ is a predicate that holds of a state that can be decomposed in two disjoint parts, one satisfying H_1 and another satisfying H_2.

A Separation Logic triple is written $^{\mathsf{SL}}\{H\}\, t\, \{\lambda x.H'\}$. Such a triple is equivalent to the proposition: $\forall H''.\ ^{\mathsf{HOARE}}\{H \star H''\}\, t\, \{\lambda x.H' \star H''\}$. This equivalence captures the property that a Separation Logic triple is a specification that remains valid in any extension of the input heap over which the program t operates, with the guarantee that the evaluation of t does not alter values from this extension. This property is reflected by the *frame rule*:

$$\frac{{}^{\text{SL}}\{H\}\, t\, \{\lambda x.\, H'\}}{{}^{\text{SL}}\{H \star H''\}\, t\, \{\lambda x.\, H' \star H''\}} \; \text{FRAME}$$

Three other Separation Logic operators are useful for the purpose of this paper. The construct $[P]$ lifts a pure proposition P of type Prop into a predicate of type Heap $\rightarrow$ Prop. The construct $\exists x.\, H$ denotes existential quantification over heap predicates. The construct $\text{RO}(H)$ denotes a read-only version of the predicate H. Read-only predicates are provided by an extension of Separation Logic [8] that features the following read-only-frame rule:

$$\frac{{}^{\text{SL}}\{H \star \text{RO}(H'')\}\, t\, \{\lambda x.\, H'\}}{{}^{\text{SL}}\{H \star H''\}\, t\, \{\lambda x.\, H' \star H''\}} \; \text{RO-FRAME}$$

We employ read-only predicates in our translation from GOSPEL to Separation Logic. All that the reader needs to know is that read-only predicates are duplicatable at will; that they may be discarded at any time (*i.e.*, they are not linear, but affine); and that they may appear only in preconditions, not in postconditions.

3.3   Example Translations of Mutable Queue Specifications

Before presenting the general translation scheme from GOSPEL to Separation Logic, we first provide concrete instances of the translation for some queue operations from Sect. 2. Recall that a queue has a single mutable model field of type 'a seq. As a consequence, we introduce a *representation predicate* R of type loc $\rightarrow$ 'a seq $\rightarrow$ Heap $\rightarrow$ Prop. Here, loc denotes the type of pointers in Separation Logic. Concretely, given a pointer q and a sequence L, the heap predicate R q L captures the piece of state and invariants involved in the memory representation of a mutable queue at address q with contents L.

The translations for the specifications of the queue operations push, pop, is_empty, and create are shown below.[1] Thereafter, variable v has type 'a, variable L type 'a seq, variable b type bool, and variable u type unit.

$\{\, (\text{R q L})\, \}$ push v q $\{\, \lambda u.\, \exists L'.\, (\text{R q L'}) \star [L' = v::L]\, \}$

$\{\, (\text{R q L}) \star [L \neq \text{nil}]\, \}$ pop q $\{\, \lambda v.\, \exists L'.\, (\text{R q L'}) \star [L = L' \mathbin{+\mkern-8mu+} v::\text{nil}]\, \}$

$\{\, \text{RO}\,(\text{R q L})\, \}$ is_empty q $\{\, \lambda b.\, [b = \text{true} \leftrightarrow L = \text{nil}]\, \}$

$\{\, [\text{True}]\, \}$ create u $\{\, \lambda q.\, \exists L.\, (\text{R q L}) \star [L = \text{nil}]\, \}$

Observe in particular how the function is_empty takes as argument a read-only description of the queue. The corresponding triple implicitly asserts that the queue is returned unmodified in the postcondition.

We next present the translation for the three variants of the concatenation function from Sect. 2.

---

[1] The triples are obtained by applying our translation scheme; more concise triples may be derived for push and create by eliminating existential quantifiers.

```
{ (R q1 L1) * (R q2 L2) }
in_place_concat q1 q2
{ λu. ∃L1' L2'. (R q1 L1') * (R q2 L2') * [L1' = nil ∧ L2' = L1++L2] }
```

```
{ (R q1 L1) * (R q2 L2) }
in_place_destructive_concat q1 q2
{ λu. ∃L2'. (R q2 L2') * [L2' = L1++L2] }
```

```
{ RO (R q1 L1) * RO (R q2 L2) }
nondestructive_concat q1 q2
{ λq3. ∃L3'. (R q3 L3') * [L3' = L1++L2] }
```

The first function clears the contents of its first argument, whereas the second function consumes the representation predicate for its first argument. The third function differs in that it takes two read-only arguments.

3.4   General Translation Scheme from GOSPEL to Separation Logic

To keep things concise and readable, we define the general pattern of the translation by considering an example that captures the various possible cases. Without lack of generality, let us assume a type t with two mutable model fields called left and right. Their types are irrelevant to what follows.

```
type t
(*@ mutable model left:  type1 *)
(*@ mutable model right: type2 *)
```

To specify values of type t in Separation Logic, we introduce a representation predicate, called T, of type loc → type1 → type2 → Heap → Prop. Concretely, a heap predicate of the form T p X Y describes the memory layout of a structure of type t at address p, whose left and right model fields are described by X and Y, respectively. If invariants were attached to the data type t (as illustrated for example in Sect. 2.5), predicate T would capture those invariants.

Consider now the function f specified as follows, for the sake of example.

```
val f: t -> t -> t -> t -> int -> t * t * int
(*@ p5, p6, m, [h: integer] = f p1 p2 p3 p4 n [g: integer]
    requires P
    modifies p1, p2.left   consumes p3
    ensures  Q *)
```

Argument p1 appears in the modifies clause, thus both its model fields may be modified; argument p2 has only its left field modifiable, thus its right model field remains unchanged; argument p3 is declared in the consumes clause, thus it gets lost during the call; argument p4 is not declared in the modifies clause, thus it is read-only.

Additionally, a precondition P and a postcondition Q are declared. The precondition P is a logical proposition that may refer to the left and right projections of p1, p2, p3, and p4, as well as to n and g. The postcondition Q may refer to the same set of variables, minus p3 (which is consumed), plus the old values of the modified model fields (namely, old p1.left, old p1.right, and old p2.left), plus the left and right projections of the return values p5 and p6, as well as to the return values m and h.

We translate the specification for the function f into the following Separation Logic statement, where the variables Xi (resp. Yi) refer to the values of the left (resp. right) model fields.

$\forall$p1 p2 p3 p4 n g X1 Y1 X2 Y2 X3 Y3 X4 Y4,
{ [P] $\star$ (T p1 X1 Y1) $\star$ (T p2 X2 Y2) $\star$ (T p3 X3 Y3) $\star$ RO (T p4 X4 Y4) }
f p1 p2 p3 p4 n
{ λ(p5,p6,m). $\exists$h X1' Y1' X2' X5' Y5' X6' Y6'. [Q] $\star$
               (T p1 X1' Y1') $\star$ (T p2 X2' Y2) $\star$ (T p5 X5' Y5') $\star$ (T p6 X6' Y6') }

Observe in particular how the postcondition first binds the return values, then quantifies existentially: (1) the ghost return value h, (2) the updated model fields associated with the represented arguments, and (3) the model fields associated with the represented return values. Observe also how the read-only predicate for p4 appears only in the precondition (as discussed in Sect. 3.2).

The above example illustrates the general scheme behind our translation. Two other minor aspects are worth mentioning. First, if an argument features an immutable model field, then we treat this field like a mutable model field not declared in the modifies clause. Second, for a polymorphic function, we need to quantify the appropriate type variables in the Separation Logic statement.

4   Implementation and Application

We next describe GOSPEL tools and applications: its parser, its type-checker, its mathematical library, its connection with verification tools, and its application to the specification and verification of a general-purpose library of data structures and algorithms.

Parsing and Type-Checking of GOSPEL Specifications. As explained in Sect. 2.1, GOSPEL specifications appear in comments in an OCaml interface file. The GOSPEL parser proceeds in two stages. First, the parser from the OCaml compiler is invoked to parse the structure of the file. It produces a parse tree that features, in particular, type and prototype declarations. The GOSPEL comments are stored as *attributes* to these definitions, with payloads represented as strings.[2] Second, a dedicated GOSPEL parser is used to parse the attributes that correspond to GOSPEL specifications, and to integrate them with the corresponding OCaml declarations. The use of two distinct parsers is a deliberate choice, aimed at making the framework easily maintainable in the face of evolution of either the OCaml syntax or the GOSPEL syntax.

---

[2] We patched the parser from the OCaml compiler so as to process comments of the form (*@ ...*) as if they were written as OCaml attributes of the form [@@gospel "..."]. The OCaml parser already processes documentation comments in this way.

After being parsed, GOSPEL specifications are type checked. We developed a type checker independent from that of the OCaml compiler to handle, *e.g.*, types associated with model fields. Our type checker performs ML-style type inference, allowing the user to quantify variables without providing their types, and to apply polymorphic functions without explicit instantiations. The GOSPEL type-checker verifies in particular the well-formedness of the specification clauses. For example, it checks that only legitimate variables appear in the `requires`, `consumes`, `modifies`, and `ensures` clauses (as explained in Sect. 3.1).

The GOSPEL Library. The purpose of the GOSPEL library is twofold. First, the library provides mathematical theories to be used in specifications, covering unbounded integers, sequences, sets, bags, and maps. For example, a queue is specified using a sequence, a priority queue is specified using a bag, etc. Second, the library provides logical models for built-in OCaml data types, such as machine integers, lists, arrays, and strings. The GOSPEL library takes the form of regular OCaml .mli files, containing only GOSPEL declarations. These libraries may contain symbols that are left uninterpreted. For instance, the library currently does not give any definition for what a "set" is. For the moment, it appears more practical to leave a collection of mathematical symbols abstract and to provide, for each verification tool, a mapping from these abstract symbols towards their corresponding realization (*e.g.*, in SMT theories or Coq mathematical theories).

Program Verification w.r.t. GOSPEL Specifications. In Sect. 3, we have provided GOSPEL with a formal semantics. The existence of this semantics means that GOSPEL specifications make sense independently of which verification tool is used to carry out the proofs. Thus, for a given program, we are free to use the most suitable verification tool. For example, if the code is purely functional, it makes sense to verify it directly using Coq. If the code features advanced pointer manipulations, then CFML [5,6], with its interactive proofs in Separation Logic, would be the tool of choice. If mutability is limited, then the Why3 tool [13] provides convenient support for automated proofs, by leveraging SMT provers. Thanks to the existence of the common specification language GOSPEL, it is even possible to build modular proofs where different components are verified using distinct tools.

Implementing a verification tool to handle GOSPEL specifications can be achieved in several ways. In the case of Why3, the GOSPEL specification is translated into Why3's specification language; the source code is written in WhyML, proved to satisfy the specification, then extracted into OCaml code.[3] In the case of CFML, the GOSPEL specification is translated into CFML's specification language; the OCaml source to be verified is parsed by CFML and converted into a *characteristic formula* expressed in higher-order logic; one then proves that the characteristic formula entails the desired specification.

---

[3] More details about the Why3 workflow may be found in Pereira's PhD thesis [30].

Application to the VOCaL Library. A collection of general-purpose data structures and algorithms is an essential ingredient for the successful construction of a large-scale software. When it comes to formal verification, it thus makes sense to start with the verification of such libraries. This observation has motivated efforts in the deductive verification community to verify programming libraries [11,31]. OCaml is a programming language that lends itself particularly well to formal verification, in particular thanks to its simple semantics. Moreover, OCaml is used to implement several tools whose soundness is critical, *e.g.*, proof assistants [35], static analysis tools [9,20], SMT solvers [2]. Thus, there would be strong benefits in developing a verified library for OCaml.

The recent VOCaL project precisely aims at developing a "mechanically Verified *OCa*ml Library" of efficient general-purpose data structures and algorithms. The public GitHub repository of the project already includes several OCaml modules, such as resizable arrays, priority queues, and union-find.[4] These libraries have been verified using Why3 or CFML. As a contribution of the present work, we provide GOSPEL specifications for all these verified libraries.

The VOCaL library may be looked at in different ways, depending on one's needs. First, one could choose to ignore all the GOSPEL annotations and simply be interested in using VOCaL as a *trustworthy* library of OCaml code. Second, one could be interested in reading GOSPEL annotations from the VOCaL libraries in order to *unambiguously* understand what is the semantics of the operations that it provides. Third, one might be interested in producing a *formally verified* OCaml program, by leveraging the VOCaL libraries. In this case, the user would engage in verification proofs and would reason about interactions with the VOCaL libraries by exploiting their GOSPEL specifications.

5   Related Work

In recent years, a number of behavioral specification languages [15] have been proposed for various state-of-the-art programming languages, such as JML for Java [23] and ACSL for C [1]. The SPARK [3] programming and specification language is a subset of the Ada language targeting verification. Several verification tools, such as VeriFast [17], Viper [27], Why3 [13], and Dafny [24], come with their own specification languages.

Three important aspects influence the design of specification languages. The first aspect is whether specifications are meant to be executable or not. For example, JML and SPARK specifications are executable [22]. ACSL specifications are not executable, but contains an executable subset called E-ACSL [33]. Requiring executable specifications severely constrains expressivity. For this reason, we chose to not impose executable specifications in GOSPEL. A second aspect is whether specifications are meant to be entirely discharged by automated tools. For example, Dafny emits proof obligations for SMT solvers (Z3, in particular). Targeting fully automated proofs may impose a certain presentation style for

---

[4] https://github.com/vocal-project/vocal.

specifications. GOSPEL is agnostic to the verification tool. Both SMT-based and interactive-proofs-based approaches can be used.

The third aspect of a specification language is how it treats the *frame problem*, and how it describes the *separation* of arguments and the *freshness* of return values. Specifications languages such as SPARK, JML, or ACSL require explicit freshness assertions. Dafny [24] exploits Dynamic Frames [19], an approach that is flexible but that leads to relatively verbose specifications [18]. Chalice [25] leverages Implicit Dynamic Frames [34]. This approach, partially inspired by Separation Logic, aims at providing first-order tool support. Its assertions are interpreted with non-separating conjunctions, like in Separation Logic, yet with explicit accessibility predicates. For more details on Dynamic Frames technique, we refer to Kassios' tutorial [18], and to an article by Parkinson and Summers [29] which formally explores the relationship between Implicit Dynamic Frames and Separation Logic. In contrast, GOSPEL is firmly grounded on Separation Logic: accessibility predicates, disjointness and freshness assertions are always implicit.

Why3 [13] is a deductive verification tool with a dedicated programming and specification language called WhyML. A number of aspects of GOSPEL are based on WhyML. There are, however, important differences. A first important difference is that the semantics of GOSPEL is given by means of Separation Logic, whereas WhyML is given a more traditional semantics in terms of weakest-precondition calculus and first-order logic [12]. A second difference is that GOSPEL targets a mainstream programming language used in the development of large and complex software systems. Although WhyML has many features similar to OCaml, it remains a verification-oriented language, with many OCaml features missing. In contrast, GOSPEL intends to introduce, lightly and incrementally, ideas of formal methods into the OCaml community. For instance, GOSPEL may be used in large projects to specify and verify a number of critical core components, while leaving other components unverified.

Compared with writing specifications directly in Separation Logic, the use of GOSPEL significantly improves the practical experience of writing and reading specifications. The example from Sect. 3.4 gives an idea of how much more concise a GOSPEL specification might be relative to its Separation Logic counterpart. We next summarize the key design choices that we have made w.r.t. plain Separation Logic.

In Separation Logic, one has the possibility to introduce several representation predicates for a same type. This possibility may be useful in rare cases for specifying advanced access patterns in complex data structures. In practice, the vast majority of data structures are naturally specified with a unique representation predicate. In GOSPEL, we leave the representation predicates implicit, and instead refer directly to the names of the model fields. (We could add support for multiple representation predicates in the future, while keeping the current behavior as a default). Furthermore, in GOSPEL, unlike in Separation Logic, we do not need to provide names for the model fields that are not explicitly involved in the specification.

Another difference is that in Separation Logic, permissions (representation predicates) have to be provided even for read accesses. Yet, it would serve little purpose to provide a function with a pointer if not providing at least the corresponding read permission. Thus, we have chosen for GOSPEL a design that assumes implicit read permissions for all the arguments provided to a function. For arguments that require write access, Separation Logic specifications require to repeat the permission both in the precondition and the postcondition. One exception is in the rare case where an argument is consumed. In GOSPEL, we only require a list of the names of the modified arguments to appear either in the `modifies` clause or in the `consumes` clause. This design avoids repetitions and significantly reduces the clutter.

VeriFast [17] is a verification tool targeting C and Java programs. It features a specification language based on Separation Logic. As recently demonstrated [4], it is possible to encode model fields in VeriFast, although with some overheads. On the contrary, GOSPEL provides builtin support for representation predicates. Thus, it can leverage dedicated features for manipulating and referring to model fields, and indicating which ones may be modified. This design enables important gains in conciseness.

Viper [27] is an intermediate verification language, which features front-ends for several programming languages, including Java, Python, and Rust. Viper's specification language is based on permissions, which are explicitly manipulated both in contracts and in the code. To indicate that a method has access to a field, the specification must include an explicit *accessibility predicate*. Moreover, to distinguish between read and write accesses, Viper relies on *fractional permissions*: only a full permission (*i.e.*, a fraction equal to 1) enables write access. In contrast, GOSPEL design makes read-access permissions implicit for all fields, and write-access permissions are simply listed in the `modifies` clause. Furthermore, GOSPEL design takes advantage of read-only permissions, whose benefits over fractional permissions are discussed in details in the paper that introduces read-only permissions [8] (§1.3 and §5.4).

6   Conclusion and Future Work

We have presented GOSPEL, a behavioral specification language for OCaml. So far, a subset of OCaml was identified for which GOSPEL specifications can be translated to Separation Logic. We expect to extend GOSPEL to a larger subset of OCaml in the future, to support other constructs such as signature constraints (`with type`) and inclusion (`include`). GOSPEL can also be extended in other directions, *e.g.*, to allow specifying the asymptotic cost of each function [7,14,28].

We have developed verification frameworks on top of GOSPEL and successfully applied them to the verification of an algorithms and data structures library. So far, these frameworks are based on Why3 and CFML. It would be interesting to also try and target the Viper ecosystem [27]. One could hope for a straightforward translation from GOSPEL to Viper, which is based on Separation Logic.

There are several other interesting directions for future work for GOSPEL. It could be extended to include invariants for, *e.g.*, loops. It could be exploited for runtime assertion checking, by identifying an executable subset. It could be integrated with a property-based testing framework, for example leveraging the qcheck [10] tool that generates random test values satisfying given invariants.

Acknowledgments. We are grateful to X. Leroy, F. Pottier, A. Guéneau, and A. Paskevich for discussions and comments during the preparation of this paper.

References

1. Baudin, P., Filliâtre, J.C., Marché, C., Monate, B., Moy, Y.,Prevosto, V.: ACSL: ANSI/ISO C Specification Language, version 1.4 (2009). http://frama-c.cea.fr/acsl.html
2. Bobot, F., Conchon, S., Contejean, E., Iguernelala, M., Lescuyer, S., Mebsout, A.: The Alt-Ergo automated theorem prover (2008). http://alt-ergo.lri.fr/
3. Carré, B., Garnsworthy, J.: SPARK–an annotated Ada subset for safety-critical programming. In: Proceedings of the Conference on TRI-Ada 1990, New York, NY, USA, pp. 392–402. ACM Press (1990)
4. Cauderlier, R., Sighireanu, M.: A verified implementation of the bounded list container. In: Beyer, D., Huisman, M. (eds.) TACAS 2018. LNCS, vol. 10805, pp. 172–189. Springer, Cham (2018). https://doi.org/10.1007/978-3-319-89960-2_10
5. Charguéraud, A.: Characteristic Formulae for Mechanized Program Verification. PhD thesis, Université Paris (2010). http://www.chargueraud.org/arthur/research/2010/thesis/
6. Charguéraud, A.: Characteristic formulae for the verification of imperative programs. In: Manuel, M.T., Chakravarty, Hu, Z., Danvy, O. (eds.) Proceeding of the 16th ACM SIGPLAN International Conference on Functional Programming (ICFP), Tokyo, Japan, pp. 418–430. ACM, September 2011
7. Charguéraud, A., Pottier, F.: Verifying the correctness and amortized complexity of a union-find implementation in separation logic with time credits. J. Autom. Reasoning (2017)
8. Charguéraud, A., Pottier, F.: Temporary read-only permissions for separation logic. In: Yang, H. (ed.) ESOP 2017. LNCS, vol. 10201, pp. 260–286. Springer, Heidelberg (2017). https://doi.org/10.1007/978-3-662-54434-1_10
9. Cousot, P.,Cousot, R., Feret, J., Mauborgne, L., Miné, A., Monniaux, D., Rival, X.: The ASTRÉE analyzer. In: ESOP, number 3444 in Lecture Notes in Computer Science, pp. 21–30 (2005)
10. Cruanes, S., Grinberg, R., Deplaix, J.-P., Midtgaard, J.: Qcheck (2019). https://github.com/c-cube/qcheck
11. de Gouw, S., de Boer, F.S., Bubel, R., Hähnle, R., Rot, J., Steinhöfel, D.: Verifying OpenJDK's sort method for generic collections. J. Autom. Reasoning (2017)
12. Filliâtre, J.-C.: One logic to use them all. In: Bonacina, M.P. (ed.) CADE 2013. LNCS (LNAI), vol. 7898, pp. 1–20. Springer, Heidelberg (2013). https://doi.org/10.1007/978-3-642-38574-2_1
13. Filliâtre, J.-C., Paskevich, A.: Why3 — where programs meet provers. In: Felleisen, M., Gardner, P. (eds.) ESOP 2013. LNCS, vol. 7792, pp. 125–128. Springer, Heidelberg (2013). https://doi.org/10.1007/978-3-642-37036-6_8
14. Guéneau, A., Charguéraud, A., Pottier, F.: A fistful of dollars: formalizing asymptotic complexity claims via deductive program verification. In: Ahmed, A. (ed.) ESOP 2018. LNCS, vol. 10801, pp. 533–560. Springer, Cham (2018). https://doi.org/10.1007/978-3-319-89884-1_19

15. Hatcliff, J., Leavens, G.T., Leino, K.R.M., Müller, P., Parkinson, M.: Behavioral interface specification languages. ACM Comput. Surv. **44**(3), 16:1–16:58 (2012)
16. Hoare, C.A.R.: An axiomatic basis for computer programming. Commun. ACM **12**(10), 576–580, 583 (1969)
17. Jacobs, B., Smans, J., Philippaerts, P., Vogels, F., Penninckx, W., Piessens, F.: VeriFast: a powerful, sound, predictable, fast verifier for C and java. In: Bobaru, M., Havelund, K., Holzmann, G.J., Joshi, R. (eds.) NFM 2011. LNCS, vol. 6617, pp. 41–55. Springer, Heidelberg (2011). https://doi.org/10.1007/978-3-642-20398-5_4
18. Kassios, I.T.: Dynamic frames and automated verification (2011). Tutorial for the 2nd COST Action IC0701 Training School, Limerick 6/11, Ireland
19. Kassios, I.T.: The dynamic frames theory. Formal Aspects Comput. **23**(3), 267–288 (2011)
20. Kirchner, F., Kosmatov, N., Prevosto, V., Signoles, J., Yakobowski, B.: Frama-c: a software analysis perspective. Formal Aspects Comput. **27**(3), 573–609 (2015)
21. Klein, G., et al.: seL4: formal verification of an OS kernel. Commun. ACM **53**(6), 107–115 (2010)
22. Kosmatov, N., Marché, C., Moy, Y., Signoles, J.: Static versus dynamic verification in Why3, Frama-C and SPARK 2014. In: Margaria, T., Steffen, B. (eds.) ISoLA 2016. LNCS, vol. 9952, pp. 461–478. Springer, Cham (2016). https://doi.org/10.1007/978-3-319-47166-2_32
23. Leavens, G.T., Baker, A.L., Ruby, C.: Preliminary design of JML: A behavioral interface specification language for Java. Technical Report 98–06i, Iowa State University (2000)
24. Leino, K.R.M.: Dafny: an automatic program verifier for functional correctness. In: Clarke, E.M., Voronkov, A. (eds.) LPAR 2010. LNCS (LNAI), vol. 6355, pp. 348–370. Springer, Heidelberg (2010). https://doi.org/10.1007/978-3-642-17511-4_20
25. Leino, K.R.M., Müller, P.: A basis for verifying multi-threaded programs. In: Castagna, G. (ed.) ESOP 2009. LNCS, vol. 5502, pp. 378–393. Springer, Heidelberg (2009). https://doi.org/10.1007/978-3-642-00590-9_27
26. Leroy, X.: A formally verified compiler back-end. J. Autom. Reasoning **43**(4), 363–446 (2009)
27. Müller, P., Schwerhoff, M., Summers, A.J.: Viper: a verification infrastructure for permission-based reasoning. In: Jobstmann, B., Leino, K.R.M. (eds.) VMCAI 2016. LNCS, vol. 9583, pp. 41–62. Springer, Heidelberg (2016). https://doi.org/10.1007/978-3-662-49122-5_2
28. Mével, G., Jourdan, J.-H., Pottier, F.: Time credits and time receipts in iris. In: Caires, L. (ed.) ESOP 2019. LNCS, vol. 11423, pp. 3–29. Springer, Cham (2019). https://doi.org/10.1007/978-3-030-17184-1_1
29. Parkinson, M.J., Summers, A.J.: The relationship between separation logic and implicit dynamic frames. Log. Methods Comput. Sci. **8**(3) (2012)
30. Pereira, M.J.P.: Tools and Techniques for the Verification of Modular Stateful Code. PhD thesis, Université Paris-Saclay (2018)
31. Polikarpova, N., Tschannen, J., Furia, C.A.: A fully verified container library. Formal Aspects Comput. **30**(5), 495–523 (2018)
32. Reynolds, J.C.: Separation logic: a logic for shared mutable data structures. In: 17th Annual IEEE Symposium on Logic in Computer Science. IEEE (2002)

33. Signoles, J., Kosmatov, N., Vorobyov, K.: E-ACSL, a Runtime Verification Tool for Safety and Security of C Programs (Tool Paper). In: International Workshop on Competitions, Usability, Benchmarks, Evaluation, and Standardisation for Runtime Verification Tools (RV-CuBES 2017), September 2017

34. Smans, J., Jacobs, B., Piessens, F.: Implicit dynamic frames: combining dynamic frames and separation logic. In: Drossopoulou, S. (ed.) ECOOP 2009. LNCS, vol. 5653, pp. 148–172. Springer, Heidelberg (2009). https://doi.org/10.1007/978-3-642-03013-0_8

35. The Coq Development Team. The Coq Proof Assistant Reference Manual - Version V8.9 (2019). http://coq.inria.fr

Unification in Matching Logic

Andrei Arusoaie[(✉)] and Dorel Lucanu

Alexandru Ioan Cuza University, Iaşi, Romania
{arusoaie.andrei,dlucanu}@info.uaic.ro

Abstract. Matching Logic is a framework for specifying programming language semantics and reasoning about programs. Its formulas are called *patterns* and are built with variables, symbols, connectives and quantifiers. A pattern is a combination of structural components (term patterns), which must be matched, and constraints (predicate patterns), which must be satisfied. Dealing with more than one structural component in a pattern could be cumbersome because it involves multiple matching operations. A source for getting patterns with many structural components is the conjunction of patterns. Here, we propose a method that uses a syntactic unification algorithm to transform conjunctions of structural patterns into equivalent patterns having only one structural component and some additional constraints. We prove the soundness and the completeness of our approach, and we provide sound strategies to generate certificates for the equivalences.

Keywords: Matching Logic · Syntactic term unification · Semantic unification · Certification

1 Introduction

Matching Logic [21] (hereafter shorthanded as ML) is a novel framework which is currently used for specifying programming languages semantics [8,11,12,19] and for reasoning about programs [5,10,14,22,24–26]. Inspired by the domain of programming language semantics, the logic uses the operational semantics of a programming language for both *execution* and *verification* of programs.

The ML formulas, called *patterns*, are built using variables, symbols, connectives and quantifiers. A pattern is evaluated to the set of values that it *matches*. ML makes no distinction between function and predicate symbols. Not having this distinction increases the expressivity of the language, where various notions (e.g., *function*, *equality*) can be specified using symbols that satisfy some axioms.

For example, the next ML formula φ_1 matches over the set of lists that start at address $p + 2$ and store the sequence a, which contains an even number on the third position:

$$\varphi_1 \triangleq \mathtt{list}(p + 2, a) \wedge \exists k.(select\ a\ 3) = 2 * k$$

Basically, the novelty in ML w.r.t. first-order logics is that *structural* components are formulas as well. In our example, φ_1 is a conjunction of a structural component $\mathtt{list}(p + 2, a)$ – a list that starts at address $p + 2$ and stores a sequence

© Springer Nature Switzerland AG 2019
M. H. ter Beek et al. (Eds.): FM 2019, LNCS 11800, pp. 502–518, 2019.
https://doi.org/10.1007/978-3-030-30942-8_30

implemented as an array (encoded using the *select-store* axioms), – together with the constraint $\exists k.(select\ a\ 3) = 2 * k$. In ML, the structural components are called *term patterns*, whereas the constraints are called *predicate patterns*.

The conjunction of two ML patterns may produce a new pattern with more than one structural component, as shown in this example:

$$\underbrace{\overbrace{\texttt{list}(p+2,a)}^{\text{structure}} \wedge \overbrace{\exists k.(select\ a\ 3) = 2 * k}^{\text{constraint}}}_{\varphi_1} \wedge \underbrace{\overbrace{\texttt{list}(q,(store\ b\ 3\ y))}^{\text{structure}} \wedge \overbrace{y > 2}^{\text{constraint}}}_{\varphi_2}$$

Finding a set of elements that matches the conjunction $\varphi_1 \wedge \varphi_2$ is not necessarily an easy task, mainly because both structural components ($\texttt{list}(p+2,a)$) and ($\texttt{list}(q,(store\ b\ 3\ y))$) need to be matched simultaneously. In theory, this set is the *intersection* of the sets matched by φ_1 and φ_2 independently.

In practice, dealing with multiple structural components in one formula is cumbersome. The issue comes from the fact that reasoning in ML could generate conjunctions with many structural components. Therefore, an implementation of a ML prover needs to handle conjunctions in an efficient way.

Let us explain what produces large conjunctions. ML is designed to reason about programs using the semantics of programming languages. Inspired from Rewriting Logic, where programming language semantics can be encoded using rewrite rules, in ML the semantics can be encoded by axioms of the form $t_1 \wedge \phi_1 \rightarrow \bullet(t_2 \wedge \phi_2)$ (as shown in [1]). Here, t_1 and t_2 are term patterns that are meant to match over program states, and ϕ_1 and ϕ_2 are predicate patterns, i.e., constraints over program states. Also, $\bullet$ is a special symbol called *one-path next* [9], which is interpreted as a transition relation. The formula $\bullet(t_2 \wedge \phi_2)$ matches all states that have at least one next state (w.r.t. the transition relation) that is matched by $t_2 \wedge \phi_2$. The implication $t_1 \wedge \phi_1 \rightarrow \bullet(t_2 \wedge \phi_2)$ can be understood as an inclusion of the set that matches $t_1 \wedge \phi_1$ into the set that matches $\bullet(t_2 \wedge \phi_2)$.

These axioms are used to perform symbolic execution of programs, which is essential in a ML prover implementation: it increases the level of automation. A symbolic execution is a sequence of symbolic steps $t \wedge \phi \Rightarrow t' \wedge \phi'$, where the next symbolic configuration $t' \wedge \phi'$ is obtained from the current one $t \wedge \phi$ by applying a semantics axiom $t_1 \wedge \phi_1 \rightarrow \bullet(t_2 \wedge \phi_2)$. Now, $t' \wedge \phi'$ is computed such that only the states matched by $(t_1 \wedge \phi_1) \wedge (t \wedge \phi) \wedge \bullet(t_2 \wedge \phi_2)$ transition to states matched by $t' \wedge \phi'$. It is easy to see now where the conjunction of patterns occurs: it is used to compute the symbolic successors of $t \wedge \phi$. The size of the conjunction grows when repeatedly applying symbolic steps, and thus, it becomes unfeasible to compute symbolic successors from conjunctions that have multiple structural components. Computing a convenient form $t' \wedge \phi'$ for conjunctions also enables the use of SMT solvers (e.g., Z3 [18], CVC4 [7]): if such a solver finds that ϕ' is not satisfiable, then the current symbolic execution path is unfeasible, and thus, it is not worth exploring it.

In ML, the semantics of $\varphi_1 \wedge \varphi_2$ is the largest set of elements matching φ_1 and φ_2. The conjunction of two patterns can be seen as a *semantic* unification of the patterns [21]. So, it makes sense to relate syntactic unification to this notion of semantic unification. Let us consider the particular case when $\varphi_i \triangleq t_i \wedge \phi_i$, where t_i is a term pattern and ϕ_i is a predicate pattern, $i \in \{1, 2\}$. Using ML reasoning, the conjunction $\varphi_1 \wedge \varphi_2$ can be written in an equivalent form $t_1 \wedge (t_1 = t_2) \wedge \phi_1 \wedge \phi_2$. The predicate patterns expressing the equality of two term patterns $t_1 = t_2$ cannot be handled, e.g., by SMT solvers. Thus, it would be convenient to reduce it to an equivalent predicate $\phi^{t_1=t_2}$, which can be handled by SMT solvers. Also, it would be worth producing a proof certificate of the equivalence of $t_1 = t_2$ and $\phi^{t_1=t_2}$.

At a first sight, unification of terms seems to be useful here. If σ is the most general unifier of t_1 and t_2, seen as first-order terms, then $t_1\sigma = t_2\sigma$. Unifiers are substitutions, and substitutions can be expressed as ML formulas [4].

In our list example, $\text{list}(p + 2, a)$ and $\text{list}(q, (\text{store } b \; 3 \; y))$ have $\sigma = \{q \mapsto p + 2, a \mapsto (\text{store } b \; 3 \; y)\}$ as the most general unifier. Translating σ to a formula results in $\phi^\sigma \triangleq (q = p + 2) \wedge (a = (\text{store } b \; 3 \; y))$. The equality $\text{list}(p + 2, a) = \text{list}(q, (\text{store } b \; 3 \; y))$ is now equivalent to ϕ^σ. Moreover, the semantic unifier $\varphi_1 \wedge \varphi_2$ is equivalent to $\text{list}(p + 2, a) \wedge \phi^\sigma \wedge (\exists k.(\text{select } a \; 3) = 2 * k) \wedge y > 0$. This form is now convenient since it has only one structural component and a constraint manageable by an SMT solver.

Contributions. First, we show that $\phi^{t_1=t_2}$ is equivalent to a ϕ^σ obtained using the most general unifier σ of t_1 and t_2, whenever it exists. The proof of the equivalence between $t_1 = t_2$ and ϕ^σ is not trivial and, surprisingly, it depends on the algorithm used to compute the most general unifier. Our proof uses the syntactic unification algorithm proposed by Martelli and Montanari [16].

Second, we find the minimal requirements, expressed as ML axiom patterns, such that this algorithm is *sound* for semantic unification in ML:

1. if the syntactic unification algorithm returns a most general unifier σ for term patterns t_1 and t_2, then t_1 and t_2 are unifiable in ML as well, and σ can be encoded as a predicate pattern.
2. if the algorithm returns that t_1 and t_2 are not syntactically unifiable, then they are not unifiable in ML.

Third, the completeness of syntactic unification is proved in a similar manner:

1. if t_1 and t_2 are unifiable in ML, then t_1 and t_2 are syntactically unifiable;
2. if t_1 and t_2 are not unifiable in ML, then they are not syntactically unifiable.

Finally, a *provableness* property of the Martelli-Montanari unification algorithm is shown: we provide a sound strategy to generate a proof certificate of the equivalence between $t_1 \wedge t_2$ and $t_1 \wedge \phi^\sigma$, where σ is the most general unifier of t_1 and t_2. This proof uses the original ML proof system [21].

Paper Organisation. In Sect. 2.1 we recall the main notions and notations from the unification theory that we use in this paper. Section 2.2 includes a concise presentation of Matching Logic based on [21]. In Sect. 3 we show how to find the convenient representation of our semantic unifiers using the syntactic unification algorithm. We prove that the unification algorithm is sound and complete for semantic unification. In Sect. 4 we describe sound strategies for generating proofs that can be further used to generate proof certificates. The last section includes concluding remarks and how this research can be continued.

2 Preliminaries

2.1 Syntactic Unification

We recall from [6] the notions related to unification that we use in this paper, and from [16], the algorithm for finding the *most general unifier* (mgu).

Let S be a set of sorts. We consider a (countably) infinite S-indexed set of variables *Var* and a *signature* Σ, i.e., a (finite or countably infinite) S-indexed set of function symbols. To keep the presentation simple (as in [6]), we do not explicitly show the sorts of the terms unless they cannot be inferred from context. This does not restrict in any way the generality and will be handled properly when transferring all these to Matching Logic.

We use the typical conventions and notations. Letters x, y, z denote variables and c, f, g denote function symbols. Terms are either variables $x \in Var$, or compound terms of the form $f(t_1, \ldots, t_n)$. If $n = 0$ then $f()$ is a constant denoted by f. The membership $f \in \Sigma_{s_1 \ldots s_n, s}$ means that f has *arity* $s_1 \ldots s_n, s$, that is, for each $i = \overline{1, n}$, the subterm t_i has sort s_i, and $f(t_1, \ldots, t_n)$ has sort s.

By $var(t)$ we denote the set of variables occurring in t. For substitutions we use σ, η, θ or directly a set of bindings $\{x_1 \mapsto t_1, \ldots, x_n \mapsto t_n\}$. Substitutions σ are extended to terms in the usual way; $t\sigma$ denotes the term obtained after applying σ to variables in t. The *composition* of substitutions σ and η is denoted as $\sigma\eta$. Two substitutions σ and η are equal, written $\sigma = \eta$, if they are extensionally equal: $x\sigma = x\eta$ for every x. We say that σ is *more general* than η, written as $\sigma \leq \eta$, if there is θ such that $\sigma\theta = \eta$.

Definition 1 (Unifier, Most General Unifier). *A substitution σ is a unifier of two terms t and t' if $t\sigma = t'\sigma$. A unifier σ is a most general unifier (mgu) if for every unifier σ' of t and t' we have $\sigma \leq \sigma'$.*

Example 1. If $t \triangleq f(g(x, c), y)$ and $t' \triangleq f(z, y')$ are terms then $\sigma = \{z \mapsto g(x, c), y \mapsto y'\}$ is a unifier of t and t': $t\sigma = f(g(x, c), y') = t'\sigma$.

Whenever there exists a unifier for two given terms we say that the terms are *syntactically unifiable.* In the particular context of syntactic unification, for every two syntactically unifiable terms there exists a most general unifier, which is unique up to a composition with a renaming substitution.

Delete:	$P \cup \{t \doteq t\} \Rightarrow P$
Decomposition:	$P \cup \{f(t_1, \ldots, t_n) \doteq f(t'_1, \ldots, t'_n)\} \Rightarrow P \cup \{t_1 \doteq t'_1, \ldots, t_n \doteq t'_n\}$
Orient:	$P \cup \{f(t_1, \ldots, t_n) \doteq x\} \Rightarrow P \cup \{x \doteq f(t_1, \ldots, t_n)\}$
Elimination:	$P \cup \{x \doteq t\} \Rightarrow P\{x \mapsto t\} \cup \{x \doteq t\}$ if $x \notin var(t), x \in var(P)$
Symbol clash:	$P \cup \{f(t_1, \ldots, t_n) \doteq g(t'_1, \ldots, t'_n)\} \Rightarrow \bot$
Occurs check:	$P \cup \{x \doteq f(t, \ldots, t)\} \Rightarrow \bot$, if $x \in var(f(t, \ldots, t))$

Fig. 1. Syntactic unification algorithm

Definition 2 (Unification problem, Solution, Solved form). *A unification problem P is either a set of pairs of terms $\{t_1 \doteq t'_1, \ldots, t_n \doteq t'_n\}$ or a special symbol $\bot$. A substitution σ is a* solution *of a $P = \{t_1 \doteq t'_1, \ldots, t_n \doteq t'_n\}$ if σ is a unifier of t_i and t'_i, for every $i = \overline{1, n}$. A unification problem P is in* solved form *if $P = \bot$ or $P = \{x_1 \doteq t'_1, \ldots, x_n \doteq t'_n\}$ with $x_i \notin var(t_j)$ for all $i, j = \overline{1, n}$.*

Let $unifiers(P) = \{\sigma \mid \sigma \text{ is a solution of } P\}$ denote the set of solutions of P. If $P = \bot$ then $unifiers(P) = \emptyset$. Each unification problem $P = \{x_1 \doteq t'_1, \ldots, x_n \doteq t'_n\}$ in solved form defines a solution $\sigma_P = \{x_1 \mapsto t'_1, \ldots, x_n \mapsto t'_n\}$.

A well-known algorithm for finding the mgu is presented in [16]. It consists of a set of transformations $P \Rightarrow P'$, where the relation $\Rightarrow$ is defined in Fig. 1.

Remark 1. If P is a unification problem then the following facts hold (cf. [6]):

1. *Progress*: If P is not in solved form, then there exists P' such that $P \Rightarrow P'$;
2. *Solution preservation*: If $P \Rightarrow P'$ then $unifiers(P) = unifiers(P')$;
3. *Termination*: There is no infinite sequence $P \Rightarrow P_1 \Rightarrow P_2 \Rightarrow \cdots$;
4. *Most general unifier*: If θ is a solution for P, then for any maximal sequence of transformations that starts with P and ends with P', either P' is $\bot$ or $\sigma_{P'} \le \theta$. There is no solution for P iff P' is $\bot$.

A direct consequence of Remark 1 is that the unification algorithm produces the mgu whenever it exists.

Example 2. Recall $t \triangleq f(g(x, c), y)$ and $t' \triangleq f(z, y')$ from Example 1. Consider the unification problem $P = \{t \doteq t'\}$. Using the unification algorithm we obtain:

$$
\begin{aligned}
P = \{t \doteq t'\} \triangleq \{f(g(x, c), y) \doteq f(z, y')\} &\Rightarrow \quad \textbf{(Decomposition)} \\
\{g(x, c) \doteq z, y \doteq y'\} &\Rightarrow \quad \textbf{(Orient)} \\
\{z \doteq g(x, c), y \doteq y'\} &\triangleq P'
\end{aligned}
$$

The obtained unification problem P' is in solved form; the corresponding substitution $\sigma_{P'} = \{z \mapsto g(x, c), y \mapsto y'\}$ is the most general unifier of t and t'.

$P \Rightarrow^* P'$ denotes that P' is obtained by applying zero or more rules from Fig. 1 to P. We use $P \Rightarrow^! P'$ to further denote that P' is in solved form.

2.2   Matching Logic

Matching Logic [21] started as a logic over a particular case of constrained terms [5,10,14,22–25], but now it is developed as a solid logical framework. We recall from [21] the definitions and notions that we use in the paper.

ML formulas are defined over a *many-sorted signature* (S, Σ), where Σ is a $S^* \times S$-indexed set of *symbols*. The formulas in ML are *patterns*:

Definition 3 (ML Formula). *A Σ-pattern φ_s of sort s is defined by:*
$$\varphi_s ::= x_s \mid f(\varphi_{s_1}, \ldots, \varphi_{s_n}) \mid \neg \varphi_s \mid \varphi_s \wedge \varphi_s \mid \exists x.\varphi_s$$
where s_i and s range over S, x_s ranges over the variables of sort s ($x_s \in Var_s$), f ranges over $\Sigma_{s_1 \ldots s_n, s}$, and x ranges over the set of variables (of any sort).

When sorts are not relevant or can be inferred from the context we drop the sort subscript (φ_s becomes φ). The derived patterns are defined as expected: $\top_s \triangleq \exists x.x$ (x of sort s), $\bot_s \triangleq \neg\top_s$[1], $\varphi_1 \vee \varphi_2 \triangleq \neg(\neg\varphi_1 \wedge \neg\varphi_2)$, $\varphi_1 \rightarrow \varphi_2 \triangleq \neg\varphi_1 \vee \varphi_2$, $\varphi_1 \leftrightarrow \varphi_2 \triangleq (\varphi_1 \rightarrow \varphi_2) \wedge (\varphi_2 \rightarrow \varphi_1)$.

Definition 4 (ML model). *An ML Σ-model M consist of:*
- *an S-sorted set M_s for each $s \in S$, the* carrier of sort s *of M;*
- *a function $f_M : M_{s_1} \times \cdots \times M_{s_n} \rightarrow \mathcal{P}(M_s)$ for each symbol $f \in \Sigma_{s_1 \ldots s_n, s}$ (note the use of the powerset $\mathcal{P}(M_s)$ as the co-domain).*

The functions f_M are extended to $f_M : \mathcal{P}(M_{s_1}) \times \cdots \times \mathcal{P}(M_{s_n}) \rightarrow \mathcal{P}(M_s)$ by setting $f_M(A_1, \ldots, A_n) = \bigcup\{f_M(a_1, \ldots, a_n) \mid a_i \in A_i, i = \overline{1,n}\}$.

The meaning of patterns is given by using variable *valuations* ρ as in first-order logic, but the result of the interpretation is a *set* of elements that the pattern "matches", similar to the worlds in modal logic.

Definition 5 (M-valuations). *If $\rho : Var \rightarrow M$ is a variable valuation and φ a pattern, then the extension $\overline{\rho}(\varphi)$ of ρ to patterns is inductively defined as follows:*
1. *$\overline{\rho}(x) = \{\rho(x)\}$;*
2. *$\overline{\rho}(f(\varphi_1, \ldots, \varphi_n)) = \bigcup\{f_M(v_1, \ldots, v_n) \mid v_i \in \overline{\rho}(\varphi_i), i = 1, \ldots, n\}$;*
3. *$\overline{\rho}(\neg\varphi) = M_s \setminus \overline{\rho}(\varphi)$, where the sort of φ is s;*
4. *$\overline{\rho}(\varphi_1 \wedge \varphi_2) = \overline{\rho}(\varphi_1) \cap \overline{\rho}(\varphi_2)$, where φ_1 and φ_2 have the same sort;*
5. *$\overline{\rho}(\exists x.\varphi) = \bigcup_{v \in M_s} \overline{\rho}[v/x](\varphi)$, where $x \in Var_s$ and $\overline{\rho}[v/x]$ is the valuation ρ' s.t. $\rho'(y) = \rho(y)$ for all $y \neq x$, and $\rho'(x) = v$.*

When a symbol is a constant c (case 2 in Definition 5) we have $\overline{\rho}(c) = c_M \subseteq M_s$. Additional constructs can be handled similarly (e.g. $\overline{\rho}(\varphi_1 \vee \varphi_2) = \overline{\rho}(\varphi_1) \cup \overline{\rho}(\varphi_2)$).

Example 3. Let *Nat* be a sort and Σ a signature which includes symbols $o \in \Sigma_{Nat}$ and $succ \in \Sigma_{Nat, Nat}$. Then, o, $succ(x)$, $o \vee \exists x.succ(x)$ are ML patterns.

A possible Σ-model M includes a set $M_{Nat} = \mathbb{N}$, a constant function o_M which evaluates to the singleton set $\{0\}$, and a function $succ_M : \mathbb{N} \rightarrow \mathcal{P}(\mathbb{N})$

---

[1] Note that $\bot$ is different from the (bold) symbol $\perp$ used in Sect. 3.

R1.	⊢ propositional tautologies:

P1. $\ \vdash \varphi \to (\varphi' \to \varphi)$
P2. $\ \vdash (\varphi \to (\varphi' \to \varphi'')) \to ((\varphi \to \varphi') \to (\varphi \to \varphi''))$
P3. $\ \vdash (\neg\varphi' \to \neg\varphi) \to (\varphi \to \varphi')$

R2.	Modus ponens: $\vdash \varphi_1$ and $\vdash \varphi_1 \to \varphi_2$ imply $\vdash \varphi_2$
R3.	$\vdash (\forall x.\varphi_1 \to \varphi_2) \to \varphi_1 \to (\forall x.\varphi_2)$, when x does not occur free in φ_1
R4.	Universal generalization: $\vdash \varphi$ implies $\vdash \forall x.\varphi$
R5.	Functional substitution: $\vdash (\forall x.\varphi) \wedge (\exists y.\varphi' = y) \to \varphi[\varphi'/x]$
R5′.	Functional variable: $\vdash \exists y.x = y$
R6.	Equality introduction: $\vdash \varphi = \varphi$
R7.	Equality elimination: $\vdash \varphi_1 = \varphi_2 \wedge \varphi[\varphi_1/x] \to \varphi[\varphi_2/x]$
R8.	$\vdash \forall x.x \in \varphi$ iff $\vdash \varphi$
R9.	$\vdash x \in y = (x = y)$ when $x, y \in Var$
R10.	$\vdash x \in \neg\varphi = \neg(x \in \varphi)$
R11.	$\vdash x \in \varphi_1 \wedge \varphi_2 = (x \in \varphi_1) \wedge (x \in \varphi_2)$
R12.	$\vdash (x \in \exists y.\varphi) = \exists y.(x \in \varphi)$, with x and y distinct
R13.	$\vdash x \in f(\varphi_1, .., \varphi_{i-1}, \varphi_i, \varphi_{i+1}, .., \varphi_n) = \exists y.(y \in \varphi_i \wedge f(\varphi_1, .., \varphi_{i-1}, y, \varphi_{i+1}, .., \varphi_n))$

Fig. 2. Sound and complete proof system of Matching Logic [21]

which returns a singleton set containing the successor of the given natural number. The pattern $succ(x)$ matches $\{1\}$ since $\overline{\rho}(succ(x)) = succ_M(\overline{\rho}(x)) = succ_M(\{\rho(x)\}) = succ_M(\{0\}) = \{1\}$, whenever $\rho(x) = 0$.

Here, the interpretations of the two symbols have singleton sets as results. This is not always the case. Let us enrich Σ with a new symbol $\leq \in \Sigma_{NatNat,Nat}$. We may choose the following interpretation for this symbol: $\leq_M : \mathbb{N} \times \mathbb{N} \to \mathcal{P}(\mathbb{N})$, where $\leq_M (x,y) = \mathbb{N}$ if x is less or equal than y, and $\leq_M (x,y) = \emptyset$ otherwise. The pattern $x \leq succ(x)$ matches $M_{Nat} = \mathbb{N}$, while $succ(x) \leq x$ matches $\emptyset$.

A model M *satisfies* φ_s, written $M \models \varphi_s$, if $M_s = \overline{\rho}(\varphi_s)$ for each $\rho : Var \to M$. A pattern φ is *valid* (written $\models \varphi$) iff $M \models \varphi$ for all M. In Example 3, $M \models o \vee \exists x.succ(x)$ since, for all $\rho : Var \to M$ we have $\overline{\rho}(o \vee \exists x.succ(x)) = M_{Nat}$.

A particular type of patterns are M-*predicates*. These are meant to capture the usual meaning of predicates, i.e., patterns that can be either true or false. A pattern φ_s is an M-*predicate* iff for any valuation $\rho : Var \to M$, $\overline{\rho}(\varphi_s)$ is either M_s or $\emptyset$. Also, φ_s is called a *predicate* iff φ is an M-predicate for all models M. For instance, the patterns $x \leq y$ and $o \vee \exists x.succ(x)$ (Example 3) and $o \wedge succ(o)$ are M-predicates.

Definition 6 (ML specifications). *A matching logic specification is a triple* (S, Σ, F), *where F is a set of Σ-patterns. The Σ-patterns in F are axiom patterns. We say that φ is a semantical consequence of F, written $F \models \varphi$, iff* $M \models F$ *implies* $M \models \varphi$, *for each Σ-model M.*

An important ingredient of ML is the *definedness* symbol $\lceil \_ \rceil_{s_1}^{s_2} \in \Sigma_{s_1,s_2}$: if φ is matched by *some* values of sort s_1 then $\lceil \varphi \rceil_{s_1}^{s_2}$ is $\top_{s_2}$, otherwise it is $\bot_{s_2}$. This interpretation is enforced by adding the axiom $\lceil x \rceil_{s_1}^{s_2}$ to F. Using this symbol and its axiom we may define:

- *conjunction of patterns with different sorts*: for instance, if the symbol $\leq_b \in \Sigma_{Nat\ Nat,Bool}$, then the pattern $x \wedge o \leq_b x$ is not syntactically correct, because x has sort *Nat* whereas $o \leq_b x$ has sort *Bool*. Using definedness we can now write a syntactically correct formula $x \wedge \lceil o \leq_b x \rceil_{Bool}^{Nat}$;
- *membership pattern*: $x \in_{s_1}^{s_2} \varphi \triangleq \lceil x \wedge \varphi \rceil_{s_1}^{s_2}$ with $x \in Var_{s_1}$;
- *equality pattern*: $\varphi =_{s_1}^{s_2} \varphi' \triangleq \neg \lceil \neg (\varphi \leftrightarrow \varphi') \rceil_{s_1}^{s_2}$.

In ML we can easily specify that certain symbols are interpreted as functions:

Definition 7 (Functional patterns, Term patterns). *A pattern φ is functional in a model M iff $| \overline{\rho}(\varphi) | = 1$ for any valuation $\rho: Var \to M$. The pattern φ is functional in (S, Σ, F) iff it is functional in all models M such that $M \models F$. Term patterns are formulas containing only functional symbols.*

The patterns o and $succ(x)$ (in Example 3) are functional in M_{Nat} since they are interpreted as functions (i.e., o_M and $succ_M$) which return a singleton set.

Obviously, any term pattern is functional. Moreover, given a ML specification (S, Σ, F), a pattern φ is functional in all (S, Σ, F)-models iff $F \models \exists y.(\varphi = y)$.

When functional patterns have the same sort, the proposition below holds:

Proposition 1 (Proposition 5.24 in [21]). *If φ and φ' are two functional patterns of the same sort, then $\models (\varphi \wedge \varphi') = \varphi \wedge (\varphi = \varphi')$.*

The Proof System of Matching Logic. Matching Logic provides a proof system that is sound and complete (Fig. 2). The notation $\varphi[\varphi'/x]$ denotes the pattern obtained from φ by replacing all free occurrences of x with φ'. Note that the propositional calculus reasoning is subsumed by rules *R1-R2* of the proof system. According to [2], *R1* is in fact a set of rules that includes a version of the implicational propositional calculus (proposed by Łukasievicz [15]).

Unification in Matching Logic. In [21], unification has a semantical definition. More precisely, it is defined in terms of conjunctions of patterns. Let us consider two ML patterns φ and φ'. Both patterns can be matched by (possibly infinite) sets of elements, say $\overline{\rho}(\varphi)$ and $\overline{\rho}(\varphi')$, given some valuation ρ. In this context, finding a unifier is the same as finding a pattern φ_u that matches over a set of elements included in both $\overline{\rho}(\varphi)$ and $\overline{\rho}(\varphi')$, that is, $\overline{\rho}(\varphi_u) \subseteq \overline{\rho}(\varphi) \cap \overline{\rho}(\varphi')$, for any ρ. The *most general* pattern φ_u that corresponds to the *largest* set with this property (i.e., $\overline{\rho}(\varphi) \cap \overline{\rho}(\varphi')$), is (by Definition 5) the pattern $\varphi \wedge \varphi'$.

3   Syntactic Unification and Matching Logic

The idea of transforming the pattern $t_1 \wedge t_2$ into an equivalent one $t \wedge \phi$ was suggested in [21], using an example. Here we propose a general solution that involves the unification algorithm shown in Fig. 1. Example 4 illustrates how the rules of the unification algorithm are simulated by pattern transformations.

Example 4. If $t_1 \triangleq f(x, g(1), g(z))$ and $t_2 \triangleq f(g(y), g(y), g(g(x)))$ then $t_1 \wedge t_2$ can be transformed into an equivalent formula $t \wedge \phi$:

$$
\begin{align}
t_1 \wedge t_2 &= f(x, g(1), g(z)) \wedge f(g(y), g(y), g(g(x))) \tag{1} \\
&= f(x, g(1), g(z)) \wedge (f(x, g(1), g(z)) = f(g(y), g(y), g(g(x)))) \tag{2} \\
&= f(x, g(1), g(z)) \wedge (x = g(y)) \wedge (g(1) = g(y)) \wedge (g(z) = g(g(x))) \tag{3} \\
&= f(x, g(1), g(z)) \wedge (x = g(y)) \wedge (1 = g(y)) \wedge (g(z) = g(g(x))) \tag{4} \\
&= f(x, g(1), g(z)) \wedge (x = g(y)) \wedge (1 = y) \wedge (z = g(x)) \tag{5} \\
&= f(x, g(1), g(z)) \wedge (x = g(y)) \wedge (y = 1) \wedge (z = g(x)) \tag{6} \\
&= f(x, g(1), g(z)) \wedge (x = g(1)) \wedge (y = 1) \wedge (z = g(x)) \tag{7} \\
&= \underbrace{f(x, g(1), g(z))}_{t} \wedge \underbrace{(x = g(1)) \wedge (y = 1) \wedge (z = g(g(1)))}_{\phi^\sigma} \tag{8}
\end{align}
$$

Except the step (2) - which is a direct consequence of Proposition 1 applied to (1) - the rest of the equations correspond to the steps of the algorithm: **Decomposition** for (3, 4, 5), **Orient** for (6), and **Elimination** for (7, 8). Note that ϕ^σ corresponds to the most general unifier $\sigma = \{x \mapsto g(1), y \mapsto 1, z \mapsto g(g(1))\}$ of t_1 and t_2. Moreover, ϕ^σ is also equivalent to $t_1 = t_2$ (from step (2)). In this section we answer the following questions:

1. What is the relationship between ϕ^σ and $t_1 = t_2$, when σ is a unifier of t_1 and t_2? In particular, if σ is the mgu, are ϕ^σ and $t_1 = t_2$ equivalent?
2. Is $t_1 \wedge t_2$ different from $\perp$ if t_1 and t_2 are syntactically unifiable?
3. Is $t_1 \wedge t_2$ equivalent to $\perp$ if t_1 and t_2 are not syntactically unifiable?
4. Are t_1 and t_2 syntactically unifiable if $t_1 \wedge t_2$ is different from $\perp$?
5. Are t_1 and t_2 not syntactically unifiable if $t_1 \wedge t_2$ is equivalent to $\perp$?

3.1 Encoding Syntactic Unification in ML

Terms, substitutions, and unification problems can be naturally expressed in ML as patterns provided that the following symbols and axioms are added to the specification (S, Σ, F):

1. The definedness symbols and their corresponding patterns, needed to define equality and membership;
2. An axiom $\exists y. f(x_1, \ldots, x_n) = y$ for each symbol f occurring in term patterns.

We assume that the syntactic unification algorithm is applied on terms that are encoded as term patterns in ML. Next, we encode unification problems as ML patterns:

Definition 8. *For each unification problem* $P = \{v_1 \doteq u_1, \ldots, v_n \doteq u_n\}$ *we define a corresponding ML predicate* $\phi^P \triangleq \bigwedge_{i=1}^n v_i = u_i$. *Also,* $\phi^\perp = \perp$.

Substitutions can be encoded as ML predicates called *substitution patterns*:

Definition 9. *A substitution pattern, which corresponds to a substitution* $\sigma = \{x_i \mapsto u_i \mid i = 1, \ldots, n\}$, *is a predicate of the form* $\phi^\sigma \triangleq \bigwedge_{i=1}^{n} x_i = u_i$.

For the particular case when σ_P corresponds to a unification problem $P \neq \bot$ in solved form we have $\phi^{\sigma_P} = \phi^P$.

Using this encoding, we can establish a first result relating the unification patterns and the equality of the term patterns:

Lemma 1. *If* σ *is a unifier of term patterns* t_1 *and* t_2 *then* $F \models \phi^\sigma \rightarrow (t_1 = t_2)$.

For the converse implication we need additional axioms, as shown in Sect. 3.2.

3.2 Unification Algorithms as Constraint Patterns Transformers

The syntactic unification algorithm in Fig. 1 defines a transformation relation $P \Rightarrow^! P'$ between unification problems. In Sect. 3.1, for unification problems P we define a corresponding predicate ϕ^P. In this section we establish the relationship between ϕ^P and $\phi^{P'}$. More precisely, our goal is to show that these constraint patterns are equivalent.

To prove this equivalence when $P' \neq \bot$, the next axiom has to be added to F:

Injectivity : $f(x_1, \ldots, x_n) = f(y_1, \ldots, y_n) \rightarrow x_1 = y_1 \wedge \ldots \wedge x_n = y_n$.

Injectivity is needed to handle the case when P' is reached using **Decomposition**. Lemma 2 shows that a step performed by the syntactic unification algorithm can be encoded as an implication in ML.

Lemma 2. *For all* P *and* P', *if* $P \Rightarrow P'$ *and* $P' \neq \bot$ *then* $F \models \phi^P \rightarrow \phi^{P'}$.

By applying Lemma 2 repeatedly we easily obtain the following result:

Corollary 1. *If* $\{t_1 \doteq t_2\} \Rightarrow^! P$ *and* $P \neq \bot$ *then* $F \models (t_1 = t_2) \rightarrow \phi^{\sigma_P}$.

A first contribution of this paper is given by the next result: it establishes that the equality of two term patterns is equivalent to the substitution pattern corresponding to their unifier.

Theorem 1. *If* $\{t_1 \doteq t_2\} \Rightarrow^! P$ *and* $P \neq \bot$ *then* $F \models (t_1 = t_2) \leftrightarrow \phi^{\sigma_P}$.

To obtain a similar result for the case when P' is $\bot$, we need more axioms to handle the transformation rules **SymbolClash** and **OccursCheck**.

For the **SymbolClash** case we add the following axiom, which is used in [21] to axiomatise constructors:

No confusion, different constructors:
$\neg(c(x_1, \ldots, x_m) \wedge c'(y_1, \ldots, y_n))$, with $c \neq c'$, $c \in \Sigma_{s_1..s_m,s}$, and $c \in \Sigma_{s_1..s_n,s}$.

The **Occurs check** case is more complicated because it expresses a particular property of terms. Terms can be formalised as an ML model, say TERM, which consists of:

- a carrier set TERM_s for each $s \in S$, which contains all Σ-terms of sort s;
- a function $f_{\text{TERM}} : \text{TERM}_{s_1} \times \cdots \times \text{TERM}_{s_n} \to \mathcal{P}(\text{TERM}_s)$, for all $f \in \Sigma_{s_1..s_n,s}$, where $f_{\text{TERM}}(t_1, \ldots, t_n) = \{f(t_1, \ldots, t_n)\}$.

Working only in this particular model is not practical since not all symbols are required to be functional (e.g., predicate symbols). Therefore, we need to axiomatise the property required by **Occurs check**. This property is implied by the axiom (C) from Malcev's axiomatisation of the term algebra [3], $x \neq t(x)$, where $t(x)$ is a term containing x as a variable[2]. Unfortunately this is not an ML axiom, but an axiom schema because we must have an axiom for each such term. We build a new ML specification (S^*, Σ^*, F^*), starting from (S, Σ, F), as follows:

- $S^* = S \cup \{s^*\}$, where s^* is a new sort;
- $\Sigma^* = \Sigma \cup \{<\}$ where the symbol $< \in \Sigma^*_{s^* s^*, s^*}$;
- F^* includes F and the following axioms:

$$
\begin{array}{ll}
\textbf{Supersort} & : \exists x{:}s^*.\, x = \bigvee_{s \in S} \exists y{:}s.y \\
\textbf{Basecase} & : x_i < f(x_1, .., x_i, .., x_n) \\
\textbf{Irreflexive} & : \neg(x < x) \\
\textbf{Transitivity} & : x < y \wedge y < z \to x < z \\
\textbf{Predicate} & : ((x < y) = \bot_s) \vee ((x < y) = \top_s)
\end{array}
$$

The axiomatization of $<$ is similar to that of the predicate *Sub* in [13][3]. The next result shows that these axioms solve the **OccursCheck** problem.

Lemma 3. *If* $x \in var(f(t_1, .., t_n))$ *then* $F^* \models \neg(x = f(t_1, .., t_n))$.

In the next example we show how the axioms F^* are used.

Example 5. We prove by contradiction that $F^* \models \neg(x = f(g(x,y), z))$. Assume that $F^* \models x = f(g(x,y), z)$ (♠). Then:

$$
\begin{array}{ll}
F^* \models x < g(x,y) & \text{by } \textbf{Basecase} \\
F^* \models g(x,y) < f(g(x,y), z) & \text{by } \textbf{Basecase} \text{ and funct. subst.} \\
F^* \models x < f(g(x,y), z) & \text{by } \textbf{Transitivity} \\
F^* \models x < x & \text{by ♠ and eq. elim.}
\end{array}
$$

which contradicts the **Irreflexive** axiom.

As expected, with the new set of axioms F^*, the following holds:

Lemma 4. *For all unification problems* P, *if* $P \Rightarrow \bot$ *then* $F^* \models \phi^P \to \bot$.

The next result completes the first contribution of the paper:

Theorem 2. *If* $P \Rightarrow^! \bot$ *then* $F^* \models \phi^P \to \bot$.

---

[2] The other two axioms (A) and (B) in [3] correspond to **Injectivity** and **No confusion, different constructors**.

[3] We thank to the anonymous referee for having noticed this similarity.

3.3   Soundness and Completeness

The main contributions reported in this section includes the *soundness* and the *completeness* of the syntactic unification algorithm for the semantic unification in ML. Throughout this section we assume the ML specifications (S, Σ, F) and (S^*, Σ^*, F^*) as presented in Sect. 3.2.

The first result that we present states that if the unification algorithm produces the mgu σ, then the semantic unifier $t_1 \wedge t_2$ can be expressed as $t_i \wedge \phi^\sigma$ with $i \in \{1, 2\}$, i.e., a conjunction of a term pattern and a constraint. Note that this is precisely the convenient form that we discussed in Sect. 1 of this paper.

Lemma 5. *If* $\{t_1 \doteq t_2\} \Rightarrow^! P \neq \bot$ *then* $F \models t_1 \wedge t_2 = t_i \wedge \phi^{\sigma_P}$, *where* $i \in \{1, 2\}$.

In order to state the soundness and completeness results we need to define what it means that two patterns t_1 and t_2 are semantically *unifiable* in ML:

Definition 10. *Two term patterns* t_1 *and* t_2 *are* unifiable *(in ML) iff* $F \models \lceil \exists \overline{x}.t_1 \wedge t_2 \rceil$, *where* $\overline{x} = var(t_1 \wedge t_2)$. *Obviously,* t_1 *and* t_2 *are not unifiable iff* $F \models \neg \lceil \exists \overline{x}.t_1 \wedge t_2 \rceil$.

Recall that $\lceil \exists \overline{x}.t_1 \wedge t_2 \rceil$ holds iff $\exists \overline{x}.t_1 \wedge t_2$ is matched by some values, i.e. iff t_1 and t_2 are unifiable in some model.

The next theorem states the soundness of our approach: if the syntactic unification algorithm produces a syntactic unifier for term patterns t_1 and t_2 then t_1 and t_2 are unifiable in ML as well. If the algorithm finds that t_1 and t_2 are not syntactically unifiable, then they are not unifiable in ML.

Theorem 3 (Soundness). *If* $\{t_1 \doteq t_2\} \Rightarrow^! P$ *then the following hold:*

1. *If* $P \neq \bot$ *then* $F \models \lceil \exists \overline{x}.t_1 \wedge t_2 \rceil$ *and* $F \models (t_1 \wedge t_2) = (t_1 \wedge \phi^{\sigma_P})$;
2. *If* $P = \bot$ *then* $F^* \models \neg \lceil \exists \overline{x}.t_1 \wedge t_2 \rceil$.

The next theorem states the completeness of our approach: if t_1 and t_2 are unifiable in ML, then they are syntactically unifiable; if t_1 and t_2 are not unifiable in ML, then they are not syntactically unifiable.

Theorem 4 (Completeness). *Let* t_1 *and* t_2 *be two term patterns.*

1. *If* $F^* \models \lceil \exists \overline{x}.t_1 \wedge t_2 \rceil$ *then* $\{t_1 \doteq t_2\} \Rightarrow^! P \neq \bot$ *and* σ_P *is the mgu of* t_1, t_2;
2. *If* $F \models \neg \lceil \exists \overline{x}.t_1 \wedge t_2 \rceil$ *then* $\{t_1 \doteq t_2\} \Rightarrow^! \bot$.

In the second case of Theorem 3 and the first case of the Theorem 4 we use the set of axioms F^* instead of F. The issue comes from the fact that F is not sufficient to avoid situations when patterns are unifiable in ML, but they are not syntactically unifiable. Here is an example. Let s be a sort and Σ a signature which includes only a functional symbol $f \in \Sigma_{s,s}$. Also, let M be a ML model where $f_M(a) = a$, with a the only element in M_s. We obviously have $M \models \lceil \exists x.x \wedge f(x) \rceil$, i.e., x and $f(x)$ are unifiable in ML. It is easy to see that x and $f(x)$ are not syntactically unifiable.

4 Generating Proofs

In this section we show the *provableness* property of the syntactic unification algorithm, i.e., how a formal proof can be generated from its executions. More precisely, if the executions returns a mgu σ, then a formal proof of equivalence between $t_1 \wedge t_2$ and $t_1 \wedge \phi^\sigma$ can be generated. If the algorithm returns $\perp$, then a formal proof of equivalence between $t_1 \wedge t_2$ and $\perp$ is generated. This strategy uses the rules of the ML proof system [21] and some derived rules that mimic the steps of the syntactic unification algorithm. Since the conjunction of the patterns occurs often in the proofs, the formal proofs that justify the use of the syntactic term unification algorithm are crucial when a ML prover outputs a proof certificate.

Our current approach is to generate proofs in two stages: first, we start with $t_1 \wedge t_2$ as hypothesis and we derive $t_1 \wedge \phi^\sigma$ using several derived proof rules, which are proved separately using the ML proof system; second, we start with $t_1 \wedge \phi^\sigma$ as hypothesis and we derive $t_1 \wedge t_2$ using the original proof system of ML.

Stage 1. The list of derived rules that we use in the first stage is shown here:

Δ1. $F, \varphi \wedge (t = t) \vdash \varphi$ **Delete**
Δ2. $F, \varphi \wedge (f(t_1, .., t_n) = f(t'_1, .., t'_n)) \vdash \varphi \wedge t_1 = t'_1 \wedge .. \wedge t_n = t'_n$ **Decomposition**
Δ3. $F, \varphi \wedge (f(t_1, .., t_n) = x) \vdash \varphi \wedge (x = f(t_1, .., t_n))$ **Orient**
Δ4. $F, \varphi \wedge (x = t) \vdash \varphi[t/x] \wedge (x = t)$, if $x \notin var(t), x \in var(\varphi)$ **Elimination**
Δ5. $F^*, \varphi \wedge (f(t_1, .., t_n) = g(t'_1, .., t'_n)) \vdash \perp$ **Symbol clash**
Δ6. $F^*, \varphi \wedge (x = f(t_1, .., t_n)) \vdash \perp$, if $x \in var(f(t_1, \ldots, t_n))$ **Occurs check**

For each rule we indicate the corresponding rule from the unification algorithm. Also, we used the notation $F, \varphi \vdash \varphi'$ instead of $F \cup \{\varphi\} \vdash \varphi'$. For this first stage, the proof is dictated by the syntactic unification algorithm as shown here:

$$
\begin{array}{lll}
 & \overbrace{}^{t_1} \quad \overbrace{}^{t_2} & \\
\text{i} & f(x, g(1), g(z)) \wedge f(g(y), g(y), g(g(x))) & hypothesis \\
\text{ii} & f(x, g(1), g(z)) \wedge (f(x, g(1), g(z)) = f(g(y), g(y), g(g(x)))) & Prop\,1\text{: i} \\
\text{iii} & f(x, g(1), g(z)) \wedge (x = g(y)) \wedge (g(1) = g(y)) \wedge (g(z) = g(g(x))) & \Delta2\text{: ii} \\
\text{iv} & f(x, g(1), g(z)) \wedge (x = g(y)) \wedge (1 = g(y)) \wedge (g(z) = g(g(x))) & \Delta2\text{: iii} \\
\text{v} & f(x, g(1), g(z)) \wedge (x = g(y)) \wedge (1 = y) \wedge (z = g(x)) & \Delta2\text{: iv} \\
\text{vi} & f(x, g(1), g(z)) \wedge (x = g(y)) \wedge (y = 1) \wedge (z = g(x)) & \Delta3\text{: v} \\
\text{vii} & f(x, g(1), g(z)) \wedge (x = g(1)) \wedge (y = 1) \wedge (z = g(x)) & \Delta4\text{: vi} \\
\text{viii} & \underbrace{f(x, g(1), g(z))}_{t_1} \wedge \underbrace{(x = g(1)) \wedge (y = 1) \wedge (z = g(g(1)))}_{\phi^\sigma} & \Delta4\text{:vii} \\
\end{array}
$$

Each line represents a proof step annotated with a justification specified as ⟨the applied proof rule⟩:⟨references to previous steps⟩. We intentionally omit $F \vdash$ before each proof step and we prefer to add some useful annotations at the end.

The first line is our hypothesis. The pattern derived at the second line is obtained by applying Proposition 1 to pattern i. The third line is obtained by applying Δ2 to ii, that is, **Decomposition** for symbol f. To keep the above proof simple, we silently use the associativity and commutativity of $\wedge$.

The first stage of our strategy is sound. The derived rules and Proposition 1 can be proved using the rules of the ML proof system. Some of these proofs are trivial (e.g., the proofs for $\Delta 1$ or $\Delta 3$), but others are more interesting. For example, this the proof for $\Delta 2$:

i	$\varphi \wedge (f(t_1,..,t_n) = f(t'_1,..,t'_n))$	*hypothesis*
ii	φ	R1: i
iii	$f(t_1,..,t_n) = f(t'_1,..,t'_n)$	R1: i
iv	$f(t_1,..,t_n) = f(t'_1,..,t'_n) \rightarrow t_1 = t'_1 \wedge .. \wedge t_n = t'_n$	F: **Injectivity**
v	$t_1 = t'_1 \wedge .. \wedge t_n = t'_n$	R2: iii, iv
vi	$\varphi \wedge t_1 = t'_1 \wedge .. \wedge t_n = t'_n$	R1: ii, v

As expected, the proof uses the **Injectivity** axiom. The other rules are the ones for propositional calculus which are used only to arrange the goals conveniently.

Stage 2. The strategy corresponding to this stage has five steps:

1. start with $t_1 \wedge \phi^\sigma$ as *hypothesis*;
2. use R1 to break the large conjunction in the *hypothesis* (e.g., steps ii–vii)
3. use R6 to introduce equalities $t_1 = t_1$ and $t_2 = t_2$ (e.g., steps viii, ix);
4. use R7 to replace the variables occurring in the left hand sides of the equalities (e.g., steps xi, xiv);
5. use R7 to equate the right hand sides of the equalities produced by the previous step (e.g. xv); then apply R1 ($\wedge$ introduction, e.g., xvi), and finally Proposition 1 (e.g., xvii).

Applying the above strategy on the reversed implication of our previous example we get the following proof:

	$\overbrace{\qquad\qquad t_1 \qquad\qquad}\qquad\qquad \overbrace{\qquad\qquad \phi^\sigma \qquad\qquad}$	
i	$f(x,g(1),g(z)) \wedge (x = g(1)) \wedge (y = 1) \wedge (z = g(g(1)))$	*hypothesis*
ii	$f(x,g(1),g(z))$	R1: i
iii	$(x = g(1)) \wedge (y = 1) \wedge (z = g(g(1)))$	R1: i
iv	$x = g(1)$	R1: iii
v	$(y = 1) \wedge z = g(g(1))$	R1: iii
vi	$y = 1$	R1: v
vii	$z = g(g(1))$	R1: v
viii	$f(x,g(1),g(z)) = f(x,g(1),g(z))$	R6
ix	$f(g(y),g(y),g(g(x))) = f(g(y),g(y),g(g(x)))$	R6
x	$f(g(1),g(1),g(z)) = f(x,g(1),g(z))$	R7: viii, iv
xi	$f(g(1),g(1),g(g(g(1)))) = f(x,g(1),g(z))$	R7: x, vii
xii	$f(g(1),g(y),g(g(x))) = f(g(y),g(y),g(g(x)))$	R7: ix, vi
xiii	$f(g(1),g(1),g(g(x))) = f(g(y),g(y),g(g(x)))$	R7: xii, vi
xiv	$f(g(1),g(1),g(g(g(1)))) = f(g(y),g(y),g(g(x)))$	R7: xiii, iv
xv	$f(x,g(1),g(z)) = f(g(y),g(y),g(g(x)))$	R7: xi, xiv
xvi	$f(x,g(1),g(z)) \wedge (f(x,g(1),g(z)) = f(g(y),g(y),g(g(x))))$	R1: ii, xv
xvii	$\underbrace{f(x,g(1),g(z))}_{t_1} \wedge \underbrace{f(g(y),g(y),g(g(x)))}_{t_2}$	Prop 1: xvi

This strategy essentially rebuilds the semantic unifier $t_1 \wedge t_2$ starting with $t_1 \wedge \phi^\sigma$. Because ϕ^σ has the form $\bigwedge_{i=1}^n x_i = u_i$ the step 2 will always produce equalities of the form $x_i = u_i$ for all $i = \overline{1,n}$. In the left hand sides of the equalities introduced by step 3 we can always substitute x_i by u_i. Since σ is the most general unifier, the left hand sides will become equal after substitutions performed by step 4. Finally, we can always apply $R7$, $R1$, and Proposition 1 conveniently to obtain $t_1 \wedge t_2$. This strategy is sound since it uses only rules from the original proof system of ML and Proposition 1.

5   Conclusions

Previous verification efforts with ML [5,10,14,17,20,22–26] were based on unification. However, unification was always considered a trusted component.

In this paper we finally tackle down this issue by proposing a sound method for unification which involves a syntactic unification algorithm. More precisely, we show that, under the presence of certain axioms (cf. Sect. 3.2), the syntactic unification algorithm proposed by Martelli and Montanari [16] is *sound* and *complete* for semantic unification in ML. Finally, we show a *provableness* property: we provide a sound strategy to generate proof certificates. This strategy uses some derived rules and the rules of the original ML proof system [21].

Related Work. The closest related work is Kore [2]: an implementation of ML which is currently under development [1]. They handle conjunctions via a set of transformations over patterns intended to serve a more general purpose, for instance, to deal with partiality and injections (subsort relations). Here, we focus on how the syntactic unification algorithms can be used to help reasoning in ML.

In this paper unification is used to tackle conjunctions of ML patterns. On the other hand, disjunctions of patterns can be tackled using anti-unification. This is almost completely treated in [21] using the Plotkin's algorithm for anti-unification. What is missing in [21] is the generation of a formal proof.

Future Work. The fact that the proof of the soundness of our approach depends on the unification algorithm is intriguing. We intend to explore whether there is an independent proof, which uses only the definition of the most general unifier.

Recently, in [9] a new proof system for ML together with a deduction theorem is presented. We intend to adapt our proof generation strategy to use this new proof system instead. The fixpoint constructs from modal μ-logic increase the expressivity of the logic and it is challenging to investigate whether the axiomatisation proposed in this paper can be improved in the new framework.

It also interesting to test how efficient is our approach. The results we obtained for several small experiments are promising, but a deeper investigation is needed, especially for the **OccursCheck** rule.

Finally, a completely new ground to explore is unification modulo axioms (e.g., commutativity, associativity). Obviously, it is more challenging to use the existing unification modulo axioms algorithms in the same manner as we have done for syntactic unification. Another possible direction is to study the unification in many/order sorted algebras.

Acknowledgements. We thank the anonymous reviewers for their insightful comments. We would like to especially thank the Kore developers and researchers: Phillip Harris, Traian Şerbănuţă and Virgil Şerbănuţă for their valuable assistance and feedback. They helped us with our proof generation strategy and they suggested improvements for our current work. We also want to specially thank Grigore Roşu for the fruitful discussions that we had about this topic at FROM 2018. This work was supported by a grant of the "Alexandru Ioan Cuza" University of Iaşi, within the Research Grants program, Grant UAIC, ctr. no. 6/01-01-2017.

References

1. The Kore language (GitHub repository). https://github.com/kframework/kore. Accessed 07 Nov 2018
2. The semantics of K (online document). https://github.com/kframework/kore/blob/master/docs/semantics-of-k.pdf. Accessed 07 Nov 2018
3. Chapter 23 axiomatizable classes of locally free algebras of various types. In: Mal'cev, A.I. (ed.) The Metamathematics Algebraic Systems, Studies in Logic and the Foundations of Mathematics, vol. 66, pp. 262–281. Elsevier (1971). https://doi.org/10.1016/S0049-237X(08)70560-3
4. Arusoaie, A., Lucanu, D., Rusu, V.: Symbolic execution based on language transformation. Comput. Lang. Syst. Struct. **44**, 48–71 (2015)
5. Arusoaie, A., Nowak, D., Rusu, V., Lucanu, D.: A certified procedure for RL verification. In: SYNASC 2017, pp. 129–136. IEEE CPS, Timişoara, Romania, September 2017. https://hal.inria.fr/hal-01627517
6. Baader, F.: Unification theory. In: Schulz, K.U. (ed.) IWWERT 1990. LNCS, vol. 572, pp. 151–170. Springer, Heidelberg (1992). https://doi.org/10.1007/3-540-55124-7_5
7. Barrett, C., et al.: CVC4. In: Gopalakrishnan, G., Qadeer, S. (eds.) CAV 2011. LNCS, vol. 6806, pp. 171–177. Springer, Heidelberg (2011). https://doi.org/10.1007/978-3-642-22110-1_14
8. Bogdanas, D., Roşu, G.: K-Java: a complete semantics of Java. In: Proceedings of the 42nd Annual ACM SIGPLAN-SIGACT Symposium on Principles of Programming Languages, POPL 2015, pp. 445–456. ACM, New York (2015). https://doi.org/10.1145/2676726.2676982
9. Chen, X., Roşu, G.: Matching mu-logic. In: Proceedings of the 34th Annual ACM/IEEE Symposium on Logic in Computer Science (LICS 2019) (2019, to appear)
10. Ştefănescu, A., Ciobâcă, Ş., Mereuta, R., Moore, B.M., Şerbănuţă, T.F., Roşu, G.: All-path reachability logic. In: Dowek, G. (ed.) RTA 2014. LNCS, vol. 8560, pp. 425–440. Springer, Cham (2014). https://doi.org/10.1007/978-3-319-08918-8_29
11. Ellison, C., Rosu, G.: An executable formal semantics of C with applications. In: Proceedings of the 39th Annual ACM SIGPLAN-SIGACT Symposium on Principles of Programming Languages, POPL 2012, pp. 533–544. ACM, New York (2012). https://doi.org/10.1145/2103656.2103719
12. Hathhorn, C., Ellison, C., Roşu, G.: Defining the undefinedness of C. In: Proceedings of the 36th ACM SIGPLAN Conference on Programming Language Design and Implementation, PLDI 2015, pp. 336–345. ACM, New York (2015). https://doi.org/10.1145/2737924.2737979

13. Kovács, L., Robillard, S., Voronkov, A.: Coming to terms with quantified reasoning. In: Proceedings of the 44th ACM SIGPLAN Symposium on Principles of Programming Languages, POPL 2017, pp. 260–270. ACM, New York (2017). https://doi.org/10.1145/3009837.3009887

14. Lucanu, D., Rusu, V., Arusoaie, A., Nowak, D.: Verifying reachability-logic properties on rewriting-logic specifications. In: Martí-Oliet, N., Ölveczky, P.C., Talcott, C. (eds.) Logic, Rewriting, and Concurrency. LNCS, vol. 9200, pp. 451–474. Springer, Cham (2015). https://doi.org/10.1007/978-3-319-23165-5_21

15. Łukasiewicz, J.: The shortest axiom of the implicational calculus of propositions. Proc. R. Irish Acad. Sect. Math. Phys. Sci. **52**, 25–33 (1948). http://www.jstor.org/stable/20488489

16. Martelli, A., Montanari, U.: An efficient unification algorithm. ACM Trans. Program. Lang. Syst. **4**(2), 258–282 (1982). https://doi.org/10.1145/357162.357169

17. Moore, B., Peña, L., Rosu, G.: Program verification by coinduction. In: Ahmed, A. (ed.) ESOP 2018. LNCS, vol. 10801, pp. 589–618. Springer, Cham (2018). https://doi.org/10.1007/978-3-319-89884-1_21

18. de Moura, L., Bjørner, N.: Z3: an efficient SMT solver. In: Ramakrishnan, C.R., Rehof, J. (eds.) TACAS 2008. LNCS, vol. 4963, pp. 337–340. Springer, Heidelberg (2008). https://doi.org/10.1007/978-3-540-78800-3_24

19. Park, D., Ştefănescu, A., Roşu, G.: KJS: a complete formal semantics of JavaScript. In: Proceedings of the 36th ACM SIGPLAN Conference on Programming Language Design and Implementation, PLDI 2015, pp. 346–356. ACM, New York (2015). https://doi.org/10.1145/2737924.2737991

20. Park, D., Zhang, Y., Saxena, M., Daian, P., Roşu, G.: A formal verification tool for ethereum VM bytecode. In: Proceedings of the 2018 26th ACM Joint Meeting on European Software Engineering Conference and Symposium on the Foundations of Software Engineering, ESEC/FSE 2018, pp. 912–915. ACM, New York (2018). https://doi.org/10.1145/3236024.3264591

21. Roşu, G.: Matching logic. Log. Methods Comput. Sci. **13**(4), 1–61 (2017). http://arxiv.org/abs/1705.06312

22. Roşu, G., Ştefănescu, A.: From Hoare logic to matching logic reachability. In: Giannakopoulou, D., Méry, D. (eds.) FM 2012. LNCS, vol. 7436, pp. 387–402. Springer, Heidelberg (2012). https://doi.org/10.1007/978-3-642-32759-9_32

23. Roşu, G., Ştefănescu, A.: Matching logic: a new program verification approach. In: Proceedings of the 33rd International Conference on Software Engineering, ICSE 2011, Waikiki, Honolulu, HI, USA, 21–28 May 2011, pp. 868–871 (2011). https://doi.org/10.1145/1985793.1985928

24. Roşu, G., Ştefănescu, A., Ştefan Ciobâcă, Moore, B.M.: One-path reachability logic. In: 28th Annual ACM/IEEE Symposium on Logic in Computer Science, LICS 2013, New Orleans, LA, USA, 25–28 June 2013, pp. 358–367 (2013). https://doi.org/10.1109/LICS.2013.42

25. Rusu, V., Arusoaie, A.: Proving reachability-logic formulas incrementally. In: Lucanu, D. (ed.) WRLA 2016. LNCS, vol. 9942, pp. 134–151. Springer, Cham (2016). https://doi.org/10.1007/978-3-319-44802-2_8

26. Ştefănescu, A., Park, D., Yuwen, S., Li, Y., Roşu, G.: Semantics-based program verifiers for all languages. In: Proceedings of the 2016 ACM SIGPLAN International Conference on Object-Oriented Programming, Systems, Languages, and Applications, OOPSLA 2016, pp. 74–91. ACM, New York (2016). https://doi.org/10.1145/2983990.2984027

Embedding High-Level Formal Specifications into Applications

Philipp Körner$^{(\boxtimes)}$ ⓘ, Jens Bendisposto ⓘ, Jannik Dunkelau ⓘ,
Sebastian Krings ⓘ, and Michael Leuschel ⓘ

Institut für Informatik, Universität Düsseldorf,
Universitätsstr. 1, 40225 Düsseldorf, Germany
{p.koerner,jens.bendisposto,jannik.dunkelau,
sebastian.krings,michael.leuschel}@hhu.de

Abstract. The common formal methods workflow consists of formalising a model followed by applying model checking and proof techniques. Once an appropriate level of certainty is reached, code generators are used in order to gain executable code.

In this paper, we propose a different approach: instead of generating code from formal models, it is also possible to embed a model checker or animator into applications in order to use the formal models themselves at runtime. We present the enabling technology PROB 2.0, a Java API to the PROB animator and model checker. We describe several case studies that use PROB 2.0 to interact with a formal specification at runtime.

1 Introduction

When designing safety-critical software, the use of formal methods is highly recommended [13] to ensure correctness. This is often done by combining (manual and automatic) proof with model checking.

Once a formal model has been found to be correct, it is required to translate the model into a traditional programming language. Low-level formalisms are usually close enough that code can be generated easily. When using high-level formalisms though, the model has to be gradually refined to an implementation level so that it only uses a restricted version of the specification language, disallowing high-level constructs which require, e.g., constraint solving techniques or unconstrained memory for execution. The alternative to code generation is manual implementation, which is known to be error-prone.

In this paper, we investigate another approach: we assume that a high-level specification is written to be *executable*, in the sense that a tool like an animator or model checker is able to compute all state transitions. Can we then implement a program interfacing with, e.g., a model checker that also simulates the environment and executes the model by choosing a traversing transition?

This paper is a mixture of a position, tool and application paper: in the following, we briefly introduce two high-level specification languages, B and Event-B, as well as PROB, an animator and model checker for these languages. Afterwards, we present the enabling technology PROB 2.0, a Java API for interaction

© Springer Nature Switzerland AG 2019
M. H. ter Beek et al. (Eds.): FM 2019, LNCS 11800, pp. 519–535, 2019.
https://doi.org/10.1007/978-3-030-30942-8_31

with PROB in Sect. 2. Following, we evaluate our approach by implementing and discussing several new case studies based on PROB 2.0 in Sect. 3, summarising its use in existing industrial applications and insights gained from implementation work. Finally, we argue for using formal models as runtime artefacts and discuss similar approaches in Sect. 4.

1.1 B, Event-B and ProB

Both B [3] and its successor, Event-B [2], are state-based specification languages that allow for high levels of abstraction. They are based on Zermelo-Fraenkel set theory with the axiom of choice [17,18], using sets for data modelling. Further, they make use of generalised substitution for state modifications, and of refinement calculus [4,5] to describe models at different levels of abstraction [9].

The highest level of abstraction includes, besides set theory, formulation of quantified formulae over arbitrary domains, functional composition and lambda expressions, as well as non-deterministic assignments[1].

In the following, we describe several projects that make use of PROB [33], an animator and model checker for both B and Event-B. Its core is developed mainly in SICStus Prolog [11], with some parts being implemented in C and Java, and makes use of co-routines and SICStus' CLP(FD) library [10]. Besides B, PROB offers support for several other formalisms as well, including TLA[+] [30] (via translation to B [22]), Z [38,42], CSP [8,25] and more. Hence, the approach discussed in this article is immediately applicable to languages other than B and Event-B.

2   ProB 2.0

As PROB is written in Prolog, which admittedly is neither the most popular nor the easiest language to pick up, it is hard for formal method experts to use anything but the default animation and model checking capabilities. Thus, a main design goal of PROB 2.0 was to offer access to the API of PROB via a scripting language that allows easy embedding of domain specific languages (DSLs). For this, we picked and embraced Groovy, a dynamic programming language running on the JVM, which is (almost) a superset of Java. PROB 2.0 is available on GitHub[2].

A general overview of PROB 2.0 is given in Fig. 1. For each B model that is interacted with, an instance of the PROB-CLI (command line interface), which actually loads the model, is started in socket-mode. This means that the PROB-CLI listens on a socket for commands to execute whitelisted Prolog code. The whitelist offers fine-grained access to PROB's constraint solving, animation and model checking capabilities as well as PROB's preferences and machine components.

---

[1] Cf. https://www3.hhu.de/stups/prob/index.php/Summary_of_B_Syntax.
[2] https://github.com/bendisposto/prob2.

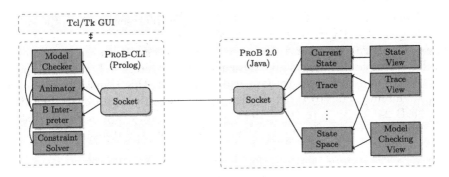

Fig. 1. Overview of the PROB ecosystem

Each command on the whitelist has a corresponding implementation in PROB 2.0. This offers an API that is fairly low-level and intended for PROB and PROB 2.0 developers. It is complemented by a high-level API that is built on top and abstracts away from PROB's internals in Prolog. The high-level API allows easy animation of the model, exploration of the state space, solving custom constraints over the variables in the state space, or registration of listeners subscribed to custom formulae which are notified once a new state is reached.

The State Space acts as the central interface to the PROB-CLI. It is a representation of the underlying labelled transition system. Exploring the state space by executing operations adds transitions and newly encountered states. It allows animation of the model, evaluation of predicates in arbitrary states, extraction of states that match a given predicate, and, in general, execution of arbitrary PROB 2.0 commands.

The Model is an in-memory version of the loaded B machine. PROB 2.0 offers convenient access to the contents of the specification. This includes invariants, variables, operations and their preconditions, etc. Upon that, it is possible to expand on loaded machines by adding further invariants or operations, resulting in a dynamically altered version with stricter semantics [14].

The Trace keeps track of the path throughout the state space starting from the initialisation of the machine. Traces behave like a browser history in the sense that they are append-only, but it is possible to "go back in time" and start a new fork. Executing an operation during animation automatically appends the successor state to the currently active trace.

The State objects are linked to their corresponding state space. They store outgoing transitions as well as map abstractions of variables and formulas to abstractions of values. For example, it is possible to retrieve the value of a given state variable but also to add expressions and predicates which are automatically evaluated in every state and are kept track of.

Value Translation is required to give a meaningful representation to the values of state variables. By default, PROB provides a string representation of each value to PROB 2.0. However, they can be translated into Java data structures as well: For example, B integers are translated into BigIntegers, B sets correspond to Java sets and sequences to Java lists. Naturally, this translation does not work for infinite sets. To avoid duplication of the entire state space in PROB and PROB 2.0, only up to 100 states are cached in Java. If a non-cached state is required, it is retrieved via a handle (a unique state ID) from the PROB-CLI.

Trace Synchronisation is a tool that is provided by PROB 2.0. It allows coupling of multiple traces, even on different machines. One example is that a refined machine is synchronised with a more abstract version upon the shared operations, in order to ensure that it is a valid refinement. Another example is synchronisation of two entirely different machines that are two components in a system.

3   Examples

In this section, we describe different use cases based on several examples. The first couple of examples we discuss are student projects implementing two well-known games: Pac-Man and Chess. Additionally, the approach found use in two more complex projects, namely a timetable planner for university courses, and a safety critical, industrial application for the ETCS Hybrid Level 3 concept.

In all four examples we use the state that is translated into Java data structures in order to provide an (interactive) visualisation.

3.1   Real-Time Animation: Pac-Man

Our first example application is based on a formal model of Pac-Man[3].

The formal model itself is written in Event-B. It specifies all valid positions on the board that the Pac-Man and the ghosts can be in. There are state transitions that describe valid moves, though in the model itself ghosts are allowed to turn around. The model also manages the duration and targets of super pills (so that ghosts may be eaten, but only once per pill), and encounters of the Pac-Man with pills and ghosts. Finally, it keeps tracks of the Pac-Man's lives and deadlocks the game once none of Pac-Man's lives are left. It is possible to play a turn-based version of Pac-Man in the animator.

Note that the model is non-deterministic in the sense that there are multiple available operations, one for each direction the Pac-Man and each ghost may move.

Additional to the model, we implemented a plugin in PROB 2.0 that allows to play the game via traditional controls instead of executing transitions by clicking in the operation view. On the press of an arrow key, the following actions happen (Fig. 2):

---

[3] Available at: https://github.com/pkoerner/EventBPacman-Plugin.

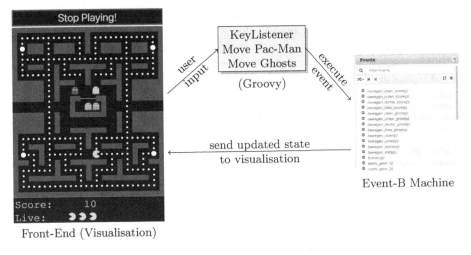

Fig. 2. Architecture of a Pac-Man game based on a formal model

- In the current state, it is evaluated whether the Pac-Man may move into that direction and the operation to move him is executed if allowed. Operations that result in eating a pill are preferred. This yields a new Trace object.
- For each ghost, it is evaluated whether enough time has passed to leave the monster pen. If so, the transition to move the ghost in a direction mandated by a heuristic is executed. New Trace objects are generated for each ghost and are extended by the next movement operation.
- It is verified whether the Pac-Man or some of the ghosts have to jump to the other side of the board via the tunnel. If the operation is enabled, it is executed.
- If available, operations that catch a ghost or the Pac-Man are executed.
- The GUI inspects the current state of the Trace and updates based on the new state values. The positions of the ghosts and the Pac-Man, the remaining pills, the score and the amount of remaining lives are extracted from the animation state.

For this kind of application, as the calculation of the next-state function is very fast, we did not encounter any performance issues when executing the model. We found that, even though the visualisation is in Java, depending on the operating system and JDK implementation, the game can run smoothly or just below acceptable performance[4]. Yet, we find it especially note-worthy that it is indeed possible to create real-time applications that depend on user input based on formal models, as at least five events per tick are executed, one to move the Pac-Man and four to move the ghosts. Plain animation in PROB could not capture this, instead it would turn Pac-Man into a turn-based game.

---

[4] On a Mac, it runs smoothly. On more powerful Linux PCs, it runs with stutters. We suspect that the socket communication is slower depending on the OS.

Main Contribution: Real-Time Animation. The Pac-Man case study shows that our approach is feasible for real-time applications as long as the computation of successor states is reasonably complex. The application is able to timely react to user input, directly embedding the formal model in the application does not lead to a noticeable performance decline.

Lessons Learned: Non-determinism. The case study made obvious that it is hard to get the amount of non-determinism right. The formal model itself has to incorporate certain aspects non-deterministically, e.g. we have to take into account every key the player might press. Simultaneously, the model has to be as deterministic as possible. As at least the ghosts are to be moved automatically, the computer controlled aspects of Pac-Man have to be modelled deterministically in order to avoid ambiguity and to avoid having to implement how to decide between different options.

3.2   Predicting the Future: Chess

In the chess example[5], we have two use cases. Firstly, we want two (human) players to be able to play against each other. Secondly, a (simple) chess AI should be available to play against.

As with Pac-Man, we use the formal specification in order to specify the rules of the game. The model offers all valid moves as enabled actions, checkmate is encoded as an invariant violation. Then, we can use the vanilla PROB animator to play chess (preferably with an additional visualisation of the current state).

The more interesting part is that an AI is hard to specify but somewhat easy to implement. Thus, the AI was written in Java using PROB 2.0: we implemented a Minimax algorithm with alpha-beta pruning [27]. The calculated tree has the current state at its root and its children are the successor states representing all valid turns by the AI. Their children again are their corresponding successor states where each state represents a turn by the human player and so forth. For termination, we limit the depth of the state space that should be explored, i.e. the amount of turns the AI is able to look ahead. Hence, this depth determines the AI's strength.

The Java side hereby is responsible for two things. It decides which child states need to be expanded and picks the most beneficial action for the AI opponent based on the explored game tree. Figure 3 visualises the execution. After the user's turn, the state space is explored, uncovering all possible courses the game could take. Then, the best action is chosen and the current chess state is updated accordingly. Note that the calculation of successor states happens on PROB side, as the game logic is fully implemented in B.

In order to assign a weight to each state, we use a more sophisticated evaluation function that only depends on a single state. It incorporates both the amount of pieces on the board and their positions and is also specified in B.

---

[5] Available at: https://github.com/pkoerner/b-chess-example.

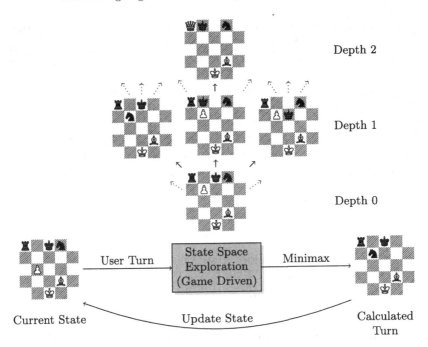

Fig. 3. Architecture of chess based on a formal model

Then, after checking states until a given depth, the turn suggested by Minimax is picked for the opponent. This strategy is very similar to bounded model checking [6], though execution is kept explicit instead of resorting to symbolic means. However, regarding this chess implementation we are not particularly concerned with violated invariants other than for identifying a checkmate state (which the AI accounts for). Instead, all possible outcomes are generated via execution of the model. Afterwards, a trace is chosen based on its Minimax value, eventually leading to an action that guarantees the most favourable outcome.

This case study offers worse results than Pac-Man. Due to the state space explosion caused by the sheer amount of possible moves, generating all successor states as deep as required by a strong chess engine is infeasible. An implementation in, e.g., plain C or Java is orders of magnitudes faster. Modern chess engines usually make use of additional heuristics, and opening and end game databases in order to improve performance. Using our approach following a somewhat naive implementation, only a small part of the state space from a given board position can be generated in reasonable time, which results in the AI being a rather weak opponent.

Main Contribution: Game-Driven Model Exploration. In this case study, we replaced the common exploration strategies of PROB (breadth-first, depth-first and random) by an exploration strategy based on the current state of a game. The Minimax algorithm is used to drive the model checker, with the aim of expanding the most promising states, rather than exhaustively analysing the state space. Hence, we were able to implement a heuristic-based model checking approach.

Although PROB offers support for directed model checking [32] with a custom heuristic function already, our game-driven model exploration offers a huge advantage. Specifying an exploration heuristic in B is limited to the closed world of the calculated state. For each state the heuristic provides a value after which it is sorted into a priority queue. It is not possible to argue about the heuristic values of, e.g., sister nodes in the search tree. By animating the model externally in PROB 2.0 however, we are able to do exactly that: comparing heuristic values of different nodes to decide which states do not need to be explored further by alpha-beta pruning.

Lessons Learned: Model Complexity. Fully encoding all possible moves on a chessboard has lead to a model that is very complex and features a very large state space. Even though our traversal strategy avoids exhaustively expanding it, debugging and partial exploration were extremely difficult. Furthermore, the high complexity prevented our proof efforts. Further investigation into a refinement-based implementation of chess might help to overcome the difficulties.

3.3   ProB as a Constraint Solver: PlüS

PlüS[6] is an application for planning university timetables [40, 41]. The goal is to show that it is possible for students to finish their studies in legal standard time for all courses or combinations of major and minor subjects. If a course or a combination is found to be infeasible, the smallest conflicting set of classes and timeframes should be provided such that it can be fixed manually. This process is started from the current timetables. Complete re-generation of timetables is avoided due to informal agreements, e.g., lecturers prefer given timeslots or are unavailable on certain days.

A database stores information about all courses, e.g., for which subject they can be attributed, whether they are mandatory or if other courses are required to be completed beforehand. From this database, a B model is compiled. This is included in another B machine that allows checking for feasibility of a subject, move lectures etc. from one time-slot to another and to calculate the unsatisfiable core if applicable.

The formal model is the foundation for a GUI in JavaFX. The initial state is the initial timetable setup. Each course and combination can be checked individually, which triggers the state transition that checks feasibility. If the B model returns that there are conflicts, they are highlighted in the GUI. Then, the user can move courses to different timeslots and re-calculate. This is done via drag-and-drop and, again, triggers the corresponding operation in the B machine.

---

[6] Available at: https://plues.github.io/en/index/.

If a course works out with the current scheduling, the state variable that represents the timetable is used to generate PDF files containing a default timetable that can be given to students so they know in what semester they should attend which courses.

In this application, the interaction with PROB is hidden from the user, i.e., they do not need to know about formal methods, states and transitions. It is currently used by the University of Düsseldorf.

Main Contribution: Improving the B Eco-System. PlüS was one of the earlier projects that used PROB 2.0 extensively in the way presented. In particular, the value translator that translates B values into Java data structures, which is used in the other case studies, was created during the development of PlüS. Furthermore, certain shortcomings of B were identified: if-then-else statements are only available for substitutions, but not in the predicate and expression sublanguage. Similarly, it is not possible to use `let`-like syntax to locally capture values for any identifier. These have been addressed in newer versions of PROB, which extend the syntax of B in these ways.

Lastly, it is hard to express function-like constructs that calculate values that can be used in predicates. B offers definitions, which offer a macro system similar to the C-preprocessor with all its shortcomings, e.g. shadowing of variable identifiers, which are unacceptable in a formal language. Currently, we work on a language extension for PROB that allows a more sophisticated construct to implement pure functions.

Lessons Learned: Model Interaction. Interacting with the model can be quite cumbersome: in particular, feeding information from scratch into the model can be slow or very complex. Instead, it is easier to generate a large model containing all information.

Initially, the idea was to work on pure predicates without a state machine in order to find scheduling conflicts. However, the aforementioned shortcomings in the language resulted in large predicates with many repetitions that were hard to debug. We found that incorporating the information into a state machine with given operations for manipulation of the schedule is more sensible. Additionally, this offers a simple undo-feature by reverting the trace to an earlier state.

3.4   Real Time Animation: ETCS Hybrid Level 3 Concept

We also used PROB 2.0 in an industrial project, for a demonstrator of the ETCS (European Train Control System) HL3 (hybrid level 3) principles. HL3 is a novel approach to increase the capacity of the railway infrastructure, by allowing multiple trains to occupy the same track section. This is achieved by dividing the track sections into virtual subsections (VSS). While the status of the track sections is determined by existing wayside infrastructure (axle counters or track circuits), the status of the VSS is computed from train position reports.

Fig. 4. Screenshot from a video of Deutsche Bahn https://www.youtube.com/watch? v=FjKnugbmrP4 showing a formal Event-B model in action

In this application, the formal model was used as a component at runtime to control real trains in real time. This can be seen in Fig. 4, where in the lower center one can see the PROB 2.0 visualisation of the formal model. The visualisation shows that two trains occupy the same occupied track section, but occupy disjoint virtual subsections. The ETCS hybrid level 3 principles were independently used as a case study for ABZ 2018 [23]. Due to page constraints, we can only give a high-level overview here. More details can be found in [23].

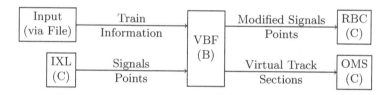

Fig. 5. Architecture of the HL3 prototype

When considering railroad tracks, they are usually divided in subsections. On the boundaries, usually there are sensors like axle counters in order to determine whether a train is occupying the corresponding subsection. The main idea is that by using a Virtual Block Function (VBF), the capacity of existing railroad networks can be increased. The VBF subdivides the tracks into virtual subsections without having to install further sensors or other hardware onto the tracks. As main part of the demonstration, the VBF was written as a B model, managing the status of said virtual subsections.

For the overall demonstrator, the VBF was interfaced with other hardware components (Fig. 5):

– an interlocking (IXL) which manages the signals and the status of the track sections,

- a Thales Radio Block Centre (RBC) which communicates with the trains and grants movement authorities,
- and an Operation and Maintenance Server (OMS).

These three components feed information into the model via PROB 2.0 in order to drive the formal model.

The model itself is non-deterministic. Based on the inputs from the external sources, the corresponding operation is chosen. After updating the state of the model, the successor state is passed to a consumer in Java that in turn sends information to the IXL, OMS and RBC. The VBF application, comprising PROB, PROB 2.0 and the B formal model, performs well enough on a regular notebook computer for a real-life demonstration involving the management of actual trains on their VSS.

Though we cannot disclose the model and the application itself, the overall architecture of the VBF demonstrator is very similar to the Pac-Man example. The Pac-Man board can be seen equivalent to the railtrack topology, and the Pac-Man behaves similar to trains, as they move based on external input. Instead of only visualising the model state to the user, additionally the application reacts to it and communicates with other components.

Main Contribution: Application Based on Model Alone. The ETCS case study fully relies on an embedded model rather than on code generation. By doing so, it has proven our approach to be both feasible and efficient in a real-world application. The overall development time was low when compared to manual or automated code generation. In addition, the formal model was very close to the HL3 natural language requirements. Changes to the requirements and model could be quickly carried out. Indeed, the use of our demonstrator has uncovered over 40 issues in the original HL3 principles paper, which were corrected in the official document along with our formal model. Of course, a fully refinement-based approach ending with code generation would be able to prove the system correctness and hence deliver a higher level of certainty than our approach does. However, we believe that for prototypes and demonstrators, a model-checked and well-tested specification that is directly executed can beat non-formal software development by a wide margin in terms of development time and costs.

Lessons Learned: Full-Stack Debugging Workflow. One important benefit of our approach was that we could store the formal model's behaviour in log files and later replay these traces in the PROB animator. This allowed us to analyse suspect behaviours, fix the HL3 specification and model, and then check that the corrected model solved the uncovered issues by replaying the trace again. I.e., we automatically got record and replay capabilities of debuggers as in [35].

4 Discussion and Related Work

When thinking of executing formal specifications, one usually has animation or code generation (cf. [20,44]) in mind. Yet, we will first discuss whether the approach itself makes sense: in the past, there has been thorough discussion [19, 21,24] whether specifications should be executable in the first place.

4.1 Soundness of Approach

Some argue [24] that formal specifications should not be executable for several reasons:

- Proof is more important than (finite) execution,
- Forms of usable specifications are restricted,
- Executable specifications tend to be over-specified,
- Execution is inefficient.

We deliberately go against this judgement and use a formal specification language, B, that has powerful tooling such as animators, model checkers, PO generators, etc.

This does not mean that we disagree with these arguments; firstly, we find formal proof to be very important. However, we have observed that for most formal specifications, which are more involved and are written to be executable, it is very hard and cumbersome to discharge any proof obligation. On the other hand, models written to be proven usually are not executable either. Yet, proof should always be complemented by animation in order to verify that not only the model is consistent in itself, but also describes the desired behaviour.

Secondly, B is a language that is very high-level and allows writing non-executable specifications (as one could encode a non-decidable problem in a single state transition). Instead, we embrace specifications an animator can handle and execute.

Thirdly, over-specification does not seem to be an issue for our use case. An example from [24] is a sorting algorithm. In B, this can be calculated by the constraint solver by purely specifying the *property* what it means for a sequence to be sorted. An example for a valid B predicate that can be solved by PROB in order to yield a sorted sequence is given in Fig. 6. Note that no concrete implementation is specified, as the problem is solved in a declarative manner.

In the typical workflow of the B-Method, a concrete implementation happens during refinement. Thus, the writer of the specification is usually *able to choose* the level of abstraction herself.

The last argument concerning performance is carefully reviewed for each of our case studies individually in Sect. 3 and overall in Sect. 5.

Being able to execute specifications also gives rise to techniques such as animation and model checking. Both of them have proven to be vital during creation and debugging of a formal specification, as errors can be caught early on.

$$input = [12, -3, 42, 7] \wedge \qquad \text{(input sequence)}$$
$$output \in 1..size(input) \rightarrow ran(input) \wedge \qquad \text{(type of output)}$$
$$\forall e \in ran(input) \cdot (card(input \rhd \{e\}) = card(output \rhd \{e\}))) \wedge \qquad \text{(keep elements)}$$
$$\forall i \cdot 1 \leq i < size(input) \implies output(i) \leq output(i+1) \qquad \text{(ordering)}$$

Fig. 6. Sorting predicate

4.2 Animation

As mentioned above, animation of a formal specification is an important means to quickly find errors by executing certain scenarios. This can either be done manually or even replaying a given trace in an automated manner. Executing a longer trace by hand and verifying each encountered state is correct is very cumbersome and might be aided by state visualisations.

In contrast to the approach we presented earlier, the user interacts with the formal model directly. This also means that all events have been chosen by hand, even ones that should be picked by the environment. In our examples, that includes movement of the ghosts in Pac-Man, moving the chess pieces of the enemy and providing the input of signals, points, etc.

Another approach [37] executes several example runs on probabilistic models. Yet, it is not possible to let an environment interact with the model itself. On the other hand, this approach encourages non-deterministic models.

4.3 Visualisation

All the presented projects include a GUI which displays a visualisation of the current state. State visualisation by itself is a useful tool to understand the application state more easily and is often used during the development of a model, debugging, and also to explain it to a domain expert.

BMotionWeb [28,29] is a tool for state visualisation based on web technologies. It also builds upon ProB 2.0 API and allows simple interaction with the model. The chess example from Sect. 3.2 uses this tool both for visualisation and embedding the script that controls the AI. A heavy disadvantage however is the complex technology stack: BMotionWeb builds upon ProB 2.0 and uses Groovy, SVG, JavaScript and HTML5, where each component of the stack may go wrong, rendering development very cumbersome.

State visualisation is not unique to the B formalisms: e.g., another tool that allows visualisations based on web technologies is WebASM [45], which works on top of CoreASM [16]. CoreASM is a tool that can be used to execute abstract state machines (ASM).

4.4 Code Generation

A more traditional approach is to generate (low-level) code based on the specification. Translation tools usually cannot work on most constructs that high-level formalisms have to offer, e.g. calculation of an appropriate parameter for an operation, set comprehensions or solving quantifications usually require constraint solving techniques which are infeasible to generate.

A popular implementation-level subset of B is named B0 [1,15], from which translation into an imperative language is fairly straightforward. Many features of the B language are missing though, including many operators on functions, relations and sets as well as quantifications.

For B and Event-B, several code generators exist. One such code generator is C4B which is integrated in Atelier B [15]. It allows generation of C code from the implementation level subset of B (i.e. B0). However, refining a model of industrial size down to B0 is a notably cumbersome task to do. Another code generator that is capable to cope with a subset of B0 is b2llvm [7] that generates LLVM code. A notable toolset Event-B is EB2ALL [34], which allows code generation to several languages including C and Java.

Currently, we explore which level of abstraction is required to render it feasible to generate code from higher-level specifications [43]. Supporting more constructs from B that are not included in B0 might make an approach using code generation more feasible. This work is aligned with EventB2Java [12,39] that also translates higher-level constructs.

4.5   Other Approaches

Another formal specification language is part of the Vienna Development Method (VDM) [26]. A well-known tool for VDM is Overture [31], which implements an interpreter in Java. In [36], an extension to the VDM language and Overture was presented. It allows execution of Java code from VDM specifications and, in turn, to control the interpreter to evaluate expressions in the current state. The goal is to add visualisation of the current state to the model and to integrate models with legacy systems, as we did, e.g., in Sect. 3.4.

5   Conclusions

In this paper, we presented PROB 2.0, which offers a Java API to the PROB model checker. PROB 2.0 renders it possible to write applications that interact with a formal model at runtime, offering declarative programming, rapid prototyping and easy debugging. Furthermore, we embedded formal models into actual applications and investigated this approach via four different case studies. We also considered counterarguments regarding executable specifications and re-evaluated them given the gained experiences.

Overall, we can draw the following conclusions:

– We think that specifications can and should indeed be executable, as it allows verification of an interpretation or an implementation against the specification. Given a suitable high-level specification language, many counterarguments such as over-specification do not hold. With a tool as presented in

Sect. 2 or in [36], it is possible and (often) viable to use that specification as a library in an application, allowing embedment of declarative programming into traditional, imperative programming languages.

- Development of complex components is significantly eased by the level of abstractions a high-level specification language, such as B, can provide. Integration with existing code, that may be written in other programming languages or running on different machines, is very powerful. In particular, when re-iterating on the formal model, changes can immediately be re-evaluated by a test scenario in the context of an entire application. Otherwise, an implementation has to be changed as well, which allows introduction of new bugs. Tool support such as model checking or animation proved to be invaluable to uncover errors early on which may otherwise have gone unnoticed for a longer time.
- The main concern for real-life applications, as already stated in 1989 by [24], is performance. Low-level applications written in traditional imperative, functional or even logical programming languages can be orders of magnitudes faster because they can work at lower levels of abstraction. Hence, for many time-critical applications the execution of formal specifications is not the way to go yet. However, as long as performance requirements are reasonable (e.g., if data sets are rather small), utilising formal models at runtime allows us to quickly deploy complex applications that can make use of the eco-system associated with formal methods, from proof to animation and model checking.

Acknowledgement. We thank Christoph Heinzen and David Geleßus for authoring and improving the presented Pac-Man application, as well as Philip Höfges for the chess model, AI and GUI. Additionally, we want to thank the many people who were involved in the development of both PROB and PROB 2.0, the Slot Tool and the ETCS Hybrid Level 3 case study.

References

1. Abrial, J.-R.: The B-Book: Assigning Programs to Meanings. Cambridge University Press, Cambridge (1996)
2. Abrial, J.-R.: Modeling in Event-B: System and Software Engineering, 1st edn. Cambridge University Press, Cambridge (2010)
3. Abrial, J.-R., Lee, M.K.O., Neilson, D.S., Scharbach, P.N., Sørensen, I.H.: The B-method. In: Prehn, S., Toetenel, H. (eds.) VDM 1991. LNCS, vol. 552, pp. 398–405. Springer, Heidelberg (1991). https://doi.org/10.1007/BFb0020001
4. Back, R.: On correct refinement of programs. J. Comput. Syst. Sci. **23**(1), 49–68 (1981)
5. Back, R.-J., Wright, J.: Refinement Calculus: A Systematic Introduction. Springer, Heidelberg (2012)
6. Biere, A., Cimatti, A., Clarke, E.M., Strichman, O., Zhu, Y., et al.: Bounded model checking. Adv. Comput. **58**(11), 117–148 (2003)
7. Bonichon, R., Déharbe, D., Lecomte, T., Medeiros, V.: LLVM-based code generation for B. In: Braga, C., Martí-Oliet, N. (eds.) SBMF 2014. LNCS, vol. 8941, pp. 1–16. Springer, Cham (2015). https://doi.org/10.1007/978-3-319-15075-8_1

8. Butler, M., Leuschel, M.: Combining CSP and B for specification and property verification. In: Fitzgerald, J., Hayes, I.J., Tarlecki, A. (eds.) FM 2005. LNCS, vol. 3582, pp. 221–236. Springer, Heidelberg (2005). https://doi.org/10.1007/11526841_16

9. Cansell, D., Méry, D.: Foundations of the B method. Comput. Inf. **22**(3–4), 221–256 (2012)

10. Carlsson, M., Ottosson, G., Carlson, B.: An open-ended finite domain constraint solver. In: Glaser, H., Hartel, P., Kuchen, H. (eds.) PLILP 1997. LNCS, vol. 1292, pp. 191–206. Springer, Heidelberg (1997). https://doi.org/10.1007/BFb0033845

11. Carlsson, M., et al.: SICStus Prolog User's Manual, vol. 3. Swedish Institute of Computer Science Kista, Sweden (1988)

12. Cataño, N., Rivera, V.: EventB2Java: a code generator for Event-B. In: Rayadurgam, S., Tkachuk, O. (eds.) NFM 2016. LNCS, vol. 9690, pp. 166–171. Springer, Cham (2016). https://doi.org/10.1007/978-3-319-40648-0_13

13. CENELEC. Railway Applications - Communication, signalling and processing systems - Software for railway control and protection systems. Technical report EN50128, European Standard (2011)

14. Clark, J., Bendisposto, J., Hallerstede, S., Hansen, D., Leuschel, M.: Generating Event-B specifications from algorithm descriptions. In: Butler, M., Schewe, K.-D., Mashkoor, A., Biro, M. (eds.) ABZ 2016. LNCS, vol. 9675, pp. 183–197. Springer, Cham (2016). https://doi.org/10.1007/978-3-319-33600-8_11

15. ClearSy: Atelier B, User and Reference Manuals. Aix-en-Provence, France (2016). http://www.atelierb.eu/

16. Farahbod, R., Gervasi, V., Glässer, U.: CoreASM: an extensible ASM execution engine. Fundamenta Informaticae **77**(1–2), 71–103 (2007)

17. Fraenkel, A.: Zu den Grundlagen der Cantor-Zermeloschen Mengenlehre. Math. Ann. **86**(3), 230–237 (1922)

18. Fraenkel, A.A., Bar-Hillel, Y., Levy, A.: Foundations of Set Theory, vol. 67. Elsevier, Amsterdam (1973)

19. Fuchs, N.E.: Specifications are (preferably) executable. Softw. Eng. J. **7**(5), 323–334 (1992)

20. Ghezzi, C., Kennerer, R.A.: Executing formal specifications: the ASTRAL to TRIO translation approach. In: Proceedings of the Symposium on Testing, Analysis, and Verification, TAV4, pp. 112–122. ACM (1991)

21. Gravell, A., Henderson, P.: Executing formal specifications need not be harmful. Softw. Eng. J. **11**(2), 104–110 (1996)

22. Hansen, D., Leuschel, M.: Translating TLA$^+$ to B for Validation with PROB. In: Derrick, J., Gnesi, S., Latella, D., Treharne, H. (eds.) IFM 2012. LNCS, vol. 7321, pp. 24–38. Springer, Heidelberg (2012). https://doi.org/10.1007/978-3-642-30729-4_3

23. Hansen, D., et al.: Using a formal B model at runtime in a demonstration of the ETCS hybrid level 3 concept with real trains. In: Butler, M., Raschke, A., Hoang, T.S., Reichl, K. (eds.) ABZ 2018. LNCS, vol. 10817, pp. 292–306. Springer, Cham (2018). https://doi.org/10.1007/978-3-319-91271-4_20

24. Hayes, I.J., Jones, C.B.: Specifications are not (necessarily) executable. Softw. Eng. J. **4**(6), 330–339 (1989)

25. Hoare, C.A.R.: Communicating sequential processes. In: Hansen, P.B. (ed.) The Origin of Concurrent Programming, pp. 413–443. Springer, New York (1978). https://doi.org/10.1007/978-1-4757-3472-0_16

26. Jones, C.B.: Systematic Software Development Using VDM, vol. 2. Princeton, Citeseer (1990)

27. Knuth, D.E., Moore, R.W.: An analysis of alpha-beta pruning. Artif. Intell. **6**(4), 293–326 (1975)
28. Ladenberger, L.: Rapid creation of interactive formal prototypes for validating safety-critical systems. Ph.D. thesis (2017)
29. Ladenberger, L., Leuschel, M.: BMotionWeb: a tool for rapid creation of formal prototypes. In: De Nicola, R., Kühn, E. (eds.) SEFM 2016. LNCS, vol. 9763, pp. 403–417. Springer, Cham (2016). https://doi.org/10.1007/978-3-319-41591-8_27
30. Lamport, L.: Specifying Systems: the TLA+ Language and Tools for Hardware and Software Engineers. Addison-Wesley Longman Publishing Co., Inc., Boston (2002)
31. Larsen, P.G., Battle, N., Ferreira, M., Fitzgerald, J., Lausdahl, K., Verhoef, M.: The overture initiative integrating tools for VDM. ACM SIGSOFT Softw. Eng. Notes **35**(1), 1–6 (2010)
32. Leuschel, M., Bendisposto, J.: Directed model checking for B: an evaluation and new techniques. In: Davies, J., Silva, L., Simao, A. (eds.) SBMF 2010. LNCS, vol. 6527, pp. 1–16. Springer, Heidelberg (2011). https://doi.org/10.1007/978-3-642-19829-8_1
33. Leuschel, M., Butler, M.: ProB: a model checker for B. In: Araki, K., Gnesi, S., Mandrioli, D. (eds.) FME 2003. LNCS, vol. 2805, pp. 855–874. Springer, Heidelberg (2003). https://doi.org/10.1007/978-3-540-45236-2_46
34. Méry, D., Singh, N.K.: Automatic code generation from event-B models. In: Proceedings SoICT, pp. 179–188. ACM (2011)
35. Narayanasamy, S., Pokam, G., Calder, B.: BugNet: continuously recording program execution for deterministic replay debugging. In: ACM SIGARCH Computer Architecture News, vol. 33, pp. 284–295. IEEE Computer Society (2005)
36. Nielsen, C.B., Lausdahl, K., Larsen, P.G.: Combining VDM with executable code. In: Derrick, J., et al. (eds.) ABZ 2012. LNCS, vol. 7316, pp. 266–279. Springer, Heidelberg (2012). https://doi.org/10.1007/978-3-642-30885-7_19
37. Nummenmaa, T.: Executable formal specifications in game development: design, validation and evolution. Ph.D. thesis (2013)
38. Plagge, D., Leuschel, M.: Validating Z specifications using the PROB animator and model checker. In: Davies, J., Gibbons, J. (eds.) IFM 2007. LNCS, vol. 4591, pp. 480–500. Springer, Heidelberg (2007). https://doi.org/10.1007/978-3-540-73210-5_25
39. Rivera, V., Cataño, N., Wahls, T., Rueda, C.: Code generation for Event-B. STTT **19**(1), 31–52 (2017)
40. Schneider, D.: Constraint modelling and data validation using formal specification languages. Ph.D. thesis. Heinrich-Heine-Universität Düsseldorf (2017)
41. Schneider, D., Leuschel, M., Witt, T.: Model-based problem solving for university timetable validation and improvement. Formal Aspects Comput. **30**, 545–569 (2018)
42. Spivey, J.M., Abrial, J.: The Z Notation. Prentice Hall, Hemel Hempstead (1992)
43. Vu, F.: A high-level code generator for safety critical B models. Bachelor's thesis, Heinrich Heine Universität Düsseldorf, August 2018
44. Wahls, T., Leavens, G.T., Baker, A.L.: Executing formal specifications with concurrent constraint programming. Autom. Softw. Eng. **7**(4), 315–343 (2000)
45. Zenzaro, S., Gervasi, V., Soldani, J.: WebASM: an abstract state machine execution environment for the web. In: Ait Ameur, Y., Schewe, K.D. (eds.) Abstract State Machines, Alloy, B, TLA, VDM, and Z. ABZ 2014. LNCS, vol. 8477, pp. 216–221. Springer, Heidelberg (2014). https://doi.org/10.1007/978-3-662-43652-3_19

Reasoning Techniques

Value-Dependent Information-Flow Security on Weak Memory Models

Graeme Smith[1,2]([✉]), Nicholas Coughlin[2], and Toby Murray[3]

[1] Defence Science and Technology Group, Brisbane, Australia
[2] School of Information Technology and Electrical Engineering,
The University of Queensland, Brisbane, Australia
smith@itee.uq.edu.au
[3] School of Computing and Information Systems,
The University of Melbourne, Melbourne, Australia

Abstract. Weak memory models implemented on modern multicore processors are known to affect the correctness of concurrent code. They can also affect whether or not it is secure. This is particularly the case in programs where the security levels of variables are *value-dependent*, i.e., depend on the values of other variables. In this paper, we illustrate how instruction reordering allowed by contemporary multicore processors leads to vulnerabilities in such programs, and present a compositional, timing-sensitive information-flow logic which can be used to detect such vulnerabilities. The logic allows step-local reasoning (one instruction at a time) about a thread's security by tracking information about dependencies between instructions which guarantee their order of occurrence. Program security can then be established from individual thread security using rely/guarantee reasoning.

1 Introduction

Modern multicore processors utilise *weak memory models* which, for reasons of efficiency, allow instructions to take effect in an order different to that in the program text [25]. Such instruction reordering is constrained by basic principles, the key one being that the sequential semantics of each thread in the original code should be preserved [6,7]. This ensures the effects of weak memory models can largely be ignored by programmers whose code is either not concurrent, or is concurrent but data-race free.[1] However, these effects do need to be considered by programmers writing efficient low-level code for device drivers and data structures. Such code is generally concurrent and *non-blocking*, i.e., using no, or minimal, locking, and hence inherently not data-race free [16]. It is well known that this affects the correctness of such code on weak memory models [2]. As shown by Vaughan and Milstein [26] (for the weak memory model TSO) and Mantel et al. [14] (for TSO, PSO and IBM-370), it also leads to security violations which are not detectable using the standard approaches to information-flow security.

---

[1] The recently discovered Meltdown [12], Spectre [11] and Foreshadow [4] vulnerabilities show that this is not strictly the case.

© Commonwealth of Australia 2019
M. H. ter Beek et al. (Eds.): FM 2019, LNCS 11800, pp. 539–555, 2019.
https://doi.org/10.1007/978-3-030-30942-8_32

While TSO [24] is widely used (by chip manufacturers Intel and AMD), PSO and IBM-370 are not supported on recent processors. More relevant weak memory models are ARM [9,22] and IBM POWER [23]; the former being widely used in mobile devices [8]. These memory models are significantly weaker (allowing more kinds of reordering) than those studied by the papers above, yet have received little attention from the security community.

Additionally, the effects of weak memory models on programs with security levels that are *value-dependent* [13,18,27] have not been explored to date. In such programs, the security level of a variable may depend on the values of one or more other variables. Hence, it may change as the program changes the state.

Building on Mantel et al.'s compositional information-flow logic for concurrent programs [15], Murray et al. [19,20] provide two information-flow logics for concurrent programs which are compositional and also handle dynamic, value-dependent security levels. The latter of these has been successfully applied to a non-trivial concurrent program running on an embedded device which facilitates secure interaction with multiple classified networks.

In this paper, we take this work further by incorporating the effects of weak memory models. Our logic specifically captures the effects of the revised version of ARMv8 [22], the latest version of ARM.[2] This memory model has much in common with prior versions of ARM [9], and with IBM POWER [23]. Our logic has been proven sound with respect to a recent operational semantics of ARMv8 [6] which has been validated against approximately 10,000 litmus tests run on actual hardware.

We begin with an overview of weak memory models in Sect. 2 and demonstrate how they can lead to security vulnerabilities in value-dependent security systems in Sect. 3. In Sect. 4, we present a formal framework for our logic which is presented in full in Sect. 5. We discuss the issue of timing sensitivity in Sect. 6 and conclude in Sect. 7.

2   Weak Memory Models

Hardware weak memory models, as exemplified by TSO [24], ARM [9,22] and IBM POWER [23], aim at optimising assembly code by restricting accesses to global shared memory: a well known cause of inefficiency in multicore systems. This can be achieved, for example, by buffering writes to memory and letting the hardware control when those writes actually occur, or by allowing *speculative execution* of code occurring in a branch of the program before evaluating whether that branch should be taken (which may require access to shared memory). It can also be achieved by propagating writes to other cores rather than the shared memory (referred to as *non-multi-copy atomicity* since different cores may receive a particular write at different times).

The effects of such optimisations can lead to the instructions of one thread appearing to occur out-of-order from the perspective of threads running on other

---

[2] We will refer to this as simply ARMv8 in the remainder of this paper.

cores. For example, if a thread t buffers the writes to variables x and y while executing the code x := 1; y := 2 and then the hardware flushes the value assigned to y first, it appears to threads running on other cores as if t executed the code y := 2; x := 1.

Colvin and Smith [6,7] define four constraints related to this perceived reordering of assignments on weak memory models. These constraints, which are common to all contemporary weak memory models, ensure that the sequential semantics of the thread on which the reordering occurs is unchanged. An assignment x := e can be reordered with an assignment y := f if, and only if, (i) x and y are distinct variables; (ii) x is not referred to in f; (iii) y is not referred to in e; and (iv) e and f do not reference any common global variables.

Constraint (i) is obviously required as x := 1; x := 2 has a different final value of x (and hence different behaviour) than x := 2; x := 1. Constraint (ii) is required since x := 1; y := x will result in a different value for y than y := x; x := 1 when the initial value of x is not 1. Similarly, constraint (iii) is required since x := y; y := 1 can result in a different value for x than y := 1; x := y. Finally, constraint (iv) is required so that the order of updates and accesses of each global variable, considered individually, is maintained: x := z; y := z will not behave the same as y := z; x := z in an environment which modifies z since the former will never result in y having an earlier value of z than x.

In contemporary processors, constraint (ii) is weakened by *forwarding* which allows a program such as x := e; y := x to be reordered to y := e; x := e when e does not refer to global variables, i.e., the effect of the first assignment is taken into account when determining whether the second can be reordered with it.

Specific memory models may add additional constraints, e.g., TSO does not allow a write to a global variable to be reordered with a subsequent write to a global variable. They will also have reordering constraints related to other types of instructions such as branch instructions and fences (see Sect. 3.1 for the branch constraints on ARM). Fences are a means by which the programmer can enforce ordering where necessary in their program. For example, letting fence denote a full fence (e.g., the instruction DMB on ARM), the program x := 1; fence; y := 2 ensures the write to x is seen by other threads before the write to y. A full set of reordering constraints for TSO, ARM and POWER which have been validated against existing test suites on hardware is provided in [6,7].

3 Weak Memory Models and Security

We are interested in evaluating the security of assembly code running on ARMv8 processors [9]. For ease of presentation, we adopt a high-level language to represent assembly commands (as in [6,7]). The syntax of a command, i.e., a program, c in this language is as follows:

$$c ::= \text{skip} \mid c \; ; \; c \mid \text{if } (b) \text{ then } c \text{ else } c \mid \text{while } (b) \text{ do } c \mid x := e \mid \text{fence}$$

where x is a (global or local) variable, b a Boolean condition, and e an expression. In our examples, we also allow do c while (b) as a shorthand for c ; while (b) do c.

This simple language has only one kind of fence (a full fence which requires all updates to be seen by all threads before proceeding). ARM additionally supports store fences (which maintain an order on stores only) and a control fence (for restricting speculative execution beyond branch points). Extending our approach to cater for such additional constructs is beyond the scope of this paper which focusses on the interplay between value-dependent security levels and instruction reordering in weak memory models.

To illustrate this interplay we introduce the example of Fig. 1. In this example, the four operations are of an IO-driver object which receives input data from an IO device, such as a keyboard, and stores it in the variable x. This variable is intended to be an abstract representation of an input buffer.

As well as a simple write operation, the object has a secret_write operation. This is used when the user indicates (via the keyboard or another input device) that the information to be input is classified. The operation sets a variable z, which is initially 0, to an odd number by incrementing it before allowing the input data to be assigned to x. After the data is read (how this is detected is elided in the abstract representation of Fig. 1), the operation enters some unclassified data in x (the value 0) before setting z back to an even number by incrementing it again. As we will see, the setting of z ensures that the classified input is not readable by all applications running on the computer to which the keyboard is attached.

```
write:              read:
  x := data           do
                        do
                          r1:= z;
secret_write:             while (r1 % 2 ≠ 0)
  z := z+1;               r2 := x;
  x := secret;          while (z ≠ r1)
  ...                     y := r2
  x := 0;
  z := z+1            secret_read:
                        y := x
```

Fig. 1. An IO-driver object with operations for accepting input from a keyboard at unclassified (write) and classified (secret_write) levels, and for reading input data at unclassified (read) and classified (secret_read) levels.

We call z a *control variable* because it controls the security level of x; when it is even x may only contain unclassified data, but when it is odd it may also contain classified data. The use of such control variables provides us with *value-dependent security* [13,18,27].

Next consider the operations which read from the buffer. We have a secret_read operation which only applications which are allowed access to classified information can call, as well as a general read operation which all applications can call. To avoid leaks of classified data, the latter should not read the variable x when z is odd; this is the only time when x can contain classified data. A naive approach would be to use an if statement in read to disallow reading x when z is odd: if $(z \% 2 = 0)$ then $y := x$ else skip where y is a variable which the application calling the operation can access. Obviously, this will not work in a concurrent setting since the check of z's value could be made before z is incremented for the first time by secret_write and subsequently the assignment to y made immediately after x is assigned the classified data.

To avoid this undesirable behaviour, we could ensure mutual exclusion between the operations secret_write and read using a lock; each of these operations would acquire the lock as it first step and release it as its last. This, however, would be highly inefficient. Firstly, there may be many applications running and wishing to access the keyboard data, and requiring each to acquire the lock before reading would create an obvious bottleneck. Secondly, the secret_write operation should preferably not be made to acquire a lock as it needs to react without delay in order to accept (real-time) keyboard input.

A better solution is to use a *non-blocking algorithm* [16]. Such algorithms allow threads to run concurrently on the same object with no, or minimal, use of locking. For example, consider the implementation of read in Fig. 1 where r1 and r2 are local variables. This operation waits in a loop until z is even (and hence x does not contain classified information) and then reads x into r2. It then checks that z has not changed (and hence has been even the entire time since it was checked) before copying the value of r2 to y. Since z can only stay at its current value or increase, if its value is the same as at some earlier time t, we can deduce that z has not changed since time t.

This algorithm allows the secret_write operation to operate without locking or delay, and allows multiple threads to call the read operation simultaneously. It is based on a Linux read-write mechanism called seqlock [3], and is a typical example of a non-blocking algorithm.

3.1   Value-Dependent Security and Reordering

The implementation in Fig. 1 is secure on a *sequentially consistent* memory model, i.e., one that does not allow instruction reordering. It is also secure on a memory model such as TSO where writes are seen by other threads in the order in which they occur. For weaker memory models such as ARM and POWER, this is not the case. These memory models allow writes by a thread to be seen out-of-order by other threads since no additional constraints are added to the four common constraints presented in Sect. 2.

For example, consider the operation secret_write. If from the perspective of threads running read, the assignment of the classified data to x occurred before the first assignment to z then that classified data could be read into the variable y. To avoid this situation, a fence is required between these two assignments. Similarly, if the second assignment to z occurred before the assignment of 0 to x then again the classified data in x could be read into y. The solution again is to maintain the order by placing a fence between these assignments. A secure version of secret_write is given in Fig. 2.

Similar issues arise with the read operation. To understand these, we first provide the rules for reordering involving branch instructions on ARM processors [6,7].

1. An assignment x := e following a branch instruction with branching condition b can be reordered with the branch instruction if, and only if, x is a local

variable and does not appear free in b, and b and e do not reference common global variables.

2. An assignment x := e preceding a branch with branching condition b can be reordered with the branch if, and only if, x does not appear free in b, and b and e do not reference common global variables.

3. Two branch instructions can be reordered if, and only if, their branching conditions do not reference common global variables.

In case 1 the assignment is speculatively executed (before the branch condition is evaluated). It is therefore restricted to assignments to local variables since if it is later determined that the branch should not be executed, it is necessary to discard the results of such assignments. This cannot be done with assignments to global variables.

In the read operation two problems arise due to these reorderings. Firstly, since r2 is a local variable, the assignment to r2 could be reordered with the first branch instruction (case 1) and further reordered with the assignment to r1. This results in reading a value of x into r2 before checking that z is even. If this value is classified and subsequently z is made even by secret_write, the check will pass and the classified information in r2 will be able to be passed into y. A fence before the assignment to r2 will prevent this reordering.

Secondly, if the assignment to r2 is reordered with the second branch condition (case 2) then it is possible that a secret_write operation begins after the check of that branch condition and hence r2 is loaded with classified data. Again, a fence can prevent the reordering. A secure version of read is included in Fig. 2.

```
secret_write:        read:
z := z+1;            do
fence;                   do
x := secret;                 r1:= z;
...                      while (r1 % 2 ≠ 0)
x := 0;                  fence;
fence;                   r2 := x;
z := z+1                 fence;
                     while (z ≠ r1)
                     y := r2
```

Fig. 2. Versions of the operations (secret_write) and (read) which are secure when run on the ARMv8 memory model.

4   Formal Framework

In this section, we provide a formal framework on which we build our logic in Sect. 5. We let *Var* be the set of all program variables. Variables are partitioned into global (i.e. shared) variables *Global*, and local variables *Local*, i.e., $Var = Global \cup Local$ and $Local \cap Global = \varnothing$. We let $var(e)$ denote the set of variables which occur free in an expression e.

4.1   Assumptions and Guarantees

An important issue when reasoning about concurrent systems is compositionality. For scalability, we want to reason about individual threads in isolation and combine this reasoning to deduce properties of the entire program. One way to do this is to utilise rely/guarantee reasoning [5,10]. Reasoning done on an individual thread will be valid in the wider context of its execution if all of its assumptions are matched by a guarantee from all other threads. For example, if the thread assumes that no other thread writes to z then all other threads must guarantee that they do not.

Mantel et al. [15] adopt this approach in their concurrent information-flow logic by assigning variables referenced by a thread to one or more of the following *modes*.

- *AssNoRW* - the variable is not read or written to by another thread
- *AssNoW* - the variable is not written to by another thread (but may be read by another thread)
- *GuarNoW* - this thread does not write to the variable (but may read it)
- *GuarNoRW* - this thread does not read or write to the variable.

In our logic, such modes are represented by a function $M : Mode \to \mathcal{P} Var$ mapping each mode to the set of variables which have that mode. Local variables are always non-readable and non-writable by other threads, i.e., $Local \subseteq M(AssNoRW)$.

4.2   Value-Dependent Security Levels

Murray et al. [19,20] extend the approach of Mantel et al. [15] to include value-dependent security levels. As in that work, we adopt a two-point lattice of security levels with values Low and $High$ such that $Low \sqsubseteq High$ and $High \not\sqsubseteq Low$ (meaning that information classified $High$ should not flow to a variable classified Low).

Also following [19,20], we let $\mathcal{L}(x)$, for a variable x, be a predicate which is true precisely when x has security level Low. For example, $\mathcal{L}(\mathsf{x}) = (\mathsf{z} \% 2 = 0)$ in the example of Sect. 3, i.e., the security level of x depends on the parity of z. $\mathcal{L}$ is provided by the user and is independent of the program's state. In order to determine the security level of a variable in our logic, we introduce the following.

- A partial function $\Gamma : Var \nrightarrow \{Low, High\}$ whose domain is the set of *stable* variables, i.e., variables in $M(AssNoRW) \cup M(AssNoW)$, and which returns the security level of data held by those variables. This data can be at a lower level than the variable's security level, i.e., a variable with a $High$ security level may hold Low data. The data referred to by Γ at any point in the execution of a program assumes that precisely the instructions up to that point have been executed, i.e., instruction reordering due to a weak memory model is not considered.
- A predicate P on the program's variables (capturing the current state). We let $low_P(x) \widehat{=} P \vdash \mathcal{L}(x)$ denote that x's security level is provably Low when P holds, and $high_P(x) \widehat{=} P \vdash \neg \mathcal{L}(x)$ denote that x's security level is provably $High$ when P holds. As for Γ, at any point in the execution of a program, P assumes that precisely the instructions up to that point have been executed, i.e., instruction reordering is not considered.

Based on these we define the following shorthand for determining the security level t of an expression e (as the highest level of any free variable in e).

$$\Gamma, P \vdash e : t \;\;\widehat{=}\;\; t = \bigsqcup_{x \in var(e)} \Gamma_P(x)$$

$$\text{where} \quad \Gamma_P(x) \;\;\widehat{=}\;\; \begin{cases} \Gamma(x) & \text{if } x \in \text{dom } \Gamma \\ Low & \text{if } x \notin \text{dom } \Gamma \text{ and } low_P(x) \\ High & \text{otherwise} \end{cases}$$

Note that when the security level of one or more variables in an expression is unknown (i.e., neither specified in Γ nor derivable from P), Γ_P will default to security level $High$ for those variables. This ensures that an expression which we are assigning to a variable is given its highest possible security level.

When determining the security level of a variable x to which we assign a value, on the other hand, we want to default to Low.

$$eval_P(x) \;\;\widehat{=}\;\; \begin{cases} High & \text{if } high_P(x) \\ Low & \text{otherwise} \end{cases}$$

Following Murray et al. [19, 20], we assume control variables are always Low, i.e., $\mathcal{L}(z) = true$ for each control variable z. As a result, it is not necessary to include them in Γ when they are stable.

4.3 Weak Memory Models

Γ and P ignore the effects of reordering possible under a weak memory model. This is not a problem for Γ under the defined reordering constraints, as it is only consulted for the reads of an instruction. If an instruction containing such an expression e is reordered before a prior write to a variable x then, according to the constraints in Sect. 2, either (i) x is not in e, or (ii) x is in e and the reordering involves forwarding. In case (i), the assignment does not affect the value of Γ for any of the variables in e and hence does not affect the evaluation of e's security level. In case (ii), since forwarding involves taking into account the prior assignment's effect, using the updated value for x in Γ is appropriate.

P, on the other hand, cannot be used directly to determine the security level of a variable or expression. To use P we need to consider guarantees on the ordering of program instructions. To capture these guarantees in our logic, we introduce a function $known_W$ where, for a given instruction a, $known_W(a)$ is the set of variables whose most recent prior write in the program is known to have occurred. Hence, these variables' values in P can be used when determining the security level of x (using $eval_P(x)$) and the expression assigned to x (using $\Gamma, P \vdash e : t$).

The value of $known_W(a)$ evolves as the program progresses. For example, given the code z := x; y := x; z := 0; y := x where z, y and x are global variables, after the first assignment $known_W$ (y := x) contains z since the first assignment must occur before the second due to constraint (iv) of Sect. 2. However, after the third assignment $known_W$ (y := x) does not contain z since the fourth assignment can be reordered before the third.

We similarly introduce a function $known_R(a)$ to denote the set of variables whose most recent prior read in the program is known to have occurred. This set is required in cases where a read of a variable may be reordered with an instruction which changes the variable's security level (see Sect. 5 for details).

We define $known_W$ and $known_R$ in terms of four other functions each of type $Var \rightarrow \mathcal{P} Var$ capturing the dependencies between writes and reads:

- $W_w(x)$ returns the set of variables whose prior writes, if any, have occurred when we reach an instruction which writes to x;
- $W_r(x)$ returns the set of variables whose prior writes, if any, have occurred when we reach an instruction which reads x;
- $R_w(x)$ returns the set of variables whose prior reads, if any, have occurred when we reach an instruction which writes to x; and
- $R_r(x)$ returns the set of variables whose prior reads, if any, have occurred when we reach an instruction which reads x.

Given these definitions, we define $known_\psi(a)$ where ψ stands for either W or R as

$$known_\psi(a) = \begin{cases} Var & \text{if } a = \text{fence} \\ \bigcup_{y \in wr(a)} \psi_w(y) \cup \bigcup_{y \in rd(a)} \psi_r(y) & \text{otherwise} \end{cases}$$

where $wr(a)$ is the set of variables written to by instruction a and $rd(a)$ the set of variables read by a.

Initially the functions W_w, W_r, R_w and R_r map all variables to Var. At other points in the program their values are defined in terms of allowable instruction reorderings. We define $later_w(a)$ to return the set of variables whose *writes* cannot be reordered before a. Similarly, we define $later_r(a)$ to return the set of variables whose *reads* cannot be reordered before a. For example, $y \in later_w(x := e)$ implies writes of y cannot be reordered before the instruction $x := e$. This will be the case when $y = x$ (due to constraint (i) of Sect. 2) or $y \in var(e)$ (due to constraint (iii) of Sect. 2). Similarly, $y \in later_r(x := e)$ implies reads of y cannot be reordered before $x := e$. This will be the case when $y = x$ and e contains global variables (due to the weakened constraint (ii) of Sect. 2) or $y \in var(e) \cap Global$ (due to constraint (iv) of Sect. 2). The full definitions are:

$$later_w(Fence) = Var$$
$$later_w(x := e) = \{x\} \cup var(e)$$
$$later_w(b) = var(b) \cup Global$$

$$later_r(Fence) = Var$$
$$later_r(b) = var(b) \cap Global$$

$$later_r(x := e) = \begin{cases} \{x\} \cup (var(e) \cap Global) & \text{if } var(e) \cap Global \neq \varnothing \\ \varnothing & \text{otherwise} \end{cases}$$

where an argument b denotes the guard of an if or while instruction. The 'otherwise' case of the definition of $later_r(x := e)$ allows for forwarding.

Let $f[a]$ denote the update of function f (which may be W_w, W_r, R_w or R_r) when instruction a occurs, and ψ stand for either W or R. Then

$$\psi_w[a](x) = \begin{cases} \psi_w(x) \cup known_\psi(a) & \text{if } x \in later_w(a) \\ \psi_w(x) \setminus kill_\psi(a) & \text{otherwise} \end{cases}$$

$$\psi_r[a](x) = \begin{cases} \psi_r(x) \cup known_\psi(a) & \text{if } x \in later_r(a) \\ \psi_r(x) \setminus kill_\psi(a) & \text{otherwise} \end{cases}$$

where $kill_W(a) = wr(a)$ and $kill_R(a) = rd(a)$.

For example when an instruction a occurs, for any instruction a_1, $known_W(a_1)$ is updated by changes to $W_w(y)$ for any variable y written in a_1, and $W_r(y)$ for any variable y read in a_1. These changes reflect the instruction reorderings captured in $later_w(a)$ and $later_r(a)$. If the instruction a_1 cannot be reordered before a (due to a variable written or read in a_1 being in $later_w(a)$ or $later_r(a)$, respectively) then any writes that are known to have occurred before a will also be known to have occurred before a subsequent instruction a_1. Hence, they are added into $W_w(y)$ or $W_r(y)$. If, on the other hand, a_1 can be reordered before a then any writes in a are removed from those known to have occurred before a_1 (by removing them from both $W_w(y)$ and $W_r(y)$).

5   The Logic

In this section, we present our logic in which a thread c is secure when a judgement $\Gamma, P, D \{c\}_M \Gamma', P', D'$ can be derived from the logic's rules under modes M where D is the tuple (W_w, W_r, R_w, R_r) capturing the dependencies between instructions. Initially, $\Gamma(x)$ is Low for those stable variables x for which $\mathcal{L}(x)$ is true and $High$ otherwise, P is $true$, and all functions in D map each variable to Var. In the logic, we let $\mathcal{C} \subseteq Var$ represent the set of control variables.

The rules for skip, sequential composition, if statements and while loops (see Fig. 3) are based on those of Murray et al. [19,20]. The most significant modification is the introduction of P_a, a version of P restricted to the writes which are guaranteed to have occurred prior to reaching instruction a. We define $P_a = P \mid_{known_W(a)}$, where

$$P \mid_S \ \widehat{=} \ \exists y_1, ... y_n \cdot P \text{ where } \{y_1, .., y_n\} = Var \setminus S$$

As in Murray et al. [19,20], rules with branching conditions restrict the expression to be Low. This is necessary to ensure our logic is timing-sensitive (see Sect. 6). Additionally, we introduce an update to D based on an instruction a, $D[a]$, which updates all of its components as described in Sect. 4.

These rules also uses the notation $[b]_M$, which is the condition b with all free occurrences of unstable variables removed.

$$[b]_M \ \widehat{=} \ \exists y_1, ... y_n \cdot b$$
$$\text{where } \{y_1, ..., y_n\} = Var \setminus (M(AssNoRW) \cup M(AssNoW))$$

$$\text{SKIP} \; \frac{}{\Gamma, P, D \; \{\text{skip}\}_M \; \Gamma, P, D}$$

$$\text{SEQ} \; \frac{\Gamma, P, D \; \{c_1\}_M \; \Gamma', P', D' \qquad \Gamma', P', D' \; \{c_2\}_M \; \Gamma'', P'', D''}{\Gamma, P, D \; \{c_1; \; c_2\}_M \; \Gamma'', P'', D''}$$

$$\text{IF} \; \frac{\Gamma, P_b \vdash b : Low \qquad \begin{array}{l} \Gamma, P \wedge [b]_M, D[b] \; \{c_1\}_M \; \Gamma', P', D' \\ \Gamma, P \wedge [\neg \, b]_M, D[b] \; \{c_2\}_M \; \Gamma', P', D' \end{array}}{\Gamma, P, D \; \{\text{if } (b) \text{ then } c_1 \text{ else } c_2\}_M \; \Gamma', P', D'}$$

$$\text{WHILE} \; \frac{\Gamma, P_b \vdash b : Low \qquad \Gamma, P \wedge [b]_M, D[b] \; \{c\}_M \; \Gamma, P, D}{\Gamma, P, D \; \{\text{while } (b) \text{ do } c\}_M \; \Gamma, P \wedge [\neg \, b]_M, D[b]}$$

$$\text{REWRITE} \; \frac{\Gamma_1, P_1, D_1 \; \{c\}_M \; \Gamma_1', P_1', D_1' \qquad \begin{array}{ll} \Gamma_2 \geq \Gamma_1 & \Gamma_1' \geq \Gamma_2' \\ P_2 \Rightarrow P_1 & P_1' \Rightarrow P_2' \\ D_2 \supseteq D_1 & D_1' \supseteq D_2' \end{array}}{\Gamma_2, P_2, D_2 \; \{c\}_M \; \Gamma_2', P_2', D_2'}$$

$$\text{ASSIGN} \; \frac{x \notin C \qquad \Gamma, P_{x:=e} \vdash e : t \qquad x \notin M(AssNoRW) \Rightarrow t \sqsubseteq eval_{P_{x:=e}}(x)}{\Gamma, P, D \; \{x := e\}_M \; \Gamma[x \mapsto t], P[x := e]_M, D[x := e]}$$

$$\text{ASSIGNC} \; \frac{x \in C \qquad \Gamma, P_{x:=e} \vdash e : Low \qquad secure\_update_{\Gamma, P_{x:=e}, D, M}(x := e)}{\Gamma, P, D \; \{x := e\}_M \; \Gamma, P[x := e]_M, D[x := e]}$$

$$\text{FENCE} \; \frac{}{\Gamma, P, D \; \{\text{fence}\}_M \; \Gamma, P, D[\text{fence}]}$$

Fig. 3. Rules of the logic.

The removal of free occurrences of unstable variables is required as these variables may be changed by another thread at any time (invalidating the relationship between them and stable variables). For example, if variables x and y are stable but z is not, the guard expression $x = y + z$ should add the predicate $\exists z \cdot x = y + z$ to P, rather than $x = y + z$.

The REWRITE rule is typically required when using the IF and WHILE rules to ensure both branches have corresponding analysis states and to establish loop invariants, respectively. The rule allows for the introduction of stronger Γ, P and D on the left-hand side, and weaker Γ', P' and D' on the right. To express this, we introduce a relation $\supseteq$ between values of D.

$$D \supseteq D' \triangleq \forall x : Var \cdot \psi_w(x) \supseteq \psi_w'(x) \wedge \psi_r(x) \supseteq \psi_r'(x) \qquad \text{where } \psi \in \{W, R\}$$

Additionally, we introduce a relation $\geq$ between values of Γ. This relation constrains the entries in the weaker Γ to be higher or equal to those in the stronger, as any expressions that pass the logic's rules with a *High* read will also succeed with a *Low* read. Such a rewriting property allows for branches that consider the same variable at different security levels to merge, rewriting to the highest level.

$$\Gamma \geq \Gamma' \;\widehat{=}\; \mathrm{dom}\,\Gamma = \mathrm{dom}\,\Gamma' \wedge \forall x : \mathrm{dom}\,\Gamma \cdot \Gamma(x) \sqsubseteq \Gamma'(x)$$

While the use of the REWRITE rule requires user interaction, its application can be automated based on the context, e.g., through the introduction of a specialised IF rule as in Murray et al. [19, 20].

There are two rules for assignment. The first rule, ASSIGN, corresponds to the assignment of an expression e to a non-control variable x. If another thread can read x, the expression's security level should not be higher than x's security level when considered under $P_{x:=e}$.

Γ, P and D are updated to reflect the assignment. The notation $\Gamma[x \mapsto t]$ denotes reassignment, where the function Γ is updated so that x maps to t provided $x \in \mathrm{dom}\,\Gamma$. For P we use a shorthand that denotes the strongest postcondition, sp, of the assignment $x := e$ from a state satisfying P with all free occurrences of unstable variables removed.

$$P[x := e]_M \;\widehat{=}\; sp(x := e, P)\,|_{M(AssNoRW) \cup M(AssNoW)}$$

The second assignment rule, ASSIGNC, corresponds to an assignment to a control variable. In this case, the expression must have a Low security level to conform with the restriction on control variables introduced in Sect. 4.2. Moreover, the effect of the assignment on the security level of controlled variables must be taken into account. If the security level of a readable controlled variable y falls from $High$ to Low, it is necessary that any earlier writes to y are guaranteed to have occurred, and that the final such write has set y to Low.

If, on the other hand, the security level of y rises from Low to $High$, it is necessary that any earlier reads of y are guaranteed to have occurred. To see why this is required, consider the code z = 0; x = y; z = 1 where $\mathcal{L}(y) = (z = 0)$ and $\mathcal{L}(x) = true$. If the assignment z = 1 occurs before x = y then another thread may update y to a $High$ value before x = y occurs. This would result in a $High$ value being passed to x which has a Low security level.

The required condition for assignment to control variables is captured by the shorthand $secure\_update_{\Gamma,P,D,M}(x := e)$ defined below.

$$\begin{aligned}
secure\_update&_{\Gamma,P,D,M}(x := e) \;\widehat{=} \\
&(\forall y : falling(x, P, P') \setminus M(AssNoRW) \cdot \\
&\quad y \in known_W(x := e) \wedge \Gamma, P' \vdash y : Low) \wedge \\
&(\forall y : rising(x, P, P') \cdot y \in known_R(x := e))
\end{aligned}$$

where $P' = P[x := e]_M$ is the predicate after the assignment and

$$\begin{aligned}
falling(x, P, P') &\;\widehat{=}\; \{y : Var \mid x \in var(\mathcal{L}(y)) \wedge \neg\,(low_P(y)) \wedge \neg\,(high_{P'}(y))\} \\
rising(x, P, P') &\;\widehat{=}\; \{y : Var \mid x \in var(\mathcal{L}(y)) \wedge \neg\,(high_P(y)) \wedge \neg\,(low_{P'}(y))\}
\end{aligned}$$

The sets *falling* and *rising* identify all variables that could change security level due to the modification of a control variable x. As not all information may be available in P or P' to determine security levels, for soundness the definitions default to assume a change has occurred.

The final rule is for fences. After a fence, it is guaranteed that the earlier reads and writes of all variables have occurred.

5.1 Soundness

The logic has been encoded in Isabelle/HOL [21] and proved sound with respect to an encoding of the operational semantics of ARMv8 [6]. The soundness proof follows the structure of prior proofs for sequentially consistent logics [15,19,20] and proves that programs that pass the logic's rules will satisfy a compositional non-interference property. That compositional property requires showing that whenever two copies of the program each perform an execution step from states that agree on the values of *Low* variables, then the resulting states also agree on their *Low* variables. The main extra complexity of the proof concerns the case in which one copy performs a step that is out-of-order. In this case we must prove that the other copy must also perform this out-of-order step. To do so, we encode into the operational semantics the assumption that the choice about *when* to reorder instructions never depends on sensitive information, akin to prior work that made a similar assumption about the thread schedule [19,20] by quantifying over all deterministic interleavings of threads. The theories are available at https://bitbucket.org/wmmif/wmm-if.

5.2 Example Revisited

The sequential composition rule allows us to step through a program one line at a time. The values of Γ, P and D following a given line can be calculated from the applied rule. If we reach a line of code that no rule can be applied to, this indicates a potential security leak. For example, consider the writer_thread in Fig. 4 for which we will assume $M(AssNoW) = \{z,x\}$. This thread initialises the variables z and x and then

```
writer_thread:
1   z := 0;
2   x := 0;
3   while (true)
4       z := z+1;
5       fence;
6       x := secret;
        ...
7       x := 0;
8       fence;
9       z := z+1
```

```
reader_thread:
10  while(true)
11      do
12          do
13              r1:= z;
14          while (r1 % 2 ≠ 0)
15          fence;
16          r2 := x;
17          fence;
18      while (z ≠ r1)
19      y := r2
```

Fig. 4. Writer and reader threads using the operation secret_write and read of Fig. 2.

repeatedly calls the secret_write operation of Fig. 2. Applying rules AssignC and Assign to lines 1 and 2, respectively, shows that the code up to line 2 is secure. Following line 2, we have $\Gamma = \{z \mapsto Low, x \mapsto Low\}$, $P = (z = 0 \wedge x = 0)$, and D comprises $W_w = \{z \mapsto \{z\}, x \mapsto \{x\}\}$, $W_r = \{x \mapsto \varnothing, z \mapsto \varnothing\}$ and $R_w = R_r = \{z \mapsto \{x, z\}, x \mapsto \{x, z\}\}$.

The REWRITE rule can then be applied to weaken P to $z\%2 = 0 \wedge x = 0$ and leave Γ and D unchanged. These values become the starting point for evaluating lines 4 to 9. We can show that these lines are also secure by applying rules ASSIGNC, FENCE and ASSIGN. Note that without the fence at line 5, z would not be a member of $known_W(x := \mathsf{secret})$ and hence not in $P_{x:=secret}$. Therefore, ASSIGN would not be applicable (since the value of z is required to be odd for this assignment to be secure). Hence, no rule would be applicable for line 6. This demonstrates how the leak of x would be detected by the logic if lines 4 and 6 could be reordered.

Similarly, without the fence at line 8, no rule would be applicable to line 9. In this case, since z becomes even at line 9, the variable x must hold *Low* data to satisfy $secure\_update_{\Gamma, P_{z := z+1}, D, M}$. This could not be ascertained, however, since x would not be in $known_W(z := z + 1)$. This demonstrates how the leak of x would be detected by the logic if lines 7 and 9 could be reordered.

The situation for the reader_thread is not as straightforward. Even with the fences (as suggested in Sect. 3), the logic cannot be used to show that the code is secure. This is because z is not stable and hence the assignment at line 16 cannot guarantee that r2's value is *Low*. Although the logic is sound, it is not precise enough to determine that reader_thread's code is secure.

5.3   A More Precise Logic

The reason that the reader_thread of Fig. 4 is secure, is that it only reaches line 19 when z is stable from line 13 (when it is assigned to r1) until line 18 (where it is checked to be equal to r1). The algorithm works on the principle that there is a high chance of z being stable while these lines are executed, and hence the reader_thread will reach line 19 without too many iterations of the outer do-loop. This reliance on stability is common among non-blocking algorithms.

To allow for us to check the security of such algorithms, we allow non-blocking loops, such as the outer loop in reader_thread, to be annotated with a variable which we expect to be stable (z in this example). The annotation allows local reasoning to assume that the nominated variable is stable using the following rule (where c can be a while or do loop).

$$\text{NONBLOCKING} \quad \frac{\Gamma, P \mid_{known_W(z)} \vdash z : t \qquad \Gamma \cup \{z \mapsto t\}, P, D \ \{c\}_{M^z} \ \Gamma' \cup \{z \mapsto t'\}, P', D'}{\Gamma, P, D \ \{c^z\}_M \ \Gamma', P', D'}$$

where Γ is updated with a value for z (based on what is known to have occurred if the variable were read) and M is extended to $M^z = M[AssNoW \mapsto M(AssNoW) \cup \{z\}, GuarNoW \mapsto M(GuarNoW) \cup Global]$.

The extension of $GuarNoW$ in M^z ensures that, while in the loop, no writes can be made by the thread to any global variables. This is required in such non-blocking algorithms so that the execution can be discarded and restarted when z is discovered not to be stable.

For the rule to be sound, we also require that the loop cannot be exited unless the variable is stable from the time that it is entered. This check requires reasoning about the functionality of the code and is outside of the scope of the logic (similar to the obligation that assumptions are matched by guarantees on other threads). In the case of reader_thread, the proof follows from the fact that the value of z is never decreased (as described in Sect. 3).

6 Timing Sensitivity

In earlier work on information-flow security on weak memory models [14,26], an auxiliary variable is introduced (called wt in [26] and pt in [14]) to record the lowest security level of a pending write, i.e., one that has occurred locally but has not necessarily been flushed to global memory. This is argued to be necessary to prevent *Low* variables being flushed on a *High* path (i.e., a path entered depending on the value of a *High* variable) and thus revealing that the program has taken that path. In our logic, we do not allow *High* paths and hence do not require such a variable.

Our justification for this restriction is based on the fact that a compositional information-flow logic must be *timing-sensitive*, i.e., information should not be leaked to an attacker who is able to time the execution of a program. As argued in [19], this is not possible in the presence of *High* paths. For example, consider the program in Fig. 5 in which *high* is a *High* variable and *low* and *output* are *Low* variables. Both threads are timing-insensitive secure since *low* is never

Thread 1:
```
low := 0;
if (high=0)
then while (high < 1000) high++;
else skip;
low := 1;
```

Thread 2:
```
output=low;
```

Fig. 5. Example illustrating the need for timing-sensitive security.

dependent on the value of *high*. However, when they are composed the value written to *output* is more likely to be 0 than 1 when *high* is 0. Hence, although the threads are timing-insensitive secure, their composition is not. This does not require a probabilistic argument: under a round-robin scheduler with time slices less than the time it takes to execute the loop, the result *output* = 1 would indicate that *high* = 1.

The first thread is obviously not timing-sensitive secure (as its execution time depends directly on *high*) and hence under timing-sensitive security the issue with compositionality does not arise. Eliminating *High* paths from code can be achieved using program transformations as described, for example, in [1,17].

7 Conclusion

In this paper, we have presented the first information-flow logic for the ARMv8 weak memory model; a memory model which is significantly weaker than those such as TSO for which prior information-flow logics have been considered. Our logic supports dynamic, value-dependent security levels and is compositional and timing-sensitive. It has been proven sound with respect to an operational semantics of ARMv8 which has been validated against extensive test suites.

This work, focusing on instruction reordering, is a first step towards a more extensive logic in terms of its coverage of both ARM instructions and behaviours, and potential security vulnerabilities. We also anticipate improving the completeness of the logic, in particular by supporting more general rely/guarantee conditions, and adapting it for other weak memory models including those of IBM POWER and prior versions of ARM.

References

1. Almeida, J.B., Barbosa, M., Barthe, G., Dupressoir, F., Emmi, M.: Verifying constant-time implementations. In: Holz, T., Savage, S. (eds.) 25th USENIX Security Symposium, USENIX Security 16, pp. 53–70. USENIX Association (2016)
2. Atig, M.F., Bouajjani, A., Burckhardt, S., Musuvathi, M.: On the verification problem for weak memory models. In: Hermenegildo, M.V., Palsberg, J. (eds.) Proceedings of the 37th ACM SIGPLAN-SIGACT Symposium on Principles of Programming Languages, POPL 2010, pp. 7–18. ACM (2010)
3. Boehm, H.: Can seqlocks get along with programming language memory models? In: Zhang, L., Mutlu, O. (eds.) Proceedings of the 2012 ACM SIGPLAN Workshop on Memory Systems Performance and Correctness: Held in Conjunction with PLDI 2012, pp. 12–20. ACM (2012)
4. Bulck, J.V., et al.: Foreshadow: extracting the keys to the Intel SGX kingdom with transient out-of-order execution. In: Enck, W., Felt, A.P. (eds.) 27th USENIX Security Symposium, USENIX Security 2018, pp. 991–1008. USENIX Association (2018)
5. Chandy, K.M., Misra, J.: Asynchronous distributed simulation via a sequence of parallel computations. Commun. ACM **24**(4), 198–206 (1981)
6. Colvin, R.J., Smith, G.: A high-level operational semantics for hardware weak memory models. CoRR, abs/1812.00996 (2018)
7. Colvin, R.J., Smith, G.: A wide-spectrum language for verification of programs on weak memory models. In: Havelund, K., Peleska, J., Roscoe, B., de Vink, E. (eds.) FM 2018. LNCS, vol. 10951, pp. 240–257. Springer, Cham (2018). https://doi.org/10.1007/978-3-319-95582-7_14
8. Fitzpatrick, J.: An interview with Steve Furber. Commun. ACM **54**(5), 34–39 (2011)
9. Flur, S., et al.: Modelling the ARMv8 architecture, operationally: concurrency and ISA. In: Bodík, R., Majumdar, R. (eds.), Proceedings of the 43rd Annual ACM SIGPLAN-SIGACT Symposium on Principles of Programming Languages, POPL 2016, pp. 608–621. ACM (2016)
10. Jones, C.B.: Specification and design of (parallel) programs. In: IFIP Congress, pp. 321–332 (1983)
11. Kocher, P., et al.: Spectre attacks: exploiting speculative execution. CoRR, abs/1801.01203 (2018)
12. Lipp, M., et al.: Meltdown: reading kernel memory from user space. In: Enck, W., Felt, A.P. (eds.) 27th USENIX Security Symposium, USENIX Security 2018, pp. 973–990. USENIX Association (2018)

13. Lourenço, L., Caires, L.: Dependent information flow types. In: Rajamani, S.K., Walker, D. (eds.) Proceedings of the 42nd Annual ACM SIGPLAN-SIGACT Symposium on Principles of Programming Languages, POPL 2015, pp. 317–328. ACM (2015)

14. Mantel, H., Perner, M., Sauer, J.: Noninterference under weak memory models. In: IEEE 27th Computer Security Foundations Symposium, CSF 2014, pp. 80–94. IEEE Computer Society (2014)

15. Mantel, H., Sands, D., Sudbrock, H.: Assumptions and guarantees for compositional noninterference. In: Proceedings of the 24th IEEE Computer Security Foundations Symposium, CSF 2011, pp. 218–232. IEEE Computer Society (2011)

16. Moir, M., Shavit, N.: Concurrent data structures. In: Mehta, D.P., Sahni, S. (eds.), Handbook of Data Structures and Applications. Chapman and Hall/CRC (2004)

17. Molnar, D., Piotrowski, M., Schultz, D., Wagner, D.: The program counter security model: automatic detection and removal of control-flow side channel attacks. In: Won, D.H., Kim, S. (eds.) ICISC 2005. LNCS, vol. 3935, pp. 156–168. Springer, Heidelberg (2006). https://doi.org/10.1007/11734727_14

18. Murray, T.C.: Short paper: on high-assurance information-flow-secure programming languages. In: Clarkson, M., Jia, L. (eds.), Proceedings of the 10th ACM Workshop on Programming Languages and Analysis for Security, PLAS@ECOOP 2015, pp. 43–48. ACM (2015)

19. Murray, T.C., Sison, R., Engelhardt, K.: COVERN: a logic for compositional verification of information flow control. In: 2018 IEEE European Symposium on Security and Privacy, EuroS&P 2018, pp. 16–30. IEEE (2018)

20. Murray, T.C., Sison, R., Pierzchalski, E., Rizkallah, C.: Compositional verification and refinement of concurrent value-dependent noninterference. In: IEEE 29th Computer Security Foundations Symposium, CSF 2016, pp. 417–431. IEEE Computer Society (2016)

21. Nipkow, T., Paulson, L.C., Wenzel, M.: Isabelle/HOL - A Proof Assistant for Higher-Order Logic. LNCS, vol. 2283. Springer, Heidelberg (2002). https://doi.org/10.1007/3-540-45949-9

22. Pulte, C., Flur, S., Deacon, W., French, J., Sarkar, S., Sewell, P.: Simplifying ARM concurrency: multicopy-atomic axiomatic and operational models for ARMv8. PACMPL 2(POPL), 19:1–19:29 (2018)

23. Sarkar, S., Sewell, P., Alglave, J., Maranget, L., Williams, D.: Understanding POWER multiprocessors. In: Hall, M.W., Padua, D.A. (eds.), Proceedings of the 32nd ACM SIGPLAN Conference on Programming Language Design and Implementation, PLDI 2011, pp. 175–186. ACM (2011)

24. Sewell, P., Sarkar, S., Owens, S., Nardelli, F.Z., Myreen, M.O.: x86-TSO: a rigorous and usable programmer's model for x86 multiprocessors. Commun. ACM 53(7), 89–97 (2010)

25. Sorin, D.J., Hill, M.D., Wood, D.A.: A Primer on Memory Consistency and Cache Coherence. Synthesis Lectures on Computer Architecture. Morgan & Claypool Publishers, San Rafael (2011)

26. Vaughan, J.A., Millstein, T.D.: Secure information flow for concurrent programs under Total Store Order. In: Chong, S. (ed), 25th IEEE Computer Security Foundations Symposium, CSF 2012, pp. 19–29. IEEE Computer Society (2012)

27. Zheng, L., Myers, A.C.: Dynamic security labels and static information flow control. Int. J. Inf. Sec. 6(2–3), 67–84 (2007)

Reasoning Formally About Database Queries and Updates

Jon Haël Brenas[1], Rachid Echahed[2], and Martin Strecker[3(✉)]

[1] UTHSC - ORNL, Memphis, TN, USA
[2] CNRS and University Grenoble Alpes, Grenoble, France
[3] Toulouse, France
http://martin-strecker.org/

Abstract. This paper explores formal verification in the area of database technology, in particular how to reason about queries and updates in a database system. The formalism is sufficiently general to be applicable to relational and graph databases. We first define a domain-specific language consisting of nested query and update primitives, and give its operational semantics. Queries are in full first-order logic. The problem we try to solve is whether a database satisfying a given precondition will satisfy a given post-condition after execution of a given sequence of queries and updates. We propose a weakest-precondition calculus and prove its correctness. We finally examine a restriction of our framework that produces formulas in the guarded fragment of predicate logic and thus leads to a decidable proof problem.

Keywords: Automated theorem proving · Modal logic ·
Graph transformations · Program verification

1 Introduction

1.1 Context and Contributions

The work reported here has initially grown out of an effort to verify graph-manipulating programs that owe much to a traditional imperative programming style. The transformation language presented in this paper is inspired by query and update primitives found in graph databases such as Cypher [27], but we do not try to mimic a specific DB language, and our language is sufficiently general that it is also interesting for relational DBs. The structure of the language is in principle very simple, consisting of nested match constructs (however with queries that are full first-order logic formulas) and addition and deletion of relations. We are here interested in structural aspects, dealing only with uninterpreted relations. The transformation language (syntax and well-formedness constraints and semantics) will be defined in Sect. 2.

The transformation language has a clearly imperative (as opposed to functional) flavour, with a notion of DB state that coincides with a non-standard

© Springer Nature Switzerland AG 2019
M. H. ter Beek et al. (Eds.): FM 2019, LNCS 11800, pp. 556–572, 2019.
https://doi.org/10.1007/978-3-030-30942-8_33

notion of interpretation of formulas. The main focus of the paper is on verifying whether a DB satisfying a given pre-condition will satisfy a given post-condition after the transformation. These conditions are again full first-order formulas. It is important to emphasise that we are dealing with the verification of the correctness of transformations as such, and not the validation of the satisfaction of constraints for particular instances of a DB (thus a kind of model checking problem). The program correctness calculus (a particular form of weakest pre-condition calculus) is described in Sect. 3. The resulting proof obligations are undecidable in general. However, in Sect. 4, we restrict our attention to the Guarded Fragment of predicate logic. By imposing suitable restrictions on the formulas occurring in assertions and selection statements, we identify a natural class of transformations that give rise to decidable proof obligations.

A particular challenge of our formalism is to take into account contextual information stemming from nested `match` statements, and to deal with relational update (an essentially second-order construct) in a first-order framework.

Related Work. The view of a database transformation as an imperative program, with pre- and post-conditions, seems to be new.

Work in the context of deductive DBs ([8,26], also see [23] for an overview) mainly seems to address the problem of maintaining the consistency of DB *w.r.t.* specific constraints after individual updates, and not deductive verification. Consistency maintenance is then often enforced by Prolog-like inference rules. The more general question of DB updates as theory updates, for example in [11], has triggered an extensive amount of work, including investigations in non-monotonic logics. This line of research is not at all related to our approach that is situated in classical logic, with the credo that updates modify models and not theories.

A notable exception to the above is the work by Benedikt, Griffin and Libkin [5] that considers the problem of definability of database transactions for a very abstract notion of transformation language, leading mainly to negative decidability results. Contrary to this, we start with a specific (and, in particular in Sect. 4, restricted) language, to arrive at a proposal for a practically useful verification framework.

XML transformations [19,22] are transformations of particular tree-like structures, and the powerful type systems developed for them can be assimilated with program correctness assertions. However, XML transducers have a functional flavour, the verification method is not comparable to ours.

As mentioned before, our work has its origin in the verification of graph transformations. The landscape is heterogeneous, ranging from approaches based on category theory [16] to work in Monadic Second Order logic [10,20]. The graph decompositions inherent to this latter approach are often not compatible with updates performed naturally in graph structures (insertion or deletion of arcs, updates of attributes).

Our own work [6,7,9] has so far concentrated on particular decidable logics (modal or description logics). We have evoked the problem of the procedural transformation language; we mention in particular the difficulty with loops whose verification requires an annotation with invariants, so the verification approach is not fully automatic. Work that is very similar in spirit, also based on description logics and consistency management in ontologies, is [1–3]. The limitation of expressiveness of description logics leads to unpleasant circumlocutions: the logics are often not closed under simple operations like substitutions of relational expressions, with the consequence that extraction of proof obligations and proof procedures are intertwined. In order to have a clearer picture of the underlying mechanisms, we choose a plain first-order setting in this paper.

The modification of databases in conjunction with an imperative programming language is described in [21], with a verification procedure based on two-variable first order logic. To obtain decidability, severe restrictions on the domains (bounded domains and only one unbounded domain) have to be imposed.

As mentioned in the outset, we want to capture the spirit of DB languages like Cypher, without reproducing these languages in detail; our nested `match` statements seem to go beyond what is currently available in Cypher, and there are a huge number of features we do not cover, in particular paths. We are aware of a formal definition of the semantics of Cypher [12] and hope that a merger of this semantics and our language might make it possible to formally reason about integrity constraints in languages like Cypher.

1.2 Introductory Example

Before starting with the technical development, we present an example that informally introduces the principal notions and gives an overview of the verification methodology.

We consider the scenario of a database of a service provider for subscription of potential clients to its services. The database maintains some integrity constraints:

– *ValidClient*: All clients C registered in the database have to have their subscription approved (*Valid*) by an employee (E) of the company: ($\forall c.C(c) \longrightarrow \exists e.E(e) \land Valid(e,c)$)
– *ActiveIfSubscr*: A service is activated for a client only if the client has previously subscribed to it: ($\forall s\,c.\ Active(s,c) \longrightarrow Subscr(s,c)$). The provider may suspend a service, so the inverse is not necessarily the case.

After registering at the service provider and subscribing to some services, the potential clients first get the status of applicants (A). At regular intervals, the database runs the program of Fig. 1 to integrate applicants into its standard client base. This program proceeds as follows: it first retrieves all the applicants a that have their subscription approved (outer `match`) and adds these applicants as clients (first `add` statement). It then retrieves all the services s a given applicant a has subscribed to and activates these services (inner `match`). Finally, it removes the selected applicants from the set A (`del` statement).

The program is annotated with a pre-condition (the integrity constraint mentioned before) and a post-condition: the integrity constraint and the knowledge that all applicants remaining in A have not had their demand validated so far.

```
Pre:  ValidClient ∧ ActiveIfSubscr
    match   a  where  A(a) ∧ ∃ e. E(e) ∧ Valid(e, a)  {
        add(C(a));
        match  s  where  S(s) ∧ Subscr(s, a)  {
            add(Active(s, a))
        };
        del(A(a))
    }
Post: ValidClient∧ ActiveIfSubscr∧ (∀ a. A(a)  ⟶  ¬∃ e. E(e) ∧ Valid(e,a))
```

Fig. 1. An example program

Let us run the program on a particular instance of a DB (the operational semantics in full generality is defined in Sect. 2.3). The extensions of the unary predicates are sets of elements; and of the binary relations are sets of pairs. At the start of the program, we assume:

$$A \quad = \{a_1, a_2, a_3\} \qquad\qquad E = \{e_1, e_2\}$$
$$C \quad = \{c_1, c_2\} \qquad\qquad\quad S = \{s_1, s_2\}$$
$$Valid = \{(e_1, c_1), (e_1, c_2), (e_1, a_1), (e_2, a_2)\}$$
$$Subscr = \{(s_1, c_1), (s_2, c_2), (s_1, a_1), (s_2, a_1), (s_2, a_2)\}$$
$$Active = \{(s_1, c_1)\}$$

Before looking in more detail at the execution of the program, it is important to understand the notion of a *state* of a program, which coincides with our non-standard notion of *interpretation* of a formula, which is set-based and not instance-based, as explained in the following. An interpretation is made up of three components: a domain (in this case, the set $\{a_1, a_2, \ldots s_1, s_2\}$) and an interpretation of the predicate symbols (as above); all this is standard. The difference is in the way individual variables are interpreted: instead of having a single function mapping variables into the domain, we take a set of such functions. We are in particular interested in *maximal* interpretations that contain all the individual interpretation functions satisfying certain requirements.

As the precondition contains no free variables, the maximal interpretation set is initially the set of all functions mapping the set of variables to elements of the domain. The first **match** restricts the set of variable interpretations to those that map variable a to a_1 or a_2, as only these satisfy the condition of the match (the relation interpretations are not modified by **match**, and the domain remains invariant for all operations). The first **add** operation has an effect on the interpretation of relation C, adding the elements a_1, a_2 so that it will then become $\{c_1, c_2, a_1, a_2\}$ (here, the individual interpretations are not modified). The inner **match** limits the set of admissible individual interpretations still further to the set $\{(a \mapsto a_1, s \mapsto s_1), (a \mapsto a_1, s \mapsto s_2), (a \mapsto a_2, s \mapsto s_2)\}$. These pairs are then added to *Active*, whose extension is $\{(s_1, c_1), (s_1, a_1), (s_2, a_1), (s_2, a_2)\}$ at the end of the inner **match** statement. Note in particular that we do not simply take the cross-product of the elements $\{s_1, s_2\}$ bound to s and the elements $\{a_1, a_2\}$ bound to a: the pair (s_1, a_2) is not added to *Active*. We finally execute the **del** statement, which sets A to $\{a_3\}$. The net effect of the program is therefore an update of the relations A, C and $Active$ in the DB.

Reasoning about these programs proceeds by backwards propagation of post-conditions, by computing weakest pre-conditions (wp). There are in particular two challenges for wp reasoning: taking into account contextual information (given by the conditions in the match clauses), and reasoning about sets and relations, instead of individuals.

When reasoning backwards, we first have to take the effect of $del(A(a))$ into account. We look up the contextual information about variable a. Its defining clause is $A(a) \wedge \exists e.E(e) \wedge Valid(e, a)$, so we symbolically remove from A in the post-condition all the elements satisfying this predicate. The subformula $(\forall a.A(a) \longrightarrow \neg\exists e.E(e) \wedge Valid(e, a))$ then becomes $(\forall a.(A(a) \wedge \neg(A(a) \wedge \exists e.E(e) \wedge Valid(e, a))) \longrightarrow \neg\exists e.E(e) \wedge Valid(e, a))$, which reduces to true. The subformula $ValidClient \wedge ActiveIfSubscr$ is not affected by the delete statement.

We next examine the effective of $add(Active(s, a))$ on the remaining post-condition. The contextual information for variable a is as before, and for variable s is $S(s) \wedge Subscr(s, a)$. In $ActiveIfSubscr$, we replace $Active(s, c)$ by a formula describing the union of $Active$ and the conjunction of the characterising formulas of a and s, which yields $\forall s\, c.\ (Active(s, c) \vee A(c) \wedge (\exists e.E(e) \wedge Valid(e, c)) \wedge S(s) \wedge Subscr(s, c)) \longrightarrow Subscr(s, c)$. It is easy to see that this formula is implied by $ActiveIfSubscr$ in the precondition of the program. In a similar spirit, we reason about $add(C(a))$, replacing $C(c)$ in the precondition $ValidClient$ by $C(c) \vee A(c) \wedge \exists e.E(e) \wedge Valid(e, c)$.

2 Transformation Language

This section defines the syntax of the transformation language (Sect. 2.1); it presents two notions of interpretation of formulas that are also instrumental for the concept of program state (Sect. 2.2); and it gives the operational semantics of programs (Sect. 2.3). The rest of this paper uses a semi-formal, mathematical style. A fully formal development in the Isabelle proof assistant is under way.[1]

2.1 Syntax

The syntax of statements $stmt$ and programs $prog$ is defined by the following grammar, where boldface $\mathbf{v}$ stands for a list of variables $v_1, \ldots, v_n$:

$$
\begin{aligned}
stmt ::= {}&\texttt{Skip} \\
| {}&\texttt{add}(R(\mathbf{v})) \\
| {}&\texttt{del}(R(\mathbf{v})) \\
| {}&\texttt{match}\ \mathbf{v}\ \texttt{where}\ form\ \{\ stmt\ \} \\
| {}&stmt;\ stmt \\
prog ::= {}&\texttt{Pre}: form\ stmt\ \texttt{Post}: form
\end{aligned}
$$

---

[1] Parts of the development can be found in the repository https://bitbucket.org/Martin_Strecker/db_queries_updates/.

Formulas *form* are occurring in `match` clauses and the pre- and post-conditions. They are formulas of standard first-order logic, defined by

$$form ::= \perp \mid R(\mathbf{v}) \mid x = y \mid \neg form \mid form \wedge form \mid \forall v.form$$

featuring constant symbol $\perp$, relational application $R(\mathbf{v})$, equality $x = y$ between individual variables, negation, binary connectors, first-order quantification over individual variables v. Other connectors and quantifiers than those shown are defined as usual.

Renaming individual variable x by y in formula ϕ is written $\phi[x := y]$. In formula manipulations like these, we assume that bound variables are correctly renamed to avoid clashes.

We assume that relation symbols have a fixed arity which can be enforced by typing or a naming convention; we do not describe the details here. Well-typing of a statement c in a context (list of variables) Γ, written $\Gamma \vdash c$, is defined by:

- $\Gamma \vdash$ `add`$(R(\mathbf{v}))$ if $\mathbf{v} \subseteq \Gamma$ and similarly for `del`
- $\Gamma \vdash$ `match v where` b $\{c\}$ if $\Gamma \cap \mathbf{v} = \{\}$ and $\Gamma@\mathbf{v} \vdash c$ and $fv(b) \subseteq \Gamma@\mathbf{v}$, where @ is list concatenation and $fv(b)$ is the set of free individual variables of b. In particular, `match` binds the variables $\mathbf{v}$ in b and c, and these variables should not occur in the context.
- $\Gamma \vdash c_1; c_2$ if $\Gamma \vdash c_1$ and $\Gamma \vdash c_2$

Pre- and post-conditions and statements may contain free individual variables, whose declaration constitutes the initial context for type checking. Since the programs we present in the examples are all closed, we have omitted the variable declaration clauses.

Apart from typing, we have to impose another restriction on the programs we analyse: There are no modifications of defining relations before use.

Example 1. Before defining this notion, we will look at a counter-example:

```
match   a where   A(a)  {
    match   b where   B(b)  {
        add(A(b))
    };
    del(C(a))
}
```

When reasoning about relation updates (`add` or `del`), we describe the changes induced *w.r.t.* the defining properties of the variables. Before the `add` in Example 1, the defining properties of a and b are $A(a)$ and $B(b)$ respectively. Intuitively and using a set-theoretic notation, the effect of the `add` is that the new A becomes $A^0 \cup B$, where A^0 is the original value of A. Computing this effect is not difficult.

The problem is the following `del`$(C(a))$, where we cannot proceed in a similar fashion. We cannot say that new C is $C^0 - A$ by looking up how a was defined in the corresponding `match` statement, because relation A has been modified between definition and use of a, but the variable a is still bound to the original values: before the `del` statement, $A(a)$ is not true any more. In fact, it should be that $C = C^0 - A^0$. Intuitively speaking, it seems that our analysis would become considerably more complex if it were necessary to precisely track which property was true for a variable in the execution history of the program, instead of taking its defining value.

We give a series of definitions that are reminiscent of the notion of definition-use chains in compiler technology [24], whence the name of *DU-stability* introduced below.

Definition 1 (DU-stability). *For a statement* `match v where` P, *we say that the* $v \in \mathbf{v}$ *are* defined *by this statement, and we say that* P *is their* defining property. *Note that in a well-typed program, a variable occurs in at most one* `match`, *so this notion is well-defined. The set of* defining relations *of a variable* v, $def\_rels(v)$, *is the set of relation symbols* R *that occur in the defining property of* v. *We say that a variable is* used *in the predicate of a* `match` *or in an* `add` *or* `del` *statement if it is among the free variables of the respective predicates. We say that a relation* R *is* modified *by an update if this update is* `add(R(v))` *or* `del(R(v))`. *We say that a variable* v *defined in a* `match` *is* DU-stable *if in none of the execution paths leading from the definition to a use of* v, *any of the defining relations of* v *is modified. We say that a program is* DU-stable *if all its variables are.*

In order to avoid clutter, these definitions have been kept semi-formal in the sense that they are not defined inductively over the syntax and some parameters (such as the underlying program) remain implicit. Some related, more formal definitions are provided in Sect. 3.2.

The program of Example 1 is not DU-stable because the defining relation A is modified between the use of a in `del(C(a))` and its definition. The program in Fig. 1 is DU-stable, but it would not be if swapping `add(C(a))` and `del(A(a))`, because then, the defining relation A of variable a would be modified before the uses of a.

Note that the restriction to property-preserving bindings is not a limitation, at least in principle and disregarding questions of efficiency of execution. Indeed, any breach of DU-stability can be avoided by storing values in an auxiliary relation and then retrieving this copy instead of referring to the modified relation.

2.2   Interpretations

We will introduce two kinds of semantics:

- an individual semantics that is the traditional logical semantics;
- a set-based semantics allowing to reason about sets of assignments of individual variables.

The *individual semantics* is given by interpretations $\iota = (\iota_d, \iota_r, \iota_i)$ where ι_d is a domain, ι_r is a function that assigns to each n-ary relation symbol of the language a subset of ι_d^n, and ι_i a function that assigns to each individual variable an element of ι_d. The relation $\iota \models \phi$ (interpretation ι is a model of formula ϕ) is defined as usual:

- $\iota \not\models \bot$
- $\iota \models R(\mathbf{v})$ if $\iota_i(\mathbf{v}) \in \iota_r(R)$, where $\iota_i(\mathbf{v})$ is the obvious mapping of ι_i on a vector of variables.
- $\iota \models x = y$ if $\iota_i(x) = \iota_i(y)$
- $\iota \models \neg\psi$ if $\iota \not\models \psi$
- $\iota \models \psi \wedge \phi$ if $\iota \models \psi$ and $\iota \models \phi$
- $\iota \models \forall v.\psi$ (first-order quantification) if for all $vi \in \iota_d$, we have $\iota^{v:=vi} \models \psi$. Here, if $\iota = (\iota_d, \iota_r, \iota_i)$, then $\iota^{v:=vi} = (\iota_d, \iota_r, \iota_i(v := vi))$ and $\iota_i(v := vi)$ is the update of function ι_i at variable v with value vi.

The *set-based semantics* is given by interpretations $\sigma = (\sigma_d, \sigma_r, \sigma_i)$ where σ_d and σ_r are as for the individual semantics, and σ_i is a set of individual assignments. We write $\iota \in \sigma$ if $\iota = (\iota_d, \iota_r, \iota_i)$ with $\iota_d = \sigma_d$ and $\iota_r = \sigma_r$ and $\iota_i \in \sigma_i$.

For instance, in the example of Sect. 1.2, we considered a set-based interpretation σ with a domain σ_d and relational assignment σ_r as defined there, and $\sigma_i = \{(a \mapsto a_1, s \mapsto s_1), (a \mapsto a_1, s \mapsto s_2), (a \mapsto a_2, s \mapsto s_2)\}$. One of the individual interpretations $\iota \in \sigma$ has the same domain and relational assignment, and individual variable assignment $\iota_i = (a \mapsto a_1, s \mapsto s_1)$.

The model relation[2] for the set-based semantics is defined by $\sigma \models \phi$ iff for all $\iota \in \sigma$, $\iota \models \phi$. The intuitive meaning of $\sigma \models \phi$ is that σ is a result for a query ϕ, where σ_i is the (not necessarily maximal) set of solutions, *i.e.* assignments to the free variables that satisfy ϕ, given the extension of the database as defined by σ_r.

A possibly bewildering consequence of this definition is that also formulas that are inconsistent (according to the individual semantics) have a model in the set-based semantics. Indeed, $(\sigma_d, \sigma_r, \{\}) \models \bot$. This choice is motivated by the intended behaviour of the operational semantics, which should be non-blocking: execution can always proceed after a `match` statement, even for an inconsistent match condition, but then with an empty solution set.

As usual, a formula is called *valid* if it is true under every interpretation. The notions coincide for the two semantics:

Lemma 1. *A formula is valid under the individual semantics iff it is valid under the set-based semantics.*

---

[2] We use the same relation symbol $\models$ and disambiguate individual and set-based semantics with the designation of the model (ι resp. σ).

$$
\text{(ADD)} \ \frac{\sigma' = add\_rel\_si \ R \ \mathbf{v} \ \sigma}{(\mathtt{add}(R(\mathbf{v})), \sigma) \Rightarrow \sigma'} \qquad\qquad \text{(DEL)} \ \frac{\sigma' = del\_rel\_si \ R \ \mathbf{v} \ \sigma}{(\mathtt{del}(R(\mathbf{v})), \sigma) \Rightarrow \sigma'}
$$

$$
\text{(MATCH)} \ \frac{(c, max\_model \ b \ \sigma) \Rightarrow \sigma'' \quad \sigma' = \sigma'' (\!| i := \sigma.i |\!)}{(\mathtt{match} \ \mathbf{v} \ \mathtt{where} \ b \ \{c\}, \sigma) \Rightarrow \sigma'}
$$

$$
\text{(SKIP)} \ (\mathtt{Skip}, \sigma) \Rightarrow \sigma \qquad\qquad \text{(SEQ)} \ \frac{(c_1, \sigma) \Rightarrow \sigma'' \quad (c_2, \sigma'') \Rightarrow \sigma'}{(c_1; c_2, \sigma) \Rightarrow \sigma'}
$$

Fig. 2. Big-step semantics rules

2.3 Operational Semantics

The operational semantics defines how the program state evolves when executing the instructions of a program. In our case, a program state is precisely a set-based interpretation in the sense of Sect. 2.2. Intuitively, in an interpretation $\sigma = (\sigma_d, \sigma_r, \sigma_i)$, the component σ_r corresponds to the extension of the database that is manipulated by $\mathtt{add}$ and $\mathtt{del}$ statements, and the component σ_i corresponds to variable bindings established by the $\mathtt{match}$ clauses. The domain σ_d remains unchanged throughout the program.

The rules of the operational semantics have the form $(c, \sigma) \Rightarrow \sigma'$, meaning that execution of statement c transforms state σ to state σ'. The inductive definition of the transition relation is given in Fig. 2.

Before commenting on these rules, we introduce some more notation for manipulating interpretations. In an interpretation $\sigma = (\sigma_d, \sigma_r, \sigma_i)$, we retrieve the component σ_d, σ_r, resp. σ_i with $\sigma.d$, $\sigma.r$, resp. $\sigma.i$. Component update is written in banana brackets. Thus, $\sigma'' (\!| i := \sigma.i |\!)$ (as in rule MATCH) is the interpretation $(\sigma''_d, \sigma''_r, \sigma_i)$.

The rule for the $\mathtt{add}$ statement is defined with the aid of an auxiliary function that adds to relation R the values bound to variables $\mathbf{v}$ in state σ. The precise definition of $add\_rel\_si \ R \ \mathbf{v} \ \sigma$ is: $\sigma (\!| r := \sigma.r(R := (\sigma.r(R) \cup ((\lambda ii.\mathtt{map} \ ii \ \mathbf{v}) \triangleright \sigma.i))) |\!)$.

In a similar spirit, the definition of $del\_rel\_si \ R \ \mathbf{v} \ \sigma$ is: $\sigma (\!| r := \sigma.r(R := (\sigma.r(R) - ((\lambda ii.\mathtt{map} \ ii \ \mathbf{v}) \triangleright \sigma.i))) |\!)$.

Let us decipher the definition of add_rel_si: We update the relational interpretation of σ for relation R, so that the new interpretation of R becomes $(\sigma.r(R) \cup ((\lambda ii.\mathtt{map} \ ii \ \mathbf{v}) \triangleright \sigma.i))$. This is the old interpretation of relation R, plus new elements resulting from mapping the individual interpretations on the variable vector $\mathbf{v}$. Here, $\mathtt{map}$ is the mapping of a function on a list, and $\triangleright$ is the image of a set under a function. For example, if the relation to be updated is $Active$ with interpretation $\sigma.r(Active) = \{(s_1, c_1)\}$ and the individual variable interpretation $\sigma.i = \{(a \mapsto a_1, s \mapsto s_1), (a \mapsto a_1, s \mapsto s_2), (a \mapsto a_2, s \mapsto s_2)\}$, the expression $((\lambda ii.\mathtt{map} \ ii \ (s, a)) \triangleright \sigma.i)$ yields $\{(s_1, a_1), (s_2, a_1), (s_2, a_2)\}$ which are added to $\sigma.r(Active)$ (cf. example of Sect. 1.2).

For executing the `match` statement, we first compute the maximal model satisfying condition b in σ. Note that σ already incorporates the cumulative effect of surrounding `match` statements. The auxiliary function is defined as $max\_model\ b\ \sigma := fusion\ \sigma\ \{\iota \in \sigma \mid \iota \models b\}$, where $fusion\ \sigma\ I := (\sigma_d, \sigma_r, \bigcup \iota \in I.\{\iota.i\})$. "Maximality" of a set-based interpretation is here understood as "containing the maximum of individual interpretations". If σ is the maximal interpretation satisfying the surrounding `match` conditions, then $max\_model\ b\ \sigma$ is the maximal model satisfying in addition the current condition. Note that for a condition b that is inconsistent with the surrounding conditions, $max\_model\ b\ \sigma = (\sigma_d, \sigma_r, \{\})$.

Starting from this model, we execute the body c of the `match` statement, to reach a state σ''. We finally obtain the result state by restoring the individual variable bindings of the outer scope; of course, we keep the modifications induced by c on the relational assignment σ_r. The rules for `Skip` (no-op) and sequential composition are standard.

3   Program Logic

In this section, we show how to reason about the programs introduced in Sect. 2. For the programming language, we introduce extended Hoare triples (Sect. 3.1) that take contextual information into account, and establish a correspondence with the operational semantics, in the form of a soundness result (Sect. 3.2). We then show how to derive weakest pre-conditions (Sect. 3.3).

3.1   Hoare Triples: Definition

As is common practice in program logics, we reason about programs with Hoare triples $\{P\}\ c\ \{Q\}$ which express that when started in a program state that satisfies condition P, execution of statement c ends up in a program state satisfying condition Q. The programs of our language always terminate, never get stuck, and the language is deterministic, so there is no need to distinguish between partial and total correctness of programs.

To this triple, we add a context β that is the list of conditions accumulated while diving into nested `match` statements. This list dynamically grows or shrinks as we move into or out of a `match` statement. The conjunction of these formulas can be assumed to hold at the given point of the program. Indeed, in formulas (such as $R(\mathbf{v}) \vee \beta$), β does not stand for a list of formulas, but for the conjunction of the elements of the list. The inductive definition of the relation $\beta \vdash \{P\}\ c\ \{Q\}$ is given in Fig. 3. At the start of a program, the context is assumed to be empty: $\beta = []$. In spite of its four components, we continue speaking about Hoare triples.

Again, the rules SKIP and SEQ are standard, and so is CONSEQ that permits to weaken pre- respectively post-conditions and that is provided to ensure completeness of the calculus.

The MATCH rule adds the match condition b to the list of bindings β (list concatenation $\beta@[b]$) and then computes the pre-condition P for the body of the

(ADD) $\beta \vdash \{Q[R := \lambda\mathbf{v}.(R(\mathbf{v}) \vee \beta)]\}$ add$(R(\mathbf{v}))$ $\{Q\}$

(DEL) $\beta \vdash \{Q[R := \lambda\mathbf{v}.(R(\mathbf{v}) \wedge \neg\beta)]\}$ del$(R(\mathbf{v}))$ $\{Q\}$

(MATCH) $\dfrac{\beta@[b] \vdash \{P\}\, c\, \{Q\}}{\beta \vdash \{\forall\mathbf{v}.(b \longrightarrow P)\}\ (\text{match v where } b\ \{c\})\ \{Q\}}$

(SKIP) $\beta \vdash \{P\}$ Skip $\{P\}$ (SEQ) $\dfrac{\beta \vdash \{P\}\, c_1\, \{R\} \quad \beta \vdash \{R\}\, c_2\, \{Q\}}{\beta \vdash \{P\}\, c_1; c_2\, \{Q\}}$

(CONSEQ) $\dfrac{P \longrightarrow P' \quad \beta \vdash \{P'\}\, c\, \{Q'\} \quad Q' \longrightarrow Q}{\beta \vdash \{P\}\, c\, \{Q\}}$

Fig. 3. Hoare triples

match statement. Whereas Q is outside the scope of the variables $\mathbf{v}$ bound by match, these variables could appear in P. The pre-condition of match therefore discharges the local condition b and abstracts over the local variables $\mathbf{v}$.

In rules ADD and DEL, we use relation update:

Definition 2. *The* update of relation R *by relation* S *in formula* Q *is written as* $Q[R := \lambda\mathbf{v}.S]$, *where the variables* $\mathbf{v}$ *may occur in* S. *It is defined recursively with base case* $R(a_1, \ldots, a_n)[R := \lambda v_1, \ldots, v_n.S] = (\lambda v_1, \ldots, v_n.S)(a_1, \ldots, a_n) = S[v_1 := a_1, \ldots v_n := a_n]$ *and* $R'(a_1, \ldots, a_n)[R := \lambda v_1, \ldots, v_n.S] = R'(a_1, \ldots, a_n)$ *for* $R \neq R'$. *The propagation of update* $[R := \lambda\mathbf{v}.S]$ *through Boolean connectives is standard, with variable renaming in* $(\forall v.\psi)[R := \lambda\mathbf{v}.S] = (\forall v'.\psi[v := v'][R := \lambda\mathbf{v}.S])$ *to avoid free variable capture.*

Please refer back to Sect. 1.2 for an illustration: For example, for statement add$(Active(s, a))$, the context β is the conjunction of $A(a) \wedge \exists e.E(e) \wedge Valid(e, a)$ and $S(s) \wedge Subscr(s, a)$, and relation update $(\forall s\, c.\ Active(s, c) \longrightarrow Subscr(s, c))[Active := \lambda s\, a.Active(s, a) \vee \beta]$ yields $\forall s\, c.\ (Active(s, c) \vee A(c) \wedge (\exists e.E(e) \wedge Valid(e, c)) \wedge S(s) \wedge Subscr(s, a)) \longrightarrow Subscr(s, c)$.

3.2   Hoare Triples: Soundness

The proof of soundness follows a general approach that is relatively standard, see for example [25]. We first define a semantic notion of validity of a Hoare triple and then show that the inductively defined relation of Fig. 3 implies semantic validity. We first define a simplified variant of validity (Definition 3), from which soundness is not directly provable. For the induction to go through and to take into account the notion of DU-stability, we have to define a more complex notion of validity (Definition 6) with a more involved soundness lemma (Lemma 2) of which the desired theorem (Theorem 1) is an instance.

Definition 3 (Validity of Hoare Triples). *For formulas P and Q and statement c, we define the relation $\models \{P\}\, c\, \{Q\}$ as: For all states σ, σ', if $(c, \sigma) \Rightarrow \sigma'$ and $\sigma \models P$, then $\sigma' \models Q$.*

Theorem 1 (Soundness). *Let c be a well-typed and DU-stable program. If $[] \vdash \{P\}\, c\, \{Q\}$, then $\models \{P\}\, c\, \{Q\}$.*

We prove this theorem later and first introduce additional notation.

An *exclusion set* X is a set of variables, with the intended meaning that if $v \in X$ at a particular point in program execution, then there exists an R that is a defining relation of v (see Definition 1) and R has been modified since the definition of v. Intuitively, this has as a consequence that if $P(v)$ is the defining property of v, then there is a risk that $P(v)$ is not true at this point any more.

To keep track of how exclusion sets evolve during execution of a program, we define a relation of exclusion propagation.

Definition 4 (Exclusion Propagation). *For statement c and exclusion sets X, X', we inductively define the relation of exclusion propagation $(c, X) \xrightarrow{\times} X'$ by:*

- $(\texttt{Skip}, X) \xrightarrow{\times} X$
- $(\texttt{add}(R(\mathbf{v})), X) \xrightarrow{\times} X \cup D(R)$ *where $D(R)$ is the set of variables v such that R is a defining relation of v*
- $(\texttt{del}(R(\mathbf{v})), X) \xrightarrow{\times} X \cup D(R)$
- $(\texttt{match } \mathbf{v} \texttt{ where } b\; \{c\}, X) \xrightarrow{\times} (X' - \mathbf{v})$ *if $(c, X) \xrightarrow{\times} X'$*
  Note that the local variables $\mathbf{v}$ are not visible outside of c and can therefore be removed after the match.
- $((c_1; c_2), X) \xrightarrow{\times} X'$ *if $(c_1, X) \xrightarrow{\times} X''$ and $(c_2, X'') \xrightarrow{\times} X'$*

Example 2. Let us look back at the introductory example in Fig. 1. When starting exclusion propagation with an empty set at the beginning of the program, it remains empty most of the time, until after the del statement, when it becomes $\{a\}$, so the defining property of a is not usable in the following, but this is not problematic as there are no further statements (*a fortiori*, statements where a is used).

Now please refer back to the program of Example 1. When starting exclusion propagation with an empty set, after the add statement, the exclusion set is $\{a\}$, and it remains so until the del statement. The problem is that variable a is still used at this point.

Definition 5 (Admissible Predicates). *For a list of formulas β and an exclusion set X, the set of admissible predicates is $adm(\beta, X) = \{b \in \beta \mid fv(b) \cap X = \{\}\}$. Taken as a formula, $adm(\beta, X)$ is understood to be the conjunction of the formulas contained in the set.*

Consider an exclusion propagation of a program that starts with an empty exclusion set. Assume that at a point before a statement $\texttt{add}(R(\mathbf{v}))$ (or similarly del), there is a $v \in \mathbf{v}$ that is also contained in the current exclusion set. Then this would contradict DU-stability of v and thus of the whole program. Differently said, in a DU-stable program, the variables of an add or del do not occur in an exclusion set.

Definition 6 (Validity of Hoare Triples with Exclusion Sets). *For a list of formulas β, exclusion set X, formulas P and Q and statement c, we define the relation $\beta, X \models \{P\}\ c\ \{Q\}$ as: For all states σ, σ', if $(c, \sigma) \Rightarrow \sigma'$ and $\sigma \models adm(\beta, X) \wedge P$, for all X', if $(c, X) \xrightarrow{\times} X'$, then $\sigma' \models adm(\beta, X') \wedge Q$.*

Lemma 2 (Soundness with Exclusion Sets). *Let c be a sub-statement of a well-typed and DU-stable program. If $\beta \vdash \{P\}\ c\ \{Q\}$, then $\beta, X \models \{P\}\ c\ \{Q\}$ for all X.*

A proof of this lemma is given in the formal Isabelle development.

Proof. (of Theorem 1): The theorem is an instance of Lemma 2, for $\beta = []$ and $X = \{\}$.

3.3   Weakest Pre-conditions

The weakest pre-condition wp for a given post-condition Q and statement c is a pre-condition that is implied by any other pre-condition. We compute the wp with function $wp(\beta, c, Q)$ that also takes into account the local bindings. The recursive definition of wp is given in Fig. 4.

$$
\begin{aligned}
&wp(\beta, \texttt{Skip}, Q) = Q \\
&wp(\beta, \texttt{add}(R(\mathbf{v})), Q) = Q[R := \lambda \mathbf{v}.(R(\mathbf{v}) \vee \beta)] \\
&wp(\beta, \texttt{del}(R(\mathbf{v})), Q) = Q[R := \lambda \mathbf{v}.(R(\mathbf{v}) \wedge \neg \beta)] \\
&wp(\beta, \texttt{match v where } b\ \{c\}, Q) = \forall \mathbf{v}.b \longrightarrow wp(\beta@[b], c, Q) \\
&wp(\beta, c_1; c_2, Q) = wp(\beta, c_1, wp(\beta, c_2, Q))
\end{aligned}
$$

Fig. 4. Weakest pre-conditions

The correspondence between the weakest pre-conditions and the program calculus of Sect. 3.1 is established by the following lemma, whose proof is by an easy induction over c.

Lemma 3. $\beta \vdash \{wp(\beta, c, Q)\}\ c\ \{Q\}$.

Initially, β is assumed to be empty. Proving the correctness of a program $\{Pre\}\ prog\ \{Post\}$ therefore amounts to showing that $Pre \longrightarrow wp([], prog, Post)$ is valid, by an application of rule CONSEQ.

Let us emphasise one point: in Sect. 2.2, we have defined two semantics. Because the notion of validity of Hoare triples is defined with reference to the set-based semantics, the whole soundness argument is carried out in this semantics. Showing that $Pre \longrightarrow wp([], prog, Post)$ is valid can be done *w.r.t.* the set-based semantics, but according to Lemma 1, it is equivalent to the standard individual semantics, so it is more convenient to switch to this semantics here to be able to use standard proof procedures of predicate logic.

4 Guarded Fragment

The results established in the previous section are sound for programs containing full first-order formulas, but application of the wp calculus to such programs will in general produce proof problems that are undecidable. The Guarded Fragment (GF) is a fragment of first-order predicate logic that has been introduced by Andréka, Németi and van Benthem [4] and studied in depth [14,15]. The aspect of interest for us is that GF is decidable; several decision procedures have been described [13,17] and implemented [18].

We summarise the essential features of GF: An *atomic formula* or *atom* is defined as an equality $x = y$ or the application of a relation symbol to a tuple of variables, $R(\mathbf{v})$. On this basis, we define GF:

Definition 7 (Guarded Fragment, GF).

- *All quantifier-free first-order formulas are formulas of GF.*
- *If ψ and ϕ are formulas of GF, then so are $\neg\psi$ and $(\psi \wedge \phi)$.*
- *If $\psi(\mathbf{x},\mathbf{y})$ is a formula of GF and $\alpha(\mathbf{x},\mathbf{y})$ is an atom and $fv(\psi(\mathbf{x},\mathbf{y})) \subseteq$ $fv(\alpha(\mathbf{x},\mathbf{y}))$, then $\exists\mathbf{y}.\alpha(\mathbf{x},\mathbf{y}) \wedge \psi(\mathbf{x},\mathbf{y})$ and $\forall\mathbf{y}.\alpha(\mathbf{x},\mathbf{y}) \longrightarrow \psi(\mathbf{x},\mathbf{y})$ are formulas of GF. Here, we call $\alpha(\mathbf{x},\mathbf{y})$ the guard and $\psi(\mathbf{x},\mathbf{y})$ the body of a quantified formula.*

We say that a formula is guarded if it belongs to the guarded fragment of first-order logic. The definitions of *ValidClient* and *ActiveIfSubscr* of Sect. 1.2 are examples of guarded formulas.

Definition 8 (Guarded statement and program). *We say that a formula b is a* quasi-guard *if it can be written as $\alpha_1(\mathbf{v_1}) \wedge \ldots \wedge \alpha_n(\mathbf{v_n}) \wedge \psi$, where ψ is a guarded formula and the α_i are atoms, where different $\mathbf{v_i}, \mathbf{v_j}$ are disjoint.*

We say that a match clause match v where b *is guarded if b is a quasi-guard.*

We say that a statement is guarded if all its match clauses are guarded. We say that a program is guarded if its pre- and post-conditions and its constituting statement are guarded.

For example, the program of Fig. 1 is guarded. A program with a clause match v_1, v_2 where $(\exists x.R(x,v_1)) \wedge (\exists y.R(y,v_2))$ is not guarded.

Theorem 2. *If c is a guarded statement, Q a guarded formula and β a list of quasi-guards, then $wp(\beta, c, Q)$ is a guarded formula.*

Proof. The proof is by induction on the structure of the statement. The proposition is evident for Skip. For a sequence $c_1; c_2$ of instructions and guarded Q, by induction hypothesis, we obtain a guarded formula for $wp(\beta, c_2, Q)$. Similarly, for a match statement, $wp(\beta@[b], c, Q)$ is a guarded formula G. If match v where b is guarded and b a quasi-guard, we can write $\forall\mathbf{v}.b \longrightarrow G$ as $\forall\mathbf{v_1}.\alpha_1(\mathbf{v_1}) \longrightarrow \ldots \longrightarrow \forall\mathbf{v_n}.\alpha_n(\mathbf{v_n}) \longrightarrow \psi \longrightarrow G$, which is again guarded.

The main concern is therefore preservation of guardedness in relation update; we first discuss the case $Q[R := \lambda\mathbf{v}.(R(\mathbf{v})\vee\beta)]$. We reason by induction on Q. The only critical cases are existential and universal quantification; we only look at the latter, the former is similar. Thus, assume Q is of the form $\forall \mathbf{y}. \alpha(\mathbf{x}, \mathbf{y}) \longrightarrow \psi(\mathbf{x}, \mathbf{y})$. The case where $\alpha \neq R$ poses no problem, so assume Q of the form $\forall \mathbf{y}. R(\mathbf{x}, \mathbf{y}) \longrightarrow \psi(\mathbf{x}, \mathbf{y})$, with $Q[R := \lambda \mathbf{v}.(R(\mathbf{v}) \vee \beta)] = \forall \mathbf{y}.(R(\mathbf{x}, \mathbf{y}) \vee \beta[\mathbf{v} := \mathbf{x}, \mathbf{y}]) \longrightarrow \psi'$, where ψ' is the result of the relation update in $\psi(\mathbf{x}, \mathbf{y})$. This formula is not guarded any longer, but we can rewrite it to a conjunction of $\forall \mathbf{y}. R(\mathbf{x}, \mathbf{y}) \longrightarrow \psi'$ (which is guarded) and $\forall \mathbf{y}. \beta[\mathbf{v} := \mathbf{x}, \mathbf{y}] \longrightarrow \psi'$, with β a list of quasi-guards, which can be turned into a guarded formula in a similar form as seen for the `match` statement.

The reasoning for a relation update $Q[R := \lambda \mathbf{v}.(R(\mathbf{v}) \wedge \neg \beta)]$ for a delete statement proceeds along the same line, but is slightly simpler: the intermediate formula $\forall \mathbf{y}.(R(\mathbf{x}, \mathbf{y}) \wedge \neg \beta[\mathbf{v} := \mathbf{x}, \mathbf{y}]) \longrightarrow \psi'$ can directly be rewritten to the guarded $\forall \mathbf{y}. R(\mathbf{x}, \mathbf{y}) \longrightarrow (\neg \beta[\mathbf{v} := \mathbf{x}, \mathbf{y}]) \longrightarrow \psi'$.

From this theorem, the fact that a program $\{Pre\}\ c\ \{Post\}$ yields a proof obligation $Pre \longrightarrow wp([], c, Post)$, and the decidability of GF, we obtain:

Corollary 1.

- *Application of the weakest pre-condition calculus of Sect. 3.3 to a guarded program produces a guarded proof obligation.*
- *The correctness problem of guarded programs is decidable.*

5 Conclusions

This paper has presented a language combining queries and updates that can be used for graph and relational databases. The focus of the paper is on verifying assertions in the form of pre- and post-conditions, the operational aspect of the language was secondary. It might nevertheless be interesting to make this language executable, which is not possible when bluntly taking the operational semantics as it stands, because the semantics is manipulating possibly infinite sets of individual interpretations. We are however convinced that it is easy to derive a realistic operational semantics, by a restriction to relevant variables (the variables occurring in the program).

Our current efforts concentrate on formally verifying the theory developed in this paper in the Isabelle proof assistant, in order to obtain a fully verified proof obligation generator. Completeness of the calculus presented here is an open question. Further steps in the theory are extensions of the logic permitting to reason about paths in graphs, leading us to consider logics with transitive closure.

Acknowledgements. We are grateful to Lison Kardassevitch for implementing a prototype of the verification framework.

References

1. Ahmetaj, S., Calvanese, D., Ortiz, M., Simkus, M.: Managing change in graph-structured data using description logics. In: Proceedings of the 28th AAAI Conference on Artificial Intelligence (AAAI 2014), pp. 966–973. AAAI Press (2014). http://www.inf.unibz.it/~calvanese/papers-html/AAAI-2014-graph-dbs.html
2. Ahmetaj, S., Calvanese, D., Ortiz, M., Simkus, M.: Managing change in graph-structured data using description logics. ACM Trans. Comput. Log. 18(4), 27:1–27:35 (2017). https://doi.org/10.1145/3143803
3. Ahmeti, A., Calvanese, D., Polleres, A.: Updating RDFS ABoxes and TBoxes in SPARQL. In: Mika, P., et al. (eds.) ISWC 2014. LNCS, vol. 8796, pp. 441–456. Springer, Cham (2014). https://doi.org/10.1007/978-3-319-11964-9_28
4. Andréka, H., Németi, I., van Benthem, J.: Modal languages and bounded fragments of predicate logic. J. Philos. Log. 27(3), 217–274 (1998). http://www.fenrong.net/teaching/Andreka.pdf
5. Benedikt, M., Griffin, T., Libkin, L.: Verifiable properties of database transactions. Inf. Comput. 147(1), 57–88 (1998). https://core.ac.uk/download/pdf/82337092.pdf
6. Brenas, J.H., Echahed, R., Strecker, M.: Ensuring correctness of model transformations while remaining decidable. In: Sampaio, A., Wang, F. (eds.) ICTAC 2016. LNCS, vol. 9965, pp. 315–332. Springer, Cham (2016). https://doi.org/10.1007/978-3-319-46750-4_18
7. Brenas, J.H., Echahed, R., Strecker, M.: A Hoare-like calculus using the SROIQ$^\sigma$ logic on transformations of graphs. In: Diaz, J., Lanese, I., Sangiorgi, D. (eds.) TCS 2014. LNCS, vol. 8705, pp. 164–178. Springer, Heidelberg (2014). https://doi.org/10.1007/978-3-662-44602-7_14
8. Bry, F., Decker, H., Manthey, R.: A uniform approach to constraint satisfaction and constraint satisfiability in deductive databases. In: Schmidt, J.W., Ceri, S., Missikoff, M. (eds.) EDBT 1988. LNCS, vol. 303, pp. 488–505. Springer, Heidelberg (1988). https://doi.org/10.1007/3-540-19074-0_69
9. Chaabani, M., Echahed, R., Strecker, M.: Logical foundations for reasoning about transformations of knowledge bases. In: Eiter, T., Glimm, B., Kazakov, Y., Krötzsch, M. (eds.) DL - Description Logics. CEUR Workshop Proceedings, vol. 1014, pp. 616–627. CEUR-WS.org (2013)
10. Courcelle, B., Engelfriet, J.: Graph Structure and Monadic Second-Order Logic, a Language Theoretic Approach. Cambridge University Press (2011). http://www.labri.fr/perso/courcell/Book/TheBook.pdf
11. Fagin, R., Ullman, J.D., Vardi, M.Y.: On the semantics of updates in databases. In: Proceedings of the 2nd ACM SIGACT-SIGMOD Symposium on Principles of Database Systems, pp. 352–365. ACM (1983)
12. Francis, N., et al.: Cypher: An evolving query language for property graphs. In: Proceedings of the 2018 International Conference on Management of Data, SIGMOD Conference 2018, Houston, TX, USA, 10–15 June 2018, pp. 1433–1445 (2018). https://doi.org/10.1145/3183713.3190657. https://doi.org/10.1145/3183713.3190657
13. Grädel, E.: Decision procedures for guarded logics. In: Ganzinger, H. (ed.) CADE 1999. LNCS, vol. 1632, pp. 31–51. Springer, Heidelberg (1999). https://doi.org/10.1007/3-540-48660-7_3
14. Grädel, E.: On the restraining power of guards. J. Symb. Log. 64, 1719–1742 (1999). http://www.logic.rwth-aachen.de/pub/graedel/Gr-jsl99.ps

15. Grädel, E.: Decidable fragments of first-order and fixed-point logic. From prefix-vocabulary classes to guarded logics. In: Proceedings of Kalmár Workshop on Logic and Computer Science, Szeged (2003). http://www.logic.rwth-aachen.de/pub/graedel/Gr-kalmar03.ps

16. Habel, A., Pennemann, K.-H., Rensink, A.: Weakest preconditions for high-level programs. In: Corradini, A., Ehrig, H., Montanari, U., Ribeiro, L., Rozenberg, G. (eds.) ICGT 2006. LNCS, vol. 4178, pp. 445–460. Springer, Heidelberg (2006). https://doi.org/10.1007/11841883_31

17. Hirsch, C.: Guarded logics: algorithms and bisimulation. Ph.D. thesis, RWTH Aachen (2002). http://www.logic.rwth-aachen.de/pub/hirsch/hirsch.pdf

18. Hladik, J.: Implementation and optimisation of a tableau algorithm for the guarded fragment. In: Egly, U., Fermüller, C.G. (eds.) TABLEAUX 2002. LNCS, vol. 2381, pp. 145–159. Springer, Heidelberg (2002). https://doi.org/10.1007/3-540-45616-3_11

19. Hosoya, H.: XML Processing - The Tree-Automata Approach. Cambridge University Press, Cambridge (2011)

20. Inaba, K., Hidaka, S., Hu, Z., Kato, H., Nakano, K.: Graph-transformation verification using monadic second-order logic. In: International ACM SIGPLAN Symposium on Principles and Practice of Declarative Programming (PPDP), pp. 17–28, July 2011. http://dl.acm.org/authorize?442117

21. Itzhaky, S., et al.: On the automated verification of web applications with embedded SQL. In: Benedikt, M., Orsi, G. (eds.) 20th International Conference on Database Theory (ICDT 2017). Leibniz International Proceedings in Informatics (LIPIcs), vol. 68, pp. 16:1–16:18. Schloss Dagstuhl-Leibniz-Zentrum fuer Informatik, Dagstuhl, Germany (2017). https://doi.org/10.4230/LIPIcs.ICDT.2017.16. http://drops.dagstuhl.de/opus/volltexte/2017/7050

22. Martens, W., Neven, F.: Frontiers of tractability for typechecking simple XML transformations. J. Comput. Syst. Sci. **73**(3), 362–390 (2007)

23. Martinenghi, D., Christiansen, H., Decker, H.: Integrity checking and maintenance in relational and deductive database and beyond. In: Intelligent Databases: Technologies and Applications, pp. 238–285. IGI Global (2007)

24. Muchnick, S.: Advanced Compiler Design and Implementation. Morgan Kaufmann, Burlington (1997)

25. Nipkow, T., Klein, G.: Concrete Semantics (2014). http://concrete-semantics.org/

26. Olivé, A.: Integrity constraints checking in deductive databases. In: VLDB, pp. 513–523. Citeseer (1991)

27. openCypher Project: Cypher Query Language Reference, version 9 edn. (2018). http://www.opencypher.org/

Abstraction and Subsumption in Modular Verification of C Programs

Lennart Beringer$^{(\boxtimes)}$ and Andrew W. Appel

Princeton University, Princeton, NJ 08544, USA
{eberinge,appel}@cs.princeton.edu

Abstract. Representation predicates enable *data abstraction* in separation logic, but when the same concrete implementation may need to be abstracted in different ways, one needs a notion of *subsumption*. We demonstrate *function-specification subtyping*, analogous to subtyping, with a *subsumption* rule: if ϕ is a funspec_sub of ψ, that is $\phi <: \psi$, then $x : \phi$ implies $x : \psi$, meaning that any function satisfying specification ϕ can be used wherever a function satisfying ψ is demanded. We extend previous notions of Hoare-logic sub-specification, which already included parameter adaption, to include *framing* (necessary for separation logic) and impredicative bifunctors (necessary for higher-order functions, i.e. function pointers). We show intersection specifications, with the expected relation to subtyping. We show how this enables compositional modular verification of the functional correctness of C programs, in Coq, with foundational machine-checked proofs of soundness.

Keywords: Foundational program verification · Separation logics · Specification subsumption

1 Introduction

Even in the 21st century, the world still runs on C: operating systems, runtime systems, network stacks, cryptographic libraries, controllers for embedded systems, and large swaths of critical infrastructure code are either directly hand-coded in C or employ C as intermediate target of compilation or code synthesis. Analysis methods and verification tools that apply to C thus remain a vital area of research. The Verified Software Toolchain (VST) [4] is a semi-automated proof system for functional-correctness verification of C programs that integrates two long-standing lines of research: (i) program logics with machine-checked proofs of soundness; (ii) practical verification tools for industry-strength programming languages. VST consists of three main components:

Verifiable C [3] is a higher-order impredicative concurrent separation logic covering almost all the control-flow and data-structuring features of C (we currently omit goto and by-copy whole-struct assignment);

© Springer Nature Switzerland AG 2019
M. H. ter Beek et al. (Eds.): FM 2019, LNCS 11800, pp. 573–590, 2019.
https://doi.org/10.1007/978-3-030-30942-8_34

VST-Floyd [7] is a library of lemmas, definitions, and automation tactics that assist the user in applying the program logic to a program, using forward symbolic execution, with separation logic assertions as symbolic states;

The semantic model justifies the proof rules, exploiting the theories of step-indexing, impredicative quantification, separation algebras, and concurrent ghost state. The semantic model is the basis of a machine-checked proof [4], in Coq, that the Verifiable C program logic is sound w.r.t. the operational semantics of CompCert Clight. Thus the user's Coq proof *in* Verifiable C composes with our soundness proof *of* Verifiable C and with Leroy's CompCert compiler correctness proof [15] to yield an end-to-end proof of the functional correctness of the assembly-language program.

VST's key feature—distinguishing it from tools such as VCC [8], Frama-C [11], or VeriFast [9]—is that it is *entirely* implemented in the Coq proof assistant. A user imports C code into the Coq development environment and applies VST-Floyd's automation—computational decision procedures from Coq's standard library, plus custom-built tactics for forward symbolic execution and entailment checking—to construct formal derivations in the Verifiable C program logic. The full power of Coq and its libraries are available to manipulate application-specific mathematics. The semantic validity of the proof rules—machine-checked by Coq's kernel—connects these derivations to Clight, i.e. CompCert's representation of parsed and determinized C code.

Recent applications of VST include the verification of cryptographic primitives from OpenSSL [2,6] and mbedTLS [24], an asynchronous communication mechanism [17], and an internet-facing server component [13]. Ongoing efforts elsewhere include a generational garbage collector and a malloc-free library.

Motivated by these applications, we now add support for data abstraction, a key enabler of scalability. As shown in previous work [21], separation logic can easily express data abstraction, using abstract predicates: just as the client program of an abstract data type (ADT) can be written without knowing the representation, verification of the client can proceed without knowing the representation. In type theory, this is the principle of *existential types* [18].

But in real-life modular programming, the same function may want more than one specification. For example, a function may expose a concrete specification to "friend" functions that know the representation of internal data and a more abstract specification for clients that do not. In this case, one should not have to verify the function-body twice, once for each specification; instead, one should verify the function-body with respect to the concrete specification, then prove the concrete implies the abstract. Again, type theory provides an appropriate notion: *subtyping* [22]. In other cases, it may be desirable to specify different use cases of a function—applying, for example, to different input configurations, or to different control flow paths—using different specifications, perhaps using different abstract predicates. Yet again, type theory provides a useful analogue: *intersection types*, a form of ad-hoc polymorphism.

These observations motivate the use of type-theoretic principles as guidelines for developing specification mechanisms and automation features for abstraction. We now take a step in this direction, focusing primarily on the notion of subtyping. The observation that Hoare's original rule of consequence is insufficiently powerful in languages with (recursive) procedures motivated research into *parameter adaptation*, by (among others) Kleymann, Nipkow, and Naumann [12,19,20]. Indeed, Kleymann observed that ([12], p. 9).

- *in proving that the postcondition has been weakened, one may also assume the precondition of the conclusion holds...*
- *one may adjust the auxiliary variables in the premise. Their value may depend on the value of auxiliary variables in the conclusion and the value of all program variables in the initial state.*

But these developments were carried out for small languages and predate the emergence of separation logic. The present article hence revisits these ideas in the context of VST, by developing a powerful notion of function-specification subtyping for higher-order impredicative separation logic. Our treatment improves on previous work in several regards:

- We support function-specifications of function pointers, as part of our support for almost the entire C language. Kleymann only considers a single (anonymous, parameterless, but possibly recursive) procedure, while Nipkow supports mutual recursion between named procedures.
- Our notion of subtyping avoids direct quantification over states, thus permitting a higher-order impredicative separation logic in the style of VST and Iris [10], where "assertion" must be an abstract type with a step-indexed model rather than simply state→Prop. This is necessary to fully support function pointers and higher-order resource invariants (for concurrent programming). In contrast, Kleymann's and Nipkow's assertions are predicates over states, and the side conditions of their adaptation rules explicitly quantify over states. Naumann's formulation using predicate transformers captures the same relationship in a slighty more abstract manner.
- VST associates function specifications to globally named functions in its proof context Δ and includes a separation logic assertion func_at that attaches specifications to function-pointer values. Our treatment integrates subsumption coherently into proof contexts, func_at, and the soundness judgment. We support subsumption at function call sites but also incorporate subsumption in a notion of (proof) context subtyping that is reminiscent of record subtyping [22]. This will allow bundling function specifications into specifications of objects or modules that can be abstractly presented to client programs and are compatible with behavioral subtyping [14,16,23].
- We introduce intersection specifications and show that their interaction with subsumption precisely matches that of intersection types.

Our presentation is example-driven: we illustrate several use cases of subsumption on concrete code fragments in Verifiable C. Technical adaptations of the model that support these verifications have been machine-checked for soundness, but in the paper we only sketch them. The full Coq proofs of our example are in the VST repo, github.com/PrincetonUniversity/VST in directory progs/pile.

2 Function Specifications in Verifiable C

Our main example is an abstract data type (ADT) for *piles*, simple collections of integers. Figure 1 (on the next page) shows a modular C program that throws numbers onto a pile, then adds them up.

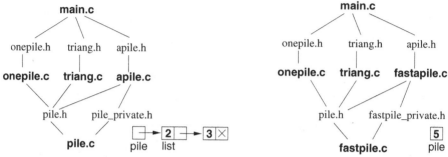

The diagram at left shows that pile.c is imported by onepile.c (which manages a single pile), apile.c (which manages a single pile in a different way), and triang.c (which computes the nth triangular number). The latter three modules are imported by main.c. Onepile.c and triang.c import the abstract interface pile.h; apile.c imports also the low-level concrete interface pile_private.h that exposes the representation—a typical use case for this organization might be when apile.c implements representation-dependent debugging or performance monitoring.

When—as shown on the right—pile.c is replaced by a faster implementation fastpile.c (code in Fig. 3) using a different data structure, apile.c must be replaced with fastapile.c, but the other modules need not be altered, *and neither should their specification or verification.*

Figure 2 presents the specification of the pile module, in the Verifiable C separation logic. Each C-language function identifier (such as _Pile_add) is bound to a funspec, a function specification in separation logic.

Before specifying the functions (with preconditions and postconditions), we must first specify the data structures they receive as arguments and return as results. Linked lists are specified as usual in separation logic: listrep is a recursive definition over the abstract ("mathematical") list value σ, specifying how it is laid out in a memory footprint rooted at address p. Then pilerep describes a memory location containing a pointer to a listrep.

A funspec takes the form, WITH $\vec{x} : \vec{\tau}$ PRE ... POST .... For example, take Pile_add_spec from Fig. 2: the $\vec{x}$ are bound Coq variables visible in both the precondition and postcondition, in this case, p:val, n:Z, σ:list Z, gv:globals, where p is the address of a pile data structure, n is the number to be added to the pile, σ is the sequence currently represented by the pile, and gv is a way to access all named global variables. The PREcondition is parameterized by the C-language formal parameter names _p and _n. An assertion in Verifiable C takes the form, PROP(*propositions*) LOCAL(*variable bindings*) SEP(*spatial conjuncts*). In

```
/* pile.h */
typedef struct pile *Pile;
Pile Pile_new(void);
void Pile_add(Pile p, int n);
int Pile_count(Pile p);
void Pile_free(Pile p);
```

```
/* onepile.h */
void Onepile_init(void);
void Onepile_add(int n);
int Onepile_count(void);
```

```
/* apile.h */
void Apile_add(int n);
int Apile_count(void);
```

```
/* triang.h */
int Triang_nth(int n);
```

```
/* triang.c */
#include "pile.h"
int Triang_nth(int n) {
  int i,c;
  Pile p = Pile_new();
  for (i=0; i<n; i++)
    Pile_add(p,i+1);
  c = Pile_count(p);
  Pile_free(p);
  return c;
}
```

```
/* onepile.c */
#include "pile.h"
Pile the_pile;
void Onepile_init(void)
  {the_pile = Pile_new();}
void Onepile_add(int n)
  {Pile_add(the_pile, n);}
int Onepile_count(void)
  {return Pile_count(the_pile);}
```

```
/* pile_private.h */
struct list {int n; struct list *next;};
struct pile {struct list *head;};
```

```
/* pile.c */
#include <stddef.h>
#include "stdlib.h"
#include "pile.h"
#include "pile_private.h"
Pile Pile_new(void) {
  Pile p = (Pile)surely_malloc(sizeof *p);
  p→head=NULL;
  return p;
}
void Pile_add(Pile p, int n) {
  struct list *head = (struct list *)
    surely_malloc(sizeof *head);
  head→n=n;
  head→next=p→head;
  p→head=head;
}
int Pile_count(Pile p) {
  struct list *q;
  int c=0;
  for(q=p→head; q; q=q→next)
    c += q→n;
  return c;
}
void Pile_free(Pile p) { ... }
```

```
/* apile.c */
#include "pile.h"
#include "pile_private.h"
#include "apile.h"
struct pile a_pile = {NULL};
void Apile_add(int n)
  {Pile_add(&a_pile, n);}
int Apile_count(void)
  {return Pile_count(&a_pile);}
```

Fig. 1. The pile.h abstract data type has operations *new, add, count, free.* The triang.c client adds the integers 1–n to the pile, then counts the pile. The pile.c implementation represents a pile as header node (struct pile) pointing to a linked list of integers. At bottom, there are two modules that each implement a single "implicit" pile in a module-local global variable: onepile.c maintains a pointer to a pile, while apile.c maintains a struct pile for which it needs knowledge of the representation through pile_private.h.

(* spec_pile.v *)
(* representation of linked lists in separation logic *)
Fixpoint listrep (σ: list Z) (x: val) : mpred :=
match σ **with**
| $h::hs \Rightarrow$ EX y:val, !! $(0 \leq h \leq$ Int.max_signed) &&
   data_at Ews tlist (Vint (Int.repr h), y) x
   * malloc_token Ews tlist x * listrep hs y
| nil $\Rightarrow$!! (x = nullval) && emp
end.

(* representation predicate for piles *)
Definition pilerep (σ: list Z) (p: val) : mpred :=
EX x:val, data_at Ews tpile x p * listrep σ x.

Definition pile_freeable (p: val) :=
   malloc_token Ews tpile p.

Definition Pile_new_spec :=
DECLARE _Pile_new
WITH gv: globals
PRE [ ] PROP() LOCAL(gvars gv) SEP(mem_mgr gv)
POST[tptr tpile]
   EX p: val,
      PROP() LOCAL(temp ret_temp p)
      SEP(pilerep nil p; pile_freeable p; mem_mgr gv).

Definition Pile_add_spec :=
DECLARE _Pile_add
WITH p: val, n: Z, σ: list Z, gv: globals
PRE [_p OF tptr tpile, _n OF tint]
   PROP($0 \leq n \leq$ Int.max_signed)
   LOCAL(temp _p p; temp _n (Vint (Int.repr n));
            gvars gv)
   SEP(pilerep σ p; mem_mgr gv)
POST[tvoid]
   PROP() LOCAL()
   SEP(pilerep ($n::\sigma$) p; mem_mgr gv).

Definition sumlist : list Z $\rightarrow$ Z := List.fold_right Z.add 0.

Definition Pile_count_spec :=
DECLARE _Pile_count
WITH p: val, σ: list Z
PRE [_p OF tptr tpile]
   PROP($0 \leq$ sumlist $\sigma \leq$ Int.max_signed) LOCAL(temp _p p)
   SEP(pilerep σ p)
POST[tint]
   PROP() LOCAL(temp ret_temp (Vint (Int.repr (sumlist σ))))
   SEP(pilerep σ p).

Notation key

mpred   predicate on memory

EX   existential quantifier
!!   injects Prop into mpred
&&   nonseparating conjunction
data_at π τ v p is $p \mapsto v$,
   separation-logic mapsto
   at type τ, permission π

malloc_token π τ x represents
   "capability to deallocate x"

Ews   the "extern write share"
   gives write permission

_Pile_new is a C identifier

WITH   quantifies variables
   over PRE/POST of funspec

The C function's return type,
   tptr tpile,   is "pointer
   to **struct** pile"

PROP(...) are pure propositions
   on the WITH-variables

LOCAL(... temp _p p ...)
   associates C local var _p
   with Coq value p

gvars gv establishes gv as
   mapping from C global
   vars to their addresses

SEP(R_1; R_2)   are separating
   conjuncts $R_1 * R_2$

mem_mgr gv represents
   different states of the
   malloc/free system in
   PRE and POST of
   any function that
   allocates or frees

Fig. 2. Specification of the pile module (Pile_free_spec not shown).

this case the PROP asserts that n is between 0 and max-int; LOCAL asserts[1] that address p is the current value of C variable _p, integer n is the value of C variable _n, and gv is the global-variable access map. The precondition's SEP clause has two conjuncts: the first one says that there's a *pile* data structure at address p representing sequence σ; the second one represents the memory-manager library. The spatial conjunct (mem_mgr gv) represents the private data structure of the memory-manager library, that is, the global variables in which the malloc-free system keeps its free lists.

The SEP clause of the POSTcondition says that the *pile* at address p now represents the list $n::\sigma$, and that the memory manager is still there.

Verifying that pile.c's functions satisfy the specifications in Fig. 2 using VST-Floyd is done by proving Lemmas like this one (in file verif_pile.v):

Lemma body_Pile_new: semax_body Vprog Gprog f_Pile_new Pile_new_spec.
Proof. ... *(∗7 lines of Coq proof script∗)*.... **Qed**.

This says, in the context Vprog of global-variable types, in the context Gprog of function-specs (for functions that Pile_new might call), the function-body f_Pile_new satisfies the function-specification Pile_new_spec.

Linking

A modular proof of a modular program is organized as follows: CompCert parses each module M.c into the AST file M.v. Then we write the specification file spec_M.v containing funspecs as in Fig. 2. We write verif_M.v which imports spec files of all the modules from which M.c calls functions, and contains semax_body proofs of correctness (such as body_Pile_new at the end of Sect. 2), for each of the functions in M.c.

What's special about the main() function is that its separation-logic precondition has all the initial values of the global variables, merged from the global variables of each module. In spec_main we merge the ASTs (global variables and function definitions) of all the M.v by a simple, computational, syntactic function. This is illustrated in the Coq files in VST/progs/pile.

VST's main soundness statement is that, when running main() in CompCert's operational semantics, in the initial memory induced from all global-variable initializers, the program is safe and correct—with a notion of partial correctness in interacting with the world via effectful external function calls [13] and returning the "right" value from main.

3   Subsumption of Function Specifications

We now turn to the replacement of pile.c by a more performant implementation, fastpile.c, and its specification—see Fig. 3. As fastpile.c employs a differ-

---

[1] A LOCAL clause temp _p p asserts that the current value of C local variable _p is the Coq value p. If n is a mathematical integer, then Int.repr n is its projection into 32-bit machine integers, and Vint projects machine integers into the type of scalar C-language values.

```
/* fastpile_private.h */
struct pile { int sum; };

/* fastpile.c */
#include . . .
#include "pile.h"
#include "fastpile_private.h"
Pile Pile_new(void)
    {Pile p = (Pile)surely_malloc(sizeof *p); p→sum=0; return p; }
void Pile_add(Pile p, int n)
    {int s = p→sum; if (0≤n && n≤INT_MAX-s) p→sum = s+n; }
int Pile_count(Pile p) {return p→sum;}
void Pile_free(Pile p) {free(p);}
```

(* spec_fastpile.v *)
Definition pilerep (σ: list Z) (p: val) : mpred :=
  EX s:Z, !! ($0 \leq s \leq$ Int.max_signed $\land$ Forall (Z.le 0) $\sigma \land$
              ($0 \leq$ sumlist $\sigma \leq$ Int.max_signed $\rightarrow s$=sumlist σ))
  && data_at Ews tpile (Vint (Int.repr s)) p.

Definition pile_freeable := (* looks identical to the one in fig.2 *)
Definition Pile_new_spec := (* looks identical to the one in fig.2 *)
Definition Pile_add_spec := (* looks identical to the one in fig.2 *)
Definition Pile_count_spec := (* looks identical to the one in fig.2 *)

Fig. 3. fastpile.c, a more efficient implementation of the pile ADT. Since the only query function is count, there's no need to represent the entire list, just the sum will suffice. In the verification of a client program, the pilerep separation-logic predicate has the same signature: list Z $\rightarrow$ val $\rightarrow$ mpred, even though the representation is a single number rather than a linked list.

ent data representation than pile.c, its specification employs a different representation predicate pilerep. As pilerep's type remains unchanged, the function specifications look virtually identical[2]; however, the VST-Floyd proof scripts (in file verif_fastpile.v) necessarily differ. Clients importing only the pile.h interface, like onepile.c or triang.c, cannot tell the difference (except that things run faster and take less memory), and are specified and verified only once (files spec_onepile.v/verif_onepile.v and spec_triang.v/verif_triang.v).

But we may also equip fastpile.c with a more low-level specification (see Fig. 4) in which the function specifications refer to a different representation predicate, countrep. In reasoning about clients of this low-level interface, we do not need a notion of "sequence"—in contrast to pilerep in Fig. 3. The new specification is less abstract than the one in Fig. 3, and closer to the implementation. The subsumption rule (to be introduced shortly) allows us to exploit this relationship:

---

[2] Existentially abstracting over the internal representation predicates would further emphasize the uniformity between fastpile.c and pile.c—a detailed treatment of this is beyond the scope of the present article.

(* spec_fastpile_concrete.v *)
Definition countrep (s: Z) (p: val) : mpred := EX s':Z,
   !! ($0 \leq s \land 0 \leq s' \leq$ Int.max_signed $\land$ ($s \leq$ Int.max_signed $\rightarrow s'=s$)) &&
   data_at Ews tpile (Vint (Int.repr s')) p.

Definition count_freeable (p: val) := malloc_token Ews tpile p.

Definition Pile_new_spec := ...

Definition Pile_add_spec :=
 DECLARE _Pile_add
 WITH p: val, n: Z, s: Z, gv: globals
 PRE [_p OF tptr tpile, _n OF tint]
   PROP($0 \leq n \leq$ Int.max_signed)
   LOCAL(temp _p p; temp _n (Vint (Int.repr n)); gvars gv)
   SEP(countrep s p; mem_mgr gv)
 POST[tvoid]
   PROP() LOCAL() SEP(countrep ($n + s$) p; mem_mgr gv).

Definition Pile_count_spec := ...

Fig. 4. The fastpile.c implementation could be used in applications that simply need to keep a running total. That is, a *concrete* specification can use a predicate countrep: Z $\rightarrow$ val $\rightarrow$ mpred that makes no assumption about a sequence (list Z). In countrep, the variable s' and the inequalities are needed to account for the possibility of integer overflow.

we only need to explicitly verify the code against the low-level specification and can establish satisfaction of the high-level specification by recourse to subsumption. This separation of concerns extends from VST specifications to model-level reasoning: for example, in our verification of cryptographic primitives we found it convenient to verify that the C program implements a *low-level functional model* and then separately prove that the low-level functional model implements a high-level specification (e.g. cryptographic security).[3] In our running example, fastpile.c's low-level functional model is *integer* (the Coq Z type), and its high level specification is list Z.

To formally state the desired subsumption lemma, observe that notation like DECLARE _Pile_add WITH ... PRE ... POST ... is merely VST's syntactic sugar

---

[3] For example: in our proof of HMAC-DRBG [24], before VST had function-spec subsumption, we had two different proofs of the function f_mbedtls_hmac_drbg_seed, one with respect to a more concrete specification drbg_seed_inst256_spec and one with respect to a more abstract specification drbg_seed_inst256_spec_abs. The latter proof was 202 lines of Coq, at line 37 of VST/hmacdrbg/drbg_protocol_proofs.v in commit 3e61d2991e3d70f5935ae69c88d7172cf639b9bc of https://github.com/ PrincetonUniversity/VST. Now, instead of reproving the function-body a second time, we have a funspec_sub proof that is only 60 lines of Coq (at line 42 of the same file in commit c2fc3d830e15f4c70bc45376632c2323743858ef).

for a pair that ties the identifier _Pile_add to the funspec WITH...PRE...POST.
For _Pile_add we have two such specifications,

spec_fastpile.Pile_add_spec: ident∗funspec   *(* in Figure 3 *)*
spec_fastpile_concrete.Pile_add_spec: ident∗funspec   *(* in Figure 4 *)*.

and our notion of *funspec subtyping* will satisfy the following lemma.

Lemma sub_Pile_add: funspec_sub (snd spec_fastpile_concrete.Pile_add_spec)
                    (snd spec_fastpile.Pile_add_spec).

and similarly for Pile_new and Pile_count. Specifically, we permit related specifications to have different WITH-lists, in line with Kleymann's adaptation-complete
rule of consequence

$$\frac{\vdash \{P'\}c\{Q'\}}{\vdash \{P\}c\{Q\}} \forall Z. \forall \sigma. \, PZ\sigma \to \forall \tau. \, \exists Z'.(P'Z'\sigma \land (Q'Z'\tau \to QZ\tau))$$

where assertions are binary predicates over auxiliary and ordinary states, and
Z, Z' are the WITH values.[4]

Our subsumption applies to function specifications, not arbitrary statements
c. In the rule for function calls, it ensures that a concretely specified function
can be invoked where callers expect an abstractly specified one, just like the
subsumption rule of type theory: $\dfrac{\Gamma \vdash e : \sigma \quad \sigma <: \tau}{\Gamma \vdash e : \tau}$. It is also reflexive and transitive.

Support for Framing. An important principle of separation logic is the frame
rule:

$$\frac{\{P\}c\{Q\}}{\{P * R\}c\{P * R\}}(\text{modifiedvars}(c) \cap \text{freevars}(R) = \emptyset)$$

We have found it useful to explicitly incorporate framing in funspec_sub, because
abstract specifications may have useless data. Consider a function that performs
some action (e.g., increment a variable) using some auxiliary data (e.g., an array
of 10 integers):

int incr1(int i, unsigned int ∗auxdata)   {auxdata[i%10] += 1; **return** i+1;}

The function specification makes clear that the private contents of the auxdata
is, from the client's point of view, unconstrained; the implementation is free to
store anything in this array:

Definition incr1_spec := DECLARE _incr1
WITH i: Z, a: val, π: share, *private*: list val
  PRE [_i OF tint, _auxdata OF tptr tuint]
    PROP $(0 \leq i < \text{Int.max\_signed}$; writable_share $\pi)$

---

[4] We give Kleymann's rule for total correctness here. VST is a logic for partial correctness, but its preconditions also guarantee safety; Kleymann's partial-correctness
adaptation rule cannot guarantee safety.

LOCAL(temp _i (Vint (Int.repr i))); temp _auxdata a)
  SEP(data_at sh (tarray tuint 10) *private* a)
POST [tint]
  EX *private'*: list val, PROP() LOCAL(temp ret_temp (Vint (Int.repr $(i+1)$))))
              SEP(data_at π (tarray tuint 10) *private'* a).

You might think the auxdata is useless, but (i) real-life interfaces often have useless or vestigial fields; and (ii) this might be where the implementation keeps profiling statistics, memoization, or other algorithmically useful information.

Here is a different implementation that should serve any client just as well:

int incr2(**int** i, **unsigned int** *auxdata)   {**return** i+1;}

Its natural specification has an empty SEP clause:

Definition incr2_spec := DECLARE _incr2
  WITH i: Z
  PRE [_i OF tint, _auxdata OF tptr tuint]
      PROP ($0 \leq i <$ Int.max_signed) LOCAL(temp _i (Vint (Int.repr i))) SEP()
  POST [tint]
      PROP() LOCAL(temp ret_temp (Vint (Int.repr $(i+1)$)))) SEP().

The *formal* statement that incr2 serves any client just as well as incr1 is another case of subsumption:

Lemma sub_incr12: funspec_sub (snd incr2_spec) (snd incr1_spec).

In the proof, we use (data_at π (tarray tuint 10) *private* a) as the *frame*.

If the auxdata is a global variable instead of a function parameter, all the same principles apply:

int global_auxdata[10];
int incr3(**int** i)   {global_auxdata[i%10] += 1; **return** i+1;}
int incr4(**int** i)   {**return** i+1;}

We define a funspec for incr3 whose SEP clause mentions the auxdata, we define a funspec for incr4 whose SEP clause is empty, and we can prove,

Lemma sub_incr34: funspec_sub (snd incr4_spec) (snd incr3_spec).

For another example of framing, consider again Fig. 2, the specification of pilerep, pile_freeable, Pile_new_spec, etc. One might think to combine pile_freeable (the memory-deallocation capability) with pile_rep (capability to modify the contents) yielding a single combined predicate pilerep'. That way, proofs of client programs would not have to manage two separate conjuncts.

That would work for clients such as triang.c and onepile.c, but not for apile.c which has an initialized global variable (a_pile) that satisfies pilerep but *not* pile_freeable (since it was not obtained from the malloc-free system). Furthermore, the specifications of pile_add and pile_count do not mention pile_freeable in their pre- or postconditions, since they have no need for this capability.

By using funspec_sub (with its framing feature), we can have it both ways. One can easily make a more abstract spec in which the funspecs of pile_new, pile_add, pile_count, pile_free all take pilerep' in their pre- and postconditions; onepile and triang will still be verifiable using these specs. But in proving funspec_sub, therefore, specifications for pile_add and pile_count now *do* implicitly take pile_freeable in their pre- and postconditions, even though they have no use for it; this is the essence of the frame rule.

4   Definitions of Funspec Subtyping

Except in certain higher-order cases, we use this notion of function specification:

NDmk_funspec (f: funsig) (cc: calling_convention)
       (A: Type) (Pre Post: $A \to$ environ $\to$ mpred): funspec.

To construct a *nondependent* (ND) function spec, one gives the function's C-language type signature (funsig), the calling convention (usually cc=cc_default), the precondition, and the postcondition. A gives the type of variable (or tuple of variables) "shared" between the precondition and postcondition. Pre and Post are each applied to the shared value of type A, then to a local-variable environment (of type environ) containing the formal parameters or result-value (respectively), finally yielding an mpred, a spatial predicate on memory.

For example, to specify an increment function with formal parameter _p pointing to an integer in memory, we let $A = $ int, so that

$$\mathsf{Pre} = \lambda i : A. \, \lambda \rho. \, \rho(\_\mathsf{p}) \mapsto i \quad \text{and} \quad \mathsf{Post} = \lambda i : A. \, \lambda \rho. \, \rho(\_\mathsf{p}) \mapsto (i+1).$$

This form suffices for most C programming. But sometimes in the presence of higher-order functions, one wants impredicativity: A may be a tuple of types that includes the type mpred. If this is done naively, it cannot typecheck in CiC (there will be universe inconsistencies); see the Appendix.

General Funspec. Higher-order function specs are (mostly) beyond the scope of this paper. When precondition and postcondition must predicate over predicates, we must ensure that each is a *bifunctor*, that is, we must keep track of *covariant* and *contravariant* occurrences, and so on. This approach was outlined by America and Rutten [1] and has been implemented both in Iris [10] and VST.[5]

VST's most general form of function spec is,

Inductive funspec :=
     mk_funspec: forall (f: funsig) (cc: calling_convention) (A: TypeTree)
     (P Q: forall ts, dependent_type_functor_rec ts (AssertTT A) mpred)
     (P_ne: super_non_expansive P) (Q_ne: super_non_expansive Q), funspec.

Here, super_non_expansive is a proof that the precondition (or postcondition) is a nonexpansive (in the step-indexing sense) bifunctor; see the Appendix. The *nondependent* (ND) form of mk_funspec shown above is simply a derived form of dependent mk_funspec.

---

[5] Bifunctor function-specs in VST were the work of Qinxiang Cao, Robert Dockins, and Aquinas Hobor.

Too-Special Funspec Subtyping. Let's consider the obvious notion of funspec subtyping: ϕ_1 is a subtype of ϕ_2 if the precondition of ϕ_2 entails the precondition of ϕ_1, and the postcondition of ϕ_1 entails the postcondition of ϕ_2.

Definition far_too_special_NDfunspec_sub $(f_1\ f_2$: funspec$)$:=
let Δ := funsig_tycontext (funsig_of_funspec f_1) **in**
match $f_1,\ f_2$ **with**
 NDmk_funspec $fsig_1\ cc_1\ A_1\ P_1\ Q_1$, NDmk_funspec $fsig_2\ cc_2\ A_2\ P_2\ Q_2$ $\Rightarrow$
  $fsig_1 = fsig_2 \wedge cc_1 = cc_2 \wedge A_1 = A_2 \wedge (\forall x : A_1,\ \Delta,\ P_2$ nil $x \vdash P_1$ nil $x) \wedge$
  $(\forall x : A_1,\ ($ret0_tycon $\Delta),\ Q_1$ nil $x \vdash Q_2$ nil $x)$
end.

We write $\Delta,\ P_2$ nil $x \vdash P_1$ nil x, where P_1 and P_2 are the preconditions of f_1 and f_2, nil expresses that these are nondependent funspecs (no bifunctor structure), and x is the value shared between precondition and postcondition. The type-context Δ provides the additional guarantee that the formal parameters are well typed, and ret0_tycon Δ guarantees that the return-value is well typed.

This notion of funspec-sub is sound (w.r.t. subsumption), but barely useful: (1) it requires that the witness types of the two funspecs be the same ($A_1 = A_2$), (2) it doesn't support framing, and (3) it requires $Q_1 \vdash Q_2$ even when P_2 is not satisfied. *Each* of these omissions prevents the practical use of funspec-sub in real verifications, but only (1) and (3) were addressed in previous work [12,20].

Useful, Ordinary Funspec Subtyping. If NDmk_funspec were a constructor, we could define,

Definition NDfunspec_sub $(f_1\ f_2$: funspec$)$:=
let Δ := funsig_tycontext (funsig_of_funspec f_1) **in**
match $f_1,\ f_2$ **with**
 NDmk_funspec $fsig_1\ cc_1\ A_1\ P_1\ Q_1$, NDmk_funspec $fsig_2\ cc_2\ A_2\ P_2\ Q_2$ $\Rightarrow$
  $fsig_1 = fsig_2 \wedge cc_1 = cc_2 \wedge$
  $\forall x_2 : A_2,$
   $\Delta,\ P_2$ nil $x_2 \vdash$
    EX $x_1{:}A_1$, EX $F{:}$mpred, $(((\lambda\rho.F) * P_1$ nil $x_1)$ &&
     !! $(($ret0_tycon $\Delta),\ (\lambda\rho.F) * Q_1$ nil $x_1 \vdash Q_2$ nil $x_2))$
end.

Here, each of the three deficiencies is remedied: the witness value $x_1 : A_1$ is existentially derived from $x_2 : A_2$, the frame F is existentially quantified, and the entailment $Q_1 \vdash Q_2$ is conditioned on the precondition P_2 being satisfied.

This version of funspec-sub is, we believe, fully general for NDmk_funspec, that is, for function specifications whose witness types A do not contain (covariant or contravariant) occurrences of mpred. We present the general, dependent funspec-sub in the Appendix, with its constructor mk_funspec, and show the construction of NDmk_funspec as a derived form. And actually, since NDmk_funspec is not really a constructor (it is a function that applies the constructor mk_funspec), we must define NDfunspec_sub as a pattern-match on mk_funspec; see the Appendix.

5   The Subsumption Rules

The purpose of funspec_sub is to support subsumption rules.

Our Hoare-logic judgment takes the form $\Delta \vdash \{P\}c\{Q\}$ where the context Δ describes the types of local and global variables and the funspecs of global functions. We say $\Delta <: \Delta'$ if Δ is at least as strong as Δ'; in Verifiable C this is written tycontext_sub $\Delta \Delta'$. Again, this relation is reflexive and transitive.

Definition *(glob_specs):* If i is a global identifier, write (glob_specs Δ)!i to be the option(funspec) that is either None or Some ϕ.

Lemma *funspec_sub_tycontext_sub:* **Suppose** Δ agrees with Δ' on types attributed to global variables, types attributed to local variables, current function return type (if any), and differs only in *specifications* attributed to global functions, in particular: For every global identifier i, if (glob_specs Δ)!i = Some ϕ then (glob_specs Δ')!i = Some ϕ' and funspec_sub $\phi \phi'$. **Then** $\Delta <: \Delta'$.

Proof. Trivial from the definition of $\Delta <: \Delta'$.

Theorem *(semax_Delta_subsumption):*

$$\frac{\Delta <: \Delta' \qquad \Delta' \vdash \{P\}c\{Q\}}{\Delta \vdash \{P\}c\{Q\}}$$

Proof. Nontrivial. Because this is a logic of higher-order recursive function pointers, our Coq proof[6] in the modal step-indexed model uses the Löb rule to handle recursion, and unfolds our rather complicated semantic definition of the Hoare triple [4].

But this is not the only subsumption rule we desire. Because C has function-pointers, the general function-call rule is for $\Delta \vdash \{P\}e_f(e_1, \ldots, e_n)\{Q\}$ where e_f is an expression that evaluates to a function-pointer. Therefore, we cannot simply look up e_f as a global identifier in Δ. Instead, the precondition P must associate the value of e_f with a funspec. Without subsumption, the rules are:

$$\frac{\begin{array}{c}(\text{glob\_specs } \Delta)!f = \text{Some } \phi \\ \Delta \vdash f \Downarrow v \\ \Delta \vdash \{\text{func\_ptr } v\, \phi \ \wedge \ P\}c\{Q\}\end{array}}{\Delta \vdash \{P\}c\{Q\}} \qquad \frac{\begin{array}{c}\Delta \vdash e_f \Downarrow v \\ \Delta \vdash e_1 \Downarrow v_1 \ldots \Delta \vdash e_n \Downarrow v_n \\ P * F \vdash \text{func\_ptr } v\, \phi \\ \phi(w) = \{P\}\{Q\}\end{array}}{\Delta \vdash \{P * F\}e_f(e_1, e_2, \ldots, e_n)\{Q * F\}}$$

The rule semax_fun_id at left says, if the global context Δ associates identifier f with funspec ϕ, and if f evaluates to the address v, then for the purposes of proving $\{P\}c\{Q\}$ we can assume the stronger precondition in which address v has the funspec ϕ.

The semax_call rule says, if e_f evaluates to address v, and the precondition factors into conjuncts $P * F$ that imply address v has the funspec ϕ, then choose a

---

[6] See file veric/semax_lemmas.v in the VST repo.

witness w (for the WITH clause), instantiate the witness of ϕ with w, and match the precondition and postcondition of $\phi(w)$ with P and Q; then the function-call is proved. (Functions can return results, but we don't show that here.)

To turn semax_call into a rule that supports subsumption, we simply replace the hypothesis $\phi(w) = \{P\}\{Q\}$ with $\phi <: \phi' \land \phi'(w) = \{P\}\{Q\}$.

To reconcile semax_Delta_subsumption and semax_fun_id, we build $<:$ into the definition of the predicate func_ptr v ϕ, i.e. permit ϕ to be more abstract than the specification associated with address v in VST's semantic model ("rmap").

6   Intersection Specifications

In some of our verification examples, we found it useful to separate different use cases of a function into separate function specifications. One can easily do this using a pattern that discriminates on a boolean value from the WITH list jointly in the pre- and postcondition:

WITH $b : bool, \vec{x} : \vec{\tau}$ PRE if b then P_1 else P_2 POST if b then Q_1 else Q_2.

To attach different WITH-lists to different cases, we may use Coq's sum type to define a type such as Variant T := case1: int | case2: string. and use it in a specification

WITH $\vec{x} : \vec{\tau}, t : T, \vec{y} : \vec{\sigma}$
PRE [...] **match** t **with** case1 i $\Rightarrow P_1(\vec{x}, i, \vec{y})$ | case2 s $\Rightarrow P_2(\vec{x}, s, \vec{y})$ **end**
POST [...] **match** t **with** case1 i $\Rightarrow Q_1(\vec{x}, i, \vec{y})$ | case2 s $\Rightarrow Q_2(\vec{x}, s, \vec{y})$ **end**.

which amounts to the *intersection* of
WITH $\vec{x} : \vec{\tau}, i : int, \vec{y} : \vec{\sigma}$ PRE [...] P_1 $(\vec{x}, i, \vec{y})$ POST [...] $Q_1(\vec{x}, i, \vec{y})$ and
WITH $\vec{x} : \vec{\tau}, s : string, \vec{y} : \vec{\sigma}$ PRE [...] $P_2(\vec{x}, i, \vec{y})$ POST [...] $Q_2(\vec{x}, i, \vec{y})$.

Generalizing to arbitrary index sets, we may—for a given function signature and calling convention—combine specifications into specification *families*. (We show the nondependent (ND) case; the Coq proofs cover the general case.)

Definition funspec_Pi_ND sig cc (I:Type) (A : I $\rightarrow$ Type)
　　　　(Pre Post: forall i, A i $\rightarrow$ environ $\rightarrow$ mpred): funspec := ...

In previous work [5] we showed how relational (2-execution) specifications can be encoded as unary VDM-style specifications. Intersection specifications internalize VDM's "sets of specifications" feature.

The interaction between this construction and subtyping follows precisely that of intersection types in type theory: the lemmas

Lemma funspec_Pi_ND_sub: forall fsig cc I A Pre Post i,
　　funspec_sub (funspec_Pi_ND fsig cc I A Pre Post)
　　　　　　(NDmk_funspec fsig cc (A i) (Pre i) (Post i)).

Lemma funspec_Pi_ND_sub3: forall fsig cc I A Pre Post g (i:I)
　　　　(HI: forall i, funspec_sub g (NDmk_funspec fsig cc (A i) (Pre i) (Post i))),
　　funspec_sub g (funspec_Pi_ND fsig cc I A Pre Post).

are counterparts of the typing rules $\wedge_{j \in I} \tau_j <: \tau_i$ (for all $i \in I$) and $\dfrac{\forall i,\ \sigma <: \tau_i}{\sigma <: \wedge_{i \in I} \tau_i}$, the specializations of which to the binary case appear on page 206 of TAPL [22]. We expect these rules to be helpful for formalizing Leavens and Naumann's treatment of specification inheritance in object-oriented programs [14].

7   Conclusion

Even without funspec subtyping, separation logic easily expresses data abstraction [21]. But real-world code is modular (as in our running example) and reconfigurable (as in the substitution of fastpile.c for pile.c). Therefore a notion of specification re-abstraction is needed. We have demonstrated how to extend Kleymann's notion from commands to functions, and from first-order Hoare logic to higher-order separation logic with framing. We have a full soundness proof for the extended program logic, in Coq. Our funspec_sub integrates nicely with our existing proof automation tools and our existing methods of verifying individual modules. As a bonus, one's intuition that function-specs are like the "types" of functions is borne out by our theorems relating funspec_sub to intersection types.

Future Work: When a client module respects data abstraction, such as onepile.c and triang.c in our example, its Coq proof script does not vary if the implementation of the abstraction changes (such as changing pile.c to fastpile.c). But our current proofs need to rerun the proof scripts on the modified definition of pilerep. As footnote 2 suggests, this could be avoided by the use of existential quantification, in Coq, to describe data abstraction at the C module level.

Acknowlegdements. This work was funded by the National Science Foundation under the awards 1005849 (*Verified High Performance Data Structure Implementations*, Beringer) and 1521602 *Expedition in Computing: The Science of Deep Specification*, Appel). We are grateful to the members of both projects for their feedback, and we greatly appreciate the reviewers' comments and suggestions.

Appendix: Fully General funspec_sub

NDfunspec_sub as introduced in Sect. 4 specializes the "real" subtype relation $\phi <: \psi$ in two regards: first, it only applies if ϕ and ψ are of the NDfunspec form, i.e. the types of their WITH-lists ("witnesses") are trivial bifunctors as they do not contain co- or contravariant occurrences of mpred. Second, it fails to exploit step-indexing and is hence unnecessarily strong.

The technical report (www.cs.princeton.edu/~eberinge/funspec_sub.pdf) contains a brief appendix presenting the fully general funspec_sub_si.

References

1. America, P., Rutten, J.: Solving reflexive domain equations in a category of complete metric spaces. J. Comput. Syst. Sci. **39**(3), 343–375 (1989)
2. Appel, A.W.: Verification of a cryptographic primitive: SHA-256. ACM Trans. on Program. Lang. Syst. **37**(2), 7:1–7:31 (2015)
3. Appel, A.W., Beringer, L., Cao, Q., Dodds, J.: Verifiable C: applying the verified software toolchain to C programs (2019). https://vst.cs.princeton.edu/download/VC.pdf
4. Appel, A.W., et al.: Program Logics for Certified Compilers. Cambridge University Press, Cambridge (2014)
5. Beringer, L.: Relational decomposition. In: van Eekelen, M., Geuvers, H., Schmaltz, J., Wiedijk, F. (eds.) ITP 2011. LNCS, vol. 6898, pp. 39–54. Springer, Heidelberg (2011). https://doi.org/10.1007/978-3-642-22863-6_6
6. Beringer, L., Petcher, A., Ye, K.Q., Appel, A.W.: Verified correctness and security of OpenSSL HMAC. In: 24th USENIX Security Symposium, pp. 207–221. USENIX Assocation, August 2015
7. Cao, Q., Beringer, L., Gruetter, S., Dodds, J., Appel, A.W.: VST-Floyd: a separation logic tool to verify correctness of C programs. J. Autom. Reason. **61**(1–4), 367–422 (2018)
8. Cohen, E., et al.: VCC: a practical system for verifying concurrent C. In: Berghofer, S., Nipkow, T., Urban, C., Wenzel, M. (eds.) TPHOLs 2009. LNCS, vol. 5674, pp. 23–42. Springer, Heidelberg (2009). https://doi.org/10.1007/978-3-642-03359-9_2
9. Jacobs, B., Smans, J., Philippaerts, P., Vogels, F., Penninckx, W., Piessens, F.: VeriFast: a powerful, sound, predictable, fast verifier for C and Java. In: Bobaru, M., Havelund, K., Holzmann, G.J., Joshi, R. (eds.) NFM 2011. LNCS, vol. 6617, pp. 41–55. Springer, Heidelberg (2011). https://doi.org/10.1007/978-3-642-20398-5_4
10. Jung, R., Krebbers, R., Jourdan, J.-H., Bizjak, A., Birkedal, L., Dreyer, D.: Iris from the ground up: a modular foundation for higher-order concurrent separation logic. J. Funct. Program. **28** (2018)
11. Kirchner, F., Kosmatov, N., Prevosto, V., Signoles, J., Yakobowski, B.: Frama-C: a software analysis perspective. Formal Aspects Comput. **27**(3), 573–609 (2015)
12. Kleymann, T.: Hoare logic and auxiliary variables. Formal Aspects Comput. **11**(5), 541–566 (1999)
13. Koh, N., et al.: From C to interaction trees: specifying, verifying, and testing a networked server. In: Proceedings of the 8th ACM SIGPLAN International Conference on Certified Programs and Proofs, pp. 234–248. ACM (2019)
14. Leavens, G.T., Naumann, D.A.: Behavioral subtyping, specification inheritance, and modular reasoning. ACM Trans. Program. Lang. Syst. **37**(4), 13:1–13:88 (2015)
15. Leroy, X.: Formal verification of a realistic compiler. Commun. ACM **52**(7), 107–115 (2009)
16. Liskov, B., Wing, J.M.: A behavioral notion of subtyping. ACM Trans. Program. Lang. Syst. **16**(6), 1811–1841 (1994)
17. Mansky, W., Appel, A.W., Nogin, A.: A verified messaging system. In: Proceedings of the 2017 ACM International Conference on Object Oriented Programming Systems Languages & Applications, OOPSLA 2017. ACM (2017)
18. Mitchell, J.C., Plotkin, G.D.: Abstract types have existential type. ACM Trans. Program. Lang. Syst. **10**(3), 470–502 (1988)

19. Naumann, D.A.: Deriving sharp rules of adaptation for Hoare logics. Technical report 9906, Department of Computer Science, Stevens Institute of Technology (1999)
20. Nipkow, T.: Hoare logics for recursive procedures and unbounded nondeterminism. In: Bradfield, J. (ed.) CSL 2002. LNCS, vol. 2471, pp. 103–119. Springer, Heidelberg (2002). https://doi.org/10.1007/3-540-45793-3_8
21. Parkinson, M.J., Bierman, G.M.: Separation logic and abstraction. In: 32nd ACM SIGPLAN-SIGACT Symposium on Principles of Programming Languages (POPL 2005), pp. 247–258 (2005)
22. Pierce, B.C.: Types and Programming Languages. MIT Press, Cambridge (2002)
23. Pierik, C., de Boer, F.S.: A proof outline logic for object-oriented programming. Theor. Comput. Sci. **343**(3), 413–442 (2005)
24. Ye, K.Q., Green, M., Sanguansin, N., Beringer, L., Petcher, A., Appel, A.W.: Verified correctness and security of mbedTLS HMAC-DRBG. In: Proceedings of the 2017 ACM SIGSAC Conference on Computer and Communications Security (CCS 2017). ACM (2017)

Modelling Languages

IELE: A Rigorously Designed Language and Tool Ecosystem for the Blockchain

Theodoros Kasampalis[1]([✉]), Dwight Guth[2], Brandon Moore[2],
Traian Florin Șerbănuță[2,3], Yi Zhang[1], Daniele Filaretti[2], Virgil Șerbănuță[2],
Ralph Johnson[2], and Grigore Roșu[1,2]

[1] University of Illinois at Urbana-Champaign, Urbana, USA
kasampa2@illinois.edu
[2] Runtime Verification, Urbana, USA
[3] University of Bucharest, Bucharest, Romania

Abstract. This paper proposes IELE, an LLVM-style language, together with a tool ecosystem for implementing and formally reasoning about smart contracts on the blockchain. IELE was designed by specifying its semantics formally in the K framework. Its implementation, a IELE virtual machine (VM), as well as a formal verification tool for IELE smart contracts, were automatically generated from the formal specification. The automatically generated formal verification tool allows us to formally verify smart contracts without any gap between the verifier and the actual VM. A compiler from Solidity, the predominant high-level language for smart contracts, to IELE has also been (manually) implemented, so Ethereum contracts can now also be executed on IELE.

1 Introduction

Ethereum [5], with more that 500,000 daily transactions [13] is the largest blockchain network supporting smart contracts. The smart contracts used in the context of Ethereum transactions are written in the language of the Ethereum Virtual Machine (EVM) [38], a stack-based assembly-level language.

Unfortunately, recent exploits on EVM smart contracts have led to losses in the range of hundreds of millions USD [1,4,7,34,35]. In response, KEVM [15] was developed, a formal semantics of the EVM in K [29], to provide formal verification assistance to the EVM smart contract world [26,32]. We and others in the Ethereum community have embraced and adopted KEVM, as a more rigorous and thus precise alternative to the Yellow paper [38]. Through our own experience with KEVM and the reports of others, we became aware of the limitations of EVM as a language: it includes features that are easily exploitable and its low-level nature makes formal verification efforts tedious and time-consuming. On the positive side, as reported in [15], the EVM interpreter automatically generated from KEVM by the K framework [29] was only one order of magnitude slower than the official EVM client written in C++ [10]. Since the node client

© Springer Nature Switzerland AG 2019
M. H. ter Beek et al. (Eds.): FM 2019, LNCS 11800, pp. 593–610, 2019.
https://doi.org/10.1007/978-3-030-30942-8_35

code takes only a small fraction of the total execution time on a blockchain, the KEVM performance was considered acceptable by IOHK (http://iohk.io), the company that is in charge of the Ethereum Classic blockchain, to deploy a testnet that is entirely powered by the auto-generated KEVM client [17].

In response to these limitations of EVM, we have designed and implemented IELE, a new language for smart contracts. IELE is a low-level language with syntax similar to that of LLVM [22]. It is designed to be both human readable and suitable as a compilation target for more high-level languages. IELE has various high-level features, such as function calls/returns, static jumps, arbitrary-precision integer arithmetic among others, that both make automatic formal verification more straight-forward and the language itself more secure.

IELE was designed using a formal specification, and its implementation was automatically generated from its specification using the same technology that was used to generate the implementation of KEVM [15], namely K [29]. In contrast, other languages have separate specifications and implementations, and it is hard to keep them from differing. Sometimes the specification is informal, like that of LLVM [22] and sometimes formal, like that of SML [23], but in either case the implementation is separate so it is not possible to execute test cases against the specification. To bridge the gap between specification and tools, K provides support for developing language semantic definitions as well as a host of tools for such a definition, such as parser, interpreter, deductive verifier, and more. These tools are automatically generated so any change to the formal semantics is automatically propagated to the tools. For IELE, we use the generated parser/interpreter to obtain a IELE Virtual Machine (IELE VM) tool (also reference implementation). We also use the capability of K to generate sound and relatively complete deductive program verifiers for the defined languages [6], to obtain a IELE smart contract formal verification tool. As a result, IELE is formally specified and its implementation and verifier are correct by construction and remain correct, with zero effort, in the presence of updates to the language.

We have deployed the IELE VM in a testnet supported by IOHK, a major blockchain company [16]. To do so, we have built appropriate infrastructure around the IELE VM: a full compiler for Solidity [11], a popular high-level language for smart contracts that until now could only be compiled to EVM, as well as integration with the Mantis Ethereum client [18]. This allows us to run real-world Solidity contracts on IELE (see appendix B in [20] for more details).

In summary, our contributions are:

- IELE, a smart contract language designed from the ground up using formal methods with the goals of security, verification, human-readability, and portability in mind, using the K framework. IELE is publicly available [33].
- Useful tools for IELE: A IELE virtual machine that was deployed as a testnet by a major blockchain company and a IELE smart contract verifier automatically generated by the K framework from the IELE formal semantics.

More details can be found on Github [33] and on the IELE testnet [16].

2 Background

We briefly discuss the K framework, Ethereum and the EVM, as well as other smart contract languages currently under development.

The K Language Semantic Framework. K [29] is a rewriting-/reachability-based framework for defining executable semantic specifications of programming languages. Given the syntax and semantics of a language, K automatically generates a parser, an interpreter, as well as formal analysis tools such as a deductive verifier. This avoids duplication while improving efficiency and consistency. For example, using the interpreter, one can test the semantics immediately, which significantly increases the efficiency of and confidence in semantics development. There exists a rich literature on using K for formalizing existing languages, such as C [9, 14], Java [3] and JavaScript [25], among others. K has also been used to formally specify the Ethereum Virtual Machine (EVM) [15], the current smart contract language for Ethereum. In fact, the process of formalizing EVM as an executable semantics uncovered various inconsistencies and unspecified behaviors in its original English specification (the Yellow paper) [38].

Blockchain and Ethereum. A blockchain is an append-only ledger that is commonly used for synchronization in distributed protocols. Cryptocurrencies such as Bitcoin [24], refer to such protocols that allow a set of clients to transfer and maintain a balance of virtual coins. A cryptocurrency network consists of accounts (essentially encrypted client IDs) with cryptocurrency balances, a blockchain of verified transactions, and a set of so-called miners, computation resources that process pending transactions and append them in the blockchain.

Ethereum [5] is a blockchain-based network that provides a decentralized, replicated computer for distributed applications and uses a blockchain to store its global state. Ethereum supports a programming language for writing *smart contracts*, which are programs associated with Ethereum accounts. Ethereum accounts interact with each other using transactions over a cryptocurrency called Ether. When an Ethereum account associated with a smart contract receives a transaction, execution of its smart contract code is triggered. Such transactions can both transfer Ether and pass input data to the smart contract.

Ethereum smart contracts often manage large monetary amounts, in the range of 100M USD. Ethereum's popularity is largely due to the fact that there is no need for a trusted third party (such as a bank) to verify the transactions; the trust comes from the consensus algorithm and the fact that smart contract code is binding. Ethereum transactions are irreversible and the source code of the involved smart contracts is public and immutable. Moreover, any transaction can be replicated through the information stored in the blockchain.

EVM. Currently, Ethereum contracts should be translated to the language of the Ethereum Virtual Machine (EVM) [38]. The EVM is a stack-based VM with an assembly-level language with no code/data separation or function-level calls/returns. The language is loosely specified in the Yellow Paper [38], but has been recently formally specified as a K definition in KEVM [15]. KEVM provides a reference implementation that is considered for adoption by the Ethereum Foundation, a deductive verifier that has been used to verify real-world contracts [26,32], and the Jello Paper [21], an English language specification of EVM generated from the documentation of the KEVM semantics definition.

Other Smart Contract Languages. Several smart contract programming languages have been proposed either as alternatives to EVM or as higher-level, more programmer-friendly options. Solidity [11] and Vyper [12] are popular high-level languages for Ethereum contracts that are typically compiled down to EVM. Plutus [19] is a high-level functional language that offers increased security due to features such as type safety. Rholang [28] is a functional, concurrency-oriented language that powers RChain, an evolution of traditional blockchain networks that allows for concurrent transactions. We believe that IELE could serve as a compilation target of all these languages. In fact, we have implemented a Solidity-to-IELE compiler as part of our evaluation (see appendix B.1 in [20]). Intermediate-level smart contract languages include Michelson [36], a stack-based, but also statically typed language, Scilla [39], a language that offers clear separation between in-contract computation and inter-contract communication to facilitate formal reasoning about smart contracts, and Simplicity [2], a language designed to have simple semantics which lend themselves to static analysis and formal reasoning. IELE shares the goals of enhanced security and ease of formal verification with these languages. We believe that the novelty in the design of IELE, compared to those efforts, stems from the fact that its formal specification and its de-facto implementation are one and the same artifact: any change to IELE's specification is automatically propagated to the implementation of the language execution engine and verification tools.

3   The IELE Language

Based on experience with KEVM and formal verification of EVM smart contracts, we identified five desired properties for an ideal blockchain low-level language and designed IELE around them. Our design was done using formal semantics, and the implementation was generated automatically [16,33].

Security. Smart contracts often manage large monetary amounts and have been targets of attackers that seek to exploit any vulnerabilities in their code [1]. Very often, language design weaknesses such as undefined behaviors, execution of arbitrary data as code, and silent integer overflow act as enablers for attackers to exploit corresponding bugs. IELE avoids all of the above (and more) design weaknesses and hence eliminates many possible attack vectors by design.

Formal Verification. No matter how many insecure features are avoided at the language definition level, software bugs can always allow for exploits. The three most expensive exploits of Ethereum smart contracts are all due to software errors [4,7,35]. A strong defense against such exploits is formal correctness verification and IELE is designed with the goal of formal verification in mind.

Human Readable. Smart contracts act as binding agreements between human end-users. Being human readable reinforces this intention, as it is easier for the agreeing parties to trust a formal agreement they can read and understand. Ideally smart contracts should be human readable at the exact level they are stored in the blockchain and executed. This is true for IELE contracts, since the IELE syntax was designed to be almost identical to that of LLVM [22], a state-of-the-art intermediate language designed to be human readable.

Determinism. Ethereum's blockchain stores transactions that can be replicated by any Ethereum client and many of these transactions require execution of smart contract code to be replayed. For this reason it is important that the underlying smart contract language and its implementation are deterministic. The IELE specification contains no undefined and/or implementation-defined behaviors, as well as no by-design non-deterministic features.

Gas Model. The philosophy behind IELE's gas model is simple: no limitations in code execution, but costs are analogous to the resource consumption. For example, IELE programs have access to an unlimited number of registers, but more used registers incur steeper gas charges. Similarly IELE uses unbounded integer arithmetic, but the larger the numbers at runtime, the more gas required. A detailed discussion of IELE's gas model can be found in appendix A in [20].

Listing 1 shows a simple forwarder contract in IELE. The contract forwards any amount of Ether[1] sent to it to the account that created the contract. The @init function of the contract is executed when a transaction creates this contract. The built-in @iele.caller returns the account address of the account that posted the transaction, which is the creator of this contract. This address is saved in the account storage of the forwarder. The @deposit function is a public function meaning it can be invoked by incoming transactions. The built-in @iele.callvalue returns the amount of Ether that was sent to the forwarder with the incoming transaction. This amount is forwarded to the creator account by invoking its own @deposit function with the IELE instruction call .. at. Note that the forwarder specifies an upper limit of gas to spend at the creator during the account call. If the forwarding fails (e.g., due to lack of gas), the built-in @iele.invalid is called that reverts any global state change made so far, including the Ether receipt for the forwarder account.

The full formal semantics of the IELE language, given as an executable K definition that also serves as a reference implementation, can be found in [33]. In the remainder of this section we give a high-level presentation of IELE and discuss the improvements over the state-of-the-art EVM.

3.1   IELE Contracts

A IELE contract is the main compilation unit of code that can be associated with a blockchain account. A IELE contract has a name and contains one or more

---

[1] IELE can be used in any Ethereum-style blockchain, where the cryptocurrency may be called differently. We use Ether throughout the paper for the sake of concreteness.

functions, global variables, and external contract declarations. Public functions can be invoked from other accounts while private functions only from within the contract. Global variables are accessible from anywhere within the contract and hold a constant value. The Listing 1 contract has one global variable, @creator, one private function, @init, and one public function, @deposit.

Account Storage. An account includes a storage that is an unbounded sparse array of arbitrary-precision signed integers. The storage is persistent, i.e., it holds its contents throughout the account's lifetime. As such the storage contents of all accounts are part of the global state and any modification on them is recorded in the blockchain. IELE code associated with an account can access the account storage through the dedicated sload and sstore instructions. IELE global variables are typically used to hold specific storage addresses, so that the contract code can refer to those addresses by the name of the variable. See, e.g., how the global variable @creator is used in the contract of Listing 1.

Listing 1. Forwarder contract in IELE

```
// Contract forwards any funds it receives to its creator account
contract Forwarder {
  // account storage index holding the creator account address
  @creator = 1
  // initializes a forwarder
  define @init() {
    // get the address of the creator account
    %creator = call @iele.caller()
    // store the creator's address in the storage
    sstore %creator, @creator
  }
  // forwards the received funds to the creator of this account
  define public @deposit() {
    // get the received funds
    %value = call @iele.callvalue()
    // get the creator account address from the storage
    %creator = sload @creator
    // forward funds by calling deposit at the creator account
    %status = call @deposit at %creator () send %value ,
                   gaslimit 2300
    br %status, throw // contract call failed
    ret void
  throw:
    call @iele.invalid()
  }
}
```

Contract Creation. An account can be created and associated with a IELE contract manually by an end user, by posting of an appropriate transaction, or dynamically by another executing IELE contract, using IELE's create instruction. We say that a new contract created this way is deployed, since an executable object (including smart contract code and state) is literally stored in the blockchain. Listing 2 shows a contract that dynamically creates accounts associated with the Forwarder contract shown in Listing 1. The create instruction dynamically creates a new account, deploys the Forwarder smart contract, and finally returns the new account's address. The send attribute specifies that no initial amount of Ether is sent to the new account.

The smart contract code to be associated with a newly created account should be available at creation time. In case of dynamic account creation, we chose to design IELE with the stricter requirement that the code should have been available at creation time of the creator contract. For this purpose, a IELE contract contains a list of external contracts that it is allowed to create at runtime, and the code for each of these contracts should be available when the contract itself is created. Recursively, the code of each contract that these contracts may create should also be available. Hence, all code that can be stored in the blockchain is available at the time when some end user posts an account creation transaction.

In Listing 2, the `Wallet` contract declares the `Forwarder` contract as external. This means that if a new `Wallet` contract is to be created and deployed, at that time both the code of the `Wallet` contract and the code of the `Forwarder` contract should be provided and will be stored in the blockchain as part of the creation transaction. Later, during execution, the `Wallet` contract is able to dynamically create `Forwarder` contracts using the available `Forwarder` code.

Listing 2. Wallet contract that creates Forwarder contracts

```
// Wallet contract that creates new accounts that forward funds sent to them to this wallet.
contract Wallet {
  external contract Forwarder
  define @init() {}

  // @deposit is empty: any received funds are simply added the associated account's balance
  define public @deposit() {}

  // creates a new account that simply forwards any funds sent to it to this wallet and
  // returns the address of the created forwarder account
  define public @newForwarder() {
    // ensure that the caller is the account associated with the wallet
    %caller = call @iele.caller()
    %owner = call @iele.address()
    %isnotowner = cmp ne %caller , %owner
    br %isnotowner , throw
    // create a new account associated with a Forwarder contract and return its address
    %status, %addr = create Forwarder () send 0
    br %status , throw
    ret %addr
  throw:
    call @iele.invalid()
  }
}
```

Dynamic contract creation is thus guaranteed to only use code that has already become available in the blockchain; *no dynamic code generation is allowed*. This design has two major advantages. Expensive code validation checks (well-formedness, formal verification, etc.) need only take place when account creation transactions are posted and never during code execution. Also code can be stored in the blockchain separately from the account it is associated with: contracts can be stored in a separate storage (with no duplicate contract code) and accounts need only store a pointer to their associated code. This allows for cheap dynamic account creation that doesn't generate duplicate code in the blockchain.

Contract Initialization. A special private `@init` function can be defined and will be executed at contract creation time. This function typically contains initialization code, e.g. initialization of the account storage. It is not callable and it can only be invoked at contract creation time. This way, IELE guarantees that the state of an already deployed contract cannot be reset maliciously by invoking initialization code after contract creation, thus avoiding a weakness of the current Ethereum design that has been exploited in the past [4].

3.2   IELE Functions

IELE functions are the main structural units of a IELE contract. A function definition includes the function signature, the function body and whether or not the function is public. A function signature includes a function name and names of formal arguments. A public function can be called by other accounts, while a private one can only be called by other functions within the same contract. Listing 3 shows a simple implementation of the factorial as a IELE function.

Listing 3. IELE function for factorial

```
define public @factorial(%n) {
  // ensure %n >= 0
  %lt = cmp lt %n, 0
  br %lt, throw
  %result = 1
condition:
  %cond = cmp le %n, 0
  br %cond, after_loop
loop_body:
  %result = mul %result, %n
  %n      = sub %n, 1
  br condition
after_loop:
  ret %result
throw:
  call @iele.invalid()
}
```

Control Flow. The function body code is organized in labeled blocks. The execution falls through from the last instruction of a block to the first of the next one, or jumps to the start of a specific block. IELE supports jumps to statically known targets only: The branch instruction accepts a block label as an argument for the target of the jump. This differs from the EVM, where jumps amount to pushing a possibly computed number on the stack and then jumping to it regarded as an address. IELE ensures a statically known control flow graph and thus makes static analysis and formal verification easier.

Function Calls. A public function can be invoked manually by an end user posting a transaction, or dynamically by another executing contract using IELE's account call instruction, `call .. at`. The address of the callee and the name of the called function are provided at call time. The call may be accompanied with an Ether amount to be transferred from the caller to the callee. IELE defines a simple call/return convention: Called functions expect a specific number of arguments (the number of formal arguments) and return a specific number of return values (the number of return values at `ret` plus an exit status). If an ABI error occurs (e.g. incorrect number of arguments, function not found or not public, etc), a corresponding erroneous exit status is returned.

For reference, in EVM the caller just sends an arbitrary bytestream containing the call arguments. There is an externally defined ABI convention that most EVM compilers follow, but it is not enforced. EVM does not have a notion of callable function; instead, the execution always starts at the contract's first instruction. The higher abstraction level of IELE's calls and its more structured design makes IELE contracts more readable and less tedious to formally verify.

EVM supports another type of account call, namely `delegatecall`, that differs from the normal call, in that the code of the callee is executed in the environment of the caller. This essentially means that the storage of the caller account becomes accessible and writable from the callee code. EVM offers this feature to avoid code duplication: typically library code is associated with a single account and invoked with `delegatecall` by multiple clients. IELE offers a different solution to the code duplication problem as discussed in Sect. 3.1. For this reason and because `delegatecall` poses serious security concerns and has been exploited in the past [35], we decided to drop `delegatecall` in IELE.

Deposit Handler. A special public function, `@deposit`, can be defined for a IELE contract and it is invoked whenever the account receives a payment that is not accompanied with a specific function call. A contract can forbid such payments by refusing to define a `@deposit` function.

3.3   IELE Instructions

IELE instructions take the form of opcodes that accept a specific number of arguments and return a specific number of values. There are various families of instructions, including arithmetic, bitwise, comparison, and hashing operations. There are also dedicated instructions for accessing the local memory, accessing the account storage, and appending to the account log. Finally there are branch instructions, the function call/return instructions, and the account create/selfdestruct instructions. In addition to instructions, IELE supports a number of useful intrinsics that can be called like private functions and provide functionality such as querying the local or network state, cryptographic functions, etc.

IELE is register-based: Instructions operate on and store their output in virtual registers. An infinite number of virtual registers is available, but the actual number of registers used by the function can be determined statically by counting the different register names used in its code. We chose to design IELE as a register-based language, unlike the stack-based EVM, for two reasons. First, it makes IELE code significantly more human-readable. Second, IELE formal verification tools do not need to reason about the size of the operation stack (bounded to 1024 words, a tedious requirement for verifying EVM programs).

3.4   IELE Datatypes

IELE uses arbitrary-precision signed integers. All virtual registers and account storage locations hold values of this type. They can also be stored in and loaded from the local memory. Arbitrary-precision arithmetic removes arithmetic overflows thus making specification and formal verification less tedious, as well as making attacks like [27] that exploit arithmetic overflow bugs not viable.

4 Formal IELE Language Definition in K

Here we describe the formal semantics of IELE, from which several of our IELE tools are generated automatically by the K framework, such as an interpreter, a well-formedness checker, and a program verifier. In total, the IELE semantics consists of 3122 lines of K code (not including literate comments), including 729 productions (for syntactic or semantic constructs) and 1255 semantic rules [33]. For comparison, the K EVM semantics in [15] consists of 2628 lines of K code, including 510 productions and 1025 semantic rules; these total less than 20% the size of the VM code component of the official EVM client implemented in C++ (about 15k LOC) [10]. A similar save would be seen if IELE had a conventional VM implementation in C++, although such an implementation was never needed because the IELE VM was automatically generated from the formal semantics.

Listing 4. K syntax productions for IELE contracts

```
syntax ContractDefinition  ::= "contract" IeleName "{" TopLevelDefinitions "}"
syntax TopLevelDefinitions ::= List{TopLevelDefinition, ""}
syntax TopLevelDefinition  ::= FunctionDefinition
                             | GlobalDefinition
                             | ContractDeclaration
syntax GlobalDefinition    ::= GlobalName "=" IntConstant
syntax ContractDeclaration ::= "external" "contract" IeleName
syntax FunctionDefinition  ::= "define" FunctionSignature "{" Blocks "}"
                             | "define" "public" FunctionSignature "{" Blocks "}"
syntax FunctionSignature   ::= GlobalName "(" FunctionParameters ")"
syntax FunctionParameters  ::= LocalNames
syntax GlobalName          ::= "@" IeleName
syntax LocalName           ::= "%" IeleName
syntax LocalNames          ::= List{LocalName, ","}
```

4.1 IELE Formal Semantics Overview

The formal semantics of IELE [33] is spread among several files: `iele-syntax.md` contains a quick introduction to the various features of the language along with their syntactical definitions. `iele.md` contains the semantics of the various language features and the specification of the program execution state. `iele-gas.md` contains the semantics of the gas model of IELE. `welformdness.md` contains a formal definition of a well-formed IELE contract, a syntactically valid IELE contract free from type errors and other malformed instructions and/or functions. Finally, `data.md` contains the semantics of various data structures and utilities used in the rest of the specification. In the following paragraphs, we discuss examples from the formal specification of IELE along with features of K as needed.

Syntax. The syntax of IELE is specified as a collection of EBNF-style productions. As an example, the productions shown in Listing 4 define the syntax for a IELE contract and its contents. The left-hand side of each syntax production defines a K sort and the right-hand side of the production gives one or more syntactically valid ways to construct a value of the sort. The keywords enclosed in double quotes represent terminal symbols. K uses these productions to automatically derive a parser for the language.

Execution State (Configuration). The execution state of a IELE program is defined as a K configuration, that is an ordered list of potentially nested cells, specified with an XML-like notation. At any given time during execution, each cell contains a corresponding value that reflects the current execution state. When declaring a K configuration, initial values for the cell contents are supplied. Among other components, the configuration for IELE contains a description of the local state and the network state.

(1) The local state is created when a transaction is sent to a specific account and contains information about the smart contract code associated with the account, the intra-contract call stack, the amount of gas remaining, and the state of the local memory and virtual register file (see Listing 5).

Listing 5. Configuration for local state

```
<id>      0 </id>      // Currently executing account
<caller> 0 </caller> // Account that called current account
<gas>     0 </gas>     // Current gas remaining
<program>
  <functions>
    <function multiplicity="*" type="Map">
      <funcId>    deposit </funcId>   // Name of the function
      <nparams>    0          </nparams>  // Number of parameters
      <jumpTable> .Map      </jumpTable> // Jump table
      <nregs>      0          </nregs>    // Number of registers
      <instructions>
        (.Instructions .LabeledBlocks):Blocks
      </instructions>                      // The blocks of the function
    </function>
  </functions>
  // ... more cells ...
</program>
<localCalls> .List   </localCalls> // Intra-contract call stack
<regs>          .Array </regs>       // Current values of registers
<localMem>    .Map   </localMem>   // Current values of local memory
```

The `id` cell contains the address of the currently executing account and the `caller` cell contains the address of the account that initiated the transaction. The `program` cell and its nested cells contain the code of the currently executing smart contract. The code is contained in one or more `function` cells, one for each function of the smart contract. These cells in turn contain the code for the corresponding function as a list of blocks and other information, such as the function name and number of formal parameters, and a jump table mapping label names to corresponding blocks. The `gas` cell contains the amount of gas remaining. This cell is initialized upon receiving the transaction to the amount of gas sent from the caller and is being reduced while the smart contract code executes. Finally, the cells `regs` and `localMem` map virtual register names and local memory addresses to their containing values, while the cell `localCalls` contains a stack of frames for all the functions in the current call stack.

(2) The network state contains information about the Ethereum network, such as active accounts, their balance in Ether, their storage contents, whether or not they are associated with code, pending transactions, and more. The Ethereum network state at any point in time can be reached by replaying all the transactions that are stored in the blockchain up to this point. Instead of specifying the network state as a transaction log, we choose to describe only the current network state, as only it is relevant for the rest of the formal specification.

Listing 6 shows part of the network state that describes the state of active Ethereum accounts. The `accounts` cell contains one cell per account in the network. Active accounts have their address in the `acctID` cell and their balance in the `balance` cell. The `code` cell contains any associated smart contract code. The `storage` cell maps storage addresses to their current contents for the account's storage. The `nonce` cell contains a monotonically increasing integer that counts the number of transactions performed by this account.

Listing 6. Configuration for network state

```
<network>
  <accounts>
    <account multiplicity="*" type="Map">
      <acctID>    0             </acctID>    // ID of account
      <balance>   0             </balance>   // Funds in account
      <code>      #emptyCode </code>         // Contract of account
      <storage>   .Map          </storage>   // Permanent storage
      <nonce>     0             </nonce>     // Nonce of account
    </account>
  </accounts>
  // ... more cells ...
</network>
```

Transition Rules. Transition rules define valid rewrites of the current configuration to a next one. Each rule consists of a left-hand side that is a pattern over one or more configurations (meaning it may contain variables) and a right-hand side that describes how a matched configuration should be rewritten to the next valid configuration. A pattern matches an actual configuration when there exists an assignment of its variables that makes it equal to the configuration. The derived interpreter that K generates matches patterns found in the left-hand side of rules with the contents of the current configuration, and rewrites it according to the right-hand side. The program verifier does the same, except that it applies the rules symbolically, using unification instead of matching.

The k cell of the configuration drives the execution: It contains at any time a list of execution steps to be matched and rewritten. The IELE semantics defines a set of internal operators that represent different such execution steps and maintains a list of such operators inside the k cell during execution.

As an example, Listing 7 shows the rules that specify the behavior of the `div` instruction. The syntax production defines the internal operator `#exec`, which represents the execution of a single IELE instruction. Both rules match a configuration where the top of the k cell contains the `#exec` operator with a division instruction. The first rule matches when the denominator is different from zero, as specified in the `requires` clause. Then, the top of the k cell is rewritten to another internal operator, `#load`, that loads the result of the division to the left-hand side virtual register. The `/Int` and `=/=Int` operators are K built-in operators for arbitrary-precision signed integers.

Listing 7. Rules for the `div` instruction

```
syntax InternalOp ::= "#exec" Instruction
// -----------------------------------------------
rule <k> #exec REG = div W0 , W1 => #load REG W0 /Int W1  ... </k>
     requires W1 =/=Int 0
rule <k> #exec REG = div W0 , 0 => #exception USER_ERROR ... </k>
```

The second rule matches in the case of division by zero and rewrites the top of the k cell to an `#exception` with the appropriate error code (here USER_ERROR is a macro that stands for corresponding error code). Other parts of the specification provide rules that handle exceptions by reverting all account state changes since the account started execution for the current transaction and returning the error code to the caller. The ellipses (. . .) is K syntax for a pattern that matches the rest of the k cell, which is a list of internal operators.

Listing 8. Rules for the `#load` internal operator

```
syntax InternalOp ::= "#load" LValue Int
                    | "#load" Int Int Int [klabel(#loadAux)]
// ------------------------------------------------------------
rule <k> #load % REG VALUE => #load REG VALUE {REGS [ REG ]} ...</k>
     <regs> REGS </regs>
rule <k> #load REG VALUE OLD => .  ... </k>
     <regs> REGS => REGS [ REG <- VALUE ] </regs>
     <currentMemory>
       CURR => CURR -Int intSize(OLD) +Int intSize(VALUE)
     </currentMemory>
```

The rules shown in Listing 8 specify the behavior of the `#load` internal operator, used to store values in virtual registers. Note that the syntax for a virtual register (after desugaring) is `%` `Int` and the integer that is the name of the register is used as an index in the register file to look up its value.

The first rule accesses the current register file in the `regs` cell and looks up the old value of the register to be updated. It then rewrites the `#load` operator to an auxiliary operator that matches the second rule. The second rule updates the register file using the K built-in operator `_[_<-_]` for writing array elements. It also updates the total size of the register file in the `currentMemory` cell; this information is needed to compute the gas cost of the operation. The top of the k cell is rewritten to ".", which is a K idiom for the empty string.

As a last example, `intSize`, used above to compute the size in 64-bit words of the given arbitrary-precision signed integer, is defined as shown in Listing 9.

Listing 9. Rules for the `intSize` operator

```
syntax Int ::= intSize ( Int ) [function]
// -----------------------------------------
rule intSize(N) => (log2Int(N) +Int 2) up/Int 64 requires N >Int 0
rule intSize(0) => 1
rule intSize(N) => intSize(~Int N) requires N <Int 0
```

The syntax production specifies the pattern `intSize(_)` as a member of the `Int` sort (the arbitrary-precision signed integers) and attaches the `function` attribute to it. This attribute informs K that the pattern is "pure", as in the rules for rewriting it do not depend on any context other than its argument. The K rewrite engine will attempt to rewrite these pattern as much as possible when they appear anywhere in the current configuration.

5   Formal Verifier of IELE Smart Contracts

K provides a sound and relatively complete language-parametric program verifier. That is, given a language semantics as input, K yields a program verifier for that language that can prove, modulo a domain reasoning oracle (currently Z3 [8]), any reachability property about any program in that language. This important capability of K, that generalizes and eliminates the need for Hoare logic, has already been demonstrated with languages that are much larger than IELE, such as C, Java and JavaScript, and shown to offer the same level of automation and performance as program verifiers crafted specifically for the languages in question (e.g., VCC for C) [6]. Here we briefly explain how the K verifier works with IELE as input language, to verify IELE smart contracts. We emphasize how it compares with the same generic verifier instantiated with the EVM semantics [15], which has been used extensively as part of commercial services [26,32].

As discussed in Sect. 3, formal verification of smart contracts was one of the main forces driving the design of IELE, often in sharp contrast to the design of the EVM: statically known jumps allow us to write and compose code properties modularly; eliminating stack bounds for arithmetic expression evaluation allows us to soundly focus only on functional properties of code and write simpler, higher-level properties; eliminating the ABI encoding conventions allow us to reason about any programs, not only about those that obey the conventions; unbounded integers eliminate the need to reason about arithmetic overflow; etc.

We now discuss how to verify in IELE the most popular smart contract, ERC20 [37], which provides functionality for maintaining and exchanging tokens. Details about the verification of ERC20 in EVM can be found in [26,32].

Formal Specification. We start with ERC20-K [30], a complete language-independent formalization of the high level business logic of the ERC20 standard. ERC20-K clarifies what data (e.g., balances and allowances) are handled by the various ERC20 functions and the precise meaning of those functions on such data. More importantly, ERC20-K clarifies the meaning of all the corner cases that the ERC20 standard omits to discuss, such as transfers to itself and transfers that result in arithmetic overflow. From ERC20-K, we can easily derive the specification for the ERC20 contract written in IELE by mapping ERC20-K to the configuration of IELE. We follow the same approach and DSL used for EVM [26], but taking the specifics of IELE into account. Mathematically, the ERC20 specification consists of a set of reachability formulae of the form $\phi \Rightarrow \psi$, with the meaning that the set of states satisfying/matching the pattern ϕ will either reach a state in ψ or not terminate when executed with IELE.

Listing 10 shows a snippet of the specification for two possible behaviors of transfer. For each case, it specifies the function name (fid), the function parameters (`callData` and `regs`), the return value (`output`), whether an exception occurred (`k`), the log generated (`log`), the storage update (`storage`), and the path-condition (`requires`). The success case ([`transfer-success`]) specifies that the function succeeds in transferring the `VALUE` tokens from the `FROM` account to the `TO` account, with generating the corresponding log message, and returns 1 (i.e., true), provided that the `FROM` account has sufficient balance. The failure case ([`transfer-failure`]) specifies that the function throws an exception without modifying the account balances, if the `FROM` balance is insufficient.

Listing 10. Formal specification of ERC20 `transfer`

```
[transfer-success]
k: #execute => #end ...
callData: TO, VALUE, .Ints
output: _ => (1, .Ints)
regs: (0 |-> TO_ID  1 |-> VALUE   .Map) => _
fid: transfer
log: ... (. => #eventLog(FROM, #topics(TransferEvent, FROM, TO), Int2Bytes(VALUE)))
storage: #mapKey({BALANCE}, FROM) |-> (BAL_FROM => BAL_FROM -Int VALUE)
         #mapKey({BALANCE}, TO)   |-> (BAL_TO   => BAL_TO   +Int VALUE)
         ...
requires: andBool 0 <=Int VALUE
          andBool FROM =/=Int TO
          andBool VALUE <=Int BAL_FROM

[transfer-failure]
k: #execute => #exception(4) ...
callData: TO, VALUE, .Ints
output: _ => _
regs: (0 |-> TO_ID  1 |-> VALUE   .Map) => _
fid: transfer
log: ...
storage: #mapKey({BALANCE}, FROM) |-> BAL_FROM
         #mapKey({BALANCE}, TO)   |-> BAL_TO
         ...
requires: andBool 0 <=Int VALUE
          andBool FROM =/=Int TO
          andBool VALUE >Int BAL_FROM
```

Formal Verification. We verified the hand-written IELE implementation of ERC20 at [31], following the same automatic process used for EVM-level verification described in [26]. All 15 high-level ERC20 properties were seamlessly proved, automatically. It is insightful to compare the IELE and EVM verification experiences. We found that most of the EVM-level verification challenges described in [26] are addressed by the IELE language design. For example:

(Arithmetic Overflow). Since EVM performs modular arithmetic (i.e., mod 2^{256}), detecting arithmetic overflow is critical for preventing security attacks. When writing EVM-level specifications, one needs to reverse engineer constraints on the input such that the arithmetic overflow checks in the program pass. For example, in case `transfer-success`, one needs to add constraints to make sure that the balance of `TO` account does not overflow. This is not only tedious, but also imposes non-trivial proof obligations on SMT solvers. In contrast, IELE arithmetic instructions admit unbounded integers, which not only makes the smart contract more secure but also makes it much easier to specify correctly.

(**Hash Collision**). Due to the storage limitation of EVM, compilers such as Solidity and Vyper use SHA3 hash to implement the builtin map. However, SHA3 is not cryptographically collision free. The contract developers simply assume collisions will not occur during normal execution and SHA3 hash is modeled as an injective function during the verification of EVM smart contracts. Unfortunately, that is unsound: one can derive false, using the pigeonhole principle. In contrast, IELE provides *infinite* memory and storage, so injective functions can be defined to map different keys to different locations instead of SHA3 hashing.

6 Conclusion

We presented IELE, a new low-level language for smart contracts. The full formal specification of IELE is available as a K specification, serving at the same time as the implementation as well as a formal documentation of the language. The specification/implementation of IELE is in par with the state of the art in the world of smart contract virtual machines. With the support of a Solidity to IELE compiler (see appendix B.1 in [20]) and a fully functional Ethereum client that is based on Mantis and powered by the IELE virtual machine (see appendix B.2 in [20]), we were able to deploy and execute IELE contracts in a real-world blockchain testnet. This makes IELE the first practical language to be defined and implemented directly as a formal semantics specification and significantly raises the bar for how virtual machines for the blockchain must be developed. In this new and disruptive field where security and correctness are paramount, it is in our view unjustified to adopt any lower standards anymore.

Acknowledgements. We are grateful to IOHK (http://iohk.io) for funding the IELE project, as well as for insightful discussions, encouragements and constructive criticisms along the way. The work on the K framework and its tooling was supported in part by NSF grant CNS 16-19275 and by the United States Air Force and DARPA under Contract No. FA8750-18-C-0092.

References

1. Atzei, N., Bartoletti, M., Cimoli, T.: A survey of attacks on Ethereum smart contracts. IACR Cryptology ePrint Archive 2016, 1007 (2016). https://eprint.iacr.org/2016/1007.pdf
2. Blockstream: Simplicity blog post and resources (2019). https://blockstream.com/2018/11/28/en-simplicity-github/
3. Bogdanas, D., Rosu, G.: K-Java: a complete semantics of Java. In: Proceedings of the 42nd Symposium on Principles of Programming Languages (POPL2015), pp. 445–456. ACM, January 2015. https://doi.org/10.1145/2676726.2676982
4. Breidenbach, L., Daian, P., Juels, A., Sirer, E.G.: An in-depth look at the parity multisig bug (2017). http://hackingdistributed.com/2017/07/22/deep-dive-parity-bug/
5. Buterin, V., Ethereum Foundation: Ethereum White Paper (2013). https://github.com/ethereum/wiki/wiki/White-Paper

6. Ştefănescu, A., Park, D., Yuwen, S., Li, Y., Roşu, G.: Semantics-based program verifiers for all languages. In: Proceedings of the 31th Conference on Object-Oriented Programming, Systems, Languages, and Applications (OOPSLA 2016), pp. 74–91. ACM, November 2016. https://doi.org/10.1145/2983990.2984027

7. Daian, P.: DAO attack (2016). http://hackingdistributed.com/2016/06/18/analysis-of-the-dao-exploit/

8. de Moura, L., Bjørner, N.: Z3: an efficient SMT solver. In: Ramakrishnan, C.R., Rehof, J. (eds.) TACAS 2008. LNCS, vol. 4963, pp. 337–340. Springer, Heidelberg (2008). https://doi.org/10.1007/978-3-540-78800-3_24

9. Ellison, C., Rosu, G.: An executable formal semantics of C with applications. In: Proceedings of the 39th ACM SIGPLAN-SIGACT Symposium on Principles of Programming Languages (POPL 2012), pp. 533–544. ACM, January 2012. https://doi.org/10.1145/2103656.2103719

10. Ethereum: Ethereum C++ Client (2019). https://github.com/ethereum/cpp-ethereum

11. Ethereum: Solidity documentation (2019). http://solidity.readthedocs.io

12. Ethereum: Vyper documentation (2019). https://vyper.readthedocs.io

13. Etherscan: Ethereum Transaction Growth (2019). https://etherscan.io/chart/tx

14. Hathhorn, C., Ellison, C., Rosu, G.: Defining the undefinedness of C. In: Proceedings of the 36th ACM SIGPLAN Conference on Programming Language Design and Implementation (PLDI 2015), pp. 336–345. ACM, June 2015. https://doi.org/10.1145/2813885.2737979

15. Hildenbrandt, E., et al.: KEVM: a complete semantics of the Ethereum virtual machine. In: 2018 IEEE 31st Computer Security Foundations Symposium, pp. 204–217. IEEE (2018). https://doi.org/10.1109/CSF.2018.00022

16. IOHK: IELE Testnet (2019). https://testnet.iohkdev.io/iele/

17. IOHK: KEVM Testnet (2019). https://testnet.iohkdev.io/kevm/

18. IOHK: Mantis Ethereum Classic Client (2019). https://iohk.io/blog/mantis-ethereum-classic-beta-release

19. IOHK: Plutus testnet (2019). https://testnet.iohkdev.io/plutus/

20. Kasampalis, T., et al.: IELE: a rigorously designed language and tool ecosystem for the blockchain. Technical report, University of Illinois, July 2019. http://hdl.handle.net/2142/104601

21. KEVM: Jello paper (2019). https://jellopaper.org/

22. Lattner, C., Adve, V.: LLVM: a compilation framework for lifelong program analysis & transformation. In: Proceedings of the International Symposium on Code Generation and Optimization: Feedback-directed and Runtime Optimization, CGO 2004, p. 75. IEEE Computer Society, Washington, DC, USA (2004). http://llvm.org

23. Milner, R., Tofte, M., Harper, R., MacQueen, D.: The Definition of Standard ML: Revised. MIT Press, Cambridge (1997)

24. Nakamoto, S.: Bitcoin: a peer-to-peer electronic cash system (2008). https://bitcoin.org/bitcoin.pdf

25. Park, D., Stefanescu, A., Rosu, G.: KJS: a complete formal semantics of JavaScript. In: Proceedings of the 36th ACM SIGPLAN Conference on Programming Language Design and Implementation (PLDI 2015), pp. 346–356. ACM, June 2015. https://doi.org/10.1145/2737924.2737991

26. Park, D., Zhang, Y., Saxena, M., Daian, P., Roşu, G.: A Formal verification tool for Ethereum VM bytecode. In: Proceedings of the 26th ACM Joint European Software Engineering Conference and Symposium on the Foundations of Software Engineering (ESEC/FSE 2018). ACM, November 2018. https://doi.org/10.1145/3236024.3264591

27. PeckShield: New batchOverflow Bug in Multiple ERC20 Smart Contracts (CVE-2018-10299) (2018). https://medium.com/coinmonks/alert-new-batchoverflow-bug-in-multiple-erc20-smart-contracts-cve-2018-10299-511067db6536

28. RChain Cooperative: Rchain and rholang documentation (2019). https://architecture-docs.readthedocs.io/

29. Rosu, G., Serbanuta, T.F.: An overview of the K semantic framework. J. Logic Algebraic Program. **79**(6), 397–434 (2010). http://kframework.org

30. RuntimeVerification: ERC20-K: Formal Executable Specification of ERC20 (2017). https://github.com/runtimeverification/erc20-semantics

31. RuntimeVerification: ERC20 Token in IELE (2019). https://github.com/runtimeverification/iele-semantics/blob/master/iele-examples/erc20.iele

32. RuntimeVerification: Formal Smart Contract Verification (2019). https://runtimeverification.com/smartcontract/

33. RuntimeVerification: The formal semantics for IELE – source code (2019). https://github.com/runtimeverification/iele-semantics

34. Solana, J.: $500K hack challenge backfires on blockchain lottery Smart-Billions (2017). https://calvinayre.com/2017/10/13/bitcoin/500k-hack-challenge-backfires-blockchain-lottery-smartbillions/

35. Steiner, J.: Security is a process: a postmortem on the parity multi-sig library self-destruct (2017). http://goo.gl/LBh1vR

36. Tezos: Michelson documentation (2019). https://tezos.gitlab.io/master/index.html

37. The Ethereum Foundation: ERC20 token standard (2019). https://github.com/ethereum/EIPs/blob/master/EIPS/eip-20-token-standard.md

38. Wood, G.: Ethereum: a secure decentralised generalised transaction ledger. Ethereum Proj. Yellow Pap. **151**, 1–32 (2014)

39. Zilliqa: Scilla language webpage (2019). https://scilla-lang.org/

APML: An Architecture Proof Modeling Language

Diego Marmsoler$^{(\boxtimes)}$ (ID) and Genc Blakqori

Technische Universität München, Munich, Germany
`diego.marmsoler@tum.de`

Abstract. To address the increasing size and complexity of modern software systems, compositional verification separates the verification of single components from the verification of their composition. In architecture-based verification, the former is done using Model Checking, while the latter is done using interactive theorem proving (ITP). As of today, however, architects are usually not trained in using a full-fledged interactive theorem prover. Thus, to bridge the gap between ITP and the architecture domain, we developed APML: an architecture proof modeling language. APML allows one to sketch proofs about component composition at the level of architecture using notations similar to Message Sequence Charts. With this paper, we introduce APML: We describe the language, show its soundness and completeness for the verification of architecture contracts, and provide an algorithm to map an APML proof to a corresponding proof for the interactive theorem prover Isabelle. Moreover, we describe its implementation in terms of an Eclipse/EMF modeling application, demonstrate it by means of a running example, and evaluate it in terms of a larger case study. Although our results are promising, the case study also reveals some limitations, which lead to new directions for future work.

Keywords: Compositional verification ·
Interactive Theorem Proving · Architecture-based Verification ·
FACTum · Isabelle

1 Introduction

Software intensive systems are becoming increasingly big and complex, which makes their verification a challenge. To address this challenge, compositional verification techniques separate the verification of single components from the verification of their composition. In architecture-based verification (ABV) [30], for example, verification of such systems is split into two parts: First, suitable contracts are identified for the involved components and their implementation is verified against these contracts. Since a single component is usually of limited complexity, in ABV this step is fully automated using Model Checking [2]. In a second step, component contracts are combined to verify overall system properties. Reasoning about the composition of contracts, however, might be difficult

© Springer Nature Switzerland AG 2019
M. H. ter Beek et al. (Eds.): FM 2019, LNCS 11800, pp. 611–630, 2019.
https://doi.org/10.1007/978-3-030-30942-8_36

and sometimes requires manual interaction [29]. Thus, in ABV, it is done using interactive theorem provers, such as Isabelle [34].

A full-fledged interactive theorem prover, however, can be quite complex and its usage usually requires expertise which is not always available in the architecture context [28]. Thus, in an effort to bridge the gap between interactive theorem proving and the architecture domain, we developed APML: a language to specify proofs for the composition of contracts using abstractions an architect is familiar with. APML comes with a *graphical notation*, similar to Message Sequence Charts [15], to sketch proofs at the architecture level and it is shown to be *sound* and *complete* regarding the verification of architecture contracts. It is *implemented in Eclipse/EMF* [41], where it can be used to model proofs for architecture contracts and synthesize corresponding proofs for Isabelle's structured proof language Isar [43,44].

The aim of this paper is to introduce APML. To this end, we provide the following contributions: (i) We provide a formal description of APML, including a formal semantics for architecture contracts. (ii) We show soundness and completeness of APML for the verification of architecture contracts. (iii) We present an algorithm to map an APML proof to a corresponding proof in Isabelle/Isar. (iv) We describe its implementation in terms of an Eclipse/EMF modeling application. (v) We demonstrate the approach by means of a running example and report on the outcome of a case study in which we applied APML for the verification of a railway control system. Thereby, to the best of our knowledge, *this is the first attempt to synthesize proofs for an interactive theorem prover from an architecture description.*

Our presentation is structured as follows: In Sect. 2, we provide some background to clarify our understanding of architecture in general and specifically our notion of architecture contract. In Sect. 3, we describe our running example, a reliable calculator. In Sect. 4, we introduce APML, demonstrate it by verifying a property for our running example, and present our soundness and completeness results. In Sect. 5, we present our algorithm to map an APML proof to a corresponding proof in Isabelle/Isar and demonstrate it by means of the running example. In Sect. 6, we describe the implementation of APML in terms of an Eclipse/EMF modeling application and in Sect. 7 we describe our effort to evaluate APML by means of a larger case study. In Sect. 8, we discuss related work before we conclude the paper in Sect. 9 with a brief summary and a discussion of future work.

2   Background

2.1   Basic Mathematical Notations

For a function $f \colon D \to R$, we shall use $f|_{D'} \colon D' \to R$ to denote the restriction of f to domain $D' \subseteq D$. In addition, we shall use partial functions $f \colon D \dashrightarrow R$ for which we denote with $\mathrm{dom}\,(f) \subseteq D$ its domain and with $\mathrm{ran}\,(f) \subseteq R$ its range.

We will also use finite as well as infinite *sequences* of elements. Thereby, we denote with $(E)^*$ the set of all finite sequences over elements of a given set E, by $(E)^\infty$ the set of all infinite sequences over E, and by $(E)^\omega$ the set of all finite and infinite sequences over E. The n-th element of a sequence s is denoted with $s(n-1)$ and the first element is $s(0)$. Moreover, we shall use $\#s \in \mathbb{N}_\infty$ to denote the length of s. For a sequence $s \in (D \to R)^\infty$ of functions we shall use $s|_{D'}$ to denote the sequence of all restrictions $s(n)|_{D'}$.

2.2 Architecture Model

In our model [27, 33], components communicate to each other by exchanging *messages* over *ports*. Thus, we assume the existence of set $\mathcal{M}$, containing all messages, and set $\mathcal{P}$, containing all ports, respectively. Moreover, we postulate the existence of a type function

$$T \colon \mathcal{P} \to \wp(\mathcal{M}) \tag{1}$$

which assigns a set of messages to each port.

Ports are means to exchange messages between a component and its environment. This is achieved through the notion of port valuation. Roughly speaking, a valuation for a set of ports is an assignment of messages to each port.

Definition 1 (Port Valuation). *For a set of ports $P \subseteq \mathcal{P}$, we denote with $\overline{P}$ the set of all possible, type-compatible port valuations, formally:*

$$\overline{P} \stackrel{def}{=} \left\{ \mu \in (P \to \mathcal{M}) \mid \forall p \in P \colon \mu(p) \in T(p) \right\}$$

Components communicate through interfaces by receiving messages on its input ports and sending messages through its output ports.

Definition 2 (Interface). *An interface is a pair (I, O), consisting of disjoint sets of input ports $I \subseteq \mathcal{P}$ and output ports $O \subseteq \mathcal{P}$. For an interface f, we denote by $in(f)$ the set of input ports, $out(f)$ the set of output ports, and $port(f)$ the set of all ports. A set of interfaces is called disjoint iff its interfaces do not share any ports. For such sets of interfaces, we shall use the same notation as introduced for single interfaces, to denote their input, output, and all ports.*

In addition, a component has a behavior which is given in terms of a *non-empty* set of sequences of port valuations over its interface.

In our model, an architecture connects input and output ports of a set of interfaces. Thereby, the types of connected ports must be compatible.

Definition 3 (Architecture). *An architecture is a pair (F, N), consisting of a disjoint set of interfaces F and a connection $N \colon in(F) \dashrightarrow out(F)$, such that*

$$\forall p \in \mathrm{dom}\,(N) : T(N(p)) \subseteq T(p) \tag{2}$$

Note that a connection is modeled as a *partial* function from input to output ports, meaning that not every input port of an architecture is connected to a corresponding output port and vice versa. Thus, ports of an architecture can be classified as either *connected* (given by $\mathrm{dom}\,(N) \cup \mathrm{ran}\,(N)$) or *disconnected* (given by $(in(F) \setminus \mathrm{dom}\,(N)) \cup (out(F) \setminus \mathrm{ran}\,(N))$).

2.3   Composition

The interface of an architecture with its environment is given by its disconnected ports.

Definition 4 (Architecture Interface). *For an architecture $A = (F, N)$, its interface is defined as $_A\otimes = (I, O)$, consisting of input ports $I = in(F)\backslash \mathrm{dom}\,(N)$ and output ports $O = out(F) \setminus \mathrm{ran}\,(N)$.*

Note that, since F is required to be disjoint, an architecture's input and output ports are guaranteed to be disjoint, too. Thus, an architecture interface fulfills all the requirements of Definition 2 and thus represents a valid interface. Hence, we can use the same notation as introduced for interfaces to access its ports.

We can now define a notion of composition to obtain the behavior of an architecture from the behavior of its components.

Definition 5 (Architecture Behavior). *Given an architecture $A = (F, N)$ and a non-empty behavior $\mathcal{B}_f \subseteq (\overline{port(f)})^\infty$ for all of its interfaces $f \in F$. The behavior of the composition is given by a set of traces $_A\otimes \mathcal{B} \subseteq (\overline{port(_A\otimes)})^\infty$, defined as follows:*

$$_A\otimes \mathcal{B} \stackrel{def}{=} \{t|_{port(_A\otimes)} \mid t \in (\overline{port(F)})^\infty \wedge \tag{3}$$

$$\left(\forall f \in F: t|_{port(f)} \in \mathcal{B}_f\right) \wedge \tag{4}$$

$$(\forall (i, o) \in N,\ n \in \mathbb{N}: t(n)(i) = t(n)(o))\} \tag{5}$$

Roughly speaking, the behavior of a composition is defined as all traces over the architecture's interface (Eq. (3)), which respect the behavior of each component (Eq. (4)) and the connections imposed by the architecture (Eq. (5)).

2.4   Contracts

In the following, we are considered with the specification of architectures (as they were described in the previous section). To this end, we assume the existence of a set of predicates $\Gamma(P)$ to specify valuations for a set of ports $P \subseteq \mathcal{P}$.

Our notion of contract is inspired by Dwyer's work on specification patterns [18] which is often found in practice [24]. Thereby, contracts have the form: "if P is true then Q happens after d time points".

Definition 6 (Contracts). *A contract for an interface (I, O) is a triple (tg, gr, d), consisting of a (possibly empty) trigger $tg \in (\Gamma(I) \times \mathbb{N})^*$, a guarantee $gr \in \Gamma(O)$, and a duration $d \in \mathbb{N}$. For every entry e of a trigger, we denote by $state(e)$ its predicate and with $time(e)$ its time point. Moreover, we require the following conditions for a contract:*

- *The time point of the first trigger is 0: $time(tg(0)) = 0$ (if $\#tg > 0$).*
- *Triggers are ordered by their time points: $\forall j, j' < \#tg : j \leq j' \implies time(tg(j)) \leq time(tg(j'))$.*
- *The guarantee is after the last trigger: $d > time(tg(\#tg - 1))$ (or $d > 0$ if $tg = \langle\rangle$).*

Moreover, since they are specified over interfaces, contracts can be specified for components as well as for architectures. They are best expressed graphically using a notation similar to Message Sequence Charts [15] (see Figs. 4 or 5 for an example).

In the following, we define what it means for a behavior of a component (or architecture) to satisfy a corresponding contract. Thereby, we denote with $\mu \models \gamma$ that a valuation $\mu \in \overline{P}$ satisfies a predicate $\gamma \in \Gamma(P)$.

Definition 7 (Satisfaction). *A behavior $\mathcal{B}$ for an interface satisfies a contract $k = (tg, gr, d)$ for that interface, written $\mathcal{B} \models k$, whenever for all $t \in \mathcal{B}$, satisfaction of the triggers implies satisfaction of the guarantee:*

$$\forall n \in \mathbb{N} \colon \Big(\big(\forall j < \#tg \colon t(n + time(tg(j))) \models state(tg(j)) \big) \implies t(n + d) \models gr \Big)$$

Again, the same definition can be applied for component contracts as well as for architecture contracts.

2.5 Isabelle

Isabelle [34] is a generic proof assistant which allows mathematical formulæ to be expressed in a formal language and which provides tools for proving those formulas in a logical calculus. The version of Isabelle used for the work presented in this paper is Isabelle/HOL, which includes tools to support the specification of datatypes, inductive definitions, and recursive functions.

Specifications in Isabelle are grouped into so-called theories, which may import other theories. To modularize results, Isabelle supports the development of abstract specifications by means of locales [3]. Figure 1 shows how such a locale usually looks like: It consists of a name, a list of parameters, and a list of assumptions about these parameters. In previous work [29], we show how to map an architecture specification to a corresponding Isabelle locale. Thereby, ports are mapped to corresponding locale parameters and specifications to locale assumptions.

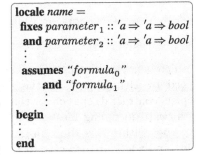

locale *name* =
fixes *parameter$_1$* :: $'a \Rightarrow 'a \Rightarrow bool$
and *parameter$_2$* :: $'a \Rightarrow 'a \Rightarrow bool$
$\vdots$
assumes *"formula$_0$"*
and *"formula$_1$"*
$\vdots$
begin
$\vdots$
end

Fig. 1. A typical Isabelle locale.

In Isabelle, proofs can be expressed in a natural way using Isabelle's structured proof language Isar [44]. A typical Isar proof is depicted in Fig. 2: It consists of a sequence of proof steps, which are discharged by some proof methods. For example, Isabelle's

proof
  assume $label_0$: "$formula_0$"
  from $label_0$ **have** $label_1$: "$formula_1$" **by** *blast*
  $\vdots$
  from $label_0$, $label_1$, ... **show** "$formula_n$" **by** *blast*
qed

Fig. 2. A typical Isabelle/Isar proof.

classical reasoner *blast* can perform long chains of reasoning steps to prove formulas. Or the simplifier *simp* can reason with and about equations. Moreover, external, first-order provers can be invoked through *sledgehammer*.

3 Running Example: A Reliable Adder

As a running example, let us consider a simple system which calculates the sum of two numbers in a redundant way. Its architecture is depicted in Fig. 3: It consists of a dispatcher component which receives two numbers as input from its environment and forwards copies of these numbers to two different adder components. The adder components then calculate the sum of the two numbers and communicate their result to a merger component. The merger component compares the two results and forwards the final result to its environment.

Fig. 3. Architecture for a reliable adder.

The behavior of each component is specified in terms of contracts (as introduced by Definition 6) by the sequence diagrams depicted in Fig. 4: Fig. 4a depicts contract `dispatch` for the dispatcher component. It requires a dispatcher to forward incoming messages received at ports i1 and i2, on its output ports o1 − o4, within one time unit. The contracts for the two adder components, `add1` and `add2`, are depicted in Fig. 4b and c, respectively. They both require an adder to calculate the sum of the numbers obtained on its input ports i1 and i2 and output it on its output port o. For our example, we assume that the two components use different algorithms to calculate the sum, which is why Adder1 requires four time units while Adder2 requires only three time units to output its result. Figure 4d, e, and f, depict three different contracts for the merger component. Contract `merge1` requires the merger component to compare the messages received on its input ports i1 and i2, and for the case they coincide, to forward the message after two time units on its output port o. Contracts `merge2` and `merge3` require the merger component to cope with a potential delay of one time unit for messages received on its input ports i2 and i1, respectively.

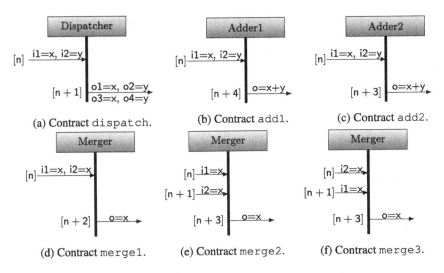

(a) Contract `dispatch`.   (b) Contract `add1`.   (c) Contract `add2`.

(d) Contract `merge1`.   (e) Contract `merge2`.   (f) Contract `merge3`.

Fig. 4. Contracts for components of reliable adder.

Among other things, we expect the resulting system to output the sum of two numbers it receives on its input ports i1 and i2 after seven time units on its output port o. This can be expressed in terms of a contract over its architecture as specified by the sequence diagram depicted in Fig. 5.

Note that our running example is deliberately oversimplified, since its main purpose is
to demonstrate our concepts and ideas rather
than evaluating the approach in a real world
scenario. For details about how the approach
works on a real example, we refer to the
description of the case study in Sect. 7.

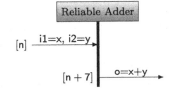

Fig. 5. Contract for reliable adder.

4   Modeling Architecture Proofs

An architecture contract can be verified from a set of contracts for its components through a sequence of proof steps.

Definition 8 (Proof Step). *A* proof step *for an architecture* (F, N) *and corresponding contracts* K_f *for its interfaces* $f \in F$, *is a 4-tuple* $s = (tp, \gamma, r, rf)$, *consisting of*

- a time point $tp \in \mathbb{N}$ denoted $time(s)$,
- an architecture state $\gamma \in \Gamma(out(f))$ (for some $f \in F$) denoted $state(s)$,
- a rationale $r = (tg, gr, d) \in K_f$ (for some $f \in F$) denoted $rat(s)$,
- a (possibly empty) sequence of references $rf \in (R)^*$ denoted $ref(s)$, such that $\#rf = \#tg$ and where R is a non-empty set of elements $\mathbb{N} \cup (\mathbb{N} \times \wp(N))$.

Note that an element of R is either a reference to an assumption $\mathbb{N}$ of the architecture contract we want to prove, or a reference to another proof step $\mathbb{N}$ and a set of connections $\wp(N)$. An architecture proof is given by a sequence of corresponding proof steps.

Definition 9 (Architecture Proof). *Given an architecture $A = (F, N)$ and corresponding contracts K_f for its interfaces $f \in F$. An architecture proof for a contract (tg, gr, d) over the architecture's interface $_A\otimes$ is a finite, non-empty sequence ps of proof steps, such that the state of the last entry implies the guarantee of the architecture contract:*

$$state(ps(\#ps - 1)) \implies gr \qquad (6)$$

the time of the last entry corresponds to the duration of the architecture contract:

$$time(ps(\#ps - 1)) = d \qquad (7)$$

and for all entries $0 \leq i < \#ps$, such that $rat(ps(i)) = (tg', gr', d')$:

1. *$ps(i)$ refers only to triggers of the architecture contract or previous proof steps:*

$$\forall j < \#ref(ps(i)):$$
$$\big(\forall k \in ref(ps(i))(j): k < \#tg\big) \ \wedge \ \big(\forall(k, n) \in ref(ps(i))(j): k < i\big)$$

   Note that this implies that $ref(ps(0))$ contains only references to triggers tg of the architecture contract.

2. *The time points of the referenced entries respect the time points of the triggers of the rationale. Thus, we first introduce a function time (for $\#ref(ps(i)) > 0$) to return the relative time point of a reference:*

$$time(ref(ps(i))(j)) = \begin{cases} time(tg(k)) & if \ k \in ref(ps(i))(j) \\ time(ps(k)) & if \ (k, n) \in ref(ps(i))(j) \end{cases}$$

   Now we can use this function to formalize the condition (note that by Definition 8, $\#ref(ps(i)) = \#tg'$):

$$\forall j < \#ref(ps(i)): time(ref(ps(i))(j)) = time(ref(ps(i))(0)) + time(tg'(j))$$

   Note that this condition implies that for all $j < \#ref(ps(i))$, the referenced time points of all entries $e \in ref(ps(i))(j)$ is the same.

3. *The referenced entries imply the corresponding triggers of the rationale:*

$$\forall j < \#ref(ps(i)): \left(\bigwedge_{k \in ref(ps(i))(j)} state(tg(k)) \right) \wedge$$

$$\left(\bigwedge_{(k,n) \in ref(ps(i))(j)} state(ps(k)) \wedge \bigwedge_{(p_i, p_o) \in n} p_i = p_o \right) \implies state(tg'(j))$$

4. *The time of the current entry respects the duration of the rationale (note that the time of* $ref(ps(i))(0)$ *corresponds to the time point of the first trigger of the rationale):*

$$time(ps(i)) = time(ref(ps(i))(0)) + d'$$

5. *The guarantee of the rationale implies the current state:*

$$gr' \implies state(ps(i))$$

Similar as for contracts, architecture proofs are best expressed graphically using a notation similar to Message Sequence Charts (see Fig. 6 for an example).

4.1 Verifying Reliable Adder

Table 1 shows an architecture proof for the contract of our running example depicted in Fig. 5. It consists of four steps: 0. First, we apply contract dispatch of the dispatcher component to trigger 0 of the architecture contract, to obtain a valuation of the dispatcher's output ports at time point 1 with messages x and y, respectively. 1. Then, we use connections $(a1i1, do1)$ and $(a1i2, do2)$ to pass messages x and y to the corresponding input ports of Adder1 and apply contract add1 to obtain a new state for time point 5, in which the output port of Adder1 contains the sum of x and y. 2. Similarly, we can use connections $(a2i1, do3)$ and $(a2i2, do4)$ to apply contract add2 to the architecture state given by step 0, to obtain a new state for time point 4, in which the output port of Adder2 contains the sum of x and y. 3. Finally, we can use connections $(mi1, a1o)$ and $(mi2, a2o)$ to pass the calculated sums to the input of the merger component and apply contract merge3 to forward it on its output port. Note that the proof is only valid, since we chose contract merge3 for the merger component. If we had chosen merge1 or merge2, the proof would have violated condition 2 of Definition 9.

As mentioned above, architecture proofs can also be expressed graphically using a notation similar to Message Sequence Charts. For example, the proof from Table 1, could also be expressed graphically as depicted in Fig. 6.

Table 1. Architecture proof for reliable adder.

	tp	γ	r	rf
0	1	$do1 = x \wedge do2 = y$	dispatch	$\{0\}$
1	5	$a1o = x + y$	add1	$\{(0, \{(a1i1, do1), (a1i2, do2)\})\}$
2	4	$a2o = x + y$	add2	$\{(0, \{(a2i1, do3), (a2i2, do4)\})\}$
3	7	$mo = x + y$	merge3	$\{(1, \{(mi1, a1o)\}), (2, \{(mi2, a2o)\})\}$

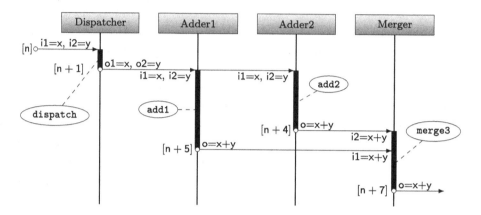

Fig. 6. Architecture proof by means of Message Sequence Chart.

4.2 Soundness and Completeness

In the following, we provide two theoretical results for APML. The first one ensures that if we can prove an architecture contract from the contracts of its components using APML, then, an architecture in which the components satisfy the corresponding contracts is indeed guaranteed to satisfy the architecture contract.

Theorem 1 (Soundness). *Given an architecture $A = (F, N)$ and corresponding contracts K_f for each interface $f \in F$, such that $\forall f \in F: \mathcal{B}_f \models K_f$. If there exists an architecture proof ps for an architecture contract $k = (tg, gr, d)$, we have $_A \otimes \mathcal{B} \models k$.*

Proof (The full proof is provided in [31]). According to Definition 7 we have to show that for all $t \in {}_A \otimes \mathcal{B}$ and all $n \in \mathbb{N}$, $(\forall j < \#tg: t(n + time(tg(j))) \models state(tg(j))) \implies t(n + d) \models gr$. Thus, we assume $\forall j < \#tg: t(n + time(tg(j))) \models state(tg(j))$ and we show by *complete* induction over the length of the proof sequence that $\forall i < \#ps: t(n + time(ps(i))) \models state(ps(i))$. Thus, $t(n + time(ps(\#ps - 1))) \models state(ps(\#ps - 1))$ and, by Eqs. (6) and (7), we can conclude $t(n + d) \models gr$. □

The second result guarantees that, whenever the satisfaction of contracts for components of an architecture leads to the satisfaction of a corresponding contract for the architecture, then it is possible to find a corresponding APML proof.

Theorem 2 (Completeness). *Given an architecture $A = (F, N)$ and corresponding contracts K_f for each interface $f \in F$. For each architecture contract k, such that for all possible behaviors $\mathcal{B}$:*

$$(\forall f \in F \colon \mathcal{B}_f \models K_f) \implies {}_A \otimes \mathcal{B} \models k \tag{8}$$

there exists an architecture proof ps for $k = (tg, gr, d)$.

Proof (The full proof is provided in [31]). For the proof we construct a "maximal" architecture proof ps, according to Definition 9, by repeatedly applying all feasible contracts. If we eventually reach an entry such that $state(ps(\#ps - 1)) \implies gr$ and $time(ps(\#ps - 1)) = d$ then we are done. If not, then we build an architecture trace $t \in \overline{(port(F))}^{\infty}$, such that $\forall j < \#tg \colon t(time(tg(j))) \models state(tg(j))$ and $\forall i < \#ps \colon t(time(ps(i))) \models state(ps(i))$ and $t(d) \not\models gr$ and for all other n, we choose $t(n)$, such that the projection to every interface $f \in F$ does not satisfy the assumptions of any contract K_f. Now, we can show that $\forall f \in F \colon \mathcal{B}_f \models K_f$ and thus, by Eq. (8) we can conclude ${}_A \otimes \mathcal{B} \models k$. Thus, since $\forall j < \#tg \colon t(time(tg(j))) \models state(tg(j))$, we can conclude $t(d) \models gr$ which is a contradiction to $t(d) \not\models gr$.   □

Algorithm 1. Mapping an APML proof to a corresponding proof in Isabelle/Isar

Input: a proof ps according to definition 9 and a function $toIsabelle$ to convert port predicates

Output: a proof in Isabelle/Isar [43]

```
 1: i = 0
 2: while i < #ps do
 3:    (tp, γ, r, rf) := ps(i); (tg, gr, d) := r;
 4:    if rf = ⟨⟩ then print "have s" + i + ": " + toIsabelle(γ, tp) + " by simp" else
 5:       i' = 0
 6:       while i' < #rf do
 7:          if i' > 0 then print "moreover " end if
 8:          print "from "
 9:          for all i'' ∈ rf(i') do print "a" + i'' + " " end for
10:          for all (i'', n') ∈ rf(i') do print "s" + i'' + " " end for
11:          print "have " + toIsabelle(state(tg(i')), time(tg(i'))) + " "
12:          if rf(i') \ ℕ ≠ ∅ then print "using " end if
13:          for all (i'', n') ∈ rf(i') and (p_i, p_o) ∈ n' do print "p_i-p_o " end for
14:          print " by simp"
15:          i' + +
16:       end while
17:       if i' = 1 then print "hence " else
18:       if i' > 1 then print "ultimately have " end if
19:       print "s" + i + ": " + toIsabelle(γ, tp) + " using " + r + " by blast" end if
20:       i + +
21: end while
22: print "thus ?thesis by auto"
```

5   From APML to Isabelle

To verify soundness of an APML proof, Algorithm 1 shows how an APML proof can be mapped to a corresponding Isar proof for the interactive theorem prover Isabelle.

Let us see how the algorithm can be applied to generate an Isar proof for the APML proof of our running example, described in Sect. 4.1. First, we create an Isabelle locale for the architecture as described in Fig. 3:

---

locale *rsum* =
  fixes
    — Dispatcher: $di1$::$nat{\Rightarrow}nat$ **and** $di2$::$nat{\Rightarrow}nat$
    and $do1$::$nat{\Rightarrow}nat$ **and** $do2$::$nat{\Rightarrow}nat$ **and** $do3$::$nat{\Rightarrow}nat$ **and** $do4$::$nat{\Rightarrow}nat$
    — Adder1: **and** $a1i1$::$nat{\Rightarrow}nat$ **and** $a1i2$::$nat{\Rightarrow}nat$ **and** $a1o$::$nat{\Rightarrow}nat$
    — Adder2: **and** $a2i1$::$nat{\Rightarrow}nat$ **and** $a2i2$::$nat{\Rightarrow}nat$ **and** $a2o$::$nat{\Rightarrow}nat$
    — Merger: **and** $mi1$::$nat{\Rightarrow}nat$ **and** $mi2$::$nat{\Rightarrow}nat$ **and** mo::$nat{\Rightarrow}nat$
    — Contracts:
  assumes *dispatch*: $\bigwedge n \; x \; y.$ $[\![di1 \; n = x; \; di2 \; n = y]\!] \Longrightarrow$
    $do1 \; (n{+}1) = x \land do2 \; (n{+}1) = y \land do3 \; (n{+}1) = x \land do4 \; (n{+}1) = y$
    and *add1*: $\bigwedge n \; x \; y.$ $[\![a1i1 \; n = x; \; a1i2 \; n = y]\!] \Longrightarrow a1o \; (n{+}4) = x + y$
    and *add2*: $\bigwedge n \; x \; y.$ $[\![a2i1 \; n = x; \; a2i2 \; n = y]\!] \Longrightarrow a2o \; (n{+}3) = x + y$
    and *merge1*: $\bigwedge n \; x.$ $[\![mi1 \; n = x; \; mi2 \; n = x]\!] \Longrightarrow mo \; (n{+}2) = x$
    and *merge2*: $\bigwedge n \; x.$ $[\![mi1 \; n = x; \; mi2 \; (n{+}1) = x]\!] \Longrightarrow mo \; (n{+}3) = x$
    and *merge3*: $\bigwedge n \; x.$ $[\![mi2 \; n = x; \; mi1 \; (n{+}1) = x]\!] \Longrightarrow mo \; (n{+}3) = x$
    — Connections
    and *do1-a1i1*: $\bigwedge n.$ $a1i1 \; n = do1 \; n$ **and** *a1i2-do2*: $\bigwedge n.$ $a1i2 \; n = do2 \; n$
    and *do3-a2i1*: $\bigwedge n.$ $a2i1 \; n = do3 \; n$ **and** *a2i2-do4*: $\bigwedge n.$ $a2i2 \; n = do4 \; n$
    and *a1o-mi1*: $\bigwedge n.$ $mi1 \; n = a1o \; n$ **and** *mi2-a2o*: $\bigwedge n.$ $mi2 \; n = a2o \; n$

Note that each contract, as presented in Fig. 4, results in a corresponding locale assumption. Now, we can create a theorem for the architecture contract described by Fig. 5:

---

theorem *sum*:
  fixes $n \; x \; y$ **assumes** *a0*: $di1 \; n = x \land di2 \; n = y$
  shows $mo \; (n{+}7) = x + y$

Finally, we can apply Algorithm 1 to create an Isar proof for the theorem from the APML proof described in Table 1:

proof –
  from *a0* **have** *di1 n = x ∧ di2 n = y* **by** *auto*
  hence *s1: do1 (n+1) = x ∧ do2 (n+1) = y ∧ do3 (n+1) = x ∧ do4 (n+1) = y*
    using *dispatch* **by** *blast*
  from *s1* **have** *a1i1 (n+1) = x ∧ a1i2 (n+1) = y*
    using *do1-a1i1 a1i2-do2* **by** *auto*
  hence *s2: a1o (n+5) = x + y* **using** *add1* **by** *blast*
  from *s1* **have** *a2i1 (n+1) = x ∧ a2i2 (n+1) = y*
    using *do3-a2i1 a2i2-do4* **by** *auto*
  hence *s3: a2o (n+4) = x + y* **using** *add2* **by** *blast*
  from *s2* **have** *mi1 (n+5) = x + y* **using** *a1o-mi1* **by** *auto*
  moreover from *s3* **have** *mi2 (n+4) = x + y* **using** *mi2-a2o* **by** *auto*
  ultimately have *mo (n+7) = x+y* **using** *merge3* **by** *blast*
  thus *?thesis* **by** *auto*
qed

6 Modeling Architecture Proofs in FACTum Studio

To support the development of APML proofs in practice, we implemented the language in FACTum Studio [32]: an architecture modeling application based on Eclipse/EMF [41]. FACTum Studio now supports the user in the development of "correct" APML proofs by means of three key features: (i) It analyses the structure of a given APML proof and checks it for syntactical errors. (ii) It uses so-called validators to check for violations of the conditions described in Definition 8 and, to a limited extent, also the ones described in Definition 9. (iii) The textual development of APML proofs in Xtext [5] is complemented by corresponding graphical notations using Sirius [35]. To support the verification of single proof steps, we implemented Algorithm 1 in FACTum Studio. Thus, after specifying an APML proof, a user can automatically generate a corresponding Isar proof for Isabelle.

Figure 7 depicts the specification of our running example in FACTum Studio: First, the architecture is specified graphically in terms of interfaces (represented as gray rectangles) and connections between their input (empty circles) and output (filled circles) ports. Then, contracts can be added for each component using a textual notation.

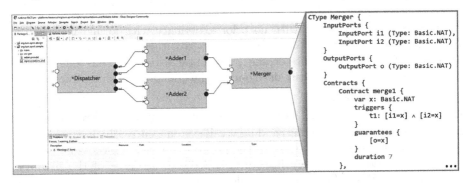

Fig. 7. Specification of reliable adder in FACTum Studio.

Figure 8 shows how we can verify the adder system using FACTUM Studio's APML implementation: After specifying the contract, we can provide a corresponding proof in terms of a sequence of proof steps as described in Definition 8.

As mentioned above, FACTUM Studio performs several checks to ensure consistency of proofs: (i) For each step it checks whether enough rationales are provided (last condition of Definition 8). (ii) It verifies that only existing connections are used in the "with" clause (last condition of Definition 8). (iii) It ensures that each step only refers to triggers of the contract or previous proof steps (condition 1 of Definition 9) (iv) It ensures consistency of the time points of contracts with those of rationales (conditions 2 and 4 of Definition 9).

```
Contract sum {
    var x: Basic.NAT,
    var y: Basic.NAT
    triggers {
        t1: [Dispatcher.i1=x] ∧ [Dispatcher.i2=y]
    }
    guarantees {
        [Merger.o=Basic.add[x,y]]
    }
    duration 7
    proof {
        s0: at 1
            have [Dispatcher.o1=x] ∧ [Dispatcher.o2=y]
            from [
                t1
            ]
            using Dispatcher.dispatch,
        s1: at 5
            have
                [Adder1.o=Basic.add[x,y]]
            from [
                s0 with [
                    (Adder1.i1, Dispatcher.o1),
                    (Adder1.i2, Dispatcher.o2)
                ]
            ]
            using Adder1.add1,              ...
```

Fig. 8. APML proof in FACTUM Studio.

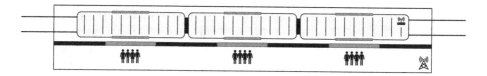

Fig. 9. Automatic Train Control System

7 Case Study: Trainguard MT Control System

We evaluated our approach by applying it for the verification of a railway-control system. To investigate whether the approach can indeed be used to apply interactive theorem proving by users not trained in using this technology, verification was performed by a subject with no prior experience with formal methods in general and specifically with the use of interactive theorem provers. The subject holds a Bachelor of Science degree in computer science and has four years of industrial experience as software developer in the domain of business information systems.

Study Context. Trainguard MT (TGMT) is an automatic train control system for metros, rapid transit, commuter, and light rail systems currently in development by one of our industrial partners. For the purpose of this case study, we focused on the verification of one key feature of TGMT: controlling of the platform screen doors (PSDs). The situation is depicted by Fig. 9: In an effort to make train stations safer for the passengers, modern stations protect their rail zone with a wall (represented by a black line) with several doors (represented by gray lines), the so-called PSDs. When a train arrives at the station, its onboard control unit communicates with the Wayside control unit to control opening/closing of the PSDs.

Study Setup. To model the PSD functionality, the company provided four documents as input, which were taken directly from the PSD development: a high-level system requirements specification (59 pages), a more detailed system architecture specification (299 pages), a performance specification (57 pages), and a glossary (42 pages). Based on the documents, we specified a corresponding architecture for the PSD functionality, consisting of 33 components with 36 contracts in total.

Study Execution. The subject then verified five architecture contracts: (P1) If the train is moving, the PSDs are closed. (P2) If the train is at standstill and the position of the train doors match the position of the PSDs, the PSDs are opened. (P3) If the train doors open on the right hand side, the platform must be on the right hand side. (P4) If door release is permissive and the train is at standstill, its doors are open. (P5) When the train indicates that the doors are closed, the PSDs are closed.

Results. After a study of the architecture and a brief introduction into APML, the subject was able to verify versions of all the properties with no further guidance. Figure 10 depicts the verification effort in terms of APML proof steps required for each property. In total, the subject required roughly 25 working hours to develop the proofs. Sometimes, however, the original contracts needed to be adapted to fit the structure of a contract as defined by Definition 6. This was mainly due to two reasons: (i) Some of the contracts

Fig. 10. Number of proof steps for each property.

required to express statements of the form "whenever x happens, after n time points y happens *and in between z holds*". (ii) In addition, some components required contracts combined by disjunction rather than conjunction. Moreover, the proofs for properties P1 and P5 share a common proof sequence of 8 proof steps, which is more than 50% of the steps required to proof the properties. Finally, some of the proof steps could only be discharged by adapting the generated Isabelle script to tune the simplifier and the logical reasoner, respectively.

Conclusions. From our results, we derive the following conclusions:

C1 The approach can be used to support users with no prior experience with formal methods in the development of proofs for interactive theorem provers.

C2 Some of the properties sometimes required in a practical setting cannot yet be expressed by the notion of contract used in this paper.

C3 The verification of properties can involve considerable, redundant proof sequences.

C4 Some initial setup may be required to automatically discharge generated proof steps.

8 Related Work

Related work can be found in two different areas: verification of contract-based specifications and interactive verification of component-based systems.

Verification of Contract-Based Specifications. Verification of contract-based specifications is not a new topic, at all. First works in this area go back to Pnueli's work about modular model checking [37] and Clarke's work on compositional model checking [14], in which they investigated possibilities to leverage assumptions about a component's environment for the verification of its implementation. Later on, attempts were made to automatically synthesize minimal assumptions from a component's implementation [7,19,20,36]. In all these studies, the focus is mainly on the verification of component implementations under the presence of assumptions about its environment. In contrary, the focus of the work presented in this paper, is on the verification of contract-composition, without even considering component implementations.

Another line of research in this area is work which focuses on the analysis of contract compatibility. In parametric AG reasoning [39], there may even be many assumptions and guarantees for each component. An example of work in this area is Damm et al. [16], in which the authors describe an approach for virtual integration testing based on rich components. Another example is the work of Chilton et al. [11], which provides an approach to AG reasoning for safety properties. Later on, Kugele and Marmsoler [25] provide an approach to check compatibility of AG contracts using SMT solvers [17]. Finally, Broy [8] provides a detailed characterization about compatible assumptions and guarantees for FOCUS [9]. While the work in this line of research also focuses on the verification at the level of contracts, the focus is mainly on the verification of contract compatibility. With our work, however, we focus on a related, though different problem: verification of refinement of contracts.

Work in this area of research which is most closely related to our work is Cimatti's work on OCRA [12,13]. Here, the author proposes an approach based on bounded model checking [6] to verify refinement of LTL-based contracts. With our work, we follow a similar goal by applying an alternative approach based on interactive theorem proving, which is why we actually complement Cimatti's work.

Interactive Verification Component based Systems. There exists some work which investigates the application of interactive theorem proving (ITP) for the verification of component-based systems. Fensel and Schnogge [21], for example, apply the KIV interactive theorem prover [38] to verify architectures in the area of knowledge-based systems. More recently, some attempts were made to apply ITP for the verification of architectural connectors: Li and Sun [26], for example, apply the Coq proof assistant [4] to verify connectors specified in Reo [1].

Moreover, there exists work on the formalization of OCL [42] in Isabelle [10]. In addition, Spichkova [40] provides a framework for the verification of component-based systems in Isabelle and Marmsoler [28] extends the work to deal with dynamic reconfiguration. Also the mechanization of UTP [23] in Isabelle, due by Foster et al. [22], belongs to this line of research. However, while most of these works focus on the interactive verification of component based systems, verification is usually done at the level of the prover. With the work presented in this paper, we aim to contribute to this line of research by exploring possibilities and limitations of synthesizing proofs for the provers from architectural descriptions.

Summary. Concluding, to the best of our knowledge, this is the first attempt to synthesize proof for an interactive theorem prover for the verification of contract composition from architectural descriptions.

9   Conclusion

With this paper, we introduced APML: an architecture proof modeling language. To this end, we first introduced a formal semantics for component contracts as well as architecture contracts. Then, we described APML and showed soundness and completeness of it for the verification of architecture contracts. Moreover, we presented an algorithm to map an APML proof to a corresponding proof in Isabelle/Isar and discussed its implementation in Eclipse/EMF. Finally, we demonstrated the approach by means of a running example and evaluated it by means of a larger case study from the railway domain.

Our theoretical results (Sect. 4.2) show that APML can indeed be used to specify abstract proofs for the composition of contracts using a notation similar to Message Sequence Charts. Moreover, as indicated by C1 of our case study, it supports users with no prior experience in interactive theorem proving in the development of proofs. Thus, APML indeed contributes to the overall goal of bridging the gap between software architecture and interactive theorem proving. Nevertheless, the case study also revealed some limitations of the approach, which should be addressed by future work: As indicated by C2, future work should investigate possibilities to enhance expressiveness of the contracts. Specifically, the support for until-like contracts and disjunction of contracts should be investigated. Moreover, as indicated by C3, future work should investigate possibilities to support reuse of proof sequences. To this end, a proof step should be allowed to reference to already verified contracts. Finally, as indicated by C4, future work should investigate possibilities to increase automation at the level of interactive theorem proving.

Acknowledgments. We would like to thank Simon Foster and Mario Gleirscher for inspiring discussions about APML. Parts of the work on which we report in this paper was funded by the German Federal Ministry of Education and Research (BMBF) under grant no. 01Is16043A.

References

1. Arbab, F.: Reo: a channel-based coordination model for component composition. Math. Struct. Comput. Sci. **14**(03), 329–366 (2004)
2. Baier, C., Katoen, J., Larsen, K.: Principles of Model Checking. MIT Press (2008). https://books.google.de/books?id=nDQiAQAAIAAJ
3. Ballarin, C.: Locales and locale expressions in Isabelle/Isar. In: Berardi, S., Coppo, M., Damiani, F. (eds.) TYPES 2003. LNCS, vol. 3085, pp. 34–50. Springer, Heidelberg (2004). https://doi.org/10.1007/978-3-540-24849-1_3
4. Barras, B., et al.: The Coq proof assistant reference manual: version 6.1. Ph.D. thesis, Inria (1997)
5. Bettini, L.: Implementing Domain-specific Languages with Xtext and Xtend. Packt Publishing Ltd., Birmingham (2016)
6. Biere, A., Cimatti, A., Clarke, E., Zhu, Y.: Symbolic model checking without BDDs. In: Cleaveland, W.R. (ed.) TACAS 1999. LNCS, vol. 1579, pp. 193–207. Springer, Heidelberg (1999). https://doi.org/10.1007/3-540-49059-0_14
7. Gheorghiu Bobaru, M., Păsăreanu, C.S., Giannakopoulou, D.: Automated assume-guarantee reasoning by abstraction refinement. In: Gupta, A., Malik, S. (eds.) CAV 2008. LNCS, vol. 5123, pp. 135–148. Springer, Heidelberg (2008). https://doi.org/10.1007/978-3-540-70545-1_14
8. Broy, M.: Theory and methodology of assumption/commitment based system interface specification and architectural contracts. Formal Methods Syst. Des. **52**(1), 33–87 (2018). https://doi.org/10.1007/s10703-017-0304-9
9. Broy, M., Stølen, K.: Specification and Development of Interactive Systems: Focus on Streams, Interfaces, and Refinement. Springer, Heidelberg (2012)
10. Brucker, A.D., Wolff, B.: A proposal for a formal OCL semantics in Isabelle/HOL. In: Carreño, V.A., Muñoz, C.A., Tahar, S. (eds.) TPHOLs 2002. LNCS, vol. 2410, pp. 99–114. Springer, Heidelberg (2002). https://doi.org/10.1007/3-540-45685-6_8
11. Chilton, C., Jonsson, B., Kwiatkowska, M.: Assume-guarantee reasoning for safe component behaviours. In: Păsăreanu, C.S., Salaün, G. (eds.) FACS 2012. LNCS, vol. 7684, pp. 92–109. Springer, Heidelberg (2013). https://doi.org/10.1007/978-3-642-35861-6_6
12. Cimatti, A., Dorigatti, M., Tonetta, S.: OCRA: a tool for checking the refinement of temporal contracts. In: 2013 28th IEEE/ACM International Conference on Automated Software Engineering (ASE), pp. 702–705, November 2013
13. Cimatti, A., Tonetta, S.: Contracts-refinement proof system for component-based embedded systems. Sci. Comput. Program. **97**(P3), 333–348 (2015). https://doi.org/10.1016/j.scico.2014.06.011
14. Clarke, E.M., Long, D.E., McMillan, K.L.: Compositional model checking. In: 1989 Proceedings of Fourth Annual Symposium on Logic in Computer Science, pp. 353–362. IEEE (1989)
15. Damm, W., Harel, D.: LSCs: breathing life into message sequence charts. Formal Methods Syst. Des. **19**(1), 45–80 (2001)
16. Damm, W., Hungar, H., Josko, B., Peikenkamp, T., Stierand, I.: Using contract-based component specifications for virtual integration testing and architecture design. In: 2011 Design, Automation & Test in Europe, pp. 1–6. IEEE (2011)
17. De Moura, L., Bjørner, N.: Satisfiability modulo theories: introduction and applications. Commun. ACM **54**(9), 69–77 (2011). https://doi.org/10.1145/1995376.1995394

18. Dwyer, M.B., Avrunin, G.S., Corbett, J.C.: Patterns in property specifications for finite-state verification. In: Proceedings of the 1999 International Conference on Software Engineering (IEEE Cat. No. 99CB37002), pp. 411–420. IEEE (1999)

19. Elkader, K.A., Grumberg, O., Păsăreanu, C.S., Shoham, S.: Automated circular assume-guarantee reasoning. In: Bjørner, N., de Boer, F. (eds.) FM 2015. LNCS, vol. 9109, pp. 23–39. Springer, Cham (2015). https://doi.org/10.1007/978-3-319-19249-9_3

20. Emmi, M., Giannakopoulou, D., Păsăreanu, C.S.: Assume-guarantee verification for interface automata. In: Cuellar, J., Maibaum, T., Sere, K. (eds.) FM 2008. LNCS, vol. 5014, pp. 116–131. Springer, Heidelberg (2008). https://doi.org/10.1007/978-3-540-68237-0_10

21. Fensel, D., Schnogge, A.: Using KIV to specify and verify architectures of knowledge-based systems. In: Automated Software Engineering, pp. 71–80, November 1997

22. Foster, S., Zeyda, F., Woodcock, J.: Isabelle/UTP: a mechanised theory engineering framework. In: Naumann, D. (ed.) UTP 2014. LNCS, vol. 8963, pp. 21–41. Springer, Cham (2015). https://doi.org/10.1007/978-3-319-14806-9_2

23. Hoare, C.A.R., Jifeng, H.: Unifying Theories of Programming, vol. 14. Prentice Hall, Englewood Cliffs (1998)

24. Huber, F., Schätz, B., Schmidt, A., Spies, K.: AutoFocus—a tool for distributed systems specification. In: Jonsson, B., Parrow, J. (eds.) FTRTFT 1996. LNCS, vol. 1135, pp. 467–470. Springer, Heidelberg (1996). https://doi.org/10.1007/3-540-61648-9_58

25. Kugele, S., Marmsoler, D., Mata, N., Werther, K.: Verification of component architectures using mode-based contracts. In: 2016 ACM/IEEE International Conference on Formal Methods and Models for System Design, MEMOCODE 2016, Kanpur, India, 18–20 November 2016, pp. 133–142. IEEE (2016). https://doi.org/10.1109/MEMCOD.2016.7797758

26. Li, Y., Sun, M.: Modeling and analysis of component connectors in Coq. In: Fiadeiro, J.L., Liu, Z., Xue, J. (eds.) FACS 2013. LNCS, vol. 8348, pp. 273–290. Springer, Cham (2014). https://doi.org/10.1007/978-3-319-07602-7_17

27. Marmsoler, D., Gleirscher, M.: On activation, connection, and behavior in dynamic architectures. Sci. Ann. Comput. Sci. **26**(2), 187–248 (2016)

28. Marmsoler, D.: A framework for interactive verification of architectural design patterns in Isabelle/HOL. In: Sun, J., Sun, M. (eds.) ICFEM 2018. LNCS, vol. 11232, pp. 251–269. Springer, Cham (2018). https://doi.org/10.1007/978-3-030-02450-5_15

29. Marmsoler, D.: Hierarchical specification and verification of architectural design patterns. In: Russo, A., Schürr, A. (eds.) FASE 2018. LNCS, vol. 10802, pp. 149–168. Springer, Cham (2018). https://doi.org/10.1007/978-3-319-89363-1_9

30. Marmsoler, D.: Verifying dynamic architectures using model checking and interactive theorem proving. In: Becker, S., Bogicevic, I., Herzwurm, G., Wagner, S. (eds.) Software Engineering and Software Management 2019, pp. 167–169. Gesellschaft für Informatik e.V., Bonn (2019). https://doi.org/10.18420/se2019-52

31. Marmsoler, D., Blakqori, G.: APML: An architecture proof modeling language. https://arxiv.org/abs/1907.03723, July 2019. Extended preprint

32. Marmsoler, D., Gidey, H.K.: FACTUM studio: a tool for the axiomatic specification and verification of architectural design patterns. In: Bae, K., Ölveczky, P.C. (eds.) FACS 2018. LNCS, vol. 11222, pp. 279–287. Springer, Cham (2018). https://doi.org/10.1007/978-3-030-02146-7_14

33. Marmsoler, D., Gleirscher, M.: Specifying properties of dynamic architectures using configuration traces. In: Sampaio, A., Wang, F. (eds.) ICTAC 2016. LNCS, vol. 9965, pp. 235–254. Springer, Cham (2016). https://doi.org/10.1007/978-3-319-46750-4_14

34. Nipkow, T., Wenzel, M., Paulson, L.C. (eds.): Isabelle/HOL: A Proof Assistant for Higher-Order Logic. LNCS, vol. 2283. Springer, Heidelberg (2002). https://doi.org/10.1007/3-540-45949-9

35. Obeo: Sirius. https://www.eclipse.org/sirius/

36. Păsăreanu, C.S., Dwyer, M.B., Huth, M.: Assume-guarantee model checking of software: a comparative case study. In: Dams, D., Gerth, R., Leue, S., Massink, M. (eds.) SPIN 1999. LNCS, vol. 1680, pp. 168–183. Springer, Heidelberg (1999). https://doi.org/10.1007/3-540-48234-2_14. http://dl.acm.org/citation.cfm?id=64 5879.672067

37. Pnueli, A.: In transition from global to modular temporal reasoning about programs. In: Apt, K.R. (ed.) Logics and Models of Concurrent Systems. NATO ASI Series (Series F: Computer and Systems Sciences), vol. 13, pp. 123–144. Springer, Berlin (1985). https://doi.org/10.1007/978-3-642-82453-1_5

38. Reif, W.: The Kiv-approach to software verification. In: Broy, M., Jähnichen, S. (eds.) KORSO: Methods, Languages, and Tools for the Construction of Correct Software. LNCS, vol. 1009, pp. 339–368. Springer, Heidelberg (1995). https://doi.org/10.1007/BFb0015471

39. Reussner, R.H., Becker, S., Firus, V.: Component composition with parametric contracts. In: Tagungsband der Net. ObjectDays 2004, pp. 155–169 (2004)

40. Spichkova, M.: Focus on Isabelle: from specification to verification. In: 21st International Conference on Theorem Proving in Higher Order Logics, p. 104. Citeseer (2008)

41. Steinberg, D., Budinsky, F., Merks, E., Paternostro, M.: EMF: Eclipse Modeling Framework. Pearson Education, London (2008)

42. Warmer, J.B., Kleppe, A.G.: The Object Constraint Language: Precise Modeling with UML. Addison-Wesley Object Technology Series (1998)

43. Wenzel, M.: The Isabelle/Isar reference manual (2004)

44. Wenzel, M.: Isabelle/Isar - a generic framework for human-readable proof documents. In: From Insight to Proof - Festschrift in Honour of Andrzej Trybulec, vol. 10, no. 23, pp. 277–298 (2007)

Learning-Based Techniques and Applications

Learning Deterministic Variable Automata over Infinite Alphabets

Sarai Sheinvald$^{(\boxtimes)}$

Department of Software Engineering, Braude College of Engineering, Karmiel, Israel
sarai@braude.ac.il

Abstract. Automated reasoning about systems with infinite domains requires an extension of automata, and in particular, finite automata, to *infinite alphabets*. One such model is Variable Finite Automata (VFA). VFAs are finite automata whose alphabet is interpreted as variables that range over an infinite domain. On top of their simple and intuitive structure, VFAs have many appealing properties. One such property is a *deterministic* fragment (DVFA), which is closed under the Boolean operations, and whose containment and emptiness problems are decidable. These properties are rare amongst the many different models for automata over infinite alphabets. In this paper, we continue to explore the advantages of DVFAs, and show that they have a canonical form, which proves them to be a particularly robust model that is easy to reason about and use in practice. Building on these results, we construct an efficient learning algorithm for DVFAs, based on the L* algorithm for regular languages.

1 Introduction

Automata-based formal methods are successfully applied in automated reasoning about systems. When the systems are finite-state, their behaviors and specifications can be modeled by finite automata. Infinite-state systems, and in particular systems over infinite data domains, such as communication and e-commerce systems or large databases, require models that can handle languages over infinite alphabets.

Many types of automata over infinite alphabets have been defined and studied, with varying closure and decidability properties. We briefly survey some of these models.

A *register automaton* [SF94] has a finite set of registers, each of which may contain a letter from the infinite alphabet. The transitions of a register automaton compare and store the input letter in a register. Several variants of this model have been studied. For example, [KF94] forces the inequality in the registers content, [NSV01] adds alternation and two-wayness, and [KZ08] allows the registers to change their content nondeterministically during the run.

A *pebble automaton* [NSV01] places pebbles on the input word in a stack-like manner. The transitions of a pebble automaton compare the letter in the

© Springer Nature Switzerland AG 2019
M. H. ter Beek et al. (Eds.): FM 2019, LNCS 11800, pp. 633–650, 2019.
https://doi.org/10.1007/978-3-030-30942-8_37

input with the letters in positions marked by the pebbles. Several variants of this model have been studied. For example, [NSV01] studies alternating and two-way pebble automata, and [Tan09] introduces top-view weak pebble automata.

A *data automaton* [BMS+06, BMSS09] runs on *data words*, which are words over the alphabet $\Sigma \times F$, where Σ is infinite and F is a finite auxiliary alphabet. A data automaton consists of two components. The first is a letter-to-letter transducer that runs on the projection of the input word on F and generates words over yet another alphabet Γ. The second is a regular automaton that runs on subwords (determined by the equivalence classes of letter equality) of the word generated by the transducer.

Symbolic automata allow the transitions to carry predicates over an infinite alphabet, determining the subset from which the letter that is read along the transition is taken. Different theories lead to different types of languages, and [DD17, AD18] study learning of symbolic automata.

Variable finite automata (VFA) [GKS10], are a special case of nondeterministic register automata, in which some of the registers are preassigned values that do not change during the run, and one register is allowed free assignments. VFAs are especially convenient to work with, as they can be easily modeled by standard nondeterministic finite automata (NFA). A VFA is an NFA A over a *pattern alphabet*, which consists of constant letters, *bound variables*, which may be assigned the same unique letter throughout the run, and a *free variable*, which is freely assigned during the run. Thus, every word in the *pattern language* of A induces a set of words over the infinite alphabet. Modeling VFAs as NFAs allows using standard methods for NFAs for various computations for VFAs. For example, checking the emptiness of a VFA amounts to checking the emptiness of the underlying pattern NFA. VFAs have further appealing properties: they are closed under union and intersection, and their emptiness is NL-complete,

[GKS10] also identified a deterministic fragment of VFA, called DVFA, in which every word over the infinite alphabet has a single run. DVFAs are the focus of this paper. It does not suffice for the pattern NFA of a DFA to be a deterministic finite automaton, as a word w may have several different pattern words, which differ in the variables that are assigned the letters of w. However, [GKS10] shows that syntactic conditions on the pattern NFA do exist, and can be easily checked. DVFAs are closed under the Boolean operations, and their emptiness and universality problems are NL-complete. These qualities are rare in the realm of automata over infinite alphabets, which, in general, tend to be highly undecidable.

In [FGS18], VFAs were generalized to *alternating variable automata*, which were shown to model a fragment of first order LTL, an extension of LTL that expresses properties of systems over infinite data. The full capacity of VFAs is not always needed, and in many useful cases such properties can be modeled by VFAs and DVFAs. For example, the property "Every communication interaction begins and ends by transmitting the same interaction ID" can be modeled by DVFA.

Session automata were introduced in [BHLM14]. Like VFA, session automata are a special case of register automata, in which registers may be reassigned with fresh values only. [BHLM14] showed that session automata are a decidable and closed model. Moreover, session automata have a canonical form, which enables an L*-based learning algorithm for them. Session automata are incomparable with DVFA. For example, session automata are able to express the language of all words whose letters are different which DVFAs cannot express, but are unable to express the language of all words whose first and last letters are similar, which DVFAs can express.

The automata learning algorithm L*, first introduced in [Ang87], consists of two entities: a *learner*, whose goal is to construct an automaton for a language $\mathcal{L}$, and a *teacher*, who helps the learner by answering *membership queries* – " is $w \in L$?", and *equivalence queries* – " is A an automaton for $\mathcal{L}$?". In case that A does not accept $\mathcal{L}$, the teacher also returns a counterexample: a word which is accepted by A and is not in $\mathcal{L}$, or vice versa. [Ang87] presented a learning algorithm for regular languages, in which the learner constructs a minimal finite automaton for $\mathcal{L}$, which runs in polynomial time in the number of states in the automaton and in the length of the longest counterexample that is returned by the teacher in the process.

Automata learning has useful applications in system verification. For example, [PGB+08] uses learning of regular languages in order to find a minimal component in an assume-guarantee style compositional verification.

In this paper, we show that on top of their previously known advantages, and much like session automata, DVFAs have a canonical form, called *ordered* DVFA, which allows a standard representation to every language that is expressible by a DVFA. Essentially, an ordered DVFA dictates an order of using the bound variables, so that every word has a single possible pattern word. As in the case of regular languages, this ordered form is based on an equivalence relation that is defined over the language. In the case of DVFAs, the relation is over the pattern language. The ordered form enables finding an equivalent ordered DVFA that is not only minimal in the number of states, but also uses a minimal number of variables.

We then exploit the canonical form of DVFAs to construct a learning algorithm for them, called DVL*, that is based on the L* algorithm. In our case, not only the state space of the DVFA is unknown in advance, but also its set of variables. DVL* manages finding both the minimal ordered DVFA and the minimal set of variables needed to express the language $\mathcal{L}$ that it learns.

A run of DVL* proceeds in iterations. In every iteration, an ordered DVFA is constructed, based on the current pattern alphabet and the current answers of the teacher to the membership and equivalence queries. Membership queries are submitted for concrete words over the infinite alphabet, which are translated by DVL* to pattern words over the current pattern alphabet. Once it is recognized that the current number of variables does not suffice to distinguish between two words w_1, w_2 that do not agree on their membership to $\mathcal{L}$, then more variables are added in a way that distinguishes between the pattern words of w_1 and w_2, and a new iteration begins.

We prove the correctness of DVL*, and demonstrate its details with an example.

2   Preliminaries

A *nondeterministic finite automaton* (NFA) is a tuple $A = \langle \Gamma, Q, q_0, \delta, F \rangle$, where Γ is a finite alphabet, Q is a finite set of *states*, $q_0 \in Q$ is an initial state, $\delta : Q \times \Gamma \to 2^Q$ is a *transition function*, and $F \subseteq Q$ is a set of *accepting states*. If $\delta(q, a) \neq \emptyset$, we say that a *exits* q. A *run of A* on a word $w = \sigma_1 \sigma_2 \dots \sigma_n$ in Γ^* is a sequence of states $r = r_0, r_1, \dots, r_n$ such that $r_0 = q_0$ and for every $1 \leq i \leq n$ it holds that $r_i \in \delta(r_{i-1}, \sigma_i)$. If $r_n \in F$ then r is *accepting*. Note that a run may not exist. If a run does exist, we say that w is *read along A*. If a run of A on w reaches a state q, we denote $q \in \delta^*(q_0, w)$. The language of A, denoted $L(A)$, is the set of words w for which there exists an accepting run of A on w.

An NFA is *deterministic* (DFA) if for every $q \in Q$ and every $a \in \Gamma$, there is a single state q' such that $q' \in \delta(q, a)$. Consequently, a DFA has exactly one run over every word over Γ.

Let Σ be an infinite alphabet, and let $\Gamma = \Sigma_A \cup X \cup \{y\}$, where $\Sigma_A \subset \Sigma$ is a finite set of *constant letters*, X is a finite set of *bound variables* and y is a *free variable*. The variables range over $\Sigma \setminus \Sigma_A$. We refer to Γ as a *pattern alphabet*.

Consider a word $u = u_1 u_2 \dots u_n \in \Gamma^*$, and a word $w = w_1 w_2 \dots w_n \in \Sigma^*$. We say that w is a *legal instance of u* if

- $u_i = w_i$ for every $u_i \in \Sigma_A$,
- For $u_i, u_j \in X$, it holds that $w_i = w_j$ iff $u_i = u_j$, and $w_i, w_j \notin \Sigma_A$, and
- For $u_i = y$ and $u_j \neq y$, it holds that $w_i \neq w_j$.

Intuitively, a legal instance of u leaves all occurrences of $u_i \in \Sigma_A$ unchanged, associates all occurrences of $u_j \in X$ with the same unique letter, not in Σ_A, and associates every occurrence of y freely with letters from $\Sigma \setminus \Sigma_A$, different from those associated with X variables.

We say that a word $u \in \Gamma^*$ is a *pattern word* for a word $w \in \Sigma^*$ if w is a legal instance of u. We sometimes refer to $w \in \Sigma^*$ as a *concrete word*. Note that u may be the pattern word for infinitely many words in Σ^*, and that a word in Σ^* may have several pattern words (or have none). The *language* of u, denoted $L(u)$, is the set of all legal instances of u. We denote the set of variables that occur in u by $var(u)$.

A *variable finite automaton* (VFA) is a pair $\mathcal{A} = \langle \Sigma, A \rangle$, where Σ is an infinite alphabet and A is an NFA over a pattern alphabet Γ, which we call the *pattern automaton* of $\mathcal{A}$, and its language (over Γ) is the *pattern language* of $\mathcal{A}$. The language of $\mathcal{A}$, denoted $L(\mathcal{A})$, is $\bigcup_{u \in L(A)} L(u)$. That is, $L(\mathcal{A})$ is the set of words in Σ^* for which there exists a pattern word in $L(A)$.

For a word $w \in \Sigma^*$, a *run of $\mathcal{A}$ on w* is a run of A on a pattern word for w.

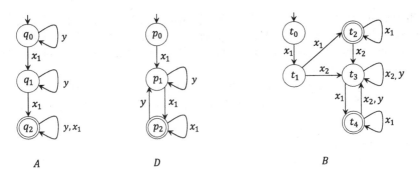

Fig. 1. The pattern automata for $\mathcal{A}$, $\mathcal{D}$, and $\mathcal{B}$.

Example 1. Let $\mathcal{A} = \langle \Sigma, A \rangle$ where A is the NFA appearing in Fig. 1. Then, $L(\mathcal{A})$ is the language of all words in Σ^* in which some letter appears at least twice. By deleting the x_1 labels from the self loop in q_2, we get the language of all words in which some letter appears exactly twice.

A VFA $\mathcal{A} = \langle \Sigma, A \rangle$ is *deterministic* (DVFA, for short), if for every word $w \in \Sigma^*$, there exists exactly one run of $\mathcal{A}$ on w.

Note that, equivalently, a VFA is deterministic if for every word in Σ^* there is exactly one pattern word on which there is a single run in the pattern automaton.

Example 2. Consider the VFA $\mathcal{D} = \langle \Sigma, D \rangle$, where D is the DFA appearing in Fig. 1. The language of $\mathcal{D}$ is the set of all words over Σ in which the first letter equal to the last letter. To see that $\mathcal{D}$ is deterministic, consider a word $w = w_1 w_2 \ldots w_n$ in Σ^*. A pattern word for w is over x_1 and y. Since only x_1 exits the initial state, then x_1 must be assigned w_1, and all other occurrences of other letters must be assigned to y. Therefore, every word w has a single pattern word u that is read along D. Since D is deterministic, every pattern word has a single run in D. It follows that $\mathcal{D}$ is deterministic.

It is not enough for the pattern automaton to be deterministic for a VFA $\mathcal{A}$ to be deterministic, since there can be several different pattern words to the same word w. However, a syntactic characterization does exists, as shown in [GKS10]. A VFA with a pattern automaton $A = \langle \Gamma, Q, q_0, \delta, F \rangle$ is deterministic iff the following hold.

1. For every $\sigma \in \Gamma_A$ and every $q \in Q$, exactly one transition labeled σ exits q,
2. For every $z \in X \cup \{y\}$ and every $q \in Q$, at most one transition labeled z exits q,
3. For every $q \in Q$ and every $z \in X \cup \{y\}$ that occurs along a path from q_0 to q, it holds that z exits q,
4. For every $q \in Q$, either y exits q, or a variable $x \in X$ that does not occur along a path from q_0 to q exits q (but not both).

These conditions make sure that from every state q there is exactly one transition with every letter in Σ_A, one transition with every letter that has been read up to q, and one transition with a new letter. The latter is ensured by condition 4.

DVFAs are closed under the Boolean operations. Moreover, their emptiness, universality and containment problems are NL-complete, and membership is in P.

We say that a language $\mathcal{L}$ over Σ^* is *deterministic* if there exists a DVFA $\mathcal{D}$ such that $L(\mathcal{D}) = \mathcal{L}$.

3   A Canonical Form for DVFA

In this section we show that deterministic languages have a canonical form, much like regular languages. The form is based on an ordering on the variables in a way that ensures that every word over the infinite alphabet Σ has a single ordered pattern word.

Let Σ_A be a set of constant letters. For $k \in \mathbb{N}$, we denote the pattern alphabet $\Sigma_A \cup \{x_1, x_2, \ldots x_k, y\}$ by Γ_k.

Definition 1. *Let u be a pattern word over Γ_k. We say that u is Γ_k-ordered if the following hold.*

1. *For every $1 \le i < j \le k$, the first occurrence of x_i in u precedes the first occurrence of x_j in u.*
2. *y occurs in u only after x_k first occurs in u.*

Example 3. For $\Sigma_A = \{a\}$,

- $x_1 a x_2 x_1 y x_1$ is Γ_2-ordered.
- $x_1 y a x_2$ is not Γ_k-ordered for every $k \in \mathbb{N}$, since y occurs before x_2 first occurs.
- $x_1 x_3 x_1$ is not Γ_k-ordered for every $\Gamma_k \in \mathbb{N}$, since x_3 occurs before x_2 first occurs.

We denote by $\mathcal{O}(\Gamma_k)$ the set of all Γ_k-ordered words over Γ_k. We match every word $w \in \Sigma^*$ with a pattern word $o_{\Gamma_k}(w) \in \mathcal{O}(\Gamma_k)$, which we call the Γ_k-*ordering* of w, as follows. Let $\sigma_1, \sigma_2, \ldots \sigma_j$ be the letters in $\Sigma \setminus \Sigma_A$ that occur in w, ordered by their first occurrence in w. The word $o_{\Gamma_k}(w)$ is obtained from w by replacing every occurrence of σ_i with x_i for $1 \le i \le k$, and by y for $k < i \le j$.

It is easy to see that for every $w \in \Sigma^*$, it holds that $w \in L(o_{\Gamma_k}(w))$, and that $o_{\Gamma_k}(w)$ is the only Γ_k-ordered pattern word for w.

Example 4. For $\Sigma_A = a$ and $w = cddaefcg$, we have

- $o_{\Gamma_0}(w) = yyyayyyy$
- $o_{\Gamma_1}(w) = x_1 yyayyx_1 y$
- $o_{\Gamma_2}(w) = x_1 x_2 x_2 ayyx_1 y$

Lemma 1. *Let* $D = \langle \Gamma_k, Q, q_0, \delta, F \rangle$ *be an NFA that meets the following conditions.*

1. *For every state* $q \in Q$ *and every* $\alpha \in \Gamma_k$, *at most one transition labeled* α *exits* q,
2. *For every* $u \in \Gamma_k^*$, *it holds that* u *is read along* D *iff* $u \in \mathcal{O}(\Gamma_k)$.

Let $\mathcal{D}$ *be a VFA whose pattern automaton is* D. *Then the following hold.*

1. $\mathcal{D}$ *is a DVFA,*
2. *For every state* $q \in Q$ *there exists* $0 \leq i \leq k$ *such that every word* u *for which* $q \in \delta^*(q_0, u)$, *it holds that* $var(u) = \{x_1, \ldots x_i\}$, *and if* $i = k$, $var(u)$ *may also contain* y.

Intuitively, every word $w \in \Sigma^*$ has exactly one run in $\mathcal{D}$, on its Γ_k-ordering. Moreover, for two pattern words u_1, u_2 that reach the same state q, for every letter a that exits q, it must hold that both $u_1 \cdot a$ and $u_2 \cdot a$ are ordered, which is possible only if they contain the same set of bound variables.

We call a DVFA that meets the conditions of Lemma 1 a Γ_k-*ordered DVFA*. We call a DVFA that is Γ_k-ordered for some k an *ordered DVFA*. For example, in Fig. 1, the DVFA $\mathcal{D}$ whose pattern automaton D is Γ_1-ordered, and the DVFA $\mathcal{B}$ whose pattern automaton is B is Γ_2-ordered.

According to Lemma 1, for a state q in a Γ_k-ordered DVFA $\mathcal{D}$, all words that are read along $\mathcal{D}$ from the initial state to q have the same set of bound variables $\{x_1, x_2, \ldots x_i\}$, for some $0 \leq i \leq k$. We then say that q is in *level* i in $\mathcal{D}$.

We now show that every DVFA has an equivalent ordered DVFA.

Theorem 1. *Let* $\mathcal{D} = \langle D, \Sigma \rangle$ *be a DVFA over* Γ_k. *Then there exists an equivalent* Γ_k'-*ordered DVFA* $\mathcal{D}' = \langle D', \Sigma \rangle$, *where* Γ_k' *is a pattern alphabet over* Σ_A *with* k *bound variables.*

Proof. Let $D = \langle \Gamma_k, Q, q_0, \delta, F \rangle$. Intuitively, we unwind D while maintaining a function that assigns new variable names to the variables of D.

Let $\Gamma_k' = \Sigma_A \cup Z \cup \{y'\}$, where $Z = \{z_1, z_2, \ldots z_k\}$ is a set of bound variables, and y' is a free variable. The states of D' are $Q \times G$, where $G = \{x_1, x_2, \ldots x_k, y\}^{\{z_1, z_2, \ldots z_k\}}$ is the set of one-to-one partial functions from $\{z_1, z_2, \ldots z_k\}$ to $\{x_1, x_2, \ldots x_k, y\}$. We denote the domain of a partial function $g \in G$ by $Dom(g)$, its range by $Range(g)$, and the maximal index of a bound variable in Z in $Dom(g)$ by $max(g)$. If $g = \emptyset$, then $max(g) = 0$. The initial state of D' is $s_0 = \langle q_0, \emptyset \rangle$. We construct the transition relation δ' of D' in two stages. In the first stage, we translate the transitions in D over X to transitions of D' over Z, in increasing order of variable indices. We add transitions to δ' as follows.

1. For every $\langle q, a, q' \rangle \in \delta$, where $a \in \Sigma_A$, we add $\langle \langle q, g \rangle, a, \langle q', g \rangle \rangle$ to δ' for every $g \in G$.
2. For every $\langle q, x_i, q' \rangle \in \delta$, we add $\langle \langle q, g \rangle, z_j, \langle q', g \rangle \rangle$ to δ' for every $g \in G$ such that $x_i \in Range(g)$ and $g(z_j) = x_i$.

3. For every $\langle q, x_i, q' \rangle \in \delta$, we add $\langle \langle q, g \rangle, z_j, \langle q', g' \rangle \rangle$ to δ' for every $g \in G$ such that $x_i \notin Range(g)$, where $j = max(g) + 1$, and $g' = g \cup \{(z_j, x_i)\}$.
4. For every $\langle q, y, q' \rangle \in \delta'$, we add $\langle \langle q, g \rangle, y', \langle q', g \rangle \rangle$ for every $g \in G$.

Notice that in every state $\langle q', g \rangle$ of D', the Z-variables in $Dom(g)$ are $z_1, z_2, \ldots z_i$ for some $1 \leq i \leq k$. Therefore, z_j in (3) is always well defined, as $j \leq k$. Also, if $\langle \langle q, g \rangle, \alpha, \langle q', g' \rangle \rangle \in \delta'$ for some q, q', α, g, g', then $g \subseteq g'$. Accordingly, along every path in D', for $j > i$, it holds that z_j does not first occur before z_i first occurs. Also, since D is deterministic, along every path, y does not occur before a variable in X first occurs. Accordingly, along every path in D', the free variable y' does not occur before a variable in Z first occurs.

However, there may be a path along D' in which y' first occurs not after all the variables in Z occur, since no extension of the matching path in D makes use of all the variables in X. In the second stage, we fix δ' so that y' only occurs after z_k first occurs.

Intuitively, along every path, we transform the premature y' transitions to a sequence of Z-transitions, until all variables in Z occur along the path. We say that a state $\langle q, g \rangle$ such that $max(g) < k$ and y' exits $\langle q, g \rangle$ is *premature*.

For every transition $\langle \langle q, g \rangle, y', \langle q', g \rangle \rangle$ such that $\langle q, g \rangle$ is premature, we remove the transition and add the transition $\langle \langle q, g \rangle, z_j, \langle q', g' \rangle \rangle$, where $j = max(g) + 1$, and where $g' = g \cup \{(z_j, y)\}$. In addition, we add $\langle \langle q, g \rangle, z_i, \langle q', g \rangle \rangle$ to δ' for every z_i such that $g(z_i) = y$.

Once all premature transitions have been removed, every word that is read along D' is ordered.

It holds that for every state $s = \langle q, g \rangle$ in Q', the set of bound variables along every path that reaches s is exactly $Dom(g)$. Since q satisfies the determinism conditions in $\mathcal{D}$, it holds that every constant in Σ_A and every variable in $Dom(g)$ exits s exactly once, as well as a new variable or y.

For every pattern word u that is read along D, the VFA D' matches the i'th occuring bound variable in u with z_i and maintains this match in reachable states. Therefore, there exists a bijection from the runs of D to the runs of D', and every such run induces the same set of concrete words.

Example 5. Consider the DVFA $\mathcal{A}$ seen in Fig. 2, over the pattern alphabet $\Gamma_2 = \{x_1, x_2, y\}$. While $\mathcal{A}$ is deterministic[1], it is not ordered. For example, along the path (q_0, q_1, q_2, q_2), the variable x_2 does not occur at all yet y occurs, and along the path (q_0, q_3, q_4, q_5), the variable x_2 first occurs before x_1. The translation of $\mathcal{A}$ to a Γ'_2-ordered DVFA $\mathcal{D}$ also appears in Fig. 2. Note that q_4 has two copies in $\mathcal{D}$: one in which z_1 represents x_1, and one in which z_1 represents x_2. This is due to the two different paths that lead to q_4, which have a different order of X variables. As a result, q_5 has three copies in $\mathcal{D}$: two that follow q_4 after both z_1, z_2 have been seen, and one that follows q_4 after only z_1 has been seen. The state q_2 also has two copies in $\mathcal{D}$, to account for the missing bound variable along the path (q_0, q_1, q_2, q_2).

---

[1] we omit the transitions labeled a from every state, for clarity of presentation.

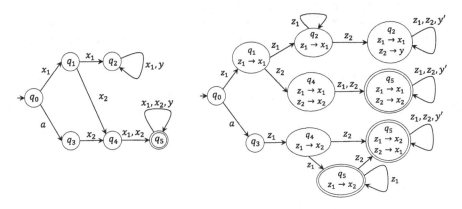

Fig. 2. A pattern automaton for $\mathcal{A}$ (on the left), and its translation to an ordered DVFA $\mathcal{D}$.

Let $\mathcal{L}$ be a language over Σ. We define a relation $\sim_{\mathcal{L},\Gamma_k}$ over $\mathcal{O}(\Gamma_k)$, as follows. For every $u_1, u_2 \in \mathcal{O}(\Gamma_k)$, we define $u_1 \sim_{\mathcal{L},\Gamma_k} u_2$ iff for every $u \in \Gamma_k^*$, it holds that $u_1 \cdot u$ is Γ_k-ordered iff $u_2 \cdot u$ is Γ_k-ordered, and if both $u_1 \cdot u$ and $u_2 \cdot u$ are Γ_k-ordered, then either $L(u_1 \cdot u) \subseteq \mathcal{L}$ and $L(u_2 \cdot u) \subseteq \mathcal{L}$,

or $L(u_1 \cdot u) \cap \mathcal{L} = \emptyset$ and $L(u_2 \cdot u) \cap \mathcal{L} = \emptyset$.

It is easy to see that $\sim_{\mathcal{L},\Gamma_k}$ is an equivalence relation.

Example 6. Consider the language $L(\mathcal{D})$ of the DVFA whose pattern automaton is D of Fig. 1, which is the language of all words over Σ whose first and last letters are equal. Then for $\Sigma_A = \emptyset$, it holds that $x_1 yy \sim_{L(\mathcal{D}),\Gamma_1} x_1 y$. Indeed, since x_1 occurs in both words, for every word u over Γ_1 it holds that $x_1 yy \cdot u$ and $x_1 y \cdot u$ are Γ_1-ordered. Moreover, if u ends with x_1 then both $L(x_1 yy \cdot u)$ and $L(x_1 y \cdot u)$ are contained in $L(\mathcal{D})$, and if u ends with y then both $L(x_1 yy \cdot u)$ and $L(x_1 y \cdot u)$ are disjoint from $L(\mathcal{D})$,

Lemma 2. *If $u_1 \sim_{\mathcal{L},\Gamma_k} u_2$, then the sets of bound variables in u_1 and u_2 are equal.*

Proof. Assume the contrary. Then, without loss of generality, u_1 contains more variables than u_2. Let x_j be the highest indexed variable that occurs in u_1. If $j = k$, then let $u = y$. Otherwise, let $u = x_{j+1}$. In either case, $u_1 \cdot u$ is Γ_k-ordered and $u_2 \cdot u$ is not, a contradiction.

We say that $\mathcal{L}$ is Γ_k-*ordered* if for every $w \in \mathcal{L}$, it holds that $L(o_{\Gamma_k}(w)) \subseteq \mathcal{L}$, and for every $w \notin \mathcal{L}$, it holds that $L(o_{\Gamma_k}(w)) \cap \mathcal{L} = \emptyset$. We say that $\mathcal{L}$ is *finitely* Γ_k-*ordered* if it is Γ_k-ordered, and $rank(\sim_{\mathcal{L},\Gamma_k})$ is finite. If $\mathcal{L}$ is finitely Γ_k-ordered for some k, we say that $\mathcal{L}$ is *finitely ordered*.

Lemma 3. *If $\mathcal{L}$ is finitely Γ_k-ordered, then $\mathcal{L}$ is deterministic.*

Proof. We construct a DVFA $\mathcal{D} = \langle D, \Sigma \rangle$ over the pattern alphabet Γ_k such that $L(\mathcal{D}) = \mathcal{L}$, as follows. The set of states of D is the set E of equivalence classes of $\sim_{\mathcal{L}, \Gamma_k}$. The initial state is $[\epsilon]$. For every $[u] \in E$ and $\alpha \in \Gamma_k$ such that $u \cdot \alpha$ is Γ_k-ordered, we add a transition $\langle [u], \alpha, [u \cdot \alpha] \rangle$ to the transition relation of D. A state $[u]$ is accepting iff $L([u]) \subseteq \mathcal{L}$.

It follows from Theorem 1 that if $\mathcal{L}$ is deterministic, then it is finitely ordered. Indeed, the equivalence classes of $\mathcal{L}$ match the Myhill-Nerode equivalence classes of the pattern automaton of an equivalent ordered DVFA (restricted to ordered words). Together with Lemma 3, we conclude the following.

Theorem 2. *$\mathcal{L}$ is deterministic iff $\mathcal{L}$ is finitely ordered.*

3.1 Finding a Minimal Set of Variables

Once we construct a Γ_k-ordered DVFA $\mathcal{D}$ for a deterministic language $\mathcal{L}$, we can find a minimal equivalent Γ_k-ordered DVFA by applying the classic Myhill-Nerode minimization for DFAs on its pattern automaton (while considering only the relevant transitions from each state, according to its level). Indeed, the resulting pattern DFA accepts an equivalent pattern language, and is therefore a DVFA that accepts $\mathcal{L}$.

However, it might be the case that $\mathcal{L}$ can be expressed by an ordered DVFA with fewer than k bound variables. We can find the minimal k' for which $\mathcal{L}$ is $\Gamma_{k'}$-ordered, as follows[2].

Let $D = \langle \Gamma_k, Q, q_0, \delta, F \rangle$ be the pattern automaton of $\mathcal{D}$, and let A be the pattern automaton obtained from D by replacing every occurrence of x_k with y. Notice that A may be nondeterministic, since states in level k may now have two transitions labeled y that exit them. Also notice that the set of words on which A runs is exactly $\mathcal{O}(\Gamma_{k-1})$.

Let w be a word over Σ^*. Then $o_{\Gamma_{k-1}}(w)$ is obtained from $o_{\Gamma_k}(w)$ by replacing all occurrences of x_k with y. Notice that if $o_{\Gamma_k}(w)$ contains no occurrences of x_k, then $o_{\Gamma_k}(w) = o_{\Gamma_{k-1}}(w)$, and so both D and A have a single identical run on $o_{\Gamma_{k-1}}(w)$.

We then have the following. For every $w \in \Sigma^*$, if $w \in \mathcal{L}$, then $o_{\Gamma_k}(w) \in L(D)$, and therefore there exists an accepting run on $o_{\Gamma_{k-1}}$ in A. If $w \notin \mathcal{L}$, then $o_{\Gamma_k}(w) \notin L(D)$, and therefore there exists a rejecting run on $o_{\Gamma_{k-1}}(w)$ in A.

Moreover, $k - 1$ bound variables suffice to express $\mathcal{L}$ by an ordered DVFA iff there exist no two words w_1, w_2 such that $w_1 \in \mathcal{L}, w_2 \notin \mathcal{L}$, such that $o_{\Gamma_{k-1}}(w_1) = o_{\Gamma_{k-1}}(w_2)$. Two such words exist iff $o_{\Gamma_{k-1}}(w_1)$ has two runs in A, one is accepting and the other rejecting.

As a corollary to the above, in order to construct a Γ_{k-1}-ordered DVFA for $\mathcal{L}$, we apply the standard subset construction on A to obtain a Γ_{k-1}-ordered DVFA $\mathcal{D}'$. If one of the subsets includes two states such that one is accepting and the other rejecting, we conclude that Γ_k is minimal, and otherwise, we have that $L(\mathcal{D}') = L(\mathcal{D}) = \mathcal{L}$.

We can now repeat the process until reaching a minimal set $\Gamma_{k'}$.

---

[2] It may be the case that $\mathcal{L}$ can be expressed with even fewer than k' variables, by a non-ordered VFA. Here, we only consider ordered DVFA.

Example 7. Consider the ordered DVFA $\mathcal{B}$ whose pattern automaton B appears in Fig. 1. Its language is the set of all words whose first and last letters are equal. The VFA B' obtained from B by replacing all transitions labeled x_2 with y is deterministic, and is therefore equivalent to its subset construction. We then have that B' is equivalent to $\mathcal{B}$, but uses fewer variables.

4   A Learning Algorithm for DVFA

In this section we exploit the canonical form defined in Sect. 3 to construct a learning algorithm for DVFAs. Our algorithm, DVL*, is based on the L* algorithm for learning regular languages, and we use some of the terminology and mechanisms of [Ang87].

Let $\mathcal{L}$ be a deterministic language with a set of constants Σ_A. DVL* learns an ordered DVFA that accepts $\mathcal{L}$, with a minimal set of variables and a minimal set of states. Much like L*, DVL* consists of a learner and a teacher. The learner constructs an ordered DVFA by submitting a sequence of membership ("is the word w in $\mathcal{L}$?") and equivalence ("does the DVFA A accept $\mathcal{L}$?") queries. We only expect the teacher to handle concrete words, and so the membership queries, as well as the counterexamples provided by the teacher, are concrete.

The run maintains a pattern alphabet $\Gamma_k = \Sigma_A \cup X \cup \{y\}$, where initially $X = \emptyset$. The run proceeds in iterations, which gradually increase the number of variables in X. In every iteration, a set of tables $\mathcal{T} = \{T_0, T_1, \ldots T_k\}$ is constructed and maintained for the current Γ_k (we sometimes refer to $\mathcal{T}$ itself as a table).

The rows of the tables are words from a set $S \cup S \cdot \Gamma_k$ of Γ_k-ordered words, where S is prefix-closed, and the columns of the tables are from a set E of suffix-closed words over Γ_k. The rows of T_m are denoted S_m, and the columns of T_m are denoted E_m. For every $s \in S_m$, it holds that $var(s) = \{x_1, \ldots x_m\}$, and words in S_k may also contain y. For every T_m, a word $e \in E$ is in E_m only if $s \cdot e$ is Γ_k-ordered for every $s \in S_m$ (notice that since all the words in S_m use the same set of bound variables, either $s \cdot e \in \mathcal{O}(\Gamma_k)$ for every $s \in S_m$, or for none). Every $s \in S \cup S \cdot \Gamma_k$ and $e \in E$ are assigned concrete words $w(s)$ and $w(e)$, respectively. These words are used for membership queries.

For $1 \leq m \leq k$, the table T_m matches each $s \in S_m$ and $e \in E_m$ with a truth value in $\{0, 1\}$, such that $T_m(s, e) = 1$ iff $w(s) \cdot w(e) \in \mathcal{L}$. We denote by $\mathcal{T}(s, e)$ the truth value for $T_m(s, e)$.

Notice that $T_m(s, e) = 1$ does not necessarily imply that $L(s \cdot e) \subseteq \mathcal{L}$, since we only have $L(s \cdot e) \cap \mathcal{L} \neq \emptyset$. Dually, $T_m(s, e) = 0$ does not mean that $L(s \cdot e) \cap \mathcal{L} = \emptyset$. Recall that if $\mathcal{L}$ is Γ_k-ordered, for every ordered word u, either $L(u) \subseteq \mathcal{L}$ or $L(u) \cap \mathcal{L} = \emptyset$. In case that $L(s \cdot e)$ does not satisfy either condition, there are two words w_1, w_2 in $L(s \cdot e)$ that do not agree on membership to $\mathcal{L}$, yet have the same Γ_k-ordering. Adding bound variables will enable to distinguish between w_1 and w_2. During the run, counterexamples for such s, e are produced by the teacher, and accordingly lead to an update of Γ_k.

In order to maintain the consistency in the assignments to the words assigned by w, every bound variable x_i is always assigned the same letter a_i in Σ. Moreover, in $S \cup S \cdot \Gamma_k$, the variable y is always assigned the same letter.

For $s \in S \cup S \cdot \Gamma_k$, we refer to $row(s)$ as the vector of truth values in the table in which s is a row.

We say that T_m is *consistent* if for every $s_1, s_2 \in S_m$ such that $row(s_1) = row(s_2)$, for every $a \in \Gamma_k$ such that $s_1 \cdot a, s_2 \cdot a$ are Γ_k-ordered, it holds that $row(s_1 \cdot a) = row(s_2 \cdot a)$. Notice that $s_1 \cdot a, s_2 \cdot a$ may either both be in T_m, or both be in T_{m+1} (the latter in case that $a = x_{m+1}$).

We say that T_m is *closed* if for every $s \cdot a \in (S \cdot \Gamma_k \cap S_m)$ there exists $s' \in S \cap S_m$ such that $row(s) = row(s')$.

We say that $\mathcal{T}$ is *refined* if for every s, s', e, e' such that $s \in S_m, e \in E_m$, $s' \in S_{m'}, e' \in T_{m'}$ such that $s \cdot e = s' \cdot e'$, it holds that $T_m(s, e) = T_{m'}(s', e')$. That is, $\mathcal{T}$ is consistent for similar Γ_k-ordered words.

During the run, the tables in $\mathcal{T}$ are filled by submitting membership queries of the type $w(s) \cdot w(e)$ to the teacher.

Initially, the pattern alphabet is Γ_0. We construct a single table T_0, and initially set $S = E = \{\epsilon\}$. Accordingly, $S \cdot \Gamma_k = \Sigma_A \cup \{y\}$. We set $S_0 = S \cup S \cdot \Gamma_k$, and $E_0 = E$. We set $w(y) = a$ for some $a \in \Sigma$, and fill the entries in T_0 by membership queries.

In later iterations, for a pattern alphabet Γ_k with $k > 0$, we construct a set of tables $\{T_0, \ldots, T_k\}$, and initially set $S = \{\epsilon, x_1, x_1 x_2, \ldots, x_1 x_2 \cdots x_k\}$. The set $S \cdot \Gamma_k$ is calculated accordingly. The words in $S \cup S \cdot \Gamma_k$ are distributed along $S_0, S_1, \ldots S_k$ according to the variables they contain, and $E_m = \{\epsilon\}$ for every $0 \leq m \leq k$. We assign words $w(s)$ and $w(e)$ in $L(s)$ and $L(e)$ for every $s \in S \cdot \Gamma_k$ and $e \in E$ as described above, and fill the tables accordingly.

We now describe how to fix the tables in case that $\mathcal{T}$ is not consistent, closed or refined.

If some table T_m is not consistent, then there exist two words $s_1, s_2 \in S_m \cap S$ such that $row(s_1) = row(s_2)$, and $a \in \Gamma_k$ such that $s_1 \cdot a, s_2 \cdot a$ are Γ_k-ordered, such that $row(s_1 \cdot a) \neq row(s_2 \cdot a)$. Let e be a word for which $\mathcal{T}(s_1 \cdot a \cdot e) \neq \mathcal{T}(s_2 \cdot a \cdot e)$. Then $a \cdot e$ is a separating word for s_1, s_2. We add $a \cdot e$ to E_m, assign it a word $w(a \cdot e)$ that preserves the previous assignment to a and e, and fill the table accordingly. Notice that since $\mathcal{T}$ was suffix-closed for E, it remains so also after adding $a \cdot e$. Also, now $row(s_1) \neq row(s_2)$.

If some table T_m is not closed, then there exists a word $s \cdot a \in S_m \cap (S \cdot \Gamma_k)$ for which there exists no $s' \in S_m \cap S$ such that $row(s \cdot a) = row(s')$. In this case, we add $s \cdot a$ to S, and add words of the type $s \cdot a \cdot b$ for every b for which $s \cdot a \cdot b$ is Γ_k-ordered to $S \cdot \Gamma_k$, and either to S_m (if $b \neq x_{m+1}$) or S_{m+1} (otherwise). We fill the table entries accordingly. Notice that since S was prefix-closed, it remains so also after adding $s \cdot a$.

If $\mathcal{T}$ is not refined, then there are $s \in S_m, s' \in S_{m'}$ and $e \in E_m, e' \in E_{m'}$ such that $s \cdot e = s' \cdot e'$, but $T_m(s \cdot e) = 1$ yet $T_{m'}(s' \cdot e') = 0$. This means that $L(s \cdot e) \not\subseteq \mathcal{L}$, and yet $L(s \cdot e) \cap \mathcal{L} \neq \emptyset$. To distinguish between $w(s) \cdot w(e)$ and $w(s') \cdot w(e')$, the pattern alphabet must be refined by adding more bound variables such that the ordering of these two words will be different. We do so by calculating k', the minimal required number of bound variables for which $o_{\Gamma_{k'}}(w(s) \cdot w(e)) \neq o_{\Gamma_{k'}}(w(s') \cdot w(e'))$. For example, 3 bound variables are needed to distinguish between $abcd$ and $abcc$. The minimal number of bound variables that is needed to distinguish between two words w_1 and w_2 is calculated as follows. Let j be the minimal index for which there exists $i < j$ such that $w_1(i) = w_1(j)$, yet $w_2(i) \neq w_2(j)$. Then the number of bound variables needed to distinguish between w_1 and w_2 is the index, in order of first occurrences, of $w_1(i)$.

We then begin a new iteration with $\Gamma_{k'}$, the updated pattern alphabet.

Once $\mathcal{T}$ is closed, consistent and refined, it can be translated to a DVFA $\mathcal{A}_{\mathcal{T}}$ whose pattern automaton is $A_{\mathcal{T}} = \langle \Gamma_k, Q, q_0, \delta, F \rangle$, as follows.

- $Q = \{\langle row(s), m \rangle | s \in S_m \cap S, 1 \leq m \leq k\}$,
- $q_0 = \langle row(\epsilon), 0 \rangle$,
- Let $s \cdot a \in S_m \cap (S \cdot \Gamma_k)$. Then $s \in S_{m'}$ where either $m' = m$, or $m' = m - 1$ (if $a = x_{m+1}$). Since $\mathcal{T}$ is closed, there exists $s' \in S_m \cap S$ such that $row(s') = row(s \cdot a)$. Then we set $\delta(\langle row(s), m' \rangle, a) = \langle row(s'), m \rangle$.
- $F = \{\langle row(s), m \rangle | T_m(s, \epsilon) = 1, 1 \leq m \leq k\}$.

Since $\mathcal{T}$ is consistent, it holds that for $s_1, s_2 \in S \cup S \cdot \Gamma_k$, if $row(s_1) = row(s_2)$ then both $s_1 \cdot a$ and $s_2 \cdot a$ are Γ_k-ordered (since s_1, s_2 are in the same table). Also, since $\mathcal{T}$ is consistent, we have that $row(s_1) = row(s_2)$ implies $row(s_1 \cdot a) = row(s_2 \cdot a)$, and so δ is well defined.

The learner constructs $\mathcal{A}_{\mathcal{T}}$, and submits an equivalence query. The teacher either confirms that $L(\mathcal{A}_{\mathcal{T}}) = \mathcal{L}$, thus terminating the run, or returns a counterexample w' which $\mathcal{A}_{\mathcal{T}}$ accepts although $w' \notin \mathcal{L}$, or rejects although $w' \in \mathcal{L}$.

In case of a counterexample, we add $o_{\Gamma_k}(w')$ and all its suffixes to E, and distribute them to E_m according to their variables. We attach a word $v(u) \in L(u)$ to every such suffix u, as follows. Let $b_i b_{i+1} \ldots b_n$ the suffix of w' that induces u. The word $v(u)$ is consistent with w (that is, every x_i is assigned a_i), and $v(u)_j = v(u)_{j'}$ iff $b_j = b_{j'}$. Notice that since $w' \in L(u)$, the latter two conditions are consistent. The words $b_i b_{i+1} \ldots b_n$ and $v(u)$ are then equivalent up to letter identity. For every new suffix u, we set $w(u) = v(u)$, add u to the appropriate tables and fill the missing table entries. For every suffix u that is already in $\mathcal{T}$, we proceed as follows. For every m such that $u \in E_m$, for every $s \in S_m$, we run a membership query for $w(s) \cdot v(u)$. If some membership query returns a different answer from $T_m(s, u)$, we conclude that more variables must be added. Indeed, $w(s) \cdot w(u)$ and $w(s) \cdot v(u)$ have the same Γ_k-ordering, yet one is in $\mathcal{L}$ and the other is not. As with the case of a non-refined table, we add the minimal number of variables needed to distinguish between $w(s) \cdot w(u)$ and $w(s) \cdot v(u)$, and start a new iteration.

As we show next, DVL* finds a minimal DVFA for $\mathcal{L}$. Our main theorem is the following.

Theorem 3. *If $\mathcal{T}$ is closed, consistent and refined, then $\mathcal{A}_{\mathcal{T}}$ is a minimal ordered DVFA that is consistent with $\mathcal{T}$.*

We prove Theorem 3 by the following sequence of lemmas.

Lemma 4. *Let $\mathcal{T}$ be a closed, consistent and refined table, and let $A_{\mathcal{T}}$ be the pattern automaton for its matching DVFA. Then the following hold.*

1. *For every word $s \in S$, it holds that $\delta^*(q_0, s) = \langle row(s), m \rangle$, where $s \in S_m$.*
2. *For every $1 \leq m \leq k$, for every $s \in S_m$ and $e \in E_m$, it holds that $\delta^*(q_0, s \cdot e) \in F$ iff $T_m(s, e) = 1$.*
3. *Let n be the number of states in $A_{\mathcal{T}}$. Then every Γ_k-ordered DVFA with n or fewer states that is consistent with $\mathcal{T}$ is isomorphic to $\mathcal{A}_{\mathcal{T}}$.*

Lemma 4 is proved in a similar way to similar lemmas in [Ang87], with some added technicalities due to the more complicated nature of $\mathcal{T}$.

Lemma 4 holds for DVFAs that are consistent with $\mathcal{T}$ and use the same pattern alphabet. However, we need to show that DVL* eventually converges to the minimal number of required variables.

We first show that upon termination, $A_{\mathcal{T}}$ uses a minimal pattern alphabet.

Lemma 5. *Let $\mathcal{T}$ be a closed, consistent and refined table with k bound variables. Then an ordered DVFA for $\mathcal{L}$ must use at least k bound variables.*

Proof. Assume by contradiction that an ordered DVFA $\mathcal{A}$ for $\mathcal{L}$ uses $k' < k$ variables. DVL* begins with a free variable only. Recall that new variables are added when the run finds two words w, w' in $L(u)$ for some pattern word u in $\mathcal{T}$ such that $w \in \mathcal{L}$ and $w' \notin \mathcal{L}$, in which case the new number of variables is the minimal number for which the ordering of w, w' is different. Let w, w' be the last pair of words that led to the last increase in the number of variables in $\mathcal{T}$. Since k is the minimal number of variables needed to distinguish between w and w', we have that $o_{\Gamma_{k'}}(w) = o_{\Gamma_{k'}}(w')$, and therefore $\mathcal{A}$ cannot accept $\mathcal{L}$, a contradiction.

Finally, we show that as long as the minimal number of required variables has not been reached, DVL* does not produce a larger DVFA than the minimal one for $\mathcal{L}$.

Lemma 6. *Let $\mathcal{T}$ be a closed, consistent and refined table over Γ_k, and let n be the number of states in $A_{\mathcal{T}}$. Then every ordered DVFA with more than k bound variables that is consistent with $\mathcal{T}$ with respect to the concrete words assigned by w has at least n states.*

Proof. Let $\mathcal{A}$ be an ordered DVFA that is consistent with $\mathcal{T}$ whose pattern automaton is $\langle \Gamma_{k'}, Q', q_0, F', \delta' \rangle$, where $k' > k$.

We define a function $f : Q \rightarrow Q'$ by $f(\langle row(s), m \rangle) = \delta'^*(q_0', w(s))$. We show that f is one-to-one. Let $s_1, s_2 \in S$. If s_1, s_2 are in different tables $T_m, T_{m'}$, they are not mapped to the same state in $\mathcal{A}_{\mathcal{T}}$, and $var(s_1) \neq var(s_2)$. Since only words in S_k contain y, at most one of s_1, s_2 can contain y. Assume, without loss of generality, that $var(s_1) \subset var(s_2)$. Then $w(s_1)$ contains $j < k$ different letters, and $w(s_2)$ contains more than j different letters. Since $k' > k$, we have that $o_{\Gamma_{k'}}(w(s_1)), o_{\Gamma_{k'}}(w(s_2))$ have different sets of bound variables. Therefore, $\delta'^*(q_0', o_{\Gamma_{k'}}(w(s_1)))$ and $\delta'^*(q_0', o_{\Gamma_{k'}}(w(s_2)))$ are in different levels in Q', and so are not the same state.

If $s_1, s_2 \in S_m$ such that $row(s_1) \neq row(s_2)$, then there exists a word $e \in E$ such that $T_m(s_1, e) \neq T_m(s_2, e)$. Therefore, $w(s_1) \cdot w(e) \in \mathcal{L}$ and $w(s_2) \cdot w(e) \notin \mathcal{L}$, or vice versa. Let $q_1 = \delta'^*(q_0', w(s_1))$, and $q_2 = \delta'^*(q_0', w(s_2))$. Since $\mathcal{A}$ is consistent with T, we have that either $w(s_1) \cdot w(e) \in L(\mathcal{A})$ and $w(s_2) \cdot w(e) \notin L(\mathcal{A})$, or vice versa. Since $\mathcal{A}$ is deterministic, it must be the case that $q_1 \neq q_2$, otherwise, since $w(e)$ has a single run from every state in Q', both $w(s_1) \cdot w(e)$ and $w(s_2) \cdot w(e)$ are accepted by $\mathcal{A}$, or both are rejected by $\mathcal{A}$, a contradiction.

Notice that in every change in T, we either add at least one state to $\mathcal{A}_T$, or add at least one bound variable to the pattern alphabet. Together with the lemmas above, we conclude that DVL^* always converges to a minimal ordered DVFA for $\mathcal{L}$.

The size of every table in T is polynomial in n, the number of states of a minimal ordered DVFA for $\mathcal{L}$, and m, the length of the longest counterexample provided by the teacher. The number of tables in T is at most k, the minimal number of bound variables for $\mathcal{L}$. Checking for consistency, closure and refinement are all polynomial in the size of T, and so every iteration of DVL^*, much like L^*, runs in time polynomial in n, m and k. The total number of iterations is at most k. Therefore, DVL^* runs in time polynomial in n, m, and k.

Example Run. Let $\mathcal{L}$ be the language of all words over Σ^* in which the first and second letters are different, and the second and last letters are equal. $\mathcal{L}$ is deterministic, and an ordered DVFA for $\mathcal{L}$ needs two bound variables, to keep the first and second letters.

We demonstrate the first iterations of a run of DVL^* on $\mathcal{L}$. As standard in these cases, the upper rows of the tables are the words in S, and the lower are the words in $S \cdot \Gamma$.

Initially the pattern alphabet is $\Gamma_0 = \{y\}$. Figure 3 describes the stages of constructing T for Γ_0. In stage (1), S_0 consists of $S = \{\epsilon\}$ and $S \cdot \Gamma_0 = \{y\}$. Both are assigned concrete words by w, and the table is filled. T is now is closed, consistent and refined, and $\mathcal{A}_T$ is a single rejecting state with a self loop labeled y. An equivalence query is then submitted to the teacher. The teacher returns a counterexample abb.

The Γ_0-ordering of abb is yyy, and so in stage (2), yyy and all its suffixes are added to E_0. Each suffix is assigned a concrete word by w that is consistent with abb, and the table is filled.

Since T_0 is not closed in stage (2), In stage (3) y is added to S, and consequently yy is added to $S \cdot \Gamma_0$, and the missing entries are filled. At this point, due to the concrete words w has assigned, we have that $T_0(y, yyy) \neq T_0(yy, yy)$, that is, T is not refined. As we have explained, this means that the pattern alphabet must contain more variables. The minimal number of bound variables needed to distinguish between $w(y) \cdot w(yyy) = aabb$ and $w(yy) \cdot w(yy) = abbb$ is one, and so a new iteration begins with the new alphabet Γ_1.

T_0	$\epsilon\,(\epsilon)$
$\epsilon\,(\epsilon)$	0
$y\,(a)$	0

T_0	$\epsilon\,(\epsilon)$	$y\,(b)$	$yy(bb)$	$yyy(abb)$
$\epsilon\,(\epsilon)$	0	0	0	1
$y\,(a)$	0	0	1	0

T_0	$\epsilon\,(\epsilon)$	$y\,(b)$	$yy(bb)$	$yyy(abb)$
$\epsilon\,(\epsilon)$	0	0	0	1
$y\,(a)$	0	0	1	0
$yy\,(ab)$	0	1	1	0

(1)   (2)   (3)

Fig. 3. $\mathcal{T}$ for Γ_0.

T_0	$\epsilon\,(\epsilon)$
$\epsilon\,(\epsilon)$	0

T_1	$\epsilon\,(\epsilon)$
$x_1\,(a)$	0
$x_1x_1\,(aa)$	0
$x_1y\,(ab)$	0

(1)

T_0	$\epsilon\,(\epsilon)$	$x_1yy\,(abb)$
$\epsilon\,(\epsilon)$	0	1

(2)

T_1	$\epsilon\,(\epsilon)$	$y\,(b)$	$yy\,(bb)$	$x_1yy\,(abb)$
$x_1\,(a)$	0	0	1	0
$x_1x_1\,(aa)$	0	0	0	0
$x_1y\,(ab)$	0	1	1	1
$x_1yy\,(abb)$	1	1	1	1
$x_1x_1x_1\,(aaa)$	0	0	0	0
$x_1x_1y\,(aab)$	0	0	0	0
$x_1yx_1\,(aba)$	0	1	1	1
$x_1yyy\,(abbb)$	1	1	1	1
$x_1yyx_1\,(abba)$	0	1	1	1

Fig. 4. Reconstructing $\mathcal{T}$ after adding a variable x_1.

Figure 4 describes the second iteration of DVL* on $\mathcal{L}$. In stage (1) of this iteration, $S = \{\epsilon, x_1\}$, which are distributed to S_0, S_1, respectively. $S \cdot \Gamma_1$ is calculated and distributed accordingly, in this case, to S_1. Concrete words are then assigned to S, E by w, and the tables entries are filled. Since all entries are 0, once again $\mathcal{A}_\mathcal{T}$ is empty. This time, since $\mathcal{A}_\mathcal{T}$ is Γ_1-ordered, there are two rejecting states, one that reads x_1 and one with a self-loop labeled x_1, y. An equivalence query returns a counterexample bcc.

Since $o_{\Gamma_1}(bcc) = x_1yy$, we construct a matching word $v(x_1yy) = abb$, add x_1yy and all of its prefixes to the appropriate tables: x_1yy is added to T_0, T_1 (recall that we add a word to E_m only if its concatenation with S_m is ordered), and the rest are added to T_1. The tables are filled accordingly. Stage (2) of Fig. 4 describes T_0 and T_1 after filling the entries and closing $\mathcal{T}$ by adding x_1x_1, x_1y and later x_1yy to S. At this point, $\mathcal{T}$ is closed, consistent and refined, $\mathcal{A}_\mathcal{T}$ is constructed and a new equivalence query is submitted.

The teacher then returns a counterexample dfe, which is in $L(\mathcal{A}_\mathcal{T})$ but is not in $\mathcal{L}$. Since $o_{\Gamma_1}(dfe) = x_1yy$, we construct $v(x_1yy) = abc$, which is consistent with both the assignments of w and with the structure of dfe. For $s = \epsilon$, we have that $T_0(\epsilon, x_1yy) = 1$, whereas $w(\epsilon) \cdot v(u) \notin \mathcal{L}$. Therefore, bound variables need to be added. The minimal number of bound variables needed to distinguish between abb and abc is 2, and so a new iteration begins with Γ_2. Since Γ_2 suffices to express $\mathcal{L}$, this is the final iteration. From here, the run continues much like L*, with respect to the concrete words assigned by w.

5   Summary and Future Work

We have presented ordered DVFAs, and proved them to be a canonical form for DVFAs. We have further presented a use for this canonical form in an L^*-based learning algorithm for DVFAs.

DVFAs are a special restrictive form of register automata. As future work, we would like to push the boundaries of this fragment and find richer models for which a canonical form exists, in which the registers have a more free behavior. It was shown in [GKS10] that VFAs are in general not determinizable, hence further fragments would need to be in between DVFA and VFA, or, like session automata, incomparable to these models.

VFAs and DVFAs are used for modeling both infinite state systems whose control is finite and whose source of infinite state space is the data, and specifications for these systems. In the future, in a similar manner to [PGB+08], we plan to use DVL^* as basis for compositional verification procedures for such infinite state systems.

References

[AD18] Argyros, G., D'Antoni, L.: The learnability of symbolic automata. In: Chockler, H., Weissenbacher, G. (eds.) CAV 2018. LNCS, vol. 10981, pp. 427–445. Springer, Cham (2018). https://doi.org/10.1007/978-3-319-96145-3_23

[Ang87] Angluin, D.: Learning regular sets from queries and counterexamples. Inf. Comput. **75**(2), 87–106 (1987)

[BHLM14] Bollig, B., Habermehl, P., Leucker, M., Monmege, B.: A robust class of data languages and an application to learning. Logical Methods Comput. Sci. **10**, 11 (2014)

[BMS+06] Bojanczyk, M., Muscholl, A., Schwentick, T., Segoufin, L., David, C.: Two-variable logic on words with data. In: LICS, pp. 7–16. IEEE Computer Society (2006)

[BMSS09] Bojańczyk, M., Muscholl, A., Schwentick, T., Segoufin, L.: Two-variable logic on data trees and XML reasoning. J. ACM **56**(3), 1–48 (2009)

[DD17] Drews, S., D'Antoni, L.: Learning symbolic automata. In: Legay, A., Margaria, T. (eds.) TACAS 2017. LNCS, vol. 10205, pp. 173–189. Springer, Heidelberg (2017). https://doi.org/10.1007/978-3-662-54577-5_10

[FGS18] Frenkel, H., Grumberg, O., Sheinvald, S.: An automata-theoretic approach to model-checking systems and specifications over infinite data domains. J. Autom. Reasoning, 1–25 (2018). https://doi.org/10.1007/s10817-018-9494-0

[GKS10] Grumberg, O., Kupferman, O., Sheinvald, S.: Variable automata over infinite alphabets. In: Dediu, A.-H., Fernau, H., Martín-Vide, C. (eds.) LATA 2010. LNCS, vol. 6031, pp. 561–572. Springer, Heidelberg (2010). https://doi.org/10.1007/978-3-642-13089-2_47

[KF94] Kaminski, M., Francez, N.: Finite-memory automata. Theoret. Comput. Sci. **134**(2), 329–363 (1994)

[KZ08] Kaminski, M., Zeitlin, D.: Extending finite-memory automata with nondeterministic reassignment. In: Csuhaj-Varjú, E., Ézik, Z. (eds.) AFL, pp. 195–207 (2008)

[NSV01] Neven, F., Schwentick, T., Vianu, V.: Towards regular languages over infinite alphabets. In: Sgall, J., Pultr, A., Kolman, P. (eds.) MFCS 2001. LNCS, vol. 2136, pp. 560–572. Springer, Heidelberg (2001). https://doi.org/10.1007/3-540-44683-4_49

[PGB+08] Pasareanu, C.S., Giannakopoulou, D., Bobaru, M.G., Cobleigh, J.M., Barringer, H.: Learning to divide and conquer: applying the L* algorithm to automate assume-guarantee reasoning. Formal Methods Syst. Des. **32**, 175–205 (2008)

[SF94] Shemesh, Y., Francez, N.: Finite-state unification automata and relational languages. Inf. Comput. **114**, 192–213 (1994)

[Tan09] Tan, T.: Pebble automata for data languages: separation, decidability, and undecidability. Ph.D. thesis, Technion - Computer Science Department (2009)

L^*-Based Learning of Markov Decision Processes

Martin Tappler[1(✉)], Bernhard K. Aichernig[1], Giovanni Bacci[3],
Maria Eichlseder[2], and Kim G. Larsen[3]

[1] Institute of Software Technology, Graz University of Technology, Graz, Austria
{martin.tappler,aichernig}@ist.tugraz.at
[2] Institute of Applied Information Processing and Communications, Graz University
of Technology, Graz, Austria
maria.eichlseder@iaik.tugraz.at
[3] Department of Computer Science, Aalborg University, Aalborg, Denmark
{giovbacci,kgl}@cs.aau.dk

Abstract. Automata learning techniques automatically generate system models from test observations. These techniques usually fall into two categories: passive and active. Passive learning uses a predetermined data set, e.g., system logs. In contrast, active learning actively queries the system under learning, which is considered more efficient.

An influential active learning technique is Angluin's L^* algorithm for regular languages which inspired several generalisations from DFAs to other automata-based modelling formalisms. In this work, we study L^*-based learning of deterministic Markov decision processes, first assuming an ideal setting with perfect information. Then, we relax this assumption and present a novel learning algorithm that collects information by sampling system traces via testing. Experiments with the implementation of our sampling-based algorithm suggest that it achieves better accuracy than state-of-the-art passive learning techniques with the same amount of test data. Unlike existing learning algorithms with predefined states, our algorithm learns the complete model structure including the states.

Keywords: Model inference · Active automata learning ·
Markov decision processes

1 Introduction

Automata learning automatically generates models from system observations such as test logs. Hence, it enables model-based verification for black-box software systems [1,22], e.g. via model checking. Automata learning techniques generally fall into two categories: passive and active learning. Passive algorithms take a given sample of system traces as input and generate models consistent with the sample. The quality and comprehensiveness of learned models therefore largely depend on the given sample. In contrast, active algorithms actively query the system under learning (SUL) to sample system traces. This enables to steer

© Springer Nature Switzerland AG 2019
M. H. ter Beek et al. (Eds.): FM 2019, LNCS 11800, pp. 651–669, 2019.
https://doi.org/10.1007/978-3-030-30942-8_38

the trace generation towards parts of the SUL's state space that have not been thoroughly covered, potentially finding yet unknown aspects of the SUL.

Many active automata learning algorithms are based on Angluin's L^* algorithm [4]. It was originally proposed for learning deterministic finite automata (DFA) accepting regular languages and later applied to learn models of reactive systems, by considering system traces to form regular languages [23]. L^* has been extended to formalisms better suited for modelling reactive systems such as Mealy machines [30,35] and extended finite state-machines [14]. Most L^*-based work, however, targets deterministic models, with the exceptions of algorithms for non-deterministic Mealy machines [25] and non-deterministic input-output transition systems [43]. Both techniques are based on testing, but abstract away the observed frequency of events, thus they do not use all available information.

Here, we present an L^*-based approach for learning models of stochastic systems with transitions that happen with some probability depending on non-deterministically chosen inputs. More concretely, we learn deterministic Markov decision processes (MDPs), like IOALERGIA [28,29], a state-of-the-art passive learning algorithm. Such models are commonly used to model randomised distributed algorithms [8], e.g. in protocol verification [26,32]. We present two learning algorithms: the first takes an ideal view assuming perfect knowledge about the exact distribution of system traces. The second algorithm relaxes this assumption, by sampling system traces to estimate their distribution. We refer to the former as *exact learning algorithm* $L^*_{\text{MDP}^e}$ and to the latter as *sampling-based learning algorithm* L^*_{MDP}. We implemented L^*_{MDP} and evaluated it by comparing it to IOALERGIA [28,29]. Experiments showed favourable performance of L^*_{MDP}, i.e. it produced more accurate models than IOALERGIA given approximately the same amount of data. Generally, models learned by L^*_{MDP} converge in the limit to an MDP observationally equivalent to the SUL. To the best of our knowledge, L^*_{MDP} is the first L^*-based learning algorithm for MDPs that can be implemented via testing. Our contributions span the algorithmic development of learning algorithms, the implementation and the evaluation of learning algorithms. The full technical report on L^*_{MDP} [38] additionally includes convergence proofs, further experiments and implementation details.

The rest of this paper is structured as follows. We introduce notational conventions, preliminaries on MDPs and active automata learning in Sect. 2. Section 3 discusses semantics of MDPs and presents the exact learning algorithm $L^*_{\text{MDP}^e}$. Section 4 describes the sampling-based L^*_{MDP}. Section 5 discusses the evaluation and in Sect. 6, we discuss related work. We provide a summary and concluding remarks in Sect. 7.

2   Preliminaries

Notation and Auxiliary Definitions. Let S be a set. We denote the concatenation of two sequences s and s' in S^* by $s \cdot s'$, the length of a sequence s by $|s|$ and the empty sequence by ϵ. We implicitly lift elements in S to sequences of length one. Sequence s is a prefix of s' if there exists an s'' such that $s \cdot s'' = s'$, denoted by $s \ll s'$. The pairwise concatenation of sets of sequences $A, B \subseteq S^*$ is $A \cdot B = \{a \cdot b \mid a \in A, b \in B\}$. A set of sequences $A \subseteq S^*$ is prefix-closed, iff for every $a \in A$, A also contains all prefixes of a. Suffixes and suffix-closedness are defined analogously. For a sequence s in S^*, $s[i]$ is the element at index i, with indexes starting at 1, $s[\ll i]$ is the prefix of s with length i and $prefixes(s) = \{s' \mid s' \in S^* : s' \ll s\}$ is the set of all prefixes of s. Given a multiset $\mathcal{S}$, we denote the multiplicity of x in $\mathcal{S}$ by $\mathcal{S}(x)$. $Dist(S)$ denotes the set of probability distributions over S, i.e. for all $\mu : S \to [0,1]$ in $Dist(S)$ we have $\sum_{s \in S} \mu(s) = 1$. In the remainder of this paper, distributions μ may be partial functions, in which case we implicitly set $\mu(e) = 0$ if μ is not defined for e. For $A \subseteq S$, $\mathbf{1}_A$ denotes the indicator function of A, i.e. $\mathbf{1}_A(e) = 1$ if $e \in A$ and $\mathbf{1}_A(e) = 0$ otherwise.

Markov Decision Processes

Definition 1 (Markov decision process (MDP)). *A labelled Markov decision process (MDP) is a tuple* $\mathcal{M} = \langle Q, \Sigma^{\mathrm{I}}, \Sigma^{\mathrm{O}}, q_0, \delta, L \rangle$ *where Q is a finite non-empty set of states, Σ^{I} and Σ^{O} are finite sets of inputs and outputs, $q_0 \in Q$ is the initial state, $\delta : Q \times \Sigma^{\mathrm{I}} \to Dist(Q)$ is the probabilistic transition function, and $L : Q \to \Sigma^{\mathrm{O}}$ is the labelling function. An MDP is* deterministic *if $\forall q \in Q, \forall i : \delta(q,i)(q') > 0 \wedge \delta(q,i)(q'') > 0 \to q' = q'' \vee L(q') \neq L(q'')$.*

We learn deterministic labelled MDPs as learned by passive learning techniques like IOALERGIA [29]. Such MDPs define at most one successor state for each source state and input-output pair. In the following, we refer to these models uniformly as MDPs. We use $\Delta : Q \times \Sigma^{\mathrm{I}} \times \Sigma^{\mathrm{O}} \to Q \cup \{\bot\}$ to

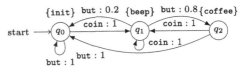

Fig. 1. MDP model of a faulty coffee machine

compute successor states. The function is defined by $\Delta(q, i, o) = q' \in Q$ with $L(q') = o$ and $\delta(q,i)(q') > 0$ if there exists such a q', otherwise Δ returns $\bot$. Figure 1 shows an MDP model of a faulty coffee machine [3]. Outputs in curly braces label states and inputs with corresponding probabilities label edges. After providing the inputs coin and but, the coffee machine MDP produces the output coffee with probability 0.8, but with probability 0.2, it resets itself, producing the output init.

Execution. A path ρ through an MDP is an alternating sequence of states and inputs starting in the initial state q_0, i.e. $\rho = q_0 \cdot i_1 \cdot q_1 \cdot i_2 \cdot q_2 \cdots i_{n-1} \cdot q_{n-1} \cdot i_n \cdot q_n$. In each state q_k, the next input i_{k+1} is chosen non-deterministically and based on that, the next state q_{k+1} is chosen probabilistically according to $\delta(q_k, i_{k+1})$. The execution of an MDP is controlled by a so-called scheduler, resolving the non-deterministic choice of inputs by specifying a distribution over the next input given the current execution path. The composition of an MDP and a scheduler induces a Markov chain with a corresponding probability measure, see e.g. [19].

Sequences of Observations. During the execution of a finite path ρ, we observe a trace $L(\rho) = t$, i.e. an alternating sequence of inputs and outputs starting with an output, with $t = o_0 i_1 o_1 \cdots i_{n-1} o_{n-1} i_n o_n$ and $L(q_i) = o_i$. Since we consider deterministic MDPs, L is invertible, thus each trace in $\Sigma^O \times (\Sigma^I \times \Sigma^O)^*$ corresponds to at most one path. We say that a trace t is *observable* if there exists a path ρ with $L(\rho) = t$. In a deterministic MDP $\mathcal{M}$, each observable trace t uniquely defines a state of $\mathcal{M}$ reached by executing t from the initial state q_0. We compute this state by $\delta^*(t) = \delta^*(q_0, t)$ defined by $\delta^*(q, L(q)) = q$ and

$$\delta^*(q, o_0 i_1 o_1 \cdots i_{n-1} o_{n-1} i_n o_n) = \Delta(\delta^*(q, o_0 i_1 o_1 \cdots i_{n-1} o_{n-1}), i_n, o_n).$$

If t is not observable, then there is no path ρ with $t = L(\rho)$, denoted by $\delta^*(t) = \bot$. We denote the last output o_n of a trace $t = o_0 \cdots i_n o_n$, by $last(t)$.

We use three types of observation sequences with short-hand notations:

- *Traces:* abbreviated by $\mathcal{TR} = \Sigma^O \times (\Sigma^I \times \Sigma^O)^*$
- *Test sequences:* abbreviated by $\mathcal{TS} = (\Sigma^O \times \Sigma^I)^*$
- *Continuation sequences:* abbreviated by $\mathcal{CS} = \Sigma^I \times \mathcal{TS}$

These sequence types alternate between inputs and outputs, thus they are related among each other. In slight abuse of notation, we use $A \times B$ and $A \cdot B$ interchangeably for the remainder of this paper. Furthermore, we extend the sequence notations and the notion of prefixes to Σ^O, Σ^I, $\mathcal{TR}$, $\mathcal{TS}$ and $\mathcal{CS}$, e.g., test sequences and traces are related by $\mathcal{TR} = \mathcal{TS} \cdot \Sigma^O$.

As noted, a trace in $\mathcal{TR}$ leads to a unique state of an MDP $\mathcal{M}$. A test sequence in $s \in \mathcal{TS}$ of length n consists of a trace in $t \in \mathcal{TR}$ with n outputs and an input $i \in \Sigma^I$ with $s = t \cdot i$; thus executing test sequence $s = t \cdot i$ puts $\mathcal{M}$ into the state reached by t and tests $\mathcal{M}$'s reaction to i. Extending the notion of observability, we say that the test sequence s is observable if t is observable. A continuation sequence $c \in \mathcal{CS}$ begins and ends with an input, i.e. concatenating a trace $t \in \mathcal{TR}$ and c creates a test sequence $t \cdot c$ in $\mathcal{TS}$. Informally, continuation sequences test $\mathcal{M}$'s reaction in response to multiple consecutive inputs.

Active Automata Learning. We consider active automata learning in the minimally adequate teacher (MAT) framework [4], introduced by Angluin for the L^* algorithm. It assumes the existence of a MAT, which is able to answer queries. L^* learns a DFA representing an unknown regular language L over some alphabet A and therefore requires two types of queries: *membership* and *equivalence* queries. First, L^* repeatedly selects strings in A^* and checks if they are in L via *membership* queries. Once the algorithm has gained sufficient information, it forms a hypothesis DFA consistent with the membership query results. It then poses an *equivalence* query checking for equivalence between L and the language accepted by the hypothesis. The teacher responds either with *yes* signalling equivalence; or with a counterexample to equivalence, i.e. a string in the symmetric difference between L and the language accepted by the hypothesis. After processing a counterexample, L^* starts a new round of learning, consisting of membership queries and a concluding equivalence query. Once an equivalence query returns *yes*, learning stops with the final hypothesis as output.

L^* has been extended to learn models of reactive systems such as Mealy machines [35]. In practice, queries for learning models of black-box systems are usually implemented via testing [2]. Therefore, equivalence queries are generally only approximated as complete testing for black-box systems is impossible unless there is an upper bound on the number of system states.

3   Exact Learning of MDPs

This section presents $L^*_{\mathrm{MDP}^e}$, an exact active learning algorithm for MDPs, the basis for the sampling-based algorithm presented in Sect. 4. In contrast to sampling, $L^*_{\mathrm{MDP}^e}$ assumes the existence of a teacher with perfect knowledge about the SUL that is able to answer two types of queries: *output distribution* queries and *equivalence* queries. The former asks for the exact distribution of outputs following a test sequence in the SUL. The latter takes a hypothesis MDP as input and responds either with *yes* iff the hypothesis is observationally equivalent to the SUL or with a counterexample to equivalence. A counterexample is a test sequence leading to different output distributions in hypothesis and SUL. First, we describe how we capture the semantics of MDPs.

Semantics of MDPs. We can interpret an MDP as a function $M : \mathcal{TS} \to Dist(\Sigma^O) \cup \{\bot\}$, mapping test sequences s to output distributions or undefined behaviour for non-observable s. This follows the interpretation of Mealy machines as functions from input sequences to outputs [36]. Viewing MDPs as reactive systems, we consider two MDPs to be equivalent, if their semantics are equal, i.e. we make the same observations on both.

Definition 2 (MDP Semantics). *Given an MDP* $\langle Q, \Sigma^I, \Sigma^O, q_0, \delta, L \rangle$, *its semantics is a function* M, *defined for* $i \in \Sigma^I$, $o \in \Sigma^O$, $t \in \mathcal{TR}$ *as follows:*

$$M(\epsilon)(L(q_0)) = 1$$
$$M(t \cdot i) = \bot \ \mathit{if} \ \delta^*(t) = \bot$$
$$M(t \cdot i)(o) = p \ \mathit{otherwise} \ \mathit{if} \ \delta(\delta^*(t), i)(q) = p > 0 \land L(q) = o$$

MDPs $\mathcal{M}_1$ *and* $\mathcal{M}_2$ *with semantics* M_1 *and* M_2 *are output-distribution equivalent, denoted* $\mathcal{M}_1 \equiv_{od} \mathcal{M}_2$, *iff* $M_1 = M_2$.

Definition 3 (*M*-Equivalence of Traces). *Two traces* $t_1, t_2 \in \mathcal{TR}$ *are equivalent with respect to* $M : \mathcal{TS} \to Dist(\Sigma^O) \cup \{\bot\}$, *denoted* $t_1 \equiv_M t_2$, *iff* $last(t_1) = last(t_2)$ *and for all continuations* $v \in \mathcal{CS}$ *it holds that* $M(t_1 \cdot v) = M(t_2 \cdot v)$.

A function M defines an equivalence relation on traces, like the Myhill-Nerode equivalence for formal languages [31] (see also [38]). Two traces are M-equivalent if they end in the same output and if their behaviour in response to future inputs is the same. Two traces leading to the same MDP state are in the same equivalence class of $\equiv_M$, as in Mealy machines [36].

Queries. We are now able to define queries focusing on the observable behaviour of MDPs. Assume that we want to learn a model of a black-box deterministic MDP $\mathcal{M}$, with semantics M. Output distribution queries (**odq**) and equivalence queries (**eq**) are then defined as follows:

- *output distribution (**odq**):* an **odq**(s) returns $M(s)$ for input $s \in \mathcal{TS}$.
- *equivalence (**eq**):* an **eq** query takes a hypothesis MDP $\mathcal{H}$ with semantics H as input and returns *yes* if $\mathcal{H} \equiv_{\mathrm{od}} \mathcal{M}$; otherwise it returns an $s \in \mathcal{TS}$ such that $H(s) \neq M(s)$ and $M(s) \neq \bot$.

Observation Tables. Like L^*, we store information in observation table triples $\langle S, E, T \rangle$, where:

- $S \subset \mathcal{TR}$ is a prefix-closed set of traces, initialised to $\{o_0\}$, with o_0 being the initial SUL output,
- $E \subset \mathcal{CS}$ is a suffix-closed set of continuation sequences, initialised to Σ^{I},
- $T : (S \cup Lt(S)) \cdot E \rightarrow Dist(\Sigma^{\mathrm{O}}) \cup \{\bot\}$ is a mapping from test sequences to output distributions or $\bot$ denoting undefined behaviour. This mapping basically stores a finite subset of M. The set $Lt(S) \subseteq S \cdot \Sigma^{\mathrm{I}} \cdot \Sigma^{\mathrm{O}}$ is given by $Lt(S) = \{s \cdot i \cdot o | s \in S, i \in \Sigma^{\mathrm{I}}, o \in \Sigma^{\mathrm{O}}, \mathbf{odq}(s \cdot i)(o) > 0\}$.

We can view an observation table as a two-dimensional array with rows labelled by traces in $S \cup Lt(S)$ and columns labelled by E. We refer to traces in S as short traces and to their extensions in $Lt(S)$ as long traces. An extension $s \cdot i \cdot o$ of a short trace s is in $Lt(S)$ if $s \cdot i \cdot o$ is observable. Analogously to traces, we refer to rows labelled by S as short rows. The table cells store the mapping defined by T. To represent rows labelled by traces s we use functions $row(s) : E \rightarrow Dist(\Sigma^{\mathrm{O}}) \cup \{\bot\}$ for $s \in S \cup Lt(S)$ with $row(s)(e) = T(s \cdot e)$. Equivalence of rows labelled by traces s_1, s_2, denoted $\mathbf{eqRow}_E(s_1, s_2)$, holds iff $row(s_1) = row(s_2) \wedge last(s_1) = last(s_2)$ and approximates M-equivalence $s_1 \equiv_M s_2$, by considering only continuations in E, i.e. $s_1 \equiv_M s_2$ implies $\mathbf{eqRow}_E(s_1, s_2)$. The observation table content defines the structure of hypothesis MDPs based on the following principle: we create one state per equivalence class of $S/\mathbf{eqRow}_E$, thus we identify states with traces in S reaching them and we distinguish states by their future behaviour in response to sequences in E (as is common in active automata learning [36]). The long traces $Lt(S)$ serve to define transitions. Transition probabilities are given by the distributions in the mapping T.

Table 1 shows a part of the observation table created during learning of the coffee machine shown in Fig. 1. The set S has a trace for each state of the MDP. Note that these traces are pairwise inequivalent with respect to $\mathbf{eqRow}_E$, where $E = \Sigma^{\mathrm{I}} = \{\mathtt{but}, \mathtt{coin}\}$. We only show one element of $Lt(S)$, which gives rise to the self-loop in the initial state with the input $\mathtt{but}$ and probability 1.

Definition 4 (Closedness). *An observation table $\langle S, E, T \rangle$ is closed if for all $l \in Lt(S)$ there is an $s \in S$ such that $\mathbf{eqRow}_E(l, s)$.*

Table 1. Parts of observation table for learning the faulty coffee machine (Fig. 1).

		but	coin
S	init	$\{\texttt{init} \mapsto 1\}$	$\{\texttt{beep} \mapsto 1\}$
	init $\cdot$ coin $\cdot$ beep	$\{\texttt{coffee} \mapsto 0.8, \texttt{init} \mapsto 0.2\}$	$\{\texttt{beep} \mapsto 1\}$
	init $\cdot$ coin $\cdot$ beep $\cdot$ but $\cdot$ coffee	$\{\texttt{init} \mapsto 1\}$	$\{\texttt{beep} \mapsto 1\}$
$Lt(S)$	init $\cdot$ but $\cdot$ init	$\{\texttt{init} \mapsto 1\}$	$\{\texttt{beep} \mapsto 1\}$
	$\ldots$	$\ldots$	$\ldots$

Algorithm 1. Making an observation table closed and consistent

```
 1: function MAKECLOSEDANDCONSISTENT(⟨S, E, T⟩)
 2:     if ⟨S, E, T⟩ is not closed then
 3:         l ← l′ ∈ Lt(S) such that ∀s ∈ S : row(s) ≠ row(l′) ∨ last(s) ≠ last(l′)
 4:         S ← S ∪ {l}
 5:     else if ⟨S, E, T⟩ is not consistent then
 6:         for all s₁, s₂ ∈ S such that eqRow_E(s₁, s₂) do
 7:             for all i ∈ Σ^I, o ∈ Σ^O do
 8:                 if T(s₁ · i)(o) > 0 and ¬eqRow_E(s₁ · i · o, s₂ · i · o) then
 9:                     e ← e′ ∈ E such that T(s₁ · i · o · e′) ≠ T(s₂ · i · o · e′)
10:                     E ← E ∪ {i · o · e}
11:     return ⟨S, E, T⟩
```

Definition 5 (Consistency). *An observation table $\langle S, E, T \rangle$ is consistent if for all $s_1, s_2 \in S, i \in \Sigma^I, o \in \Sigma^O$ such that $\mathbf{eqRow}_E(s_1, s_2)$ it holds either that (1) $T(s_1 \cdot i)(o) = 0 \wedge T(s_2 \cdot i)(o) = 0$ or (2) $\mathbf{eqRow}_E(s_1 \cdot i \cdot o, s_2 \cdot i \cdot o)$.*

Closedness and consistency are required to derive well-formed hypotheses, analogously to L^* [4]. We require closedness to create transitions for all inputs in all states and we require consistency to be able to derive deterministic hypotheses. During learning, we apply Algorithm 1 repeatedly to establish closedness and consistency of observation tables. The algorithm adds a new short trace if the table is not closed and adds a new column if the table is not consistent.

We derive a hypothesis $\mathcal{H} = \langle Q_h, \Sigma^I, \Sigma^O, q_{0h}, \delta_h, L_h \rangle$ from a closed and consistent observation table $\langle S, E, T \rangle$, denoted $\mathcal{H} = \text{hyp}(S, E, T)$, as follows:

- $Q_h = \{\langle last(s), row(s) \rangle | s \in S\}$
- $q_{0h} = \langle o_0, row(o_0) \rangle$, $o_0 \in S$ is the trace consisting of the initial SUL output
- for $s \in S, i \in \Sigma^I$ and $o \in \Sigma^O$:
  $\delta_h(\langle last(s), row(s) \rangle, i)(\langle o, row(s \cdot i \cdot o) \rangle) = p$ if $T(s \cdot i)(o) = p > 0$
- for $s \in S$: $L_h(\langle last(s), row(s) \rangle) = last(s)$

Learning Algorithm. Algorithm 2 implements $L^*_{\text{MDP}^e}$ using queries **odq** and **eq**. First, the algorithm initialises the observation tables and fills the table cells with output distribution queries (Lines 1 to 3). The main loop in Lines 4 to 15 makes the observation table closed and consistent, derives a hypothesis $\mathcal{H}$ and performs an equivalence query **eq**($\mathcal{H}$). If a counterexample *cex* is found, all its prefix traces are added as short traces to S, otherwise the final hypothesis is

Algorithm 2. The main algorithm implementing $L^*_{\mathrm{MDP}^e}$

Input: Σ^I, exact teacher capable of answering **odq** and **eq**
Output: learned model $\mathcal{H}$ (final hypothesis)
  1: $o_0 \leftarrow o$ such that $\mathbf{odq}(\epsilon)(o) = 1$
  2: $S \leftarrow \{o_0\}, E \leftarrow \Sigma^I$
  3: FILL(S, E, T)
  4: **repeat**
  5:      **while** $\langle S, E, T \rangle$ not closed or not consistent **do**
  6:           $\langle S, E, T \rangle \leftarrow$ MAKECLOSEDANDCONSISTENT$(\langle S, E, T \rangle)$
  7:           FILL(S, E, T)
  8:      $\mathcal{H} \leftarrow \mathrm{hyp}(S, E, T)$
  9:      $eqResult \leftarrow \mathbf{eq}(\mathcal{H})$
10:      **if** $eqResult \neq yes$ **then**
11:           $cex \leftarrow eqResult$
12:           **for all** $(t \cdot i) \in prefixes(cex)$ with $i \in \Sigma^I$ **do**
13:                $S \leftarrow S \cup \{t\}$
14:           FILL(S, E, T)
15: **until** $eqResult = yes$
16: **return** $\mathrm{hyp}(S, E, T)$
17: **procedure** FILL(S, E, T)
18:      **for all** $s \in S \cup Lt(S), e \in E$ **do**
19:           **if** $T(s \cdot e)$ undefined **then**   ▷ we have no information about $T(s \cdot e)$ yet
20:                $T(s \cdot e) \leftarrow \mathbf{odq}(s \cdot e)$

---

returned, as it is output-distribution equivalent to the SUL. Whenever the table contains empty cells, the FILL procedure assigns values to these cells via **odq**.

Theorem 1. $L^*_{\mathrm{MDP}^e}$ *terminates and learns an MDP $\mathcal{H}$ that is output-distribution equivalent to the SUL and minimal in the number of states [38, Theorem 3].*

4   Learning MDPs by Sampling

The sampling-based L^*_{MDP} is based on $L^*_{\mathrm{MDP}^e}$, but samples SUL traces instead of posing exact queries. Distribution comparisons are consequently approximated through statistical tests. While using similar data structures, L^*_{MDP} has a slightly different algorithm structure allowing to stop before reaching exact equivalence.

Queries. The sampling-based teacher maintains a multiset of traces $\mathcal{S}$ for the estimation of output distributions that grows during learning. It offers an equivalence query and three queries relating to output distributions and samples $\mathcal{S}$.

- *frequency (**fq**):* given a test sequence $s \in \mathcal{TS}$, $\mathbf{fq}(s) : \Sigma^O \rightarrow \mathbb{N}_0$ are output frequencies observed after s, where $\mathbf{fq}(s)(o) = \mathcal{S}(s \cdot o)$ for $o \in \Sigma^O$.
- *complete (**cq**):* given a test sequence $s \in \mathcal{TS}$, $\mathbf{cq}(s)$ returns **true** if sufficient information is available to estimate an output distribution from $\mathbf{fq}(s)$; returns **false** otherwise.
- *refine (**rfq**):* instructs the teacher to refine its knowledge of the SUL by testing it directed towards rarely observed samples. Traces sampled by **rfq** are added to $\mathcal{S}$, increasing the accuracy of subsequent probability estimations.

– *equivalence (eq)*: given a hypothesis $\mathcal{H}$, **eq** tests for output-distribution equivalence between the SUL and $\mathcal{H}$; returns a counterexample from $\mathcal{TS}$ showing non-equivalence, or returns *none* if no counterexample was found.

To implement these queries, we require the ability to reset the SUL, to perform a single input on the SUL and to observe the SUL output.

4.1 Learner Implementation

Observation Table. L^*_{MDP} also uses observation tables. They carry similar information as in Sect. 3, but instead of output distributions in $Dist(\Sigma^O)$, we store integral output frequencies ($\Sigma^O \to \mathbb{N}_0$), from which we estimate distributions.

Definition 6. (Sampling-based Observation Table). *An observation table is a tuple $\langle S, E, \widehat{T} \rangle$, consisting of a prefix-closed set of traces $S \subset \mathcal{TR}$, a suffix-closed set of continuation sequences $E \subset \mathcal{CS}$, and a mapping $\widehat{T} : (S \cup Lt(S)) \cdot E \to (\Sigma^O \to \mathbb{N}_0)$, where $Lt(S) = \{s \cdot i \cdot o \,|\, s \in S, i \in \Sigma^I, o \in \Sigma^O : \mathbf{fq}(s \cdot i)(o) > 0\}$.*

Hypothesis Construction. As in Sect. 3, observation tables need to be closed and consistent for a hypothesis to be constructed. Here, we test statistically if cells and rows are approximately equal, referred to as compatible. The statistical tests applied in Definition 7 are based on Hoeffding bounds, as in [13]. Definition 8 serves as basis for adapted notions of closedness and consistency.

Definition 7. (Different). *Two sequences s and s' in $\mathcal{TS}$ produce statistically different output distributions with respect to $f : \mathcal{TS} \to (\Sigma^O \to \mathbb{N}_0)$, denoted diff$_f(s, s')$, iff (1) $\mathbf{cq}(s) \wedge \mathbf{cq}(s') \wedge n_1 > 0 \wedge n_2 > 0$ where $n_1 = \sum_{o \in \Sigma^O} f(s)(o)$, $n_2 = \sum_{o \in \Sigma^O} f(s')(o)$, and (2) one of the following conditions holds:*

2a. $\exists o \in \Sigma^O : \neg(f(s)(o) > 0 \Leftrightarrow f(s')(o) > 0)$, *or*

2b. $\exists o \in \Sigma^O : \left| \frac{f(s)(o)}{n_1} - \frac{f(s')(o)}{n_2} \right| > \left(\sqrt{\frac{1}{n_1}} + \sqrt{\frac{1}{n_2}} \right) \cdot \sqrt{\frac{1}{2} \ln \frac{2}{\alpha}}$, *where α specifies the confidence level $(1 - \alpha)^2$ for testing each o separately based on a Hoeffding bound [13, 21].*

Definition 8. (Compatible). *Two cells labelled by $c = s \cdot e$ and $c' = s' \cdot e'$ are compatible, denoted $\mathbf{compatible}(c, c')$, iff $\neg diff_{\widehat{T}}(c, c')$. Two rows labelled by s and s' are compatible, denoted $\mathbf{compatible}_E(s, s')$ iff $last(s) = last(s')$ and the cells corresponding to all $e \in E$ are compatible, i.e. $\mathbf{compatible}(s \cdot e, s' \cdot e)$.*

Compatibility Classes. In Sect. 3, we formed equivalence classes of traces with respect to $\mathbf{eqRow}_E$ creating one hypothesis state per equivalence class. Now we partition rows labelled by S based on compatibility. Compatibility given by Definition 8, however, is not an equivalence relation, as it is not transitive in general. As a result, we cannot simply create equivalence classes. We apply the heuristic implemented by Algorithm 3 to partition S.

Algorithm 3. Creating compatibility classes

1: **for all** $s \in S$ **do**
2: | rank$(s) \leftarrow \sum_{i \in \Sigma^{\mathrm{I}}} \sum_{o \in \Sigma^{\mathrm{O}}} \widehat{T}(s \cdot i)(o)$
3: $unpartitioned \leftarrow S$, $R \leftarrow \emptyset$
4: **while** $unpartitioned \neq \emptyset$ **do**
5: | $r \leftarrow m$ where $m \in unpartitioned$ with largest rank(m)
6: | $R \leftarrow R \cup \{r\}$
7: | $cg(r) \leftarrow \{s \in unpartitioned \mid \mathbf{compatible}_E(s, r)\}$
8: | **for all** $s \in cg(r)$ **do**
9: | | $rep(s) \leftarrow r$
10: | $unpartitioned \leftarrow unpartitioned \setminus cg(r)$

First, we assign a rank to each trace in S. Then, we partition S by iteratively selecting the trace r with the largest rank and computing a *compatibility class* $cg(r)$ for r. The trace r is the (canonical) representative for s in $cg(r)$, which we denote by $rep(s)$ (Line 9). Each r is stored in the set of representative traces R. In contrast to equivalence classes, elements in a compatibility class need not be pairwise compatible and an s may be compatible to multiple representatives, where the unique representative $rep(s)$ of s has the largest rank.

Definition 9. (Sampling Closedness). *An observation table* $\langle S, E, \widehat{T} \rangle$ *is closed if for all* $l \in Lt(S)$ *there is a representative* $s \in R$ *with* $\mathbf{compatible}_E(l, s)$.

Definition 10. (Sampling Consistency). *An observation table* $\langle S, E, \widehat{T} \rangle$ *is consistent if for all compatible pairs of short traces* s, s' *in* S *and all input-output pairs* $i \cdot o \in \Sigma^{\mathrm{I}} \cdot \Sigma^{\mathrm{O}}$, *we have that (1) at least one of their extensions has not been observed yet, i.e.* $\widehat{T}(s \cdot i)(o) = 0$ *or* $\widehat{T}(s' \cdot i)(o) = 0$, *or (2) both extensions are compatible, i.e.* $\mathbf{compatible}_E(s \cdot i \cdot o, s' \cdot i \cdot o)$.

Given a closed and consistent observation table $\langle S, E, \widehat{T} \rangle$, we derive hypothesis MDP $\mathcal{H} = \mathrm{hyp}(S, E, \widehat{T})$ through the steps below. Note that extensions $s \cdot i \cdot o$ of s in S define transitions. Some extensions may have few observations, i.e. $\widehat{T}(s \cdot i)$ is low and $\mathbf{cq}(s \cdot i) = \mathbf{false}$. In case of such uncertainties, we add transitions to a special sink state labelled by "chaos", an output not in the original alphabet[1]. A hypothesis is a tuple $\mathcal{H} = \langle Q_h, \Sigma^{\mathrm{I}}, \Sigma^{\mathrm{O}} \cup \{\mathrm{chaos}\}, q_{0h}, \delta_h, L_h \rangle$ where:

- representatives for long traces $l \in Lt(S)$ are given by (see Algorithm 3):
  $rep(l) = r$ where $r \in \{r' \in R \mid \mathbf{compatible}_E(l, r')\}$ with largest rank(r)
- $Q_h = \{\langle last(s), row(s) \rangle \mid s \in R\} \cup \{q_{\mathrm{chaos}}\}$,
  - for $q = \langle o, row(s) \rangle \in Q_h \setminus \{q_{\mathrm{chaos}}\}$: $L_h(q) = o$
  - for q_{chaos}: $L_h(q_{\mathrm{chaos}}) = \mathrm{chaos}$ and for all $i \in \Sigma^{\mathrm{I}}$: $\delta_h(q_{\mathrm{chaos}}, i)(q_{\mathrm{chaos}}) = 1$
- $q_{0h} = \langle L(q_0), row(L(q_0)) \rangle$
- for $q = \langle last(s), row(s) \rangle \in Q_h \setminus \{q_{\mathrm{chaos}}\}$ and $i \in \Sigma^{\mathrm{I}}$ (note that $\Sigma^{\mathrm{I}} \subseteq E$):
  - If $\neg \mathbf{cq}(s \cdot i)$:
    $\delta(q, i)(q_{\mathrm{chaos}}) = 1$, i.e. move to chaos
  - Otherwise estimate a distribution $\mu = \delta_h(q, i)$ over the successor states:
    for $o \in \Sigma^{\mathrm{O}}$ with $\widehat{T}(s \cdot i)(o) > 0$: $\mu(\langle o, row(rep(s \cdot i \cdot o)) \rangle) = \dfrac{\widehat{T}(s \cdot i)(o)}{\sum_{o' \in \Sigma^{\mathrm{O}}} \widehat{T}(s \cdot i)(o')}$

---

[1] This is inspired by the introduction of chaos states in **ioco**-based learning [43].

Algorithm 4. The main algorithm implementing L^*_{MDP}

Input: sampling-based teacher capable of answering **fq, rfq, eq** and **cq**
1: $S \leftarrow \{L(q_0)\}, E \leftarrow \Sigma^I, \widehat{T} \leftarrow \{\}$ ▷ initialise observation table
2: perform **rfq**($\langle S, E, \widehat{T} \rangle$)   ▷ sample traces for initial observation table
3: **for all** $s \in S \cup Lt(S), e \in E$ **do**
4: | $\widehat{T}(s \cdot e) \leftarrow$ **fq**($s \cdot e$)   ▷ update observation table with frequency information
5: $round \leftarrow 0$
6: **repeat**
7: | $round \leftarrow round + 1$
8: | **while** $\langle S, E, \widehat{T} \rangle$ not closed or not consistent **do**
9: | | $\langle S, E, \widehat{T} \rangle \leftarrow$ MAKECLOSEDANDCONSISTENT($\langle S, E, \widehat{T} \rangle$)
10: | $\mathcal{H} \leftarrow$ hyp($S, E, \widehat{T}$)   ▷ create hypothesis
11: | $\langle S, E, \widehat{T} \rangle \leftarrow$ TRIM($\langle S, E, \widehat{T} \rangle, \mathcal{H}$)   ▷ remove rows that are not needed
12: | $cex \leftarrow$ **eq**($\mathcal{H}$)
13: | **if** $cex \neq none$ **then**   ▷ we found a counterexample
14: | | **for all** $(t \cdot i) \in prefixes(cex)$ with $i \in \Sigma^I$ **do**
15: | | | $S \leftarrow S \cup \{t\}$ ▷ add all prefixes of the counterexample
16: | perform **rfq**($\langle S, E, \widehat{T} \rangle$)   ▷ sample traces to refine knowledge about SUL
17: | **for all** $s \in S \cup Lt(S), e \in E$ **do**
18: | | $\widehat{T}(s \cdot e) \leftarrow$ **fq**($s \cdot e$)   ▷ update observation table with frequency information
19: **until** STOP($\langle S, E, \widehat{T} \rangle, \mathcal{H}, round$)
20: **return** hyp($S, E, \widehat{T}$)   ▷ output final hypothesis

---

Updating the Observation Table. Analogously to Sect. 3, we make observation tables closed by adding new short rows and we establish consistency by adding new columns. While Algorithm 2 needs to fill the observation table after executing MAKECLOSEDANDCONSISTENT, this is not required in the sampling-based setting due to the adapted notions of closedness and consistency.

Trimming the Observation Table. Observation table size greatly affects learning performance, therefore it is common to avoid adding redundant information [24, 33]. Due to inexact information, this is hard to apply in a stochastic setting. We instead remove rows via a function TRIM, once we are certain that this does not change the hypothesis. We remove rows that are (1) not prefixes of representatives $r \in R$, (2) that are compatible to exactly one $r \in R$, and (3) that are not prefixes of counterexamples to equivalence between SUL and hypothesis.

Learning Algorithm. Algorithm 4 implements L^*_{MDP}. It first initialises an observation table $\langle S, E, \widehat{T} \rangle$ with the initial SUL output as first row and with the inputs Σ^I as columns (Line 1). Lines 2 to 4 perform a refine query and then update $\langle S, E, \widehat{T} \rangle$, which corresponds to output distribution queries in $L^*_{\text{MDP}^e}$. Here, the teacher resamples the only known trace $L(q_0)$.

After that, we perform Lines 6 to 19 until a stopping criterion is reached. We establish closedness and consistency of $\langle S, E, \widehat{T} \rangle$ in Line 9 to build a hypothesis $\mathcal{H}$ in Line 10. After that, we remove redundant rows of the observation table via TRIM in Line 11. Then, we perform an equivalence query, testing for equivalence between SUL and $\mathcal{H}$. If we find a counterexample, we add all its prefix traces as rows to the observation table like in $L^*_{\text{MDP}^e}$. Finally, we sample new system traces via **rfq** to gain more accurate information about the SUL (Lines 16 to 18). Once we stop, we output the final hypothesis.

Stopping. The exact learner $L^*_{\text{MDP}^e}$ stops upon reaching equivalence to the SUL, i.e. once there is no counterexample. In the sampling-based setting, we may not find a counterexample due to inaccurate hypotheses. Our stopping criterion therefore takes uncertainty into account, which we quantify with r_{unamb}, the relative number of (unambiguous) traces in $S \cup Lt(S)$ compatible to exactly one representative in R. Additionally, we check if the chaos state is reachable.

Consequently, we stop when (1) $r_{\text{unamb}} \geq t_{\text{unamb}}$ where t_{unamb} is a user-defined threshold, (2) the chaos state is unreachable, and (3) at least r_{min} rounds have been executed. We also stop after a maximum of r_{max} rounds.

4.2   Teacher Implementation

Due to space constraints, we discuss each query only briefly. An accurate description can be found in the full technical report [38].

- *frequency (fq):* returns output frequencies observed in the sampled traces S.
- *complete (cq):* complete queries are based on threshold n_c. We consider test sequences complete that have been sampled at least n_c times.
- *refine (rfq):* refine queries take an observation table $\langle S, E, \widehat{T} \rangle$ and resample incomplete sequences in $(S \cup Lt(S)) \cdot E$. The parameter n_{resample} defines how often we resample.
- *equivalence (eq):* we apply two strategies for equivalence queries. *First*, we test for structural equivalence between hypothesis $\mathcal{H}$ and SUL. The testing strategy inspired by [2] performs random walks on $\mathcal{H}$ and has three parameters: n_{test}, the maximum number of tests, p_{stop}, the stop probability, and p_{rand}, the probability of choosing inputs uniformly at random. *Second*, we check for conformance between the collected samples S and $\mathcal{H}$ via *diff$_{\text{fq}}$*.

Note that we return no counterexample if trivial counterexamples containing chaos are observable in the hypothesis. This prompts L^*_{MDP} to issue further *refine* queries, causing the chaos state to be unreachable eventually. Otherwise, the observation table might grow unnecessarily which is detrimental to performance.

Convergence. We have examined convergence of the sampling-based L^*_{MDP} in the limit with respect to the following setup. We configure equivalence testing such that each input is chosen uniformly at random and the length of each test is geometrically distributed. This resembles the sampling regime assumed for IoA-LERGIA [29]. Likewise, we consider a data-dependent $\alpha_n = \frac{1}{n^r}$ with $r > 2$, where n is the number of samples collected so far. Finally, we consider L^*_{MDP} without trimming of observation tables. Informally, letting the number of rounds and thus the sample size n approach infinity, we eventually learn the correct MDP.

Theorem 2. L^*_{MDP} *as configured above creates hypotheses $\mathcal{H}_n$ that are minimal in the number of states and output-distribution equivalent to the SUL in the limit (see Theorem 4 and its proof in [38]).*

5   Experiments

We evaluate the sampling-based L^*_{MDP} and compare it to the passive IOALER-GIA [29] by learning a gridworld model with both techniques. Experimental results and the implementation can be found in the evaluation material [37]. We treat the known true MDP model $\mathcal{M}$ as a black box for learning and measure similarity to this model using two criteria: (1) the discounted bisimilarity distance [6,7] between $\mathcal{M}$ and the learned MDPs and (2) the difference between probabilistic model-checking results for $\mathcal{M}$ and learned MDPs. We compute maximal probabilities of manually defined temporal properties with all models using PRISM 4.4 [27].

Measurement Setup. As in [29], we use a data-dependent $\epsilon_N = \frac{10000}{N}$ for IOA-LERGIA, where N is the combined length of all learning traces. This parameter serves a role analogous to the α parameter of L^*_{MDP}. In contrast, we observed that L^*_{MDP} performs better with a fixed $\alpha = 0.05$. We sample traces for IOALERGIA with a length geometrically distributed with parameter p_l and inputs chosen uniformly at random, also as in [29]. The number of traces is chosen such that IOALERGIA and L^*_{MDP} learn from approximately the same amount of data.

We implemented L^*_{MDP} and IOALERGIA in Java. Additionally, we use the MDPDIST library [5] for bisimilarity distances, adapted to labelled MDPs. We performed the experiments with a Lenovo Thinkpad T450 with 16 GB RAM, an Intel Core i7-5600U CPU with 2.6 GHz and running Xubuntu Linux 18.04.

Gridworld. Models similar to our gridworld have, e.g., been considered in the context of learning control strategies [20]. Basically, a robot moves around in a world of tiles of different terrains. It may make errors in movement, e.g. move south west instead of south with an error probability depending on the target terrain. Our aim is to learn an environment model, i.e. a map. Figure 2 shows our gridworld. Black tiles are walls and other terrains are represented by different shades of grey and letters (Sand, Mud, Grass & Concrete). A circle marks the initial location and a double circle marks a goal location. Four inputs enable movement in four directions. Observable outputs include the different terrains, walls, and a label indicating the goal. The true model of this gridworld has 35 different states. All terrains except Concrete have a distinct positive error probability.

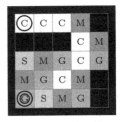

Fig. 2. The evaluation gridworld

We configured sampling by $n_{\text{resample}} = 300$, $n_{\text{test}} = 50$, $p_{\text{stop}} = 0.25$ and $p_{\text{rand}} = 0.25$, and stopping by $t_{\text{unamb}} = 0.99$, $r_{\text{min}} = 500$ and $r_{\text{max}} = 4000$. Finally, we set $p_l = 0.25$ for IOALERGIA.

Results. Table 2 shows the measurement results for learning the gridworld. Our active learning stopped after 1147 rounds, sampling 391530 traces (Row 2) with a combined number of outputs of 3101959 (Row 1). The bisimilarity distance

Table 2. Results for learning the gridworld example.

	True model	L^*_{MDP}	IoALERGIA
# outputs	-	3 101 959	3 103 607
# traces	-	391 530	387 746
time [s]	-	118.3770	21.4420
# states	35	35	21
$\delta_{0.9}$	-	0.1442	0.5241
$\mathbb{P}_{\max}(F^{\leq 11}(\text{goal}))$	0.9622	0.9651	0.2306
$\mathbb{P}_{\max}(\neg G\ U^{\leq 14}(\text{goal}))$	0.6499	0.6461	0.1577
$\mathbb{P}_{\max}(\neg S\ U^{\leq 16}(\text{goal}))$	0.6912	0.6768	0.1800

discounted with $\lambda = 0.9$ to the true model is 0.144 for L^*_{MDP} and 0.524 for IoA-
LERGIA (Row 5); thus it can be assumed that model checking the L^*_{MDP} model
produces more accurate results. This is indeed true for our three evaluation
queries in the last three rows. These model-checking queries ask for the maximum probability (quantified over all schedulers) of reaching the goal within a
varying number of steps. The first query does not restrict the terrain visited
before the goal, but the second and third require to avoid G and S, respectively.
The absolute difference to the true values is at most 0.015 for L^*_{MDP}, but the
results for IoALERGIA differ greatly from the true values. One reason is that the
IoALERGIA model with 21 states is significantly smaller than the minimal true
model, while the L^*_{MDP} model has as many states as the true model. IoALERGIA
is faster than L^*_{MDP}, which applies time-consuming computations during equivalence queries. However, the runtime of learning-specific computations is often
negligible in practical applications, such as learning of protocol models [34,39], as
the communication with the SUL usually dominates the overall runtime. Given
the smaller bisimilarity distance and the lower difference to the true probabilities
computed with PRISM, we conclude that the L^*_{MDP} model is more accurate.

Due to space constraints, we only present the intuitive gridworld experiment.
The full technical report includes further experiments with a larger gridworld
(72 states), a consensus protocol (272 states) and a slot machine model (109
states) [38]. They also confirm the favourable accuracy of L^*_{MDP}.

6   Related Work

In the following, we discuss techniques for learning both model structure and
transition probabilities in case of probabilistic systems. There are many learning
approaches for models with a given structure, e.g., for learning control strategies [20]. Covering these approaches is beyond the scope of this paper.

We build upon Angluin's L^* [4], thus our work shares similarities with other
L^*-based work like active learning of Mealy machines [30,35]. Interpreting MDPs

as functions from test sequences to output distributions is similar to the interpretation of Mealy machines as functions from input sequences to outputs [36].

Volpato and Tretmans presented an L^*-based technique for non-deterministic input-output transition systems [43]. They simultaneously learn an over- and an under-approximation of the SUL with respect to the input output conformance (ioco) relation [40]. Inspired by that, we apply completeness queries and we add transitions to a chaos state in case of incomplete information. Beyond that, we consider systems to behave stochastically rather than non-deterministically. Early work on ioco-based learning for non-deterministic systems has been presented by Willemse [44]. Khalili and Tacchella [25] addressed non-determinism by presenting an L^*-based algorithm for non-deterministic Mealy machines.

Most sampling-based learning algorithms for stochastic systems are passive. Notable early works are ALERGIA [12] and rlips [13], which identify stochastic regular languages. Both also apply Hoeffing bounds [21] for testing for difference between probability distributions. We compare L^*_{MDP} to IoALERGIA, an extension of ALERGIA by Mao et al. [28,29]. It basically creates a tree-shaped representation of given system traces and repeatedly merges compatible nodes, creating an automaton. Normalised observed output frequencies estimate transition probabilities. IoALERGIA also converges in the limit. Chen and Nielsen applied it in an active setting [16], by sampling new traces to reduce uncertainty in the data. In contrast to this, we base our sampling not only on data collected so far (refine queries), but also on observation tables and derived hypothesis MDPs (refine & equivalence queries), taking information about the SUL's structure into account. In previous work, we presented a different approach to active learning via IoALERGIA which takes reachability objectives into account with the aim at maximising the probability of reaching desired events [3].

Feng et al. [17] learn assumptions for compositional verification in the form of probabilistic finite automata with an L^*-style method. Their method requires queries returning exact probabilities, hence it is not applicable in a sampling-based setting. It shares similarities with an L^*-based algorithm for learning multiplicity automata [10], a generalisation of deterministic automata. Further query-based learning in a probabilistic setting has been described by Tzeng [41]. He presented a query-based algorithm for learning probabilistic automata and an adaptation of Angluin's L^* for learning Markov chains. Castro and Gavaldà review passive learning techniques for probabilistic automata with a focus on convergence guarantees and present them in a query framework [15]. Unlike MDPs, the learned automata cannot be controlled by inputs.

7   Conclusion

We presented L^*-based learning of MDPs. For our exact learning algorithm $L^*_{\text{MDP}^e}$, we assumed an ideal setting that allows to query information about the SUL with exact precision. Subsequently, we relaxed our assumptions, by approximating exact queries through sampling SUL traces via directed testing. These traces serve to infer the structure of hypothesis MDPs, to estimate transition probabilities and to check for equivalence between SUL and learned hypotheses. The resulting sampling-based L_{MDP}^* iteratively learns approximate MDPs which converge to the correct MDP in the large sample limit. We implemented L_{MDP}^* and compared it to IOALERGIA [29], a state-of-the-art passive learning algorithm for MDPs. The evaluation showed that L_{MDP}^* is able to produce more accurate models. To the best of our knowledge, L_{MDP}^* is the first L^*-based algorithm for MDPs that can be implemented via testing. Further details regarding the implementation, convergence proofs and extended experiments can be found in the technical report [38] and the evaluation material [37].

The evaluation showed promising results, therefore we believe that our technique can greatly aid the black-box analysis of reactive systems such as communication protocols. While deterministic active automata learning has successfully been applied in this area [18,39], networked environments are prone to be affected by uncertain behaviour that can be captured by MDPs. A potential direction for future work is an analysis of L_{MDP}^* with respect to probably approximately correct (PAC) learnability [15,42] to provide stronger convergence guarantees. A challenge towards this goal will be the identification of a distance measure suited to verification [29]. Furthermore, L_{MDP}^* provides room for experimentation, e.g. different testing techniques could be applied in equivalence queries.

Acknowledgment. The work of B. Aichernig, M. Eichlseder and M. Tappler has been carried out as part of the TU Graz LEAD project "Dependable Internet of Things in Adverse Environments". The work of K. Larsen and G. Bacci has been supported by the Advanced ERC Grant nr. 867096 (LASSO).

References

1. Aichernig, B.K., Mostowski, W., Mousavi, M.R., Tappler, M., Taromirad, M.: Model learning and model-based testing. In: Bennaceur et al. [9], pp. 74–100. https://doi.org/10.1007/978-3-319-96562-8_3
2. Aichernig, B.K., Tappler, M.: Efficient active automata learning via mutation testing. J. Autom. Reasoning (2018). https://doi.org/10.1007/s10817-018-9486-0
3. Aichernig, B.K., Tappler, M.: Probabilistic black-box reachability checking (extended version). Formal Methods Syst. Des. (2019). https://doi.org/10.1007/s10703-019-00333-0
4. Angluin, D.: Learning regular sets from queries and counterexamples. Inf. Comput. **75**(2), 87–106 (1987). https://doi.org/10.1016/0890-5401(87)90052-6
5. Bacci, G., Bacci, G., Larsen, K.G., Mardare, R.: MDPDist library. http://people.cs.aau.dk/~giovbacci/tools/bisimdist.zip. Accessed 28 June 2019
6. Bacci, G., Bacci, G., Larsen, K.G., Mardare, R.: Computing behavioral distances, compositionally. In: Chatterjee, K., Sgall, J. (eds.) MFCS 2013. LNCS, vol. 8087, pp. 74–85. Springer, Heidelberg (2013). https://doi.org/10.1007/978-3-642-40313-2_9
7. Bacci, G., Bacci, G., Larsen, K.G., Mardare, R.: The BISIMDIST library: efficient computation of bisimilarity distances for Markovian models. In: Joshi, K., Siegle, M., Stoelinga, M., D'Argenio, P.R. (eds.) QEST 2013. LNCS, vol. 8054, pp. 278–281. Springer, Heidelberg (2013). https://doi.org/10.1007/978-3-642-40196-1_23

8. Baier, C., Katoen, J.: Principles of Model Checking. MIT Press, Cambridge (2008)
9. Bennaceur, A., Hähnle, R., Meinke, K. (eds.): Machine Learning for Dynamic Software Analysis: Potentials and Limits. LNCS, vol. 11026. Springer, Cham (2018). https://doi.org/10.1007/978-3-319-96562-8
10. Bergadano, F., Varricchio, S.: Learning behaviors of automata from multiplicity and equivalence queries. SIAM J. Comput. **25**(6), 1268–1280 (1996). https://doi.org/10.1137/S009753979326091X
11. Bernardo, M., Issarny, V. (eds.): Formal Methods for Eternal Networked Software Systems - 11th International School on Formal Methods for the Design of Computer, Communication and Software Systems, SFM 2011, Bertinoro, Italy, 13–18 June 2011, Advanced Lectures. LNCS, vol. 6659. Springer, Heidelberg (2011). https://doi.org/10.1007/978-3-642-21455-4
12. Carrasco, R.C., Oncina, J.: Learning stochastic regular grammars by means of a state merging method. In: Carrasco, R.C., Oncina, J. (eds.) ICGI 1994. LNCS, vol. 862, pp. 139–152. Springer, Heidelberg (1994). https://doi.org/10.1007/3-540-58473-0_144
13. Carrasco, R.C., Oncina, J.: Learning deterministic regular grammars from stochastic samples in polynomial time. ITA **33**(1), 1–20 (1999). https://doi.org/10.1051/ita:1999102
14. Cassel, S., Howar, F., Jonsson, B., Steffen, B.: Active learning for extended finite state machines. Formal Aspects Comput. **28**(2), 233–263 (2016). https://doi.org/10.1007/s00165-016-0355-5
15. Castro, J., Gavaldà, R.: Learning probability distributions generated by finite-state machines. In: Heinz, J., Sempere, J.M. (eds.) Topics in Grammatical Inference, pp. 113–142. Springer, Heidelberg (2016). https://doi.org/10.1007/978-3-662-48395-4_5
16. Chen, Y., Nielsen, T.D.: Active learning of Markov decision processes for system verification. In: 11th International Conference on Machine Learning and Applications, ICMLA, Boca Raton, FL, USA, 12–15 December 2012, vol. 2, pp. 289–294. IEEE (2012). https://doi.org/10.1109/ICMLA.2012.158
17. Feng, L., Han, T., Kwiatkowska, M.Z., Parker, D.: Learning-based compositional verification for synchronous probabilistic systems. In: Bultan, T., Hsiung, P.-A. (eds.) ATVA 2011. LNCS, vol. 6996, pp. 511–521. Springer, Heidelberg (2011). https://doi.org/10.1007/978-3-642-24372-1_40
18. Fiterău-Broștean, P., Janssen, R., Vaandrager, F.: Combining model learning and model checking to analyze TCP implementations. In: Chaudhuri, S., Farzan, A. (eds.) CAV 2016. LNCS, vol. 9780, pp. 454–471. Springer, Cham (2016). https://doi.org/10.1007/978-3-319-41540-6_25
19. Forejt, V., Kwiatkowska, M.Z., Norman, G., Parker, D.: Automated verification techniques for probabilistic systems. In: Bernardo and Issarny [11], pp. 53–113. https://doi.org/10.1007/978-3-642-21455-4_3
20. Fu, J., Topcu, U.: Probably approximately correct MDP learning and control with temporal logic constraints. In: Fox, D., Kavraki, L.E., Kurniawati, H. (eds.) Robotics: Science and Systems X, University of California, Berkeley, USA, 12–16 July 2014 (2014). http://www.roboticsproceedings.org/rss10/p39.html
21. Hoeffding, W.: Probability inequalities for sums of bounded random variables. J. Am. Stat. Assoc. **58**(301), 13–30 (1963). http://www.jstor.org/stable/2282952
22. Howar, F., Steffen, B.: Active automata learning in practice - an annotated bibliography of the years 2011 to 2016. In: Bennaceur et al. [9], pp. 123–148. https://doi.org/10.1007/978-3-319-96562-8_5

23. Hungar, H., Niese, O., Steffen, B.: Domain-specific optimization in automata learning. In: Hunt Jr., W.A., Somenzi, F. (eds.) CAV 2003. LNCS, vol. 2725, pp. 315–327. Springer, Heidelberg (2003). https://doi.org/10.1007/978-3-540-45069-6_31
24. Isberner, M., Howar, F., Steffen, B.: The TTT algorithm: a redundancy-free approach to active automata learning. In: Bonakdarpour, B., Smolka, S.A. (eds.) RV 2014. LNCS, vol. 8734, pp. 307–322. Springer, Cham (2014). https://doi.org/10.1007/978-3-319-11164-3_26
25. Khalili, A., Tacchella, A.: Learning nondeterministic Mealy machines. In: Clark, A., Kanazawa, M., Yoshinaka, R. (eds.) Proceedings of the 12th International Conference on Grammatical Inference, ICGI 2014, Kyoto, Japan, 17–19 September 2014. JMLR Workshop and Conference Proceedings, vol. 34, pp. 109–123. JMLR.org (2014). http://jmlr.org/proceedings/papers/v34/khalili14a.html
26. Kwiatkowska, M.Z., Norman, G., Parker, D.: Analysis of a gossip protocol in PRISM. SIGMETRICS Perform. Eval. Rev. 36(3), 17–22 (2008). https://doi.org/10.1145/1481506.1481511
27. Kwiatkowska, M.Z., Norman, G., Parker, D.: PRISM 4.0: verification of probabilistic real-time systems. In: Gopalakrishnan, G., Qadeer, S. (eds.) CAV 2011. LNCS, vol. 6806, pp. 585–591. Springer, Heidelberg (2011). https://doi.org/10.1007/978-3-642-22110-1_47
28. Mao, H., Chen, Y., Jaeger, M., Nielsen, T.D., Larsen, K.G., Nielsen, B.: Learning Markov decision processes for model checking. In: Fahrenberg, U., Legay, A., Thrane, C.R. (eds.) Proceedings Quantities in Formal Methods, QFM 2012, Paris, France, 28 August 2012. EPTCS, vol. 103, pp. 49–63 (2012). https://doi.org/10.4204/EPTCS.103.6
29. Mao, H., Chen, Y., Jaeger, M., Nielsen, T.D., Larsen, K.G., Nielsen, B.: Learning deterministic probabilistic automata from a model checking perspective. Mach. Learn. 105(2), 255–299 (2016). https://doi.org/10.1007/s10994-016-5565-9
30. Margaria, T., Niese, O., Raffelt, H., Steffen, B.: Efficient test-based model generation for legacy reactive systems. In: Ninth IEEE International High-Level Design Validation and Test Workshop 2004, pp. 95–100. IEEE Computer Society (2004). https://doi.org/10.1109/HLDVT.2004.1431246
31. Nerode, A.: Linear automaton transformations. Proc. Am. Math. Soc. 9, 541–544 (1958)
32. Norman, G., Shmatikov, V.: Analysis of probabilistic contract signing. J. Comput. Secur. 14(6), 561–589 (2006). http://content.iospress.com/articles/journal-of-computer-security/jcs268
33. Rivest, R.L., Schapire, R.E.: Inference of finite automata using homing sequences. Inf. Comput. 103(2), 299–347 (1993). https://doi.org/10.1006/inco.1993.1021
34. de Ruiter, J., Poll, E.: Protocol state fuzzing of TLS implementations. In: Jung, J., Holz, T. (eds.) 24th USENIX Security Symposium, USENIX Security 15, Washington, D.C., USA, 12–14 August 2015, pp. 193–206. USENIX Association (2015). https://www.usenix.org/conference/usenixsecurity15/technical-sessions/presentation/de-ruiter
35. Shahbaz, M., Groz, R.: Inferring Mealy machines. In: Cavalcanti, A., Dams, D.R. (eds.) FM 2009. LNCS, vol. 5850, pp. 207–222. Springer, Heidelberg (2009). https://doi.org/10.1007/978-3-642-05089-3_14
36. Steffen, B., Howar, F., Merten, M.: Introduction to active automata learning from a practical perspective. In: Bernardo and Issarny [11], pp. 256–296. https://doi.org/10.1007/978-3-642-21455-4_8
37. Tappler, M.: Evaluation material for L^*-based learning of Markov decision processes. https://doi.org/10.6084/m9.figshare.7960928.v1

38. Tappler, M., Aichernig, B.K., Bacci, G., Eichlseder, M., Larsen, K.G.: L^*-based learning of Markov decision processes (extended version). CoRR arXiv:1906.12239 (2019), http://arxiv.org/abs/1906.12239

39. Tappler, M., Aichernig, B.K., Bloem, R.: Model-based testing IoT communication via active automata learning. In: 2017 IEEE International Conference on Software Testing, Verification and Validation, ICST 2017, Tokyo, Japan, 13–17 March 2017, pp. 276–287. IEEE Computer Society (2017). https://doi.org/10.1109/ICST.2017. 32

40. Tretmans, J.: Test generation with inputs, outputs and repetitive quiescence. Softw. Concepts Tools **17**(3), 103–120 (1996)

41. Tzeng, W.: Learning probabilistic automata and Markov chains via queries. Mach. Learn. **8**, 151–166 (1992). https://doi.org/10.1007/BF00992862

42. Valiant, L.G.: A theory of the learnable. Commun. ACM **27**(11), 1134–1142 (1984). https://doi.org/10.1145/1968.1972

43. Volpato, M., Tretmans, J.: Approximate active learning of nondeterministic input output transition systems. ECEASST **72** (2015). https://doi.org/10.14279/tuj. eceasst.72.1008

44. Willemse, T.A.C.: Heuristics for **ioco**-based test-based modelling. In: Brim, L., Haverkort, B., Leucker, M., van de Pol, J. (eds.) FMICS 2006. LNCS, vol. 4346, pp. 132–147. Springer, Heidelberg (2007). https://doi.org/10.1007/978-3-540-70952- 7_9

Star-Based Reachability Analysis
of Deep Neural Networks

Hoang-Dung Tran[1], Diago Manzanas Lopez[1], Patrick Musau[1],
Xiaodong Yang[1], Luan Viet Nguyen[2], Weiming Xiang[1],
and Taylor T. Johnson[1]($\boxtimes$)

[1] Institute for Software Integrated Systems, Vanderbilt University,
Nashville, TN, USA
taylor.johnson@vanderbilt.edu
[2] Department of Computer and Information Science, University of Pennsylvania,
Philadelphia, PA, USA

Abstract. This paper proposes novel reachability algorithms for both
exact (sound and complete) and over-approximation (sound) analysis of
deep neural networks (DNNs). The approach uses star sets as a symbolic representation of sets of states, which are known in short as stars
and provide an effective representation of high-dimensional polytopes.
Our star-based reachability algorithms can be applied to several problems in analyzing the robustness of machine learning methods, such as
safety and robustness verification of DNNs. The star-based reachability
algorithms are implemented in a software prototype called the neural network verification (NNV) tool that is publicly available for evaluation and
comparison. Our experiments show that when verifying ACAS Xu neural
networks on a multi-core platform, our exact reachability algorithm is on
average about 19 times faster than Reluplex, a satisfiability modulo theory (SMT)-based approach. Furthermore, our approach can visualize the
precise behavior of DNNs because the reachable states are computed in
the method. Notably, in the case that a DNN violates a safety property,
the exact reachability algorithm can construct a complete set of counterexamples. Our star-based over-approximate reachability algorithm is
on average 118 times faster than Reluplex on the verification of properties for ACAS Xu networks, even without exploiting the parallelism
that comes naturally in our method. Additionally, our over-approximate
reachability is much less conservative than DeepZ and DeepPoly, recent
approaches utilizing zonotopes and other abstract domains that fail to
verify many properties of ACAS Xu networks due to their conservativeness. Moreover, our star-based over-approximate reachability algorithm
obtains better robustness bounds in comparison with DeepZ and Deep-
Poly when verifying the robustness of image classification DNNs.

1 Introduction

Deep neural networks (DNNs) have become one of the most powerful techniques
to deal with challenging and complex problems such as image processing [15]

© Springer Nature Switzerland AG 2019
M. H. ter Beek et al. (Eds.): FM 2019, LNCS 11800, pp. 670–686, 2019.
https://doi.org/10.1007/978-3-030-30942-8_39

and natural language translation [9,16] due to its learning ability on large data sets. Recently, the power of DNNs has inspired a new generation of intelligent autonomy which makes use of DNNs-based learning enable components such as autonomous vehicles [5] and air traffic collision avoidance systems [11]. Although utilizing DNNs is a promising approach, assuring the safety of autonomous applications containing neural network components is difficult because DNNs usually have complex characteristics and behavior that are generally unpredictable. Notably, it has been proved that well-trained DNNs may not be robust and are easily to be fooled by a slight change in the input [18]. Several recent incidents in autonomous driving (e.g., Tesla and Uber) raises an urgent need for techniques and tools that can formally verify the safety and robustness of DNNs before utilizing them in safety-critical applications.

Safety verification and robustness certification of DNNs have attracted a huge attention from different communities such as machine learning [1,2,13, 17,20,25,26,31], formal methods [6,10,12,19,23,28–30], and security [7,24,25], and a recent survey of the area is available [27]. Analyzing the behavior of a DNN can broadly be categorized into exact and over-approximate analyses. For the exact analysis, the SMT-based [12] and polyhedron-based approaches [23, 28] are notable representatives. For the over-approximate analysis, the mixed-integer linear program (MILP) [6], interval arithmetic- [24,25], zonotope- [20], input partition- [30], linearization- [26], and abstract-domain- [21] based are fast and efficient approaches. While the over-approximate analysis is usually faster and more scalable than the exact analysis, it guarantees only the soundness of the result. In contrast, the exact analysis is usually more time-consuming and less scalable. However, it guarantees both the soundness and completeness of the result [12]. Although the over-approximate analysis is fast and scalable, it is unclear how good the over-approximation is in term of conservativeness since the exact result is not available for comparison. Importantly, if an over-approximation approach is too conservative for neural networks with small or medium sizes, it will potentially produce huge conservative results for DNNs with a large number of layers and thousands of neurons since the over-approximation error is accumulated quickly over layers. Therefore, a scalable, exact reachability analysis is crucial not only for formal verification of DNNs, but also for estimating the conservativeness of current and up-coming over-approximation approaches.

In this paper, we propose a fast and scalable approach for the *exact* and *over-approximate* reachability analysis of DNN with ReLU activation functions using the concept of *star* sets [3], or shortly "star". Star fits perfectly for the reachability analysis of DNNs due to its following essential characteristics: (1) an efficient (exact) representation of large input sets; (2) fast and cheap affine mapping operations; (3) inexpensive intersections with half-spaces and checking empty. *By utilizing star, we avoid the expensive affine mapping operation in polyhedron-based approach* [23] *and thus, reduce the verification time significantly.* Our approach performs reachability analysis for feedforward DNNs layer-by-layer. In the case of exact analysis, the output reachable set of each layer is a union of a set of stars. Based on this observation, *the star-based exact reachability algorithm naturally can be designed for efficient execution on multi-core platforms* where each layer can handle multiple input sets at the same time. In the case of over-approximate analysis, the output reachable set of each layer is a single star which can be constructed by doing *point-wise* over-approximation of the reachable set at all neurons of the layer.

We evaluate the proposed algorithms in comparison with the polyhedron approach [23], Reluplex [12], zonotope [20] and abstract domain [21] approaches on safety verification of the ACAS Xu neural networks [11] and robust certification of image classification DNN. The experimental results show that our exact reachability algorithm can achieve 19 times faster than Reluplex when running on multi-core platform and >70 times faster than the polyhedron approach. Notably, our exact algorithm can visualize the precise behavior of the ACAS Xu networks and can construct the complete set of counter example inputs in the case that a safety property is violated. Our over-approximate reachability algorithm is averagely 118 times faster than Reluplex. It successfully verifies many safety properties of ACAS Xu networks while the zonotope and abstract domain approaches fail due to their large over-approximation errors. Our over-approximate reachability algorithm also provides a better robustness certification for image classification DNN in comparison with the zonotope and abstract domain approaches. In summary, the main contributions of this paper are: (1) propose novel, fast and scalable methods for the exact and over-approximate reachability analysis of DNNs; (2) implement the proposed methods in NNV toolbox that is available online for evaluation and comparison; (3) provide a thorough evaluation of the new methods via real-world case studies.

2   Preliminaries

2.1   Machine Learning Models and Symbolic Verification Problem

A feed-forward neural network (FNN) consists of an input layer, an output layer, and multiple hidden layers in which each layer comprises of neurons that are connected to the neurons of preceding layer labeled using weights. Given an input vector, the output of an FNN is determined by three components: the weight matrices W_k, representing the weighted connection between neurons of two consecutive layers $k-1$ and k, the bias vectors b_k of each layer, and the activation function f applied at each layer. Mathematically, the output of a neuron i is defined by:

$$y_i = f(\Sigma_{j=1}^n \omega_{ij} x_j + b_i),$$

where x_j is the jth input of the ith neuron, ω_{ij} is the weight from the jth input to the ith neuron, b_i is the bias of the ith neuron. In this paper, we are interested in FNN with ReLU activation functions defined by $ReLU(x) = max(0, x)$.

Definition 1 (Reachable Set of FNN). *Given a bounded convex polyhedron input set defined as* $\mathcal{I} \triangleq \{x \mid Ax \leq b, x \in \mathbb{R}^n\}$, *and an k-layers feed-forward* *neural network* $F \triangleq \{L_1, \cdots, L_k\}$, *the reachable set* $F(\mathcal{I}) = \mathcal{R}_{L_k}$ *of the neural network* F *corresponding to the input set* I *is defined incrementally by:*

$$\mathcal{R}_{L_1} \triangleq \{y_1 \mid y_1 = ReLU(W_1 x + b_1), \ x \in \mathcal{I}\},$$
$$\mathcal{R}_{L_2} \triangleq \{y_2 \mid y_2 = ReLU(W_2 y_1 + b_2), \ y_1 \in \mathcal{R}_{L_1}\},$$
$$\vdots$$
$$\mathcal{R}_{L_k} \triangleq \{y_k \mid y_k = ReLU(W_k y_{k-1} + b_k) \ y_{k-1} \in \mathcal{R}_{L_{k-1}}\},$$

where W_k *and* b_k *are the weight matrix and bias vector of the* k^{th} *layer* L_k, *respectively. The reachable set* $\mathcal{R}_{L_k}$ *contains all outputs of the neural network corresponding to all input vectors* x *in the input set* $\mathcal{I}$.

Definition 2 (Safety Verification of FNN). *Given a k-layers feed-forward neural network* F, *and a safety specification* $\mathcal{S}$ *defined as a set of linear constraints on the neural network outputs* $\mathcal{S} \triangleq \{y_k \mid Cy_k \leq d\}$, *the neural network* F *is called to be safe corresponding to the input set* $\mathcal{I}$, *we write* $F(\mathcal{I}) \vDash S$, *if and only if* $\mathcal{R}_{L_k} \cap \neg \mathcal{S} = \emptyset$, *where* $\mathcal{R}_{L_k}$ *is the reachable set of the neural network with the input set* $\mathcal{I}$, *and* $\neg$ *is the symbol for logical negation. Otherwise, the neural network is called to be unsafe* $F(\mathcal{I}) \nvDash S$.

2.2 Generalized Star Sets

Definition 3 (Generalized Star Set [3]). *A generalized star set (or simply star)* Θ *is a tuple* $\langle c, V, P \rangle$ *where* $c \in \mathbb{R}^n$ *is the center,* $V = \{v_1, v_2, \cdots, v_m\}$ *is a set of m vectors in* $\mathbb{R}^n$ *called basis vectors, and* $P : \mathbb{R}^m \to \{\top, \bot\}$ *is a predicate. The basis vectors are arranged to form the star's* $n \times m$ *basis matrix. The set of states represented by the star is given as:*

$$[\![\Theta]\!] = \{x \mid x = c + \Sigma_{i=1}^m (\alpha_i v_i) \text{ such that } P(\alpha_1, \cdots, \alpha_m) = \top\}. \tag{1}$$

Sometimes we will refer to both the tuple Θ *and the set of states* $[\![\Theta]\!]$ *as* Θ. *In this work, we restrict the predicates to be a conjunction of linear constraints,* $P(\alpha) \triangleq C\alpha \leq d$ *where, for p linear constraints,* $C \in \mathbb{R}^{p \times m}$, α *is the vector of m-variables, i.e.,* $\alpha = [\alpha_1, \cdots, \alpha_m]^T$, *and* $d \in \mathbb{R}^{p \times 1}$. *A star is an empty set if and only if* $P(\alpha)$ *is empty.*

Proposition 1. *Any bounded convex polyhedron* $\mathcal{P} \triangleq \{x \mid Cx \leq d, x \in \mathbb{R}^n\}$ *can be represented as a star.*[1]

Proposition 2 *[Affine Mapping of a Star]. Given a star set* $\Theta = \langle c, V, P \rangle$, *an affine mapping of the star* Θ *with the affine mapping matrix* W *and offset vector* b *defined by* $\bar{\Theta} = \{y \mid y = Wx + b, \ x \in \Theta\}$ *is another star with the following characteristics.*

$$\bar{\Theta} = \langle \bar{c}, \bar{V}, \bar{P} \rangle, \ \bar{c} = Wc + b, \ \bar{v} = \{Wv_1, Wv_2, \cdots, Wv_m\}, \ \bar{P} \equiv P.$$

---

[1] Proofs appear in the appendix of the extended version of this paper [22].

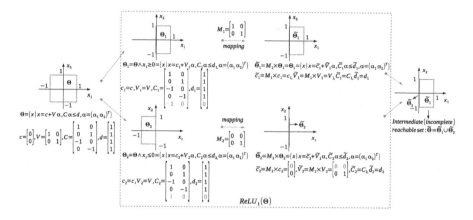

Fig. 1. An example of a stepReLU operation on a layer with two neurons.

Proposition 3 (Star and Half-space Intersection). *The intersection of a star* $\Theta \triangleq \langle c, V, P \rangle$ *and a half-space* $\mathcal{H} \triangleq \{x \mid Hx \leq g\}$ *is another star with following characteristics.*

$$\bar{\Theta} = \Theta \cap \mathcal{H} = \langle \bar{c}, \bar{V}, \bar{P} \rangle, \quad \bar{c} = c, \quad \bar{V} = V, \quad \bar{P} = P \wedge P',$$

$$P'(\alpha) \triangleq (H \times V_m)\alpha \leq g - H \times c, V_m = [v_1 \ v_2 \cdots v_m].$$

3   Star-Based Reachability Analysis of FNNs

3.1   Exact and Complete Analysis

Since any bounded convex polyhedron can be represented as a star (Proposition 1), we assume the input set $\mathcal{I}$ of an FNN is a star set. From Definition 1, one can see that the reachable set of an FNN is derived layer-by-layer. Since the affine mapping of a star is also a star (Proposition 2), the core step in computing the exact reachable set of a layer with a star input set is applying the ReLU activation function on the star input set, i.e., compute $ReLU(\Theta)$, $\Theta = \langle c, V, P \rangle$. For a layer L with n neurons, the reachable set of the layer can be computed by executing a sequence of n stepReLU operations as follows $\mathcal{R}_L = ReLU_n(ReLU_{n-1}(\cdots ReLU_1(\Theta)))$.

The stepReLU operation on the ith neuron, i.e., $ReLU_i(\cdot)$, works as follows. First, the input star set Θ is decomposed into two subsets $\Theta_1 = \Theta \wedge x_i \geq 0$ and $\Theta_2 = \Theta \wedge x_i < 0$. Note that from Proposition 3, Θ_1 and Θ_2 are also stars. Let assume that $\Theta_1 = \langle c, V, P_1 \rangle$ and $\Theta_2 = \langle c, V, P_2 \rangle$. Since the later set has $x_i < 0$, applying the ReLU activation function on the element x_i of the vector $x = [x_1 \cdots x_i \ x_{i+1} \cdots x_n]^T \in \Theta_2$ will lead to the new vector $x' = [x_1 \ x_2 \cdots 0 \ x_{i+1} \cdots x_n]^T$. This procedure is equivalent to mapping Θ_2 by the mapping matrix $M = [e_1 \ e_2 \cdots e_{i-1} \ 0 \ e_{i+1} \cdots e_n]$. Also, applying the ReLU activation function on the element x_i of the vector $x \in \Theta_1$ does

Algorithm 3.1. Star-based exact reachability analysis for one layer.

Input: $I = [\Theta_1 \ \cdots \ \Theta_N]$, W, b ▷ star input sets, weight matrix, bias vector
Output: R ▷ exact reachable set
1: **procedure** R = LAYERREACH(I, W, b)
2:     $R = \emptyset$
3:     **parfor** $i = 1 : N$ **do** ▷ parallel for loop
4:         $I_1 = W * \Theta_i + b = \langle Wc_i + b, WV_i, P_i \rangle$
5:         $R_1 = reachReLU(I_1)$, $R = R \cup R_1$
6:     **end parfor**
7: **procedure** R_1 = REACHRELU(I_1)
8:     $In = I_1$
9:     $[lb, ub] = In.getRange$ ▷ get ranges of all input variables
10:     $map = find(lb < 0)$ ▷ construct computation map
11:     $m = length(map)$ ▷ minimized number of stepReach operations
12:     **for** $i = 1 : m$ **do**
13:         $In = stepReLU(In, map(i), lb(i), ub(i))$ ▷ stepReLU operation
14:     $R_1 = In$
15: **procedure** $\tilde{R}$ = STEPRELU($\tilde{I}, i, lb_i, ub_i$)
16:     $\tilde{R} = \emptyset$, $\tilde{I} = [\tilde{\Theta}_1 \ \cdots \ \tilde{\Theta}_k]$ ▷ intermediate star input and output sets
17:     **for** $j = 1 : k$ **do**
18:         $\mathcal{R}_1 = \emptyset$, $M = [e_1 \ e_2 \ \cdots e_{i-1} \ 0 \ e_{i+1} \ \cdots \ e_n]$
19:         **if** $lb_i \geq 0$ **then** $\mathcal{R}_1 = \tilde{\Theta}_j = \langle \tilde{c}_j, \tilde{V}_j, \tilde{P}_j \rangle$
20:         **if** $ub_i \leq 0$ **then** $R_1 = M * \tilde{\Theta}_j = \langle M\tilde{c}_j, M\tilde{V}_j, \tilde{P}_j \rangle$
21:         **if** $lb_i < 0$ & $ub_i > 0$ **then**
22:             $\tilde{\Theta}'_j = \tilde{\Theta}_j \wedge x[i] \geq 0 = \langle \tilde{c}_j, \tilde{V}_j, \tilde{P}'_j \rangle$, $\tilde{\Theta}''_j = \tilde{\Theta}_j \wedge x[i] < 0 = \langle \tilde{c}_j, \tilde{V}_j, \tilde{P}''_j \rangle$
23:             $\mathcal{R}_1 = \tilde{\Theta}'_j \cup M * \tilde{\Theta}''_j$
24:         $\tilde{R} = \tilde{R} \cup R_1$

not change the set since we have $x_i \geq 0$. Consequently, the result of the stepReLU operation on input set Θ at the ith neuron is a union of two star sets $ReLU_i(\Theta) = \langle c, V, P1 \rangle \cup \langle Mc, MV, P2 \rangle$. A concrete example of the first stepReLU operation on a layer with two neurons is depicted in Fig. 1.

The number of stepReLU operation can be reduced if we know beforehand the ranges of all states in the input set. For example, if we know that x_i is always larger than zero, then we have $ReLU_i(\Theta) = \Theta$, or in other words, we do not need to execute the stepReLU operation on the ith neuron. Therefore, to minimize the number of stepReLU operations and the computation time, we first determine the ranges of all states in the input set which can be done efficiently by solving n-linear programming problems.

The star-based exact reachability algorithm given in Algorithm 3.1. works as follows. The layer takes the star output sets of the preceding layer as input sets $I = [\Theta_1, \cdots, \Theta_N]$. The main procedure in the algorithm is *layerReach* which processes the input sets I in parallel. On each input element $\Theta_i = \langle c_i, V_i, P_i \rangle$, the main procedure maps the element with the layer weight matrix W and bias vector b which results a new star $I_1 = \langle Wc_i + b, WV_i, P_i \rangle$. The reachable set

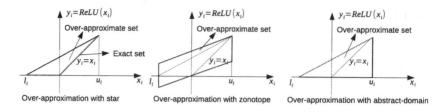

Fig. 2. Over-approximation of ReLU functions with different approaches.

of the layer corresponding to the element Θ_i is computed by *reachReLU* sub-procedure which executes a *minimized sequence* of stepReLU operations on the new star I_1, i.e., iteratively calls *stepReLU* sub-procedure. Note that that the *stepReLU* sub-procedure is designed to handle multiple star input sets since the number of star sets may increase after each stepReLU operation.

Lemma 1. *The worst-case complexity of the number of stars in the reachable set of an N-neurons FNN computed by Algorithm 3.1. is $\mathcal{O}(2^N)$.*

Lemma 2. *The worst-case complexity of the number of constraints of a star in the reachable set of an N-neuron FNN computed by Algorithm 3.1. is $\mathcal{O}(N)$.*

Theorem 1 (Verification complexity). *Let F be an N-neuron FNN, Θ be a star set with p linear constraints and m-variables in the predicate, S be a safety specification with s linear constraints. In the worst case, the safety verification or falsification of the neural network $F(\Theta) \models S$? is equivalent to solving 2^N feasibility problems in which each has $N + p + s$ linear constraints and m-variables.*

Remark 1. Although in the worst-case, the number of stars in the reachable set of an FNN is 2^N, in practice, the actual number of stars is usually much smaller than the worst-case result which enhances the applicability of the star-based exact reachability analysis for practical DNNs.

Theorem 2 (Safety and complete counter input set). *Let F be an FNN, $\Theta = \langle c, V, P \rangle$ be a star input set, $F(\Theta) = \cup_{i=1}^{k} \Theta_i$, $\Theta_i = \langle c_i, V_i, P_i \rangle$ be the reachable set of the neural network, and S be a safety specification. Denote $\bar{\Theta}_i = \Theta_i \cap \neg S = \langle c_i, V_i, \bar{P}_i \rangle$, $i = 1, \cdots, k$. The neural network is safe if and only if $\bar{P}_i = \emptyset$ for all i. If the neural network violates its safety property, then the complete counter input set containing all possible inputs in the input set that lead the neural network to unsafe states is $C_\Theta = \cup_{i=1}^{k} \langle c, V, \bar{P}_i \rangle$, $\bar{P}_i \neq \emptyset$.*

3.2   Over-Approximate Analysis

Although the exact reachability analysis can compute the exact behavior of FNN, the number of stars grows exponentially with the number of layers and leads to

---

Algorithm 3.2. Star-based over-approximate reachability analysis for one layer.

Input: $I = \Theta = \langle c, V, P \rangle$, W, b ▷ star input set, weight matrix, bias vector
Output: R ▷ over-approximate reachable set
1: **procedure** R = ApproxLayerReach(I, W, b)
2:     $I_1 = W * \Theta + b = \langle Wc + b, WV, P \rangle$
3:     $In = I_1$
4:     **for** $i = 1 : n$ **do** ▷ n is the number of neurons of the layer
5:         $In = approxStepReLU(In, i)$ ▷ i^{th} approximate-stepReLU operation
6:     $R_1 = In$
7: **procedure** $\tilde{R}$ = ApproxStepReLU$(\tilde{I}, i)$
8:     $\tilde{I} = \tilde{\Theta} = \langle \tilde{c}, \tilde{V}, \tilde{P} \rangle$
9:     $[l_i, u_i] = \tilde{\Theta}.getRange(i)$ ▷ range of $x[i]$, i.e., $l_i \leq x[i] \leq u_i$
10:     $M = [e_1\ e_2\ \cdots e_{i-1}\ 0\ e_{i+1}\ \cdots\ e_n]$
11:     **if** $l_i \geq 0$ **then** $\tilde{R} = \tilde{\Theta} = \langle \tilde{c}, \tilde{V}, \tilde{P} \rangle$
12:     **if** $u_i \leq 0$ **then** $\tilde{R} = M * \tilde{\Theta} = \langle M\tilde{c}, M\tilde{V}, \tilde{P} \rangle$
13:     **if** $l_i < 0$ & $u_i > 0$ **then**
14:         $\tilde{P}(\alpha) \triangleq \tilde{C}\alpha \leq \tilde{d}$, $\alpha = [\alpha_1, \alpha_2, \cdots, \alpha_m]^T$ ▷ input set's predicate
15:         $\alpha' = [\alpha_1, \cdots, \alpha_m, \alpha_{m+1}]^T$ ▷ new variable α_{m+1}
16:         $C_1 = [0\ 0\ \cdots\ 0\ \text{-}1] \in \mathbb{R}^{1 \times m+1}$, $d_1 = 0$ ▷ $\alpha_{m+1} \geq 0 \Leftrightarrow C_1\alpha' \leq d_1$
17:         $C_2 = [V[i, :]\ \text{-}1] \in \mathbb{R}^{1 \times m+1}$, $d_2 = -\tilde{c}[i]$ ▷ $\alpha_{m+1} \geq x[i] \Leftrightarrow C_2\alpha' \leq d_2$
18:         $C_3 = [\frac{-u_i}{u_i - l_i} \times V[i, :]\ 1]$, $d_3 = \frac{u_i l_i}{u_i - l_i} \times (1 - \tilde{c}[i])$ ▷ $\alpha_{m+1} \leq \frac{u_i(x[i]-l_i)}{u_i-l_i} \Leftrightarrow C_3\alpha' \leq d_3$
19:         $C_0 = [\tilde{C}\ 0_{m \times 1}]$, $d_0 = \tilde{d}$
20:         $C' = [C_0; C_1; C_2; C_3]$, $d' = [d_0; d_1; d_2; d_3]$
21:         $P'(\alpha') \triangleq C'\alpha' \leq d'$ ▷ output set's predicate
22:         $c' = M\tilde{c}$, $V' = M\tilde{V}$, $V' = [V'\ e_i]$ ▷ $y[i] = ReLU(x[i]) = \alpha_{m+1}$
23:         $\tilde{R} = \langle c', V', P' \rangle$

---

an increase in computation cost that limits scalability. In this section, we propose an over-approximation reachability algorithm for FNNs. The main benefit of this approach is that the reachable set of each layer is only a single star that can be constructed efficiently by using an over-approximation of the ReLU activation function at all neurons in the layer. Importantly, our star-based over-approximate reachability algorithm is much less conservative than the zonotope-based [20] and abstract domain [21] based approaches in the way of approximating the ReLU activation function, shown in Fig. 2. The zonotope-based approach [20] over-approximates the ReLU activation function by a minimal parallelogram while the abstract-domain approach [21] over-approximates the ReLU activation function by a triangle. Our star-based approach also over-approximates the ReLU activation function with a triangle as in the abstract-domain approach. However, the abstract-domain approach only uses lower bound and upper bound constraints for the output $y_i = ReLU(x_i)$ to avoid the state space explosion [21], for example, in Fig. 2, these constraints are $y_i \geq 0$, $y_i \leq u_i(x_i - l_i)/(u_i - l_i)$. To obtain a tighter over-approximation, our approach uses three constraints for the output y_i instead. The over-approximation rule for a single neuron is given as follows,

---

Algorithm 3.3. Reachability analysis for a FNN.

Input: $I = \Theta = \langle c, V, P \rangle$, $L = [L_1 \ L_2 \ \cdots \ L_k]$, *scheme* ▷ star input set, network's layers, reachabiltiy scheme

Output: R ▷ reachable set

1: **procedure** R = REACH($I, L, scheme$)
2:     $In = I$
3:     **for** $i = 1 : k$ **do** ▷ k is the number of layers on the network
4:         **if** *scheme* = *exact* **then** $In = L_i.LayerReach(In)$
5:         **else if** *scheme* = *approx* **then** $In = L_i.ApproxLayerReach(In)$
6:     $R = In$

$$\begin{cases} y_i = x_i & \text{if } l_i \geq 0 \\ y_i = 0 & \text{if } u_i \leq 0 \\ y_i \geq 0, \ y_i \leq \frac{u_i(x_i - l_i)}{u_i - l_i}, \ y_i \geq x_i & \text{if } l_i < 0 \text{ and } u_i > 0 \end{cases}$$

where l_i and u_i is the lower and upper bounds of x_i.

Similar to the exact approach, the over-approximate reachable set of a Layer with n neurons can be computed by executing a sequence of n *approximate-stepReLU* operations performing the above over-approximation rule. The over-approximate reachability algorithm for a single layer of FNN using star set given in Algorithm 3.2. works as follows. Given a star input set Θ, the algorithm computes the affine mapping of the input set using the layer's weight matrix and bias vector. The resulting star set is the input of a sequence of n $approximate - stepReLU$ operations. An approximate-stepReLU operation first computes the lower and upper bounds of the state variable $x[i]$ w.r.t the ith neuron. If the lower bound is not negative (line 11), the approximate-stepReLU operation returns a new intermediate reachable set which is exactly the same as its input set. If the upper bound is not positive (line 12), the approximate-stepReLU operation returns a new intermediate reachable set which is the same as its input set except the ith state variable is zero. If the lower bound is negative and the upper bound is positive (line 13), the approximate-stepReLU operation introduces a new variable α_{m+1} to capture the over-approximation of ReLU function at the ith neuron. As a result, the obtained intermediate reachable set has one more variable and three more linear constraints in the predicate in comparison with the corresponding input set. From this observation, we can see that in the worst case, the over-approximate reachability algorithm will obtain a reachable set with $N + m_0$ variables and $3N + n_0$ constraints in the predicate, where m_0, n_0 respectively are the number of variables and linear constraints of the predicate of the input set and N is the total number of neurons of the FNN.

3.3 Reachability Algorithm for FNNs

The reachability analysis of a FNN is done layer-by-layer in which the output set of the previous layer is the input set of the next layer. The reachability algorithm for a FNN is summarized in Algorithm 3.3.

4 Evaluation

In this section, we evaluate the proposed star-based reachability algorithms in comparison to existing state-of-the-art approaches including exact (sound and complete) SMT-based (Reluplex [12]) and polyhedron-based [23] approaches, as well as over-approximate approaches, such as those using zonotopes [20] and abstract domains [21]. To clarify intuitively the benefit of our approach, we re-implement the zonotope- and abstract-domain based approaches in our tool called NNV. This allows the visualization of the over-approximate reachable set of these approaches. The evaluation and comparison are done by verifying safety of the ACAS Xu DNNs [11] and the robustness of image classification

Table 1. Safety verification results of ACAS Xu networks. Notation: TO is 'Timeout', **Rel** states for 'Reluplex', **Poly** is the Polyhedron method, UN states for unknown (due to over-approximation error), VT is the verification time in seconds, and r_{ES}^1, r_{ES}^2 are the verification time improvement of the exact, star-based method compared with Reluplex and the polyhedron-based methods; r_Z, r_{AD} and r_{AS} respectively are the verification time improvement of the zonotope-, abstract domain- and over-approximate star-based methods compared with Reluplex. The computation time limitation for polyhedron-based method (run on Amazon cloud) was set to be 1 h while for Reluplex, it was set at 24 h.

Prop.	ID	\multicolumn Exact methods						\multicolumn Over-approximation methods								
		Res.	Rel	Poly	Star			\multicolumn Zonotope			\multicolumn Abstract-domain			\multicolumn Star		
			VT	VT	VT	r_{ES}^1	r_{ES}^2	Res.	VT	r_Z	Res.	VT	r_{AD}	Res.	VT	r_{AS}
ϕ_1	N_{1_1}	Safe	5986	TO	1481.2	**4.04x**	–	Safe	0.07	**85514x**	Safe	6.22	**962.4x**	Safe	13.79	**434.1x**
ϕ_2	N_{1_3}	Safe	1102	TO	77.3	**14.3x**	**> 47x**	UN	0.06	**18367x**	UN	6.3	**174.9x**	UN	6.01	**183.4x**
	N_{2_1}	Safe	1173	TO	51.57	**22.8x**	**> 70x**	UN	0.062	**18919x**	UN	5.72	**205.1x**	Safe	5.91	**198.5x**
	N_{2_2}	Safe	634	TO	35.8	**17.7x**	**> 101x**	UN	0.084	**7548x**	UN	5.83	**108.8x**	Safe	5.8	**109.3x**
	N_{2_3}	Safe	1014	TO	36.1	**28.1x**	**> 100x**	UN	0.073	**13890x**	UN	5.89	**172.2x**	UN	5.79	**175.7x**
	N_{5_1}	Safe	1097	TO	17.76	**61.8x**	**> 202x**	UN	0.081	**13543x**	UN	5.85	**187.5x**	UN	5.76	**190.5x**
ϕ_3	N_{1_5}	Safe	393	1520.29	33.39	**11.8x**	**45.5x**	UN	0.0796	**4937x**	UN	6.1	**64.4x**	Safe	5.89	**66.7x**
	N_{2_2}	Safe	451	TO	43.66	**10.3x**	**> 83x**	UN	0.056	**8054x**	UN	5.57	**81x**	Safe	5.66	**79.7x**
	N_{2_3}	Safe	293	2759	37.23	**7.8x**	**74.1x**	UN	0.08	**3663x**	UN	6.04	**74.7x**	Safe	5.66	**79.7x**
	N_{2_8}	Safe	653	1152.6	31.04	**21x**	**37.1x**	Safe	0.102	**6401x**	Safe	6.36	**102.7x**	Safe	7.47	**87.4x**
	N_{2_9}	Safe	61	233	6.33	**9.63x**	**36.8x**	Safe	0.065	**938.5x**	Safe	5.76	**10.6x**	Safe	5.88	**10.4x**
	N_{3_7}	Safe	357	1115.6	14	**25.5x**	**79.7x**	UN	0.085	**4200x**	Safe	5.88	**60.7x**	Safe	6	**59.5x**
	N_{3_8}	Safe	149	770	15.2	**9.8x**	**50.7x**	UN	0.08	**1862x**	UN	5.53	**26.9x**	Safe	5.83	**25.6x**
	N_{3_9}	Safe	715	1664.4	40.9	**17.5x**	**40.7x**	UN	0.076	**9408x**	UN	6.25	**114.4x**	Safe	6.13	**116.6x**
	N_{4_9}	Safe	489	1098.7	22.2	**22x**	**49.49x**	Safe	0.049	**9980x**	Safe	5.3	**92.3x**	Safe	5.57	**87.8x**
	N_{5_1}	Safe	585	1005.3	18.43	**31.74x**	**54.5x**	UN	0.069	**8479x**	UN	5.8	**100.9x**	Safe	5.83	**100.3x**
	N_{5_7}	Safe	42	275.1	7.69	**5.5x**	**35.8x**	Safe	0.054	**778x**	Safe	5.5	**7.6x**	Safe	5.54	**7.6x**
\multicolumn **Average time improvement**					**≈ 18.9x**	**> 70x**		\multicolumn **≈ 12734x**			\multicolumn **≈ 150x**			\multicolumn **≈ 118.4x**	

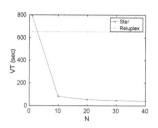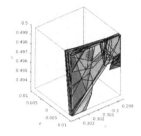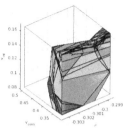

(a) Verification times for property ϕ_3 on N_{2_8} network with different number of cores.

(b) The (normalized) complete counter input set for property ϕ'_3 on N_{2_8} network is a part of the normalized input set (red boxes).

Fig. 3. Verification time reduction with parallel computing and complete counter input set construction. (Color figure online)

DNN against adversarial attacks. All results presented in this section and their corresponding scripts are available online[2].

4.1   Safety Verification for ACAS Xu DNNs

The ACAS Xu networks are DNN-based advisory controllers that map the sensor measurements to advisories in the Airborne Collision Avoidance System X [11]. It consists of 45 DNNs which are trained to replace the traditional memory-consuming lookup table. Each DNN denoted by N_{x_y} has 5 inputs, 5 outputs, and 6 hidden layers of 50 neurons. The detail about ACAS Xu networks and their safety properties are given in the appendix [22]. The experiments in this case study are done using Amazon Web Services Elastic Computing Cloud (EC2), on a powerful `m5a.24xlarge` instance with 96 cores and 384 GB of memory. The verification results are presented in Table 1. We used 90 cores for the exact reachability analysis of the ACAS Xu networks using the polyhedron- and star-based approaches, and only 1 core for the over-approximate reachability analysis approaches.

Verification Results and Timing Performance. Safety verification using star-based reachability algorithms consists of two major steps. The first step constructs the whole reachable set of the networks. The second step checks the intersection of the constructed reachable set with the unsafe region. The verification time (VT) in our approach is the sum of the reachable set computation time (RT) and the safety checking time (ST). The reachable set computation time dominates (averagely 95% of) the verification time in all cases and the verification time varies for different properties. The detail of the reachable set computation time and the safety checking time can be found in the verification results.

---

[2] https://github.com/verivital/nnv/tree/fm2019/nnv/examples/Submission/FM2019.

Exact Star-Based Method. The experimental results show that the exact star-based approach is on average >70 times faster than the polyhedron-based approach and 18.9 times faster than Reluplex when using parallel computing. Impressively, it can even achieve 61.8 faster than Reluplex when verifying property ϕ_2 on N_{5_1} network. This improvement comes from the fact that star set that is very efficient in affine mapping and intersection with half-spaces which are crucial operations for reachable set computation and safety checking. Therefore, the exact star-based method is much more efficient than the polyhedron-based approach [23]. In addition, the exact star-based algorithm is well-designed and optimized (i.e., minimize the number of stepReLU operations) for efficiently running on multi-core platforms while Reluplex does not exploit the power of parallel-computing. Figure 3a describes the benefits of parallel computing. The figure shows that when a single core is used for a verification task, our approach takes 790.07 s which is a little bit slower than Reluplex with 653 s. However, our verification time drops quickly to 80.45 s, which is 8 times faster than Reluplex, when we use 10 cores for the computation.

Zonotope-Based Method [20]. The experimental results show that the over-approximate, zonotope-based method is significantly faster than the exact methods. In some cases, it can verify the safety of the networks with less than 0.1 s, for example, the zonotope-based method successfully verifies property ϕ_3 on N_{5_7} network in 0.054 s and the corresponding reachable set is depicted in Fig. 4a. Although the zonotope-based method is time-efficient (on average 12734 times faster than Reluplex), it is unable to verify the safety of many networks due to its huge over-approximation error, i.e., if the over-approximate reachable set reaches an unsafe region, we do not know whether or not the actual reachable set reaches the unsafe region. For example, Fig. 4b describes the reachable set obtained by the zonotope-based method for N_{3_8} network w.r.t property ϕ_3. As shown in the figure, the obtained reachable set is too conservative and can not be used for safety verification of the network. The main reason that makes the zonotope approach fast is that, to do reachability analysis, we need to compute the lower and upper bounds of each state $x[i]$ of all neurons in each layer. This information can be obtained straightforwardly in the zonotope method while in the other approaches, i.e., abstract-domain and star-based approaches, this is equivalent to solving n linear optimization problems where n is the number of neurons at that layer. The time for solving these optimization problems increase over layers since the number of constraints in the reachable set increases. Therefore, despite the a large over-approximation error, the zonotope-based method is *time-efficient* when dealing with large and deep neural networks.

Abstract-Domain Based Method [21]. The over-approximation method using abstract-domain is 150 times faster than Reluplex on average. It is also much less conservative than the zonotope-based method as can be seen from Fig. 4. However, the reachable set computed by the abstract-domain based method is still too conservative, which makes this approach unable to verify the safety properties of many ACAS Xu networks.

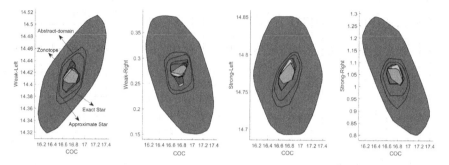

(a) Reachable sets of N_{5_7} network w.r.t property ϕ_3 with different methods. All methods successfully verify the property.

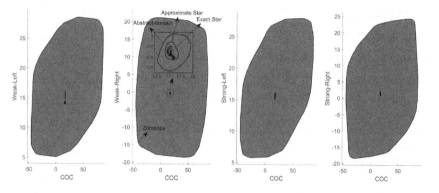

(b) Reachable sets of N_{3_8} network w.r.t property ϕ_3 with different methods. The zonotope (used in DeepZ [20]) and abstract-domain (used in DeepPoly [21]) methods cannot verify the property due to large over-approximation error.

Fig. 4. Conservativeness of the reachable sets obtained by different methods.

Over-Approximate Star-Based Method. The experiments show that our over-approximate star-based approach can obtain tight reachable sets for many networks compared to the exact sets. Therefore, our over-approximate approach successfully verifies safety properties of most of ACAS Xu networks. Notably, it is on average 118.4 times faster than Reluplex. Impressively, it is 434 times faster than Reluplex when verifying property ϕ_1 on N_{1_1} network. In comparison with the zonotope and abstract-domain approaches, our method is timing-comparable with the abstract-domain method and slower than the zonotope method. However, our results is much less conservative than those obtained by the zonotope and abstract-domain methods which are shown in Fig. 4. This makes our approach applicable for safety verification of many ACAS Xu networks where the zonotope and abstract-domain methods cannot verify.

Benefits of Computing the Reachable Set. The reachable set computed in our NNV tool are useful for intuitively checking the safety properties of the net-

Table 2. Maximum robustness values (δ_{max}) of image classification networks with different methods in which k is the number of hidden layers of the network, N is the total number of neurons, Tol is the tolerance error in searching.

Net	Parameters	Tol	δ_{max}			
			Zonotope	Approximate-Star	Abstract-Domain	Exact-Star
N_1	k = 5, N = 140	0.0001	0.0046	0.0048	0.0046	$\geq$0.0058
N_2	k = 5, N = 250	0.0001	0.0087	0.0101	0.0095	TimeOut
N_3	k = 2, N = 1000	0.0001	0.0072	0.0089	0.0084	TimeOut
N_4	k = 1, N = 2000	0.0001	0.0027	0.0027	0.0027	TimeOut
N_5	k = 1, N = 4000	0.0001	0.0034	0.0034	0.0034	TimeOut

work. For example, Fig. 4a describes the behaviors of N_{5_7} network corresponding to property ϕ_3 requiring that the output COC is not the minimal score. From the figure, one can see that the COC is not the minimal score and thus, property ϕ_3 holds on N_{5_7} network. Importantly, as shown in the figure, via visualization, one can intuitively observe the conservativeness of different over-approximation approaches in comparison to the exact ones which is impossible if we use $ERAN$, a C-$Python$ implementation of the zonotope and abstract-domain-based methods. Last but not least, the reachable set is useful in the case that we need to verify a set of safety properties corresponding to the same input set. In this case, once the reachable set is obtained, it can be re-used to check different safety properties without rerunning the whole verification procedure as Reluplex does, and thus helps saving a significant amount of time.

Complete Counter Example Input Set Construction. Another strong advantage of our approach in comparison with other existing approaches is, in the case that a neural network violates its safety specification, our exact, star-based method can construct a *complete counter input set* that leads the neural network to the unsafe region. The complete counter input set can be used as a adversarial input generator [4,8] for robust training of the network. We note that finding a single counter input falsifying a safety property of a neural network can be done efficiently using only random simulations. However, constructing a complete counter input set that contains all counter inputs is very challenging because of the non-linearity of a neural network. To the best of our knowledge, our exact star-based approach is the only approach that can solve this problem. For example, assume that we want to check the following property $\phi_3' \triangleq \neg(COC \geq 15.8 \wedge StrongRight \leq 15.09)$ on N_{2_8} network with the same input constraints as in property ϕ_3. Using the available reachable set of N_{2_8} network, we can verify that the above property ϕ_3' is violated in which 60 stars in 421 stars of the reachable set reach the unsafe region. Using Theorem 2, we can construct a complete counter input set which is a union of 60 stars in 0.9893 s. This counter input set depicted in Fig. 3b is a part of the input set that contains all counter inputs that make the neural network unsafe.

4.2   Maximum Robustness Certification of Image Classification DNNs

Robustness certification of DNNs becomes more an more important as many safety-critical applications using image classification DNNs can be fooled easily by slightly perturbing a correctly classified input. A network is said to be δ-locally-robust at input point x if for every x' such that $\|x - x'\|_\infty \leq \delta$, the network assigns the same label to x and x'. In this case study, instead of proving the robustness of a network corresponding to a given robustness certification δ, we focus on finding the maximum robustness certification value δ_{max} that a verification method can provide a robustness guarantee for the network. We investigate this interesting problem on a set of image classification DNN with different architectures trained (with an accuracy of 98%) using the well-known MNIST data set consisting of 60000 images of handwritten digits with a resolution of 28×28 pixels [14]. The trained networks have 784 inputs and a single output with expected value from 0 to 9. We find the maximum robustness verification value δ_{max} for the networks on an image of digit one with the assumption that there is a δ_{max}-bounded disturbance modifying the (normalized) values of the input vector x at all pixels of the image, i.e., $|x[i] - x'[i]| \leq \delta_{max}$. The result are presented in Table 2. We note that the polyhedron and Reluplex approaches are not applicable for these networks because they cannot deal with high dimensional input space. The table shows that our approximate star approach produces larger upper bounds of the robustness values of the networks with many layers. For single layer networks, our approach gives the same results as the zonotope [20] and the abstract domain [21] methods. The exact-star method can prove that the network N_1 is robust with the bounded disturbance $\delta = 0.0058$. When $\delta > 0.0058$, we ran into the "out of memory" issue in parallel computation since the number of the reachable sets becomes too large. The exact star method reaches timeout (set as 1 h) when finding the maximum robustness value for the other networks.

5   Conclusion and Future Work

We have proposed two reachability analysis algorithms for DNNs using star sets, one that is exact (sound and complete) but has scalability challenges and one that over-approximates (sound) with better scalability. The exact algorithm can compute and visualize the exact behaviors of DNNs. The exact method is more efficient than standard polyhedra approaches, and faster than SMT-based approaches when running on multi-core platforms. The over-approximate algorithm is much faster than the exact one, and notably, it is much less conservative than recent zonotope and abstract-domain based approaches. Our algorithms are applicable for real world applications as shown in the safety verification of ACAS Xu DNNs and robustness certification of image classification DNNs. In future work, we are extending the proposed methods for convolutional neural networks (CNN) and recurrent neural networks (RNN), as well as improving scalability for other types of activation functions such as tanh and sigmoid.

Acknowledgments. We thank Gagandeep Singh from ETH Zurich for his help on explaining DeepZ and DeepPoly methods as well as running his tool ERAN. We also thank Shiqi Wang from Columbia University for his explanation about his interval propagation method, and Guy Katz from The Hebrew University of Jerusalem for his explanation about ACAS Xu networks and Reluplex. The discussions with Gagandeep Singh, Shiqi Wang, and Guy Katz is the main inspiration of our work in this paper. The material presented in this paper is based upon work supported by the Air Force Office of Scientific Research (AFOSR) through contract number FA9550-18-1-0122, and the Defense Advanced Research Projects Agency (DARPA) through contract number FA8750-18-C-0089. The U.S. government is authorized to reproduce and distribute reprints for Governmental purposes notwithstanding any copyright notation thereon. Any opinions, findings, and conclusions or recommendations expressed in this publication are those of the authors and do not necessarily reflect the views of AFOSR or DARPA.

References

1. Akintunde, M., Lomuscio, A., Maganti, L., Pirovano, E.: Reachability analysis for neural agent-environment systems. In: Sixteenth International Conference on Principles of Knowledge Representation and Reasoning (2018)
2. Akintunde, M.E., Kevorchian, A., Lomuscio, A., Pirovano, E.: Verification of RNN-based neural agent-environment systems. In: Proceedings of the 33th AAAI Conference on Artificial Intelligence (AAAI19), Honolulu, HI, USA. AAAI Press (2019, to appear)
3. Bak, S., Duggirala, P.S.: Simulation-equivalent reachability of large linear systems with inputs. In: Majumdar, R., Kunčak, V. (eds.) CAV 2017. LNCS, vol. 10426, pp. 401–420. Springer, Cham (2017). https://doi.org/10.1007/978-3-319-63387-9_20
4. Bastani, O., Ioannou, Y., Lampropoulos, L., Vytiniotis, D., Nori, A., Criminisi, A.: Measuring neural net robustness with constraints. In: Advances in Neural Information Processing Systems, pp. 2613–2621 (2016)
5. Bojarski, M., et al.: End to end learning for self-driving cars. arXiv preprint arXiv:1604.07316 (2016)
6. Dutta, S., Jha, S., Sanakaranarayanan, S., Tiwari, A.: Output range analysis for deep neural networks. arXiv preprint arXiv:1709.09130 (2017)
7. Gehr, T., Mirman, M., Drachsler-Cohen, D., Tsankov, P., Chaudhuri, S., Vechev, M.: Ai 2: safety and robustness certification of neural networks with abstract interpretation. In: 2018 IEEE Symposium on Security and Privacy (SP) (2018)
8. Goodfellow, I.J., Shlens, J., Szegedy, C.: Explaining and harnessing adversarial examples. arXiv preprint arXiv:1412.6572 (2014)
9. Hinton, G., et al.: Deep neural networks for acoustic modeling in speech recognition: the shared views of four research groups. IEEE Signal Process. Mag. **29**(6), 82–97 (2012)
10. Huang, X., Kwiatkowska, M., Wang, S., Wu, M.: Safety verification of deep neural networks. In: Majumdar, R., Kunčak, V. (eds.) CAV 2017. LNCS, vol. 10426, pp. 3–29. Springer, Cham (2017). https://doi.org/10.1007/978-3-319-63387-9_1
11. Julian, K.D., Kochenderfer, M.J., Owen, M.P.: Deep neural network compression for aircraft collision avoidance systems. arXiv preprint arXiv:1810.04240 (2018)
12. Katz, G., Barrett, C., Dill, D.L., Julian, K., Kochenderfer, M.J.: Reluplex: an efficient SMT solver for verifying deep neural networks. In: Majumdar, R., Kunčak, V. (eds.) CAV 2017. LNCS, vol. 10426, pp. 97–117. Springer, Cham (2017). https://doi.org/10.1007/978-3-319-63387-9_5

13. Kouvaros, P., Lomuscio, A.: Formal verification of CNN-based perception systems. arXiv preprint arXiv:1811.11373 (2018)
14. LeCun, Y.: The MNIST database of handwritten digits (1998). http://yann.lecun.com/exdb/mnist/
15. Litjens, G., et al.: A survey on deep learning in medical image analysis. Med. Image Anal. **42**, 60–88 (2017)
16. Liu, W., Wang, Z., Liu, X., Zeng, N., Liu, Y., Alsaadi, F.E.: A survey of deep neural network architectures and their applications. Neurocomputing **234**, 11–26 (2017)
17. Lomuscio, A., Maganti, L.: An approach to reachability analysis for feed-forward ReLU neural networks. arXiv preprint arXiv:1706.07351 (2017)
18. Moosavi-Dezfooli, S.M., Fawzi, A., Frossard, P.: DeepFool: a simple and accurate method to fool deep neural networks. In: Proceedings of the IEEE Conference on Computer Vision and Pattern Recognition, pp. 2574–2582 (2016)
19. Pulina, L., Tacchella, A.: An abstraction-refinement approach to verification of artificial neural networks. In: Touili, T., Cook, B., Jackson, P. (eds.) CAV 2010. LNCS, vol. 6174, pp. 243–257. Springer, Heidelberg (2010). https://doi.org/10.1007/978-3-642-14295-6_24
20. Singh, G., Gehr, T., Mirman, M., Püschel, M., Vechev, M.: Fast and effective robustness certification. In: Advances in Neural Information Processing Systems, pp. 10825–10836 (2018)
21. Singh, G., Gehr, T., Püschel, M., Vechev, M.: An abstract domain for certifying neural networks. Proc. ACM Program. Lang. **3**(POPL), 41 (2019)
22. Tran, H.D., et al: Star-based reachability analysis of deep neural networks: extended version. In: 23rd International Symposium on Formal Methods (2019). http://www.taylortjohnson.com/research/tran2019fm_extended.pdf
23. Tran, H.D., et al.: Parallelizable reachability analysis algorithms for feed-forward neural networks. In: 7th International Conference on Formal Methods in Software Engineering (FormaliSE 2019), Montreal, Canada (2019)
24. Wang, S., Pei, K., Whitehouse, J., Yang, J., Jana, S.: Efficient formal safety analysis of neural networks. In: Advances in Neural Information Processing Systems, pp. 6369–6379 (2018)
25. Wang, S., Pei, K., Whitehouse, J., Yang, J., Jana, S.: Formal security analysis of neural networks using symbolic intervals. arXiv preprint arXiv:1804.10829 (2018)
26. Weng, T.W., et al.: Towards fast computation of certified robustness for ReLU networks. arXiv preprint arXiv:1804.09699 (2018)
27. Xiang, W., et al.: Verification for machine learning, autonomy, and neural networks survey. CoRR abs/1810.01989 (2018)
28. Xiang, W., Tran, H.D., Johnson, T.T.: Reachable set computation and safety verification for neural networks with ReLU activations. arXiv preprint arXiv:1712.08163 (2017)
29. Xiang, W., Tran, H.D., Johnson, T.T.: Output reachable set estimation and verification for multilayer neural networks. IEEE Trans. Neural Netw. Learn. Syst., 1–7 (2018)
30. Xiang, W., Tran, H.D., Johnson, T.T.: Specification-guided safety verification for feedforward neural networks. In: AAAI Spring Symposium on Verification of Neural Networks (2019)
31. Zhang, H., Weng, T.W., Chen, P.Y., Hsieh, C.J., Daniel, L.: Efficient neural network robustness certification with general activation functions. In: Advances in Neural Information Processing Systems, pp. 4944–4953 (2018)

Refactoring and Reprogramming

SOA and the Button Problem

Sung-Shik Jongmans[1,2(✉)], Arjan Lamers[1,3], and Marko van Eekelen[1,4]

[1] Department of Computer Science, Open University of the Netherlands,
Heerlen, The Netherlands
ssj@ou.nl
[2] CWI, Netherlands Foundation of Scientific Research Institutes,
Amsterdam, The Netherlands
[3] First8, Nijmegen, The Netherlands
[4] Institute for Computing and Information Sciences,
Radboud University Nijmegen, Nijmegen, The Netherlands

Abstract. Service-oriented architecture (SOA) is a popular architectural style centered around services, loose coupling, and interoperability. A recurring problem in SOA development is the *Button Problem*; how to ensure that whenever a "button is pressed" on some service—no matter what—the performance of other key services remains unaffected? The Button Problem is especially complex to solve in systems that have devolved into hardly comprehensible spaghettis of service dependencies.

In a collaborative effort with industry partner First8, we present the first formal framework to help SOA developers solve the Button Problem, enabling automated reasoning about service sensitivities and candidate refactorings. Our formalization provides a rigorous foundation for a tool that was already successfully evaluated in industrial case studies, and it is built against two unique requirements: "whiteboard level of abstraction" and non-quantitative analysis.

1 Introduction

Context. Service-oriented architecture (SOA) is a popular architectural style centered around services, loose coupling, and interoperability [19].

A recurring problem in SOA development is the *Button Problem*: how to ensure that whenever a "button is pressed" (i.e., an operation is invoked; a resource is requested) on some service—no matter what—the performance of other key services remains unaffected? For instance, increased activity on an accounting service of an e-commerce system should never slow down the front-end service; sales are lost otherwise [1]. The Button Problem occurs in all stages of SOA development, from initial analysis (when dependencies among services are still reasonably well-understood) to final maintenance (when dependencies have often devolved into a hardly comprehensible spaghetti).

To solve the Button Problem, SOA developers need to engage in two kinds of activities: (1) they need to analyze dependencies among services to determine whether or not a service is indeed *sensitive* to button-presses on other services; if so, (2) they need to invent a series of *refactorings* that eliminate the sensitivity,

© Springer Nature Switzerland AG 2019
M. H. ter Beek et al. (Eds.): FM 2019, LNCS 11800, pp. 689–706, 2019.
https://doi.org/10.1007/978-3-030-30942-8_40

but without changing the system's functional behavior. Especially in cases where services and their dependencies are plentiful, these two activities are challenging to carry out by hand: both service sensitivities and candidate refactorings are easily missed, leading to suboptimal architecture and deployment decisions.

Contribution. In a collaborative effort with industry partner First8, we present the first formal framework to help SOA developers solve the Button Problem, enabling automated reasoning about service sensitivities and candidate refactorings in the form of tool support. Our formalization is built against two unique requirements derived from First8's experience with large enterprise systems (Sect. 2): "whiteboard level of abstraction" and non-quantitative analysis. We provide an extensible core library of refactorings and prove their correctness; this facilitates mechanical exploration of a system's design space toward given insensitivity goals. Our formalization provides a rigorous foundation for a decision support tool (Sect. 2) that we developed and recently demonstrated at ICSOC 2018 [16].

In Sect. 2, we explain the background of this research project. In Sect. 3, we present our formalization of architectures and refactorings. In Sect. 4, we present our formalization of deployments and sensitivities. In Sect. 5, we explain the implementation of our formal framework. In Sect. 6, we discuss related work and future work. *Proofs of theorems appear in a separate technical report* [9].

2   Background

First8. First8 (https://www.first8.nl), subsidiary of Conclusion (https://www.conclusion.nl), is a software company specialized in custom business-critical systems, including SOA, in all stages of the software life cycle. SOA developers at First8 regularly encounter and struggle with the Button Problem. In general, the industry-wide practice of manually reasoning about service sensitivities and candidate refactorings has three major issues. *First*, it is an intellectually demanding activity that often requires SOA developers to make simplifying assumptions. This leads to imprecise refactoring proposals, which may be more costly, more risky, and less effective than necessary. *Second*, as refactoring proposals are based on experience and best-practices, SOA developers can easily overlook less-intuitive refactorings that may well be most-effective for a given system. *Third*, predicting how multiple refactorings will affect each other is hard.

The aim of this research project is to develop a decision support tool (open source), built on top of a rigorous foundation, that helps SOA developers (First8 or otherwise) solve the Button Problem. Based on extensive experience with large enterprise systems, First8 imposed two unique requirements on the tool and its underlying formalization that give our project a novel position among existing computer-aided software engineering tools (see also Sect. 6):

– **"Whiteboard level of abstraction":** Finding a technical solution to the Button Problem is one thing; convincing business executives that this solution is truly worth pursuing and implementing is a whole different challenge.

Decisions are often made in meetings where there is neither time nor expertise on the executives' side to go through all the technical intricacies; instead, high-level whiteboard drawings are the main artifacts to explain service sensitivities and candidate refactorings, their consequences, and their trade-offs. To truly contribute to executives' decision-making, it is therefore imperative that our tool and its foundation are based on the simple whiteboard-style notation that executives intuitively understand and are accustomed to.

- **Non-quantitative analysis:** Ultimately, every Button Problem is about coarse-grained predictability of performance; it is *never* about reducing latency by x milliseconds, or increasing throughput by y transactions per hour. Although it is possible to try to solve the Button Problem using fine-grained quantitative approaches in terms of absolute latencies and throughputs (e.g., [3,5,13,15,22]), it is excessive (i.e., not the right tool for the job) and impractical. One issue is collecting the measurements to instantiate a quantitative model, which can be cumbersome or even impossible (i.e., if the system has not been deployed yet). Another issue is that measurements are implementation-specific and deployment-specific, and therefore brittle: changes in a service implementation or deployment can greatly impact absolute performance and immediately render a previously instantiated quantitative model obsolete. To solve the Button Problem *effectively*, using automated tool support, a non-quantitative approach is needed.

The Elmo Tool. Elmo is the decision support tool that is developed in this research project (open source; https://bitbucket.org/arjanl/elmo-tool), recently demonstrated at ICSOC 2018 [10,16] and built on top of the formalization presented in this paper. Leveraging a whiteboard-style notation for architectures and deployments, Elmo's main features are (1) automated non-quantitative analysis of service sensitivities and (2) automated inference of series of candidate refactorings that are guaranteed to be behavior-preserving and achieve given insensitivity goals. If multiple different series of candidate refactorings achieve the specified goals, Elmo automatically computes a comparison of other attributes of the final system designs for the user to inspect. Moreover, Elmo also supports an interactive mode that enables users to manually explore a system's design space by selecting and applying candidate refactorings from a list. (Elmo does not actually carry out refactorings, though; the tool is geared toward providing decision support to solve the Button Problem.)

We successfully evaluated Elmo in two case studies involving systems of First8 clients that suffer(ed) from the Button Problem:

1. In an e-commerce system at an undisclosed client, performance issues arose in key services when the load on seemingly unrelated services increased. First8 was consulted to solve this Button Problem, but Elmo did not yet exist at the time. Due to the sheer size and complexity of the system, the SOA developers involved ultimately proposed a broad, coarse-grained refactoring approach that affected the whole system; they were unable to manually find a more targeted series of refactorings to solve the problem more locally. The project revealed the need for a decision support tool to deal with this complexity.

Recently, we modeled the system in Elmo and automatically found a much more localized series of refactorings that achieves the same goals. Moreover, SOA developers that worked on the project are of the opinion that if Elmo had existed at the time of the project, this would have resulted in performance improvements much earlier in the process and with more confidence.

2. JoinData is a digital highway for farm-generated data, used nation-wide in the Netherlands. It allows for data exchange in the agricultural sector. For example, milking-robots on the farm, animal feed suppliers, or soil laboratories can exchange information with accountancy firms, governmental organisations, or farm management systems. Due to expected growth, the scalability of the messaging component, called EDI-Circle, needed to improve by solving the Button Problem of one of its constituent services.

   We compared (i) the manual analysis and proposed course of action by the lead architect of EDI-Circle with (ii) Elmo's automated analysis. Whereas the architect proposed "to change the whole system, since everything is connected", Elmo proposed a much more localized series of refactorings.

Details of case study 1 are protected by NDA; details of case study 2 are in [16].

In the rest of this paper, we present the rigorous foundation on top of which Elmo is built. We shall formalize systems at the abstraction level of their architectures and deployments. Refactorings are subsequently defined over formal architecture models; sensitivities are derived from formal deployment models.

3   Architectures and Refactorings

3.1   Architecture Models

Our formalization of architectures closely follows the proven whiteboard-style notation used by First8's SOA developers to effectively communicate with clients and business executives. The notation comprises graphical diagrams where services are drawn as nodes and calls between services as edges. Services are annotated with the *types* of information they *produce* and *consume*. Calls come in two flavors: *pushes* and *pulls*. A push by service s_1 to service s_2 entails a single communication from s_1 to s_2 (there is no subsequent acknowledgment from s_2 to s_1[1]); a pull by s_1 from s_2 entails a request for information from s_1 to s_2, and a subsequent response from s_2 to s_1. We formalize these diagrams as architecture models. Let $\mathbb{S}$ denote the set of all services, ranged over by s, and let $\mathbb{T}$ denote the set of all types of information, ranged over by t.

Definition 1. *An **architecture model** A is a tuple $(S, T, \Pi, \Gamma, \longrightarrow, \longrightarrow\!\!\prec)$ where:*

- *$S \subseteq \mathbb{S}$ and $T \subseteq \mathbb{T}$ denote sets of services and types;*
- *$\Pi, \Gamma : T \to 2^S$ denote indexed sets of producers and consumers;*

---

[1] In terms of the OSI transport layer, TCP/IP packets involved in a push *are* acknowledged (as part of the TCP/IP protocol), but this is at a lower level of abstraction.

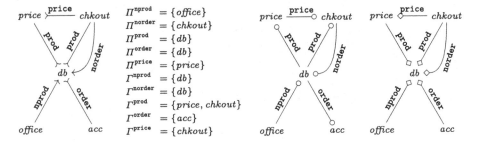

Fig. 1. Example architecture model   **Fig. 2.** Example directions/initiatives

$- \longrightarrow, \longleftarrow\, :\, T\, \rightarrow\, 2^{S \times S}$ *denote indexed push and pull relations such that* $(s_1, s_2) \in \longrightarrow(t)$ *implies* $s_1 \neq s_2$, *and* $(s_1, s_2) \in \longleftarrow(t)$ *implies* $s_1 \neq s_2$.

Arch denotes the set of all architecture models.

In words, $s \in \Pi(t)$ and $s \in \Gamma(t)$ mean that service s respectively produces and consumes information of type t (the utility of these sets becomes clear when we define well-formedness, shortly); we write Π^t and Γ^t instead of $\Pi(t)$ and $\Gamma(t)$. In words, $(s_1, s_2) \in \longrightarrow(t)$ and $(s_1, s_2) \in \longleftarrow(t)$ mean that service s_1 respectively pushes and pulls information of type t to and from service s_2; we write $s_1 \overset{t}{\longrightarrow} s_2$ and $s_1 \overset{t}{\longleftarrow} s_2$ instead of $(s_1, s_2) \in \longrightarrow(t)$ and $(s_1, s_2) \in \longleftarrow(t)$. The *domain* of an architecture model A is its set of services, denoted by $\mathrm{Dom}(A)$.

Example 1. Figure 1 shows an architecture model for a webshop system; it is a simplified version of the e-commerce system discussed in Sect. 2.

The database service, called *db*, manages information about products and orders. The front-end service, called *chkout*, is used by customers to order products; it calls the database service to pull product information and push new orders, while it pulls from a pricing service, called *price*, for calculating final prices (including additional fees and transport costs). The accounting service, called *acc*, checks if orders have been paid for; it calls the database service to pull order information. Finally, the back-office service, called *office*, maintains the product catalog; it calls the database service to push updated product information.

We note that we distinguish between new order/product information (**nprod** and **norder**), produced by *chkout*/*office*, and existing order/product information (**prod** and **order**), produced (i.e., "owned") by *db*. □

Architecture models (Definition 1) specify precisely the *direction* (i.e., from pusher to "pushee", but from "pullee" to puller) and the *initiative* (i.e., pushers and pullers; services that start information flows) of information flows; they abstract from call specifics (e.g., operations that are invoked; resources that are accessed), quantitative aspects of communication (e.g., call frequencies; latency; throughput), and transport characteristics (e.g., synchronous vs. asynchronous; reliable vs. lossy; unordered vs. order-preserving). Direction and initiative serve

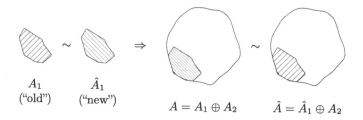

A_1 $\hat{A}_1$
("old")   ("new") $A = A_1 \oplus A_2$ $\hat{A} = \hat{A}_1 \oplus A_2$

Fig. 3. Refactoring framework

key purposes in our work: in this section, we use direction to reason about candidate refactorings; in the next section, we use initiative to reason about service sensitivities. We elicit these notions formally as follows. Let $f_1 \uplus f_2 = \{x \mapsto f_1(x) \mid x \in X_1 \setminus X_2\} \cup \{x \mapsto f_2(x) \mid x \in X_2 \setminus X_1\} \cup \{x \mapsto f_1(x) \cup f_2(x) \mid x \in X_1 \cap X_2\}$ denote the pointwise union of functions $f_1 : X_1 \to 2^{Y_1}$ and $f_2 : X_2 \to 2^{Y_2}$.

Definition 2. $\multimap, \multimapdotinv$: $\mathbb{A}\mathrm{rch} \to (\mathbb{T} \to 2^{\mathbb{S} \times \mathbb{S}})$ *denote the (doubly) indexed direction and initiative relations defined by the following equations:*

$$\multimap((S, T, \Pi, \Gamma, \longrightarrow, \longleftarrow)) = \{t \mapsto \longrightarrow(t) \cup \longleftarrow(t)^{-1} \mid t \in T\}$$
$$\multimapdotinv((S, T, \Pi, \Gamma, \longrightarrow, \longleftarrow)) = \longrightarrow \uplus \longleftarrow$$

In words, $(s_1, s_2) \in \multimap(A)(t)$ and $(s_1, s_2) \in \multimapdotinv(A)(t)$ means that flow of information of type t is directed and initiated from service s_1 to service s_2 in architecture model A; we write $s_1 \overset{t}{\multimap}_A s_2$ and $s_1 \overset{t}{\multimapdotinv}_A s_2$ instead of $(s_1, s_2) \in \multimap(A)(t)$ and $(s_1, s_2) \in \multimapdotinv(A)(t)$. Figure 2 exemplifies these relations for Fig. 1.

An architecture model is *well-formed* if every flow of information of type t starts at a producer of t (i.e., information should not emerge out of nowhere) and ends at a consumer of t (i.e., information should not be discarded unused). Formally, if $A = (S, T, \Pi, \Gamma, \longrightarrow, \longleftarrow)$ and $s_1 \overset{t}{\multimap}_A s_2$, then there exist services s_p and s_c such that: $\Pi^t \ni s_\mathrm{p} \overset{t}{\multimap}{}^*_A s_1$ and $s_2 \overset{t}{\multimap}{}^*_A s_\mathrm{c} \in \Gamma^t$. Well-formedness is an important sanity condition that models need to satisfy; it catches modeling inconsistencies and redundancies regarding information availability (which is also why producers/consumers are explicit elements of the model and not derived).

3.2   Refactoring Framework

We define a rigorous refactoring framework in terms of *composition* ($\oplus$) and *equivalence* ($\sim$) of architecture models (Fig. 3). The idea is to represent an architecture A as the composition of an "old part" A_1 and a "remaining part" A_2 (formally: $A = A_1 \oplus A_2$). Refactoring, then, amounts to substituting the old part with an equivalent "new part" $\hat{A}_1$ (formally: $A_1 \sim \hat{A}_1$). If the equivalence is in fact a *congruence* for composition, substitution of equivalent parts is guaranteed to yield equivalent wholes, which means that all existing information flows are preserved by substitution and no spurious new ones are introduced. This congruence property is pivotal: because of it, to show that a refactoring is correct, we need to prove only the equivalence of the old part and the new part, while we can safely ignore the remaining part. We now explain the details.

To compose architecture models A_1 and A_2, we "glue" them together on their shared services; through these services, information can subsequently flow from A_1 to A_2 and back, in accordance with the original push and pull relations. Such composition of architecture models corresponds roughly to union of graphs with overlapping vertex sets but disjoint edge sets.

Definition 3. $\oplus$: $\mathbb{Arch} \times \mathbb{Arch} \to \mathbb{Arch}$ *denotes the* ***composition function*** *defined by the following equation:*

$$A_1 \oplus A_2 = (S_1 \cup S_2, T_1 \cup T_2, \Pi_1 \uplus \Pi_2, \Gamma_1 \uplus \Gamma_2, \longrightarrow_1 \uplus \longrightarrow_2, \longrightarrow_1 \uplus \longrightarrow_2)$$

$$where \ A_i = (S_i, T_i, \Pi_i, \Gamma_i, \longrightarrow_i, \longrightarrow_i)$$

The following theorem states that composition of architecture models preserves the direction of information flows.

Theorem 1. $\longrightarrow^{\circ}_{A_1 \oplus A_2} = \longrightarrow^{\circ}_{A_1} \uplus \longrightarrow^{\circ}_{A_2}$

Two architecture models are equivalent iff the direction of every flow of information in the one can be mimicked in the other, including production and consumption of information, and vice versa. We note that we do not require mimicry of initiative; the idea is that it does not matter which service initiates sharing of information, so long as all information reaches the right services.

Definition 4. $\preceq, \sim$: $2^{\mathbb{S} \times \mathbb{S}} \to 2^{\mathbb{Arch} \times \mathbb{Arch}}$ *denote the indexed* ***preorder and equivalence relations*** *defined by the following equations:*

$$\preceq(R) = \left\{ (A, \hat{A}) \left| \begin{array}{l} \forall t, s, s'. \left[s \xrightarrow{t}_A s' \Rightarrow \exists \hat{s}, \hat{s}'. \left[\hat{s} \xrightarrow{t}_{\hat{A}} \hat{s}' \land s R \hat{s} \land s' R \hat{s}' \right] \right] \\ \land \ \forall t, s. \left[s \in \Pi^t \Rightarrow \exists \hat{s}. \left[\hat{s} \in \hat{\Pi}^t \land s R \hat{s} \right] \right] \\ \land \ \forall t, s. \left[s \in \Gamma^t \Rightarrow \exists \hat{s}. \left[\hat{s} \in \hat{\Gamma}^t \land s R \hat{s} \right] \right] \\ \land \ A = (S, T, \Pi, \Gamma, \longrightarrow, \longrightarrow) \land \hat{A} = (\hat{S}, \hat{T}, \hat{\Pi}, \hat{\Gamma}, \longrightarrow, \longrightarrow) \end{array} \right. \right\}$$

$$\sim(R) = \preceq(R) \cap \preceq(R^{-1})^{-1}$$

In words, $(A, \hat{A}) \in \preceq(R)$ means that relation R associates every service s in A with a set of services $\hat{S} = \{ \hat{s} \mid s R \hat{s} \}$ in $\hat{A}$ that *collectively*[2] *simulate* s (i.e., every information flow from s to some service s' in A can be mimicked as an information flow from some service $\hat{s} \in \hat{S}$ to some service $\hat{s}'$ in $\hat{A}$; every information production or consumption by s can be mimicked as an information production or consumption by some service $\hat{s} \in \hat{S}$). In words, $(A, \hat{A}) \in \sim(R)$ means that services in A and in $\hat{A}$ simulate each other under the same relation R. We write $A \preceq_R \hat{A}$ and $A \sim_R \hat{A}$ instead of $(A, \hat{A}) \in \preceq(R)$ and $(A, \hat{A}) \in \sim(R)$.

---

[2] Individual services in $\hat{S}$ may contribute only partially to the simulation (see also Example 2). This is where our definition of simulation differs significantly from the classical one in concurrency theory (e.g., [17]). It is also why $s R \hat{s}$ appears as a conjunct on the right-hand side of the implication instead of on the left-hand side.

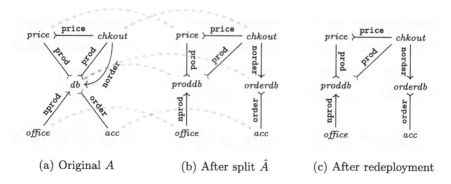

(a) Original A (b) After split $\hat{A}$ (c) After redeployment

Fig. 4. Equivalent architecture models (and deployment models) of the example web-shop systems before and after refactoring. Blue dashed lines indicate the simulation relation; sets of producers and consumers are omitted to save space. (Color figure online)

Example 2. Figure 4a and b show two equivalent architecture models of the example webshop system (Example 1), before and after refactoring; we discuss Fig. 4c, the gray boxes around services, and the parenthetical mentioning of "deployment models" in the caption in Sect. 4. Architecture model A in Fig. 4a is the original (cf. Fig. 1).

Architecture model $\hat{A}$ in Fig. 4b results from "splitting" service db in A into two new services: one that stores only product information, and one that stores only order information. To see that A and $\hat{A}$ are equivalent, observe that $\mathtt{prod}$ information flows from db to services $chkout$ and $price$ in A, while $\mathtt{prod}$ information flows from service $proddb$ to $chkout$ and $price$ in $\hat{A}$. Thus, db in A is partially simulated by $proddb$ in $\hat{A}$; likewise, with respect to $\mathtt{order}$ information flows, db in A is partially simulated by service $orderdb$ in $\hat{A}$. Thus, db in A is collectively simulated by $proddb$ and $orderdb$ in $\hat{A}$. Similarly, we can argue that $\hat{A}$ is simulated by A.   □

Example 3. To further illustrate (the intricacies of) Definition 4, suppose well-formed architecture A precisely consists of $\Pi^t \ni s \xrightarrow{t} s' \xrightarrow{t} s'' \in \Gamma^t$, while well-formed architecture $\hat{A}$ precisely consists of $\Pi^t \ni s \xrightarrow{t} s'_a \in \Gamma^t$ and $\Pi^t \ni s'_b \xrightarrow{t} s'' \in \Gamma^t$. These architectures are *not* equivalent: no relation R exists such that $A \sim_R \hat{A}$. Notably, $A \not\sim_{R^\dagger} \hat{A}$ for $R^\dagger = \{(s,s), (s',s'_a), (s',s'_b), (s'',s'')\}$, because s'_a (resp. s'_b) in $\hat{A}$ is consumer (resp. producer), but s' in A is not. Also, $A \not\sim_{R^\ddagger} \hat{A}$ for $R^\ddagger = \{(s,s), (s,s'_b), (s'',s'_a), (s'',s'')\}$, because s' is missing from $R^\ddagger$. This also shows that well-formedness does not imply production/consumption mimicry.

But, $A \sim_{R^\dagger} \hat{A}$ *does hold* after updating A such that $s' \in \Pi^t \cap \Gamma^t$. In that case, splitting s' into s'_a and s'_b means the consumption and production responsibilities of s' are divided over two new services; this can be perfectly fine in practice. □

$$\text{flip}\left(\begin{matrix} s_1 \\ t \downarrow \\ s_2 \end{matrix}\right) = t\uparrow\begin{matrix} s_1 \\ \\ s_2 \end{matrix} \qquad \text{split}\left(\begin{matrix} s_1 \quad s_2 \\ t_1 \diagdown \; t_2 \\ s_3 \end{matrix}; s_3, s_{3a}, s_{3b}, \{t_1\}\right) = \begin{matrix} s_1 \quad s_2 \\ t_1\downarrow \quad \downarrow t_2 \\ s_{3a}\; s_{3b} \end{matrix}$$

$$\text{flip}\left(\begin{matrix} s_1 \\ t \uparrow \\ s_2 \end{matrix}\right) = t\downarrow\begin{matrix} s_1 \\ \\ s_2 \end{matrix} \qquad \text{merge}\left(\begin{matrix} s_1 \quad s_2 \\ t_1\downarrow \quad \downarrow t_2 \\ s_{3a}\; s_{3b} \end{matrix}; \{s_{3a}, s_{3b}\}, s_3\right) = \begin{matrix} s_1 \quad s_2 \\ t_1 \diagdown \; t_2 \\ s_3 \end{matrix}$$

$$\text{addqueue}(s_1 \xrightarrow{t} s_2 ; t, s_1, s_2, s_q) = s_1 \xrightarrow{t} s_q \overset{t}{\rightarrowtail} s_2$$

$$\text{addcache}(s_1 \overset{t}{\rightarrowtail} s_2 ; t, s_1, s_2, s_c, s_{rd}) = s_1 \overset{t}{\rightarrowtail} s_c \overset{t}{\leftarrowtail} s_{rd} \overset{t}{\rightarrowtail} s_2$$

Fig. 5. Basic instances of example refactorings

The following theorem states that the equivalence relation $\sim$ (Definition 4) is a congruence relation for the composition operation $\oplus$ (Definition 3). To prove the theorem, we need additional assumptions beside equivalence of the parts. These additional assumptions state that *after substitution*, the services on the "boundary" between the old/new parts and the remaining part (set S_B in the theorem) must be indistinguishable from those *before substitution* (in terms of their names and information flows). In other words, the interface must remain the same: services on the boundary may not be renamed, added, or removed by a refactoring.

Theorem 2.

$$\begin{bmatrix} A_1 \sim_{R_1} \hat{A}_1 \\ \wedge \; S_B = \text{Dom}(A_1) \cap \text{Dom}(A_2) \\ \wedge \; S_B = \text{Dom}(\hat{A}_1) \cap \text{Dom}(A_2) \\ \wedge \; \forall s, \hat{s}.\big[[s \; R_1 \; \hat{s} \; \wedge \; s \in S_B] \Rightarrow s = \hat{s}\big] \\ \wedge \; \forall s, \hat{s}.\big[[s \; R_1 \; \hat{s} \; \wedge \; \hat{s} \in S_B] \Rightarrow s = \hat{s}\big] \end{bmatrix} \Rightarrow \exists R.\big[A_1 \oplus A_2 \sim_R \hat{A}_1 \oplus A_2\big]$$

3.3   Core Library of Refactorings

Now, every refactoring in our framework (Fig. 3) is defined by a predicate–function pair (P, f): predicate P identifies (sub)architectures that can take on the role of A_1 (the old part), while function f describes the transformation of A_1 into $\hat{A}_1$ (the new part). An *instance* of a refactoring, then, is the transformation of a concrete A_1 that satisfies P into $\hat{A}_1$ according to f. We call refactoring (P, f) *correct* if, for all A_1, satisfaction of P by A_1 implies that A_1 and $f(A_1)$ are equivalent. Subsequently, Theorem 2 ensures that a correct refactoring for A_1 can safely be applied in any architecture that contains A_1.

We defined a core library of provably correct refactorings: *Flip, Split, Merge, AddQueue,* and *AddCache.* These refactorings were selected to form a minimal

Let $A = (S, \Pi, \Gamma, \longrightarrow, \longrightarrow\!\!\!\!\prec)$. Predicates Flip?, Split?, Merge?, AddQueue?, AddCache? are the smallest relations induced by the following rules:

$$\frac{}{\mathsf{Flip?}(A)} \qquad \frac{s \in S \,\wedge\, s_1, s_2 \notin S}{\mathsf{Split?}(A; s, s_1, s_2, T_1)} \qquad \frac{S' \subseteq S \,\wedge\, s \notin S}{\mathsf{Merge?}(A; S', s)}$$

$$\frac{s_1 \xrightarrow{\;t\;} s_2 \,\wedge\, s \notin S}{\mathsf{AddQueue?}(A; t, s_1, s_2, s)} \qquad \frac{s_1 \xrightarrow{\;t\;}\!\!\!\prec s_2 \,\wedge\, s, s' \notin S}{\mathsf{AddCache?}(A; t, s_1, s_2, s, s')}$$

Fig. 6. Predicates of refactorings in the core library

set of primitive building blocks to support our two case studies (Sect. 2); due to the generality of our framework, the core library can straightforwardly be extended in future work, by need. Figure 5 shows basic instances of these refactorings; notationally, we use a semicolon to distinguish the old architecture to which a refactoring is applied from additional information that is used to compute the refactoring. Refactoring *Flip* converts pushes between corresponding "reverse-pulls" and vice versa. Refactoring *Split* divides the responsibilities of a single old service s_3 over multiple new services s_{3a} and s_{3b} (practically, such splitting is usually subject to additional constraints, such as information dependencies, which can be manually added as model annotations in the implementation; Sect. 5, footnote 4). Dually, refactoring *Merge* combines the responsibilities of multiple old services s_{3a} and s_{3b} into a single new service s_3. Refactoring *Add-Queue* introduces a special service s_q to replace a push from service s_1 to service s_2; the idea is that "producer" s_1 now pushes information to "queue" s_q (instead of directly to s_2), while "consumer" s_2 pulls that information from s_q (at its own pace, independent of s_1). Refactoring *AddCache* introduces special services s_c and s_{rd} to replace a pull from service s_1 to service s_2; the idea is that "consumer" s_1 pulls information from "cache" s_c, which is eagerly filled through pushes from "reader" s_{rd}, which gets the information by pulling from "producer" s_2.

Let $X[y/Y]$ denote the substitution in X of element y for every element from set Y (i.e., $X[y/Y] = X$ if $X \cap Y = \emptyset$, and $X[y/Y] = (X \setminus Y) \cup \{y\}$ otherwise), and let $\circ : 2^{X \times Y} \times 2^{Y \times Z} \to 2^{X \times Z}$ denote relational composition. Figures 6 and 7 show the predicates and functions that formally define the refactorings in the core library. The following theorem states their correctness.

Theorem 3.

- $\mathsf{Flip?}(A) \;\Rightarrow\; \exists R. \big[A \sim_R \mathsf{flip}(A)\big]$
- $\mathsf{Split?}(A; s, s_1, s_2, T_1) \;\Rightarrow\; \exists R. \big[A \sim_R \mathsf{split}(A; s, s_1, s_2, T_1)\big]$
- $\mathsf{Merge?}(A; S, s) \;\Rightarrow\; \exists R. \big[A \sim_R \mathsf{merge}(A; S, s)\big]$
- $\mathsf{AddQueue?}(A; s_q) \;\Rightarrow\; \exists R. \big[A \sim_R \mathsf{addqueue}(A; s_q)\big]$
- $\mathsf{AddCache?}(A; s_c, s_{rd}) \;\Rightarrow\; \exists R. \big[A \sim_R \mathsf{addcache}(A; s_c, s_{rd})\big]$

Together, Theorems 2 and 3 support the refactoring framework shown in Fig. 3. We note, though, that to apply Theorem 2 with *Split* and *Merge* (i.e., to satisfy the boundary condition), not only the split/merged service s must be in the old/new parts, but also the services that s calls and those that call s.

4   Deployments and Sensitivities

The whiteboard-style architecture models and rigorous refactoring framework presented in Sect. 3 offer a formal means of defining and reasoning about (the correctness of) refactorings. However, the formalism so far does not tell us which refactorings are "good" and which ones are "bad"; what is missing is a mechanism to evaluate the effectiveness of a refactoring. In this section, we define non-quantitative sensitivity indicators based on which SOA developers can make informed choices between candidate refactorings to solve the Button Problem.

Example 4. To illustrate core concepts, we shall continue to develop the example webshop system (Example 1) It actually suffers from exactly the same Button Problem as the e-commerce system on which our simplified version is based.

Specifically, services *chkout* and *price* (in the system as modeled in Fig. 4a) are sensitive to button-presses on service *acc*: once *acc* starts checking whether orders have been paid for, the performance of *chkout* and *price* decreases, as service *db* is unable to process the additional calls from *acc* without affecting the calls from *chkout* and *price*. Checking payment statuses is, however, only a low-priority task—it does not matter whether it happens immediately or in a few hours—and it should definitely not hinder the high-priority front-end of the system (which directly affects business). Refactoring the system to make *chkout* and *price* insensitive to *acc* is therefore an important improvement.   □

We start by observing that the sensitivity of a service to button-presses on other services does not depend solely on its incoming push and pull calls, but also on the machine on which it is deployed: if two architecturally independent services are deployed on the same machine, an increased load on the one will affect the performance of the other. To reason about service sensitivities, we therefore need to take into account deployments as well. Let $\mathbb{M}$ denote the set of all machines, ranged over by M.

Definition 5. *A deployment model D is a tuple $(A, M, \mathcal{M})$ where:*

- $A \in \mathrm{Arch}$ *denotes an architecture model;*
- $M \subseteq \mathbb{M}$ *denotes a set of machines;*
- $\mathcal{M} : \mathrm{Dom}(A) \to M$ *denotes a service–machine allocation.*

$\mathbb{D}$ *denotes the set of all deployment models.*

Example 5. Reconsider Fig. 4; it actually shows deployment models, where gray boxes around services represent machines. Thus, in Fig. 4a and b, there are three machines (from top to bottom: a front-end machine, a database machine, and an administration machine), whereas in Fig. 4c, there are four machines.   □

Let $A = (S, \Pi, \Gamma, \longrightarrow, \longrightarrow\!\!\!\!\prec)$. Functions flip, split, merge, addqueue, addcache are defined by the following equations:

$$\mathsf{flip}(A) = (S, \Pi, \Gamma, \{t \mapsto (\xrightarrow{t}\!\!\!\!\prec)^{-1} \mid t \in \mathbb{T}\}, \{t \mapsto (\xrightarrow{t})^{-1} \mid t \in \mathbb{T}\})$$

$$\mathsf{split}(A; s, s_1, s_2, T_1) = ((S \setminus \{s\}) \cup \{s_1, s_2\}, \hat{\Pi}, \hat{\Gamma}, \xrightarrow{\;}, \xrightarrow{\;}\!\!\!\!\prec)$$
$$\hat{\Pi} = \{t \mapsto \Pi^t[s_1/\{s\}] \mid t \in T_1\} \cup \{t \mapsto \Pi^t[s_2/\{s\}] \mid t \notin T_1\}$$
$$\hat{\Gamma} = \{t \mapsto \Gamma^t[s_1/\{s\}] \mid t \in T_1\} \cup \{t \mapsto \Gamma^t[s_2/\{s\}] \mid t \notin T_1\}$$
$$\xrightarrow{\;} = \{t \mapsto \{(s_1, s)\} \circ \xrightarrow{t} \circ \{(s, s_1)\} \mid t \in T_1\} \cup$$
$$\{t \mapsto \{(s_2, s)\} \circ \xrightarrow{t} \circ \{(s, s_2)\} \mid t \notin T_1\}$$
$$\xrightarrow{\;}\!\!\!\!\prec = \{t \mapsto \{(s_1, s)\} \circ \xrightarrow{t}\!\!\!\!\prec \circ \{(s, s_1)\} \mid t \in T_1\} \cup$$
$$\{t \mapsto \{(s_2, s)\} \circ \xrightarrow{t}\!\!\!\!\prec \circ \{(s, s_2)\} \mid t \notin T_1\}$$

$$\mathsf{merge}(A; S', s) = ((S \setminus S') \cup \{s\}, \hat{\Pi}, \hat{\Gamma}, \xrightarrow{\;}, \xrightarrow{\;}\!\!\!\!\prec)$$
$$\hat{\Pi} = \{t \mapsto \Pi^t[s/S'] \mid t \in \mathbb{T}\}$$
$$\hat{\Gamma} = \{t \mapsto \Gamma^t[s/S'] \mid t \in \mathbb{T}\}$$
$$\xrightarrow{\;} = \{t \mapsto (s \times S') \circ \xrightarrow{t} \circ (S' \times s) \mid t \in \mathbb{T}\}$$
$$\xrightarrow{\;}\!\!\!\!\prec = \{t \mapsto (s \times S') \circ \xrightarrow{t}\!\!\!\!\prec \circ (S' \times s) \mid t \in \mathbb{T}\}$$

$$\mathsf{addqueue}(A; t, s_1, s_2, s) = (S \cup \{s\}, \Pi, \Gamma, \xrightarrow{\;}, \xrightarrow{\;}\!\!\!\!\prec)$$
$$\xrightarrow{\;} = (\longrightarrow \setminus \{t \mapsto \xrightarrow{t}\}) \cup \{t \mapsto (\xrightarrow{t} \setminus \{(s_1, s_2)\}) \cup \{(s_1, s)\}\}$$
$$\xrightarrow{\;}\!\!\!\!\prec = (\longrightarrow\!\!\!\!\prec \setminus \{t \mapsto \xrightarrow{t}\!\!\!\!\prec\}) \cup \{t \mapsto \xrightarrow{t}\!\!\!\!\prec \cup \{(s_2, s)\}\}$$

$$\mathsf{addcache}(A; t, s_1, s_2, s, s') = (S \cup \{s, s'\}, \Pi, \Gamma, \xrightarrow{\;}, \xrightarrow{\;}\!\!\!\!\prec)$$
$$\xrightarrow{\;} = (\longrightarrow \setminus \{t \mapsto \xrightarrow{t}\}) \cup \{t \mapsto \xrightarrow{t} \cup \{(s', s)\}\}$$
$$\xrightarrow{\;}\!\!\!\!\prec = (\longrightarrow\!\!\!\!\prec \setminus \{t \mapsto \xrightarrow{t}\!\!\!\!\prec\}) \cup$$
$$\{t \mapsto (\xrightarrow{t}\!\!\!\!\prec \setminus \{s_1, s_2\}) \cup \{(s_1, s), (s', s_2)\}\}$$

Fig. 7. Functions of refactorings in the core library

Based on a deployment model of a system, we can compute two non-quantitative indicators that we shortly use to formalize sensitivity: *stress* and *delay*. The stress of a service is a non-quantitative abstraction of the number of incoming calls that it needs to process. The higher the number of calls, the higher the stress of the service and the lower its performance. The delay of a service is a non-quantitative abstraction of the number of outgoing pulls whose processing (by other services) it needs to await. The higher the number of pulls, the higher the delay of the service and the lower its performance. The *stress set* of a service s contains the services that affect the stress of s (including itself): if the stress of a service in its stress set increases, then so does the stress of s. The *delay set* of a service s contains the services that affect the delay of s.

Definition 6. Stress, Delay : $\mathbb{D} \times \mathbb{S} \to 2^{\mathbb{S}}$ *denote the indexed* **stress and delay** *sets defined by the following equations:*

$$\mathsf{Stress}(D, s) \quad = \{s\} \cup \bigcup\{\mathsf{Stress}(D, s') \mid s' \xrightarrow{t}\!\!\!\diamond_A s \ \vee \ \mathcal{M}(s') = \mathcal{M}(s)\}$$
$$\mathsf{Delay}(D, s) \quad = \bigcup\{\mathsf{Stress}(D, s') \cup \mathsf{Delay}(D, s') \mid s \xrightarrow{t}\!\!\!\!\prec s'\}$$

where $D = (A, M, \mathcal{M})$ *and* $A = (S, T, \Pi, \Gamma, \longrightarrow, \longrightarrow\!\!\!\!\prec)$.

Note that the delay set of a service s contains the stress set of every service s' from which s pulls information. This is because the services in the stress set of s' may negatively affect the rate at which s' can process pulls by s: if the services in the stress set of s' heavily stress s', then this rate goes down.

We can now formalize (in)sensitivity to button-presses as follows:

- If service s_1 is affected by service s_2 regardless of s_1's calls to s_2, then s_1 is *forcibly sensitive* to s_2 (i.e., s_1 is forcibly sensitive to s_2 if s_2 stresses s_1).
- If service s_1 is affected by service s_2 because s_1 requires information from s_2 by means of a pull, then s_1 is *voluntarily sensitive* to s_2 (i.e., s_1 is voluntarily sensitive to s_2 if s_2 delays s_1).
- If service s_1 is unaffected by service s_2, it is *insensitive* to s_2.

Definition 7. $\mathcal{I}, \mathcal{V}, \mathcal{F} : \mathbb{D} \rightarrow \mathbb{S} \times \mathbb{S}$ *denote the indexed* **sensitivity relations** *defined by the following equations:*

$$\mathcal{F}(D) = \{(s, s') \mid s' \in \mathsf{Stress}(D, s)\}$$
$$\mathcal{V}(D) = \{(s, s') \mid s' \notin \mathsf{Stress}(D, s) \wedge s' \in \mathsf{Delay}(D, s)\}$$
$$\mathcal{I}(D) = \{(s, s') \mid s' \notin \mathsf{Stress}(D, s) \wedge s' \notin \mathsf{Delay}(D, s)\}$$

Remark: $\{\mathcal{F}(D), \mathcal{V}(D), \mathcal{I}(D)\}$ *partitions* $\mathrm{Dom}(A) \times \mathrm{Dom}(A)$ *for* $D = (A, M, \mathcal{M})$.

Example 6. Recall from Example 4 that front-end services *chkout* and *price* suffer from the Button Problem in the example webshop system as modeled in Fig. 4a. We shall apply two changes to alleviate this problem, but first, we show that the deployment model in Fig. 4a indeed confirms these undesirable sensitivities.

Let D denote the deployment model in Fig. 4a. Because services *chkout* and *price* are deployed on the same machine (and because they receive no external calls), their stress set under D is $\{chkout, price\}$. However, because *chkout* and *price* both pull from service *db*, their delay set contains all services that stress *db*, including service *acc*. Thus, $acc \in \mathsf{Delay}(D, chkout)$ and $acc \in \mathsf{Delay}(D, price)$: according to the model high-priority *chkout* and *price* are both voluntarily sensitive to low-priority *acc*. Intuitively, if service *acc* pulls intensely from service *db* (increasing the stress of *db*), the rate at which *db* can process pulls by *chkout* and *price* is negatively affected (increasing the delay of *chkout*).

The first change is the application of refactoring *Split* to divide the responsibilities of existing service *db* over new services *proddb* and *orderdb*; let $\hat{D}$ denote the resulting deployment model in Fig. 4b (Example 2). Intuitively, this refactoring should make services *chkout* and *price* insensitive to button-presses on service *acc* (because the only pulls they perform are directed to *proddb*, which is architecturally independent of *acc*), but because *proddb* and *orderdb* are still deployed on the same machine, the voluntary sensitivities actually remain: *acc* can still stress *orderdb*, which subsequently affects the processing speed of *proddb*.

The second change is a *redeployment* that puts each of services *proddb* and *orderdb* on its own machine; let $\hat{D}$ denote the resulting deployment model in Fig. 4c. A redeployment is not a refactoring, it does not change information flows among services, and thus it is trivially behavior-preserving; it only changes the service–machine allocation. By redeploying services according to $\hat{D}$, stress is no longer shared between *proddb* and *orderdb*; as a result, services *chkout* and *price* become insensitive to *acc*, solving the Button Problem. Reasoning with sensitivities in this way thus provides a formal justification to refactor.   □

5   Implementation

Engine. We now explain how the formalization presented in the previous section provides a rigorous foundation for the Elmo tool. To safeguard a tight correspondence between the tool and its formalization, the lead developer of the tool is closely involved in the formalization as well. Essentially, Elmo's implementation consists of two key components: data structures to store architecture models and deployment models and a reasoning engine. The engine has two capabilities:

1. Computation of stress sets, delay sets, (in)sensitivities, and secondary performance indicators (e.g., network depth)
2. Exploration of a system's design space toward one or more insensitivity goals

These capabilities are invoked in Elmo's two usage modes.

Interactive Mode. In interactive mode, after drawing an initial deployment model of the system in Elmo, Capability 1 is invoked to get an overview of services that potentially suffer from the Button Problem. The user can subsequently refactor the model to evaluate and compare manually devised candidate solutions. Interactive mode is particularly suitable to get quick feedback on candidate solutions (e.g., during live meetings with project members to explore the options), without having to work out all details manually, which is laborious and error-prone. It is therefore important that computation of performance indicators is fast. To give an indication, the computation of stress sets, delay sets, and (in)sensitivities in the model of the full e-commerce system (case study 1; Sect. 2), which consists of 60 services with 125 calls, takes less than a second (on regular hardware).

Automatic Mode. In automatic mode, if service s suffers from the Button Problem (e.g., found using Capability 1), the user can declaratively formulate a solution to the problem as a set of target insensitivities from s to other services; then, Capability 2 is invoked to let Elmo automatically look for series of refactorings that achieve the specified insensitivity goals by exploring the *design space*.

The design space of a system is essentially a directed graph, where vertices are deployment models, and edges are refactorings (from the core library; Sect. 3.3) and redeployments that transform (the architecture model of) a "source" deployment model into (the architecture model of) a "target" deployment model. To generate a system's design space, starting from an initial deployment model, refactorings are applied and sensitivities are computed for the resulting models to check if the specified insensitivity goals have been achieved (using Capability 1). In this way, the entire design space is generated and exhaustively explored;

solutions are reported as soon as they are found, so if a satisfactory one is discovered early, the rest of the search may be user-aborted long before exhaustive exploration is done (it can also be bounded to a fixed depth from the start). We employ a breadth-first exploration policy, as it finds solutions of few refactorings (generally more attractive for businesses) sooner than those of many refactorings (generally more expensive). A similar level of automation to explore a system's design space is very difficult to achieve when quantitative models are used, as it is unclear how to get new quantitative data to instantiate refactored models.

The design space generated from an initial deployment model D_0 is finite: there are finitely many services and calls in D_0, there are only finitely many ways in which refactorings create additional services and calls,[3] and the number of machines is bounded by the number of services. As a result, under our formalization, the Button Problem is decidable in the sense that Elmo can exhaustively explore the entire design space for solutions. Design spaces do tend to get very large, though, so even if they can be explored in finite time in theory, it may not always be feasible in practice. As a result, pending future optimizations (see below), Elmo's automatic mode is useful in two scenarios:

- **Live meetings:** A question that typically arises during discussions among project members is whether no "easy solutions" (i.e., those that require few refactorings) are overlooked. In this case, Elmo's automatic mode can be effectively used with an explicit depth bound (i.e., maximum number of refactorings that candidate solutions may consist of), significantly reducing the design space to explore. If an easy solution is subsequently found that was previously overlooked, this is of course valuable information; moreover, if no new easy solution is found, this is valuable information, too, as it gives the project team confidence (*and objective data*) to convince executives that a "hard solution" is fundamentally needed. To give an indication, it takes only ten minutes to automatically explore the design space of the full e-commerce system (case study 1; Sect. 2) up to depth 2.
- **Off-line:** In the absence of short deadlines, Elmo's automatic mode can perfectly be run unrestricted, to fully explore the potentially huge design space. A crucial observation is that the size of the design space is not a modeling artifact, but an inherent characteristic of the problem. *Without tool support, SOA developers just have to plow through it by hand*, which seems infeasible; instead, only the more obvious directions are followed, based on experience and best-practices, leaving a large part of the space unexplored and (potentially better) solutions hidden. Our case studies confirm this (Sect. 2): for both systems, Elmo found better solutions that SOA developers did not find.

We are working on a number of optimizations to reduce the design space wherever possible and speed up the exploration: (1) model annotations to fur-

---

[3] More precisely, the only services that create additional services or calls are *Split*, *AddQueue*, and *AddCache*. The number of times a service can be split is bound by the number of types, while the services and calls added through *AddQueue* and *AddCache* carry annotations that inform Elmo to not refactor them any further.

ther constrain which candidate solutions are truly acceptable;[4] (2) partial order reduction to prune away commuting refactorings [20]; (3) parallelization.

6   Conclusion

Related Work. Other tools exist that aid in refactoring existing architectures. These tools help to visualize architectures, detect code smells like dependency cycles, or validate architectural rules (e.g. [4,6,11,21]). However, these tools work at the implementation/code level and do not take deployment into account, nor can they evaluate performance sensitivities like Elmo does. Moreover, a key strength of Elmo is its rigorous foundation and formal correctness (i.e., the core contribution of this paper); these other tools do not provide such guarantees.

Application performance monitoring tools (e.g. [2,7,8,18]) provide a quick insight in interactions between services and aid in detecting performance problems. However, they can only do this when software is actually deployed; not during design. These tools can identify bottlenecks, but they have only very limited support for finding solutions. Based on the formalization presented in this paper, in contrast, Elmo can automatically compute series of refactorings.

UML component diagrams allow developers to document dependencies between components/services. A key difference with our approach is that component diagrams do not distinguish between pushes and pulls [14] (i.e., component diagrams model dependencies between components, but they do not model the direction and initiative of information flows that push and pull operations additionally convey); in our model, this is vital information to reason about refactorings and sensitivities. To provide such information in UML, complementary behavioral diagrams (e.g., UML sequence diagrams) can be used, but then the level of detail becomes too low for our purpose, while at the same time a maintenance burden emerges. Also, mixing different types of diagrams is cumbersome.

Future Work. We are currently working along three axes: theory, implementation, and case studies. Along the theory axis, to better support situations where the specified insensitivity goals are inconsistent (i.e., impossible to achieve), we

---

[4] Elmo may find designs that solve the specified insensitivity goals, but that are still unacceptable to SOA developers due to external constraints (e.g., the number of machines exceeds the budget; some services should not be merged because it requires reorganization of development teams). Instead of letting Elmo first explore the entire design space and then filtering the unacceptable solutions, SOA developers can specify additional model annotations upfront to constrain which refactorings Elmo will try to apply; corners of unacceptable solutions in the design space are skipped.

Specifically, in the initial deployment model, users can indicate that a service must remain intact (i.e., it cannot be split, merged, or modified); that some services cannot be merged; that some sets of types cannot be split; that a call must remain intact (i.e., it cannot be flipped or replaced by a queue/cache); that some sets of services must be collocated; that the number of machines must not exceed some limit.

are developing notions of *Pareto efficiency* of deployment models. The idea is to devise formal machinery to compute *Pareto frontiers*: sets of deployment models such that no deployment model in the set can be be further refactored to eliminate an undesirable sensitivity without simultaneously (re)introducing one. We are also considering to incorporate a form of simulation to provide quantitative feedback on refactorings (e.g., [12]); this may be useful to analyze and reason about, for instance, latency (currently not supported).

Along the implementation axis, we are working on the optimizations stated in Sect. 5 (model annotations; partial order reduction; parallellization).

References

1. Akamai Technologies Inc.: Akamai Online Retail Performance Report | Akamai (2017). Accessed 28 June 2019. https://www.akamai.com/uk/en/about/news/press/2017-press/akamai-releases-spring-2017-state-of-online-retail-performance-report.jsp
2. AppDynamics LLC: Application Performance Monitoring and Management | AppDynamics (nd). Accessed 28 June 2019. https://www.appdynamics.com
3. Bertoli, M., Casale, G., Serazzi, G.: JMT: performance engineering tools for system modeling. SIGMETRICS Perform. Eval. Rev. **36**(4), 10–15 (2009)
4. Bischofberger, W., Kühl, J., Löffler, S.: Sotograph – a pragmatic approach to source code architecture conformance checking. In: Oquendo, F., Warboys, B.C., Morrison, R. (eds.) EWSA 2004. LNCS, vol. 3047, pp. 1–9. Springer, Heidelberg (2004). https://doi.org/10.1007/978-3-540-24769-2_1
5. Brebner, P.: Real-world performance modelling of enterprise service oriented architectures: delivering business value with complexity and constraints (abstracts only). SIGMETRICS Perform. Eval. Rev. **39**(3), 12 (2011)
6. Caracciolo, A., Lungu, M.F., Nierstrasz, O.: A unified approach to architecture conformance checking. In: WICSA, pp. 41–50. IEEE Computer Society (2015)
7. Datadog Inc.: Modern monitoring and analytics | Datadog (nd). Accessed 28 June 2019. https://www.datadoghq.com
8. Dynatrace LLC: Software intelligence for the enterprise cloud | Dynatrace (nd). Accessed 28 June 2019. https://www.dynatrace.com
9. van Eekelen, M., Jongmans, S.S., Lamers, A.: Non-Quantitative Modeling of Service-Oriented Architectures, Refactorings, and Performance. Technical Report TR-OU-INF-2017-02, Open University of the Netherlands (2017)
10. Elmo Demo (2018). Accessed 28 June 2019. https://youtu.be/Oi9kxqh_GBs
11. Headway Software Technologies Ltd.: Structure101 Home – Structure101 (nd). Accessed 28 June 2019. https://structure101.com
12. Johnsen, E.B., Pun, K.I., Tapia Tarifa, S.L.: A formal model of cloud-deployed software and its application to workflow processing. In: SoftCOM, pp. 1–6. IEEE (2017)
13. Juan Ferrer, A., et al.: OPTIMIS: a holistic approach to cloud service provisioning. Future Gener. Comp. Syst. **28**(1), 66–77 (2012)
14. Kobryn, C.: Modeling components and frameworks with UML. Commun. ACM **43**(10), 31–38 (2000)
15. Kounev, S.: Performance modeling and evaluation of distributed component-based systems using queueing petri nets. IEEE Trans. Softw. Eng. **32**(7), 486–502 (2006)

16. Lamers, A., van Eekelen, M., Jongmans, S.-S.: Improved architectures/ deployments with elmo. In: Liu, X., et al. (eds.) ICSOC 2018. LNCS, vol. 11434, pp. 419–424. Springer, Cham (2019). https://doi.org/10.1007/978-3-030-17642-6_36
17. Milner, R.: Communication and concurrency. PHI Series in computer science. Prentice Hall, New Jersey (1989)
18. New Relic Inc.: New Relic | Deliver more perfect software (nd). Accessed 28 June 2019. https://www.newrelic.com
19. Pautasso, C., Zimmermann, O., Amundsen, M., Lewis, J., Josuttis, N.M.: Microservices in practice, part 1: reality check and service design. IEEE Software **34**(1), 91–98 (2017)
20. Peled, D.: Partial-order reduction. In: Clarke, E., Henzinger, T., Veith, H., Bloem, R. (eds.) Handbook of Model Checking, pp. 173–190. Springer, Cham (2018). https://doi.org/10.1007/978-3-319-10575-8_6
21. SonarSource SA: Continuous Inspection | SonarQube (nd). Accessed 28 June 2019. https://www.sonarqube.org
22. Zhu, L., Liu, Y., Bui, N.B., Gorton, I.: Revel8or: model driven capacity planning tool suite. In: ICSE, pp. 797–800. IEEE Computer Society (2007)

Controlling Large Boolean Networks with Temporary and Permanent Perturbations

Cui Su[1], Soumya Paul[2], and Jun Pang[1,2(✉)]

[1] Interdisciplinary Centre for Security, Reliability and Trust,
University of Luxembourg, Esch-sur-Alzette, Luxembourg
jun.pang@uni.lu
[2] Faculty of Science, Technology and Communication, University of Luxembourg,
Esch-sur-Alzette, Luxembourg

Abstract. A salient objective of studying gene regulatory networks (GRNs) is to identify potential target genes whose perturbations would lead to effective treatment of diseases. In this paper, we develop two control methods for GRNs in the context of asynchronous Boolean networks. Our methods compute a minimal subset of nodes of a given Boolean network, such that temporary or permanent perturbations of these nodes drive the network from an initial state to a target steady state. The main advantages of our methods include: (1) temporary and permanent perturbations can be feasibly conducted with techniques for genetic modifications in biological experiments; and (2) the minimality of the identified control sets can reduce the cost of experiments to a great extent. We apply our methods to several real-life biological networks *in silico* to show their efficiency in terms of computation time and their efficacy with respect to the number of nodes to be perturbed.

1 Introduction

Cellular reprogramming has opened up an unprecedented opportunity for pathological studies and regenerative medicine. It can rejuvenate somatic cells to pluripotent state, or even convert somatic cells directly to other differentiated cells [1–3]. Yet the identification of potential target genes and reprogramming paths remains a major hurdle in *in vivo* cellular reprogramming [4]. Combinatorial complexity of potential drug targets and the high cost of experimental tasks make an experimental approach [5] infeasible. This reinforces the need for efficient control methods based on mathematical modelling.

Many control methods have been developed in recent years to solve the problem. However, most of them are not applicable to real-life biological networks due to different reasons. First, biological networks have a specific control objective [5,6]: finding a set of nodes, such that the control of these nodes can drive the system from a steady state to any other steady state. Biologically admissible steady states are observable phenotypes [7] and only the control of these states is meaningful. This rules out the methods based on classical controllability [8].

© Springer Nature Switzerland AG 2019
M. H. ter Beek et al. (Eds.): FM 2019, LNCS 11800, pp. 707–724, 2019.
https://doi.org/10.1007/978-3-030-30942-8_41

Second, some modelling frameworks are not suitable for biological networks. For example, linear dynamical networks fail to capture the non-linearity of biological networks, thus rendering control strategies for such networks inapplicable [8–10]. Lack of biological information prohibits the modelling of biological systems with networks of ordinary differential equations (ODEs) [11]. This further limits the application of control methods based on ODE networks [12,13]. Compared to the above modelling frameworks, Boolean networks (BNs) are well suited to model discrete and nonlinear dynamical biological systems. In BNs, genes are modelled as binary variables, being either 'expressed' or 'not expressed' and activation/inhibition regulations between genes are described by Boolean functions. The dynamics of a BN is determined by Boolean functions together with the update mode, either *synchronous* or *asynchronous*. The steady states of biological systems are described as *attractors* in BNs, to one of which the network eventually settles down. Recently, Kim et al. [14] and Zhao et al. [15] developed methods to drive a synchronous BN towards a desired attractor. However, the synchronous update mode is considered less realistic than the asynchronous update mode as only the latter allows for different time-scales of biological processes [16]. For asynchronous BNs, Zañudo et al. [6] developed a promising method to identify attractors and drug targets based on stable motifs. However, this method does not guarantee the minimality of perturbations.

Owing to various shortcomings of the existing control methods, we aim to develop a minimal and realistic control strategy for the control of asynchronous BNs. Given a BN, a source state and a target attractor, our idea is to identify an *exact minimal* set C of nodes of the BN, such that by perturbing the nodes in C, the dynamics of the BN is driven from the source state to the desired target attractor. One key factor to make this strategy realistic is to adopt physically admissible and experimentally feasible perturbations [17]. Rapid development of biomolecular techniques enables us to perturb expressions of nodes for different classes of time periods (instantaneously, temporarily or permanently) in both directions: from 'expressed' to 'not expressed' and/or from 'not expressed' to 'expressed' [18]. In [19], we developed such a method for perturbations that are instantaneous and showed that it is well suited for certain biological networks [17]. In this work, we develop methods for identifying a minimal set C of control nodes for asynchronous BNs whose perturbations can be long-term (temporary) or even permanent. The application of control C reshapes the BN to a new one, where the Boolean functions of the nodes in C are fixed to either ON or OFF. Permanent control leads to a permanent shift of the dynamics, whereas, for the temporary control, the perturbations of the identified set C of nodes are maintained for sufficient time until the network reaches a state, from which there only exist paths towards the target in the original BN.

We have implemented our temporary and permanent control methods and evaluated them on a variety of real-life biological networks modelled as BNs. We show that: (1) both temporary and permanent control sets can be efficiently computed on BNs that model real-life GRNs; (2) our methods not only capture the essential genes identified in the literature (e.g, see [20]), but also give other solutions for potential applications; (3) both methods can greatly reduce the number of control nodes compared to the instantaneous control [19]. The control nodes computed by the two methods form a relatively small set even for large-scale networks. This agrees with the empirical findings that the control of a few nodes is sufficient to control cell fate determination processes [21, 22].

2 Preliminaries

In this section, we give preliminary notions of Boolean networks in Sects. 2.1, 2.2 and 2.3 and precisely formulate our control problems in Sect. 2.4.

2.1 Boolean Networks

Let $[n]$ denote the set of positive integers $\{1, 2, \ldots, n\}$. A Boolean network (BN) describes elements of a dynamical system with binary-valued nodes and interactions between elements with Boolean functions. It is formally defined as:

Definition 1 (Boolean networks). *A Boolean network is a tuple* $\mathsf{BN} = (\mathbf{x}, \mathbf{f})$ *where* $\mathbf{x} = \{x_1, x_2, \ldots, x_n\}$ *such that each* $x_i, i \in [n]$ *is a Boolean variable and* $\mathbf{f} = \{f_1, f_2, \ldots, f_n\}$ *is a set of Boolean functions over* $\mathbf{x}$.

A Boolean network $\mathsf{BN} = (\mathbf{x}, \mathbf{f})$ has an associated directed graph $\mathcal{G}_{\mathsf{BN}} = (V, E)$, where $V = \{v_1, v_2 \ldots, v_n\}$ is the set of vertices or nodes and for every $i, j \in [n]$ there is a directed edge from v_j to v_i if and only if f_i depends on x_j. For the rest of the exposition, we assume that an arbitrary but fixed network $\mathsf{BN} = (\mathbf{x}, \mathbf{f})$ of n variables is given to us. For all occurrences of x_i and f_i, we assume x_i and f_i are elements of $\mathbf{x}$ and $\mathbf{f}$ resp.

A state $\mathbf{s}$ of BN is an element in $\{0, 1\}^n$. Let $\mathbf{S}$ be the set of states of BN. For any state $\mathbf{s} = (s_1, s_2, \ldots, s_n)$, and for every $i \in [n]$, the value of s_i, often denoted as $\mathbf{s}[i]$, represents the value that the variable x_i takes when the BN 'is in state $\mathbf{s}$'. For some $i \in [n]$, suppose f_i depends on $x_{i_1}, x_{i_2}, \ldots, x_{i_k}$. Then $f_i(\mathbf{s})$ will denote the value $f_i(\mathbf{s}[i_1], \mathbf{s}[i_2], \ldots, \mathbf{s}[i_k])$. For two states $\mathbf{s}, \mathbf{s}' \in \mathbf{S}$, the Hamming distance between $\mathbf{s}$ and $\mathbf{s}'$ will be denoted as $\mathsf{hd}(\mathbf{s}, \mathbf{s}')$ and $\arg \mathsf{hd}(\mathbf{s}, \mathbf{s}') \subseteq [n]$ will denote the set of indices in which $\mathbf{s}$ and $\mathbf{s}'$ differ. It will be convenient to view $\arg \mathsf{hd}(\mathbf{s}, \mathbf{s}')$ as a tuple of two disjoint sets $(\mathbb{1}, \mathbb{0})$, where $\mathbf{s}'[i] = 1$ if $i \in \mathbb{1}$ and $\mathbf{s}'[i] = 0$ if $i \in \mathbb{0}$. For a state $\mathbf{s}$ and a subset $\mathbf{S}' \subseteq \mathbf{S}$, the Hamming distance between $\mathbf{s}$ and $\mathbf{S}'$ is defined as the minimum of the Hamming distances between $\mathbf{s}$ and all the states in $\mathbf{S}'$, i.e. $\mathsf{hd}(\mathbf{s}, \mathbf{S}') = \min_{\mathbf{s}' \in \mathbf{S}'} \mathsf{hd}(\mathbf{s}, \mathbf{s}')$. Let $\arg \mathsf{hd}(\mathbf{s}, \mathbf{S}')$ denote the set of tuples, such that $(\mathbb{1}, \mathbb{0}) \in \arg \mathsf{hd}(\mathbf{s}, \mathbf{S}')$ if and only if $\mathbb{1} \cup \mathbb{0}$ is a set of indices of the variables that realise the minimum Hamming distance.

2.2 Dynamics of Boolean Networks

We assume that the Boolean network evolves in discrete time steps. It starts initially in a state $\mathbf{s}_0$ and its state changes in every time step according to the update functions $\mathbf{f}$. The updating may happen in various ways [23, 24]. Every such way of updating gives rise to a different dynamics for the network. In this work, we shall be interested primarily in the asynchronous update mode.

Definition 2 (Asynchronous dynamics of Boolean networks). *Suppose* $s_0 \in S$ *is an initial state of* BN. *The asynchronous evolution of* BN *is a function* $\xi_{BN} : \mathbb{N} \to \wp(S)$ *such that* $\xi_{BN}(0) = \{s_0\}$ *and for every* $j \geq 0$, *if* $s \in \xi_{BN}(j)$ *then* $s' \in \xi_{BN}(j+1)$ *is a possible* next state *of* s *iff either* $hd(s, s') = 1$ *and* $s'[i] = f_i(s)$ *where* $s'[i] = 1 - s[i]$ *or* $hd(s, s') = 0$ *and there exists* i *such that* $s'[i] = f_i(s)$.

Note that the asynchronous dynamics is non-deterministic – the value of exactly one variable is updated in a single time-step whose index is not known in advance. Henceforth, when we talk about the dynamics of BN, we shall mean the asynchronous dynamics as defined above. The dynamics of a Boolean network can be represented as a *state transition graph* or a *transition system (TS)*.

Definition 3 (Transition system of BN). *The transition system of* BN, *denoted as* TS$_{BN}$ *is a tuple* $(S, \to_{BN})$, *where the vertices are the set of states* S *and for any two states* s *and* s' *there is a directed edge from* s *to* s', *denoted* $s \to_{BN} s'$ *iff* s' *is a possible next state of* s *according to the asynchronous evolution function* ξ_{BN} *of* BN.

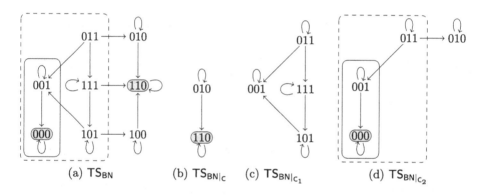

(a) TS$_{BN}$ (b) TS$_{BN|C}$ (c) TS$_{BN|C_1}$ (d) TS$_{BN|C_2}$

Fig. 1. The transition systems of BN.

Example 1. Consider a network BN $= (\mathbf{x}, \mathbf{f})$, where $\mathbf{x} = \{x_1, x_2, x_3\}$, $\mathbf{f} = \{f_1, f_2, f_3\}$, and $f_1 = ((\neg x_3) \wedge x_1) \vee x_2$, $f_2 = ((\neg x_3) \wedge x_2) \vee ((\neg x_3) \wedge x_1)$, $f_3 = 0$. The transition system of the network TS$_{BN}$ is given in Fig. 1a.

Definition 4 (Control). *A control* C *is a tuple* $(\mathbb{1}, \mathbb{0})$ *where* $\mathbb{1}, \mathbb{0} \subseteq [n]$, $\mathbb{1}$ *and* $\mathbb{0}$ *are mutually disjoint (possibly empty) set of indices of variables of* BN. *The size of control* C *is defined as* size(C) $= |\mathbb{1}| + |\mathbb{0}|$. *Given two states* $s, s' \in S$, *let* $C^{s \to s'} = (\mathbb{1}, \mathbb{0})$, *where* $\mathbb{1} = \{i \in [n] \mid s'[i] = 1 = 1 - s[i]\}$ *and* $\mathbb{0} = \{i \in [n] \mid s'[i] = 0 = 1 - s[i]\}$.

Intuitively, $\mathbb{1}$ and $\mathbb{0}$ represent the indices of variables of BN whose values are held fixed to 1 and 0 respectively under the control C. For $C^{s \to s'}$, $\mathbb{1} \cup \mathbb{0}$ are the set of indices in which $\mathbf{s}$ and $\mathbf{s}'$ differ, out of which $\mathbb{1}$ and $\mathbb{0}$ are the indices which have a value 1 and 0 in $\mathbf{s}'$, respectively. The application of a control C to $\mathsf{BN} = (\mathbf{x}, \mathbf{f})$ has the effect of reducing the state space of BN to those which have the values of the variables in $\mathbb{1}$ and $\mathbb{0}$ set respectively to 1 and 0 and modifying the update functions accordingly. This results in a new Boolean network derived from BN defined as follows.

Definition 5 (BN under control). *Let $\mathsf{C} = (\mathbb{1}, \mathbb{0})$ be a control. Then the Boolean network BN under control C, denoted $\mathsf{BN}|_\mathsf{C}$, is defined as a tuple $\mathsf{BN}|_\mathsf{C} = (\hat{\mathbf{x}}, \hat{\mathbf{f}})$ where the elements of $\hat{\mathbf{x}}$ and $\hat{\mathbf{f}}$ are given as, for all $i \in [n]$:*

- *$\hat{x}_i = 1$ if $i \in \mathbb{1}$, $\hat{x}_i = 0$ if $i \in \mathbb{0}$, and $\hat{x}_i = x_i$ otherwise.*
- *$\hat{f}_i = 1$ if $i \in \mathbb{1}$, $\hat{f}_i = 0$ if $i \in \mathbb{0}$, and $\hat{f}_i = f_i$ otherwise.*

The state space of $\mathsf{BN}|_\mathsf{C}$, denoted $\mathbf{S}|_\mathsf{C}$ is derived by fixing the values of the variables in the set C to their respective values and is defined as $\mathbf{S}|_\mathsf{C} = \{\mathbf{s} \in \mathbf{S} \mid \mathbf{s}[i] = 1, i \in \mathbb{1} \text{ and } \mathbf{s}[j] = 0, j \in \mathbb{0}\}$. Note that $\mathbf{S}|_\mathsf{C} \subseteq \mathbf{S}$. For any subset $\mathbf{S}'$ of $\mathbf{S}$ we let $\mathbf{S}'|_\mathsf{C} = \mathbf{S}' \cap \mathbf{S}|_\mathsf{C}$. The asynchronous dynamics and the transition system of $\mathsf{BN}|_\mathsf{C}$ are defined similarly to Definitions 2 and 3 by replacing $\mathsf{BN} = (\mathbf{x}, \mathbf{f})$ with $\mathsf{BN}|_\mathsf{C} = (\hat{\mathbf{x}}, \hat{\mathbf{f}})$. We omit the definitions to avoid duplications.

Definition 6 (Application and release of control). *Let $\mathbf{s} \in \mathbf{S}$ be a state of BN and let $\mathsf{C} = (\mathbb{1}, \mathbb{0})$ be a control. The* instantaneous application *or* 0-step application *of C to $\mathbf{s}$ results in a state $\mathbf{s}'$ such that $\mathbf{s}'[i] = 1$ for all $i \in \mathbb{1}$, $\mathbf{s}'[j] = 0$ for all $j \in \mathbb{0}$ and $\mathbf{s}'[k] = \mathbf{s}[k]$ otherwise. We will often denote this as $\mathbf{s} \overset{\mathsf{C}}{\sim} \mathbf{s}'$ and denote $\mathbf{s}'$ as $\mathsf{C}(\mathbf{s})$. The application of C to $\mathbf{s}$ for $t \geq 1$ time steps results in a sequence $\mathbf{s}_0, \mathbf{s}_1, \mathbf{s}_2, \ldots, \mathbf{s}_t$, where $\mathbf{s}_0 = \mathsf{C}(\mathbf{s})$ and for every $k \in [t], \mathbf{s}_k \in \xi_{\mathsf{BN}|_\mathsf{C}}(\mathbf{s}_{k-1})$. When $t \to \infty$, we shall call it a* permanent application *of C to $\mathbf{s}$ or a* permanent control *of $\mathbf{s}$.*

Suppose BN under control C is in state $\mathbf{s} \in \mathbf{S}|_\mathsf{C}$ and has been evolving according to $\xi_{\mathsf{BN}|_\mathsf{C}}$. The release *of control at $\mathbf{s}$ is performed instantaneously and it restores the update dynamics to ξ_{BN}. We often denote it as $\mathbf{s} \overset{\mathsf{C}^{-1}}{\sim} \mathbf{s} \to_{\mathsf{BN}} \cdots$*

Thus suppose BN starts evolving from an initial state $\mathbf{s}_0 \in \mathbf{S}$ and after t_1 steps a control C is applied to it. Suppose the control lasts for t_2 steps and then it is released and then BN goes back to evolving according to its original update dynamics. This will result in a sequence that can be represented as:

$$\underbrace{\mathbf{s}_0 \to_{\mathsf{BN}} \mathbf{s}_1 \to_{\mathsf{BN}} \cdots \to_{\mathsf{BN}} \mathbf{s}_{t_1}}_{t_1 \text{ steps}} \overset{\mathsf{C}}{\sim} \underbrace{\mathbf{s}'_0 \to_{\mathsf{BN}|_\mathsf{C}} \mathbf{s}'_1 \to_{\mathsf{BN}|_\mathsf{C}} \cdots \to_{\mathsf{BN}|_\mathsf{C}} \mathbf{s}'_{t_2}}_{t_2 \text{ steps under control } \mathsf{C}} \overset{\mathsf{C}^{-1}}{\sim} \mathbf{s}''_0 \to_{\mathsf{BN}} \mathbf{s}''_1 \to_{\mathsf{BN}} \cdots$$

Intuitively, on the application of control C for t_2 steps, the behaviour of BN is given according to $\mathsf{TS}_{\mathsf{BN}|_\mathsf{C}}$ for t_2 time steps. After that, when C is released, the behaviour goes back to $\mathsf{TS}_{\mathsf{BN}}$. The release of C does not change the value of any variable, thus $\mathbf{s}''_0 = \mathbf{s}'_{t_2}$.

Example 2. For Example 1, given a control $\mathsf{C} = (\mathbb{1}, \mathbb{0})$, where $\mathbb{1} = \{2\}$ and $\mathbb{0} = \{3\}$, the transition system $\mathsf{TS}_{\mathsf{BN}|_\mathsf{C}}$ of $\mathsf{BN}|_\mathsf{C}$ is described in Fig. 1b.

2.3 Attractors and Basins

In what follows we shall use the generic notation TS to represent either the full transition system $\mathsf{TS_{BN}}$ of BN or the transition system $\mathsf{TS_{BN|c}}$ of BN under a control C. Similarly we let '$\rightarrow$' stand for either $\rightarrow_{BN}$ or $\rightarrow_{BN|c}$. We define several notions on TS below which can be interpreted both on $\mathsf{TS_{BN}}$ and $\mathsf{TS_{BN|c}}$. The state space, transitions etc. will correspond either to $\mathsf{TS_{BN}}$ or $\mathsf{TS_{BN|c}}$ (or both) depending on the context.

A path ρ from a state $\mathbf{s}$ to a state $\mathbf{s}'$ is a (possibly empty) sequence of transitions from $\mathbf{s}$ to $\mathbf{s}'$ in TS. Thus, $\rho = \mathbf{s}_0 \rightarrow \mathbf{s}_1 \rightarrow \ldots \rightarrow \mathbf{s}_k$, where $\mathbf{s}_0 = \mathbf{s}$ and $\mathbf{s}_k = \mathbf{s}'$. A path from a state $\mathbf{s}$ to a subset $\mathbf{S}'$ of $\mathbf{S}$ is a path from $\mathbf{s}$ to any state $\mathbf{s}' \in \mathbf{S}'$. An infinite path ρ from $\mathbf{s}$ is an infinite sequence of transitions from $\mathbf{s}$. Let $\mathsf{Path}_\infty(\mathbf{s})$ denote the set of infinite paths from $\mathbf{s}$. Let $\rho = \mathbf{s}_0 \rightarrow \mathbf{s}_1 \rightarrow \ldots$ be an infinite path from $\mathbf{s}_0$. A state $\mathbf{s} \in \mathbf{S}$ appears *infinitely often* in ρ if for every $i \geq 0$ there exits $j \geq i$ such that $\mathbf{s}_j = \mathbf{s}$. $\mathbf{s}$ appears *finitely often* in ρ otherwise.

Definition 7 (Fairness). *Let $\mathbf{s}_0 \in \mathbf{S}$. An infinite path $\rho = \mathbf{s}_0 \rightarrow \mathbf{s}_1 \rightarrow \ldots$ is said to be* unfair *if for every state $\mathbf{s}$ that occurs infinitely often in ρ, there exists a possible next state $\mathbf{s}'$ of $\mathbf{s}$ which occurs only finitely often in ρ. ρ is said to be* fair *otherwise.*

It is important to impose the restriction of fairness because otherwise, the $\mathsf{TS_{BN}}$ would have pseudo-attractors (defined shortly) which would not correspond to any meaningful phenotypes of the GRN being modelled. Fairness ensures that the attractors of TS are exactly the ones that are experimentally observed. Henceforth, we shall assume that the evolution of BN is always fair, and hence consider only fair paths. Therefore, let $\mathsf{Path}_\infty(\mathbf{s})$ denote the set of all infinite fair paths from a state $\mathbf{s} \in \mathbf{S}$.

For any state $\mathbf{s} \in \mathbf{S}$, let $\mathsf{pre_{TS}}(\mathbf{s}) = \{\mathbf{s}' \in \mathbf{S} \mid \mathbf{s}' \rightarrow \mathbf{s}\}$ and let $\mathsf{post_{TS}}(\mathbf{s}) = \{\mathbf{s}' \in \mathbf{S} \mid \mathbf{s} \rightarrow \mathbf{s}'\}$ where $\rightarrow \in \{\rightarrow_{BN}, \rightarrow_{BN|c}\}$ depending on the context. $\mathsf{pre_{TS}}(\mathbf{s})$ contains all the states that can reach $\mathbf{s}$ by performing a single transition in TS and $\mathsf{post_{TS}}(s)$ contains all the states that can be reached from $\mathbf{s}$ by a single transition in TS. $\mathsf{pre_{TS}}(\mathbf{s})$ and $\mathsf{post_{TS}}(\mathbf{s})$ are often called the set of *predecessors* and *successors* of $\mathbf{s}$. Note that, by definition, $\mathsf{hd}(\mathbf{s}, \mathsf{pre_{TS}}(\mathbf{s})) \leq 1$ and $\mathsf{hd}(\mathbf{s}, \mathsf{post_{TS}}(\mathbf{s})) \leq 1$. $\mathsf{pre_{TS}}$ and $\mathsf{post_{TS}}$ can be lifted to a subset $\mathbf{S}'$ of $\mathbf{S}$ as: $\mathsf{pre_{TS}}(\mathbf{S}') = \bigcup_{\mathbf{s} \in \mathbf{S}'} \mathsf{pre_{TS}}(\mathbf{s})$ and $\mathsf{post_{TS}}(\mathbf{S}') = \bigcup_{\mathbf{s} \in \mathbf{S}'} \mathsf{post_{TS}}(\mathbf{s})$. We define $\mathsf{pre_{TS}}^{i+1}(\mathbf{S}') = \mathsf{pre_{TS}}(\mathsf{pre_{TS}}^i(\mathbf{S}'))$ and $\mathsf{post_{TS}}^{i+1}(\mathbf{S}') = \mathsf{post_{TS}}(\mathsf{post_{TS}}^i(\mathbf{S}'))$ where $\mathsf{pre_{TS}}^0(\mathbf{S}') = \mathsf{post_{TS}}^0(\mathbf{S}') = \mathbf{S}'$. For a state $\mathbf{s} \in \mathbf{S}$, $\mathsf{reach_{TS}}(\mathbf{s})$ denotes the set of states $\mathbf{s}'$ such that there is a path from $\mathbf{s}$ to $\mathbf{s}'$ in TS and can be defined as the fixpoint of the successor operation which is often denoted as $\mathsf{post_{TS}^*}$. Thus, $\mathsf{reach_{TS}}(\mathbf{s}) = \mathsf{post_{TS}^*}(\mathbf{s})$.

Definition 8 (Attractor). *An attractor A of TS is a minimal non-empty subset of states of $\mathbf{S}$ such that for every $\mathbf{s} \in A, \mathsf{reach_{TS}}(\mathbf{s}) = A$.*

Any state which is not part of an attractor is a transient state. An attractor A of TS is said to be reachable from a state $\mathbf{s}$ if $\mathsf{reach_{TS}}(\mathbf{s}) \cap A \neq \emptyset$. Attractors represent the stable behaviour of the BN according to the dynamics. The network starting at any initial state $\mathbf{s}_0 \in \mathbf{S}$ will eventually end up in one of the attractors of TS and remain there forever unless perturbed.

Observation 1. Any attractor of TS is a bottom strongly connected component of TS.

Let $\mathbf{S}'$ be a subset of states of $\mathbf{S}$. We define subsets of states of $\mathbf{S}$ called the weak and strong basins of $\mathbf{S}'$, denoted as $\mathsf{bas}_{\mathsf{TS}}^W(\mathbf{S}')$ and $\mathsf{bas}_{\mathsf{TS}}^S(\mathbf{S}')$, respectively.

Definition 9 (Basin). *Let* $\mathbf{S}' \subseteq \mathbf{S}$.

- **Weak basin:** *The weak basin of $\mathbf{S}'$ with respect to* TS, *is defined as* $\mathsf{bas}_{\mathsf{TS}}^W(\mathbf{S}') = \{\mathbf{s} \in \mathbf{S} \mid \mathsf{reach}_{\mathsf{TS}}(\mathbf{s}) \cap \mathbf{S}' \neq \emptyset\}$ *which equals the fixpoint of the predecessor operation on $\mathbf{S}'$ and is often denoted as* $\mathsf{pre}_{\mathsf{TS}}^*(\mathbf{S}')$. *Thus,* $\mathsf{bas}_{\mathsf{TS}}^W(\mathbf{S}') = \mathsf{pre}_{\mathsf{TS}}^*(\mathbf{S}')$. *In other words, since all paths in* $\mathsf{Path}_\infty(\mathbf{s})$ *are fair,*

$$\mathsf{bas}_{\mathsf{TS}}^W(\mathbf{S}') = \{\mathbf{s} \in \mathbf{S} \mid \exists \rho = \mathbf{s}_0 \to \mathbf{s}_1 \to \ldots \in \mathsf{Path}_\infty(\mathbf{s}), \exists j \geq 0, \mathbf{s}_j \in \mathbf{S}'\}$$

- **Strong basin:** *The strong basin of $\mathbf{S}'$ with respect to* TS, *is defined as*

$$\mathsf{bas}_{\mathsf{TS}}^S(\mathbf{S}') = \{\mathbf{s} \in \mathbf{S} \mid \forall \rho = \mathbf{s}_0 \to \mathbf{s}_1 \to \ldots \in \mathsf{Path}_\infty(\mathbf{s}), \exists j \geq 0, \mathbf{s}_j \in \mathbf{S}'\}$$

We say that a path $\rho = \mathbf{s}_0 \to \mathbf{s}_1 \to \ldots$ *eventually* reaches $\mathbf{S}'$ if there exits $j \geq 0$ such that $\mathbf{s}_j \in \mathbf{S}'$. Intuitively, the weak basin of $\mathbf{S}'$ consists of all states from which there is at least one path to $\mathbf{S}'$, whereas the strong basin of $\mathbf{S}'$ consists of all states from which all paths eventually reach $\mathbf{S}'$. Clearly thus, $\mathsf{bas}_{\mathsf{TS}}^S(\mathbf{S}') \subseteq \mathsf{bas}_{\mathsf{TS}}^W(\mathbf{S}')$. If $\mathbf{S}'$ is an attractor A (say), $\mathsf{bas}_{\mathsf{TS}}^W(A)$ and $\mathsf{bas}_{\mathsf{TS}}^S(A)$ will also be referred to as weak and strong *basins of attractions* with respect to A. Thus the weak basin of attraction of A is the set of all states $\mathbf{s}$ from which there is a path to A. It is possible that there are paths from $\mathbf{s}$ to some other attractor $A' \neq A$. However, the notion of a strong basin does not allow this. Thus, it is easy to see that,

Observation 2. *If* $\mathbf{s} \in \mathsf{bas}_{\mathsf{TS}}^S(A)$ *then* $\mathbf{s} \notin \mathsf{bas}_{\mathsf{TS}}^W(A')$ *for any other attractor A'. Therefore,* $\mathsf{bas}_{\mathsf{TS}}^S(A) = \mathsf{bas}_{\mathsf{TS}}^W(A) \setminus (\bigcup_{A'} \mathsf{bas}_{\mathsf{TS}}^W(A'))$ *where the union is over all attractors $A' \neq A$ of* TS.

Note that if $\mathbf{S}'$ is an attractor A, then if ρ eventually reaches A, it gets stuck in A forever. That is, for every $i \geq 0$, $\mathbf{s}_i \in A$ implies $\mathbf{s}_j \in A$ for all $j > i$. This follows directly from Definition 8. We need the notion of strong basin to *ensure* that every fair sequence under a given update dynamics *always* reaches the target attractor. The following observation will be crucial for the control algorithms developed in this paper.

Observation 3. *Let* $\mathbf{s} \in \mathbf{S}$ *and* $\mathbf{S}' \subseteq \mathbf{S}$. *Every path* $\rho \in \mathsf{Path}_\infty(\mathbf{s})$

1. *possibly eventually reaches $\mathbf{S}'$ if and only if* $\mathbf{s} \in \mathsf{bas}_{\mathsf{TS}}^W(\mathbf{S}')$,
2. *always eventually reaches $\mathbf{S}'$ if and only if* $\mathbf{s} \in \mathsf{bas}_{\mathsf{TS}}^S(\mathbf{S}')$.

Example 3. To continue with the example given in Example 1, TS_{BN} has two attractors $A_1 = \{(110)\}$ and $A_2 = \{(000)\}$ shown by dark grey rectangles in Fig. 1a. The weak basin and the strong basin of A_2 are shown by the dashed and solid rectangles, respectively. The state $s_1 = \{(011)\}$ is in the weak basin $\mathsf{bas}^W_{TS|BN}(A_2)$ but not in the strong basin $\mathsf{bas}^S_{TS|BN}(A_2)$ of A_2 as there exist paths from s_1 to the other attractor A_1. Starting from the state s_1, BN can reach either A_1 or A_2 eventually. The state $s_2 = \{(001)\}$ is in the strong basin $\mathsf{bas}^S_{TS|BN}(A_2)$ of A_2. Starting from s_2, BN always eventually reaches A_2.

2.4   The Control Problem

As described in the introduction (Sect. 1), the attractors of a Boolean network represent the cellular phenotypes. Some of these attractors may be diseased, weak or undesirable while others are healthy and desirable. Curing a disease is thus, in effect, moving the dynamics of the network from an undesired 'source' attractor to a desired 'target' attractor.

This can be achieved by applying control (as defined in Sect. 2.2) to the network. There can be various strategies of applying such a control. These can be broadly classified based on the number of parameters of the network controlled at the same time and the amount of time the control is applied. In terms of the number of parameters controlled at the same time, we have: (1) simultaneous control – the perturbation is applied to all the parameters at once; and (2) sequential control – the perturbation is applied to the required parameters over a sequence of steps. Based on the amount of time that the control is applied, we have: (a) permanent control – the control is applied for all the following time steps, i.e., the parameters are changed forever; and (b) temporary control – the control is applied for a finite (possibly zero) number of steps and then removed.

In this work we shall be interested in simultaneous control that is applied both temporarily and permanently. Moreover, we aim to compute the exact *minimum* number of parameters needed to be controlled in each case. The control problems that we shall deal with in this work are defined as follows.

Definition 10 (Control problems). *Given a source state* $s \in S$ *and an attractor* A *of* TS_{BN} *of BN, a:*

1. **Permanent control:** *is a control* $C = (\mathbb{1}, \mathbb{0})$ *such that the dynamics of BN always eventually reaches* A *on the permanent application of* C *to* s. *(Here we assume implicitly that* A *is also an attractor of the transition system under control* $TS_{BN|_C}$.)
2. **Temporary control:** *is a control* $C = (\mathbb{1}, \mathbb{0})$ *such that there exists a* $t_0 \geq 0$ *such that for all* $t \geq t_0$, *the dynamics of BN always eventually reaches* A *on the application of* C *to* s *for* t *steps.*

In addition, if in each case C *is* minimal, *in the sense that, for every control* C' *that achieves one of the above objectives,* $\mathsf{size}(C) \leq \mathsf{size}(C')$, *we call* C *a* minimal permanent (resp. temporary) control. *The control problems are then, given a source state* $s \in S$ *and an attractor* A *of* TS_{BN} *of BN, find a minimal permanent or temporary control.*

Note that the constraint of minimality in the above definition makes the problems non-trivial. Otherwise, one can simply choose a control C such that $C(s) \in A$ in each case. In [19,25], we developed a method for the efficient *minimal simultaneous control* of Boolean networks, where given a source state s and an attractor of TS_{BN} of BN the control C is applied simultaneously and instantaneously to s so that the dynamics of BN eventually reaches A and C is minimal. Such a control is a special case of the temporary control defined above with $t = 0$. Since the minimal simultaneous control problem of [19,25] is computationally difficult (PSPACE-hard), the control problems that we study here, defined above, are also computationally difficult (at least PSPACE-hard). Thus, efficient algorithms to solve these problems are highly unlikely. However, we showed in [19,25], that if the BNs are structurally well-behaved (e.g., the graph of the BN has small strongly connected components (SCCs), with a small number of interdependencies between the SCCs etc.), we can have relatively efficient methods to compute the attractors and basins of such BNs. Since it is known that real-life BNs corresponding to GRNs are reasonably well-behaved, this led us to develop efficient algorithms for computing the weak and strong basins of desired target attractors of such BNs by decomposing the BNs based on the SCCs of their graphs. The algorithms we develop here will crucially use the procedures developed in [19,25] for the computation of the weak and strong basins of the target attractors, denoted as $COMP\_WB(A)$ and $COMP\_SB(A)$ [19,25], respectively. These then applied to real-life networks can result in a significant level of efficiency as will be demonstrated later.

3 Results

In this section, we develop algorithms to solve the control problems described in Definition 10. These algorithms are based on the key observation made in Observation 3. Indeed, given a source state s and a target attractor A of TS_{BN} of BN, if after the application of a control C to s, the resulting state $C(s)$ lies in the strong basin of A w.r.t. the transition system under control, $TS_{BN|c}$, then the dynamics will always eventually reach A. One needs to be careful though as the attractors and their structure in $TS_{BN|c}$ might be different from TS_{BN}. However, we note that the application of C to TS does not create any additional edges except for self loops.

Lemma 1. *Let* C *be a control. If* s $\rightarrow_{BN|c}$ s′ *is in* $TS_{BN|c}$ *then* s $\neq$ s′ *implies* s $\rightarrow_{BN}$ s′ *is in* TS_{BN}.

3.1 Permanent Control

We now develop an algorithm to solve the problem of permanent control. For the sake of simplicity, we use $bas_{BN}^{S(W)}(.)$ and $bas_{BN|c}^{S(W)}(.)$ to represent $bas_{TS_{BN}}^{S(W)}(.)$ and $bas_{TS_{BN|c}}^{S(W)}(.)$, respectively. The following proposition will be useful.

Proposition 1. *Let* C *be a control and* A *be an attractor of* $\mathsf{TS}_{\mathsf{BN}}$ *such that* A *is also an attractor of* $\mathsf{TS}_{\mathsf{BN}|_{\mathsf{C}}}$. *For any* $\mathbf{s} \in \mathbf{S}$, *if* $\mathbf{s} \in \mathsf{bas}_{\mathsf{BN}|_{\mathsf{C}}}^{W}(A)$ *then* $\mathbf{s} \in \mathsf{bas}_{\mathsf{BN}}^{W}(A)$.

The converse of Proposition 1 may not hold as shown by the following example.

Example 4. Let $\mathsf{C}_1 = \{\mathbb{1}_1, \mathbb{0}_1\}$ with $\mathbb{1}_1 = \{3\}$ and $\mathbb{0}_1 = \emptyset$ and $\mathsf{C}_2 = \{\mathbb{1}_2, \mathbb{0}_2\}$ with $\mathbb{1}_2 = \emptyset$ and $\mathbb{0}_2 = \{1\}$ be two controls of the BN of Example 1. The original transition system $\mathsf{TS}_{\mathsf{BN}}$ and the two transition systems under control $\mathsf{TS}_{\mathsf{BN}|_{\mathsf{C}_1}}$ and $\mathsf{TS}_{\mathsf{BN}|_{\mathsf{C}_2}}$ are given in Fig. 1. The application of C_1 fixes $\mathbf{f}_3$ to 1 and neither of the attractors is preserved in $\mathsf{TS}_{\mathsf{BN}|_{\mathsf{C}_1}}$. The application of C_2 fixes $\mathbf{f}_1$ to 0. In $\mathsf{TS}_{\mathsf{BN}|_{\mathsf{C}_2}}$, the attractor $A_2 = \{(000)\}$ is the attractor of $\mathsf{TS}_{\mathsf{BN}}$ and $\mathsf{TS}_{\mathsf{BN}|_{\mathsf{C}_2}}$. The state $\mathbf{s} = \{(111)\}$ is in $\mathsf{bas}_{\mathsf{BN}}^{W}(A_2)$ but not in $\mathsf{bas}_{\mathsf{BN}|_{\mathsf{C}_2}}^{W}(A_2)$.

The intuition for the algorithm for the problem of permanent control that we shall develop in this section is as follows. Suppose $\mathbf{s} \in \mathbf{S}$ is an initial state and A is the target attractor of $\mathsf{TS}_{\mathsf{BN}}$ that we want the dynamics of BN to always eventually reach. The following is a straightforward corollary of Observation 3.

Corollary 1. *A control* C *is a permanent control from* $\mathbf{s}$ *to* A *iff* A *is an attractor of* $\mathsf{TS}_{\mathsf{BN}|_{\mathsf{C}}}$ *and* $\mathsf{C}(\mathbf{s}) \in \mathsf{bas}_{\mathsf{BN}|_{\mathsf{C}}}^{S}(A)$.

Thus, we want to find a control C such that the condition $\mathsf{C}(\mathbf{s}) \in \mathsf{bas}_{\mathsf{BN}|_{\mathsf{C}}}^{S}(A)$ is satisfied. Now, since we want the control C to be minimal, we proceed as follows. We start with a state $\mathbf{s}' \in \mathsf{bas}_{\mathsf{BN}}^{W}(A)$ that has the minimal Hamming distance with $\mathbf{s}$. We first check if A is an attractor of $\mathsf{TS}_{\mathsf{BN}|_{\mathsf{C}^{\mathbf{s} \rightarrow \mathbf{s}'}}}$ since otherwise, $\mathsf{C}^{\mathbf{s} \rightarrow \mathbf{s}'}$ cannot be a permanent control (by definition). If A is indeed an attractor of $\mathsf{TS}_{\mathsf{BN}|_{\mathsf{C}^{\mathbf{s} \rightarrow \mathbf{s}'}}}$, we check if $\mathbf{s}' \in \mathsf{bas}_{\mathsf{BN}|_{\mathsf{C}^{\mathbf{s} \rightarrow \mathbf{s}'}}}^{S}(A)$. If so, we are done. Otherwise, we remove $\mathbf{s}'$ from $\mathsf{bas}_{\mathsf{BN}}^{W}(A)$ and select a state $\mathbf{s}''$ from $(\mathsf{bas}_{\mathsf{BN}}^{W}(A) \setminus \{\mathbf{s}'\})$ having the minimal Hamming distance with $\mathbf{s}$. We repeat the same procedure this time with $\mathsf{C}^{\mathbf{s} \rightarrow \mathbf{s}''}$. We iterate till we find a state $\mathbf{s}^* \in \mathsf{bas}_{\mathsf{BN}}^{W}(A)$ such that $\mathbf{s}^* \in \mathsf{bas}_{\mathsf{BN}|_{\mathsf{C}^{\mathbf{s} \rightarrow \mathbf{s}^*}}}^{S}(A)$.

The procedure described above, in the worst case, explores all possible states in $\mathsf{bas}_{\mathsf{TS}_{\mathsf{BN}}}^{W}(A)$. By Proposition 1 we know that for any control C, $\mathsf{bas}_{\mathsf{BN}|_{\mathsf{C}}}^{W}(A) \subseteq \mathsf{bas}_{\mathsf{BN}}^{W}(A)$. Thus, it is enough to explore only the states in $\mathsf{bas}_{\mathsf{BN}}^{W}(A)$ and it will eventually find the required control. $\mathsf{C}^{\mathbf{s} \rightarrow \mathbf{s}^*}$ is then the required minimal permanent control. Algorithm 1 describes this procedure in pseudo-code.

3.2   Temporary Control

The algorithm for computing a minimal temporary control is slightly more involved than that for computing a minimal permanent control developed in Sect. 3.1. We first prove the following proposition with the help of Lemma 1.

Proposition 2. *Let* A *be an attractor of* $\mathsf{TS}_{\mathsf{BN}}$ *and* C *be any control.*

1. *For any state* $\mathbf{s} \in \mathsf{bas}_{\mathsf{BN}}^{S}(A)$, $\mathsf{reach}_{\mathsf{TS}_{\mathsf{BN}}}(\mathbf{s}) \subseteq \mathsf{bas}_{\mathsf{BN}}^{S}(A)$.
2. *For any state* $\mathbf{s} \in (\mathsf{bas}_{\mathsf{BN}}^{S}(A)|_{\mathsf{C}})$, $\mathsf{reach}_{\mathsf{TS}_{\mathsf{BN}|_{\mathsf{C}}}}(\mathbf{s}) \subseteq (\mathsf{bas}_{\mathsf{BN}}^{S}(A)|_{\mathsf{C}})$.

Algorithm 1. Minimal permanent control

1: **procedure** COMP_PERM_CONTROL($\mathcal{G}, \mathbf{f}, \mathbf{s}, A$) % **s**: *the source state; A: the target*
2: WB :=COMP_WB($A, \mathbf{f}$)   % *the weak basin of A in* $\mathsf{TS_{BN}}$ *[19, 25]*
3: isMin := false
4: **while** isMin = false and WB $\neq \emptyset$ **do**
5:   C $\in$ arg hd(**s**, WB), $\mathbf{s}' := C(\mathbf{s})$ % *a possible minimal control from* **s** *to A*
6:   **if** $\{\mathbf{s}'\}|_C = A|_C$ **then**   % *A is preserved in* $\mathsf{TS_{BN|C}}$
7:    $\mathbf{f}_C$:=COMP_FN_CONTR($\mathbf{f}, C$)   % **f** *in* $\mathsf{BN|_C}$ *(see Algorithm 2)*
8:    SB$_C$:=COMP_SB($A, \mathbf{f}_C$)   % *the strong basin of A in* $\mathsf{TS_{BN|C}}$ *[19, 25]*
9:    **if** $\mathbf{s}' \in$ SB$_C$ **then**
10:     isMin := true
11:   **if** isMin = false **then**
12:    WB := WB $\setminus \{\mathbf{s}'\}$
13: **return** C

Algorithm 2. Helper functions

1: **procedure** COMP_FN_CONTR($\mathbf{f}, C$) %   10: **procedure** COMP_STATE_CONTR($\mathbf{S}, C$)
   $C = (1, 0)$ 11: $\mathbf{S}|_C := \mathbf{S}$
2: $\mathbf{f}_C := \mathbf{f}$ 12: **for** $\mathbf{s} \in \mathbf{S}$ **do**
3: **for** $i \in 1$ **do**   13:   **for** $i \in 1$ **do**
4:   $\mathbf{f}_C[i] := 1$ 14:   **if** $\mathbf{s}[i] \neq 1$ **then**
5: **for** $i \in 0$ **do**   15: $\mathbf{S}|_C := \mathbf{S}|_C \setminus \{\mathbf{s}\}$
6:   $\mathbf{f}_C[i] := 0$ 16:   **for** $j \in 0$ **do**
7: **return** $\mathbf{f}_C$ 17:   **if** $\mathbf{s}[j] \neq 0$ **then**
8:                         18: $\mathbf{S}|_C := \mathbf{S}|_C \setminus \{\mathbf{s}\}$
9:                         19: **return** $\mathbf{S}_C$

Using Observation 3 and Proposition 2, we can prove the following theorem.

Theorem 4. *Let* $\mathbf{s} \in \mathbf{S}$ *be a source state and A be the target attractor of* $\mathsf{TS_{BN}}$. *A control C is a temporary control from* **s** *to A if and only if* $\mathsf{bas}_{BN}^S(A)|_C \neq \emptyset$ *and* $C(\mathbf{s}) \in \mathsf{bas}_{BN|_C}^S(\mathsf{bas}_{BN}^S(A)|_C)$.

Theorem 4 forms the basis for our algorithm for computing the temporary control C, given a source state **s** and a target attractor A. Intuitively, on the application of C, we want the dynamics to move to a state $C(\mathbf{s})$ which is in the strong basin (w.r.t the restricted transition system $\mathsf{TS_{BN|_C}}$) of the strong basin (w.r.t the original transition system $\mathsf{TS_{BN}}$) of the target attractor A, restricted to states in $\mathbf{S}|_C$. Then if we hold the control C for long enough, the dynamics will eventually reach the strong basin of A in $\mathsf{TS_{BN}}$. By Proposition 2, we know that once in the strong basin, the dynamics cannot escape it. This means that finally when the control C is released, the dynamics is in the strong basin of A and hence will eventually reach A which is the target.

How can we ensure that we indeed compute a temporary control C that is minimal? Once again, we proceed as before. We start with a state $\mathbf{s}' \in \mathsf{bas}_{BN}^W(A)$ that has the minimal Hamming distance with **s**. We check if

---

Algorithm 3. Minimal temporary control

1: **procedure** COMP_TEMP_CONTROL$(\mathcal{G}, \mathbf{f}, \mathbf{s}, A)$ % **s**: *the source state; A: the target*
2:     WB :=COMP_WB$(A, \mathbf{f})$ % *the weak basin of A in* $\mathsf{TS_{BN}}$
3:     SB :=COMP_SB$(A, \mathbf{f})$ % *the strong basin of A in* $\mathsf{TS_{BN}}$
4:     isMin := false
5:     **while** isMin = false **and** WB $\neq \emptyset$ **do**
6:         $C \in$ arg hd$(\mathbf{s}, \text{WB})$, $\mathbf{s}' = C(\mathbf{s})$ % *a possible minimal control from* **s** *to A*
7:         **if** $\mathbf{s}' \in$ SB **then**
8:             isMin := true   % *instantaneous perturbation*
9:         **else**
10:             $\mathbf{f}_C$:=COMP_FN_CONTR$(\mathbf{f}, C)$ % **f** *in* $\mathsf{BN}|_C$ *(see Algorithm 2)*
11:             SB$|_C$:=COMP_STATE_CONTR(SB, C) % *SB in* $\mathsf{TS_{BN|_C}}$ *(see Algorithm 2)*
12:             **if** SB$|_C \neq \emptyset$ **then**
13:                 bas$^S_{\mathsf{BN}|_C}$(SB$|_C$) :=COMP_SB$(\text{SB}|_C, \mathbf{f}_C)$
14:                 **if** $\mathbf{s}' \in$ bas$^S_{\mathsf{BN}|_C}$(SB$|_C$) **then**
15:                     isMin := true
16:             **if** isMin = false **then**
17:                 WB := WB $\setminus \{\mathbf{s}'\}$
18:     **return** C

$\mathbf{s}' \in$ bas$^S_{\mathsf{BN}|_{C^{\mathbf{s} \to \mathbf{s}'}}}$(bas$^S_{\mathsf{BN}}(A)|_{C^{\mathbf{s} \to \mathbf{s}'}}$). If so, we are done. Otherwise, we remove $\mathbf{s}'$ from bas$^W_{\mathsf{BN}}(A)$ and select a state $\mathbf{s}''$ from (bas$^W_{\mathsf{BN}}(A) \setminus \{\mathbf{s}'\}$) having the minimal Hamming distance with **s**. We repeat the same procedure this time with $C^{\mathbf{s} \to \mathbf{s}''}$. We iterate till we find a state $\mathbf{s}^* \in$ bas$^W_{\mathsf{BN}}(A)$ such that $\mathbf{s}^* \in$ bas$^S_{\mathsf{BN}|_{C^{\mathbf{s} \to \mathbf{s}^*}}}$(bas$^S_{\mathsf{BN}}(A)|_{C^{\mathbf{s} \to \mathbf{s}^*}}$). Once again, by Proposition 1 we know that for any control C, bas$^W_{\mathsf{BN}|_C}(A) \subseteq$ bas$^W_{\mathsf{BN}}(A)$. Thus, it is enough to explore only the states in bas$^W_{\mathsf{BN}}(A)$ and it will eventually find the required control. $C^{\mathbf{s} \to \mathbf{s}^*}$ is then the required minimal temporary control. Algorithm 3 describes this procedure in pseudo-code.

Notice that the amount of time for the application of C depends on the specific system and the detailed perturbations. Biologists can determine when to release the control case by case based on experimental settings. As long as the control is released in finite steps, holding it longer will not affect its effectiveness.

Constraints on the control sets. Constraints encoding practical requirements can eliminate perturbations of certain nodes, for instance essential genes for cell survival [26]. We implement the constraints by slightly modifying our algorithms as follows. Let R_1, R_0 be two sets of indices of nodes, where the state of a node with index $i \in R_1(R_0)$ cannot be perturbed to 0 (1). The above constraints can be realised by removing the states $\{\mathbf{s}' \in$ bas$^W_{\mathsf{BN}}(A)|$ for $i \in R_1, \mathbf{s}'[i] = 0$ or for $j \in R_0, \mathbf{s}'[j] = 1\}$ from bas$^W_{\mathsf{BN}}(A)$ before the main loop of Algorithms 1 and 3.

4   Case Studies

To demonstrate the efficacy and efficiency of our control methods, we apply our minimal temporary and permanent controls (Algorithms 1 and 3) to 10 biological networks [20,27–34]. The results are compared with the minimal instantaneous control method developed in [19]. These three algorithms are implemented as part of the software ASSA-PBN [23]. All the experiments are performed on a computer with a CPU of Intel Core i7 @3.1 GHz and 8 GB of DDR3 RAM. An overview of the networks is given in Table 1.

Table 1. An overview of the networks and the evaluation results. I, T and P stand for the instantaneous, temporary and permanent controls, respectively.

network	# nodes	# edges	#A	range of $|C|$			time (seconds)		
				$|C_I|$	$|C_T|$	$|C_P|$	T_I	T_T	T_P
myeloid	11	30	6	1–5	1–3	1–3	0.015	0.059	0.056
cardiac	15	39	6	1–9	1–4	1–4	0.233	0.885	0.842
ERBB	20	52	3	1–9	1–3	1–3	0.054	0.179	0.251
tumour	32	158	9	1–10	1–4	1–4	6.726	35.207	34.065
PC12	33	62	7	1–11	1–4	1–4	0.394	2.150	2.634
hematopoietic	33	88	5	1–13	1–3	1–3	1.749	11.356	16.080
MAPK_r3	53	105	20	1–19	1–5	1–5	112.429	213.111	230.871
HGF	66	103	18	1–31	1–5	1–5	234.373	441.541	417.897
bortezomib	67	135	5	1–21	1–3	1–4	46.062	145.111	106.268
CD4$^+$	188	380	12	1–5	1–4	1–4	8536.420	15930.900	16007.500

Table 2. The number of perturbations computed for the cardiac network.

	A_1			A_2			A_3			A_4			A_5			A_6		
	$|C_I|$	$|C_T|$	$|C_P|$	$|C_I|$	$|C_T|$	$|C_P|$	$|C_I|$	$|C_T|$	$|C_P|$	$|C_I|$	$|C_T|$	$|C_P|$	$|C_I|$	$|C_T|$	$|C_P|$	$|C_I|$	$|C_T|$	$|C_P|$
A_1	–	–	–	1	1	1	1	1	1	2	2	2	1	1	1	2	2	2
A_2	2	1	1	–	–	–	4	2	3	1	1	1	1	1	1	2	2	2
A_3	1	1	1	2	2	2	–	–	–	1	1	1	2	2	2	1	1	1
A_4	4	2	2	1	1	1	3	1	2	–	–	–	2	2	2	1	1	1
A_5	8	3	3	6	2	2	9	4	4	6	3	3	–	–	–	1	1	1
A_6	8	4	4	7	3	3	6	2	2	4	2	2	1	1	1	–	–	–

Efficiency. We compute a minimal control C with the three methods for each pair of source and target attractors. The total execution time is summarised in the last three columns of Table 1. We do not give detailed time costs for each pair due to the page limit. The temporary and permanent controls have similar performance in terms of efficiency. Both of them are less efficient than the instantaneous control as it may take several iterations to compute a valid control set

Table 3. The control sets for the myeloid differentiation network computed by the temporary and permanent controls. The sets in grey are only required by the temporary control. Underlined genes are switched to OFF, otherwise to ON.

	Megakaryocyte	Erythrocyte	Granulocyte	Monocyte
Megakaryocyte	–	{EKLF} {Fli1}	{C/EBPα, PU1, Gfi1} {C/EBPα, Gfi1, GATA1}	{EgrNab, C/EBPα, GATA1} {EgrNab, C/EBPα, PU1}
Erythrocyte	{EKLF} {Fli1}	–	{C/EBPα, PU1, Gfi1} {C/EBPα, Gfi1, GATA1}	{EgrNab, C/EBPα, GATA1} {EgrNab, C/EBPα, PU1}
Granulocyte	{GATA2, Fli1} {GATA1, Fli1} {Fli1, PU1}	{GATA2, EKLF} {GATA1, EKLF}	–	{EgrNab} {Gfi1}
Monocyte	{GATA2, Fli1} {GATA1, Fli1} {Fli1, PU1}	{GATA2, EKLF} {GATA1, EKLF}	{PU1} {Gfi1},{cJun},{EgrNab}	–

(see Algorithms 1 and 3). Despite that, both methods are still very efficient. For instance, for the CD4$^+$ T-cell network, the computation time for each case is in the range of (38–212), (84–581) and (63–718) s for the instantaneous, temporary and permanent controls, respectively.

Efficacy. The number of perturbations are summarised in Table 1. By extending the application time of control, the number of perturbations can be greatly reduced, which in turn reduces the cost of biological experiments. Especially for the model of bortezomib responses, the number of perturbations can be reduced from 21 to 3 and 4 by the temporary and permanent controls, respectively.

Table 2 summarises the number of perturbations for the cardiac network. The first column and the first row represent the source and target attractors, respectively. For most cases, the temporary and permanent controls require the same number of perturbations, while the temporary control can further reduce it for a few cases (e.g., $A_2 \to A_3$ and $A_4 \to A_3$). In general, the instantaneous control needs to control more nodes to guarantee the reachability.

We take the myeloid differentiation network as an example to compare our results with the perturbations found in [20]. Four of the six attractors of this network correspond to megakaryocytes, erythrocytes, granulocytes or monocytes. Table 3 gives the minimal control sets computed by our temporary and permanent controls for these four attractors. In general, our results are consistent with the conclusions of [20].

1. Reprogramming of EKLF or Fli1 can achieve a conversion between erythrocytes and megakaryocytes [20].
2. Simultaneous perturbations of C/EBPα and PU1 can convert the network from MegE lineage (megakaryocytes and erythrocytes) to GM lineage (granulocytes and monocytes) [20], but to reach a specific state (granulocyte or monocyte), one more gene is required. Besides, our methods also identified other paths to realise the reprogramming.

3. We also spotted the pivotal role of GATA1 and GATA2 in the transdifferentiation from GM lineage to MegE lineage [20]. However, the over-expression of GATA2 can only be applied with temporary perturbations, since the permanent over-expression of GATA2 leads to absence of MegE lineage.

5   Discussion and Future Work

In this paper, we have developed the temporary and permanent control methods to identify a minimal set of nodes, such that the temporary or permanent perturbations of these nodes guide the network from a source state to a desired target attractor. Together with the instantaneous control [19], we have been working on bridging the gap between computational control methods and practical reprogramming of GRNs from three perspectives.

First, we have explored three kinds of perturbations: instantaneous, temporary and permanent perturbations. All of them are feasible to conduct in biological experiments. Besides that, each kind of perturbations has its own merits and demerits. (1) Permanent perturbations have a permanent influence on the dynamics of the system and thus are more invasive than instantaneous and temporary perturbations. (2) Temporary and permanent perturbations alter the dynamics of networks either for sufficient time or permanently, thus less number of perturbations are required to achieve the goal compared to instantaneous perturbations. Indeed, there is no universal standard of good perturbations for different biological networks. We provide control methods for different kinds of perturbations, so that biologists can choose suitable strategies to deal with different biological networks.

Second, considering the expensive cost and other difficulties in performing biological experiments, practical constraints are encoded to make our control strategies more realistic and applicable. Two problems commonly arise in biological experiments. One is that some genes are essential for cell survival and thus cannot be turned off. The other is that some genes are harder or more expensive to perturb. For instance, GATA1 and GATA2 are part of a family of transcription factors that may have different functions but may have similar structural features to be recognised by the 'perturbation tool'. Hence, we adapt our methods to avoid (1) perturbing certain nodes from 'expressed' to 'not expressed' and/or (2) perturbing certain nodes from 'not expressed' to 'expressed'.

Third, so far we have focused on identifying a minimal set of perturbations to fulfil the control purpose with 100% success rate. Apart from that, given an upper bound of perturbations, our methods can compute all the control sets within the upper bound efficiently for different kinds of perturbations. Incorporated with practical constraints, our methods can compute a rich set of restricted solutions, which will be beneficial to biological applications.

Currently, we are working a sequential control method, where other attractors (observable biological phenotypes) can act as intermediates [35]. We want to drive the network from a source state to a target attractor through intermediate attractors by applying a sequence of instantaneous or temporary or permanent perturbations. Such a sequential method can provide more potential reprogramming solutions and may further reduce the number of required perturbations. Other than that, we plan to extend our work to the control of probabilistic Boolean networks (PBNs) [36,37] and explore if and how to adapt the instantaneous, temporary and permanent control strategies to such networks.

Acknowledgements. The work was partially supported by the research project SEC-PBN funded by the University of Luxembourg and the ANR-FNR project AlgoReCell (INTER/ANR/15/11191283). We also want to thank Loïc Paulevé for discussions.

References

1. Takahashi, K.: Cellular reprogramming. Cold Spring Harb. Perspect. Biol. **6**(2), a018606 (2014)
2. Sol, A.D., Buckley, N.: Concise review: a population shift view of cellular reprogramming. Stem Cells **32**(6), 1367–1372 (2014)
3. Graf, T., Enver, T.: Forcing cells to change lineages. Nature **462**(7273), 587–594 (2009)
4. Srivastava, D., DeWitt, N.: In vivo cellular reprogramming: the next generation. Cell **166**(6), 1386–1396 (2016)
5. Wang, L.Z., et al.: A geometrical approach to control and controllability of nonlinear dynamical networks. Nat. Commun. **7**, 11323 (2016)
6. Zañudo, J.G.T., Albert, R.: Cell fate reprogramming by control of intracellular network dynamics. PLoS Comput. Biol. **11**(4), e1004193 (2015)
7. Kauffman, S.A.: Homeostasis and differentiation in random genetic control networks. Nature **224**, 177–178 (1969)
8. Liu, Y.Y., Slotine, J.J., Barabási, A.L.: Controllability of complex networks. Nature **473**, 167–73 (2011)
9. Gao, J., Liu, Y.Y., D'Souza, R.M., Barabási, A.L.: Target control of complex networks. Nat. Commun. **5**, 5415 (2014)
10. Czeizler, E., Gratie, C., Chiu, W.K., Kanhaiya, K., Petre, I.: Target controllability of linear networks. In: Bartocci, E., Lio, P., Paoletti, N. (eds.) CMSB 2016. LNCS, vol. 9859, pp. 67–81. Springer, Cham (2016). https://doi.org/10.1007/978-3-319-45177-0_5
11. Bornholdt, S.: Less is more in modeling large genetic networks. Science **310**(5747), 449–451 (2005)
12. Mochizuki, A., Fiedler, B., Kurosawa, G., Saito, D.: Dynamics and control at feedback vertex sets. II: a faithful monitor to determine the diversity of molecular activities in regulatory networks. J. Theor. Biol. **335**, 130–146 (2013)
13. Zañudo, J.G.T., Yang, G., Albert, R.: Structure-based control of complex networks with nonlinear dynamics. Proc. Natl. Acad. Sci. **114**(28), 7234–7239 (2017)
14. Kim, J., Park, S., Cho, K.: Discovery of a kernel for controlling biomolecular regulatory networks. Sci. Rep. **3**, 2223 (2013)
15. Zhao, Y., Kim, J., Filippone, M.: Aggregation algorithm towards large-scale Boolean network analysis. IEEE Trans. Autom. Control **58**(8), 1976–1985 (2013)
16. Papin, J.A., Hunter, T., Palsson, B.O., Subramaniam, S.: Reconstruction of cellular signalling networks and analysis of their properties. Nat. Rev. Mol. Cell Biol. **6**(2), 99 (2005)

17. Cornelius, S.P., Kath, W.L., Motter, A.E.: Realistic control of network dynamics. Nat. Commun. **4**, 1942 (2013)
18. Germini, D., Tsfasman, T., Zakharova, V.V., Sjakste, N., Lipinski, M., Vassetzky, Y.: A comparison of techniques to evaluate the effectiveness of genome editing. Trends Biotechnol. **36**(2), 147–159 (2018)
19. Paul, S., Su, C., Pang, J., Mizera, A.: A decomposition-based approach towards the control of Boolean networks. In: Proceedings 9th ACM Conference on Bioinformatics, Computational Biology, and Health Informatics, pp. 11–20. ACM Press (2018)
20. Krumsiek, J., Marr, C., Schroeder, T., Theis, F.J.: Hierarchical differentiation of myeloid progenitors is encoded in the transcription factor network. PLOS one **6**(8), e22649 (2011)
21. Müller, F., Schuppert, A.: Few inputs can reprogram biological networks. Nature **478**(7369), E4 (2011)
22. Takahashi, K., Yamanaka, S.: Induction of pluripotent stem cells from mouse embryonic and adult fibroblast cultures by defined factors. Cell **126**(4), 663–676 (2006)
23. Mizera, A., Pang, J., Su, C., Yuan, Q.: ASSA-PBN: a toolbox for probabilistic Boolean networks. IEEE/ACM Trans. Comput. Biol. Bioinform. **15**(4), 1203–1216 (2018)
24. Zhu, P., Han, J.: Asynchronous stochastic Boolean networks as gene network models. J. Comput. Biol. **21**(10), 771–783 (2014)
25. Paul, S., Su, C., Pang, J., Mizera, A.: An efficient approach towards the source-target control of Boolean networks. IEEE/ACM Trans. Comput. Biol. Bioinform. (2019)
26. Zhang, R., Lin, Y.: Deg 5.0, a database of essential genes in both prokaryotes and eukaryotes. Nucleic Acids Res. **37**, D455–D458 (2008). (Database issue)
27. Herrmann, F., Groß, A., Zhou, D., Kestler, H.A., Kühl, M.: A Boolean model of the cardiac gene regulatory network determining first and second heart field identity. PLOS one **7**(10), 1–10 (2012)
28. Sahin, O., et al.: Modeling ERBB receptor-regulated G1/S transition to find novel targets for de novo trastuzumab resistance. BMC Syst. Biol. **3**(1), 1 (2009)
29. Cohen, D.P.A., Martignetti, L., Robine, S., Barillot, E., Zinovyev, A., Calzone, L.: Mathematical modelling of molecular pathways enabling tumour cell invasion and migration. PLoS Comput. Biol. **11**(11), e1004571 (2015)
30. Offermann, B., et al.: Boolean modeling reveals the necessity of transcriptional regulation for bistability in PC12 cell differentiation. Front. Genet. **7**, 44 (2016)
31. Collombet, S., et al.: Logical modeling of lymphoid and myeloid cell specification and transdifferentiation. Proc. Natl. Acad. Sci. **114**(23), 5792–5799 (2017)
32. Grieco, L., Calzone, L., Bernard-Pierrot, I., Radvanyi, F., Kahn-Perles, B., Thieffry, D.: Integrative modelling of the influence of MAPK network on cancer cell fate decision. PLoS Comput. Biol. **9**(10), e1003286 (2013)
33. Singh, A., Nascimento, J.M., Kowar, S., Busch, H., Boerries, M.: Boolean approach to signalling pathway modelling in HGF-induced keratinocyte migration. Bioinformatics **28**(18), 495–501 (2012)
34. Conroy, B.D., et al.: Design, assessment, and in vivo evaluation of a computational model illustrating the role of CAV1 in CD4+ T-lymphocytes. Front. Immunol. **5**, 599 (2014)
35. Mandon, H., Su, C., Haar, S., Pang, J., Paulevé, L.: Sequential reprogramming of Boolean networks made practical. In: Proceedings 17th International Conference on Computational Methods in Systems Biology. LNCS, Springer-Verlag (2019)

36. Shmulevich, I., Dougherty, E.R.: Probabilistic Boolean Networks: The Modeling and Control of Gene Regulatory Networks. SIAM Press, Philadelphia (2010)
37. Trairatphisan, P., Mizera, A., Pang, J., Tantar, A.A., Schneider, J., Sauter, T.: Recent development and biomedical applications of probabilistic Boolean networks. Cell Commun. Signal. **11**, 46 (2013)

I-Day Presentations

Formal Methods Applicability on Space Applications Specification and Implementation Using MORA-TSP

Daniel Silveira[1]([⊠]), Andreas Jung[2], Marcel Verhoef[2],
and Tiago Jorge[1]

[1] GMV, Tres Cantos, Spain
{daniel.silveira,tiago.jorge}@gmv.com
[2] ESA, Paris, France
{andreas.jung,marcel.verhoef}@esa.int

Abstract. The usage of formal methods in Model Driven Engineering (MDE) has already been demonstrated with a significant boost in both productivity and quality in the design and analysis of software and systems. However, the integration of applicable tools and techniques for formal analysis needs improvement in order to create a practical MDE environment for FM, suitable for use in an industrial setting. This paper presents the European Space Agency (ESA) MORA-TSP (Multicore implementation of the On-Board Software Reference Architecture with Time and Space Partitioning capability) study. MORA-TSP comprises to develop a MDE toolset suitable to apply FM for early analysis, correctness and validation of the modeled software, in the context of space flight software.

Keywords: Model Validation · Model transformation · FSM · MDE · OSRA · TASTE · AIR

1 Introduction

ESA's SAVOIR-FAIRE (SF) working group led an analysis of the issues faced by onboard software (OBSW) developers now and in the future, resulting into a set of requirements [1]. The intention of SF was that these requirements would be addressed through the use of appropriate technologies, and the specification of an On-board Software Reference Architecture (OSRA) with an accompanying development process [2].

OSRA applies the principles of MDE to address the user needs captured by SAVOIR-FAIRE. Consequently, the OSRA specification is founded on the principles of component-based software engineering (CBSE), where a software application consists entirely of software entities called components.

All of the information relating to the available component and interface types, and the way they are instantiated and assembled in a system, together with their non-functional properties, is captured in a model. A developer uses model information to generate documentation and to perform analysis on the system, including the validation of various system properties, even before the functional software is complete.

© Springer Nature Switzerland AG 2019
M. H. ter Beek et al. (Eds.): FM 2019, LNCS 11800, pp. 727–737, 2019.
https://doi.org/10.1007/978-3-030-30942-8_42

Similar to OSRA, TASTE [3] also follows CBSE and same principles, and while OSRA focuses on Requirements/Architecture, TASTE supports the detailed design process, also relying on formal languages for specification, and the synthesis down to source code generation and full application build. The basic idea is that OSRA and TASTE cover the entire software engineering process, fully model based, heavily relying on model analysis, synthesis and automation in order to close the design loop as early as possible. Recall that in particular in the space domain, the typically used hardware is usually available very late (and also very short) in the development process, the ability to start the validation and verification process well before the software meets the hardware is critical for success.

OSRA and TASTE use techniques of model transformation, finite state machines (FSM) and validation where the implemented infrastructure is suited to the introduction of FM to execute the stated system correctness, analysis and validation. The OSRA and TASTE is an intuitive toolchain bridges MDE with FM being capable to reduce the FM problem of overcoming the usage of complex notations.

The OSRA and TASTE are independent initiatives developed and supported by ESA and European industry, it is open source, uses open standards, has short time-to-market. Furthermore, the benefits of the tools, especially TASTE have been used in several activities [22], although Europe is not the dominant space market force, there is an European consensus for an accepting and adopting the tools.

The ESA's MORA TSP reference study has particular relevance for the space industry because its objective was to demonstrate the feasibility and performance evaluation of an end-to-end process, tools and building blocks from application level specification using OSRA and later TASTE, down to representative implementation running on the future space on-board computers board using Time and Space Partitioning (TSP), also known as IMA [21], paradigm on multi-core processors, such as the NGMP (LEON4-N2X, GR740). This process is achieved through the following toolchain:

- OSRA with respective editor, detailed in Sect. 3.
- TASTE toolchain, detailed in Sect. 4.
- AIR [4] toolchain, detailed in Sect. 6.

Each element of the toolchain is available for download and further information can be retrieved in the respective websites [23–26].

In Fig. 1 it is presented a data flow showing the MORA-TSP process:

- The user starts to define the software component models comprised by core OSRA model related to space OBSW and external model containing additional information such as the TSP data.
- Then a model transformation engine named to OSRA-to-TASTE automatically validates and transforms the OSRA models into TASTE models (shown as AADL and ASN1 blocks) and some source code.
- The TASTE buildsupport tool is invoked, transforms the TASTE models into source code, makefiles and TSP configuration data.
- Then as last step the AIR configuration builds the source code using also the respective configuration data and generates an executable.

2 MORA-TSP Suitability to Formal Methods

The relevance of MORA-TSP, is the provision of an easy to use and intuitive software modelling tools (OSRA and TASTE) that provides the usage of several methodologies that are capable of being improved through the application of FM. MORA-TSP is a full model-based framework and using known open standards, naturally making a consistent (properly integrated) and iterative adoption of FMs techniques into the framework/workflow more practical and easy. The following three approaches are identified: Model Transformation; Model Validation and FSM. These are detailed in the following sections.

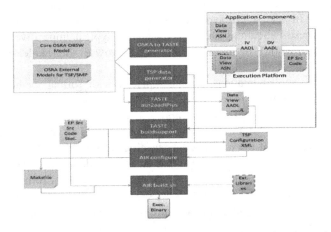

Fig. 1. MORA-TSP process showing the toolchain produced data inputs/outputs

2.1 Model Transformation

OSRA and TASTE use OBSW component modelling with a domain-specific meta-model, which allows the possibility to generate multiple outputs for different purposes and analysis through model transformation. MORA-TSP uses model transformation from OSRA to TASTE AADL models, models to source code, transformation within TASTE models, and other.

OSRA uses Meta Object Facility Model to Text Transformation Language (MOFM2T) [5] to express transformations. The OSRA component models are transformed in source code, SAE standardized AADL language models [18] used by TASTE and documentation. While TASTE uses its own "build support" tool capable of transforming its own AADL models.

The usage of MOFM2T or build support is applicable to make model transformation and create new models with proper formal semantics, endowing OSRA/TASTE modeling languages with a precise, executable behavior which can be subjected to formal analysis and validation of the models. An example is the application tridimensional classification [6], where the component model is transformed so it is possible to apply a formal verification of component model properties; also another example is the formalization in Isabelle/HOL [7] of a component model, focusing on the structure and lemmas to handle component structure. At the level of the transformed TASTE AADL model, formal analysis of the schedulability is already feasible at an early stage, and robustness of the design can be analysed by extending the AADL model (adding error models for the sensors and actuators), such that they can be analysed using COMPASS[1] [15]. Also through model transformation it is possible to generate FSMs.

2.2   Model Validation

OSRA, TASTE and AIR include a set of functionalities executing a set of checks ensuring the correctness of the used models aiming the anticipation of possible errors that could occur in later stages avoiding higher cost respective corrections.

Currently, these validations are implemented in typical imperative programming languages (Java/Python) or through OCL that browse the model structure and properties.

The existing implementations can be replaced with formal methodologies. An example is the usage of the formal B-Method [8] capable of validation the correctness of a component based system, further improved with a priori gluing algorithm which helps in the integration of mismatching components and in the implementation of missing functionalities of the requirements specifications of the software system.

In addition, another interesting example is using a divide & conquer validation technique through component-based analysis and verification of formal requirements specifications expressed through Software Cost Reduction models [9], the division approach is through partitioning which is already applied in OSRA/TASTE models.

The replacement of the purpose built validations by application of more generic formal techniques is part of the on-going research in the MORA-TSP study.

2.3   Component Behavior Definition with FSM

Each component at implementation model level in OSRA and each function component at interface level in TASTE can have their functional behavior specified through FSM. This feature was implemented within ESA's VERICOCOS activity [10] using TASTE OpenGEODE, an FSM editor using SDL (ITU-T Z.100 standard) language with source code generation capability in C and Ada.

FSM are used to formally test communication protocols [11], it is also applicable for formal verifications demonstrated in an automatic translation of the FSM into a Timed Automaton specification being applied by UPPAAL model checker tool [12]. As the OSRA components are service based, with well-defined formal protocols (specified in SDL and ASN.1 in TASTE), this provides a wide range of possible consistency checks that can be performed, already at the model level. As an aside, it also allows to generate fully consistent documentation from this single source, which is typically a major (maintenance) concern in traditional software development.

---

[1] The toolset can be found at http://www.compass-toolset.org.

3 OSRA

OSRA is a single, commonly agreed reference framework for the (component-based) definition of the OBSW of future ESA missions. OSRA comprises three layers: the component layer, the interaction layer and the execution platform (see Fig. 2). In addition, it provides a process that defines how these models can (or should) be constructed. The application functions are components, which exist in the Component Layer, along with the specification of the needed non-functional properties. The containers which envelope components, and the connectors which bind component interfaces, exist at the Interaction Layer. Both of these layers are dependent on the application function and rely on the underlying Execution Platform for application-independent services.

The ESA's COrDeT [14] activities implement the component model named "Space Component Model" (SCM). It consists of a domain specific realized Ecore metamodel, giving the advantage of keeping the metamodel simpler and its entities as close as possible to the concepts of the component model. The implemented SCM metamodel with associated editor (the OSRA editor) demonstrated the OSRA's feasibility.

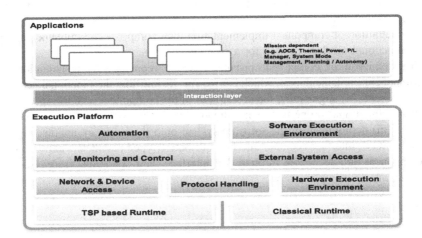

Fig. 2. OSRA layers.

3.1 OSRA Process Description

OSRA lays its foundations in MDE centering on the use of models to increase the abstraction level of design, while delegating a sizeable part of implementation to automated code generation. The greater abstraction level of models permits to:

Focus on the essential parts of the solution design, without being distracted by technology or implementation details that are not essential for the its understanding; Express the design in a manner that is economical (with lower effort than traditional approaches) yet precise enough to enable predictive analysis of the solution (e.g., in terms of correctness, coherence,...), as well as code generation of part of the implementation.

It is possible to split the OSRA software development process down into three basic stages: Specification and design; Construction; and Integration.

The OSRA Reference Development Process overlays the classical V-cycle process.

- The specification and design phase corresponds: (i) architecture definition using SCM; (ii) optional behavior modelling with dedicated models; (iii) detailed design;
- The construction phase corresponds to manual code development (after generation of business code skeletons) and possibly to behavioral code automated generation, and possibly the integration of existing (re-used) code artifacts.
- The integration corresponds to join the software components with architecture.

Verification and validation is included in each of the three stages.

3.2   The OSRA Specification/Architecture

The OSRA component model was designed to support (among others) the following:

- A specification of interfaces as first-class entities in a design step that precedes the definition of components
- The definition of component types, whose concerns are exclusively their functional relationship with the rest of the system
- The definition of component implementation, that comprises the implementation of all functional services defined for a component type
- The definition of component instances, which represent the instantiation of a component implementation, which is used for: (i) fulfilling the functional needs of a component; (ii) augmenting the description of the component with the specification of non-functional properties in the dimension of timing, space, concurrency and QoS; (iii) deployment of the software system onto the hardware architecture.
- In the SCM, interfaces contain interface attributes (typed parameters exposed by the component and accessible through that interface) and operations (services offered by an interface implementer.

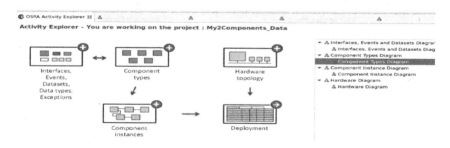

Fig. 3. The OSRA editor showing OSRA workflow

3.3   OSRA Editor

The OSRA editor is built on top of the SCM metamodel under the Eclipse eco-system. The editor provides facilities to model everything that is considered belonging to OSRA core model. Hence it supports the Design Views shown in Fig. 3.

An OSRA workflow support was implemented, it guides the user through all implementation step, which are simplified thanks to a robust rationalization of the number of graphical diagrams and tables. It also provides two alternative Eclipse viewpoints, one for preliminary evaluation of the tools (advanced features are hidden) and one (termed Expert) which provides all available features.

4 TASTE

TASTE[2] is an open source development environment dedicated to embedded, real-time systems and was created under the initiative of the ESA's ASSERT activity. TASTE relies on formal languages to create constituent models for all system aspects to build "correct by construction" software, by exposing these models to rigorous analysis, and by continuous integration and test to ensure that, the full path towards the actual application can be supported from day one. This approach ensures that potential errors are captured as early as possible and alleviates the user from tedious and error-prone repetitive tasks that typically hinders the rapid evolution of the design and implementation.

TASTE can be divided in three steps for the construction of the software.

The first step consists to generate the logical architecture of the software composed of elements called "functions" which interface through a set of provided/required interfaces. This step is done in the in interface view (IV) GUI being specified in AADL language. The ASN.1 is used to provide a description of the data structures.

The second step is the "functions" behaviour description. From the IV, TASTE is capable of generating the application skeleton, identifying where user defines the "function" behaviour according to the interfaces instantiations and associated input. The user can specify the behaviour programming in Ada and C language, or alternatively using SDL FSM that is then converted to Ada or C (Fig. 4).

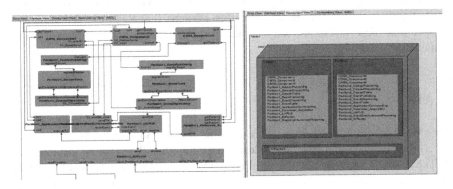

Fig. 4. TASTE IV - Interface view (left) and DV - Deployment view (right)

---

[2] The entire toolset is available through https://taste.tools.

Last step is deployment view, here the hardware platforms are bind to the IV "functions". This view is a hierarchy of "nodes" composed by "processors" which are then composed by "partitions", using the AADL as the underlying description language.

The IV/DV represent hardware and software system specifications at a high-level. Even if they describe system requirements, they do not bind both aspects (how the software is executed, which resources are used, etc.). Combining these two aspects is done with a specific tool called "build support" that transforms the IV and DV into a concurrency view that describes resources usage and software/hardware association. The concurrency view also performs scheduling analysis providing 2 tools by using Cheddar [16] and MAST [17] via an exporting tool from AADL to MAST. Additionally it is also possible to perform a scheduling simulation function using Marzhin [18].

5   Model Transformation OSRA to TASTE

TASTE includes four main layers: Application Layer, Glue Layer, Middleware Layer and OS/BSP Layer. Component instances defined in the OSRA Editor are translated into TASTE Functions, from those code skeletons can be generated automatically. With the associated behavior defined, it makes the Application Layer. TASTE also generates the glue code (i.e., Glue Layer) which adapts the application layer code to the lower parts of the system. Besides the Application and Glue layers, TASTE includes:

– Middleware Layer (Ocarina and PolyORB-HI): It provides transparent distribution of services for applications running on the same or different computer, and adapts the glue code according to the selected target platform. Moving from one target to another (simulator to target hardware) is nearly opaque from the point of view of the user.
– OS/BSP: It is the target execution environment. TASTE supports a wide range of run-times (i.e. Ada Ravenscar), operating systems (i.e. RTEMS) and simulators. Note that these layers are fully automatically generated and configured through models.

6   AIR

The growth in complexity of software systems functionalities associated with more powerful on board computers (OBC), leads to a complex task for the system integrator.

The aviation industry set the need to create a concept to achieve an integrated system architecture that preserves fault containment properties while creating a clear separation between software modules that share the common hardware. This concept uses time and space partitioning (TSP) to share the computing platform between possibly multiple applications with different levels of criticality. A partition is an allocation of application resources in terms of memory space, CPU time, I/O device access, CPU privilege mode and communication via ports. ESA has already identified the benefits of incorporating software TSP into the spacecraft avionics architecture to manage the growth of mission functions implemented in the OBSW [19] namely: reduced integration effort; resource savings; system fault containment; mixed criticality; security [20].

AIR is an hypervisor based on TSP that allows a single computer to simultaneously execute several independent Real Time Operating Systems (RTOS) partitions following a preconfigured schedule. AIR architecture is composed of the following modules:

Partition Management Kernel (PMK): it holds the main functionality of the hypervisor and implements the TSP; Partition Operating System (POS): it holds the para-virtualized RTOS, it corresponds to the guest OS of TSP System Executive Platform; LIBIOP: Integrated I/O into a single dedicated system partition, clearing the need for kernel reconfiguration or reimplementation and the partition can be handled the same way an application partition does.

In MORA-TSP, AIR is used as the TSP kernel with RTEMS 5 as the guest OS with SMP feature enabled. A 4 core LEON4-N2X board is the target to demonstrate several scheduling scenarios of partitions and tasks. One of the scenarios is presented in Fig. 5, it exemplifies the multitude of scheduling options system designers have while using a single multi-core on-board computer.

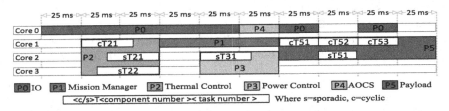

Fig. 5. MORA TSP scenario using TSP with AIR

7   Conclusions

The MORA-TSP presents an end-to-end OBSW development in the space industry. This process goes through a toolchain where conditions were set to apply formal methods, by integrating languages to create well-defined models, which are exposed to rigorous analysis and for the basis for consistent elaboration and synthesis, all the way down to the executable.

The MORA-TSP toolchain uses Component Based Modelling approach taking all advantages of MDE, it is achieved with OSRA, TASTE and AIR tools that provides early application development.

The tools provide a development environment to employ formal methods to ensure early error avoidance, complete software validation and analysis.

The following techniques used in the OSRA/TASTE/AIR allow FM applicability:

– Model Transformation to proper FM semantics leading the performance of formal analysis and validation, such as the usage of tridimensional classification or the usage of Isabelle/HOL formalization.

- Model Validation using methods of correctness of the model system or formal requirement validation with the Software Cost Reduction models.
- Usage of FSM in component model behavior, where formal tests can be executed with Timed Automatons and UPPAAL model checker. Also to improve software and system analysis/quality with Abstract State Machine formal methods.

References

1. SAVOIR FAIRE Working Group: Space onboard software reference architecture. In: Proceedings of the Data Systems in Aerospace Conference DASIA (2010)
2. Panunzio, M., Vardanega, T.: A component model for on-board software applications. In: Institute of Electrical and Electronics Engineers (IEEE) (September 2010)
3. TASTE. http://download.tuxfamily.org/taste
4. Rufino, J., Craveiro, J., Schoofs, T., Tatibana, C., Windsor, J.: AIR technology: a step towards IMA in space. In: DASIA (2009)
5. Object Management Group: MOF model to text transformation language (2008). https://www.omg.org/spec/MOFM2T/About-MOFM2T/
6. Amrani, M., et al.: Formal verification techniques for model transformations: a tridimensional classification. In: Journal of Object Technology - Published by AITO
7. de Boer, F.S., Bonsangue, M., Hallerstede, S., Leuschel, M.: Formal Methods for Components and Objects. Springer, Cham (2010). https://doi.org/10.1007/978-3-642-17071-3
8. Khan, A., Mottahir, A.M., Qayyum, N.-u., Khan, U.: Validation of component based software development model using formal B-method. Int. J. Comput. Appl. **67**, 24–39 (2013). https://doi.org/10.5120/11423-6768
9. Desovski, D., Cukic, B.: A component-based approach to verification and validation of formal software models. In: de Lemos, R., Gacek, C., Romanovsky, A. (eds.) WADS 2006. LNCS, vol. 4615, pp. 89–114. Springer, Heidelberg (2007). https://doi.org/10.1007/978-3-540-74035-3_5
10. Alaña, E., et al.: Verification of computer-controlled systems. DASIA (2017)
11. Bosik, B.S., Uyar, M.: Finite state machine based formal methods in protocol conformance testing. Comput. Netw. ISDN Syst. **22**(1), 7–33 (1991)
12. Salem, P.: Practical programming, validation and verification with finite-state machines: a library and its industrial application, pp. 51–60 (2016). https://doi.org/10.1145/2889160.2889226
13. Riccobene, E., Scandurra, P.: Combining formal methods and MDE techniques for model-driven system design and analysis (2019)
14. Rodriguez, A., et al.: The component layer of COrDeT on-board software architecture (2012)
15. Bozzano, M., Bruintjes, H., Cimatti, A., Katoen, J.-P., Noll, T., Tonetta, S.: COMPASS 3.0. In: Vojnar, T., Zhang, L. (eds.) TACAS 2019. LNCS, vol. 11427, pp. 379–385. Springer, Cham (2019). https://doi.org/10.1007/978-3-030-17462-0_25
16. Singhoff, F., Legrand, J., Nana, L., Marcé, L.: Cheddar: a flexible real-time scheduling framework. ACM SIGAda Ada Lett. **24**(4), 1–8 (2004). ACM Press
17. Harbour, M.G., Garcia, J.G., Gutierrez, J.P., Moyano, J.D.: MAST: modeling and analysis suite for real time applications. In: Proceedings 13th Euromicro Conference on Real-Time Systems, pp. 13–15. IEEE (June 2001)

18. Dissaux, P., Marc, O.: Executable AADL real time simulation of AADL models. In: CEUR Workshop Proceedings (2014)
19. Windsor, J., Hjortnaes, K.: Time and space partitioning in spacecraft avionics. In 2009 Third IEEE International Conference on Space Mission Challenges for Information Technology. Institute of Electrical and Electronics Engineers (IEEE) (July 2009)
20. Gaska, T., Watkin, C., Chen, Y.: Integrated modular avionics - past, present, and future. IEEE Aerosp. Electron. Syst. Mag. **30**(9), 12–23 (2015)
21. ARINC Specification: 653-1, Avionics Application Standard Interface. Aeronautical Radio Inc. Software, Annapolis (2003)
22. Perrotin, M., et al.: TASTE in action (2016)
23. OSRA - onboard software reference architecture. https://essr.esa.int/project/osra-onboard-software-reference-architecture
24. TASTE. https://taste.tools/
25. AIR Git Repository. https://spass-git-ext.gmv.com/AIR/AIR
26. AIR. https://www.gmv.com/en/Products/air/

Industrial Application of Event-B to a Wayside Train Monitoring System: Formal Conceptual Data Analysis

Robert Eschbach[(⊠)]

ITK Engineering GmbH, Rülzheim, Germany
robert.eschbach@itk-engineering.de

Abstract. The experience gained in the application of Event-B to a subsystem of a wayside train monitoring system (WTMS) will be presented in this paper. The WTMS configuration management system (CMS) supports the creation and management of configuration data for the WTMS. Consistency of system data is one of the most important quality properties of a CMS since inconsistency may lead to critical malfunctioning. Therefore, the development of the data handling part of a CMS requires the use of high integrity methods in order to ensure the highest quality. Event-B, with its set-theoretic basis for modelling, its approach of refinement and the use of formal proof to ensure consistency of refinement steps, is used in this study for the conceptual modelling of system data and system operations. Due to the Agile-structured development process, the conceptual model has been created in several iterations by a changing team of developers. The challenge was to guarantee completeness and consistency of this model and to keep it aligned with the goals of all relevant stakeholders. This has been achieved by producing an incremental, refinement-based creation of a formal conceptual model together with an appropriate formalization of the conceptual data constraints. The relationship between the conceptual model and the formal conceptual model has been realized by using an appropriate traceability model. This paper describes how the application of Event-B can successfully address these challenges.

Keywords: Formal conceptual data model · Formal verification · Refinement · Event-B

1   Introduction

The purpose of a wayside train monitoring system (WTMS) is to detect early threats that may lead to hazards and damages by monitoring trains and environmental conditions [4]. Typical examples are the detection of hot box, brake-locking or load displacements. A WTMS is a highly distributed system that, from a system data perspective, gathers, analyzes and exchanges different kinds of measurement and status data. A central part of a WTMS is the configuration management system (CMS). It is responsible for the correct data exchange between connected devices and control and management service points.

© Springer Nature Switzerland AG 2019
M. H. ter Beek et al. (Eds.): FM 2019, LNCS 11800, pp. 738–745, 2019.
https://doi.org/10.1007/978-3-030-30942-8_43

The goal of our project was the development of a server-based subsystem of the CMS. A relevant part of its functionality can be compared to a ticket system with user accounts, technical areas for discussions, technical experts assigned to these areas and tickets with related workflows (see entity ticket of the CDM in Fig. 1). A data configuration task can be mapped to one or more tickets and can be accomplished with the aid of associated users and technical experts.

A conceptual data model (CDM) has been defined as an extended entity relationship model with entities, relationships, data constraints and initial data requirements for this ticket system. The CDM was the basis for discussions between stakeholders and development team and has been aligned with stakeholder expectations and development needs in regular meetings. The underlying Agile development process was organized according to SCRUM. Due to SCRUM, the CDM has been created incrementally in several iterations by a changing team of developers. The challenge was to guarantee the overall completeness and consistency of this model and to keep it aligned with stakeholder and development team goals.

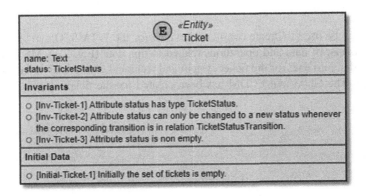

Fig. 1. CDM entity ticket

This challenge was met through the use of an incremental refinement-based creation of a formal conceptual model (FCDM) together with an appropriate formalization of the conceptual data constraints. The basic development principles are part of our Smart Engineering approach (see [3]). Event-B (see [1, 2]) with its set-theoretic basis for modelling, its approach of refinement and the use of formal proof ensuring consistency of refinement steps has been used for the conceptual modelling of system data and system operations (Fig. 2). Formal methods, especially Event-B have been applied successfully in many safety-critical railway systems [6–9]. The success of Event-B and the B method has even an influence on the definition of CENELEC standard EN50128 [10]. A state-of-the-art of methods and tools for the verification of interlocking systems can be found in [11]. The relationship between the conceptual model and the formal conceptual model has been realized by an appropriate traceability model. In the following it will be described how the application of Event-B can successfully address these challenges.

```
MACHINE
      admin1
SEES
    ctx1
VARIABLES
    Ticket
    Ticket_Status
    ticket_status_transition
    ticket_status
    ticket_status_old
INVARIANTS
    inv1:   Ticket ⊆ 1_MAX_TICKET not theorem
    inv2:   Ticket_Status ⊆ 1_MAX_TICKET_STATUS not theorem
    inv3:   ticket_status ∈ Ticket → Ticket_Status not theorem  [Inv-Ticket-1], [Inv-Ticket-3]
    inv4:   ticket_status_old ∈ Ticket → Ticket_Status not theorem  [Inv-Ticket-3]
    inv5:   {new,open,pending,on_hold,closed,solved} ⊆ Ticket_Status not theorem  [Inv-TicketStatus-1]
    inv6:   ticket_status_transition ⊆ Ticket_Status × Ticket_Status not theorem  [Inv-TicketStatusTransition-1]
    inv7:   {new↦open,open↦pending,open↦on_hold,open↦closed,
            open↦solved, pending↦open,on_hold↦open,closed↦open}
            ⊆ ticket_status_transition not theorem  [Inv-TicketStatusTransition-2]
    inv8:   ∀t·t∈Ticket ⇒ ticket_status_old(t)↦ticket_status(t)
            ∈ ticket_status_transition not theorem  [Inv-Ticket-2]
```

Fig. 2. Screenshot Event-B, rodin

2   Formal Conceptual Data Model of the Ticket System

2.1   CMS Architecture

The CMS can be used to create configuration data for the WTMS. On an abstract level the CMS consist of data and operations related to this data (Fig. 3). CMS data can be further divided into data for the ticket system and technical configuration data related to the WTMS. The CDM and FCDM has been created for the ticket system.

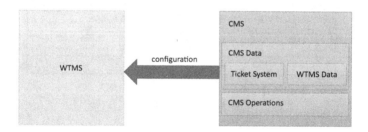

Fig. 3. Conceptual view

2.2   Entity and Relationship Analysis

Entities and relationships of the ticket system and associated data constraints were identified together with all stakeholders of the CMS. In the following we will focus on a representative part of the CDM in order to illustrate our approach.

Central entity of the ticket system is a ticket. On the highest abstraction level, a ticket has a name and a status. In subsequent refinement steps, further attributes can be added. All entities will be specified with invariants and initial data requirements. All of these have unique identifiers in order to make these elements traceable. For example, permitted ticket status transitions are specified in relation TicketStatusTransition (see Fig. 4). There are two invariants [Inv-TicketStatusTransition-1] and [Inv-TicketStatusTransition-2] and one initial data requirement [Initial-TicketStatusTransition-1].

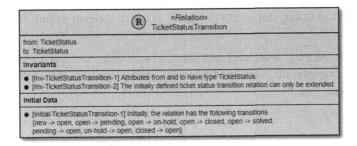

Fig. 4. Relation TicketStatusTransition

These and further entities and relations have been discussed and elaborated with all stakeholders. The conceptual data model has been refined to a so-called logical data model (LDM). The LDM has been aligned with the expectations of all stakeholders. From the LDM a concrete SQL database scheme has been derived. The FCDM has been built on top of this conceptual data model.

2.3 Formal Conceptual Data Model

The FCDM assigns to each entity of the CDM an finite set. For example, the set of tickets is specified as

$$\text{Ticket} \subseteq 1 \cdot \cdot \text{MAX\_TICKET}$$

where MAX_TICKET denotes a constant specified as

$$\text{MAX\_TICKET} \in \mathbb{N} \wedge \text{MAX\_TICKET} > 0$$

Relationships of the CDM will be formalized as relations of the FCDM. For example, the ticket status transition relation will be defined as

$$\text{ticket\_status\_transition} \subseteq \text{Ticket\_Status} \times \text{Ticket\_Status}$$

with trace information [Inv-Ticket-1], [Inv-Ticket-3]. The relation will be initialized as

$$\text{ticket\_status\_transition} := \{\text{new} \mapsto \text{open}, \text{open} \mapsto \text{pending}, \text{open} \mapsto \text{on\_hold},$$
$$\text{open} \mapsto \text{closed}, \text{open} \mapsto \text{solved}, \text{pending} \mapsto \text{open},$$
$$\text{on\_hold} \mapsto \text{open}, \text{closed} \mapsto \text{open}\}$$

with trace information [Initial-TicketStatusTransition-1]. Invariant [Inv-Ticket-2] is formalized as

$$\forall t \cdot t \in Ticket \Rightarrow ticket\_status\_old(t) \mapsto ticket\_status(t) \in ticket\_status\_transition$$

Events for creating, modifying and deleting were defined or each entity and each relation. For example, the event **modify_ticket_status** specifies the modification of a ticket status (see Fig. 5).

```
modify_ticket_status: not extended ordinary
ANY
 o    t
 o    st
WHERE
 o    grd1:    t ∈ Ticket not theorem
 o    grd2:    ticket_status(t)↦st ∈ ticket_status_transition not theorem [Imp-Ticket-2]
THEN
 o    act1:    ticket_status(t) := st
 o    act2:    ticket_status_old(t) := ticket_status(t)
END
```

Fig. 5. Event modify_ticket_status

A database trigger has been derived from event **modify_ticket_status/grd2** (see Fig. 6).

```
-- [Imp-Ticket-2] begin
-- Ensures invariant [Inv-Ticket-2].
 CREATE TRIGGER trigger_ticket_attr_status_update BEFORE UPDATE OF sta-tus_id ON ticket
BEGIN
   SELECT CASE WHEN
           NOT EXISTS (
             SELECT 1 FROM ticket_status_transition
               WHERE
                 OLD.status_id = ticket_status_transition.current_ticket_status_id AND
                 NEW.status_id = ticket_status_transition.next_ticket_status_id
                 )
         THEN
           RAISE (FAIL, 'ERROR: Ticket status change is not allowed.')
   END;
END;
-- [Imp-Ticket-2] end
```

Fig. 6. Trigger derivation

As soon as the trigger is created in the database, the SELECT-Statement will be performed automatically before an update statement on table `ticket` will be executed. The SELECT-Statement checks whether the corresponding status transition is permitted using table `ticket_status_transition`. If the transition is not permitted, an exception will be raised.

The FCDM consists of five refinement steps. Each refinement step adds new variables, invariants and events and corresponds to a user story that must be implemented in a sprint.

3 Challenges and Solutions

This chapter presents the main challenges facing the development of CMS. Since a CMS is responsible for correct data exchange, data integrity is very important. Other challenges are related to faults. Any non-trivial system possesses faults. From an engineering point of view, it is important to deal systematically with faults. At the beginning of the system development, it is important to prevent faults. By deriving checklists and database-specific information from our formal model, it was possible to prevent faults related to data operations. Strategies for fault tolerance help to avoid failures during system execution by means of error detection and recovery mechanisms. Using database constraints and triggers based on our formal model as well as SQL statements involved in transactions with roll-back mechanisms, a specific kind of fault tolerance has been achieved. The underlying Agile development process leads to an incremental development of the conceptual data model (CDM). Since developers may change from increment to increment, keeping the CDM consistent and complete is a big challenge. The chosen traceability model between the CDM and the formal model helps to understand the impact of changes, for example, when new entities or relationships are modelled, or existing entities and relationships need to be adapted.

3.1 Data Integrity

Data integrity and especially data consistency of system data is one of the most important quality properties of a CMS since inconsistency may lead to critical malfunctioning. Therefore, the development of a CMS requires the use of high integrity methods in order to ensure the highest quality. To this extent, the formal conceptual data model (FCDM) has been constructed to be traceably correct in alignment with the CDM, i.e. each modelling decision like the definition of constants, variables or invariants of the FCDM can be traced back to relevant parts of the informal CDM. Furthermore, each derived concrete database constraint and each derived trigger can be traced back to the FCDM.

3.2 Fault Prevention

During system development, it is important to prevent as many faults as possible. A fault may cause errors during system execution and may lead to critical situations. Different techniques for fault prevention exist. For example, coding guidelines or systematic code reviews may help software developers to prevent faults. In our project, checklists and concrete SQL constraints and triggers based on the FCDM were extracted and discussed with the developers before they started to implement the corresponding data operations.

3.3 Fault Tolerance

Another important quality attribute required for the CMS is fault tolerance. Since each non-trivial system has faults, it is very important to deal with faults systematically. Fault tolerance covers different techniques for error detection as well as for system recovery. A special way to recover a consistent system state in a CMS is to remove inconsistent data and roll back to an earlier consistent and saved data restoration point. In our project, interrelated database statements of a data operations are always part of a transaction with associated rollback mechanisms. Whenever an exception occurs (for example, by violating a unique or foreign key constraint), the database will roll back to the last saved restoration point. The calling data operation will check whether the execution of the transaction was successful or not and will trigger a warning in the latter case.

3.4 Agile Development

Due to the Agile-structured development process, the conceptual model has been created in several iterations by a changing team of developers. With each increment of the model, ensuring consistency and completeness is a challenge. In our project, increments have been mapped to Event-B refinement steps. According to [5, 8 and 12] we have used Event-B in the inception and construction phases and passed the derived database triggers to the developers. An extension or modification of the CDM will lead to an appropriate adaption of the FCDM. Since each refinement step and invariant will be formally verified, it becomes clear how to adapt the FCDM. When all proof obligations have been verified, the FCDM is in a consistent state and can be used to derive information for the CDM or the database. Each change of the CDM must be aligned with stakeholders and the development team. Since the cause of the change can be traced back to the FCDM, it is easy to understand the impact of a change and to provide convincing arguments for the change within stakeholder and team discussions.

4 Conclusion

The knowledge gained in the application of Event-B to the configuration management system of a wayside train monitoring system has been presented in this paper. The configuration management system supports the creation and management of configuration data for the wayside train monitoring system. The biggest challenges for system development have been presented and show how the formal conceptual data model, together with its precise traceability model, succeeds in rising to these challenges. Requirements for data integrity, fault prevention and fault tolerance as well as iterative and incremental characteristics of the Agile development process has led to these hard challenges. All of these can be addressed using Smart Engineering principles [3] and Event-B [1, 2] as formal technique. Especially the integration of formal specifications and formal verification, as well as the refinement concept, lends Event-B to a practical and powerful formal technique useful in industrial projects.

References

1. Abrial, J.-R.: Modeling in Event-B - System and Software Engineering. Cambridge University Press, Cambridge (2010)
2. Abrial, J.-R.: The B-book: Assigning Programs to Meanings. Cambridge University Press, New York (1996)
3. Smart Engineering – Effiziente Softwareentwicklung in der Bahntechnik, Robert Eschbach, Harald Laub, Thomas Freissler, Tobias Hofbaur, ZEVrail, 2017 (Jahrgang 141), Ausgabe 11/12
4. Bracciali, A.: Wayside train monitoring systems: a state-of-the-art and running safety implications. Int. J. Railw. Technol. 1(1), 231–247 (2012)
5. Edmunds, A., et al.: Using the Event-B formal method for disciplined agile delivery of safety-critical systems. In: SOFTENG (2016)
6. Lecomte, T., Servat, T., Pouzancre, G.: Formal methods in safety-critical railway systems (2007)
7. ter Beek, M.H., Fantechi, A., Ferrari, A., Gnesi, S., Scopigno, R.: Formal methods for the railway sector. In: ERCIM News 2018(112) (2018)
8. Ferrari, A., et al.: Survey on formal methods and tools in railways: the ASTRail approach. In: Collart-Dutilleul, S., Lecomte, T., Romanovsky, A. (eds.) RSSRail 2019. LNCS, vol. 11495, pp. 226–241. Springer, Cham (2019). https://doi.org/10.1007/978-3-030-18744-6_15
9. ASTRail. http://www.astrail.eu/
10. Fantechi, A., Fokkink, W., Morzenti, A.: Some trends in formal methods applications to railway signaling. In: Gnesi, S., Margaria, T. (eds.) Formal Methods for Industrial Critical Systems, pp. 61–84. Wiley, Hoboken (2012)
11. Haxthausen, A.E., Peleska, J.: Model checking and model-based testing in the railway domain. In: Drechsler, R., Kühne, U. (eds.) Formal Modeling and Verification of Cyber-Physical Systems, pp. 82–121. Springer, Wiesbaden (2015). https://doi.org/10.1007/978-3-658-09994-7_4
12. Wolff, S.: Scrum goes formal: agile methods for safety-critical systems. In: 2012 First International Workshop on Formal Methods in Software Engineering: Rigorous and Agile Approaches (FormSERA), Zurich, pp. 23–29 (2012)

Property-Driven Software Analysis
(Extended Abstract)

Mathieu Comptier, David Déharbe[(⊠)], Paulin Fournier,
and Julien Molinero-Perez

CLEARSY Systems Engineering, Aix-en-Provence, France
david.deharbe@clearsy.com

Keywords: Formal methods · Formal proof · Software specification

Context. Software in industrial products, such as in the railway industry, constantly evolves to meet new or changing requirements. For projects with a lifetime spanning decades (such as the control software for energy plants, for railway lines, etc.), keeping track of the original design rationale through time is a significant challenge. The software provider may eventually lose some technical control over its product, which may then become unnecessarily complex. This may hinder beneficial architectural changes, result in the integration of overprotective measures and lead to increased costs. For safety critical systems, the risk is that the software eventually degrades up to a point where safety is no longer guaranteed in some corner cases.

Typically, for any requirement that is introduced or modified for a new version of the software, the development follows all the activities in the V cycle, from high-level requirements up to integration testing. Figure 1 zooms in on the initial design activities of the V-cycle. These are precisely the activities that are verified by property-driven software analysis: a *systematic* and *complete* analysis approach to prove mathematically that a software implementation conforms to a high-level (safety or functional) requirement. This activity detects errors early in the V-cycle, before any testing needs to be conducted, resulting in increased confidence in the design and offering the possibility to revert the loss of technical control.

Technical Insights. A property-driven software analysis establishes a direct and formal link between software source and the properties expected of the system integrating the software. Any discrepancy introduced in the design phase is detected, be it in the high-level algorithmic specification of the solution, or in its implementation. Technically, the approach first identifies, in collaboration with the customer, the *key properties* that must be preserved. These are system *invariant* properties relating physical objects and logical (software) variables. The analysis then proceeds and naturally uncovers a modular and layered vision of the software and of the represented entities. Each variable contributing to the implementation of the requirement is identified, its role is expressed by

© Springer Nature Switzerland AG 2019
M. H. ter Beek et al. (Eds.): FM 2019, LNCS 11800, pp. 746–750, 2019.
https://doi.org/10.1007/978-3-030-30942-8_44

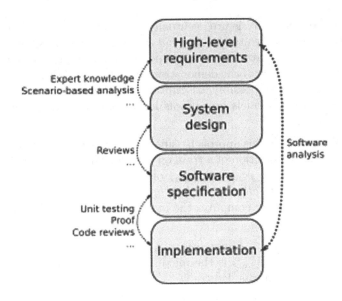

Fig. 1. Position of the activity in the design process.

connecting properties relating it to the concrete environment elements interacting with the software. The demonstration then consists in showing that (a) the key properties derive from the set of connecting properties, (b) every action of the software preserves the connecting properties, and (c) every evolution of the physical elements preserves the connecting properties.

The analysis team requires as inputs the high-level requirements, usually safety properties stemming from the analysis of the undesirable events and a faithful representation of the code implementing the feature (the software specification, or a formal model of the code, if it exists, or the code itself). It is also desirable that a product expert is available part-time for one-off discussions.

Although this approach can be conducted with pen and paper with good results, we find it yields even greater benefits when the safety demonstration is carried out with a tool able to support both formal modeling of the system and mechanical verification of the demonstration. Indeed, using tools

1. guarantees that the safety demonstration is free from logical flaws;
2. uncovers all domain-specific hypotheses necessary to the demonstration;
3. requires expressing properties at the right level of detail and precision.

To formalize the system model and the safety demonstration, we have used different tools in different projects: Event-B [1] support in Atelier [2], as well as HLL [4]. We also found it beneficial to employ Pro-B [3] animation and verification features to tune the system model. Nevertheless, the presented method does not depend on this specific tooling. All that is needed is a formalism that is expressive enough, with support for machine-controlled reasoning (i.e., interactive and automatic theorem proving).

The results of the analysis are eventually delivered as a series of documents describing the scope of the study, listing all the hypotheses made upon the environment of the studied feature, the key properties and the connection properties, a natural language version of the demonstration that the code is safe with respect to the key property, and, possibly, description of scenarios leading to unsafe situations. When formal models and proofs have been developed, these are also part of the deliverables.

Example. We illustrate this approach using the safety critical software responsible for calculating the position of a train on a track. The outputs of the software are two ordered positions p_{min} and p_{max} on the track; the key safety property is: *the physical train is totally included in the portion bounded by p_{min} and p_{max}.* Assume that this software computes the maximal and minimal positions (p_{max} and p_{min}) as follows:

- $p_{max} = p_{beacon} + V_{max} \cdot T$ where p_{beacon} is the position with respect to the last detected beacon, V_{max} is the maximal speed of the train, and T is the time since the beacon was detected.
- $p_{min} = p_{beacon} - R - Lg - err$ where R is the maximal movement backwards of a train, Lg is the train length and err the localization error.

Note that the result depends on the position of the last activated beacon. To ensure the key property we thus have to ensure that this position is correct (up to the localization error). Moreover, all possible train movements must be taken into account. We derive the following connecting properties:

1. A train detects a beacon activation only if its head is near the position (known by the train) of the beacon;
2. The correction added to compute maximal and minimal position covers all possible movements of the train.

Any implementation that ensures these two properties will ensure that the key safety property is satisfied. Then to show that these two properties hold in this particular setting, the proof will rely on several sub-properties that are either hypotheses, or constraints, or exported constraints such as:

(a) The position of the beacon known by the train includes the correction due to the distance between the position of the detector and the head of the train;
(b) A beacon is active only if it is located at the right position (*i.e.* if a beacon is dragged by a train it can no longer be active);
(c) Beacon can be activated at most at a distance bounded by err;
(d) Trains speed is bounded by V_{max};
(e) Trains cannot go backward by a distance greater than R;
(f) T is an over approximation of the time elapsed since beacon activation;
(g) The real length of the train is smaller than Lg.

In summary, the initial high level requirement is first refined in two properties that combine the key property with the design principles, based on beacon placement and over approximation of the train movement. Next, the analysis yields a set of simple properties sufficient to prove the initial requirement is met.

Industrial Applications. This method is proposed when traditional verification and validation activities are lacking, either when case-base analysis would be incomplete for systems that contain too many states, or when defects are detected too late in the development cycle. The method has been applied on a SIL4 system for the railways, on a feature corresponding to over 100 pages of software specification and a 12kloc implementation. It has also been applied to an anti-theft device in the automotive domain, and to show compliance of smart cards with the Common Criteria level 5+ specifications.

The approach is pragmatic, with a rapid delivery of concrete results. In the traditional V-cycle, such results are eventually achieved by testing scenarios *if* the corresponding scenarios were initially identified and selected. Property-oriented analysis improves qualitatively (it is complete) and quantitatively (it applies earlier). Having a property-oriented analysis of safety-critical software-based systems presents a real gain both for the provider and for the operator of that system. On the one hand, for the provider in charge of developing the system, this method provides added robustness and reduces the risk of facing problems during service. It ensures the sustainability of the knowledge of design decisions, by facilitating skill transmission. Also the safety demonstration is an important asset to obtain the certificate for the required safety level. On the other hand, the operator is also liable for the product in service and, as such, benefits from applying this approach, especially in case the product is part of a larger, multi-supplier system where it plays the role of integrator.

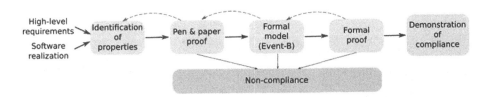

Fig. 2. Synthesis of the process for property-oriented analysis

Synthesis. We have described an application of formal methods that has seen increasing interest from different industrial partners to address the challenge of verifying systematically safety-related product features implemented in software. This rigorous approach follows the process presented in Fig. 2; it is driven by the identification of properties relating software entities and physical elements from the environment, which proves essential to establish key safety and functional requirements. The study of the possible changes affecting these elements provides a systematic and complete procedure to verify that these requirements are met, in all possible situations. Our experience shows that formal methods equipped with tool support, such as Event-B, can be used to support this analysis with success and provide added guarantee and effectiveness to the methodology.

References

1. Abrial, J.R.: Modeling in Event-B - System and Software Engineering. Cambridge University Press, Cambridge (2010)
2. Atelier, B.: CLEARSY Systems Engineering. http://atelierb.eu
3. Leuschel, M., Butler, M.: ProB: a model checker for B. In: Araki, K., Gnesi, S., Mandrioli, D. (eds.) FME 2003. LNCS, vol. 2805, pp. 855–874. Springer, Heidelberg (2003). https://doi.org/10.1007/978-3-540-45236-2_46. https://www3.hhu.de/stups/prob/
4. Ordioni, J., Breton, N., Colaço, J.L.: HLL vol 2.7 Modelling Language Specification. Technical Report STF-16-01805, RATP, May 2018

Practical Application of SPARK
to OpenUxAS

M. Anthony Aiello[1], Claire Dross[2], Patrick Rogers[1], Laura Humphrey[3(✉)],
and James Hamil[4]

[1] AdaCore Technologies, Inc., New York, NY 10001, USA
[2] AdaCore SAS, 75009 Paris, France
[3] Air Force Research Laboratory, Dayton, OH 45433, USA
`laura.humphrey@us.af.mil`
[4] LinQuest Corporation, Beavercreek, OH 45431, USA

Abstract. This paper presents initial, positive results from using
SPARK to prove critical properties of OpenUxAS, a service-oriented
software framework developed by AFRL for mission-level autonomy
for teams of cooperating unmanned vehicles. Given the intended use
of OpenUxAS, there are many safety and security implications; however, these considerations are unaddressed in the current implementation. AFRL is seeking to address these considerations through the use
of formal methods, including through the application of SPARK, a programming language that includes a specification language and a toolset
for proving that programs satisfy their specifications. Using SPARK, we
reimplemented one of the core services in OpenUxAS and proved that
a critical part of its functionality satisfies its specification. This successful application provides a foundation for further applications of formal
methods to OpenUxAS.

Keywords: OpenUxAS · SPARK · Formal methods · Autonomy

1 Introduction

This paper presents initial, positive results from using SPARK to prove critical
properties of OpenUxAS, a software framework for mission-level autonomy for
teams of cooperating unmanned vehicles.

Efficient and effective use of unmanned vehicles requires greater levels of
autonomy than employed today. Currently, command and control of a single
vehicle requires multiple human operators to perform lower-level tasks such as
path planning, piloting, sensor steering, and so forth. Automating these lower-
level tasks would ideally allow multiple vehicles to be managed by a single operator, increasing efficiency and allowing the operator to focus on tactical and

DISTRIBUTION STATEMENT A: Distribution unlimited; approved for public release;
case number 88ABW-2017-1985.

This is a U.S. government work and not under copyright protection in the U.S.; foreign copyright
protection may apply 2019

M. H. ter Beek et al. (Eds.): FM 2019, LNCS 11800, pp. 751–761, 2019.
https://doi.org/10.1007/978-3-030-30942-8_45

strategic aspects of the mission rather than low-level execution details. Toward this end, additional automation could build off of these tasks to provide the operator with a high-level interface to command and control multiple vehicles. Additionally, communication channels between vehicles are often unreliable, so services must function with only intermittent communication between vehicles.

The United States Air Force Research Laboratory (AFRL) has explored solutions to this problem through the research and development of decentralized cooperative control approaches [4]. AFRL has developed a service-oriented architecture called Unmanned Systems Autonomy Services (UxAS) that provides services handling many of the low-level details necessary for decentralized cooperative control and tasks[1] implementing high-level command and control, thus accelerating research and development in this area. (Although the main focus of UxAS is aircraft, the 'x' in UxAS indicates support for other vehicles).

AFRL has created a public-release, open-source version of UxAS, called OpenUxAS, and has made OpenUxAS[2] and a compatible multi-vehicle simulation environment (OpenAMASE[3]) available on github. UxAS is implemented in C++ 11, but the messages used for communication between services are described using AFRL's language-neutral Lightweight Message Construction Protocol (LMCP), allowing UxAS tasks and services to be written in other languages. LMCP is also available on github[4].

Given the intended use of UxAS, there are many safety and security implications. Because UxAS was developed initially to accelerate internal research and development, these considerations are currently left unaddressed. However, as interest in UxAS grows, both within AFRL and also in the broader community, addressing the safety and security of UxAS becomes increasingly important.

The known limitations of testing [1], especially for autonomy, make the application of formal methods to UxAS a priority for AFRL. Because UxAS was originally intended to facilitate research, the design and implementation of UxAS does not always lend itself well to the application of formal methods. For example, in addition to being implemented in C++, UxAS makes frequent use of pointers and does not define application-specific ranges for numeric values.

AFRL and AdaCore have therefore collaborated to rewrite parts of OpenUxAS in Ada 2012 and SPARK 2014 so that SPARK can prove critical properties of core services. In this paper, we describe our implementation approach, present initial results, and identify our next objectives.

---

[1] For the remainder of the paper, we use "task" to refer to a component of a mission in UxAS (see: [3]). When we refer to an Ada task, we will clearly indicate it as such.

[2] https://github.com/afrl-rq/OpenUxAS.

[3] https://github.com/afrl-rq/OpenAMASE.

[4] https://github.com/afrl-rq/LmcpGen.

2   Background

2.1   OpenUxAS

UxAS is designed to be highly extensible and configurable: depending on the configuration of loaded services and tasks, which perform mission-specific activities such as area, line or point surveillance [3], UxAS can perform a variety of missions, including decentralized surveillance [4] or ground-intruder isolation. At the heart of UxAS is the task-assignment pipeline, which is implemented as a set of cooperating services [5]. The role of the task-assignment pipeline is to take tasks, with associated task orderings or dependencies, and distribute them amongst eligible vehicles. The goal of the distribution is to be time-optimal: all tasks should be completed by the eligible vehicles as quickly as possible. Services and tasks communicate by exchanging messages, defined using LMCP, over the message bus, which is implemented using ZeroMQ[5].

For this work, we focus on the Automation Request Validator service, which validates and serializes new Automation Request messages. Automation Request messages describe missions by referencing tasks, eligible vehicles, and operating regions by their IDs, which must have been previously defined by other received messages. The service thus acts as a gatekeeper, performing two functions: (1) ensure that the Automation Request can be carried out, by checking that the ID of every vehicle, task and operating region referenced has previously been defined; and then (2) ensure that only one resulting actionable request, in the form of a Unique Automation Request message, is fed into the rest of the system at a time. Our focus for the application of SPARK is on the first function.

2.2   SPARK

SPARK is both a programming language with a specification language and a toolset that is supported by specific development and verification processes [2]. Here, we focus on the latest generation of SPARK, SPARK 2014, in which the specification language and the programming language have been unified as a subset of Ada 2012. SPARK excludes features not amenable to sound static verification, principally access types (pointers), function side effects, and exception handling. Constraints on both program data and control can be specified using type contracts (predicates and invariants) and function contracts (preconditions and postconditions), respectively. The SPARK verification toolset can automatically prove that an implementation conforms to its specification and is free from run-time exceptions.

3   Approach

Our approach is to translate the Automation Request Validator service from C++ to Ada and SPARK. We use Ada to implement the message-based communication classes above ZeroMQ the object-oriented class hierarchy for the service

---

[5] http://zeromq.org.

classes. Both Ada and SPARK are used to implement the concrete Automation Request Validator service subclass. In particular, SPARK is used to implement the critical functionality of the service, i.e., the part that validates the Automation Request messages.

We follow the C++ design closely so that any errors encountered will not be due to a design change we introduced. Some changes are required for SPARK, and are described below. As noted in Sect. 4.1, more substantial changes would improve the quality of the code and reduce the effort required for proof.

3.1   Service Class Hierarchy

All services in UxAS inherit from a common abstract class named Service_Base that provides facilities for creating and configuring services. In particular, Service_Base creates a new service instance given only the name of the required service. This dynamic creation is necessary because UxAS instances are configured using service names listed in an XML configuration file and explains the use of pointers to designate dynamically allocated services.

Service_Base is a subclass of LMCP_Object_Network_Client_Base, the root abstract base class for all LMCP network-oriented client subclasses. This class provides the means for communicating LMCP messages over the network, and includes a thread, implemented as an Ada task, that actively sends and receives the messages.

Rather than defining Ada bindings to the C++ code, we implemented these classes in Ada because we want to be able to apply Ada features such as contracts and, in the future, extend the scope of the SPARK analysis to a larger portion of the code. To that end, although we follow the C++ design closely, we make changes for SPARK when necessary. For example, all state-changing functions in C++ are converted into procedures in Ada because SPARK does not allow functions to have side-effects. Similarly, we use bounded data types in place of unbounded types, e.g., String. We use a formally proven "dynamic bounded array" abstract data type for several of these replacements and use contracts extensively in the message serializer/deserializer class, requiring us to think through the intended usage scenarios and providing checks at run-time for our understanding.

3.2   Properties of Interest

Although a high-level description of the Automation Request Validator service exists on the OpenUxAS wiki[6], we found that there was insufficient detail there to identify meaningful properties. Instead, we examined the C++ code for the Automation Request Validator service to identify intent based on the current implementation. For the identification of intent, we restricted our focus to high-level understanding of the code and comments, rather than focusing on the details of the implementation.

---

[6] https://github.com/afrl-rq/OpenUxAS/wiki/Core-Services-Description.

The identified properties focus on the validation of specific, critical aspects of Automation Requests. A request contains several pieces of data: a list of entities, a list of operating regions, and a list of tasks. For a request to be valid, all these data should be checked to make sure that they have been previously declared and configured appropriately. This is done in a C++ function named isCheckAutomationRequestRequirements. This function takes an automation request and checks whether it is valid or not. Additionally, if the request is invalid, it computes and sends an error message to describe why the request was rejected. This function is translated in SPARK as a procedure (because a function cannot have side effects, including sending messages).

To describe the functional behavior of isCheckAutomationRequestRequirements, we have introduced a SPARK function named Valid_Automation_Request that describes when an automation request should be valid. This function does not care about error messages; it simply describes validity in as concise a way as possible. Additionally, this function is specification-only, which means that it should not be used in the final executable. To make sure that this restriction is enforced, Valid_Automation_Request is annotated with the Ghost aspect (ghost code is removed by the compiler when assertion checking is disabled). To ensure that the definition stays in the specification part of the program, and is available for verification, we have defined Valid_Automation_Request directly as an expression function:

```
function Valid_Automation_Request
  (This    : Configuration_Data ;
   Request : My_UniqueAutomationRequest) return Boolean
is
     -- Check entities
  (Check_For_Required_Entity_Configurations
   ( ... )

     -- Check operating regions
   and then Check_For_Required_Operating_Region_And_Keepin_Keepout_Zones
   (Operating_Region  => Get_OperatingRegion_From_OriginalRequest (Request),
      Operating_Regions => This . Available_Operating_Regions ,
      KeepIn_Zones_Ids  => This . Available_KeepIn_Zones_Ids ,
      KeepOut_Zones_Ids => This . Available_KeepOut_Zones_Ids )

     -- Check tasks
   and then Check_For_Required_Tasks_And_Task_Requirements
   ( ... )
with Ghost , Global => null ;
```

The three subproperties are translated in the same way. For example, here is the function that checks the validity of operating regions:

```
function Check_For_Required_Operating_Region_And_Keepin_Keepout_Zones
  (Operating_Region  : Int64 ;
   Operating_Regions : Operating_Region_Maps ;
   KeepIn_Zones_Ids  : Int64_Set ;
   KeepOut_Zones_Ids : Int64_Set ) return Boolean
is
     -- if there is an operating region , it should be listed in Operating_Regions
  (if Operating_Region ≠ 0 then Contains (Operating_Regions , Operating_Region )

     -- and all its associated keepin areas should be in KeepIn_Zones_Ids
   and then All_Elements_In
     (Element (Operating_Regions , Operating_Region ) . KeepInAreas ,
      KeepIn_Zones_Ids )
```

```
   — and all its associated keepout areas should be in KeepOut_Zones_Ids
   and then All_Elements_In
       (Element (Operating_Regions, Operating_Region).KeepOutAreas,
         KeepOut_Zones_Ids))
with Ghost;
```

That is, the requested operating region should have been previously stored in the operating-region map of the Automation Request Validator service, and its keep-in/keep-out areas should all be stored in the their respective sets.

3.3   Ada-SPARK Boundaries

The concrete Automation_Request_Validator_Service inherits from Service_Base, which inherits from LMCP_Object_Network_Client_Base. Both use constructs outside the SPARK subset, primarily pointers. Moreover, the Automation Request Validator service directly processes LMCP messages, which contain pointers and use container packages that are not amenable to formal analysis.

While changes are therefore required to enable analysis with SPARK, we avoid propagating these changes throughout the application and allow other parts of the application to use the full expressivity of Ada, in particular retaining the use of pointers. This approach promotes efficiency and stays as close as possible to the C++ code. Because the SPARK restrictions are mostly localized to the implementation of the Automation Request Validator service, this approach also simplifies modifying the integration between SPARK and Ada, for example if we change containers or take advantage of enhancements to SPARK.

The complexity of this approach lies in the interface between SPARK and Ada. When a SPARK function is called by Ada to validate a message, we must build a SPARK-compatible abstraction of the message. Rather than copying the message, we preserve the Ada types (including pointers and standard containers) and build abstractions on top of them so that they can be used in SPARK. These abstractions handle objects (e.g., messages, tasks, etc.) as black boxes and extract from them the required information in a SPARK-compatible way (e.g., translate standard containers to formal containers[7] or dereference pointers).

For example, the received Automation Request message is a pointer to an object of the Object inheritance class and is hidden from SPARK in a private type, with functions for converting to and from the pointer type and dereferencing:

```
package avtas.lmcp.object.SPARK_Boundary with SPARK_Mode is
   pragma Annotate (GNATprove, Terminating, SPARK_Boundary);

   type My_Object_Any is private;
   function Deref (X : My_Object_Any) return Object'Class with
      Global ⇒ null, Inline;
   function Wrap (X : Object_Any) return My_Object_Any with
      Global      ⇒ null, Inline,
      SPARK_Mode ⇒ Off;
```

---

[7] In addition to standard containers defined by Ada in the form of generic packages, SPARK includes a library of formal containers that have been designed specifically to facilitate proof.

```
function Unwrap (X :  My_Object_Any) return Object_Any with
     Global        ⇒ null, Inline ,
     SPARK_Mode ⇒ Off;
private
   pragma SPARK_Mode (Off);
   type My_Object_Any is new Object_Any;
   (...)
end avtas.lmcp.object.SPARK_Boundary;
```

The SPARK code can dereference objects of type My_Object_Any using the Deref function. The functions to construct/destruct the abstractions (Wrap and Unwrap) are only accessible by the Ada code (they are marked SPARK_Mode ⇒Off).

4   Results

We developed a complete demonstration of the reimplemented, proven Automation Request Validator service, which is available on github[8]. We adapted an existing UxAS example that illustrates a UAV searching a waterway. The example includes a UxAS instance and the OpenAMASE simulator running as separate programs and communicating using ZeroMQ. Rather than integrate the Ada/SPARK into the C++ UxAS program, we run the service in a separate program. Our service receives messages from ZeroMQ and processes the Automation Request messages as if in the same UxAS instance as the C++ code.

Normally, a UxAS instance includes the Automation Request Validator service, which in this case would conflict with the Ada version since both would respond to Automation Request messages. Therefore, we disable the original Automation Request Validator service in OpenUxAS by removing it from the instance's XML configuration file. The C++ instance still receives Automation Request messages as they are injected but because none of its services process them, the intended UAV never begins the search. However, the XML file for the Ada version does include the Automation Request Validator service, so an instance is created, which validates Automation Request messages and then responds with Unique Automation Request messages. The UAV then performs the expected search.

4.1   Verification Results

Our goal was to verify both that the code fulfills its specification and that no errors can occur during its execution. We entirely achieved the first goal. We mostly achieved the second goal, with two notable exceptions.

First, we did not attempt to verify correct usage of the bounded strings and formal containers APIs. More precisely, we did not verify: the possible overflow of the error message string that is generated in response to an invalid request; the possible overflow of the data structures used to store messages and declared objects; or the uniqueness of keys in data structures, which requires reasoning about uniqueness of identifiers. These could be verified if we provided additional

---

[8] https://github.com/AdaCore/OpenUxAS, in the 'ada' branch.

annotations and assumptions on inputs. We did not seek completeness because we believe these properties are insufficiently interesting to pollute other verification tasks with these concerns.

Second, the tool is unable to verify correctness of the part of the code in which, in C++, a classwide task object is cast to a specific task type depending on a string ID (its name). Ensuring the correctness of this code would require verifying globally the complete type hierarchy for all tasks, to make sure that each ID is never reused for a different task type. This problem may be seen as an incentive to refactor the code to use Ada membership tests instead of comparing string IDs, so that no such global invariant is required to ensure correctness.

During our process of reverse engineering the specifications from the C++ code base and comments, we found only one error: a nested loop was used to find a match in two maps but both loops where iterating on the same map! We corrected this bug when we found it but demonstrated that it would have been detected by a formalization of the validity criteria.

Overall, the results we obtained using formal verification on the Automation Request Validator service are encouraging. However, the verification effort required to achieve this goal was significant because of two key challenges.

First, there was no appropriate high-level functional specification of what the service was supposed to do; we had to reverse engineer the specification from the C++ code and comments. Our specifications were validated by stakeholders.

Second, the code was not designed to be easily verified using SPARK; we had to abstract incompatible features, as detailed above. The abstractions could have been avoided by a global redesign of the code to more systematically use the formal containers and to eliminate pointers. Alternatively, the abstractions could have been avoided by improving the support in SPARK for excluded Ada features, such as pointers.

Because of these challenges, significant effort was required to define and express appropriate specifications in SPARK. Furthermore, actually verifying that the code conforms to its specification using the SPARK proof tool was challenging, because: (1) the code contains several loops, each requiring the use of a manually crafted loop invariant to act as a cut point for the tool; and (2) even with the code annotated and all the invariants supplied, we ran into provability issues. Indeed, the tool was overwhelmed by the amount of information it had to carry, mostly due to the number of different container instances employed. As a result, we had to manually guide the proof tool to complete the proofs by adding manual assertions in the code, sometimes at the expense of readability.

To help the provers, we primarily relied on two techniques.

First, we often restated the property we were trying to establish at several points in the program using pragma Assert_And_Cut. These pragmas not only check the property and add it to the context of subsequent checks like pragma Assert but also use the expression provided as a cut point. After the cut, the provers forget everything before the pragma and only remember the supplied property. For example, the code that checks that entities are properly configured is 175 lines long and includes 14 if statements and five loops, some of which are nested.

At the conclusion of this code, we state that the IsReady flag really is the result of the expected computation using a pragma Assert_And_Cut:

```
pragma Assert_And_Cut
   (IsReady = Check_For_Required_Entity_Configurations
   (Entity_Ids       ⇒ EntityIds ,
    Configurations   ⇒ This . Configs . Available_Configuration_Entity_Ids ,
    States           ⇒ This . Configs . Available_State_Entity_Ids ,
    Planning_States  ⇒ Get_PlanningStates_Ids ( Request ))) ;
```

Thus we verify the property and help the verification of the remaining checks by forgetting the intermediate steps required by the computation up to that point.

Second, we introduced lemmas for often-reused reasoning. For example, the code sometimes performs computations that are hidden from the analysis, such as sending messages to the outside world. While these computations modify the internal state of the service, they do not modify the configuration data such as the available entities. Unfortunately, the only mechanism provided by SPARK to state that a part of an object is unchanged by a subprogram call is Ada equality, which is fairly complex. Equality on an array, for instance, is the equality of elements: two arrays can be equal even if they have different bounds. As a result, proving that properties are preserved because two objects are equal can be nontrivial. For example, consider the contract of Send_Error_Response, which is used to send an error message if the request is invalid:

```
procedure Send_Error_Response
   ( This              :  in out Automation_Request_Validator_Service ;
     Request           :  My_UniqueAutomationRequest ;
     ReasonForFailure  :  Bounded_Dynamic_Strings . Sequence ;
     ErrResponseID     :  out Int64 )
with Post ⇒ This . Configs 'Old = This . Configs
and Same_Requests
   (Model ( This . Requests_Waiting_For_Tasks ) ,
    Model ( This . Requests_Waiting_For_Tasks ) 'Old)
   and Same_Requests
     (Model ( This . Pending_Requests ) ,
      Model ( This . Pending_Requests ) 'Old) ;
```

This contract states that both configuration data (This.Configs) and the request queues are left unchanged by the procedures.[9] When we call this procedure from our SPARK code, we would like to be able to deduce that if all requests were valid in the data configuration before the call, then they will be valid after the call. Unfortunately, this reasoning involves complex computations, as it relies on Ada equality for complicated data structures. Moreover, the validity of requests itself contains several (nested) quantified expressions. To help with these proofs, we introduced axioms in the form of ghost procedures with no effects; these axioms are used as lemmas in proofs. The premises are stated using preconditions; the conclusions are stated using postconditions. For example:

---

[9] We do not use Ada equality on the request queues: the requests contain parts which are hidden from SPARK, so SPARK does not know the meaning of equality for these queues; this is not the case, however, for the data configuration where we took care to only store SPARK-compatible information.

```
procedure Prove_Validity_Preserved
 (Data1, Data2 : Configuration_Data;
  R : My_UniqueAutomationRequest)
with
 Ghost,
 Global ⇒ null,
 Pre    ⇒ Data1 = Data2,
 Post   ⇒ Valid_Automation_Request (Data1, R) =
               Valid_Automation_Request (Data2, R);
```

This lemma states that if two configurations are equal, a request will have the same validity status in both. To use the lemma, we call it explicitly in the code:

```
declare
 ErrResponseID : Int64;
 Old_Confs : constant Configuration_Data := This.Configs with Ghost;
begin
 Send_Error_Response (This, Request, ReasonForFailure, ErrResponseID);
 Prove_Validity_Preserved (Old_Confs, This.Configs, Request);
end;
```

The use of both of these techniques made the proofs tractable *without* requiring a major redesign of the program. However, these techniques are costly in terms of lines of code. Check_Automation_Request_Requirements is about 200 lines of C++. Our verified version is approximately 410 lines long. Of these, the specification and contract is 20 lines, but depends on 130 lines of expression functions that help to express the property so that it is as readable as possible. The implementation contains roughly 45 lines of loop invariants and just over 100 lines of ghost code, including regular Assert pragmas, Assert_And_Cut pragmas, and calls to ghost lemmas with associated ghost state. The remainder – about 250 lines – is the Ada code, which we translated as closely as possible from the C++ version. In addition, we have some 50 lines of lemmas, most of which are automatically verified by the tool and do not require additional annotation.

5   Conclusion

We applied SPARK to OpenUxAS, AFRL's service-oriented architecture that provides core services supporting cooperative control and high-level command and control. In our application, we defined a partial specification for the Automation Request Validator service. We successfully proved that the implementation of the procedure intended to perform request validation satisfies the specification and additionally proved the absence of most run-time exceptions.

This work provides a foundation upon which we intend to build. In future work, we intend to extend the application of SPARK and Ada to additional services in UxAS and to investigate recently added support for ownership pointers to help simplify the application of SPARK. Ultimately, our goal is to provide a sufficient framework to enable us to formalize and prove interesting, application-relevant composition properties across the architecture.

References

1. Butler, R.W., Finelli, G.B.: The infeasibility of experimental quantification of life-critical software reliability. SIGSOFT Softw. Eng. Notes **16**(5), 66–76 (1991). https://doi.org/10.1145/123041.123054
2. Dross, C., et al.: Climbing the software assurance ladder-practical formal verification for reliable software (2018). https://www.adacore.com/uploads/techPapers/spark_avocs_2018.pdf
3. Kingston, D., Rasmussen, S., Humphrey, L.: Automated UAV tasks for search and surveillance. In: 2016 IEEE Conference on Control Applications (CCA), pp. 1–8 (September 2016). https://doi.org/10.1109/CCA.2016.7587813
4. Kingston, D., Beard, R.W., Holt, R.S.: Decentralized perimeter surveillance using a team of UAVs. IEEE Trans. Robot. **24**(6), 1394–1404 (2008)
5. Rasmussen, S., Kingston, D., Humphrey, L.: A brief introduction to unmanned systems autonomy services (UxAS), pp. 257–268 (June 2018). https://doi.org/10.1109/ICUAS.2018.8453287

Adopting Formal Methods in an Industrial Setting: The Railways Case

Maurice H. ter Beek[1](✉)(iD), Arne Borälv[3],
Alessandro Fantechi[1,2](✉)(iD), Alessio Ferrari[1](✉)(iD), Stefania Gnesi[1](✉)(iD),
Christer Löfving[3], and Franco Mazzanti[1](✉)(iD)

[1] ISTI–CNR, Pisa, Italy
{terbeek,ferrari,gnesi,mazzanti}@isti.cnr.it
[2] Università di Firenze, Florence, Italy
alessandro.fantechi@unifi.it
[3] Trafikverket, Göteborg, Sweden
christer.lofving@trafikverket.se

Abstract. The railway sector has seen a large number of successful applications of formal methods and tools. However, up-to-date, structured information about the industrial usage and needs related to formal tools in railways is limited. Two Shift2Rail projects, X2Rail-2 and ASTRail, have addressed this issue by performing a systematic search over the state of the art of formal methods application in railways to identify the best used practices. As part of the work of these projects, questionnaires on formal methods and tools have been designed to gather input and guidance on the adoption of formal methods in the railway domain. Even though the questionnaires were developed independently and distributed to different audiences, the responses show a certain convergence in the replies to the questions common to both. In this paper, we present a detailed report on such convergence, drawing some indications about methods and tools that are considered to constitute the most fruitful approaches to industrial adoption.

1 Introduction

The benefits that can be expected from using formal methods depend on several factors and can vary considerably depending on the scope and purpose, the quality and maturity of the tools that are used, the knowledge of users of the formal methods and tools, and so on.

Considering *formal specification* of requirements, formal methods provide a better insight and understanding, compared to specifying requirements in natural language. Formal specifications may be processed automatically by software tools, allowing the requirements to be debugged during development. Besides such benefits, a formal specification can be used as basis to prove that a system (model) satisfies its requirements using formal verification.

Formal verification enables exhaustive verification that critical properties related to safety and security are satisfied, which traditional methods based

© Springer Nature Switzerland AG 2019
M. H. ter Beek et al. (Eds.): FM 2019, LNCS 11800, pp. 762–772, 2019.
https://doi.org/10.1007/978-3-030-30942-8_46

on test and simulation cannot. This makes it possible to accurately identify meaningful errors, and to provide strong guarantees for correctness. In addition, formal verification is often (but not always) automated which can reduce the effort and time for proving the correctness of systems considerably. In the last decade or two, formal verification has matured considerably, thanks to more sophisticated algorithms for formal verification and more powerful computers.

The largest benefits can be expected from *formal development*, that is, integrating formal methods in the development process, so that safer software can be produced with lower costs. Formal development may replace existing processes, but this requires a large commitment and investment, including a learning curve to become proficient in a new process.

Successful applications of formal methods in industry (automotive, avionics, etc.) have demonstrated these benefits to varying degree, and have shown that the number of defects in the code can be significantly reduced [1,4,10,11]. However, formal methods do not pervade critical software industry, and this happens also in the railway domain, despite several success stories [3,6,7] and even though formal methods are highly recommended by the CENELEC standards [5].

The Shift2Rail Joint Undertaking (S2R JU) has identified the use of formal methods as one of the key concepts to enable reducing the time it takes to develop and deliver railway signalling systems, and to reduce high costs for procurement, development and maintenance. Formal methods have been recognized as needed to ensure correct behaviour, interoperability and safety, at the same time reducing long-term life cycle costs. In this S2R JU initiative, two complementary projects, one proposed by the JU Members themselves, the other one as a result of an open call, respectively X2Rail-2[1] and ASTRail[2], have been funded having as one of the objectives common to both, that is, to perform a search over the state of the art of formal methods application in railways to identify the best used practices. As part of the work of the two projects, questionnaires on formal methods and tools have been designed to gather input and guidance on the adoption of formal methods in the railway domain. The purpose was to validate existing know-how and experience in the subject matter and to gain insight into expectations by the railway industry regarding what formal methods can and should bring. Even though the questionnaires were developed independently and distributed to different audiences by the two projects, the responses show a certain convergence in the replies to the questions common to both.

In this paper, we present a detailed report on such convergence, drawing some indications about methods and tools that are considered to constitute the most fruitful approaches to industrial adoption. Indeed, the main aim of the questionnaires was, in both cases, to investigate:

- The most relevant functionality of formal methods applications among, e.g., formal verification, requirement traceability, test case generation and simulation, etc.

---

[1] https://projects.shift2rail.org/s2r_ip2_n.aspx?p=X2RAIL-2.
[2] http://www.astrail.eu.

- The system development phases that can benefit most from using formal tools.
- The most important quality aspect of formal tools, such as maturity, easy to learn, easy to integrate in a CENELEC process, etc.

This paper is organized as follows: the questionnaires are presented in Sect. 2. The results of the questionnaires are shown in Sect. 3, after an elaboration aimed to cumulate and harmonize the raw results of the different questionnaires. Lessons learned and conclusions are summarized in Sect. 4.

2 Questionnaires

Three questionnaires were defined, two by the X2Rail-2 project [12] and one by the ASTRail project [2,8]. In the following, we will distinguish them by the names X2Rail2-a, X2Rail2-b and ASTRail.

The questionnaires were independently distributed to different audiences by the two projects in order to gather feedback on the usage of formal methods in the railway domain, both from academic and industrial stakeholders. Below we summarize the main characteristics of the respondents.

X2Rail2-a:

- 17 out of 22 invited individuals answered the questionnaire.
- The respondents had on average 10 years of experience in railway signalling and 9 years in formal methods.
- One third of the respondents were affiliated with a supplier company, one third with a research institution, and one quarter were from an infrastructure manager.
- Most respondents had experience from projects using formal methods, with such projects delivering systems in revenue service or as pilots.
- The most common signalling subsystem type of such projects has been interlocking, followed by on-board software.

X2Rail2-b:

- 86 out of 500 invited individuals answered the questionnaire.
- The respondents had on average 20 years of experience in railway signalling.
- 38% of the respondents were affiliated with an infrastructure manager, 16% with a supplier company, 28% with engineering firms, 5% with a research institution, and 5% with safety assessment.
- More than half of the respondents were familiar with formal methods for development of railway signalling systems (formal specification, formal verification, semi-formal methods).
- More than half of the respondents had used formal methods (directly or indirectly).

ASTRail:

- The questionnaire was proposed to the participants of the RSSRail'17 conference. The 44 respondents were balanced between academics (50%) and practitioners (50%, of which 47.7% from railway companies and 2.3% from aerospace and defense).
- A large percentage of respondents had several years of experience in railways (68% more than 3 years and 39% more than 10 years) and in formal methods (75% more than 3 years, 52% more than 10 years).

3   Cumulated Results of the Two Projects' Questionnaires

In order to extend the validity of the results obtained by the different questionnaires, we considered the integration of their results, focusing on those questions that are common, or similar, between them. Even in the case of the same or similar questions, sometimes the questionnaires proposed a different set of closed form replies: this required a harmonization effort which in some case has necessarily reduced the information provided by one of the questionnaires.

Products. Both projects included questions on the type of railway signalling systems to which formal methods were applied by respondents or their institution; however, X2Rail2-a also distinguished between equipments belonging to ERTMS, CBTC or conventional signaling applications. Figure 1 shows a summary of the results expressed as the percentage of the respondents to ASTRail, while for X2Rail2-a the percentages are given for each application category (multiple answers were allowed, so the sum is not 100).

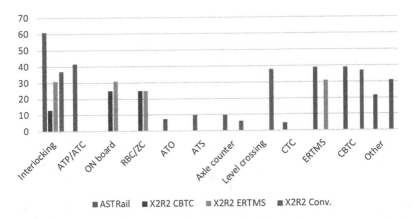

Fig. 1. Usage of formal methods in the railway sector – type of products

Phases. Another common question of ASTRail and X2Rail2-a regarded the phases of the development process in which formal methods were applied. Unfortunately, the two questionnaires proposed a different granularity in the definition of the phases, and we were therefore unable to meaningfully synthesize the results beyond the mere juxtaposition presented in Table 1, in which the location of the entries hints at some rough correspondences between the two cases, and where the numbers give the percentage of interested respondents for each questionnaire.

Table 1. Phases in the process in which formal methods are applied

Phase	ASTRail	X2Rail2-a
Specification	73.8	
User requirements		6
Prototyping		13
System level user requirements		31
Software user requirements		69
System configuration		13
Design		63
Simulation	40.5	
Model analysis	50.0	
Formal verification	73.8	
Design verification		50
Code generation	32.0	
Coding		38
Testing	32.0	
Code verification		25
Unit testing		25
Integration testing		13
Static analysis	7.1	
Safety assessment		19
Other	2.4	13

Formal Tools. Tools based on formal methods, for short *formal tools*, have been the key to success stories of industrial application of formal methods [9, 11]. The questionnaires therefore addressed the industrial diffusion of formal tools, without providing any specific list of tools in advance, nor any predefined definition of what constitutes a formal tool. ASTRail and X2Rail2-a differ for the classification of used tools (X2Rail2-b did not include a question asking for tool identification):

- In X2Rail2-a there are separate questions related to formal verification, formal specification and formal development.
- In ASTRail only the name of used tools where asked, irrespective of the phase in which they were used.

To harmonize the results, we ignored the phase distinction made in X2Rail2-a: we simply merged the three values given by respondents to X2Rail2-a by assuming that who has indicated the use of a tool in a phase is one of those that indicated the use of the same tool for another phase, that is, it is more likely that someone adopting a tool for one phase has adopted the same tool for another phase. Under this assumption, for each tool we took the maximum of the numbers of users given for each phase. Moreover, to simplify the presentation, we merged values related to tools that form the *B ecosystem*, merged values referring to Petri Net tools and removed from X2Rail2-a the answers on semi-formal tools (cf. next paragraph). We then ordered the tools in Fig. 2 by the sum of the resulting ASTRail and X2Rail2-a values, removing all tools mentioned only once in one of the questionnaires, in order to contain the size of the figure.[3]

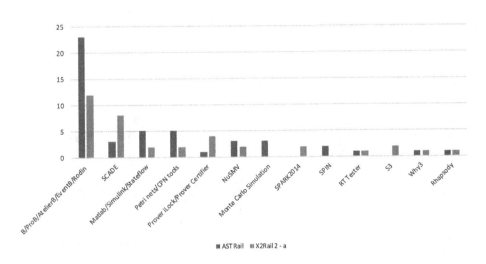

Fig. 2. Tools cited in the questionnaires

We notice that the industrial perception of what constitutes a formal method or a formal tool is rather liberal, including some tools and languages that may not be considered 'formal' according to canonical definitions of formal methods. For example, typical commercial *model-based design* tools like SCADE and Simulink

---

[3] The list of tools gaining only one mention is: ABS, Astah, CADP, CNL, CryptoVerif, Datalog, F*, iUML-B, FDR4, Markov Chains, Maude, mCRL2, Moebius, MoMuT, PRISM, ProVerif, QA, RAISE, RobustRails, SafeCap, SAL, SAT, SMT, TAMARIN, UMC, UPPAAL, and XILINK.

were cited among tools offering formal verification capabilities, and therefore in this respect are considered formal. In line with [9], we extend this liberal notion of formal tools to Rhapsody as well (in spite of what will be said later about UML) since, although not offering formal verification, it provides simulation and automatic test generation capabilities to support the design, construction and analysis of systems. Moreover, such features are considered among the most relevant ones requested from formal tools, as we will show later in Fig. 4. On the other hand, respondents also listed generic names of verification techniques (SAT, Monte Carlo simulation, etc.) rather than specific tools.

Semi-formal Tools. Semi-formal methods refer to formalisms and languages that are not considered fully 'formal'. Examples include UML and dialects thereof, in which requirements are expressed using graphical diagrams. Although semi-formal, such diagrams can convey the meaning of requirements more clearly than natural language. Advocates consider the use of semi-formal methods worthwhile, for instance due to easier adoption during earlier phases such as when defining and eliciting the user and system requirements. Using semi-formal methods simply defers the task of completing the semantics to a later stage. Semi-formal tools were cited only in X2Rail2-a, whose results are reported in Fig. 3.

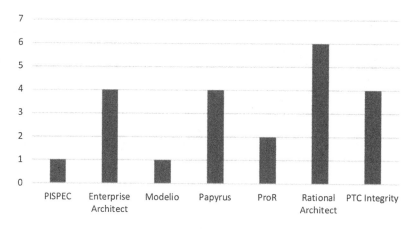

Fig. 3. Semi-formal tools

Figures 2 and 3 already show a convergence towards a limited set of tools. This trend is even more marked if we cross these results with those coming from other sources, that is, the systematic literature review conducted in the ASTRail project, and the associated study of European industrial research projects related to the application of formal methods in railway signalling [2,8].

Expectations on Tools. The respondents to all three questionnaires were asked, according to their experience, what they considered to be the most relevant functionalities that formal (or semi-formal) methods and tools should support. Figure 4 depicts the compared results, which exhibit a substantial agreement: verification is by far the functionality that is asked most from a formal tool.

Another question common to the three questionnaires concerns the most relevant quality aspects that (semi-)formal tools should have in order to be used in the railway industry. The results depicted in Fig. 5 show that maturity, easy learning and easy integration in a CENELEC development process are the qualities that scored highest. We note that ASTRail and X2Rail2-b show a more substantial agreement, while X2Rail2-a scores differently some aspects (e.g., the importance of the tools' cost).

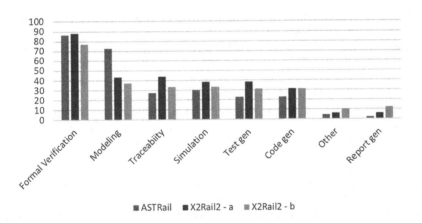

Fig. 4. Most relevant features

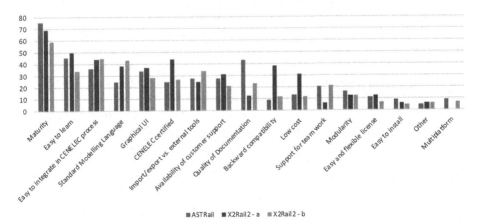

Fig. 5. Relevant quality aspects

4 Conclusion

Formal methods have been largely applied to railway problems for more than three decades. However, structured information is limited about their current application in industry, and about the most relevant features that practitioners expect from tools supporting formal development. In this paper, we merge the information elicited through three different questionnaires involving practitioners and academics with experience in formal methods and railway systems. The questionnaires were performed in the contexts of two ongoing Horizon 2020 research projects funded through the Shift2Rail initiative, namely ASTRail and X2Rail-2. Both projects include tasks specifically dedicated to collect information about the application of formal methods in railways. The results of the questionnaires show the following:

1. Most of the applications of formal methods in industrial projects are focused on interlocking systems.
2. Formal methods àre mainly used for formal specification and formal verification, mostly in the early development phases, as requirements and design.
3. The B-family is the dominant set of tools, followed by tools with simulation capabilities such as SCADE and Simulink.
4. The most relevant functionalities are formal verification and support for formal modelling, followed by traceability, simulation, test and code generation.
5. The most relevant quality features are related to the maturity, usability and learnability of the tools.

This paper consolidates the body of knowledge in formal methods for railway system development by confirming some trends (e.g., dominance of the B-method, focus on early development phases) that are visible to the interested practitioners and academics, by means of an empirical inquiry. The conducted study has also shown a certain gap in the industrial perception of what formal methods and tools are, with respect to more canonical definitions of these terms.

There is an obvious threat to the validity of the conclusions of this work, due to the possible low representativity of the replies to the questionnaires; however, the questionnaires were by their nature targeted to a specific niche of professionals, with a good coverage of the main stakeholders involved in the design and production of railway signalling systems.

We are also aware of the limits of the proposed questionnaires, which aimed mainly at a rapid collection of data, in the end providing only superficial data on the quite diverse background and experience of the respondents. No definition of formal methods, nor of formal (specification, development, verification) tools was given in advance to the respondents. While this allowed to probe the rather broad understanding of how formal methods are conceived in industry, at the same time it has reduced the importance of the results of the questionnaires by spreading the scores over a wide and variegated area of techniques and tools, which has required weakening the canonical definitions of formal methods and tools. The questionnaires also lacked a precise definition of terms that could easily be given different meanings by the respondents (e.g., "maturity", which could mean that the tool has been around for a while, appears polished, or is stable in the sense that it does not crash a lot).

Surely, more investigation is needed to refine the obtained results. An extended format for the questionnaires addressing the above limits should be prepared and proposed to a larger, more controlled, audience. Moreover, the latest conclusions drawn from the integration of the three questionnaires, regarding the most used tools and related expectations in terms of most relevant features and relevant quality aspects, have triggered our interest in understanding to what extent currently available tools, such as those cited in the questionnaires, actually satisfy the expectations: a specific investigation among professionals in this regard could form a solid base for subsequent research on the definition of readily available development processes that integrate formal and semi-formal tools, providing industry with clear paths to follow in different situations, with minimum friction and maximum benefit. The recent overview of the status of formal tools presented in [9] perfectly summarizes the current difficulties faced by users of such tools. However, the authors also propose a number of directions for improvement, both for the individual tool developer and for the academic community as a whole.

Acknowledgements. This work has been partially funded by the ASTRail and the X2Rail-2 projects. These projects received funding from the Shift2Rail Joint Undertaking under the European Union's Horizon 2020 research and innovation programme under grant agreement No. 777561 and No. 777465.

References

1. Ameur, Y.A., Boniol, F., Wiels, V.: Toward a wider use of formal methods for aerospace systems design and verification. Int. J. Softw. Tools Technol. Transfer **12**(1), 1–7 (2010)
2. Basile, D., et al.: On the industrial uptake of formal methods in the railway domain. In: Furia, C.A., Winter, K. (eds.) IFM 2018. LNCS, vol. 11023, pp. 20–29. Springer, Cham (2018). https://doi.org/10.1007/978-3-319-98938-9_2
3. Butler, M.J., et al.: Formal modelling techniques for efficient development of railway control products. RSSRail. LNCS, vol. 10598, pp. 71–86. Springer, Cham (2017). https://doi.org/10.1007/978-3-319-68499-4_5
4. Davis, J.A., et al.: Study on the barriers to the industrial adoption of formal methods. In: Pecheur, C., Dierkes, M. (eds.) FMICS 2013. LNCS, vol. 8187, pp. 63–77. Springer, Heidelberg (2013). https://doi.org/10.1007/978-3-642-41010-9_5
5. European Committee for Electrotechnical Standardization: CENELEC EN 50128 – Railway applications - communication, signalling and processing systems - software for railway control and protection systems (1 June 2011)
6. Fantechi, A.: Twenty-five years of formal methods and railways: what next? In: Counsell, S., Núñez, M. (eds.) SEFM 2013. LNCS, vol. 8368, pp. 167–183. Springer, Cham (2014). https://doi.org/10.1007/978-3-319-05032-4_13
7. Fantechi, A., Ferrari, A., Gnesi, S.: Formal methods and safety certification: challenges in the railways domain. In: Margaria, T., Steffen, B. (eds.) ISoLA 2016. LNCS, vol. 9953, pp. 261–265. Springer, Cham (2016). https://doi.org/10.1007/978-3-319-47169-3_18

8. Ferrari, A., et al.: Survey on formal methods and tools in railways: The ASTRail approach. In: Collart-Dutilleul, S., Lecomte, T., Romanovsky, A. (eds.) RSSRail 2019. LNCS, vol. 11495, pp. 226–241. Springer, Cham (2019). https://doi.org/10.1007/978-3-030-18744-6_15

9. Garavel, H., Mateescu, R.: Reflections on Bernhard Steffen's physics of software tools. In: Margaria, T., Graf, S., Larsen, K.G. (eds.) Models, Mindsets, Meta: The What, the How, and the Why Not?. LNCS, vol. 11200, pp. 186–207. Springer, Cham (2019). https://doi.org/10.1007/978-3-030-22348-9_12

10. Nyberg, M., Gurov, D., Lidström, C., Rasmusson, A., Westman, J.: Formal verification in automotive industry: enablers and obstacles. In: Margaria, T., Steffen, B. (eds.) ISoLA 2018. LNCS, vol. 11247, pp. 139–158. Springer, Cham (2018). https://doi.org/10.1007/978-3-030-03427-6_14

11. Plat, N., van Katwijk, J., Toetenel, H.: Application and benefits of formal methods in software development. Softw. Eng. J. 7(5), 335–346 (1992)

12. X2Rail-2 - Deliverable D5.1, Formal Methods (Taxonomy and Survey), Proposed Methods and Applications (16 May 2018). https://projects.shift2rail.org/download.aspx?id=b4cf6a3d-f1f2-4dd3-ae01-2bada34596b8

Author Index